250040

Classics in World
LITERATURE

AMERICA READS   **CLASSIC EDITION**

AMERICA READS CLASSIC EDITION

BEGINNINGS IN LITERATURE
Alan L. Madsen
Sarah Durand Wood
Philip M. Connors

DISCOVERIES IN LITERATURE
L. Jane Christensen
Edmund J. Farrell

EXPLORATIONS IN LITERATURE
Nancy C. Millett
Raymond J. Rodrigues

PATTERNS IN LITERATURE
Edmund J. Farrell
Ouida H. Clapp
Karen J. Kuehner

TRADITIONS IN LITERATURE
Helen McDonnell
James E. Miller, Jr.
Russell J. Hogan

THE UNITED STATES IN LITERATURE
The Red Badge of Courage Edition
Three Long Stories Edition
James E. Miller, Jr.
Kerry M. Wood
Carlota Cárdenas de Dwyer

ENGLAND IN LITERATURE
Macbeth edition
Hamlet edition
John Pfordresher
Gladys V. Veidemanis
Helen McDonnell

CLASSICS IN WORLD LITERATURE
Kerry M. Wood
Helen McDonnell
John Pfordresher
Mary Alice Fite
Paul Lankford

The authors and editors wish to thank the following consultants for reading and teaching editorial material and proposed selections for America Reads.
■ Barbara E. Anderson, Junior Level Coordinator and Teacher, James B. Conant High School, Hoffman Estates, Illinois
■ Anita Arnold, Chairman, English Department, Thomas Jefferson High School, San Antonio, Texas
■ Pat Dudley, Principal, Jane Long Elementary School, Abilene ISD, Abilene, Texas
■ Dr. V. Pauline Hodges-McLain, Coordinator, Language Arts, Jefferson County Public Schools, Golden, Colorado
■ Rance Howe, English/Language Arts Consultant K–12, Anoka-Hennepin ISD 11, Coon Rapids, Minnesota
■ Lisbeth Johnson, English Teacher, Capital High School, Olympia, Washington
■ Daniel Lane, Supervisor of Humanities, Holmdel Twp. Public Schools, Holmdel, New Jersey
■ May Lee, English Teacher, Baldwin Senior High School, Baldwin, New York
■ Richard T. Martin, English Department Chairman, Burrillville Junior-Senior High School, Harrisville, Rhode Island
■ Barbara McCormick, Systemwide Chairman of English, Greenville Public Schools, Greenville, Mississippi
■ James McCullough, English Teacher, Carmel High School, Mundelein, Illinois
■ Cathy Nufer, Teacher, Grade 6, Elm School, Hinsdale, Illinois
■ Marlyn Payne, Teacher, Grade 7, Nichols Middle School, Evanston, Illinois
■ Sally P. Pfeifer, English Department Chair, Lewis and Clark High School, Spokane, Washington
■ James B. Phillips, Instructor in English and Reading, Norwood Senior High School, Norwood, Massachusetts
■ John Pratt, Language Arts Chairperson, Edison High School, Stockton, California
■ Cora Wolfe, English Department Chairperson, Antelope Union High School, Wellton, Arizona

Classics in World
LITERATURE

AMERICA READS　　　　　　**CLASSIC EDITION**

Kerry M. Wood
Helen McDonnell
John Pfordresher
Mary Alice Fite
Paul Lankford

S C O T T ,　　F O R E S M A N

Scott, Foresman and Company　Editorial Offices: Glenview, Illinois
Regional Offices:
Sunnyvale, California　Tucker, Georgia　Glenview, Illinois　Oakland, New Jersey　Dallas, Texas

Kerry M. Wood

English teacher at Woodside High School in Woodside, California. Formerly: coordinator of the Advanced Placement English program, Sequoia Union High School District, California. Consultant of the University of California Bay Area Writing Project. Teacher of a course in Scholastic Aptitude Test preparation for College Admissions Preparatory Service on the San Francisco Peninsula.

Helen McDonnell

Professor of English (adjunct faculty) at Manatee Community College, South Campus, Venice, Florida. Formerly: English Supervisor of the Ocean Township Junior and Senior High Schools, Oakhurst, New Jersey; member of the Commission on Literature, National Council of Teachers of English. Member and former chairman of the Committee on Comparative and World Literature, NCTE. Coeditor, *Teacher's Guide to World Short Stories*, NCTE.

John Pfordresher

Professor of English Literature, Georgetown University, Washington, D.C. Editor of *Variorum Edition of the Idylls of the King* and coauthor of *Matthew Arnold, Prose Writings: The Critical Heritage*. Author of articles in the *English Journal, Studies in Short Fiction,* and *Studies in Bibliography*. Currently a member of the National Council of Teachers of English Commission on Literature.

Mary Alice Fite

John V. Chapman Distinguished Chair of English. English Department Chair, Columbus School for Girls, Columbus, Ohio. Formerly English Adjunct Instructor, Park College Residence Center, Rickenbacker Air Force Base, Ohio. Member of the NCTE Comparative and World Literature Committee and former member of the Otterbein College English Festival Advisory Board.

Paul Lankford

English Department Chairman, Green Run High School, Virginia Beach, Virginia. Formerly English teacher, Bayside High School, Virginia Beach, and Franklin High School, Franklin, Virginia. Chairman of the NCTE Committee on Comparative and World Literature. City and State English Teacher of the Year in 1982.

Cover: Claude Lorrain, *The Arrival of Aeneas at Pallanteum* (detail). 1675. National Trust, Anglesey Abbey.

Pronunciation key and dictionary entries are from *Scott, Foresman Advanced Dictionary* by E. L. Thorndike and Clarence L. Barnhart. Copyright © 1988 Scott, Foresman and Company. Acknowledgments continued on page 1060.

ISBN: 0-673-29385-8

Copyright © 1991, 1989
Scott, Foresman and Company, Glenview, Illinois
All Rights Reserved. Printed in the United States of America.

8 9 10 RRC 02 01 00

CONTENTS

THINKING CRITICALLY ABOUT LITERATURE

3   **3**

UNIT 3   THE MIDDLE AGES   800–1400

THINKING CRITICALLY ABOUT LITERATURE

UNIT 4   THE RENAISSANCE   1300–1650

UNIT 5   NEOCLASSICISM   1650–1780

THINKING CRITICALLY ABOUT LITERATURE

UNIT 6   ROMANTICISM AND REALISM   1780–1880

UNIT 7   MODERNISM   1880–1940

THINKING CRITICALLY ABOUT LITERATURE

UNIT 8 RECENT LITERATURE 1940–

THINKING CRITICALLY ABOUT LITERATURE

READING LITERATURE

COMMENTS

READER'S NOTES

THEMES IN WORLD LITERATURE

THE HISTORY OF LANGUAGE

HANDBOOK OF LITERARY TERMS

WRITER'S HANDBOOK

GLOSSARY OF LITERARY TERMS 1012

PREVIEW

Classics in World Literature has eight chronological units presenting a survey of major authors and literary works from the time of the earliest surviving writings until the present day.

UNIT ORGANIZATION

Units 2–8 begin with a **time line** showing the chronological sequence of some of the important historical and literary events of the period surveyed. (Unit 1 is divided into three parts, each with its own time line.) This is followed by a **unit preview.** Next a **background** article (or in the case of Unit 1, three background articles) provides political, social, and literary history, so that the works of literature can be read in a more meaningful context.

Author biographies precede most selections. The exceptions are anonymous selections or groups of selections, which are preceded by introductions. Each biography or introduction portrays a writer or a literary work or group of works in the appropriate historical setting.

Many selections contain **footnotes** or **sidenotes** to define and pronounce words or to help clarify passages. A **date** on the right following a selection indicates the year in which the work was published. If there is a date on the left, it indicates the year the work was written. The abbreviation c. with a date means "approximately."

Think and Discuss questions follow each selection or group of selections. They are divided into three levels: *Understanding, Analyzing,* and *Extending.* You may find it helpful to study the questions as a guide before you read a selection.

Many selections are preceded by a **handbook reference** that directs you to an article in the Handbook of Literary Terms at the back of the text. There you will learn about or review a literary term before you read the selection. Then, following the selection, **Applying/Reviewing** questions about that literary term help ensure that you understand the literary techniques involved. After a term has been introduced, it may appear in boldface type in the editorial material accompanying subsequent selections.

Vocabulary exercises focus on selected words in a piece of writing and help you learn or review techniques for determining the meanings of unfamiliar words as well as for increasing your vocabulary. You may be tested on the words in these exercises.

Thinking Skills exercises will help you learn to think about literature in new ways by *classifying, generalizing, synthesizing* (putting together parts and elements to form new ideas), and *evaluating.*

Composition assignments and ideas follow most selections. You can refer to the Writer's Handbook at the back of this text for more help with some of these assignments.

Enrichment sections occasionally provide ideas for class projects, research, and speaking and listening activities.

OTHER FEATURES

Five types of articles occur from time to time throughout the text.

Comment articles provide interesting sidelights on a work, an author, or a period. (See, for example, "Homer and History," page 133.)

Reader's Note articles provide help in reading certain works, or present a critical insight into an author's technique or style. (See, for example, *Antigone*, page 873.) One Reader's Note in each unit is devoted to comparing several translations of a specific work. (See, for example, "Translating 'The Loreley,'" page 620.)

A **Themes in World Literature** article in each unit explores major themes in the writings of different periods. (See, for example, "Men and Women," page 830.)

The History of Language articles in each unit discuss significant events in the development of speech and writing. (See, for example, "The Origin of Writing," page 103.)

Reading Literature articles in most units provide additional background on specific types of literature as well as helpful hints on how to approach them. (See, for example, "Reading a Medieval Allegory," page 315.)

UNIT REVIEWS

Each unit ends with a review entitled **Thinking Critically About Literature.** It is divided into three parts.

A short work typical of the period appears in the **Concept Review.** It is accompanied by sidenotes to guide your reading. Questions then measure your understanding of the work and review applicable literary terms that you have studied in the unit.

In the **Content Review,** classifying, generalizing, synthesizing, and evaluating questions help you review the selections in the unit.

A **Composition Review** provides topics for writing about the period or the literary genres you have studied.

END-OF-BOOK MATERIAL

The **Handbook of Literary Terms** contains brief lessons about the important terms you need in order to understand and discuss the literature. Handbook references preceding selected writings refer you to specific articles, to be studied before reading the selections.

The **Writer's Handbook** contains lessons on the writing process and on writing about various types of literature. Some of the composition assignments will refer you to these lessons.

A **Glossary of Literary Terms** provides definitions and examples of many terms in addition to those taught in the Handbook.

A dictionary-type **Glossary** contains all words featured in Vocabulary exercises, plus other words you will encounter in your reading.

The various types of literature included in this text have been written during a period of nearly four thousand years by a wide variety of authors. An understanding of this vast literary heritage provides both insights into the greatly differing cultures that produced these works and the very real enjoyments they continue to offer.

PREVIEW

UNIT 1 THE ANCIENT EAST 3000 B.C.–A.D. 1700

Authors or Works

The Epic of Gilgamesh	Omar Khayyám	*Shakuntala*	Tu Fu
Egyptian Poetry	Rumi	Babur	Po Chü-i
Genesis	Sadi	Confucius	Sei Shōnagon
Ruth	Hafiz	Chuang Tzu	Seami
Psalms	*Rig Veda*	T'ao Ch'ien	Bashō
Firdausi	*Bhagavad Gita*	Li Po	

Features

Comment: The Gods of Mesopotamia
Comment: Amarna Art
Reading Biblical Poetry
Reader's Note: Translating the *Rubáiyát*
Comment: Sufism
Comment: The Last Moghul
Comment: Confucianism and the Cultural
   Revolution
Reader's Note: Literary Criticism in Ancient
   China
Comment: Lady Murasaki's Diary
Reader's Note: Seami on the Art of the *No*
The History of Language: The Origin of
   Writing
Themes in World Literature: Appearance and
   Reality

Application of Literary Terms

figurative language	hyperbole
archetype	personification
imagery	setting
theme	apostrophe
metaphor	simile
rhyme	satire
paradox	tone
irony	

Review of Literary Term

theme

Vocabulary Skills

context
archaic words
etymology

Thinking Skills

classifying	generalizing
evaluating	synthesizing

Composition Assignments Include

Analyzing Patterns of Imagery
Writing a Dialogue
Analyzing Archetypes
Writing a Fable
Writing About Theme
Describing Your Setting
Creating a Utopia
Writing a Narrative
Creating a Collection

Enrichment

Researching Mesopotamian Archaeology
Interpreting Egyptian Poetry
Reading the Story of Sohrab and Rustum
Examining Moghul Art
Reading *Haiku*

Thinking Critically About Literature

Concept Review
Content Review
Composition Review

BACKGROUND

THE ANCIENT EAST   3000 B.C.–A.D. 1700

During the last century, finely observed and skillfully executed images of animals were discovered on the walls of caves in France and Spain. Although these beautiful paintings and engravings are far from *primitive*—in the sense of "rude" or "undeveloped"—they were the work of ice-age hunters fifteen to twenty thousand years ago. They provide striking evidence that far back in the past human beings were already responding to their world through the creation of art.

Like the pictorial arts, the art of words must have existed among stone-age peoples. (It certainly does among those peoples, like the Australian aborigines, whose stone-age culture has survived unchanged.) But since it was unrecorded, ancient oral literature such as ritual chant or tribal lore vanished with the people who created it. Only after the development of systems of writing could literature be recorded and therefore stand a chance—and a remote one at that—of surviving to the present day. The study of literature, as has been said of history, is one in which it is impossible to begin at the be-

ginning. The study of literature begins not with the appearance of language, but of written language. The first systems of writing were developed by the peoples of several river-valley civilizations in Mesopotamia, Egypt, India, and China at different times from around 3000 B.C. to around 1500 B.C.

In Unit 1 you will examine the ancient literature of these regions, as well as several others that had cultural ties to them. These seven cultures have been arranged in three groups. The first is the Near East, and includes Mesopotamia, Egypt, and Israel. Persia and India, which make up the second region, share a common ancestry in the cultural traditions of the Aryan-speaking peoples who invaded both areas. The third region is the Far East, and includes China and Japan. There is a separate introduction for each of the three regions. The introduction for the Near East begins on page 4. The introduction for Persia and India begins on page 38. The introduction for the Far East begins on page 70.

This painting of a horse, found in the Lascaux (las kō′) Cave in southern France, was made by Cro-Magnon hunters perhaps twenty thousand years ago.

THE NEAR EAST   3000 B.C.–200 B.C.

3000	2750	2500	2250	2000	1750

HISTORY AND ARTS

- Old Kingdom begins
- Pyramids built
  - Sargon I unites Sumeria
  - Jews migrate to Canaan
  - Hammurabi reunites Sumeria •

PEOPLE

- Menes
  - Gilgamesh
  - Sargon I
  - Abraham
  - Hammurabi •

LITERATURE

- Sumerians develop cuneiform
- Egyptians develop hieroglyphics
  - Scribal schools in Sumeria
  - *Gilgamesh* composed
  - Hammurabi's Code •

Victory tablet of the pharaoh
Narmer (or Menes). c. 3100 B.C.

Bronze head believed to be
Sargon I. After 2500 B.C.

Head of Queen Nefertiti
Painted limestone. c. 1370 B.C.

1500	1250	1000	750	500	250

- New Kingdom begins
  - Amarna period
    - Jewish exodus from Egypt
- Rise of Assyria begins
  - Solomon's Temple built
  - Israel falls to Assyrians
- Jewish exile in Babylon

- Akhenaton
  - Moses
- David
  - Solomon
- Ashurbanipal
  - Nebuchadnezzar
  - Cyrus

- Earliest parts of
  Old Testament composed
- Ruth composed
  - Old
    Testament
    assembled

Cuneiform tablet containing
Deluge story. c. 650 B.C.

Panel of polychrome glazed
brick from Babylon. 605–562 B.C.

Partially unrolled Dead Sea
scroll. 1st century B.C.

THE NEAR EAST

MESOPOTAMIA

Ancient Greek geographers gave the name *Mesopotamia* (mes′ə pə tā′mē ə), "the land between the rivers," to the region of the Tigris and Euphrates, which flow through what is now Iraq to empty into the Persian Gulf. (See the map on page 5.) Mesopotamia formed one horn of the "Fertile Crescent," a semicircle of rich farming and grazing land extending from the southeastern corner of the Mediterranean Sea to the head of the Persian Gulf. In ancient times a succession of peoples invaded the Fertile Crescent from the surrounding deserts and mountains. In varying degrees these different peoples contributed to the development of a characteristic Mesopotamian civilization.

The first and most influential of these invaders were the Sumerians (sü mir′ē ənz). About 3500 B.C. they moved down from the Zagros Mountains and occupied the fertile, marshy lowlands where the Tigris and Euphrates flowed into the Persian Gulf. They established a number of independent city-states that continually warred among themselves. Each city-state was a theocracy: the local god, believed to be the real ruler, had an earthly representative who served as both high priest and city governor.

Sumerian cities were small by modern standards. At its height the city of Ur may have had fifty thousand inhabitants. But they represented a new magnitude in human settlement. Large populations and effective administration enabled the Sumerians to undertake ambitious building projects. Their cities were defended by massive walls of sun-baked brick. Those at the city of Uruk, which were supposed to have been built by the Sumerian king Gilgamesh, were nearly six miles around.

Before 3000 B.C. the Sumerians had developed a simple pictographic system of writing. It probably originated in the markings appearing on the counters used to keep track of quantities of livestock or goods. (See page 103.) The Sumerians gradually improved and simplified this system into a script of wedged-shaped characters that stood for the syllables of their language rather than objects like sheep or jars

of oil. An eighteenth-century English traveler gave this script the name *cuneiform* (kyü nē′ə-fôrm), from the Latin word *cuneus*, "wedge." By about 2500 B.C. most Sumerian cities had a "tablet house," or writing school, where clever boys—the future administrators of the city-state—learned to inscribe cuneiform script with a wedge-shaped reed stylus on clay tablets. Although their cuneiform script continued to be used until almost the beginning of the Christian era, the Sumerians themselves were completely forgotten until their cities were discovered by modern archaeologists.

About 2300 B.C. the Sumerian city-states were united by Sargon I, an invader from northern Mesopotamia. He built the first empire of which any record survives. It extended east to the highlands of Iran, north to the Black Sea, and west to the Mediterranean. Sargon's descendants ruled after him for nearly two hundred years and did much to spread throughout the Near East the civilization of the conquered Sumerians, including cuneiform and the cycle of tales about their hero-king Gilgamesh. These tales formed the basis for *The Epic of Gilgamesh*, the greatest surviving work of Mesopotamian literature. The decline of Sargon's empire was followed by invasions of barbarians from the Zagros Mountains. About 1700 B.C. Mesopotamia was reunited by Hammurabi (ham′ù rä′bē), who established the capital of his empire at Babylon on the Euphrates. Hammurabi is chiefly remembered as the creator of a written code of laws that shows the legal system developed by the Sumerians.

Hammurabi's empire was occupied by a series of invaders. Around 1100 B.C. the Assyrians (ə sir′-ē ənz), who came from the highlands north of the Tigris, began a long series of attacks on their neighbors, eventually creating an empire that included the entire Fertile Crescent. A ruthless and effective military power, Assyria nevertheless helped insure the survival of Mesopotamian civilization. One of their greatest kings, Ashurbanipal (ä′shür bä′nē päl′), who reigned from 668 to 627 B.C., systematically organized the creation of a reference library at his palace at Nineveh

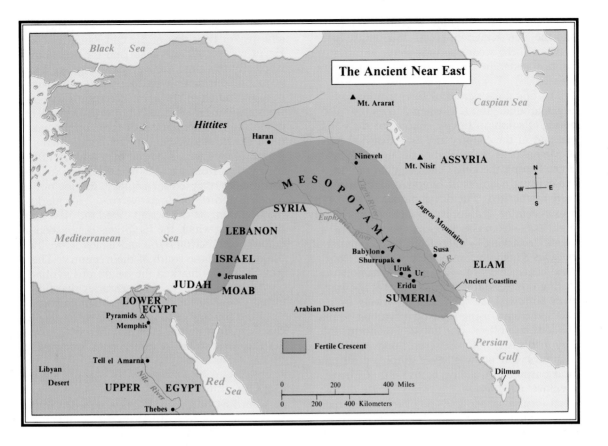

The Ancient Near East

Black Sea

Caspian Sea

▲ Mt. Ararat

Hittites

Haran •

Nineveh •
▲ Mt. Nisir   **ASSYRIA**

M E S O P O T A M I A

Tigris River

Zagros Mountains

SYRIA

Euphrates River

Mediterranean   *Sea*

LEBANON

Babylon •   Susa •
Shurrupak •
Uruk •
Ur •   **ELAM**

ISRAEL
• Jerusalem
Eridu •
JUDAH   **MOAB**

Ancient Coastline

SUMERIA

LOWER
EGYPT
Pyramids △   Arabian Desert
Memphis •

Persian
Gulf

☐ Fertile Crescent

Libyan
Desert   Tell el Amarna •

UPPER   **EGYPT**   *Red*
Nile River   *Sea*

Dilmun •

0   200   400 Miles

0   200   400 Kilometers

Thebes •

on the Tigris. It was in the long buried ruins of Ashurbanipal's library that nineteenth-century archaeologists discovered much of what we know about Mesopotamian civilization, including the tablets containing *The Epic of Gilgamesh.*

Mesopotamian literature offers a bleak vision of human life. This was partly the result of the rigors of the climate. Fierce winds created terrible dust storms, and destructive floods were frequent. "The god of the storm," says *The Epic of Gilgamesh*, "turned daylight to darkness, when he smashed the land like a cup." The Sumerians had a tradition that their earliest city, Eridu, had been destroyed in a vast flood. Created amid such violence, Mesopotamian civilization had a dark mood: "Mere man—his days are numbered; whatever he may do, he is but wind."

EGYPT

At about the same time Mesopotamian civilization was being shaped by the harshness of the Tigris-Euphrates region, that of Egypt was developing in the gentler environment of the Nile Valley. (See the map above.) The Nile's annual flooding renewed the fertility of the Egyptian fields by covering them with a layer of nutrient-rich silt carried downstream by the river from the highlands of central Africa. The dependability of the Nile flood and a sunny climate insured an ample food supply. The deserts and mountains surrounding Egypt both served as natural barriers to invasion and isolated the Egyptians culturally. These factors contributed to making the Egyptians, in the estimate of one historian, "perhaps the most self-confident people the world has known." Between 4000 and 3000 B.C. the necessity of digging and maintaining irrigation canals forced Egyptian villages to develop the rudiments of government. One of the earliest Egyptian titles was "Canal Digger," and the individuals who organized this all-important work gradually became local rulers.

Historians divide Egyptian history into three major periods: the Old Kingdom (3100–2200

B.C.); the Middle Kingdom (2000–1800 B.C.); and the New Kingdom (1600–1100 B.C.). In between these secure periods were centuries of political instability, social disorder, and foreign invasion.

The first great period of Egyptian history began around 3100 B.C. when Menes (mē′nēz), a king of southern Egypt, conquered the northern part of the country and established the city of Memphis as the capital of his united kingdom. During the long Old Kingdom period the essential features of Egyptian civilization were established. The development of the Egyptian system of writing, called *hieroglyphics* (hī′ər-ə glif′iks)—from Greek, *hieros* "sacred" and *glyphe* "a carving"—dates from the beginning of the Old Kingdom. Since there was close cultural contact between Egypt and Mesopotamia during this period, it is probable that the Egyptians borrowed the basic idea of writing from the Sumerians, using their own symbols to put the idea into effect. But unlike cuneiform, the Egyptian system of over seven hundred hieroglyphic characters was never simplified for practical purposes. A cursive equivalent of hieroglyphic, called *hieratic* ("priestly"), was developed for use on papyrus (pə pī′rəs), the paper the Egyptians manufactured from the reeds of the Nile.

In government, religion, science, and the arts, the Egyptians of the Old Kingdom developed characteristic ideas and patterns that were modified over the next two thousand years, but never fundamentally changed. One of the characteristic features of Egyptian civilization was a preoccupation with life after death. In contrast to the gloomy underworld of the Sumerians, the Egyptians pictured a peaceful afterlife in "the West," the sunset region of the dead. Because of their paramount importance to the very survival of Egypt, the fertilizing Nile and the ever-present sun assumed a corresponding importance in Egyptian thought. Egyptian literature is full of references to the life-giving river and sun, deified as the gods Osiris and Re.

Around 2200 B.C. famine and civil war brought the collapse of the Old Kingdom, and for nearly two hundred years rival leaders fought one another. Eventually princes from the city of Thebes reunified the country, beginning the period known as the Middle Kingdom. The government of the Middle Kingdom was generally weaker than that of the Old Kingdom, but Egypt was prosperous again and the arts flourished. By this time the Egyptian language had acquired considerable flexibility and expressiveness and much of the finest literature surviving from ancient Egypt dates from the Middle Kingdom. Shortly after 1800 B.C. the central government again collapsed and Egypt endured another period of civil war, followed by a century of rule by invaders from western Asia. Once more Theban leaders reunited the country, driving out the invaders and restoring native rule. This marked the beginning of the period called the New Kingdom, during which the Egyptians established an empire, conquering Syria and Israel, as well as the regions to the south of their country. The New Kingdom marked the height of Egyptian power and prosperity. The centuries that followed saw a slow ebbing of Egyptian greatness, until the country once again suffered foreign conquest, first by the Persians, then by Alexander the Great, later by the Romans, and finally by the Arabs.

ISRAEL

According to Jewish tradition recorded in the Bible, their ancestor Abraham was an inhabitant of the Mesopotamian city of Ur. (See the map on page 5.) This tradition suggests the probable route by which the nomadic tribes that would become the Jewish people reached the region that would become their homeland. Following the path of the Fertile Crescent, these nomads first migrated north, apparently settling in Haran about 1800 B.C. From there they went south and west and eventually occupied Canaan, a fertile strip of land on the eastern shore of the Mediterranean. Canaan formed part of "the Way of the Sea," the traditional route of armies moving north out of Egypt or south from the empires of the Hittites or the Assyrians.

The history of the Jews was a long struggle to escape domination by their powerful neighbors and preserve their political and religious independence. This struggle was occasionally successful, notably during the reigns of the great Jewish kings David (c. 1000–965 B.C.) and his son Solomon (c. 965–929 B.C.). But thereafter internal divisions weakened the Jewish state, which split into independent north-

A panel from a bas-relief picturing Jews forced into exile by the Assyrian king Sennacherib in 701 B.C.

ern and southern kingdoms. Israel, the northern kingdom, fell to the Assyrians in 722 B.C. Jerusalem, the capital of the southern kingdom, Judah, was destroyed in 586 B.C. by Nebuchadnezzar (neb'yə kəd nez'ər), king of Babylon. In the words of one historian, the king "carried off the noblest, richest, and ablest of the citizens to exile by the waters of Babylon." Before the Babylonian captivity the Jews already possessed the first five books of the Old Testament (called the *Torah*, or "Law"), which Jewish tradition ascribed to their greatest leader, Moses. In exile the Jewish community in Babylon studied their ancient writings and began to compare texts and establish the form of their sacred books.

The Jews were able to return to their homeland when the Persians under Cyrus the Great conquered Babylon around 538 B.C. But they were rarely politically independent thereafter, finally becoming part of the Roman empire. The Jews had little gift for conquest or government. Their lasting contribution to civilization was contained in their religious literature. As the poet Heinrich Heine observed of the Bible, "That one book is to the Jews their country." Through the Bible, the Jewish conception of a single, transcendent, invisible God whose divine will is manifest in human history has had an enormous impact on the development of human thought.

THINKING ABOUT GRAPHIC AIDS
Using the Time Line
The time line on pages 2–3 shows the chronological sequence of the historical and literary events discussed in Part 1. Use the time line to answer the following questions.

1. Who founded the Old Kingdom in Egypt? (**a**) Akhenaton; (**b**) Menes; (**c**) Cyrus
2. Who of the following could have seen the Pyramids? (**a**) Menes; (**b**) Moses; (**c**) Akhenaton
3. Who ended the Jewish exile in Babylon? (**a**) David; (**b**) Cyrus; (**c**) Solomon
4. During how long a period was the Old Testament taking shape? (**a**) less than 300 years; (**b**) around 400 years; (**c**) more than 500 years
5. At least how old a work was *The Epic of Gilgamesh* when Ashurbanipal added it to his royal library? (**a**) 1,300 years; (**b**) 1,500 years; (**c**) 2,000 years

Using the Map
The map on page 5 shows the geographical area occupied by the three civilizations that are discussed in Part 1. Use the map to answer the following questions.

1. What direction would you travel from Upper Egypt to Lower Egypt? (**a**) north; (**b**) south; (**c**) west
2. Which of the following places is *not* located in the Fertile Crescent? (**a**) Ur; (**b**) Jerusalem; (**c**) Thebes
3. Approximately how many miles would a traveler cover in a journey from Ur to Jerusalem along the Fertile Crescent? (**a**) 500; (**b**) 1,200; (**c**) 2,000
4. Would Gilgamesh have a longer or shorter journey to reach the seacoast today than in his own time?
5. What natural defenses against invasion did ancient Egypt possess?

The Epic of Gilgamesh

Detail of an Assyrian relief showing Gilgamesh holding a lion cub. 8th century B.C. Louvre

In London on the evening of December 3, 1872, a shy, thirty-two-year-old scholar named George Smith lectured to an overflow audience of the Biblical Archaeological Society that included Prime Minister Gladstone. What attracted the crowd was a discovery that Smith had recently made at the British Museum. He was deciphering the cuneiform inscriptions on some clay tablets that had been found in the ruins of the royal library of the Assyrian king Ashurbanipal. What Smith found was an ancient Mesopotamian account of a great flood that was remarkably similar to the story of Noah and the Ark in the Old Testament. He was so elated by his discovery that he began to dance around the room, astonishing his fellow scholars.

Smith's "Deluge Tablets" became a journalistic sensation, and one of the London newspapers put up the money to enable him to go to Mesopotamia and search for the tablets containing a missing portion of the narrative. He was no explorer, and the Near East in the nineteenth century was a difficult and dangerous place to conduct archaeological digs. Despite these obstacles, he succeeded almost immediately in finding the missing tablets. But Smith's good fortune then deserted him, and he became ill and died on his return journey.

The Deluge Tablets were part of the greatest surviving work of Mesopotamian literature, *The Epic of Gilgamesh*. Its author is unknown. Originally composed in the Babylonian language about 2000 B.C., *The Epic of Gilgamesh* was based on an earlier cycle of Sumerian poems whose hero was Gilgamesh (gēl'gä mesh), a legendary king of Uruk. The deeds of this king made him so famous that he became the supreme hero of Sumerian literature. Poems about the adventures of Gilgamesh were composed not only in Sumerian and Babylonian, but also in most of the other major languages of western Asia. Ashurbanipal, who lived in the seventh century B.C., was very interested in what was already in his day ancient literature. He had the writings of the earlier peoples of Mesopotamia, including *The Epic of Gilgamesh*, collected and translated into Akkadian, the language of his empire. Some three thousand lines in length, the Akkadian version of *The Epic of Gilgamesh* covered twelve large tablets in Ashurbanipal's library.

The Epic of Gilgamesh has been described as "a protest against death." Like other epics, the poem contains stories of heroic adventures, but the central episode is the quest of Gilgamesh to discover the secret of everlasting life. He fails in his search, and the epic expresses a heroic but somber view of human life that was a basic part of the civilization of the Mesopotamian peoples. Their mythology and cultural values in turn influenced the spiritual development of both Israel and Greece.

from The Epic of Gilgamesh

translated by **N. K. Sandars**

The Epic of Gilgamesh opens with a prologue that introduces the hero and summarizes the action of the whole poem. The narrative itself begins with an account of how Gilgamesh first fights and then befriends the wild man Enkidu (en′kē dü). Together, Gilgamesh and Enkidu perform a series of heroic deeds. They destroy a giant named Humbaba who lives in the cedar forests of Lebanon. They also kill the Bull of Heaven, a monster sent against them by the fierce goddess of love and war, Ishtar (ēsh′tär), who is angry with Gilgamesh for rejecting her love. She revenges herself on the hero by cursing his friend, who falls ill and dies.

The Prologue

 will proclaim to the world the deeds of Gilgamesh. This was the man to whom all things were known; this was the king who knew the countries of the world. He was wise, he saw mysteries and knew secret things, he brought us a tale of the days before the flood. He went on a long journey, was weary, worn-out with labor, returning he rested, he engraved on a stone the whole story.

When the gods created Gilgamesh they gave him a perfect body. Shamash the glorious sun endowed him with beauty, Adad the god of the storm endowed him with courage, the great gods made his beauty perfect, surpassing all others, terrifying like a great wild bull. Two thirds they made him god and one third man.

In Uruk he built walls, a great rampart, and the temple of blessed Eanna[1] for the god of the firmament Anu, and for Ishtar the goddess of love. Look at it still today: the outer wall where the cornice runs, it shines with the brilliance of copper; and the inner wall, it has no equal. Touch the threshold, it is ancient. Approach Eanna the dwelling of Ishtar, our lady of love and war, the like of which no latter-day king, no man alive can equal. Climb upon the wall of Uruk; walk along it, I say; regard the foundation terrace and examine the masonry: is it not burnt brick and good? The seven sages[2] laid the foundations. . . .

The Lament for Enkidu

Ten days Enkidu lay and his suffering increased, eleven and twelve days he lay on his bed of pain. Then he called to Gilgamesh, "My friend, the great goddess cursed me and I must die in shame. I shall not die like a man fallen in battle; I feared to fall, but happy is the man who falls in the battle, for I must die in shame." And Gilgamesh wept over Enkidu. With the first light

---

1. *Eanna* (e ä′nä), the name given at Uruk to the area that held the temples of Anu and Ishtar.
2. *seven sages*, wise men who brought civilization to the seven oldest cities of Mesopotamia.

Comment

The Gods of Mesopotamia

Like the Greeks and Romans, the peoples of ancient Mesopotamia worshiped similar gods under different names. The beautiful, treacherous goddess that the Greeks called *Aphrodite* and the Romans *Venus*, the Sumerians called *Inanna* (ē nä′nä) and the Babylonians *Ishtar* (ēsh′tär). The gods in *The Epic of Gilgamesh* have their Babylonian names. The following figures appear in the sections of the epic you are reading.

Adad (ä′däd), a storm god
Annunaki (ä nü nä′kē), gods of the underworld who judge the dead

Anu (ä′nü), god of the "firmament"—the heavens, the region above the sky
Ea (e′ä), god of wisdom
Enlil (en′lēl), god of air and wind
Ennugi (en nü′gē), god of canals
Hanish (hä′nēsh), a storm god
Ishtar, Queen of Heaven, goddess of love and war
Nergal (nėr′gäl), god of the underworld
Ninurta (nē nür′tä), a war god
Shamash (shä′mäsh), sun god
Shullat (shül′lät), a storm god

---

of dawn he raised his voice and said to the counsellors of Uruk:

"Hear me, great ones of Uruk,
I weep for Enkidu, my friend,
Bitterly moaning like a woman mourning
I weep for my brother.
5 O Enkidu, my brother,
You were the axe at my side,
My hand's strength, the sword in my belt,
The shield before me,
A glorious robe, my fairest ornament;
10 An evil Fate has robbed me.
The wild ass and the gazelle
That were father and mother,
All long-tailed creatures that nourished you
Weep for you,
15 All the wild things of the plain and pastures;
The paths that you loved in the forest of cedars
Night and day murmur.
Let the great ones of strong-walled Uruk
Weep for you;
20 Let the finger of blessing
Be stretched out in mourning;
Enkidu, young brother. Hark,
There is an echo through all the country
Like a mother mourning.
25 Weep all the paths where we walked together;
And the beasts we hunted, the bear and hyena,
Tiger and panther, leopard and lion,
The stag and the ibex, the bull and the doe.
The river along whose banks we used to walk,
30 Weeps for you,
Ula of Elam[3] and dear Euphrates
Where once we drew water for the water-skins.
The mountain we climbed where we slew the
    Watchman,[4]
Weeps for you.
35 The warriors of strong-walled Uruk
Where the Bull of Heaven was killed,
Weep for you.
All the people of Eridu
Weep for you, Enkidu.
40 Those who brought grain for your eating
Mourn for you now;
Who rubbed oil on your back
Mourn for you now;
Who poured beer for your drinking
45 Mourn for you now.
The harlot who anointed you with fragrant
    ointment
Laments for you now;
The women of the palace, who brought you a
    wife,
A chosen ring of good advice,

---

3. *Ula of Elam.* The river Ula (ü′lä) flowed down from the Zagros Mountains in Elam (ē′läm), the region east of Sumeria.
4. *the Watchman,* the giant Humbaba, the guardian of the cedar forest of Lebanon.

50 Lament for you now.
And the young men your brothers
As though they were women
Go long-haired in mourning.
What is this sleep which holds you now?
55 You are lost in the dark and cannot hear me."

He touched his heart but it did not beat, nor did he lift his eyes again. When Gilgamesh touched his heart it did not beat. So Gilgamesh laid a veil, as one veils the bride, over his friend. He began to rage like a lion, like a lioness robbed of her whelps. This way and that he paced round the bed, he tore out his hair and strewed it around. He dragged off his splendid robes and flung them down as though they were abominations.

In the first light of dawn Gilgamesh cried out, "I made you rest on a royal bed, you reclined on a couch at my left hand, the princes of the earth kissed your feet. I will cause all the people of Uruk to weep over you and raise the dirge of the dead. The joyful people will stoop with sorrow; and when you have gone to the earth I will let my hair grow long for your sake, I will wander through the wilderness in the skin of a lion." The next day also, in the first light, Gilgamesh lamented; seven days and seven nights he wept for Enkidu, until the worm fastened on him. Only then he gave him up to the earth, for the Anunnaki, the judges, had seized him. . . .

Bitterly Gilgamesh wept for his friend Enkidu; he wandered over the wilderness as a hunter, he roamed over the plains; in his bitterness he cried, "How can I rest, how can I be at peace? Despair is in my heart. What my brother is now, that shall I be when I am dead. Because I am afraid of death I will go as best I can to find Utnapishtim whom they call the Faraway, for he has entered the assembly of the gods." So Gilgamesh travelled over the wilderness, he wandered over the grasslands, a long journey, in search of Utnapishtim, whom the gods took after the deluge; and they set him to live in the land of Dilmun, in the garden of the sun; and to him alone of men they gave everlasting life.[5]

---

5. *Utnapishtim . . . life.* Utnapishtim (üt nä pēsh′tēm) was an immortal being who lived in the remote island of paradise of Dilmun (dēl′mün), beyond the waters of death.

THINK AND DISCUSS
Understanding
1. What qualities and deeds of Gilgamesh are emphasized by being included in the Prologue?
2. What reflection on the death of Enkidu causes Gilgamesh to despair?

Analyzing
3. The Prologue mentions that Gilgamesh, on returning from his journey, "engraved on a stone the whole story." What does this reference suggest about the place of writing in Mesopotamian civilization?
4. In his Lament for Enkidu, how does Gilgamesh universalize the grief he feels for his friend?

Extending
5. Discuss how this first section of *The Epic of Gilgamesh* might be described as "a protest against death."

APPLYING: Figurative Language HT
See Handbook of Literary Terms, p. 947.
   Figurative language is language used in a nonliteral way to express a suitable relationship between essentially unlike things. In the Prologue to *The Epic of Gilgamesh*, for example, the hero is described as "terrifying like a wild bull." This phrase employs figurative language to convey the quality of fearsomeness shared by the hero and a wild beast. Examine lines 6–9 of the Lament for Enkidu.

1. To what different things does Gilgamesh compare his dead friend?
2. How does each of these comparisons provide a suitable and appropriate description of the relationship between the two men?

ENRICHMENT
Researching Mesopotamian Archaeology
   For more information on George Smith and his discovery of the Deluge Tablets, consult Brian M. Fagan's *Return to Babylon: Travelers, Archaeologists, and Monuments in Mesopotamia.* (Little, Brown, 1979)

The Epic of Gilgamesh 11

Horrified by the prospect of his own death, Gilgamesh flees Uruk, in search of the secret of everlasting life. His quest brings him at last to Utnapishtim (üt nä pēsh′tēm), an immortal being who lives in a remote island paradise beyond the waters of death. Utnapishtim and his family were the only survivors of a great flood sent by the gods to destroy humanity. Utnapishtim tells Gilgamesh the story of the flood.

The Story of the Flood

"You know the city Shurrupak,[6] it stands on the banks of Euphrates? That city grew old and the gods that were in it were old. There was Anu, lord of the firmament, their father, and warrior Enlil their counsellor, Ninurta the helper, and Ennugi watcher over canals; and with them also was Ea. In those days the world teemed, the people multiplied, the world bellowed like a wild bull, and the great god was aroused by the clamor. Enlil heard the clamor and he said to the gods in council, 'The uproar of mankind is intolerable and sleep is no longer possible by reason of the babel.' So the gods agreed to exterminate mankind. Enlil did this, but Ea because of his oath[7] warned me in a dream. He whispered their words to my house of reeds, 'Reed-house, reed-house! Wall, O wall, hearken reed-house, wall reflect; O man of Shurrupak, son of Ubara-Tutu; tear down your house and build a boat, abandon possessions and look for life, despise worldly goods and save your soul alive. Tear down your house, I say, and build a boat. These are the measurements of the barque as you shall build her: let her beam equal her length, let her deck be roofed like the vault that covers the abyss;[8] then take up into the boat the seed of all living creatures.'

"When I had understood I said to my lord, 'Behold, what you have commanded I will honor and perform, but how shall I answer the people, the city, the elders?' Then Ea opened his mouth and said to me, his servant, 'Tell them this: I have learnt that Enlil is wrathful against me, I dare no longer walk in his land nor live in his city; I will go down to the Gulf[9] to dwell with Ea my lord. But on you he will rain down abundance, rare fish and shy wild-fowl, a rich harvest-tide. In the evening the rider of the storm[10] will bring you wheat in torrents.'

"In the first light of dawn all my household gathered round me, the children brought pitch and the men whatever was necessary. On the fifth day I laid the keel and the ribs, then I made fast the planking. The ground-space was one acre, each side of the deck measured one hundred and twenty cubits,[11] making a square. I built six decks below, seven in all, I divided them into nine sections with bulkheads between. I drove in wedges where needed, I saw to the punt-poles, and laid in supplies. The carriers brought oil in baskets, I poured pitch into the furnace and asphalt and oil; more oil was consumed in caulking, and more again the master of the boat took into his stores. I slaughtered bullocks for the people and every day I killed sheep. I gave the shipwrights wine to drink as though it were river water, raw wine and red wine and oil and white wine. There was feasting then as there is at the time of the New Year's festival; I myself anointed my head. On the seventh day the boat was complete.

"Then was the launching full of difficulty; there was shifting of ballast above and below till two thirds was submerged. I loaded into her all that I

---

6. Shurrupak (shür′rü päk), one of the oldest cities of Mesopotamia, located northwest of Uruk.
7. because of his oath. Utnapishtim is under the special protection of the god Ea. In order not to violate the agreement of the gods, Ea does not speak directly to Utnapishtim, but gives the message to the walls of his protege's house.
8. vault . . . abyss, the firmament, the vault of the sky.
9. the Gulf, the Persian Gulf.
10. the rider of the storm, the god Adad.
11. one hundred and twenty cubits, 180 feet.

had of gold and of living things, my family, my kin, the beasts of the field both wild and tame, and all the craftsmen. I sent them on board, for the time that Shamash had ordained was already fulfilled when he said, 'In the evening, when the rider of the storm sends down the destroying rain, enter the boat and batten her down.' The time was fulfilled, the evening came, the rider of the storm sent down the rain. I looked out at the weather and it was terrible, so I too boarded the boat and battened her down. All was now complete, the battening and the caulking; so I handed the tiller to Puzur-Amurri the steersman, with the navigation and the care of the whole boat.

"With the first light of dawn a black cloud came from the horizon; it thundered within where Adad, lord of the storm was riding. In front over hill and plain Shullat and Hanish, heralds of the storm, led on. Then the gods of the abyss rose up; Nergal pulled out the dams of the nether waters, Ninurta the war-lord threw down the dykes, and the seven judges of hell, the Annunaki, raised their torches, lighting the land with their livid flame. A stupor of despair went up to heaven when the god of the storm turned daylight to darkness, when he smashed the land like a cup. One whole day the tempest raged, gathering fury as it went, it poured over the people like the tides of battle; a man could not see his brother nor the people be seen from heaven. Even the gods were terrified at the flood, they fled to the highest heaven, the firmament of Anu; they crouched against the walls, cowering like curs. Then Ishtar the sweet-voiced Queen of Heaven cried out like a woman in travail: 'Alas the days of old are turned to dust because I commanded evil; why did I command this evil in the council of all the gods? I commanded wars to destroy the people, but are they not my people, for I brought them forth? Now like the spawn of fish they float in the ocean.' The great gods of heaven and of hell wept, they covered their mouths.

"For six days and six nights the winds blew, torrent and tempest and flood overwhelmed the world, tempest and flood raged together like warring hosts. When the seventh day dawned the storm from the south subsided, the sea grew calm, the flood was stilled; I looked at the face of the world and there was silence, all mankind was turned to clay. The surface of the sea stretched as flat as a roof-top; I opened a hatch and the light fell on my face. Then I bowed low, I sat down and I wept, the tears streamed down my face, for on every side was the waste of water. I looked for land in vain, but fourteen leagues distant there appeared a mountain, and there the boat grounded; on the mountain of Nisir[12] the boat held fast, she held fast and did not budge. One day she held, and a second day on the mountain of Nisir she held fast and did not budge. A third day, and a fourth day she held fast on the mountain and did not budge; a fifth day and a sixth day she held fast on the mountain. When the seventh day dawned I loosed a dove and let her go. She flew away, but finding no resting-place she returned. Then I loosed a swallow, and she flew away but finding no resting-place she returned. I loosed a raven, she saw that the waters had retreated, she ate, she flew around, she cawed, and she did not come back. Then I threw everything open to the four winds, I made a sacrifice and poured out a libation on the mountain top. Seven and again seven cauldrons I set up on their stands, I heaped up wood and cane and cedar and myrtle. When the gods smelled the sweet savor, they gathered like flies over the sacrifice. Then, at last, Ishtar also came, she lifted her necklace with the jewels of heaven that once Anu had made to please her. 'O you gods here present, by the lapis lazuli round my neck I shall remember these days as I remember the jewels of my throat; these last days I shall not forget. Let all the gods gather round the sacrifice, except Enlil. He shall not approach this offering, for without reflection he brought the flood; he consigned my people to destruction.'

"When Enlil had come, when he saw the boat, he was wroth and swelled with anger at the gods, the host of heaven, 'Has any of these mortals escaped? Not one was to have survived the destruction.' Then the god of the wells and canals Ninurta opened his mouth and said to the warrior Enlil, 'Who is there of the gods that can devise

---

12. *Nisir* (nē'sēr), "mountain of salvation," equivalent to Mt. Ararat in Genesis.

without Ea? It is Ea alone who knows all things.' Then Ea opened his mouth and spoke to warrior Enlil, 'Wisest of gods, hero Enlil, how could you so senselessly bring down the flood?

Lay upon the sinner his sin,
Lay upon the transgressor his transgression,
Punish him a little when he breaks loose,
Do not drive him too hard or he perishes;
5 Would that a lion had ravaged mankind
Rather than the flood,
Would that a wolf had ravaged mankind
Rather than the flood,
Would that famine had wasted the world
10 Rather than the flood,
Would that pestilence had wasted mankind
Rather than the flood.

It was not I that revealed the secret of the gods; the wise man learned it in a dream. Now take your counsel what shall be done with him.'

"Then Enlil went up into the boat, he took me by the hand and my wife and made us enter the boat and kneel down on either side, he standing between us. He touched our foreheads to bless us saying, 'In time past Utnapishtim was a mortal man; henceforth he and his wife shall live in the distance at the mouth of the rivers.' Thus it was that the gods took me and placed me here to live in the distance, at the mouth of the rivers."

Utnapishtim said, "As for you, Gilgamesh, who will assemble the gods for your sake, so that you may find that life for which you are searching?"

The Return

Then Gilgamesh and Urshanabi[13] launched the boat on to the water and boarded it, and they made ready to sail away; but the wife of Utnapishtim the Faraway said to him, "Gilgamesh came here wearied out, he is worn out; what will you give him to carry him back to his own country?" So Utnapishtim spoke, and Gilgamesh took a pole and brought the boat in to the bank. "Gilgamesh, you came here a man wearied out, you have worn yourself out; what shall I give you to carry you back to your own country? Gilgamesh, I shall reveal a secret thing, it is a mystery of the gods that I am telling you. There is a plant that grows under the water, it has a prickle like a thorn, like a rose; it will wound your hands, but if you succeed in taking it, then your hands will hold that which restores his lost youth to a man."

When Gilgamesh heard this he opened the sluices so that a sweet-water current might carry him out to the deepest channel; he tied heavy stones to his feet and they dragged him down to the water-bed. There he saw the plant growing; although it pricked him he took it in his hands; then he cut the heavy stones from his feet, and the sea carried him and threw him on to the shore. Gilgamesh said to Urshanabi the ferryman, "Come here, and see this marvellous plant. By its virtue a man may win back all his former strength. I will take it to Uruk of the strong walls; there I will give it to the old men to eat. Its name shall be 'The Old Men Are Young Again'; and at last I shall eat it myself and have back all my lost youth." So Gilgamesh returned by the gate through which he had come, Gilgamesh and Urshanabi went together. They travelled their twenty leagues and then they broke their fast; after thirty leagues they stopped for the night.

Gilgamesh saw a well of cool water and he went down and bathed; but deep in the pool there was lying a serpent, and the serpent sensed the sweetness of the flower. It rose out of the water and snatched it away, and immediately it sloughed its skin and returned to the well. Then Gilgamesh sat down and wept, the tears ran down his face, and he took the hand of Urshanabi; "O Urshanabi, was it for this that I toiled with my hands, is it for this I have wrung out my heart's blood? For myself I have gained nothing; not I, but the beast of the earth has joy of it now. Already the stream has carried it twenty leagues back to the channels where I found it. I found a sign and now I have lost it. Let us leave the boat on the bank and go."

After twenty leagues they broke their fast, after thirty leagues they stopped for the night; in three days they had walked as much as a journey of a

---

13. *Urshanabi* (ŭr shä nä′bē), boatman who ferries daily across the waters of death; reminiscent of Charon in classical mythology.

month and fifteen days. When the journey was accomplished they arrived at Uruk, the strong-walled city. Gilgamesh spoke to him, to Urshanabi the ferryman, "Urshanabi, climb up on to the wall of Uruk, inspect its foundation terrace, and examine well the brickwork; see if it is not of burnt bricks; and did not the seven wise men lay these foundations? One third of the whole is city, one third is garden, and one third is field, with the precinct of the goddess Ishtar. These parts and the precinct are all Uruk."

This too was the work of Gilgamesh, the king, who knew the countries of the world. He was wise, he saw mysteries and knew secret things, he brought us a tale of the days before the flood. He went on a long journey, was weary, worn out with labor, and returning engraved on a stone the whole story.

c. 2000 B.C.

THINK AND DISCUSS

Understanding
1. How does Utnapishtim acquire immortality?
2. How does Gilgamesh find and lose the miraculous plant?
3. What does Gilgamesh show to Urshanabi when they reach Uruk?

Analyzing
4. Why do the gods repent their decision to destroy humanity?
5. Why does Gilgamesh show Urshanabi the walls of Uruk?

Extending
6. One widespread ancient belief held that people were responsible for the misdeeds of their parents. How does this view contrast with the one expressed by the god Ea in *The Epic of Gilgamesh*: "Lay upon the sinner his sin/Lay upon the transgressor his transgression"?

APPLYING: Archetype **H⫶**
See Handbook of Literary Terms, p. 941.

An **archetype** is an image, story-pattern, or character that recurs frequently in literature and evokes strong, often unconscious, associations in the reader. Traditional literature like *The Epic of Gilgamesh* is often rich in archetypal elements. Gilgamesh himself is the first example in literature of one archetype, the strong man who performs a series of heroic deeds, like Samson or Hercules. Identify elements in *The Epic of Gilgamesh* that correspond to the following archetypes:

1. the hero's companion in adventure (like Little John in the Robin Hood stories)
2. the only survivor of a great flood (like Noah)
3. a garden where death does not exist (like Eden)

VOCABULARY

Context
Use context clues to determine the meaning of the italicized word in each of the following passages from *The Epic of Gilgamesh*. Write the meaning of each word on a separate sheet of paper and use each of the italicized words in a sentence of your own that shows you understand its meaning.

1. ". . . And the beasts we hunted, the bear and the hyena,/Tiger and panther, leopard and lion,/The stag and the *ibex*, the bull and the doe."
2. "The uproar of mankind is intolerable and sleep is no longer possible by reason of the *babel*."
3. "Tear down your house, I say, and build a boat. These are the measurements of the *barque* as you shall build her . . ."
4. "O you gods here present, by the *lapis lazuli* round my neck I shall remember these days as I remember the jewels of my throat . . ."
5. "Lay upon the sinner his sin,/Lay upon the transgressor his *transgression* . . ."

Egyptian Poetry

The cultural self-confidence created by the long peace and prosperity of the Old Kingdom period is attested to by the simplicity and grandeur of the Pyramids. These colossal structures were built as a combination of temple and tomb for the kings of Egypt, the *pharaohs* (fer'ōz), who were worshipped as gods. Old Kingdom literature was largely sacred and impersonal in character, the official hymns of the theocratic Egyptian state. It was not until the stability of the Old Kingdom had given way to a period of social disorder that a new type of literature appeared. During these hard times and the Middle Kingdom period that followed, people begin to express their personal feelings about the world in which they live. As a result, Middle Kingdom literature often lacks the serenity of much of the writing of the Old Kingdom. It is sometimes bitter or fearful in tone. One example of this new sensibility is "A Dialogue of a Man with His Soul" (page 17). A dialogue is a literary work in the form of a conversation between two or more people. The conversation here is between an unhappy man and his soul, or *ba*, conceived by the Egyptians as a bird with a human head. (See the illustration on page 17.) In the portion of the dialogue included here, the man is speaking.

One of the most remarkable and controversial figures in Egyptian history was the New Kingdom Pharaoh Amenhotep IV, who reigned from 1379 to 1362 B.C. He appears to have rejected the polytheism of official Egyptian religion in favor of the worship of a single god, whom he identified with the *Aton*, the disk of the sun. Changing his name to *Akhenaton* (ä ke nä'tn), "It is well with Aton," he also moved his court from the ancient capital of Thebes to a new site, which is today called Tell el-Amarna. (See the map on page 5.) During the brief, weak reign of his successor, Tutankhamun (tü'tängk ä'mən), the official priesthood reasserted its control over the state religion and wiped out the effects of Akhenaton's theological revolution. The poem that appears on page 18 is one of his hymns to the sun.

Several small collections of love poems have survived from the New Kingdom period. Scholars date these texts to between 1300 and 1100 B.C. In all of these poems, the speaker, the "I" who addresses the reader, is a young person. In "I Was Simply Off to See Nefrus My Friend" (page 20), the speaker is a young woman; in "I Think I'll Go Home and Lie Very Still" (page 20), the speaker is a young man.

This illustration from a papyrus scroll shows the soul-bird, or *ba*, hovering over a mummified body. 1250 B.C. British Museum

from A Dialogue of a Man with His Soul

translated by **John A. Wilson**

With whom can I speak today?
One's companions are evil;
The friends of today do not love.
With whom can I speak today?
5 Hearts are filled with greed;
Every man seizes his neighbor's goods.
With whom can I speak today?
The gentle man has disappeared,
But the violent is accepted every-
    where. . . .
10 With whom can I speak today?
I am weighted down with misery
For lack of an intimate friend.
With whom can I speak today?
The evil which roams the earth,
15 It is without end.

Death is in my sight today
Like the recovery of a sick man,
Like the first going-out after an illness.
Death is in my sight today
20 Like the fragrance of myrrh,
Like sitting under an awning on a breezy
    day. . . .

Death is in my sight today
Like the passing-away of rain clouds,
Like the homecoming of men from a
    trip. . . .
25 Death is in my sight today
Like the longing of a man to see his
    home
After long years spent in captivity.

Why surely, he who is yonder[1]
Will be a living god,
30 Able to punish the sins of wrongdoers.
Why surely, he who is yonder
Will stand in the boat of the sun-god,
Assigning the best therefrom to the
    temples.
Why surely, he who is yonder
35 Will be a man of wisdom,
Free to voice his appeal to Re.[2]

c. 2000 B.C.

---

1. *yonder*, the world of the dead.
2. *Re* (rā), the sun-god of line 32.

from Akhenaton's Hymn to the Sun

translated by **John A. Wilson**

When thou settest in the western horizon,
The land is in darkness as if in death.
Men sleep in a room with heads wrapped up,
And no eye sees another.
5 Though all their goods under their heads be
    stolen,
Yet would they not perceive it.
Every lion comes forth from his den,
And all creeping things sting.
Darkness is a shroud and the earth is still,
10 For he who made them rests in his
    horizon.

At daybreak, when thou risest on the
    horizon,
When thou shinest as the sun disk by day,
Thou drivest away darkness and givest thy
    rays;
Then the Two Lands[1] are in daily festivity:
15 Men awake and stand upon their feet,
For thou hast raised them up.
They wash their bodies and take their
    clothing,
Their arms raised in praise at thy appearing.
And all the world, they do their work. . . .

20 How manifold it is,
What thou hast made!
It is hidden from the face of man.
Thou sole god, without thy like,
Thou didst create the world after thy desire,
25 Whilst thou wert alone:
All mankind, cattle and wild beasts,
Whatever goes by foot upon the earth,
Whatever flies on high with wings. . . .
The world came into being by thy hand,
30 According as thou didst make them all.
When thou hast risen they live,

A relief from the temple of Aton at Tell el-Amarna
showing Akhenaton, Queen Nefertiti, and one of their
daughters adoring the sun. Egyptian Museum, Cairo

When thou settest then they die.
Thou art lifetime thy own self,
For we live only through thee.
35 Eyes are fixed on beauty until thou settest,
All work is laid aside when thou settest in
    the west.
But when thou risest again,
Then everything is made to flourish. . . .

c. 1375 B.C.

---

1. *Two Lands,* Upper and Lower Egypt, united by Menes
around 3100 B.C.

A tomb painting of an ornamental fishpond. c. 1400 B.C. British Museum

Amarna Art

The religious revolution of the pharaoh Akhenaton (see page 16) was reflected in the art created for his new capital, Akhetaton ("The Horizon of Aton"), located on the Nile about halfway between Memphis and Thebes at a site known today as Tell el-Amarna. The central importance of the pharaoh as the living incarnation of *Aton*, the divine sun, is demonstrated by the frequency of the depiction of Akhenaton and his family in the paintings, sculptured reliefs, and other decorative art done for his capital. However, in a dramatic departure from the formal, idealized royal portraits typical of previous Egyptian art, the pharaoh, his wife, and his two daughters are portrayed in a variety of casual, domestic scenes and in a highly naturalistic manner, creating what is referred to as the Amarna style.

As one historian remarks, "No artist's subject was ever better fitted for naturalistic treatment than Akhenaton himself, for he was a strange-looking man with a scrawny neck, a pear-shaped torso, thin unmuscular legs, and a soft, sensitive mouth." These characteristics are evident in the relief that appears on the opposite page, which shows the pharaoh and his family worshiping the sun. The famous portrait sculpture of Akhenaton's beautiful queen, Nefertiti (see page 2), also displays the sensitive, closely observed naturalism of the Amarna style. According to one inscription, Bak, Akhenaton's chief sculptor, was instructed in the creation of this style by the pharaoh himself. But the delight in natural form that appears in the painting above, from a tomb that slightly antedates Akhenaton's reign, suggests that some of the cultural values that went to shape the Amarna style were already present in Egyptian art. The influence of Akhenaton's cultural revolution survived briefly into the short reign of his successor, Tutankhamun. The illustration on page 20 shows Tutankhamun and his queen, Ankhesenamun, who was one of Akhenaton's daughters. This scene of the young queen rubbing scented oil on her husband still shows the freedom of Amarna art in the depiction of family life and affection.

A golden panel from the back of the throne of Tutankhamun showing the young pharaoh and his wife. c. 1350 B.C. Egyptian Museum, Cairo

I Was Simply Off to See Nefrus My Friend

translated by **John L. Foster**

I was simply off to see Nefrus my friend,
Just to sit and chat at her place
                (about men),
When there, hot on his horses, comes Mehy
    (Oh god, I said to myself, it's Mehy!)
Right over the crest of the road
             wheeling along with the boys.

5 O Mother Hathor,[1] what shall I do?
    Don't let him see me!
                Where can I hide?
Make me a small creeping thing
    to slip by his eye
        (sharp as Horus')[2]
                    unseen.

Oh, look at you, feet—
    (this road is a river!)
        you walk me right out of my depth!
Someone, silly heart, is exceedingly ignorant
    here—
    aren't you a little too easy near Mehy?

If he sees that I see him, I know
    he will know how my heart flutters (Oh,
                 Mehy!)
10 I know I will blurt out,
    "Please take me!"
                (I mustn't)
No, all he would do is brag out my name,
    just one of the many . . . (I know) . . .
Mehy would make me just one of the girls
    for all of the boys in the palace
              (oh Mehy).

c. 1150 B.C.

---

1. *Mother Hathor* (hath'ôr), the goddess of love and joy.
2. *Horus* (hôr'əs), a sun god, child of Osiris and Isis. Horus was represented as having the head of a hawk.

I Think I'll Go Home and Lie Very Still

translated by **John L. Foster**

I think I'll go home and lie very still,
                feigning terminal illness.
Then the neighbors will all troop over to stare,
           my love, perhaps, among them.
How she'll smile while the specialists
              snarl in their teeth!—

        she perfectly well knows what ails me.
1300–1100 B.C.

THINK AND DISCUSS
Understanding
1. What problem does the speaker describe in the first stanza of "A Dialogue of a Man with His Soul"?
2. What account of the creation of the world does Akhenaton give in the last two stanzas of his "Hymn to the Sun"?
3. What scene does the speaker imagine in "I Think I'll Go Home and Lie Very Still"?
4. What portion of "I Was Simply Off to See Nefrus My Friend" describes what actually occurs? What portion describes the speaker's reaction?

Analyzing
5. What solution to his problem does the speaker contemplate in the second stanza of "A Dialogue of a Man with His Soul"?
6. Does Akhenaton indicate that the Sun-god cares about the fate of the beings he has created?
7. What "ails" the speaker in "I Think I'll Go Home and Lie Very Still"?
8. How does the speaker in "I Was Simply Off to See Nefrus My Friend" use **figurative language** in line 7?

Extending
9. How is the Mesopotamian view of the nature of the gods exhibited by *The Epic of Gilgamesh* like the Egyptian views expressed in "A Dialogue of a Man with His Soul" and Akhenaton's "Hymn to the Sun"? How is it different?
10. How are the personalities revealed by the speakers in the two love poems alike? How are they different?

APPLYING: Imagery HT
See Handbook of Literary Terms, p. 953.

Imagery is the sensory detail that provides vividness in a literary work. "Death is in my sight today/Like the fragrance of myrrh,/Like sitting under an awning on a breezy day. . . ." Concrete images like these tend to arouse feelings in readers that abstract language does not. The Egyptian poetry of the Middle and New Kingdom often conveys its quality of intense personal emotion through the use of vivid images drawn from everyday life.

1. In the first stanza of "A Dialogue of a Man with His Soul," the speaker defines the character of the world he sees through the use of abstract words like "evil," "greed," and "violent." How does the speaker's method change in the second stanza?
2. What qualities are shared by the images the speaker employs in the second stanza?
3. What feelings about death does the imagery of the second stanza express?

COMPOSITION ✒
Analyzing Patterns of Imagery
The images in a literary work often form a pattern. In one stanza of a poem, for example, the images might evoke spring, and in the next stanza, autumn. In a brief paper (2–3 paragraphs) examine Akhenaton's "Hymn to the Sun," for such patterns in the use of imagery. See "The Writing Process" in the Writer's Handbook.

Writing a Dialogue
Suppose the following: the speaker in "I Think I'll Go Home and Lie Very Still" is the "Mehy" of the other love poem; the speaker in "I Was Simply Off to See Nefrus My Friend" is the girl beloved by the speaker of the other poem; neither speaker is aware of the other's feelings. Write some dialogue that might be exchanged if they met by accident.

ENRICHMENT
Interpreting Egyptian Poetry
Select one of the Egyptian poems for oral interpretation. In preparing, be sure to consider the age, sex, and mood of the speaker in the poem. Notice changes of mood in the speaker that you can signal in your delivery of the lines.

The Old Testament

The Bible is not one book but a collection of many books including many different types of literature. Some individual portions of the Bible (often called "books") are themselves collections. The Book of Psalms contains 150 sacred songs; the Book of Proverbs includes over 500 wise sayings. Christians divide the Bible into two sections, the Old Testament, containing the laws, history, and literature of the Jews, and the New Testament. Jews do not include the New Testament in their Bibles. They divide the books of the Old Testament into three groups. The first group is made up of the five books traditionally ascribed to Moses. Referred to as the Torah (tôr′ə, from Hebrew, "law") or the Pentateuch (pen′tə-tük, from Greek, "five books"), these books contain the early history of the Jews and an account of their religious laws. The second group, called "the Prophets," continues the history of the Jews down to the time of the Babylonian exile and includes the sermons and visions attributed to various members of a unique class of Jewish religious reformers, the prophets. The third group, called simply "the Writings," is a miscellaneous collection that includes psalms, proverbs, moral tales, and love songs.

Despite these different categories, the subject of all these works is basically the same—the divine order of human events, the way in which God operates in history. But because these different works were composed at different times between the tenth and fifth centuries B.C., the vision of the divine order the Old Testament presents as a whole is an evolving one. The Jewish conception of God grows from a vengeful deity exclusively concerned with a single people, to a universal spirit of justice and mercy.

Nineteenth-century biblical scholars decided that the five books of the Torah were not the work of Moses, but rather of a number of different writers working from a variety of oral and written traditions several centuries after him. The first of these five books is called Genesis (jen′ə sis, from Greek, "be born") and most of it is devoted to the history of the tribal ancestors of the Jews, the patriarchs Abraham, Isaac, and Jacob. In order to set this history in the widest possible context, the first chapters of Genesis (page 23) give an account of the creation of the world and of the parents of the human race, Adam and Eve.

The brief Book of Ruth (page 27) is one of the miscellaneous group of "the Writings." It tells a simple story which the German writer Goethe described as the finest example in world literature of the brief, charming picture of country life called an idyll. The book was probably written after the Babylonian exile, but it is set over five hundred years earlier, in the time "when the judges ruled." The judges were the tribal military leaders of Israel in the period before the kingship was established under Saul, David, and Solomon. Ruth herself is presented as an ancestor of David—his great-grandmother. She is not a Jew, but a foreigner from the neighboring region of Moab. (See the map on page 5.) By recalling a tradition that the greatest of Jewish kings was the descendant of a foreigner, the Book of Ruth argues against religious intolerance and narrow nationalism.

The collection of the Psalms (page 33) is the hymn-book of the Jewish religion. Although 73 of the 150 lyrics were traditionally ascribed to David, most modern scholars date them to a far later period, the years immediately preceding and following the Babylonian exile. The range of ideas and feelings expressed in the Psalms is very wide. Psalms 8 and·19 are celebrations of the creative power of God. Psalms 23 and 90 are expressions of humility and trust in God. Psalm 137 recalls the anguish of exile "by the waters of Babylon."

from Genesis

The King James Translation

Chapter 1

n the beginning God created the heaven and the earth. And the earth was without form, and void; and darkness was upon the face of the deep. And the Spirit of God moved upon the face of the waters. And God said, "Let there be light": and there was light. And God saw the light, that it was good: and God divided the light from the darkness. And God called the light Day, and the darkness he called Night. And the evening and the morning were the first day.

And God said, "Let there be a firmament in the midst of the waters, and let it divide the waters from the waters." And God made the firmament, and divided the waters which were under the firmament from the waters which were above the firmament: and it was so. And God called the firmament Heaven. And the evening and the morning were the second day.

And God said, "Let the waters under the heaven be gathered together unto one place, and let the dry land appear": and it was so. And God called the dry land Earth; and the gathering together of the waters called he Seas: and God saw that it was good. And God said, "Let the earth bring forth grass, the herb yielding seed, and the fruit tree yielding fruit after his kind, whose seed is in itself,

upon the earth": and it was so. And the earth brought forth grass, and herb yielding seed after his kind, and the tree yielding fruit, whose seed was in itself, after his kind: and God saw that it was good. And the evening and the morning were the third day.

And God said, "Let there be lights in the firmament of the heaven to divide the day from the night; and let them be for signs, and for seasons, and for days, and years: and let them be for lights in the firmament of the heaven to give light upon the earth": and it was so. And God made two great lights; the greater light to rule the day, and the lesser light to rule the night: he made the stars also. And God set them in the firmament of the heaven to give light upon the earth. And to rule over the day and over the night, and to divide the light from the darkness: and God saw that it was good. And the evening and the morning were the fourth day.

And God said, "Let the waters bring forth abundantly the moving creature that hath life, and fowl that may fly above the earth in the open firmament of heaven." And God created great whales, and every living creature that moveth, which the waters brought forth abundantly, after their kind, and every winged fowl after his kind: and God saw that it was good. And God blessed them, saying,

"Be fruitful, and multiply, and fill the waters in the seas, and let fowl multiply in the earth." And the evening and the morning were the fifth day.

And God said, "Let the earth bring forth the living creature after his kind, cattle, and creeping thing, and beast of the earth after his kind": and it was so. And God made the beast of the earth after his kind, and cattle after their kind, and every thing that creepeth upon the earth after his kind: and God saw that it was good.

And God said, "Let us make man in our image,[1] after our likeness; and let them have dominion over the fish of the sea, and over the fowl of the air, and over the cattle, and over all the earth, and over every creeping thing that creepeth upon the earth." So God created man in his own image, in the image of God created he him; male and female created he them. And God blessed them, and God said unto them, "Be fruitful, and multiply, and replenish the earth, and subdue it: and have dominion over the fish of the sea, and over the fowl of the air, and over every living thing that moveth upon the earth."

And God said, "Behold, I have given you every herb bearing seed, which is upon the face of all the earth, and every tree, in the which is the fruit of a tree yielding seed; to you it shall be for meat. And to every beast of the earth, and to every fowl of the air, and to every thing that creepeth upon the earth, wherein there is life, I have given every green herb for meat": and it was so.

And God saw every thing that he had made, and behold, it was very good. And the evening and the morning were the sixth day.

Chapter 2

Thus the heavens and the earth were finished, and all the host of them. And on the seventh day God ended his work which he had made; and he rested on the seventh day from all his work which he had made. And God blessed the seventh day, and sanctified it: because that in it he had rested from all his work which God created and made.

These are the generations of the heavens and of the earth when they were created, in the day that the Lord God made the earth and the heavens, and every plant of the field before it was in

the earth, and every herb of the field before it grew: for the Lord God had not caused it to rain upon the earth, and there was not a man to till the ground. But there went up a mist from the earth, and watered the whole face of the ground. And the Lord God formed man of the dust of the ground,[2] and breathed into his nostrils the breath of life; and man became a living soul.

And the Lord God planted a garden eastward in Eden; and there he put the man whom he had formed. And out of the ground made the Lord God to grow every tree that is pleasant to the sight, and good for food; the tree of life[3] also in the midst of the garden, and the tree of knowledge of good and evil. . . .

And the Lord God took the man, and put him into the garden of Eden to dress it and to keep it. And the Lord God commanded the man, saying, "Of every tree of the garden thou mayest freely eat: but of the tree of the knowledge of good and evil, thou shalt not eat of it: for in the day that thou eatest thereof thou shalt surely die."

And the Lord God said, "It is not good that the man should be alone; I will make him an helpmeet for him." And out of the ground the Lord God formed every beast of the field, and every fowl of the air; and brought them unto Adam to see what he would call them: and whatsoever Adam called every living creature, that was the name thereof. And Adam gave names to all cattle, and to the fowl of the air, and to every beast of the field; but for Adam there was not found an helpmeet for him.

And the Lord God caused a deep sleep to fall upon Adam, and he slept: and he took one of his ribs, and closed up the flesh instead thereof; and the rib, which the Lord God had taken from man, made he a woman, and brought her unto the man.

And Adam said, "This is now bone of my bones, and flesh of my flesh: she shall be called Woman, because she was taken out of Man."

Therefore shall a man leave his father and his mother, and shall cleave unto his wife: and they

---

1. *us . . . our image.* This may refer to lesser beings in God's heavenly court.
2. *man . . . ground.* In the original Hebrew, the word for ground is *adamah* and the word for mankind is *adam.*
3. *tree of life.* Its fruit was believed to bring eternal life.

shall be one flesh. And they were both naked, the man and his wife, and were not ashamed.

Chapter 3

Now the serpent was more subtil than any beast of the field which the Lord God had made.

And he said unto the woman, "Yea, hath God said, 'Ye shall not eat of every tree of the garden'?"

And the woman said unto the serpent, "We may eat of the fruit of the trees of the garden: but of the fruit of the tree which is in the midst of the garden, God hath said, 'Ye shall not eat of it, neither shall ye touch it, lest ye die.' "

And the serpent said unto the woman, "Ye shall not surely die: for God doth know that in the day ye eat thereof, then your eyes shall be opened, and ye shall be as gods, knowing good and evil."

And when the woman saw that the tree was good for food, and that it was pleasant to the eyes, and a tree to be desired to make one wise, she took of the fruit thereof, and did eat, and gave also unto her husband with her; and he did eat. And the eyes of them both were opened, and they knew that they were naked; and they sewed fig leaves together, and made themselves aprons.

And they heard the voice of the Lord God walking in the garden in the cool of the day: and Adam and his wife hid themselves from the presence of the Lord God amongst the trees of the garden.

And the Lord God called unto Adam, and said unto him, "Where art thou?"

And he said, "I heard thy voice in the garden, and I was afraid, because I was naked; and I hid myself."

And he said, "Who told thee that thou wast naked? Has thou eaten of the tree, whereof I commanded thee that thou shouldest not eat?"

And the man said, "The woman whom thou gavest to be with me, she gave me of the tree, and I did eat."

And the Lord God said unto the woman, "What is this that thou hast done?"

And the woman said, "The serpent beguiled me, and I did eat."

And the Lord God said unto the serpent, "Because thou hast done this, thou art cursed above all cattle, and above every beast of the field; upon

An ivory plaque in the Phoenician style from the city of Megiddo showing a winged sphinx in a lotus thicket. 12th century B.C. The Cherubim set to guard Eden would have been conceived as similar creatures.

thy belly shalt thou go, and dust shalt thou eat all the days of thy life: and I will put enmity between thee and the woman, and between thy seed and her seed;[4] it shall bruise thy head, and thou shalt bruise his heel."

Unto the woman he said, "I will greatly multiply thy sorrow and thy conception; in sorrow thou shalt bring forth children; and thy desire shall be to thy husband, and he shall rule over thee."

And unto Adam he said, "Because thou hast hearkened unto the voice of thy wife, and hast eaten of the tree, of which I commanded thee, saying, 'Thou shalt not eat of it': cursed is the ground for thy sake; in sorrow shalt thou eat of it all the days of thy life. Thorns also and thistles shall it bring forth to thee; and thou shalt eat the herb of the field; in the sweat of thy face shalt thou eat bread, till thou return unto the ground; for out of it wast thou taken: for dust thou art, and unto dust shalt thou return."

And Adam called his wife's name Eve;[5] because she was the mother of all living. Unto Adam also

---

4. *seed,* children, descendants.
5. *Eve,* very close to the Hebrew word for "living."

and to his wife did the Lord God make coats of skins, and clothed them.

And the Lord God said, "Behold, the man is become as one of us, to know good and evil: and now, lest he put forth his hand, and take also of the tree of life, and eat, and live for ever": therefore the Lord God sent him forth from the garden of Eden, to till the ground from whence he was taken.

So he drove out the man; and he placed at the east of the garden of Eden Cherubims,[6] and a flaming sword which turned every way, to keep the way of the tree of life.

---

6. **Cherubims** (cher'ə bimz), winged angels.

THINK AND DISCUSS
Understanding
1. What exists before the creation of the world?
2. What repeated phrase describes God's response to what has been created?
3. What reason does God give for creating woman?
4. How do the animals receive their names?
5. How is the serpent characterized?
6. What is the first consequence of Adam and Eve's eating of the forbidden fruit?
7. How does Adam explain his disobedience? How does Eve explain hers?
8. Why does God exile Adam and Eve from Eden?

Analyzing
9. The first two chapters of Genesis contain differing accounts of the creation of human beings. How do the accounts differ?
10. How are the punishments God pronounces on Adam and Eve appropriate to each of them?

Extending
11. Eve's answer to the serpent (page 25) includes an addition to God's original command. Devise an explanation for how this addition was introduced.
12. Some have argued that it was unfair of God to place a tempting but forbidden tree in the Garden. Others feel that without the presence of the tree and the possibility of disobeying God, Adam and Eve would not have been fully human. What are your views?

13. Compare and contrast the role of the serpent as an **archetype** in *The Epic of Gilgamesh* and in Genesis.

THINKING SKILLS
Classifying
To classify things is to arrange them into classes or groups according to some system. For example, living things are classified as animals or vegetables; animals as mammals, birds, reptiles, insects, and so on.

1. Classify each of the things that God creates in Chapter 1 of Genesis according to the day on which it is created.
2. What is similar about the things created on the first and fourth days? on the second and fifth days? on the third and sixth days?

COMPOSITION
Writing a Dialogue
Write a brief dialogue between God and the serpent in which the latter defends its conduct. Recall your answers to questions 5 and 7 above in devising the serpent's explanation for its actions.

Analyzing Archetypes
The cultural traditions of many peoples contain archetypes of sacred trees like the Tree of Knowledge and the Tree of Life in Genesis. Write a three-paragraph paper comparing and contrasting these archetypes with a sacred tree from another culture. You might find the *Standard Dictionary of Folklore, Mythology, and Legend* (Funk & Wagnalls, 1949) helpful.

Ruth

The King James Translation

Chapter 1

ow it came to pass in the days when the judges ruled that there was a famine in the land. And a certain man of Bethlehem-Judah went to sojourn in the country of Moab,[1] he, and his wife, and his two sons.

And the name of the man was Elimelech, and the name of his wife Naomi,[2] and the name of his two sons Mahlon and Chilion, Ephrathites of Bethlehem-Judah. And they came into the country of Moab and continued there.

And Elimelech, Naomi's husband died; and she was left, and her two sons.

And they took them wives of the women of Moab; the name of the one was Orpah, and the name of the other Ruth: and they dwelled there about ten years.

And Mahlon and Chilion died also, both of them; and the woman was left of her two sons and her husband.

Then she arose with her daughters-in-law, that she might return from the country of Moab: for she had heard in the country of Moab how that the Lord had visited his people in giving them bread.

Wherefore she went forth out of the place where she was, and her two daughters-in-law with her; and they went on the way to return unto the land of Judah.

And Naomi said unto her two daughters-in-law, "Go, return each to her mother's house: the Lord deal kindly with you, as ye have dealt with the dead and with me. The Lord grant you that ye may find rest, each of you in the house of her husband."

Then she kissed them; and they lifted up their voice and wept.

And they said unto her, "Surely we will return with thee unto thy people."

And Naomi said, "Turn again, my daughters: why will ye go with me? Are there yet any more sons in my womb, that they may be your husbands?

"Turn again, my daughters, go your way; for I am too old to have a husband. If I should say I have hope, if I should have a husband also tonight and should also bear sons, would ye tarry for them till they were grown? Would ye stay for them from having husbands? Nay, my daughters; for it grieveth me much for your sakes that the hand of the Lord is gone out against me."

And they lifted up their voice and wept again: and Orpah kissed her mother-in-law, but Ruth clave unto her.

And she said, "Behold, thy sister-in-law is gone back unto her people and unto her gods: Return thou after thy sister-in-law."

And Ruth said, "Entreat me not to leave thee or to return from following after thee: for whither thou goest, I will go; and where thou lodgest, I will lodge: thy people shall be my people, and thy God my God: where thou diest, will I die, and there will I be buried: the Lord do so to me,[3] and more also, if ought but death part thee and me."

---

1. **Moab** (mō′ab), a country east of the Dead Sea; its people were often unfriendly to Israel.
2. **Naomi,** (nā ō′mē).
3. *do so to me,* punish me.

When she saw that she was steadfastly minded to go with her, then she left speaking unto her.

So they two went until they came to Bethlehem. And it came to pass, when they were come to Bethlehem, that all the city was moved about them, and they said, "Is this Naomi?"

And she said unto them, "Call me not Naomi, call me Mara:[4] for the Almighty hath dealt very bitterly with me. I went out full, and the Lord hath brought me home again empty: why then call ye me Naomi, seeing the Lord hath testified against me, and the Almighty hath afflicted me?"

So Naomi returned, and Ruth the Moabitess, her daughter-in-law, with her, which returned out of the country of Moab: and they came to Bethlehem in the beginning of barley harvest.

Chapter 2

And Naomi had a kinsman of her husband's, a mighty man of wealth, of the family of Elimelech; and his name was Boaz.[5]

And Ruth the Moabitess said unto Naomi, "Let me now go to the field and glean[6] ears of corn after him in whose sight I shall find grace." And she said unto her, "Go, my daughter."

And she went, and came, and gleaned in the field after the reapers: and her hap was to light on a part of the field belonging unto Boaz, who was of the kindred of Elimelech.

And, behold, Boaz came from Bethlehem and said unto the reapers, "The Lord be with you." And they answered him, "The Lord bless thee."

Then said Boaz unto his servant that was set over the reapers, "Whose damsel is this?"

And the servant that was set over the reapers answered and said, "It is the Moabitish damsel that came back with Naomi out of the country of Moab. And she said, 'I pray you, let me glean and gather after the reapers among the sheaves': so she came, and hath continued even from the morning until now, that she tarried a little in the house."

Then said Boaz unto Ruth, "Hearest thou not, my daughter? Go not to glean in another field, neither go from hence, but abide here fast by my maidens. Let thine eyes be on the field that they do reap, and go thou after them: have I not charged the young men that they shall not touch thee? And when thou art athirst, go unto the vessels, and drink of that which the young men have drawn."

Then she fell on her face and bowed herself to the ground and said unto him, "Why have I found grace in thine eyes, that thou shouldest take knowledge of me, seeing I am a stranger?"

And Boaz answered and said unto her, "It hath fully been showed me all that thou hast done unto thy mother-in-law since the death of thine husband: and how thou hast left thy father and thy mother, and the land of thy nativity and art come unto a people which thou knewest not heretofore. The Lord recompense thy work, and a full reward be given thee of the Lord God of Israel, under whose wings thou art come to trust."

Then she said, "Let me find favor in thy sight, my lord; for that thou hast comforted me, and for that thou hast spoken friendly unto thine handmaid, though I be not like unto one of thine handmaidens."

And Boaz said unto her, "At mealtime come thou hither, and eat of the bread, and dip thy morsel in the vinegar." And she sat beside the reapers: and he reached her parched corn, and she did eat, and was sufficed, and left.

And when she was risen up to glean, Boaz commanded his young men, saying, "Let her glean even among the sheaves, and reproach her not. And let fall also some of the handfuls on purpose for her, and leave them, that she may glean them, and rebuke her not."

So she gleaned in the field until even, and beat out that she had gleaned: and it was about an ephah[7] of barley.

And she took it up and went into the city: and her mother-in-law saw what she had gleaned: and she brought forth and gave to her what she had reserved after she was sufficed.

And her mother-in-law said unto her, "Where hast thou gleaned today? and where wroughtest thou? Blessed be he that did take knowledge of

---

4. **Naomi . . . Mara.** In Hebrew, *Naomi* means "pleasant"; *Mara* means "bitter."
5. **Boaz** (bō′az).
6. **glean**, gather fallen grains which, according to Jewish law, were left by the reapers for the poor.
7. **ephah** (ē′fə), about a bushel.

A detail from a miniature in a French illuminated manuscript of the Old Testament showing scenes from the story of Ruth. c. A.D. 1250. Pierpont Morgan Library, New York

thee." And she showed her mother-in-law with whom she had wrought, and said, "The man's name with whom I wrought today is Boaz."

And Naomi said unto her daughter-in-law, "Blessed be he of the Lord, who hath not left off his kindness to the living and to the dead." And Naomi said unto her, "The man is near of kin unto us, one of our next kinsmen."

And Ruth the Moabitess said, "He said unto me also, 'Thou shalt keep fast by my young men, until they have ended all my harvest.'"

And Naomi said unto Ruth her daughter-in-law, "It is good my daughter, that thou go out with his maidens, that they meet thee not in any other field."

So she kept fast by the maidens of Boaz to glean unto the end of barley harvest and of wheat harvest; and dwelt with her mother-in-law.

Chapter 3

Then Naomi her mother-in-law said unto her, "My daughter, shall I not seek rest for thee, that it may be well with thee? And now is not Boaz of our kindred,[8] with whose maidens thou wast? Behold, he winnoweth barley tonight in the threshingfloor.

Wash thyself therefore, and anoint thee, and put thy raiment upon thee, and get thee down to the floor: but make not thyself known unto the man, until he shall have done eating and drinking. And it shall be, when he lieth down, that thou shalt mark the place where he shall lie, and thou shalt go in and uncover his feet and lay thee down; and he will tell thee what thou shalt do."

And she said unto her, "All that thou sayest unto me I will do."

And she went down unto the floor and did according to all that her mother-in-law bade her.

And when Boaz had eaten and drunk and his heart was merry, he went to lie down at the end of the heap of corn: and she came softly and uncovered his feet and laid her down.

And it came to pass at midnight, that the man was afraid and turned himself: and, behold, a woman lay at his feet.

And he said, "Who art thou?" And she answered, "I am Ruth thine handmaid: spread

---

8. **kindred.** Since Ruth's husband left no brother to marry her, Jewish law required his nearest unmarried relative to wed her.

therefore thy skirt over thine handmaid; for thou art a near kinsman."

And he said, "Blessed be thou of the Lord, my daughter: for thou hast showed more kindness in the latter end than at the beginning, inasmuch as thou followedst not young men, whether poor or rich. And now, my daughter, fear not; I will do to thee all that thou requirest: for all the city of my people doth know that thou art a virtuous woman. And now it is true that I am thy near kinsman: howbeit, there is a kinsman nearer than I. Tarry this night, and it shall be in the morning that if he will perform unto thee the part of a kinsman, well; let him do the kinsman's part: but if he will not do the part of a kinsman to thee, then will I do the part of a kinsman to thee, as the Lord liveth: lie down until the morning."

And she lay at his feet until the morning: and she rose up before one could know another. And he said, "Let it not be known that a woman came into the floor."

Also he said, "Bring the vail[9] that thou hast upon thee, and hold it." And when she held it, he measured six measures of barley and laid it on her: and she went into the city.

And when she came to her mother-in-law, she said, "Who art thou, my daughter?" And she told her all that the man had done to her.

And she said, "These six measures of barley gave he me; for he said to me, 'Go not empty unto thy mother-in-law.' "

Then said she, "Sit still, my daughter, until thou know how the matter will fall: for the man will not be in rest until he have finished the thing this day."

Chapter 4

Then went Boaz up to the gate[10] and sat him down there: and, behold, the kinsman of whom Boaz spake came by; unto whom he said, "Ho, such a one! turn aside, sit down here." And he turned aside and sat down.

And he took ten men of the elders of the city and said, "Sit ye down here." And they sat down.

And he said unto the kinsman, "Naomi, that is come again out of the country of Moab, selleth a parcel of land, which was our brother Elimelech's.

And I thought to advertise thee, saying, Buy it before the inhabitants and before the elders of my people. If thou wilt redeem it, redeem it: but if thou wilt not redeem it, then tell me, that I may know: for there is none to redeem it beside thee; and I am after thee." And he said, "I will redeem it."

Then said Boaz, "What day thou buyest the field of the hand of Naomi, thou must buy it also of Ruth the Moabitess, the wife of the dead, to raise up the name of the dead upon his inheritance."

And the kinsman said, "I cannot redeem it for myself, lest I mar mine own inheritance: redeem thou my right to thyself; for I cannot redeem it."

Now this was the manner in former time in Israel concerning redeeming and concerning changing, for to confirm all things; a man plucked off his shoe, and gave it to his neighbor: and this was a testimony in Israel.

Therefore the kinsman said unto Boaz, "Buy it for thee." So he drew off his shoe.

And Boaz said unto the elders and unto all the people, "Ye are witnesses this day, that I have bought all that was Elimelech's, and all that was Chilion's and Mahlon's, of the hand of Naomi. Morover, Ruth the Moabitess, the wife of Mahlon, have I purchased[11] to be my wife, to raise up the name of the dead upon his inheritance, that the name of the dead be not cut off from among his brethren and from the gate of his place: ye are witnesses this day."

And all the people that were in the gate and the elders said, "We are witnesses. The Lord make the woman that is come into thine house like Rachel and like Leah,[12] which two did build the house of Israel: and do thou worthily in Ephratah, and be famous in Bethlehem. And let thy house be like the house of Pharez,[13] whom Tamar bare unto Judah,

---

9. *vail*, cloak.
10. *gate*, where legal agreements were made before witnesses.
11. *Ruth . . . have I purchased*, that is, purchased the right to marry Ruth.
12. *Rachel . . . Leah*, wives of Jacob, "mothers of Israel."
13. *Pharez*. Judah's son Pharez was an ancestor of Boaz, born to a widow who, like Ruth, claimed the right of kinship.

of the seed which the Lord shall give thee of this young woman."

So Boaz took Ruth, and she was his wife: and when he went in unto her, the Lord gave her conception, and she bare a son.

And the women said unto Naomi, "Blessed be the Lord, which hath not left thee this day without a kinsman, that his name may be famous in Israel. And he shall be unto thee a restorer of thy life and a nourisher of thine old age: for thy daughter-in-law, which loveth thee, which is better to thee than seven sons, hath born him."

And Naomi took the child and laid it in her bosom and became nurse unto it.

And the women her neighbors gave it a name, saying, "There is a son born to Naomi"; and they called his name Obed: he is the father of Jesse, the father of David.

Now these are the generations of Pharez: Pharez begat Hezron, and Hezron begat Ram, and Ram begat Amminadab, and Amminadab begat Nahshon, and Nahshon begat Salmon, and Salmon begat Boaz, and Boaz begat Obed, and Obed begat Jesse, and Jesse begat David.

THINK AND DISCUSS
Understanding
1. Why does Naomi's family leave Israel? Why does she return?
2. Why does Naomi say that she should be known as "Mara"?
3. For what two reasons does Ruth go to glean grain in the fields?
4. What advice does Naomi give to Ruth?
5. What must Boaz do before he can marry Ruth?

Analyzing
6. The author of Ruth sets the story "in the days when the judges ruled." What other evidence is there to indicate that this story takes place in a remote period?
7. Ruth's eloquent refusal to leave Naomi is one of the most famous speeches in the Old Testament. What feature characterizes the construction of this passage?
8. What do you think is the moment of greatest suspense in this story? What techniques are used to increase the tension of this moment?
9. Why do you think the story of Ruth concludes with a genealogy?

Extending
10. Do you think Ruth is correct in valuing her relationship to her mother-in-law more than her ties to her homeland?

APPLYING: Theme HⱫ
See Handbook of Literary Terms, page 975.

The **theme** is the underlying meaning of a literary work. A theme may be directly stated, but more often it is implied. Examine the response of Boaz to Ruth's question, "Why have I found grace in thine eyes, that thou shouldest take knowledge of me, seeing I am a stranger?" (See page 28.)

1. Does Boaz appear to admire or condemn Ruth for preferring Naomi to her homeland?
2. Does his response suggest that God's care extends only to the people of Israel?
3. What is the theme of the story of Ruth?
4. Is this theme directly stated or implied?

VOCABULARY
Archaic Words
Because the King James version of the Bible was done early in the seventeenth century, many of the words that the translators used have become *archaic;* that is, they are no longer employed in ordinary language. The following list contains some of the archaic words you encountered in the King James translation of Ruth. Look up in the Glossary the meanings of any words you do not know, and then on a separate sheet of paper write a sentence using each of the words.

howbeit	hap	fast
clave	damsel	spake

Reading BIBLICAL POETRY

Among the many types of literature included in the Old Testament is a great deal of poetry. Some of it is in collections, like the Psalms. Some of it is included in other books, like the Song of Deborah, which is part of the Book of Judges. One brief book, the Song of Songs, is formed of a single poem. The following are a few things to notice in reading the poetry of the Bible.

Notice the style of biblical poetry. The Old Testament contains a great variety of poetry. Some biblical poetry is simple and direct, like Deborah's fierce song of victory, which is one of the earliest poems in the Bible. Some is elaborate and sophisticated, like the love poetry of the Song of Songs. But despite great differences in purpose, feeling, and artistry, all biblical poetry shares two basic characteristics—the use of imagery and of repetition.

Notice the use of imagery. The poetry of the Old Testament is rich in **imagery,** the sensory details that provide vividness in a literary work. In many cases this imagery has a pastoral quality, offering idealized pictures of rural life, as in the famous opening lines of Psalm 23:

> The Lord is my shepherd;
> I shall not want.
> He maketh me to lie down in green pastures;
> He leadeth me beside the still waters.

Imagery in Old Testament poetry is often employed in making comparisons, as in the following description of the sun from Psalm 19:

> Which is as a bridegroom coming out of his
>   chamber,
> And rejoiceth as a strong man to run a race.
> His going forth is from the end of the heaven,
> And his circuit unto the ends of it:
> And there is nothing hid from the heat
>   thereof.

Imagery is also frequently employed in making contrasts, as in the following lines from the Book of Proverbs:

> Better is a dinner of herbs where love is,
> Than a stalled ox and hatred therewith.

Notice the use of repetition. Biblical poetry employs several kinds of repetition, or parallelism: (**a**) the use of the same word or phrase two or more times; (**b**) the use of the same sentence structure with different words; (**c**) the use of the same idea with different words. The following are examples of each of these types of repetition:

(**a**) *Repetition of words*

> A time to weep and a time to laugh,
> A time to mourn and a time to dance.
>   Ecclesiastes 3:4

(**b**) *Repetition of sentence structure*

> The law of the Lord is perfect, converting the
>   soul:
> The testimony of the Lord is sure, making
>   wise the simple.
>   Psalm 19:7

(**c**) *Repetition of idea*

> If I forget thee, O Jerusalem,
> Let my right hand forget her cunning.
> If I do not remember thee,
> Let my tongue cleave to the roof of my
>   mouth . . .
>   Psalm 137: 5–6

from Psalms

The King James Translation

Psalm 8

O Lord our Lord, how excellent is thy name
    in all the earth!
Who hast set thy glory above the heavens.
Out of the mouth of babes and sucklings hast
    thou ordained strength because of thine
    enemies,
That thou mightest still the enemy and the
    avenger.
5 When I consider thy heavens, the work of
    thy fingers,
The moon and the stars, which thou hast
    ordained;
What is man, that thou art mindful of him?
And the son of man, that thou visitest him?
For thou hast made him a little lower than
    the angels,
10 And hast crowned him with glory and honor.
Thou madest him to have dominion over the
    works of thy hands;
Thou hast put all things under his feet:
All sheep and oxen,
Yea, and the beasts of the field;
15 The fowl of the air, and the fish of the sea,
And whatsoever passeth through the paths
    of the seas.
O Lord our Lord, how excellent is thy name
    in all the earth!

Terra-cotta plaque of a harpist. 1792–1595 B.C. Oriental Institute of Chicago

Psalm 23

The Lord is my shepherd;
I shall not want.
He maketh me to lie down in green pastures:
He leadeth me beside the still waters.
5 He restoreth my soul:
He leadeth me in the paths of righteousness
    for his name's sake.
Yea, though I walk through the valley of the
    shadow of death, I will fear no evil: for
    thou art with me;
Thy rod and thy staff they comfort me.
Thou preparest a table before me in the
    presence of mine enemies:
10 Thou anointest my head with oil;[1] my cup
    runneth over.
Surely goodness and mercy shall follow me
    all the days of my life:
And I will dwell in the house of the Lord for
    ever.

---

1. *anointest . . . oil,* a sign of God's blessing.

Psalm 19

The heavens declare the glory of God
And the firmament showeth his handywork.
Day unto day uttereth speech,
And night unto night showeth knowledge.
5 There is no speech or language where their
  voice is not heard.
Their line[1] is gone out through all the earth,
And their words to the end of the world.
In them he hath set a tabernacle for the sun,
Which is as a bridegroom coming out of his
  chamber,
10 And rejoiceth as a strong man to run a race.
His going forth is from the end of the heaven,
And his circuit unto the ends of it:
And there is nothing hid from the heat[2] thereof.
The law of the Lord is perfect, converting the
  soul:
15 The testimony of the Lord is sure, making wise
  the simple.
The statutes of the Lord are right, rejoicing the
  heart:
The commandment of the Lord is pure,
  enlightening the eyes.
The fear of the Lord is clean, enduring for ever:
The judgments of the Lord are true and
  righteous altogether.
20 More to be desired are they than gold, yea, than
  much fine gold:
Sweeter also than honey and the honeycomb.
Moreover by them is thy servant warned:
And in keeping of them there is great reward.
Who can understand his errors?
25 Cleanse thou me from secret faults.
Keep back thy servant also from presumptuous
  sins;
Let them not have dominion over me:
Then shall I be upright,
And I shall be innocent from the great
  transgression.
30 Let the words of my mouth, and the meditation
  of my heart,
Be acceptable in thy sight, O Lord, my
  strength, and my redeemer.

1. *line,* a rule of conduct, a precept.
2. *heat,* one trial in a race.

Psalm 90

Lord, thou hast been our dwelling place in all
  generations.
Before the mountains were brought forth,
Or ever thou hadst formed the earth and the
  world,
Even from everlasting, thou art God.
5 Thou turnest man to destruction:
And sayest, Return ye children of men.
For a thousand years in thy sight are but as
  yesterday when it is past
And as a watch in the night.
Thou carriest them away as with a flood;
10 They are as a sleep:
In the morning they are like grass which
  groweth up.
In the morning it flourisheth, and groweth up;
In the evening it is cut down, and withereth.
For we are consumed by thine anger,
15 And by thy wrath are we troubled.
Thou hath set our iniquities before thee,
Our secret sins in the light of thy countenance.
For all our days are passed away in thy wrath:
We spend our years as a tale that is told.
20 The days of our years are threescore years and ten;
And if by reason of strength they be fourscore
  years,
Yet is their strength labor and sorrow;
For it is soon cut off, and we fly away.
Who knoweth the power of thine anger?
25 Even according to thy fear, so is thy wrath.
So teach us to number our days,
That we may apply our hearts unto wisdom.
Return, O Lord, how long?
And let it repent thee concerning thy servants.
30 O satisfy us early with thy mercy;
That we may rejoice and be glad all our days.
Make us glad according to the days wherein
  thou hast afflicted us,
And the years wherein we have seen evil.
Let thy work appear unto thy servants,
35 And thy glory unto their children.
And let the beauty of the Lord our God be
  upon us:
And establish thou the work of our hands upon us;
Yea, the work of our hands establish thou it.

Psalm 137

By the rivers of Babylon, there we sat down,
Yea, we wept, when we remembered Zion.
We hanged our harps upon the willows in the
    midst thereof.
For there they that carried us away captive
    required of us a song;
5 And they that wasted us required of us mirth,
Saying, Sing us one of the songs of Zion.
How shall we sing the Lord's song in a strange
    land?
If I forget thee, O Jerusalem,
Let my right hand forget her cunning.
10 If I do not remember thee,
Let my tongue cleave to the roof of my mouth;

If I prefer not Jerusalem above my chief joy.
Remember, O Lord, the children of Edom[1] in
    the day of Jerusalem;
Who said, Raze it, raze it, even to the
    foundation thereof.
15 O daughter of Babylon, who art to be
    destroyed;
Happy shall he be, that rewardeth thee as thou
    has served us.
Happy shall he be, that taketh and dasheth thy
    little ones against the stones.

---

1. **Edom**, an ancient country south of Israel. Traditional enemies of the Jews, the Edomites joined forces with the Babylonian army besieging Jerusalem in 587 B.C.

THINK AND DISCUSS
Understanding
1. Psalm 8 sketches a kind of scale of creation. Beginning with God, describe this scale in descending order.
2. Psalm 19 celebrates God's works in two distinct areas. What are they?
3. What different **images** in Psalm 23 suggest safety, comfort, and trust?
4. What images of the swift passage of time occur in Psalm 90?
5. What historical situation forms the background of Psalm 137?

Analyzing
6. In Psalm 19, how is the presentation of God's creation of the material universe linked to his establishment of the moral law?
7. Describe the different emphasis in each of the following sections of Psalm 23: lines 1–6; lines 7–8; lines 9–12.
8. Contrast the feeling conveyed by lines 1–12 of Psalm 137 with that of lines 13–17.

Extending
9. Compare the way in which God the creator is presented in Psalm 19 with the way

Akhenaton describes the Aton in his "Hymn to the Sun" (page 18).
10. Compare the attitude toward exile expressed in Psalm 137 with that of the Book of Ruth.

APPLYING: Metaphor HI
See Handbook of Literary Terms, p. 957.

A **metaphor** is a figure of speech that expresses a likeness between things that are essentially unlike. "You were the axe at my side," laments the hero of *The Epic of Gilgamesh* for his dead friend. The friend and the axe were different in most ways, but alike in being dependable and treasured. The comparison between a valued comrade and a valued weapon is a metaphor because it does not employ any of the words that commonly signal a comparison, such as *like* or *as*. When a metaphor is developed at length, throughout the whole or a great part of a literary work, it is called an extended metaphor. One of the most famous extended metaphors in literature is contained in Psalm 23.

1. What is the basic comparison being made here?
2. How is this metaphor extended throughout Psalm 23?

PERSIA AND INDIA 1500 B.C.–A.D. 1500

1500 B.C.	1250	1000	750	500	250	0

HISTORY AND ARTS

- Aryans destroy Indus civilization
- Cyrus conquers Babylon
- Zoroastrianism becomes state religion
- Asoka conquers India

PEOPLE

- Zarathustra
- Cyrus
- Buddha
- Asoka

LITERATURE

- *Rig Veda*
- *Mahabharata*
- *Ramayana*
- Edicts of Asoka

Carved seal from Mohenjo-Daro. c. 3000–1500 B.C.

Lion capital from one of Asoka's pillars. 242–232 B.C.

Detail of seated Buddha. 2nd–3rd century A.D.

PART TWO

UNIT 1

A.D. 250	500	750	1000	1250	1500

• Islam reaches India

• Guptas unite northern India

• Moslems invade India

• Babur conquers northern India

• Arabs conquer Persia

• Mongols invade Persia

• Abbasids seize power

• Abbasids build Baghdad

• Mongols capture Baghdad

• Chandragupta II

• Kalidasa

• Mohammed

• Harun al-Rashid

• Firdausi

• Mahmud of Ghazni

• Omar Khayyám

• Genghis Khan

• Sadi

• Rumi

• Hafiz

• Tamerlane

• Babur

• Kalidasa: *Shakuntala*

• *Koran*

• Firdausi: *Shah-nama*

• Rumi: *Mathnavi*

• Sadi: *Gulistan*

• Hafiz: *Divan*

• *Babur-nama*

Persian silver plate showing hunting scene. 5th century A.D.

Detail from a *Koran* in kufic script. 8th–9th century A.D.

Detail of a Persian miniature of Genghis Khan

PERSIA AND INDIA

THE ARYAN-SPEAKING TRIBES

Sometime after 2000 B.C., nomadic tribes whose homeland was the steppes of southern Russia began migrating south. These peoples spoke a common language, often called Aryan (ėr′ē ən), which was the remote ancestor of the Indo-European family of languages to which English belongs. They had domesticated the horse, and their use of mounted warriors in battle allowed them to overwhelm the native populations of the lands they reached. Some of these Aryan-speaking tribes invaded northern India through the passes of the Hindu Kush Mountains. Their speech became the ancestor of Sanskrit, the ancient language of northern India. Other Aryan-speaking tribes occupied the mountainous region of Iran, or Persia, as it has been called throughout much of its long history. (See the map on page 39.) Their Aryan speech gradually evolved into the earliest surviving form of the Iranian language, Old Persian.

ANCIENT PERSIA

Old Persian was one of the official languages of the first great Persian empire, that of Cyrus the Great and his successors. Around 538 B.C., Cyrus conquered Babylon and its empire. By the time of his death in 529, the territory he ruled extended east to the borders of India, west to Asia Minor, and south to the edge of Egypt, which was itself added to the empire during the reign of his son.

The chief cultural achievement of the ancient Persians lay in the organization and administration of this vast empire. But although like another military power, the Assyrians, much of their culture was derived from earlier Near Eastern civilizations, they did leave an original and enduring legacy in the Zoroastrian religion. Founded by the teacher Zarathustra—called Zoroaster (zôr′ō as′tər) by the Greeks—in the seventh century B.C., Zoroastrianism was spread throughout the Persian empire from the time of Cyrus onward and became the state religion about 500 B.C. Zoroaster's ideas of the existence of a single true God, of a struggle between good and evil principles, of a last judgment, and of eternal rewards and punishments were to influence both Judaism and Christianity. The Greek and Roman myth of a series of ages or epochs—gold, silver, bronze, and iron—marked by decreasing human strength and virtue, came to the west from Persia.

ISLAMIC PERSIA

The second religion to exercise a major influence on Persian culture was Islam. Within twenty years of the death of its founder, the prophet Mohammed, in A.D. 632, Moslem Arabs had conquered Persia. While most Persians accepted conversion to Islam, some of the Zoroastrians fled to India, where they established the still surviving community of the Parsis (pär′sēz). According to one historian, the impact on Persian culture of the Arab invaders was "comparable with that which the landing of the Normans in England inflicted on Saxon tradition."

The requirement that Moslems read the Islamic sacred writings, called the *Koran* (kô-rän′), in Mohammed's own language resulted in a flood of Arabic words into Persian. Despite this influx, the Persians managed to retain their own language basically unchanged, unlike other conquered peoples, such as the Syrians or Egyptians, who adopted Arabic. Even in Persia, however, Arabic became for a time (like Norman French in England) the language of government, scholarship, and literature. The Arabs in turn borrowed many elements from the far older and richer literary tradition of Persia. Many of the stories in the famous collection of tales called the *Arabian Nights* are clearly Persian in origin.

In 750 the dynasty ruling the Islamic empire was overthrown by rebels. The new dynasty, the Abbasids (ab′ə sēdz), moved the capital eastward from the ancient city of Damascus in Syria to a magnificent new city—Baghdad—which they built on the Tigris River in Iraq. The period of the Abbasid *caliphs* (kā′lifs), as the Muslim rulers were called, was the Islamic Golden Age. For the next five hundred years, under

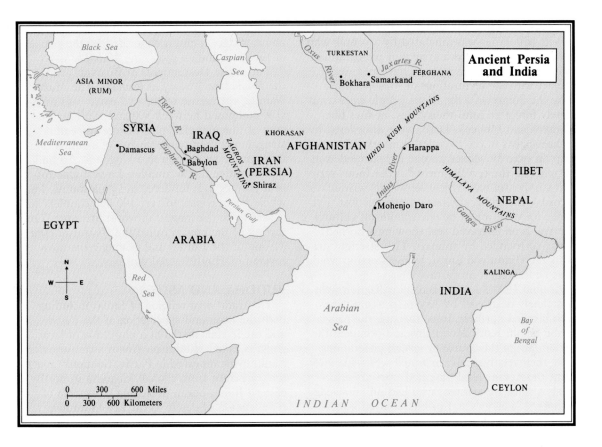

Ancient Persia and India

rulers like the famous eighth-century caliph Harun al-Rashid (hä rün′ äl rä shēd′), Baghdad was a great world center of ideas, trade, and government.

By the middle of the tenth century, the power of the Abbasids had greatly declined, and native princes had established control over much of Persia. One result of this reawakening of nationalist feeling was a revival of Persian literature, particularly in areas remote from Baghdad like the northeastern province of Khorasan. Here around 940 was born the poet Firdausi, author of the *Shah-nama*, or "Book of Kings," a long epic poem that is the greatest work of Persian literature.

Early in the thirteenth century, Persia was shattered by the invasion of the Mongols under Genghis Khan (jeng′gis kän). "City after city was reduced to ashes," observes one modern historian; "pyramids of skulls marked the trail of the ferocious horsemen." In 1258 a grandson of Genghis Khan captured and burned Baghdad. He massacred 100,000 citizens and had the last Abbasid caliph put in a bag and trampled to death. Despite the chaos and destruction caused by the Mongols, this period was marked by the works of Persia's greatest lyric poets—Rumi, Sadi, and Hafiz.

THE INDUS CIVILIZATION

The ancient civilization of India differs from those of Mesopotamia and Egypt in that its cultural tradition has survived largely unbroken down to the present. As one historian observes, "To this day legends known to the humblest Indian recall the names of shadowy chieftains who lived nearly a thousand years before Christ, and the orthodox brahman in his daily worship repeats hymns composed even earlier." India's past does contain a lost civilization, however.

By about 2500 B.C. the region of the Indus River and its tributaries was inhabited by a people who built cities and created a system of pictographic writing. These people seem to have had some contact with the civilizations of Mesopotamia. Like the Sumerians, the Indus people were completely forgotten until their cities, at sites like Harappa and Mohenjo Daro, were discovered by archaeologists in the twentieth century. (See the map on page 39.) Since no one has succeeded in deciphering the few fragments of the Indus script that survive, in one critical sense—its written records—the Indus civilization remains lost. Evidence for what might be one significant cultural survival is an engraved seal showing a horned figure surrounded by animals. This strongly suggests the Hindu god Shiva, whose worship would thus be the oldest on earth.

Around 1500 B.C., the Indus civilization was completely destroyed by Aryan-speaking tribes who invaded northern India through the passes of the Hindu Kush Mountains and occupied the region during the course of several generations. Like their relatives who migrated westward into Iran, the Aryans used mounted warriors effectively against the natives, who had no knowledge of horses. Warriors and priests enjoyed a privileged position within Aryan society, and these groupings eventually developed, with much elaboration, into the Indian system of hereditary castes.

THE *VEDAS* AND THE EPICS

If the Indus people possessed a literature, no knowledge of it survives; Indian literature begins with the Aryan-speaking invaders. Their speech developed into Sanskrit (san'skrit), the ancient language of northern India. The oldest literary works in Sanskrit, which were composed between 2000 and 800 B.C., are the collections of sacred literature known as the *Vedas* (vā'dəz), meaning "knowledge" or "lore." The *Vedas* are the result of a slow, thousand-year-long accumulation of oral religious poetry. The oldest and most sacred of the Vedic literature is the collection known as the *Rig Veda*, which contains the traditional hymns and prayers of the Aryan-speaking tribes.

The Vedic period of Sanskrit literature ends about 500 B.C., and is succeeded by the period of the great Indian epics, the *Mahabharata* ("War of the Descendants of Bharata") and the *Ramayana* ("Story of Rama"). The *Mahabharata*, the earlier of the two epics, was probably composed between 500 and 300 B.C. The core of this immense poem is the story of a struggle between two branches of a ruling family over the succession to a kingdom. Around this narrative has accumulated a vast amount of myth, legend, folklore, and philosophy. The whole poem comes to over 100,000 couplets and is said to be the longest in world literature. One section of the epic is called the *Bhagavad Gita* ("Song of the Lord") and is among the most revered of Hindu sacred writings.

BUDDHA AND ASOKA

The traditional religion of India, including both the profound speculation of the *Vedas* and the livelier myths of a multitude of local gods, is called Hinduism. About a century after Zarathustra appeared in Persia, Gautama (gou'tə-mə), a prince from a small kingdom in northeastern India, began preaching a doctrine of renunciation of desire as the key to human salvation. Called the Buddha ("Enlightened One") and eventually deified by his followers, Gautama became the founder of one of the world's great religions, Buddhism, which spread throughout the Far East during the next thousand years.

Buddhism's most notable convert was Asoka (ə sō'kə), who in the third century B.C. ruled an empire that included most of India. It was Asoka's ambition that his government should embody the Buddhist ideal of *dharma* (där'mə), "righteousness." Like Hammurabi he had his laws inscribed on stone at various points throughout his empire. In a vast region like India, including such various climates and peoples, political division rather than unity was the rule. Following Asoka's death, his empire fragmented, and in the centuries that followed, internal warfare and a series of invasions by Central Asian tribes left little of his heritage beyond the memory of a united India ruled by a great king.

THE GUPTAS AND THE MOGHULS

Around A.D. 320 northern India was unified by the Gupta dynasty. The greatest of these kings, Chandragupta II (chun′drə gup′tə), who ruled from around 375 to 415, was also a patron of the arts. There was a revival of the ancient classics, particularly the *Mahabharata*, which was revised, one historian observes, "to the glory of unified India under godlike emperors." From the Gupta period dates the work of the greatest Sanskrit poet, Kalidasa, author of the verse play *Shakuntala*, one of the masterpieces of Indian drama. Northern India, united for two hundred years by the Gupta kings, fell apart in the sixth century; the southern part of the country had not been united since Asoka's time. Centuries of small, feudal kingdoms followed, during which Hinduism experienced a revival, due to the translation of its classics from Sanskrit into the regional languages of India. During this period the influence of Buddhism declined, until it was confined to the edges of India, the Himalayan regions of Tibet and Nepal to then north, and the island of Ceylon to the south.

A third major religion, Islam, had appeared in India by the eighth century A.D. Islam eventually came to dominate the northern part of the country, which was invaded by Moslems from Afghanistan in the late tenth and early eleventh centuries. The Moslem invader who left the most enduring impact on India was Babur, the founder of the Moghul ("Mongol") dynasty in India. Descended from both Genghis Khan and Tamerlane, Babur had conquered northern India by the time of his death in 1530. He also left a vivid, thoughtful account of his life, called the *Babur-nama* ("Book of Babur"), which is a masterpiece of autobiography.

THINKING ABOUT GRAPHIC AIDS
Using the Time Line

The time line on pages 36–37 shows the chronological sequence of the historical and literary events discussed in Part 2. Use the time line to answer the following questions.

1. For approximately how long was Zoroastrianism the dominant religion of Persia? (a) around 500 years; (b) around 800 years; (c) around 1,100 years
2. At whose court might the poet Firdausi have been present? (a) Chandragupta II; (b) Harun al-Rashid; (c) Mahmud of Ghazni
3. How old was Baghdad when it was captured by the Mongols? (a) nearly 300 years; (b) nearly 500 years; (c) nearly 800 years
4. Which of the following conquerors could the poet Hafiz have met? (a) Genghis Khan; (b) Tamerlane; (c) Babur
5. Which of the following poets were contemporaries? (a) Firdausi; (b) Omar Khayyám; (c) Rumi; (d) Sadi; (e) Hafiz

Using the Map

The map on page 39 shows the geographical area occupied by the two civilizations discussed in Part 2. Use the map to answer the following questions.

1. What is similar about the geographical sites of Babylon, Mohenjo Daro, and Harappa?
2. Which of the following places in Persia would Mongol invaders from Central Asia have reached first? (a) Shiraz; (b) Khorasan; (c) Baghdad
3. The Oxus River was the traditional northeastern boundary of the Persian Empire. What region lies immediately beyond the Oxus?
4. Locate Babur's kingdom of Ferghana. (It is north of India.) The conquest of what city would have been a natural ambition for him?
5. What mountain range would Babur have crossed to invade India?

Persian Poetry

Detail of a miniature showing Firdausi at the court of Mahmud of Ghazni. c. 1573. British Library

The Persians traditionally regarded poetry as a higher form of literary art than prose. Four medieval poets—Firdausi, Rumi, Sadi, and Hafiz—are revered as Persia's greatest writers. Of these four, Firdausi (940?–1020?) was the earliest. There is very little certainty about the events of his life, and a variety of conflicting traditions exist concerning the poet. The dates of his birth and death are uncertain, and even his personal name—usually given as Mansur—is unknown. His pen name, *Firdausi* (fĕr dou′sē), means "from Paradise." He was born in the province of Khorasan, an area where—far from the Arabic influences of Baghdad—native Persian traditions were very strong. Early in life Firdausi conceived of creating a vast epic poem that would tell the stories of the Persian kings from the creation of the world to the Islamic conquest in the seventh century A.D. Firdausi did not invent, but instead collected and transmitted in verse form the legends of his country that were being submerged by Arabic influences. He worked on this project for over thirty years. When it was completed in 1010, the *Shah-nama* (shä′ nä mä′), or "Book of Kings," contained over 60,000 verses. As one scholar observes, "There is in the *Shah-nama* an amalgamation of the Persian equivalents of chapters of Genesis, *The Odyssey, Paradise Lost,* Chaucer's *Canterbury Tales,* and Shakespeare. . . . Drama, comedy, tragedy—all are here." In the passage from the *Shah-nama* that appears on page 44, Firdausi laments the death of his son.

The Persian poet best known to European and American readers is certainly Omar Khayyám (ō′mär kī yäm′). This is not due to his reputation in his own country, but to the enormous popularity of Edward FitzGerald's nineteenth-century English translation, *The Rubáiyát of Omar Khayyám.* (See Reader's Note: Translating the *Rubáiyát,* page 46.) Omar Khayyám (1050?–1123?) was not known to his contemporaries as a poet, but as a distinguished scientist and mathematician. He published no poetry and was probably the author of only a small portion of the hundreds of poems that came to be attributed to him after his death. These poems were in one of the basic forms of Persian verse—the *rubai* (rü′bä ē′), "quatrain," a stanza of four lines. *Rubáiyát* (rü′bē yät′), "quatrains," is the plural of *rubai.* In the estimate of one critic, the philosophy expressed in *The Rubáiyát of Omar Khayyám* is skeptical, but not despairing. "The poet is incredulous, but not defiant; disillusioned, but compassionate." Nine quatrains from FitzGerald's version of the *Rubáiyát* appear on page 45.

The greatest mystical poet of Persia was Jalal al-Din (1207–1273), known by his pen name, *Rumi* (rü′me). While he was still a young man, his family fled westward from invading Mongols, eventually settling in Asia Minor. In medieval times the Arabs called this area *Rum* ("Rome") because it was part of the Byzantine Empire. Jalal al-Din became known as *Rumi* ("of Rome") after his adopted home. Rumi was strongly influenced by Sufism, the mystical movement within Islam. (See Comment: Sufism, page 47.) Rumi's greatest work, the *Mathnavi* (mäth nä′vē), or "Couplets," is

a huge collection of Sufi sermons and fables in verse. Called "the Persian *Koran*," the *Mathnavi* is regarded as second only to the *Shah-nama* as a masterpiece of Persian literature. Passages from the *Mathnavi* appear on pages 48–50.

Firdausi, Omar Khayyám, and Rumi all came from the eastern edge of Persia. Sadi and Hafiz both came from Shiraz, the capital of the southern province of Fars (from which the name *Persia* comes). By surrendering to the Mongols, Shiraz escaped the destruction that had befallen many cities in Persia and Iraq Sadi (sä′dē) was born in Shiraz around 1184. While he retained a lifelong association with his native city, he also traveled widely, visiting—by his own account—Arabia, Egypt, Morocco, Ethiopia, Central Asia, and India. His masterpiece, the *Gulistan* (gül′ə-stän), or "Rose Garden," a book of moral fables in prose mixed with verse, has remained one of Persia's most popular classics. Sadi's combination of wit, common sense, and piety, coupled with a charming literary style, has made him perhaps the most beloved of Persian poets. Some fables from the *Gulistan* appear on pages 52–53.

Unlike Sadi, Hafiz (hä′fəz) spent nearly all his life in his native city of Shiraz, where he was born about 1326. The most famous story told of Hafiz associates him with the ferocious Turkish conqueror Tamerlane. In a celebrated poem Hafiz had written that he would surrender Bokhara and Samarkand, the chief cities of Tamerlane's empire, to win the love of a Turkish girl from Shiraz. Tamerlane is supposed to have summoned Hafiz and demanded to know how a poor poet could dare to make such an offer. Hafiz replied that it was just such generosity that had made him poor. Hafiz is honored as Persia's greatest lyric poet. He employs the images of wine, love, and roses in his poetry. But these images do not stand for religious equivalents as in Sufi poetry. In the poetry of Hafiz, it is in these things themselves that spirituality is to be found. In the estimate of one scholar, "his poems project at once the sweetness of the joys of the world and its inadequacies." Two poems by Hafiz appear on page 54.

(top) Detail of a miniature from an illuminated manuscript of the *Gulistan* showing Sadi. 1581. British Library
(bottom) Detail of a miniature from an illuminated manuscript of the *Divan* showing Hafiz. 18th century. British Library

Detail of an illustration showing the combat of Sohrab and Rustum from an illuminated manuscript of the *Shah-nama*. c. 1605–1607. Metropolitan Museum of Art

Lament for His Son

Firdausi *from the* **Shah-nama**
translated by **Reuben Levy**

My years have passed sixty and five and no purpose now would be served for me by striving after wealth. Perhaps I should take my own counsel and give a thought to the death of my son. It was my turn to have gone, but it was the younger man who departed and in my agony for him I am a body without a soul. I hasten about dreaming that perchance I may find him; and if I find him I will hasten to him with reproaches, telling him that it was my turn to go and demanding why he has gone, robbing me of hope and tranquillity. He had ever been one to take me by the hand when distresses came and now he has taken a path far from his old fellow-wayfarer. Have you perchance found younger companions on the way, since you have so swiftly gone ahead of me? When this young man reached the age of thirty-seven, the world no longer went according to his liking. He has gone and what remains is my grief and sorrow for him; he has steeped my heart and eyes in blood.

Now that he is departed, going towards the light, he would surely choose out a place for his father? Long is the time that has passed over me and none of my fellow-wayfarers have returned. Surely he awaits me and is angry at my tarrying? May the All-possessor keep your spirit ever in brightness! May wisdom ever be the shield that guards your soul!

c. 1005

THINK AND DISCUSS
Understanding
1. What does the speaker say prompts him to reflect on his son's death?
2. For what does the speaker imagine reproaching his son?

Analyzing
3. At two points in his lament, the speaker directly addresses his dead son. What effect does each of these have?
4. Another concern is intermixed with the speaker's grief for his son. What is this other concern and how is it coupled with the death of the speaker's son?

Extending
5. How do the feelings expressed in Firdausi's lament for the death of his son differ from those expressed by Gilgamesh in his lament for Enkidu? Be sure to consider how old each speaker is in discussing this question.

ENRICHMENT
Reading the Story of Sohrab and Rustum
Firdausi's lament recalls that of another father, the Persian hero Rustum, who also mourns the untimely death of his son, Sohrab, in what is probably the most familiar episode from the *Shah-nama*. A famous nineteenth century retelling of this story is Matthew Arnold's long narrative poem "Sohrab and Rustum." A recent prose version is included in Louis Untermeyer's collection of legends, *The Firebringer and Other Great Stories* (M. Evans, 1968).

from The Rubáiyát of Omar Khayyám

translated by Edward FitzGerald

1

Wake! For the Sun, who scattered into flight
The Stars before him from the Field of
    Night,
　　Drives Night along with them from
    Heaven, and strikes
The Sultán's Turret with a Shaft of Light.

12

A Book of Verses underneath the Bough,
A Jug of Wine, a Loaf of Bread—and Thou
　　Beside me singing in the Wilderness—
Oh, Wilderness were Paradise enow![1]

13

Some for the Glories of This World; and
    some
Sigh for the Prophet's Paradise[2] to come;
　　Ah, take the Cash, and let the Credit go,
Nor heed the rumble of a distant Drum!

17

Think, in this battered Caravanserai[3]
Whose Portals are alternate Night and Day,
　　How Sultán after Sultán with his Pomp
Abode his destined Hour, and went his way.

19

I sometimes think that never blows so red
The Rose as where some buried Caesar bled;
　　That every Hyacinth the Garden wears
Dropt in her Lap from some once lovely
    Head.[4]

27

Myself when young did eagerly frequent
Doctor and Saint,[5] and heard great argument
　　About it[6] and about: but evermore
Came out by the same door where in I went.

28

With them the seed of Wisdom did I sow,
And with mine own hand wrought to make it
    grow;
　　And this was all the Harvest that I reaped—
"I came like Water, and like Wind I go."

71

The Moving Finger[7] writes; and, having writ,
Moves on: nor all your Piety nor Wit
　　Shall lure it back to cancel half a Line,
Nor all your Tears wash out a Word of it.

99

Ah Love! could you and I with Him conspire
To grasp this sorry Scheme of Things entire,
　　Would not we shatter it to bits—and then
Remold it nearer to the Heart's Desire!

---

1. *enow* (i nou′), an archaic form of *enough*.
2. *the Prophet's Paradise,* that promised by the Prophet Mohammed.
3. *Caravanserai* (kar′ə van′sə rī′), a large inn where caravans in the Orient put up for the night.
4. *Hyacinth . . . Head.* In Greek mythology, Hyacinthus, a beautiful young man, was accidentally killed by the god Apollo, who caused a flower (the hyacinth) to grow from the dead youth's blood.
5. *Doctor and Saint,* philosopher and religious teacher.
6. *About it,* about life and death.
7. *Moving Finger,* of destiny, recording human fates.

THINK AND DISCUSS

Understanding
1. What event is being described in quatrain 1?
2. What is "this battered Caravanserai" in quatrain 17?

Analyzing
3. What point is being made in quatrain 19?
4. In quatrains 27, 28, and 71, what effect do learning and religion have on life?

Extending
5. What things in today's world might be described as "the Cash" and what things as "the Credit" in the sense in which these words are used in quatrain 13?

APPLYING: Rhyme H
See Handbook of Literary Terms, p. 965.

Rhyme is the repetition of similar or identical sounds. The most common form of rhyme used in poetry is end rhyme, the rhyming of words at the ends of lines of verse. The pattern of rhymes in a stanza is called the rhyme scheme. The rhyme scheme of a poem is expressed by using a different letter to stand for each rhyme. Edward FitzGerald employed the traditional rhyme scheme of the Persian *rubai* form in his translation.

1. Which of the following correctly expresses the *rubai* rhyme scheme? (**a**) *abab;* (**b**) *aaba;* (**c**) *abcd.*
2. Which of the verse translations of quatrain 12 on page 47 uses the traditional rhyme scheme employed by FitzGerald?

Reader's Note

Translating the *Rubáiyát*

"I suppose very few people have ever taken such pains in translation as I have," writes Edward FitzGerald to a friend in 1859, "though certainly not to be literal." While much admired as poetry, FitzGerald's famous version of the *Rubáiyát* has also been much criticized as translation, with some scholars claiming that many of his most brilliant images have no prototypes in the Persian original. As the Argentine writer Jorge Luis Borges put it, from the unlikely encounter between the medieval Persian and the Victorian Englishman "emerges an extraordinary poet who does not resemble either of them."

One basic difference between the Persian poems and FitzGerald's English versions is suggested by his description of his method of translation. Many of Omar Khayyám's quatrains, FitzGerald writes, "are mashed together" in

his version of the *Rubáiyát.* An examination of FitzGerald's most famous lines, the stanza beginning "A Book of Verses underneath the Bough," shows this process at work. In this case, FitzGerald has taken two very similar poems from his Persian original and collapsed them into one. Compare FitzGerald's version (quatrain 12) with the far more literal prose translation of Justin Huntly McCarthy on the opposite page. In each of McCarthy's stanzas, the poet has listed his simple requirements for happiness. The two lists are similar—bread and wine appear on both. From the remaining items FitzGerald has selected the more delicate **image** of a book of verse, and dropped the earthier one of a leg of mutton. He has also transformed the meditative passivity of "a little idleness" into the rapture of "singing in the wilderness."

According to Robert Graves and Omar Ali Shah, FitzGerald made an even more basic alteration. In FitzGerald's version, it is apparent that "Thou" is the poet's girlfriend. (This is clear in the other versions on page 47 as well.) Graves and Ali Shah claim that in Omar Khayyám's original poem the companion is not a girl but another member of the Islamic mystical order of the Sufis (see page 49) to which Omar Khayyám belonged. Rather than the poet and a pretty girl, they say, the poem pictures two Sufis meditating over a book of verse. Consistent with their view of the essentially religious nature of the retirement pictured by the poet, Graves and Ali Shah describe his other requirements in a much less luxurious way than the version of Peter Avery and John Heath-Stubbs. The cosy "corner of a garden" in the translation of Avery and Heath-Stubbs is replaced by the bareness of a "wide plain" in the other version. The "two casks of wine" shrink to a mere gourdful.

Detail of a miniature showing lovers in a garden. c. 1527. Harvard University Museums

E. H. Whinfield (1883)

Give me a skin of wine, a crust of bread,
A pittance bare, a book of verse to read;
    With thee, O love, to share my solitude,
I would not take the Sultan's realm instead!

So long as I possess two maunds of wine,
Bread of the flower of wheat, and mutton chine,
    And you, O Tulip-cheeks, to share my cell,
Not every Sultan's lot can vie with mine.

Justin Huntly McCarthy (1932)

Give me a flagon of red wine, a book of verses, a loaf of bread, and a little idleness. If with such store I might sit by thy dear side in some lonely place, I should deem myself happier than a king in his kingdom.

When the hand possesses a loaf of wheaten bread, two measures of wine, and a piece of flesh, when seated with tulip-cheeks in some lonely spot, behold such joy as is not given to all sultans.

Robert Graves and Omar Ali Shah (1968)

A gourd of red wine and a sheaf of poems—
A bare subsistence, half a loaf, not more—
Supplied us two alone in the free desert:
What Sultan could we envy on his throne?

Should our day's portion be one mancel loaf,
A haunch of mutton and a gourd of wine
Set for us two alone on the wide plain,
No Sultan's bounty could evoke such joy.

Peter Avery and John Heath-Stubbs (1979)

I need a jug of wine and a book of poetry,
Half a loaf for a bite to eat,
Then you and I, seated in a deserted spot,
Will have more wealth than a Sultan's realm.

If chance supplied a loaf of white bread,
Two casks of wine and a leg of mutton,
In the corner of a garden with a tulip-cheeked
    girl
There'd be enjoyment no Sultan could outdo.

The Man Who Fled from Azrael

Rumi *from the* **Mathnavi**
translated by **R. A. Nicholson**

One forenoon a freeborn nobleman arrived and ran into Solomon's hall of justice,[1] his countenance pale with anguish and both lips blue. Then Solomon said, "Good sir, what is the matter?"

He replied, "Azrael[2] cast on me such a look, so full of wrath and hate."

"Come," said the king, "what boon do you desire now? Ask!" "O protector of my life," said he, "command the wind to bear me from here to India. Maybe, when thy slave is come thither he will save his life."

Solomon commanded the wind to bear him quickly over the water to the uttermost part of India. Next day, at the time of conference and meeting, Solomon said to Azrael: "Didst thou look with anger on that Moslem in order that he might wander as an exile far from his home?"

Azrael said, "When did I look on him angrily? I saw him as I passed by, and looked at him in astonishment, for God had commanded me, saying, 'Hark, today do thou take his spirit in India.' From wonder I said to myself, 'Even if he has a hundred wings, 'tis a far journey for him to be in India today.'"

---

1. *Solomon's hall of justice.* Solomon, a great king of Israel in the Old Testament, is also mentioned in the *Koran*. Renowned for his wisdom, he is a venerated figure in both Jewish and Islamic tradition.
2. *Azrael* (az'rā el), in Jewish and Islamic tradition, the angel of death.

The Elephant in the Dark House

Rumi *from the* **Mathnavi**
translated by **R. A. Nicholson**

The elephant was in a dark house: some Hindus had brought it for exhibition.

In order to see it, many people were going, every one, into that darkness.

As seeing it with the eye was impossible, each one was feeling it in the dark with the palm of his hand.

The hand of one fell on its trunk: he said, "This creature is like a waterpipe."

The hand of another touched its ear: to him it appeared to be like a fan.

Since another handled its leg, he said, "I found the elephant's shape to be like a pillar."

Another laid his hand on its back: he said, "Truly, this elephant was like a throne."

Similarly, when any one heard a description of the elephant, he understood it only in respect of the part that he had touched. If there had been a candle in each one's hand, the difference would have gone out of their words.

Persian miniature of elephants. 13th century. Pierpont Morgan Library, New York

The Soul of Goodness in Things Evil

Rumi *from the* **Mathnavi**
translated by **R. A. Nicholson**

Fools take false coins because they are like
    the true.
If in the world no genuine minted coin
Were current, how would forgers pass the
    false?
Falsehood were nothing unless truth were
    there,
5 To make it specious. 'Tis the love of right
Lures men to wrong. Let poison but be
    mixed
With sugar, they will cram it into their
    mouths.
Oh, cry not that all creeds are vain! Some
    scent

Of truth they have, else they would not
    beguile.
10 Say not, "How utterly fantastical!"
No fancy in the world is all untrue.
Amidst the crowd of dervishes hides one,
One true fakir.[1] Search well and thou wilt
    find!

---

1. *dervishes . . . fakir.* A dervish (dèr′vish) is a member
of a Moslem religious order. A fakir (fə kir′) is a Moslem
holy man who lives by begging.

Comment

Sufism

In its first years Islam was spread throughout the Near East by Arab armies. A century later, a religious counter-movement began among the now-Moslem inhabitants of the conquered countries, particularly Syria and Persia. In place of Islamic orthodoxy, this movement stressed the attainment of a mystical union with God through contemplation and other practices. The movement also embraced poverty and those belonging to it frequently wore a patched cloak of rough wool as a sign of their membership. They became known as *Sufis* (sü′fēz), from the Arabic word *suf*, "wool," and the movement is referred to historically as *Sufism* (süf′iz əm). The works of Omar Khayyám, Rumi, Sadi, and Hafiz all exhibit—in very different ways—the influence of Sufism and its notions of the oneness of the universe and the unknowability of God.

In the introduction to his translation of the *Rubáiyát*, Peter Avery observes that "Sufism's motive force is love. This love cannot be quite equated with agape [kindliness]. Nor is it simply eros [sexual love]. The dichotomy between these two does not seem to have been present to the Persian mind. What the Persians call *'Ishq*, the passion of love, was directed in Sufism solely toward God the Creator." The result of this total concentration in Sufism on God gives much of Sufi poetry a quality which in the West would be called "pantheistic." But, Avery goes on, "in Persian thought it is not so much a matter of 'pantheism' as of the sense that all the elements of God's creation—of nature—are inextricably and sympathetically combined."

The Greek and the Chinese Artists, on the Difference Between Theologians and Mystics

Rumi *from the* **Mathnavi**
translated by **A. J. Arberry**

If you desire a parable of the hidden knowledge,[1] tell the story of the Greeks and the Chinese.

"We are the better artists," the Chinese declared.

"We have the edge on you," the Greeks countered.

"I will put you to the test," said the Sultan. "Then we shall see which of you makes good your claim."

"Assign to us one particular room, and you Greeks another," said the Chinese.

The two rooms faced each other, door to door, the Chinese taking one and the Greeks the other. The Chinese demanded of the king a hundred colors, so that worthy monarch opened up his treasury and every morning the Chinese received of his bounty their ration of colors from the treasury.

"No hues or colors are suitable for our work," said the Greeks. "all we require is to get rid of the rust."

So saying, they shut their door and set to work polishing; smooth and unsullied as the sky they became.

There is a way from multicolority to colorlessness; color is like the clouds, colorlessness is a moon. Whatever radiance and splendor you see in the clouds, be sure that it comes from the stars, the moon, and the sun.

When the Chinese had completed their work they began drumming for joy. The king came in and saw the pictures there; the moment he encountered that sight, it stole away his wits. Then he advanced toward the Greeks, who thereupon removed the intervening curtain so that the reflection of the Chinese masterpieces struck upon the

Detail of a Persian miniature showing dancing dervishes of the order founded by Rumi. c. 1490. Metropolitan Museum of Art

walls they had scoured clean of rust. All that the king had seen in the Chinese room showed lovelier here, so that his very eyes were snatched out of their sockets.

The Greeks, my father, are the Sufis; without repetition and books and learning, yet they have scoured their breasts clean of greed and covetousness, avarice and malice. The purity of the mirror without doubt is the heart, which receives images innumerable. The reflection of every image, whether numbered or without number, shines forth forever from the heart alone, and forever every new image that enters upon the heart shows forth within it free of all imperfection. They who have burnished their hearts have escaped from scent and color; every moment, instantly, they behold Beauty.

c. 1258–1270

---

1. *a parable of the hidden knowledge,* a story to illustrate the nature of mystical truth.

THINK AND DISCUSS
Understanding
1. In "The Man Who Fled from Azrael," why does the man flee?
2. Why is Azrael surprised to see him?
3. In "The Elephant in the Dark House," why can each of the Hindus perceive only a portion of the elephant?
4. What different images of good and evil appear in "The Soul of Goodness in Things Evil"?
5. In "The Greek and the Chinese Artists," what method do the Chinese artists use in decorating the room assigned to them? What method do the Greek artists employ?

Analyzing
6. What point about fate is made in "The Man Who Fled from Azrael"?
7. What might the elephant represent in "The Elephant in the Dark House"?
8. According to Rumi's poem "The Soul of Goodness in Things Evil," why are people deceived by various evils?
9. The title "The Greek and the Chinese Artists, on the Difference Between Theologians and Mystics" suggests that one group of artists is to be associated with the theologians, the other with the mystics. Which artists are the theologians and which are the mystics? Explain.

Extending
10. "The Greek and the Chinese Artists" illustrates two basic methods of approach to art and life. One approach stresses mastery of details, the other the discovery of an underlying nature. Rumi associates the first of these approaches with theologians, the second with mystics, but other parallels could be found. For example, there is one approach to acting which emphasizes the small details—such as accent and gesture—of a part to be played. There is another approach in which the actor attempts to "become" the character. Discuss other areas such as music or writing in which these two different approaches might be taken.

APPLYING: Paradox HƗ
See Handbook of Literary Terms, p. 960.

A **paradox** is an apparently contradictory statement that is nevertheless true in some sense. Wordsworth's line, "The Child is father to the Man," expresses a paradox. Influenced by Sufism, Rumi often used paradox to express mystical truths. Look at his poem "The Soul of Goodness in Things Evil."

1. List two paradoxical statements that Rumi makes in this poem.
2. What basic point is he attempting to make in this poem?

COMPOSITION
Writing a Fable
The playwright Oscar Wilde was famous for the witty paradoxes in his comedies and other writings; for example, "Ambition is the last refuge of the failure" or "Charity creates a multitude of sins." Using one of Wilde's paradoxes (any good dictionary of quotations will provide a sampling) or inventing one of your own, write a brief fable to illustrate it.

Writing About Theme
One **theme** that unites the selections from Rumi that you have just read might be called "the limitations of knowledge." How much can human beings know about the nature of reality? What good does this knowledge do them? In a paper of two or three paragraphs, describe how Rumi deals with these questions. See "Writing About Theme" in the Writer's Handbook.

See IRONY in the Handbook of Literary Terms, page 955.

The Padshah and the Slave

Sadi *from the* **Gulistan**
translated by **Edward Rehatsek**

A padshah[1] was in the same boat with a Persian slave who had never before been at sea and experienced the inconvenience of a vessel. He began to cry and to tremble to such a degree that he could not be pacified by kindness, so that at last the king became displeased as the matter could not be remedied. In that boat there happened to be a philosopher, who said: "With thy permission I shall quiet him." The padshah replied: "It will be a great favor." The philosopher ordered the slave to be thrown into the water so that he swallowed some of it, whereon he was caught and pulled by his hair to the boat, to the stern of which he clung with both his hands. Then he sat down in a corner and became quiet. This appeared strange to the king who knew not what wisdom there was in the proceeding and asked for it. The philosopher replied: "Before he had tasted the calamity of being drowned, he knew not the safety of the boat; thus also a man does not appreciate the value of immunity from a misfortune until it has befallen him."

O thou full man, barley-bread pleases thee not.
She is my sweetheart who appears ugly to thee.
To the huris of paradise[2] purgatory seems hell.
Ask the denizens of hell. To them purgatory is
    paradise.

There is a difference between him whose friend is
    in his arms
And him whose eyes of expectation are upon the
    door.

A Vision of the Sultan Mahmud

Sadi *from the* **Gulistan**
translated by **Edward Rehatsek**

One of the kings of Khorasan had a vision in a dream of Sultan Mahmud,[3] one hundred years after his death. His whole person appeared to have been dissolved and turned to dust, except his eyes, which were revolving in their orbits and looking about. All the sages were unable to give an interpretation, except a dervish who made his salutation and said: "He is still looking amazed how his kingdom belongs to others."

Many famous men have been buried under ground
Of whose existence on earth not a trace has
    remained
And that old corpse which had been surrendered
    to the earth
Was so consumed by the soil that not a bone
    remains.
The glorious name of Nushirvan[4] survives in good
    repute
Although much time elapsed since he passed away.
Do good, O man, and consider life as a good fortune,
The more so, as when a shout is raised, a man
    exists no more.

---

1. *padshah* (päd'shäh), great king, emperor.
2. *huris of paradise.* The huris (hùr'ēz) were young, eternally beautiful women of the Moslem paradise.
3. *Sultan Mahmud* (mä müd'). Mahmud of Ghazni (971?–1030) ruled an Islamic empire that included Afghanistan and northeastern Persia. Firdausi's home, the province of Khorasan, was part of Mahmud's empire and the poet was at his court.
4. *Nushirvan* (nü'shər vän), one of the most famous kings of pre-Islamic Persia, renowned for his benevolence.

Nushirvan the Just

Sadi *from the* **Gulistan**
translated by **Edward Rehatsek**

Someone had brought information to Nushirvan the just that an enemy of his had been removed from this world by God the most high. He asked: "Hast thou heard anything about his intending to spare me?"

There is no occasion for our rejoicing at a foe's
    death
Because our own life will also not last for ever.

A Pious Child

Sadi *from the* **Gulistan**
translated by **Edward Rehatsek**

I remember, being in my childhood pious, rising in the night, addicted to devotion and abstinence. One night I was sitting with my father, remaining awake and holding the beloved Quran[1] in my lap, whilst the people around us were asleep. I said: "Not one of these persons lifts up his head or makes a genuflection. They are as fast asleep as if they were dead." He replied: "Darling of thy father, would that thou wert also asleep rather than disparaging people."

The pretender sees no one but himself
Because he has the veil of conceit in front.
If he were endowed with a God-discerning eye
He would see that no one is weaker than himself.
1258

---

1. *Quran,* Koran.

THINK AND DISCUSS

Understanding

1. At the beginning of Sadi's fable, "The Padshah and the Slave," of what is the slave afraid? What is he afraid of at the end?
2. In "A Vision of the Sultan Mahmud," what interpretation does the dervish give to the vision?
3. In "Nushirvan the Just," why does Nushirvan not rejoice in the death of his enemy?
4. How does the father in "A Pious Child" react to his son's criticism of those who would rather sleep than pray?

Analyzing

5. What point about the human conception of happiness and misery does Sadi illustrate in "The Padshah and the Slave"?
6. What point about ambition does he make in "A Vision of the Sultan Mahmud"?

Extending

7. Both Rumi and Sadi tell moral fables. In what ways do they differ? For example, who tells you more about himself? Who is more exclusively concerned with God?

APPLYING: Irony

See Handbook of Literary Terms, p. 955.

Irony is the term broadly used to describe a contrast between what appears to be and what really is. One kind of irony, sometimes called "irony of situation," refers to a state of affairs that is the opposite of what is expected. Sadi often employs this type of irony in his fables.

1. In "Nushirvan the Just," what kind of response does the courtier who delivers the news of the death of Nushirvan's enemy probably expect?
2. What response does he get?
3. How is irony of situation employed in "A Pious Child"?

If That Shirazi Turk

Hafiz *from the* **Divan**
translated by **R. H. Rehder**

If that Shirazi Turk will take my heart in her
    hand
I will give up for her Bokhara and
    Samarkand.
Give me, Saqi,[1] the last of the wine,
For in Paradise we will not find
5 The waters of Ruknabad or the meadows of
    Mosalla.
Alas these Luliyan[2] torment the city with
    their sweet work,
Taking patience from the heart as the Turks
    plunder.
Her beauty is independent of my incomplete
    love.
What line, perfume, or color does beauty
    need?
10 I, before that ever-increasing beauty which
    Joseph had,
Know the love which separated Zuleika[3]
    from her veils.
If you curse me or swear, I am content;
The bitter answer fits your red, sugar-eating
    lip.
Hear, O Soul, advice from the wise man who
    knows,
15 Which is dearer than soul to the young who
    possess joy.
Speak music, talk wine, and as for Fortune's
    mystery—
As philosophy does not unravel or untie that
    tangle.
Your song is spoken. The pearls are strung.
    Sweetly, Hafiz, sing
20 That heaven on your poem may scatter knots
    of stars.

The Crier

Hafiz *from the* **Divan**
translated by **Walter Leaf**

Send the criers round the market, call the
    royst'rers' band to hear,
Crying, "O yes! all ye good folk through the
    Loved One's realm,[4] give ear!

"Lost, a handmaid! Strayed a while since!
    Lost, the Vine's wild daughter, lost!
Raise the hue and cry to seize her! Danger
    lurks where she is near.

5 "Round her head she wears a foam-crown;
    all her garb glows ruby-hued;
Thief of wits is she; detain her, lest ye dare
    not sleep for fear.

"Whoso brings me back the tart maid, take
    for sweetmeat all my soul!
Though the deepest hell conceal her, go ye
    down, go hale her here.

"She's a wastrel, she's a wanton, shame-
    abandoned, rosy-red;
10 If ye find her, send her forthright back to
    HAFIZ, Balladier."

14th century

---

1. *Saqi* (sä′kē), a cupbearer.
2. *Luliyan* (lü′lē yän), gypsies.
3. *Joseph . . . Zuleika* (zü lī′kə). Joseph, the son of the Patriarch Jacob in the Old Testament, also appears in the *Koran*. Both the Old Testament and the *Koran* tell the story of how Joseph resisted the love of his master's wife, called *Zuleika* in the *Koran*. In Islamic literature, Joseph became an archetypal lover.
4. *the Loved One's Realm*, Islam.

THINK AND DISCUSS

Understanding

1. What extravagant offer does Hafiz make in "If That Shirazi Turk"?
2. Whom does he address in lines 12–13 of this poem?
3. What two types of **imagery** does Hafiz employ describing his lost beloved in "The Crier"?
4. What is paradoxical about the attitude toward his beloved that Hafiz expresses in "The Crier"?

Analyzing

5. Both "If That Shirazi Turk" and "The Crier" are examples of the *ghazal* (gaz′əl), the form of Persian lyric poetry for which Hafiz is most famous. In the typical *ghazal*, the first two lines **rhyme,** and this rhyme is picked up in all the succeeding even-numbered lines. (The rhyme scheme is *aa, ba, ca, da,* etc.) Which of the two translations you have just read strictly follows the traditional *ghazal* form? How does the other translation depart from this traditional form?
6. "His poems project at once the sweetness of the joys of the world and its inadequacies." Discuss how the two poems by Hafiz you have just read support this estimate of his poetry.

Extending

7. Both Rumi and Hafiz employ **paradox** in their poetry. Compare the use Hafiz makes of paradox in "The Crier" with Rumi's use of it in "The Soul of Goodness in Things Evil."

APPLYING: Hyperbole H𝒵

See Handbook of Literary Terms, p. 952.

Hyperbole is an exaggerated statement used especially as a figure of speech to heighten effect. Written to express strong feeling, love poetry is often characterized by hyperbolic offers to climb the highest mountain or swim the deepest river to win the beloved. The love poetry of Hafiz shares this extravagance.

1. How does Hafiz employ hyperbole in "If That Shirazi Turk"?
2. What feeling about the power of love is he attempting to convey through his use of hyperbole in this poem?

VOCABULARY

Etymology

In most dictionaries an etymology, or word history, is included along with the definitions of many words. The etymology traces the development of a word back in history, giving recent sources first. Use the etymologies in your Glossary to answer the following questions.

1. The words that are sources of *fakir* and *dervish* share a common meaning. What is it?
2. Which of these words comes from Persian and which from Arabic?
3. Both *shah* and *sultan* refer to a ruler. Which of these words comes from Persian and which from Arabic?
4. A *huri* is one of the beautiful women who inhabit the Moslem paradise. Is the original source of this word Persian or Arabic?
5. What was the original meaning of *huri?*

Indian Literature

The nomadic peoples who invaded northern India around 1500 B.C. made two important contributions to the development of Indian literature. The first was their Aryan speech, which became the ancestor of Sanskrit. The second contribution was their traditional religious poetry. The hymns with which the Aryans praised their many gods, prayed for their help, and offered them sacrifice became the earliest Indian literature that has survived. These hymns were composed by many different authors over a period of centuries—from as early as 2000 B.C. to as late as 800 B.C. Together they form a great collection of religious poetry known as the *Rig Veda* (rig vä′də), or "hymn lore." These hymns exhibit great differences in their literary style and quality. Many are simple, matter-of-fact requests to the gods to protect crops or herds or to give long life or relief from sickness. But the best of them express an exalted and reverent sympathy with nature through noble imagery, vivid descriptions, and simple, concrete language. Here, in the estimate of one historian, the hymns of the *Rig Veda* "reach to the eloquence and beauty of the Psalms." Several of the hymns appear on pages 58–59.

The hymns of the *Rig Veda* are divided into ten books. "Hymn of the Thoughts of Men" comes from Book IX, which is dedicated to the worship of Soma, the god associated with the intoxicating juice of an unknown plant used by the Aryans in their religious rituals. Both "Prayer in Sickness" and "Night" come from Book X. Like many of the hymns in the *Rig Veda*, "Hymn of the Thoughts of Men" is addressed to all the gods in general. "Night" is one of the few hymns addressed to a goddess.

The first English translation from Sanskrit appeared in 1785. It was the philosophical dialogue known as the *Bhagavad Gita* (bug′ə vəd gē′tə), or "Song of the the Lord." This dialogue forms part of the *Mahabharata* (mä-hä′bä′rə tə), a vast epic poem that was probably composed between 500 and 300 B.C., though some portions may date from as early as 1000 B.C. The central plot of the epic concerns a great struggle between two families of royal cousins for control of a kingdom in northern India. Upon the death of the reigning king, his brother succeeded him, and the five sons of the old ruler were driven into exile by the hundred sons of the new king. The third of the five exiled princes, Arjuna (är′jü nə), is the hero of the epic. After years of banishment, the five princes return to defeat and kill their cousins with the aid of the Hindu god Krishna (krish′nə), who serves as Arjuna's charioteer in the final battle. The most famous section of the *Mahabharata* is the *Bhagavad Gita*, a philosophical dialogue between Arjuna and Krishna that takes place just as the two forces are preparing to fight. With his warriors arrayed for battle, Arjuna hesitates, fearing that to undertake this slaughter of his kinsmen to gain a worldly end must be sinful. Krishna reassures him with a long discourse in eighteen chapters in which he explains that a disinterested performance of duty in the world involves no desire and hence no sin. This reconciliation of

Copper figure in the shape of a man. Vedic period (c. 1000 B.C.). National Museum, New Delhi

Detail from the wall paintings of the Ajanta caves. A.D. 400–700

Detail of a miniature from a manuscript of the *Babur-nama* showing Babur at a feast. 17th century. National Museum, New Delhi

work and necessary activity in this world with the idea that the world is a mere illusion to be ignored is central to Hinduism. Often printed separately from the rest of the *Mahabharata*, the *Bhagavad Gita* is one of Hinduism's most sacred texts. The passages from the *Bhagavad Gita* on page 60 are from the first two chapters.

Tragedy was not permitted in Indian drama. In the Hindu theater, according to one historian, "happy endings are unavoidable; faithful love must always triumph, virtue must always be rewarded, if only to balance reality." To the Hindu, defeat and death in this world could have no tragic meaning.

The masterpiece of Sanskrit drama, *Shakuntala* (shä kün′tə lə), is not a revenge tragedy like Shakespeare's *Hamlet*, but a romantic play about lovers meeting in a wood that often recalls one of Shakespeare's pastoral comedies. Nothing survives about the life of the traditional author of *Shakuntala*, the poet Kalidasa (kä lē dä′sə), but legends and what can be learned from the works attributed to him. Like Shakespeare, he was equally gifted in narrative, lyric, and dramatic poetry. He wrote other comedies, epic poems based on myths from the *Ramayana*, and a cycle of love lyrics. The plot of *Shakuntala* was taken from the *Mahabharata* and tells of the love of King Dushyanti (düsh yän′tē) for the beautiful, half-divine Shakuntala, whom he has encountered at the forest hermitage of a Hindu sage. The six brief passages from *Shakuntala* on pages 62–63 are all spoken by the lovelorn king at various points in the play.

The traditional enemies of the Persians were the Turkish peoples who lived beyond the Oxus River, the eastern border of Persia, in the vast mountainous region called Turkestan. (See the map on page 39.) Here was located the small kingdom of Ferghana (fèr gä′nä), home of Zahir-ud-din Muhammed, known by his Mongol nickname, *Babur* (bä′ber), "tiger." Babur was born the eldest son of the ruler of Ferghana, and was descended from both the Turkish conqueror Tamerlane and the Mongol Genghis Khan. His father died while Babur was still a boy, and the young king of Ferghana immediately plunged into the career of military adventuring that would occupy the rest of his life. Although brave, intelligent, energetic, and prudent, Babur experienced many reverses, suffering defeat, exile, and privation. In 1526, with a small force, he invaded and conquered the whole of northern India, the region called Hindustan (hin′də stän′). He established the Moghul (mō′gul), or "Mongol" dynasty that would last for over three hundred years. (See Comment: The Last Moghul, page 66.) Babur was a gifted writer as well as a brilliant soldier. His great literary work is the *Babur-nama* ("Book of Babur"), a frank and vivid account of his life that has been called the greatest autobiography in Oriental literature. The passage from the *Babur-nama* on page 64 is the opening of his memoir, in which he describes his place of birth, his family, and the circumstances under which he became king. The passage on page 65 describes an attempt on his life that took place after his conquest of Hindustan. Babur had defeated and killed the region's ruler, Sultan Ibrahim. Afterward the Sultan's mother attempted to have Babur poisoned.

Hymn of the Thoughts of Men

from the **Rig Veda**
translated by **Jean Le Mee**

Our thoughts wander in all directions
And many are the ways of men:
The cartwright hopes for accidents,
The physician for the cripple,
5 And the priest for a rich patron.
    For the sake of Spirit, O Mind,
    Let go of all these wandering thoughts!

With his dry grass and feather fan
And all his tools of fashioned stone,[1]
10 The blacksmith seeks day after day
The customer endowed with gold.
    For the sake of Spirit, O Mind,
    Let go of all these wandering thoughts!

I'm a singer, father's a doctor,
15 Mother grinds flour with a millstone.
Our thoughts all turn upon profit
And cowlike we all plod along.
    For the sake of Spirit, O Mind,
    Let go of all these wandering thoughts!

---

1. *dry grass . . . fashioned stone*, tools of the blacksmith's trade.

Night

from the **Rig Veda**
translated by **Henry W. Wells**

With myriad eyes the Goddess Night
Looks down on earth when day is done,
Putting all her glories on.

Her deathless being fills the waste;
5 The Goddess pierces depth and height,
Conquering darkness with her light.

The Goddess as she enters, goes,
Yields Dawn her place, as ritual says,
Then all darkness vanishes.

10 Dear, favor us this night with rest,
Whose transit we delight to see
As birds their nest upon a tree!

The villagers have sought their homes,
With birds and beasts at close of day—
15 Even the falcons, fain for prey!

Keep off the she-wolf and her mate,
Turn the roving thief aside,
In quietness let the evening glide!

Quietly she comes to my tired eyes
20 With richest sheen and starry frets—
Morning will cancel them like debts.

Dear Night, accept my hymn, a gift
In sacrifice to you and for
True service to my conqueror!

Prayer in Sickness

from the **Rig Veda**
translated by **Henry W. Wells**

Our gods, raise him once more whom you have
    humbled,
The man whom you have stricken and brought
    low,
Restore again to life the evil doer
Whom you have smitten with so heavy a blow!

5 Two separate winds are blowing from the
    Ocean
Where the beneficent in life holds sway;
May one bring strong, new energy upon you,
May one blow your malignancy away!

"I come with balms to bring you rest and safety,
10 I come to drive off ills, to give you ease.
Here let the gods deliver him, and the Maruts[1]
And all things free him from his foul disease!

Waters, with your healing powers flow on him,
Waters, caress him, fair tongues bless all such!
15 Then, with the ten-fold branching of our
    hands,
Release and stroke him with our gentle touch!"

---

1. *Maruts* (mə rüts'), storm gods in the mythology of the *Vedas.*

THINK AND DISCUSS

Understanding
1. In line 3 of "Hymn of the Thoughts of Men," why might the cartwright hope for accidents?
2. What rhyme schemes are employed in "Prayer in Sickness" and "Night"?
3. What petition is made in "Night"?
4. What problem of peasant life is alluded to in line 21 of "Night"?
5. How does the way in which Night is addressed suggest a warmth and intimacy between the worshiper and the goddess?

Analyzing
6. What two directions of the mind are being contrasted in "Hymn of the Thoughts of Men"?
7. In "Prayer in Sickness" who is the speaker and who is spoken to in stanza one? In stanza two? In the last two stanzas?

Extending
8. How are the structure of "Night" and the emotions the poem conveys similar to those of Akhenaton's "Hymn to the Sun" (page 18)? How do the two poems differ?

APPLYING: Personification
See Handbook of Literary Terms, p. 961.

    Personification is figurative language which represents abstractions, ideas, animals, or inanimate objects as human beings by endowing them with human qualities. When Psalm 19 describes the rising sun as "a bridegroom coming out of his chamber" (page 34), this is an example of personification. In the hymn "Night" from the *Rig Veda*, the starlit night is personified.

1. What do the stars represent figuratively here?
2. What human behavior is suggested by line 3, "putting all her glories on"?

from the Bhagavad Gita

translated by **Juan Mascaró**

hen Arjuna saw in both armies fathers, grandfathers, sons, grandsons; fathers of wives, uncles, masters; brothers, companions and friends.

When Arjuna thus saw his kinsmen face to face in both lines of battle, he was overcome by grief and despair and thus he spoke with a sinking heart.

Arjuna: When I see all my kinsmen, Krishna, who have come here on this field of battle,

Life goes from my limbs and they sink, and my mouth is sear and dry; a trembling overcomes my body, and my hair shudders in horror;

My great bow Gandiva falls from my hands, and the skin over my flesh is burning; I am no longer able to stand, because my mind is whirling and wandering.

And I see forebodings of evil, Krishna. I cannot foresee any glory if I kill my own kinsmen in the sacrifice of battle.

Because I have no wish for victory, Krishna, nor for a kingdom, nor for its pleasures. How can we want a kingdom, Govinda,[1] or its pleasures or even life,

When those for whom we want a kingdom, and its pleasures, and the joys of life, are here in this field of battle about to give up their wealth and their life?

Facing us in the field of battle are teachers, fathers and sons; grandsons, grandfathers, wives' brothers; mothers' brothers and fathers of wives.

These I do not wish to slay, even if I myself am slain. Not even for the kingdom of the three worlds:[2] how much less for a kingdom of the earth!

If we kill these evil men, evil shall fall upon us: what joy in their death could we have, O Janardana,[3] mover of souls?

O day of darkness! What evil spirit moved our minds when for the sake of an earthly kingdom we came to this field of battle ready to kill our own people?

Better for me indeed if the sons of Dhritarashtra,[4] with arms in hand, found me unarmed, unresisting, and killed me in the struggle of war.

Thus spoke Arjuna in the field of battle, and letting fall his bow and arrows he sank down in his chariot, his soul overcome by despair and grief.

Then arose the Spirit of Krishna and spoke to Arjuna, his friend, who with eyes filled with tears, thus had sunk into despair and grief.

Krishna: Whence this lifeless dejection, Arjuna, in this hour, the hour of trial? Strong men know not despair, Arjuna, for this wins neither heaven nor earth.

Fall not into degrading weakness, for this becomes not a man who is a man. Throw off this ignoble discouragement, and arise like a fire that burns all before it. . . .

Thy tears are for those beyond tears; and are thy words words of wisdom? The wise grieve not for those who live; and they grieve not for those who die—for life and death shall pass away.

Because we all have been for all time: I, and thou, and those kings of men. And we all shall be for all time, we all for ever and ever.

As the Spirit of our mortal body wanders on in childhood, and youth and old age, the Spirit wanders on to a new body: of this the sage has no doubts.

From the world of the senses, Arjuna, comes heat and comes cold, and pleasure and pain. They come and they go: they are transient. Arise above them, strong soul.

---

1. *Govinda,* another name for Krishna.
2. *three worlds,* heaven, earth, and *Patala,* the collective name for the seven underworlds in Hindu mythology.
3. *Janardana,* another name for Krishna.
4. *Dhritarashtra* (drit′ə rash′trə), the blind king whose hundred sons are Arjuna's opponents.

The man whom these cannot move, whose soul is one, beyond pleasure and pain, is worthy of life in Eternity.

The unreal never is: the Real never is not. This truth indeed has been seen by those who can see the true.

Interwoven in his creation, the Spirit is beyond destruction. No one can bring to an end the Spirit which is everlasting.

For beyond time he dwells in these bodies, though these bodies have an end in their time; but he remains immeasurable, immortal. Therefore, great warrior, carry on thy fight.

If any man thinks he slays, and if another thinks he is slain, neither knows the ways of truth. The Eternal in man cannot kill: the Eternal in man cannot die.

He is never born, and he never dies. He is in Eternity: he is for evermore. Never-born and eternal, beyond times gone or to come, he does not die when the body dies.

When a man knows him as never-born, everlasting, never-changing, beyond all destruction, how can that man kill a man, or cause another to kill?

As a man leaves an old garment and puts on one that is new, the Spirit leaves his mortal body and wanders on to one that is new.

Weapons cannot hurt the Spirit and fire can never burn him. Untouched is he by drenching waters, untouched is he by parching winds.

Beyond the power of sword and fire, beyond the power of waters and winds, the Spirit is everlasting, omnipresent, never-changing, never-moving, ever One.

Invisible is he to mortal eyes, beyond thought and beyond change. Know that he is, and cease from sorrow.

But if he were born again and again, and again and again he were to die, even then, victorious man, cease thou from sorrow.

For all things born in truth must die, and out of death in truth comes life. Face to face with what must be, cease thou from sorrow.

Invisible before birth are all beings and after death invisible again. They are seen between two unseens. Why in this truth find sorrow?

A manuscript in Sanskrit of the *Mahabharata*. 1841. Scenes from the story of Krishna are painted on the inside of the wooden covers. Library of Congress

One sees him in a vision of wonder, and another gives us words of his wonder. There is one who hears of his wonder; but he hears and knows him not.

The Spirit that is in all beings is immortal in them all: for the death of what cannot die, cease thou to sorrow.

Think thou also of thy duty and do not waver. There is no greater good for a warrior than to fight in righteous war.

There is a war that opens the doors of heaven, Arjuna! Happy the warriors whose fate is to fight such war.

But to forgo this fight for righteousness is to forgo thy duty and honor: is to fall into transgression.

Men will tell of thy dishonor both now and in times to come. And to a man who is in honor, dishonor is more than death.

The great warriors will say that thou hast run from the battle through fear; and those who thought great things of thee will speak of thee in scorn.

And thine enemies will speak of thee in contemptuous words of ill-will and derision, pouring scorn upon thy courage. Can there be for a warrior a more shameful fate?

In death thy glory in heaven, in victory thy glory on earth. Arise therefore, Arjuna, with thy soul ready to fight.

Prepare for war with peace in thy soul. Be in peace in pleasure and pain, in gain and in loss, in victory or in the loss of a battle. In this peace there is no sin.

500–300 B.C.

THINK AND DISCUSS

Understanding

1. What does Arjuna see that halts him just before he is to go into battle?
2. What does Arjuna say he would prefer to fighting?
3. To what different things does Krishna compare the movement of the Spirit from body to body?
4. What does Krishna say is the greatest good for a warrior?

Analyzing

5. Why does Arjuna feel he must not fight?
6. Explain Krishna's argument that it is impossible to kill or be killed.
7. Why does Krishna feel that Arjuna must fight?

Extending

8. Both "Hymn of the Thoughts of Men" and the *Bhagavad Gita* discuss the importance of spiritual values in relation to the responsibilities of various walks of life. Compare and contrast the views presented in these two selections. Which one is concerned with the lives of the aristocracy and which with those of ordinary people? Which argues that spirituality must be sought apart from one's ordinary duties? In which are these duties the highest ethical norm?

COMPOSITION ◄━●

Writing a Dialogue

In Unit 1 you have read portions of two philosophical dialogues—an Egyptian poem on the validity of suicide (page 17) and an Indian one on the validity of war. Pick any arguable subject—serious or light—that interests you. Create arguments for the various positions on the subject and then try to imagine an appropriate speaker to represent each of these positions.

Writing a Letter of Advice

Imagine you are an advice columnist and Arjuna's problem is presented to you in a letter. How would you answer him? Would you use Krishna's arguments about Arjuna's duty as a soldier and the immortality of the soul or would you take another approach? Write a reply in no more than three paragraphs. See "Developing Your Style" in the Writer's Handbook.

from Shakuntala

translated by **A. W. Ryder**

1

It is my body leaves my love, not I;
  My body moves away, but not my mind;
For back to her my struggling fancies fly
  Like silken banners borne against the
    wind.

2

Her glance was loving—but 'twas not for me;
Her step was slow—'twas grace, not coquetry;
Her speech was short—to her detaining
  friend.
In things like these love reads a selfish end!

3

She seems a flower whose fragrance none has
    tasted,
  A gem uncut by workman's tool,
A branch no desecrating hands have wasted,
  Fresh honey, beautifully cool.
No man on earth deserves to taste her
    beauty,
  Her blameless loveliness and worth,
Unless he has fulfilled man's perfect duty—
  And is there such a one on earth?

4

'Twas love that caused the burning pain;
'Tis love that eases it again;
As when, upon a sultry day,
Rain breaks, and washes grief away.

5

Her face, adorned with soft eye-lashes,
Adorable with trembling flashes
Of half-denial, in memory lingers;
The sweet lips guarded by her fingers,
The head that drooped upon her shoulder—
Why was I not a little bolder?

6

As my heart ponders whether I could ever
  Have wed this woman that has come to
    me
In tortured loveliness, as I endeavor
  To bring it back to mind, then like a bee
That hovers round a jasmine flower at dawn,
  While frosty dews of morning still
    o'erweave it,
And hesitates to sip ere they be gone,
  I cannot taste the sweet, and cannot leave
    it.

5th century A.D.

THINK AND DISCUSS
Understanding
1. To what does Dushyanti compare his thoughts in lyric 1?
2. What images of untouched loveliness and sweetness appear in lyric 3?
3. What image suggesting indecision does the king present in lyric 6?
4. What rhyme scheme is employed in lyric 1? In lyric 5?

Analyzing
5. In lyric 5 why does Dushyanti wish he had been "a little bolder"?
6. Does the king's view of his situation in lyric 6 represent a **paradox**? Explain.

Extending
7. Compare these lyrics from *Shakuntala* to the two Egyptian love poems that appear on page 20. Discuss the character of the speakers, the thoughts and feelings they express about love, and the literary style of the poems.

COMPOSITION
Writing About Poetry and Poetic Devices
    In a paper of two or three paragraphs, compare and contrast lyric 3 from *Shakuntala* with quatrain 12 from *The Rubáiyát of Omar Khayyám* (page 45). Discuss their use of **imagery** and **rhyme** and the attitudes toward love, happiness, and duty they express. See "Writing About Poetry and Poetic Devices" in the Writer's Handbook.

Writing About Theme
    One **theme** expressed in these lyrics from *Shakuntala* you have just read might be called "thinking against yourself." In his reflections about his feelings for Shakuntala, Dushyanti is constantly making things more difficult for himself. In a paper of two or three paragraphs describe how several of these lyrics express this theme. See "Writing About Theme" in the Writer's Handbook.

from the Babur-nama

translated by **John Leyden** *and* **William Erskine**

The Year 1494

In the month of Ramzan,[1] in the year fourteen hundred and ninety-four, and in the twelfth year of my age, I became King of Ferghana.

The country of Ferghana is situated on the extreme boundary of the habitable world. It is of small extent, and is surrounded with hills on all sides except the west.

The country abounds in grains and fruits, its grapes and melons are excellent and plentiful, and it is noted for pomegranates and apricots. The people have a way of taking the stones out of the apricot and putting in almonds in their place, which is very pleasant.

It is abundantly supplied with running water, and is extremely pleasant in spring.

There are many gardens overlooking the rivers where tulips and roses grow in great profusion, and there are meadows of clover, sheltered and pleasant, where travellers love to rest. They are called the mantle of lambskins.

It abounds in birds and beasts of game; its pheasants are so fat that four persons may dine on one and not finish it, and the game and venison are excellent.

It is a good sporting country; the white deer, mountain goat, stag, and hare are found in great plenty, and there is good hunting and hawking.

In the hills are mines of turquoises, and in the valleys people weave cloth of a purple color.

The revenues of Ferghana suffice to maintain 4,000 troops.

My father, Omer-Sheikh-Mirza, was a prince of high ambition and magnificent pretensions, and was always bent on some scheme of conquest. He several times led an army against Samarkand,[2] and was repeatedly defeated.

At this time, 1494, the Sultan Mahomed Khan and the Sultan Ahmed Mirza, having taken offense at his conduct, concluded an alliance, and one marched an army from the north, the other from the south, against his dominions.

At this crisis a singular incident occurred. The Fort of Akhsi is situated on a steep precipice, on the edge of which some of its buildings are raised.

On the fourth day of Ramzan, 1494, my father was engaged in feeding his pigeons, when the platform slipped, precipitating him from the top of the rock, and with his pigeons and pigeon-house he took his flight to the other world.

My father was of low stature, had a short bushy beard, and was fat. He used to wear his tunic extremely tight, insomuch that as he was wont to contract his waist when he tied the strings; when he let himself out again the strings often burst. He was not particular in food or dress, and wore his turban without folds, allowing the ends to hang down. His generosity was large, and so was his whole soul, yet brave withal and manly. He was only a middling shot with the bow, but had uncommon force with his fists, and never hit a man without knocking him flat to the ground.

He was a humane man, and played a great deal at backgammon.

---

1. **Ramzan** (räm zän′), or *Ramadan* (ram′ə dän′), Islamic month of fasting.
2. **Samarkand** (sam′ər kand′), a city in Turkestan.

He had three sons and five daughters. Of the sons, I, Muhammed Babur, was the eldest.

My mother was Kutlak Khanum.

The Year 1526

A very important incident happened on Friday, the 16th of Rabia-ul-Awal,[3] in this year. The circumstances are these:—The mother of Ibrahim,[4] an ill-fated lady, had heard that I had eaten some things from the hand of natives of Hindustan. It happened in this way. Three or four months ago, never having seen any of the dishes of Hindustan, I desired Ibrahim's cooks to be called, and out of fifty or sixty cooks, four were chosen and retained. The lady, having heard the circumstance, sent a person to Etaweh to call Ahmed, the taster, and delivered into the hands of a female slave an ounce of poison, wrapped up in a folded paper, desiring it to be given to the taster Ahmed. Ahmed gave it to a Hindustani cook who was in my kitchen, seducing him with the promise of four districts, and desiring him, by some means or other, to throw it into my food. She sent another female slave after the one whom she had desired to carry the poison to Ahmed, in order to observe if the first slave delivered the poison or not. It was fortunate that the poison was not thrown into the pot, it was thrown into the tray. He did not throw it into the pot, because I had strictly enjoined the tasters to watch the Hindustanis, and they had tasted the food in the pot while it was cooking. When they were dishing the meat, my graceless tasters were inattentive, and he threw it upon a plate of thin slices of bread; he did not throw above one half of the poison that was in the paper upon the bread, and put some meat fried in butter upon the slices of bread. If he had thrown it above the fried meat, or into the cooking pot, it would have been still worse; but in his confusion, he spilt the better half of it on the fireplace.

On Friday, when afternoon prayers were past, they dished the dinner. I was very fond of hare, and ate some, as well as a good deal of fried carrot. I was not, however, sensible of any disagreeable taste; I likewise ate a morsel or two of smoke-dried meat, when I felt nausea. The day before, while eating some smoke-dried flesh, I had felt

Late 16th-century Moghul miniature showing Babur laying out a Persian garden at Kabul in 1508. Victoria and Albert Museum

an unpleasant taste in a particular part of it. I ascribed my nausea to that incident. The nausea again returned, and I was seized with so violent a retching, two or three times while the tray was before me, that I had nearly vomited. At last, perceiving that I could not check it, I went out. While on the way my heart rose, and I had again nearly vomited. When I had got outside I vomited a great deal.

---

3. *Rabia-ul-Awal* (rä bē'ä ul ä wäl'), third month of the Islamic year.
4. *Ibrahim* (ib'rə him), sultan of Hindustan, whom Babur defeated and killed at the battle of Panipat in 1526.

Comment

The Last Moghul

In the spring of 1857, an uprising began among the native troops that formed the bulk of the British army in India. These soldiers, called *sepoys* (sē'poiz), complained that a new cartridge issued to them was smeared with the fat of cows and pigs. This outraged both the Hindus among them, to whom the cow was sacred, and the Moslems, to whom the pig was unclean. Only after fighting of extraordinary ferocity, marked by atrocities committed by both sides, did the British restore order. One of the many casualties of the Indian Mutiny, as this event is generally called, was the last Moghul emperor, Bahadur Shah II, who had been persuaded to support the rebels. An aged man, who before the Mutiny had devoted himself largely to literature, Bahadur Shah II was tried by the British and convicted of treason and rebellion. His property was confiscated and he and his household were exiled to the city of Rangoon in Burma. In exile he continued to write poetry. He died of a stroke in 1862 at the age of eighty-seven. "A few hours after he died," observes a recent historian, "he was buried without public ceremony, with neither tomb nor cenotaph, in a patch of earth surrounded by a simple bamboo fence that soon followed the last Moghul emperor into oblivion."

I had never before vomited after my food, and not even after drinking wine. Some suspicions crossed my mind. I ordered the cooks to be taken into custody, and desired the meat to be given to a dog, which I directed to be shut up. Next morning about the first watch, the dog became sick, his belly swelled, and he seemed distressed. Although they threw stones at him, and shoved him, they could not make him rise. He remained in this condition till noon, after which he rose and recovered. Two young men had also eaten of this food. Next morning they too vomited much, one of them was extremely ill, but both in the end escaped.

A calamity fell upon me, but I escaped in safety,
Almighty God bestowed a new life upon me,—
I came from the other world,—
I was again born from my mother's womb.

I was broken and dead, but am again raised to life;
Now, in the salvation of my life, I recognize the
   hand of God.

I ordered Muhammed Bakhshi to guard and examine the cooks, and at last all the particulars came to light, as they have been detailed.

On Monday, being a court day, I directed all the grandees and chief men, the Begs and Vazirs, to attend the Diwan.[5] I brought in the two men and the two women, who, being questioned, detailed the whole circumstances of the affair in all its particulars. The taster was ordered to be cut to pieces. I commanded the cook to be flayed alive. One of the women was ordered to be trampled to death by an elephant; the other I commanded to be shot with a matchlock. The lady I directed to be thrown into custody. She too, pursued by her guilt, will one day meet with due retribution. On Saturday I drank a bowl of milk. I also drank some of the makhtum flower, brayed and mixed in spirits. The milk scoured my inside extremely. Thanks be to God, there are now no remains of illness! I did not fully comprehend before that life was so sweet a thing. The poet says,

Whoever comes to the gates of death, knows the
   value of life.

Whenever these awful occurrences pass before my memory, I feel myself involuntarily turn faint. The mercy of God has bestowed a new life on

---

5. *Begs and Vazirs . . . Diwan.* Begs (begz) and Vazirs (və zirz') were officials and advisers at an Islamic court. The Diwan (dē wän') was the meeting of an Islamic ruler with his counselors and the rest of his court.

me, and how can my tongue express my gratitude? Having resolved with myself to overcome
my repugnance, I have written fully and circum-
stantially everything that happened. Although the
occurrences were awful, and not to be expressed
by the tongue or lips, yet by the favor of Almighty
God, other days awaited me, and have passed in
happiness and health.

THINK AND DISCUSS

Understanding
1. How does Babur come to be king while still
   only a boy?
2. What kind of individual is Babur's father?
3. After Babur is taken ill, what steps does he
   take to determine if he has been poisoned?

Analyzing
4. Describe Babur's attitude toward his father as
   it is suggested by the opening of the *Babur-
   nama*.
5. What does Babur's reference to his mother
   suggest about the position of women within
   the society from which he came?
6. Why might Ibrahim's mother have escaped
   immediate punishment for her role in the
   attempt on Babur's life?

Extending
7. Compare the feelings Babur expresses after
   surviving the attempt on his life with the
   moral of Sadi's story of the padshah and the
   Persian slave (page 52).

APPLYING: Setting   HT
See Handbook of Literary Terms, p. 969.

The **setting** of a narrative is the time and
place in which the action occurs. That a story
takes place, for example, in the present or far
in the past, in an American city or on a remote
island in the Pacific, can be very important to
the development of the action, the characters,
and the atmosphere.

1. What setting is described in the opening of
   the *Babur-nama*?
2. What does his description of Ferghana suggest about Babur?
3. How do the mountains of Ferghana contribute to the development of the action in
   the *Babur-nama*?

THINKING SKILLS

Evaluating
To evaluate is to make a judgment based
on some sort of standard. For example, a jury
makes judgments on the facts presented in a
court case employing their standards of morality
and common sense.

1. Babur was generally known as a merciful
   ruler. Considering his reputation for clemency, what might account for the savagery of
   the punishments he imposed in the poisoning
   episode?
2. Given the times in which he lived and his
   particular circumstances in India, do you
   think these punishments were valid?

COMPOSITION   ━●

Writing About Characters
In a paper of two or three paragraphs, write
a character sketch of Babur as he is revealed in
the two passages from the *Babur-nama* you have
just read. See "Writing About Characters" in the
Writer's Handbook.

Describing Your Setting
In a brief sketch, describe the setting of your
own life—your time and place—as if you were
communicating to a reader far in the future.

ENRICHMENT

Examining Moghul Art
The artists of the Moghul Period in India
created beautiful paintings and a great variety
of exquisitely decorated jewelry, weapons, and
other objects. Both of the following books by
art historian Stuart Cary Welch would help you
to better visualize the world of Babur: *Imperial
Mughul Painting* (George Braziller, 1978) and
India: Art and Culture 1300–1900 (Metropolitan
Museum of Art, 1985).

THE FAR EAST   1000 B.C.–A.D. 1700

1000 B.C.	750	500	250	0	A.D. 250	

HISTORY AND ARTS

- Zhou invade China
- Period of Warring States
  - Qin conquer China
  - Great Wall built
  - Han dynasty established
- Han dynasty falls

PEOPLE

- Lao Tzu
  - Confucius
- Mencius
  - Chuang Tzu
  - Shi Huangdi

T'ao Ch'ien •

LITERATURE

- Age of the Hundred Schools
  - Confucius: *Analects*
  - Lao Tzu: *Tao Te Ching*
  - *Chuang Tzu*
- Buddhism reaches China

Chinese bronze ceremonial
vessel. 11th–10th century B.C.

The Great Wall of China, begun
in the 3rd century B.C.

Camel of glazed earthenware.
Tang dynasty. 8th century A.D.

PART THREE

UNIT 1

500	750	1000	1250	1500	1750

- Sui dynasty
- Tang dynasty established
- Yamato chief becomes emperor
- Nara built
- Rebellion of An Lu-shan
- Capital moved to Kyoto
- Beginning of Heian period

- Fall of Tang dynasty
- Civil war in Japan
- End of Heian period
- Yoritomo becomes shogun
- Kublai Khan attempts invasions of Japan
- Sesshu paints landscapes

- Christianity reaches Japan

- Prince Shotoku
- Li Po
- Tu Fu
- Po Chü-i

- Murasaki Shikibu
- Sei Shōnagon
- Yoritomo
- Kublai Khan

- Seami Motokiyo
- Sesshu

- Bashō

- Buddhism reaches Japan
- *Manyoshu*
- *kana* develops
- Murasaki Shikibu: *The Tale of Genji*

- Sei Shōnagon: *The Pillow Book*
- *No* drama develops
- Seami: *The Damask Drum*

- *haiku* develops

Portrait of Yoritomo. Color on silk. Late 12th century A.D.

Portrait of Kublai Khan. 13th century A.D.

Samurai armor. Muromachi Period (1333–1600)

THE FAR EAST

CHINA

Even more than India, China possesses a cultural tradition that has had an unbroken development from ancient times. "Every Chinese is born at least thirty-five hundred years old," observes one recent historian of the Far East. "More than any other people, the Chinese have a long continuous history until the present century unbroken by major cultural revolutions." There was no serious challenge to the traditional culture of China until the attacks on classical Chinese literature that took place during the Cultural Revolution launched by the Communist government of Mao Zedong in the late 1960s. (See Comment: Confucianism and the Cultural Revolution, page 76.)

The earliest Chinese written records are those inscribed on "oracle bones." These were animal bones used in religious rites performed at the royal capital of China over three thousand years ago. Various questions were inscribed on the oracle bones, which were then heated, causing them to crack. The pattern of the cracks was interpreted by a priest, who provided answers to the questions. Modern archaeologists have discovered the names of rulers of the earliest Chinese dynasties, the Shang, inscribed on the oracle bones. It was during the Shang period that the Chinese developed their pictographic script. By 1400 B.C. the Chinese already possessed a highly advanced system of writing containing a vocabulary of over three thousand characters. It seems improbable that the development of the Chinese system of writing was influenced by either Mesopotamian cuneiform or Egyptian hieroglyphics. All three scripts use symbols denoting words or syllables; none is an alphabet. But at that point their similarity ends.

Around the eleventh century B.C., the plain of North China was invaded by a Central Asian people, the Zhou (jō), who overthrew the Shang but adopted their civilization. Later tradition presents the Zhou as establishing the authority of the emperor and the system of imperial administration. But as the centuries passed, the power of the Zhou emperors, challenged by new waves of invading peoples on the frontiers and by rebellious nobles at home, grew very weak. Despite the frequency of wars, the latter part of the Zhou era was the golden age of philosophy in China.

The period from about 550 to 250 B.C. is referred to as the Age of the Hundred Schools because of the large number of philosophers who were then teaching. The first and most influential of these thinkers was Kong Fuzi (c. 551–479 B.C.), known to the West as Confucius (kən fyü′shəs), a Latinized version of his Chinese name first used by a sixteenth-century Christian missionary. The great Indian contemporary of Confucius, Buddha, had been primarily concerned with the nature of reality. The teachings of Confucius are a code of social conduct. Confucianism had a great influence on the later development of Chinese culture. After 202 B.C. a knowledge of his works was a prerequisite for government service, and Confucianism retained this official preeminence until the Cultural Revolution of the 1960s. The great philosophical rival of Confucianism was Taoism (dou′iz′əm), traditionally founded by Lao Tzu (lou′ dzù′), who may have been a contemporary of Confucius. Like Buddhism, the school of Lao Tzu and his principal disciple Chuang Tzu (chung′ dzù′), who lived in the fourth century B.C., advocated withdrawal from worldly concerns. The name of the school comes from its doctrine of the tao, "the way," the cosmic order. When Buddhist missionaries from India reached China in the first century A.D., the Taoist school merged with the new religion.

The final centuries of Zhou decline, called the Period of Warring States, ended when the state of Qin (chin) conquered all its rivals around 221 B.C. The Qin dynasty lasted only until 206 B.C., but left a number of significant legacies. The only important Qin emperor, Shi Huangdi (shėr′ hwäng′dē′), was an extraordinarily energetic ruler who combined great vision with

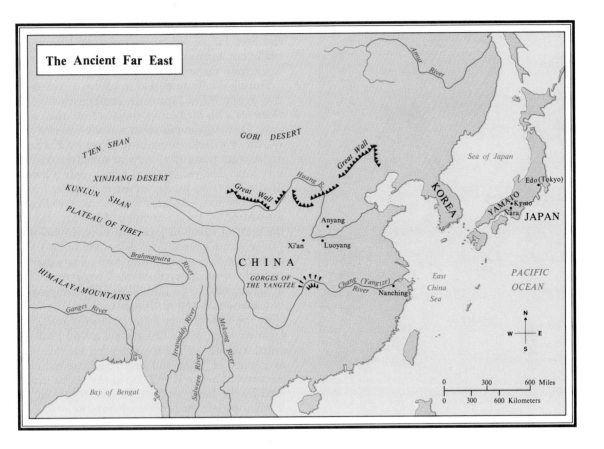

The Ancient Far East

great brutality. He strengthened the central government by ending the power of the nobles. He then divided China into 36 military provinces, each governed by an appointed official. With a few changes, this basic form of government lasted for more than two thousand years. To protect the northern and western border areas from the frequent invasions of Central Asian nomads, Shi Huangdi repaired, strengthened, and linked together already existing defensive walls into a barrier fourteen hundred miles long—the Great Wall of China. "For this colossal work," reports one historian, "he used the forced labor of conscripted peasants, war captives, beggars, criminals, and slaves. The building of the Great Wall is believed to have cost a million lives."

The short-lived Qin dynasty was succeeded by the Hans, who governed China for the next four hundred years. During Han rule, China grew as large and prosperous as the Roman Empire of the same period. The fall of the Han dynasty in A.D. 220 was followed by centuries of disorder like the Warring States Period. "The land was divided like a melon," lamented one writer. China's first great lyric poet, T'ao Ch'ien (A.D. 365–427) wrote during this period. China was reunited in 581 by another short-lived dynasty, the Sui, who were succeeded in 618 by the Tang (täng). For almost three hundred years the Tangs gave China a golden age. The country was prosperous and free from invasion. Its people made progress in education, literature, and the arts. At its height, Tang China was the strongest, most advanced, and best governed country in the world. The lyric poets of the Tang period—Li Po, Tu Fu, Po Chü-i, and others—are regarded as China's greatest poets.

Detail of a landscape done in ink on paper by Sesshu (1420–1506). Seattle Art Museum

JAPAN

The history and culture of the mountainous chain of offshore islands that forms Japan were strongly influenced by geographical factors. Located five hundred miles off the coast of China, Japan was close enough so that the influence of the older, richer culture of the mainland was inevitable. But the distance was also great enough so that Japan was able to preserve its independence, both politically and culturally. In the estimate of one historian, it was their long experience with China that taught the Japanese the valuable lesson of how "to take over and apply to their own purposes what impressed them as desirable in a foreign culture." The mountainousness of the Japanese islands worked against the development of a centralized state like Han or Tang China. Instead, Japan throughout much of its history has been essentially a feudal society composed of a number of separate and frequently hostile clans. The culture of Japan has also been influenced by the mountain landscape, whose combination of barrenness and delicacy has helped shape the Japanese sense of beauty.

During the Tang period in China, a civilization developed in Japan that combined native elements with many importations from the mainland. One such importation was the Chinese system of writing, brought to Japan by Korean immigrants possibly as early as the fifth century A.D. (The peninsula of Korea, only a hundred miles from Japan, served to transmit Chinese influences.) Another import was Buddhism, introduced by Prince Shotoku (574–622), one of the greatest rulers in Japan's history. In 600 the prince sent a large official delegation to China containing a number of young aristocrats eager to study mainland civilization. They returned home as converts to Buddhism and champions of Chinese arts and institutions.

By the fifth century A.D. the chief of one Japanese clan, who ruled a small inland plain called Yamato (yä′mä tō), extended his rule over much of Japan and became recognized as emperor. (*Yamato* is still one of the poetic names used by the Japanese for their country.) The Yamato regime made some attempt to introduce a centralized government modeled on Tang China. But despite some success—including the building of Japan's first city, Nara—the effort failed and the power of the emperors gradually declined. In 784 the imperial capital was moved from Nara to the city later known as Kyoto (kyō′tō), marking the beginning of the Heian (hā′än) period. During the next four centuries, the Japanese developed a distinct culture of their own free of Chinese dominance.

They also evolved a way of life which, for a fortunate minority—the emperor and his court at Kyoto—was one of the most delightful known to history. These nobles led a sheltered and privileged life, spending their days in an endless round of ceremonies and festivities connected with court life. They also devoted themselves to the cultivation of elegance in a variety of artistic pursuits like poetry and calligraphy. Heian court life was memorably captured around 1000 in the masterpiece of Japanese literature, *The Tale of Genji*, a novel by the noblewoman known as Lady Murasaki. A lady-in-waiting to the empress at the imperial court at Kyoto, Lady Murasaki created a vast narrative of aristocratic life, containing a cast of five hundred characters spanning three generations, and set in a Japan which was wealthy, cultured, and at peace. *The Tale of Genji* has had an enormous impact on Japanese culture. In addition to affecting all subsequent literature, its influence on Japanese ideas of manhood and femininity, on their attitude toward the beauty of landscape, and even on fashions in clothing and interior design, continues to the present day.

By the middle of the twelfth century, the emperor had authority in name only. In 1156, outright civil war burst out between two great clans, the Taira and the Minamoto. "Earthquakes of exceptional violence," observes one historian about the terrible period that followed, "plague, famine, and private banditry on the part of 'Buddhist' soldier-monks aggravated the horrors of a civil war, which ended only in 1185 with the annihilation of the Taira in a sea battle of appalling ferocity." In 1192, the chief of the victorious Minamoto clan, Yoritomo, had the emperor name him the *shogun* (shō'gun), or supreme general of the entire country. This office became hereditary, and the emperor continued as a mere figurehead at Kyoto. Japan remained a feudal society governed by a series of shogunates until modern times. The power of Japan's military rulers was based on the loyalty of their warriors, called *samurai* (sam'u rī). Like the knights of European feudalism, the samurai pledged complete loyalty to their lord.

In the late thirteenth century, the Mongol ruler of China, Kublai Khan, made two unsuccessful attempts to invade Japan. While the Chinese were defeated, the effort exhausted Japan, and the power of the shogunate established by Yoritomo declined rapidly. In 1333 a new military group seized power. This new shogunate was not as powerful as its predecessor, and a number of local nobles, called *daimyo* (dī'myō) struggled with each other for more power and territory. Despite the turmoil, Japan enjoyed one of its most productive eras in the arts. During the fourteenth and fifteenth centuries, the Japanese developed their characteristic dramatic form, the *No* play. The greatest figure in the tradition of the *No* drama was Seami Motokiyo (1363–1443), who both wrote and performed in *No* plays. Another glory of this period was its painting. Charming landscapes, vigorous battle-scenes, and realistic sketches of everyday life were the chief subjects. The most famous artist of the period was a Buddhist monk named Sesshu (1420–1506).

THINKING ABOUT GRAPHIC AIDS
Using the Time Line

The time line on pages 68–69 shows the chronological sequence of the historical and literary events discussed in Part 3. Use the time line to answer the following questions.

1. What Chinese dynasty was in power when Buddhism reached China?
2. Could the shogun Yoritomo have organized the Japanese defenses against either of Kublai Khan's two invasion fleets?
3. Was the Japanese court located at Nara when the *kana* system of writing was developed?
4. Which of the following writers could not have been affected by the rebellion of An Lu-shan? (a) T'ao Ch'ien; (b) Tu Fu; (c) Po Chü-i
5. What dynasty was ruling China at the time of the visit of Prince Shotoku's delegation?

Using the Map

The map on page 71 shows the geographical area occupied by the two civilizations discussed in Part 3. Use the map to answer the following questions.

1. What natural defenses against invasion does China possess?
2. What do the locations of the early imperial capitals—Anyang, Luoyang, Xi'an—indicate about the geographical focus of the development of Chinese civilization?
3. What lies to the north of the Great Wall?
4. What country's geographical position made it a cultural bridge between China and Japan?
5. Do the locations of its early capitals—Nara and Kyoto—suggest that Japan was dominated by its northern or its southern part?

Chinese Philosophy

Rubbing of a portrait of Confucius cut in stone. 1734. Field Museum of Natural History, Chicago

Philosophical thought in China begins amid the social disorder of the final centuries of the Zhou era. The violence of the period is reflected in the debate between Confucianism, which stressed the need to reform a corrupt and collapsing society, and Taoism, which advocated withdrawal from this society. Almost nothing is known with certainty about the lives of either of the two great founders of Chinese philosophy, Confucius and Lao Tzu. According to tradition they were contemporaries who lived at the end of the sixth and the beginning of the fifth centuries B.C. The great ambition of Confucius was to find a ruler who would employ him and put his theories of government into practice. "If only someone would make use of me, even for a single year," he laments in the *Analects* ("Sayings"), "I could do a great deal; and in three years I could finish off the whole work." But though he apparently traveled from province to province seeking an official appointment, he found no ruler sufficiently interested in reform to employ him. In the end, he retired to teaching, hoping to change Chinese society through his pupils. The influence of Confucianism on Chinese civilization has been enormous. By "Confucianism" is meant not only the teachings of Confucius, but those of his chief disciple, Mencius (men′-shē əs), who lived in the fourth century B.C., and those of their followers in other periods. "A practicable moral philosophy that teaches the rules of personal cultivation and the virtues of human relationships," observes one historian, "Confucianism has molded the Chinese national character and pervaded every aspect of Chinese society, the family, literature, and the arts." At the heart of Confucianism is an ideal of the moral order of society. To sustain this moral order, Confucius urged moderation, benevolence, and a respect for tradition. Several passages from the *Analects*, a collection of his sayings made soon after his death, appear on page 75.

There is a famous story that describes a visit that Confucius made to Lao Tzu to ask for advice. Lao Tzu bluntly tells him to abandon his cultivation of rulers and his ambition to reform society, and then dismisses him. The meeting probably never took place, but the story illustrates both the essentially antisocial nature of Lao Tzu's thought and the rivalry that existed between his followers and those of Confucius. Lao Tzu is the traditional founder of the philosophical school known as Taoism. Tradition also attributes to him the authorship of the *Tao Te Ching* (dou′ də king), sometimes translated "The Classic of the Way and Its Power." The *Tao Te Ching* is a brief, enigmatic, mystical work that combines prose and verse. Its basic subject is the paradoxical nature of the *tao* (dou), or "way," the cosmic order, manifest in all things yet utterly hidden and unknowable. Unlike the *Analects*, the political philosophy of the *Tao Te Ching* is anti-intellectual and anarchic: "Drop wisdom, abandon cleverness, and the people will be benefited a hundredfold." Far more elegant in style than the *Tao Te Ching* are the fables of Lao Tzu's most important disciple, Chuang Chou (c. 365–c. 290 B.C.), or as he is usually called Chuang Tzu (chung′ dzu), "Master Chuang." Two of his fables appear on pages 76–77.

from the Analects

Confucius
translated by **Arthur Waley**

he Master[1] said, He who rules by moral force is like the pole-star, which remains in its place while all the lesser stars do homage to it.

The Master said, Govern the people by regulations, keep order among them by chastisements, and they will flee from you, and lose all self-respect. Govern them by moral force, keep order among them by ritual[2] and they will keep their self-respect and come to you of their own accord.

Mêng Wu Po[3] asked about the treatment of parents. The Master said, Behave in such a way that your father and mother have no anxiety about you, except concerning your health.

The Master said, High office filled by men of narrow views, ritual performed without reverence, the forms of mourning observed without grief—these are the things I cannot bear to see!

Wealth and rank are what every man desires; but if they can only be retained to the detriment of the Way he professes, he must relinquish them. Poverty and obscurity are what every man detests; but if they can only be avoided to the detriment of the Way he professes, he must accept them. The gentleman who ever parts company with Goodness does not fulfil that name. Never for a moment does a gentleman quit the way of Goodness. He is never so harried but that he cleaves to this; never so tottering but that he cleaves to this.

The Master said, Mêng Chih-fan is no boaster. When his people were routed he was the last to flee; but when they neared the city-gate, he whipped up his horses, saying, It was not courage that kept me behind. My horses were slow.

Chi Wên Tzu used to think thrice before acting. The Master hearing of it said, Twice is quite enough.

The Master said, Learn as if you were following someone whom you could not catch up, as though it were someone you were frightened of losing.

Jan Jung asked about Goodness. The Master said, Behave when away from home as though you were in the presence of an important guest. Deal with the common people as though you were officiating at an important sacrifice. Do not do to others what you would not like yourself. Then there will be no feelings of opposition to you, whether it is the affairs of a State that you are handling or the affairs of a Family.[4] Jan Jung said, I know that I am not clever; but this is a saying that, with your permission, I shall try to put into practice.

Tzu-kung asked about government. The Master said, sufficient food, sufficient weapons, and the confidence of the common people. Tzu-kung said, Suppose you had no choice but to dispense with one of these three, which would you forgo? The Master said, Weapons. Tzu-kung said, Suppose you were forced to dispense with one of the two that were left, which would you forgo? The Master said, Food. For from of old death has been the lot of all men; but a people that no longer trusts its rulers is lost indeed.

5th century B.C.

---

1. *Master*, Confucius.
2. *ritual*, traditional religious observances.
3. *Mêng Wu Po*, a government official in Confucius's home state, Lu. The other names mentioned in these passages from the *Analects* are also those of officials of Lu in Confucius's time.
4. *Family*, a ruling clan.

Comment

Confucianism and the Cultural Revolution

In 1966, the Chinese leader Mao Zedong began the "Great Proletarian Cultural Revolution," a campaign against intellectuals and members of other elite groups within the Communist society of the People's Republic. The schools were closed and mobs of young people, called the Red Guards, were encouraged to attack teachers, party officials, and others who held to "old ideas, old customs, and old habits."

Among these "old ideas" were those of Confucianism. Confucius was denounced for his defense of the value of tradition. His moral principles of moderation and benevolence were said to lead to submission and passivity. Since sexual equality was one of the goals of the People's Republic, Confucius was also attacked for his low opinion of women. His views on the superiority of the intellectual work of the scholar to the manual labor of ordinary people were denounced as elitist.

Soon the Cultural Revolution got out of hand. Anyone with an education was attacked. Eventually Mao was forced to use the army to restore order. The schools were reopened and the Red Guards disbanded. Since Mao's death in 1976, there has been a modest attempt by the Chinese government to rehabilitate Confucianism by integrating its principles with those of Marxism.

Chuang Tzu and the Butterfly

from the **Chuang Tzu**
translated by **Burton Watson**

Once Chuang Chou[1] dreamt he was a butterfly, a butterfly flitting and fluttering around, happy with himself and doing as he pleased. He didn't know he was Chuang Chou. Suddenly he woke up and there he was, solid and unmistakable Chuang Chou. But he didn't know if he was Chuang Chou who had dreamt he was a butterfly, or a butterfly dreaming he was Chuang Chou. Between Chuang Chou and a butterfly there must be *some* distinction! This is called the Transformation of Things.

---

1. *Chuang Chou,* Chuang Tzu.

The Cook Ting

from the **Chuang Tzu**
translated by **Burton Watson**

Your life has a limit but knowledge has none. If you use what is limited to pursue what has no limit, you will be in danger. If you understand this and still strive for knowledge, you will be in danger for certain! If you do good, stay away from fame. If you do evil, stay away from punishments. Follow the middle; go by what is constant, and you can stay in one piece, keep yourself alive, look after your parents, and live out your years.

Cook Ting was cutting up an ox for Lord Wen-hui.[2] At every touch of his hand, every heave of his shoulder, every move of his feet, every thrust of his knee—zip! zoop! He slithered the knife along with a zing, and all was in perfect rhythm, as though he were performing the dance of the Mulberry Grove or keeping time to the Ching-shou music.[3]

---

2. *Lord Wen-hui* (wen hwā′), ruler of the state of Wei.
3. *Mulberry Grove . . . Ching-shou music,* traditional Chinese music.

"Ah, this is marvelous!" said Lord Wen-hui. "Imagine skill reaching such heights!"

Cook Ting laid down his knife and replied, "What I care about is the Way, which goes beyond skill. When I first began cutting up oxen, all I could see was the ox itself. After three years I no longer saw the whole ox. And now—now I go at it by spirit and don't look with my eyes. Perception and understanding have come to a stop and spirit moves where it wants. I go along with the natural makeup, strike in the big hollows, guide the knife through the big openings, and follow things as they are. So I never touch the smallest ligament or tendon, much less a main joint.

"A good cook changes his knife once a year—because he cuts. A mediocre cook changes his knife once a month—because he hacks. I've had this knife of mine for nineteen years and I've cut up thousands of oxen with it, and yet the blade is as good as though it had just come from the grindstone. There are spaces between the joints, and the blade of the knife has really no thickness. If you insert what has no thickness into such spaces, then there's plenty of room—more than enough for the blade to play about in. That's why after nineteen years the blade of my knife is still as good as when it first came from the grindstone.

"However, whenever I come to a complicated place, I size up the difficulties, tell myself to watch out and be careful, keep my eyes on what I'm doing, work very slowly, and move the knife with the greatest subtlety, until—flop! the whole thing comes apart like a clod of earth crumbling to the ground. I stand there holding the knife and look all around me, completely satisfied and reluctant to move on, and then I wipe off the knife and put it away.

"Excellent!" said Lord Wen-hui. "I have heard the words of Cook Ting and learned how to care for life!"

4th century B.C.

THINK AND DISCUSS
Understanding
1. Describe Confucius's view of the role of traditional rituals in Chinese society.
2. What point is Confucius making in his observations about Chi Wên Tzu and Mêng Chih-fan?
3. What happens in the story of Chuang Tzu and the butterfly?
4. In Chuang Tzu's story, why is Cook Ting able to continually use the same knife without blunting it?

Analyzing
5. Is the view of human nature implied by the *Analects* a positive or negative one?
6. Describe what Confucius means by a "gentleman."

Extending
7. Asked about the nature of goodness, Confucius says, "Do not do to others what you would not like yourself." Relate this maxim to the moral principle known as the "golden rule"—Do to others what you would have them do to you. Which moral ideal is more challenging? Which is wiser? Explain.
8. Compare Chuang Tzu's use of **paradox** with that of Rumi (pages 48–50).

THINKING SKILLS
Generalizing
To generalize is to infer a general rule from particular data. For example, an archaeologist examines the artifacts surviving from an ancient culture and infers their level of technology.

1. Using the passages from the *Analects* as your data, infer the attitude of Confucius toward political ambition.
2. Using the fables of Chuang Tzu as your data, infer his view of the nature of physical reality.

Chinese Poetry

Unlike the Persians, who traditionally regarded poetry as the highest literary art, the Chinese reserved this distinction for history. They thought of poetry as an ordinary, everyday activity, a scholar's pastime. A common saying during the Tang era held that "whoever was a man, was a poet." The greatest achievements of Chinese poetry are not in narrative forms—as in India—but in lyric ones. There is no Chinese epic like the *Mahabharata* or the *Ramayana;* instead, Chinese poetry is generally brief and written on simple, personal themes. They are songs expressing love of natural beauty and peaceful rural life. They deal with the joys and sorrows of family life, and especially, of friendship. They express the sufferings of ordinary people in the frequent wars and famines. The Chinese valued brevity as an essential characteristic of poetry. Four- and eight-line verse forms were popular. Within this limited scope, however, Chinese poets exercised high literary craftsmanship, weighing each word carefully for artistic effect.

T'ao Ch'ien (dou' chē'en) [A.D. 365–427], China's first great poet of rural life, lived during the troubled years between the Han and Tang dynasties. Chinese critics characterize his subject matter as "fields and gardens," to distinguish it from another type of nature poetry, "mountains and water." Much of his work deals with life on his small farm, to which he retired at the age of forty. He resigned his post as a minor public official, rather than, as he puts it, "cringe for five pecks of rice." As one literary historian observes, T'ao Ch'ien "aspired to attune himself to the cycle of nature in Taoist fashion, but also felt, true to the Confucian tradition, that he had a political destiny to fulfill." Two of his poems appear on pages 79–80. He also wrote one of the most famous pieces of Chinese prose, "The Peach-Blossom Fountain," which appears on page 80. This brief tale is one of the earliest pictures in world literature of a utopia, an ideal society.

The golden age of Chinese poetry was the period of the Tang dynasty (618–906). Even the amount of Tang poetry that has survived—nearly fifty thousand poems by some 2,300 poets—is an impressive indication of both the creative fertility of the period and the high regard its literary works have enjoyed in the more than ten centuries since then. Out of this vast body of work, the most highly regarded is that by Li Po (701–762) and his younger contemporary and friend, Tu Fu (712–770). Li Po represents for China the spirit of romance. He never took to the conservative Confucian teaching of his childhood, but was fascinated by Taoist mysticism and the simple, natural life. He had a reputation for improvising verses any place, any time, and especially when he had had his fill of wine. For some twenty years he wandered about from place to place, staying with friends or relatives, taking odd jobs, or living as a recluse. For a short period he served at the imperial court, where he became a favorite of the Emperor. But because of his enemies or his irresponsibility—or perhaps both—he was dismissed from the Emperor's service and again became a wanderer. Several of his poems appear on pages 84–86.

Portrait of Li Po in ink on paper. Early 13th century. Tokyo National Museum

Chinese scholars consider Tu Fu their greatest poet, although Li Po has always been more popular, both with ordinary Chinese and with foreigners. Born into a poor family, he was a precocious student, but failed to obtain appointment to public office. Devoted to Confucianism, he was forced like Confucius to wander through the provinces of China in search of an official post. Despite constant travel and frequent hardship, Tu Fu committed himself to exacting standards of literary craft. Two of his poems appear on page 87.

In 755 the rebellion of An Lu-shan, a Turkish general in command of imperial troops, plunged Tang China into a bloody and destructive civil war from which it never fully recovered. Later Tang poetry reflects the disorder and uncertainty of the period. The best known of the later Tang poets was Po Chü-i (bō′ jü′ē) [772–846], who used his poetry to attack the social evils he observed. His clear style, avoiding learned allusions and philosophical ambiguities, earned him during his lifetime an extraordinary popularity among his contemporaries of all classes. Several of his poems appear on pages 88–91.

 Review THEME in the Handbook of Literary Terms, page 975.

I Built My Cottage Among the Habitations of Men

T'ao Ch'ien
translated by **Liu Wu-chi**

I built my cottage among the habitations of
  men,
And yet there is no clamor of carriages and
  horses.
You ask: "Sir, how can this be done?"
"A heart that is distant creates its own
  solitude."
5 I pluck chrysanthemums under the eastern
  hedge,
Then gaze afar towards the southern hills.
The mountain air is fresh at the dusk of day;
The flying birds in flocks return.
In these things there lies a deep meaning;
10 I want to tell it, but have forgotten the words.

Two Poems on Returning to Dwell in the Country

T'ao Ch'ien
translated by **William Acker**

1

In youth I had nothing
  that matched the vulgar tone,
For my nature always
  loved the hills and mountains.
Inadvertently I fell
  into the Dusty Net,
Once having gone
  it was more than thirteen years.
5 The tame bird
  longs for his old forest—
The fish in the house-pond
  thinks of his ancient pool.

I too will break the soil
    at the edge of the southern moor,
I will guard simplicity
    and return to my fields and garden.
My land and house—
    a little more than ten acres,
10 In the thatched cottage—
    only eight or nine rooms.
Elms and willows
    shade the back verandah,
Peach and plum trees
    in rows before the hall.
Hazy and dimly seen
    a village in the distance,
Close in the foreground
    the smoke of neighbors' houses.
15 A dog barks
    amidst the deep lanes,
A cock is crowing
    atop a mulberry tree.
No dust and confusion
    within my doors and courtyard;
In the empty rooms,
    more than sufficient leisure.
Too long I was held
    within the barred cage.
20 Now I am able
    to return again to Nature.

2

Long I have loved to stroll among the hills
    and marshes,
And take my pleasure roaming the woods and
    fields.
Now I hold hands with a train of nieces and
    nephews,
Parting the hazel growth we tread the untilled
    wastes—
5 Wandering to and fro amidst the hills and
    mounds
Everywhere around us we see dwellings of
    ancient men.
Here are vestiges of their wells and
    hearthstones,
There the rotted stumps of bamboo and
    mulberry groves.
I stop and ask a faggot-gatherer:[1]
10 "These men—what has become of them?"
The faggot-gatherer turns to me and says:
"Once they were dead that was the end of
    them."
In the same world men lead different lives;
Some at the court, some in the marketplace.
15 Indeed I know these are no empty words:
The life of man is like a shadow-play
Which must in the end return to nothingness.
After A.D. 405

---

1. *faggot-gatherer*, someone who collects faggots, bundles of sticks or twigs tied together for fuel.

The Peach-Blossom Fountain

T'ao Ch'ien
translated by **Herbert Giles**

owards the close of the fourth century A.D., a certain fisherman of Wu-ling, who had followed up one of the river branches without taking note whither he was going, came suddenly upon a grove of peach trees in full bloom, extending some distance on each bank, with not a tree of any other kind in sight. The beauty of the scene and the exquisite perfume of the flowers filled the heart of the fisherman with surprise, as he proceeded onwards, anxious to reach the limit of this lovely grove. He found

Painting of the Peach-Blossom
Fountain. Ink and color on paper.
1646. Metropolitan Museum of Art

that the peach trees ended where the water began, at the foot of a hill; and there he espied what seemed to be a cave with light issuing from it. So he made fast his boat, and crept in through a narrow entrance, which shortly ushered him into a new world of level country, of fine houses, of rich fields, of fine pools, and of luxuriance of mulberry and bamboo. Highways of traffic ran north and south; sounds of crowing cocks and barking dogs were heard around; the dress of the people who passed along or were at work in the fields was of a strange cut; while young and old alike appeared to be contented and happy.

One of the inhabitants, catching sight of the fisherman, was greatly astonished; but, after learning whence he came, insisted on carrying him home, and killed a chicken and placed some wine before him. Before long, all the people of the place had turned out to see the visitor, and they informed him that their ancestors had sought refuge here, with their wives and families, from the troublous times of the house of Ch'in,[2] adding that they had thus become finally cut off from the rest of the human race. They then enquired about the politics of the day, ignorant of the establishment of the Han dynasty,[3] and of course of the later dynasties which had succeeded it. And when the fisherman told them the story, they grieved over the vicissitudes of human affairs.

Each in turn invited the fisherman to his home and entertained him hospitably, until at length the latter prepared to take his leave. "It will not be worth while to talk about what you have seen to the outside world," said the people of the place to the fisherman, as he bade them farewell and returned to his boat, making mental notes of his route as he proceeded on his homeward voyage.

When he reached home, he at once went and reported what he had seen to the Governor of the district, and the Governor sent off men with him to seek, by the aid of the fisherman's notes, to discover this unknown region. But he was never able to find it again. Subsequently, another desperate attempt was made by a famous adventurer to pierce the mystery; but he also failed, and died soon afterwards of chagrin, from which time forth no further attempts were made.

Early 5th Century

---

2. **Ch'in,** or Qin (chin), short-lived dynasty that ruled China at the end of the third century B.C.
3. **Han dynasty,** one of the greatest Chinese dynasties, ruling from 202 B.C. to A.D. 220; successors of the Qin.

THINK AND DISCUSS
Understanding
1. What paradoxical situation does T'ao Ch'ien present at the opening of "I Built My Cottage Among the Habitations of Men"?
2. In the first of his "Two Poems on Returning to Dwell in the Country," to what does T'ao Ch'ien compare himself in his longing to escape to his farm?
3. In the second of these poems, what does T'ao Ch'ien discover on his walks with his nieces and nephews?
4. In "The Peach-Blossom Fountain," where had the inhabitants of the country discovered by the fisherman come from? When had they arrived?

Analyzing
5. In his poem "I Built My Cottage Among the Habitations of Men," what does T'ao Ch'ien mean when he says, "A heart that is distant creates its own solitude" (line 4)?
6. In the first of his "Two Poems on Returning to Dwell in the Country," what does T'ao Ch'ien mean by his **metaphors** "the Dusty Net" (line 3) and "the barred cage" (line 19)?
7. When the fisherman is about to leave the country he has found in "The Peach-Blossom Fountain," why do its inhabitants caution him, "It will not be worth while to talk about what you have seen to the outside world"?

Extending
8. How do you think that T'ao Ch'ien's young relatives in the second of his "Two Poems on Returning to Dwell in the Country" might have reacted to the discovery of the ancient dwellings? Would they have had the same sort of response as their uncle? Explain.
9. Like many Chinese poets, T'ao Ch'ien's work exhibits the influence of both Confucianism (with its emphasis on duty and tradition) and Taoism (with its emphasis on simplicity and nature). Does T'ao Ch'ien seem more influenced by Confucianism or Taoism? Explain.

REVIEWING: Theme
See Handbook of Literary Terms, p. 975.

The **theme** is the underlying meaning of a literary work. A theme may be directly stated, but more often it is implied. In the first of his "Two Poems on Returning to Dwell in the Country," T'ao Ch'ien states his theme in the final four lines: "Too long I was held/within the barred cage./Now I am able/to return again to Nature."

1. In the second of these two poems, is the theme directly stated or implied?
2. What is the theme?

COMPOSITION
Creating a Utopia
In "The Peach-Blossom Fountain," T'ao Ch'ien creates a picture of an ideal society. In a paper of no more than five paragraphs, sketch your own vision of a perfect society. You can choose whether or not to frame your utopia in a simple story, as T'ao Ch'ien did.

Writing About Theme
In a paper of two or three paragraphs, describe how T'ao Ch'ien develops the theme in either of his "Two Poems on Returning to Dwell in the Country." Whichever poem you choose, be sure to discuss T'ao Ch'ien's use of **imagery** and **setting**.

Literary Criticism in Ancient China

A concern with the way in which language is used was part of the Confucian tradition. Confucius had taught that all wisdom lay in learning to call things by their right names. This idea, which he called "the rectification of names," involved both precision in language and correctness of moral judgment. China's first important literary critic was Lu Chi (A.D. 261–303). A member of a distinguished military family, he was forced to go into exile when the ruler whom he served was overthrown. While in exile he studied both philosophical texts and literary history. Three years before his death he wrote the *Wen Fu,* a series of meditations on the nature, process, and purpose of writing. Three sections from the *Wen Fu* appear below.

Beginning

Eyes closed, he hears an inner music; he is lost in thoughts and questions—

His spirit rides to the eight corners of the universe, his mind a thousand miles away.

And then the inner voice grows clearer as objects become defined,

And he pours forth the essence of words, savoring their sweetness.

He drifts in a heavenly lake, he dives to the depths of seas.

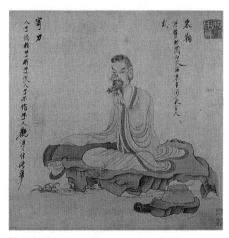

Detail of an imaginary portrait of T'ao Ch'ien. 1650. Honolulu Academy of Arts

And he brings up living words like fishes hooked in their gills, leaping from the deep;

And beauty is brought down like a bird on an arrowstring shot from passing clouds.

He gathers his words and images from those unused by previous generations, his music comes from melodies unplayed for a thousand years or more.

The morning blossoms bloom; soon the night buds will unfold.

He sees past and present commingle; he sees the whole Four Seas in the single blink of an eye.

Revision

Looking back, one finds the disharmonious image; anticipating what will come, one seeks the smooth transition.

Even with right reason, the words will sometimes clang; sometimes the language flows, though the ideas tend to be trivial.

Knowing one from the other, the writing is made clearer; confuse the two, and everything will suffer.

The General inspects his soldiers for every minutest detail, down to a single hair.

When corrections are precise, the building stands square and plumb.

Conclusion

Consider the use of letters, for all principles demand them.

Though they travel a thousand miles and more, nothing in the world can stop them; they traverse ten thousand years.

Look at them one way, and they clarify laws for the future; look at them another, and they provide models from old masters.

The art of letters has saved governments from certain ruin and propagates proper morals.

Through letters there is no road too distant to travel, no idea too confusing to be ordered.

It comes like rain from clouds; it renews the vital spirit.

Inscribed on bronze and marble, it honors every virtue; it sings through flute and strings, and every day is made newer.

The River-Merchant's Wife: A Letter

Li Po
translated by **Ezra Pound**

While my hair was still cut straight across my
    forehead
I played about the front gate, pulling flowers.
You came by on bamboo stilts, playing horse,
You walked about my seat, playing with blue
    plums.
5 And we went on living in the village of Chōkan:
Two small people, without dislike or suspicion.

At fourteen I married My Lord you.
I never laughed, being bashful.
Lowering my head, I looked at the wall.
10 Called to, a thousand times, I never looked
    back.

At fifteen I stopped scowling,
I desired my dust to be mingled with yours
Forever and forever and forever.
Why should I climb the look out?

15 At sixteen you departed,
You went into far Ku-tō-en, by the river of
    swirling eddies.
And you have been gone five months.
The monkeys make sorrowful noise overhead.
You dragged your feet when you went out.
20 By the gate now, the moss is grown, the
    different mosses,
Too deep to clear them away!
The leaves fall early this autumn, in wind.
The paired butterflies are already yellow with
    August
Over the grass in the West garden;
25 They hurt me. I grow older.
If you are coming down through the narrows of
    the river Kiang,[1]
Please let me know beforehand,
And I will come out to meet you
                  As far as Chō-fū-Sa.

---

1. *narrows . . . Kiang,* the gorges of the Yangtze River,
site of the rapids mentioned in line 16.

Addressed Humorously to Tu Fu

Li Po
translated by **Shigeyoshi Obata**

Here! is this you on the top of Fan-ko Mountain,
Wearing a huge hat in the noon-day sun?
How thin, how wretchedly thin, you have grown!
You must have been suffering from poetry again.

Fighting South of the Ramparts

Li Po
translated by **Arthur Waley**

Last year we were fighting at the source of the
    Sang-kan;[1]
This year we are fighting on the Onion River[2]
    road.
We have washed our swords in the surf of
    Parthian seas;[3]
We have pastured our horses among the snows
    of the T'ien Shan,[4]
5 The King's armies have grown grey and old
Fighting ten thousand leagues away from
    home.
The Huns have no trade but battle and
    carnage;
They have no fields or ploughlands,
But only wastes where white bones lie among
    yellow sands.
10 Where the House of Ch'in built the great wall
    that was to keep away the Tartars,
There, in its turn, the House of Han lit beacons
    of war.
The beacons are always alight, fighting and
    marching never stop.
Men die in the field, slashing sword to
    sword;
The horses of the conquered neigh piteously to
    Heaven.
15 Crows and hawks peck for human guts,
Carry them in their beaks and hang them on
    the branches of withered trees.
Captains and soldiers are smeared on the bushes
    and grass;
The General schemed in vain.
Know therefore that the sword is a cursed
    thing
20 Which the wise man uses only if he must.

Terra-cotta statue of an infantryman, one of the
7,500 clay figures found in the tomb of the emperor
Shi Huangdi, who died in 210 B.C. Museum of Qin
Figures, Lintong, Shaanxi Province

1. **Sang-kan,** a river north of the Great Wall of China.
2. **Onion River,** a river in Turkestan.
3. **Parthian seas,** Parthia was an ancient country in Asia
southeast of the Caspian Sea, now a part of Iran.
4. **T'ien Shan,** mountains in a remote region of China.

Parting at a Wine-Shop in Nan-king

Li Po
translated by **Witter Bynner**

A wind, bringing willow-cotton, sweetens the shop,
And a girl from Wu, pouring wine, urges me to share it
With my comrades of the city who are here to see me off;
And as each of them drains his cup, I say to him in parting,
5 Oh, go and ask this river running to the east
If it can travel farther than a friend's love!

THINK AND DISCUSS
Understanding
1. How old is the speaker in "The River-Merchant's Wife: A Letter"? Why does she remark on her age in line 25?
2. In line 25 of this poem, who are "they"? Why do they "hurt" the speaker?
3. In his poem "Addressed Humorously to Tu Fu," to what does Li Po attribute his friend's gauntness?
4. Who is the speaker in "Fighting South of the Ramparts"?
5. Why does the speaker feel it is useless to fight the Huns?

Analyzing
6. The speaker in "The River-Merchant's Wife: A Letter" never directly tells her husband that she loves him. In what ways is this love revealed?
7. What signs indicate the husband's love?
8. Is the **theme** of "Fighting South of the Ramparts" stated directly or implied? What is the theme?

Extending
9. Even though "Parting at a Wine-Shop in Nan-king" has a sad subject, would you characterize it as a sad poem? Explain.

APPLYING: Apostrophe HT
See Handbook of Literary Terms, p. 941.

An **apostrophe** is a figure of speech in which an absent or dead person, an inanimate object, or an abstract concept is addressed directly. Edwin Muir's poem beginning "O Merlin in your crystal cave" is an example of apostrophe.

1. Which of the poems by Li Po you have read exhibit apostrophe?
2. To whom is each addressed?

COMPOSITION
Writing a Narrative
Li Po's "The River-Merchant's Wife: A Letter" is a capsule summary of how a love grew. It says little but implies much. Write a prose narrative of no more than three paragraphs describing the course of this marriage—how it came about, what it has come to mean to both the young woman and her husband. Explore the reasons for the girl's changing feelings, her love, her fears, her yearnings.

Writing a Letter
Imagine you are the young husband in Li Po's poem. Compose a brief letter (two or three paragraphs) to your wife, speaking of your travels and reassuring her.

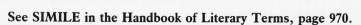

HT See SIMILE in the Handbook of Literary Terms, page 970.

Sent to Li Po as a Gift

Tu Fu
translated by **Florence Aysough**
and **Amy Lowell**

Autumn comes,
We meet each other.
You still whirl about as a thistledown in the
    wind.
Your Elixir of Immortality is not yet
    perfected
5 And, remembering Ko Hung,[1] you are
    ashamed.
You drink a great deal,
You sing wild songs,
Your days pass in emptiness.
Your nature is a spreading fire,
10 It is swift and strenuous.
But what does all this bravery amount to?
745

---

1. ***Ko Hung,*** Chinese official who tried to make the Elixir
of Immortality.

A Night Abroad

Tu Fu
translated by **Witter Bynner**

A light wind is rippling at the grassy
    shore. . . .
Through the night, to my motionless tall
    mast,
The stars lean down from open space,
And the moon comes running up the river,

5 . . . If only my art might bring me fame
And free my sick old age from office!—
Flitting, flitting, what am I like
But a sand-snipe[1] in the wide, wide world!
768

---

1. ***sand-snipe,*** a sandpiper, a small long-billed shore bird.

THINK AND DISCUSS
Understanding
1. What criticisms does Tu Fu make of his friend in "Sent to Li Po as a Gift"?
2. What is the **setting** of "A Night Abroad"?
3. To what does Tu Fu compare himself in this poem?

Analyzing
4. In "Sent to Li Po as a Gift," what do Tu Fu's criticisms of his friend tell you about Tu Fu?
5. How is the setting of "A Night Abroad" appropriate to the comparison that Tu Fu makes in lines 7–8?

Extending
6. Using the poems you have read by Li Po and Tu Fu, discuss the ways in which the two friends were alike and different as poets.

APPLYING: Simile
See Handbook of Literary Terms, p. 970.

A **simile** is a figure of speech involving a comparison using *like* or *as*. On leaving the girl with whom he has fallen in love, the king in *Shakuntala* laments that his thoughts keep flying back to her "like silken banners borne against the wind." The use of the word *like* in this comparison marks it as a simile. (A comparison not employing *like* or *as* is called a metaphor.) The use of figurative comparisons such as similes is not characteristic of Chinese poetry. However, two such comparisons are contained in Tu Fu's "Sent to Li Po as a Gift."

1. What are the two comparisons?
2. Identify each as a simile or metaphor.

HT   **See SATIRE in the Handbook of Literary Terms, page 968.**

Lao Tzu

Po Chü-i
translated by **Arthur Waley**

"Those who speak know nothing;
Those who know are silent."
These words, as I am told,
Were spoken by Lao Tzu.
5 If we are to believe that Lao Tzu
    Was himself *one who knew,*
How comes it that he wrote a book
    Of five thousand words?[1]

---

1. *book . . . words.* Lao Tzu's *Tao Te Ching* is sometimes called "the book of five thousand words."

The Red Cockatoo

Po Chü-i
translated by **Arthur Waley**

Sent as a present from Annam[1]—
A red cockatoo.
Colored like the peach-tree blossom,
Speaking with the speech of men.
5 And they did to it what is always done
To the learned and eloquent.
They took a cage with stout bars
And shut it up inside.

---

1. *Annam,* a region in Southeast Asia, now part of Vietnam.

Detail of a painting on silk by the Emperor Hui-tsung (1082–1135) showing women preparing newly woven silk. Museum of Fine Arts, Boston

Remembering Golden Bells

Po Chü-i
translated by **Arthur Waley**

Ruined and ill,—a man of two score;
    Pretty and guileless,—a girl of three.
Not a boy,—but still better than nothing:[1]
To soothe one's feeling,—from time to time a
    kiss!
There came a day,—they suddenly took her
    from me;
5 Her soul's shadow wandered I know not
    where.
And when I remember how just at the time
    she died
She lisped strange sounds, beginning to learn
    to talk,
Then I know that the ties of flesh and blood
Only bind us to a load of grief and sorrow.

10 At last, by thinking of the time before she was
    born,
By thought and reason I drove the pain away.
Since my heart forgot her, many days have
    passed
And three times winter has changed to
    spring.
This morning, for a little, the old grief came
    back,
15 Because, in the road, I met her foster-nurse.

---

1. *Not a boy . . . nothing.* Girls were considered inferior to boys in China.

Golden Bells

Po Chü-i
translated by **Arthur Waley**

        When I was almost forty
I had a daughter whose name was Golden
    Bells.
Now it is just a year since she was born;
She is learning to sit and cannot yet talk.
5 Ashamed,—to find that I have not a sage's
    heart:
I cannot resist vulgar thoughts and feelings.
Henceforward I am tied to things outside
    myself:
My only reward,—the pleasure I am getting
    now.
If I am spared the grief of her dying young,
10 Then I shall have the trouble of getting her
    married.
My plan for retiring and going back to the
    hills
Must now be postponed for fifteen years!

Chu-ch'ēn Village

Po Chü-i
translated by **Arthur Waley**

In Hsü-chou, in the District of Ku-fōng
There lies a village whose name is Chu-ch'ēn[1]—
A hundred miles away from the county-town,
Amid fields of hemp and green of mulberry-
    trees.
5 Click, click goes the sound of the spinning-
    wheel;
Mules and oxen pack the village-streets.
The girls go drawing the water from the brook;
The men go gathering firewood on the hill.
So far from the town Government affairs are
    few;
10 So deep in the hills, man's ways are simple.
Though they have wealth, they do not traffic
    with it;
Though they reach the age, they do not enter the
    Army.
Each family keeps to its village trade;
Grey-headed, they have never left the gates.

15 Alive, they are the people of Ch'ēn Village;
Dead, they become the dust of Ch'ēn Village.
Out in the fields old men and young
Gaze gladly, each in the other's face.
In the whole village there are only two clans;
20 Age after age Chus have married Ch'ēns.
Near or distant, they have kinsmen in every
    house;
Young or old, they have friends wherever they
    go.
On white wine and roasted fowl they fare
At joyful meetings more than "once a week."
25 While they are alive, they have no distant
    partings;

To choose a wife they go to a neighbor's house.
When they are dead,—no distant burial;
Round the village graves lie thick.
They are not troubled either about life or
    death;

30 They have no anguish either of body or soul.
And so it happens that they live to a ripe age
And great-great-grandsons are often seen.

I was born in the Realms of Etiquette;
In early years, unprotected and poor.
35 Alone, I learnt to distinguish between Evil and
    Good;
Untutored, I toiled at bitter tasks.
The World's Law honors Learning and Fame;
Scholars prize marriages and Caps.
With these fetters I gyved my own hands;
40 Truly I became a much-deceived man.
At ten years old I learnt to read books;
At fifteen, I knew how to write prose.
At twenty I was made a Bachelor of Arts;
At thirty I became a Censor at the Court.
45 Above, the duty I owe to Prince and parents;
Below, the ties that bind me to wife and child.
The support of my family, the service of my
    country—
For these tasks my nature is not apt.
I reckon the time that I first left my home;
50 From then till now,—fifteen Springs!
My lonely boat has thrice sailed to Ch'u;
Four times through Ch'in[2] my lean horse has
    passed.
I have walked in the morning with hunger in
    my face;
I have lain at night with a soul that could not
    rest.
55 East and West I have wandered without pause,
Hither and thither like a cloud astray in the
    sky.
In the civil-war my old home was destroyed;

---

1. *Chu-ch'en,* (chü′chen).

2. *Ch'u . . . Ch'in.* Ch'u was an ancient state that occupied the area on both sides of the Yangtze River almost to
the coast. Ch'in was a frontier state north and west of Ch'u
and west of the Huang River.

Of my flesh and blood many are scattered and
    lost.
    North of the River, and South of the
        River[3]—
60 In both lands are the friends of all my life;
    Life-friends whom I never see at all,—
    Whose deaths I hear of only after the lapse of
        years.

Sad at morning, I lie on my bed till dusk;
Weeping at night, I sit and wait for dawn.
65 The fire of sorrow has burnt my heart's core;
    The frost of trouble has seized my hair's roots.
    In such anguish has my whole life passed;
    Long I have envied the people of Ch'ēn Village.
    811

---

3. *the River*, the Yangtze.

THINK AND DISCUSS
Understanding
1. In "The Red Cockatoo" what talent does the bird possess?
2. What are the "vulgar thoughts and feelings" to which the speaker refers in line 6 of "Golden Bells"?
3. What occurrence has caused the speaker to recall his dead infant daughter in "Remembering Golden Bells"?
4. In "Chu-ch'ēn Village" the speaker presents a kind of utopia embodying all that is simple and good in the world. What details does he employ to create the **setting** of an ideal society?
5. How has the life of the speaker differed from that of the people in Chu-ch'ēn Village?

Analyzing
6. What kind of father does the speaker reveal himself to be in "Golden Bells" and "Remembering Golden Bells"?
7. Like T'ao Ch'ien, Po Chü-i exhibits the influence of both Confucianism (with its emphasis on scholarship and social order) and Taoism (with its emphasis on simplicity and the natural order). Point out places in his poetry where Po Chü-i shows both these influences.

Extending
8. In the concluding line of "Chu-ch'ēn Village," the speaker says that he has "long envied the people of Ch'ēn Village." Do you think the speaker could really be happy there? Or is he, in a manner typical of human nature, indulging in an edifying but purely romantic dream?

APPLYING: Satire H⁊
See Handbook of Literary Terms, p. 968.

Satire is the use of sarcasm, irony, or wit to ridicule a subject. The subjects of satire can include personality types, social classes, institutions, ideas, habits, customs. In his satirical poem "Lao Tzu," Po Chü-i uses irony, pointing to the inconsistency between what the philosopher said and what he did.

1. What is Po Chü-i satirizing in "The Red Cockatoo"?
2. Which of these two poems—"Lao Tzu" and "The Red Cockatoo"—seems the more valid in its satirical attack?

THINKING SKILLS
Synthesizing
To synthesize is to put together parts and elements so as to form a whole, a new pattern or structure not evident before. Synthesis can involve personal experience and imagination. For example, when the poet W. H. Auden named the period after World War II "the Age of Anxiety," he was synthesizing his knowledge of the events and literature of this period, his own experiences, and his feelings for words.

Using what you know about the poetry of Li Po, Tu Fu, and Po Chü-i, and the period in which they wrote, create a descriptive name for the period of the Tang poets.

Chinese Poetry 91

Japanese Literature

Japan has an old and rich literary tradition. As one historian observes, its varied forms include "some of the world's longest novels and shortest poems, plays which are miracles of muted suggestion and others filled with the most extravagant bombast." Like the Chinese, the Japanese excelled in the use of short poetic forms, such as the *tanka* (tän′kä), which contains thirty-one syllables arranged in five lines (5-7-5-7-7). By the eighth century, when the first great anthology of Japanese poetry, the *Manyoshu* (män-yō′shù), or "Book of Ten Thousand Leaves," was collected, the *tanka* form had already been in existence for several hundred years.

Japan's earliest prose literature appeared during the Heian Era (794–1192). It was written almost entirely by women. One reason was that the men of the imperial court were taught to write in Japanese by using the complicated Chinese characters. For formal writing, educated Japanese men used the Chinese language, much as the scholars of medieval Europe used Latin in preference to their native languages. Japanese women, however, did not generally learn to use either the Chinese characters or the Chinese language. Instead, they wrote in their native language using *kana* (kä′nä), an alphabetic representation of the forty-seven syllables of the Japanese language that had developed in the ninth century. Using *kana*, court women wrote diaries, letters, essays, and novels. The most famous work of *kana* prose, and the masterpiece of Japanese literature, is Lady Murasaki's long novel of life at the imperial court, *The Tale of Genji*. Another lady of the Heian court and a contemporary of Lady Murasaki, Lady Sei Shōnagon (sā′ē shō′nä gōn), also provided a brilliant picture of aristocratic life in her journal, *The Pillow Book*. Little is known about her life except what can be learned from *The Pillow Book*. One scholar observes that its title, "whether or not Shōnagon used it herself, was probably a generic term used to describe a type of informal book of notes which men and women composed when they retired to their rooms in the evening and which they kept near their sleeping place, possibly in the drawers of their wooden pillows, so that they might record stray impressions." Completed about 1002, *The Pillow Book* reveals a fascinating personality—witty and naive, snobbish and irreverent. Some selections from *The Pillow Book* appear on pages 94–97. A passage from the diary of Lady Murasaki, in which she describes Shōnagon, appears on page 95.

One of the principal forms of classical Japanese theater, the *No* (nō) drama developed from traditional religious festivals in the fourteenth and fifteenth centuries. A highly stylized form of theater, the *No* drama is as much a dance as it is a play, and the music—employing flute and drums—is also an important element. *No* plays were staged with little scenery and few props, and performed by all-male casts wearing symbolic masks and magnificent costumes. Unlike classical Indian drama, the *No* plays generally had tragic themes. The audience was the aristocracy and the plays were presented as part of dramatic programs that lasted all day.

Portrait of Bashō.
Early 19th century.
Collection Kimiko
and John Powers

The greatest master of the *No* drama was Seami (or Zeami) Motokiyo (sā-ä mē mō tō kē yō), who lived from 1363 to 1443. Like Shakespeare and Molière, he was both a playwright and an actor, first appearing on the stage as a child. One of his 240 *No* plays, *The Damask Drum*, begins on page 98. Seami was also known for his critical writing on the *No* drama, a passage from which appears on page 101.

In the sixteenth century, the brief *tanka* form was further compressed into the *haiku*, in which seventeen syllables are arranged in three lines (5-7-5). The greatest writer of *haiku*, Matsuo Munefusa (1644–1694), who used the pseudonym *Bashō*, was born into a samurai family. While he wrote throughout most of his life, he did not reach the peak of his ability until the last ten years of his life. Though some of Bashō's poems have a mystical character (possibly influenced by Zen Buddhism, which he embraced late in life), most are simple descriptions of real scenes and real events, with just enough detail to communicate an emotion to a reader. Nine of Bashō's *haiku* appear on page 102.

Illustration from a scroll
of *The Tale of Genji.*
Early 17th century.
The Mary and Jackson
Burke Collection

See TONE in the Handbook of Literary Terms, page 976.

from The Pillow Book

Sei Shōnagon
translated by **Ivan Morris**

In Spring It Is the Dawn

n spring it is the dawn that is most beautiful. As the light creeps over the hills, their outlines are dyed a faint red and wisps of purplish cloud trail over them.

In summer the nights. Not only when the moon shines, but on dark nights too, as the fireflies flit to and fro, and even when it rains, how beautiful it is!

In autumn the evenings, when the glittering sun sinks close to the edge of the hills and the crows fly back to their nests in threes and fours and twos; more charming still is a file of wild geese, like specks in the distant sky. When the sun has set, one's heart is moved by the sound of the wind and the hum of the insects.

In winter the early mornings. It is beautiful indeed when snow has fallen during the night, but splendid too when the ground is white with frost; or even when there is no snow or frost, but it is simply very cold and the attendants hurry from room to room stirring up the fires and bringing charcoal, how well this fits the season's mood! But as noon approaches and the cold wears off, no one bothers to keep the braziers alight, and soon nothing remains but piles of white ashes.

When I Make Myself Imagine

When I make myself imagine what it is like to be one of those women who live at home, faithfully serving their husbands—women who have not a single exciting prospect in life yet who believe that they are perfectly happy—I am filled with scorn. Often they are of quite good birth, yet have had no opportunity to find out what the world is like. I wish they could live for a while in our society, even if it should mean taking service as Attendants, so that they might come to know the delights it has to offer.

I cannot bear men who believe that women serving in the Palace are bound to be frivolous and wicked. Yet I suppose their prejudice is understandable. After all, women at Court do not spend their time hiding modestly behind fans and screens, but walk about, looking openly at people they chance to meet. Yes, they see everyone face to face, not only ladies-in-waiting like themselves, but even Their Imperial Majesties (whose august names I hardly dare mention), High Court Nobles, senior courtiers, and other gentlemen of high rank. In the presence of such exalted personages the women in the Palace are all equally brazen, whether they be the maids of ladies-in-waiting, or the relations of Court ladies who have come to visit them, or housekeepers, or latrine-cleaners, or women who are of no more value than a roof-tile or a pebble. Small wonder that the young men regard them as immodest! Yet are the gentlemen themselves any less so? They are not exactly bashful when it comes to looking at the great people in the Palace. No, everyone at Court is much the same in this respect. . . .

Hateful Things

One is in a hurry to leave, but one's visitor keeps chattering away. If it is someone of no importance,

Comment

Lady Murasaki's Diary

In addition to *The Tale of Genji*, Lady Murasaki also left a brilliant record of Heian court life in her diary. In the following passage she describes one of her contemporaries, Lady Sei Shōnagon.

Lady Sei Shōnagon. A very proud person. She values herself highly, and scatters her Chinese writings all about. Yet should we study her closely, we should find that she is still imperfect. She tries to be exceptional, but naturally persons of that sort give offence. She is piling up trouble for her future. One who is too richly gifted, who indulges too much in emotion, even when she ought to be reserved, and cannot turn aside from anything she is interested in, in spite of herself will lose self-control. How can such a vain and reckless person end her days happily!

---

one can get rid of him by saying, "You must tell me all about it next time"; but, should it be the sort of visitor whose presence commands one's best behavior, the situation is hateful indeed.

One finds that a hair got caught in the stone on which one is rubbing one's inkstick, or again that gravel is lodged in the inkstick, making a nasty, grating sound.

Someone has suddenly fallen ill and one summons the exorcist. Since he is not at home, one has to send messengers to look for him. After one has had a long fretful wait, the exorcist finally arrives, and with a sigh of relief one asks him to start his incantations. But perhaps he has been exorcising too many evil spirits recently; for hardly has he installed himself and begun praying when his voice becomes drowsy. Oh, how hateful!

A man who has nothing in particular to recommend him discusses all sorts of subjects at random as though he knew everything.

An elderly person warms the palms of his hands over a brazier and stretches out the wrinkles. No young man would dream of behaving in such a fashion; old people can really be quite shameless. I have seen some dreary old creatures actually resting their feet on the brazier and rubbing them against the edge while they speak. These are the kind of people who in visiting someone's house first use their fans to wipe away the dust from the mat and, when they finally sit on it, cannot stay still but are forever spreading out the front of their hunting costume or even tucking it up under their knees. One might suppose that such behavior was restricted to people of humble station; but I have observed it in quite well-bred people, including a Senior Secretary of the Fifth Rank in the Ministry of Ceremonial and a former Governor of Suruga.

I hate the sight of men in their cups who shout, poke their fingers in their mouths, stroke their beards, and pass on the wine to their neighbors with great cries of "Have some more! Drink up!" They tremble, shake their heads, twist their faces, and gesticulate like children who are singing, "We're off to see the Governor." I have seen really well-bred people behave like this and I find it most distasteful.

To envy others and to complain about one's own lot; to speak badly about people; to be inquisitive about the most trivial matters and to resent and abuse people for not telling one, or, if one does manage to worm out some facts, to inform everyone in the most detailed fashion as if one had known all from the beginning—oh, how hateful!

One is just about to be told some interesting piece of news when a baby starts crying.

A flight of crows circle about with loud caws.

An admirer has come on a clandestine visit, but a dog catches sight of him and starts barking. One feels like killing the beast. . . .

Things That Make One's Heart Beat Faster

Sparrows feeding their young. To pass a place where babies are playing. To sleep in a room where some fine incense has been burnt. To notice that one's elegant Chinese mirror has become a little cloudy. To see a gentleman stop his carriage before

Portrait of a poet. 17th century. The Mary and Jackson Burke Collection

one's gate and instruct his attendants to announce his arrival. To wash one's hair, make one's toilet, and put on scented robes; even if not a soul sees one, these preparations still produce an inner pleasure.

It is night and one is expecting a visitor. Suddenly one is startled by the sound of rain-drops, which the wind blows against the shutters.

Things That Arouse a Fond Memory of the Past

Dried hollyhock. The objects used during the Display of Dolls. To find a piece of deep violet or grape-colored material that has been pressed between the pages of a notebook.

It is a rainy day and one is feeling bored. To pass the time, one starts looking through some old papers. And then one comes across the letters of a man one used to love.

Last year's paper fan. A night with a clear moon.

A Preacher Ought To Be Good-Looking

A preacher ought to be good-looking. For, if we are properly to understand his worthy sentiments, we must keep our eyes on him while he speaks; should we look away, we may forget to listen. Accordingly an ugly preacher may well be the source of sin. . . .

But I really must stop writing this kind of thing. If I were still young enough, I might risk the consequence of putting down such impieties, but at my present stage of life I should be less flippant.

Some people, on hearing that a priest is particularly venerable and pious, rush off to the temple where he is preaching, determined to arrive before anyone else. They, too, are liable to bring a load of sin on themselves and would do better to stay away. . . .

Elegant Things

A white coat worn over a violet waistcoat.

Duck eggs.

Shaved ice mixed with liana syrup and put in a new silver bowl.[1]

A rosary of rock crystal.

Wistaria blossoms. Plum blossoms covered with snow.

A pretty child eating strawberries.

---

1. *Shaved ice . . . silver bowl.* In Heian Japan, ice was stored in ice-chambers and eaten during the summer (for instance in sherbets) or used to preserve perishable food. The stems and leaves of the liana, a wild vine, were used as a sweetener. Sugar was not introduced into Japan until several centuries after the Heian period.

Things That Cannot Be Compared

Summer and winter. Night and day. Rain and sunshine. Youth and age. A person's laughter and his anger. Black and white. Love and hatred. The little indigo plant and the great philodendron. Rain and mist.

When one has stopped loving somebody, one feels that he has become someone else, even though he is still the same person.

In a garden full of evergreens the crows are all asleep. Then, towards the middle of the night, the crows in one of the trees suddenly wake up in a great flurry and start flapping about. Their unrest spreads to the other trees, and soon all the birds have been startled from their sleep and are cawing in alarm. How different from the same crows in daytime!

c. 990–1002

THINK AND DISCUSS
Understanding
1. *The Pillow Book* might be described as "a collection of collections." Describe the different categories of things Shōnagon assembles in her journal.
2. What does Shōnagon say in "When I Make Myself Imagine" about the charge of worldliness directed at the women who served at the imperial court?
3. Why does Shōnagon feel that "a preacher should be good-looking"?

Analyzing
4. "In Spring It Is the Dawn" begins with a picture of unqualified loveliness. How does Shōnagon qualify this perfection in the succeeding seasons?
5. How does Shōnagon **satirize** ostentatious piety in "A Preacher Ought to be Good-Looking"?

Extending
6. Are you convinced by Shōnagon's expression of scorn for women living away from the palace in "When I Make Myself Imagine"? Explain.
7. Contrast the way Sei Shōnagon observes nature with the manner in which T'ao Ch'ien does. Discuss how their different ways of life—she a lady-in-waiting at the imperial court, he a public official turned small farmer—might affect their ways of seeing nature.
8. The passage you have read from *The Pillow Book* and Lady Murasaki's diary picture a brilliant, strong-willed, and independent woman. Consider Sei Shōnagon from the position of contemporary feminism. Was she a "liberated" woman in a male-dominated society? Discuss.

APPLYING: Tone H✏
See Handbook of Literary Terms, p. 976.

Tone is the author's attitude toward his or her subject and toward the audience. Sei Shōnagon's tone can be sharp and satirical, as when she pictures people making a show of their piety. Her tone can also be tender and lyrical, as when she describes "Things That Make One's Heart Beat Faster."

1. How does the tone of "In Spring It Is the Dawn" change at the end?
2. Sei Shōnagon was writing for a small, aristocratic audience. How does this affect her tone?

COMPOSITION ✒
Creating a Collection
In the passages from *The Pillow Book* you have read, Sei Shōnagon records five of her curious collections. Using one of her groupings or creating a new one, make up a collection of your own in two or three paragraphs.

Writing About Character
Using the indications about Sei Shōnagon's personality in *The Pillow Book* and the diary of Lady Murasaki, do a character sketch of Shōnagon in three paragraphs. See "Writing About Characters" in the Writer's Handbook.

The Damask Drum

Seami
translated by **Arthur Waley**

PERSONS

A COURTIER
AN OLD GARDENER
THE PRINCESS

COURTIER. I am courtier at the Palace of Kino-maru in the country of Chikuzen. You must know that in this place there is a famous pond called the Laurel Pond, where the royal ones often take their walks; so it happened that one day the old man who sweeps the garden here caught sight of the Princess. And from that time he has loved her with a love that gives his heart no rest.

Someone told her of this, and she said, "Love's equal realm knows no divisions," and in her pity she said, "By that pond there stands a laurel tree, and on its branches there hangs a drum. Let him beat the drum, and if the sound is heard in the Palace, he shall see my face again."

I must tell him of this.

Listen, old Gardener! The worshipful lady has heard of your love and sends you this message: "Go and beat the drum that hangs on the tree by the pond, and if the sound is heard in the Palace, you shall see my face again." Go quickly now and beat the drum!

GARDENER. With trembling I receive her words. I will go and beat the drum.

COURTIER. Look, here is the drum she spoke of. Make haste and beat it!

(*He leaves the* GARDENER *standing by the tree and seats himself at the foot of the "Waki's pillar."*)[1]

GARDENER. They talk of the moon-tree, the laurel that grows in the Garden of the Moon. . . . But for me there is but one true tree, this laurel by the lake. Oh, may the drum that hangs on its branches give forth a mighty note, a music to bind up my bursting heart.

Listen! the evening bell to help me chimes;
But then tolls in
A heavy tale of day linked on to day,

CHORUS (*speaking for the* GARDENER). And hope stretched out from dusk to dusk.

But now, a watchman of the hours, I beat
The longed-for stroke.

GARDENER. I was old, I shunned the daylight,
I was gaunt as an aged crane;
And upon all that misery
Suddenly a sorrow was heaped,
The new sorrow of love.
The days had left their marks,
Coming and coming, like waves that beat on a
    sandy shore . . .

CHORUS. Oh, with a thunder of white waves
The echo of the drum shall roll.

GARDENER. The afterworld draws near me,
Yet even now I wake not
From this autumn of love that closes
In sadness the sequence of my years.

CHORUS. And slow as the autumn dew
Tears gather in my eyes, to fall
Scattered like dewdrops from a shaken flower
On my coarse-woven dress.
See here the marks, imprint of tangled love,
That all the world will read.

GARDENER. I said "I will forget,"

CHORUS. And go worse to torment so
Than by remembrance. But all in this world

---

1. *"Waki's pillar,"* a support on stage used in *Nō* plays.

Is as the horse of the aged man of the land of
  Sai;[2]
And as a white colt flashes
Past a gap in the hedge, even so our days pass.
And though the time be come,
Yet can none know the road that he at last must
  tread,
Goal of his dewdrop life.
All this I knew; yet knowing,
Was blind with folly.
GARDENER. "Wake, wake," he cries,—
CHORUS. The watchman of the hours,—
  "Wake from the sleep of dawn!"
And batters on the drum.
For if its sound be heard, soon shall he see
Her face, the damask of her dress . . .
Aye, damask! He does not know
That on a damask drum he beats,
Beats with all the strength of his hands, his aged
  hands,
But hears no sound.
"Am I grown deaf?" he cries, and listens,
  listens:
Rain on the windows, lapping of waves on the
  pool—
Both these he hears, and silent only
The drum, strange damask drum.
Oh, will it never sound?
I thought to beat the sorrow from my heart,
Wake music in a damask drum; an echo of love
From the voiceless fabric of pride!
GARDENER. Longed for as the moon that hides
  In the obstinate clouds of a rainy night
  Is the sound of the watchman's drum,
  To roll the darkness from my heart.
CHORUS. I beat the drum. The days pass and the
  hours.
  It was yesterday, and it is today.
GARDENER. But she for whom I wait
CHORUS. Comes not even in dream. At dawn and
  dusk
GARDENER. No drum sounds.
CHORUS. She has not come. Is it not sung that
  those
Whom love has joined
Not even the god of Thunder can divide?
Of lovers, I alone

Am guideless, comfortless.
Then weary of himself and calling her to witness
  of his woe,
"Why should I endure," he cried,
"Such life as this?" and in the waters of the pond
He cast himself and died.
  (GARDENER *leaves the stage.*)
  Enter the PRINCESS.
COURTIER. I would speak with you, madam.
    The drum made no sound, and the aged Gar-
  dener in despair has flung himself into the pond
  by the laurel tree, and died. The soul of such
  a one may cling to you and do you injury. Go
  out and look upon him.
PRINCESS (*speaking wildly, already possessed by the*
  GARDENER'*s angry ghost, which speaks through*
  her). Listen, people, listen!
In the noise of the beating waves
I hear the rolling of a drum.
Oh, joyful sound, oh joyful!
The music of a drum.
COURTIER. Strange, strange!
  This lady speaks as one
  By fantasy possessed.
  What is amiss, what ails her?
PRINCESS. Truly, by fantasy I am possessed.
  Can a damask drum give sound?
  When I bade him beat what could not ring,
  Then tottered first my wits.
COURTIER. She spoke, and on the face of the eve-
  ning pool
  A wave stirred.
PRINCESS. And out of the wave
COURTIER. A voice spoke.
  (*The voice of the* GARDENER *is heard; as he grad-*
  ually advances along the hashigakari[3] *it is seen that*
  he wears a "demon mask," leans on a staff and
  carries the "demon mallet" at his girdle.)
GARDENER'S GHOST. I was driftwood in the pool,
  but the waves of bitterness
CHORUS. Have washed me back to the shore.

---

2. *the horse . . . Sai.* According to a Japanese tale, a
man's horse bolted and consequently was saved from being
requisitioned by the government during a revolutionary
period. After the revolution the man found his horse. The
moral is as follows: what appears to be bad luck is sometimes good luck and vice versa.
3. *hashigakari*, runway.

GHOST. Anger clings to my heart,
   Clings even now when neither wrath nor
     weeping
   Are aught but folly.
CHORUS. One thought consumes me,
   The anger of lust denied
   Covers me like darkness.
   I am become a demon dwelling
   In the hell of my dark thoughts,
   Storm cloud of my desires.
GHOST. "Though the waters parch in the fields
   Though the brooks run dry,
   Never shall the place be shown
   Of the spring that feeds my heart."[4]
   So I had resolved. Oh, why so cruelly
   Set they me to win
   Voice from a voiceless drum,
   Spending my heart in vain?
   And I spent my heart on the glimpse of a moon
    that slipped
   Through the boughs of an autumn tree.
CHORUS. This damask that hangs on the laurel
   tree
GHOST. Will it sound, will it sound?
   (*He seizes the* PRINCESS *and drags her towards the drum.*)
    Try! Strike it!
CHORUS. "Strike!" he cries;
   "The quick beat, the battle-charge!
   Loud, loud! Strike, strike," he rails,
   And brandishing his demon stick
   Gives her no rest.
   "Oh woe!" the lady weeps,
   "No sound, no sound. Oh misery!" she wails.
   And he, at the mallet stroke, "Repent, repent!"
   Such torments in the world of night
   Abōrasetsu, chief of demons, wields,
   Who on the Wheel of Fire
   Sears sinful flesh and shatters bones to dust.
   Not less her torture now!
   "Oh, agony!" she cries, "What have I done,
   By what dire seed this harvest sown?"
GHOST. Clear stands the cause before you.
CHORUS. Clear stands the cause before my eyes;
                    I know it now.
   By the pool's white waters, upon the laurel's
    bough

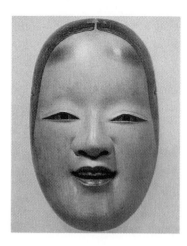

No mask of a princess. Painted wood. Early 16th century. Tokyo National Museum

The drum was hung.
He did not know his hour, but struck and struck
Till all the will had ebbed from his heart's core;
Then leapt into the lake and died.
And while his body rocked
Like driftwood on the waves,
His soul, an angry ghost,
Possessed the lady's wits, haunted her heart
   with woe.
The mallet lashed, as these waves lash the shore,
Lash on the ice of the eastern shore.
The wind passes; the rain falls
On the Red Lotus, the Lesser and the Greater.[5]
The hair stands up on my head.
"The fish that leaps the falls
To a fell snake is turned,"[6]
I have learned to know them;
Such, such are the demons of the World of
   Night.
"O hateful lady, hateful!" he cried, and sank
   again
Into the whirlpool of desire.

14th century

---

4. *"Though the waters . . . feeds my heart,"* a quotation from a poem in one of the ancient collections of Japanese verse.
5. *the rain . . . Greater.* In Buddhism the *Red Lotus* is an emblem of paradise, whereas *the Lesser and the Greater* are the names of two cold hells. Accordingly the rain falls on both the virtuous and the evil.
6. *"The fish . . . turned."* According to a legend, the fish that successfully cleared a certain waterfall became a dragon. Thus, the Gardener's efforts to attain equality with the Princess have turned him into an evil spirit.

Seami on the Art of the *No*

Part of Seami's pre-eminence in the tradition of the *No* drama is due to his critical writings. Seami's thinking, according to one scholar, reflects "the influence of Zen Buddhism, with its emphasis on intuitive understanding." The Zen form of Buddhism, which incorporated Taoist elements, had been introduced into Japan from China in the 12th and 13th centuries. The following passage is from Seami's critical writing on the *No* play.

The One Mind Linking All Powers

Sometimes spectators of the *No* say that the moments of "no action" are the most enjoyable. This is one of the actor's secret arts. Dancing and singing, movements on the stage, and the different types of miming are all acts performed by the body. Moments of "no action" occur in between. When we examine why such moments without action are enjoyable, we find that it is due to the underlying spiritual strength of the actor which unremittingly holds the attention. He does not relax the tension when the dancing or singing comes to an end or at intervals between the dialogue and the different types of miming, but maintains an unwavering inner strength. This feeling of inner strength will faintly reveal itself and bring enjoyment. However, it is undesirable for the actor to permit this inner strength to become obvious to the audience. If it is obvious, it becomes an act, and is no longer "no action." The actions before and after an interval of "no action" must be linked by entering the state of mindlessness in which the actor conceals even from himself his own intent. The ability to move audiences depends, thus, on linking all the artistic powers with one mind.

Life and death, past and present—
Marionettes on a toy stage.
When the strings are broken,
Behold the broken pieces!

This is a metaphor describing human life as it transmigrates between life and death. Marionettes on a stage appear to move in various ways, but in fact it is not they who really move—they are manipulated by strings. When these strings are broken, the marionettes fall and are dashed to pieces. In the art of the *No* too, the different types of miming are artificial things. What holds the parts together is the mind. This mind must not be disclosed to the audience. If it is seen, it is just as if a marionette's strings were visible. The mind must be made the strings which hold together all the powers of the art.

THINK AND DISCUSS
Understanding
1. What background does the Courtier provide at the beginning of *The Damask Drum?*
2. Why doesn't the drum make a sound?
3. What finally causes the Princess to hear the sound of the drum?

Analyzing
4. What are the functions of the Courtier and the Chorus?

5. One speech of the Chorus concludes: "I thought to beat the sorrow from my heart,/Wake music in a damask drum; an echo of love/From the voiceless fabric of pride!" Discuss the **metaphors** in this passage and relate them to the meaning of the play.

Extending
6. In his first speech, the Courtier speaks of the Princess's "pity." Is she really compassionate? Has she learned compassion by the end of the play?

Haiku

Bashō
translated by **Harold G. Henderson**

The Sun Path

The sun's way:
  hollyhocks turn toward it
    through all the rain of May.
1690

The Poor Man's Son

Poverty's child—
  he starts to grind the rice,
    and gazes at the moon.
1687

Darkness

    On a withered branch
a crow has settled—
    autumn nightfall.
1679

Leaves of Grass

Summer grass:
  of stalwart warriors' splendid dreams
    the aftermath.
1689

Summer Voices

So soon to die,
  and no sign of it showing—
    locust-cry.
1690

Persistence

Did it yell
  till it became *all* voice?
  Cicada-shell!
Date unknown

Clouds

Clouds come from time to time—
  and bring to men a chance to rest
    from looking at the moon.
1685

Lightning at Night

A lightning gleam:
  into darkness travels
    a night heron's scream.
1694

In a Wide Wasteland

On the moor: from things
  detached completely—
    how the skylark sings!
1687

THINK AND DISCUSS
Understanding
1. Characterize the **images** that Bashō uses in these *haiku*. Are they drawn from the court or the countryside?

Analyzing
2. In Japanese, the pattern of syllables in a *haiku* is tightly structured. What sound device of English poetry has the translator often chosen to substitute for this syllable pattern?

Extending
3. A literal translation of "Persistence" might read "Voice to all/cry-itself-out?/cicada-shell." Do you agree with the interpretation the translator has given it in his English version? Could another reading be given to the literal English translation?

ENRICHMENT
Reading *Haiku*
A number of excellent collections of Japanese *haiku* are available, including *An Introduction to Haiku* by Harold G. Henderson (Doubleday, 1958).

The Origin of Writing

History Begins at Sumer observes the title of a famous book about ancient Mesopotamia. The study of literature begins there as well. The appearance of the cuneiform script in Sumeria around 5,000 years ago marks the great dividing line in the knowledge that human beings have about their past. What is known of the period before the invention of writing must be inferred from the material remains of our ancestors—their bones and possessions. But the coming of written records allowed ancient peoples to speak directly to their descendents. How did this decisive event come about? The evidence of archaeology suggests that cuneiform was not a sudden innovation. Instead, it was the result of several thousand years of slow development in the way in which the people of the ancient Near East kept track of their goods.

Archaeologists distinguish several stages in this process. The first stage began about 8000 B.C. and coincided with the beginnings of farming and the appearance of villages. This new, settled, agricultural way of life required some means for counting quantities of grain or livestock. Pebbles had probably been the first objects used as counters, and sufficed as long as human beings remained nomadic hunters and gatherers. But then the world's first farmers began to mold counters out of clay in simple geometric shapes—spheres, disks, or cones. The different shapes of these clay tokens stood for different types of goods —bushels of grain or flocks of sheep or goats. This simple system of tokens was used largely unchanged for thousands of years by the villagers of ancient Mesopotamia.

The appearance of the second stage coincided with the rise of cities in this region between 4000 and 3000 B.C. Larger concentrations of people meant larger numbers of goods to keep track of. In addition, the needs of organized civilization—taxes, for example—require record-keeping as well as enumeration. Around 3000 B.C. tokens began to be stored in clay "envelopes." These envelopes were simply hollowed-out balls of clay. Tokens representing a certain number of bushels of grain, for example, were placed inside an envelope and sealed up. In order to indicate the kind and number of the tokens inside the envelope, various kinds of markings were made on the outside. These markings were often done by simply pressing the tokens themselves into the outside of the clay envelope.

Very soon the Sumerians realized that the signs on the outside of the envelopes were all they needed for their record-keeping. It was unnecessary to keep the tokens themselves. In the estimate of one archaeologist, this third stage—the substitution of signs for tokens—"was no less than the invention of writing." The final transition from tokens to cuneiform script came when the Sumerians discovered that they could better create the signs that represented the tokens by inscribing them with a wedge-shaped stylus than by simply using the impression of the counters themselves. By 3100 B.C. clay tablets appear with both impressed and inscribed signs.

Sumerian clay counters. c. 3000 B.C. Louvre

Themes IN WORLD LITERATURE

APPEARANCE AND REALITY

We are such stuff as dreams are made on.
    Shakespeare, *The Tempest*

What is the relationship between the way things appear and the way they are? Are they like they seem to most of us most of the time; that is, fairly solid and familiar? Or do they, as Shakespeare's magician Prospero suggests (pages 466–467, lines 148–158), have no more substance than a dream? Perhaps because literature is itself "made-up"—constructed out of such immaterial, "unreal" things as words and thoughts and feelings—the question of the distinction between appearance and reality has frequently occurred to writers. The following article discusses some of their responses.

The Oriental Vision

Like Prospero, many Oriental writers have felt that appearance and reality are hard to distinguish. The Persian mystic Rumi's poem "The Soul of Goodness in Things Evil" (page 49) begins with a series of **paradoxes** touching on this distinction and leading to the extraordinary statement, " 'Tis the love of right/Lures men to wrong." Rumi's tale "The Man Who Fled from Azrael" (page 48) is as much a statement about the confusion between appearance and reality as it is one about the ironic nature of fate. In "The Elephant in the Dark House" (page 48), this confusion is traced to the incompleteness of human knowledge. In the famous Chinese fable of Chuang Tzu's dream (page 76), the confusion about the nature of reality goes even deeper. On awaking, Chuang Tzu is no longer sure if he is a dreamer or a dream. The hero of "The Circular Ruins" (page 847), a short story by the modern Argentine writer Jorge Luis Borges, suffers from a similar uncertainty.

The answer provided by the Hindu *Bhagavad Gita* (page 60) to the question of the relationship between appearance and reality is more confident than that of Chuang Tzu or Borges, if just as radical in its denial of any permanent substance in the things we see. Only the immortal Spirit is real; all else, including our bodies, is illusion: "As a man leaves an old garment and puts on one that is new, the Spirit leaves his mortal body and wanders on to one that is new." Psalm 90 (page 34) makes a similar point about the insubstantiality of the things of the material world: "They are as a sleep:/In the morning they are like grass which groweth up./In the morning it flourisheth, and groweth up;/In the evening it is cut down, and withereth."

Faith and Doubt

Who has not been carried away into fantasies by stories or movies? *Don Quixote* (page 406) is a man who reads so many medieval romances about knightly chivalry that he decides to imitate them by going off to perform his own deeds of derring-do. The narrator claims that Don Quixote is mentally disturbed, but readers do not want to agree. Perhaps this is because of the man's idealism, which contrasts with the materialism of Sancho Panza. Or perhaps it is because we think it makes sense to confuse appearance and reality. When Don Quixote sees windmills and calls them giants, do we say he is entirely wrong? Perhaps the modern equivalent of windmills would be atomic reactors. Are they atomic reactors or are they giants?

Whereas Don Quixote seems confused because of his idealism, the character in La Fontaine's fable "The Acorn and the Pumpkin" (page 509) is confused for another reason: He has no faith. He thus presumes to question God's ordering of the universe and to imagine a redesigning of it according to his own ideas. But an experience teaches him that appearances deceive us unless we have faith in the goodness of God's works.

The goodness of God's works is also the subject of *An Essay on Man* (page 570), in which

Pope deals with the question of how evil can exist in a world created by a God who is good. Pope, like La Fontaine, asserts that people must have faith in God's ordered universe, and not call appearance imperfection simply because they fail to see the reality of order. He who would break this great chain of order is a "Vile Worm," and Pope addresses such a person in the lines, "All Nature is but Art, unknown to thee; . . . All partial Evil, universal Good: . . . One truth is clear: 'Whatever Is, is Right.' "

Voltaire's *Candide* (page 575) is a parody of ideas such as these. Whenever a character in *Candide* makes reference to "this best of all possible worlds," he is alluding to the kind of optimism in *An Essay on Man*. The butt of Voltaire's **satire** is Dr. Pangloss, who is the source of all such ideas in the novel. His influence in the book makes *Candide* a study in the conflict between reality and philosophy. Pangloss's philosophy is all appearance, and he is a fool not to realize it, since the events of the novel continue to discredit his views. But Candide begins to see through those views, wondering, "If this is the best of all possible worlds, what are the others like?"

Behind the Hedge

When you see a painting of a hedge, do you wonder what is behind that hedge? The answer, of course, is that there is nothing behind it except canvas, because the hedge is art, not reality; and we should ask questions about it that are appropriate to art, not to reality.

The same principle applies to literature. In Maupassant's "The False Gems" (page 689), for example, the author does not tell us how Lantin's wife acquires her jewelry. By withholding this information, he makes us curious about her character, and whether there is a discrepancy between her appearance and her reality. But in literature we know only what the author gives us; and here the author does not give us the truth about the woman. So we would be wiser to concentrate on Lantin himself when we are asking questions about his fate.

Similarly, in *The Metamorphosis* (page 785), Kafka withholds from us the information that we most want to know: Why did this change

Detail of a painting by Ch'en Hung-shou (1598–1652). Ink and color on silk. Honolulu Academy of Arts

occur? He never answers this question. Instead, he devotes most of the story to such physical details as Gregor's difficulties in moving about the floor. This emphasis may make you think Gregor's actions have no human significance. But his *thoughts* have human significance, even though he has to devote those thoughts to problems that are nonhuman. His difficulties in moving become his new reality; his thoughts, though human, might as well be appearance.

Oedipus the King (page 165) is famous for the way in which Sophocles allows the truth to emerge, with each character revealing part of the truth and the combined testimonies of all the characters being necessary to reveal all of it. But of course it is Sophocles himself who is doing the revealing, in such a way that the gradual but inevitable unfolding of the facts will show the inescapable character of reality. There has probably never been a play in which the contrast between reality and appearance is so important. This is partly because of Oedipus's unwillingness to see. Given normal sight, he is blind to reality. This fact explains the importance of Tiresias, the blind seer, and it helps us to understand the fate of Oedipus, who at the end sees better than when he had eyes.

UNIT 1   THE ANCIENT EAST

■ CONCEPT REVIEW

Below on the left are a series of quatrains from Edward FitzGerald's translation, *The Rubáiyát of Omar Khayyám*. In this section of the poem, the speaker overhears a discussion in which a number of pots speculate on the nature of the potter who created them and on what their destiny might be. The figures of the pot and the potter, representing the relationship between human beings and God, are **archetypal** ones occurring in many literatures.

Below on the right are notes to help you read this section of *The Rubáiyát* and to review some of the literary terms and thinking skills that have appeared in Unit 1. Page numbers in the notes refer to an application. A more extensive discussion of these terms is in the Handbook of Literary Terms. On a separate sheet of paper write your answers to the questions following the poems.

from The Rubáiyát of Omar Khayyám

translated by **Edward FitzGerald**

82

As under cover of departing Day
Slunk hunger-stricken Ramazán away,
   Once more within the Potter's house alone
I stood, surrounded by the Shapes of Clay.

83

5 Shapes of all Sorts and Sizes, great and small,
That stood along the floor and by the wall;
   And some loquacious Vessels were; and some
Listened perhaps, but never talked at all.

■ **Ramazán** (räm′ə zän′): Islamic month of fasting; often called *Ramadan*. Each day's fast ends at sundown.
■ **Setting** (page 67): Note the details of time and place in lines 1–4.
■ **Personification** (page 59): Note the human characteristics given to the month of Ramazán.
■ **loquacious:** talkative

Moghul miniature of a poet in a garden. Early 17th century. Museum of Fine Arts, Boston

84

Said one among them—"Surely not in vain
My substance of the common Earth was ta'en
   And to this Figure molded, to be broke,
Or trampled back to shapeless Earth again."

85

Then said a Second—"Ne'er a peevish Boy
Would break the Bowl from which he drank in joy;
   And He that with his hand the Vessel made
Will surely not in after Wrath destroy."

86

After a momentary silence spake
Some Vessel of a more ungainly Make;
   They sneer at me for leaning all awry:
"What! did the Hand then of the Potter shake?"

■ **ta'en** (tān): contraction of *taken.*

■ **Rhyme** (page 46): The standard rhyme scheme of the Persian *rubai* ("quatrain") is *aaba.*

87

Whereat some one of the loquacious Lot—
I think a Súfi pipkin—waxing hot—
    "All this of Pot and Potter—Tell me, then,
Who is the Potter, pray, and who the Pot?"

88

25 "Why," said another, "some there are who tell
Of one who threatens he will toss to Hell
    The luckless Pots he marred in making—Pish!
He's a Good Fellow, and 't will all be well."

89

"Well," murmured one, "let whoso make or buy,
30 My Clay with long Oblivion is gone dry:
    But fill me with the old familiar Juice,
Methinks I might recover by and by."

90

So, while the Vessels one by one were speaking,
The little Moon looked in that all were seeking:
35   And then they jogged each other, "Brother! Brother!
Now for the Porter's shoulder-knot a-creaking!"

■ **Súfi** (sü′fē): One of the basic notions of the Islamic mystical movement called Sufism is the oneness of the universe.

■ **Satire** (page 91): A *pipkin* is a small pot. This quatrain sketches a comic portrait of a short, vehement Sufi preacher.

■ **Evaluating:** Note how the quality of trust in God expressed in quatrain 88 differs from that expressed in quatrain 85.

■ **Imagery** (page 21): The "old familiar Juice" (line 31) is wine.

■ **little Moon:** the new moon that signals the end of the month of fasting.
■ **Porter's . . . a-creaking:** the sound made by a porter carrying a cask of wine to an inn.

THINK AND DISCUSS
Understanding
1. Why does the pot in quatrain 84 feel that the potter will not allow it to be broken?
2. What characterizes the pot in quatrain 86?
3. What attitude does the pot in quatrain 88 express toward the potter?
4. Why are all the pots eager to see the new moon?

Analyzing
5. What is the problem addressed by quatrain 86?
6. What answer would the "Súfi pipkin" give to the question it asks in line 24?

Extending
7. Compare the point made in quatrain 87 with that expressed in Rumi's poem "The Soul of Goodness in Things Evil."

8. The speaker, the "I" in quatrain 82 who is listening to the pots, never makes a statement of his own position. What do you think he might say if, like the pots, he were to give a brief expression of his feelings about his destiny?

REVIEWING LITERARY TERMS
Setting
1. How does the setting contribute to the development of this section of *The Rubáiyát?*

Personification
2. What is appropriate about the manner in which Ramazán is personified?

Rhyme
3. Does FitzGerald employ the standard rhyme scheme of the Persian *rubai* in his translation?

4. Why does he use the contraction *ta'en* in line 10?

Satire

5. What is being satirized in quatrain 87?

Imagery

6. Influenced by Sufism, Persian poets sometimes employed the imagery of wine in a figurative sense in religious verse; other poets, like Hafiz, were more literal in their use of such imagery. Which seems to be the intention in these quatrains?

■ CONTENT REVIEW
THINKING SKILLS
Classifying

1. Identify each of the following as either a system of writing or as a literary form:
   (**a**) cuneiform; (**b**) hieroglyphics; (**c**) psalm;
   (**d**) rubai; (**e**) kana; (**f**) haiku
2. The work of which of the following writers might be described as primarily religious or philosophical in intent? (**a**) Akhenaton;
   (**b**) Rumi; (**c**) Hafiz; (**d**) Kalidasa; (**e**) Babur;
   (**f**) Confucius; (**g**) Sei Shōnagon

Generalizing

3. What is the subject basic to all the different writings contained in the Old Testament?
4. Identify Sufism and explain its importance in the history of Persian literature.
5. Describe the position of women in ancient China as suggested by Li Po's "The River-Merchant's Wife: A Letter" and Po Chü-i's "Golden Bells."

Synthesizing

6. The oldest literary work in this unit, *The Epic of Gilgamesh*, was composed around four thousand years ago. Even the most recent works included, the haiku of Bashō, are over three hundred years old. Forgetting for a moment their actual dates of composition, which of the works you have read in this unit seem the most modern in the thoughts and feelings they express? Which seem the least contemporary, the most remote?

Evaluating

7. Contrast the attitudes toward death expressed by *The Epic of Gilgamesh* and the *Bhagavad Gita*.
8. The Garden of Eden in Genesis and T'ao Ch'ien's "Peach-Blossom Fountain" are both conceptions of paradise. How are they alike? What do the differences between them suggest about the differences between ancient Israel and ancient China?
9. Discuss the similarities and differences in the pictures of aristocratic life contained in the *Babur-nama* and *The Pillow Book*. Which court seems more "civilized"—the Moghul or the Heian?

■ COMPOSITION REVIEW
Analyzing Poetry

In a three-paragraph paper discuss the impact of Confucianism and Taoism on the poetry of T'ao Ch'ien. In your first paragraph contrast the two philosophies. In the second paragraph describe several ways in which the works of T'ao Ch'ien you have read exhibit Confucian or Taoist influences. In the third paragraph draw a conclusion as to which influence was dominant.

Comparing Elegies

An elegy is a lament for the dead. Both the lament for Enkidu in *The Epic of Gilgamesh* and Firdausi's lament for his son in the *Shah-nama* are examples of this type of literature. In a three-paragraph paper discuss the similarities and differences of these two elegies. Be sure to address the following questions: How does each speaker characterize his dead loved one? How does he characterize himself? Does he include others in his grief?

Contrasting Cultures

Unit 1 provided a brief introduction to seven ancient Oriental cultures—Mesopotamia, Egypt, Israel, Persia, India, China, and Japan. Select the two cultures that seem to you the most dissimilar (or simply the most interesting) and contrast them in a three-paragraph paper. Be sure to use examples from the literature you have read to support your statements.

THE CLASSICAL WORLD

750 B.C.	650	550	450	350

HISTORY AND ARTS

• Olympic Games begin
    • Traditional founding of Rome

              • Second Peloponnesian War
                • Gauls sack Rome
      • Tribunes appointed   • Latin War
    • Persian War
        • First Peloponnesian War
          • Parthenon built
        • Law of the Twelve Tables

PEOPLE

• Homer

• Archilochus   • Sappho

Death of Socrates •   • Alexander the Great conquers Persia

Death of Pericles •

Plato founds Academy •

Tarquin expelled •   Ptolemy founds Library of Alexandria •

LITERATURE

• Greeks acquire alphabet
    • Homer: *Iliad*
    • Homer: *Odyssey*

Herodotus: *Histories* •

Euripides: *Medea* •

Thucydides: *History of the Peloponnesian War* •

    • Aeschylus: *Agamemnon*
      • Sophocles: *Oedipus the King*
    • Plato: *The Apology*
    • Aristotle: *Poetics*

Archaic Greek sculpture from Acropolis. Marble. c. 530 B.C.

Athenian coin showing owl. Silver. 5th century B.C.

Roman mosaic showing Alexander at the battle of Issus

750 B.C.–A.D. 150

250	150	50	A.D. 50	150

• Battle of Cannae   • Social War   • Eruption of Vesuvius

• Italy completely Roman   • Conquest of Gaul   • Romans conquer Britain

• First Punic War   • Battle of Actium   • Fire of Rome

• Second Punic War   • Hadrian's Wall built

• Coliseum built

• Hannibal invades Italy   • Caesar crosses Rubicon

Assassination of Caesar •   • Titus captures Jerusalem

• Birth of Jesus

Augustus becomes emperor •   • Death of Augustus

Virgil: *Georgics* •   • Ovid: *Metamorphoses*

• Cicero: *Philippics*   • Tacitus: *Annals*

• Horace: *Odes*

Catullus: *Carmina* •   • Virgil: *Aeneid*

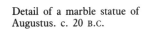

Roman decorated plate showing war elephants. 3rd century B.C.

Detail of a marble statue of Augustus. c. 20 B.C.

Sculptured relief from Roman Britain. Late 2nd century A.D.

PREVIEW

UNIT 2 THE CLASSICAL WORLD 750 B.C.–A.D. 150

Authors

Homer	Sophocles	Cicero	Virgil
Archilochus	Thucydides	Catullus	Ovid
Sappho	Plato	Horace	Tacitus

Features
Reading a Classical Epic
Comment: Homer and History
Reader's Note: Translating Homer
Reading a Greek Tragedy
Comment: The Delphic Oracle
Reader's Note: Aristotle on Tragedy
Reader's Note: The Art of Catullus's Poetry
Reader's Note: The Sounds of Virgil's Latin
The History of Language: The Origin
   of the Alphabet
Themes in World Literature: Heroism

Application of Literary Terms

narrative poetry	inference
foreshadowing	plot
characterization	analogy
lyric	allusion
protagonist	

Review of Literary Terms
tone
imagery
metaphor

Vocabulary Skills
word analogies
context
Latin roots

Thinking Skills
classifying
evaluating
generalizing
synthesizing

Composition Assignments Include
Writing a Letter
Writing About Characters
Describing Odysseus's Palace
Justifying the Actions of Odysseus
Writing About Theme
Finishing a Lyric Poem
Explaining Sappho's Values
Analyzing a Speech
Writing an Editorial
Writing About Drama
Analyzing Dramatic Irony
Writing A Narrative
Imagining a Reaction to Pericles' Speech
Analyzing Pericles' Leadership
Analyzing Catullus's Imagery

Enrichment
Readers Theater
Researching Pictures
Imagining a Greek Chorus
Comparing Pericles and Lincoln
Making and Listening to a Speech
Contrasting Horace and Owen
Filming the Fall of Troy
Comparing Shakespeare and Ovid
Researching Other Disastrous Fires

Thinking Critically About Literature
Concept Review
Content Review
Composition Review

THE CLASSICAL WORLD   750 B.C.–A.D. 150

EARLY GREEK HISTORY

Some ancient literatures, like those of India and China, come from empires spread over broad land masses. Characteristically, these nations developed strong, centralized governments and strict religious codes to control their large populations. The Greeks, by contrast, settled on scattered islands in the Aegean Sea, and on a peninsula divided by steep mountains and deep valleys. (See the map on page 115.) This environment encouraged the Greeks to create small, independent communities, or "city-states," free to develop in different directions. Each individual "state," or *polis,* had a central town where political and religious events took place; surrounding it was open countryside dominated by the *polis* and farmed by its members.

Division fostered rivalry between cities which sometimes led to healthy competition and sometimes to war. Yet the Greeks always considered themselves bound together by a shared *hellenikon,* a "Greekness." They recognized a common ancestry and shared the same Indo-European language. They called alien peoples *barbaroi* ("stammerers"), because foreign languages sounded like childish babble. The Greeks worshipped the same cluster of gods and goddesses and they followed similar customs. For example, every four years, starting as far back as 776 B.C., the Olympic games brought athletes from all over the Greek world to share in a panhellenic competition honoring Zeus (züs), the chief Greek god.

Greek civilization spread throughout the Mediterranean from 600 to 300 B.C., but the history of its development goes much further back in time. Migrating south from central Europe, the first Greek peoples settled in the Pelopon-nesus (pel′ə pə nē′səs) around 2100 B.C. At that time Minoan civilization, based on the island of Crete, dominated the eastern Mediterranean. The first Greeks built a heavily fortified palace at Mycenae (mī sē′nē), and at other sites. Mycenaean Greece was a feudal culture of warrior kings and their retainers, seeking victory on the battlefield and weapons and treasure won through fighting. By 1450 B.C. Mycenaean Greeks overran the Minoans, destroying Knossos (nos′əs), the capital of Crete. Soon they were spreading throughout the Aegean. Quite possibly in their expansion they captured the city of Troy around 1220 B.C., an event recalled five hundred years later in the epic poems of Homer.

Such Mycenaean attacks may have been the result of pressure on their own territory. By 1150 B.C., most Mycenaean towns had been destroyed —no one is quite sure by whom. Another, more belligerent Greek tribe, the Dorians, migrated south into the Greek peninsula around 1000 B.C. While the citizens of Athens may have held out, many others fled the Dorians, to settle the coast of Ionia and its offshore islands. For the next 250 years, through killing, enslavement, separate development, or amalgamation, rival clusters of Greek-speaking people evolved their system of city-states. By 800 B.C. many had grown to the point where expanding population, depleted natural resources, and a mounting desire for greater wealth and power led to an era of colonization, with Greeks settling throughout the Mediterranean basin from Spain and North Africa all the way to what is now Russian Crimea.

It was during this era of vigorous growth and frequent contact with other peoples around 750 B.C. that the Greeks acquired a system of alphabetic writing from the Phoenicians, their neighbors to the southeast. (See page 262.) This constituted a critical moment in Greek culture. Life in the Greek *polis* was far more collective than it is in modern times. People gathered in the marketplace to do business, and talk politics. They went to the temples to perform religious rituals. They exercised at gymnasiums, joining friends in the evening for wine and entertainment. Before the alphabet, Greek literature was entirely oral and public, the sharing of stories—myths about the gods and hero-tales of past adventure—and the singing of poems. These poems included both short lyrics about victories in athletic contests, the wedding of friends, the kindness of a local god, and longer stories of the heroic past chanted in metrical language by professional bards whose special task it was to preserve in their memories the history of the Greek people. With the advent of the written word the Greeks acquired the power to record this oral culture.

THE HOMERIC EPICS

The first known works of Greek literature to be written down are the epic poems of Homer. They illustrate the crucial shift from the spoken to the written word. Homer (c. 725 B.C.) was probably a professional bard from Ionia, where a tradition of oral storytelling had transmitted an account of the Mycenaean victory at Troy, and the return of the hero Odysseus to his home after the war. Homer transformed these materials into the long, complex, and richly detailed epic poems called the *Iliad* and the *Odyssey*. With the advent of writing, Homer's words could be transcribed, to become the foundation for later Greek culture.

During the five hundred years between the Mycenaean era and Homer, much had changed, and the ancient heroes had come to represent an ideal long past. Their courage, their persistence, and the clarity with which they understood the tragedy of human limitations became a model for conduct. Soon the Greeks were studying Homer as children and memorizing long passages from his works. Artists depicted scenes from the Homeric epics on pottery and in statuary. Two hundred and fifty years after the composition of the Homeric epics, when the drama flourished in Athens, playwrights drew their plots and characters from this rich source.

Homer is an impersonal poet. He presents his characters and their experiences objectively, and rarely intrudes his own feelings or judgments into the narrative. During the next hundred years, a very different kind of poetry flourished throughout the islands of the Aegean sea, as new generations of poets adapted the meters and melodies of hymns and folk songs into short lyric poems which speak in a very personal voice. Archilochus (7th century B.C.), the wandering soldier with a chip on his shoulder, and Sappho (6th century B.C.), with her ecstatic delight in the beauty of the visible world, illustrate how rich and diverse were these new experiments in self-expression.

At the beginning of the fifth century the freedom of the Greek world was suddenly threatened from the East. The Persian empire under Darius had been steadily extending its power, and the independence of the Greek city-states presented a challenge the Persians would not tolerate. In 490 they invaded the Greek mainland, only to be stopped by the Athenians at Marathon. Ten years later, Xerxes (zėrk′sēs′), the son of Darius, mounted an even larger campaign, but the Spartans held the Persians back at Thermopylae, and then the Athenians destroyed their fleet in a naval battle off Salamis. The following year under Spartan leadership, the Greeks utterly defeated the Persian army at Platea.

THE GOLDEN AGE OF GREECE

Victory over Persia made it clear that two very different city-states—Athens and Sparta—now dominated Greece. The Spartans, descendants of Dorian invaders, had a rigid, unchanging form of government based on a standing army. Boys left their families at the age of seven for rigorous military training which went on until they were men. Even as adults, male Spartans ate at a mess hall. Their king was also the commander in chief and personally led his 9,000 troops into battle. The principal reason for this militaristic system is that daily work in Sparta was done by slaves, the *helots*, descendants of people the Spartans had first overrun, and the helots vastly outnumbered their masters.

Athens was very different. Spartan power grew from a land-based army. The Athenians defeated the Persians at sea. In 478 B.C., two

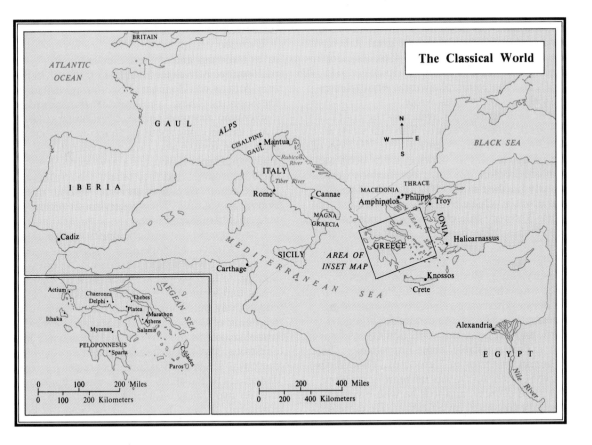

The Classical World

years after their naval victory at Salamis, the Athenians organized the Delian League, an anti-Persian alliance of cities scattered throughout the Aegean, with Athens at its head. Controlling and using the taxes collected by this league, Athens became not only powerful, but wealthy. At the same time, urged by the orator and general Pericles (per′ə klēz′) [490?–429 B.C.], the Athenians were dramatically altering their system of government to achieve the world's first notable experiment in democracy. By 450 B.C. an assembly of all adult male citizens governed this *polis*, and at its meetings anyone was free to speak. Juries, policy-making committees, general-ships—all governmental positions were open to any citizen. This was a culture of brilliant amateurs, since a farmer or stonemason might be asked to lead an army or direct the construction of a temple. Athenians prided themselves on their ability to adapt to new challenges, and to do all things well.

It is these Athenian Greeks who invented the drama for western civilization. Drama evolved out of rituals celebrating events such as a military victory or a good harvest, and Greek plays remained closely connected with both religious and political issues. Plays were performed during the annual festival of the wine-god Dionysus (dī′ə nī′səs). The ancient rites commemorating this god had employed wine and frenzied dancing to arouse ecstatic emotions of divine awe. The same cultivation of strong emotions, of fear or reckless delight, became a central feature of Greek drama. Athenian playwrights used ancient myths and hero tales as their subject matter, but shaped these materials to represent the issues of the moment. During the days of the dramatic festival, work stopped, and citizens were actually paid by the state to attend. Going to the theater became a civic responsibility in which writer and actor through their art helped the people confront current political or religious problems.

Greek drama was at its height in the fifth century, an era in which the three great Athenian tragedians, Aeschylus (c. 525–456 B.C.), Sophocles (c. 496–406 B.C.), and Euripides (c. 484–406 B.C.), and the comic playwright Aristophanes (c. 450–c. 385 B.C.), all wrote.

The fifth century B.C. was also the era of the great Greek historians. The first work of Greek prose to survive intact is the *Histories* of Herodotus (c. 484–c. 420 B.C.). His book was published before 425 B.C., but sections were already finished in the 440s. For the Greeks, prose was a vehicle to record investigation into facts. The very title chosen by Herodotus means "researches." His book is a study of the Persian invasions. Coming as he did from the city of Halicarnassus in Ionia, with its long tradition of storytelling, Herodotus based his history on tales which he collected during his travels. While he does evaluate the reliability of some of his information, Herodotus cannot resist a good yarn, and his book is a collection of vivid narratives, some reliable, some improbable. The Athenian successor of Herodotus, Thucydides (c. 455–c. 399 B.C.), was far more scrupulous about his sources, and it is he who invented scientific historical investigation. He quite self-consciously set out to revolutionize the writing of history, by striving to record objectively the tragic events that closed the fifth century.

After the victories over Persia, Athenian power seemed threatening to her neighbor city-states, and in two destructive wars they tried to diminish her influence. The two Peloponnesian Wars, the first from 461 to 451, the second from 431 to 404, were going on just as Athens was achieving some of her greatest cultural successes. During this threatening period, the Athenians produced their greatest achievements in sculpture and architecture, establishing a "classical style" in both of these areas whose influence has endured to the present. Thucydides describes the second of these wars, examining political and military power and how human nature expresses itself in political action. As the events it chronicles proceed, his *History of the Peloponnesian War* shows how Sparta and Athens destroyed themselves because they could not live together in peace.

GREEK PHILOSOPHY

If the uncertainties of this era are not reflected in its buildings and statues, they are in its philosophy. Advanced thought in mid-fifth century Athens was dominated by a group called the Sophists. These "professional" thinkers liked challenging accepted norms, questioning traditional assumptions about right and wrong, even expressing doubts about the gods themselves. They sometimes advocated a new spirit of personal selfishness, and they taught their students how to argue any side of an issue, without questioning its validity. Their relativism fit nicely with such dangerous times.

The principal foe of the Sophists was Socrates (470–399 B.C.), self-appointed "gadfly" of Athenian society, who sought, through acute questioning, to lead people to find a truth for themselves that would be clear and unshakable. He had nothing but scorn for the brilliant but empty reasoning of the Sophists. But Socrates seemed a troublemaker to those who could not answer his questions, and when the wars ended in 404 B.C. there was a revulsion against people considered dangerous to the state. Socrates was brought to trial on two charges, introducing new gods and corrupting the minds of the young, and was condemned to death.

Stung by this injustice, Socrates' pupil Plato (429–347 B.C.) began writing the first surviving books of Greek philosophy, works on freedom of thought like the *Apology* and ideal government like the *Republic* which became foundation-stones in western thought. In 387 B.C., when he was in mid-life, Plato founded his own philosophical school in Athens, the Academy. There he taught Aristotle (384–322 B.C.), who arrived in 367. Aristotle was to take philosophy in different, significant directions toward the end of the fourth century, in books such as his study of literature, the *Poetics* (335 B.C.). These philosophers worked in the afterglow of Athenian achievement. The great dramatists, poets, historians were gone.

Historical events now overtook the Greeks. Philip, king of Macedonia (mas'ə dō'nē ə), the region to the north of Greece, was written off by the Greeks as a crude outsider, a barbarian. Nevertheless, Philip harbored dreams of a Greek empire of his own, to rival the Persians. He be-

The Parthenon, the temple of Athena *Parthenos* ("Virgin"), was built between 447 and 432 B.C. It is located on the Acropolis, the citadel of Athens.

gan capturing Greek cities in 357. By 338 he had defeated Thebes and Athens at the fateful battle of Chaeronea, and had won the right to be called King of the Greeks. Philip was about to invade Persia when he was assassinated in 336 B.C. His son Alexander the Great (356–323 B.C.) completed this project. Relying on his control over the formerly independent city-states, Alexander left Greece, and invaded Asia, conquering both Persia and Egypt by 331. He then led his army east, reaching India before his troops forced him to turn back. He died in Babylon in 323 at the age of thirty-two, and his empire was divided into three parts, each ruled by one of his generals. These kingdoms (called *Hellenistic*) lasted for almost 200 years after Alexander's death.

THE HERITAGE OF ROME

Rome has had a unique influence on the development of both Europe and the United States. The Roman Empire was so enormous, it endured for so long, and it was so successful in engineering, in the arts, and especially in law and government, that Rome came to seem an ideal civilization and other nations strove to copy it. In A.D. 800, Pope Leo III crowned Charlemagne as

"Emperor and Augustus," reviving the titles of the rulers of the Roman empire. A thousand years later, when Napoleon crowned himself emperor, French coins pictured him as a Roman. The name of Rome's most famous family, the Caesars, became the title of the German Kaiser and the Russian Czar. The individuals who crafted the Constitution of the United States turned to the example of the Roman Republic, naming the members of one House of Congress "senators." Official buildings and monuments throughout the United States employ a Roman architectural style to express ideals of patriotism and order. Newspapers style themselves "tribunes," borrowing the title of Roman officials who were the guardians of the rights of the common people. With its brutal wars of conquest and periods of social decay at home, Roman civilization also had its dark side. But it was as an ideal state, combining supreme power with reason and virtue, that Rome has continued to inspire artists, writers, and statesmen over the centuries since its fall.

EARLY ROMAN HISTORY

The Italian peninsula, the birthplace of this success story, is geographically very different from Greece. (See the map on page 115.) Though divided by a spine of mountains, Italy opens into broad plains of fertile soil, freely inviting travel to the north and south. Around 800 B.C., this entire area was sparsely settled by a variety of different peoples competing for power. On the northwest coast of Italy, the Etruscans built fortified cities. Greek colonies dotted the southern coast and the island of Sicily. Across the Mediterranean on the northern shore of Africa, the Phoenicians founded the maritime empire of Carthage. In the center of the peninsula, the native Italic peoples were building small towns. One of these, located on the Tiber River, was to become the city of Rome.

Legends obscure the facts of early Roman history. One tradition held that Aeneas, a Trojan prince, escaped from his burning city and fled to Italy, where he married the daughter of a local king. Eight generations later, one of their descendants became the mother, by Mars, the god of war, of twin sons, Romulus and Remus. Abandoned as infants, they were nursed by a wolf. When they grew to manhood they returned to the spot where they had been reared, on the banks of the Tiber, and founded the town that would be Rome.

Archaeology and modern historical research suggest that people were living in this area as early as 1000 B.C., but tradition places the founding of the city at 753 B.C. For the first centuries, Rome was a monarchy ruled by Etruscan kings. But in 509 B.C. the Roman people expelled the last of them, Tarquin the Proud, and established a republic.

THE ROMAN REPUBLIC

At first the Roman Republic was an oligarchy, ruled by an elite of landed aristocrats called patricians. Three hundred patricians made up the senate, which annually elected the two chief magistrates, the consuls, who governed the republic. The mass of the citizens, called plebeians, had their own assembly that passed laws for their class. With the passage of time, the plebeians gained more power. After 494 B.C. they appointed officials called tribunes, who had the right to veto any senate bill not in the interest of the plebeians. About 450 B.C. the plebeians won the right to have laws put in writing. The laws were inscribed on a dozen bronze tablets, the Twelve Tables, and set up in the Forum, the market place used for public assemblies. The Law of the Twelve Tables was the first landmark in the long history of Roman law, and Roman schoolchildren were required to memorize it.

The early history of the Roman Republic is a story of territorial expansion. Surrounded by warlike neighbors, Rome's first victories were the consequence of defense. In the Latin War (340–338 B.C.), Rome destroyed an alliance of neighboring tribes, and by 270 B.C., the entire Italian peninsula had become Roman. During this period Carthage was also growing in power. A struggle for the control of the western Mediterranean became inevitable. In the first two Punic Wars (264–241 B.C. and 218–201 B.C.) Rome built a fleet, drove the Carthaginians out of Sicily, Sardinia, and Spain, and finally completely defeated them.

Nevertheless, Rome knew defeat. In 390 B.C. a swarm of barbarians from Gaul (modern France) actually took the city and destroyed

A marble relief from the arch erected in A.D. 81 to commemorate the victories of the emperor Titus. This panel shows part of the triumphal procession displaying the spoils taken in the conquest of Jerusalem in A.D. 70.

it. During the Second Punic War the brilliant Carthaginian general Hannibal came close to doing the same thing again. Assembling an army in Spain, Hannibal crossed the Alps and invaded Italy. At the battle of Cannae in 216 B.C., he wiped out a Roman force of seventy thousand men. But Hannibal lacked the troops and supplies to lay siege to Rome itself, and was eventually forced to withdraw. As the war with Hannibal indicated, Roman armies were persistent, if not invincible. As time passed the span of the empire spread inexorably over Spain, North Africa, Egypt, Syria, Asia Minor, Greece, and finally Gaul and Britain.

One key to success was the Roman inclination to permit, with the passage of time, subject peoples to become citizens of the empire, even of Rome itself. As Rome got bigger, citizenship meant not only a measure of security but also a chance to share in the enormous wealth which accompanied imperial power. Between 91 and 88 B.C. Rome quelled a rebellion of neighboring tribes, called the Social War, by offering her enemies citizenship, something they found so attractive that they put down their arms.

With success came problems that proved insoluble. The newly conquered territories became Roman provinces, governed by officials called praetors—who were next to consuls in rank—and taxed for tribute in the form of goods, money, and slaves. Wealth flooded the capital, corrupting magistrates and soldiers who began to assume that a generalship or a term as praetor entitled them to a fortune. The traditional citizen-soldier could not remain in distant countries on campaigns which lasted for years, and had to be replaced with professionals who expected booty while serving, and gifts of land when they returned from a successful campaign. The city of Rome swelled to a population of over a million people, sharply divided by wealth. The rich lived luxurious lives in their urban palaces and country villas. The Roman "mob" of unemployed workers, farmers driven off the land, freed slaves, and former soldiers became a dangerous force, willing to riot when their will was thwarted, demanding free food and lavish public entertainments.

This was the setting for the last, convulsive century of the Republic (133–31 B.C.). For three generations powerful military leaders set off to defend and extend the empire at its extreme limits in Spain, North Africa, Asia Minor, Egypt, and Gaul. They would put down rebellion, fend off attackers, and take new territory. At the same time, supporters back in Rome would fight for their interests within the government. When these military leaders returned to the city they expected political positions, power, and wealth. But since there were always several of these strongmen jockeying for power, they would, at times, join in secret agreements in an attempt to carve up the empire for their mutual benefit. In every case these alliances fell apart with the former partners attacking each other. Only death ended their rivalries.

CIVIL WAR

The climax to these cycles of political violence came with Julius Caesar, the brilliant general who conquered Gaul between 58 and 51 B.C. When he proposed to bring his army back to Rome, a practice forbidden by law, he was opposed by a rival general, Pompey (pom′pē). Caesar defied Pompey, crossed the border—a small river called the Rubicon (rü′bə kən)—in 49 B.C., and started a civil war. One year later, he met and defeated Pompey's army at Pharsalus (fär sā′ləs) in central Greece; eventually, he returned to Rome, evidently planning to create a monarchy, with himself as king. Fearing this, senators loyal to the Republic assassinated him on March 15, 44 B.C.

Now Caesar's followers, led by his friend Mark Antony and his adopted son Octavian, pursued the Republicans Brutus and Cassius to Philippi (fi lip′ī), a remote spot north of Greece, where they defeated them in 42 B.C. Subsequently the victorious allies Antony and Octavian turned on each other. Antony joined forces with Cleopatra, the queen of Egypt, hoping to create a new power center in the East. Octavian attacked them, and with Antony's defeat at the battle of Actium (ak′tē əm) in 31 B.C. and his joint suicide with Cleopatra the following year, Octavian took control of the Roman government. He occupied several crucial elected positions at once, and through this appearance of legality masked the fact that the Republic had finally become a monarchy. After so many years of exhausting struggle, few seemed to mind. In 27 B.C. the Roman people renamed him *Augustus* ("Revered") and began to treat him as a god.

LATIN LITERATURE

Ironically, Roman culture flourished during these years of danger and confusion. Literature in Latin had started much earlier, during the era of territorial expansion around 240 B.C. But the early Roman writers had felt themselves too crude, too practical, their efforts overshadowed by the literary sophistication of the Greeks. The poet Horace (65–8 B.C.) later described their feelings of cultural inadequacy: "To the Greeks the muse gave genius, the Greeks she endowed/With eloquent speech and greed for nothing but praise./Our Roman lads learn arithmetic and divide/The unit into its hundreds. . . . When once the corrosive concern/For petty cash has tainted our minds, can we hope to write poems. . . ?"

The first Latin literature that has survived, the comic plays of Plautus (c. 254–184 B.C.) and Terence (195–159 B.C.), are in fact translations of Greek originals, with only slight adaptation for the Roman stage. When truly independent writers appeared later, during the last years of the Republic, they continued to base themselves on a thorough training in Greek culture, which often included travel to Greece for study with celebrated teachers. Their challenge became the problem of transformation, taking what they had mastered and making it Roman. The poet Catullus (84?–54? B.C.) did this by adapting Greek meters and stanza forms for use in Latin lyrics. Virgil (70–19 B.C.), in seeking to create a Roman epic, closely modeled his *Aeneid* upon Homer.

But these authors were no longer simple imitators. The Latin writers of the era of the civil wars, and of the reign of Augustus, became classic authors of the first magnitude. It would be difficult to properly estimate their subsequent influence on European civilization. Latin remained the second language of priests, lawyers, scholars, and scientists until the nineteenth century. It was the language every student learned. Consequently Latin literature was accessible to any person with an education, and the general estimation among educated Europeans for nearly two thousand years was that Latin authors were the greatest in history, despite the fact that they were "pagans." Indeed, because they did not subscribe to the official religions of Christian Europe, Roman writers had a special authority. The orator and philosopher Cicero (106–43 B.C.) seemed to represent the wisdom people could achieve without divine illumination. Medieval readers believed that a poem by Virgil prophesied the birth of Christ.

In our time these may no longer be grounds for praise. Instead, the writers of Rome's "golden age" now matter because they touch upon universal human feelings and values. It is Cicero's perception of how friendship makes life worth living, Catullus's intensity of feeling, Horace's balance of a love for life with a sense of its brevity, the wit and charm of the poet Ovid (43 B.C.–A.D. 17?), and the grave concern of the historian Tacitus (A.D. 55?–120?) at human folly that move us now. Above all, it is Virgil's unified vision in the *Aeneid* of human history, divine destiny, and the perilous, even tragic, life of a man called upon against his will to be a leader and hero, that makes Roman literature endlessly rewarding to the reader.

This highly creative period was relatively brief, beginning with Cicero's celebrated orations around 70 B.C. and ending with Ovid's banishment in A.D. 8. Of course Romans went on writing, and the poets of the so-called "Silver Age" have their admirers. But of the later writers, it is only in history, in works such as Tacitus's *Annals*, that Roman literature remained vital.

The fiber of the nation itself was disintegrating. Many of the emperors were incompetent; some were vicious. Economic decline and political instability weakened the empire, but it was so immense and so powerful that it took centuries to die. Culturally, however, it became sterile much sooner. The energy of invention went elsewhere—into the remote, "barbaric" lands the Romans once conquered—to reappear in the early Middle Ages in a dazzling spectrum of new languages.

THINKING ABOUT GRAPHIC AIDS
Using the Time Line

The time line on pages 110–111 shows the chronological sequence of the historical and literary events discussed in Unit 2. Use the time line to answer the following questions.

1. The Greeks dated events from the beginning of the Olympic Games, the Romans from the founding of their city. Which of these events occurred first?
2. Which of the following was not a contemporary of the others? (**a**) Pericles; (**b**) Sophocles; (**c**) Homer; (**d**) Euripides
3. Which is the older structure—the Parthenon or the Coliseum?
4. Was Jesus born during the reign of Augustus or Titus?
5. Which of the following literary works could not have been part of the original collection of the Library of Alexandria? (**a**) the *Odyssey;* (**b**) *Oedipus the King;* (**c**) the *Aeneid;* (**d**) the *Annals;* (**e**) the *Apology*

Using the Map

The map on page 115 shows the locations of many of the places discussed in Unit 2. Use the map to answer the following questions.

1. Odysseus came from Ithaka, Agamemnon from Mycenae, Menelaos from Sparta. Which of these three commanders of the Greek army at Troy was fighting the farthest from his home?
2. In what direction did the Greek expedition have to travel to reach Troy?
3. Which of the following battles took place in Italy? (**a**) Actium; (**b**) Philippi; (**c**) Cannae
4. *Magna Graecia* was the name given to a region of Greek colonies. Where was this area located?
5. Relative to Italy, is Cisalpine Gaul on the near or the far side of the Alps?

Greek tradition attributed the *Iliad* and the *Odyssey* to the same writer, a man named Homer. In ancient times, many stories grew up about his exile, his poverty, and his blindness. But modern critical analysis has questioned every detail of the old biographies. It is not even certain that the same person wrote both epics. Whoever Homer was, his personal characteristics have been lost forever. During the last two centuries, however, there has been an intensive study of the way Homer writes, to determine at least how he worked. The results have revolutionized our understanding of the Homeric poems, and of the culture which created them.

Homer probably did not write at all. He was an oral poet, a singer of tales. Before the spread of alphabetic writing, Greek society preserved accounts of the past largely by memory. The patterns of metrical language help keep the words of an account together, so the practice of narrating old stories in poetic form developed. Homer and his predecessors in this tradition handed down the recollection of a great episode in Greek tradition, when heroic warriors defeated a distant city, Troy, and then overcame terrible obstacles in their efforts to return home.

Singers such as Homer knew the stories of these feats from boyhood. They also possessed a variety of stock expressions that fit neatly into the verse patterns they used. Homer had, as a result, a set of verbal formulas to describe the dawn or the sea or a warrior throwing a spear, which fit easily into his poem's meter. He built up his epics not so much with individual words as with clusters of words frequently repeated. (This aspect of Homeric style is hard to sense in translated versions.) All told, one fifth of Homer consists of repeated lines.

Homer's words come from several different parts of Greece, and from several different eras because the formulaic phrases he uses evolved over a long period of time and in different places. While Greeks understood him, his language was a special blending of words old and new, familiar and odd, that no one would have used in conversation, but which seemed appropriate to his ancient, heroic subject matter. The great asset in this special vocabulary is that it offers a large number of alternate words for naming things. Homer has three words for sword, four for helmet, five for spear, fifty for different parts of the body, and fifty-five for different sounds. This richness of choice helps a poet who is improvising orally to find a word that fits the meter.

Almost certainly there was a person we now call Homer, someone very special among the bards of Ionia. Around 725 B.C., when the Greek alphabet itself was first coming into use, someone must have decided to set down his particular version of the ancient songs, about the Trojan War, so that they would not be lost.

THE STORY OF ODYSSEUS

In order to understand the following selection from the *Odyssey* it is necessary, first, to know the events that lead up to it. When the Trojan prince Paris kidnaps Helen, wife of the Akhaian king Menelaos (men′ə-lā′əs), all the Akhaian leaders, including Odysseus, join in an attack on Troy, seeking to get Helen back. *Akhaians* (ə kī′ənz) is one of the principal names used for the Greeks in the Homeric epics. For ten years Akhaians and Trojans fight. It is Odysseus who suggests the plan that finally ends the war. The Akhaians construct an enormous wooden horse, and then pretend to sail away. The Trojans, believing the horse to be a sacred idol, drag it into their walled city. They do not realize that inside the horse is a picked band of Akhaian warriors—including Odysseus. During the night these men escape from the horse, open the city gates to their comrades, who have returned in the darkness, and together they slaughter the Trojans and destroy their city.

The gods, angered at Akhaian savagery, direct Poseidon, ruler of the sea, to punish them. With a terrible storm he scatters the Akhaian ships across the Mediterranean. When the storm ceases, Odysseus and his men are far off course. After ten years of wandering and adventure, only Odysseus remains alive. Finally, through the aid of friendly sailors, he finds himself put ashore on his island kingdom, Ithaka (ith′ə kə). But he is not to be welcomed with open arms by his people.

During his years of wandering it is generally believed that Odysseus is dead. A group of young men come to his palace, seeking to marry his wife Penélopê. She refuses their proposals. To force her decision the suitors remain, eating and drinking, making life uncomfortable for her and dangerous for her growing son, Telémakhos. On reaching manhood, Telémakhos sets off on a journey to learn if his father might still be alive. During his absence the suitors set up an ambush, planning to kill him when he returns. But Telémakhos learns about this plot, and has his men put him on shore in a deserted area, so that he can avoid the killers and return to the city on foot.

The goddess Athena favors Odysseus, and it is she who brings son and father together. Knowing of the dangers posed by the murderous suitors, she transforms Odysseus's appearance, making him look like an old, crippled beggar. In this disguise he seeks the help of his faithful swineherd Eumaios. At his cabin the returning Telémakhos meets Odysseus. Odysseus secretly identifies himself to his son, and together they plan how to deal with the suitors. (The text of the *Odyssey* begins on page 126.)

PRINCIPAL CHARACTERS IN THE *ODYSSEY*

The list below identifies the principal characters in Books XVII–XXIII of the *Odyssey*. Since the Latin equivalents for some of these names may be more familiar, they appear in brackets at the end of certain entries.

Amphínomos (am fin'ō məs), a suitor. He is kinder than most, arguing against a plot to assassinate Telémakhos, and offering food to the disguised Odysseus.

Antínoös (an tin'ō əs), a suitor. Aggressive and brutal, he takes the lead in an effort to assassinate Telémakhos and acts with cruelty to Odysseus.

Aphroditê (af'rə dī'tē), goddess of love. [Venus]

Artemis (är'tə mis), goddess of the hunt and of the moon. She is also the protector of women. [Diana]

Athena (ə thē'nə), goddess of wisdom. She is a daughter of Zeus and protector of Odysseus. In battle she carries the magic shield of Zeus called the *aegis* (ē'gis). [Minerva]

Eumaios. (yü mā'əs), Odysseus's faithful swineherd, sometimes called a forester. He shelters Odysseus on his secret return to Ithaka and helps in the attack on the suitors.

Eurýkleia (yü'ri klē'ə), Odysseus's old nurse who has served Penélopê during his absence.

Eurýmakhos (yü rim'ə kəs), a suitor. Cunning and treacherous, he presses Penélopê to give up her hope of Odysseus's return and agree to marry. He throws a footstool at Odysseus.

Eurýnomê (yü ron'ō mē), servant of Penélopê.

Hêlios (hē'lē os), god of the sun.

Kronos (krō'nəs), a Titan, father of Zeus. [Saturn]

Laërtês (lā er'tēz), Odysseus's father. An old man at the time of this story, he is living on a farm, grieving the loss of his son. Odysseus is sometimes given the epithet *Laërtiadês* (lā er'tē'ə-dēz), "son of Laërtês."

Leódês (lā ō'dēz), a suitor. He observes the smoke rising from sacrifices to the gods and tries to read in it omens for the future.

Medon (mā'don), a suitor. He is their crier, announcing events.

Melánthios (mel an'thē əs), a goatherd serving the suitors. He is particularly abusive to the disguised Odysseus.

Melántho (mel an'thō), one of Penélopê's maids. She insults the disguised Odysseus.

Mentor (men'tor), an old citizen of Ithaka asked by Odysseus to advise Penélopê.

Odysseus (ō dis'ē əs), hero of the ten-year Trojan war, forced by the anger of the gods to wander for another ten years before returning to his homeland. [Ulysses]

Penélopê (pə nel'ə pē), Odysseus's faithful wife, who has waited twenty years for his return.

Phemios (fēm'ē əs), a harper who entertains the suitors.

Philoítios (fil oi'tē əs), a cattle herder loyal to Odysseus.

Poseidon (pə sīd'n), god of the sea. [Neptune]

Telémakhos (tə lem'ə kəs), Odysseus's son, who has just reached manhood when his father returns.

Zeus (züs), king of the gods. As ruler of the sky he frequently sends omens in thunder and lightning, or in flights of birds. [Jupiter]

Detail of a terra-cotta relief showing Odysseus and Penélopê. 460–450 B.C. Louvre

124   *The Classical World*

Reading A CLASSICAL EPIC

The Bard and His Audience In the eighth book of the *Odyssey*, Homer describes a blind poet seated at a banquet, plucking the strings of his "taut harp," inspired by the heavenly Muse to chant "a song/of heroes whose great fame rang under heaven . . . ." The audience already knows the story he tells. In fact, it is about one of them—Odysseus. As the hero listens to this poem describing his own past life, "the secret tears . . . started to his eyes." Knowing what will happen does not diminish his emotional involvement with the story. The same is true for the Greek audiences who first heard Homer sing. They came not to be surprised by a new story, but to hear a familiar tale told in a way which would move them once again.

Homer as Narrator Since Homer's tale is well known to his audience, the *Odyssey* does not conceal the fact that Odysseus will kill the suitors. There are many hints of what lies ahead: divine omens, promises from the goddess Athena, and observations made by the poem's narrator. In reading the *Odyssey* one should always keep clearly in mind how the story will end, so as to observe the way in which Odysseus achieves his goal. That is Homer's emphasis.

As a narrator, Homer rarely employs lengthy descriptions of people or places. Instead, he will focus upon one or two specific details, and the reader must use imagination to fill out the picture. Similarly, Homer does not spend time explaining a person's character. Rather, he uses what people say, and what they do, to define them. More than anything else, Homer values action. It is in doing, rather than in saying or thinking, that his people fulfill themselves. Consequently, the reader must constantly consider the implications of action within the poem.

Heroic Society Epics traditionally describe a world that is history for their audience, a time when the poet thinks human nature was finer than it is now. They deal with people caught up in great historical moments, such as the Trojan War, and they look for heroic conduct. The epic world adheres to a code that springs from the lives of its warrior aristocrats. Bravery in battle, a high sense of personal honor, loyalty to one's word and one's friends, these are the ethical norms of such a culture. Homer and his audience used the poem to examine their values, and modern people must try to read epics in a similar way. What matters in the *Odyssey* is not that Odysseus wins in his fight with the suitors, but rather how he wins, and the justifications for his winning. Homer's poems picture a feudal society of warrior-kings, their bands of retainers who provide military service in exchange for food, weapons, and treasure, and groups of workers and servants. But he is no partisan for one particular group, and readers must be prepared to find in the poorest and most humble people virtues absent from others far wealthier and more powerful.

The Role of the Gods One dimension of Homer's world that surprises modern readers is the frequent interference of the gods. Homer assumes the gods take sides in human affairs. They freely adopt the shape of specific people, talk and act, even joining in battle when they choose. While they may be instrumental in deciding someone's fate, Homer does not depict the gods as governed by moral imperatives. Consequently, one of the major issues that faces Homer's reader is the significance of what people do when they encounter these mysterious, and at times arbitrary, forces suddenly intruding into their lives.

from the Odyssey

Homer   *translated by* **Robert Fitzgerald**

from Book Seventeen

When the young Dawn came bright into the East
spreading her finger tips of rose, Telémakhos
the king's son, tied on his rawhide sandals
and took the lance that bore his handgrip. Burning
5 to be away, and on the path to town,
he told the swineherd:

                "Uncle, the truth is
I must go down myself into the city.
Mother must see me there, with her own eyes,
or she will weep and feel forsaken still,
10 and will not set her mind at rest. Your job
will be to lead this poor man down to beg. . . ."
At once Odysseus the great tactician
spoke up briskly:

              "Neither would I myself
care to be kept here, lad. A beggar man
15 fares better in the town. Let it be said
I am not yet so old I must lay up
indoors and mumble, 'Aye, Aye' to a master.
Go on, then. As you say, my friend can lead me
as soon as I have had a bit of fire
20 and when the sun grows warmer. These old rags
could be my death, outside on a frosty morning,
and the town is distant, so they say." . . .

                    Meanwhile,
swaggering before Odysseus' hall,
the suitors were competing at the discus throw
25 and javelin, on the level measured field.
But when the dinner hour drew on, and beasts
were being driven from the fields to slaughter—
as beasts were, every day—Medôn spoke out:
Medôn, the crier, whom the suitors liked;
30 he took his meat beside them.

           "Men," he said,
"each one has had his work-out and his pleasure,
come in to Hall now; time to make our feast.
Are discus throws more admirable than a roast
when the proper hour comes?"

                    At this reminder
35 they all broke up their games, and trailed away
into the gracious, timbered hall. There, first,
they dropped their cloaks on chairs; then came their
    ritual:
putting great rams and fat goats to the knife—
pigs and a cow, too.

              So they made their feast.
40 During these hours, Odysseus and the swineherd
were on their way out of the hills to town.
The forester had got them started, saying:
"Friend, you have hopes, I know, of your adventure
into the heart of town today. My lord
45 wishes it so, not I. No, I should rather
you stood by here as guardian of our steading.
But I owe reverence to my prince, and fear
he'll make my ears burn later if I fail.
A master's tongue has a rough edge. Off we go.
50 Part of the day is past; nightfall will be
early, and colder, too."

                 Odysseus,
who had it all timed in his head, replied:
"I know, as well as you do. Let's move on.
You lead the way—the whole way. Have you got
55 a staff, a lopped stick, you could let me use
to put my weight on when I slip? This path
is hard going, they said."

                Over his shoulders

he slung his patched-up knapsack, an old bundle
tied with twine. Eumaios found a stick for him,
60 the kind he wanted, and the two set out,
leaving the boys and dogs to guard the place.
In this way good Eumaios led his lord
down to the city.

             And it seemed to him
he led an old outcast, a beggar man,
65 leaning most painfully upon a stick,
his poor cloak, all in tatters, looped about him.
Down by the stony trail they made their way
as far as Clearwater, not far from town—
a spring house where the people filled their jars. . . .
70   Well, here the son of Dólios
crossed their path—Melánthios.

                      He was driving
a string of choice goats for the evening meal,
with two goatherds beside him; and no sooner
had he laid eyes upon the wayfarers
75 than he began to growl and taunt them both
so grossly that Odysseus' heart grew hot;
"Here comes one scurvy type leading another!
God pairs them off together, every time.
Swineherd, where are you taking your new pig,
80 that stinking beggar there, licker of pots?
How many doorposts has he rubbed his back on
whining for garbage, where a noble guest
would rate a cauldron or a sword? . . .
Well, I can tell you this for sure:
85 in King Odysseus' hall, if he goes there,
footstools will fly around his head—good shots
from strong hands. Back and side, his ribs will
      catch it
on the way out!"

             And like a drunken fool
he kicked at Odysseus' hip as he passed by.
90 Not even jogged off stride, or off the trail,
the Lord Odysseus walked along, debating
inwardly whether to whirl and beat
the life out of this fellow with his stick,
or toss him, brain him on the stony ground.
95 Then he controlled himself, and bore it quietly. . . .

Reaching the gate, Odysseus and the forester
halted and stood outside, for harp notes came
around them rippling on the air
as Phêmios picked out a song. Odysseus

Detail of a terra-cotta relief showing Eumaios.
460–450 B.C. Metropolitan Museum of Art

100 caught his companion's arm and said:

                            "My friend,
here is the beautiful place—who could mistake it?
here is Odysseus' hall; no hall like this! . . .
You go in first, and leave me here a little.
But as for blows and missiles,
105 I am no tyro[1] at these things. I learned
to keep my head in hardship—years of war
and years at sea. Let this new trial come.
The cruel belly, can you hide its ache?
How many bitter days it brings! Long ships
110 with good stout planks athwart—would fighters rig
      them
to ride the barren sea, except for hunger?
Seawolves—woe to their enemies!"

                            While he spoke
an old hound, lying near, pricked up his ears
and lifted up his muzzle. This was Argos,
115 trained as a puppy by Odysseus,

---

1. **tyro**, an inexperienced beginner.

but never taken on a hunt before
his master sailed for Troy. The young men, afterward,
hunted wild goats with him, and hare, and deer,
but he had grown old in his master's absence.
120 Treated as rubbish now, he lay at last
upon a mass of dung before the gates—
manure of mules and cows, piled there until
fieldhands could spread it on the king's estate.
Abandoned there, and half destroyed with flies,
125 old Argos lay.

          But when he knew he heard
Odysseus' voice nearby, he did his best
to wag his tail, nose down, with flattened ears,
having no strength to move nearer his master.
And the man looked away,
130 wiping a salt tear from his cheek; but he
hid this from Eumaios. Then he said:
"I marvel that they leave this hound to lie
here on the dung pile;
he would have been a fine dog, from the look of him,
135 though I can't say as to his power and speed
when he was young. You find the same good build
in house dogs, table dogs landowners keep
all for style."

          And you replied, Eumaios:
"A hunter owned him—but the man is dead
140 in some far place. If this old hound could show
the form he had when Lord Odysseus left him,
going to Troy, you'd see him swift and strong.
He never shrank from any savage thing
he'd brought to bay in the deep woods; on the scent
145 no other dog kept up with him. Now misery
has him in leash. His owner died abroad,
and here the women slaves will take no care of
    him. . . .
Eumaios crossed the court and went straight forward
into the mégaron[2] among the suitors;
150 but death and darkness in that instant closed
the eyes of Argos, who had seen his master,
Odysseus, after twenty years.

          Long before anyone else
Telémakhos caught sight of the grey woodsman
coming from the door, and called him over
155 with a quick jerk of his head. Eumaios'
narrowed eyes made out an empty bench
beside the one the carver used—that servant

who had no respite, carving for the suitors.
This bench he took possession of, and placed it
160 across the table from Telémakhos
for his own use. Then the two men were served
cuts from a roast and bread from a bread basket.
At no long interval, Odysseus came
through his own doorway as a mendicant,
165 humped like a bundle of rags over his stick.
He settled on the inner ash wood sill,
leaning against the door jamb—cypress timber
the skilled carpenter planed years ago
and set up with a plumbline.

          Now Telémakhos
170 took an entire loaf and a double handful
of roast meat; then he said to the forester:
"Give these to the stranger there. But tell him
to go among the suitors, on his own;
he may beg all he wants. This hanging back
175 is no asset to a hungry man."
The swineherd rose at once, crossed to the door,
and halted by Odysseus.

          "Friend," he said,
"Telémakhos is pleased to give you these,
but he commands you to approach the suitors;
180 you may ask all you want from them. He adds,
your shyness is no asset to a beggar."
The great tactician, lifting up his eyes,
cried:

          "Zeus aloft! A blessing on Telémakhos!
Let all things come to pass as he desires!"
185 Palms held out, in the beggar's gesture, he
received the bread and meat and put it down
before him on his knapsack—lowly table!—
then he fell to, devouring it. Meanwhile
the harper in the great room sang a song.
190 Not till the man was fed did the sweet harper
end his singing—whereupon the company
made the walls ring again with talk.

          Unseen,
Athena took her place beside Odysseus
whispering in his ear:

          "Yes, try the suitors.
195 You may collect a few more loaves, and learn
who are the decent lads, and who are vicious—

---

2. *mégaron* (meg′ə ron), a Greek palace with a large
central hall supported by four columns.

although not one can be excused from death!"
So he appealed to them, one after another,
going from left to right, with open palm,
as though his lifetime had been spent in beggary.
And they gave bread, for pity—wondering, though,
at the strange man. Who could this beggar be,
where did he come from? each would ask his neighbor;
till in their midst the goatherd, Melánthios,
raised his voice:

"Hear just a word from me,
my lords who court our illustrious queen!

This man,
this foreigner, I saw him on the road;
the swineherd here was leading him this way;
who, what, or whence he claims to be, I could not
say for sure."

At this, Antínoös
turned on the swineherd brutally, saying:

"You famous
breeder of pigs, why bring this fellow here?
Are we not plagued enough with beggars,
foragers and such rats?

You find the company
too slow at eating up your lord's estate—
is that it? So you call this scarecrow in?"
The forester replied:

"Antínoös,
well born you are, but that was not well said.
Who would call in a foreigner?—unless
an artisan with skill to serve the realm,
a healer, or a prophet, or a builder,
or one whose harp and song might give us joy.
All these are sought for on the endless earth,
but when have beggars come by invitation?
Who puts a field mouse in his granary? My lord,
you are a hard man, and you always were,
more so than others of this company—hard
on all Odysseus' people and on me.
But this I can forget
as long as Penélopê lives on, the wise and tender
mistress of this hall; as long
as Prince Telémakhos—"

But he broke off
at a look from Telémakhos, who said:

"Be still.
Spare me a long-drawn answer to this gentleman.
With his unpleasantness, he will forever make

strife where he can—and goad the others on."
He turned and spoke out clearly to Antínoös:
"What fatherly concern you show me! Frighten
this unknown fellow, would you, from my hall
with words that promise blows—may God forbid it!
Give him a loaf. Am I a niggard? No,
I call on you to give. And spare your qualms
as to my mother's loss, or anyone's—
not that in truth you have such care at heart:
your heart is all in feeding, not in giving."
Antínoös replied:

"What high and mighty
talk, Telémakhos! Control your temper.
If every suitor gave what I may give him,
he could be kept for months—kept out of sight!"
He reached under the table for the footstool
his shining feet had rested on—and this
he held up so that all could see his gift.
But all the rest gave alms,
enough to fill the beggar's pack with bread
and roast meat.

So it looked as though Odysseus
had had his taste of what these men were like
and could return scot free to his own doorway—
but halting now before Antínoös
he made a little speech to him. Said he:
"Give a mite, friend. I would not say, myself,
you are the worst man of the young Akhaians.
The noblest, rather; kingly, by your look;
therefore you'll give more bread than others do.
Let me speak well of you as I pass on
over the boundless earth!

I, too, you know,
had fortune once, lived well, stood well with men,
and gave alms, often, to poor wanderers
like this one that you see—aye, to all sorts,
no matter in which dire want. I owned
servants—many, god knows—and all the rest
that goes with being prosperous, as they say.
But Zeus the son of Kronos brought me down. . . ."
But here Antínoös broke in, shouting:

"God!
What evil wind blew in this pest?

Get over,
stand in the passage! Nudge my table, will you? . . .
These men have bread to throw away on you
because it is not theirs. Who cares? Who spares

Odyssey—Book Seventeen **129**

another's food, when he has more than plenty?"
With guile Odysseus drew away, then said:
280 "A pity that you have more looks than heart.
You'd grudge a pinch of salt from your own larder
to your own handy man. You sit here, fat
on others' meat, and cannot bring yourself
to rummage out a crust of bread for me!"
285 Then anger made Antínoös' heart beat hard,
and, glowering under his brows, he answered:

                                        "Now!

You think you'll shuffle off and get away
after that impudence? Oh, no you don't!"
The stool he let fly hit the man's right shoulder
290 on the packed muscle under the shoulder blade—
like solid rock, for all the effect one saw.
Odysseus only shook his head, containing
thoughts of bloody work, as he walked on,
then sat, and dropped his loaded bag again
295 upon the door sill. . . .
But now the rest were mortified, and someone
spoke from the crowd of young bucks to rebuke him:
"A poor show, that—hitting this famished tramp—
bad business, if he happened to be a god.
300 You know they go in foreign guise, the gods do,
looking like strangers, turning up
in towns and settlements to keep an eye
on manners, good or bad."

                          But at this notion
Antínoös only shrugged.

                          Telémakhos,
305 after the blow his father bore, sat still
without a tear, though his heart felt the blow.
Slowly he shook his head from side to side,
containing murderous thoughts. . . .

from **Book Eighteen**

And now heart-prompting from the grey-eyed goddess
came to the quiet queen, Penélopê:
a wish to show herself before the suitors;
for thus by fanning their desire again
5 Athena meant to set her beauty high
before her husband's eyes, before her son.
Knowing no reason, laughing confusedly,
she said:

              "Eurýnomê, I have a craving
I never had at all—I would be seen

10 among those ruffians, hateful as they are.
I might well say a word, then, to my son,
for his own good—tell him to shun that crowd;
for all their gay talk, they are bent on evil."
Mistress Eurýnomê replied:

                    "Well said, child,
15 now is the time. Go down, and make it clear,
hold nothing back from him.

                    But you must bathe
and put a shine upon your cheeks—not this way,
streaked under your eyes and stained with tears.
You make it worse, being forever sad,
20 and now your boy's a bearded man! Remember
you prayed the gods to let you see him so."
Penélopê replied:

                    "Eurýnomê,
it is a kind thought, but I will not hear it—
to bathe and sleek with perfumed oil. No, no,
25 the gods forever took my sheen away
when my lord sailed for Troy in the decked ships.
Only tell my Autonoë to come,
and Hippodameía; they should be attending me
in hall, if I appear there. I could not
30 enter alone into that crowd of men."
At this the good old woman left the chamber
to tell the maids her bidding. But now too
the grey-eyed goddess had her own designs.
Upon the quiet daughter of Ikários
35 she let clear drops of slumber fall, until
the queen lay back asleep, her limbs unstrung,
in her long chair. And while she slept the goddess
endowed her with immortal grace to hold
the eyes of the Akhaians. With ambrosia[3]
40 she bathed her cheeks and throat and smoothed her
          brow—
ambrosia, used by flower-crowned Kythereia[4]
when she would join the rose-lipped Graces[5] dancing.
Grandeur she gave her, too, in height and form,
and made her whiter than carved ivory.

---

3. *ambrosia* (am brō′zhə), literally, "immortality," a marvelous substance commonly represented as the food of the
gods, sometimes as their drink, and also as a richly perfumed ointment with beautifying and healing properties.
4. *Kythereia* (kith′er ē′ə), another name for Aphrodite.
5. *Graces*, three sister goddesses who give beauty, charm,
and joy to people and nature. Their names are Aglaia
(ə glā′ə), Thalia (thə lī′ə), and Euphrosyne (yü fros′n ē).

45 Touching her so, the perfect one was gone.
Now came the maids, bare-armed and lovely, voices
breaking into the room. The queen awoke
and as she rubbed her cheek she sighed:

                "Ah, soft
that drowse I lay embraced in, pain forgot!
50 If only Artemis the Pure would give me
death as mild, and soon! No heart-ache more,
no wearing out my lifetime with desire
and sorrow, mindful of my lord, good man
in all ways that he was, best of the Akhaians!"

55 She rose and left her glowing upper room,
and down the stairs, with her two maids in train,
this beautiful lady went before the suitors.
Then by a pillar of the solid roof
she paused, her shining veil across her cheek,
60 the two girls close to her and still;
and in that instant weakness took those men
in the knee joints, their hearts grew faint with lust;
not one but swore to god to lie beside her.
But speaking for her dear son's ears alone
65 she said:

        "Telémakhos, what has come over you?
Lightminded you were not, in all your boyhood.
Now you are full grown, come of age; a man
from foreign parts might take you for the son
of royalty, to go by your good looks;
70 and have you no more thoughtfulness or manners?
How could it happen in our hall that you
permit the stranger to be so abused?
Here, in our house, a guest, can any man
suffer indignity, come by such injury?
75 What can this be for you but public shame?"
Telémakhos looked in her eyes and answered,
with his clear head and his discretion:

                "Mother,
I cannot take it ill that you are angry.
I know the meaning of these actions now,
80 both good and bad. I had been young and blind.
How can I always keep to what is fair
while these sit here to put fear in me? —princes
from near and far whose interest is my ruin;
are any on my side? . . .

                  Thus Penélopê
85 reproached her son, and he replied. Now, interrupting,
Eurýmakhos called out to her:

             "Penélopê,
deep-minded queen, daughter of Ikários,
if all Akhaians in the land of Argos
only saw you now! What hundreds more
90 would join your suitors here to feast tomorrow!
Beauty like yours no woman had before,
or majesty, or mastery."

             She answered:
"Eurýmakhos, my qualities—I know—
my face, my figure, all were lost or blighted
95 when the Akhaians crossed the sea to Troy,
Odysseus my lord among the rest.
If he returned, if he were here to care for me,
I might be happily renowned!
But grief instead heaven sent me—years of pain.
100 Can I forget?—the day he left this island,
enfolding my right hand and wrist in his,
he said:

        'My lady, the Akhaian troops
will not easily make it home again
full strength, unhurt, from Troy. They say the
      Trojans
105 are fighters too; good lances and good bowmen,
horsemen, charioteers—and those can be
decisive when a battle hangs in doubt.
So whether God will send me back, or whether
I'll be captive there, I cannot tell.
110 Here, then, you must attend to everything.
My parents in our house will be a care for you
as they are now, or more, while I am gone.
Wait for the beard to darken our boy's cheek;
then marry whom you will, and move away.'
115 The years he spoke of are now past; the night
comes when a bitter marriage overtakes me,
desolate as I am, deprived by Zeus
of all the sweets of life.

              How galling, too,
to see newfangled manners in my suitors!
120 Others who go to court a gentlewoman,
daughter of a rich house, if they are rivals,
bring their own beeves and sheep along; her friends
ought to be feasted, gifts are due to her;
would any dare to live at her expense?"
125 Odysseus' heart laughed when he heard all this—
her sweet tones charming gifts out of the suitors
with talk of marriage, though she intended none,
Eupeithês' son, Antínoös, now addressed her:
"Ikários' daughter, O deep-minded queen!

130 If someone cares to make you gifts, accept them!
It is no courtesy to turn gifts away.
But we go neither to our homes nor elsewhere
until of all Akhaians here you take
the best man for your lord."

Pleased at this answer,
135 every man sent a squire to fetch a gift— . . .
Penélopê then mounted the stair again,
her maids behind, with treasure in their arms.

And now the suitors gave themselves to dancing,
to harp and haunting song, as night drew on;
140 black night indeed came on them at their pleasure.
But three torch fires were placed in the long hall
to give them light. On hand were stores of fuel,
dry seasoned chips of resinous wood, split up
by the bronze hatchet blade—these were mixed in
145 among the flames to keep them flaring bright;
each housemaid of Odysseus took her turn.
Now he himself, the shrewd and kingly man,
approached and told them:

"Housemaids of Odysseus,
your master so long absent in the world,
150 go to the women's chambers, to your queen.
Attend her, make the distaff whirl, divert her,
stay in her room, comb wool for her.

I stand here
ready to tend these flares and offer light
to everyone. They cannot tire me out,
155 even if they wish to drink till Dawn.
I am a patient man."

But the women giggled,
glancing back and forth—laughed in his face;
and one smooth girl, Melántho, spoke to him
most impudently. She was Dólios' daughter,
160 taken as ward in childhood by Penélopê
who gave her playthings to her heart's content
and raised her as her own. Yet the girl felt
nothing for her mistress, no compunction,
but slept and made love with Eurýmakhos.
165 Her bold voice rang now in Odysseus' ears:
"You must be crazy, punch drunk, you old goat.
Instead of going out to find a smithy
to sleep warm in—or a tavern bench—you stay
putting your oar in, amid all our men.
170 Numbskull, not to be scared! The wine you drank
has clogged your brain, or are you always this way,

boasting like a fool? . . .

But Odysseus
glared at her under his brows and said:

"One minute:
let me tell Telémakhos how you talk
175 in hall, you slut; he'll cut your arms and legs off!"
This hard shot took the women's breath away
and drove them quaking to their rooms, as though
knives were behind: they felt he spoke the truth.
So there he stood and kept the firelight high
180 and looked the suitors over, while his mind
roamed far ahead to what must be accomplished.
They, for their part, could not now be still
or drop their mockery—for Athena wished
Odysseus mortified still more.

Eurýmakhos,
185 the son of Pólybos, took up the baiting,
angling for a laugh among his friends. . . .

"Friend, you have a mind to work,
do you? Could I hire you to clear stones
from wasteland for me—you'll be paid enough—
190 collecting boundary walls and planting trees?
I'd give you a bread ration every day,
a cloak to wrap in, sandals for your feet.
Oh no: you learned your dodges long ago—
no honest sweat. You'd rather tramp the country
195 begging, to keep your hoggish belly full."
The master of many crafts replied:

"Eurýmakhos, . . .
You thick-skinned menace to all courtesy!
You think you are a great man and a champion,
but up against few men, poor stuff, at that.
200 Just let Odysseus return, those doors
wide open as they are, you'd find too narrow
to suit you on your sudden journey out."
Now fury mounted in Eurýmakhos,
who scowled and shot back:

"Bundle of rags and lice!
205 By god, I'll make you suffer for your gall,
your insolent gabble before all our men."
He had his footstool out: but now Odysseus
took to his haunches by Amphínomos' knees,
fearing Eurýmakhos' missile, as it flew.
210 It clipped a wine steward on the serving hand,
so that his pitcher dropped with a loud clang
while he fell backward, cursing, in the dust.
In the shadowy hall a low sound rose—of suitors

murmuring to one another.

                        "Ai!" they said,

215 "This vagabond would have done well to perish
somewhere else, and make us no such rumpus.
Here we are, quarreling over tramps; good meat
and wine forgotten; good sense gone by the board."
Telémakhos, his young heart high, put in:

220 "Bright souls, alight with wine, you can no longer
hide the cups you've taken. Aye, some god
is goading you. Why not go home to bed?—
I mean when you are moved to. No one jumps
at my command."

                     Struck by his blithe manner,

225 the young men's teeth grew fixed in their under lips,
but now the son of Nísos, Lord Amphínomos
of Aretíadês, addressed them all:
"O friends, no ruffling replies are called for;
that was fair counsel.

                    Hands off the stranger, now,

230 and hands off any other servant here

in the great house of King Odysseus. Come,
let my own herald wet our cups once more,
we'll make an offering, and then to bed.
The stranger can be left behind in hall;

235 Telémakhos may care for him; he came
to Telémakhos' door, not ours."

                    This won them over.
The soldier Moulios, Doulíkhion herald,
comrade in arms of Lord Amphínomos,
mixed the wine and served them all. They tipped out

240 drops for the blissful gods,[6] and drank the rest,
and when they had drunk their thirst away
they trailed off homeward drowsily to bed.

(*The text of the* Odyssey *continues on page 135.*)

---

6. *drops for the blissful gods*. The ancient Greeks had a custom of pouring out several drops of wine, water, or some other beverage about to be drunk, as an offering to the gods. Both the custom and the spilled liquid are known as a *libation* (lī bā′shən).

Comment

Homer and History

For centuries the Homeric epics were thought to be pure invention. Their mingling of pagan gods, fantastic monsters, and heroic men and women made them seem no more credible than fairy tales.

But in the nineteenth century, a challenger to this view emerged in the figure of a German grocer and self-made millionaire named Heinrich Schliemann (1822–1890). This unlikely innovator had no advanced education, but his zealous reading of Homer's poems convinced him they were based on historical fact. He went to northwestern Turkey and, following the passages of description in the *Iliad*, he decided that the site of ancient Troy must be near a hill called Hisarlik. In April of 1870 he began the excavation of the area, and almost at once discovered the remains of an ancient, ruined city. As he dug deeper Schliemann found that time and again people had settled on this site; in fact, nine cities, each from a different historical period, had been built there. Schliemann

was sure this was the actual setting of Homer's epic. Subsequent investigations have borne out his hunch, and today most archaeologists agree that the city built at level VIIA, despite heavy fortifications, succumbed to an attack and burned to the ground during the era when Homer's heroes might have lived.

Excited by his success, Schliemann went to the Greek mainland, where he began digging at Mycenae, the legendary city of Agamemnon, the king Homer describes leading the Akhaians in the Trojan war. In November of 1876 Schliemann opened up a series of ancient graves filled with gold, armor, and jewels. Schliemann announced to the world that he had uncovered the burial site of Agamemnon.

Subsequent work has questioned Schliemann's inclination to link whatever he dug up with people and events in Homer. The graves at Mycenae come from around 1600 B.C., whereas the city built at Hisarlik on level VIIA fell around 1220 B.C. But Schliemann's findings do suggest that Homer's poems may be grounded in historical fact. The kings of Mycenae dominated the Aegean in the fifteenth and fourteenth centuries B.C., and they probably would have been able to mount an attack against a city in Asia Minor even in the thirteenth century. As a recent study of this period observes, "The sack of Troy was remembered because it was the last fling of the Mycenaean world."

What must be kept in mind is that the Homeric poems were written down five hundred years after these events took place. Homer was not trying to write history in the modern sense. His epics were probably based upon tales inspired by a prolonged battle at "Troy," tales which had been handed down from generation to generation, over such a long span of time that though the central events, such as the burning of a distant city, might still be accurately recalled, details about people, battle strategy, and so on must have altered.

Homer, then, may well have based his poems on real events, but thanks to the intervening centuries, and the transforming power of the human imagination, the account of those events came to transcend its origins, becoming a tale of men who strove with gods.

THINK AND DISCUSS

Understanding

1. How do the suitors treat Odysseus when he arrives, disguised as a beggar?
2. What prompts Penélopê to come down among the suitors?
3. Why do the suitors decide to bring Penélopê gifts?

Analyzing

4. How does Odysseus's dog Argos illustrate the poem's contrast between past and present?
5. In what ways do Athena's interventions advance Odysseus's plan for revenge?
6. At what points does Telémakhos indicate his own growing self-confidence?
7. Compare and contrast the way people treat strangers in these books. How do their actions illustrate personal values?
8. Odysseus comes home after a twenty-year absence. How do his feelings, and the way he expresses them, illustrate his character?
9. Point out the speeches by Odysseus which hint at his real power. What is the effect of including such hints?

Extending

10. Evaluate the kinds of loyalty that Homer illustrates. Is this sort of conduct still necessary today, or was it appropriate only for the more primitive times that the poem describes?
11. What do you think Homer implies when he describes the actions of Athena? Does the text suggest that he literally believes a goddess acted in this manner, or is she rather representing something else?

APPLYING: Narrative Poetry H 7
See Handbook of Literary Terms, p. 959.

Homer's *Odyssey* tells, or narrates, a story, and it does so in the medium of poetry, so that we call it **narrative poetry**. Narrative poetry has a teller, or *narrator*, who presents everything to the reader. A narrative poem presents scenes that occur at different times and places, and the narrator freely shifts the reader's attention from one to the next, depending on the requirements of the story. Within scenes the narrator will use both description and the speeches of characters to build up the reader's sense of what is happening.

1. How does the Homeric narrator indicate his own feelings in Book 17, line 62?
2. Describe how the narrator shifts place in Book 17, lines 39–40.
3. Examine the scene in which Melánthios meets Odysseus and Eumaios (Book 17, lines 70–95), and explain how Homer uses description and the speech of a character to imply what things are like at the palace.

COMPOSITION

Writing a Letter

Imagine that you are one of the suitors staying in Odysseus's palace, and write a letter to a friend back home describing your experiences and feelings. Invent your own character. On a scratch sheet, make some notes about your character—background, personality, and so on. Use these notes while writing to keep your character consistent. Now draft the letter, devoting at least one paragraph to each of these topics: what the writer hopes to achieve at the court; how the writer reacts to the appearance of the old beggar; and what the writer expects will happen.

Writing About Characters

Homer's narrative poem frequently builds the reader's sense of a character through the way that person talks. In Book Eighteen of the *Odyssey* he presents Penélopê with her servant Eurýnome, her son Telémakhos, and the suitor Eurýmakhos. Analyze her personality through the kinds of speech she uses with each of them. Present your conclusions in an essay written for someone who has read the *Odyssey*. Organize your essay into at least four paragraphs, dividing your ideas according to categories such as how Penélopê recalls the past; her attitude toward her current plight; what she hopes for in the future; how she faces adversity; the ways that she talks to servants, enemies, and friends.

 See **FORESHADOWING** in the Handbook of Literary Terms, page 950.

from **Book Nineteen**

Now by Athena's side in the quiet hall
studying the ground for slaughter, Lord Odysseus
turned to Telémakhos.
               "The arms," he said.
"Harness and weapons must be out of sight
5 in the inner room. . . ."
               Then he fell silent,
and Telémakhos obeyed his father's word.
He called Eurýkleia, the nurse, and told her:
"Nurse, go shut the women in their quarters
while I shift Father's armor back
10 to the inner rooms—these beautiful arms
    unburnished,
caked with black soot in his years abroad.
I was a child then. Well, I am not now.
I want them shielded from the draught and smoke."
And the old woman answered:
               "It is time, child,
15 you took an interest in such things. I wish
you'd put your mind on all your house and chattels.

But who will go along to hold a light?
You said no maids, no torch-bearers."
                    Telémakhos
looked at her and replied:
               "Our friend here.
20 A man who shares my meat can bear a hand,
no matter how far he is from home."
               He spoke so soldierly
her own speech halted on her tongue. Straight back
she went to lock the doors of the women's hall.
And now the two men sprang to work—father
25 and princely son, loaded with round helms
and studded bucklers, lifting the long spears,
while in their path Pallas Athena
held up a golden lamp of purest light.
Telémakhos at last burst out:
               "Oh, Father,
30 here is a marvel! All around I see
the walls and roof beams, pedestals and pillars,
lighted as though by white fire blazing near.

Odyssey—Book Nineteen   **135**

One of the gods of heaven is in this place!"
Then said Odysseus, the great tactician,
35 "Be still; keep still about it: just remember it.
The gods who rule Olympos make this light.
You may go off to bed now. Here I stay
to test your mother and her maids again.
Out of her long grief she will question me."
40 Telémakhos went across the hall and out
under the light of torches—crossed the court
to the tower chamber where he had always slept.
Here now again he lay, waiting for dawn,
while in the great hall by Athena's side
45 Odysseus waited with his mind on slaughter.
Presently Penélopê from her chamber
stepped in her thoughtful beauty.

          So might Artemis
or golden Aphroditê have descended;
and maids drew to the hearth her own smooth chair
50 inlaid with silver whorls and ivory. . . .
She turned away and said to the housekeeper:
"Eurýnomê, a bench, a spread of sheepskin,
to put my guest at ease. Now he shall talk
and listen, and be questioned."

                    Willing hands
55 brought a smooth bench, and dropped a fleece upon it.
Here the adventurer and king sat down;
then carefully Penélopê began:
"Friend, let me ask you first of all:
who are you, where do you come from, of what nation
60 and parents were you born?"

                  And he replied:
"My lady, never a man in the wide world
Should have a fault to find with you. Your name
has gone out under heaven like the sweet
honor of some god-fearing king, who rules
65 in equity over the strong . . .

                O my dear lady.
this being so, let it suffice to ask me
of other matters—not my blood, my homeland.
Do not enforce me to recall my pain.
My heart is sore; but I must not be found
70 sitting in tears here, in another's house:
it is not well forever to be grieving.
One of the maids might say—or you might think—
I had got maudlin over cups of wine."
And Penélopê replied:

"Stranger, my looks,
75 my face, my carriage, were soon lost or faded
when the Akhaians crossed the sea to Troy,
Odysseus my lord among the rest.
If he returned, if he were here to care for me,
I might be happily renowned!
80 But grief instead heaven sent me—years of pain. . . .
Can I give proper heed to guest or suppliant
or herald on the realm's affairs?

                    How could I?
wasted with longing for Odysseus, while here
they press for marriage.

                  Ruses served my turn
85 to draw the time out—first a close-grained web
I had the happy thought to set up weaving
on my big loom in hall. I said, that day:
'Young men—my suitors, now my lord is dead,
let me finish my weaving before I marry,
90 or else my thread will have been spun in vain.
It is a shroud I weave for Lord Laërtês
when cold Death comes to lay him on his bier.
The country wives would hold me in dishonor
if he, with all his fortune, lay unshrouded.'
95 I reached their hearts that way, and they agreed.
So every day I wove on the great loom,
but every night by torchlight I unwove it;
and so for three years I deceived the Akhaians.
But when the seasons brought a fourth year on,
100 as long months waned, and the long days were spent,
through impudent folly in the slinking maids
they caught me—clamored up to me at night;
I had no choice then but to finish it.
And now, as matters stand at last,
105 I have no strength left to evade a marriage,
cannot find any further way; my parents
urge it upon me, and my son
will not stand by while they eat up his property.
He comprehends it, being a man full grown,
110 able to oversee the kind of house
Zeus would endow with honor.

                But you too
confide in me, tell me your ancestry.
You were not born of mythic oak or stone."[1]

---

1. *mythic oak or stone.* One Greek myth told that, after
a disastrous flood that had destroyed the human race, the
Titan Prometheus had recreated it from stones.

And the great master of invention answered:

15 "O honorable wife of Lord Odysseus,
must you go on asking about my family?
Then I will tell you, though my pain
be doubled by it: and whose pain would not
if he had been away as long as I have

20 and had hard roving in the world of men?
But I will tell you even so, my lady.
One of the great islands of the world
in midsea, in the winedark sea, is Krete:
spacious and rich and populous, with ninety

25 cities and a mingling of tongues. . . .
and one among their ninety towns is Knossos.
Here lived King Minos whom great Zeus received
every ninth year in private council—Minos,
the father of my father, Deukálion.

30 Two sons Deukálion had: Idómeneus,
who went to join the Atreidai[2] before Troy
in the beaked ships of war; and then myself,
Aithôn by name—a stripling next my brother.
But I saw with my own eyes at Knossos once

35 Odysseus.
             Gales had caught him off Cape Malea,
driven him southward on the coast of Krete,
when he was bound for Troy. At Ámnisos,
hard by the holy cave of Eileithuía,
he lay to, and dropped anchor, in that open

40 and rough roadstead riding out the blow.
Meanwhile he came ashore, came inland, asking
after Idómeneus: dear friends he said they were;
but now ten mornings had already passed,
ten or eleven, since my brother sailed.

45 So I played host and took Odysseus home,
saw him well lodged and fed, for we had plenty;
then I made requisitions—barley, wine,
and beeves for sacrifice—to give his company
abundant fare along with him.
                                Twelve days

50 they stayed with us, the Akhaians, while that wind
out of the north shut everyone inside—
even on land you could not keep your feet,
such fury was abroad. On the thirteenth,
when the gale dropped, they put to sea."

55 Now all these lies he made appear so truthful
she wept as she sat listening. The skin
of her pale face grew moist the way pure snow
softens and glistens on the mountains, thawed
by Southwind after powdering from the West,

160 and, as the snow melts, mountain streams run full:
so her white cheeks were wetted by these tears
shed for her lord—and he close by her side.
Imagine how his heart ached for his lady,
his wife in tears; and yet he never blinked;

165 his eyes might have been made of horn or iron
for all that she could see. He had this trick—
wept, if he willed to, inwardly.
                                Well, then,
as soon as her relieving tears were shed
she spoke once more:
                      "I think that I shall say, friend,

170 give me some proof, if it is really true
that you were host in that place to my husband
with his brave men, as you declare. Come, tell me
the quality of his clothing, how he looked,
and some particular of his company."

175 Odysseus answered, and his mind ranged far:
"Lady, so long a time now lies between,
it is hard to speak of it. Here is the twentieth year
since that man left the island of my father.
But I shall tell what memory calls to mind.

180 A purple cloak, and fleecy, he had on—
a double thick one. Then, he wore a brooch
made of pure gold with twin tubes for the prongs,
and on the face a work of art: a hunting dog
pinning a spotted fawn in agony

185 between his forepaws—wonderful to see
how being gold, and nothing more, he bit
the golden deer convulsed, with wild hooves flying.
Odysseus' shirt I noticed, too—a fine
closefitting tunic like dry onion skin,

190 so soft it was, and shiny. . . ."
Now hearing these details—minutely true—
she felt more strangely moved, and tears flowed
until she had tasted her salt grief again.
Then she found words to answer:
                                  "Before this

195 you won my sympathy, but now indeed
you shall be our respected guest and friend.
With my own hands I put that cloak and tunic

---

2. *Atreidai* (a trā′ə dī), Agamemnon and Menelaos, the sons
of Atreus and commanders of the Greek force that attacked
Troy.

upon him—took them folded from their place—
and the bright brooch for ornament.

                               Gone now,
200 I will not meet the man again
returning to his own home fields. Unkind
the fate that sent him young in the long ship
to see that misery at Ilion,[3] unspeakable!"
And the master improviser answered:

                              "Honorable
205 wife of Odysseus Laërtiadês, . . .
I have a thing to tell you, something true.
I heard but lately of your lord's return,
heard that he is alive, not far away, . . .
Between this present dark and one day's ebb,
210 after the wane, before the crescent moon,
Odysseus will come."

               Penélopê,
the attentive queen, replied to him:

                      "Ah, stranger,
if what you say could ever happen!
You would soon know our love! Our bounty, too:
215 men would turn after you to call you blessed.
But my heart tells me what must be.
Odysseus will not come to me; no ship
will be prepared for you. We have no master
quick to receive and furnish out a guest
220 as Lord Odysseus was.

                Or did I dream him?
Maids, maids: come wash him, make a bed for him,
bedstead and colored rugs and coverlets
to let him lie warm into the gold of Dawn.
In the morning light you'll bathe him and anoint him
225 So that he'll take his place beside Telémakhos
feasting in hall. . . ."
Warily Odysseus answered:

                   "Honorable lady,
wife of Odysseus Laërtiadês,
a weight of rugs and cover? Not for me.
230 I've had none since the day I saw the mountains
of Krete, white with snow, low on the sea line
fading behind me as the long oars drove me north.
Let me lie down tonight as I've lain often,
many a night unsleeping, many a time
235 afield on hard ground waiting for pure Dawn.
No: and I have no longing for a footbath
either; none of these maids will touch my feet,

unless there is an old one, old and wise,
one who has lived through suffering as I have:
240 I would not mind letting my feet be touched
by that old servant."

              And Penélopê said:
"Dear guest, no foreign man so sympathetic
ever came to my house, no guest more likeable,
so wry and humble are the things you say.
245 I have an old maidservant ripe with years,
one who in her time nursed my lord. She took him
into her arms the hour his mother bore him.
Let her, then, wash your feet, though she is frail.
Come here, stand by me, faithful Eurýkleia,
250 and bathe—bathe your master, I almost said,
for they are of an age, and now Odysseus'
feet and hands would be enseamed like his.
Men grow old soon in hardship."

                           Hearing this,
the old nurse hid her face between her hands
255 and wept hot tears, and murmured:

                        "Oh, my child!
I can do nothing for you! How Zeus hated you,
no other man so much! No use, great heart, . . .
There is no day of homecoming for you.
Stranger, some women in some far off place
260 perhaps have mocked my lord when he'd be home
as now these strumpets mock you here. No wonder
you would keep clear of all their whorishness
and have no bath. But here am I. The queen
Penélopê, Ikários' daughter, bids me;
265 so let me bathe your feet to serve my lady—
to serve you, too.

               My heart within me stirs,
mindful of something. Listen to what I say:
strangers have come here, many through the years,
but no one ever came, I swear, who seemed
270 so like Odysseus—body, voice and limbs—
as you do."

              Ready for this, Odysseus answered:
"Old woman, that is what they say. All who have seen
the two of us remark how like we are,
as you yourself have said, and rightly, too."
275 Then he kept still, while the old nurse filled up
her basin glittering in firelight; she poured

---

3. *Ilion* (il'ē ən), another name for Troy.

Vase painting showing Odysseus and Eurýkleia. c. 440 B.C. Museo Nazionale, Chiusi

cold water in, then hot.
                    But Lord Odysseus
whirled suddenly from the fire to face the dark.
The scar: he had forgotten that. She must not
80 handle his scarred thigh, or the game was up.
But when she bared her lord's leg, bending near,
she knew the groove at once.
                              An old wound
a boar's white tusk inflicted, on Parnassos[4]
years ago. . . .
85 she traced it under her spread hands, then let go,

and into the basin fell the lower leg
making the bronze clang, sloshing the water out.
Then joy and anguish seized her heart; her eyes
filled up with tears; her throat closed, and she
    whispered,
290 with hand held out to touch his chin:
                                        "Oh yes!
You are Odysseus! Ah, dear child! I could not
see you until now—not till I knew

---

4. **Parnassos** (pär nas′əs), a mountain in central Greece.

my master's very body with my hands!"
Her eyes turned to Penélopê with desire
295 to make her lord, her husband, known—in vain,
because Athena had bemused the queen,
so that she took no notice, paid no heed.
At the same time Odysseus' right hand
gripped the old throat; his left hand pulled her near,
300 and in her ear he said:

"Will you destroy me,
nurse, who gave me milk at your own breast?
Now with a hard lifetime behind I've come
in the twentieth year home to my father's island.
You found me out, as the chance was given you.
305 Be quiet; keep it from the others, else
I warn you, and I mean it, too,
if by my hand god brings the suitors down
I'll kill you, nurse or not, when the time comes—
when the time comes to kill the other women."
310 Eurýkleia kept her wits and answered him:
"Oh, what mad words are these you let escape you!
Child, you know my blood, my bones are yours;
no one could whip this out of me. I'll be
a woman turned to stone, iron I'll be.
315 And let me tell you too—mind now—if god
cuts down the arrogant suitors by your hand,
I can report to you on all the maids,
those who dishonor you, and the innocent."
But in response the great tactician said:
320 "Nurse, no need to tell me tales of these.
I will have seen them, each one, for myself.
Trust in the gods, be quiet, hold your peace."
Silent, the old nurse went to fetch more water,
her basin being all spilt.

When she had washed
325 and rubbed his feet with golden oil, he turned,
dragging his bench again to the fire side
for warmth, and hid the scar under his rags.
Penélopê broke the silence, saying:

"Friend,
allow me one brief question more. You know,
330 the time for bed, sweet rest, is coming soon,
if only that warm luxury of slumber
would come to enfold us, in our trouble. But for me
my fate at night is anguish and no rest.
By day being busy, seeing to my work,
335 I find relief sometimes from loss and sorrow;
but when night comes and all the world's abed

I lie in mine alone, my heart thudding,
while bitter thoughts and fears crowd on my
grief. . . .

Listen:
340 interpret me this dream: From a water's edge
twenty fat geese have come to feed on grain
beside my house. And I delight to see them.
But now a mountain eagle with great wings
and crooked beak storms in to break their necks
345 and strew their bodies here. Away he soars
into the bright sky; and I cry aloud—
all this in dream—I wail and round me gather
softly braided Akhaian women mourning
because the eagle killed my geese.

Then down
350 out of the sky he drops to a cornice beam
with mortal voice telling me not to weep.
'Be glad,' says he, 'renowned Ikários' daughter:
here is no dream but something real as day,
something about to happen. All those geese
355 were suitors, and the bird was I. See now,
I am no eagle but your lord come back
to bring inglorious death upon them all!'
As he said this, my honeyed slumber left me.
peering through half-shut eyes, I saw the geese
360 in hall, still feeding at the self-same trough."
The master of subtle ways and straight replied:
"My dear, how can you choose to read the dream
differently? Has not Odysseus himself
shown you what is to come? Death to the suitors,
365 sure death, too. Not one escapes his doom."
Penélopê shook her head and answered:

"Friend,
many and many a dream is mere confusion,
a cobweb of no consequence at all.
Two gates for ghostly dreams there are: one gateway
370 of honest horn, and one of ivory.
Issuing by the ivory gate are dreams
of glimmering illusion, fantasies,
but those that come through solid polished horn
may be borne out, if mortals only know them.
375 I doubt it came by horn, my fearful dream—
too good to be true, that, for my son and me.
But one thing more I wish to tell you: listen
carefully. It is a black day, this that comes.
Odysseus' house and I are to be parted.
380 I shall decree a contest for the day.

We have twelve axe heads. In his time, my lord
could line them up, all twelve, at intervals
like a ship's ribbing; then he'd back away
a long way off and whip an arrow through.
385 Now I'll impose this trial on the suitors.
The one who easily handles and strings the bow
and shoots through all twelve axes I shall marry,
whoever he may be—then look my last
on this my first love's beautiful brimming house.
390 But I'll remember, though I dream it only."
Odysseus said:

        "Dear honorable lady,
wife of Odysseus Laërtiadês,
let there be no postponement of the trial.
Odysseus, who knows the shifts of combat,
395 will be here: aye, he'll be here long before
one of these lads can stretch or string that bow
or shoot to thread the iron!"

        Grave and wise,
Penélopê replied:

        "If you were willing
to sit with me and comfort me, my friend,
400 no tide of sleep would ever close my eyes.
But mortals cannot go forever sleepless.
This the undying gods decree for all
who live and die on earth, kind furrowed earth.
Upstairs I go, then, to my single bed,
405 my sighing bed, wet with so many tears
after my Lord Odysseus took ship
to see that misery at Ilion, unspeakable.
Let me rest there, you here. You can stretch out
on the bare floor, or else command a bed."
410 So she went up to her chamber softly lit,
accompanied by her maids. Once there, she wept
for Odysseus, her husband, till Athena
cast sweet sleep upon her eyes.

from Book Twenty

Outside in the entry way he made his bed—
raw oxhide spread on level ground, and heaped up
fleeces, left from sheep the Akhaians killed.
And when he had lain down, Eurýnomê
5 flung out a robe to cover him. Unsleeping
the Lord Odysseus lay, and roved in thought
to the undoing of his enemies.

        Now came a covey of women

laughing as they slipped out, arm in arm,
as many a night before, to the suitors' beds;
10 and anger took him like a wave to leap
into their midst and kill them, every one—. . .

        His rage
held hard in leash, submitted to his mind,
while he himself rocked, rolling from side to side,
as a cook turns a sausage, big with blood
15 and fat, at a scorching blaze, without a pause,
to broil it quick: so he rolled left and right,
casting about to see how he, alone,
against the false outrageous crowd of suitors
could press the fight.

        And out of the night sky
20 Athena came to him; out of the nearby dark
in body like a woman; came and stood
over his head to chide him:

        "Why so wakeful,
most forlorn of men? Here is your home,
there lies your lady; and your son is here,
25 as fine as one could wish a son to be."
Odysseus looked up and answered:
"Aye,
goddess, that much is true; but still
I have some cause to fret in this affair.
30 I am one man; how can I whip those dogs?
They are always here in force. Neither
is that the end of it, there's more to come.
If by the will of Zeus and by your will
I killed them all, where could I go for safety?
35 Tell me that!"

        And the grey-eyed goddess said:
"Your touching faith! Another man would trust
some villainous mortal, with no brains—and what
am I? Your goddess-guardian to the end
in all your trials. Let it be plain as day:
40 if fifty bands of men surrounded us
and every sword sang for your blood,
you could make off still with their cows and sheep.
Now you, too, go to sleep. This all night vigil
wearies the flesh. You'll come out soon enough
45 on the other side of trouble."

        Raining soft
sleep on his eyes, the beautiful one was gone
back to Olympos. Now at peace, the man
slumbered and lay still. . . .

(*The text of the* Odyssey *continues on page 143.*)

THINK AND DISCUSS

Understanding

1. How does Penélopê describe her own personal appearance? According to her explanation, what has made her look this way?
2. Explain the trick she uses to postpone a second marriage.
3. How does Eurýkleia recognize her master?

Analyzing

4. How do the properties of snow and stream fit the weeping Penélopê, in the extended **simile** of Book 19, lines 156–162?
5. Penélopê intends to marry whoever wins the trial described in Book 19, lines 380–384. But what kind of man can pass this test? How does her plan suggest her own intentions?
6. Why do both Penélopê and Odysseus refuse to accept hopeful omens?

Extending

7. The events of Book 19 do little to advance the epic's story. Why does Homer describe at length the conversation between Odysseus and Penélopê, and the nurse's recognition of her master?
8. In your judgment, should Odysseus continue to lie to Penélopê?

APPLYING: Foreshadowing   H𝕋
See Handbook of Literary Terms, p. 950.

When Homer hints at what will come later in his narrative, he uses the technique called **foreshadowing**. Since his audience already knew the story, Homer can quite freely refer to what will happen later on.

1. Penélopê's dream in Book 19, lines 340–357, foreshadows the events to come. Who is the eagle in the dream and who are the geese?
2. What does the dream hint will happen to the suitors?

COMPOSITION

Describing Odysseus's Palace

The narrator of the *Odyssey* never stops to give the reader a detailed description of Odysseus's palace. We must use the scattered hints he provides as he goes on telling the story. To help your classmates visualize this celebrated building, write a narrative description picturing its principal elements. In preparing, skim through what you have read of the poem so far, noting all the relevant details. Organize your paper according to the route a visitor might take on first arriving, starting with the road approaching the building, then the entrance, the main hall, and finally the private rooms where the family lives and the storerooms where food, clothing, and weapons are kept. When Homer leaves something vague, use your imagination to fill in the gaps.

Writing About Characters

Write an essay in which you explain to the general reader a few of the ways that Homer makes a legendary figure into a particular and specific person. Choose a scene in which Odysseus dominates to be the focus of your analysis. Read it through with care, looking for the ways that Homer uses (1) physical description, (2) speech, (3) action, (4) the reaction of other people, and (5) (if applicable) descriptions of inner thoughts and feelings, and devote a paragraph to each.

ENRICHMENT

Readers Theater

There are passages in the *Odyssey* so dependent upon dialogue they seem closer to drama than to epic narrative. A good example of this is the night scene involving Odysseus, Penélopê, and Eurýkleia (Book 19, lines 56–413). You and your classmates can perform this scene as Readers Theater by assigning the parts of the three characters to different students, while having a fourth student take the lines of narrative that connect the speeches.

from **Book Twenty-One**

Upon Penélopê, most worn in love and thought,
Athena cast a glance like a grey sea
lifting her. Now to bring the tough bow out and bring
the iron blades. Now try those dogs at archery
5 to usher bloody slaughter in.

     So moving stairward
the queen took up a fine doorhook of bronze,
ivory-hafted, smooth in her clenched hand,
and led her maids down to a distant room,
a storeroom where the master's treasure lay:
10 bronze, bar gold, black iron forged and wrought.
In this place hung the double-torsion bow
and arrows in a quiver, a great sheaf—
quills of groaning. . . . Herb scented robes
lay there in chests, but the lady's milkwhite arms
went up to lift the bow down from a peg
15 in its own polished bowcase.

       Now Penélopê
sank down, holding the weapon on her knees,
and drew her husband's great bow out, and sobbed
and bit her lip and let the salt tears flow.
Then back she went to face the crowded hall
20 tremendous bow in hand, and on her shoulder hung
the quiver spiked with coughing death. Behind her
maids bore a basket full of axeheads, bronze
and iron implements for the master's game.
Thus in her beauty she approached the suitors,
25 and near a pillar of the solid roof
she paused, her shining veil across her cheeks,
her maids on either hand and still,
then spoke to the banqueters:

       "My lords, hear me:
suitors indeed, you commandeered this house
30 to feast and drink in, day and night, my husband
being long gone, long out of mind. You found
no justification for yourselves—none
except your lust to marry me. Stand up, then:
we now declare a contest for that prize.
35 Here is my lord Odysseus' hunting bow.
Bend and string it if you can. Who sends an arrow

through iron axe-helve sockets, twelve in line?
I join my life with his, and leave this place, my home,
my rich and beautiful bridal house, forever
40 to be remembered, though I dream it only."
Then to Eumaios:

      "Carry the bow forward.
Carry the blades."

      Tears came to the swineherd's eyes
as he reached out for the big bow. He laid it
down at the suitors' feet. Across the room
45 the cowherd sobbed, knowing the master's weapon.
Antínoös growled, with a glance at both:

       "Clods.
They go to pieces over nothing.

      You two, there,
why are you sniveling? To upset the woman
even more? Has she not pain enough
50 over her lost husband? *Sit down.*
Get on with dinner quietly, or cry about it
outside, if you must. Leave us the bow.
A clean-cut game, it looks to me.
Nobody bends that bowstave easily
55 in this company. Is there a man here
made like Odysseus? I remember him
from childhood: I can see him even now."
That was the way he played it, hoping inwardly
to span the great horn bow with corded gut
60 and drill the iron with his shot—he, Antínoös,
destined to be the first of all to savor
blood from a biting arrow at his throat,
a shaft drawn by the fingers of Odysseus
whom he had mocked and plundered, leading on
65 the rest, his boon companions. Now they heard
a gay snort of laughter from Telémakhos,
who said then brilliantly:

      "A queer thing, that!
Has Zeus almighty made me a half-wit?
For all her spirit, Mother has given in,
70 promised to go off with someone—and
is that amusing? What am I cackling for?

Step up, my lords, contend now for your prize.
I myself should like to try that bow.
Suppose I bend it and bring off the shot,
75 my heart will be less heavy, seeing the queen my
        mother
go for the last time from this house and hall,
if I who stay can do my father's feat."
He moved out quickly, dropping his crimson cloak,
and lifted sword and sword belt from his shoulders.
80 His preparation was to dig a trench,
heaping the earth in a long ridge beside it
to hold the blades half-bedded. A taut cord
aligned the socket rings. And no one there
but looked on wondering at his workmanship,
85 for the boy had never seen it done.
                        He took his stand then
on the broad door sill to attempt the bow.
Three times he put his back into it and sprang it,
three times he had to slack off. Still he meant
to string that bow and pull for the needle shot.
90 A fourth try, and he had it all but strung—
when a stiffening in Odysseus made him check.
Abruptly then he stopped and turned and said:
"Blast and damn it, must I be a milksop
all my life? Half-grown, all thumbs,
95 no strength or knack at arms, to defend myself
if someone picks a fight with me.
                        Take over,
O my elders and betters, try the bow,
run off the contest."
                        And he stood the weapon
upright against the massy-timbered door
100 with one arrow across the horn aslant,
then went back to his chair. Antínoös
gave the word:
                "Now one man at a time
rise and go forward. Round the room in order;
left to right from where they dip the wine."
105 As this seemed fair enough, up stood Leódês
the son of Oinops. This man used to find
visions for them in the smoke of sacrifice.
He kept his chair well back, retired by the winebowl,
for he alone could not abide their manners
110 but sat in shame for all the rest. Now it was he
who had first to confront the bow,
standing up on the broad door sill. He failed.
The bow unbending made his thin hands yield,

no muscle in them. He gave up and said:
115 "Friends, I cannot. Let the next man handle it.
Here is a bow to break the heart and spirit
of many strong men. Aye. And death is less
bitter than to live on and never have
the beauty that we came here laying siege to
120 so many days. Resolute, are you still,
to win Odysseus' lady Penélopê?
Pit yourselves against the bow, and look
among Akhaians for another's daughter.
Gifts will be enough to court and take her.
125 Let the best offer win."
                With this Leódês
thrust the bow away from him, and left it
upright against the massy-timbered door,
with one arrow aslant across the horn.
As he went down to his chair he heard Antínoös'
130 voice rising:
                "What is that you say?
It makes me burn. You cannot string the weapon,
so 'Here is a bow to break the heart and spirit
of many strong men.' Crushing thought!
You were not born—you never had it in you—
135 to pull that bow or let an arrow fly.
But here are men who can and will."
He called out to the goatherd, Melánthios:
"Kindle a fire there, be quick about it,
draw up a big bench with a sheepskin on it,
140 and bring a cake of lard out of the stores.
Contenders from now on will heat and grease the bow.
We'll try it limber, and bring off the shot."
Melánthios darted out to light a blaze,
drew up a bench, threw a big sheepskin over it,
145 and brought a cake of lard. So one by one
the young men warmed and greased the bow for
        bending,
but not a man could string it. They were whipped.
Antínoös held off; so did Eurýmakhos,
suitors in chief, by far the ablest there.
150 Two men had meanwhile left the hall:
swineherd and cowherd, in companionship,
one downcast as the other. But Odysseus
followed them outdoors, outside the court,
and coming up said gently:
                        "You, herdsman,
155 and you, too, swineherd, I could say a thing to you,
or should I keep it dark?

No, no; speak,
my heart tells me. Would you be men enough
to stand by Odysseus if he came back?
Suppose he dropped out of a clear sky, as I did?
Suppose some god should bring him?
Would you bear arms for him, or for the suitors?"
The cowherd said:

"Ah, let the master come!
Father Zeus, grant our old wish! Some courier
guide him back! Then judge what stuff is in me
and how I manage arms!"

Likewise Eumaios
fell to praying all heaven for his return,
so that Odysseus, sure at least of these,
told them:

"I am at home, for I am he.
I bore adversities, but in the twentieth year
I am ashore in my own land. I find
the two of you, alone among my people,
longed for my coming. Prayers I never heard
except your own that I might come again.
So now what is in store for you I'll tell you:
If Zeus brings down the suitors by my hand
I promise marriages to both, and cattle,
and houses built near mine. And you shall be
brothers-in-arms of my Telémakhos.
Here, let me show you something else, a sign
that I am he, that you can trust me, look:
this old scar from the tusk wound that I got
boar hunting on Parnassos—
Autólykos' sons and I."

Shifting his rags
he bared the long gash. Both men looked, and knew,
and threw their arms around the old soldier, weeping,
kissing his head and shoulders. He as well
took each man's head and hands to kiss, then said—
to cut it short, else they might weep till dark—
"Break off, no more of this.
Anyone at the door could see and tell them.
Drift back in, but separately at intervals
after me.

Now listen to your orders:
when the time comes, those gentlemen, to a man,
will be dead against giving me bow or quiver.
Defy them. Eumaios, bring the bow
and put it in my hands there at the door.
Tell the women to lock their own door tight.

Tell them if someone hears the shock of arms
or groans of men, in hall or court, not one
must show her face, but keep still at her weaving.
Philoítios, run to the outer gate and lock it.
Throw the cross bar and lash it."

He turned back
into the courtyard and the beautiful house
and took the stool he had before. They followed
one by one, the two hands loyal to him.
Eurýmakhos had now picked up the bow.
He turned it round, and turned it round
before the licking flame to warm it up,
but could not, even so, put stress upon it
to jam the loop over the tip
though his heart groaned to bursting.
Then he said grimly:

"Curse this day.
What gloom I feel, not for myself alone,
and not only because we lose that bride.
Women are not lacking in Akhaia,
in other towns, or on Ithaka. No, the worst
is humiliation—to be shown up for children
measured against Odysseus—we who cannot
even hitch the string over his bow.
What shame to be repeated of us, after us!"
Antínoös said:

"Come to yourself. You know
that is not the way this business ends.
Today the islanders held holiday, a holy day,
no day to sweat over a bowstring.

Keep your head.
Postpone the bow. I say we leave the axes
planted where they are. No one will take them.
No one comes to Odysseus' hall tonight.
Break out good wine and brim our cups again,
we'll keep the crooked bow safe overnight,
order the fattest goats Melánthios has
brought down tomorrow noon, and offer thighbones
burning
to Apollo, god of archers,
while we try out the bow and make the shot."
As this appealed to everyone, heralds came
pouring fresh water for their hands, and boys
filled up the winebowls. Joints of meat went round,
fresh cuts for all, while each man made his offering,
tilting the red wine to the gods, and drank his fill.
Then spoke Odysseus, all craft and gall:

"My lords, contenders for the queen, permit me:
240 a passion in me moves me to speak out.
I put it to Eurýmakhos above all
and to that brilliant prince, Antínoös. Just now
how wise his counsel was, to leave the trial
and turn your thoughts to the immortal gods! Apollo
245 will give power tomorrow to whom he wills.
But let me try my hand at the smooth bow!
Let me test my fingers and my pull
to see if any of the oldtime kick is there,
or if thin fare and roving took it out of me."

250 Now irritation beyond reason swept them all,
since they were nagged by fear that he could string it.
Antínoös answered, coldly and at length:
"You bleary vagabond, no rag of sense is left you.
Are you not coddled here enough, at table
255 taking meat with gentlemen, your betters,
denied nothing, and listening to our talk?
When have we let a tramp hear all our talk?
The sweet goad of wine has made you rave! . . .
Make no contention here with younger men."

260 At this the watchful queen Penélopê
interposed:

"Antínoös, discourtesy
to a guest of Telémakhos—whatever guest—
that is not handsome. What are you afraid of?
Suppose this exile put his back into it
265 and drew the great bow of Odysseus—
could he then take me home to be his bride?
You know he does not imagine that! No one
need let that prospect weigh upon his dinner!
How very, very improbable it seems." . . .

270 Telémakhos now faced her and said sharply:
"Mother, as to the bow and who may handle it
or not handle it, no man here
has more authority than I do—not one lord . . .
Return to your own hall. Tend your spindle.
275 Tend your loom. Direct your maids at work.
This question of the bow will be for men to settle,
most of all for me. I am master here."

She gazed in wonder, turned, and so withdrew,
her son's clearheaded bravery in her heart.
280 But when she had mounted to her rooms again
with all her women, then she fell to weeping
for Odysseus, her husband. Grey-eyed Athena
presently cast a sweet sleep on her eyes.
The swineherd had the horned bow in his hands

285 moving toward Odysseus, when the crowd
in the banquet hall broke into an ugly din,
shouts rising from the flushed young men:

"Ho! Where
do you think you are taking that, you smutty slave?"
"What is this dithering?"

"We'll toss you back alone
290 among the pigs, for your own dogs to eat,
if bright Apollo nods and the gods are kind!"
He faltered, all at once put down the bow, and stood
in panic, buffeted by waves of cries,
hearing Telémakhos from another quarter
295 shout:
"Go on, take him the bow!

Do you obey this pack?
You will be stoned back to your hills! Young as I am
my power is over you! I wish to God
I had as much the upper hand of these!
300 There would be suitors pitched like dead rats
through our gate, for the evil plotted here!"
Telémakhos' frenzy struck someone as funny,
and soon the whole room roared with laughter at him,
so that all tension passed. Eumaios picked up
305 bow and quiver, making for the door,
and there he placed them in Odysseus' hands.
Calling Eurýkleia to his side he said:

"Telémakhos
trusts you to take care of the women's doorway.
Lock it tight. If anyone inside
310 should hear the shock of arms or groans of men
in hall or court, not one must show her face,
but go on with her weaving."

The old woman
nodded and kept still. She disappeared
into the women's hall, bolting the door behind her.
315 Philoítios left the house now at one bound,
catlike, running to bolt the courtyard gate.
A coil of deck-rope of papyrus fiber
lay in the gateway; this he used for lashing,
and ran back to the same stool as before,
320 fastening his eyes upon Odysseus.

And Odysseus took his time,
turning the bow, tapping it, every inch,
for borings that termites might have made
while the master of the weapon was abroad.
The suitors were now watching him, and some
325 jested among themselves:

"A bow lover!"
"Dealer in old bows!"
                              "Maybe he has one like it
at home!"
              "Or has an itch to make one for himself."
"See how he handles it, the sly old buzzard!"
And one disdainful suitor added this:
330 "May his fortune grow an inch for every inch he bends
          it!"
But the man skilled in all ways of contending,
satisfied by the great bow's look and heft,
like a musician, like a harper, when
with quiet hand upon his instrument
335 he draws between his thumb and forefinger
a sweet new string upon a peg: so effortlessly
Odysseus in one motion strung the bow.
Then slid his right hand down the cord and plucked
          it,
so the taut gut vibrating hummed and sang
340 a swallow's note.
                    In the hushed hall it smote the suitors
and all their faces changed. Then Zeus thundered
overhead, one loud crack for a sign.
And Odysseus laughed within him that the son
of crooked-minded Kronos had flung that omen down.
345 He picked one ready arrow from his table
where it lay bare: the rest were waiting still
in the quiver for the young men's turn to come.
He nocked it, let it rest across the handgrip,
and drew the string and grooved butt of the arrow,
350 aiming from where he sat upon the stool.
                              Now flashed
arrow from twanging bow clean as a whistle
through every socket ring, and grazed not one,
to thud with heavy brazen head beyond.
                              Then quietly
Odysseus said:
                    "Telémakhos, the stranger
355 you welcomed in your hall has not disgraced you.
I did not miss, neither did I take all day
stringing the bow. My hand and eye are sound,
not so contemptible as the young men say.
The hour has come to cook their lordships' mutton—
360 supper by daylight. Other amusements later,
with song and harping that adorn a feast."
He dropped his eyes and nodded, and the prince
Telémakhos, true son of King Odysseus,

belted his sword on, clapped hand to his spear,
365 and with a clink and glitter of keen bronze
stood by his chair, in the forefront near his father.

from **Book Twenty-Two**

Now shrugging off his rags the wiliest fighter of the
          islands
leapt and stood on the broad door sill, his own bow
          in his hand.
He poured out at his feet a rain of arrows from the
          quiver
and spoke to the crowd:
                    "So much for that. Your clean-cut game is over.
5 Now watch me hit a target that no man has hit before,
if I can make this shot. Help me, Apollo."[1]
He drew to his fist the cruel head of an arrow for
          Antínoös
just as the young man leaned to lift his beautiful
          drinking cup,
embossed, two-handled, golden: the cup was in his
          fingers:
10 the wine was even at his lips: and did he dream of
          death?
How could he? In that revelry amid his throng of
          friends
who would imagine a single foe—though a strong foe
          indeed—
could dare to bring death's pain on him and darkness
          on his eyes?
Odysseus' arrow hit him under the chin
15 and punched up to the feathers through his throat.
Backward and down he went, letting the winecup fall
from his shocked hand. Like pipes his nostrils jetted
crimson runnels, a river of mortal red,
and one last kick upset his table
20 knocking the bread and meat to soak in dusty blood.
Now as they craned to see their champion where he
          lay
the suitors jostled in uproar down the hall,
everyone on his feet. Wildly they turned and scanned
the walls in the long room for arms; but not a shield,
25 not a good ashen spear was there for a man to take
          and throw.

---

1. *Apollo* (ə pol′ō), one of the greatest of the Olympian
gods, son of Zeus and the Titan Leto. He was associated
with, among other things, archery.

Vase painting showing
Odysseus shooting his
bow. c. 450–440 B.C.
Staatliche Museen,
Berlin

All they could do was yell in outrage at Odysseus:
"Foul! to shoot at a man! That was your last shot!"
"Your own throat will be slit for this!"

                  "Our finest lad is down!
You killed the best on Ithaka."

                    "Buzzards will tear your eyes out!"
30 For they imagined as they wished—that it was a wild
      shot,
an unintended killing—fools, not to comprehend
they were already in the grip of death.
But glaring under his brows Odysseus answered:
"You yellow dogs, you thought I'd never make it
35 home from the land of Troy. You took my house to
      plunder,
twisted my maids to serve your beds. You dared
bid for my wife while I was still alive.
Contempt was all you had for the gods who rule wide
      heaven,
contempt for what men say of you hereafter.
40 Your last hour has come. You die in blood."
As they all took this in, sickly green fear
pulled at their entrails, and their eyes flickered
looking for some hatch or hideaway from death.
Eurýmakhos alone could speak. He said:

45 "If you are Odysseus of Ithaka come back,
all that you say these men have done is true.
Rash actions, many here, more in the countryside.
But here he lies, the man who caused them all.
Antínoös was the ringleader, he whipped us on
50 to do these things. He cared less for a marriage
than for the power Kroníon[2] has denied him
as king of Ithaka. For that
he tried to trap your son and would have killed him.
He is dead now and has his portion. Spare
55 your own people. As for ourselves, we'll make
restitution of wine and meat consumed,
and add, each one, a tithe of twenty oxen
with gifts of bronze and gold to warm your heart.
Meanwhile we cannot blame you for your anger."
60 Odysseus glowered under his black brows
and said:

          "Not for the whole treasure of your fathers,
all you enjoy, lands, flocks, or any gold
put up by others, would I hold my hand.
There will be killing till the score is paid.

---

2. **Kroníon** (krō nē′ən), Zeus, son of Kronos.

You forced yourselves upon this house. Fight your
   way out,
or run for it, if you think you'll escape death.
I doubt one man of you skins by."
They felt their knees fail, and their hearts—but heard
Eurýmakhos for the last time rallying them.
"Friends," he said, "the man is implacable.
Now that he's got his hands on bow and quiver
he'll shoot from the big door stone there
until he kills us to the last man.

                          Fight, I say,
let's remember the joy of it. Swords out!
Hold up your tables to deflect his arrows.
After me, everyone: rush him where he stands.
If we can budge him from the door, if we can pass
into the town, we'll call out men to chase him.
This fellow with his bow will shoot no more."
He drew his own sword as he spoke, a broadsword of
   fine bronze,
honed like a razor on either edge. Then crying hoarse
   and loud
he hurled himself at Odysseus. But the kingly man let
   fly
an arrow at that instant, and the quivering feathered
   butt
sprang to the nipple of his breast as the barb stuck in
   his liver.
The bright broadsword clanged down. He lurched and
   fell aside,
pitching across his table. His cup, his bread and meat,
were spilt and scattered far and wide, and his head
   slammed on the ground.
Revulsion, anguish in his heart, with both feet kicking
   out,
he downed his chair, while the shrouding wave of mist
   closed on his eyes.
Amphínomos now came running at Odysseus,
broadsword naked in his hand. He thought to make
the great soldier give way at the door.
But with a spear throw from behind Telémakhos hit
   him
between the shoulders, and the lancehead drove
clear through his chest. He left his feet and fell
forward, thudding, forehead against the ground.
Telémakhos swerved around him, leaving the long
   dark spear
planted in Amphínomos. If he paused to yank it out

someone might jump him from behind or cut him
   down with a sword
at the moment he bent over. So he ran—ran from the
   tables
to his father's side and halted, panting, saying:
"Father let me bring you a shield and spear,
a pair of spears, a helmet.
I can arm on the run myself; I'll give
outfits to Eumaios and this cowherd.
Better to have equipment."

                          Said Odysseus:
"Run then, while I hold them off with arrows
as long as the arrows last. When all are gone
if I'm alone they can dislodge me."

                          Quick
upon his father's word Telémakhos
ran to the room where spears and armor lay.
He caught up four light shields, four pairs of spears,
four helms of war high-plumed with flowing manes,
and ran back, loaded down, to his father's side.
He was the first to pull a helmet on
and slide his bare arm in a buckler strap.
The servants armed themselves, and all three took their
   stand
beside the master of battle.

                          While he had arrows
he aimed and shot, and every shot brought down
one of his huddling enemies.
But when all barbs had flown from the bowman's fist,
he leaned his bow in the bright entry way
beside the door, and armed: a four-ply shield
hard on his shoulder, and a crested helm,
horsetailed, nodding stormy upon his head,
then took his tough and bronze-shod spears. . . .
At this moment that unmanning thunder cloud,
the aegis,[3] Athena's shield,
took form aloft in the great hall.

                          And the suitors mad with fear
at her great sign stampeded like stung cattle by a river
when the dread shimmering gadfly strikes in summer,
in the flowering season, in the long-drawn days.
After them the attackers wheeled, as terrible as falcons

---

3. *aegis* (ē′jis), a shield or breastplate used by Zeus or
Athena. The snaky head of the Gorgon Medusa, which
caused anyone who looked at it to turn to stone, was fixed
on the aegis.

from eyries in the mountains veering over and diving
     down
135 with talons wide unsheathed on flights of birds,
     who cower down the sky in chutes and bursts along
          the valley—
     but the pouncing falcons grip their prey, no frantic
          wing avails,
     and farmers love to watch those beakèd hunters.
     So these now fell upon the suitors in that hall,
140 turning, turning to strike and strike again,
     while torn men moaned at death, and blood ran
          smoking over the whole floor.
                              Now there was one
     who turned and threw himself at Odysseus' knees—
     Leódês, begging for his life:
                                        "Mercy,
145 mercy on a suppliant, Odysseus!
     Never by word or act of mine, I swear,
     was any woman troubled here. I told the rest
     to put an end to it. They would not listen,
     would not keep their hands from brutishness,
150 and now they are all dying like dogs for it.
     I had no part in what they did: my part
     was visionary—reading the smoke of sacrifice.
     Scruples go unrewarded if I die."
     The shrewd fighter frowned over him and said:
155 "You were diviner to this crowd? How often
     you must have prayed my sweet day of return
     would never come, or not for years!—and prayed
     to have my dear wife, and beget children on her.
     No plea like yours could save you
160 from this hard bed of death. Death it shall be!"
     He picked up Ageláos' broadsword
     from where it lay, flung by the slain man,
     and gave Leódês' neck a lopping blow
     so that his head went down to mouth in dust. . . .
165 And Odysseus looked around him, narrow-eyed,
     for any others who had lain hidden
     while death's black fury passed.
                              In blood and dust
     he saw that crowd all fallen, many and many slain.
     Think of a catch that fishermen haul in to a halfmoon
          bay
170 in a fine-meshed net from the white-caps of the sea:
     how all are poured out on the sand, in throes for the
          salt sea,
     twitching their cold lives away in Hêlios' fiery air:

so lay the suitors heaped on one another.
Odysseus at length said to his son:
175 "Go tell old Nurse I'll have a word with her.
What's to be done now weighs on my mind."
Telémakhos knocked at the women's door and called:
"Eurýkleia, come out here! Move, old woman.
You kept your eye on all our servant girls.
180 Jump, my father is here and wants to see you."
His call brought no reply, only the doors
were opened, and she came. Telémakhos
led her forward. In the shadowy hall
full of dead men she found his father
185 spattered and caked with blood like a mountain lion
when he has gorged upon an ox, his kill—
with hot blood glistening over his whole chest,
smeared on his jaws, baleful and terrifying—
even so encrimsoned was Odysseus
190 up to his thighs and armpits. As she gazed
from all the corpses to the bloody man
she raised her head to cry over his triumph,
but felt his grip upon her, checking her.
Said the great soldier then:
                              "Rejoice
195 inwardly. No crowing aloud, old woman.
To glory over slain men is no piety.
Destiny and the gods' will vanquished these,
and their own hardness. They respected no one,
good or bad, who came their way.
200 For this, and folly, a bad end befell them.
Your part is now to tell me of the women,
those who dishonored me, and the innocent."
His own old nurse Eurýkleia said:
                              "I will, then.
Child, you know you'll have the truth from me.
205 Fifty all told they are, your female slaves,
trained by your lady and myself in service,
wool carding and the rest of it, and taught
to be submissive. Twelve went bad,
flouting me, flouting Penélopê, too.
210 Telémakhos being barely grown, his mother
would never let him rule the serving women—
but you must let me go to her lighted rooms
and tell her. Some god sent her a drift of sleep."
But in reply the great tactician said:
215 "Not yet. Do not awake her. Tell those women
who were the suitors' harlots to come here."
She went back on this mission through his hall.

Then he called Telémakhos to his side
and the two herdsmen. Sharply Odysseus said:
"These dead must be disposed of first of all.
Direct the women. Tables and chairs will be
scrubbed with sponges, rinsed and rinsed again.
When our great room is fresh and put in order,
take them outside, these women,
between the roundhouse and the palisade,
and hack them with your swordblades till you cut
the life out of them, and every thought of sweet
Aphroditê under the rutting suitors,
when they lay down in secret."

As he spoke
here came the women in a bunch, all wailing,
soft tears on their cheeks. They fell to work
to lug the corpses out into the courtyard
under the gateway, propping one
against another as Odysseus ordered,
for he himself stood over them. In fear
these women bore the cold weight of the dead.
The next thing was to scrub off chairs and tables
and rinse them down. Telémakhos and the herdsman
scraped the packed earth floor with hoes, but made
the women carry out all blood and mire.
When the great room was cleaned up once again,
at swordpoint they forced them out, between
the roundhouse and the palisade, pell-mell
to huddle in that dead end without exit.
Telémakhos, who knew his mind, said curtly:
"I would not give the clean death of a beast
to trulls who made a mockery of my mother
and of me too—you sluts, who lay with suitors."
He tied one end of a hawser to a pillar
and passed the other about the roundhouse top,
taking the slack up, so that no one's toes
could touch the ground. They would be hung like
    doves
or larks in springès triggered in a thicket,
where the birds think to rest—a cruel nesting.
So now in turn each woman thrust her head
into a noose and swung, yanked high in air,
to perish there most piteously.
Their feet danced for a little, but not long. . . .
As their own hands and feet called for a washing,
they went indoors to Odysseus again.
Their work was done. He told Euríkleia:
    "Bring me

brimstone and a brazier—medicinal
fumes to purify my hall. Then tell
Penélopê to come, and bring her maids.
All servants round the house must be called in."
His own old nurse Euríkleia replied:
"Aye, surely that is well said, child. But let me ·
find you a good clean shirt and cloak and dress you.
You must not wrap your shoulders' breadth again
in rags in your own hall. That would be shameful."
Odysseus answered:

                    "Let me have the fire.
The first thing is to purify this place."
With no more chat Euríkleia obeyed
and fetched out fire and brimstone. Cleansing fumes
he sent through court and hall and storage chamber.
Then the old woman hurried off again
to the women's quarters to announce her news,
and all the servants came now, bearing torches
in twilight, crowding to embrace Odysseus,
taking his hands to kiss, his head and shoulders,
while he stood there, nodding to every one,
and overcome by longing and by tears.

Now, the battle over and the Great Hall cleansed,
Penélopê returns to face the stranger.

---

from **Book Twenty-Three**

Crossing the door sill she sat down at once
in firelight, against the nearest wall,
across the room from the lord Odysseus.

                                    There
leaning against a pillar, sat the man
and never lifted up his eyes, but only waited
for what his wife would say when she had seen him.
And she, for a long time, sat deathly still
in wonderment—for sometimes as she gazed
she found him—yes, clearly—like her husband,
but sometimes blood and rags were all she saw.
Telémakhos' voice came to her ears:

                                    "Mother,
cruel mother, do you feel nothing,
drawing yourself apart this way from Father?
Will you not sit with him and talk and question him?
What other woman could remain so cold?

Who shuns her lord, and he come back to her
from wars and wandering, after twenty years?
Your heart is hard as flint and never changes!"
Penélopê answered:

                    "I am stunned, child.
20 I cannot speak to him. I cannot question him.
I cannot keep my eyes upon his face.
If really he is Odysseus, truly home,
beyond all doubt we two shall know each other
better than you or anyone. There are
25 secret signs we know, we two."

                              A smile
came now to the lips of the patient hero, Odysseus,
who turned to Telémakhos and said:
"Peace: let your mother test me at her leisure. . . .

                      Strange woman,
30 the immortals of Olympos made you hard,
harder than any. Who else in the world
would keep aloof as you do from her husband
if he returned to her from years of trouble,
cast on his own land in the twentieth year?
35 Nurse, make up a bed for me to sleep on.
Her heart is iron in her breast."

                     Penélopê
spoke to Odysseus now. She said:

                    "Strange man,
if man you are . . . This is no pride on my part
nor scorn for you—not even wonder, merely.
40 I know so well how you—how he—appeared
boarding the ship for Troy. But all the same . . .
Make up his bed for him, Eurýkleia.
Place it outside the bedchamber my lord
built with his own hands. Pile the big bed
45 with fleeces, rugs, and sheets of purest linen."
With this she tried him to the breaking point,
and he turned on her in a flash raging:
"Women, by heaven you've stung me now!
Who dared to move my bed?
50 No builder had the skill for that—unless
a god came down to turn the trick. No mortal
in his best days could budge it with a crowbar.
There is our pact and pledge, our secret sign,
built into that bed—my handiwork
55 and no one else's!

                An old trunk of olive
grew like a pillar on the building plot,
and I laid out our bedroom round that tree,

lined up the stone walls, built the walls and roof,
gave it a doorway and smooth-fitting doors.
60 Then I lopped off the silvery leaves and branches,
hewed and shaped that stump from the roots up
into a bedpost, drilled it, let it serve
as model for the rest. I planed them all,
inlaid them all with silver, gold and ivory,
65 and stretched a bed between—a pliant web
of oxhide thongs dyed crimson.

                      There's our sign!
I know no more. Could someone's else's hand
have sawn that trunk and dragged the frame away?"
Their secret! as she heard it told, her knees
70 grew tremulous and weak, her heart failed her.
With eyes brimming tears she ran to him,
throwing her arms around his neck, and kissed him,
murmuring:

               "Do not rage at me, Odysseus!
No one ever matched your caution! Think
75 what difficulty the gods gave: they denied us
life together in our prime and flowering years,
kept us from crossing into age together.
Forgive me, don't be angry. I could not
welcome you with love on sight! I armed myself
80 long ago against the frauds of men,
impostors who might come—and all those many
whose underhanded ways bring evil on! . . .
But here and now, what sign could be so clear
as this of our own bed?
85 No other man has ever laid eyes on it—
only my own slave, Aktoris, that my father
sent with me as a gift—she kept our door.
You make my stiff heart know that I am yours."
Now from his breast into his eyes the ache
90 of longing mounted, and he wept at last,
his dear wife, clear and faithful, in his arms,
longed for
as the sunwarmed earth is longed for by a swimmer
spent in rough water where his ship went down
under Poseidon's blows, gale winds and tons of sea.
95 Few men can keep alive through a big surf
to crawl, clotted with brine, on kindly beaches
in joy, in joy, knowing the abyss behind:
and so she too rejoiced, her gaze upon her husband,
her white arms round him pressed as though
     forever. . . .

c. 725 B.C.

152   *The Classical World*

THINK AND DISCUSS

Understanding

1. What does Penélopê's test, the stringing of the bow, prove?
2. Why does Odysseus reveal his identity to Eumaios and Philoítios?
3. What justification does Odysseus give Eurýkleia for the deaths of the suitors?
4. How does Odysseus finally convince Penélopê that he is her husband?

Analyzing

5. Homer says that Antínoös will die, before he tries to string the bow (Book 21, lines 60–65). What effect does this have on the scene that follows?
6. Why does Homer use a **metaphor** that compares the sound of Odysseus's bow to the song of a bird (Book 21, lines 338–340)?
7. Describe how Homer as epic narrator pictures the deaths of the suitors.
8. Explain how Homer traces the shifting emotions of the suitors as they discover they will die.
9. How does the last scene between Odysseus and Penélopê work against our expectations? Why are they so cautious?

Extending

10. What are the values and ideals suggested by the ending of Homer's epic?
11. Do you find the conclusion to the action of the story appropriate or anticlimactic?

APPLYING: Characterization H𝒯
See Handbook of Literary Terms, p. 944.

Characterization means the methods an author uses to develop the personality of a character in a literary work. An author may develop a character through describing the character's physical appearance, speech, actions, and inner thoughts, or by revealing attitudes and reactions of other characters.

1. How does Odysseus define himself through action when he begins to kill the suitors?
2. What do we learn about Telémakhos as a character when, following the defeat of the suitors, his speech accuses his mother of being "cruel" in drawing "apart this way from Father" (Book 23, lines 11–18)?

THINKING SKILLS

Classifying

To classify things is to arrange them into categories or groups according to some system. The reader of Homer's *Odyssey* tends to classify the numerous characters found in the epic into groups of people who aid or oppose Odysseus during his efforts to regain his home and his wife.

1. List Odysseus's allies and enemies.
2. Subdivide these two groups, classifying individuals according to whether they are active or passive in helping or hurting Odysseus.

COMPOSITION

Justifying the Actions of Odysseus

Some readers might feel that Odysseus takes too brutal a revenge on his return home. Write an essay listing his reasons for killing the suitors, justifying his actions. In preparing, jot down a list of all the motives which you can think of, and then reorder them starting with the least persuasive and ending with what you consider the most significant. Be sure to consider practical issues such as the possibility the suitors will try to kill him, Odysseus's personal emotions, and his sense of honor.

Writing About Theme

Heroism can take many forms. Write a paper to be read by your fellow classmates in which you seek to persuade them that three particular traits define most specifically the heroism which Odysseus embodies. Take a sheet of scratch paper and note down those things about Odysseus that strike you as most clearly heroic. When you have a useful list of heroic traits, return to the poem, looking for examples that will illustrate them. In outlining the essay, name the three traits that will be your focus, and match them up with the evidence you have gathered.

Translating Homer

Until this century, educated people could usually read Latin but not Greek, and as a result, since the Renaissance numerous translations of Homer's works have appeared in modern languages. The first English translation to achieve lasting fame was by George Chapman (1559–1634), a poet and playwright contemporary with Shakespeare. Chapman's Homer appeared between 1598 and 1616. A little more than a century later, in 1726, Alexander Pope (1688–1744) published an *Odyssey* that dominated his century. In our own time, when few people read classical languages at all, many new translations of Homer have appeared, such as the version by Robert Fitzgerald used in this book and that of Richmond Lattimore.

The passage in Homer's original Greek at the bottom of the page describes the effect a vision of the goddess Athena has on the suitors during the combat in the Great Hall. It is translated by Fitzgerald on pages 149–150, lines 127–142. Translations of this same passage by Chapman, Pope, and Lattimore appear on the opposite page. Both Chapman and Pope, convinced that Homer's heroic style required an equally elevated English verse form, chose to write in English couplets, even though Homer's Greek never uses rhyme. While Homer's original passage takes only thirteen lines, Pope uses seventeen and Chapman twenty-five. These early translators elaborate on Homer's simple manner of expression, adding their own words and phrases. In describing Athena's action, Homer says that she "held up her man-destroying aegis high from the roof." Pope expands this in his first three lines, including moral judgments—"guilty heads"—and further images—"arm of vengeance"—not in the original. At times, Chapman goes even further. To be sure that his readers will understand his subject, he weaves explanations into the translation. While Homer just has the term *aegis*, Chapman describes what it is—"Her Snake-fring'd shield . . . ." Later he adds whole lines such as "Ulysses and his sonne the Flyers chac'st" to help his readers follow the action.

With a text as ancient as the *Odyssey*, there can be problems just knowing what Homer means. In this example he compares the fleeing suitors to birds attacked by vultures. Pope understood the scene to describe how hunters use the vultures to frighten birds into nets strung up on the ground, whereas all the other translators read the passage to say that the vultures pursue the birds on their own, and the earth-bound observers—"farmers" in Fitzgerald's version—simply watch.

Even when Homer's meaning can be positively known, many characteristics of his poetry remain beyond translation. Here he makes a triple parallel between the panicked suitors, cows driven wild by insect bites, and birds pursued by vultures. Homer makes sure the Greek reader sees the parallelism by beginning each phase of the comparison at the start of a line, and with the same word. Even if you cannot sound the Greek letters, your eye can easily recognize the repeated words at the start of lines 3, 6, and 9. This neat symmetry does not appear in any of these English versions. Again, if you look at Homer's original, the first word in line 12 and the second word in line 13 are different forms of the same term, which means "to hit or beat." This is the verb that describes the blows which shatter the heads of the suitors. The single translator who tries to echo this dramatic repetition is Fitzgerald, whose "to strike and strike again" only approximates Homer's effect.

δὴ τότ' Ἀθηναίη φθισίμβροτον αἰγίδ' ἀνέσχεν
ὑψόθεν ἐξ ὀροφῆς· τῶν δὲ φρένες ἐπτοίηθεν.
οἱ δ' ἐφέβοντο κατὰ μέγαρον βόες ὣς ἀγελαῖαι·
τὰς μέν τ' αἰόλος οἶστρος ἐφορμηθεὶς ἐδόνησεν
5   ὥρῃ ἐν εἰαρινῇ, ὅτε τ' ἤματα μακρὰ πέλονται.
οἱ δ' ὥς τ' αἰγυπιοὶ γαμψώνυχες ἀγκυλοχεῖλαι,
ἐξ ὀρέων ἐλθόντες ἐπ' ὀρνίθεσσι θόρωσι·
ταὶ μέν τ' ἐν πεδίῳ νέφεα πτώσσουσαι ἵενται,
οἱ δέ τε τὰς ὀλέκουσιν ἐπάλμενοι, οὐδέ τις ἀλκὴ
10   γίγνεται οὐδὲ φυγή· χαίρουσι δέ τ' ἀνέρες ἄγρῃ·
ὣς ἄρα τοὶ μνηστῆρας ἐπεσσύμενοι κατὰ δῶμα
τύπτον ἐπιστροφάδην· τῶν δὲ στόνος ὤρνυτ' ἀεικὴς
κράτων τυπτομένων, δάπεδον δ' ἅπαν αἵματι θῦε.

George Chapman (1614)

And now man-slaughtering Pallas tooke in hand
Her Snake-fring'd shield, and on that beam took
    stand
In her true forme, where Swallow-like she sat.
And then in this way of the house and that
5 The wooers (wounded at the heart with feare)
Fled the encounter. As in Pastures, where
Fat Herds of Oxen feede, about the field
(As if wilde madnesse their instincts impeld)
The high-fed Bullockes flye, whom in the Spring
10 (When days are long) Gadbees or Breezes sting,
Ulysses and his sonne the Flyers chac'st;
As when with crooked Beakes and Seres a cast
Of hill-bred Eagles, cast off at some game,
That yet their strengths keepe, but (put up) in flame
15 The Eagles' stoopes—from which along the field
The poore Foules make wing, this and that way yield
Their hard-flowne Pinions, then the clouds assay
For scape or shelter, their forlorne dismay
All spirit exhaling all wings' strength to carry
20 Their bodies forth; and (trust up) to the Quarry
Their Faulconers ride in, and rejoyce to see
Their Hawkes performe a flight so fervently:
So (in their flight) Ulysses with his Heire
Did stoope and cuffe the wooers, that the aire
25 Broke in vaste sighes—whose heads they shot and cleft,
The Pavement boyling with the soules they reft.

Marble statue of Athena *Promachos* ("Defender"). The goddess is shown holding the *aegis,* her "Snake-fring'd shield." National Museum, Naples

Alexander Pope (1726)

Now *Pallas* shines confess'd; aloft she spreads
The arm of vengeance o'er their guilty heads;
The dreadful *Aegis* blazes in their eye;
Amaz'd they see, they tremble, and they fly:
5 Confus'd, distracted, thro' the rooms they fling,
Like oxen madden'd by the breeze's sting,
When sultry days, and long, succeed the gentle spring.
Not half so keen, fierce vulturs of the chace
Stoop from the mountains on the feather'd race,
10 When the wide field extended snares beset,
With conscious dread they shun the quiv'ring net:
No help, no flight; but wounded ev'ry way,
Headlong they drop: the fowlers seize the prey.
On all sides thus they double wound on wound,
15 In prostrate heaps the wretches beat the ground,
Unmanly shrieks precede each dying groan,
And a red deluge floats the reeking stone.

Richmond Lattimore (1965)

And now Athene waved the aegis, that blights
    humanity,
from high aloft on the roof, and all their wits were
    bewildered;
and they stampeded about the hall, like a herd of cattle
set upon and driven wild by the darting horse fly
5 in the spring season, at the time when the days grow
    longer;
but the other men, who were like hook-clawed, beak-
    bent vultures,
descending from the mountains to pounce upon the
    lesser birds;
and these on the plain, shrinking away from the clouds,
    speed off,
but the vultures plunge on them and destroy them,
    nor is there any
10 defense, nor any escape, and men are glad for the
    hunting;
so these men, sweeping about the palace, struck down
the suitors, one man after another; the floor was
    smoking
with blood, and the horrible cries rose up as their heads
    were broken.

BIOGRAPHY

Archilochus

c. 680–c. 640 B.C.

The Greek lyric poetry that appears in the seventh century B.C. is frequently as personal as the Homeric epics of the preceding century were universal. So it is appropriate that the first Greek poems we can connect with a specific, historical person, and with a particular date, are the lyrics of the belligerent rebel Archilochus (är kil′ə kəs), who probably lived from about 680 to 640 B.C. He came from the island of Paros, one of the group called the Cyclades (sik′lə dēz′) in the Aegean Sea southeast of Athens. The illegitimate son of an aristocrat and a slave woman, Archilochus became a mercenary soldier and joined in the invasion of Thasos, an island just off the coast of Thrace, a country northeast of Greece. There he lived the barracks-room life of a soldier—his name means "first sergeant"—and fought in battles with the natives. He fell in love with a local girl named Neoboule, whose father opposed their marriage. Archilochus revenged himself on them so savagely in his poetry that the humiliated family supposedly committed suicide. The poetry of Archilochus's native island was traditionally rough and abusive. Its typical meter, iambic, suggested anger to Greek readers—a mood appropriate for this writer, whose favorite subjects are battle scenes, curses, and uncontrollable passion. Archilochus lived in an era of widespread colonization which brought constant warfare and rapid social change. An outsider because of his birth, Archilochus reflects in his poetry a time in which traditions were under challenge.

H⫪ See TONE in the Handbook of Literary Terms, page 976.

Loss of Shield

translated by **Richmond Lattimore**

Some barbarian is waving my shield, since I
    was obliged to
  leave that perfectly good piece of equipment
    behind
under a bush. But I got away, so what does it
    matter?
  Let the shield go; I can buy another one
    equally good.

c. 650 B.C.

Miserable with Desire

translated by **Guy Davenport**

Miserable with desire
I lie lifeless,
My bones shot through
With a godsend of anguish
5 As sharp as thorns.

c. 650 B.C.

Attribute All to the Gods

translated by **Guy Davenport**

Attribute all to the gods.
They pick a man up,
Stretched on the black loam,
And set him on his two feet,
5 Firm, and then again
Shake solid men until
They fall backward
Into the worst of luck,
Wandering hungry,
10 Wild of mind.

c. 650 B.C.

Vase painting
showing Greek
soldier.
c. 480 B.C.
British Museum

Soul, Soul

translated by **Guy Davenport**

Soul, soul,
Torn by perplexity,
On your feet now!
Throw forward your chest
5 To the enemy;
Keep close in the attack;
Move back not an inch.
But never crow in victory,
Nor mope hangdog in loss.
10 Overdo neither sorrow nor joy:
A measured motion governs man.

c. 650 B.C.

Erxias, Defender

translated by **Guy Davenport**

Erxias, Defender, how can we muster
Our scattered troops? The campfires
Lift their smoke around the city.
The enemy's sharp arrows grow
5 Like bristles on our ships. The dead
Parch in the sun. The charges are bolder,
Knifing deep into the Naxos lines.
We scythe them down like tall grass
But they hardly feel our attacks.
10 The people will believe that we accept
With indifference these locust men
Who stamp our parents' fields to waste.
My heart must speak, for fear
And grief keep my neighbors silent.
15 Listen, hear me. Help comes from Thasos,
Too long held back by Toronaios;
And from Paros in the fast ships.
The captains are furious, and rage
To attack as soon as the auxiliaries
20 Are here. Smoke hangs over the city.
Send us men, Erxias. The auguries
Are good. I know you will come.

c. 650 B.C.

How Many Times

translated by **Guy Davenport**

How many times,
How many times,
On the gray sea,
The sea combed
5 By the wind
Like a wilderness
Of woman's hair,
Have we longed,
Lost in nostalgia,
10 For the sweetness
Of homecoming.

c. 650 B.C.

The Doublecross

translated by **Willis Barnstone**

Let brawling waves beat his ship
against the shore, and have the mop-haired
    Thracians
take him naked at Salmydessos,
and he will suffer a thousand calamities
5 as he chews the bread of slaves.
His body will stiffen in freezing surf
as he wrestles with slimy seaweed,
and his teeth will rattle like a helpless dog,
flopped on his belly in the surge,
10 puking out the brine. Let me watch him
    grovel
in mud—for the wrong he did me:
as a traitor he trampled on our good faith,
he who was once my comrade.

c. 650 B.C.

THINK AND DISCUSS

Understanding

1. Why is the speaker of "Miserable with Desire" unhappy?
2. What is the speaker waiting for in "Erxias, Defender"?
3. Describe the motivation for the curse in "The Doublecross."

Analyzing

4. Explain the speaker's use of the word "god-send" in "Miserable with Desire."
5. What does the dominant **metaphor** in "Soul, Soul" suggest?
6. When the speaker of "Erxias, Defender" uses **figurative language** to describe his enemies, what does it suggest about his attitudes?
7. What are the emotional effects of the repetitions in "How Many Times"?

Extending

8. Do you agree with the ideas of Archilochus on how we should deal with adversity?
9. Describe the kind of a soldier who might speak these poems.

REVIEWING: Tone HZ
See Handbook of Literary Terms, p. 976.

Tone is the author's attitude, stated or implied, toward a subject or audience. The choice of particular words, phrases, and figures of speech can evoke a specific tone. The soldier speaking in "Loss of Shield" acknowledges that he has left his shield on the battlefield, and then says, "But I got away, so what does it matter?"

1. How formal and warrior-like are the two phrases that he uses here?
2. What does his language suggest about his attitude toward the code of battlefield heroism?

The homeland of Sappho (saf′ō) was the island of Lesbos off the coast of Asia Minor. Her family were aristocrats, and political disturbances during her childhood forced them into exile in Sicily, perhaps sometime between 604 and 596 B.C. Later they returned to their native island where Sappho married and raised her children. Some of her poems are addressed to her daughter Cleis (klā′əs).

In the native dialect of Lesbos, Sappho composed lyrics of strong personal feeling as well as more formal wedding songs. Many of her poems were addressed to women who were her close friends and were perhaps performed at gatherings of these women. Few of Sappho's poems have survived intact. Some fragments are so small they resemble the Japanese *haiku*. (See page 102.) Yet even in their damaged state such lines still suggest the brilliance of her art.

H/T See LYRIC in the Handbook of Literary Terms, page 956.

World

translated by **Willis Barnstone**

I could not hope
to touch the sky
with my two arms.

6th century B.C.

Then

translated by **Willis Barnstone**

In gold sandals
dawn like a thief
fell upon me.

6th century B.C.

Marble gravestone
showing a woman
and her servant.
c. 400 B.C.
Metropolitan Museum
of Art

To Her Daughter When Sappho Was Dying

translated by **Willis Barnstone**

It would be wrong for us. It is not right
for mourning to enter a home of poetry.

6th century B.C.

Age and Light

translated by **Willis Barnstone**

Here are fine gifts, children,
O friend, singer on the clear tortoise lyre,

all my flesh is wrinkled with age,
my black hair has faded to white,

5 my legs can no longer carry me,
once nimble like a fawn's,

but what can I do?
It cannot be undone,

no more than can pink-armed Dawn
10 not end in darkness on earth,

or keep her love for Tithonos,[1]
who must waste away;

yet I love refinement, and beauty and light
are for me the same as desire for the sun.

6th century B.C.

---

1. *Dawn . . . Tithonos* (ti thō′nəs). The goddess of dawn, Eos, was said to have loved a mortal man, Tithonos. She made him immortal but not unchanging, so that he wasted away with age but could not die.

Someone, I Tell You

translated by **Willis Barnstone**

Someone, I tell you
will remember us.

We are oppressed by
fears of oblivion

5 yet are always saved
by judgment of good men.

6th century B.C.

To Aphrodite of the Flowers, at Knossos

translated by **Willis Barnstone**

Leave Krete and come to this holy temple
where the graceful grove of apple trees
circles an altar smoking with frankincense.

Here roses leave shadow on the ground
5 and cold springs babble through apple
        branches
where shuddering leaves pour down profound
        sleep.

In our meadow where horses graze
and wild flowers of spring blossom,
anise shoots fill the air with aroma.

10 And here, Queen Aphrodite, pour
heavenly nectar into gold cups
and fill them gracefully with sudden joy.

6th century B.C.

THINK AND DISCUSS
Understanding
1. What does the speaker ask of the goddess in "To Aphrodite of the Flowers"?
2. List the details that suggest the age of the speaker in "Age and Light."

Analyzing
3. Describe how the speaker of "To Aphrodite of the Flowers" tries to persuade the goddess.
4. Characterize the dilemma facing the speaker of "Age and Light."
5. Analyze the way Sappho uses **imagery** dealing with light in her poetry.

Extending
6. Why do you think Sappho wishes Aphrodite to come to her temple?
7. Evaluate the various attitudes toward death found in these poems.

APPLYING: Lyric   H✍
See Handbook of Literary Terms, p. 956.
A **lyric** is a relatively short poem expressing the ideas and feelings of its speaker, and usually creating a unified impression on the reader.

1. What basic emotion or state of mind about aging does "Age and Light" express?
2. How do the images of Sappho's "To Aphrodite of the Flowers" give that lyric emotional unity?

COMPOSITION   ◆━━
Finishing a Lyric Poem
Many of Sappho's lyric fragments make the reader wonder about the complete work from which they came. At times a word or image evokes in the mind a hint of the larger poem now lost. Look back over the fragments "World," "Then," "To Her Daughter When Sappho Was Dying," and "Someone, I Tell You," and choose one that appeals to you.

Then, try to imagine how it might grow, like a seed, in different directions and in different ways if it had the chance, and let your imagination follow that growth. When you have a number of ideas, write your own lyric poem based on the fragment, and incorporating the fragment.

Explaining Sappho's Values
In her complete poems, and in the fragments that have survived, Sappho frequently describes what she values most. To understand her mind and spirit better, write a five-paragraph essay in which you explain to your classmates what she praises in the poems reprinted here, and her reasons for that praise. To do this well, begin with a review of the poems, listing for yourself instances in which she writes about (**1**) aspects of the natural world, (**2**) human feelings, (**3**) personal goals and ideals, and (**4**) the gods. Then in your essay devote a paragraph to each of these topics, ending with a paragraph on the values her poetry evokes.

ENRICHMENT
Researching Pictures
In "To Aphrodite of the Flowers" Sappho invites the goddess of love to come and reside in a temple nearby. The poet uses an elaborate description of the temple's setting to persuade the goddess. The poem thus raises the question: what kind of setting is so wonderful that even a goddess would wish to live there? If you were in Sappho's position, what kind of context would you think fit for a goddess? Do some picture research in your school library or at home. Use magazines that have color photos, and art books that present paintings of landscape, seeking for visual depictions of your own ideal setting. Then get together with your classmates and share with each other the pictures you have found.

BIOGRAPHY

Sophocles

c. 496–406 B.C.

Sophocles, one of the three greatest writers of Greek tragedy, was the son of a wealthy manufacturer. He lived his entire life in Athens, at the height of that city's political and cultural success. Like many of his fellow citizens, Sophocles took on important public responsibilities. In 443 B.C. he served his city as treasurer of the league organized to resist Persia. He was a military leader under Pericles during the Samian War (441–439 B.C.). In his old age, Sophocles introduced the cult of the mythical healer Asclepius (as klē′pē əs) to Athens which, as a recent historian observes, "effectively means the founding of the first public hospital."

The young Sophocles studied what we would now call theater arts, and when he was fifteen he led the hymns celebrating the victory of Athens over the Persians at Salamis. He entered the annual theatrical competitions sacred to the god Dionysus, both as an actor and as a playwright. In 468 his play won first prize and soon, because of his relatively weak voice, he gave up performing. During his long career Sophocles wrote 123 plays; 24 of them won first prize, and the rest second. Sophocles was a conscious innovator in the theater. He was the first playwright to have three actors on stage at once, thus allowing for the development of dramatically complex scenes. He increased the number of singers in the chorus and wrote a theoretical essay on its use. Breaking with past tradition, he turned from the tradition of writing three interconnected plays featuring a diversity of characters to writing single dramas of concentrated action that focus upon a dominant individual.

Sophocles' plays are about a quasi-mythical heroic era of Greek history, yet they do not evade contemporary problems. Rather, they scrutinize them through the ancient tales. *Oedipus the King* probably appeared during the decade 430–420 B.C. Athens was in the midst of the Second Peloponnesian War with her neighbors, led by Sparta. Enemy troops plundered the countryside while cautious Athenians remained protected behind the city's walls. In the summer of 430 a disastrous plague struck. The bodies of its victims lay heaped in the streets and the government seemed powerless to control the virtual anarchy that overtook the city.

It is easy to see how Sophocles' tragedy, set in ancient Thebes, is based on this Athenian crisis. The play opens with a terrible plague, which swiftly leads to a challenge for the city's political leadership that must be resolved if Thebes is to survive. The play's first speech could have just as appropriately been uttered by the great Athenian leader Pericles as by Oedipus.

Sophocles lived until 406, and his last play, *Oedipus at Colonus* premiered posthumously. He had praise and success during his lifetime, and after his death his plays were frequently performed. So popular did they become that strolling actors took them into the provinces, and began to tinker with their texts, adding and cutting passages by whim. It appears that, like Shakespeare, Sophocles had made no effort to leave an official version of his works for posterity. Worried about the danger to this part of their heritage, Athenians had a careful reconstruction of the originals made in 330 B.C., and copies were kept in the library at Alexandria. But only seven of his tragedies have survived to the present. They remain some of the most frequently performed and highly admired plays of all time.

THE STORY OF OEDIPUS

The audience that first saw *Oedipus the King* knew the story before they entered the theater. A modern reader too should know certain crucial facts to understand how Sophocles uses an old tale to create scenes of high drama and, at times, of intense **irony.**

Oedipus was a royal prince, son of Laius, king of Thebes, and his queen, Jocasta. After his birth, there was a prophecy that Oedipus would kill his father and wed his mother. Horrified, Laius had a rivet driven between the baby's ankles and ordered a servant to take him to Mount Cithaeron and leave him there to be killed by exposure to the elements. The servant, pitying the child, instead gave him to a shepherd, who took Oedipus to another city-state, Corinth, where the childless king Polybus adopted him as his own. Oedipus grew up, and as a young man again heard the prophecy that he would kill his father and marry his mother. To prevent this he fled Corinth for a life of wandering. One day, journeying through central Greece, he got into a fight with a belligerent old man and killed both him and his servants. Traveling on he reached Thebes, which at the moment was being destroyed by a monster, the Sphinx, which posed a riddle no one could answer: "What walks on four legs at dawn, two legs at noon, and three legs at nightfall." Oedipus, solver of riddles, knew the answer: man. With the Sphinx repulsed, the joyful Thebans declared Oedipus their king and offered him their widowed queen as his wife. Years pass, and they have their own children. But now a plague falls upon the city. To the Thebans, this seems a terrible punishment from the gods. A decisive ruler, Oedipus sends his wife's brother, Creon, to Apollo's oracle at Delphi to learn what they must do to save the city. At this point, the play begins.

Tragic and comic masks.
3rd century A.D.
Capitoline Museum, Rome

Reading A GREEK TRAGEDY

The Greek Stage *Oedipus the King*, like all Greek plays, was written for the annual Athenian spring festival of Dionysus. The god's statue overlooked a large open-air theater built into the southeast slope of the Acropolis that held fourteen to fifteen thousand spectators. Festival events began at dawn with a procession, followed by daylong performances in the open of both tragedies and comedies. The performance took place on a circular stone pavement called the orchestra backed by a small wooden building in which the players could change costume. There were scarcely any sets or props. The audience used its imagination to provide setting and atmosphere. After four days the festival concluded with awards given to the best plays.

Greek drama was not entertainment; it had links with sacred ritual and with the Athenian social and political system. The practice of performing plays seems to have begun with choral singing and dancing, perhaps during celebrations of military victories or at seasonal festivals such as harvest time. Formal Greek dramas continued to use the dramatic convention of a chorus of people who interrupted the action at regular intervals to sing and dance in grave, ritualistic ways.

The Role of the Chorus In reading a play such as *Oedipus* it is important to observe how the chorus reacts to events. They frequently seem to represent the people of a town, and their ideas and feelings thus serve as a barometer of popular opinion. The near-constant presence of the chorus on stage keeps the audience aware that everything which happens to Oedipus matters not just to him, but to the people of an entire society, since he is their king. Thus Sophocles' play is about a social crisis, and a political problem, as well as about the tragedy of a particular man.

As Greek drama evolved, individual persons stepped out of the chorus to act as specific characters. Sophocles was the first writer to use three actors simultaneously, because his plays focus on dramatic confrontation among several persons. Dialogue, not physical action, is the principal form of dramatic expression in *Oedipus*. Our sense of character and motivation develops from people talking to each other at crucial moments. Oedipus comes alive for us as he encounters problems and challenges, and we get to know him as a person through the manner in which he deals with them. As is typical of Greek tragedy, acts of violence happen offstage, and messengers come to describe them.

The Conventions of Greek Drama Because the Greek outdoor theater was so large, actors —only men performed—could not depend upon subtle facial expression or vocal inflection. In fact, they wore stylized masks and high boots to make them taller. We presume that they moved their audience by the skillful use of large physical gestures, and by their ability to declaim Sophocles' poetry. The original texts of Greek plays rarely have stage directions, and the modern translator of our version has invented his own to help readers picture what might have happened in a specific performance.

The Impact of *Oedipus* Sophocles' audience knew the whole story of Oedipus before they came to the theater. As the drama unfolded, the playwright was thus able to deal with his materials in two different ways. Since everyone knows that Oedipus will discover his own guilt and be driven from the city, every time he boasts of his skill as a solver of riddles, every time he threatens someone else, like Creon, there is a strong undercurrent of irony. Yet at the same time Sophocles is able to make us identify ourselves emotionally with Oedipus, perhaps because he has so many good points, and because his plight is so pitiful. This complex emotional situation is one of Sophocles' greatest achievements, and careful readers will want to follow the ways he combines irony with pity in fashioning his tragedy.

See **PROTAGONIST** in the Handbook of Literary Terms, page 964.

Oedipus the King

Sophocles   *translated by* **Robert Fagles**

CHARACTERS

OEDIPUS (ed′ə pəs), *King of Thebes.*
PRIEST *of Zeus.*
CREON (krē′on), *brother of Jocasta.*
CHORUS *of Theban citizens and their leader.*
TIRESIAS (tī rē′sē əs) *a blind prophet.*
JOCASTA (jō cas′tə), *the queen, wife of Oedipus.*
MESSENGER *from Corinth.*

SHEPHERD.
MESSENGER *from inside the palace.*
ANTIGONE (an tig′ə nē)⎫ *daughters of Oedipus*
ISMENE (is mā′nē) ⎭ *and Jocasta.*
GUARDS.
ATTENDANTS.
PRIESTS *of Thebes.*

TIME AND SCENE. The royal house of Thebes. Double doors dominate the façade: a stone altar stands at the center of the stage.
    Many years have passed since OEDIPUS *solved the riddle of the Sphinx and ascended the throne of Thebes, and now a plague has struck the city. A procession of priests enters; suppliants, broken and despondent, they carry branches wound in wool and lay them on the altar.*
    The doors open. Guards assemble. OEDIPUS *comes forward, majestic but for a telltale limp, and slowly views the condition of his people.*

OEDIPUS. Oh my children, the new blood of ancient Thebes,°
   why are you here? Huddling at my altar,
   praying before me, your branches wound in wool.°
   Our city reeks with the smoke of burning incense,
5 rings with cries for the Healer° and wailing for the dead.
   I thought it wrong, my children, to hear the truth
   from others, messengers. Here I am myself—
   you all know me, the world knows my fame:
   I am Oedipus.   *(Helping a Priest to his feet.)*
          Speak up, old man. Your years,
10 your dignity—you should speak for the others.
   Why here and kneeling, what preys upon you so?
   Some sudden fear? some strong desire?
   You can trust me; I am ready to help,
   I'll do anything. I would be blind to misery
15 not to pity my people kneeling at my feet.

Thebes (thēbz), a city in central Greece.
branches . . . wool, carried by those requesting divine aid. Such suppliants carried branches of olive or laurel, which had tufts of wool tied around them. The branches were laid on the altar of the god or gods whose aid was being requested, and were left there until the worshippers' prayer was answered.
Healer, the god Apollo (ə-pol′ō), who both brought and averted plagues. Apollo was the father of the god of medicine, Asclepios, whose cult Sophocles introduced to Athens.

Sophocles **165**

PRIEST. Oh Oedipus, king of the land, our greatest power!
　　You see us before you, men of all ages
　　clinging to your altars. Here are boys,
　　still too weak to fly from the nest,
20　　and here the old, bowed down with the years,
　　the holy ones—a priest of Zeus° myself—and here
　　the picked, unmarried men, the young hope of Thebes.
　　And all the rest, your great family gathers now,
　　branches wreathed, massing in the squares,
25　　kneeling before the two temples of queen Athena°
　　or the river-shrine where the embers glow and die
　　and Apollo sees the future in the ashes.° Our city—
　　look around you, see with your own eyes—
　　our ship pitches wildly, cannot lift her head
30　　from the depths, the red waves of death . . .
　　Thebes is dying. A blight on the fresh crops
　　and the rich pastures, cattle sicken and die,
　　and the women die in labor, children stillborn,
　　and the plague, the fiery god of fever hurls down
35　　on the city, his lightning slashing through us—
　　raging plague in all its vengeance, devastating
　　the house of Cadmus!° And Black Death luxuriates
　　in the raw, wailing miseries of Thebes.
　　Now we pray to you. You cannot equal the gods,
40　　your children know that, bending at your altar.
　　But we do rate you first of men,
　　both in the common crises of our lives
　　and face-to-face encounters with the gods.
　　You freed us from the Sphinx;° you came to Thebes
45　　and cut us loose from the bloody tribute we had paid
　　that harsh, brutal singer. We taught you nothing,
　　no skill, no extra knowledge, still you triumphed.
　　A god was with you, so they say, and we believe it—
　　you lifted up our lives. So now again,
50　　Oedipus, king, we bend to you, your power—
　　we implore you, all of us on our knees:
　　find us strength, rescue! Perhaps you've heard
　　the voice of a god or something from other men,
　　Oedipus . . . what do you know?°
55　　The man of experience—you see it every day—
　　his plans will work in a crisis, his first of all.
　　Act now—we beg you, best of men, raise up our city!
　　Act, defend yourself, your former glory!
　　Your country calls you savior now
60　　for your zeal, your action years ago.
　　Never let us remember of your reign:
　　you helped us stand, only to fall once more.

166 *The Classical World*

Zeus (züs), king of the gods.

Athena (ə thē′nə), daughter of Zeus; goddess of wisdom.

river-shrine . . . ashes. There was an oracular shrine of Apollo by the Theban river, the Ismenus, where the future was foretold by priests who interpreted as prophetic any unusual circumstances accompanying the burning of the sacrifices they offered.

Cadmus (kad′məs), traditional founder of Thebes.

Sphinx (sfingks), a monster with the head of a woman, the body of a lion, and wings.

what do you know? This question in the original Greek (*oistha pou*) has a punning resemblance to the Greek form of the name of the hero (*Oidipous*), the man who seems to know everything but does not in fact even know who he is.

Oh raise up our city, set us on our feet.
The omens were good that day you brought us joy—
65 be the same man today!
Rule our land, you know you have the power,
but rule a land of the living, not a wasteland.
Ship and towered city are nothing, stripped of men
alive within it, living all as one.

OEDIPUS.   My children,
70 I pity you. I see—how could I fail to see
what longings bring you here? Well I know
you are sick to death, all of you,
but sick as you are, not one is sick as I.
Your pain strikes each of you alone, each
75 in the confines of himself, no other. But my spirit
grieves for the city, for myself and all of you.
I wasn't asleep, dreaming. You haven't wakened me—
I've wept through the nights, you must know that,
groping, laboring over many paths of thought.
80 After a painful search I found one cure:
I acted at once, I sent Creon,
my wife's own brother, to Delphi—°
Apollo the Prophet's oracle—to learn
what I might do or say to save our city.
85 Today's the day. When I count the days gone by
it torments me . . . what is he doing?
Strange, he's late, he's gone too long.
But once he returns, then, then I'll be a traitor
if I do not do all the god makes clear.

90 **PRIEST.** Timely words. The men over there
are signaling—Creon's just arriving.

OEDIPUS (*sighting* CREON, *then turning to the altar*). Lord Apollo,
let him come with a lucky word of rescue,
shining like his eyes!

PRIEST. Welcome news, I think—he's crowned, look,
95 and the laurel wreath° is bright with berries.

OEDIPUS. We'll soon see. He's close enough to hear—
          (*Enter* CREON *from the side; his face is shaded with a wreath.*)
Creon, prince, my kinsman, what do you bring us?
What message from the god?

CREON.   Good news.
I tell you even the hardest things to bear,
100 if they should turn out well, all would be well.

OEDIPUS. Of course, but what were the god's *words*? There's no hope
and nothing to fear in what you've said so far.

CREON. If you want my report in the presence of these . . .
          (*Pointing to the priests while drawing* OEDIPUS *toward the palace.*)
I'm ready now, or we might go inside.

Terra-cotta statuette
of a masked actor.
British Museum

1 This is the first of
a series of images
of Oedipus as physician.
Note how this image
recurs and alters.
Delphi (del′fī), site of the
greatest oracular shrine of
Apollo in the Greek world.
See page 173.

laurel wreath. The laurel
was sacred to Apollo and
symbolic of triumph.

2 Why might Creon
want to deliver his
message inside?

OEDIPUS.   Speak out,
105   speak to us all. I grieve for these, my people,
     far more than I fear for my own life.
CREON.   Very well,
     I will tell you what I heard from the god.
     Apollo commands us—he was quite clear—
     "Drive the corruption° from the land,
110   don't harbor it any longer, past all cure,
     don't nurse it in your soil—root it out!"
OEDIPUS. How can we cleanse ourselves—what rites?
     What's the source of the trouble?
CREON. Banish the man, or pay back blood with blood.
115   Murder sets the plague-storm on the city.
OEDIPUS.   Whose murder?
     Whose fate does Apollo bring to light?
CREON.   Our leader,
     my lord, was once a man named Laius,
     before you came and put us straight on course.
OEDIPUS.   I know—
     or so I've heard. I never saw the man myself.
120 **CREON.** Well, he was killed, and Apollo commands us now—
     he could not be more clear,
     "Pay the killers back—whoever is responsible."
OEDIPUS. Where on earth are they? Where to find it now,
     the trail of the ancient guilt so hard to trace?
125 **CREON.** "Here in Thebes," he said.
     Whatever is sought for can be caught, you know,
     whatever is neglected slips away.
     OEDIPUS.   But where,
     in the palace, the fields or foreign soil,
     where did Laius meet his bloody death?
130 **CREON.** He went to consult an oracle, he said,
     and he set out and never came home again.
OEDIPUS. No messenger, no fellow-traveler saw what happened?
     Someone to cross-examine?
CREON.   No,
     they were all killed but one. He escaped,
135   terrified, he could tell us nothing clearly,
     nothing of what he saw—just one thing.
OEDIPUS.   What's that?
     One thing could hold the key to it all,
     a small beginning give us grounds for hope.
CREON. He said thieves attacked them—a whole band,
140   not single-handed, cut King Laius down.
OEDIPUS.   A thief,
     so daring, wild, he'd kill a king? Impossible,
     unless conspirators paid him off in Thebes.

168   *The Classical World*

corruption. The Greek word is *miasma*, which means "a stain." The blood of the murdered man is thought of as something that pollutes not only the killer but all those who come in contact with him.

3 | Does this ignorance of Oedipus concerning his predecessor's fate seem unlikely?

4 | Note that though Creon says "thieves" (line 139) attacked Laius, Oedipus immediately speaks of "A thief" (line 140). What does this suggest about Oedipus?

CREON. We suspected as much. But with Laius dead
    no leader appeared to help us in our troubles.

OEDIPUS. Trouble? Your *king* was murdered—royal blood!
    What stopped you from tracking down the killer
    then and there?

CREON.   The singing, riddling Sphinx.
    She . . . persuaded us to let the mystery go
    and concentrate on what lay at our feet.

OEDIPUS.   No,
    I'll start again—I'll bring it all to light myself!
    Apollo is right, and so are you, Creon,
    to turn our attention back to the murdered man.
    Now you have *me* to fight for you, you'll see:
    I am the land's avenger by all rights
    and Apollo's champion too.
    But not to assist some distant kinsman, no,
    for my own sake I'll rid us of this corruption.
    Whoever killed the king may decide to kill me too,
    with the same violent hand—by avenging Laius
    I defend myself. *(To the priests.)* Quickly, my children.
    Up from the steps, take up your branches now. *(To the guards.)*
    One of you summon the city here before us,
    tell them I'll do everything. God help us,
    we will see our triumph—or our fall.

               (OEDIPUS and CREON enter the palace, followed by the guards.)

PRIEST. Rise, my sons. The kindness we came for
    Oedipus volunteers himself.
    Apollo has sent his word, his oracle—
    Come down, Apollo, save us, stop the plague.

       (The priests rise, remove their branches and exit to the side. Enter
       a CHORUS, *the citizens of Thebes, who have not heard the news that*
       CREON *brings. They march around the altar, chanting.)*

CHORUS.°   Zeus!
    Great welcome voice of Zeus,° what do you bring?
    What word from the gold vaults of Delphi
    comes to brilliant Thebes? I'm racked with terror—
                   terror shakes my heart
    and I cry your wild cries, Apollo, Healer of Delos°
    I worship you in dread . . . what now, what is your price?
    some new sacrifice? some ancient rite from the past
    come round again each spring?
             what will you bring to birth?
    Tell me, child of golden Hope
        warm voice that never dies!
    You are the first I call, daughter of Zeus
    deathless Athena—I call your sister Artemis,°
    heart of the market place enthroned in glory,

Chorus. The chorus was an essential element of Greek drama, though its function varied widely in the hands of different dramatists. In Sophocles the chorus provides an emotive link between successive episodes, reinforcing the content of the preceding scene and preparing the audience for what is to follow.

5 The Chorus requests the aid of different gods and goddesses. Which god is their aid invoked against?

voice of Zeus. Though Apollo spoke through the oracle of Delphi, he was considered to speak for his father, Zeus.

Delos (dē′los). Apollo was supposed to have been born on Delos, a very small island in the Cyclades. It was a famous center of his worship.

Artemis (är′tə mis), sister of Apollo; goddess of the hunt, of the forest, of wild animals, and of the moon.

guardian of our earth—
I call Apollo, Archer astride the thunderheads of heaven—
185 O triple shield against death, shine before me now!
If ever, once in the past, you stopped some ruin
launched against our walls
you hurled the flame of pain
far, far from Thebes—you gods
190 come now, come down once more!

No, no
the miseries numberless, grief on grief, no end—
too much to bear, we are all dying
O my people . . .
Thebes like a great army dying
195 and there is no sword of thought to save us, no
and the fruits of our famous earth, they will not ripen
no and the women cannot scream their pangs to birth—
screams for the Healer, children dead in the womb
and life on life goes down
200 you can watch them go
like seabirds winging west, outracing the day's fire
down the horizon, irresistibly
streaking on to the shores of Evening
Death
so many deaths, numberless deaths on deaths, no end—
205 Thebes is dying, look, her children
stripped of pity . . .
generations strewn on the ground
unburied, unwept, the dead spreading death
and the young wives and gray-haired mothers with them
210 cling to the altars, trailing in from all over the city—
Thebes, city of death, one long cortege°
and the suffering rises
wails for mercy rise
and the wild hymn for the Healer blazes out
215 clashing with our sobs our cries of mourning—
O golden daughter of god,° send rescue
radiant as the kindness in your eyes!
Drive him back!—the fever, the god of death
that raging god of war°
220 not armored in bronze, not shielded now, he burns me,
battle cries in the onslaught burning on—
O rout him from our borders!
Sail him, blast him out to the Sea-queen's chamber°
the black Atlantic gulfs
225 or the northern harbor, death to all
where the Thracian surf comes crashing.
Now what the night spares he comes by day and kills—

Terra-cotta statuette
of an actor.
British Museum

cortege (kôr tezh′), a procession; often, a funeral
procession.
golden daughter of God,
Athena.
god of war, Ares (ar′ēz),
who is often associated
with the country of
Thrace, north of Greece
(line 226). Ares is not
generally associated with
plague. The reference here
may reflect the situation
of Athens at the time
Sophocles wrote *Oedipus
the King*—plague inside
the city and a Spartan
army outside.
Sea-queen's chamber. The
goddess Amphitrite (am fi-
trē′tā) was the wife of
Poseidon (pə sī′dən), god
of the sea.

the god of death.
                    O lord of the stormcloud,
you who twirl the lightning, Zeus, Father,
thunder Death to nothing!
Apollo, lord of the light, I beg you—
              whip your longbow's golden cord
showering arrows on our enemies—shafts of power
champions strong before us rushing on!
Artemis, Huntress,
torches flaring over the eastern ridges—
                        ride Death down in pain!
God of the headdress gleaming gold, I cry to you—
your name and ours are one,° Dionysus—
            come with your face aflame with wine
                    your raving women's cries°
        your army on the march! Come with the lightning
come with torches blazing, eyes ablaze with glory!
Burn that god of death that all gods hate!
(OEDIPUS *enters from the palace to address the* CHORUS, *as if addressing the
                                        entire city of Thebes.*)

OEDIPUS. You pray to the gods? Let me grant your prayers.
    Come, listen to me—do what the plague demands:
    you'll find relief and lift your head from the depths.
    I will speak out now as a stranger to the story,
    a stranger to the crime. If I'd been present then,
    there would have been no mystery, no long hunt
    without a clue in hand. So now, counted
    a native Theban years after the murder,
    to all of Thebes I make this proclamation:
    if any one of you knows who murdered Laius,
    the son of Labdacus, I order him to reveal
    the whole truth to me. Nothing to fear,
    even if he must denounce himself,
    let him speak up
    and so escape the brunt of the charge—
    he will suffer no unbearable punishment,
    nothing worse than exile, totally unharmed.
                        (OEDIPUS *pauses, waiting for a reply.*)
    Next, if anyone knows the murderer is a stranger,
    a man from alien soil, come, speak up.
    I will give him a handsome reward, and lay up
    gratitude in my heart for him besides.   (*Silence again, no reply.*)
    But if you keep silent, if anyone panicking,
    trying to shield himself or friend or kin,
    rejects my offer, then hear what I will do.
    I order you, every citizen of the state
    where I hold throne and power: banish this man—

your name . . . are one.
The wine-god Dionysus
(dī′ə nī′səs) was the son
of Zeus by a woman
of Thebes, and Thebes
was traditionally the first
Greek city that celebrated
his rites.
*your raving women's
cries,* those of the frenzied female worshippers
of Dionysus. "Your army
on the march" (line 242)
also refers to these women.

| 6 | What does Oedi-
pus mean in lines
249–251? What is the
effect of these lines?

whoever he may be—never shelter him, never
speak a word to him, never make him partner
to your prayers, your victims burned to the gods.
Never let the holy water° touch his hands,
275 Drive him out, each of you, from every home.
He is the plague, the heart of our corruption,
as Apollo's oracle has revealed to me
just now. So I honor my obligations:
I fight for the god and for the murdered man.
280 Now my curse on the murderer. Whoever he is,
a lone man unknown in his crime
or one among many, let that man drag out
his life in agony, step by painful step—
I curse myself as well . . . if by any chance
285 he proves to be an intimate of our house,
here at my hearth, with my full knowledge,
may the curse I just called down on him strike me!
These are your orders: perform them to the last.
I command you, for my sake, for Apollo's, for this country
290 blasted root and branch by the angry heavens.
Even if god had never urged you on to act,
how could you leave the crime uncleansed so long?
A man so noble—your king, brought down in blood—
you should have searched. But I am the king now,
295 I hold the throne that he held then, possess his bed
and a wife who shares our seed . . . why, our seed
might be the same, children born of the same mother
might have created blood-bonds between us
if his hope of offspring hadn't met disaster—
300 but fate swooped at his head and cut him short.
So I will fight for him as if he were my father,
stop at nothing, search the world
to lay my hands on the man who shed his blood,
the son of Labdacus descended of Polydorus,
305 Cadmus of old and Agenor,° founder of the line:
their power and mine are one. Oh dear gods,
my curse on those who disobey these orders!
Let no crops grow out of the earth for them—
shrivel their women, kill their sons,
310 burn them to nothing in this plague
that hits us now, or something even worse.
But you, loyal men of Thebes who approve my actions,
may our champion, Justice, may all the gods
be with us, fight beside us to the end!
315 **LEADER.** In the grip of your curse, my king, I swear
I'm not the murderer, cannot point him out.

172 *The Classical World*

---

holy water, used in the
lustrum, the rite of purification.

Agenor (a jē′nôr), king
of Phoenicia. His son
Cadmus founded Thebes
and became its king.
Polydorus (pol ē dôr′əs),
Labdacus (lab′də kəs),
and Laius (lā′əs) followed
him on the throne.

(*The text* of Oedipus the
King *continues on page
174.*)

The Delphic Oracle

Delphi, the most celebrated sanctuary in ancient Greece, was located on the lower slopes of Mount Parnassus. The Greeks believed the spot to be the center of the earth, saying that Zeus had released two eagles, one from the east and one from the west, and flying toward each other they had met there. The site was originally sacred to the earth-goddess Gaea (jē′ə).

The Greeks told the story of a monstrous serpent, Python, who guarded the spot. The god Apollo came to Delphi, slew Python, and established his oracle there. Apollo was called *Pythian* in memory of this deed. The priestess of Apollo who gave the oracle was called the *Pythia* or the *Pythoness*. The Delphic oracle was consulted on a variety of questions, both private and public.

Those who wished to consult the oracle first performed the rite of purification and sacrificed to Apollo. Precedence among pilgrims was generally determined by lot, although occasionally granted as a privilege. A male priest, the sole attendant of the Pythia, related the questions and interpreted the answer. The priestess, seated on the sacred tripod, gave the oracle while in a frenzied state. How this condition was induced is not completely clear. Excavation at Delphi has shown as improbable the theory that the priestess inhaled vapors issuing from a hole in the earth. Such practices as chewing laurel leaves and drinking the water from the Castalian spring which flowed near the sanctuary may have assisted, but the major cause was probably the priestess's own complete faith in the power of the god to speak through her. The influence of Delphi, felt throughout the entire Mediterranean world for several centuries, began to decline from the fourth century B.C. onward. The sanctuary was finally closed by the Christian emperor Theodosius in A.D. 390.

Vase painting showing a petitioner standing before the priestess of Delphi. The priestess is seated on her tripod and is holding a branch of laurel, sacred to her patron, the god Apollo.

As for the search, Apollo pressed it on us—
he should name the killer.
OEDIPUS.   Quite right,
but to force the gods to act against their will—
320   no man has the power.
    LEADER.   Then if I might mention
    the next best thing . . .
OEDIPUS.   The third best too—
don't hold back, say it.
    LEADER.   I still believe . . .
    Lord Tiresias sees with the eyes of Lord Apollo.
    Anyone searching for the truth, my king,
325   might learn it from the prophet, clear as day.
    OEDIPUS. I've not been slow with that. On Creon's cue
    I sent the escorts, twice, within the hour.
    I'm surprised he isn't here.
    LEADER.   We need him—
    without him we have nothing but old, useless rumors.
330 OEDIPUS. Which rumors? I'll search out every word.
    LEADER. Laius was killed, they say, by certain travelers.
    OEDIPUS. I know—but no one can find the murderer.
    LEADER. If the man has a trace of fear in him
    he won't stay silent long,
335   not with your curses ringing in his ears.
    OEDIPUS. He didn't flinch at murder,
    he'll never flinch at words.

    (*Enter* TIRESIAS, *the blind prophet, led by a boy with escorts in attendance.*
                              He remains at a distance.)

    LEADER. Here is the one who will convict him, look,
    they bring him on at last, the seer,° the man of god.
340   The truth lives inside him, him alone.
    OEDIPUS.   O Tiresias,
    master of all the mysteries of our life,
    all you teach and all you dare not tell,
    signs in the heavens, signs that walk the earth!
    Blind as you are, you can feel all the more
345   what sickness haunts our city. You, my lord,
    are the one shield, the one savior we can find.
    We asked Apollo—perhaps the messengers
    haven't told you—he sent his answer back:
    "Relief from the plague can only come one way.
350   Uncover the murderers of Laius,
    put them to death or drive them into exile."
    So I beg you, grudge us nothing now, no voice,
    no message plucked from the birds, the embers
    or the other mantic° ways within your grasp.
355   Rescue yourself, your city, rescue me—

Terra-cotta copy of a theatrical mask. British Museum

seer (sir), in Greek religion, a person skilled in reading omens.

mantic (man'tik), concerning divination, telling the future from omens.

rescue everything infected by the dead.
We are in your hands. For a man to help others
with all his gifts and native strength:
that is the noblest work.

TIRESIAS.   How terrible—to see the truth
360 when the truth is only pain to him who sees!
I knew it well, but I put it from my mind,
else I never would have come.

OEDIPUS. What's this? Why so grim, so dire?

TIRESIAS. Just send me home. You bear your burdens,
365 I'll bear mine. It's better that way,
please believe me.

OEDIPUS.   Strange response—unlawful,
unfriendly too to the state that bred and raised you;
you're withholding the word of god.

TIRESIAS.   I fail to see
that your own words are so well-timed.
370 I'd rather not have the same thing said of me . . .

OEDIPUS. For the love of god, don't turn away,
not if you know something. We beg you,
all of us on our knees.

TIRESIAS.   None of you knows—
and I will never reveal my dreadful secrets,
375 not to say your own.

OEDIPUS. What? You know and you won't tell?
You're bent on betraying us, destroying Thebes?

TIRESIAS. I'd rather not cause pain for you or me.
So why this . . . useless interrogation?
380 You'll get nothing from me.

OEDIPUS.   Nothing! You,
you scum of the earth, you'd enrage a heart of stone!
You won't talk? Nothing moves you?
Out with it, once and for all!

TIRESIAS. You criticize my temper . . . unaware
385 of the one *you* live with, you revile me.

OEDIPUS. Who could restrain his anger hearing you?
What outrage—you spurn the city!

TIRESIAS. What will come will come.
Even if I shroud it all in silence.

390 OEDIPUS. What will come? You're bound to *tell* me that.

TIRESIAS. I'll say no more. Do as you like, build your anger
to whatever pitch you please, rage your worst—

OEDIPUS. Oh I'll let loose, I have such fury in me—
now I see it all. You helped hatch the plot,
395 you did the work, yes, short of killing him
with your own hands—and given eyes I'd say
you did the killing single-handed!

7 | Note how quickly
Oedipus grows angry.

TIRESIAS. Is that so!
I charge you, then, submit to that decree
you just laid down: from this day onward
speak to no one, not these citizens, not myself.
You are the curse, the corruption of the land!

OEDIPUS. You, shameless—
aren't you appalled to start up such a story?
You think you can get away with this?

TIRESIAS. I have already.
The truth with all its power lives inside me.

OEDIPUS. Who primed you for this? Not your prophet's trade.

TIRESIAS. You did, you forced me, twisted it out of me.

OEDIPUS. What? Say it again—I'll understand it better.

TIRESIAS. Didn't you understand, just now?
Or are you tempting me to talk?

OEDIPUS. No, I can't say I grasped your meaning.
Out with it, again!

TIRESIAS. I say you are the murderer you hunt.

OEDIPUS. That obscenity, twice—by god, you'll pay.

TIRESIAS. Shall I say more, so you can really rage?

OEDIPUS. Much as you want. Your words are nothing—
futile.

TIRESIAS. You cannot imagine . . . I tell you,
you and your loved ones live together in infamy,
you cannot see how far you've gone in guilt,

OEDIPUS. You think you can keep this up and never suffer?

TIRESIAS. Indeed, if the truth has any power.

OEDIPUS. It does
but not for you, old man. You've lost your power,
stone-blind, stone-deaf—senses, eyes blind as stone!

TIRESIAS. I pity you, flinging at me the very insults
each man here will fling at you so soon.

OEDIPUS. Blind,
lost in the night, endless night that nursed you!
You can't hurt me or anyone else who sees the light—
you can never touch me.

TIRESIAS. True, it is not your fate
to fall at my hands. Apollo is quite enough,
and he will take some pains to work this out.

OEDIPUS. Creon! Is this conspiracy his or yours?

TIRESIAS. Creon is not your downfall, no, you are your own.

OEDIPUS. O power—
wealth and empire, skill outstripping skill
in the heady rivalries of life,
what envy lurks inside you! Just for this,
the crown the city gave me—I never sought it,
they laid it in my hands—for this alone, Creon,

8 | What does line 431
suggest about the
relationship of Oedipus
and Creon?

the soul of trust, my loyal friend from the start
steals against me . . . so hungry to overthrow me
440 he sets this wizard on me, this scheming quack,
this fortune-teller peddling lies, eyes peeled
for his own profit—seer blind in his craft!
Come here, you pious fraud. Tell me,
when did you ever prove yourself a prophet?
445 When the Sphinx, that chanting Fury° kept her deathwatch here,
why silent then, not a word to set our people free?
There was a riddle, not for some passer-by to solve—
it cried out for a prophet. Where were you?
Did you rise to the crisis? Not a word,
450 you and your birds,° your gods—nothing.
No, but I came by, Oedipus the ignorant,
I stopped the Sphinx! With no help from the birds,
the flight of my own intelligence hit the mark.
And this is the man you'd try to overthrow?
455 You think you'll stand by Creon when he's king?
You and the great mastermind—
you'll pay in tears, I promise you, for this,
this witch-hunt. If you didn't look so senile
the lash would teach you what your scheming means!
460 **LEADER.** I'd suggest his words were spoken in anger,
Oedipus . . . yours too, and it isn't what we need.
The best solution to the oracle, the riddle
posed by god—we should look for that.
TIRESIAS. You are the king no doubt, but in one respect,
465 at least, I am your equal: the right to reply.
I claim that privilege too.
I am not your slave. I serve Apollo.
I don't need Creon to speak for me in public.
So, you mock my blindness? Let me tell you this.
470 You with your precious eyes,
you're blind to the corruption of your life,
to the house you live in, those you live with—
who *are* your parents? Do you know? All unknowing
you are the scourge of your own flesh and blood,
475 the dead below the earth and the living here above,
and the double lash of your mother and your father's curse
will whip you from this land one day, their footfall
treading you down in terror, darkness shrouding
your eyes that now can see the light! Soon, soon
480 you'll scream aloud—what haven won't reverberate?
What rock of Cithaeron° won't scream back in echo?
That day you learn the truth about your marriage,
the wedding-march that sang you into your halls,
the lusty voyage home to the fatal harbor!

Fury. The Furies were three goddesses who pursued those who had not atoned for their crimes against blood relatives.

birds. The flight of birds was believed to predict the future.

Detail of a terra-cotta relief showing actors. National Museum, Naples

Cithaeron (si thēr'ən), a mountain near Thebes on which Oedipus was abandoned as an infant.

485 And a load of other horrors you'd never dream
     will level you with yourself and all your children.
     There. Now smear us with insults—Creon, myself
     and every word I've said. No man will ever
     be rooted from the earth as brutally as you.

490 OEDIPUS. Enough! Such filth from him? Insufferable—
     what, still alive? Get out—
     faster, back where you came from—vanish!

     TIRESIAS. I'd never have come if you hadn't called me here.

     OEDIPUS. If I thought you'd blurt out such absurdities,
495   you'd have died waiting before I'd had you summoned.

     TIRESIAS. Absurd, am I? To you, not to your parents:
     the ones who bore you found me sane enough.

     OEDIPUS. Parents—who? Wait . . . who is my father?

     TIRESIAS. This day will bring your birth and your destruction.

500 OEDIPUS. Riddles—all you can say are riddles, murk and darkness.

     TIRESIAS. Ah, but aren't you the best man alive at solving riddles?

     OEDIPUS. Mock me for that, go on, and you'll reveal my greatness.

     TIRESIAS. Your great good fortune, true, it was your ruin.

     OEDIPUS. Not if I saved the city—what do I care?

505 TIRESIAS.   Well then, I'll be going. (To his attendant.) Take me home, boy.

     OEDIPUS. Yes, take him away. You're a nuisance here.
     Out of the way, the irritation's gone.

                    (Turning his back on TIRESIAS, moving toward the palace.)

     TIRESIAS.   I will go,
     once I have said what I came here to say.
     I'll never shrink from the anger in your eyes—
510 You can't destroy me. Listen to me closely:
     the man you've sought so long, proclaiming,
     cursing up and down, the murderer of Laius—
     he is here. A stranger,
     you may think, who lives among you,
515 he soon will be revealed a native Theban
     but he will take no joy in the revelation.
     Blind who now has eyes, beggar who now is rich,
     he will grope his way toward a foreign soil,
     a stick tapping before him step by step.

                              (OEDIPUS enters the palace.)

520 Revealed at last, brother and father both
     to the children he embraces, to his mother
     son and husband both—he sowed the loins
     his father sowed, he spilled his father's blood!
     Go in and reflect on that, solve that.
525 And if you find I've lied
     from this day onward call the prophet blind.

                         (TIRESIAS and the boy exit to the side.)

     CHORUS.   Who—

178 *The Classical World*

---

9 Why is Oedipus so eager to know this?

10 What does Tiresias mean in line 499?

11 How is this image (line 519) reminiscent of the riddle of the Sphinx?

who is the man the voice of god denounces
resounding out of the rocky gorge of Delphi?
      The horror too dark to tell,
whose ruthless bloody hands have done the work?
His time has come to fly
      to outrace the stallions of the storm
               his feet a streak of speed—
Cased in armor, Apollo son of the Father
lunges on him, lightning-bolts afire!
And the grim unerring Furies
          closing for the kill.

                      Look,
the word of god has just come blazing
flashing off Parnassus' snowy heights!
      That man who left no trace—
after him, hunt him down with all our strength!
Now under bristling timber
      up through rocks and caves he stalks
               like the wild mountain bull—
cut off from men, each step an agony, frenzied, racing blind
but he cannot outrace the dread voices of Delphi
ringing out of the heart of Earth,
      the dark wings beating around him shrieking doom
              the doom that never dies, the terror—
The skilled prophet scans the birds and shatters me with terror!
I can't accept him, can't deny him, don't know what to say,
I'm lost, and the wings of dark foreboding beating—
I cannot see what's come, what's still to come . . .
and what could breed a blood feud between
      Laius' house and the son of Polybus?
I know of nothing, not in the past and not now,
no charge to bring against our king, no cause
to attack his fame that rings throughout Thebes—
      not without proof—not for the ghost of Laius,
      not to avenge a murder gone without a trace.
Zeus and Apollo know, they know, the great masters
      of all the dark and depth of human life.
But whether a mere man can know the truth,
whether a seer can fathom more than I—
there is no test, no certain proof
          though matching skill for skill
a man can outstrip a rival. No, not till I see
these charges proved will I side with his accusers.
We saw him then, when the she-hawk swept against him,
saw with our own eyes his skill, his brilliant triumph—
      there was the test—he was the joy of Thebes!
      Never will I convict my king, never in my heart.

***Now under . . . mountain
bull.*** The Chorus pictures
the unknown murderer
being hunted down in
the mountain wilderness.
Richmond Lattimore ob-
serves, "The Greek
wilderness is the moun-
tains . . . These were the
domain of emptiness, spirits, wild beasts, and tough
shepherds. . . ."

Terra-cotta copy of a
theatrical mask.
British Museum

12 Who is the she-
hawk?
The text of Oedipus the
King *continues on page
181.*

THINK AND DISCUSS

Understanding

1. What is the message from the oracle at Delphi?
2. Why didn't the Thebans pursue Laius's murderer?
3. How did Oedipus become king of Thebes?
4. Why does Tiresias keep mentioning Oedipus's parents?

Analyzing

5. Given the way this story will end, how does Oedipus's speech, lines 104–106, ironically **foreshadow** what will happen to him?
6. What is the principal request of the Theban people in the first chorus, lines 169–244?
7. Explain the **irony** in Oedipus's formal curse of Laius's killer, lines 270–288?
8. What sort of temptation lies in the praise Oedipus receives in lines 41–49?
9. Why doesn't Oedipus consider Tiresias's accusation in line 401?

Extending

10. Is Oedipus a boaster? Examine how he talks in lines 8, 154–156, and 249–251.
11. How is Tiresias the victim of the tension between free choice and fate?

APPLYING: Protagonist
See Handbook of Literary Terms, p. 964.

The **protagonist** is the chief or principal character in a story. If there is a principal opponent to the protagonist, that person is called the **antagonist.** In both cases the term is quite distinct from any positive or negative moral judgment. While the hero of a story must in some way compel our admiration, the protagonist only needs to be the central subject. Consequently, analysis of the protagonist's motivation, the justification for his or her words and actions, is frequently important, since until motivation has been determined the moral character of the protagonist may not be clear.

1. What is Oedipus's motivation for accusing Tiresias of plotting the death of Laius?

2. What does this suggest about Oedipus, the protagonist of the drama?

COMPOSITION
Analyzing a Speech

In lines 245–314 of the play, Oedipus delivers a long address to the Chorus, making the equivalent of a political speech. In a composition of no more than five paragraphs, analyze this speech as if you were the political reporter for a newspaper. In your first paragraph describe the circumstances and overall message of Oedipus's address. In succeeding paragraphs discuss what Oedipus accomplishes in each of the following sections of the speech: lines 245–269; 270–287; 288–306; 306–314.

Writing an Editorial

Assume you are a political columnist for a newspaper and write an editorial of no more than five paragraphs attacking or defending Oedipus for his actions in dealing with the plague in Thebes. See "Writing to Persuade an Audience" in the Writer's Handbook.

ENRICHMENT
Imagining a Greek Chorus

For modern readers, the most unusual dramatic convention in *Oedipus the King* is the Chorus. Try to imagine how this could have worked successfully. Begin with a discussion, in which you and your classmates go over the first speech by the Chorus (lines 169–244), analyzing what these citizens are saying, and the kinds of feelings which lie behind their words. Then imagine the physical movements and gestures which would fit with these ideas and feelings. Finally, consider the ways that a group of fifteen performers might move about the performing space using such gestures either in unison or in various combinations, in order to act out the meaning of the chorus' words.

(Enter CREON from the side.)

CREON. My fellow-citizens, I hear King Oedipus
  levels terrible charges at me. I had to come.
  I resent it deeply. If, in the present crisis,
  he thinks he suffers any abuse from me,
5 anything I've done or said that offers him
  the slightest injury, why, I've no desire
  to linger out this life, my reputation a shambles.
  The damage I'd face from such an accusation
  is nothing simple. No, there's nothing worse:
10 branded a traitor in the city, a traitor
  to all of you and my good friends.
LEADER.   True,
  but a slur might have been forced out of him,
  by anger perhaps, not any firm conviction.
CREON. The charge was made in public, wasn't it?
15 *I* put the prophet up to spreading lies?
LEADER. Such things were said . . .
  I don't know with what intent, if any.
CREON. Was his glance steady, his mind right
  when the charge was brought against me?
20 **LEADER.** I really couldn't say. I never look
  to judge the ones in power.   *(The doors open. OEDIPUS enters.)*
  Wait, here's Oedipus now.
OEDIPUS.   You—here? You have the gall
  to show your face before the palace gates?
  You, plotting to kill me, kill the king—
25 I see it all, the marauding thief himself
  scheming to steal my crown and power! Tell me,
  in god's name, what did you take me for,
  coward or fool, when you spun out your plot?
  Your treachery—you think I'd never detect it
30 creeping against me in the dark? Or sensing it,
  not defend myself? Aren't you the fool,
  you and your high adventure. Lacking numbers,
  powerful friends, out for the big game of empire—
  you need riches, armies to bring that quarry down!
35 **CREON.** Are you quite finished? It's your turn to listen
  for just as long as you've . . . instructed me.
  Hear me out, then judge me on the facts.

Terra-cotta copy of a
tragic mask representing
King Priam. c. 400 B.C.
Staatliche Museen,
Berlin

OEDIPUS. You've a wicked way with words, Creon,
    but I'll be slow to learn—from you.
40   I find you a menace, a great burden to me.
CREON. Just one thing, hear me out in this.
OEDIPUS.   Just one thing,
    don't tell me you're not the enemy, the traitor.
CREON. Look, if you think crude, mindless stubbornness
    such a gift, you've lost your sense of balance.
45 **OEDIPUS.** If you think you can abuse a kinsman,
    then escape the penalty, you're insane.
CREON. Fair enough, I grant you. But this injury
    you say I've done you, what is it?
OEDIPUS. Did you induce me, yes or no,
50   to send for that sanctimonious prophet?
CREON. I did. And I'd do the same again.
OEDIPUS. All right then, tell me, how long is it now
    since Laius . . .
CREON.   Laius—what did *he* do?
OEDIPUS.   Vanished,
    swept from sight, murdered in his tracks.
55 **CREON.** The count of the years would run you far back . . .
OEDIPUS. And that far back, was the prophet at his trade?
CREON. Skilled as he is today, and just as honored.
OEDIPUS. Did he ever refer to me then, at that time?
CREON.   No,
    never, at least, when I was in his presence.
60 **OEDIPUS.** But you did investigate the murder, didn't you?
CREON. We did our best, of course, discovered nothing.
OEDIPUS. But the great seer never accused me then—why not?
CREON. I don't know. And when I don't, *I* keep quiet.
OEDIPUS. You do know this, you'd tell it too—
65   if you had a shred of decency.
CREON.   What?
    If I know, I won't hold back.
OEDIPUS.   Simply this:
    if the two of you had never put heads together,
    we'd never have heard about *my* killing Laius.
CREON. If that's what he says . . . well, you know best.
70   But now I have a right to learn from you
    as you just learned from me.
OEDIPUS.   Learn your fill,
    you never will convict me of the murder.
CREON. Tell me, you're married to my sister, aren't you?
OEDIPUS. A genuine discovery—there's no denying that.
75 **CREON.** And you rule the land with her, with equal power?
OEDIPUS. She receives from me whatever she desires.
CREON. And I am the third, all of us are equals?

Fragment of a vase from
Tarentum showing an
actor holding a mask.
c. 340 B.C. Martin-von-
Wagner Museum, Würzburg

OEDIPUS. Yes, and it's there you show your stripes—
　　you betray a kinsman.

CREON. 　　　　　　　　Not at all.

80　Not if you see things calmly, rationally,
　　as I do. Look at it this way first:
　　who in his right mind would rather rule
　　and live in anxiety than sleep in peace?
　　Particularly if he enjoys the same authority.
85　Not I, I'm not the man to yearn for kingship,
　　not with a king's power in my hands. Who would?
　　No one with any sense of self-control.
　　Now, as it is, you offer me all I need,
　　not a fear in the world. But if I wore the crown . . .
90　there'd be many painful duties to perform,
　　hardly to my taste. How could kingship
　　please me more than influence, power
　　without a qualm? I'm not that deluded yet,
　　to reach for anything but privilege outright,
95　profit free and clear.
　　Now all men sing my praises, all salute me,
　　now all who request your favors curry mine.
　　I'm their best hope: success rests in me.
　　Why give up that, I ask you, and borrow trouble?
100　A man of sense, someone who sees things clearly
　　would never resort to treason.
　　No, I've no lust for conspiracy in me,
　　nor could I ever suffer one who does.
　　Do you want proof? Go to Delphi yourself,
105　examine the oracle and see if I've reported
　　the message word-for-word. This too:

| 13 | What is Creon's argument here? |

if you detect that I and the clairvoyant
have plotted anything in common, arrest me,
execute me. Not on the strength of one vote,
110 two in this case, mine as well as yours.
But don't convict me on sheer unverified surmise.
How wrong it is to take the good for bad,
purely at random, or take the bad for good.
But reject a friend, a kinsman? I would as soon
115 tear out the life within us, priceless life itself.
You'll learn this well, without fail, in time.
Time alone can bring the just man to light;
the criminal you can spot in one short day.
    LEADER.   Good advice,
    my lord, for anyone who wants to avoid disaster.
120 Those who jump to conclusions may be wrong.
    OEDIPUS. When my enemy moves against me quickly,
    plots in secret, I move quickly too, I must,
    I plot and pay him back. Relax my guard a moment,
    waiting his next move—he wins his objective,
125 I lose mine.
    CREON.   What do you want?
    You want me banished?
    OEDIPUS.   No, I want you dead.
    CREON. Just to show how ugly a grudge can . . .
    OEDIPUS.   So,
    still stubborn? you don't think I'm serious?
    CREON. I think you're insane.
    OEDIPUS.   Quite sane—in my behalf.
130 CREON. Not just as much in mine?
    OEDIPUS.   You—my mortal enemy?
    CREON. What if you're wholly wrong?
    OEDIPUS.   No matter—I must rule.
    CREON. Not if you rule unjustly.
    OEDIPUS.   Hear him, Thebes, my city!
    CREON. My city too, not yours alone!
    LEADER. Please, my lords.   *(Enter* JOCASTA *from the palace.)*
                  Look, Jocasta's coming,
135 and just in time too. With her help
you must put this fighting of yours to rest.
    JOCASTA. Have you no sense? Poor misguided men,
    such shouting—why this public outburst?
    Aren't you ashamed, with the land so sick,
140 to stir up private quarrels?   *(To* OEDIPUS.)
    Into the palace now. And Creon, you go home.
    Why make such a furor over nothing?
    CREON. My sister, it's dreadful . . . Oedipus, your husband,
    he's bent on a choice of punishments for me,

145 banishment from the fatherland or death.

OEDIPUS. Precisely. I caught him in the act, Jocasta,
plotting, about to stab me in the back.

CREON. Never—curse me, let me die and be damned
if I've done you any wrong you charge me with.

150 JOCASTA. Oh god, believe it, Oedipus,
honor the solemn oath he swears to heaven.
Do it for me, for the sake of all your people.

(The CHORUS *begins to chant.)*

CHORUS. Believe it, be sensible
give way, my king, I beg you!

155 OEDIPUS. What do you want from me, concessions?

CHORUS. Respect him—he's been no fool in the past
and now he's strong with the oath he swears to god.

OEDIPUS. You know what you're asking?

CHORUS.   I do.

OEDIPUS.   Then out with it!

CHORUS. The man's your friend, your kin, he's under oath—
160 don't cast him out, disgraced
branded with guilt on the strength of hearsay only.

OEDIPUS. Know full well, if that's what you want
you want me dead or banished from the land.

CHORUS.   Never—
no, by the blazing Sun, first god of the heavens!
165 Stripped of the gods, stripped of loved ones,
let me die by inches if that ever crossed my mind.
But the heart inside me sickens, dies as the land dies
and now on top of the old griefs you pile this,
your fury—both of you!

OEDIPUS.   Then let him go,
170 even if it does lead to my ruin, my death
or my disgrace, driven from Thebes for life.
It's you, not him I pity—your words move me.
He, wherever he goes, my hate goes with him.

CREON. Look at you, sullen in yielding, brutal in your rage—
175 you'll go too far. It's perfect justice:
natures like yours are hardest on themselves.

OEDIPUS. Then leave me alone—get out!

CREON.   I'm going.
You're wrong, so wrong. These men know I'm right.

(Exit to the side. The CHORUS *turns to* JOCASTA.*)*

CHORUS. Why do you hesitate, my lady
180   why not help him in?

JOCASTA. Tell me what's happened first.

CHORUS. Loose, ignorant talk started dark suspicions
and a sense of injustice cut deeply too.

JOCASTA. On both sides?

Ivory copy of
a tragic mask.
British Museum

CHORUS.   Oh yes.
JOCASTA.   What did they say?
185 CHORUS. Enough, please, enough! The land's so racked already
or so it seems to me . . .
End the trouble here, just where they left it.
OEDIPUS. You see what comes of your good intentions now?
And all because you tried to blunt my anger.
CHORUS.   My king,
190 I've said it once, I'll say it time and again—
I'd be insane, you know it,
senseless, ever to turn my back on you.
You who set our beloved land—storm-tossed, shattered—
straight on course. Now again, good helmsman,
195 steer us through the storm!
        (The CHORUS draws away, leaving OEDIPUS and JOCASTA side by side.)
JOCASTA.   For the love of god,
Oedipus, tell me too, what is it?
Why this rage? You're so unbending.
OEDIPUS. I will tell you. I respect you, Jocasta,
much more than these . . .   (Glancing at the CHORUS.)
200 Creon's to blame. Creon schemes against me.
JOCASTA. Tell me clearly, how did the quarrel start?
OEDIPUS. He says *I* murdered Laius—I am guilty.
JOCASTA. How does he know? Some secret knowledge
or simply hearsay?
OEDIPUS.   Oh, he sent his prophet in
205 to do his dirty work. You know Creon,
Creon keeps his own lips clean.
JOCASTA.   A prophet?
Well then, free yourself of every charge!
Listen to me and learn some peace of mind:
no skill in the world,
210 nothing human can penetrate the future.
Here is proof, quick and to the point.
An oracle came to Laius one fine day
(I won't say from Apollo himself
but his underlings, his priests) and it said
215 that doom would strike him down at the hands of a son,
our son, to be born of our own flesh and blood. But Laius,
so the report goes at least, was killed by strangers,
thieves, at a place where three roads meet . . . my son—
he wasn't three days old and the boy's father
220 fastened his ankles, had a henchman fling him away
on a barren, trackless mountain. There, you see?
Apollo brought neither thing to pass. My baby
no more murdered his father than Laius suffered—
his wildest fear—death at his own son's hands.

14 How should an actress playing Jocasta deliver lines 203–204?

₂₂₅ That's how the seers and their revelations
mapped out the future. Brush them from your mind.
Whatever the god needs and seeks
he'll bring to light himself, with ease.

OEDIPUS. Strange,
hearing you just now . . . my mind wandered,
₂₃₀ my thoughts racing back and forth.

JOCASTA. What do you mean? Why so anxious, startled?

OEDIPUS. I thought I heard you say that Laius
was cut down at a place where three roads meet.

JOCASTA. That was the story. It hasn't died out yet.

₂₃₅ **OEDIPUS.** Where did this thing happen? Be precise.

JOCASTA. A place called Phocis,° where two branching roads,
one from Daulia, one from Delphi,
come together—a crossroads.

OEDIPUS. When? How long ago?

₂₄₀ **JOCASTA.** The heralds no sooner reported Laius dead
than you appeared and they hailed you king of Thebes.

OEDIPUS. My god, my god—what have you planned to do to me?

JOCASTA. What, Oedipus? What haunts you so?

OEDIPUS. Not yet.
Laius—how did he look? Describe him.
₂₄₅ Had he reached his prime?

JOCASTA. He was swarthy,
and the gray had just begun to streak his temples,
and his build . . . wasn't far from yours.

OEDIPUS. Oh no no,
I think I've just called down a dreadful curse
upon myself—I simply didn't know!

₂₅₀ **JOCASTA.** What are you saying? I shudder to look at you.

OEDIPUS. I have a terrible fear the blind seer can see.
I'll know in a moment. One thing more—

JOCASTA. Anything,
afraid as I am—ask, I'll answer, all I can.

OEDIPUS. Did he go with a light or heavy escort,
₂₅₅ several men-at-arms, like a lord, a king?

JOCASTA. There were five in the party, a herald among them,
and a single wagon carrying Laius.

OEDIPUS. Ai—
now I can see it all, clear as day.
Who told you all this at the time, Jocasta?

₂₆₀ **JOCASTA.** A servant who reached home, the lone survivor.

OEDIPUS. So, could he still be in the palace—even now?

JOCASTA. No indeed. Soon as he returned from the scene
and saw you on the throne with Laius dead and gone,
he knelt and clutched my hand, pleading with me
₂₆₅ to send him into the hinterlands, to pasture,

---

15 What is Oedipus recalling in lines 228–230?

Phocis (fōs′əs), a district in central Greece, north of the Gulf of Corinth.

16 What has happened to Oedipus?

17 What can Oedipus see "clear as day" (line 258)?

far as possible, out of sight of Thebes.
I sent him away. Slave though he was,
he'd earned that favor—and much more.

    OEDIPUS. Can we bring him back, quickly?

270 JOCASTA. Easily. Why do you want him so?

    OEDIPUS.   I'm afraid,
Jocasta, I have said too much already.
That man—I've got to see him.

    JOCASTA.   Then he'll come.
But even I have a right, I'd like to think,
to know what's torturing you, my lord.

275 OEDIPUS. And so you shall—I can hold nothing back from you,
now I've reached this pitch of dark foreboding.
Who means more to me than you? Tell me,
whom would I turn toward but you
as I go through all this?

280   My father was Polybus, king of Corinth.°
My mother, a Dorian, Merope.° And I was held
the prince of the realm among the people there,
till something struck me out of nowhere,
something strange . . . worth remarking perhaps,

285   hardly worth the anxiety I gave it.
Some man at a banquet who had drunk too much
shouted out—he was far gone, mind you—
that I am not my father's son. Fighting words!
I barely restrained myself that day

290   but early the next I went to mother and father,
questioned them closely, and they were enraged
at the accusation and the fool who let it fly.
So as for my parents I was satisfied,
but still this thing kept gnawing at me,

295   the slander spread—I had to make my move. And so,
unknown to mother and father I set out for Delphi,
and the god Apollo spurned me, sent me away
denied the facts I came for,
but first he flashed before my eyes a future

300   great with pain, terror, disaster—I can hear him cry,
"You are fated to couple with your mother, you will bring
a breed of children into the light no man can bear to see—
you will kill your father, the one who gave you life!"
I heard all that and ran. I abandoned Corinth,

305   from that day on I gauged its landfall only
by the stars, running, always running
toward some place where I would never see
the shame of all those oracles come true.
And as I fled I reached that very spot

310   where the great king, you say, met his death.

Polybus (pol′ē bəs), *king of Corinth.* Corinth was located at the southern end of the Isthmus of Corinth, the narrow neck of land joining the Peloponnesus to the rest of Greece. *Merope* (mer′ō pē).

Now, Jocasta, I will tell you all.
Making my way toward this triple crossroad
I began to see a herald, then a brace of colts
drawing a wagon, and mounted on the bench . . . a man,
315 just as you've described him, coming face-to-face,
and the one in the lead and the old man himself
were about to thrust me off the road—brute force—
and the one shouldering me aside, the driver,
I strike him in anger!—and the old man, watching me
320 coming up along his wheels—he brings down
his prod, two prongs straight at my head!
I paid him back with interest!
Short work, by god—with one blow of the staff
in this right hand I knock him out of his high seat,
325 roll him out of the wagon, sprawling headlong—
I killed them all—every mother's son!
Oh, but if there is any blood-tie
between Laius and this stranger . . .
what man alive more miserable than I?
330 More hated by the gods? *I* am the man
no alien, no citizen welcomes to his house,
law forbids it—not a word to me in public,
driven out of every hearth and home.
And all these curses I—no one but I
335 brought down these piling curses on myself!
And you, his wife, I've touched your body with these,
the hands that killed your husband cover you with blood.
Wasn't I born for torment? Look me in the eyes!
I am abomination—heart and soul!
340 I must be exiled, and even in exile
never see my parents, never set foot
on native earth again. Else I'm doomed
to couple with my mother and cut my father down . . .
Polybus who reared me, gave me life. But why, why?
345 Wouldn't a man of judgment say—and wouldn't he be right—
some savage power has brought this down upon my head?
On no, not that, you pure and awesome gods,
never let me see that day! Let me slip
from the world of men, vanish without a trace
350 before I see myself stained with such corruption,
stained to the heart.
    LEADER. My lord, you fill our hearts with fear.
But at least until you question the witness,
do take hope.
    OEDIPUS.   Exactly. He is my last hope—
355 I'm waiting for the shepherd. He is crucial.
    JOCASTA. And once he appears, what then? Why so urgent?

18 | What trait do Oedipus and his father Laius share?

Terra-cotta statuette
of an actor.
British Museum

OEDIPUS. I'll tell you. If it turns out that his story
matches yours, I've escaped the worst.
JOCASTA. What did I say? What struck you so?
OEDIPUS.   You said *thieves*—
360 he told you a whole band of them murdered Laius.
So, if he still holds to the same number,
I cannot be the killer. One can't equal many.
But if he refers to one man, one alone,
clearly the scales come down on me:
365 I am guilty.
JOCASTA.   Impossible. Trust me,
I told you precisely what he said,
and he can't retract it now;
the whole city heard it, not just I.
And even if he should vary his first report
370 by one man more or less, still, my lord,
he could never make the murder of Laius
truly fit the prophecy. Apollo was explicit:
my son was doomed to kill my husband . . . my son,
poor defenseless thing, he never had a chance
375 to kill his father. They destroyed him first.
So much for prophecy. It's neither here nor there.
From this day on, I wouldn't look right or left.
OEDIPUS. True, true. Still, that shepherd,
someone fetch him—now!
380 **JOCASTA.** I'll send at once. But do let's go inside.
I'd never displease you, least of all in this.

(OEDIPUS *and* JOCASTA *enter the palace.*)

CHORUS. Destiny guide me always
Destiny find me filled with reverence
          pure in word and deed.
385 Great laws tower above us, reared on high
born for the brilliant vault of heaven—
          Olympian Sky their only father,
nothing mortal, no man gave them birth,
their memory deathless, never lost in sleep:
390 within them lives a mighty god, the god does not grow old.
Pride breeds the tyrant
violent pride, gorging, crammed to bursting
          with all that is overripe and rich with ruin—
clawing up to the heights, headlong pride
395 crashes down the abyss—sheer doom!
          No footing helps, all foothold lost and gone.
But the healthy strife that makes the city strong—
I pray that god will never end that wrestling:
god, my champion, I will never let you go.
400 But if any man comes striding, high and mighty

19 Contrast this speech by the Chorus (lines 382–425) with the speech on pages 178–179, lines 526–572.

in all he says and does,
no fear of justice, no reverence
for the temples of the gods—
   let a rough doom tear him down,
405 repay his pride, breakneck, ruinous pride!
If he cannot reap his profits fairly
   cannot restrain himself from outrage—
mad, laying hands on the holy things untouchable!
      Can such a man, so desperate, still boast
410   he can save his life from the flashing bolts of god?
        If all such violence goes with honor now
          why join the sacred dance?
Never again will I go reverent to Delphi,
   the inviolate heart of Earth
415 or Apollo's ancient oracle at Abae
or Olympia° of the fires—
   unless these prophecies all come true
for all mankind to point toward in wonder.
King of kings, if you deserve your titles
420   Zeus, remember, never forget!
You and your deathless, everlasting reign.
      They are dying, the old oracles sent to Laius,
      now our masters strike them off the rolls.
      Nowhere Apollo's golden glory now—
425   the gods, the gods go down.

(Enter JOCASTA *from the palace, carrying a suppliant's branch wound in wool.)*

JOCASTA. Lords of the realm, it occurred to me,
just now, to visit the temples of the gods,
so I have my branch in hand and incense too.
Oedipus is beside himself. Racked with anguish,
430 no longer a man of sense, he won't admit
the latest prophecies are hollow as the old—
he's at the mercy of every passing voice
if the voice tells of terror.
   I urge him gently, nothing seems to help,
435 so I turn to you, Apollo, you are nearest.

(Placing her branch on the altar, while an old herdsman enters from the side,
    not the one just summoned by the KING, *but an unexpected* MESSENGER
          from Corinth.)

I come with prayers and offerings . . . I beg you,
cleanse us, set us free of defilement!
Look at us, passengers in the grip of fear,
watching the pilot of the vessel go to pieces.
440 **MESSENGER** *(approaching* JOCASTA *and the* CHORUS*).*
Strangers, please, I wonder if you could lead us
to the palace of the king . . . I think it's Oedipus.
Better, the man himself—you know where he is?

Abae (ā'bē) . . . *Olympia.*
Abae was a city in Phocis,
site of a shrine to Apollo.
Olympia, a site in the
western Peloponnesus, was
the main sanctuary of Zeus
in Greece.

Detail of a marble
relief showing a
theatrical mask.
Museo Laterano, Rome

LEADER. This is his palace, stranger. He's inside.
But here is his queen, his wife and mother
445 of his children.
MESSENGER.   Blessings on you, noble queen,
queen of Oedipus crowned with all your family—
blessings on you always!
JOCASTA. And the same to you, stranger, you deserve it . . .
such a greeting. But what have you come for?
450 Have you brought us news?
MESSENGER.   Wonderful news—
for the house, my lady, for your husband too.
JOCASTA. Really, what? Who sent you?
MESSENGER.   Corinth.
I'll give you the message in a moment.
You'll be glad of it—how could you help it?—
455 though it costs a little sorrow in the bargain.
JOCASTA. What can it be, with such a double edge?
MESSENGER. The people there, they want to make your Oedipus
king of Corinth, so they're saying now.
JOCASTA. Why? Isn't old Polybus still in power?
460 MESSENGER. No more. Death has got him in the tomb.
JOCASTA. What are you saying? Polybus, dead?—dead?
MESSENGER.   If not,
if I'm not telling the truth, strike me dead too.
JOCASTA (to a servant). Quickly, go to your master, tell him this!
You prophecies of the gods, where are you now?
465 This is the man that Oedipus feared for years,
he fled him, not to kill him—and now he's dead,
quite by chance, a normal, natural death,
not murdered by his son.
OEDIPUS (emerging from the palace). Dearest,
what now? Why call me from the palace?
470 JOCASTA (bringing the MESSENGER closer). Listen to him, see for yourself
what all
those awful prophecies of god have come to.
OEDIPUS. And who is he? What can he have for me?
JOCASTA. He's from Corinth, he's come to tell you
your father is no more—Polybus—he's dead!
475 OEDIPUS (wheeling on the MESSENGER). What? Let me have it from your lips.
MESSENGER. Well, if that's what you want first, then here it is:
make no mistake. Polybus is dead and gone.
OEDIPUS. How—murder? sickness?—what? what killed him?
MESSENGER. A light tip of the scales can put old bones to rest.
480 OEDIPUS. Sickness then—poor man, it wore him down.
MESSENGER.   That,
and the long count of years he'd measured out.
OEDIPUS.   So!

192 *The Classical World*

Jocasta, why, why look to the Prophet's hearth,
the fires of the future? Why scan the birds
that scream above our heads? They winged me on
485 to the murder of my father, did they? That was my doom?
Well look, he's dead and buried, hidden under the earth,
and here I am in Thebes, I never put hand to sword—
unless some longing for me wasted him away,
then in a sense you'd say I caused his death.
490 But now, all those prophecies I feared—Polybus
packs them off to sleep with him in hell!°
They're nothing, worthless.

JOCASTA.   There.
Didn't I tell you from the start?

OEDIPUS. So you did. I was lost in fear.
495 **JOCASTA.** No more, sweep it from your mind forever.

OEDIPUS. But my mother's bed, surely I must fear—

JOCASTA.   Fear?
What should a man fear? It's all chance,
chance rules our lives. Not a man on earth
can see a day ahead, groping through the dark.
500 Better to live at random, best we can.
And as for this marriage with your mother—
have no fear. Many a man before you,
in his dreams, has shared his mother's bed.
Take such things for shadows, nothing at all—
505 Live, Oedipus,
as if there's no tomorrow!

OEDIPUS.   Brave words,
and you'd persuade me if mother weren't alive.
But mother lives, so for all your reassurances
I live in fear, I must.

JOCASTA.   But your father's death,
510 that, at least, is a great blessing, joy to the eyes!

OEDIPUS. Great, I know . . . but I fear *her*—she's still alive.

MESSENGER. Wait, who is this woman, makes you so afraid?

OEDIPUS. Merope, old man. The wife of Polybus.

MESSENGER. The queen? What's there to fear in her?
515 **OEDIPUS.** A dreadful prophecy, stranger, sent by the gods.

MESSENGER. Tell me, could you? Unless it's forbidden
other ears to hear.

OEDIPUS.   Not at all.
Apollo told me once—it is my fate—
I must make love with my own mother,
520 shed my father's blood with my own hands.
So for years I've given Corinth a wide berth,
and it's been my good fortune too. But still,
to see one's parents and look into their eyes

hell! Here only the world
of the dead is meant, not
a place of punishment for
the wicked.

Detail of a terra-cotta
relief showing actors.
National Museum, Naples

is the greatest joy I know.

MESSENGER.　　　　　You're afraid of that?

525　That kept you out of Corinth?

OEDIPUS.　　　　　My *father*, old man—
so I wouldn't kill my father.

MESSENGER.　　　　　So that's it.
Well then, seeing I came with such good will, my king,
why don't I rid you of that old worry now?

OEDIPUS. What a rich reward you'd have for that.

530　**MESSENGER.** What do you think I came for, majesty?
So you'd come home and I'd be better off.

OEDIPUS. Never, I will never go near my parents.

MESSENGER. My boy, it's clear, you don't know what you're doing.

OEDIPUS. What do you mean, old man? For god's sake, explain.

535　**MESSENGER.** If you ran from *them*, always dodging home . . .

OEDIPUS. Always, terrified Apollo's oracle might come true—

MESSENGER. And you'd be covered with guilt, from both your parents.

OEDIPUS. That's right, old man, that fear is always with me.

MESSENGER. Don't you know? You've really nothing to fear.

540　**OEDIPUS.** But why? If I'm their son—Merope, Polybus?

MESSENGER. Polybus was nothing to you, that's why, not in blood.

OEDIPUS. What are you saying—Polybus was not my father?

MESSENGER. No more than I am. He and I are equals.

OEDIPUS.　　　　　My father—
how can my father equal nothing? You're nothing to me!

545　**MESSENGER.** Neither was he, no more your father than I am.

OEDIPUS. Then why did he call me his son?

MESSENGER.　　　　　You were a gift,
years ago—know for a fact he took you
from my hands.

OEDIPUS.　　　No, from another's hands?
Then how could he love me so? He loved me, deeply . . .

550　**MESSENGER.** True, and his early years without a child
made him love you all the more.

OEDIPUS.　　　　　And you, did you . . .
buy me? find me by accident?

MESSENGER.　　　　　I stumbled on you,
down the woody flanks of Mount Cithaeron.

OEDIPUS.　　　　　So close,
what were you doing here, just passing through?

555　**MESSENGER.** Watching over my flocks, grazing them on the slopes.

OEDIPUS. A herdsman, were you? A vagabond, scraping for wages?

MESSENGER. Your savior too, my son, in your worst hour.

OEDIPUS.　　　　　Oh—
when you picked me up, was I in pain? What exactly?

MESSENGER. Your ankles . . . they tell the story. Look at them.

560　**OEDIPUS.** Why remind me of that, that old affliction?

20 Why is Oedipus so shocked by the messenger's revelation in line 542?

MESSENGER. Your ankles were pinned together; I set you free.

OEDIPUS. That dreadful mark—I've had it from the cradle.

MESSENGER. And you got your name° from that misfortune too,
    the name's still with you.

OEDIPUS.   Dear god, who did it?—
565   mother? father? Tell me.

MESSENGER.   I don't know.
    The one who gave you to me, he'd know more.

OEDIPUS. What? You took me from someone else?
    You didn't find me yourself?

MESSENGER.   No sir,
    another shepherd passed you on to me.

570 OEDIPUS. Who? Do you know? Describe him.

MESSENGER. He called himself a servant of . . .
    if I remember rightly—Laius.   (JOCASTA *turns sharply.*)

OEDIPUS. The king of the land who ruled here long ago?

MESSENGER. That's the one. That herdsman was *his* man.

575 OEDIPUS. Is he still alive? Can I see him?

MESSENGER. They'd know best, the people of these parts.
                (OEDIPUS *and the* MESSENGER *turn to the* CHORUS.)

OEDIPUS. Does anyone know that herdsman,
    the one he mentioned? Anyone seen him
    in the fields, in town? Out with it!
580   The time has come to reveal this once for all.

LEADER. I think he's the very shepherd you wanted to see,
    a moment ago. But the queen, Jocasta,
    she's the one to say.

OEDIPUS.   Jocasta,
    you remember the man we just sent for?
585   Is *that* the one he means?

JOCASTA.   That man . . .
    why ask? Old shepherd, talk, empty nonsense,
    don't give it another thought, don't even think—

OEDIPUS. What—give up now, with a clue like this?
    Fail to solve the mystery of my birth?
590   Not for all the world!

JOCASTA.   Stop—in the name of god,
    if you love your own life, call off this search!
    My suffering is enough.

OEDIPUS.   Courage!
    Even if my mother turns out to be a slave,
    and I a slave, three generations back,
595   *you* would not seem common.

JOCASTA.   Oh no,
    listen to me, I beg you, don't do this.

OEDIPUS. Listen to you? No more. I must know it all,
    see the truth at last.

your name. Oedipus
means "swollen foot."

JOCASTA. No, please—
for your sake—I want the best for you!

600 **OEDIPUS.** Your best is more than I can bear.

JOCASTA. You're doomed—
may you never fathom who you are!

OEDIPUS (*to a servant*). Hurry, fetch me the herdsman, now!
Leave her to glory in her royal birth.

JOCASTA. Aieeeeee—man of agony—
605 that is the only name I have for you,
that, no other—ever, ever, ever!

(*Flinging through the palace doors. A long, tense silence follows.*)

LEADER. Where's she gone, Oedipus?
Rushing off, such wild grief . . .
I'm afraid that from this silence
610 something monstrous may come bursting forth.

OEDIPUS. Let it burst! Whatever will, whatever must!
I must know my birth, no matter how common
it may be—must see my origins face-to-face.
She perhaps, she with her woman's pride
615 may well be mortified by my birth,
but I, I count myself the son of Chance,
the great goddess, giver of all good things—
I'll never see myself disgraced. She is my mother!
And the moons have marked me out, my blood-brothers,
620 one moon on the wane, the next moon great with power.
That is my blood, my nature—I will never betray it,
never fail to search and learn my birth!

CHORUS. Yes—if I am a true prophet
if I can grasp the truth,
625 by the boundless skies of Olympus,
at the full moon of tomorrow, Mount Cithaeron
you will know how Oedipus glories in you—
You, his birthplace, nurse, his mountain-mother!
And we will sing you, dancing out your praise—
630 you lift our monarch's heart!
Apollo, Apollo, god of the wild cry
may our dancing please you! Oedipus—
son, dear child, who bore you?
Who of the nymphs° who seem to live forever
635 mated with Pan,° the mountain-striding Father?
Who was your mother? who, some bride of Apollo
the god who loves the pastures spreading toward the sun?
Or was it Hermes,° king of the lightning ridges?
Or Dionysus, lord of frenzy, lord of the barren peaks—
640 did he seize you in his hands, dearest of all his lucky finds?—
found by the nymphs, their warm eyes dancing, gift
to the lord who loves them dancing out his joy!

21 | What does Oedipus think motivates Jocasta's desire to stop his search for his parentage?

Nymphs (nimfs), minor goddesses of nature, who lived in seas, rivers, fountains, springs, hills, and woods. Though very long-lived, they were not immortal like the Olympian gods, but perished with the natural things they inhabited.
Pan, god of woods and fields, patron of shepherds.
Hermes (hèr′mēz), the messenger of the gods.
The text of Oedipus the King *continues on page 200*).

196 *The Classical World*

THINK AND DISCUSS

Understanding

1. As Jocasta describes the death of Laius, which detail catches Oedipus's attention? Why?
2. What has happened to the one surviving witness to Laius's murder?
3. What is the good news that the messenger brings from Corinth?

Analyzing

4. Describe Creon's reply to the accusation that he plotted the death of Oedipus (lines 79–118).
5. Define the role that the Chorus plays in the argument between Oedipus and Creon.
6. In line 243 Jocasta asks Oedipus, "What haunts you so?" What do you guess he is thinking about?
7. Reexamine Oedipus's account of his boyhood (lines 275–326), and determine the extent to which he was free to act, and the limits where fate denied him any choice.
8. What does Jocasta mean when she says, "It's all chance,/chance rules our lives" (lines 497–498)? What is the other explanation that she rejects?

Extending

9. Creon says, "Time alone can bring the just man to light" (line 117). How does *Oedipus the King* illustrate what he says?
10. Point out how Jocasta's assertion that "nothing human can penetrate the future" (line 210) challenges Greek religious belief in oracles in Sophocles' day.

APPLYING: Inference H**Z**
See Handbook of Literary Terms, p. 954.

An **inference** is a reasonable conclusion about the behavior of a character or the meaning of an event drawn from hints or other limited information presented by an author. Works of literature, rather than explicitly stating everything, frequently expect readers to infer the meaning of a statement or an action.

1. What do you infer is going through Jocasta's mind when she rushes offstage in line 606?
2. What do you think she will do next? Note that the Chorus Leader is himself making an inference about her in lines 609–610.

COMPOSITION ◆━━

Writing About Drama

Jocasta enters making an effort to stop the quarrel between Oedipus and Creon (line 139) and she remains onstage for a considerable part of the play. During that period she discovers things about her life she never thought possible. Write a narrative essay for your classmates in which you chart the stages of discovery that Jocasta goes through, explaining what influences they have on the ideas and feelings of this tragic character. Using a scratch pad, skim over the scenes in which Jocasta appears, making notes about what she says, and what you infer her words tell us about her thoughts and feelings. When you have a useful list of significant statements, order them chronologically, and narrate them in your essay, always with an eye to what they tell us about Jocasta's growing knowledge about the truth. See "Writing About Drama" in the Writer's Handbook.

Analyzing Dramatic Irony

In the middle of *Oedipus the King* a messenger arrives from Corinth proclaiming "wonderful news" (line 450). His confidence turns out to be mistaken, and his news terrible. Sophocles achieves dramatic **irony** in the way he writes this entrance, since the audience already knows that the news Oedipus will get on this day will be anything but happy for him. Write a four-paragraph essay analyzing the rest of this scene in which you explain to your teacher some of the ways that Sophocles creates irony. Reread the scene, noting on a scratch sheet moments of speech and action that have ironic effect, such as Jocasta's remarks about divine prophecy, in line 464. See "Writing About Irony and Satire" in the Writer's Handbook.

Aristotle on Tragedy

The celebrated Greek scientist and philosopher Aristotle (384–322 B.C.) was born in Thrace, a region northwest of Greece, but came to Athens to study under Plato at the age of seventeen. He remained there for twenty years. With the death of the older philosopher, Aristotle began a career as a wandering scholar that took him to many city-states both on the Greek mainland and in Asia Minor. Between 342 and 340 B.C., he tutored the young Alexander of Macedon, who soon after set off to conquer Persia. Aristotle returned to Athens in 335 and opened his own school, called the Lyceum (lī-sē′əm), where he lectured on both scientific and philosophical subjects. His surviving works appear to be the notes and summaries that he prepared for these lectures, and so they lack the literary polish found in Plato's writings.

Aristotle's short book the *Poetics* is the earliest surviving Greek study of the art of literature and it has been the most influential book ever written about poetry and drama. Aristotle approaches his subject as a scientist might, classifying specific types of literature and investigating their essential characteristics. While he makes reference to epic and lyric poetry, those parts of the *Poetics* that have survived concentrate primarily on tragedy.

Aristotle begins with the most peculiar problem tragedy poses: why would audiences wish to observe the depiction of terrible events that ordinarily would horrify and repel them? His answer begins with a fundamental human trait:

> . . . the instinct of imitation is implanted in man from childhood, one difference between him and other animals being that he is the most imitative of living creatures; and through imitation he learns his earliest lessons; and no less universal is the pleasure felt in things imitated. We have evidence of this in the facts of experience. Objects which in themselves we view with pain, we delight to contemplate when reproduced with minute fidelity: such as the forms of the most ignoble animals and of dead bodies. The cause of this again is, that

to learn gives the liveliest pleasure, not only to philosophers but to men in general . . .

The pleasure Aristotle describes here arises in part from the fact that what we observe is not the real thing, but an imitation of it. Aristotle does not say the audience would take pleasure in a performance of a play in which an actor actually put out his eyes. We can take pleasure in *Oedipus the King* partly because it is only an imitation of an action. The source of our pleasure is that somehow we are learning something from that imitation. But what is it that tragedies imitate? Here is Aristotle's famous definition:

> Tragedy . . . is an imitation of an action that is serious, complete, and of a certain magnitude; in language embellished with each kind of artistic ornament . . . ; in the form of action, not of narrative; through pity and fear effecting the proper purgation of these emotions.

To understand this definition clearly, it will be necessary to consider its essential terms, and learn what Aristotle means by them. First, note that he defines the *form* of tragedy as "action not narrative," by which he means that plays do not have narrators, as epic poems do, but instead take the form of live movement on the stage. But Aristotle means by the earlier phrase "imitation of an action" not a specific motion or gesture but a series of events that connect together —a process or development over time—something which happens. In this sense the "action" of *Oedipus* is the process that reveals the **protagonist's** curse. Aristotle stresses this aspect of tragedy:

> . . . Tragedy is an imitation, not of men, but of an action and of life, and life consists in action . . . . Hence the incidents and the plot are the end of a tragedy . . .

The reason for this emphasis lies in what Aristotle goes on to argue:

Poetry, therefore, is a more philosophical and a higher thing than history: for poetry tends to express the universal, history the particular. By the universal I mean how a person of a certain type will on occasion speak or act, according to the law of probability or necessity; and it is this universality at which poetry aims . . .

The tragic poet writes about human experiences, "actions," that are universal, typical of what each person must face. The effective presentation of these actions is the playwright's specific end or purpose, and when it has been achieved the play will show to the audience a general truth about life.

Aristotle notes that the action must be *complete*. By this he means that the writer must consciously give that action a specific beginning, middle, and end. Good plays do not present a chaotic collection of unconnected events. Instead, they

. . . imitate one action and that a whole, the structural union of the parts being such that, if any one of them is displaced or removed, the whole will be disjointed and disturbed.

Further, the action must have a certain *magnitude* since trivial events will not compel our interest or exemplify the general truths of human experience that Tragedy seeks to present.

Aristotle's definition ends with one of the most discussed and debated statements in the history of literary criticism:

. . . through pity and fear [tragedies succeed in] effecting the proper purgation of these emotions.

The crucial Greek term used here is *catharsis* and it can mean either "purgation," "purification," or "clarification." Aristotle's sentence takes on very different significance depending on which meaning is used.

In Greek medicine *catharsis* described the process of purging sick persons of an illness or poison, thus healing them. If this is Aristotle's meaning here, then he is suggesting that when we go to see a tragedy, the play stirs up feelings of pity and fear, and somehow by the end those feelings have been expelled.

If *catharsis* means "purification," then a somewhat different process emerges. The play still evokes the emotions of pity and fear, but rather than expelling them, it transforms them from something dangerous to something helpful. Seeing human suffering within the framework and context of a work of art, our feelings become harmonious, serene, and tranquil. We have not lost our sympathy for the sufferings of the protagonist, but those sympathies have been purified by their context.

However, the third meaning of *catharsis* more closely links with Aristotle's ideas about imitation. If *catharsis* means "clarification," then Aristotle is arguing that tragedies present events which are pitiable or fearful, and in doing so they rid the audience of these strong feelings by helping them to see such events more clearly, and so to understand them better. This does not mean that what happens at the end of *Oedipus the King* is any less horrible; it does suggest that as we observe the end we understand something about human life more clearly than we did before, and we feel a pleasure in that discovery which rids us of the emotions of pity and fear. Perhaps Aristotle left this passage ambiguous intending to suggest all three meanings simultaneously.

What kind of actions evoke pity and fear? A virtuous man hurt merely shocks us, a villain punished satisfies our moral sense. But if the protagonist is

. . . a man who is not eminently good and just, yet whose misfortune is brought about not by vice or depravity, but by some error or frailty. . . ,

then the action of the play will evoke ". . . the true tragic pleasure." The "error" (in Greek *hamartia*) leads to misfortune, but it is not a serious moral fault—Oedipus's pride, for example, or his tendency to act too impulsively. This error or frailty is a weakness most people recognize in themselves. Because the protagonist's fault is so close to the audience, they respond readily to the emotional force conveyed by the tragic action.

(OEDIPUS *strains to see a figure coming from the distance. Attended by palace guards, an old* SHEPHERD *enters slowly, reluctant to approach the* KING.)

OEDIPUS. I never met the man, my friends . . . still,
if I had to guess, I'd say that's the shepherd,
the very one we've looked for all along.
Brothers in old age, two of a kind,

5   he and our guest here. At any rate
the ones who bring him in are my own men,
I recognize them. (*Turning to the* LEADER.) But you know more than I,
you should, you've seen the man before.

LEADER. I know him, definitely. One of Laius' men,

10   a trusty shepherd, if there ever was one.

OEDIPUS. You, I ask you first, stranger,
you from Corinth—is this the one you mean?

MESSENGER. You're looking at him. He's your man.

OEDIPUS (*to the* SHEPHERD). You, old man, come over here—

15   look at me. Answer all my questions.
Did you ever serve King Laius?

SHEPHERD.   So I did . . .
a slave, not bought on the block though,
born and reared in the palace.

OEDIPUS. Your duties, your kind of work?

20   SHEPHERD. Herding the flocks, the better part of my life.

OEDIPUS. Where, mostly? Where did you do your grazing?

SHEPHERD. Well, Cithaeron sometimes, or the foothills round about.

OEDIPUS. This man—you know him? ever see him there?

SHEPHERD (*confused, glancing from the* MESSENGER *to the* KING). Doing
what?—what man do you mean?

25   OEDIPUS (*pointing to the* MESSENGER). This one here—ever have dealings with
him?

SHEPHERD. Not so I could say, but give me a chance,
my memory's bad . . .

MESSENGER. No wonder he doesn't know me, master.
But let me refresh his memory for him.

30   I'm sure he recalls old times we had
on the slopes of Mount Cithaeron:
he and I, grazing our flocks, he with two
and I with one—we both struck up together,
three whole seasons, six months at a stretch

35   from spring to the rising of Arcturus° in the fall,
then with winter coming on I'd drive my herds

the rising of Arcturus (ärk-tür′əs). The reappearance of the great star Arcturus in the night sky each September was the sign to the ancient Greeks that summer was over: it was time to gather the grapes, drive the flocks to winter pasture, and beach the ships before the winter storms arrived.

to my own pens, and back he'd go with his
to Laius' folds. (*To the* SHEPHERD.) Now that's how it was,
wasn't it—yes or no?

SHEPHERD.   Yes, I suppose . . .

40 it's all so long ago.

MESSENGER.   Come, tell me,
you gave me a child back then, a boy, remember?
A little fellow to rear, my very own.

SHEPHERD. What? Why rake up that again?

MESSENGER. Look, here he is, my fine old friend—

45 the same man who was just a baby then.

SHEPHERD. Damn you, shut your mouth—quiet!

OEDIPUS. Don't lash out at him, old man—
you need lashing more than he does.

SHEPHERD.   Why,
master, majesty—what have I done wrong?

50 **OEDIPUS.** You won't answer his question about the boy.

SHEPHERD. He's talking nonsense, wasting his breath.

OEDIPUS. So, you won't talk willingly—
then you'll talk with pain.   (*The guards seize the* SHEPHERD.)

SHEPHERD. No, dear god, don't torture an old man!

55 **OEDIPUS.** Twist his arms back, quickly!

SHEPHERD.   God help us, why?—
what more do you need to know?

OEDIPUS. Did you give him that child? He's asking.

SHEPHERD. I did . . . I wish to god I'd died that day.

OEDIPUS. You've got your wish if you don't tell the truth.

60 **SHEPHERD.** The more I tell, the worse the death I'll die.

OEDIPUS. Our friend here wants to stretch things out, does he?
                    (*Motioning to his men for torture.*)

SHEPHERD. No, no, I gave it to him—I just said so.

OEDIPUS. Where did you get it? Your house? Someone else's?

SHEPHERD. It wasn't mine, no, I got it from . . . someone.

65 **OEDIPUS.** Which one of them?   (*Looking at the citizens.*)
                    Whose house?

SHEPHERD.   No—
god's sake, master, no more questions!

OEDIPUS. You're a dead man if I have to ask again.

SHEPHERD. Then—the child came from the house . . .
of Laius.

OEDIPUS. A slave? or born of his own blood?

SHEPHERD.   Oh no,

70 I'm right at the edge, the horrible truth—I've got to say it!

OEDIPUS. And I'm at the edge of hearing horrors, yes, but I must hear!

SHEPHERD. All right! His son, they said it was—his son!
But the one inside, your wife,
she'd tell it best.

75 **OEDIPUS**. My wife—
    she gave it to you?
  SHEPHERD. Yes, yes, my king.
  OEDIPUS. Why, what for?
  SHEPHERD. To kill it.
80 **OEDIPUS**. Her own child,
    how could she?
  SHEPHERD. She was afraid—
    frightening prophecies.
  OEDIPUS. What?
85 **SHEPHERD**. They said—
    he'd kill his parents.
  OEDIPUS. But you gave him to this old man—why?
  SHEPHERD. I pitied the little baby, master,
    hoped he'd take him off to his own country,
90   far away, but he saved him for this, this fate.
    If you are the man he says you are, believe me,
    you were born for pain.
  OEDIPUS.   O god—
    all come true, all burst to light!
    O light—now let me look my last on you!
95   I stand revealed at last—
    cursed in my birth, cursed in marriage,
    cursed in the lives I cut down with these hands!
      (*Rushing through the doors with a great cry. The Corinthian* MESSENGER,
                 the SHEPHERD *and attendants exit slowly to the side.*)
  CHORUS. O the generations of men
    the dying generations—adding the total
100   of all your lives I find they come to nothing . . .
          does there exist, is there a man on earth
    who seizes more joy than just a dream, a vision?
    And the vision no sooner dawns than dies
    blazing into oblivion.
105   You are my great example, you, your life,
    your destiny, Oedipus, man of misery—
    I count no man blest. You outranged all men!
          Bending your bow to the breaking-point
    you captured priceless glory, O dear god,
110   and the Sphinx came crashing down,
          the virgin, claws hooked
    like a bird of omen singing, shrieking death—
    like a fortress reared in the face of death
    you rose and saved our land.
115   From that day on we called you king
    we crowned you with honors, Oedipus, towering over all—
    mighty king of the seven gates of Thebes.
    But now to hear your story—is there a man more agonized?

Mosaic from Pompeii showing actors rehearsing for a play.
National Museum, Naples

More wed to pain and frenzy? Not a man on earth,
20   the joy of your life ground down to nothing
O Oedipus, name for the ages—
      one and the same wide harbor served you
                son and father both
son and father came to rest in the same bridal chamber.
25   How, how could the furrows your father plowed
bear you, your agony, harrowing on
in silence O so long? But now for all your power
Time, all-seeing Time has dragged you to the light,
judged your marriage monstrous from the start—
30   the son and the father tangling, both one—
O child of Laius, would to god
    I'd never seen you, never never!
      Now I weep like a man who wails the dead
and the dirge comes pouring forth with all my heart!

135   I tell you the truth, you gave me life
    my breath leapt up in you
    and now you bring down night upon my eyes.

                              (Enter a MESSENGER *from the palace.)*

    MESSENGER. Men of Thebes, always the first in honor,
    what horrors you will hear, what you will see,
140   what a heavy weight of sorrow you will shoulder . . .
    if you are true to your birth, if you still have
    some feeling for the royal house of Thebes.
    I tell you neither the waters of the Danube
    nor the Nile° can wash this palace clean.
145   Such things it hides, it soon will bring to light—
    terrible things, and none done blindly now,
    all done with a will. The pains
    we inflict upon ourselves hurt most of all.
    LEADER. God knows we have pains enough already.
150   What can you add to them?
    MESSENGER. The queen is dead.
    LEADER.   Poor lady—how?
    MESSENGER. By her own hand. But you are spared the worst,
    you never had to watch . . . I saw it all,
    and with all the memory that's in me
155   you will learn what that poor woman suffered.
    Once she'd broken in through the gates,
    dashing past us, frantic, whipped to fury,
    ripping her hair out with both hands—
    straight to her rooms she rushed, flinging herself
160   across the bridal-bed, doors slamming behind her—
    once inside, she wailed for Laius, dead so long,
    remembering how she bore his child long ago,
    the life that rose up to destroy him, leaving
    its mother to mother living creatures
165   with the very son she'd borne.
    Oh how she wept, mourning the marriage-bed
    where she let loose that double brood—monsters—
    husband by her husband, children by her child. And then—
    but how she died is more than I can say. Suddenly
170   Oedipus burst in, screaming, he stunned us so
    we couldn't watch her agony to the end,
    our eyes were fixed on him. Circling
    like a maddened beast, stalking, here, there,
    crying out to us—Give him a sword! His wife,
175   no wife, his mother, where can he find the mother earth
    that cropped two crops at once, himself and all his children?
    He was raging—one of the dark powers pointing the way,
    none of us mortals crowding around him, no,
    with a great shattering cry—someone, something leading him on—

the Nile. Sophocles' text actually mentions the Phasis, a river that, like the Danube, flows into the Black Sea; but the translator substituted the name of a more familiar river.

22 To whom does the messenger attribute the prompting of Oedipus's behavior here?

204   *The Classical World*

he hurled at the twin doors and bending the bolts back
out of their sockets, crashed through the chamber.
And there we saw the woman hanging by the neck,
cradled high in a woven noose, spinning,
swinging back and forth. And when he saw her,
giving a low, wrenching sob that broke our hearts,
slipping the halter from her throat, he eased her down,
in a slow embrace he laid her down, poor thing . . .
then, what came next, what horror we beheld!
He rips off her brooches, the long gold pins
holding her robes—and lifting them high,
looking straight up into the point,
he digs them down the sockets of his eyes, crying, "You,
you'll see no more the pain I suffered, all the pain I caused!
Too long you looked on the ones you never should have seen,
blind to the ones you longed to see, to know! Blind
from this hour on! Blind in the darkness—blind!"
His voice like a dirge, rising, over and over
raising the pins, raking them down his eyes,
And at each stroke blood spurts from the roots,
splashing his beard, a swirl of it, nerves and clots—
black hail of blood pulsing, gushing down.
These are the griefs that burst upon them both,
coupling man and woman. The joy they had so lately,
the fortune of their old ancestral house
was deep joy indeed. Now, in this one day,
wailing, madness and doom, death, disgrace,
all the griefs in the world that you can name,
all are theirs forever.

LEADER.   Oh poor man, the misery—
has he any rest from pain now?   (*A voice within, in torment.*)
MESSENGER.   He's shouting,
"Loose the bolts, someone, show me to all of Thebes!
My father's murderer, my mother's—"
No, I can't repeat it, it's unholy.
Now he'll tear himself from his native earth,
not linger, curse the house with his own curse.
But he needs strength, and a guide to lead him on.
This is sickness more than he can bear.   (*The palace doors open.*)
          Look,
he'll show you himself. The great doors are opening—
you are about to see a sight, a horror
even his mortal enemy would pity.

          (*Enter* OEDIPUS, *blinded, led by a boy. He stands at the palace steps,
          as if surveying his people once again.*)

CHORUS.   O the terror—
the suffering, for all the world to see,

23 Note that the description of Oedipus in the stage direction here—"led by a boy"—echoes that of the earlier description of Tiresias. (See page 174.)

Sophocles 205

the worst terror that ever met my eyes.
What madness swept over you? What god,
what dark power leapt beyond all bounds,
beyond belief, to crush your wretched life?—
225   godforsaken, cursed by the gods!
I pity you but I can't bear to look.
I've much to ask, so much to learn,
so much fascinates my eyes,
but you . . . I shudder at the sight.

OEDIPUS.   Oh, Ohhh—
230   the agony! I am agony—
where am I going? where on earth?
            where does all this agony hurl me?
where's my voice?—
            winging, swept away on a dark tide—
235   My destiny, my dark power, what a leap you made!

CHORUS. To the depths of terror, too dark to hear, to see.

OEDIPUS. Dark, horror of darkness
my darkness, drowning, swirling around me
crashing wave on wave—unspeakable, irresistible
240   headwind, fatal harbor! Oh again,
the misery, all at once, over and over
the stabbing daggers, stab of memory
raking me insane.

CHORUS.   No wonder you suffer
twice over, the pain of your wounds,
245   the lasting grief of pain.

OEDIPUS.   Dear friend, still here?
Standing by me, still with a care for me,
the blind man? Such compassion,
            loyal to the last. Oh it's you,
I know you're here, dark as it is
250   I'd know you anywhere, your voice—
it's yours, clearly yours.

CHORUS.   Dreadful, what you've done . . .
how could you bear it, gouging out your eyes?
What superhuman power drove you on?

OEDIPUS. Apollo, friends, Apollo—
255   he ordained my agonies—these, my pains on pains!
But the hand that struck my eyes was mine,
mine alone—no one else—
            I did it all myself!
What good were eyes to me?
260   Nothing I could see could bring me joy.

CHORUS. No, no, exactly as you say.

OEDIPUS.   What can I ever see?
What love, what call of the heart

206   *The Classical World*

can touch my ears with joy? Nothing, friends.
        Take me away, far, far from Thebes,
        quickly, cast me away, my friends—
    this great murderous ruin, this man cursed to heaven,
        the man the deathless gods hate most of all!
CHORUS. Pitiful, you suffer so, you understand so much . . .
    I wish you'd never known.
OEDIPUS.   Die, die—
    whoever he was that day in the wilds
who cut my ankles free of the ruthless pins,
    he pulled me clear of death, he saved my life
    for this, this kindness—
                Curse him, kill him!
    If I'd died then, I'd never have dragged myself,
    my loved ones through such hell.
CHORUS. Oh if only . . . would to god.
OEDIPUS.   I'd never have come to this,
    my father's murderer—never been branded
    mother's husband, all men see me now! Now,
        loathed by the gods, son of the mother I defiled
        coupling in my father's bed, spawning lives in the loins
    that spawned my wretched life. What grief can crown this grief?
            It's mine alone, my destiny—I am Oedipus!
CHORUS. How can I say you've chosen for the best?
    Better to die than be alive and blind.
OEDIPUS. What I did was best—don't lecture me,
    no more advice. I, with *my* eyes,
    how could I look my father in the eyes
    when I go down to death? Or mother, so abused . . .
    I've done such things to the two of them,
    crimes too huge for hanging. Worse yet,
    the sight of my children, born as they were born,
    how could I long to look into their eyes?
    No, not with these eyes of mine, never.
    Not this city either, her high towers,
    the sacred glittering images of her gods—
    I am misery! I, her best son, reared
    as no other son of Thebes was ever reared,
    I've stripped myself, I gave the command myself.
    All men must cast away the great blasphemer,
    the curse now brought to light by the gods,
    the son of Laius—I, my father's son!
    Now I've exposed my guilt, horrendous guilt,
    could I train a level glance on you, my countrymen?
    Impossible! No, if I could just block off my ears,
    the springs of hearing, I would stop at nothing—
    I'd wall up my loathsome body like a prison,

Ivory statuette of a
tragic actor.
Petit Palais, Paris

blind to the sound of life, not just the sight.
Oblivion—what a blessing . . .

310 for the mind to dwell a world away from pain.
O Cithaeron, why did you give me shelter?
Why didn't you take me, crush my life out on the spot?
I'd never have revealed my birth to all mankind.
O Polybus, Corinth, the old house of my fathers,

315 so I believed—what a handsome prince you raised—
under the skin, what sickness to the core.
Look at me! Born of outrage, outrage to the core.
O triple roads—it all comes back, the secret,
dark ravine, and the oaks closing in

320 where the three roads join . . .
You drank my father's blood, my own blood
spilled by my own hands—you still remember me?
What things you saw me do? Then I came here
and did them all once more! Marriages! O marriage,

325 you gave me birth, and once you brought me into the world
you brought my sperm rising back, springing to light
fathers, brothers, sons—one deadly breed—
brides, wives, mothers. The blackest things
a man can do, I have done them all! No more—

330 it's wrong to name what's wrong to do. Quickly,
for the love of god, hide me somewhere,
kill me, hurl me into the sea
where you can never look on me again.

(Beckoning to the CHORUS as they shrink away.)

Closer,

it's all right. Touch the man of sorrow.

335 Do. Don't be afraid. My troubles are mine
and I am the only man alive who can sustain them.

(Enter CREON from the palace, attended by palace guards.)

LEADER. Put your requests to Creon. Here he is,
just when we need him. He'll have a plan, he'll act.
Now that he's the sole defense of the country

340 in your place.

OEDIPUS.   Oh no, what can I say to him?
How can I ever hope to win his trust?
I wronged him so, just now, in every way.
You must see that—I was so wrong, so wrong.

CREON. I haven't come to mock you, Oedipus,

345 or to criticize your former failings.   (Turning to the guards.)

You there,

have you lost all respect for human feeling?
At least revere the Sun, the holy fire
that keeps us all alive. Never expose a thing
of guilt and holy dread so great it appalls

the earth, the rain from heaven, the light of day!
Get him into the halls—quickly as you can.
Piety demands no less. Kindred alone
should see a kinsman's shame. This is obscene.

OEDIPUS. Please, in god's name . . . you wipe my fears away,
coming so generously to me, the worst of men.
Do one thing more, for your sake, not mine.

CREON. What do you want? Why so insistent?

OEDIPUS. Drive me out of the land at once, far from sight,
where I can never hear a human voice.

CREON. I'd have done that already, I promise you.
First I wanted the god to clarify my duties.

OEDIPUS. The god? His command was clear, every word:
death for the father-killer, the curse—
he said destroy me!

CREON. So he did. Still, in such a crisis
it's better to ask precisely what to do.

OEDIPUS. You'd ask the oracle about a man like me?

CREON. By all means. And this time, I assume,
even you will obey the god's decrees.

OEDIPUS.   I will.
I will. And you, I command you—I beg you . . .
the woman inside, bury her as you see fit.
It's the only decent thing,
to give your own the last rites. As for me,
never condemn the city of my fathers
to house my body, not while I'm alive, no,
let me live on the mountains, on Cithaeron,
my favorite haunt, I have made it famous.
Mother and father marked out that rock
to be my everlasting tomb—buried alive.
Let me die there, where they tried to kill me.
Oh but this I know: no sickness can destroy me,
nothing can. I would never have been saved
from death—I have been saved
for something great and terrible, something strange.
Well let my destiny come and take me on its way!
About my children, Creon, the boys at least,
don't burden yourself. They're men;
wherever they go, they'll find the means to live.
But my two daughters, my poor helpless girls,
clustering at our table, never without me
hovering near them . . . whatever I touched,
they always had their share. Take care of them,
I beg you. Wait, better—permit me, would you?
Just to touch them with my hands and take
our fill of tears. Please . . . my king.

Grant it, with all your noble heart.
If I could hold them, just once, I'd think
I had them with me, like the early days
when I could see their eyes.

       (ANTIGONE and ISMENE, two small children, are led in from the palace
               by a nurse.)

                   What's that?

400 O god! Do I really hear you sobbing?—
my two children. Creon, you've pitied me?
Sent me my darling girls, my own flesh and blood!
Am I right?

CREON.   Yes, it's my doing.
I know the joy they gave you all these years,
405 the joy you must feel now.

OEDIPUS.   Bless you, Creon!
May god watch over you for this kindness,
better than he ever guarded me. Children, where are you?
Here, come quickly—

    (Groping for ANTIGONE and ISMENE, who approach their father cautiously,
                  then embrace him.)

             Come to these hands of mine,
your brother's hands, your own father's hands
410 that served his once bright eyes so well—
that made them blind. Seeing nothing, children,
knowing nothing, I became your father,
I fathered you in the soil that gave me life.
How I weep for you—I cannot see you now . . .
415 just thinking of all your days to come, the bitterness,
the life that rough mankind will thrust upon you.
Where are the public gatherings you can join,
the banquets of the clans? Home you'll come,
in tears, cut off from the sight of it all,
420 the brilliant rites unfinished.
And when you reach perfection, ripe for marriage,
who will he be, my dear ones? Risking all
to shoulder the curse that weighs down my parents,
yes and you too—that wounds us all together.
425 What more misery could you want?
Your father killed his father, sowed his mother,
one, one and the selfsame womb sprang you—
he cropped the very roots of his existence.
Such disgrace, and you must bear it all!
430 Who will marry you then? Not a man on earth.
Your doom is clear: you'll wither away to nothing,
single, without a child.   *(Turning to CREON.)*
           Oh Creon,
you are the only father they have now . . .

we who brought them into the world
35 are gone, both gone at a stroke—
Don't let them go begging, abandoned,
women without men. Your own flesh and blood!
Never bring them down to the level of my pains.
Pity them. Look at them, so young, so vulnerable,
40 shorn of everything—you're their only hope.
Promise me, noble Creon, touch my hand.

(*Reaching toward* CREON, *who draws back.*)

You, little ones, if you were old enough
to understand, there is much I'd tell you.
Now, as it is, I'd have you say a prayer.
45 Pray for life, my children,
live where you are free to grow and season.
Pray god you find a better life than mine,
the father who begot you.

CREON.   Enough.
You've wept enough. Into the palace now.
50 **OEDIPUS.** I must, but I find it very hard.
CREON. Time is the great healer, you will see.
OEDIPUS. I am going—you know on what condition?
CREON. Tell me. I'm listening.
OEDIPUS. Drive me out of Thebes, in exile.
55 **CREON.** Not I. Only the gods can give you that.
OEDIPUS. Surely the gods hate me so much—
CREON. You'll get your wish at once.
OEDIPUS.   You consent?
CREON. I try to say what I mean; it's my habit.
OEDIPUS. Then take me away. It's time.
60 **CREON.** Come along, let go of the children.
OEDIPUS.   No—
don't take them away from me, not now! No no no!
(*Clutching his daughters as the guards wrench them loose and take them through
the palace doors.*)

CREON. Still the king, the master of all things?
No more: here your power ends.
None of your power follows you through life.
(*Exit* OEDIPUS *and* CREON *to the palace. The* CHORUS *comes forward to
address the audience directly.*)
65 **CHORUS.** People of Thebes, my countrymen, look on Oedipus.
He solved the famous riddle with his brilliance,
he rose to power, a man beyond all power.
Who could behold his greatness without envy?
Now what a black sea of terror has overwhelmed him.
70 Now as we keep our watch and wait the final day,
count no man happy till he dies, free of pain at last. (*Exit in procession.*)
c. 420 B.C.

Terra-cotta statuette
from Tanagra of
Melpomene (mel pom′ə nē),
the Muse of Tragedy,
holding a tragic mask.
c. 300 B.C. Staatliche
Museen, Berlin

THINK AND DISCUSS
Understanding
1. Why does the Shepherd wish he had died long ago?
2. How does Jocasta die?
3. What punishment does Oedipus receive from the community?

Analyzing
4. Questioning the Shepherd, Oedipus cries out, ". . . I'm at the edge of hearing horrors, yes, but I must hear!" (line 71) How does this exemplify a crucial aspect of Oedipus's character?
5. Why does Oedipus put out his eyes?
6. In what ways does Creon differ from Oedipus as ruler of Thebes?

Extending
7. The Chorus, in its last long statement, summarizes the meaning of Oedipus's life. Is their evaluation fair?
8. As the play ends, has justice been achieved? Is Thebes purged?

APPLYING: Plot H⫶T
See Handbook of Literary Terms, p. 962.

The sequence of events or incidents consciously selected and organized by a writer which, through an integration of forces, moves from a conflict to a resolution is the **plot** in a work of literature.

Conflict, the struggle of contending forces, gives energy and forward motion to a plot. Its *resolution* provides the sense that the plot has come to its conclusion.

In large scale works such as *Oedipus the King*, the plot may be subdivided into: (**1**) *rising action*, as the complication of events begins and the contending forces appear; (**2**) *climax* or *crisis*, in which the conflict reaches its most extreme point and one of the contending forces gets the upper hand—the *turning point* in a struggle; (**3**) *falling action* as the complications begin to unravel; and (**4**) *denouement*, which explains puzzles and mysteries and works out the conclusions to the conflict, frequently through rewards and

punishments. In tragedy, this is also called the *catastrophe*.

1. Describe the fundamental conflict in *Oedipus the King*.
2. Where would you locate the crisis of this play?
3. List the principal features of its denouement.

THINKING SKILLS
Evaluating
To evaluate is to make a judgment based on some sort of standard.

1. Evaluate the characters who speak in *Oedipus the King*, using as a standard the extent to which each contributes to the discovery of the guilty one who has brought a curse upon Thebes.
2. Reevaluate the same people, this time using a different standard: how concerned is each person about Oedipus's personal feelings?

COMPOSITION ◀━◉
Writing a Narrative
In talking about his future, Oedipus makes vague reference to "something great and terrible, something strange" (line 384) that is yet to happen to him. Write a short story to be read by your classmates that will fill in this blank by inventing some kind of extraordinary end for Oedipus's life. As you plan the story, be sure that it includes at least one scene with dialogue.

Writing About Characters
As the evidence against him mounts, Oedipus begs the gods to let him slip from the world rather than see himself stained with corruption. Write an essay in which you evaluate Oedipus's guilt and analyze the degree to which he is indeed stained with corruption. Organize your essay in the form of a list of Oedipus's faults, starting with the least significant and ending with the worst. Devote a paragraph to each significant guilty act, and in every case analyze the degree of Oedipus's culpability. In your last paragraph summarize your conclusions about his moral character.

BIOGRAPHY

Thucydides

c. 455–c. 399 B.C.

Thucydides was the son of an aristocratic family that owned gold mines. As a young man he came to Athens, where he became an admirer of the political leader Pericles (c. 490–429 B.C.). When the longstanding and bitter rivalry between Sparta and Athens broke out into the Second Peloponnesian War in 431, Thucydides tells us that he began writing a history of it, "in the belief that it was going to be a great war and more worth writing about than any of those which had taken place in the past." In these words one can sense a deliberate attempt to surpass the most celebrated historian of his day, Herodotus, who had written about the Persian Wars. Thucydides from the start was a highly self-conscious writer, concerned to improve the historian's methods. He notes acidly the dangerous inclination to "accept all stories of ancient times in an uncritical way. . ." and he stresses his own efforts to acquire accurate and unbiased accounts. In the process Thucydides laid the foundation for modern, scientific history.

He had a lot of time to do so. As the war got underway Thucydides was himself given command of a small squadron of ships, and sent to protect the northern Athenian colony of Amphipolis from Spartan attack, but he arrived too late and the city was lost (424 B.C.). The Athenian assembly condemned him, and he went into exile. For the next twenty years Thucydides observed the war at a distance, gathering information, recording first-hand accounts from other people. Only when the war ended with Athens's defeat in 404 was he permitted back into the city he loved.

However, before his failure, in the early days of the war, Thucydides was in Athens. And so he heard many of the celebrated speeches delivered by the Athenian leaders as they developed the city's war policies. Thucydides decided to use accounts of these speeches as a way to show his reader the attitudes and expectations that existed on both sides as the war began.

Thucydides' friend Pericles was the leading Athenian politician during the early days of the war. Pericles' elected position was as one of Athens's ten generals, or *strategoi*. But because of his skill as an orator Pericles had far more power than his official title would suggest, and frequently he acted as the leader of the Athenian people. Thucydides probably heard Pericles deliver the annual speech honoring Athenian war dead in the winter of 430, but as he confesses on the pages of his *History,* "I have found it difficult to remember the precise words used in the speeches which I listened to myself . . . so my method has been, while keeping as closely as possible to the general sense of the words that were actually used, to make the speakers say what, in my opinion, was called for by each situation." In the following selection, Thucydides—through Pericles—defines two major **themes** of the *History:* the characteristics that have made Athens such a strong city-state economically and militarily, and the ideals that the city represents. In stating what the Athenians were fighting for, Pericles' funeral oration has become one of the central examples of Hellenic culture articulating its own priorities and values.

Thucydides 213

from the History of the Peloponnesian War

Thucydides   *translated by* **Rex Warner**

In the same winter the Athenians, following their annual custom, gave a public funeral for those who had been the first to die in the war. These funerals are held in the following way: two days before the ceremony the bones of the fallen are brought and put in a tent which has been erected, and people make whatever offerings they wish to their own dead. Then there is a funeral procession in which coffins of cypress wood are carried on wagons. There is one coffin for each tribe, which contains the bones of members of that tribe. One empty bier is decorated and carried in the procession: this is for the missing, whose bodies could not be recovered. Everyone who wishes to, both citizens and foreigners, can join in the procession, and the women who are related to the dead are there to make their laments at the tomb. The bones are laid in the public burial-place, which is in the most beautiful quarter outside the city walls. Here the Athenians always bury those who have fallen in war. The only exception is those who died at Marathon,[1] who, because their achievement was considered absolutely outstanding, were buried on the battlefield itself.

When the bones have been laid in the earth, a man chosen by the city for his intellectual gifts and for his general reputation makes an appropriate speech in praise of the dead, and after the speech all depart. This is the procedure at these burials, and all through the war, when the time came to do so, the Athenians followed this ancient custom. Now, at the burial of those who were the first to fall in the war Pericles, the son of Xanthippus, was chosen to make the speech. When the moment arrived, he came forward from the tomb and, standing on a high platform, so that he might be heard by as many people as possible in the crowd, he spoke as follows:

"Many of those who have spoken here in the past have praised the institution of this speech at the close of our ceremony. It seemed to them a mark of honor to our soldiers who have fallen in war that a speech should be made over them. I do not agree. These men have shown themselves valiant in action, and it would be enough, I think, for their glories to be proclaimed in action, as you have just seen it done at this funeral organized by the state. Our belief in the courage and manliness of so many should not be hazarded on the goodness or badness of one man's speech. Then it is not easy to speak with a proper sense of balance, when a man's listeners find it difficult to believe in the truth of what one is saying. The man who knows the facts and loves the dead may well think that an oration tells less than what he knows and what he would like to hear: others who do not know so much may feel envy for the dead, and think the orator overpraises them, when he speaks of exploits that are beyond their own capacities. Praise of other people is tolerable only up to a certain point, the point where one still believes that one could do oneself some of the things one is hearing about. Once you get beyond this point, you will find people becoming jealous and incredulous. However, the fact is that this institution was set up and approved by our forefathers, and it is my duty to follow the tradition and do my best to meet the wishes and the expectations of every one of you.

"I shall begin by speaking about our ancestors, since it is only right and proper on such an occasion to pay them the honor of recalling what they

---

1. **Marathon**, scene of a famous Athenian victory over the Persians in 490 B.C.

did. In this land of ours there have always been the same people living from generation to generation up till now, and they, by their courage and their virtues, have handed it on to us, a free country. They certainly deserve our praise. Even more so do our fathers deserve it. For to the inheritance they had received they added all the empire we have now, and it was not without blood and toil that they handed it down to us of the present generation. And then we ourselves, assembled here today, who are mostly in the prime of life, have, in most directions, added to the power of our empire and have organized our State in such a way that it is perfectly well able to look after itself both in peace and in war.

"I have no wish to make a long speech on subjects familiar to you all: so I shall say nothing about the warlike deeds by which we acquired our power or the battles in which we or our fathers gallantly resisted our enemies, Greek or foreign. What I want to do is, in the first place, to discuss the spirit in which we faced our trials and also our constitution and the way of life which has made us great. After that I shall speak in praise of the dead, believing that this kind of speech is not inappropriate to the present occasion, and that this whole assembly, of citizens and foreigners, may listen to it with advantage.

"Let me say that our system of government does not copy the institutions of our neighbors. It is more the case of our being a model to others, than of our imitating anyone else. Our constitution is called a democracy because power is in the hands not of a minority but of the whole people. When it is a question of settling private disputes, everyone is equal before the law; when it is a question of putting one person before another in positions of public responsibility, what counts is not membership of a particular class, but the actual ability which the man possesses. No one, so long as he has it in him to be of service to the state, is kept in political obscurity because of poverty. And, just as our political life is free and open, so is our day-to-day life in our relations with each other. We do not get into a state with our next-door neighbor if he enjoys himself in his own way, nor do we give

Roman copy of a marble bust of Pericles by Cresilas (fl. c. 450–430 B.C.). Cresilas's portrait follows the classical tradition of idealizing the features of its subject. Vatican Museums

him the kind of black looks which, though they do no real harm, still do hurt people's feelings. We are free and tolerant in our private lives; but in public affairs we keep to the law. This is because it commands our deep respect.

"We give our obedience to those whom we put in positions of authority, and we obey the laws themselves, especially those which are for the protection of the oppressed, and those unwritten laws which it is an acknowledged shame to break.

"And here is another point. When our work is over, we are in a position to enjoy all kinds of recreation for our spirits. There are various kinds of contests and sacrifices regularly throughout the year; in our own homes we find a beauty and a good taste which delight us every day and which drive away our cares. Then the greatness of our city brings it about that all the good things from all over the world flow in to us, so that to us it seems just as natural to enjoy foreign goods as our own local products.

"Then there is a great difference between us and our opponents, in our attitude toward military security. Here are some examples: Our city is open to the world, and we have no periodical deportations in order to prevent people observing or finding out secrets which might be of military advantage to the enemy. This is because we rely, not on secret weapons, but on our real courage and loyalty. There is a difference, too, in our educational systems. The Spartans, from their earliest boyhood, are submitted to the most laborious training in courage; we pass our lives without all these restrictions, and yet are just as ready to face the same dangers as they are. Here is a proof of this: When the Spartans invade our land, they do not come by themselves, but bring all their allies with them; whereas we, when we launch an attack abroad, do the job by ourselves, and, though fighting on foreign soil, do not often fail to defeat opponents who are fighting for their own hearths and homes. As a matter of fact none of our enemies has ever yet been confronted with our total strength, because we have to divide our attention between our navy and the many missions on which our troops are sent on land. Yet, if our enemies engage a detachment of our forces and defeat it, they give themselves credit for having thrown back our entire army; or, if they lose, they claim that they were beaten by us in full strength. There are certain advantages, I think, in our way of meeting danger voluntarily, with an easy mind, instead of with a laborious training, with natural rather than with state-induced courage. We do not have to spend our time practicing to meet sufferings which are still in the future; and when they are

actually upon us we show ourselves just as brave as these others who are always in strict training. This is one point in which, I think, our city deserves to be admired. There are also others:

"Our love of what is beautiful does not lead to extravagance; our love of the things of the mind does not make us soft. We regard wealth as something to be properly used, rather than as something to boast about. As for poverty, no one need be ashamed to admit it: the real shame is in not taking practical measures to escape from it. Here each individual is interested not only in his own affairs but in the affairs of the state as well: even those who are mostly occupied with their own business are extremely well-informed on general politics—this is a peculiarity of ours: we do not say that a man who takes no interest in politics is a man who minds his own business; we say that he has no business here at all. We Athenians, in our own persons, take our decisions on policy or submit them to proper discussions: for we do not think that there is an incompatibility between words and deeds; the worst thing is to rush into action before the consequences have been properly debated. And this is another point where we differ from other people. We are capable at the same time of taking risks and of estimating them beforehand. Others are brave out of ignorance; and, when they stop to think, they begin to fear. But the man who can most truly be accounted brave is he who best knows the meaning of what is sweet in life and of what is terrible, and then goes out undeterred to meet what is to come.

"Again, in questions of general good feeling there is a great contrast between us and most other people. We make friends by doing good to others, not by receiving good from them. This makes our friendship all the more reliable, since we want to keep alive the gratitude of those who are in our debt by showing continued goodwill to them: whereas the feelings of one who owes us something lack the same enthusiasm, since he knows that, when he repays our kindness, it will be more like paying back a debt than giving something spontaneously. We are unique in this. When we do kindnesses to others, we do not do them out of any calculations of profit or loss: we do them without afterthought, relying on our free liberality. Taking everything together then, I declare that our city is an education to Greece, and I declare that in my opinion each single one of our citizens, in all the manifold aspects of life, is able to show himself the rightful lord and owner of his own person, and do this, moreover, with exceptional grace and exceptional versatility. And to show that this is no empty boasting for the present occasion, but real tangible fact, you have only to consider the power which our city possesses and which has been won by those very qualities which I have mentioned. Athens, alone of the states we know, comes to her testing time in a greatness that surpasses what was imagined of her. In her case, and in her case alone, no invading enemy is ashamed at being defeated, and no subject can complain of being governed by people unfit for their responsibilities. Mighty indeed are the marks and monuments of our empire which we have left. Future ages will wonder at us, as the present age wonders at us now. We do not need the praises of a Homer, or of anyone else whose words may delight us for the moment, but whose estimation of facts will fall short of what is really true. For our adventurous spirit has forced an entry into every sea and into every land; and everywhere we have left behind us everlasting memorials of good done to our friends or suffering inflicted on our enemies.

"This, then, is the kind of city for which these men, who could not bear the thought of losing her, nobly fought and nobly died. It is only natural that every one of us who survive them should be willing to undergo hardships in her service. And it was for this reason that I have spoken at such length about our city, because I wanted to make it clear that for us there is more at stake than there is for others who lack our advantages; also I wanted my words of praise for the dead to be set in the bright light of evidence. And now the most important of these words has been spoken. I have sung the praises of our city; but it was the courage and gallantry of these men, and of people like them, which made her splendid. Nor would you find it true in the case of many of the Greeks, as it is true of them,

that no words can do more than justice to their deeds.

"To me it seems that the consummation which has overtaken these men shows us the meaning of manliness in its first revelation and in its final proof. Some of them, no doubt, had their faults; but what we ought to remember first is their gallant conduct against the enemy in defense of their native land. They have blotted out evil with good, and done more service to the commonwealth than they ever did harm in their private lives. No one of these men weakened because he wanted to go on enjoying his wealth: no one put off the awful day in the hope that he might live to escape his poverty and grow rich. More to be desired than such things, they chose to check the enemy's pride. This, to them, was a risk most glorious, and they accepted it, willing to strike down the enemy and relinquish everything else. As for success or failure, they left that in the doubtful hands of Hope, and when the reality of battle was before their faces, they put their trust in their own selves. In the fighting, they thought it more honorable to stand their ground and suffer death than to give in and save their lives. So they fled from the reproaches of men, abiding with life and limb the brunt of battle; and, in a small moment of time, the climax of their lives, a culmination of glory, not of fear, were swept away from us.

"So and such they were, these men—worthy of their city. We who remain behind may hope to be spared their fate, but must resolve to keep the same daring spirit against the foe. It is not simply a question of estimating the advantages in theory. I could tell you a long story (and you know it as well as I do) about what is to be gained by beating the enemy back. What I would prefer is that you should fix your eyes every day on the greatness of Athens as she really is, and should fall in love with her. When you realize her greatness, then reflect that what made her great was men with a spirit of adventure, men who knew their duty, men who were ashamed to fall below a certain standard. If they ever failed in an enterprise, they made up their minds that at any rate the city should not find their courage lacking to her, and they gave to her the best contribution that they could. They gave her their lives, to her and to all of us, and for their own selves they won praises that never grow old, the most splendid of sepulchres—not the sepulchre in which their bodies are laid, but where their glory remains eternal in men's minds, always there on the right occasion to stir others to speech or to action. For famous men have the whole earth as their memorial: it is not only the inscriptions on their graves in their own country that mark them out; no, in foreign lands also, not in any visible form but in people's hearts, their memory abides and grows. It is for you to try to be like them. Make up your minds that happiness depends on being free, and freedom depends on being courageous. Let there be no relaxation in face of the perils of the war. The people who have most excuse for despising death are not the wretched and unfortunate, who have no hope of doing well for themselves, but those who run the risk of a complete reversal in their lives, and who would feel the difference most intensely, if things went wrong for them. Any intelligent man would find a humiliation caused by his own slackness more painful to bear than death, when death comes to him unperceived, in battle, and in the confidence of his patriotism.

"For these reasons I shall not commiserate with those parents of the dead, who are present here. Instead I shall try to comfort them. They are well aware that they have grown up in a world where there are many changes and chances. But this is good fortune—for men to end their lives with honor, as these have done, and for you honorably to lament them: their life was set to a measure where death and happiness went hand in hand. I know that it is difficult to convince you of this. When you see other people happy you will often be reminded of what used to make you happy too. One does not feel sad at not having some good thing which is outside one's experience: real grief is felt at the loss of something which one is used to. All the same, those of you who are of the right age must bear up and take comfort in the thought of having more children. In your own homes these new children will prevent you from brooding over those who

are no more, and they will be a help to the city, too, both in filling the empty places, and in assuring her security. For it is impossible for a man to put forward fair and honest views about our affairs if he has not, like everyone else, children whose lives may be at stake. As for those of you who are now too old to have children, I would ask you to count as gain the greater part of your life, in which you have been happy, and remember that what remains is not long, and let your hearts be lifted up at the thought of the fair fame of the dead. One's sense of honor is the only thing that does not grow old, and the last pleasure, when one is worn out with age, is not, as the poet said, making money, but having the respect of one's fellow men.

"As for those of you here who are sons or brothers of the dead, I can see a hard struggle in front of you. Everyone always speaks well of the dead, and, even if you rise to the greatest heights of heroism, it will be a hard thing for you to get the reputation of having come near, let alone equalled, their standard. When one is alive, one is always liable to the jealousy of one's competitors, but when one is out of the way, the honor one receives is sincere and unchallenged.

"Perhaps I should say a word or two on the duties of women to those among you who are now widowed. I can say all I have to say in a short word of advice. Your great glory is not to be inferior to what God has made you, and the greatest glory of a woman is to be least talked about by men, whether they are praising you or criticizing you. I have now, as the law demanded, said what I had to say. For the time being our offerings to the dead have been made, and for the future their children will be supported at the public expense by the city, until they come of age. This is the crown and prize which she offers, both to the dead and to their children, for the ordeals which they have faced. Where the rewards of valor are the greatest, there you will find also the best and bravest spirits among the people. And now, when you have mourned for your dear ones, you must depart."

5th century B.C.

THINK AND DISCUSS
Understanding
1. What are the two principal achievements of past Athenians that Pericles recalls?
2. Why does Pericles consider the discipline of Spartan education unnecessary for Athenians?
3. Why doesn't Athens need a Homer?
4. According to Pericles, what is the price of freedom?

Analyzing
5. What attitude does Pericles have toward warfare?
6. How does Pericles connect Athenian battlefield courage with its democratic society?
7. Explain the special sort of "good feeling" that Pericles thinks Athens fosters in her relationships with others.
8. Use Pericles' description of the dead Athenian soldiers to define his ideals of heroism.

Extending
9. Evaluate Pericles' description of Athenian democracy, page 215. Does his list of characteristic qualities match your idea of democratic government?
10. Evaluate the ruling ideas that lie behind the instructions Pericles gives to those who survive.

COMPOSITION
Imagining a Reaction to Pericles' Speech
The people who listened to Pericles in the winter of 430 were undoubtedly a diverse group which had various reactions to what he said. Imagine to yourself a specific person who was there that day, and write a letter in which that person (1) describes the scene, (2) recounts the basic ideas of Pericles' speech, and (3) states his or her reactions. This Athenian may agree or disagree with the speech, but be sure the letter expresses a highly personal response. Imagine an audience for the letter—an Athenian who was not present at the speech, for example—and keep this audience in mind as you write.

Analyzing Pericles' Leadership
Thucydides presents Pericles as a "man chosen by the city for his intellectual gifts and for his general reputation." Write a two-page essay in which you use details from his speech to explain to your fellow students the kind of leadership he brought to Athens. Then analyze what Pericles says, seeking in the basic themes of his speech the specific effects he hopes to achieve in his audience. For example, when he says that "freedom depends on being courageous," he wishes to stir in his listeners a desire to fight to protect their liberty. Develop a list of at least three such significant ideas and the way they would lead people to some kind of emotional response or specific action. Prepare an outline with an introductory paragraph describing the need for direction in times of war, and then, in the body of your paper, explain how Pericles represents a specific kind of leadership through three particular ideas and their effect on his listeners. See "Writing About Theme" in the Writer's Handbook.

ENRICHMENT
Comparing Pericles and Lincoln
The American President Abraham Lincoln (1809–1865) was thinking of Pericles' speech when he drafted his own celebrated Gettysburg Address. Obtain a copy of Lincoln's speech and compare the two. When does Lincoln echo Pericles? How does he transform the words and ideas of his predecessor? Recalling that Lincoln's speech commemorated the Union war dead, discuss the reasons Lincoln might have had for making his speech resemble that of the Athenian leader.

Plato, the earliest philosopher whose written works have survived undamaged and in substantial numbers, is one of the most influential thinkers in history. The Athens of his boyhood was in the midst of an era of extraordinary cultural flowering, but also locked in a destructive war with Sparta. This came to a head in Plato's young manhood with the Spartan victory of 404 B.C., which installed an oligarchy called the Thirty who ruled Athens for a year before democracy could be restored. The intellectual confusions of the era matched its political uncertainties. Wandering, self-proclaimed thinkers called Sophists (from *sophia*, "wisdom") offered to teach aristocratic youths like Plato how to think cleverly and argue persuasively, but had no specific ideas or values of their own. An extreme example is Gorgias (c. 485–c. 380), who wrote a book "proving" that nothing exists; and if anything did exist, people couldn't understand it; and if they could, then they would not be able to explain their understanding.

In the midst of all this clever but pointless skepticism, Plato seems to have been transformed by an odd but powerful personality, the philosopher Socrates (470–399 B.C.). Famous for his ugliness—he had a snub nose, bulging eyes, thick lips, and a fat belly—and for his sloppiness—he never wore shoes, rarely washed, and wrapped himself in an ancient, soiled cloak—Socrates wandered the streets of Athens, confronting people and questioning them about their ideas and their values. He himself never wrote a word. His self-appointed function was to teach by questioning but unlike the Sophists he refused any money. He had a magnetic personality that drew young, thoughtful men to him, and Plato joined this circle.

When democracy returned in 403 there was a quiet effort to get revenge on people who had supported the thirty tyrants. Some of Socrates' aristocratic followers were in this group, and so perhaps because of this link, and perhaps because Socrates seemed a bothersome troublemaker, he suddenly found himself accused of "refusing to recognize the gods recognized by the State and introducing other, new divinities," and of "corrupting the youth." Before open court, a gathering of Athenian citizens, Socrates tried to defend himself. They were not persuaded, and he was condemned to drink poison (399 B.C.).

This outrageous legal murder of a philosopher may well have stimulated Plato to a response. Among his first philosophical works, written between 399 and 390, we find the *Apology*, depicting Socrates defending himself on the day of his trial. This is not a historical record of what was actually said, but rather a literary reconstruction in which Plato presents the reader with the Socrates he wishes the world to remember and admire—a man so passionately committed to free inquiry into the truth of things that he will die for it.

See ANALOGY in the Handbook of Literary Terms, page 940.

from the Apology

Plato *translated by* **Benjamin Jowett**

ow you, O Athenians, have been affected by my accusers, I cannot tell; but I know that they almost made me forget who I was—so persuasively did they speak; and yet they have hardly uttered a word of truth. But of the many falsehoods told by them, there was one which quite amazed me;—I mean when they said that you should be upon your guard and not allow yourselves to be deceived by the force of my eloquence. To say this, when they were certain to be detected as soon as I opened my lips and proved myself to be anything but a great speaker, did indeed appear to me most shameless—unless by the force of eloquence they mean the force of truth; for if such is their meaning, I admit that I am eloquent. But in how different a way from theirs! Well, as I was saying, they have scarcely spoken the truth at all; but from me you shall hear the whole truth: not, however, delivered after their manner in a set oration duly ornamented with words and phrases. No, by heaven! but I shall use the words and arguments which occur to me at the moment; for I am confident in the justice of my cause: at my time of life I ought not to be appearing before you, O men of Athens, in the character of a juvenile orator—let no one expect it of me. And I must beg of you to grant me a favor:—If I defend myself in my accustomed manner, and you hear me using the words which I have been in the habit of using in the agora,[1] at the tables of the money-changers, or anywhere else, I would ask you not to be surprised, and not to interrupt me on this account. For I am more than seventy years of age, and appearing now for the first time in a court of law, I am quite a stranger to the language of the place; and therefore I would have you regard me as if I were really a stranger, whom you would excuse if he spoke in his native tongue, and after the fashion of his country:—Am I making an unfair request of you? Never mind the manner, which may or may not be good; but think only of the truth of my words, and give heed to that: let the speaker speak truly and the judge decide justly. . . .

I will begin at the beginning, and ask what is the accusation which has given rise to the slander of me, and in fact has encouraged Meletus to prefer this charge against me. Well, what do the slanderers say? They shall be my prosecutors, and I will sum up their words in an affidavit: "Socrates is an evildoer, and a curious person, who searches into things under the earth and in heaven, and he makes the worse appear the better cause; and he teaches the aforesaid doctrines to others." Such is the nature of the accusation: it is just what you have yourselves seen in the comedy of Aristophanes,[2] who has introduced a man whom he calls Socrates, going about and saying that he walks in air, and talking a deal of nonsense concerning matters of which I do not pretend to know either much or little—not that I mean to speak disparagingly of any one who is a student of natural philosophy. I should be very sorry if Meletus could bring so grave a charge against me. But the

---

1. *agora* (ag′ôr ə), the open marketplace in Athens where citizens gathered daily.
2. *Aristophanes.* This famous comic playwright had poked good-natured fun at Socrates in *The Clouds.*

simple truth is, O Athenians, that I have nothing to do with physical speculations. Very many of those here present are witnesses to the truth of this, and to them I appeal. Speak then, you who have heard me, and tell your neighbors whether any of you have ever known me hold forth in few words or in many upon such matters. . . . You hear their answer. And from what they say of this part of the charge you will be able to judge of the truth of the rest. . . .

I dare say, Athenians, that some one among you will reply, "Yes, Socrates, but what is the origin of these accusations which are brought against you; there must have been something strange which you have been doing? All these rumors and this talk about you would never have arisen if you had been like other men: tell us, then, what is the cause of them, for we should be sorry to judge hastily of you." Now, I regard this as a fair challenge, and I will endeavor to explain to you the reason why I am called wise and have such an evil fame. Please to attend then. And although some of you may think that I am joking, I declare that I will tell you the entire truth. Men of Athens, this reputation of mine has come of a certain sort of wisdom which I possess. If you ask me what kind of wisdom, I reply, wisdom such as may perhaps be attained by man, for to that extent I am inclined to believe that I am wise; whereas the persons of whom I was speaking have a superhuman wisdom, which I may fail to describe, because I have it not myself; and he who says that I have, speaks falsely, and is taking away my character. And here, O men of Athens, I must beg you not to interrupt me, even if I seem to say something extravagant. For the word which I will speak is not mine. I will refer you to a witness who is worthy of credit; that witness shall be the god of Delphi[3]—he will tell you about my wisdom, if I have any, and of what sort it is. You must have known Chaerephon; he was early a friend of mine, and also a friend of yours, for he shared in the recent exile of the people, and returned with you. Well, Chaerephon, as you know, was very impetuous in all his doings, and he went to Delphi and boldly asked the oracle to tell him whether—as I was saying, I must beg you not to interrupt—he asked the oracle to

tell him whether any one was wiser than I was, and the Pythian prophetess answered, that there was no man wiser. Chaerephon is dead himself; but his brother, who is in court, will confirm the truth of what I am saying.

Why do I mention this? Because I am going to explain to you why I have such an evil name. When I heard the answer, I said to myself, What can the god mean? and what is the interpretation of his riddle? for I know that I have no wisdom, small or great. What then can he mean when he says that I am the wisest of men? And yet he is a god, and cannot lie; that would be against his nature. After long consideration, I thought of a method of trying the question. I reflected that if I could only find a man wiser than myself, then I might go to the god with a refutation in my hand. I should say to him, "Here is a man who is wiser than I am; but you said that I was the wisest." Accordingly I went to one who had the reputation of wisdom, and observed him—his name I need not mention; he was a politician whom I selected for examination—and the result was as follows: When I began to talk with him, I could not help thinking that he was not really wise, although he was thought wise by many, and still wiser by himself; and thereupon I tried to explain to him that he thought himself wise, but was not really wise, and the consequence was that he hated me, and his enmity was shared by several who were present and heard me. So I left him, saying to myself, as I went away: Well, although I do not suppose that either of us knows anything really beautiful and good, I am better off than he is,—for he knows nothing, and thinks that he knows; I neither know nor think that I know. In this latter particular, then, I seem to have slightly the advantage of him. Then I went to another who had still higher pretensions to wisdom, and my conclusion was exactly the same. Whereupon I made another enemy of him, and of many others besides him.

Then I went to one man after another, being not unconscious of the enmity which I provoked, and I lamented and feared this: but necessity was

---

3. **god of Delphi**, Apollo, patron of the oracle of Delphi. (See page 173.)

laid upon me,—the word of God, I thought, ought to be considered first. And I said to myself, Go I must to all who appear to know, and find out the meaning of the oracle. And I swear to you, Athenians, by the dog I swear!—for I must tell you the truth—the result of my mission was just this: I found that the men most in repute were all but the most foolish; and that others less esteemed were really wiser and better. I will tell you the tale of my wanderings and of the Herculean[4] labors, as I may call them, which I endured only to find at last the oracle irrefutable. After the politicians, I went to the poets; tragic, dithyrambic, and all sorts. And there, I said to myself, you will be instantly detected; now you will find out that you are more ignorant than they are. Accordingly I took them some of the most elaborate passages in their own writings, and asked what was the meaning of them—thinking that they would teach me something. Will you believe me? I am almost ashamed to confess the truth, but I must say that there is hardly a person present who would not have talked better about their poetry than they did themselves. Then I knew that not by wisdom do poets write poetry, but by a sort of genius and inspiration, they are like diviners or soothsayers who also say many fine things, but do not understand the meaning of them. The poets appeared to me to be much in the same case; and I further observed that upon the strength of their poetry they believed themselves to be the wisest of men in other things in which they were not wise. So I departed, conceiving myself to be superior to them for the same reason that I was superior to the politicians.

At last I went to the artisans. I was conscious that I knew nothing at all, as I may say, and I was sure that they knew many fine things; and here I was not mistaken, for they did know many things of which I was ignorant, and in this they certainly were wiser than I was. But I observed that even the good artisans fell into the same error as the poets;—because they were good workmen they thought that they also knew all sorts of high matters, and this defect in them overshadowed their wisdom; and therefore I asked myself on behalf of the oracle, whether I would like to be

as I was, neither having their knowledge nor their ignorance, or like them in both; and I made answer to myself and to the oracle that I was better off as I was.

This inquisition has led to my having many enemies of the worst and most dangerous kind, and has given occasion also to many calumnies. And I am called wise, for my hearers always imagine that I myself possess the wisdom which I find wanting in others: but the truth is, O men of Athens, that God only is wise; and by his answer he intends to show that the wisdom of men is worth little or nothing; he is not speaking of Socrates, he is only using my name by way of illustration, as if he said, He, O men, is the wisest, who, like Socrates, knows that his wisdom is in truth worth nothing. And so I go about the world obedient to the god, and search and make enquiry into the wisdom of any one, whether citizen or stranger, who appears to be wise; and if he is not wise, then in vindication of the oracle I show him that he is not wise; and my occupation quite absorbs me, and I have no time to give either to any public matter of interest or to any concern of my own, but I am in utter poverty by reason of my devotion to the god.

There is another thing:—young men of the richer classes, who have not much to do, come about me of their own accord; they like to hear the pretenders examined, and they often imitate me, and proceed to examine others; there are plenty of persons, as they quickly discover, who think that they know something, but really know little or nothing; and then those who are examined by them instead of being angry with themselves are angry with me: This confounded Socrates, they say; this villainous misleader of youth!—and then if somebody asks them, Why, what evil does he practice or teach? they do not know, and cannot tell; but in order that they may not appear to be at a loss, they repeat the ready-made charges which are used against all philosophers about teaching things up in the clouds and under the earth, and having no gods, and making the worse appear the better cause; for they do not like to confess that their

---

4. Herculean. Hercules was a legendary hero who won immortality by performing twelve impossible feats.

pretense of knowledge has been detected—which is the truth; and as they are numerous and ambitious and energetic, and are drawn up in battle array and have persuasive tongues, they have filled your ears with their loud and inveterate calumnies. . . .

Some one will say: And are you not ashamed, Socrates, of a course of life which is likely to bring you to an untimely end? To him I may fairly answer: There you are mistaken: a man who is good for anything ought not to calculate the chance of living or dying; he ought only to consider whether in doing anything he is doing right or wrong—acting the part of a good man or of a bad. Whereas, upon your view, the heroes who fell at Troy were not good for much, and the son of Thetis[5] above all, who altogether despised danger in comparison with disgrace; and when he was so eager to slay Hector, his goddess mother said to him, that if he avenged his companion Patroclus, and slew Hector, he would die himself—"Fate," she said, in these or the like words, "waits for you next after Hector"; he, receiving this warning, utterly despised danger and death, and instead of fearing them, feared rather to live in dishonor, and not to avenge his friend. "Let me die forthwith," he replies, "and be avenged of my enemy, rather than abide here by the beaked ships, a laughing stock and a burden of the earth." Had Achilles any thought of death and danger? For wherever a man's place is, whether the place which he has chosen or that in which he has been placed by a commander, there he ought to remain in the hour of danger; he should not think of death or of anything but of disgrace. And this, O men of Athens, is a true saying.

Strange, indeed, would be my conduct, O men of Athens, if I, who, when I was ordered by the generals whom you chose to command me at Potidaea and Amphipolis and Delium,[6] remained where they placed me, like any other man, facing death—if now, when, as I conceive and imagine, God orders me to fulfil the philosopher's mission of searching into myself and other men, I were to desert my post through fear of death, or any other fear; that would indeed be strange, and I might justly be arraigned in court for denying the existense of the gods, if I disobeyed the oracle because I was afraid of death, fancying that I was wise when I was not wise. For the fear of death is indeed the pretense of wisdom, and not real wisdom, being a pretense of knowing the unknown; and no one knows whether death, which men in their fear apprehended to be the greatest evil, may not be the greatest good. Is not this ignorance of a disgraceful sort, the ignorance which is the conceit that a man knows what he does not know? And in this respect only I believe myself to differ from men in general, and may perhaps claim to be wiser than they are:—that whereas I know but little of the world below, I do not suppose that I know: but I do know that injustice and disobedience to a better, whether God or man, is evil and dishonorable, and I will never fear or avoid a possible good rather than a certain evil. And therefore if you let me go now, and are not convinced by Anytus, who said that since I had been prosecuted I must be put to death; (or if not that I ought never to have been prosecuted at all); and that if I escape now, your sons will all be utterly ruined by listening to my words—if you say to me, Socrates, this time we will not mind Anytus, and you shall be let off, but upon one condition, that you are not to enquire and speculate in this way any more, and that if you are caught doing so again you shall die;—if this was the condition on which you let me go, I should reply: Men of Athens, I honor and love you; but I shall obey God rather than you, and while I have life and strength I shall never cease from the practice and teaching of philosophy, exhorting any one whom I meet and saying to him after my manner: You, my friend,—a citizen of the great and mighty and wise city of Athens,—are you not ashamed of heaping up the greatest amount of money and honor and reputation, and caring so little about wisdom and truth and the greatest improvement of the soul, which you never regard or heed at all? And if the person with whom I am arguing, says: Yes, but I do care; then I do not leave him or let him go

---

5. *son of Thetis.* The warrior hero Achilles was the son of the sea-nymph Thetis.
6. **Potidaea, Amphipolis, Delium,** military campaigns of the years 431, 424, and 422 B.C. in which Socrates served.

at once; but I proceed to interrogate and examine and cross-examine him, and if I think that he has no virtue in him, but only says that he has, I reproach him with undervaluing the greater, and overvaluing the less. And I shall repeat the same words to every one whom I meet, young and old, citizen and alien, but especially to the citizens, inasmuch as they are my brethren. For know that this is the command of God; and I believe that no greater good has ever happened in the State than my service to the God. For I do nothing but go about persuading you all, old and young alike, not to take thought for your persons or your properties, but first and chiefly to care about the greatest improvement of the soul. I tell you that virtue is not given by money, but that from virtue comes money and every other good of man, public as well as private. This is my teaching, and if this is the doctrine which corrupts the youth, I am a mischievous person. But if any one says that this is not my teaching, he is speaking an untruth. Wherefore, O men of Athens, I say to you, do as Anytus bids or not as Anytus bids, and either acquit me or not; but whichever you do, understand that I shall never alter my ways, not even if I have to die many times.

Men of Athens, do not interrupt, but hear me; there was an understanding between us that you should hear me to the end: I have something more to say, at which you may be inclined to cry out; but I believe that to hear me will be good for you, and therefore I beg that you will not cry out. I would have you know, that if you kill such an one as I am, you will injure yourselves more than you will injure me. Nothing will injure me, not Meletus nor yet Anytus—they cannot, for a bad man is not permitted to injure a better than himself. I do not deny that Anytus may, perhaps, kill him, or drive him into exile, or deprive him of civil rights; and he may imagine, and others may imagine, that he is inflicting a great injury upon him: but there I do not agree. For the evil of doing as he is doing—the evil of unjustly taking away the life of another—is greater far.

And now, Athenians, I am not going to argue for my own sake, as you may think, but for yours, that you may not sin against the God by condemning me, who am his gift to you. For if you kill me you will not easily find a successor to me, who, if I may use such a ludicrous figure of speech, am a sort of gadfly, given to the State by God; and the State is a great and noble steed who is tardy in his motions owing to his very size, and requires to be stirred into life. I am that gadfly which God has attached to the State, and all day long and in all places am always fastening upon you, arousing and persuading and reproaching you. You will not easily find another like me, and therefore I would advise you to spare me. I dare say that you may feel out of temper (like a person who is suddenly awakened from sleep), and you think that you might easily strike me dead as Anytus advises, and then you would sleep on for the remainder of your lives, unless God in his care of you sent you another gadfly. When I say that I am given to you by God, the proof of my mission is this:—if I had been like other men, I should not have neglected all my own concerns or patiently seen the neglect of them during all these years, and have been doing yours, coming to you individually like a father or elder brother, exhorting you to regard virtue; such conduct, I say, would be unlike human nature. If I had gained anything, or if my exhortations had been paid, there would have been some sense in my doing so; but now, as you will perceive, not even the impudence of my accusers dares to say that I have ever exacted or sought pay of any one; of that they have no witness. And I have a sufficient witness to the truth of what I say—my poverty.

Some one may wonder why I go about in private giving advice and busying myself with the concerns of others, but do not venture to come forward in public and advise the State. I will tell you why. You have heard me speak at sundry times and in divers places of an oracle or sign which comes to me, and is the divinity which Meletus ridicules in the indictment. This sign, which is a kind of voice,[7] first began to come to me when I was a child; it always forbids but never commands me to do anything which I am going to do. This

---

7. *voice.* Socrates several times makes references to a mysterious inner voice which guides his choices like a private oracle.

is what deters me from being a politician. And rightly, as I think. For I am certain, O men of Athens, that if I had engaged in politics, I should have perished long ago, and done no good either to you or to myself. And do not be offended at my telling you the truth: for the truth is, that no man who goes to war with you or any other multitude, honestly striving against the many lawless and unrighteous deeds which are done in a State, will save his life; he who will fight for the right, if he would live even for a brief space, must have a private station and not a public one. . . .

Well, Athenians, this and the like of this is all the defense which I have to offer. Yet a word more. Perhaps there may be some one who is offended at me, when he calls to mind how he himself on a similar, or even a less serious occasion, prayed and entreated the judges with many tears, and how he produced his children in court, which was a moving spectacle, together with a host of relations and friends; whereas I, who am probably in danger of my life, will do none of these things. The contrast may occur to his mind, and he may be set against me, and vote in anger because he is displeased at me on this account. Now, if there be such a person among you,—mind, I do not say that there is,—to him I may fairly reply: My friend, I am a man, and like other men, a creature of flesh and blood, and not "of wood or stone," as Homer says; and I have a family, yes, and sons, O Athenians, three in number, one almost a man, and two others who are still young; and yet I will not bring any of them hither in order to petition you for an acquittal. And why not? Not from any self-assertion or want of respect for you. Whether I am or am not afraid of death is another question, of which I will not now speak. But, having regard to public opinion, I feel that such conduct would be discreditable to myself, and to you, and to the whole State. One who has reached my years, and who has a name for wisdom, ought not to demean himself. Whether this opinion of me be deserved or not, at any rate the world has decided that Socrates is in some way superior to other men. And if those among you who are said to be superior in wisdom and courage, and any other virtue, demean themselves in this way, how shameful is their conduct!

I have seen men of reputation, when they have been condemned, behaving in the strangest manner: they seemed to fancy that they were going to suffer something dreadful if they died, and that they could be immortal if you only allowed them to live; and I think that such are a dishonor to the State, and that any stranger coming in would have said of them that the most eminent men of Athens, to whom the Athenians themselves give honor and command, are no better than women. And I say that these things ought not to be done by those of us who have a reputation; and if they are done, you ought not to permit them; you ought rather to show that you are far more disposed to condemn the man who gets up a doleful scene and makes the city ridiculous, than him who holds his peace. . . .

After Socrates finished his defense the assembled citizens found him guilty of the charges by a vote of 281 to 220. Socrates' official accuser, Meletus, had demanded his death; but now, according to Athenian custom, Socrates was asked to propose a different penalty. This is his response.

I will not say of myself that I deserve any evil, or propose any penalty. Why should I? Because I am afraid of the penalty of death which Meletus proposes? When I do not know whether death is a good or an evil, why should I propose a penalty which would certainly be an evil? Shall I say imprisonment? And why should I live in prison, and be the slave of the magistrate of the year—of the Eleven?[8] Or shall the penalty be a fine, and imprisonment until the fine is paid? There is the same objection. I should have to lie in prison, for money I have none, and cannot pay. And if I say exile (and this may possibly be the penalty which you will affix), I must indeed be blinded by the love of life if I am so irrational as to expect that when you, who are my own citizens, cannot endure my discourses and words, and have found them so grievous and odious that you will have no more of them, others are likely to

8. *the Eleven,* officials in charge of the prisons.

endure me. No, indeed, men of Athens, that is not very likely. And what a life should I lead, at my age, wandering from city to city, ever changing my place of exile, and always being driven out! For I am quite sure that wherever I go, there, as here, the young men will flock to me; and if I drive them away, their elders will drive me out at their request; and if I let them come, their fathers and friends will drive me out for their sakes.

Some one will say: Yes, Socrates, but cannot you hold your tongue, and then you may go into a foreign city, and no one will interfere with you? Now, I have great difficulty in making you understand my answer to this. For if I tell you that to do as you say would be a disobedience to the God, and therefore that I cannot hold my tongue, you will not believe that I am serious; and if I say again that daily to discourse about virtue, and of those other things about which you hear me examining myself and others, is the greatest good of man, and that the unexamined life is not worth living, you are still less likely to believe me. Yet I say what is true, although a thing of which it is hard for me to persuade you. Also, I have never been accustomed to think that I deserve to suffer any harm. Had I money I might have estimated the offense at what I was able to pay, and not have been much the worse. But I have none, and therefore I must ask you to proportion the fine to my means. Well, perhaps I could afford a mina,[9] and therefore I propose that penalty: Plato, Crito, Critobulus, and Apollodorus, my friends here, bid me say thirty minae, and they will be the sureties. Let thirty minae be the penalty; for which sum they will be ample security to you. . . .

When Socrates concluded his speech there was a second vote, this time on the penalty. 300 were for his death and 201 were opposed. Plato now describes Socrates' reaction.

And now, O men who have condemned me, I would fain prophesy to you; for I am about to die, and in the hour of death men are gifted with prophetic power. And I prophesy to you

who are my murderers, that immediately after my departure punishment far heavier than you have inflicted on me will surely await you. Me you have killed because you wanted to escape the accuser, and not to give an account of your lives. But that will not be as you suppose: far otherwise. For I say that there will be more accusers of you than there are now; accusers whom hitherto I have restrained: and as they are younger they will be more inconsiderate with you, and you will be more offended at them. If you think that by killing men you can prevent some one from censuring your evil lives, you are mistaken; that is not a way of escape which is either possible or honorable; the easiest and the noblest way is not to be disabling others, but to be improving yourselves. This is the prophecy which I utter before my departure to the judges who have condemned me.

Friends, who would have acquitted me, I would like also to talk with you about the thing which has come to pass, while the magistrates are busy, and before I go to the place at which I must die. Stay then a little, for we may as well talk with one another while there is time. You are my friends, and I should like to show you the meaning of this event which has happened to me. O my judges— for you I may truly call judges—I should like to tell you of a wonderful circumstance. Hitherto the divine faculty of which the internal oracle is the source has constantly been in the habit of opposing me even about trifles, if I was going to make a slip or error in any matter; and now as you see there has come upon me that which may be thought, and is generally believed to be, the last and worst evil. But the oracle made no sign of opposition, either when I was leaving my house in the morning, or when I was on my way to the court, or while I was speaking, at anything which I was going to say; and yet I have often been stopped in the middle of a speech, but now in nothing I either said or did touching the matter in hand has the oracle opposed me. What do I take to be the explanation of this silence? I will tell you. It is an intimation that what has happened to me is a good, and that those of

---

9. *mina* (mī′nə), plural *minae* (mī′nē), an ancient Greek weight and a sum of coined money equal to it.

us who think that death is an evil are in error. For the customary sign would surely have opposed me had I been going to evil and not to good.

Let us reflect in another way, and we shall see that there is great reason to hope that death is a good; for one of two things—either death is a state of nothingness and utter unconsciousness, or, as men say, there is a change and migration of the soul from this world to another. Now, if you suppose that there is no consciousness, but a sleep like the sleep of him who is undisturbed even by dreams, death will be an unspeakable gain. For if a person were to select the night in which his sleep was undisturbed even by dreams, and were to compare with this the other days and nights of his life, and then were to tell us how many days and nights he had passed in the course of his life better and more pleasantly than this one, I think that any man, I will not say a private man, but even the great king will not find many such days or nights, when compared with the others. Now, if death be of such a nature, I say that to die is gain; for eternity is then only a single night. But if death is the journey to another place, and there, as men say, all the dead abide, what good, O my friends and judges, can be greater than this? . . .

Wherefore, O judges, be of good cheer about death, and know of a certainty, that no evil can happen to a good man, either in life or after death. He and his are not neglected by the gods; nor has my own approaching end happened by mere chance. But I see clearly that the time had arrived when it was better for me to die and be released from trouble: wherefore the oracle gave no sign. For which reason, also, I am not angry with my condemners, or with my accusers; they have done me no harm, although they did not mean to do me any good; and for this I may gently blame them.

Still, I have a favor to ask of them. When my sons are grown up, I would ask you, O my friends, to punish them; and I would have you trouble them, as I have troubled you, if they seem to care about riches, or anything, more than about virtue; or if they pretend to be something when they are really nothing,—then reprove them, as I have reproved you, for not caring about that for which they ought to care, and thinking that they are something when they are really nothing. And if you do this, both I and my sons will have received justice at your hands.

The hour of departure has arrived, and we go our ways—I to die, and you to live. Which is better God only knows.

4th century B.C.

THINK AND DISCUSS
Understanding
1. How does Socrates explain the oracle that described him as the wisest man on earth?
2. Why does his search for a wiser man get him in trouble with his fellow citizens?
3. Why can't Socrates accept exile?

Analyzing
4. How can Socrates claim that "nothing will injure" him (page 225)?
5. How can Socrates' sons receive "justice" from society by being punished, reproved, and troubled?
6. Characterize the **tone** of Socrates' speech.
7. Using Socrates as an example, what does Plato imply is the "philosopher's mission"?

Extending
8. Would Pericles have considered Socrates to be a man as honorable as the warriors he praises?

APPLYING: Analogy H⫽
See Handbook of Literary Terms, p. 940.

A comparison between two quite different things, which serves to throw new light on the more unfamiliar of the two, is an **analogy.** Analogy appears in explanation and argument to illustrate and clarify.

1. Why does Socrates create the analogy between himself and the "son of Thetis," Achilles?
2. In what ways does this analogy suggest new ways to think about the role of the philosopher?
3. How does the comparison add to a philosopher's esteem in society?

BIOGRAPHY

Cicero
106–43 B.C.

As a young man Marcus Tullius Cicero spent three years in Greece completing his education. At the end of his stay the teacher Apollonius asked him to deliver an oration. When Cicero had done so, the old man then responded, "You have my praise and admiration, Cicero, and Greece my pity and commiseration, since those arts and that eloquence which are the only glories that remain to her, will now be transferred by you to Rome." Cicero became the greatest orator of ancient Rome, and one of its finest, and most influential, prose writers. His published works fill twenty-six volumes, and over 800 private letters still survive. He was deeply involved in government and the struggle for power during the last decades of the Republic. In the end he lost his life trying to help rebuild a fragmented political order.

Cicero came from a rural town, and was the first in his family to enter political life. He was, according to Roman slang, a "new man," one of those whose success had to spring from his own abilities. His skill as an orator soon made him the lawyer most likely to win even the most difficult cases. In the courtroom Cicero made no effort to be balanced or fair. His speeches freely slanted evidence and stirred the emotions of the audience. Many survive today, still ringing with his power to persuade. Legal victories soon brought political appointments. He became the quaestor (administrator) for Sicily in 75 B.C., praetor (magistrate) of Rome in 66, and achieved the highest elected office, consul, in 63. Cicero tried to function as a unifying force, arguing for the "concord of orders" among contending factions.

But the Roman Republic was decaying rapidly, and even a Cicero could not preserve it. When civil war came he sided with Pompey against Julius Caesar, and was defeated with him at Pharsalus in 48 B.C. Caesar forgave Cicero his error in judgment, and the orator withdrew from public life to become a philosopher, writing a series of works which include *On Friendship* (44 B.C.), excerpted here. Cicero was not an innovative thinker. He took ideas and arguments from Greek philosophers and translated them into the Latin language and into a Roman context. Since Greek had been the language of philosophy, Cicero frequently had to invent new words, and some of them became standard philosophical terms for the next seventeen hundred years. As a thinker, Cicero characteristically drops unrealistic theory in favor of common-sense conclusions based on everyday experience, illustrated by references to Roman people and events.

With the assassination of Julius Caesar in 44 B.C., Cicero reentered politics, siding with the young Octavian and attacking Mark Antony in a series of bitter speeches called the *Philippics*. Antony placed Cicero's name at the top of the list of enemies to be killed, and his henchmen caught Cicero trying to flee. They chopped off his head and right hand, which Antony nailed above the speaker's rostrum in Rome, in a futile effort to humiliate a man of ideas.

from On Friendship

Cicero   *translated by* **Frank O. Copley**

f you want a philosophical disquisition on friendship, I suggest that you ask it of those who make a profession of such things. All I can do is to urge you to put friendship ahead of all other human concerns, for there is nothing so suited to man's nature, nothing that can mean so much to him, whether in good times or in bad.

In any case, I want to say first of all that friendship can exist only between good men. Now I am not going to split hairs on this question, as do those who inquire into such matters with fine precision;[1] they say, you know, that no one can be a good man unless he is possessed of perfect wisdom. Perhaps so, but they are talking about a kind of wisdom that no man to this day has ever acquired. Our task is to look at conditions which actually exist in human life, not at those that men dream about or pray for. I should never say that even Gaius Fabricius, Manius Curius, and Tiberius Coruncanius,[2] whom our forefathers always judged to be men of true wisdom, were wise by any such standard as that. Well then, let them keep that term "wisdom" for their own uses: it is productive of nothing but ill-will and misunderstanding; let them grant only that men such as I have just mentioned were good men. Of course they won't do it; they will insist that such a concession can be made only in the case of their "truly wise" man.

As for us, I suggest that we pursue the matter with our own crude mother wit, as the saying goes. There are men who behave and live in such a way that they are regarded as models of honor, integrity, justice, and generosity, men who have no vestige of avarice, lustfulness, or insolence, men of unwavering conviction, men, in short, like those whose names I just mentioned. Such men are commonly regarded as good men; by the same sign, let us decide to call them so, for, as far as men can, it is they who follow nature as the best guide to the good life. For I believe I see quite clearly that all men are meant by nature to have some sort of companionship one with another, and that the depth and significance of this companionship varies according to the degree of relationship between them. Thus it is stronger between citizen and citizen than between citizen and foreigner, between those who are related by blood than between those who are not. In the latter case, at least, nature herself brings about a friendship, but it is not quite as firmly based as it ought to be. For the friend has this advantage over the relative: relatives may lose their goodwill, friends cannot, for once goodwill has been lost, the friend is no longer a friend, but the relative is still a relative.

We can best comprehend the power of friendship by considering the fact that nature has established social contact between countless numbers of men; yet friendship is so concentrated and restricted a thing that all the true affection in the world is shared by no more than a handful of individuals.

Now friendship is just this and nothing else: complete sympathy in all matters of importance, plus goodwill and affection, and I am inclined

---

1. *those who inquire . . . with fine precision.* Stoic philosophers sometimes argued that no one could be called good who was guilty of even the slightest evil.
2. *Gaius Fabricius, Manius Curius, Tiberius Coruncanius,* Roman consuls of the third century B.C., celebrated for their patriotism and virtue.

to think that with the exception of wisdom, the gods have given nothing finer to men than this. Some people place wealth ahead of it, some good health, some power, some honors, a good many even pleasure. This last, of course, is on the mere animal level; the others are unstable things that one can never be sure of, since they depend not upon our own efforts, but upon fickle Fortune. Those who say that virtue is man's highest good, are of course very inspiring; but it is to this very virtue that friendship owes its beginning and its identity: without virtue friendship cannot exist at all.

But now let us define virtue in terms of our own way of life and in words that we can understand, and let us not measure it by the degree to which we can speak of it in grandiose terms, as some professional philosophers do. Let us count as good men those who are commonly so considered—men like Paulus, Cato, Galus, Scipio, Philus. Ordinary people are quite content with them; let us forget about individuals who never existed anywhere on the face of the earth.

In the first place, how can there be a "life worth living," as Ennius[3] puts it, unless it rest upon the mutual love of friends? What could be finer than to have someone to whom you may speak as freely as to yourself? How could you derive true joy from good fortune, if you did not have someone who would rejoice in your happiness as much as you yourself? And it would be very hard to bear misfortune in the absence of anyone who would take your sufferings even harder than you. Finally, the other things on which we set our hearts have each of them a strictly limited utility: money, that we may spend it; power, that we may acquire a following; honors, that we may gain praise; pleasure, that we may enjoy it; health, that we may be free of pain and make full use of our physical endowments; friendship, on the other hand, brings with it many advantages. Wherever you turn, it is at your side; there is no place not open to it; it is never untimely, never in the way. In short, not even water and fire, as the saying goes, are as universally essential to us as friendship. And I am not now speaking of the friendships of everyday folk, or of ordinary people—although even these are a source of pleasure and profit—but of true and perfect friendship, the kind that was possessed by those few men who have gained names for themselves as friends. For when fortune smiles on us, friendship adds a luster to that smile; when she frowns, friendship absorbs her part and share of that frown, and thus makes it easier to bear.

Now friendship possesses many splendid advantages, but of course the finest thing of all about it is that it sends a ray of good hope into the future, and keeps our hearts from faltering or falling by the wayside. For the man who keeps his eye on a true friend, keeps it, so to speak, on a model of himself. For this reason, friends are together when they are separated, they are rich when they are poor, strong when they are weak, and—a thing even harder to explain—they live on after they have died, so great is the honor that follows them, so vivid the memory, so poignant the sorrow. That is why friends who have died are accounted happy, and those who survive them are deemed worthy of praise. Why, if the mutual love of friends were to be removed from the world, there is no single house, no single state that would go on existing; even agriculture would cease to be. If this seems a bit difficult to understand, we can readily see how great is the power of friendship and love by observing their opposites, enmity and ill will. For what house is so firmly established, what constitution is so unshakable, that it could not be utterly destroyed by hatred and internal division? From this we may judge how much good there is in friendship.

Why, at Agrigentum, so men say, there was a certain literary man[4] who composed a poem in Greek in which, like some prophet of old, he declared that in all the universe everything that was firm-fixed and everything that was in motion was brought into union by friendship and scattered to fragments by discord. And, for that matter, every man alive understands that principle and has experienced the truth of it. For if ever an

---

3. **Ennius,** Quintus Ennius (239–169 B.C.), early Latin poet.
4. *a certain literary man,* the Greek philosopher Empedocles (c. 493–433 B.C.), who argued that the force which keeps things together is *philotaes,* "love."

instance comes to light of a friend who showed his loyalty and devotion by risking his life or by sharing such a risk, who would not extol him to the skies? How the whole audience burst into a roar of applause not so long ago during the performance of my old friend Pacuvius' most recent play: the king did not know which man was Orestes; thereupon, Pylades[5] declared that he was Orestes, so that he might die in Orestes' place; but Orestes insisted that *he* was Orestes, as indeed he was. The people leaped to their feet and applauded, although it was only a play; what do you think they would have done if it had been an incident in real life? It was easy to see what nature prompts men to do.

Although they were not capable of doing such a thing themselves, they correctly judged its rightness when they saw it done by someone else. This, I believe, is all I can tell you of my feelings about friendship. If there are other things to say on the subject—and I have no doubt there are a great many—I think you had better direct your inquiries about them to those who make a practice of such disquisitions.

1st century B.C.

---

5. *Orestes . . . Pylades.* Orestes' friend Pylades helped in revenging the death of Orestes' father Agamemnon, king of Mycenae.

THINK AND DISCUSS
Understanding
1. Why does Cicero think friendship is an even closer bond than family relationship?
2. How does friendship make life worth living?

Analyzing
3. By what method does Cicero define "good men"?
4. Explain how Cicero might justify the list of **paradoxes** in paragraph eight, which begins, "friends are together when they are separated . . . ."

Extending
5. How can Cicero say, on the one hand, that "all the true affection in the world is shared by no more than a handful of individuals," and yet assert later that without friendship "no single house, no single state . . . would go on existing . . ."?
6. Do you think the concept of friendship can apply even to physics, as the last paragraph suggests?

APPLYING: Allusion   H*Z*
See Handbook of Literary Terms, page 938.
A brief reference within a text to a person or event from history or literature is an **allusion**.

1. Why does Cicero allude to the play about Orestes?
2. How does his allusion to "a certain literary man" (page 231) extend Cicero's observations about friendship?
3. What is his reason for alluding to other thinkers who "split hairs on this question" (page 230)?

ENRICHMENT
Making and Listening to a Speech
Cicero did not forget the art of the orator when he began writing philosophy. Some of the stylistic mannerisms of his famous speeches reappear in his book about friendship. To hear (in English translation) an echo of his style of presentation, have one of the class members read the final four paragraphs from this selection aloud. There is no need for exaggeration in delivery. A serious, slow, clearly articulated performance is best. The rest of the class should listen for the following things: passages which present main ideas clearly, moments when the oratory becomes especially involving emotionally, and lines which seem hard to grasp on first hearing. After the performance, all the students should enter into a discussion of how they reacted to the speech, specifically citing these three issues.

If Ennius's *Annales* had survived, we could more easily appreciate the shock which greeted the first appearance of Catullus's poetry. Quintus Ennius (239–169 B.C.), who seriously believed he was Homer reincarnated, was the first major Roman poet. A verse history of Rome, his *Annales* (most of which is now lost) described how the gods directed the founding of the city for their sacred purposes. Ennius represented the highest ideals of poetry when Catullus was a boy.

Catullus came to Rome from the provincial town of Verona in northern Italy. He seems to have been wealthy, since he owned villas in the country and yet lived in town much of the time. There is no evidence he ever worked a day in his life. The capital was becoming increasingly perilous when he got there, as the rival forces of Pompey and Julius Caesar began to pull apart the framework of the old order. One reaction to such danger was to live for the moment. *Carpe diem*—"seize the day"—is the Latin description of the attitude, and Catullus's poetry celebrates a life of drinking, lovemaking, and quarreling—everything which Ennius and the old Romans had scorned. Catullus's extremely short, highly personal verse makes no public statement, but merely expresses one man's private —often disreputable—feelings.

Catullus and his fellow poets also overturned former artistic values. Rather than long, serious poems on national and tragic themes, they adapted the forms of the Greek **lyric** for use in Latin. Catullus was the greatest of these new poets. He constantly experimented in different meters, especially those of Sappho. Just as Cicero imported the manner of Greek prose style and Greek philosophical ideas, Catullus imported the Greek lyric. Along with similar efforts by others, they helped begin a "golden age" of Latin literature, a time when tradition and innovation combined to give Rome its most persuasive artistic utterance.

Catullus's poems speak frequently in the poet's own voice. Most deal with his love, and later his hate, for a woman whom he gives the fictitious name Lesbia. She was probably Clodia, sister of one prominent Roman politician and wife of another, and notorious for her immorality. One recent literary historian observes that in Rome "upper-class women had achieved greater emancipation than at any time in the ancient world, and Clodia had not only the style to inspire sophisticated poetry, but the education to understand it." The elegy on Catullus's dead brother (lyric 101) also seems clearly rooted in actual experience. Catullus travelled to Asia Minor in 57 B.C. as a member of the staff of a provincial governor, and visited his brother's grave near Troy, a moment recalled in the poem. When Catullus died he left his work in a random state, to be gathered and ordered by someone else. The gesture is typical of this brilliant, emotional, eccentric innovator.

Wall painting of woman (sometimes identified as the Roman vegetation goddess Flora) gathering flowers. 1st century A.D. National Museum, Naples

5. Lesbia, Let Us Live and Love

translated by **Reney Myers** *and* **Robert J. Ormsby**

Lesbia, let us live and love,
And think what crabbed old men resent,
With all their talk, not worth a cent.
The sun which sets returns above,
5 But once our short-lived light shall die,
In endless darkness we must lie.
So kiss me, give me a thousand kisses,
Another thousand, hundreds more,
Then hundred thousands by the score,
10 Confusing all men with our blisses,
So they can't cast an evil spell
Who can't keep count of kisses well.

1st century B.C.

8. Wretched Catullus, Leave Off Playing the Fool

translated by **Reney Myers** *and* **Robert J. Ormsby**

Wretched Catullus, leave off playing the
    fool:
Give up as lost what is forever past.
But once, bright, golden suns beamed down
    and cast
A happiness on you when she would rule
5 Your steps and lead you into joyous play.
How much you loved her! More than any
    man
Can ever love. With her, what joy began!
That sunny world seemed yours in every
    way.
Yet now she does not want you, and alas,

10 You must not chase her nor live wretchedly,
Thus make your heart as hard as it can be.
So good-bye, baby! Catullus now will pass
You up, won't need you, nor will entertain
A thought of you nor seek your company.
15 Oh wicked thing, I'm tough as I can be!
Now who'll invite you? Where will you
    obtain
Praise of your beauty? Who'll make sorrows
    blisses?
Who'll love you now? Or bite your lips in
    kisses?
Not Catullus! He's determined to abstain.

1st century B.C.

70. My Love Says She Would Marry Only Me

translated by **Reney Myers** *and* **Robert J. Ormsby**

My love says she would marry only me,
And Jove himself could never make her care.
What women say to lovers, you'll agree,
One writes on running water or on air.
1st century B.C.

85. Love and Hate

translated by **G. P. Goold**

I hate and love. Perhaps you ask how I can
  do this?
  I know not, but I feel it so, and I am in
  agony.
1st century B.C.

101. At His Brother's Grave

translated by **G. P. Goold**

After travel over many a land and over many
  a sea
  I have come, brother, for these sad funeral
  rites,
to present you with death's last tribute
  and speak to your unanswering ashes,
    though speak in vain,
5 seeing that fate has robbed me of your living
  self,
  alas, poor brother, so cruelly stolen from
  me.
But now, naught else availing, take these
  gifts, which
  ancient custom prescribes, a forlorn
  tribute to the dead;
take them moistened with a brother's many
  tears,
10   and for all time, brother, hail and farewell!
1st century B.C.

Reader's Note

The Art of Catullus's Poetry

Catullus's lyric 85 reads this way:

Odi et amo. Quare id faciam, fortasse requiris.
  Nescio, sed fieri sentio et excrucior.

Translated literally, word for word, it reads:

I hate and I love. On what account this thing
  I do, perhaps you ask.
I do not know, but that it is happening I feel,
  and I am in torment.

Simply comparing the two suggests that one
of the beauties of Catullus's poem is its brevity.

This comes partly from a crucial difference in
structure between his language and ours. English
as an analytical language expresses changes in
grammar and syntax by using several words,
whereas Latin, an inflected language, expresses
the same changes by altering the form of a single
word. For example, the shift in English from "I
love" to "you love" is signaled by altering a separate word, a pronoun, while in Latin the same
shift is indicated by merely altering the verb *amo*
to *amas*. Catullus's poem is full of verbs: *odi* ("I
hate"), *amo* ("I love"), *faciam* ("I do"), *requiris*
("you ask"), *nescio* ("I do not know"), *sentio* ("I

feel"), *excrucior* ("I am in torment"). The condensation permitted by Latin as an inflected language enables him to elegantly weave all of these expressions of feeling into a tiny poem without the cumbersome extra words needed in English.

Further, because the changeable endings of words indicate grammatical meaning, Latin writers are much more free to order their words any way they like—the position of a word within a sentence doesn't affect its meaning. In this poem you can see that Catullus begins and ends each of his lines with a verb, and these four verbs summarize the meaning of the poem: *odi, requiris, nescio,* and *excrucior.* Ending the poem

with *excrucior* is especially dramatic, since the reader is left with a cry of pain whose very sound illustrates what the poem's speaker is going through. Further, Catullus balances two pairs of verbs, both connected by the simple conjunction *et* ("and"): *odi et amo* and *sentio et excrucior.* They begin and end the poem. It moves from the first pair, which describe emotion, to the second, which suggest immediate, physical sensation: I feel, and I hurt. Catullus was celebrated for using the simplest sorts of everyday words, rather than a heightened, "poetic" vocabulary. Here his plain talk still speaks of intense experience.

THINK AND DISCUSS
Understanding
1. What will the speaker of lyric 5 do despite the criticism of "crabbed old men"?
2. How does the speaker of lyric 8 try to resolve his love problem?
3. What is the only thing that the speaker of 101 can now do for his brother?

Analyzing
4. Why does the speaker in lyric 5 contrast himself with the sun?
5. Where does a humorous form of **hyperbole** appear in Catullus's lyrics?
6. Explain how the **tone** of the speaker's words changes during lyric 8.
7. How does **apostrophe** intensify the drama of these brief lyrics?
8. Explore the ways in which the contradictions of lyric 85 reappear in other lyrics by Catullus.

Extending
9. Characterize the kind of love which appears in these lyrics, and discuss its limitations.
10. Compare and contrast the attitude toward love expressed in the lyrics of Catullus with that of the Indian play *Shakuntala* in Unit 1. See pages 62–63.

COMPOSITION
Writing About Characters
Catullus identifies himself as the speaker in several of his love poems, but this voice is, nevertheless, primarily a literary creation. His poems, taken together, suggest both a character and the outlines of a love story. Write an essay for your classmates that explains the most significant traits of this character. Make a list of his traits such as his fear of death, his frequent scorn for himself, the kind of love he feels for Lesbia, and so on. Organize the traits in ascending order of importance, and use them as the basis for the outline of your paper. See "Writing About Characters" in the Writer's Handbook.

Analyzing Catullus's Imagery
The poems of Catullus have few **images,** but those that he uses can suggest a great many things. Write an essay for your teacher in which you explore how some of his images evoke particular reactions from the reader. Examine the images Catullus uses: light and darkness, a flame, lips, air and water, tears and ashes. Choose four that seem particularly effective to you. See "Writing About Poetry and Poetic Devices" in the Writer's Handbook.

Horace is the finest lyric poet of ancient Rome. He enjoyed praise and success during his own lifetime, and later generations so frequently read his work that he became the principal interpreter of Roman culture to those readers. His widely quoted phrases, *carpe diem* ("seize the day") and *dulce et decorum est pro patria mori* ("it is sweet and proper to die for the fatherland"), sum up two of the dominant—and conflicting—attitudes of his era.

Horace is a member of the generation that followed Cicero and Catullus, the generation that survived the civil wars and lived on to witness the unification of the Roman empire under Caesar Augustus. Horace himself participated in the crucial events of his day. His father was a freed slave who had made enough money to take Horace from their remote hometown of Venusia in southeastern Italy to Rome for a proper education. While Horace was studying there in 49 B.C., Julius Caesar crossed the Rubicon and the civil wars began. Horace traveled to Athens when he was nineteen to study philosophy, and when Brutus and his conspiracy assassinated Caesar in 44 B.C., Horace allied himself with these Republican rebels. He fought in the battle of Philippi in 42 B.C., and after the defeat found his family fortune confiscated. Thanks to a general amnesty he was able to return to Rome—though penniless—in 41 B.C.

There he began to write poetry that caught the eye of another young writer, Virgil, who introduced Horace to the wealthy patron Maecenas. For centuries, people of wealth and power in both Greece and Rome had considered it part of their social role to help support the arts. Maecenas, typical of his class, sought out and aided the best writers of his day. In 33 B.C., he gave Horace a large working farm in the Sabine hills, which permitted the poet to concentrate on his art, free from any financial anxiety. The relation between patron and poet was a genuine, close friendship, Maecenas expecting of Horace not flattery, but only dedication to his art. Through his patron, Horace met Octavian, the man who would soon be Caesar Augustus.

Horace's first three books of *Odes* appeared in 23 B.C., when the poet was 42 years old. The title can be misleading, since these are not the long, metrically varied odes that the Greek writer Pindar had written. Horace's odes are relatively brief, use repeating stanza forms, and usually take an informal tone. They illustrate a shift going on in the culture of his day. Some recall the themes of Catullus, urging a friend to enjoy the pleasures of the moment. And yet the emotional extremes of Catullus, the hating and hurting, are gone, replaced by a more stoic "steady head." However, there are other poems very different from those of Catullus and his school, such as the first six odes of Book III, which describe traditional Roman ideals. They echo Augustus's efforts as national leader to bring Rome back to a way of life that wealth and power were eroding, back to the virtues of their ancestors. In such works Horace becomes very much the public poet, engaged in the issues of his day.

Wall painting from Pompeii showing (left) two book-scrolls of papyrus; (right) a diptych, or wooden two-leafed writing tablet. Before A.D. 79

from the Odes

Horace *translated by* **Joseph P. Clancy**

I, 11

Don't ask, Leuconoë, the forbidden
    question, how long
the gods have given to you and to me: don't
    imagine
fortunetellers know. Better to take what is
    coming,
whether Jove allows us more winters, or this
    that now
5 wearies the Etruscan sea[1] as it beats on the
    cliffs
is the last. Be sensible: strain the wine: in a
    little life,
take no long looks ahead. As we talk, time
    spites us
and runs: reap today: save no hopes for
    tomorrow.

I, 23

You shy from me, Chloe, like a fawn
seeking on pathless hills its frightened
mother, scared silly
by breezes and the big woods.

5 For if spring's advances make the light
leaves tremble, if green lizards stir
the bramble bushes, its heart
knocks and its knees quiver.

Now really, I'm no ferocious tiger
10 or Moroccan lion, chasing, mauling:
stop trailing mama now,
you're ready for a man.

---

1. *Etruscan sea*, the Tyrrhenian Sea, which washes the
western coast of Italy north of Rome, where the Etruscan
people once lived.

III, 2

Let him learn to suffer poverty's strictness
gladly, a young man toughened by hard
    army
training, and he a horseman whose spear
is feared, a plague to savage Parthians,[1]

5 and spend his life under the sky in danger
and action. Watching from the enemy walls,
may the wife of the warring ruler
and the virgin who is ripe for marriage

sigh: "Ah god, our royal lover knows little
10 of battles, may he not arouse the lion
who is wild when touched, whose thirst for
    blood
drives him on through the heart of the
    slaughter."

Precious and proper is death for one's
    country.
And death comes swiftly after the runaway
15 and shows no mercy to the hamstrings
and the boneless backs of peace-loving boys.

Manhood, that has known no disgrace in
    defeat,

retains its brightness, its honors untarnished,
and does not take or leave the axes[2]
20 at the whim of the wavering public.

Manhood, that to those who do not deserve
    death
opens heaven, takes a path barred to others
and turns away on its beating wings
from the mere masses and the muddy earth.

25 And there is certain reward for the silence
that keeps faith: I will forbid one who
    broadcasts
the secret rites of Ceres[3] to stay
beneath the same roof, or cast off with me

in a thin ship; God the Father, disobeyed,
30 has often put innocent in with guilty:
seldom, with the sinner in the lead,
does Punishment fail though its feet are
    lame.

1st century B.C.

---

1. *Parthians*, an empire beyond the Euphrates in the Middle East, which the Romans fought intermittently, and without much success, during this period.
2. *the axes*, symbols of political authority carried before the magistrates in Rome.
3. *rite of Ceres* (sir′ēz), rituals of a secret cult brought from Greece and practiced by some Romans.

THINK AND DISCUSS
Understanding
1. What is the answer to the forbidden question in Ode I, 11?
2. In Ode I, 23 how is Chloe like a fawn?
3. What kind of conduct does Ode III, 2 praise?

Analyzing
4. How does the **setting** of Ode I, 11 underscore its theme?
5. Explain how Ode I, 23 uses **figurative language** concerning animals to give a specific **tone** to this invitation.

6. Explain the significance of the two warnings in Ode III, 2 about deserters (lines 14–16) and those who violate secrets (lines 26–32).

Extending
7. The speaker in Ode I, 11 argues that refusing to look ahead is sensible; but what dangers might this lead to?
8. Discuss whether Ode I, 23 is a *carpe diem* poem.
9. Explain why a poem such as Ode III, 2 would please Augustus.

REVIEWING: Imagery H⫯
See Handbook of Literary Terms, p. 953.
Imagery is the use of concrete words or details that appeal to the senses of sight, sound, touch, smell, and taste, or to internal feelings.

1. How many images are there in the second stanza of Ode I, 23?
2. What similarities do they share?
3. Together, how do they help picture Chloe?

VOCABULARY
Word Analogies
In each item below, you will find a pair of related words, followed by four additional pairs, each preceded by a letter. From among these four pairs, select the one whose relationship is the closest to that in the first pair and write its letter on your paper. The colon means "is related to."

1. sensible : foolish as (**a**) hatred : revenge; (**b**) hostility : comradeship; (**c**) lazy : idle; (**d**) tool : work.
2. ferocious : fierce as (**a**) certain : questionable; (**b**) active : passive; (**c**) unbreakable : permanent; (**d**) individual : general.
3. untarnished : spotless as (**a**) action : boredom; (**b**) success : failure; (**c**) child : adult; (**d**) saintly : virtuous.
4. quiver : tremble as (**a**) victory : battle; (**b**) timid : fearful; (**c**) book : learning; (**d**) farmer : agriculture.
5. mauling : caressing as (**a**) actor : theater; (**b**) boggy : dry; (**c**) wintry : frigid; (**d**) seasickness : voyage.

THINKING SKILLS
Generalizing
To generalize is to infer a general rule from particular data.

1. Considering the poems by Horace you have read, describe what might be his main reasons for writing poetry.
2. Horace calls these poems odes. Create a generalized description of their most common traits that you could use to explain to someone who has not read them the characteristics of the Horatian ode.

COMPOSITION ◄━━━━━━
Writing About Theme
One of the first difficulties facing the reader of Ode III, 2 is the variety of things it describes, from the woman watching a battle on the walls of an enemy town to the fool who betrays the secret rites of Ceres. Write an essay to be read by your classmates that explains how the theme of this poem unifies its various parts. Define for yourself just what the poem's theme is. Next, list in the order of their appearance all the different things which the poem describes, and connect each with its theme. Then outline how you will explain what you have discovered, devoting a paragraph to each of the following groupings: stanzas 1–3, stanzas 4–5, and stanzas 6–7.

ENRICHMENT
Contrasting Horace and Owen
The British educational system required schoolboys to translate Horace's Ode III, 2 and hoped that its military idealism would inspire each new generation with the will to defend their country. At the outbreak of World War I, with patriotic fervor at fever pitch, its celebrated assertion (of line 13) "dulce et decorum est pro patria mori,"—"sweet and fitting it is to die for the fatherland"—seemed exactly the right way to think about war. Months later, the young soldier Wilfred Owen wrote a poem using Horace's line as a title, "Dulce et Decorum Est." Find this poem in an anthology of English literature, have a member of the class read it aloud, and then discuss the shift in attitude between Horace and Owen, and the reasons for that shift.

BIOGRAPHY

Virgil
70–19 B.C.

Virgil was born on a farm near Mantua in the frontier province of Cisalpine Gaul. Unlike Catullus, who came from the same area, he never ceased to love farming, the fields, and the cycle of the seasons. Two of his major works are devoted to celebrating the countryside. He seems to have been a sickly man, awkward with other people. Whenever he could, Virgil fled the city for an isolated existence. Though the civil wars dominated the years of his youth, he avoided military service for the sake of study.

At the age of thirty-two Virgil published his first book, the *Eclogues* (37 B.C.), poems spoken by idealized shepherds living in an idealized landscape, elaborately echoing past writers. Perhaps because so many other Romans were disillusioned with city life, and longed for a rural peace they had long ago abandoned, the poem gained wide popularity. A famous actress recited some of its lyrics on stage. Virgil's reputation spread. Soon Maecenas, who was later to help Horace as well, became Virgil's patron, giving him a house in the countryside near Naples, and introducing him to Octavian.

It was in 29 B.C., when Octavian was returning to Rome after the defeat of Antony and Cleopatra, that Virgil and Maecenas met him in the south of Italy, and over four days Virgil read to both men his most recent poem, the *Georgics*. There Virgil describes work on a farm, celebrating in over 2,000 lines the rich fruitfulness of the Italian earth and the virtues of self-denial and hard work found in agricultural societies. Octavian recognized in this poem the moral values that he believed Rome lacked, and needed to relearn, and after praising Virgil, he urged him to begin an epic.

For the next ten years Virgil worked at his masterpiece, the *Aeneid*, and he died with it not quite finished. From the beginning he sought to rival Homer, dividing his epic into two halves, the first describing the journeys of the hero Aeneas, and thus imitating the *Odyssey*, the second narrating his battles to win a foothold on the Italian mainland, echoing Homer's *Iliad*. However, there were too many differences of intention to permit a close parallel. Virgil sought to describe the founding of his nation, and to glorify Rome as an eternal city created at the bidding of the gods themselves. He meant his readers to see in Aeneas founding Rome a foreshadowing of Octavian, now titled Caesar Augustus, rebuilding Rome a second time, after the civil wars. Thus from the first Virgil's poem was, in complicated ways, dedicated to public, contemporary concerns.

But Virgil was also a great poet, and his epic tells a story of adventure and bravery, with a beauty of language and style rarely equaled in world literature. Virgil's gift for characterization is subtle. His Aeneas is no brawny fool, but rather a complex, divided man who at first tries to resist his destiny, and, in the end, gains little personal reward from all the sacrifices that he has to make. For Europe during the Middle Ages and the Renaissance, the *Aeneid* was the greatest literary work of all time, the ideal every writer dreamed of equaling, though none ever did.

Virgil, like Homer, starts his epic *in medias res*—in the middle of the story, as Horace described it. Aeneas has led a group of refugees from Troy through terrible sea storms to a haven at Carthage, where the generous Queen Dido welcomes them. During a feast, she asks Aeneas to describe what has happened to him, and he begins, in Virgil's Book Two, with the destruction of Troy.

 Review METAPHOR in the Handbook of Literary Terms, page 957.

from the Aeneid

Virgil *translated by* **Rolfe Humphries**

from Book Two

"Broken in war, set back by fate, the leaders
Of the Greek host, as years went by, contrived,
With Pallas's[1] help, a horse as big as a mountain.
They wove its sides with planks of fir, pretending
5 This was an offering for their safe return,
At least, so rumor had it. But inside
They packed, in secret, into the hollow sides
The fittest warriors; the belly's cavern,
Huge as it was, was filled with men in armor.
10 There is an island, Tenedos,[2] well-known,
Rich in the days of Priam;[3] now it is only
A bay, and not too good an anchorage
For any ship to trust. They sailed there, hid
On the deserted shore. We thought they had gone,
15 Bound for Mycenae,[4] and Troy was very happy,
Shaking off grief, throwing the gates wide open.
It was a pleasure, for a change, to go
See the Greek camp, station and shore abandoned;
Why, this was where Achilles[5] camped, his minions,
20 The Dolopes, were here; and the fleet just yonder,
And that was the plain where we used to meet in
     battle.
Some of us stared in wonder at the horse,
Astounded by its vastness, Minerva's gift,
Death from the virgin goddess, had we known it.
25 Thymoetes,[6] whether in treachery, or because

The fates of Troy so ordered, was the first one
To urge us bring it in to the heart of the city,
But Capys, and some others, knowing better,
Suspicious of Greek plotting, said to throw it
30 Into the sea, to burn it up with fire,
To cut it open, see what there was inside it.
The wavering crowd could not make up its mind.
And, at that point, Laocoön came running,
With a great throng at his heels, down from the
     hilltop
35 As fast as ever he could, and before he reached us,
Cried in alarm: 'Are you crazy, wretched people?
Do you think they have gone, the foe? Do you think
     that any
Gifts of the Greeks lack treachery? Ulysses,[7]—
What was his reputation? Let me tell you,

---

1. **Pallas,** daughter of the king of the gods, named Pallas Athena in Greek, Minerva in Latin.
2. **Tenedos,** an island off the coast of Troy where the Greek fleet hid after leaving behind the huge wooden horse.
3. **Priam** (prī'əm), king of Troy.
4. **Mycenae** (mī sē'nē), one of the principal Greek kingdoms attacking Troy.
5. **Achilles** (ə kil'ēz), the strongest Greek warrior, already killed in battle before Troy.
6. **Thymoetes** (thi mē'tez), a Trojan citizen, as are Capys (kap'is) (l. 28) and Laocoön (lā ok'ō on) (l. 33).
7. **Ulysses,** Latin name for Odysseus.

40 Either the Greeks are hiding in this monster,
Or it's some trick of war, a spy, or engine,
To come down on the city. Tricky business
Is hiding in it. Do not trust it, Trojans,
Do not believe this horse. Whatever it may be,
45 I fear the Greeks, even when bringing presents.'
With that, he hurled the great spear at the side
With all the strength he had. It fastened, trembling,
And the struck womb rang hollow, a moaning sound.
He had driven us, almost, to let the light in
50 With the point of the steel, to probe, to tear, but
    something
Got in his way, the gods, or fate, or counsel,
Ill-omened, in our hearts; or Troy would be standing
And Priam's lofty citadel unshaken.
Meanwhile, some Trojan shepherds, pulling, and
    hauling,
55 Had a young fellow,[8] with his hands behind him,
Tied up, and they were dragging him to Priam.
He had let himself be taken so, on purpose,
To open Troy to the Greeks, a stranger, ready
For death or shifty cunning, a cool intriguer,
60 Let come what may. They crowd around to see him.
Take turns in making fun of him, that captive.
Listen, and learn Greek trickiness; learn all
Their crimes from one.
He stopped in the middle, frightened and defenseless,
65 Looked at the Trojan ranks,—'What land, what
    waters,
Can take me now?' he cried, 'There is nothing,
    nothing
Left for me any more, no place with the Greeks,
And here are the Trojans howling for my blood!'
Our mood was changed. We pitied him, poor fellow,
70 Sobbing his heart out. We bade him tell his story,
His lineage, his news: what can he count on,
The captive that he is? His fear had gone
As he began: . . .
'The Greeks were tired of the long war; they often
75 Wanted to sail from Troy for home. Oh, would
That they had only done it! But a storm
Would cut them off, or the wrong wind terrify them.
Especially, just after the horse was finished,
With the joined planks of maple, all the heaven
80 Roared loud with storm-clouds. In suspense and terror
We sent Eurypylus to ask Apollo[9]

What could be done; the oracle was gloomy,
Foreboding: "Blood, O Greeks, and a slain virgin[10]
Appeased the winds when first you came here; blood
85 Must pay for your return, a life be given,
An Argive life." The word came to our ears
With terror in it, our blood ran cold in our veins,
For whom was fate preparing? who would be
The victim of Apollo? Then Ulysses
90 Dragged Calchas into our midst, with a great uproar,
Trying his best to make the prophet tell us
What the gods wanted. And there were many then
Who told me what was coming, or kept silent
Because they saw, and all too well, the scheme
95 Ulysses had in mind. For ten days Calchas
Said nothing at all, hid in his tent, refusing
To have a word of his pronounce the sentence,
And all the time Ulysses kept on shouting,
Till Calchas broke, and doomed me to the altar.
100 And all assented; what each man had feared
In his own case, he bore with great composure
When turned another way.
The terrible day was almost on me; fillets
Were ready for my temples, the salted meal[11]
105 Prepared, the altars standing. But I fled,
I tore myself away from death, I admit it,
I hid all night in sedge and muddy water
At the edge of the lake, hoping, forever hoping,
They might set sail. And now I hope no longer
110 To see my home, my parents, or my children,
Poor things, whom they will kill because I fled them,
Whom they will murder for my sacrilege.
But oh, by the gods above, by any power
That values truth, by any uncorrupted
115 Remnant of faith in all the world, have pity,
Have pity on a soul that bears such sorrow,
More than I ever deserved.'
He had no need to ask us. Priam said,
Untie him, and we did so with a promise

---

8. *young fellow,* Sinon, a Greek sent to trick the Trojans
into accepting the horse.
9. *Apollo,* god who spoke through the oracle at Delphi.
See page 173.
10. *a slain virgin.* The gods forced the Greeks to kill
Iphigenia, the daughter of their leader Agamemnon, before
they could set sail for Troy.
11. *fillets . . . salted meal,* used in the ritual of sacrifice
to the gods.

120   To spare his life. Our king, with friendly words,
     Addressed him, saying, 'Whoever you are, forget
     The Greeks, from now on. You are ours; but tell me
     Why they have built this monstrous horse? who made
        it,
     Who thought of it? What is it, war-machine,
125   Religious offering?' And he, instructed
     In every trick and artifice, made answer,
     Lifting his hands, now free: 'Eternal fires,
     Inviolable godhead, be my witness,
     You altars, you accursèd swords, you fillets
130   Which I as victim wore, I had the right
     To break those solemn bonds, I had the right
     To hate those men, to bring whatever they hide
     Into the light and air; I am bound no longer
     To any country, any laws, but, Trojans,
135   Keep to the promise, if I tell the truth,
     If I pay back with interest.
     All the Greek hope, since first the war began,
     Rested in Pallas, always. But Ulysses,
     The crime-contriver, and the son of Tydeus[12]
140   Attacked Minerva's temple,[13] stole her image
     Out of the holy shrine, and slew the guards,
     And laid their bloody hands upon the goddess,
     And from that time the Danaan[14] hopes were broken,
     Faltered and failed. It was no doubtful anger
145   Pallas revealed; she gave them signs and portents.
     From her image in the camp the upraised eyes
     Shot fire, and sweat ran salty down the limbs,
     Thrice from the ground she seemed to flash and leap
     With vibrant spear and clashing shield. The priest,
150   Calchas, made prophecy: they must take to flight
     Over the sea, and Troy could not be taken
     Without new omens; they must go to Argos,
     Bring back the goddess again, whom they have taken
     In curved ships over the sea. And if they have gone,
155   They are bound for home, Mycenae, for new arms,
     New gods, new soldiers; they will be here again
     When least expected. Calchas' message warned them,
     And so they built this image, to replace
     The one they had stolen, a gigantic offering
160   For a tremendous sacrilege. It was Calchas,
     Again, who bade them build a mass so mighty
     It almost reached the stars, too big to enter
     Through any gate, or be brought inside the walls.
     For if your hands should damage it, destruction,

165   (May God avert it) would come upon the city,
     But if your hands helped bring it home, then Asia
     Would be invading Greece, and doom await
     Our children's children.'
                We believed him, we
     Whom neither Diomede nor great Achilles
170   Had taken, nor ten years, nor that armada,
     A thousand ships of war. But Sinon did it
     By perjury and guile.
              Then something else,
     Much greater and more terrible, was forced
     Upon us, troubling our unseeing spirits.
175   Laocoön, allotted priest of Neptune,[15]
     Was slaying a great bull beside the altars,
     When suddenly, over the tranquil deep
     From Tenedos,—I shudder even now,
     Recalling it—there came a pair of serpents
180   With monstrous coils, breasting the sea, and aiming
     Together for the shore. Their heads and shoulders
     Rose over the waves, upright, with bloody crests,
     The rest of them trailing along the water,
     Looping in giant spirals; the foaming sea
185   Hissed under their motion. And they reached the land,
     Their burning eyes suffused with blood and fire,
     Their darting tongues licking the hissing mouths.
     Pale at the sight, we fled. But they went on
     Straight toward Laocoön, and first each serpent
190   Seized in its coils his two young sons, and fastened
     The fangs in those poor bodies. And the priest
     Struggled to help them, weapons in his hand.
     They seized him, bound him with their mighty coils,
     Twice round his waist, twice round his neck, they
        squeezed
195   With scaly pressure, and still towered above him.
     Straining his hands to tear the knots apart,
     His chaplets stained with blood and the black poison,
     He uttered horrible cries, not even human,

---

12. *son of Tydeus* (tid′ē əs), Diomedes (dī ə mē′dēz), a Greek warrior.
13. *temple.* A Trojan temple housed a special statue of Athena, the Palladium, and legend had it the city would not fall as long as the statue remained. So Ulysses and Diomedes sneaked into the city one night and stole the statue. Sinon's description of what happened later is undoubtedly one of his lies.
14. *Danaan* (dan′ā ən), Greek.
15. *Neptune*, god of the sea. (Greek: Poseidon)

More like the bellowing of a bull, when wounded
200 It flees the altar, shaking from the shoulder
The ill-aimed axe. And on the pair went gliding
To the highest shrine, the citadel of Pallas,
And vanished underneath the feet of the goddess
And the circle of her shield.
                              The people trembled
205 Again; they said Laocoön deserved it,
Having, with spear, profaned the sacred image.
It must be brought to its place, they cried, the goddess
Must be appeased. We broke the walls, exposing
The city's battlements, and all were busy
210 Helping the work, with rollers underfoot
And ropes around the neck. It climbed our walls,
The deadly engine. Boys, unwedded girls
Sang alleluias round it, all rejoicing
To have a hand on the tow-rope. It came nearer,
215 Threatening, gliding, into the very city.
O motherland! O Ilium, home of gods,
O walls of Troy! Four times it stopped, four times
The sound of arms came from it, and we pressed on,
Unheedful, blind in madness, till we set it,
220 Ill-omened thing, on the citadel we worshipped.
And even when Cassandra[16] gave us warning,
We never believed her; so a god had ordered.
That day, our last, poor wretches, we were happy,
Garlanding the temples of the gods
225 All through the town.
                        And the sky turned, and darkness
Came from the ocean, the great shade covering earth
And heaven, and the trickery of the Greeks.
Sprawling along the walls, the Trojans slumbered,
Sleep holding their weary limbs, and the Greek
        armada,
230 From Tenedos, under the friendly silence
Of a still moon, came surely on. The flagship
Blazed at the masthead with a sudden signal,
And Sinon, guarded by the fates, the hostile
Will of the gods, swung loose the bolts; the Greeks
235 Came out of the wooden womb. The air received them
The happy captains, Sthenelus, Ulysses,
Thessandrus, Acamas, Achilles' son
Called Neoptolemus,[17] Thoas, Machaon,
Epeos, who designed the thing,—they all
240 Came sliding down the rope, and Menelaus
Was with them in the storming of a city

Illustration of the Trojan Horse from a late 15th-century manuscript. Bibliothèque Nationale, Paris

Buried in sleep and wine. The watch was murdered,
The open doors welcome the rush of comrades,
They marshal the determined ranks for battle.
245   It was the time when the first sleep begins
For weary mortals, heaven's most welcome gift.
In sleep, before my eyes, I seemed to see
Hector,[18] most sorrowful, black with bloody dust,

---

16. *Cassandra* (kə san′drə), a daughter of Priam who correctly foretold the future; however, because she refused the love of Apollo he cursed her so that no one would believe what she said.
17. *Achilles' son . . . Neoptolemus,* (nē′op tol′ē mŭs). Achilles' son joined the Greek army after his father's death. He is also (line 371) called *Pyrrhus.*
18. *Hector,* the greatest Trojan warrior. Achilles killed him, and dragged his body around the walls of Troy to revenge his dead friend, Patroclus, whom Hector had killed. Eventually Achilles returned the defiled body for burial.

Torn, as he had been by Achilles' car,
250 The thong-marks on his swollen feet. How changed
He was from that great Hector who came, once,
Triumphant in Achilles' spoil,[19] from hurling
Fire at the Grecian ships. With ragged beard,
Hair matted with his blood, wearing the wounds
255 He earned around the walls of Troy, he stood there.
It seemed that I spoke first:—'O light of Troy,
Our surest hope, we have long been waiting for you,
What shores have kept you from us? Many deaths,
Much suffering, have visited our city,
260 And we are tired. Why do I see these wounds?
What shame has caused them?' Those were foolish
  questions;
He made no answer but a sigh or a groan,
And then: 'Alas, O goddess-born![20] Take flight,
Escape these flames! The enemy has the walls,
265 Troy topples from her lofty height; enough
Has been paid out to Priam and to country.
Could any hand have saved them, Hector's would
  have.
Troy trusts to you her household gods, commending
Her holy things to you; take them, companions
270 Of destiny; seek walls for them, and a city
To be established, a long sea-wandering over.'
From the inner shrine he carried Vesta's chaplets[21]
In his own hands, and her undying fire.
  Meanwhile, the city is all confusion and sorrow;
275 My father Anchises' house, remote and sheltered
Among its trees, was not so far away
But I could hear the noises, always clearer,
The thickening din of war. Breaking from sleep,
I climb to the roof-top, listening and straining
280 The way a shepherd does on the top of a mountain
When fire goes over the corn, and the winds are
  roaring,
Or the rush of a mountain torrent drowns the fields
And the happy crops and the work of men and oxen
And even drags great trees over. And then I knew
285 The truth indeed; the craft of the Greeks was hidden
No longer from my sight. The house of a neighbor,
Deiphobus, went up in flames; next door,
Ucalegon was burning. Sigeum's water
Gave back the glow. Men shouted, and the trumpets
290 Blared loud. I grab my arms, with little purpose,
There was no sense in it, but my heart was burning

To mass a band for war, rush to the hilltop
With comrades at my side. Anger and frenzy
Hurry me on. A decent death in battle
295 Is a helpful thought, sometimes.
  And here came Panthus, running from the weapons,
Priest of Apollo, and a son of Othrys,
With holy relics in his hands, and dragging
His little grandson, here came Panthus, running
300 In madness to my door. 'How goes it, Panthus?
What stronghold still is ours?' I had hardly spoken,
When he began, with a groan: 'It has come, this day
Will be our last, and we can not escape it.
Trojans we have been, Troy has been, and glory
305 Is ours no more. Fierce Jupiter[22] has taken
Everything off to Argos,[23] and Greeks lord it
In a town on fire. The horse, high in the city,
Pours out armed men, and Sinon, arrogant victor,
Lights up more fires. The gates are standing open,
310 And men are there by the thousands, ever as many
As came once from Mycenae; others block
The narrow streets, with weapons drawn; the blades
Flash in the dark; the point is set for murder.
A few of the guards are trying, striking blindly,
315 For all the good it does.'
  His words, or the gods' purpose, swept me on
Toward fire and arms, where the grim furies call,
And the clamor and confusion, reaching heaven.
Ripheus joined me, Epytus, mighty in arms,
320 Came to my side in the moonlight, Hypanis, Dymas,
And young Coroebus, Mygdon's son, poor youngster,
Mad with a hopeless passion for Cassandra,
He wanted to help Priam, but never heeded
The warnings of his loved one.
        As they ranged
325 Themselves for battle, eager, I addressed them:
'O brave young hearts, it will do no good; no matter.

---

19. *Achilles' spoil.* At one point in the fighting Hector
seized Achilles' armor and wore it himself.
20. *goddess-born.* Aeneas is the son of Venus, goddess of
love.
21. *Vesta's chaplets.* Vesta was goddess of the hearth and
home. In every city a public fire burned constantly in her
honor. When Greek cities sent people out to create colonies they took coals from the fire with them, and preserved the vestal fire in the new city.
22. *Jupiter*, king of the gods; also called Jove.
23. *Argos*, Greek city-state on the Peloponnesus.

Reader's Note

The Sounds of Virgil's Latin

Even in Rolfe Humphries's skillful translation, much of the sound of Virgil's poetry disappears. Here is a tiny sample of his original. It describes night falling on fated Troy, lines 225–227. Beneath Virgil's Latin you will see a literal, word-for-word English translation.

Vertitur interea caelum et ruit Oceano nox
Turned meanwhile the sky and rushed down on
  Ocean the night
involvens umbra magna terramque polumque
wrapping up in shadows huge both earth and sky
Myrmidonumque dolos . . .
And the Myrmidons's trick . . .

The first half of the second line begins with a rich, ominous music that uses the rhythmic repetition of *v* in *involvens* and then similar repetitions of *m* and *a* in two short words with the same number of syllables, *umbra magna*. Both sound and rhythm suggest the steady, overwhelming movement of nighttime darkness as it wraps up everything in sight.

Virgil could choose various words to name the sky and the Greeks, and in the last two lines here he uses not the common Latin term for sky, *caelum* (which you will find in the first line), but an odd term, *polum*, which literally means "north pole." Instead of other words for the Greeks, he uses the name of one Greek tribe, the Myrmidons. He is creating a menacing pattern of sound, from the relatively high pitch of "*erra*" in *terram* to a more hollow sound in the *pol* of *polum* and then down to the deep pitched *donumque* of *Myrmidonumque*, the sounds of the words themselves echoing the image of a dark shadow covering the fated city.

Further, Virgil shows why this evening is so ominous by moving in the sequence of the words in this description from nature, earth and sky, to the *dolos* or "trick" which the Greeks have left behind. One way to say "and" in Latin is to attach the suffix *que* to the end of a word, and here Virgil does just that in order to link earth, sky, and trick, as well as to build up a rhythmic repetition, *. . . que . . . que . . . que*, which climaxes in *Myrmidonumque dolos*.

Even if your will is fixed, to follow a leader
Taking the final risk, you can't help seeing
The fortune of our state. The gods have gone,
30 They have left their shrines and altars, and the power
They once upheld is fallen. You are helping
A town already burnt. So let us die,
Rush into arms. One safety for the vanquished
Is to have hope of none.'
           They were young, and angry.
35 Like wolves, marauders in black mist, whom hunger
Drives blindly on, whose whelps, abandoned, wait
  them
Dry-jawed, so we went on, through foes, through
  weapons,
To certain death; we made for the heart of the city,
Black night around us with its hollow shadow.
40 Who could explain that night's destruction, equal

Its agony with tears? The ancient city,
A power for many years, comes down, and corpses
Lie littering the streets and homes and altars.
Not only Trojans die. The old-time valor
345 Returns to the vanquished heart, and the Greek victors
Know what it is to fall. Everywhere sorrow,
Everywhere panic, everywhere the image
Of death, made manifold. . . .
    You would ask, perhaps, about the fate of Priam?
350 When he saw the city fall, and the doors of the palace
Ripped from the hinge, and the enemy pouring in,
Old as he was, he went and found his armor,
Unused so many years, and his old shoulders
Shook as he put it on. He took his sword,
355 A useless weapon, and, doomed to die, went
  rushing
Into the midst of the foe. There was an altar

In the open court-yard, shaded by a laurel
Whose shadow darkened the household gods, and
    here
Hecuba[24] and her daughters had come thronging,
360 Like doves by a black storm driven. They were
    praying
Here at the altar, and clinging to the gods,
Whatever image was left. And the queen saw Priam
In the arms of his youth. 'O my unhappy husband,'
She cried, 'have you gone mad, to dress yourself
365 For battle, so? It is all no use; the time
Needs better help than yours; not even my Hector
Could help us now. Come to me, come to the altar;
It will protect us, or at least will let us
Die all together.' And she drew him to her.
370   Just then through darts, through weapons, come
    Polites,
A son of Priam, fleeing deadly Pyrrhus,
Down the long colonnades and empty hallways,
Wounded, and Pyrrhus after him, vicious, eager
For the last spear-thrust, and he drives it home;
375 Polites falls, and his life goes out with his blood,
Father and mother watching. And then Priam,
In the very grip of death, cried out in anger:—
'If there is any righteousness in heaven,
To care about such wickedness, the gods
380 Will have the right reward and thanks to offer
A man like this, who has made a father witness
The murder of his son, the worst pollution!
You claim to be Achilles's son. You liar!
Achilles had some reverence, respected
385 A suppliant's right and trust; he gave me back
My Hector's lifeless body for the tomb,
And let me go to my kingdom.' With the word
He flung a feeble spear, which dropped, deflected
From the rough bronze; it had hung there for a
    moment.
390 And Pyrrhus sneered: 'So, go and tell my father
The latest news: do not forget to mention,
Old messenger-boy, my villainous behavior,
And what a bastard Pyrrhus is. Now die!'
He dragged the old man, trembling, to the altar,
395 Slipping in his son's blood; he grabbed his hair
With the left hand, and the right drove home the
    sword
Deep in the side, to the hilt. And so fell Priam,

Who had seen Troy burn and her walls come down,
    once monarch,
Proud ruler over the peoples and lands of Asia.
400 He lies, a nameless body, on the shore,
Dismembered, huge, the head torn from the
    shoulders.
    Grim horror, then, came home to me. I saw
My father when I saw the king, the life
Going out with the cruel wound. I saw Creusa
405 Forsaken, my abandoned home, Iulus,
My little son. I looked around. They all
Had gone, exhausted, flung down from the walls,
Or dead in the fire, and I was left alone.
    And I saw Helen,[25] hiding, of all places,
410 At Vesta's shrine, and clinging there in silence,
But the bright flames lit the scene. That hated woman,
Fearing both Trojan anger and Greek vengeance,
A common fury to both lands, was crouching
Beside the altar. Anger flared up in me
415 For punishment and vengeance. Should she then,
I thought, come home to Sparta safe, uninjured
Walk through Mycenae, a triumphant queen?
See husband, home, parents and children, tended
By Trojan slave-girls? This, with Priam fallen
420 And Troy burnt down, and the shore soaked in blood?
Never! No memorable name, I knew,
Was won by punishing women, yet, for me,
There might be praise for the just abolition
Of this unholiness, and satisfaction
425 In vengeance for the ashes of my people.
All this I may have said aloud, in frenzy,
As I rushed on, when to my sight there came
A vision of my lovely mother, radiant
In the dark night, a goddess manifest,
430 As tall and fair as when she walks in heaven.
She caught me by the hand and stopped me:—'Son,
What sorrow rouses this relentless anger,
This violence? Do you care for me no longer?
Consider others first, your aged father,
435 Anchises; is your wife Creusa living?
Where is Iulus? Greeks are all around them,
Only my love between them, fire and sword.

---

24. **Hecuba** (hek′yə bə), Priam's wife, Queen of Troy.
25. **Helen**, Spartan queen, wife of Menelaus. Her abduction by the Trojan prince Paris was the cause of the Trojan war.

It is not for you to blame the Spartan woman,
Daughter of Tyndareus, or even Paris.
440 The gods are the ones, the high gods are relentless.
It is they who bring this power down, who topple
Troy from the high foundation. Look! Your vision
Is mortal dull, I will take the cloud away,—
Fear not a mother's counsel. Where you see
445 Rock torn from rock, and smoke and dust in billows,
Neptune is working, plying the trident, prying
The walls from their foundations. And see Juno,[26]
Fiercest of all, holding the Scaean gates,
Girt with the steel, and calling from the ships
450 Implacable companions. On the towers,—
Turn, and be certain—Pallas takes command
Gleaming with Gorgon and storm-cloud.[27] Even Jove,
Our father, nerves the Greeks with fire and spirit,
And spurs the other gods against the Trojans.
455 Hasten the flight, my son; no other labor
Waits for accomplishment. I promise safety
Until you reach your father's house.' She had spoken
And vanished in the thickening night of shadows.
Dread shapes come into vision, mighty powers,
460 Great gods at war with Troy, which, so it seemed,
Was sinking as I watched, with the same feeling
As when on mountain-tops you see the loggers
Hacking an ash-tree down, and it always threatens
To topple, nodding a little, and the leaves
465 Trembling when no wind stirs, and dies of its wounds
With one long loud last groan, and dirt from the
        ridges
Heaves up as it goes down with roots in air.
Divinity my guide, I leave the roof-top,
I pass unharmed through enemies and blazing,
470 Weapons give place to me, and flames retire.
    At last I reached the house, I found my father,
The first one that I looked for. I meant to take him
To the safety of the hills, but he was stubborn,
Refusing longer life or barren exile,
475 Since Troy was dead. 'You have the strength,' he told
        me,
'You are young enough, take flight. For me, had
        heaven
Wanted to save my life, they would have spared
This home for me. We have seen enough destruction,
More than enough, survived a captured city.
480 Speak to me as a corpse laid out for burial,

A quick farewell, and go. Death I shall find
With my own hand; the enemy will pity,
Or look for spoil. The loss of burial
Is nothing at all. I have been living too long
485 Hated by gods and useless, since the time
Jove blasted me with lightning wind and fire.'
He would not move, however we wept, Creusa,
Ascanius, all the house, insistent, pleading
That he should not bring all to ruin with him.
490 He would not move, he would not listen. Again
I rush to arms, I pray for death; what else
Was left to me? 'Dear father, were you thinking
I could abandon you, and go? what son
Could bear a thought so monstrous? If the gods
495 Want nothing to be left of so great a city,
If you are bound, or pleased, to add us all
To the wreck of Troy, the way is open for it—
Pyrrhus will soon be here; from the blood of Priam
He comes; he slays the son before the father,
500 The sire at the altar-stone; O my dear mother,
Was it for this you saved me, brought me through
The fire and sword, to see our enemies
Here in the very house, and wife and son
And father murdered in each other's blood?
505 Bring me my arms; the last light calls the conquered.
Let me go back to the Greeks, renew the battle,
We shall not all of us die unavenged.'
    Sword at my side, I was on the point of going,
Working the left arm into the shield. Creusa
510 Clung to me on the threshold, held my feet,
And made me see my little son:—'Dear husband,
If you are bent on dying, take us with you,
But if you think there is any hope in fighting,
And you should know, stay and defend the house!
515 To whom are we abandoned, your father and son,
And I, once called your wife?' She filled the house
With moaning outcry. And then something happened,
A wonderful portent. Over Iulus' head,
Between our hands and faces, there appeared
520 A blaze of gentle light; a tongue of flame,
Harmless and innocent, was playing over
The softness of his hair, around his temples.

---

26. *Juno,* queen of the gods.
27. *Gorgon and storm-cloud,* the decorations on Pallas's
war shield, the aegis.

Painted vase showing Aeneas carrying Anchises
from Troy. c. 500 B.C. Metropolitan Museum of Art

In worship of the gods and the holy star,
Crying: 'I follow, son, wherever you lead;
There is no delay, not now; Gods of my fathers,
540 Preserve my house, my grandson; yours the omen,
And Troy is in your keeping. O my son
I yield, I am ready to follow.' But the fire
Came louder over the walls, the flames rolled nearer
Their burning tide. 'Climb to my shoulders, father,
545 It will be no burden, so we are together,
Meeting a common danger or salvation.
Iulus, take my hand; Creusa, follow
A little way behind. Listen, you servants!
You will find, when you leave the city, an old temple
550 That once belonged to Ceres;[28] it has been tended
For many years with the worship of our fathers.
There's a little hill there, and a cypress tree;
And that's where we shall meet, one way or another.
And one thing more: you, father, are to carry
555 The holy objects and the gods of the household,
My hands are foul with battle and blood, I could not
Touch them without pollution.'
                                                    I bent down
And over my neck and shoulders spread the cover
Of a tawny lion-skin, took up my burden;
560 Little Iulus held my hand, and trotted,
As best he could, beside me; Creusa followed.
We went on through the shadows. I had been
Brave, so I thought, before, in the rain of weapons
And the cloud of massing Greeks. But now I trembled
565 At every breath of air, shook at a whisper,
Fearful for both my burden and companion.
    I was near the gates, and thinking we had made it,
But there was a sound, the tramp of marching feet,
And many of them, it seemed; my father, peering
570 Through the thick gloom, cried out:—'Son, they are
        coming!
Flee, flee! I see their shields, their gleaming bronze.'
Something or other took my senses from me
In that confusion. I turned aside from the path,
I do not know what happened then. Creusa
575 Was lost; she had missed the road, or halted, weary,
For a brief rest. I do not know what happened,
She was not seen again; I had not looked back,

We were afraid, we did our best to quench it
With our own hands, or water, but my father
525 Raised joyous eyes to heaven, and prayed aloud:—
'Almighty Jupiter, if any prayer
Of ours has power to move you, look upon us,
Grant only this, if we have ever deserved it,
Grant us a sign, and ratify the omen!'
530 He had hardly spoken, when thunder on the left
Resounded, and a shooting star from heaven
Drew a long trail of light across the shadows.
We saw it cross above the house, and vanish
In the woods of Ida, a wake of gleaming light
535 Where it had sped, and a trail of sulphurous odor.
This was a victory: my father rose

---

28. *Ceres* (sir′ēz), goddess of grain and the harvest.

Nor even thought about her, till we came
To Ceres' hallowed home. The count was perfect,
580 Only one missing there, the wife and mother.
Whom did I not accuse, of gods and mortals,
Then in my frenzy? What worse thing had happened
In the city overthrown? I left Anchises,
My son, my household gods, to my companions,
585 In a hiding-place in the valley; and I went back
Into the city again, wearing my armor,
Ready, still one more time, for any danger.
I found the walls again, the gate's dark portals,
I followed my own footsteps back, but terror,
590 Terror and silence were all I found. I went
On to my house. She might, just might, have gone
    there.
Only the Greeks were there, and fire devouring
The very pinnacles. I tried Priam's palace;
In the empty courtyards Phoenix and Ulysses
595 Guarded the spoils piled up at Juno's altar.
They had Trojan treasure there, loot from the altars,
Great drinking-bowls of gold, and stolen garments,
And human beings. A line of boys and women
Stood trembling there.
600 I took the risk of crying through the shadows,
Over and over, 'Creusa!' I kept calling,
'Creusa!' and 'Creusa!' but no answer.
No sense, no limit, to my endless rushing
All through the town; and then at last I saw her,
605 Or thought I did, her shadow a little taller
Than I remembered. And she spoke to me
Beside myself with terror:—'O dear husband,
What good is all this frantic grief? The gods

610 Have willed it so, Creusa may not join you
Out of this city; Jupiter denies it.
Long exile lies ahead, and vast sea-reaches
The ships must furrow, till you come to land
Far in the West; rich fields are there, and a river
Flowing with gentle current; its name is Tiber.
615 And happy days await you there, a kingdom,
A royal wife. Banish the tears of sorrow
Over Creusa lost. I shall never see
The arrogant houses of the Myrmidons,
Nor be a slave to any Grecian woman;
620 I am a Dardan woman; I am the wife
Of Venus' son; it is Cybele[29] who keeps me
Here on these shores. And now farewell, and love
Our son.' I wept, there was more to say; she left me,
Vanishing into empty air. Three times
625 I reached out toward her, and three times her image
Fled like the breath of a wind or a dream on wings.
The night was over; I went back to my comrades.
    I was surprised to find so many more
Had joined us, ready for exile, pitiful people,
630 Mothers, and men, and children, streaming in
From everywhere, looking for me to lead them
Wherever I would. Over the hills of Ida
The morning-star was rising; in the town
The Danaans held the gates, and help was hopeless.
635 I gave it up, I lifted up my father,
Together we sought the hills.''
1st century B.C.

___

29. *Cybele* (si bel′ē), a nature goddess.

THINK AND DISCUSS
Understanding
1. How does Sinon ensure the success of the wooden horse?
2. What force prevents Aeneas from killing Helen?
3. Why does Aeneas's father Anchises decide to abandon Troy?

Analyzing
4. How does the death of Laocoön (lines 189–201) **foreshadow** Troy's fall?
5. List the instances in which Aeneas sees some sort of supernatural vision. What do these examples suggest about him as a character?
6. Why does Virgil have Aeneas witness (**a**) the

death of Priam, and (**b**) Helen hiding by the shrine of Vesta?

7. What reasons does Virgil have for including the death of Aeneas's wife Creusa?

Extending

8. In what ways do the warrior virtues celebrated in Horace's Ode III, 2 appear in Aeneas's narrative?

9. Compare what Odysseus expects of life after his victory over the suitors, and what the *Aeneid* looks forward to in speeches like Creusa's in lines 611–616. How do these contrasting expectations illustrate the differences between Homer's epic and Virgil's epic?

REVIEWING: Metaphor H⫪

See Handbook of Literary Terms, p. 957.

Metaphor is a figure of speech that makes a comparison between two basically unlike things that have something in common. This comparison may be stated ("she was a stone") or implied ("her stony silence filled the room"). Unlike similes, metaphors use no connective such as *like* or *as*.

1. Troy is described as "a city/Buried in sleep and wine" (lines 241–242). To what is the city of Troy being compared in this metaphor?

2. The fire that destroys Troy is described in this way: "the fire/Came louder over the walls, the flames rolled nearer/Their burning tide" (lines 542–544). To what is the fire being compared in this metaphor?

VOCABULARY

Context

Try to infer the exact meaning of the following terms from the context where they appear. If you are still unsure of their meanings, check the Glossary. Then use each one in a sentence that illustrates its meaning.

1. citadel (line 53)
2. lineage (line 71)
3. appeased (line 84)

4. artifice (line 126)
5. portents (line 145)
6. commending (line 268)
7. marauders (line 335)
8. manifold (line 348)
9. suppliant (line 385)
10. pinnacles (line 593)

THINKING SKILLS

Synthesizing

To synthesize is to put together parts and elements to form a whole, a new pattern or structure not evident before.

1. What dominant idea interconnects the greatest number of scenes in the *Aeneid*?
2. Explain how that idea links each scene.

ENRICHMENT

Filming the Fall of Troy

Virgil's epic poem has all the materials for making an epic motion picture. But transforming his narrative onto the screen would be a formidable job. Divide the members of the class into separate production teams which will prepare for the filming of the scenes: (**1**) outside Troy, while the Trojans decide what to do with the wooden horse; (**2**) inside Troy, when the Greeks begin the attack; and (**3**) Aeneas's personal adventures during the destruction of the city. Each team will need to discuss: (**a**) how many camera positions will be needed, and where they should be located; (**b**) actors required, and who might best portray the principal roles; (**c**) the kinds of special effects that will be used, and possible ways to achieve them. When you have worked out your plans, get together with the other groups and compare your adaptations.

BIOGRAPHY

Ovid

43 B.C.–A.D. 18

Ovid's father wanted his son to go into public life, and so he sent the boy from their village home in Sulmo, ninety miles east of Rome, off to the capital for an education. Then, there was a long tour of the major cities of the ancient world in Greece, Asia Minor, and Sicily. On his return Ovid dutifully joined the legal profession and became a judge in the praetorian courts. But he did not really want that kind of a life. He wanted to be a poet. His father reminded him that Homer died poor, but Ovid would not listen.

Ovid was only twelve when Octavian defeated Antony, and the Rome he knew was untroubled by the civil wars that had so haunted the work of older writers. Perhaps as a reaction to this more secure, carefree society, Ovid's poetry usually turns to pleasure, and especially to love. His first book was the *Amores* (c. 16 B.C.), love lyrics addressed to a woman named Corinna, which he followed with the *Heroides*, a collection of fifteen fictional verse letters from famous women of the past to the men they loved. He then went on to a more theoretical study in three books called *The Art of Love* (c. 9 B.C.; second edition c. 2 B.C.).

However, Ovid's timing was not of the best. Octavian, now in control of the empire and renamed Augustus, sought to improve Roman life through a series of laws that punished adultery and other kinds of immoral conduct. Ovid seemed to be thumbing his nose at the emperor.

So he shifted the subjects of his next works. His *Fasti* is a poem about the religious holidays of the Roman calendar, which he left half completed in A.D. 4 while he worked on his masterpiece, the *Metamorphoses*. This narrative poem in fifteen books, written in the same meter as Virgil's epic the *Aeneid,* is a collection of stories of various kinds, united by the fact that in each of them, somehow, a transformation (or metamorphosis) takes place. Ovid's treatment is light-hearted and entertaining. The meter and length of his poem seem to mock Virgil's seriousness. The *Metamorphoses* became the repository for many of the most famous myths of ancient Mediterranean culture, and a favorite storybook for readers ever since it first appeared around A.D. 7.

Augustus was still struggling with Roman morals, however, especially within his own household. He had already banished his daughter Julia for flagrant immorality, and now he found that he had to do the same thing to his granddaughter, also named Julia. Somehow—though the facts of the case are not clear—Ovid was involved in the matter. Perhaps he knew too much, or saw something he should not have seen. At all events, he was also the author of those naughty books, and so Caesar Augustus banished him, at the age of 51, to the remote town of Tomis (modern-day Constanta) on the Black Sea. Caesar never let him return, though during the last ten years of his life Ovid wrote two works of poetic protest, *Tristia* ("The Book of Sorrows") and *Letters from the Black Sea*. He died in exile.

from the Metamorphoses

Ovid *translated by* **Rolfe Humphries**

The Story of Pyramus and Thisbe

Next door to each other, in the brick-walled city
Built by Semiramis,[1] lived a boy and girl,
Pyramus, a most handsome fellow, Thisbe,
Loveliest of all those Eastern girls. Their nearness
5 Made them acquainted, and love grew, in time,
So that they would have married, but their parents
Forbade it. But their parents could not keep them
From being in love: their nods and gestures showed
   it—
You know how fire suppressed burns all the fiercer.
10 There was a chink in the wall between the houses,
A flaw the careless builder had never noticed,
Nor anyone else, for many years, detected,
But the lovers found it—love is a finder, always—
Used it to talk through, and the loving whispers
15 Went back and forth in safety. They would stand
One on each side, listening for each other,
Happy if each could hear the other's breathing,
And then they would scold the wall: "You envious
   barrier,
Why get in our way? Would it be too much to ask
   you
20 To open wide for an embrace, or even
Permit us room to kiss in? Still, we are grateful,
We owe you something, we admit; at least
You let us talk together." But their talking
Was futile, rather; and when evening came
25 They would say *Good-night!* and give the good-night
   kisses
That never reached the other.
                                    The next morning
Came, and the fires of night burnt out, and sunshine
Dried the night frost, and Pyramus and Thisbe
Met at the usual place, and first, in whispers,
30 Complained, and came—high time!—to a decision.
That night, when all was quiet, they would fool
Their guardians, or try to, come outdoors,
Run away from home, and even leave the city.
And, not to miss each other, as they wandered

35 In the wide fields, where should they meet? At Ninus's
Tomb, they supposed, was best; there was a tree there,
A mulberry-tree, loaded with snow-white berries,
Near a cool spring. The plan was good, the daylight
Was very slow in going, but at last
40 The sun went down into the waves as always,
And the night rose, as always, from those waters.

And Thisbe opened her door, so sly, so cunning,
There was no creaking of the hinge, and no one
Saw her go through the darkness, and she came,
45 Veiled, to the tomb of Ninus, sat there waiting
Under the shadow of the mulberry-tree.
Love made her bold. But suddenly, here came
   something!—
A lioness, her jaws a crimson froth
With the blood of cows, fresh-slain, came there for
   water,
50 And far off through the moonlight Thisbe saw her
And ran, all scared, to hide herself in a cave,
And dropped her veil as she ran. The lioness,
Having quenched her thirst, came back to the woods,
   and saw
The girl's light veil, and mangled it and mouthed it
55 With bloody jaws. Pyramus, coming there
Too late, saw tracks in the dust, turned pale, and
   paler
Seeing the bloody veil. "One night," he cried,
"Will kill two lovers, and one of them, most surely,
Deserved a longer life. It is all my fault,
60 I am the murderer, poor girl; I told you
To come here in the night, to all this terror,
And was not here before you, to protect you.
Come, tear my flesh, devour my guilty body,
Come, lions, all of you, whose lairs lie hidden
65 Under this rock! I am acting like a coward,

---

1. *Semiramis* (sē mir′ə mis), legendary founder of Babylon, and wife of King Ninus.

Nicolas Poussin (1594–1665), *Landscape with Pyramus and Thisbe*.
Städelsches Kunstinstitut, Frankfurt-am-Main

Praying for death." He lifts the veil and takes it
Into the shadow of their tree; he kisses
The veil he knows so well, his tears run down
Into its folds: "Drink my blood too!" he cries,
70 And draws his sword, and plunges it into his body,
And, dying, draws it out, warm from the wound.
As he lay there on the ground, the spouting blood
Leaped high, just as a pipe sends water spurting
Through a small hissing opening, when broken
75 With a flaw in the lead, and all the air is sprinkled.
The fruit of the tree, from that red spray, turned
    crimson,
And the roots, soaked with the blood, dyed all the
    berries
The same dark hue.
                  Thisbe came out of hiding,
Still frightened, but a little fearful, also,
80 To disappoint her lover. She kept looking
Not only with her eyes, but all her heart,
Eager to tell him of those terrible dangers,

About her own escape. She recognized
The place, the shape of the tree, but there was
    something
85 Strange or peculiar in the berries' color.
Could this be right? And then she saw a quiver
Of limbs on bloody ground, and started backward,
Paler than boxwood, shivering, as water
Stirs when a little breeze ruffles the surface.
90 It was not long before she knew her lover,
And tore her hair, and beat her innocent bosom
With her little fists, embraced the well-loved body,
Filling the wounds with tears, and kissed the lips
Cold in his dying. "O my Pyramus,"
95 She wept, "What evil fortune takes you from me?
Pyramus, answer me! Your dearest Thisbe
Is calling you. Pyramus, listen! Lift your head!"
He heard the name of Thisbe, and he lifted
His eyes, with the weight of death heavy upon them,
100 And saw her face, and closed his eyes.
                        And Thisbe

Ovid 255

Saw her own veil, and saw the ivory scabbard
With no sword in it, and understood. "Poor boy,"
She said, "So, it was your own hand,
Your love, that took your life away. I too
105 Have a brave hand for this one thing, I too
Have love enough, and this will give me strength
For the last wound. I will follow you in death,
Be called the cause and comrade of your dying.
Death was the only one could keep you from me,
110 Death shall not keep you from me. Wretched parents
Of Pyramus and Thisbe, listen to us,
Listen to both our prayers, do not begrudge us,

Whom death has joined, lying at last together
In the same tomb. And you, O tree, now shading
115 The body of one, and very soon to shadow
The bodies of two, keep in remembrance always
The sign of our death, the dark and mournful color."
She spoke, and fitting the sword-point at her breast,
Fell forward on the blade, still warm and reeking
120 With her lover's blood. Her prayers touched the gods,
And touched her parents, for the mulberry fruit
Still reddens at its ripeness, and the ashes
Rest in a common urn.

1st century A.D.

THINK AND DISCUSS
Understanding
1. What interrupts the nighttime meeting of these lovers?
2. How do the gods commemorate their death?

Analyzing
3. What do the narrator's asides, found for example in lines 9, 13, and 30, suggest about his attitude toward the story?
4. Describe alternative, more practical reactions that Pyramus might have had to the discovery of Thisbe's veil.
5. Characterize the **tone** of Pyramus's speech, lines 58–66.
6. To what extent is the extended **simile** found in lines 74–76 ironic?

Extending
7. Given the kind of treatment that Ovid uses in "Pyramus and Thisbe," what sort of love do you think he would like to praise?

VOCABULARY
Latin Roots
Many English words have Latin roots. For example, the Latin word *solvere*, meaning "to loosen," is the root of such words as *dissolve*, *absolve*, and *absolute*. Use the Glossary to answer the following questions about the words below.

Read each question, then write on your paper the correct word from the list. (You will not use all the words.) Be sure you can spell and pronounce each word.

acquainted   recognized   embrace   urn
detected   comrade   futile

1. Which two words come from the Latin word meaning "to know"?
2. Which comes from the Latin word meaning "room"?
3. Which comes from the Latin word meaning "arm"?
4. Which comes from the Latin word meaning "to pour"?
5. Which comes from the Latin word meaning "to cover"?

ENRICHMENT
Comparing Shakespeare and Ovid
At the end of his comedy *A Midsummer Night's Dream*, William Shakespeare has a group of simple folk entertain King Theseus and his newly-wed wife Hippolyta with a theatrical version of the Pyramus and Thisbe story. Read this scene (Act Four, Scene 1, lines 108–349) in class, with students taking the various roles, and then discuss how Shakespeare adapts Ovid's approach to the story.

BIOGRAPHY

Tacitus

c. A.D. 56–117

In early Roman culture, writing history took the form of "annals," summaries of the events in a given year. At first the priests of Rome kept such records, and by the year 123 B.C. they had accumulated 80 volumes. These became the primary source of information for later attempts by writers, such as Livy (59 B.C.–A.D. 17), to establish a comprehensive history of Rome from its earliest years.

To the Romans, as to the Greeks, history was an art form, closely related to epic or tragedy or oratory. People read passages from historical works out loud, and writers sought to create dramatic scenes and persuasive speeches that would stir the emotions of an audience. It was generally believed that the purpose of history was to make a moral evaluation of the past, to pass judgment on good and bad in order to educate citizens in proper conduct. The Roman historian Tacitus is very much a part of this tradition. His major works, which appeared nearly a century after the golden age of Roman literature under Augustus, picture his own time as an era of serious decline. He felt loyal to the old traditions of the senate and the Republic, and he considered the emperors of the first century A.D. decadent. He feared that Rome was moving toward its destruction.

This celebrated and somber writer was probably born in northern Italy around A.D. 56, the son of a public official. His early training was in oratory, and like Cicero he became a successful lawyer and powerful speaker. In 77 he married the daughter of a general, Julius Agricola, and by the year 88 was named praetor. After the death of the cruel and suspicious emperor Domitian he became consul (A.D. 97), still the highest elected position in the empire, and as the years went on he was appointed governor of the provinces of Germany (A.D. 100) and Asia (A.D. 112–113).

Tacitus began his career as a writer with a short biography of his father-in-law, *Agricola*, and a study of the Germanic people, *Germania*, both published around A.D. 98. His major historical works, the *Histories* (written between A.D. 104 and 109) and the *Annals* (published A.D. 117), examine the century just ended, the period between the end of Augustus's reign around A.D. 14 and the start of a new line of emperors under Nerva in 96. In these works Tacitus focuses on the Roman emperors and examines how the dwindling authority of the senate and the rising instability of the army permit them to acquire ever greater power, which they hasten to abuse, damaging the empire in the process.

The Middle Ages largely ignored Tacitus's work, but the Renaissance rediscovered him, and he had a powerful influence on important political theorists such as Machiavelli, and essayists like Montaigne. Today, along with Livy, he is considered one of Rome's greatest historians. The passage from the *Annals* which follows describes a disastrous fire that broke out in Rome in A.D. 64 and destroyed a great part of the city.

from the Annals

Tacitus   *translated by* **George Gilbert Ramsay**

And now came a calamitous fire— whether it was accidental or purposely contrived by the Emperor, remains uncertain: for on this point authorities are divided—more violent and more destructive than any that ever befell our city. It began in that part of the Circus[1] which adjoins the Palatine and Caelian hills. Breaking out in shops full of inflammable merchandise, it took hold and gathered strength at once; and being fanned by the wind soon embraced the entire length of the Circus, where there were no mansions with protective walls, no temple-enclosures, nor anything else to arrest its course. Furiously the destroying flames swept on, first over the level ground, then up the heights, then again plunging into the hollows, with a rapidity that outstripped all efforts to cope with them, the ancient city lending itself to their progress by its narrow tortuous streets and its misshapen blocks of buildings. The shrieks of panic-stricken women; the weakness of the aged, and the helplessness of the young; the efforts of some to save themselves, of others to help their neighbors; the hurrying of those who dragged their sick along, the lingering of those who waited for them—all made up a scene of inextricable confusion.

Many persons, while looking behind them, were enveloped from the front or from the side; or having escaped to the nearest place of safety, found this too in possession of the flames, and even places which they had thought beyond their reach in the same plight with the rest. At last, not knowing where to turn, or what to avoid, they poured into the roads or threw themselves down in the fields: some having lost their all, not having even food for the day; others, though with means of escape open to them, preferred to perish for love of the dear ones whom they could not save. And none dared to check the flames; for there were many who threatened and forced back those who would extinguish them, while others openly flung in torches, saying that they had their orders;—whether it was really so, or only that they wanted to plunder undisturbed.

At this moment Nero was at Antium. He did not return to the city until the flames were approaching the mansion which he had built to connect the Palatine with the Gardens of Maecenas,[2] nor could they be stopped until the whole Palatine, including the palace and everything around it, had been consumed. Nero assigned the Campus Martius and the Agrippa monuments[3] for the relief of the fugitive and houseless multitude. He threw open his own gardens also, and put up temporary buildings for the accommodation of the destitute; he brought up provisions from Ostia[4] and the neighboring towns; and he reduced the price of corn to three sesterces the peck. But popular as these measures were, they aroused no gratitude; for a rumor had got abroad that at the moment when the city was in flames Nero had mounted upon a stage in his own house, and by way of likening modern calamities to ancient, had sung the tale of the sack of Troy.[5]

Not until the sixth day was the fire got under, at the foot of the Esquiline hill, by demolishing a vast extent of buildings, so as to present nothing but the ground, and as it were the open sky, to its continued fury. But scarcely had the alarm sub-

---

1. *Circus*, Circus Maximus, an immense, elliptical stadium for horse races and other spectacles which seated 180,000 spectators.
2. *Palatine . . . Maecenas*. Nero's imperial palace was on the Palatine hill, while the gardens built by Maecenas were to the northeast, on the Esquiline Hill.
3. *Campus Martius . . . monuments*, the Field of Mars, an open area dotted with public buildings such as the monumental public baths built by Agrippa.
4. *Ostia*, the port of Rome at the mouth of the Tiber River.
5. *Troy*, as described by Virgil in Book Two of the *Aeneid*.

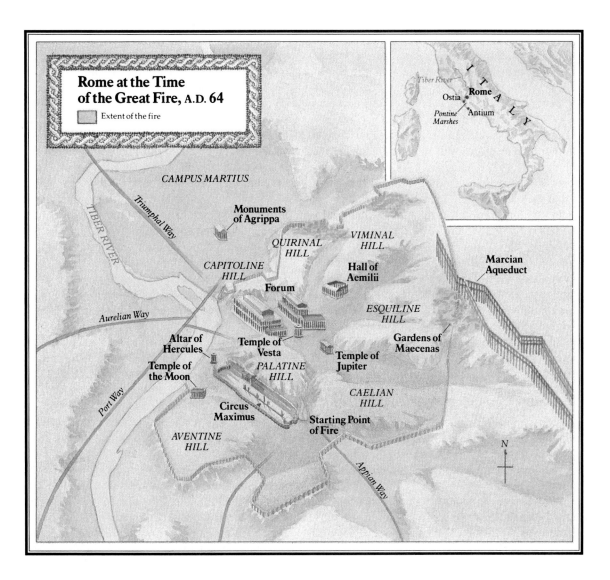

Rome at the Time of the Great Fire, A.D. 64

Extent of the fire

TIBER RIVER

Triumphal Way

CAMPUS MARTIUS

Monuments of Agrippa

QUIRINAL HILL

VIMINAL HILL

CAPITOLINE HILL

Hall of Aemilii

Marcian Aqueduct

Forum

Aurelian Way

ESQUILINE HILL

Altar of Hercules

Temple of Vesta

Gardens of Maecenas

Temple of the Moon

PALATINE HILL

Temple of Jupiter

Port Way

CAELIAN HILL

Circus Maximus

Starting Point of Fire

AVENTINE HILL

Appian Way

N

Tiber River

ITALY

Ostia **Rome**

Pontine Marshes Antium

sided, or the populace recovered from their despair, when it burst out again in the more open parts of the city; and though here the loss of life was less, the destruction of temples and porticoes of pleasure was still more complete. And the scandal attending this new fire was the greater that it broke out in the property owned by Tigellinus,[6] in the Aemilian quarter; the general belief being that Nero had the ambition to build a new city to be called after his own name. For of the four-

teen regions into which Rome was divided only four remained intact. Three were burned to the ground; in the other seven, nothing remained save a few fragments of ruined and half-burned houses.

To count up the number of mansions, of tenements, and of temples that were destroyed would be no easy matter. Among the oldest of the sacred buildings burned was that dedicated by Servius

---

6. Tigellinus (ti jel lē′nəs), second only to Nero in power.

Tullius of the Moon, and the Great Altar and fane raised by Evander to the Present Hercules. The temple vowed by Romulus to Jupiter, the Stayer of Flight; the Royal Palace of Numa; the Temple of Vesta, with the Household Gods of the Roman people, were all destroyed; added to these were the treasures won in numerous battles, and masterpieces of Greek art, as well as ancient and genuine monuments of Roman genius which were remembered by the older generation amid all the splendor of the restored city, and which could never be replaced. Some noted that the nineteenth of July, the day on which the fire began, was also the day on which the Senonian Gauls had taken and burned the city[7]; others were so curious in their calculations as to discover that the two burnings were separated from one another by exactly the same number of years, of months, and of days.

Nero profited by the ruin of his country to erect a palace in which the marvels were not to be gold and jewels, the usual and commonplace objects of luxury, so much as lawns and lakes and mock-wildernesses, with woods on one side and open glades and vistas on the other. His engineers and masters-of-works were Severus and Celer; men who had the ingenuity and the impudence to fool away the resources of the Empire in the attempt to provide by art what nature had pronounced impossible.

For these men undertook to dig a navigable canal, along the rocky shore and over the hills, all the way from Lake Avernus to the mouths of the Tiber. There was no other water for supplying such a canal than that of the Pontine marshes, and even if practicable, the labor would have been prodigious, and no object served. But Nero had a thirst for the incredible, and traces of his vain attempt to excavate the heights adjoining Lake Avernus are to be seen to this day.

The parts of the city unoccupied by Nero's palace were not built over without divisions, or indiscriminately, as after the Gallic fire, but in blocks of regular dimensions, with broad streets between. A limit was placed to the height of houses; open spaces were left; and colonnades were added to protect the fronts of tenements, Nero undertaking to build these at his own cost; and to hand over the building sites, cleared of rubbish, to the proprietors. He offered premiums also, in proportion to the rank and means of the owners, on condition of mansions or tenements being completed within a given time; and he assigned the marshes of Ostia for the reception of the rubbish, which was taken down the Tiber in the same vessels which had brought up the corn. Certain parts of the houses were to be built without beams, and of solid stone, Gabian or Alban, those stones being impervious to fire. Then as water had often been improperly intercepted by individuals, inspectors were appointed to secure a more abundant supply, and over a larger area, for public use; owners were required to keep appliances for quenching fire in some open place; party walls were forbidden, and every house had to be enclosed within walls of its own.

These useful measures added greatly to the appearance of the new city; and yet there were not wanting persons who thought that the plan of the old city was more conducive to health, as the narrow streets and high roofs were a protection against the rays of the sun, which now beat down with double fierceness upon broad and shadeless thoroughfares.

Such were the measures suggested by human counsels; after which means were taken to propitiate the Gods. The Sibylline Books[8] were consulted, and prayers were offered, as prescribed by them, to Vulcan, to Ceres, and to Proserpine. Juno was supplicated by the matrons, in the Capitol first, and afterwards at the nearest point upon the sea, from which water was drawn to sprinkle the temple and image of the Goddess; banquets to the Goddesses and all-night festivals were celebrated by married women.

But neither human aid, nor imperial bounty, nor atoning-offerings to the Gods, could remove the sinister suspicion that the fire had been brought about by Nero's order. To put an end

---

7. **Gauls . . . city,** the famous sack of Rome by barbarian tribes from Gaul in 390 B.C.
8. **Sibylline Books,** records of prophecies by Apollo's priestesses at Cumae.

therefore to this rumor, he shifted the charge on to others, and inflicted the most cruel tortures upon a body of men detested for their abominations, and popularly known by the name of Christians. This name came from one Christus, who was put to death in the reign of Tiberius by the Procurator Pontius Pilate; but though checked for the time, the detestable superstition broke out again, not in Judea only, where the mischief began, but even in Rome, where every horrible and shameful iniquity, from every quarter of the world, pours in and finds a welcome.

First those who acknowledged themselves of this persuasion were arrested; and upon their testimony a vast number were condemned, not so much on the charge of incendiarism as for their hatred of the human race. Their death was turned into a diversion. They were clothed in the skins of wild beasts, and torn to pieces by dogs; they were fastened to crosses, or set up to be burned, so as to serve the purpose of lamps when daylight failed. Nero gave up his own gardens for this spectacle; he provided also Circensian games,[9] during which he mingled with the populace, or took his stand upon a chariot, in the garb of a charioteer. But guilty as these men were and worthy of direst punishment, the fact that they were being sacrificed for no public good, but only to glut the cruelty of one man, aroused a feeling of pity on their behalf.

c. A.D. 117

---

9. *Circensian games*, chariot races in the Circus Maximus.

THINK AND DISCUSS
Understanding
1. How did Roman citizens react to the fire?
2. What finally stopped it?
3. Describe their efforts, in rebuilding Rome, to prevent another disaster of this kind.

Analyzing
4. Why does Tacitus begin his account with the uncertain possibility that Nero was responsible for the fire?
5. Explain his reasons for describing first what happened to the citizens, then what Nero may have been doing at the same time.
6. What does Tacitus imply about the significance of the fire in his list of buildings and objects that it destroyed?
7. How does Tacitus evaluate Nero's punishment of the Christians?

Extending
8. Do you find that the evidence which Tacitus provides proves Nero to be responsible for the fire?
9. Nero reportedly compared this disaster with the fall of Troy. To what extent could this be an appropriate parallel?

ENRICHMENT
Researching Other Disastrous Fires
The conflagration that destroyed much of Rome in A.D. 64 is typical of large-scale fires which, from time to time, have ravaged cities. Using the resources of your school library, look up descriptions of the Great Fire of London (1666), the Chicago Fire (1871), or the earthquake and resulting fires that destroyed San Francisco (1906). Then explain during a class discussion how the fire you investigated first began, why it was so difficult to get under control, the kinds of damage and injury it did, and how people put it out. Finally, evaluate how ordinary individuals responded to the personal challenges created by a major disaster.

The History of Language

The Origin of the Alphabet

The writing systems of the ancient Mesopotamians and Egyptians and Chinese were all basically ideographic: different symbols represented different words or ideas. One result of this approach was that these scripts needed thousands of characters in order to provide a sufficient vocabulary. Cuneiform had over two thousand characters; ancient Chinese script over three thousand.

Beginning around 1500 B.C., the Semitic peoples living at the eastern end of the Mediterranean Sea developed a radical new way of writing. They borrowed symbols from the writing systems of their neighbors, the Mesopotamians and Egyptians. But they did not use these symbols to represent ideas or words or syllables (as even the ancient ideographic scripts did sometimes), but instead the individual sounds of their language. This innovation—the first true alphabet—transformed writing. With this system it became possible to create a virtually limitless number of written words, simply by combining these new sound symbols in different patterns. And because these symbols, which the Romans would call *literae*, "letters," signified sound, not sense, the same signs could be adapted to many languages.

The cultural transmitters for this alphabet were the Phoenicians (fə nish′ənz), a Semitic people occupying a number of cities on the east coast of the Mediterranean. The Phoenicians were great sailors and traders, establishing colonies as far as Carthage and Cadiz at the western end of the Mediterranean. (See the map on page 115.) Between 1500 and 1000 B.C., the Phoenicians perfected and spread the use of the alphabet throughout the Mediterranean area.

By about 750 B.C., letters began to appear on Greek pottery. The Semitic alphabet had represented only consonants. (It was assumed that readers could provide the missing vowel sounds.) Because vowel sounds are important in the Greek language, four Semitic characters, which represented consonantal sounds not found in Greek, were used to stand for vowels. For example, the Semitic character *aleph* represented a smooth breathing sound made with a slight rush of air against the back of the mouth—a little like the *h* in "ha!" The Greeks took the sign for that sound and made it stand for the vowel sound *a*, calling it *alpha*. (The Greeks borrowed the Semitic names for the letters as well as the characters themselves, even though these names were meaningless in Greek: The Semitic name of the letter *aleph* signified "ox." In Greek *alpha* means simply "the letter a.")

Like the Phoenicians, the Greeks were great colonizers. Between 750 and 550 B.C., the Greeks planted colonies throughout much of the Mediterranean world. So many Greeks migrated to southern Italy and Sicily that the region became known as *Magna Graecia*, "Great Greece." Like the Phoenicians, these Greek colonizers took their alphabet with them. The Etruscans, a people inhabiting central and northern Italy, were using a Greek-derived alphabet by the end of the eighth century B.C. During the following century, their rivals, the Romans, also adapted the Greek alphabet to write their own language, Latin. As Roman influence spread throughout Europe, so did the use of this Latin alphabet, which is the basis for our familiar English letters.

Inscription from the tomb of a Roman cavalryman. Museo della Civiltà Romana, Rome

HEROISM

> Courage must be the firmer, heart the bolder,
> Spirit the greater, as our strength grows less.
>   The Battle of Maldon

These lines are from an Old English poem that celebrates the brave, doomed resistance of a local militia from Essex against a raiding party of Danes in August, 991. This passage is one of the most famous expressions of the heroic ideals of the Germanic tribes who occupied northern Europe as the Roman Empire declined. The Germanic view of heroism stressed courage and loyalty above all. It is the view of a warrior society. The heroic ideals in a merchant society might be wealth and prudence. The saint might be the hero of a society dominated by priests. The literatures of different societies reflect their differing heroic ideals. The following article discusses several different views of heroism.

The Code of the Warrior

One of the most positive pictures of military heroism in literature is in the *Odyssey* (page 126), which does not celebrate the glories of war, but rather the sweetness of the home that the hero struggles to return to and reclaim. Odysseus was famous less for strength and courage than for intelligence and shrewdness, qualities that appealed to Homer's Greek audience. Another of the heroic qualities of Odysseus is his perseverance. In adversity, he controls his emotions and is patient. Having killed the suitors who had dishonored his home, he does not exult over the dead. Although not known primarily as a warrior, Odysseus is a master with weapons, most notably the great bow which only he can string and which he uses to kill the suitors. Homer pictures Odysseus handling his bow like a musician playing a harp, coupling his hero's strength with grace, another quality valued by the Greeks.

Archilochus was a battle-hardened veteran like Odysseus. In his poem beginning "Soul, soul" (page 157), Archilochus expresses a heroic code that Homer might have put in the mouth of Odysseus: "Keep close in the attack; /Move back not an inch./But never crow in victory,/Nor mope hangdog in loss." Archilochus sounds less like a hero and more like the mercenary soldier that he was in his poem on the loss of his shield (page 156), concluding that survival is more important than military honor: "Let the shield go; I can buy another one equally good."

In one of his odes (page 239), the Roman poet Horace memorably sums up the heroic code of his people: "Precious and proper is death for one's country." A practical Roman, he couples this exalted expression of heroic patriotism with a down-to-earth reason for standing your ground in battle: ". . . death comes swiftly after the runaway/and shows no mercy to the hamstrings/and the boneless backs of peace-loving boys."

The heroic code of the Icelandic sagas expresses itself in an almost exuberant savagery and an almost comic grimness. In "Thorstein the Staff-Struck" (page 308), men engage in fatal duels over the slightest offenses to their honor. When the hero is bidding farewell to his father before facing a fighter they both expect to kill him, the old man can't resist a bitter joke: "Anybody who offends a more powerful man in his own district can hardly expect to wear out many more new shirts."

The medieval French epic poem the *Song of Roland* (page 284) includes religious values as well as military ones in its depiction of heroism. Rallying his Christian comrades-in-arms to face the attack of a vast Moslem army, the hero Roland exhorts them, "Right's on our side, and wrong is with these wretches!" A similar connection between military honor and spirituality is made in the *Bhagavad Gita* (page 60), a philosophical dialogue that forms part of the ancient Indian epic, the *Mahabharata*: "There is no greater good for a warrior than to fight in a righteous war."

The Tragic View of Heroism

Summer grass
  of stalwart warriors' splendid dreams
    the aftermath.

This Japanese haiku by Bashō (page 102) is not so much about the futility of war as about the futility of dreams of conquest, a strong theme in much of the recent American fiction dealing with the Vietnam War. But the futility of war has always been an important literary theme. In his poem "Fighting South of the Ramparts" (page 85), the ancient Chinese poet Li Po has such a sentiment expressed by his narrator, a veteran soldier. It is useless, he says, to fight wars of conquest far from home against barbarians who "have no trade but battle and carnage" and no cities or farms to enrich the victor. "Know therefore," the old soldier concludes, "that the sword is a cursed thing/Which the wise man uses only if he must."

Marble portrait bust of Socrates.
National Museum, Naples

One of the most negative depictions of the inhumanity of war occurs in Book II of Virgil's *Aeneid* (page 242), in which Aeneas, a Trojan refugee, describes the destruction of his city by the Greeks. In one of the most famous depictions of savagery in literature, the young Greek warrior Pyrrhus, son of the dead hero Achilles, drags the aged Priam, king of Troy, to the altar of his household gods and slaughters him there, sneering, "So, go and tell my father/The latest news: do not forget to mention,/Old messenger-boy, my villainous behavior . . . ."

The Intellectual as Hero

As was suggested earlier, there are other types of heroism besides that of soldiers. The Irish poet William Butler Yeats observed, "Why should we honor those who die on the field of battle? A man may show as reckless a courage in entering into the abyss of himself." "Know thyself" was an ideal of the ancient Greeks, but the Athenian philosopher Socrates elevated this maxim to the level of intellectual heroism in his assertion that "the unexamined life is not worth living." Socrates believed that it was the philosopher's duty to search into himself for the truth and to assist others to seek such knowledge of themselves. His method was to talk with the Athenians, questioning them about the nature of such things as knowledge, wisdom, duty, and destiny, and suggesting his own answers. But Athens was not ready for this sort of probing philosophical dialogue, and Socrates was brought to trial (and condemned to death) for corrupting the young and holding heretical religious views. The *Apology* (page 221) is an account of Socrates' defense of his way of life by his pupil Plato.

A modern picture of intellectual heroism is contained in French playwright Jean Anouilh's *Antigone* (page 874), in which his heroine's unshakable devotion to her own integrity brings about her death. "I want everything of life," she asserts. "I do; and I want it now! I want it total, complete: otherwise I reject it! I will *not* be moderate. I will *not* be satisfied with the bit of cake you offer me if I promise to be a good little girl." Of such uncompromising stuff are heroes made.

Unit 2   THE CLASSICAL WORLD

■ CONCEPT REVIEW

Below on the left begins another episode from Homer's *Odyssey*. At the end of his ten years of wandering, with all his men dead and his ship destroyed, Odysseus swims ashore near the town of the Phaiákians. There the generous king Alkínoös takes him in, and one night, after supper, asks Odysseus to tell about his adventures. The following episode, which comes at the end of his narration, explains how all his men came to be lost at sea. During his wanderings Odysseus twice hears about the dangerous island of the sun god Hêlios. Both the ancient seer Teirêsias and the enchantress Kirkê warn him that if he and his men slaughter the god's cattle found on that island, terrible results will follow. But after losing several men to the devouring monster Skylla, and barely avoiding the whirlpool Kharybdis, they need a place to moor for the night and rest. It is then that they come upon the fatal island.

On the right on the following pages are notes to help you read this episode from the *Odyssey* and to review some of the literary terms and thinking skills that have appeared in Unit 2. Page numbers in the notes refer to an application or review of literary terms in the unit. A more extensive discussion of literary terms is in the Handbook of Literary Terms. On a separate sheet of paper write your answers to the questions that follow this episode.

from the Odyssey

Homer   *translated by* **Robert Fitzgerald**

from **Book Twelve**

"Then we were coasting
the noble island of the god, where grazed
those cattle with wide brows, and bounteous flocks
of Hêlios, lord of noon, who rides high heaven.

5 From the black ship, far still at sea, I heard
the lowing of the cattle winding home
and sheep bleating; and heard, too, in my heart
the word of blind Teirêsias of Thebes
and Kirkê of Aiaia: both forbade me
10 the island of the world's delight, the Sun.
So I spoke out in gloom to my companions:
'Shipmates, grieving and weary though you are,
listen: I had forewarning from Teirêsias
and Kirkê, too; both told me I must shun
15 this island of the Sun, the world's delight.
Nothing but fatal trouble shall we find here.
Pull away, then, and put the land astern.'
That strained them to the breaking point, and, cursing,
Eurýlokhos cried out in bitterness:
20 'Are you flesh and blood, Odysseus, to endure
more than a man can? Do you never tire?
God, look at you, iron is what you're made of.
Here we all are, half dead with weariness,
falling asleep over the oars, and you
25 say "No landing"—no firm island earth
where we could make a quiet supper. No:
pull out to sea, you say, with night upon us—
just as before, but wandering now, and lost.
Sudden storms can rise at night and swamp
30 ships without a trace.

     Where is your shelter
if some stiff gale blows up from south or west—
the winds that break up shipping every time
when seamen flout the lord gods' will? I say
do as the hour demands and go ashore
35 before black night comes down.

      We'll make our supper
alongside, and at dawn put out to sea.'
Now when the rest said 'Aye' to this, I saw
the power of destiny devising ill.
Sharply I answered, without hesitation:
40 'Eurýlokhos, they are with you to a man.
I am alone, outmatched.

     Let this whole company
swear me a great oath: Any herd of cattle
or flock of sheep here found shall go unharmed;
no one shall slaughter out of wantonness
45 ram or heifer; all shall be content
with what the goddess Kirkê put aboard.'
They fell at once to swearing as I ordered,

Narrative poetry (page 134): The narrator here freely shifts time and place.

Synthesizing: The idea first expressed here will reappear throughout this episode, unifying its component parts.

Metaphor (page 252): To describe the conflict between Odysseus's sense of danger and the exhaustion of his men Homer compares their feelings with a material object.

Hyperbole: Using figurative language, Eurýlokhos contrasts Odysseus with his men in order to defy his commands.

Characterization (page 153): Through the way he argues his case Eurýlokhos gives us a clear sense of his own personality.

Inference (page 197): Here Odysseus uses rational processes to conclude that forces beyond his control determine events.

and when the round of oaths had ceased, we found
a halfmoon bay to beach and moor the ship in,
with a fresh spring nearby. All hands ashore
went about skillfully getting up a meal.
Then, after thirst and hunger, those besiegers,
were turned away, they mourned for their companions
plucked from the ship by Skylla and devoured,
and sleep came soft upon them as they mourned.
In the small hours of the third watch, when stars
that shone out in the first dusk of evening
had gone down to their setting, a giant wind
blew from heaven, and clouds driven by Zeus
shrouded land and sea in a night of storm;
so, just as Dawn with finger tips of rose
touched the windy world, we dragged our ship
to cover in a grotto, a sea cave
where nymphs had chairs of rock and sanded floors.
I mustered all the crew and said:

                  'Old shipmates,
our stores are in the ship's hold, food and drink;
the cattle here are not for our provision,
or we pay dearly for it.

              Fierce the god is
who cherishes these heifers and these sheep:
Hêlios; and no man avoids his eye.'
To this my fighters nodded. Yes. But now
we had a month of onshore gales, blowing
day in, day out—south winds, or south by east.
As long as bread and good red wine remained
to keep the men up, and appease their craving,
they would not touch the cattle. But in the end,
when all the barley in the ship was gone,
hunger drove them to scour the wild shore
with angling hooks, for fishes and sea fowl,
whatever fell into their hands; and lean days
wore their bellies thin.

              The storms continued.
So one day I withdrew to the interior
to pray the gods in solitude, for hope
that one might show me some way of salvation.
Slipping away, I struck across the island
to a sheltered spot, out of the driving gale.
I washed my hands there, and made supplication
to the gods who own Olympos, all the gods—
but they, for answer, only closed my eyes
under slow drops of sleep.

■ **Personification:** The warrior, Odysseus, thinks of hunger as an enemy attacking his men.

■ **Protagonist** (page 180): Homer has established a conflict in this story between the self-denying intelligence of Odysseus and the impulsive needs of the men he leads.

Now on the shore Eurýlokhos
made his insidious plea:

           'Comrades,' he said,
'You've gone through everything; listen to what I say.
All deaths are hateful to us, mortal wretches,
but famine is the most pitiful, the worst
95 end that a man can come to.

               Will you fight it?
Come, we'll cut out the noblest of these cattle
for sacrifice to the gods who own the sky;
and once at home, in the old country of Ithaka,
if ever that day comes—
100 we'll build a costly temple and adorn it
with every beauty for the Lord of Noon.
But if he flares up over his heifers lost,
wishing our ship destroyed, and if the gods
make cause with him, why, then I say: Better
105 open your lungs to a big sea once for all
than waste to skin and bones on a lonely island!'
Thus Eurýlokhos; and they murmured 'Aye!'
trooping away at once to round up heifers.
Now, that day tranquil cattle with broad brows
110 were grazing near, and soon the men drew up
around their chosen beasts in ceremony.
They plucked the leaves that shone on a tall oak—
having no barley meal—to strew the victims,
performed the prayers and ritual, knifed the kine
115 and flayed each carcass, cutting thighbones free
to wrap in double folds of fat. These offerings,
with strips of meat, were laid upon the fire.
Then, as they had no wine, they made libation
with clear spring water, broiling the entrails first;
120 and when the bones were burnt and tripes shared,
they spitted the carved meat.

               Just then my slumber
left me in a rush, my eyes opened,
and I went down the seaward path. No sooner
had I caught sight of our black hull, than savory
125 odors of burnt fat eddied around me;
grief took hold of me, and I cried aloud:
'O Father Zeus and gods in bliss forever,
you made me sleep away this day of mischief!
O cruel drowsing, in the evil hour!
130 Here they sat, and a great work they contrived.'
Lampetía in her long gown meanwhile
had borne swift word to the Overlord of Noon:
'They have killed your kine.'

■ **Tone** (page 158):
Notice the terms Eurý-
lokhos chooses in persuading his comrades to dis-
obey.

■ **Imagery** (page 240):
Returning from a dis-
tance, Odysseus suddenly
learns what has happened
through both sight and
smell.

■ **Apostrophe:** Odysseus
addresses his real antagonists.

■ **Lampetia** (lam pē'-
shi ə), daughter of the sun
god. She and her sister
tended his cattle.

And the Lord Hêlios

burst into angry speech amid the immortals:

135 'O Father Zeus and gods in bliss forever,
punish Odysseus' men! So overweening,
now they have killed my peaceful kine, my joy
at morning when I climbed the sky of stars,
and evening, when I bore westward from heaven.
140 Restitution or penalty they shall pay—
and pay in full—or I go down forever
to light the dead men in the underworld.'
Then Zeus who drives the stormcloud made reply:
'Peace, Hêlios: shine on among the gods,
145 shine over mortals in the fields of grain.
Let me throw down one white-hot bolt, and make
splinters of their ship in the winedark sea.'
—Kalypso later told me of this exchange,
as she declared that Hermês had told her.
150 Well, when I reached the sea cave and the ship,
I faced each man, and had it out; but where
could any remedy be found? There was none.
The silken beeves of Hêlios were dead.
The gods, moreover, made queer signs appear:
155 cowhides began to crawl, and beef, both raw
and roasted, lowed like kine upon the spits.
Now six full days my gallant crew could feast
upon the prime beef they had marked for slaughter
from Hêlios' herd; and Zeus, the son of Kronos,
160 added one fine morning.

All the gales

had ceased, blown out, and with an offshore breeze
we launched again, stepping the mast and sail,
to make for the open sea. Astern of us
the island coastline faded, and no land
165 showed anywhere, but only sea and heaven,
when Zeus Kroníon piled a thunderhead
above the ship, while gloom spread on the ocean.
We held our course, but briefly. Then the squall
struck whining from the west, with gale force, breaking
170 both forestays, and the mast came toppling aft
along the ship's length, so the running rigging
showered into the bilge.

On the after deck

the mast had hit the steersman a slant blow
bashing the skull in, knocking him overside,
175 as the brave soul fled the body, like a diver.
With crack on crack of thunder, Zeus let fly
a bolt against the ship, a direct hit,

■ **Kalypso, Hermês.**
After this disaster Odysseus was trapped on the island of the nymph Kalypso and the messenger god Hermês told her of this heavenly debate.

■ **Foreshadowing** (page 142): Note how in their hunger Odysseus's men ignore these "queer signs."

■ **Irony:** There is a significant contrast between the "queer signs" of line 154 and this description of what the men eat.

■ **Simile:** Where do you think the soul here is headed?

so that she bucked, in reeking fumes of sulphur,
and all the men were flung into the sea.
180 They came up 'round the wreck, bobbing a while
like petrels on the waves.

No more seafaring
homeward for these, no sweet day of return;
the god had turned his face from them."
c. 725 B.C.

■ **Theme:** From this point on Odysseus must make his way home alone.

THINK AND DISCUSS
Understanding
1. Why do Odysseus and his men land on the island of Hêlios?
2. How do the men manage to defy Odysseus's command?
3. What are the warning signs that trouble is ahead?
4. How do Odysseus's men die?

Analyzing
5. In what ways does Eurýlokhos exemplify what has gone wrong with Odysseus's men?
6. Why does a month-long gale suddenly come up?
7. What makes Odysseus fall asleep?
8. Explain Zeus's reasons for destroying the ship.

Extending
9. How does the contrast between Eurýlokhos and Eumaios the swineherd, who appears at the end of the *Odyssey*, define Homer's concept of the ideal retainer?
10. Discuss the extent to which Tiresias's warnings in *Oedipus the King* and this passage from the *Odyssey* illustrate the Greek belief in prophecy.

REVIEWING LITERARY TERMS
Narrative Poetry
1. Explain how the narrator shifts place to dramatize the fatal mistake of Odysseus's sailors.

Metaphor
2. In what way does the metaphor "strained to the breaking point" concretize the sailors' feelings?

Characterization
3. How does Eurýlokhos's speech (lines 20–36) imply the kind of man he is?
4. Show the way in which Odysseus's comments about his men (in lines 76–81) create a sense of his character.

Inference
5. What two kinds of information does Odysseus connect in making the inference in lines 37–38?
6. At line 90, given what you have learned so far, what could you infer about the next events in this story?

Protagonist
7. In this plot, who functions as the antagonist?

Tone
8. List the words in Eurýlokhos's speech (lines 91–106) that most immediately stir emotion, and explain the tone that they give to what he says.

Imagery
9. What dangers does the visual image of line 124 suggest?

Foreshadowing
10. What do the odd events in lines 155–156 imply about the future of Odysseus's men?
11. How does the "thunderhead" of line 167 confirm these suspicions?

■ CONTENT REVIEW

THINKING SKILLS

Classifying

1. Write down specific types of emotion found in Greek and Roman lyric poetry, and list examples.
2. Describe the different kinds of fame praised by classical writers.

Generalizing

3. Is Socrates' questioning of basic assumptions about knowledge and power common in the Greek and Roman literature in this unit?
4. Is there any hope in a reward for virtue after death in these works? How does this affect the attitude toward this life?
5. According to Greek and Roman writers, when are violence and killing acceptable?

Synthesizing

6. How does a basic element in the plot of detective fiction, the revelation of a hidden secret, appear in Homer's *Odyssey*, Sophocles' *Oedipus the King*, and Virgil's *Aeneid?*
7. Discuss how a belief in divine justice, especially as it is expressed through omens and prophecy, constitutes a recurring, dominant theme in Greek and Roman writing.
8. Explain how the virtue of self-control links together the ideas of Greek and Roman writers.

Evaluating

9. Do Greek and Roman writers such as Homer, Sophocles, and Virgil exceed the limits of good taste in describing injury and death?
10. Would you agree with Cicero that friendship makes life worth living, or do you think that another value, found in a different Greek or Roman writer, is more important?
11. Virgil modeled aspects of the *Aeneid* on Homer, but had very different purposes in mind. Define what you think epic poetry should accomplish, and decide which of these two selections most fully matches that ideal.

■ COMPOSITION REVIEW

Explaining Nature Imagery

Write a four-paragraph essay that explains how Archilochus, Sappho, and Horace use images of nature to express ideas and feelings. List for yourself specific nature images found in their poems, and the kinds of feelings that those images evoke. Cluster your evidence according to the images you find, under categories such as "images of water," "images of light," and so on. Use these categories as the topics for three different paragraphs about images and feelings. Preface them with a paragraph on the emotional range of Greek and Roman lyrics.

Analyzing How Writers Characterize Leaders

Finding suitable leaders, and then restricting their power to prevent tyranny, was a recurrent problem in Greek and Roman political life. Homer, Sophocles, Thucydides, and Virgil all depict powerful men in control of a state. Write an essay to be read by your teacher that analyzes how three of these authors characterize what power does to the man who holds it. List for yourself the specific traits in each man that connect in some way with his official position as a leader. Outline an essay that begins with a paragraph on the problems of being in command, goes on to describe in separate paragraphs what power does to your three examples, and then conclude with a paragraph that compares and contrasts them. As you write, include specific references to what your subjects say and do.

Explaining the Role of Young People

Sappho's daughter, Telémakhos, Iulus, Pyramus and Thisbe, these are just some examples of how classical writers depict the younger generation. Write a five-paragraph essay in which you explain to your teacher how three specific young people are expected to act. Choose your three characters, and skim the works where they appear, locating passages that illustrate what is expected of each of them. Outline your essay, starting with an introductory paragraph on the roles imposed upon young people as they are pictured in classical literature. After separate paragraphs devoted to each of your three examples, write a conclusion that compares your own life with the way these young people once lived.

THE MIDDLE AGES 800–1400

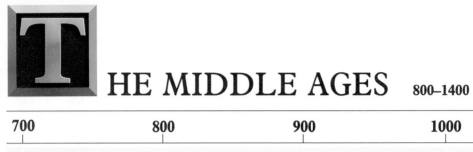

700	800	900	1000

HISTORY AND ARTS

- Battle of Roncesvalles   • Vikings invade England   Normans invade England •
   • Vikings raid England   • Vikings settle Iceland
          • Vikings raid France • Vikings settle Normandy
                          • Althing established

PEOPLE

• Charlemagne crowned emperor   William I becomes king •
         • Alfred the Great becomes king   • Canute
                                                                         becomes king

LITERATURE

• *Beowulf*   • *Lay of Thrym*

Silver reliquary bust of
Charlemagne. c. 1349

Manuscript illumination of
Alfred the Great (849–899)

Carved wooden head from a
Viking ship-burial. c. 850

1100	1200	1300	1400

- First Crusade
- Third Crusade
- Seventh Crusade
- Chartres Cathedral completed
- Norway conquers Iceland
- Eighth Crusade
- Factional struggle in Florence

Marie de France •
- **Marco Polo born** •
- **Henry II dies**
- **Richard I dies**
- **Louis IX born**
- **Death of Beatrice**
- **Dante exiled from Florence**
- **Chaucer dies**
- *Gawain*-poet

- *Song of Roland*
- Marie de France: *Lays*
- Geoffrey of Monmouth: *Historia Regum Britanniae*
- Wace: *Roman de Brut*
- *Elder Edda*
- Dante: *La Vita Nuova*
- Dante: *Commedia*
- Wycliffe's Bible
- Chaucer: *Canterbury Tales*
- *Sir Gawain and the Green Knight*

Crusaders fighting Saracens from a 14th-century chronicle

Detail of a 14th-century chronicle showing King Arthur

Detail of a 14th-century manuscript showing Marco Polo

PREVIEW

UNIT 3   THE MIDDLE AGES   800–1400

Authors or Works
Song of Roland
Marie de France
The Lay of Thrym
Thorstein the Staff-Struck
Dante Alighieri
Sir Gawain and the Green Knight

Features
Comment: Shape-Shifting
Reading a Medieval Allegory
Reader's Note: Translating Dante
Reader's Note: Who Is the Green Knight?
The History of Language: The Rise
   of the Vernacular Languages
Themes in World Literature: The Quest

Application of Literary Terms
assonance
symbol
alliteration

Review of Literary Terms
characterization
rhyme
simile
symbol
setting

Vocabulary Skills
medieval words
affixes, roots
context

Thinking Skills
generalizing
evaluating
classifying
synthesizing

Composition Assignments Include
Writing a Summary
Writing to Persuade
Analyzing Plot Structure
Writing Fables
Describing the Beasts of Opposition
Analyzing Francesca's Speech
Explaining Dante's Demonology
Analyzing Dante's Similes
Explaining What Dante Has Learned
Analyzing the Symbolism of Dante's Satan
Describing a Medieval Court
Analyzing the Ironic Reversals in *Gawain*

Enrichment
Readers Theater
Holding a Mock Court
Researching Norse Mythology
Comparing Dante's Illustrators

Thinking Critically About Literature
Concept Review
Content Review
Composition Review

THE MIDDLE AGES 800–1400

Traditionally, people have pictured the Middle Ages in terms of knights on horseback, ladies in towers, and dragons in between. Historically, the dragons are now hard to locate. There were knights and ladies, though perhaps not as clean and pretty as those in the movies. And there were many other kinds of people as well. The period is a long one, and in the process of placing its people and the literature which pictures them, it helps to understand the stages in its development. The first, which begins with the crumbling of the Roman Empire after A.D. 400, is an era of social chaos in which little that might be called literature was written. People at the time were simply preoccupied with survival. Out of that confusion emerged the outlines of new nation states, each with its own vernacular language and culture. (See page 362.) By around 1100 these countries had stabilized internally and a second stage began. Though periodic warfare between them continued, and at times a ruler and his followers would be violently replaced, there was the leisure and security to create works of literature, and the institutions to preserve them. This is the era in which medieval culture—including the knights and ladies—flourished and created some of its most characteristic products, such as the Arthurian romances and the Gothic cathedrals. But with this cultural ripeness came the seeds of change. Relative peace and quiet fostered the development of towns and commerce. With them came the growing economic and political power of merchants and artisans. Their society, based on making and selling, was very different from the world of chivalry—of the knights and ladies. But with the passage of time these less glamorous folk began fashioning the new world of the Renaissance.

BARBARIAN EUROPE

For centuries, the Roman Empire provided a common culture for an enormous span of territory inhabited by a diversity of peoples. While the empire brought wealth and power to Italy, it also created an era of peace and security for the areas it dominated, permitting widespread travel and economic prosperity for those under its protection. With its fall, Europe entered a period of confusion and bloodshed which lasted for centuries.

Out of this anarchy the Germanic peoples of northern Europe began fashioning a new political order. The barbarian conquest of Britain offers an example. In 410 the emperor Honorius sent word to Britain that Roman legions could no longer protect the province. By 449, Germanic tribes from northern Europe, the Angles, Saxons, and Jutes, began to invade and settle. For a while, local Roman and Celtic inhabitants fought back, possibly led by a general named Artorius—Arthur. But by the late 6th century the Germanic invaders controlled Britain, and the Celts took refuge in the remote hills of Wales and Scotland, as well as the region called Brittany (from *Bretagne*, "Britain") on the northwest coast of France. The Anglo-Saxons established seven separate kingdoms, that would eventually merge into Angle-land, or England.

Another Germanic tribe, the Franks, held a small portion of northeast France. Their king, Clovis, decided to expand his territory, and between 486 and 496 his military expeditions took in much of modern France. Early in the sixth century, Clovis established his capital at Paris, and over the next three hundred years his successors struggled to consolidate the kingdom. A climax to their efforts came in the late eighth century, during the reign of the Frankish king

Charlemagne (shär′lə män), who extended the borders of his realm east to the Vistula River and south through most of Italy. (See the map on page 277.) In an attempt to restore the Roman Empire, Pope Leo III crowned him "Emperor and Augustus" on Christmas Day, A.D. 800.

During this era of nation building, vernacular cultures emerged. In early eighth-century England an anonymous Anglo-Saxon poet composed the epic *Beowulf*, a synthesis of Germanic history and legend. Near the end of the century, Charlemagne founded a school at his palace at Aachen (ä′kən) that was one of Europe's earliest institutions of higher learning.

But another wave of barbarian invaders threatened this newly created political order. Vikings from Scandinavia began attacking the coast of England in 787. For nearly a hundred years these were raids for plunder; but in the late ninth century they changed character, and became an invasion. England was soon a divided land, its northeast counties ruled by Vikings from Denmark. Another, more well-organized invasion under the Danish king, Canute (kə-nüt′), in 1016 put all England under Viking rule. Viking attacks on the northern coast of France began in 840. At first these too were for booty, but by 911 the French kings found themselves forced to cede territory to the invaders, in what became the province of the Northmen, or Normandy. These Viking settlers amalgamated with their subject peoples—learning to speak French, converting to Christianity, and accepting the authority of the king of France—but in real terms, Normandy was an independent kingdom. In 1066 its Duke William—afterward called "the Conqueror"—invaded and took over England making it, for more than a century, part of an Anglo-Norman empire. Meanwhile, far to the north, other Vikings discovered Iceland about 860. By 874 some had settled there, eventually creating in that distant northern island a uniquely republican form of government.

For the rest of Europe, during the chaotic period between A.D. 400 and 900, government became some form of compromise between older, tribal patterns, and monarchy. Though from time to time powerful leaders like Charlemagne would appear, unifying a people and extending its territory, his successors invariably found it impossible to maintain centralized control over an entire country. Certain areas, like Normandy, shifted back and forth between contending parties.

The social configuration of Europe changed, and with it the physical character of the way people lived. The large cities and open countryside of the Roman Empire disappeared, replaced by a different landscape reflecting a greater need for defense and a reduced volume of trade. The center of this new medieval community became the castle of its local lord. Not the immense, stone castle of the twelfth century, but something far more simple: a moat, a drawbridge, a wooden wall, and inside, among smaller structures, a wooden tower some three or four stories tall, where the lord, his family, and his knights lived. Here he dispensed justice and ruled his lands. Close by would be a village, perhaps of fifty wooden one-room cottages, with adjoining barns and stables, and a parish church. Life was communal and interdependent. The lord owned both the land and the people who worked on it. They paid his taxes, and worked for him at certain times of the year, and in return he was to defend them from attack, and preserve justice. These communities could not depend upon trade and commerce, since travel was frequently dangerous, and so they were largely self-sufficient. Certainly there was a literary culture, but at this time it was usually an exclusively oral one, employing simple poetic forms like the *lay*, a short narrative in verse, usually on mythological or heroic themes. The Icelandic "Lay of Thrym" (page 305), which may have been composed around 900, was one of a number of such poems about the Germanic gods that were later included in the collection known as the *Elder Edda*. During this period similar oral poetry was probably circulating about Charlemagne in France and about Arthur in Wales and Brittany.

But literacy could only be expected in the Church, where it was necessary that the clergy be able to read the scriptures and the prayers of the mass. During this era of cultural fragmentation and decline, it was the Church which maintained schools for its clergy, preserved books and manuscripts in its libraries, and promoted the writing of historical chronicles, sermons,

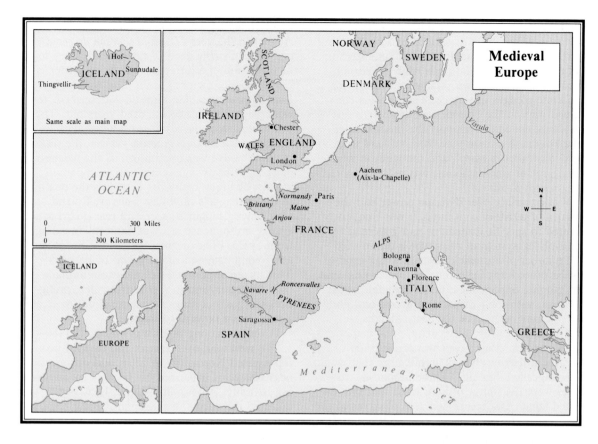

Medieval Europe

and commentaries on Scripture, as well as literary works on sacred themes. The Church also played an important social role as the common cultural bond that kept Europe together. The papacy, still centered in the old imperial capital of Rome, continued to use the language of the Roman Empire, Latin, and sent its emissaries throughout Europe, to the remotest limits of Iceland and Ireland. The popes claimed that they were God's representatives on earth, and that the Church had been given the power to decide on an individual's salvation or damnation—Christians alone would be admitted to heaven, and the Church decided who was a Christian. Popes and bishops used this power to dominate, as best they could, the secular rulers of the era.

THE HIGH MIDDLE AGES

With the twelfth and thirteenth centuries, Europe entered a new historical phase. In both England and France, powerful kings disciplined their barons and elaborated a social system called "feudalism" (fyü′dl iz′əm). Not coined until centuries later, this term refers to a society in which military service is exchanged for protection and the use of the land. Medieval feudalism in Europe had its origins in the bonds of loyalty that had united a chief and his followers in the tribal societies of the Germanic peoples. In his *Germania*, the Roman historian Tacitus had commented on the strength of this loyalty. For German warriors, he observes, "to leave a battle alive after their chief has fallen means lifelong infamy and shame. To defend and protect him, and to let him get the credit for their acts of heroism, are the most solemn obligations of their allegiance."

Feudalism developed during the decline of Rome. Cities no longer provided adequate law enforcement, and small landowners turned over their property to larger landowners in return for protection. Frankish kings had granted land to their warriors in return for military service, and this system had been developed by Charlemagne into the basis of a reliable army. These warriors became, in turn, feudal lords who passed out their lands to their own retainers in return for the same pledges of service. This process continued until at the bottom were land divisions just large enough to support the household of one knight. A person who received land from a lord was called a *vassal*, and the land, in whatever large or small amount, was called a *fief* (fēf) or a *feud* (fyüd).

While warfare over dynastic power and the control of territory continued, it was frequently limited to specific campaigns and governed by an evolving system of rules which diminished the number of battlefield casualties and established procedures for capturing, ransoming, and exchanging opponents. The savage raids of the Vikings, with their casual destruction and plunder, became a thing of the past. Thanks to this greater measure of security, great cathedrals begin to rise all over western Europe in the steep, narrow style of architecture that would later be called "gothic." These immense structures were the source of local pride and international fame. As a recent historian observes of the building of the cathedrals, "patient years were needed to complete the work; sculptors chiseled out great single figures or complex, populous groups of saints and prophets; anonymous glassworkers, leadworkers, and artists put together jewel-rich windows telling the Bible story; painters, mosaic workers, coppersmiths, and goldsmiths—all united to make for the glory of God and the honor of their city the most beautiful building in the world." The gothic cathedrals represent a unified way of looking at the world and at human life. Within their walls the ordinary churchgoer could find depicted in wall painting, sculpture and stained glass the crucial stories of sacred scripture. Pictorial symbols of virtue and vice trained the faithful in how to live. Thin, towering columns and lofty ceilings elevated and astonished the spirit, suggesting this indeed was a place where God and His people could gather.

The political ideals which dominate the start of this era appear in another kind of masterpiece, the twelfth-century French epic poem called the *Song of Roland* (page 284). Based upon an actual battle fought on the fifteenth of August in the year 778, this *chanson de geste*, or "song of noble deeds," reworked history to fit the vision of a different era. At its center is Charlemagne, pictured as an ideal warrior-king. Legend has magnified him; he is described, for example, as being two hundred years old. The poem illustrates the loyalty and love which link Charlemagne and his greatest vassals, the picked band of twelve warriors known as the *paladins*, or *peers*. It has virtually nothing to say about women or life at court. Its climax is the death of Charlemagne's mightiest warrior, Roland, after having fought a successful rear-guard action against an immense army of Saracens invading from Spain. (The original battle in 778 was actually fought against a small group of Basques.) This image of absolute devotion to a military code of honor, and to a powerful ruler, prefigures the goals of kings who were about to create a new, more powerful France.

Foremost among them was Philip II (1180–1223), who took over a weak and divided people, repossessed Normandy in 1204, and during the next two years expanded his borders by annexing Brittany, Anjou, and Maine. In 1214 he defeated the efforts of the English King John to recover Normandy, and by the time of his death he had trebled the territory of his nation. His successor, Louis IX (1226–1270), consolidated the power of the French throne during his long reign. A king of unusual virtue and strength of character, it was said that "Men feared him, because they knew that he was just." Louis joined two of the Crusades, the series of military expeditions between 1096 and 1272 in which armies from a number of European countries attempted to seize control of the Near East—and its Christian shrines—from its Moslem rulers. Defeated and imprisoned in Egypt, he refused to buy his release until he had ransomed his men. Twenty-seven years after his death of fever while on his second crusading expedition, the Church canonized him as Saint Louis.

A contemporary of Philip II, the English King Henry II (1154–1189), also brought an independent nobility under royal dominion. His successor, Richard I (1189–1199), called *Coeur de Lion*, "Lionheart," lived a more dramatic life, but frittered away Henry's political achievement. Though animated less by a piety like Louis IX's than by simple restlessness, Richard joined the Third Crusade (1189–1192), setting off to Palestine shortly after his coronation. Captured and held on his return not by the Saracens, but by a hostile European monarch, Henry VI of Germany, Richard remained imprisoned in a castle on the Danube until his people could raise his ransom.

During Richard's imprisonment Henry forced him to swear vassalage to the German throne. This is a curious and extreme example of the system of feudalism that had been evolving for centuries, and which now reached its most elaborate development. In feudal theory, the king, as a vassal of God, owned all of a nation's land; beneath him were the lords who as his vassals held his land in "fief" or in trust, and governed them on his behalf. In practical fact, the typical medieval king acquired power through the acquiescence or defeat of neighboring lords, and maintained it only as long as his actions pleased them, or until a stronger rival took over.

The medieval lord, ruling from a castle which by the twelfth or thirteenth century might be the massive stone structure of tradition and fantasy, dominated lands that he protected and that gave him wealth in return. Associated with the lord were a cluster of armed knights, his vassals, their number dependent upon his relative wealth. These men swore him fealty, or permanent loyalty, during a ceremony in which the knight, kneeling bareheaded and without weapons, placed his folded hands within the folded hands of his lord. He then received a sign of his dependent power, such as a ceremonial glove, and also, at times, the chance to rule some of the lord's lands, or to live within his castle.

Life for the medieval knight was, in a sense, an elegantly stylized version of the lives once lived by the warriors of Germanic tribes. The knight never worked, but was always to be ready for battle. He was expected to be eager to prove his skill at public tournaments, fighting other knights with the sword, or with a lance in the mounted duel called a joust. It was his duty as a gentleman, his *noblesse oblige* ("nobility obligates"), to be constantly on the lookout for insult or injustice to others weaker than himself, and to rectify such wrongs.

A peculiar aspect of this culture is its attitude

Two statues from a group at Naumberg Cathedral depicting the cathedral's founders. c. 1250–1260

toward love. Within the household of a noble family, most marriages were arranged for economic and political reasons. Wives were presumed to be discontented with their husbands, and inclined to fall in love with the younger men, the knights, who lived in the castle. The knights, in turn, were to owe such a woman complete devotion, seeking to please her through extravagant deeds of bravery and self-abnegation. This relationship between a knight and his lady, which mirrors that of a vassal to his lord, is styled "courtly love." Marie de France's "Lay of the Were-

Quentin Massys,
*The Banker and His
Wife*. 1514. Louvre

wolf" (page 297) treats this kind of situation as completely normal. A wife, who has been very happy with her husband until the story begins, has nevertheless been pursued "for a great while" by another knight, who is standing by to rescue her whenever she is ready.

These extra-marital loves, which were sometimes completely chaste, and sometimes not so completely, became a favorite subject of a new literary genre, the romance. However, the medieval romance was by no means exclusively about love, and the very term *romance* used in this context more accurately refers to tales set in remote and fantastic places, in which knights seek adventure in order to fulfill their obligations to a feudal lord, and perhaps additionally to a lady fair. The first romances, which

began to appear in the later twelfth century, used classical legends as their subject matter. But poets soon discovered the realm of Arthurian knighthood and made it the most popular literary theme of the High Middle Ages. So much so that toward the end of the twelfth century one writer exclaims, "Whither has not flying fame spread and familiarized the name of Arthur the Briton, even as far as Christendom extends." *Sir Gawain and the Green Knight* (page 340), written around 1375, a period when the Renaissance was already underway in Italy, illustrates the continuing popularity of Arthurian romances even in later centuries when the social context which they replicate had largely disappeared. *Sir Gawain and the Green Knight* also illustrates, as did the *Song of Roland*, how imagination transforms history. The legend of a fifth-century military leader who may have led the Romanized Celts of Britain against Germanic invaders had become, in medieval romances of the twelfth and thirteenth centuries, a mighty king, the ruler of a great empire, faithfully followed by a retinue of loyal men, the Knights of the Round Table.

THE LATE MIDDLE AGES

With somewhat stronger centralized governments life in Europe became more stable, and the peaceful work of merchants and artisans could flourish once again. The medieval kings did what they could to help, improving roads, opening seaports, and protecting their vessels from Moslem pirates.

A characteristic development of the eleventh and twelfth centuries is the appearance in the towns of merchant guilds, organized to control particular trades. Alongside of them appeared artisans' guilds regulating the manufacture and pricing of specific goods. These social groupings, so radically different in character from the lord and his knights gathered in their isolated castle, represent the beginnings of a new kind of collective spirit—the medieval town.

In late medieval Italy the development of urban life approached modern scale. Florence, once a Roman city destroyed by barbarian invaders, had by the thirteenth century become a manufacturing center with over three hundred small textile factories, as well as a financial center with banking houses floating loans for neighboring countries. Following bloody struggles between rival factions, its citizens had by the end of the thirteenth century developed a form of government by a small panel of "priors" elected from the city's guilds—in essence becoming a democratic city-state. It was in this context of a revived, wealthy and powerful urban center that the Italian poet Dante appeared. Thanks to the rich culture of late medieval Florence, he was able to master a broad range of knowledge, and thanks to the medieval habit of ordering and synthesizing, he was able to marshal what he knew and thought into the *Divine Comedy* (page 316), a vision of the interconnections between God and His creation that is one of the greatest legacies of medieval culture.

THINKING ABOUT GRAPHIC AIDS
Using the Time Line

The time line on pages 272–273 shows the chronological sequence of the historical and literary events discussed in Unit 3. Use the time line to answer the following questions.

1. How many years separate the Battle of Roncesvalles and the *Song of Roland?* (a) less than two hundred; (b) around three hundred; (c) more than four hundred
2. Which of the following pairs of individuals were not contemporaries? (a) Henry II and Marie de France; (b) Charlemagne and Canute; (c) Chaucer and the *Gawain*-poet
3. How long was Iceland independent? (a) nearly 200 years; (b) nearly 300 years; (c) nearly 400 years
4. Which of the following kings could have joined the Third Crusade? (a) Richard I; (b) Henry II; (c) Louis IX
5. Which of the following events in Dante's life occurred last? (a) his exile from Florence; (b) the writing of *La Vita Nuova;* (c) the death of Beatrice

Using the Map

The map on page 277 shows the locations of many of the places discussed in Unit 3. Use the map to answer the following questions.

1. Is Roncesvalles a pass in the Pyrenees Mountains or the Alps?
2. Iceland's parliament, the Althing, was held at a site in the southwest corner of the island. What is it called?
3. Charlemagne's palace at Aachen was also known by another name. What is it?
4. In what country is the province of Brittany located?
5. Which of the following cities is located on the Ebro River? (a) Ravenna; (b) Chester; (c) Saragossa

The Song of Roland

Detail of stained glass from Chartres Cathedral showing Roland splitting the rock and sounding his horn. Early 13th century

The first great work of French literature, the *Chanson de Roland*, or "Song of Roland," is about historical events. Early in the eighth century a Moslem army of Arabs and North African Berbers crossed the Strait of Gibraltar into Spain and crushed the Christian Visigothic Kingdom there. They established a powerful Islamic state that carried out intermittent wars with its Christian neighbors. In 778 the Moslem governor of Barcelona, during a quarrel with another Islamic ruler, invited Charlemagne to invade northern Spain. He did so, and laid siege to the fortified town of Saragossa. Word reached him there that Saxon tribes were attacking the other end of his empire, in Germany. Charlemagne withdrew his forces northward through a pass in the Pyrenees (pir′ə nēz′) Mountains that divide France and Spain. On August 15, 778, the rear guard of Charlemagne's army was ambushed by the local Basques. An account written about fifty years after the event reports that the attackers forced Charlemagne's troops down into a narrow valley, Roncesvalles (ron′sə valz′), where the Basques "joined battle with them and killed them to the last man." One of the dead was "Roland, Lord of the Breton Marches." Charlemagne returned several years later and recaptured some of northern Spain, which he put under French control.

Centuries passed, but the brief, disastrous battle in the valley of Roncesvalles lingered in the French imagination. By the 9th century, the story of Roland had become a legend; by the 10th, poetic versions existed. A Norman-French warrior is said to have sung of Roland while riding at the head of the forces that defeated the English at the Battle of Hastings in 1066. It is reasonable to assume that the wandering minstrels whom the French called jongleurs (jong′glərz) sang of Roland's adventures before medieval courts, whose members would see in the hero ideals they sought to emulate.

Around 1100 someone composed a poetic version of this well-known tale in the French dialect spoken in Normandy and England. He may have been called Turoldus, a name that appears in the last line of a manuscript copy of the poem. Nothing further is known about him. His masterpiece, the *Song of Roland*, began with the traditional story and created an epic. The details of the historical battle take on mythic dimensions. Charlemagne (who was actually 38 at the time of Roland's death) is described as being two hundred years old in the epic. The band of Basque attackers has become an enormous Moslem army massed against the French rear guard. The struggle is not over the booty in French wagons, but between pagan and Christian for the control of the world. As Roland expressed the contest, "Right's on our side, and wrong is with these wretches!"

Some of these transformations fit the world of 1100 when this poem was written. Christians were exalted by the success of the First Crusade, which climaxed in the capture of Jerusalem in 1099. The struggle between the

Moslem and Christian worlds commanded the attention of Europe. At the same time, the weakness of the French monarchy, challenged by the power of independent nobles, made some people look nostalgically back to a time when kings like Charlemagne seemed to rule for the good of everyone, rather than for narrow self-interest. But such contemporary issues serve only as a backdrop to the deeper and timeless concerns of the *Song of Roland*—heroism, fidelity to one's friends and one's country, and dedication to duty that may require the ultimate sacrifice.

The *Song of Roland* is a *chanson de geste*, a narrative poem about the deeds of kings and their warriors. The poet uses a stanza called a *laisse* (les). Instead of rhyming, its ten-syllable lines usually end with the same vowel sound. Like English ballads, the *Song of Roland* will sometimes go over the same situation in successive stanzas, called "similar laisses," which examine dramatic moments from various perspectives.

The poem narrates the struggle between Christian French and Islamic Saracen forces in Spain. The French king Charlemagne (also called Carlon) has gathered his twelve chief followers, called the "Peers" or "Paladins," to lead his troops. Among them are Roland, his close friend Oliver, and the warrior-bishop Turpin. Unhappily, also present is Roland's step-father Ganelon (gä′nə lon)—also called Guènes (gü′ē nez)—who for some unexplained reason hates his stepson, and to revenge himself on Roland, will betray his own king. The poem's description of their opponents has no connection with history. It pictures the Moslems as idolaters who worship a trinity of devils called Mahound (after Mohammed, the founder of Islam), Apollo (after the Greek god), and Termagant (perhaps the name of a demon). Their leader Baligant does not appear in this selection, but we do read about his subordinates Marsilion (sometimes called Marsile), his son Jurfaret, nephew Adelroth, and trusted adviser Blancandrin. In the poem these men, who have dedicated themselves to evil, will do anything to destroy the French and thereby undermine Christianity.

The narrative of the *Song of Roland* falls into four sections. In the first, Ganelon plans to betray the French; in the second, the French rear guard is destroyed and Roland dies; in the third, Charlemagne revenges Roland by defeating the Saracens, ultimately through individual combat with their leader Baligant; and in the last, Charlemagne tries and executes Ganelon. The *geste* or "deed" that comprises the whole poem is twofold: in the first half treachery leads to Roland's death; in the second half, Charlemagne, the ideal warrior-king, wins vengeance for his man, imposes justice upon a traitor, and expels the Saracens. The following selection from the *Song of Roland* comes from the poem's first half. As it begins, Charlemagne gathers with his men to debate the significance of an offer which the Saracens have sent them. They say that if the French will withdraw, taking twenty of their sons as pledges of their good word, that the Saracens will come to Charlemagne's capital at Aix (eks) and there convert to Christianity, swearing obedience to the French king. The problem which faces Charlemagne is whether to risk trust in what seems an untrustworthy enemy.

H⊼ See ASSONANCE in the Handbook of Literary Terms, page 942.

from the Song of Roland

translated by **Dorothy L. Sayers**

13

"Barons, my lords," began the Emperor Carlon,[1]
"From King Marsile[2] come envoys, seeking parley.
He makes me offers of treasure overpassing:
Of lions and bears and hounds to the leash mastered,
5 Sev'n hundred camels, and falcons mewed[3] and
  hearty,
Four hundred mules with Arab gold all chargèd,
And fifty wagons well-laden in a cart-train.
But now to France he urges my departure,
And to my palace at Aix he'll follow after,
10 There change his faith for one of more advantage,
Become a Christian and of me hold his marches.[4]
But his true purpose—for that I cannot answer."
The French all say: "We'd best be very guarded."

14

The Emperor Charles had finished all his speech.
15 The County[5] Roland, who fiercely disagrees,
Swift to oppose springs up upon his feet:
He tells the King: "Nevermore trust Marsile!
Seven years long in land of Spain we've been.
I won for you both Noples and Commibles,
20 I took Valterna, the land of Pine I seized,
And Balagate, and Seville and Tudele.
Then wrought Marsile a very treacherous deed:
He sent his Paynims[6] by number of fifteen,
All of them bearing boughs of the olive tree,
25 And with like words he sued to you for peace.
Then did you ask the French lords for their rede;[7]
Foolish advice they gave to you indeed.
You sent the Paynim two counts of your meinie:[8]
Basan was one, the other was Basile.
30 He smote their heads off in hills beneath Haltile.
This war you've started wage on, and make no cease;

To Saragossa lead your host in the field,
Spend all your life, if need be, in the siege,
Revenge the men this villain made to bleed!"

15

35 The Emperor Charles sat still with his head bended;
He stroked his beard and his moustaches gently;
Nor good nor ill he answers to his nephew.[9]
The French are silent, Guènes[10] alone excepted;
But he leaps up, strides into Carlon's presence,
40 And full of pride begins thus to address him.
He tells the King: "Trust not a brawling fellow,
Me nor another; seek only your own welfare.
If King Marsile informs you by this message
He'll set his hands in yours,[11] and fealty pledge you
45 And hold all Spain from you, at your good pleasure,
And to that faith we follow give acceptance,
The man who tells you this plea should be rejected
Cares nothing, Sire, to what death he condemns us.
Counsel of pride must not grow swollen-headed;
50 Let's hear wise men, turn deaf ears to the reckless."

---

1. *Carlon,* Charlemagne.
2. *Marsile,* the Saracen leader Marsilion.
3. *mewed* (myūd), caged.
4. *marches.* Marsilion will place control of his own lands under Charlemagne's jurisdiction.
5. *County,* Count.
6. *Paynims* (pā′nimz), pagans; here, the Saracens.
7. *rede* (rēd), counsel.
8. *meinie* (mā′ne), household.
9. *nephew,* Roland.
10. *Guènes,* alternate form for Ganelon.
11. *set his hands in yours.* The ritual of fealty at the French court dictated that the king place his folded hands over the folded hands of his men, as a sign of interdependence and subordination.

20

The Emperor said: "My free and knightly band,
Come choose me out some baron of my land
To bring my message to King Marsilion's hand."
Quoth Roland: "Guènes my step-sire is the man."
55 The French all say: "Indeed, he is most apt;
If he's passed over you will not find his match."
Count Ganelon is furious out of hand;
His great furred gown of marten he flings back
And stands before them in his silk bliaut[12] clad.
60 Bright are his eyes, haughty his countenance,
Handsome his body, and broad his bosom's span;
The peers all gaze, his bearing is so grand.
He says to Roland: "Fool! what has made thee mad?
I am thy step-sire, and all these know I am,
65 And me thou namest to seek Marsilion's camp!
If God but grant I ever thence come back
I'll wreak on thee such ruin and such wrack
That thy life long my vengeance shall not slack."
Roland replies: "This is all boast and brag!
70 Threats cannot fright me, and all the world knows that
To bear this message we must have a good man;
I'll take your place if the King says I can."

21

Quoth Ganelon: "My place thou shalt not take;
Thou'rt not my vassal, nor I thy suzerain.[13]
75 Charles for his service commands me to obey.
I'll seek Marsile in Saragossa's gates;
But rather there some deadly trick I'll play
Than not find vent from my unbounded rage."
When Roland heard him, then he laughed in his face.

28

80 Under tall olives the County Guènes rides;
The Paynim envoys he's caught up in good time,
And Blancandrin[14] drops back with him behind.
Now each other begins to speak with guile.
Blancandrin says: "Charles is a wondrous wight!
85 Pulia he's ta'en, Calabria likewise,
And unto England passed over the salt tide
To win Saint Peter the tribute[15] of the isle.
What seeks he here, warring in our confines?"
"Such is his pleasure," Count Ganelon replies;
90 "In all the world you will not find his like."

Detail of stained glass from Chartres Cathedral showing Charlemagne and his warriors. Early 13th century

30

Quoth Blancandrin: "Roland's a villain fell,
Presuming thus all folk on earth to quell,
And every land under his yoke compel!
Whom does he count on to lend his arms such
    strength?"
95 Ganelon answers: "He counts upon the French;
They'll never fail him, they love him far too well.
Silver and gold he gives them for largesse,
Horses and mules, silks and accoutrements.
And everything the Emperor wants, he gets—
100 He'll win for him all lands 'twixt east and west."

31

So long rides Guènes with Blancandrin that day
Till each to each has pledged his truth and faith
They will seek means Count Roland for to slay.
So long they ride, they come by road and way

---

12. *bliaut* (blē´ō), tunic.
13. *suzerain* (sü´zə rān), feudal lord.
14. *Blancandrin*, one of the Saracen envoys.
15. *tribute*, annual gift of money sent to the Pope (the successor of St. Peter) from England from before the reign of King Alfred the Great (871–901) until 1534, when it was abolished as a result of the split between the Church of England and the papacy. The historical Charlemagne had nothing to do with the origin of this custom.

Song of Roland 285

105 To Saragossa, and by a yew draw rein.
A faldstool[16] stood beneath a pine-tree's shade,
With silken cloth of Alexandria draped;
There sat the King that bore the rule in Spain.
Full twenty thousand Saracens stood arrayed.
110 Not one of them has any word to say,
So eagerly upon the news they wait.
And here comes Guènes and Blancandrin apace!

36

Guènes approached the King and thus addressed him:
He said to him: "You do vainly to vex you.
115 Carlon thus bids you, that hath France in possession:
The Christian faith must of you be accepted,
And one half Spain he will give you in tenure;
The other half is for Roland his nephew;
A right proud partner you'll have there for co-tenant!
120 If these conditions should by you be rejected,
In Saragossa he'll besiege and invest you,
And by main force you shall be seized and fettered.
Thence to his city of Aix you'll go directly.
You shall not ride on palfrey nor on destrier,[17]
125 Nor for the road shall you have mule nor jennet;[18]
On some poor screw of a pack-ass he'll set you;
And you will lose your head there by his sentence.
See now, the Emperor has written you this letter."
To the right hand of the Moor[19] he presents it.

38

130 Unto the orchard the King Marsile repairs:
Of his best men he takes with him a share,
And thither came Blancandrin white of hair,
And Jurfaret, who is his son and heir,
And the Caliph, his eme[20] and officer.
135 Quoth Blancandrin: "Call in that Frenchman there:
He'll serve our ends, to this I've heard him swear."
"Fetch him yourself, 'twere best," the King declares.
In his right hand[21] Count Ganelon he bare
Into the orchard where king and council were.
140 So they begin to plot the treacherous snare.

41

The Paynim said: "I marvel in my thought,
At Charlemayn, that is so old and hoar!
I know he's lived two hundred years and more.

In lands so many his body he's forworn,
145 Sharp strokes so many of lance and spear has borne,
Rich kings so many beggared and brought to naught—
When will he weary of going to the wars?"
"Never," said Guènes, "while Roland still bears sword;
There's none so valiant beneath the heavens broad,
150 Oliver too, his friend, is a brave lord;
And the Twelve Peers whom Charles so much adores
Protect the vanward with knights a thousand score;
Charles is secure, he fears no man at all."

44

"Guènes, fair sir," [the King Marsilion cries,]
155 "What must I do to bring Roland to die?"
"I'll tell you that," Count Ganelon replies.
"At Sizer Gate[22] the King will have arrived,
Leaving a rear guard to keep the pass behind.
There'll be his nephew Count Roland, the great
     knight,
160 Oliver too, on whom he most relies,
With twenty thousand good Frenchmen at their side.
An hundred thousand send of your Paynim kind,
And these shall first engage the French in fight.
Of the French force the loss will not be light—
165 Yours will be slaughtered, and that I'll not disguise!
The like assault you'll launch a second time,
And, first or last, Roland will not get by.
You will have done a deed of arms full fine;
You'll ne'er again see war in all your life.

52

170 Marsilion's hand on Guènes' shoulder lies;
He says to him: "You are both bold and wise.
Now by that faith which seems good in your eyes
Let not your heart turn back from our design.
Treasure I'll give you, a great and goodly pile,

---

16. *faldstool*, a folding chair.
17. *palfrey* (pal′frē), *destrier* (des′tri ėr), horses for women and warriors, respectively.
18. *jennet*, a she-ass.
19. *Moor* (mür), King Marsilius. The Moors were the Moslem people of mixed Arab and Berber ancestry who conquered Spain in the early eighth century.
20. *eme* (ēm), uncle.
21. *right hand*, a formal ritual of honor and acceptance.
22. *Sizer Gate*, a pass through the Pyrenees.

175 Ten mule-loads gold, digged from Arabian mines;
No year shall pass but you shall have the like.
Take now the keys of this great burg of mine,
Offer King Charles all its riches outright.
Make sure that Roland but in the rear guard rides,
180 And if in pass or passage I him find
I'll give him battle right bitter to abide."
"I think," said Guènes, "that I am wasting time."
He mounts his horse and on his journey hies.

54

Early that day the Emperor leaves his bed.
185 Matins and mass the King has now heard said;
On the green grass he stood before his tent.
Roland was with him, brave Oliver as well,
Naimon the Duke and many another yet.
Then perjured Guènes the traitor comes to them
190 And starts to speak with cunning false pretense.
He tells the King: "To you (whom God defend!)
Of Saragossa the keys I here present.
I bring you also wealth to your heart's content,
And twenty sureties:[23] see they be closely kept.
195 The valiant king, Marsile, this message sends:
The Caliph's[24] absence he prays you'll not resent.
Mine own eyes saw four hundred thousand men
In hauberk armed, some having laced their helms,
And girt with swords whose hilts were richly gemmed,
200 Attend him forth; to the seashore they went.
The faith of Christ they'd keep not, nor accept,
And for this cause they from Marsilion fled.
But ere they'd sailed four leagues, maybe, or less,
Black wind and storm and tempest on them fell;
205 They were all drowned; they'll ne'er be seen again.
Had he been living I would have had him fetched.
Now, as regards the Paynim King himself:
Believe me, sire, before a month is sped
He'll follow you to France, to your own realm.
210 There he'll receive the faith that you profess,
There with joined hands to you his fealty pledge,
And hold from you in fief the Spanish realm."
Then said the King: "The name of God be blest!
Well have you done: I shall reward you well."
215 Throughout the host a thousand trumpets swell,
The French strike camp, their goods on sumpters[25]
        set;
Home to fair France behold them all addressed.

56

The day goes down, dark follows on the day.
The Emperor sleeps, the mighty Charlemayn.
220 He dreamed he stood in Sizer's lofty gate,
Holding in hand his ashen lance full great.
Count Ganelon takes hold of it, and shakes,
And with such fury he wrenches it and breaks
That high as heaven the flinders fly away.
225 Carlon sleeps on, he sleeps and does not wake.

58

The night is past and the clear dawn is showing.
[A thousand trumpets] are sounded for the hosting.
The Emperor rides full lordly in his going.
"Barons, my lords," quoth Charlemayn, "behold
        now
230 These lofty passes, these narrows winding closely—
Say, who shall have the rear guard now to hold them?"
Quoth Ganelon: "I name my nephew Roland;
You have no baron who can beat him for boldness."
When the King heard, a stern semblance he showed
        him:
235 "A fiend incarnate you are indeed," he told him;
"Malice hath ta'en possession of you wholly!
Who then should keep the vanguard of my progress?"
Quoth Ganelon: "Ogier the Dane[26] I vote for;
You have no baron can do it with more prowess."

59

240 When Roland hears what he's appointed to,
He makes reply as knighthood bids him do:
"My noble stepsire, I owe you gratitude
That I'm assigned the rear guard at your suit.
Charles, King of France, the loss shall never rue
245 Of steed or palfrey thereby, I warrant you,
No saddle-beast, nor hinny neither mule,
Pack-horse nor sumpter thereby he shall not lose,
Save first the sword have paid the reckoning due."
Quoth Ganelon: "I know it; you speak truth."

---

23. sureties. Saracen hostages, pledges of good faith. If Marsilion breaks his word then Charlemagne is free to kill them.
24. Caliph's. The Caliph (kā′lif) is another Saracen leader.
25. sumpters, pack animals.
26. Ogier (ō′ji er) **the Dane,** one of the most famous of Charlemagne's paladins.

66

250 High are the hills, the valleys dark and deep,
Grisly the rocks, and wondrous grim the steeps.
The French pass through that day with pain and grief,
The bruit of them was heard full fifteen leagues.
But when at length their fathers' land they see,
255 Their own lord's land, the land of Gascony,
Then they remember their honors and their fiefs,
Sweethearts and wives whom they are fain to greet,
Not one there is for pity doth not weep.
Charles most of all a boding sorrow feels,
260 His nephew's left the Spanish gates to keep;
For very ruth he cannot choose but weep.

80

Oliver's climbed upon a hilly crest,
Looks to his right along a grassy cleft,
And sees the Paynims and how they ride addressed.
265 To his companion Roland he calls and says:
"I see from Spain a tumult and a press—
Many bright hauberks, and many a shining helm!
A day of wrath, they'll make it for our French.
Ganelon knew it, false heart and traitor fell;
270 When to the Emperor he named us for this stead!"
Quoth Roland: "Silence, Count Oliver, my friend!
He is my stepsire, I will have no word said."

81

Oliver's climbed a hill above the plain,
Whence he can look on all the land of Spain,
275 And see how vast the Saracen array;
All those bright helms with gold and jewels gay,
And all those shields, those coats of burnished mail;
And all those lances from which the pennons wave;
Even their squadrons defy all estimate,
280 He cannot count them, their numbers are so great;
Stout as he is, he's mightily dismayed.
He hastens down as swiftly as he may,
Comes to the French and tells them all his tale.

82

Quoth Oliver: "The Paynim strength I've seen;
285 Never on earth has such a hosting been:
A hundred thousand in van ride under shield
Their helmets laced, their hauberks all agleam

Their spears upright, with heads of shining steel.
You'll have such battle as ne'er was fought on field.
290 My lords of France, God give you strength at need!
Save you stand fast, this field we cannot keep."
The French all say: "Foul shame it were to flee!
We're yours till death; no man of us will yield."

83

Quoth Oliver: "Huge are the Paynim hordes,
295 And of our French the numbers seem but small.
Companion Roland, I pray you sound your horn,
That Charles may hear and fetch back all his force."
Roland replies: "Madman were I and more,
And in fair France my fame would suffer scorn.
300 I'll smite great strokes with Durendal[27] my sword,
I'll dye it red high as the hilt with gore.
This pass the Paynims reached on a luckless morn;
I swear to you death is their doom therefor."

87

Roland is fierce and Oliver is wise
305 And both for valor may bear away the prize.
Once horsed and armed the quarrel to decide,
For dread of death the field they'll never fly.
The counts are brave, their words are stern and high.
Now the false Paynims with wondrous fury ride.
310 Quoth Oliver: "Look, Roland, they're in sight.
Charles is far off, and these are very nigh;
You would not sound your Olifant[28] for pride;
Had we the Emperor we should have been all right.
To Gate of Spain turn now and lift your eyes,
315 See for yourself the rear-guard's woeful plight.
Who fights this day will never more see fight."
Roland replies: "Speak no such foul despite!
Curst be the breast whose heart knows cowardice!
Here in our place we'll stand and here abide:
320 Buffets and blows be ours to take and strike!"

---

27. **Durendal** (dü′ren däl), the name of Roland's sword,
which probably means "enduring."
28. **Olifant** (ol′i fant), Roland's horn, carved from a tusk
and hence called "elephant."

89

Then to their side comes the Archbishop Turpin,[29]
Riding his horse and up the hillside spurring.
He calls the French and preaches them a sermon:
"Barons, my lords, Charles picked us for this purpose;
5 We must be ready to die in our King's service.
Christendom needs you, so help us to preserve it.
Battle you'll have, of that you may be certain,
Here come the Paynims—your own eyes have observed
        them.
Now beat your breasts and ask God for His mercy:
30 I will absolve you and set your souls in surety.
If you should die, blest martyrdom's your guerdon;
You'll sit on high in Paradise eternal."
The French alight and all kneel down in worship;
God's shrift[30] and blessing the Archbishop conferreth,
35 And for their penance he bids them all strike firmly.

93

And Adelroth, (he was King Marsile's nephew),
Before the host comes first of all his fellows;
With evil words the French he thus addresses:
"Villainous Franks, with us you have to reckon!
40 You've been betrayed by him that should protect you,
Your king lacked wit who in the passes left you.
Fair France will lose her honor in this venture;
From Carlon's body the right arm will be severed."
When Roland hears him, God! but his rage is reckless!
45 He spurs his horse, gives full rein to his mettle,
His blow he launches with all his mightiest effort;
The shield he shatters, and the hauberk he rendeth,
He splits the breast and batters in the breast-bone,
Through the man's back drives out the backbone
        bended,
50 And soul and all forth on the spear-point fetches;
Clean through he thrusts him, forth of the saddle
        wrenching,
And flings him dead a lance-length from his destrier;
Into two pieces he has broken his neckbone.
No less for that he speaks to him and tells him:
55 "Out on thee, churl![31] no lack-wit is the Emperor,
He is none such, nor loved he treason ever;
Right well he did who in the passes left us,
Neither shall France lose honor by this venture.
First blood to us! Go to it, gallant Frenchmen!
60 Right's on our side, and wrong is with these wretches!"

105

The County Roland throughout the field goes riding;
With Durendal, good sword, he stabs and slices,
The toll he takes of Saracens is frightful.
Would you had seen him, dead man on dead man
        piling,
365 Seen the bright blood about his pathway lying!
Bloody his hauberk and both his arms with fighting,
His good horse bloody from crest to withers likewise;
Oliver too doth never cease from striking,
And the Twelve Peers are not a whit behindhand,
370 And all the French are hammering and smiting;
The Paynims fall, some dead and others dying.
Quoth the Archbishop: "Right blessèd be our
        knighthood";
He shouts "Mountjoy!" war-cry of Charles the mighty.

130

Said Roland then: "Full grievous is this fight.
375 I'll sound my horn, and Charles will hear the cry."
Quoth Oliver: " 'Twould ill beseem a knight.
I asked you, comrade, and you refused, for pride.
Had Charles been here, then all would have gone
        right;
He's not to blame, nor the men at his side.
380 Now by my beard (quoth he) if e'er mine eyes
Again behold my sister Aude[32] the bright,
Between her arms never you think to lie."

131

Quoth Roland: "Why so angry with me, friend?"
And he: "Companion, you got us in this mess.
385 There is wise valor, and there is recklessness:
Prudence is worth more than foolhardiness.
Through your o'erweening you have destroyed the
        French;
Ne'er shall we do service to Charles again.
Had you but given some heed to what I said,

---

29. Turpin, modeled on Tiplinus of Rheims, a warrior-priest of eighth-century France.
30. shrift, pardon.
31. churl!, a low-born person. Vilifying one's dead enemy was a customary part of such fighting.
32. Aude (ō'dä). Roland was to marry Oliver's sister Aude.

Song of Roland **289**

390 My lord had come, the battle had gone well,
And King Marsile had been captured or dead.
Your prowess, Roland, is a curse on our heads.
No more from us will Charlemayn have help,
Whose like till Doomsday shall not be seen of men.
395 Now you will die, and fair France will be shent;
Our loyal friendship is here brought to an end;
A bitter parting we'll have ere this sun set."

132

When the Archbishop thus hears them in dispute,
With his gold spurs he pricks his steed anew,
400 Draws near to them and utters this rebuke:
"Lord Oliver, and you, Lord Roland, too,
Let's have no quarrel, o' God's name, 'twixt you two.
It will not save us to sound the horn, that's true;
Nevertheless, 'twere better so to do.
405 Let the King come; his vengence will be rude;
None shall to Spain ride home with merry news.
After, our French will light them down on foot,
Seek out our bodies and limbs in sunder hewn,
Lay us on biers borne upon sumpter-mules,
410 And weep for us with grief right pitiful;
In the church-close we shall have burial due,
And not be food for dogs and swine and wolves."
Quoth Roland, "Sir, your words are right and good."

133

Roland has set Olifant to his lips,
415 Firmly he holds it and blows it with a will.
High are the mountains, the blast is long and shrill,
Thirty great leagues the sound went echoing.
King Carlon heard it and all who rode with him.
"Lo, now, our men are fighting," quoth the King.
420 Guènes retorts: "If any man said this
Except yourself, it were a lie, methinks."

134

The County Roland with pain and anguish winds
His Olifant, and blows with all his might.
Blood from his mouth comes spurting scarlet-bright
425 He's burst the veins of his temples outright.
From hand and horn the call goes shrilling high:
King Carlon hears it who through the passes rides,
Duke Naimon hears, and all the French beside.

Quoth Charles: "I hear the horn of Roland cry!
430 He'd never sound it but in the thick of fight."
"There is no battle," Count Ganelon replies;
"You're growing old, your hair is sere and white,
When you speak thus, you're talking like a child.
Full well you know Roland's o'erweening pride;
435 'Tis strange that God endures him so long time!
Took he not Noples against your orders quite?
The Paynims made a sally from inside,
And there gave battle to Roland the great knight;
So he swilled down[33] the field—a brave device
440 To keep the bloodstains from coming to your eyes!
For one small hare he'll blow from morn till night;
Now to the Peers he's showing-off in style.
Who dare attack him? No man beneath the sky!
Ride on, ride on! Why loiter here the while?
445 Our Fathers' land lies distant many a mile."

135

Count Roland's mouth with running blood is red;
He's burst asunder the temples of his head;
He sounds his horn in anguish and distress.
King Carlon hears, and so do all the French.
450 Then said the King: "This horn is long of breath."
" 'Tis blown," quoth Naimon, "with all a brave man's
    strength;
Battle there is, and that I know full well.
He that would stay you is but a traitor fell.
To arms! let sound your battle-cry to heav'n!
455 Make haste to bring your gallant household help!
You hear how Roland makes desperate lament!"

136

The Emperor Charles lets sound his horns aloft.
The French light down and arm themselves anon
With helm and hauberk and gilded swords girt on;
460 Goodly their shields, their lances stiff and strong,
Scarlet and white and blue the gonfalons.[34]
Straightway to horse the warrior lords have got;

---

33. swilled down. The manuscript is difficult to decipher here, but the line seems to describe Roland diverting local streams to wash away the blood of a battle of which Charlemagne had not approved. This episode does not appear in any other version of the Roland story.
34. gonfalons (gon′fə lənz), banners.

Swift through the passes they spur and never stop,
Each unto other they speak and make response:
5 "Might we reach Roland ere he were dead and gone,
We'ld strike good strokes beside him in the throng."
What use is that? They have delayed too long.

138

Huge are the hills and shadowy and high,
Deep in the vales the living streams run by.
0 The trumpets sound before them and behind,
All with one voice of Olifant reply.
In wrath of heart the Emperor Carlon rides,
And all the French in sorrow and in ire;
There's none but grieves and weeps from out his eyes;
5 They all pray God to safeguard Roland's life
Till they may come to battle by his side;
Once they are with him they'll make it a great fight.
What use is that? their prayers are empty quite,
Too long they've lingered, they cannot come in time.

156

80 The County Roland fights bravely as he may,
But his whole body in heat and sweat is bathed,
And all his head is racked with grievous pain
From that great blast which brake his temples' veins.
Fain would he know if Charles is bringing aid;
85 His Olifant he grasps, and blows full faint.
The Emperor halts, hearing the feeble strain:
"My lords," quoth he, "this tells a woeful tale;
Roland my nephew is lost to us this day,
That call proclaims his breath is nigh to fail.
90 Whoso would reach him must ride with desperate
      haste
Sound through the host! bid every trumpet play!"
Full sixty thousand so loud their clarions bray
The hills resound, the valleys ring again.
The Paynims hear, no lust to laugh have they:
95 "We'll soon have Charles to reckon with," they say.

160

The Paynims say: "Why were we ever born?
Woe worth the while! our day of doom has dawned.
Now have we lost our peerage and our lords,
The mighty Carlon comes on with all his force,
00 Of those of France we hear the shrilling horns,

French miniature showing (center) Roland fighting and
(bottom) dead. c. 1469–1473. Musée Condé, Chantilly

The cry 'Mountjoy!' sounds fearfully abroad.
So grim of mood is Roland in his wrath
No man alive can put him to the sword.
Let fly at him, and then give up the war."
505 So they let fly; spears, lances they outpour,
Darts and jereeds[35] and feathered shafts galore.
The shield of Roland is pierced and split and scored,
The mail-rings riven, and all his hauberk torn,
Yet in his body he is not touched at all,
510 Though under him, with thirty wounds and more,
His Veillantif[36] is stricken dead and falls.
The Paynims flee, abandoning the war;
Count Roland's left amid the field, unhorsed.

161

In wrath and grief away the Paynims fly;
515 Backward to Spain with headlong haste they hie.
The County Roland cannot pursue their flight,
Veillantif's lost, he has no steed to ride;
Will he or nill he, he must on foot abide,

---

35. *jereed*, an Arab javelin.
36. *Veillantif* (vēl'län tēf), Roland's horse. The name
means "wide awake."

He's turned to aid Archbishop Turpin's plight,
520 And from his head the gilded helm untied,
Stripped off the hauberk of subtle rings and bright,
And all to pieces has cut the bliaut fine
Wherewith to bandage his wounds that gape so wide.
Then to his breast he clasps and lifts him light
525 And gently lays him upon the green hill-side,
With fair soft speech entreating on this wise:
"Ah, noble sir, pray give me leave awhile;
These friends of ours, we loved so well in life,
We must not leave them thus lying where they died.
530 I will go seek them, find, and identify,
And lay them here together in your sight."
"Go and return," the Bishop makes reply;
"Thanks be to God, this field is yours and mine."

168

Now Roland feels that he is at death's door;
535 Out of his ears the brain is running forth.
Now for his peers he prays God call them all,
And for himself St Gabriel's aid implores;
Then in each hand he takes, lest shame befal,
His Olifant and Durendal his sword.
540 Far as a quarrel flies from a crossbow drawn,
Toward land of Spain he goes, to a wide lawn,
And climbs a mound where grows a fair tree tall,
And marble stones beneath it stand by four.
Face downward there on the green grass he falls,
545 And swoons away, for he is at death's door.

169

High are the hills and very high the trees are;
Four stones there are set there, of marble gleaming.
The County Roland lies senseless on the greensward.
A Saracen is there, watching him keenly;
550 He has feigned death, and lies among his people,
And has smeared blood upon his breast and features.
Now he gets up and runs towards him fleetly;
Strong was he, comely and of valor exceeding.
Now in his rage and in his overweening
555 He falls on Roland, his arms and body seizing;
He saith one word: "Now Carlon's nephew's beaten.
I'll take his sword, to Araby I'll reive it."
But as he draws it Roland comes to, and feels him.

170

Roland has felt his good sword being stol'n;
560 Opens his eyes and speaks this word alone:
"Thou'rt none of ours, in so far as I know."
He takes his horn, of which he kept fast hold,
And smites the helm, which was all gemmed with gold;
He breaks the steel and the scalp and the bone,
565 And from his head batters his eyes out both,
And dead on ground he lays the villain low;
Then saith: "False Paynim, and how wast thou so bold,
Foully or fairly, to seize upon me so?
A fool he'll think thee who hears this story told.
570 Lo, now! the mouth of my Olifant's broke;
Fallen is all the crystal and the gold."

171

Now Roland feels his sight grow dim and weak;
With his last strength he struggles to his feet;
All the red blood has faded from his cheeks.
575 A gray stone stands before him at his knee:
Ten strokes thereon he strikes, with rage and grief;
It grides, but yet nor breaks nor chips the steel.
"Ah!" cries the Count, "Saint Mary succor me!
Alack the day, Durendal, good and keen!
580 Now I am dying, I cannot fend for thee.
How many battles I've won with you in field!
With you I've conquered so many goodly fiefs
That Carlon holds, the lord with the white beard!
Let none e'er wield you that from the foe would flee—
585 You that were wielded so long by a good liege!
The like of you blest France shall never see."

174

Now Roland feels death press upon him hard;
It's creeping down from his head to his heart.
Under a pine-tree he hastens him apart,
590 There stretches him face down on the green grass,
And lays beneath him his sword and Olifant.
He's turned his head to where the Paynims are,
And this he doth for the French and for Charles,
Since fain is he that they should say, brave heart,
595 That he has died a conquerer at the last.

Panel from a silver reliquary showing (top right) Charlemagne weeping for his men killed at Roncesvalles. Early 13th century. Cathedral Treasury, Aachen

He beats his breast full many a time and fast,
Gives, with his glove, his sins into God's charge.

176

The County Roland lay down beneath a pine;
To land of Spain he's turned him as he lies,
00 And many things begins to call to mind:
All the broad lands he conquered in his time,
And fairest France, and the men of his line,
And Charles his lord, who bred him from a child;
He cannot help but weep for them and sigh.
05 Yet of himself he is mindful betimes;
He beats his breast and on God's mercy cries:
"Father most true, in whom there is no lie,
Who didst from death Saint Lazarus make to rise,
And bring out Daniel safe from the lions' might,
10 Save Thou my soul from danger and despite
Of all the sins I did in all my life."
His right-hand glove[37] he's tendered unto Christ,
And from his hand Gabriel accepts the sign.
Straightway his head upon his arm declines;
15 With folded hands he makes an end and dies.
God sent to him His Angel Cherubine,
And great Saint Michael to Peril-by-the-Tide;

Saint Gabriel too was with them at his side;
The County's soul they bear to Paradise.

177

620 Roland is dead, in Heaven God hath his soul.
The Emperor Charles rides in to Roncevaux.[38]
No way there is therein, nor any road,
No path, no yard, no foot of naked mold
But there some French or Paynim corpse lies strown.
625 Charles cries: "Where are you, fair nephew? Out,
    harò!
Where's the Archbishop? is Oliver laid low?
Where are Gerin, Gerier his playfellow,
And Berenger, and the good Count Othone?
Ivor and Ives, so well I loved them both?
630 Where's Engelier, the Gascon great of note?
Samson the Duke, and Anseïs the Bold?
And where is Gerard of Roussillon the Old?
Where the Twelve Peers I left to guard the host?"

---

37. glove. Roland makes the ritual gesture of resignation to his lord.
38. Roncevaux (rôns vō′), the French form of the name *Roncesvalles*. The original form of the word, *Rencesvals*, means "valley of thorns."

What use to cry? all's still as any stone.
635 "God!" says the King, "how bitter my reproach,
That I was absent when they struck the first blow!"
He plucks his beard right angerly and wroth;
Barons and knights all weep and make their moan,
Full twenty thousand swoon to the ground for woe;
640 Naimon the Duke is grieved with all his soul.

180

For Charlemayn God wrought a wondrous token:
The sun stood still in the mid-heaven holden.
The Paynims flee, the French pursue them closely.
They overtake them in Vale of Tenebrosa.
645 Toward Saragossa they drive and beat them broken,
With mighty strokes they slay them in their going,
Cut their retreat off by the highways and roadways.

The River Ebro confronts them swiftly-flowing
And very deep and most fearfully swollen;
650 There is no barge, neither lighter nor dromond.[39]
In desperation their Termagant[40] invoking,
The Paynims plunge, but their gods take no notice.
Those that are armed in heavy helm and hauberk
Sink to the bottom in numbers past all noting.
655 Others drift downstream upon the current floating;
Happiest is he who promptly gets his throatful,
They are all drowned in a welter most woeful:
The French cry: "Luckless the day you looked on
     Roland!"

c. 1100

---

39. *dromond* (drom′ənd), fast sailing galley.
40. *Termagant* (tèr′mə gənt), according to the poem, one
of the Saracen gods.

THINK AND DISCUSS
Understanding
1. What do the Saracens offer the French to persuade them to retreat?
2. Whenever he speaks, what is the strategy which Roland urges?
3. What is the tactical reason which the Saracens have for wanting to kill Roland?
4. Why is Roland appointed leader of the rear guard?
5. State Roland's reason for refusing to sound his horn when Oliver first sees the Saracen army.
6. Why do the Saracens flee the field of battle?

Analyzing
7. How do details of his physical appearance help to characterize Charlemagne?
8. Explain why Ganelon is infuriated by Roland's suggestion that he be the ambassador to the Saracens.
9. Interpret Charlemagne's dream (lines 220–225).
10. How do the descriptions of the landscape at Roncesvalles foreshadow what is to come?
11. Explain the significance of the various conclusions to the "similar laisses" 80–83.

12. What does the poet wish to illustrate in the killing of Adelroth?
13. Explain the basis for Oliver's anger at Roland on the battlefield at Roncesvalles.
14. What kind of reasoning does Archbishop Turpin use to settle the two arguments between Oliver and Roland?
15. Roland blows his horn so hard that he begins to bleed. What does this symbolize?
16. As he dies, Roland tries to shatter Durendal (lines 575–578). Why?
17. How does the **setting** for Roland's death express his significance?
18. In what ways does the French cry, the last line of this selection, explain what will destroy the pagans?

Extending
19. Where, in our own day, do you find the sort of fantastic story Ganelon tells Charlemagne in lines 197–205?
20. What purposes do such stories serve?
21. Laisses 93 and 105 exemplify a code of values which the *Song of Roland* was written, at least in part, to teach. Does that code connect in any way with life in the twentieth century?

APPLYING: Assonance
See Handbook of Literary Terms, p. 942.

When syllables in two or more different words have the same vowel sound, they link by a sound effect called **assonance**. The stanza of the *Song of Roland* employs assonance instead of rhyme at the end of most lines, an effect that Dorothy Sayers, the translator of this version, has attempted to reproduce.

1. What is the assonated vowel in the last syllables of laisse 80?
2. What words do not fit this pattern?
3. List the different letters which signify the same vowel sound in the last syllables of laisse 138.

VOCABULARY
Medieval Words

If a friend said she was going "vanward" you might think she was getting a ride in a large vehicle, but this translation uses the term in line 152 to describe being at the head of a body of troops. The translator, Dorothy Sayers, has used many medieval English words in trying to capture the flavor of language in the *Song of Roland*. But the reader must be sure to recognize the particular meaning of a term within a specific context. Find the following six words within the poem, decide exactly what they mean, using your dictionary where necessary, and then fit each into a sentence which illustrates the meaning which the word has in Sayers's translation.

1. *tenure* (line 117).
2. *flinders* (line 224).
3. *bruit* (line 253).
4. *despite* (line 317).
5. *quarrel* (line 540).
6. *mold* (line 623).

THINKING SKILLS
Generalizing

In generalizing we draw broad conclusions from a range of particular information.

1. In general, what degree of loyalty does Charlemagne enjoy in the *Song of Roland*?
2. Who is the exception to your generalization?
3. Describe the significance of women in this poem.
4. What role does religion play in the warrior ethos this poem describes?

COMPOSITION
Writing a Summary

Write a summary that will explain to someone who has not read this selection exactly what happens. Divide your summary into four paragraphs, which will cover Ganelon's secret deal with Marsilion, the decision to assign charge of the rear guard to Roland, the progress of the battle, and Roland's death. Give particular attention to a specific explanation of personal motives, when you refer to decision making. See "Writing Notes and Summaries" in the Writer's Handbook.

Writing to Persuade

In one of the most frequently discussed passages from the *Song of Roland*, the poet comments: "Roland is fierce and Oliver is wise. . ." (line 304). Some readers think this suggests that Roland's refusal to call for help when Oliver first sees the Saracens was "fierce" rather than "wise," while others defend his decision. First, make your own evaluation, then write an essay of four paragraphs in which you justify it. Plan your argument in four stages: (**1**) a summary of events as the poem describes them; (**2**) an explanation of Oliver's criticisms of Roland; (**3**) what Roland says in his own defense; (**4**) your evaluation, which should draw upon information from the preceding three paragraphs, now reshaped according to your own evaluation. See "Writing to Persuade an Audience" in the Writer's Handbook.

ENRICHMENT
Readers Theater

The poet who wrote the *Song of Roland* preserves some of the musical effects of the jongleurs who first sang this story, especially in the "similar laisses." In order to hear, clearly, the effects of repeated images and phrases, prepare a performance of laisses 133–136. Have different students read aloud the narration in each stanza. Assign other students to read the speeches by the characters, and keep the same performers throughout the performance. The result will be that you will hear both the differences of the various stanzas, and the continuity of the characters.

The earliest known woman poet to write in French, Marie de France probably lived during the era when Anglo-Norman kings ruled an empire which stretched from Scotland in the north to the Pyrenees in the south. Little is known about her, though there are many guesses. Some speculate that she was the abbess of Shaftsbury in England from 1181 to 1215, a daughter of Geoffrey Plantagenet (d. 1151) and so half-sister to King Henry II. Others place her at Henry's court for most of her life.

Her name suggests that she was from France. Her most important book, by her own description, is an effort to save and transmit a very special aspect of French culture. After setting aside an earlier plan to translate Latin stories into French, she explains that she "called to mind those lays (short lyric or narrative poems to be sung) I had heard so often. I doubted nothing—for well I know—that our fathers fashioned them, that men should bear in remembrance the deeds of those who have gone before. Many a one, on many a day, the minstrel has chanted to my ear. I would not that they should perish, forgotten, by the roadside. In my turn, therefore, I have made of them a song, rhymed as well as I am able, and often has their shaping kept me sleepless in my bed."

The lays Marie heard sung by minstrels come from the northwest corner of France, called Brittany. For centuries it had been the refuge of Celtic peoples, driven there from central Europe and from England. Their oral literature, markedly different from the Germanic culture to the east, and Latin culture to the south, describes earth gods, forest demons, elves and fairies. The songs she heard spoke of King Arthur and his court, and also of werewolves. As Marie herself makes clear, she decided to preserve this culture in her poetry, and in fact all the original Breton tales she heard have been lost. Only her retellings survive. Marie's versions run from 100 to 1200 lines of verse. She collected them in a book that she dedicates to "a most noble and courteous King," now considered to be Henry II (who reigned from 1154 to 1189). They enjoyed immediate, wide popularity. Early in the next century, a poet notes that "she is much praised and her rhyme is loved everywhere; for counts, barons, and knights greatly admire it, and hold it dear. And they love her writing so much, and take such pleasure in it, that they have it read, and often copied." Her "Lay of the Werewolf" begins on the opposite page.

Marie also wrote a collection of 103 fables titled *Ysopet*, or "Little Aesop," which she translated from English into French, and dedicated to a Count William, perhaps William Longsworth, Earl of Shrewsbury and a son of Henry II. Three of her fables appear on page 301. Toward the end of her life she also translated a Latin treatise on Purgatory into French. From an era in which a woman writer was an oddity, Marie de France still speaks, with a voice which is clearly and confidently her own.

See SYMBOL in the Handbook of Literary Terms, page 974.

The Lay of the Werewolf

Marie de France   *translated by* **Eugene Mason**

mongst the tales I tell you once again, I would not forget the Lay of the Werewolf. Such beasts as he are known in every land. Bisclavaret he is named in Brittany; whilst the Norman calls him Garwal.

It is a certain thing, and within the knowledge of all, that many a christened man has suffered this change, and ran wild in woods, as a Werewolf. The Werewolf is a fearsome beast. He lurks within the thick forest, mad and horrible to see. All the evil that he may, he does. He goeth to and fro, about the solitary place, seeking man, in order to devour him. Hearken, now, to the adventure of the Werewolf, that I have to tell.

In Brittany there dwelt a baron who was marvellously esteemed of all his fellows. He was a stout knight, and a comely, and a man of office and repute. Right private was he to the mind of his lord, and dear to the counsel of his neighbors. This baron was wedded to a very worthy dame, right fair to see, and sweet of semblance. All his love was set on her, and all her love was given again to him. One only grief had this lady. For three whole days in every week her lord was absent from her side. She knew not where he went, nor on what errand. Neither did any of his house know the business which called him forth.

On a day when this lord was come again to his house, altogether joyous and content, the lady took him to task, right sweetly, in this fashion,

"Husband," said she, "and fair, sweet friend, I have a certain thing to pray of you. Right willingly would I receive this gift, but I fear to anger you in the asking. It is better for me to have an empty hand, than to gain hard words."

When the lord heard this matter, he took the lady in his arms, very tenderly, and kissed her.

"Wife," he answered, "ask what you will. What would you have, for it is yours already?"

"By my faith," said the lady, "soon shall I be whole. Husband, right long and wearisome are the days you spend away from your home. I rise from my bed in the morning, sick at heart, I know not why. So fearful am I, lest you do aught to your loss, that I may not find any comfort. Very quickly shall I die for reason of my dread. Tell me now, where you go, and on what business! How may the knowledge of one who loves so closely, bring you to harm?"

"Wife," made answer the lord, "nothing but evil can come if I tell you this secret. For the mercy of God do not require it of me. If you but knew, you would withdraw yourself from my love, and I should be lost indeed."

When the lady heard this, she was persuaded that her baron sought to put her by with jesting words. Therefore she prayed and required him the more urgently, with tender looks and speech, till he was overborne, and told her all the story, hiding naught.

"Wife, I become Bisclavaret. I enter in the forest, and live on prey and roots, within the thickest of the wood."

After she had learned his secret, she prayed and entreated the more as to whether he ran in his raiment, or went spoiled of vesture.

"Wife," said he, "I go naked as a beast."

"Tell me, for hope of grace, what you do with your clothing?"

"Fair wife, that will I never. If I should lose my raiment, or even be marked as I quit my vesture, then a Werewolf I must go for all the days of my life. Never again should I become man, save in that hour my clothing were given back to me. For this reason never will I show my lair."

"Husband," replied the lady to him, "I love you better than all the world. The less cause have you for doubting my faith, or hiding any tittle from me. What savor is here of friendship? How have I made forfeit of your love; for what sin do you mistrust my honor? Open now your heart, and tell what is good to be known."

So at the end, outwearied and overborne by her importunity, he could no longer refrain, but told her all.

"Wife," said he, "within this wood, a little from the path, there is a hidden way, and at the end thereof an ancient chapel, where oftentimes I have bewailed my lot. Near by is a great hollow stone, concealed by a bush, and there is the secret place where I hide my raiment, till I would return to my own home."

On hearing this marvel the lady became sanguine of visage, because of her exceeding fear. She dared no longer to lie at his side, and turned over in her mind, this way and that, how best she could get her from him. Now there was a certain knight of those parts, who, for a great while, had sought and required this lady for her love. This knight had spent long years in her service, but little enough had he got thereby, not even fair words, or a promise. To him the dame wrote a letter, and meeting, made her purpose plain.

"Fair friend," said she, "be happy. That which you have coveted so long a time, I will grant without delay. Never again will I deny your suit. My heart, and all I have to give, are yours, so take me now as love and dame."

Right sweetly the knight thanked her for her grace, and pledged her faith and fealty. When she had confirmed him by an oath, then she told him all this business of her lord—why he went, and what he became, and of his ravening within the wood. So she showed him of the chapel, and of the hollow stone, and of how to spoil the Werewolf of his vesture. Thus, by the kiss of his wife, was Bisclavaret betrayed. Often enough had he ravished his prey in desolate places, but from this jour-

ney he never returned. His kinsfolk and acquaintance came together to ask of his tidings, when this absence was noised abroad. Many a man, on many a day, searched the woodland, but none might find him, nor learn where Bisclavaret was gone.

The lady was wedded to the knight who had cherished her for so long a space. More than a year had passed since Bisclavaret disappeared. Then it chanced that the King would hunt in that self-same wood where the Werewolf lurked. When the hounds were unleashed they ran this way and that, and swiftly came upon his scent. At the view the huntsman winded on his horn, and the whole pack were at his heels. They followed him from morn to eve, till he was torn and bleeding, and was all adread lest they should pull him down. Now the King was very close to the quarry, and when Bisclavaret looked upon his master, he ran to him for pity and for grace. He took the stirrup within his paws, and fawned upon the prince's foot. The King was very fearful at this sight, but presently he called his courtiers to his aid.

"Lords," cried he, "hasten hither, and see this marvellous thing. Here is a beast who has the sense of man. He abases himself before his foe, and cries for mercy, although he cannot speak. Beat off the hounds, and let no man do him harm. We will hunt no more today, but return to our own place, with the wonderful quarry we have taken."

The King turned him about, and rode to his hall, Bisclavaret following at his side. Very near to his master the Werewolf went, like any dog, and had no care to seek again the wood. When the King had brought him safely to his own castle, he rejoiced greatly, for the beast was fair and strong, no mightier had any man seen. Much pride had the King in his marvellous beast. He held him so dear, that he bade all those who wished for his love, to cross the Wolf in naught, neither to strike him with a rod, but ever to see that he was richly fed and kennelled warm. This commandment the Court observed willingly. So all the day the Wolf sported with the lords, and at night he lay within the chamber of the King. There was not a man who did not make much of the beast, so frank was he and debonair. None had reason to do him wrong, for ever was he about his master, and for his part did evil to none. Every day were these two companions together, and all perceived that the King loved him as his friend.

Hearken now to that which chanced.

The King held a high Court, and bade his great vassals and barons, and all the lords of his venery[1] to the feast. Never was there a goodlier feast, nor one set forth with sweeter show and pomp. Amongst those who were bidden, came that same knight who had the wife of Bisclavaret for dame. He came to the castle, richly gowned, with a fair company, but little he deemed whom he would find so near. Bisclavaret marked his foe the moment he stood within the hall. He ran towards him, and seized him with his fangs, in the King's very presence, and to the view of all. Doubtless he would have done him much mischief, had not the King called and chidden him, and threatened him with a rod. Once, and twice, again, the Wolf set upon the knight in the very light of day. All men marvelled at his malice, for sweet and serviceable was the beast, and to that hour had shown hatred of none. With one consent the household deemed that this deed was done with full reason, and that the Wolf had suffered at the knight's hand some bitter wrong. Right wary of his foe was the knight until the feast had ended, and all the barons had taken farewell of their lord, and departed, each to his own house. With these, amongst the very first, went that lord whom Bisclavaret so fiercely had assailed. Small was the wonder that he was glad to go.

No long while after this adventure it came to pass that the courteous King would hunt in that forest where Bisclavaret was found. With the prince came his wolf, and a fair company. Now at nightfall the King abode within a certain lodge of that country, and this was known of that dame who before was the wife of Bisclavaret. In the morning the lady clothed her in her most dainty apparel, and hastened to the lodge, since she desired to speak with the King, and to offer him a rich present. When the lady entered in the chamber, neither man nor leash might restrain the fury of the Wolf. He became as a mad dog in his hatred and malice. Breaking from his bonds he sprang at the lady's face, and bit the nose from her visage.

From every side men ran to the succor of the dame. They beat off the wolf from his prey, and for a little would have cut him in pieces with their swords. But a certain wise counsellor said to the King,

"Sire, hearken now to me. This beast is always with you, and there is not one of us all who has not known him for long. He goes in and out amongst us, nor has molested any man, neither done wrong or felony to any, save only to this dame, one only time as we have seen. He has done evil to this lady, and to that knight, who is now the husband of the dame. Sire, she was once the wife of that lord who was so close and private to your heart, but who went, and none might find where he had gone. Now, therefore, put the dame in a sure place, and question her straitly, so that she may tell—if perchance she knows thereof—for what reason this Beast holds her in such mortal hate. For many a strange deed has chanced, as well we know, in this marvellous land of Brittany."

The King listened to these words, and deemed the counsel good. He laid hands upon the knight, and put the dame in surety in another place. He caused them to be questioned right straitly, so that their torment was very grievous. At the end, partly because of her distress, and partly by reason of her exceeding fear, the lady's lips were loosed, and she told her tale. She showed them of the betrayal of her lord, and how his raiment was stolen from the hollow stone. Since then she knew not where he went, nor what had befallen him, for he had never come again to his own land. Only, in her heart, well she deemed and was persuaded, that Bisclavaret was he.

Straightway the King demanded the vesture of his baron, whether this were to the wish of the lady, or whether it were against her wish. When the raiment was brought him, he caused it to be spread before Bisclavaret, but the Wolf made as though he had not seen. Then that cunning and crafty counsellor took the King apart, that he might give him a fresh rede.[2]

"Sire," said he, "you do not wisely, nor well, to set this raiment before Bisclavaret, in the sight

---

1. *venery* (ven′ər ē), the king's huntsmen.
2. *rede* (rēd), advice.

of all. In shame and much tribulation must he lay aside the beast, and again become man. Carry your wolf within your most secret chamber, and put his vestment therein. Then close the door upon him, and leave him alone for a space. So we shall see presently whether the ravening beast may indeed return to human shape."

The King carried the Wolf to his chamber, and shut the doors upon him fast. He delayed for a brief while, and taking two lords of his fellowship with him, came again to the room. Entering therein, all three, softly together, they found the knight sleeping in the King's bed, like a little child. The King ran swiftly to the bed and taking his friend in his arms, embraced and kissed him fondly, above a hundred times. When man's speech returned once more, he told him of his adventure. Then the King restored to his friend the fief that was stolen from him, and gave such rich gifts, moreover, as I cannot tell. As for the wife who had betrayed Bisclavaret, he bade her avoid his country, and chased her from the realm. So she went forth, she and her second lord together, to seek a more abiding city, and were no more seen.

The adventure that you have heard is no vain fable. Verily and indeed it chanced as I have said. The Lay of the Werewolf, truly, was written that it should ever be borne in mind.

c. 1175

Comment

Shape-Shifting

The belief in the power of certain persons to change their form, usually into that of an animal, has been worldwide. It was accepted firmly by medieval people and even investigated by theologians. Gervase of Tilbury, who lived early in the thirteenth century, illustrates the probability that the serpent who tempted Eve in Genesis had a woman's face by pointing to the existence of werewolves in England. Marie de France, who was a contemporary of Gervase, gave literary form to existing belief in her "Lay of the Werewolf." She says that *bisclavaret* is the Breton word for werewolf, "whilst the Norman calls him *garwal*." *Bisclavaret* may come from the Breton *bleizgarv*, "wild wolf"; though *garv*, like *garou* (as in the French word for werewolf, *loup-garou*), may be Germanic in origin and itself mean "werewolf."

Detail of a manuscript illumination from the *Luttrell Psalter* showing a wild man. c. 1335–1340. British Library

Miniature from a French
manuscript, *The Book of
King Modus*, showing a
stag hunt. c. 1460.
Pierpont Morgan Library,
New York

Three Fables

Marie de France   *translated by* **Norman Shapiro**

1

A thirsty deer was standing by
A stream and drinking, when his eye—
Suddenly, as he sipped—was caught
By his reflection. "Ah!" he thought,
5 "What handsome, shapely horns have I!
No hornless beast, I vow, can vie
With likes of me. . ." And on and on
He sang his praise; until, anon,
He spied a pack of hunting hounds,
10 Spurred by the huntsman, heard the sounds
His horn blared forth, as they drew near
With one intent—to bag the deer.

Trembling, he turned to flee, and started
Into the wood. . . He dashed, he darted,
15 He flew. . . But all at once, betwixt
Branches and boughs, he stood transfixed:
A tree had caught his horns! . . . The pack
Grew closer now, would soon attack. . .
"Alas, alack!" he sighed, distraught,
20 "How true it is, as man has taught,
That we, too often, blindly prize
Those things that we had best despise;
While in our folly we abhor
Those we should well be thankful for."

2

A certain peasant—so they tell us—
Rode up to church and, duly zealous,
Wanted to pray. But first he tied
His true and trusty steed outside.
5 Once at his pew, our pious peasant
Begged that the Lord make him a present:
Another horse as fine and fair.
While he was thus engaged in prayer,
Thieves came, alas, and stole his horse.
10 The peasant—much distressed, of course,
When he came out to find it gone—
Turned on his heel and, thereupon,
Ran back to pray that God ignore
The prayer he'd uttered just before:
15 "Forget that second horse!" he cried.
"Bring back the first—my joy, my pride!"
God frowns on those whose greed is such
That they, too often, ask too much.
So don't complain about your lot:
20 Be glad to have what good you've got.

3

A fox, they say, his leisure taking—
Out for the evening, merry-making—
Started to cross a pond; when lo!
He saw the moon's reflection—though
5 He had no notion, actually,
What such a curious thing could be.
After a bit of introspection,
It struck the fox that said reflection
Must be a cheese. And so, he hung
10 His head down low, and with his tongue
Began to lap the water, thinking—
While thus he gulped and saw it sinking—
That soon the cheese was his. . . But first,
He drank, drank, drank . . . and promptly
    burst.
15 How many the men whose aims are such
That they aspire to far too much!
Reaching for goals unwisely cherished,
Many have suffered, many have perished.
c. 1175

THINK AND DISCUSS
THE LAY OF THE WEREWOLF
Understanding
1. What is the key to power over Bisclavaret?
2. How does the baron's wife gain that power?
3. Why don't the courtiers kill the wolf, when he attacks a man, and later, his wife?

Analyzing
4. Which knightly virtue saves the baron, even though he has the shape of a wolf?
5. Describe how the King recognizes in a wolf merits which the wife could not see in a man.
6. Compare the conduct of the beast, and of civilized courtiers. Which does the story favor?
7. Why does the narrator use the **simile** "like a little child" to describe the restored baron?
8. How does the punishment awarded the wife and lover fit their crime?

Extending
9. Should the wife have tolerated her original ignorance?
10. Discuss the reasons that fantastic creatures like the werewolf continue to interest contemporary people.
11. Describe other stories about monsters and beasts, which you have read or seen in films, that show people to be worse than the monster.

THINK AND DISCUSS
THREE FABLES
Understanding
1. Why does the deer get caught?
2. Describe the peasant's mistake.
3. What kills the fox?

Analyzing

4. How do these fables use reflections in the water?
5. What particular failure in judgment do these fables focus on?

Extending

6. Following the pattern of these fables, write a moral to conclude "The Lay of the Were-wolf."

APPLYING: Symbol
See Handbook of Literary Terms, p. 974.

A **symbol** in a work of literature is a person, place, event, or object which has a meaning in itself, but also suggests other meanings as well.

1. What do the horns of the deer symbolize?
2. How do the characteristics of the moon fit its symbolic function, in the fable of the fox?
3. What do the Baron's clothes symbolize, in "The Lay of the Werewolf"?

VOCABULARY
Affixes, Roots

Use the Glossary to answer the following questions about the structure of the words in the list below. Read each question, then write on your paper the correct word from the list. (You will not use all the words.) Be sure you can spell and pronounce each word.

zealous	bewailed
introspection	fearsome
adread	transfixed

1. Which has a suffix meaning "causing"?
2. Which has a prefix meaning "within"?
3. Which has a root meaning "mourn"?
4. Which has a root meaning "eagerness"?
5. Which has a prefix meaning "through"?

COMPOSITION
Writing Fables

Following the example of Marie de France, write two prose fables (each two paragraphs long) which will show your fellow students what you think about human pride. Make the principal character of the first a **personified** object, like an automobile, and for the second, a pet you might find in a typical American home.

Analyzing Plot Structure

Write a four-paragraph theme, to be read by your teacher, which will use analysis of **plot** to expose the significant themes in "The Lay of the Werewolf." Devote separate paragraphs to explaining the basic conflict in the story, the turning point in the action, and how justice emerges in the denouement. As you write, be sure to point out the motives which drive the various characters, and in a closing paragraph suggest the kinds of conclusions which the author intended her reader to draw. See "Writing About Plot and Plot Devices" in the Writer's Handbook.

ENRICHMENT
Holding a Mock Court

From your class, assemble two teams of lawyers, and assign to one the prosecution of the baron's wife, and to the other, her defense. Appoint a student judge to moderate, and empanel a jury which will hear both sides and render a verdict. Afterward, discuss as a class whether the decision might have been different in the twelfth century.

Icelandic Literature

Five hundred and twenty miles northwest of Scotland is the volcanic island known as Iceland. Steep mountain peaks and plains of lava make much of it uninhabitable. But around A.D. 874 a small group of Norwegian Vikings settled on the arable land of its southwest coast. In A.D. 930 these isolated warrior clans united into a republic governed by the Constitution of Ulfiot, which guaranteed citizens certain rights and called for an annual national meeting named the Althing. Christian missionaries reached the island about 1000, bringing with them knowledge of writing. There was already a diverse and robust oral literary culture, and during the next two centuries writers invented and set down a series of masterworks which made Icelandic the finest Scandinavian literature of the Middle Ages. In 1262 a civil war among Icelandic chieftains opened the way to annexation by Norway, and soon, it seems, the vitality and imaginative power drained out of Icelandic culture. What had been a nation became a province.

The early settlers were pagans, believing in a mythology of gods and goddesses, elves and giants. Their court poets, called *skalds*, recited lays, or narrative poems, about the gods before local tribal leaders. These poems survived even after Iceland had been Christianized. Thirty such lays appear in a manuscript collection called the *Elder Edda*, which may have been compiled around 1270. (The origin of the term *edda* is uncertain, but may be related to the Old Norse word for poetry.) Some of the poems it contains are much older, going back to the 10th century. No one knows who collected them, or for what purpose. The poems assume that the reader already knows the story being told, and the mythological characters involved, so pagan lore must have lingered a long time in Icelandic culture.

In Icelandic myth, Thor, the god of thunder, is a mighty warrior, champion of the Norse gods in their ages-long war with the giants, and his weapon is the hammer named Mjöllnir (myōl′nir). With the other gods, he lives in Asgard. In "The Lay of Thrym," his ally is Loki (lō′kē), a dangerous character who can change his shape at will and whose loyalty to the gods is equally uncertain. Thor and Loki must protect the honor of the goddess Freya (frā′ə) from Thrym (thrim), a giant who wants to wed her.

Along with the poetry of the *Edda*, Icelandic writers set down prose *sagas*, literally "things which have been said." These too come from an oral tradition, in which a semi-professional "saga man" passed on old tales to the next generation. The sagas could be brief stories, or narratives running hundreds of pages in length, and they dealt with a wide variety of subjects. One particularly realistic tradition is the "family saga," about the lives and adventures of simple Icelandic farmers. The dominant **theme** of these tales is the preservation of honor, a central issue for this individual-istic and proud people. Saga-telling is direct and simple, with little scenic description or psychological speculation. People talk briefly and frankly, and then act. The stories frequently use repeated, formulaic phrases, such as "There was a man . . .", perhaps to aid in memorizing the content. A brief saga, "Thorstein the Staff-Struck," begins on page 308.

The Lay of Thrym

from the **Elder Edda**
translated by **Paul B. Taylor** *and* **W. H. Auden**

The Hurler[1] woke, went wild with rage,
For, suddenly, he missed his sacred Hammer:
He tore his beard, tossed his red locks,
Groped about but could grasp nothing.
5 Thus, then did Thor speak:
"Loki, Loki, listen well.
Unmarked by men, unmarked by gods,
Someone has stolen my sacred Hammer."

Fast they went to Freya's quarters.
10 Then said Loki, Laufey's Son:[2]
"Freya, will you lend me your feathered cloak[3]
To fly in search of the sacred Hammer?"

"I would give it you gladly, were it gold not
feathers,
Part with it now, were it pure silver."

15 Then Loki flew—the feathers whistled—
Out of the door of the Hall of Gods
On and on to the Hall of Giants.
There, on a howe,[4] Thrym sat,
Braiding gold collars for his kennel of hounds,
20 Unteasing the manes of the mares he loved:
"How fare the gods? How fare the elves?
What brings you on this journey to Gianthome?"

"Ill fare the gods, ill fare the elves.
Have you taken and hidden the Hammer of
Thunder?"

25 "I have taken and hidden the Hammer of
Thunder
Eight miles deep, way under the ground:
Henceforth no god shall get it back
Till you fetch me Freya for my future bride."

Then Loki flew—the feathers whistled—
30 Out of the door of the Hall of Giants
On and on to the Hall of Gods.
Meeting him there in the middle court,
Thus then did Thor speak:
"Do you come with a message, not mischief
only?
35 Stand where you are. Let me hear your tidings.
He who sits is seldom truthful,
Who stretches at length a liar always."

"I come with a message, not mischief only.
Thrym stole your Hammer to hide it away.
40 Henceforth no god shall get it back
Till we fetch him Freya for his future bride."

Fast they went to Freya's quarters.
Then said Loki, Laufey's Son:
"Busk[5] yourself, Freya, in a bridal veil.
45 You must journey with me to Gianthome."

Freya snorted with fierce rage,
The hall shook and shuddered about them,
Broken to bits was the Brising Necklace:[6]
"In the eyes of the gods a whore I should seem,
50 If I journeyed with you to Gianthome."

---

1. *Hurler,* Thor. His hammer, Mjöllnir, is the lightning.
2. *Laufey's son.* Both Loki's father, Farbauti, and his
mother Laufey (lôf'ē) were giants, the enemies of the
Norse gods. Loki is the trickster of Norse mythology. He
is handsome, but is also cunning and malicious, equally
adept at getting the gods into and out of trouble.
3. *feathered cloak,* a magical garment that enables its
wearer to fly.
4. *howe* (hō), a bank of earth.
5. *busk,* dress; adorn.
6. *Brising Necklace,* Brisingamen (brē'sing ä mən'), "fire
necklace"; the necklace of Freya, made by the dwarves.

Bronze statuette of the god Thor showing him holding his hammer. c. 1000. National Museum, Iceland

Loki replied, Laufey's Son:
"Be silent, Thunderer, say no more.
Without the Hammer Asgard is lost.
The giants will dwell here, soon drive us out."

70 They busked Thor then in a bridal veil,
Hung about him the Brising Necklace,
Bound to his waist a bunch of keys,
Hid his legs in a long dress,
Broad brooches to his breast pinned,
75 With a neat cap covered his locks.

Then said Loki, Laufey's Son:
"I also shall come as your handmaid with you.
We will journey together to Gianthome."

Quickly the goats were gathered from pasture,
80 Hurried into harness:[8] eagerly they ran.
Fire scorched the earth, the fells cracked,
As Thunderer journeyed to Gianthome.

Thus, then did Thrym speak:
"Stand up giants, lay straw on the benches.
85 They may well bring me my bride now,
Njörd's Daughter, from Noatun.[9]
In my fields there graze gold-horned cattle,
All-black oxen, for my eye's delight.
Much is my treasure, many my gems;
90 Nothing I lack save lovely Freya."

Evening came: ale and food
Were brought to the benches. The bride
        quickly
Ate a whole ox and eight salmon,
The sweet dainties reserved for the women,

The gods hastened to their Hall of Judgment,
Gathered together, goddesses with them,
Sat in council to consider how
To recover the holy Hammer of Thunder.

55 Heimdal[7] said, sagest of gods,
Who could see the future as his fathers did:
"We must busk Thor in a bridal veil,
Hang about him the Brising Necklace,
Bind to his waist a bunch of keys,
60 Hide his legs in a long dress,
Broad brooches to his breast pin,
With a neat cap cover his locks."

Thus, then, did Thor speak:
"With coarse laughs you will call me a She
65 If I busk myself in a bridal veil."

7. *Heimdal* (hăm′däl), the watchman of Asgard, the home of the Norse gods. He will sound his horn to warn the gods of the advance of their enemies at the end of the world.
8. *the goats . . . harness.* Thor drives a brazen chariot drawn by two goats; the sound of thunder is the rumble of his chariot wheels.
9. *Njörd's daughter, from Noatun.* Njörd was the chief of the Vanir, godlike beings who are the allies of the gods of Asgard. Freya is Njörd's daughter. Njörd is associated with the sea, and the name of his home, *Noatun*, means "ships' haven."
10. *mead* (mēd), an alcoholic drink made from fermented honey and water.

5 And more than three measures of mead[10] drank.
Thus, then did Thrym speak:
"Was ever bride with appetite so keen,
Ever a bride who took such big mouthfuls,
When was more mead drunk by one maid
    alone?"

10 Loki, the handmaid, leaning forward,
Found the words to befuddle the giant:
"She has not eaten for eight long nights,
So wild her longing for the wedding day."

Thrym lifted her veil, leaned to kiss her,
15 Back he leaped, the full length of the hall:
"How fierce the look in Freya's eyes!
Dangerous the fire that darts out of them."

Loki, the handmaid, leaning forward,
Found the words to befuddle the giant:
20 "She has had no sleep for eight long nights,
So wild her longing for the wedding day."

The luckless sister of the luckless giant
Dared to beg for bridal gifts:
"Give me your rings of red gold,
115 The rings from your fingers, my favor to win,
My good will, my grace and blessing."

Thus, then, did Thrym speak:
"To bless the bride now bring the Hammer,
Lay Mjöllnir upon the maiden's lap
120 And wish us joy with joined hands."

Then in his heart Thunderer laughed,
The savage one, when he saw his Hammer.
First Thrym he felled to the ground,
Then all his kin he killed in turn,
125 Laid low his luckless sister
Who had dared to beg for bridal gifts:
Instead of gold she got a blow,
Instead of rings a rap on the skull.
Thus Thor came to recover his Hammer.

10th–13th century

THINK AND DISCUSS
Understanding
1. Why had Thrym stolen Thor's hammer?
2. How does Thor trick him, and so get it back?

Analyzing
3. Explain the effect of the repeated lines in this poem.
4. At what point does Thor indicate his mistrust of Loki?
5. Using context clues, explain what you can infer about the Brising Necklace (line 48) and the god Heimdal (line 55).
6. What function does Loki serve during the wedding banquet?
7. Describe the reader reaction the poet expects at the end of this Lay.

Extending
8. Using this poem as an example, describe the religious attitudes of the culture which produced it.

9. Where in contemporary culture do you find the kind of delight expressed at the end of this poem?

APPLYING: Alliteration H𝄢
See Handbook of Literary Terms, p. 938.

The repetition of consonant sounds at the start of two or more words, or in their accented syllables, is called **alliteration**. The Icelandic original of "The Lay of Thrym" used four alliterating syllables per line (with a gap, or "caesura," in the middle) to create the poem's rhythm, and the translators of this version have tried to echo its effect in English.

1. What consonant sound alliterates in line 1?
2. Describe why the alliteration of line 7 is less perfect.

Thorstein the Staff-Struck

translated by **Hermann Pálsson**

here was a man called Thorarin who lived at Sunnudale; he was old and nearly blind. He had been a fierce viking in his younger years, and even in his old age he was very hard to deal with. He had an only son, Thorstein, who was a tall man, powerful but even-tempered; he worked so hard on his father's farm that three other men could hardly have done any better. Thorarin had little money, but a good many weapons. He and his son owned some breeding horses and that was their main source of income, for the young colts they sold never failed in spirit or strength.

Bjarni of Hof[1] had a servant called Thord who looked after his riding horses and was considered very good at the job. Thord was an arrogant man and would never let anyone forget the fact that he was in the service of a chieftain. But this didn't make him a better man and added nothing to his popularity. Bjarni also had two brothers working for him who were called Thorhall and Thorvald, both great scandalmongers about any gossip they heard in the district.

Thorstein and Thord arranged a horse-fight[2] for their young stallions. During the fight, Thord's horse started giving way, and when Thord realized he was losing, he struck Thorstein's horse a hard blow on the jaw. Thorstein saw this and hit back with an even heavier blow at Thord's horse, forcing it to back away. This got the spectators shouting with excitement. Then Thord aimed a blow at Thorstein with his horse-goad, hitting him so hard on the eye-brow that the skin broke and the lid fell hanging down over the eye. Thorstein

tore a piece off his shirt and bandaged his head. He said nothing[3] about what had happened, apart from asking people to keep this from his father. That should have been the end of the incident, but Thorvald and Thorhall kept jeering at Thorstein and gave him the nickname Staff-Struck.

One morning that winter just before Christmas, when the women at Sunnudale were getting up for their work, Thorstein went out to feed the cattle. He soon came back and lay down on a bench. His father, old Thorarin, came into the room and asked who was lying there. Thorstein told him.

"Why are you up so early, son?" said Thorarin.

Thorstein answered, "It seems to me there aren't many men about to share the work with me."

"Have you got a headache, son?" said Thorarin.

"Not that I've noticed," said Thorstein.

"What can you tell me about the horse-fight last summer, son?" said Thorarin. "Weren't you beaten senseless like a dog?"

"It's no credit to me if you call it a deliberate blow, not an accident," said Thorstein.

Thorarin said, "I'd never have thought I could have a coward for a son."

"Father," said Thorstein, "Don't say anything now that you'll live to regret later."

---

1. **Bjarni** (byär'nē) **of Hof** (hōf). Bjarni of Hof was the local chieftain, and the wealthiest and most important farmer in the district. He appears in other saga literature.
2. **horse-fight**, once a very popular sport in Iceland. Two stallions were pitted against one another, and behind each stood a man equipped with a prod who urged them on.
3. **He said nothing.** An old Icelandic proverb says, "A slave takes vengeance at once; the coward never."

"I'm not going to say as much as I've a mind to," said Thorarin.

Thorstein got to his feet, seized his weapons and set off. He came to the stable where Thord was grooming Bjarni's horses, and when he saw Thord he said, "I'd like to know, friend Thord, whether it was accidental when you hit me in the horse-fight last summer, or deliberate. If it was deliberate, you'll be willing to pay me compensation."

"If only you were double-tongued," said Thord, "then you could easily speak with two voices and call the blow accidental with one and deliberate with the other. That's all the compensation you're getting from me."

"In that case don't expect me to make this claim a second time," said Thorstein.

With that he rushed at Thord and dealt him his death-blow. Then he went up to the house at Hof where he saw a woman standing outside the door. "Tell Bjarni that a bull has gored Thord, his horse-boy," he said to her, "and also that Thord will be waiting for him at the stable."

"Go back home, man," she said. "I'll tell Bjarni in my own good time."

Thorstein went back home, and the woman carried on with her work.

After Bjarni had got up that morning and was sitting at table, he asked where Thord could be, and was told he had gone to see to the horses.

"I'd have thought he'd be back by now, unless something has happened to him," said Bjarni.

The woman Thorstein had spoken to broke in. "It's true what we women are often told, we're not very clever. Thorstein the Staff-Struck came here this morning and he said Thord had been gored by a bull and couldn't look after himself. I didn't want to wake you, and then I forgot all about it."

Bjarni left the table, went over to the stable and found Thord lying there, dead. Bjarni had him buried, then brought a court action against Thorstein and had him sentenced to outlawry for manslaughter. But Thorstein stayed on at Sunnudale and worked for his father, and Bjarni did nothing more about it.

One day in the autumn when the men of Hof were busy singeing sheep's heads,[4] Bjarni lay down on top of the kitchen wall to listen to their talk. Now the brothers Thorhall and Thorvald started gossiping; "It never occurred to us when we came to live here with Killer-Bjarni[5] that we'd be singeing lambs' heads while his outlaw Thorstein is singeing the heads of wethers. It would have been better for Bjarni to have been more lenient with his kinsmen at Bodvarsdale and not to let his outlaw at Sunnudale act just like his own equal. But 'A wounded coward lies low', and it's not likely that he'll ever wipe away this stain on his honor."

One of the men said, "Those words were better left unsaid, the trolls[6] must have twisted your tongue. I think Bjarni simply isn't prepared to take the only breadwinner at Sunnudale away from Thorstein's blind father and other dependants there. I'll be more than surprised if you singe many more lambs' heads here, or tattle on much longer about the fight at Bodvarsdale."

Then they went inside to have their meal, and after that to bed. Bjarni gave no sign that he had heard anything of what had been said. But early next morning he roused Thorhall and Thorvald and told them to ride over to Sunnudale and bring him Thorstein's severed head before midmorning. "I think you're more likely than anyone else to wipe away that stain from my honor, since I haven't the courage to do it for myself," he said.

The brothers realized they had said too much, but they set off and went over to Sunnudale. Thorstein was standing in the doorway, sharpening a short sword. He asked them where they were going, and they told him they were looking for some horses. Thorstein said they didn't have very far to go. "The horses are down by the fence."

"We're not sure we'll be able to find them unless you tell us more precisely," they said.

Thorstein came outside, and as they were walk-

---

4. *singeing sheep's heads.* In Iceland, as in some other sheep-raising countries, sheep's heads are considered a great delicacy. The heads are singed over a fire to remove all traces of wool before they are cleaned and cooked.
5. *Killer-Bjarni,* a reference to the battle of Bodvarsdale, where Bjarni fought and killed some of his own kinsmen. The battle is mentioned in other saga literature.
6. *trolls* (trŏlz), an ugly dwarf or giant in Norse mythology, living underground or in caves and possessing supernatural powers.

ing together across the meadow, Thorvald raised his axe and rushed at him. But Thorstein pushed him back so hard that he fell, then ran him through with the short sword. Thorhall tried to attack Thorstein and went the same way as his brother. Thorstein tied them to their saddles, fixed the reins to the horses' manes, and drove them off.

The horses went back to Hof. Some of the servants there were out of doors and went inside to tell Bjarni that Thorvald and Thorhall had come back and their journey hadn't been wasted. Bjarni went outside and saw what had happened. He said nothing and had the two men buried. Then everything was quiet till after Christmas.

One evening after Bjarni and his wife Rannveig[7] had gone to bed, she said to him, "What do you think everyone in the district is talking about these days?"

"I couldn't say," said Bjarni. "In my opinion most people talk a lot of rubbish."

"This is what people are mainly talking about now," she continued: "They're wondering how far Thorstein the Staff-Struck can go before you bother to take revenge. He's killed three of your servants, and your supporters are beginning to doubt whether you can protect them, seeing that you've failed to avenge this. You often take action when you shouldn't and hold back when you should."

"It's the same old story," said Bjarni, "no one seems willing to learn from another man's lesson. Thorstein has never killed anyone without a good reason—but still, I'll think about your suggestion."

With that they dropped the subject and slept through the night. In the morning Rannveig woke up as Bjarni was taking down his sword and shield. She asked him where he was going.

"The time has come for me to settle that matter of honor between Thorstein of Sunnudale and myself," he said.

"How many men are you taking with you?" she asked.

"I'm not taking a whole army to attack Thorstein," he said. "I'm going alone."

"You mustn't do that," she said, "risking your life against the weapons of that killer."

"You're a typical woman," said Bjarni, "arguing against the very thing you were urging just a few hours ago! There's a limit to my patience, I can only stand so much taunting from you and others. And once my mind's made up, there's no point in trying to hold me back."

Bjarni went over to Sunnudale. He saw Thorstein standing in the doorway, and they exchanged some words.

"You'll fight me in single combat," said Bjarni, "on that hillock over there in the home-meadow."

"I'm in no way good enough to fight you," said Thorstein. "I give you my promise to leave the country with the first ship that sails abroad. I know a generous man like you will provide my father with labor to run the farm if I go away."

"You can't talk yourself out of this now," said Bjarni.

"You'll surely let me go and see my father first," said Thorstein.

"Certainly," said Bjarni.

Thorstein went inside and told his father that Bjarni had come and challenged him to a duel.

The old man said, "Anybody who offends a more powerful man in his own district can hardly expect to wear out many more new shirts. In my opinion your offenses are so serious, I can't find any excuse for you. So you'd better take your weapons and defend yourself the best you can. In my younger days I'd never have given way before someone like Bjarni, great fighting-man though he may be. I'd much rather lose you than have a coward for a son."

Thornstein went outside and walked with Bjarni up the hillock. They started fighting with determination and destroyed each other's shield. When they had been fighting for a long time, Bjarni said to Thorstein, "I'm getting very thirsty now, I'm not so used to hard work as you are."

"Go down to the stream then and drink," said Thorstein.

Bjarni did so, and laid the sword down beside him. Thorstein picked it up, examined it and said, "You can't have been using this sword at Bodvarsdale."

---

7. *Rannveig*, (rän'vīg).

Bjarni said nothing, and they went back to the hillock. After they'd been fighting for a time, it became obvious to Bjarni that Thorstein was a highly skilled fighter, and the outcome seemed less certain than he'd expected.

"Everything seems to go wrong for me today," he said. "Now my shoe-thong's loose."

"Tie it up then," said Thorstein.

When Bjarni bent down to tie it, Thorstein went into the house and brought back two shields and a sword. He joined Bjarni on the hillock and said, "Here's a sword and shield my father sends you. The sword shouldn't get so easily blunted as the one you've been using. And I don't want to stand here any longer with no shield to protect me against your blows. I'd very much like us to stop this game now, for I'm afraid your good luck will prove stronger than my bad luck. Every man wants to save his life, and I would too, if I could."

"There's no point in your trying to talk yourself out of this," said Bjarni. "The fight must go on."

"I wouldn't like to be the first to strike," said Thorstein.

Then Bjarni struck at Thorstein, destroying his shield, and Thorstein hacked down Bjarni's shield in return.

"That was a blow," said Bjarni.

Thornstein replied, "Yours wasn't any lighter."

Bjarni said, "Your sword seems to be biting much better now than it was earlier."

"I want to save myself from the foulest of luck if I possibly can," said Thorstein. "It scares me to have to fight you, so I want you yourself to settle the matter between us."

It was Bjarni's turn to strike. Both men had lost their shields. Bjarni said, "It would be a great mistake in one stroke both to throw away good fortune and do wrong. In my opinion I'd be fully paid for my three servants if you took their place and served me faithfully."

Thornstein said, "I've had plenty of opportunity today to take advantage of you, if my bad luck had been stronger than your good luck. I'll never deceive you."

"Now I can see what a remarkable man you must be," said Bjarni. "You'll allow me to go inside to see your father and tell him about this in my own words?"

"You can go if you want as far as I'm concerned," said Thorstein, "but be on your guard."

Bjarni went up to the bed-closet where Old Thorarin was lying. Thorarin asked who was there, and Bjarni told him.

"What's your news, friend Bjarni?" said Thorarin.

"The killing of Thorstein, your son," said Bjarni.

"Did he put up any defense at all?" asked Thorarin.

"I don't think there's ever been a better fighter than your son, Thorarin," said Bjarni.

"It's no wonder your opponents at Bodvarsdale found you so hard to deal with," said Thorarin, "seeing that you've overcome my son."

Bjarni said, "I want to invite you to come over to Hof and take the seat of honor there for the rest of your life. I'll be just like a son to you."

"I'm in the same position now as any other pauper," said Thorarin. "Only a fool accepts a promise gladly, and promises of chieftains like yourself aren't usually honored for more than a month after the event, while you're trying to console us. After that we're treated as ordinary paupers, though our grief doesn't grow any the less for that. Still, anyone who shakes hands on a bargain with a man of your character should be satisfied, in spite of other men's lessons. So I'd like to shake hands with you, and you'd better come into the bed-closet to me. Come closer now, for I'm an old man and trembling on my feet because of ill-health and old age. And I must admit, the loss of my son has upset me a bit."

Bjarni went into the bed-closet and shook Thorarin by the hand. Then he realized the old man was groping for a short sword with the idea of thrusting it at him. Bjarni pulled back his hand and said, "You merciless old rascal! I can promise you now you'll get what you deserve. Your son Thorstein is alive and well, and he'll come with me over to Hof, but you'll be given slaves to run the farm for you, and never suffer any want for the rest of your life."

Thorstein went with Bjarni over to Hof, and stayed in his service for the rest of his life. He was considered a man of great courage and integrity. Bjarni kept his standing and became better-liked and more self-controlled the older he grew. He was a very trustworthy man. In the last years of his life he became a devout Christian and went to Rome on pilgrimage. He died on that journey, and is buried at a town called Sutri, just north of Rome.

c. 1300

THINK AND DISCUSS
Understanding
1. What deed starts the feud?
2. Describe the agreement which Bjarni and Thorstein reach in order to settle it.

Analyzing
3. Explain how the narrator's laconic remark that Thorarin "had little money, but a good many weapons" helps **foreshadow** what is to happen in the story.
4. What do you think is on Thorstein's mind, when he lies on a bench one morning before Christmas?
5. Do Thorhall and Thorvald deserve the deaths they suffer?
6. In each episode of this story, what is the immediate cause which spurs a man to take the revenge he has postponed?
7. Discuss the implications in this repeated pattern.
8. What permits Thorstein and Bjarni to carry on such extensive conversations during their fight?
9. How does the fight alter Bjarni's attitude?

Extending
10. Compare Thorstein's courage with Roland's.
11. You may have noticed how many male names in this story echo the name of the warrior god Thor. Explain how his characteristics, found in "The Lay of Thrym," reappear in the lives of these people.

REVIEWING: Characterization HァP
See Handbook of Literary Terms, p. 944.
Writers use physical description, speeches, action, reports on inner thoughts, as well as the reaction of others, to create **characterization** in a literary work.

1. How do the contents of Thorarin's house help characterize his approach to problems?
2. When Thorarin describes his son's injury at the horse fight as being "beaten senseless like a dog," what do his words tell us about Thorarin?
3. Explain how Thorarin's reaction to the news of his son's death fits with his character.

THINKING SKILLS
Evaluating
When people evaluate, they judge worth according to some sort of standard.

1. What is the unvarying standard by which Thorarin evaluates his son Thorstein?
2. Explain how you would evaluate Thorstein's reluctance to challenge Thord. Indicate the standard which you use.
3. Apply this same standard to Bjarni's decision not to fight Thorstein to the death. How do you evaluate what he does?

ENRICHMENT
Researching Norse Mythology
Have several members of the class consult books on Norse mythology in your school library, and learn the story of Loki and Baldur. Once they feel confident that they know its details, have a story-telling session in which they narrate this tale to the other members of the class. When they are finished, ask those who have listened to compare Loki's actions in that story with what he does in "The Lay of Thrym," and evaluate the differences.

BIOGRAPHY

Dante Alighieri
1265–1321

Dante lived at the end of the Middle Ages. His masterpiece, the *Divine Comedy*, a poem as massive and intricate as a gothic cathedral, sums up the learning, the visionary intensity, and the comprehensive grasp of the medieval mind. He came from Florence, a city-state that in his day was wealthy and powerful enough to be almost constantly embroiled in political and military struggle. His father was a member of the lower nobility who had come down in the world; he may have been a money-lender. Dante's mother died when he was a boy; and his father, though he remarried, soon followed her in death. The orphaned Dante may have lived out his adolescence with a stepmother. The writings of the mature man illustrate such extensive learning that people have always wondered where Dante studied. In 1287 he may have gone to Bologna, the site of a celebrated university, but it appears that Dante was largely self-taught.

By his mid-twenties Dante had become, like the typical young Florentine of his day, deeply involved in civic life. In 1289 he fought for his city in the battle of Campaldino. Early in the next decade, he married Gemma Donati, the daughter of a powerful family, and they had at least three children. Dante entered politics, and by 1300 found himself elected to be one of the six "priors" who ruled Florence. This proved his undoing. During his time in office the priors decided to exile leaders from both sides of a feud then raging in the city. In 1301, while Dante was on an embassy to Pope Boniface VIII in Rome some of these exiles returned to Florence, took over the government, and on January 27, 1302 exiled Dante from his native city for the rest of his life.

During these years of public life, Dante had also been engaged in another, very different kind of activity. In 1292, around the time of his marriage, he had completed *La Vita Nuova* ("The New Life"). In both prose and verse, this book celebrates his love for another woman, named Beatrice. He had seen her first when they were both nine years old. Nine years later, when she was eighteen, she had greeted him on the streets of Florence. She seemed perfect to him. Her very name, "she who blesses," signified her mystical significance in his life. That she married a banker in 1287 meant little to Dante. But her death in 1290 precipitated the book about his youthful love for her, and started Dante dreaming about another book which would be more worthy of her.

During the nineteen years of exile, as Dante wandered from one aristocratic patron to another, that book took shape. By 1307 he was probably at work on his *Commedia*, so called because it ended joyfully. (It was only centuries later that it was styled the *Divine Comedy*.) It was written not in the Latin of the learned, but in an Italian vernacular that anyone could read. There Beatrice appears once more, as the figure of Divine Love who leads the wanderer Dante into paradise. The earthly man seems to have finished this poem shortly before his death in 1321.

THE *DIVINE COMEDY*

The hero tale about a journey to the land of the dead appears in Homer's *Odyssey* and Virgil's *Aeneid*. Dante took this story form and made it the basis for his entire *Commedia*. On the level of literal narrative, he describes a man who has been trapped, and must follow a difficult path to get out. Allegorically, this is that terrible moment of crisis in the life of each one of us when evil inside and outside of ourselves seems to block any hope for further constructive development. For Dante, as a medieval Christian, this had quite literal and specific implications. It was his conviction that people decide during life for good or for evil. When that choice has been made, they live with it for eternity.

He divided his poem into three sections devoted to Hell, the realm of endless punishment; Purgatory, where the pardonable evils of a lifetime are slowly atoned for, preparing an individual to meet God; and Paradise, where those who have chosen good live in endless happiness. He subdivides each of the three sections into thirty-three *cantos* or "songs," so that the whole work is ninety-nine cantos long, plus one more, the introduction, making a perfect hundred.

Dante invented a rhyme scheme called *terza rima* to match his poem's structure. The first and third lines of his three-line stanzas rhyme, while the middle line rhymes with the first and third lines of the next stanza, endlessly linking lines together. (The translator of our version rhymes the first and third lines, but does not try to connect the middle line with the next triplet.)

In the first cantos of the *Inferno*, Dante finds himself, in the middle of his life, suddenly trapped in a dark wood of evil and confusion. Beset by three allegorical beasts, the Leopard of Lust, the Lion of Pride, and the She-wolf of Avarice, he begins to despair of ever reaching the mountain of salvation in the distance. Then the specter of Virgil, the Roman poet, and Dante's literary model, appears, volunteering to take him through Hell and up the mountain of Purgatory, to teach him the hard but necessary way to salvation. Limited as a pagan must be to mere human wisdom, Virgil must halt at the borders of Paradise; but from there Beatrice, trained in

Miniature from a fifteenth-century illuminated manuscript of the *Commedia* showing Dante meeting the three allegorical beasts. Vatican Library, Rome

divine theology, will take Dante on to a vision of Heaven.

Dante accepts, and together they pass under the open gateway into Hell. The first people they encounter refused in their earthly lives to commit themselves to either God or the Devil. Now both will have nothing to do with them, and their punishment is to wander forever on the borders of Hell, ceaselessly following a meaningless banner that sways in the darkness. Beyond them is the river Acheron, which all the damned must cross, and Charon, the boatman, tries to refuse Dante passage because he still lives. Nevertheless he and Virgil cross, and begin to descend the concentric rings of the pit of Hell, each devoted to the punishment of a specific kind of sin. In the outermost ring they see the lustful, and speak with Francesca of Rimini, daughter of a house where Dante himself once stayed.

Reading A MEDIEVAL ALLEGORY

The word *allegory* (al′ə gôr′ē) means a narrative in which the setting, characters, and action represent abstract concepts apart from the literal meaning of the story. The Greeks were the first to employ the term, using it to refer to what they saw as the hidden meanings of the Homeric epics. For example, an interpretation of the *Odyssey* as an allegory might view Odysseus as a symbol of the human spirit longing for fulfillment; this fulfillment might be represented by his wife Penelope. In the Middle Ages writers began to create texts that could be understood only if the reader grasped both what was literally happening, and also the figurative, or allegorical, meaning of the narrative. The beast fables of Marie de France are typical of this new approach. While it is possible to enjoy her story of the hungry fox for its own sake, the real meaning of the tale lies in its application to human greed. Dante's *Divine Comedy* is an allegory of vast size and complexity, and to grasp this larger significance the reader must be aware of how the poet creates meaning through allegorical strategies.

Notice different levels of meaning. In Canto 1 Dante relates that, midway through life, he found himself in a dark wood, and that when he tried to reach a nearby hill, behind which the sun was just rising, his way was blocked by three wild beasts. Dante's story of his journey can be enjoyed on a literal level, simply as a tale of strange adventures; but on an allegorical level, its meaning is much greater.

Watch for symbols. Medieval allegorists like Dante employ a variety of symbols. Notice particularly the following types: (1) *Universal symbols*. Some symbols appear in so many different cultures that they can be justly called universal. When Dante embarks on a journey, it symbolizes his life, and a quest for some goal. When he crosses the threshold of hell, this gate stands for a new phase of his life. (2) *Biblical and classical symbols*. Some symbols derive from a specific cultural tradition. In medieval writers of allegory, the most frequent source for such symbolism was the Bible and classical literature. For example, in Canto III Dante meets Charon, a figure from Greek myth, who ferries the souls of the dead to the underworld. For help in interpreting this kind of symbolism, use the footnotes accompanying your text or check a dictionary. (3) *Allegorical figures*. The three beasts that halt Dante's progress through the dark wood seem to represent different human vices. For example, the lion "raging with hunger" suggests violence and the absence of restraint. But their exact meaning is not clear. They are not universal symbols like the journey or the gate, and they do not derive from a specific source, like the Bible or classical myth. Dante's readers have been speculating about their exact significance ever since his day. (4) *Symbolic people*. One of Dante's most brilliant strategies in the *Divine Comedy* was to take real people and make them, on the allegorical level, into symbols of human traits. On his journey Dante meets many historical figures, some of whom he knew in life. He speaks with these people about the details of their past experiences. But everything that Dante reveals about these people has an allegorical as well as factual significance. Thus, Francesca da Rimini, a real person, also becomes a symbol of sinful love.

Notice allegorical structure. Every location in Dante's allegory has some significance. For example, condemned lovers occupy one of the outer rings of hell because their fault is a relatively minor one. At the center of hell are the worst sinners, Judas, Brutus, and Cassius, who betrayed their benefactors. Temporal and numerical structure are also important in the *Divine Comedy*. Dante's journey through hell occupies exactly one day, from the evening of Good Friday to that of Holy Saturday. The poem is built upon the number three, because Dante believed in a God of three persons. Thus, hell has three times three, or nine circles.

from the Inferno

Dante Alighieri *translated by* **John Ciardi**

from **Canto I**

Midway in our life's journey,[1] I went astray
  from the straight road and woke to find myself
  alone in a dark wood. How shall I say

what wood that was! I never saw so drear,
5   so rank, so arduous a wilderness!
  Its very memory gives a shape to fear.

Death could scarce be more bitter than that place!
  But since it came to good, I will recount
  all that I found revealed there by God's grace.

10 How I came to it I cannot rightly say,
  so drugged and loose with sleep had I become
  when I first wandered there from the True Way.

But at the far end of that valley of evil
15   whose maze had sapped my very heart with fear!
  I found myself before a little hill[2]

and lifted up my eyes. Its shoulders glowed
  already with the sweet rays of that planet[3]
  whose virtue leads men straight on every road,

and the shining strengthened me against the fright
20   whose agony had wracked the lake of my heart
  through all the terrors of that piteous night.

Just as a swimmer, who with his last breath
  flounders ashore from perilous seas, might turn
  to memorize the wide water of his death—

25 so did I turn, my soul still fugitive
  from death's surviving image, to stare down
  that pass that none had ever left alive.

And there I lay to rest from my heart's race
  till calm and breath returned to me. Then rose
30   and pushed up that dead slope at such a pace

each footfall rose above the last. And lo!
  almost at the beginning of the rise
  I faced a spotted Leopard,[4] all tremor and flow

and gaudy pelt. And it would not pass, but stood
35   so blocking my every turn that time and again
  I was on the verge of turning back to the wood.

This fell at the first widening of the dawn
  as the sun was climbing Aries[5] with those stars
  that rode with him to light the new creation.

40 Thus the holy hour and the sweet season
  of commemoration did much to arm my fear
  of that bright murderous beast with their good
    omen.

---

1. Midway . . . journey. The Bible often speaks of the span of a human life as "threescore and ten"—seventy years. The action of the *Divine Comedy* opens in Dante's thirty-fifth year, A.D. 1300.

2. little hill. This universal symbol of aspiration may link specifically with Dante's symbolic hill of Purgatory, found in the second part of *The Divine Comedy*.

3. that planet, the sun.

4. Leopard. The Leopard is an allegorical figure, like the Lion and She-Wolf that follow. The three may represent three different kinds of sin that Hell punishes in its different divisions: in the uppermost circles selfish sins of incontinence, the "tremor and flow" of the Leopard; further down, the violent sins of savagery represented by the "raging Lion"; and at the bottom of the pit, the malicious sins involving fraud, typified by the "gaunt and craving" She-Wolf.

5. Aries, one of the constellations forming the Zodiac. The time is just before dawn on the morning of Good Friday. For Christians this begins the three-day commemoration of the death and resurrection of Jesus, and the beginning of human salvation. Dante locates the action of *The Divine Comedy* during this season to suggest symbolically that he is embarking on a spiritual resurrection into a new life.

Yet not so much but what I shook with dread
　　at sight of a great Lion that broke upon me
45　raging with hunger, its enormous head

held high as if to strike a mortal terror
　　into the very air. And down his track,
　　a She-Wolf drove upon me, a starved horror

ravening and wasted beyond all belief.
50　She seemed a rack for avarice, gaunt and craving.
　　Oh many the souls she has brought to endless
　　　grief!

She brought such heaviness upon my spirit
　　at sight of her savagery and desperation,
　　I died from every hope of that high summit.

55　And like a miser—eager in acquisition
　　but desperate in self-reproach when Fortune's
　　　wheel[6]
　　turns to the hour of his loss—all tears and attrition

I wavered back; and still the beast pursued,
　　forcing herself against me bit by bit
60　till I slid back into the sunless wood.

And as I fell to my soul's ruin, a presence
　　gathered before me on the discolored air,
　　the figure of one who seemed hoarse from long
　　　silence.

At sight of him in that friendless waste I cried:
65　"Have pity on me, whatever thing you are,
　　whether shade or living man." And it replied:

"Not man, though man I once was, and my blood
　　was Lombard, both my parents Mantuan.
　　I was born, though late, *sub Julio*, and bred

70　in Rome under Augustus in the noon
　　of the false and lying gods.[7] I was a poet
　　and sang of old Anchises' noble son

who came to Rome after the burning of Troy.[8]
　　But you—why do *you* return to these distresses
75　instead of climbing that shining Mount of Joy

which is the seat and first cause of man's bliss?"
　　"And are you then that Virgil and that fountain
　　of purest speech?" My voice grew tremulous:

"Glory and light of poets! now may that zeal
80　and love's apprenticeship that I poured out
　　on your heroic verses serve me well!

For you are my true master and first author,
　　the sole maker from whom I drew the breath
　　of that sweet style whose measures have brought me
　　　honor.

85　See there, immortal sage, the beast I flee.
　　For my soul's salvation, I beg you, guard me from
　　　her,
　　for she has struck a mortal tremor through me."

And he replied, seeing my soul in tears:
　　"He must go by another way who would escape
90　this wilderness, for that mad beast that fleers

before you there, suffers no man to pass.
　　She tracks down all, kills all, and knows no glut,
　　but, feeding, she grows hungrier than she was. . . .

you follow me and I will be your guide
95　and lead you forth through an eternal place.
　　There you shall see the ancient spirits tried

in endless pain, and hear their lamentation
　　as each bemoans the second death of souls.[9]
　　Next you shall see upon a burning mountain[10]

100　souls in fire and yet content in fire,
　　knowing that whensoever it may be
　　they yet will mount into the blessed choir.[11]

To which, if it is still your wish to climb,
　　a worthier spirit[12] shall be sent to guide you.
105　With her shall I leave you, for the King of Time,

---

6. *Fortune's wheel*. The traditional allegorical figure of
human fortune pictured a woman spinning a wheel representing success in life. Any point on the wheel, while
sometimes at the top of the circuit, must eventually come
to the bottom again.

7. *Not man . . . lying gods*. Virgil was born in the town
of Mantua in the region of Lombardy in the north of Italy.
Sub Julio ("under Julius") refers to the period when the
government of Rome was dominated by Julius Caesar. Virgil accomplished his great work as a poet during the reign
of the successor of Julius, Augustus Caesar. The "false and
lying gods" are those of Classical mythology.

8. *I was . . . of Troy*. Virgil's greatest work was the
Aeneid, which told how the Trojan hero Aeneas ("old
Anchises' noble son") fled from the destruction of his city
and came to what would be Rome.

9. *second death of souls*, their suffering in Hell.

10. *burning mountain*, Purgatory.

11. *blessed choir*, Heaven.

12. *worthier spirit*, Beatrice.

who reigns on high, forbids me to come there
    since, living, I rebelled against his law.[13]
    He rules the waters and the land and air

and there holds court, his city and his throne.
110   Oh blessed are they he chooses!" And I to him:
    "Poet, by that God to you unknown,

lead me this way. Beyond this present ill
    and worse to dread, lead me to Peter's gate[14]
    and be my guide through the sad halls of Hell."

115 And he then: "Follow." And he moved ahead
    in silence, and I followed where he led.

Canto III

I AM THE WAY INTO THE CITY OF WOE.
I AM THE WAY TO A FORSAKEN PEOPLE.
I AM THE WAY INTO ETERNAL SORROW.

120 SACRED JUSTICE MOVED MY ARCHITECT.
I WAS RAISED HERE BY DIVINE OMNIPOTENCE,
PRIMORDIAL LOVE AND ULTIMATE INTELLECT.

ONLY THOSE ELEMENTS TIME CANNOT WEAR
WERE MADE BEFORE ME, AND BEYOND TIME I
    STAND.
125 ABANDON ALL HOPE YE WHO ENTER HERE.

These mysteries I read cut into stone
    above a gate. And turning I said: "Master,
    what is the meaning of this harsh inscription?"

And he then as initiate to novice:
130   "Here must you put by all division of spirit
    and gather your soul against all cowardice.

This is the place I told you to expect.
    Here you shall pass among the fallen people,
    souls who have lost the good of intellect."[15]

135 So saying, he put forth his hand to me,
    and with a gentle and encouraging smile
    he led me through the gate of mystery.

Here sighs and cries and wails coiled and recoiled
    on the starless air, spilling my soul to tears.
140   A confusion of tongues and monstrous accents toiled

in pain and anger. Voices hoarse and shrill
    and sounds of blows, all intermingled, raised
    tumult and pandemonium that still

whirls on the air forever dirty with it
145   as if a whirlwind sucked at sand. And I,
    holding my head in horror, cried: "Sweet Spirit,

what souls are these who run through this black
        haze?"
    And he to me: "These are the nearly soulless
    whose lives concluded neither blame nor praise.

150 They are mixed here with that despicable corps
    of angels who were neither for God nor Satan,
    but only for themselves. The High Creator

scourged them from Heaven for its perfect beauty,
    and Hell will not receive them since the wicked
155   might feel some glory over them." And I:

"Master, what gnaws at them so hideously
    their lamentation stuns the very air?"
    "They have no hope of death," he answered me,

"and in their blind and unattaining state
160   their miserable lives have sunk so low
    that they must envy every other fate.

No word of them survives their living season.
    Mercy and Justice deny them even a name.
    Let us not speak of them: look, and pass on."

165 I saw a banner there upon the mist.
    Circling and circling, it seemed to scorn all pause.
    So it ran on, and still behind it pressed

a never-ending rout of souls in pain.[16]
    I had not thought death had undone so many
170   as passed before me in that mournful train.

---

13. *I rebelled . . . his law.* Virgil died still a pagan,
and so cannot enter Heaven.
14. *Peter's gate,* that of Heaven, whose porter is St.
Peter.
15. *good of intellect.* Since God is the author of truth,
those who turn from Him lose the ultimate object of
intelligence.
16. *souls in pain.* In Dante's vision, punishment always
fits the crime, and so the nature of a specific sin is revealed by the manner in which those guilty of it now suffer in Hell. In this first example, people who have refused
to commit themselves morally in life wander forever on the
edge of Hell, rejected by both God and Satan.

And some I knew among them; last of all
   I recognized the shadow of that soul
   who, in his cowardice, made the Great Denial.[17]

At once I understood for certain: these
175   were of that retrograde and faithless crew
   hateful to God and to His enemies.

These wretches never born and never dead
   ran naked in a swarm of wasps and hornets
   that goaded them the more the more they fled,

180 and made their faces stream with bloody gouts
   of pus and tears that dribbled to their feet
   to be swallowed there by loathsome worms and
      maggots.

Then looking onward I made out a throng
   assembled on the beach of a wide river,
185   whereupon I turned to him: "Master, I long

to know what souls these are, and what strange usage
   makes them as eager to cross as they seem to be
   in this infected light." At which the Sage:

"All this shall be made known to you when we stand
190   on the joyless beach of Acheron."[18] And I
   cast down my eyes, sensing a reprimand

in what he said, and so walked at his side
   in silence and ashamed until we came
   through the dead cavern to that sunless tide.

195 There, steering toward us in an ancient ferry
   came an old man[19] with a white bush of hair,
   bellowing: "Woe to you depraved souls! Bury

here and forever all hope of Paradise:
   I come to lead you to the other shore,
200   into eternal dark, into fire and ice.

And you who are living yet, I say begone
   from these who are dead." But when he saw me
      stand
   against his violence he began again:

"By other windings and by other steerage
205   shall you cross to that other shore. Not here! Not
      here!
   A lighter craft than mine must give you passage."

And my Guide to him: "Charon, bite back your
   spleen:

Illustration by William Blake showing souls in
the vestibule of Hell and at the Acheron. 1821–
1827. National Gallery of Victoria, Australia

this has been willed where what is willed must be,[20]
   and is not yours to ask what it may mean."

210 The steersman of that marsh of ruined souls,
   who wore a wheel of flame around each eye,
   stifled the rage that shook his woolly jowls.

---

17. that soul . . . Great Denial. This is a reference to
Celestine V, made pope in 1294. He was later persuaded
to renounce the papacy by a priest, who promptly became
pope as Boniface VIII and was a symbol to Dante of all
the worst corruptions of the Church. Later in the *Inferno*
Dante reveals the punishment that awaits Boniface (who
was still alive in 1300). Celestine's sin is that, through
his cowardice in refusing to shoulder the burdens of office
that God has appointed for him, so much evil entered the
Church.
18. Acheron (ak'ə ron'), one of the rivers in the Underworld in Classical mythology.
19. old man, Charon (ker'ən), boatman who ferried the
souls of the dead across the Styx (stiks), the river that bordered the Underworld in Classical mythology.
20. where what . . . must be. God has willed Dante's
journey, and so Virgil has the authority to command those
they encounter.

But those unmanned and naked spirits there
    turned pale with fear and their teeth began to
      chatter
215   at sound of his crude bellow. In despair

they blasphemed God, their parents, their time on
      earth,
    the race of Adam, and the day and the hour
    and the place and the seed and the womb that gave
      them birth.

But all together they drew to that grim shore
220   where all must come who lose the fear of God.
    Weeping and cursing they come for evermore,

and demon Charon with eyes like burning coals
    herds them in, and with a whistling oar
    flails on the stragglers to his wake of souls.

225 As leaves in autumn loosen and stream down
    until the branch stands bare above its tatters
    spread on the rustling ground, so one by one

the evil seed of Adam in its Fall
    cast themselves, at his signal, from the shore
230   and streamed away like birds who hear their call.

So they are gone over that shadowy water,
    and always before they reach the other shore
    a new noise stirs on this, and new throngs gather.

"My son," the courteous Master said to me,
235   "all who die in the shadow of God's wrath
    converge to this from every clime and country.

And all pass over eagerly, for here
    Divine Justice transforms and spurs them so
    their dread turns wish: they yearn for what they
      fear.

240 No soul in Grace comes ever to this crossing;
    therefore if Charon rages at your presence
    you will understand the reason for his cursing."

When he had spoken, all the twilight country
    shook so violently, the terror of it
245   bathes me with sweat even in memory:

the tear-soaked ground gave out a sigh of wind
that spewed itself in flame on a red sky,
and all my shattered senses left me. Blind,

like one whom sleep comes over in a swoon,[21]
250 I stumbled into darkness and went down.

from Canto V

I came to a place stripped bare of every light
    and roaring on the naked dark like seas
    wracked by a war of winds.[22] Their hellish flight

of storm and counterstorm through time foregone,
255   sweeps the souls of the damned before its charge.
    Whirling and battering it drives them on,

and when they pass the ruined gap of Hell
    through which we had come, their shrieks begin
      anew.
    There they blaspheme the power of God eternal.

260 And this, I learned, was the never ending flight
    of those who sinned in the flesh, the carnal and
      lusty
    who betrayed reason to their appetite.

As the wings of wintering starlings bear them on
    in their great wheeling flights, just so the blast
265   wherries these evil souls through time foregone.

Here, there, up, down, they whirl and, whirling,
     strain
    with never a hope of hope to comfort them,
    not of release, but even of less pain.

As cranes go over sounding their harsh cry,
270   leaving the long streak of their flight in air,
    so come these spirits, wailing as they fly.

And watching their shadows lashed by wind, I cried:
    "Master, what souls are these the very air
    lashes with its black whips from side to side?"

275 "The first of these whose history you would know,"
    he answered me, "was Empress of many tongues.[23]
    Mad sensuality corrupted her so

---

21. swoon. To mark his entrance into Hell itself, Dante pictures himself losing consciousness. When he wakes, he is on the other side of Acheron.

22. *a place . . . of winds,* the second circle of Hell, where those guilty of lust now whirl about in uncontrollable winds that represent the passions to which they submitted their free will during life.

23. *Empress of many tongues,* Semiramis (sə mir'ə mis), legendary Assyrian princess who lived about 800 B.C. and was said to have founded Babylon.

that to hide the guilt of her debauchery
  she licensed all depravity alike,
280 and lust and law were one in her decree.

She is Semiramis of whom the tale is told
  how she married Ninus and succeeded him
  to the throne of that wide land the Sultans hold.

The other is Dido;[24] faithless to the ashes
285 of Sichaeus, she killed herself for love.
  The next whom the eternal tempest lashes

is sense-drugged Cleopatra.[25] See Helen[26] there,
  from whom such ill arose. And great Achilles,[27]
  who fought at last with love in the house of prayer.

290 And Paris. And Tristan."[28] As they whirled above
  he pointed out more than a thousand shades
  of those torn from the mortal life by love.

I stood there while my Teacher one by one
  named the great knights and ladies of dim time;
295 and I was swept by pity and confusion.[29]

At last I spoke: "Poet, I should be glad
  to speak a word with those two[30] swept together
  so lightly on the wind and still so sad."

And he to me: "Watch them. When next they pass,
300 call to them in the name of love that drives
  and damns them here. In that name they will
    pause."

Thus, as soon as the wind in its wild course
  brought them around, I called: "O wearied souls!
  if none forbid it, pause and speak to us."

305 As mating doves that love calls to their nest
  glide through the air with motionless raised wings,
  borne by the sweet desire that fills each breast—

Just so those spirits turned on the torn sky
  from the band where Dido whirls across the air;
310 such was the power of pity in my cry.

"O living creature, gracious, kind, and good,
  going this pilgrimage through the sick night,
  visiting us who stained the earth with blood,

were the King of Time our friend, we would pray His
    peace
315 on you who have pitied us. As long as the wind
  will let us pause, ask of us what you please.

The town where I was born lies by the shore
  where the Po[31] descends into its ocean rest
  with its attendant streams in one long murmur.

320 Love, which in gentlest hearts will soonest bloom
  seized my lover with passion for that sweet body
  from which I was torn unshriven[32] to my doom.

Love, which permits no loved one not to love,
  took me so strongly with delight in him
325 that we are one in Hell, as we were above.

Love led us to one death. In the depths of Hell
  Caïna[33] waits for him who took our lives."
  This was the piteous tale they stopped to tell.

And when I had heard those world-offended lovers
330 I bowed my head. At last the Poet spoke:
  "What painful thoughts are these your lowered
    brow covers?"

---

24. **Dido,** widow of Sichaeus (sə kē′əs) and queen of Carthage. In his *Aeneid* Virgil tells of her fatal love for Aeneas, which is here described as an act of faithlessness to her dead husband.
25. **Cleopatra,** queen of Egypt and mistress of the Roman general Mark Antony.
26. **Helen,** whose desertion of her husband, Menelaus, for her lover, Paris, began the Trojan War.
27. **Achilles.** Besotted by his love for Polyxena, the daughter of Priam, king of Troy, Achilles deserted the Greek army during the Trojan War. While waiting to marry her in a Trojan temple, Achilles was murdered by Paris.
28. **Tristan,** in the Arthurian legend, a knight of the Round Table who was the lover of Iseult, wife of King Mark.
29. **pity and confusion.** New to Hell, Dante does not yet fully comprehend that the damned are there of their own choosing, and persist in the faults they committed during life.
30. **those two,** the lovers Paolo and Francesca. In 1275 Giovanni Malatesta made a political marriage with Francesca, daughter of Guido da Polenta of Ravenna. She fell in love with Giovanni's younger brother Paolo, and for many years they carried on a secret love affair. Around 1285 Giovanni happened upon them in Francesca's room and killed them both.
31. **Po,** a river of northern Italy.
32. **unshriven,** before she could confess her sin to a priest and gain God's forgiveness.
33. **Caïna,** (kä ē′nä). Giovanni Malatesta was still alive when Dante wrote. His fate is already decided, however, and upon his death his soul will fall to Caïna, the section deep within Hell where those are punished who performed acts of treachery against their kin.

Dante Gabriel Rossetti, *Paolo and Francesca da Rimini.* 1855. Tate Gallery, London
The Italian phrase *O Lasso!* ("Alas!") is spoken by Dante at line 332 below.

When at length I answered, I began: "Alas!
    What sweetest thoughts, what green and young
        desire
    led these two lovers to this sorry pass."

335 Then turning to those spirits once again,
    I said: "Francesca, what you suffer here
    melts me to tears of pity and of pain.

But tell me: in the time of your sweet sighs
    by what appearances found love the way
340   to lure you to his perilous paradise?"

And she: "The double grief of a lost bliss
    is to recall its happy hour in pain.
    Your Guide and Teacher knows the truth of this.

But if there is indeed a soul in Hell
345   to ask of the beginning of our love
    out of his pity, I will weep and tell:

On a day for dalliance we read the rhyme
    of Lancelot,[34] how love had mastered him.
    We were alone with innocence and dim time.

350 Pause after pause that high old story drew
    our eyes together while we blushed and paled;
    but it was one soft passage overthrew

our caution and our hearts. For when we read
    how her fond smile was kissed by such a lover,
355   he who is one with me alive and dead

breathed on my lips the tremor of his kiss.
    That book, and he who wrote it, was a pander.[35]
    That day we read no further." As she said this,

the other spirit, who stood by her, wept
360   so piteously, I felt my senses reel
    and faint away with anguish. I was swept

by such a swoon as death is, and I fell,
    as a corpse might fall, to the dead floor of Hell.
    (*The text of the* Inferno *continues on page 326.*)

---

34. *Lancelot* (lan'sə lot), knight of the Round Table who was the lover of King Arthur's wife, Guenevere.
35. *pander,* a go-between who arranges a love affair.

THINK AND DISCUSS
Understanding
1. Why does Dante agree to follow Virgil?
2. How does Charon react to Dante's appearance at Acheron?
3. Describe Dante's reaction to Francesca's story.

Analyzing
4. Explain the allegorical meaning of the choice which the beasts force on Dante in Canto I.
5. Characterize the relationship between Virgil and Dante.
6. How does the **imagery** which describes "the nearly soulless" (Canto III, line 148) explain the character of their sin?
7. What makes the damned eager to cross Acheron?
8. Both the dead, waiting Charon, and the lustful swept through the sky, blaspheme God (Canto III, line 216 and Canto V, line 259). Why?
9. In what ways does Francesca's general assertion, that "Love, which permits no loved one not to love,/Took me . . ." (Canto V, lines 323–324) explain why she is in Hell?

Extending
10. Dante gives only hints to explain why he finds himself in the dark wood. Using them, try to infer what has brought him to this point.
11. Dante swoons twice in the *Inferno,* and you have just read both examples. Why does he do it?
12. Discuss whether the principle that the punishment fit the crime should be renewed for a present-day penal system.

REVIEWING: Rhyme H⅂
See the Handbook of Literary Terms, p. 965.
Rhyme is the repetition of the same vowel sound in the stressed syllables of words which end lines of poetry. The consonants, in a "perfect rhyme," should differ.

1. Explain why the rhymes in lines 10 and 12 of Canto I are "perfect."
2. What impairs the rhyme of Canto I, lines 13 and 15?
3. Do lines 25 and 27 rhyme?
4. How does Dante employ rhyme to conclude each Canto?

COMPOSITION
Describing the Beasts of Opposition
Dante's three allegorical figures, the Leopard, the Lion, and the She-wolf, represent forces which block the poet's life. In the *Commedia* they seem to represent vices Dante must avoid or overcome. Now, think about your country, and its positions in the world today. What are the forces, within or without, which stand in the way of its development? Using your imagination, invent three allegorical figures which personify those forces, or beasts of opposition, and in a descriptive essay, to be read by your classmates, devote a paragraph to each.

Analyzing Francesca's Speech
Though their appearances are brief, Dante is able to vividly characterize the people his wanderer meets through the way they speak. Write a four-paragraph essay, to be read by your teacher, in which you analyze how her own words help characterize Francesca da Rimini. Take notes on the way she establishes a rapport with Dante, the manner in which she characterizes her solitary afternoon with Paolo, and the arguments, implicit and explicit, which she now uses to explain what she did. Make these issues the topics of three paragraphs in your paper, followed by a concluding paragraph in which you describe your own reactions to what she says, and how she says it.

Reader's Note

Translating Dante

One of the most famous passages in Dante's *Divine Comedy* is Francesca's speech describing the origin of her love for Paolo. Below you will find Dante's original; a number of different translations appear on the opposite page. (John Ciardi's translation of this passage appears on page 322, lines 341–358.)

Looking at the Italian, you can readily see the pattern of Dante's *terza rima* rhyme scheme: *felice* (line 2) linking with *radice* (line 4) and *dice* (line 6). Dante uses his rhymes, when possible, to underscore the meaning of his verse. *Felice* names the delight Paolo and Francesca once knew, and she promises to reveal its source, or "root," *radice*. Of all the translators appearing here, only Dorothy Sayers attempts the extremely difficult task of replicating Dante's *terza rima*, and its sound effects, into English. Sometimes she must strain to maintain rhymes, as in *Queen* (line 8), *then* (line 10), and *when* (line 12). Ciardi decided to rhyme only the first and third lines, and forgo Dante's interlacing of the second line with the next stanza. This allows Ciardi to stay close to the sense of Dante's Italian, and yet maintain some of the qualities of the original rhyming pattern.

However, preserving Dante's rhyme keeps both Sayers and Ciardi from reproducing other aspects of Dante's art. For example, in the first three lines of Francesca's speech, as Dante constructs it, she begins with sorrow (*dolore*), refers back to past happiness (*felice*), and then returns to even greater sorrow (*miseria*)—her sadness literally enclosing her joy in the structure of the sentence. To keep her rhymes, Sayers must start with the two kinds of unhappiness, then go on to the delight, thus losing the elegance of Dante's structure. Allan Mandelbaum's translation, though not rhyming, is much closer to Dante's original in its structure here.

One of Dante's celebrated poetic effects in this passage occurs in line 18, where Francesca discreetly hints at the start of her love affair through circumlocution, devoting an entire line to simply admitting that she and Paolo stopped reading. Of these translators, Longfellow comes closest to the lengthy way in which Francesca

says—yet doesn't say—what happened next. The others collapse her ladylike hinting into half a line, and lose some of Dante's drama.

There is a special diction problem in this passage, and the various solutions to it illustrate the different approaches of these translators. The story of Lancelot that the lovers read becomes for them, according to Francesca, a go-between. European literature traditionally treats the figure of the go-between with scorn, since they set up love affairs for others instead of themselves. In the story of Lancelot, the go-between is named Galleot or Galehalt (depending upon whether one reads an Italian or French version of the story.) *Galleoto* (line 17) is the name Francesca uses, and by it she means to condemn the book for getting her and Paolo into trouble. Most modern readers no longer know this part of the Lancelot story, and using Dante's original word will require a footnote. Cary avoids this by translating the name into plain English—"love's purveyors" (line 18). Longfellow, Sayers, and Mandelbaum employ Dante's original allusion, and risk confusing their readers. Ciardi chooses the closest English equivalent, "pander" (line 357). The origin of this word is in the story of another pair of lovers, the classical figures Troilus and Cressida. Their go-between was named Pandarus, and his name became the source of the English word *pander*. Thus Ciardi has, by changing the literary allusion Dante employs here, managed to preserve both the meaning of the original and the essential character of the **allusion**.

E quella a me: "Nessun maggior dolore
che ricordarsi del tempo felice
ne la miseria; e ciò sa 'l tuo dottore.
    Ma s'a conoscer la prima radice
5 del nostro amor tu hai cotanto affetto,
dirò come colui che piange e dice.
    Noi leggiavamo un giorno per diletto
di Lancialotto come amor lo strinse;
soli eravamo e sanza alcun sospetto.
10   Per più fïate li occhi ci sospinse
quella lettura, e scolorocci il viso;
ma solo un punto fu quel che ci vinse.

Quando leggemmo il disïato riso
esser basciato da contanto amante,
15 questi, che mai da me non fia diviso,
   la bocca mi basciò tutto tremante.
Galeotto fu 'l libro e chi lo scrisse:
quel giorno più non vi leggemmo avante."

Henry Cary (1814)

                    . . . She replied:
"No greater grief than to remember days
Of joy, when misery is at hand. That kens
Thy learn'd instructor. Yet so eagerly
5 If thou art bent to know the primal root,
From whence our love gat being, I will do
As one, who weeps and tells his tale. One day,
For our delight we read of Lancelot,
How him love thrall'd. Alone we were, and no
10 Suspicion near us. Oft-times by that reading
Our eyes were drawn together, and the hue
Fled from our alter'd cheek. But at one point
Alone we fell. When of that smile we read,
The wished smile, so rapturously kiss'd
15 By one so deep in love, then he, who ne'er
From me shall separate, at once my lips
All trembling kiss'd. The book and writer both
Were love's purveyors. In its leaves that day
We read no more."

Henry Wadsworth Longfellow (1865)

And she to me: "There is no greater sorrow
   Than to be mindful of the happy time
   In misery, and that thy Teacher knows.
But, if to recognize the earliest root
5   Of love in us thou hast so great desire,
   I will do even as he who weeps and speaks.
One day we reading were for our delight
   Of Launcelot, how Love did him enthrall.
   Alone we were and without any fear.
10 Full many a time our eyes together drew
   That reading, and drove the color from our
      faces;
   But one point only was it that o'ercame us.
Whenas we read of the much longed-for smile
   Being by such a noble lover kissed,
15 This one, who ne'er from me shall be divided,
   Kissed me upon the mouth all palpitating.
   Galeotto was the book and he who wrote it.
   That day no further did we read therein."

Dorothy L. Sayers (1949)

Then she to me: "The bitterest woe of woes
   Is to remember in our wretchedness
   Old happy times; and this thy Doctor knows;

Yet, if so dear desire thy heart possess
5   To know that root of love which wrought our
      fall,
   I'll be as those who weep and who confess.

One day we read for pastime how in thrall
   Lord Lancelot lay to love, who loved the
      Queen;
   We were alone—we thought no harm at all.

10 As we read on, our eyes met now and then,
   And to our cheeks the changing color started,
   But just one moment overcame us—when

We read of the smile, desired of lips long-
      thwarted,
   Such smile, by such a lover kissed away,
15   He that may never more from me be parted

Trembling all over, kissed my mouth. I say
   The book was Galleot, Galleot the complying
   Ribald who wrote; we read no more that day."

Allen Mandelbaum (1980)

   And she to me: "There is no greater sorrow
than thinking back upon a happy time
in misery—and this your teacher knows.
   Yet if you long so much to understand
5 the first root of our love, then I shall tell
my tale to you as one who weeps and speaks.
   One day, to pass the time away, we read
of Lancelot—how love had overcome him.
We were alone, and we suspected nothing.
10   And time and time again that reading led
our eyes to meet, and made our faces pale,
and yet one point alone defeated us.
   When we had read how the desired smile
was kissed by one who was so true a lover,
15 this one, who never shall be parted from me,
   while all his body trembled, kissed my mouth.
A Gallehault indeed, that book and he
who wrote it, too; that day we read no more."

Dante pictures Hell as a gigantic pit located directly beneath the holy
city of Jerusalem. Its walls slope downward and inward, like a cone. Dante's Hell is subdivided into nine concentric rings. In each ring there is
a punishment for a specific crime. Leaving the lustful, Dante and Virgil
move downward past gluttons, the avaricious, the wrathful, heretics, the
violent, and reach the eighth circle, *Malebolge* (mä′lā bōl′jā), "The Evil
Ditches." Here, in ten concentric ditches, God punishes those guilty of
fraud, such as panderers, flatterers, hypocrites, and so on. Virgil and
Dante observe the punishments from ridges above the ditches, and then
proceed downward by bridges spanning them. As Canto XXI begins, Virgil
and Dante, caught up in private conversation, reach the fifth ditch.

from Canto XXI

Thus talking of things which my Comedy does not
    care
    to sing, we passed from one arch to the next
    until we stood upon its summit. There

we checked our steps to study the next fosse[1]
5   and the next vain lamentations of Malebolge;
    awesomely dark and desolate it was.

As in the Venetian arsenal,[2] the winter through
    there boils the sticky pitch to caulk the seams
    of the sea-battered bottoms when no crew

10 can put to sea—instead of which, one starts
    to build its ship anew, one plugs the planks
    which have been sprung in many foreign parts;

some hammer at a mast, some at a rib;
    some make new oars, some braid and coil new
      lines;
15   one patches up the mainsail, one the jib—

so, but by Art Divine[3] and not by fire,
    a viscid pitch boiled in the fosse below
    and coated all the bank with gluey mire.

I saw the pitch; but I saw nothing in it
20   except the enormous bubbles of its boiling,

which swelled and sank, like breathing, through
    all the pit.

And as I stood and stared into that sink,
    my Master cried, "Take care!" and drew me back
    from my exposed position on the brink.

25 I turned like one who cannot wait to see
    the thing he dreads, and who, in sudden fright,
    runs while he looks, his curiosity

competing with his terror—and at my back
    I saw a figure that came running toward us
30   across the ridge, a Demon huge and black.

Ah what a face he had, all hate and wildness!
    Galloping so, with his great wings outspread
    he seemed the embodiment of all bitterness.

Across each high-hunched shoulder he had thrown
35   one haunch of a sinner, whom he held in place
    with a great talon round each ankle bone.

---

1. *fosse* (fôs), ditch.
2. *Venetian arsenal.* The arsenal in Venice was not only a
place to manufacture and store weapons, but a great center
for shipbuilding and repairing.
3. *Art Divine,* God's power.

"Blacktalons[4] of our bridge," he began to roar,
  "I bring you one of Santa Zita's Elders![5]
  Scrub him down while I go back for more:

40 I planted a harvest of them in that city:
  everyone there is a grafter except Bonturo.[6]
  There 'Yes' is 'No' and 'No' is 'Yes' for a fee."[7]

Down the sinner plunged, and at once the Demon
  spun from the cliff; no mastiff ever sprang
45 more eager from the leash to chase a felon.

Down plunged the sinner and sank to reappear
  with his backside arched and his face and both his
    feet
  glued to the pitch, almost as if in prayer.

But the Demons under the bridge, who guard that
    place
50 and the sinners who are thrown to them, bawled
    out:
  "You're out of bounds here for the Sacred Face:[8]

this is no dip in the Serchio:[9] take your look
  and then get down in the pitch. And stay below
  unless you want a taste of a grappling hook."

55 Then they raked him with more than a hundred hooks
  bellowing: "Here you dance below the covers.
  Graft all you can there; no one checks your
    books."[10]

They dipped him down into that pitch exactly
  as a chef makes scullery boys dip meat in a boiler,
60 holding it with their hooks from floating free.

And the Master said: "*You* had best not be seen
  by these Fiends till I am ready. Crouch down here.
  One of these rocks will serve you as a screen.

And whatever violence you see done to me,
65 you have no cause to fear. I know these matters:
  I have been through this once and come back
    safely."

With that, he walked on past the end of the bridge;
  and it wanted all his courage to look calm
  from the moment he arrived on the sixth ridge.

70 With that same storm and fury that arouses
  all the house when the hounds leap at a tramp
  who suddenly falls to pleading where he pauses—

so rushed those Fiends from below, and all the pack
  pointed their gleaming pitchforks at my Guide.
75 But he stood fast and cried to them: "Stand back!

Before those hooks and grapples make too free,
  send up one of your crew to hear me out,
  then ask yourselves if you still care to rip me."

All cried as one: "Let Malacoda[11] go."
80 So the pack stood and one of them came forward,
  saying: "What good does he think *this* will do?"

"Do you think, Malacoda," my good Master said,
  "you would see me here, having arrived this far
  already, safe from you and every dread,

85 without Divine Will and propitious Fate?
  Let me pass on, for it is willed in Heaven
  that I must show another this dread state."

The Demon stood there on the flinty brim,
  so taken aback he let his pitchfork drop;
90 then said to the others: "Take care not to harm
    him!"

"O you crouched like a cat," my Guide called to me,
  "among the jagged rock piles of the bridge,
  come down to me, for now you may come safely."

Hearing him, I hurried down the ledge;
95 and the Demons all pressed forward when I
    appeared,
  so that I feared they might not keep their pledge.

---

4. **Blacktalons,** a general name for the devils. Dante's
original is *Malebranche*,"Evil Claws."
5. **Santa Zita's Elders.** Santa Zita was the patron saint
of the city of Lucca, which in Dante's view was inhabited
by grafters.
6. **Bonturo.** This is an ironic reference. The politician
Bonturo Dati was the most avid grafter in Lucca.
7. **There 'Yes'** . . . *a fee.* This is the root fault of graft,
that corrupt politicians base official decisions not on justice, or the best interests of the state, but on behalf of
those who bribe them.
8. **Sacred Face,** an ancient wooden image of Christ
venerated by the people of Lucca.
9. **Serchio** (ser′kyō), a river near Lucca.
10. **books,** account books.
11. **Malacoda,** "Evil Tail."

So once I saw the Pisan infantry
   march out under truce from the fortess at
      Caprona,[12]
   staring in fright at the ranks of the enemy.

100 I pressed the whole of my body against my Guide,
   and not for an instant did I take my eyes
   from those black fiends who scowled on every side.

They swung their forks saying to one another:
   "Shall I give him a touch in the rump?" and
      answering:
105   "Sure; give him a taste to pay him for his bother."

But the Demon who was talking to my Guide
   turned round and cried to him: "At ease there,
      Snatcher!"
   And then to us: "There's no road on this side:

the arch lies all in pieces in the pit.
110   If you *must* go on, follow along this ridge;
   there's another cliff to cross by just beyond it.

In just five hours it will be, since the bridge fell,
   a thousand two hundred sixty-six years and a day;
   that was the time the big quake shook all Hell.[13]

115 I'll send a squad of my boys along that way
   to see if anyone's airing himself below:
   you can go with them: there will be no foul play.

Front and center here, Grizzly and Hellken,"
   he began to order them. "You too, Deaddog.
120   Curlybeard, take charge of a squad of ten.

Take Grafter and Dragontooth along with you.
   Pigtusk, Catclaw, Cramper, and Crazyred.
   Keep a sharp lookout on the boiling glue

as you move along, and see that these gentlemen
125   are not molested until they reach the crag
   where they can find a way across the den."

"In the name of heaven, Master," I cried, "what sort
   of guides are these? Let us go on alone
   if you know the way. Who can trust such an escort!

130 If you are as wary as you used to be
   you surely see them grind their teeth at us,
   and knot their beetle brows so threateningly."

And he: "I do not like this fear in you.
   Let them gnash and knot as they please; they
      menace only
135   the sticky wretches simmering in that stew." . . .

Canto XXII

All my attention was fixed upon the pitch:
   to observe the people who were boiling in it,
   and the customs and the punishments of that ditch.

As dolphins surface and begin to flip
140   their arched backs from the sea, warning the sailors
   to fall-to and begin to secure ship—

So now and then, some soul, to ease his pain,
   showed us a glimpse of his back above the pitch
   and quick as lightning disappeared again.

145 And as, at the edge of a ditch, frogs squat about
   hiding their feet and bodies in the water,
   leaving only their muzzles sticking out—

so stood the sinners in that dismal ditch;
   but as Curlybeard approached, only a ripple
150   showed where they had ducked back into the pitch.

I saw—the dread of it haunts me to this day—
   one linger a bit too long, as it sometimes happens
   one frog remains when another spurts away;

and Catclaw, who was nearest, ran a hook
155   through the sinner's pitchy hair and hauled him in.
   He looked like an otter dripping from the brook.

I knew the names of all the Fiends by then;
   I had made a note of them at the first muster,
   and, marching, had listened and checked them over
      again.

---

12. Pisan infantry . . . at Caprona. Dante was probably present with a Tuscan army that attacked the fortress of Caprona near Pisa in 1289. After fierce fighting, the Pisan defenders were promised a safe-conduct if they would surrender. Some accounts of the event claim that the Tuscans, despite their promise, massacred the Pisans as they came out.
13. *five hours* . . . *all Hell.* The "big quake" occurred when Jesus died on the cross. Christ died on Good Friday in A.D. 34, and it is now Holy Saturday in 1300, five hours before the time of his death.

Detail of an illustration by Gustave Doré showing the Demons threatening Virgil from an 1861 edition of the *Inferno*.

160 "Hey, Crazyred," the crew of Demons cried
    all together, "give him a taste of your claws.
    Dig him open a little. Off with his hide."

And I then: "Master, can you find out, please,
    the name and history of that luckless one
165 who has fallen into the hands of his enemies?"

My Guide approached that wraith from the hot tar
    and asked him whence he came. The wretch replied:
    "I was born and raised in the Kingdom of
      Navarre.[14]

My mother placed me in service to a knight;
170 for she had borne me to a squanderer
    who killed himself when he ran through his
      birthright.

Then I became a domestic in the service
    of good King Thibault.[15] There I began to graft,
    and I account for it in this hot crevice."

175 And Pigtusk, who at the ends of his lower lip
    shot forth two teeth more terrible than a boar's,
    made the wretch feel how one of them could rip.

The mouse had come among bad cats, but here
    Curlybeard locked arms around him crying:
180 "While I've got hold of him the rest stand clear!"

And turning his face to my Guide: "If you want to
    ask him
    anything else," he added, "ask away
    before the others tear him limb from limb."

And my Guide to the sinner: "I should like to know
185 if among the other souls beneath the pitch
    are any Italians?" And the wretch: "Just now

I left a shade who came from parts near by.
    Would I were still in the pitch with him, for then
    these hooks would not be giving me cause to cry."

190 And suddenly Grafter bellowed in great heat:
    "We've stood enough!" And he hooked the sinner's
    arm
    and, raking it, ripped off a chunk of meat.

Then Dragontooth wanted to play, too, reaching
    down
    for a catch at the sinner's legs; but Curlybeard
195 wheeled round and round with a terrifying frown,

---

14. Navarre, a kingdom that lay in what is now northern
Spain. Nothing beyond what Dante records is known about
the sinner who tells his story in lines 168–174.
15. Thibault, (tib'əlt).

and when the Fiends had somewhat given ground
   and calmed a little, my Guide, without delay,
   asked the wretch, who was staring at his wound:

"Who was the sinner from whom you say you made
200   your evil-starred departure to come ashore
   among these Fiends?" And the wretch: "It was the shade

of Friar Gomita of Gallura,[16] the crooked stem
   of every Fraud: when his master's enemies
   were in his hands, he won high praise from them.

205 He took their money without case or docket,
   and let them go. He was in all his dealings
   no petty bursar, but a kingly pocket.

With him, his endless crony in the fosse,
   is Don Michel Zanche of Logodoro;[17]
210   they babble about Sardinia without pause.

But look! See that fiend grinning at your side!
   There is much more that I should like to tell you,
   but oh, I think he means to grate my hide!"

But their grim sergeant wheeled, sensing foul play,
215   and turning on Cramper, who seemed set to strike,
   ordered: "Clear off, you buzzard. Clear off, I say!"

"If either of you would like to see and hear
   Tuscans or Lombards," the pale sinner said,
   "I can lure them out of hiding if you'll stand clear

220 and let me sit here at the edge of the ditch,
   and get all these Blacktalons out of sight;
   for while they're here, no one will leave the pitch.

In exchange for myself, I can fish you up as pretty
   a mess of souls as you like. I have only to whistle
225   the way we do when one of us gets free."

Deaddog raised his snout as he listened to him;
   then, shaking his head, said, "Listen to the grafter
   spinning his tricks so he can jump from the brim!"

And the sticky wretch, who was all treachery:
230   "Oh I am more than tricky when there's a chance
   to see my friends in greater misery."

Hellken, against the will of all the crew,
   could hold no longer. "If you jump," he said
   to the scheming wretch, "I won't come after you

235 at a gallop, but like a hawk after a mouse.
   We'll clear the edge and hide behind the bank:
   let's see if you're trickster enough for all of us."

Reader, here is new game! The Fiends withdrew
   from the bank's edge, and Deaddog, who at first
240   was most against it, led the savage crew.

The Navarrese chose his moment carefully:
   and planting both his feet against the ground,
   he leaped, and in an instant he was free.

The Fiends were stung with shame, and of the lot
245   Hellken most, who had been the cause of it.
   He leaped out madly bellowing: "You're caught!"

but little good it did him; terror pressed
   harder than wings; the sinner dove from sight
   and the Fiend in full flight had to raise his breast.

250 A duck, when the falcon dives, will disappear
   exactly so, all in a flash, while he
   returns defeated and weary up the air.

Grizzly, in a rage at the sinner's flight,
   flew after Hellken, hoping the wraith would escape,
255   so he might find an excuse to start a fight.

And as soon as the grafter sank below the pitch,
   Grizzly turned his talons against Hellken,
   locked with him claw to claw above the ditch.

But Hellken was sparrowhawk enough for two
260   and clawed him well; and ripping one another,
   they plunged together into the hot stew.

The heat broke up the brawl immediately,
   but their wings were smeared with pitch and they
     could not rise.
   Curlybeard, upset as his company,

265 commanded four to fly to the other coast
   at once with all their grapples. At top speed
   the Fiends divided, each one to his post.

---

16. *Friar Gomita* (gwä´mē tä) *of Gallura*, the administrator of a district in Sardinia, which in 1300 was a possession of Pisa. The Friar was hanged by the Pisan governor for taking bribes to let prisoners escape.
17. *Michel Zanche* (mē kel´ zän´ke) *of Logodoro*. He connived to have the Queen of Sardinia divorce her husband when the King was captured in war and did not return. He then married her himself. He was later murdered by his son-in-law, whom Dante encounters lower down in Hell.

Some on the near edge, some along the far,
  they stretched their hooks out to the clotted pair
0 who were already cooked deep through the scar

of their first burn. And turning to one side
we slipped off, leaving them thus occupied.

(*The text of the* Inferno *continues on page 332.*)

THINK AND DISCUSS
Understanding
1. How does Virgil hold off the Demons?
2. Why do Dante and Virgil follow the Demon squad?
3. How does the Navarrese grafter escape?

Analyzing
4. A successful grafter takes money for political favors in secret. In what ways does the punishment of the fifth ditch fit their crimes?
5. Explain how the Demons at their jobs resemble a certain kind of public official in ordinary society. What does Dante mean through this parallel?
6. How does the Navarrese demonstrate that he is still a dedicated grafter?

Extending
7. Dante puts corrupt public officials near the center of Hell to illustrate how heinous he thinks their crimes to be. Do you share his views, or do you think a certain amount of corruption is an unavoidable byproduct of government?
8. If you wanted to picture creatures of absolute evil, how would you describe them?

REVIEWING: Simile H𝓣
See Handbook of Literary Terms, p. 970.

A **simile** is a figure of speech involving a comparison using *like* or *as*.

1. Explain how the simile of Canto XXI, lines 58–60 illustrates the degree of control which the Demons have over the grafters.

2. How does the simile in Canto XXI, lines 97–99 elevate the picture of Dante cowering?
3. Explain how the characteristics of the creatures to which the grafters are compared in Canto XXII, lines 145–147 affect your conception of the sinners.

COMPOSITION ◆━
Explaining Dante's Demonology
Write an essay of four paragraphs in which you explain to your classmates how the Demons in Cantos XXI–XXII of Dante's *Inferno* embody specific kinds of sin. Discuss how the characteristics of their speech, the way they react to situations, and the motives that drive them illustrate certain kinds of evil. Use your concluding paragraph to summarize your sense of what Dante wished to attack through his depiction of the demons in these two cantos.

Analyzing Dante's Similes
When Dante's narrator compares something he is observing with something else, he frequently uses the characteristic qualities of the thing compared to illustrate his reaction to the thing he sees. Grafters compared with frogs associates all the qualities of frogs with the men. Examine the **similes** found in Canto I, lines 22–24; Canto III, lines 225–227; and Canto XXI, lines 70–73, and then write a four-paragraph essay, to be read by your teacher, in which you explain how similes illustrate Dante's feelings about the thing described. See "Writing About Poetry and Poetic Devices" in the Writer's Handbook.

As Virgil and Dante continue downward they pass the ditches where hypocrites, thieves, evil counselors, and other sinners find punishment. Then they encounter a ring of giants and titans, a barrier to the center of hell. One of them, Antaeus, lifts Dante and Virgil over and down onto the ninth circle, Cocytus (co si′təs), a vast sheet of ice. The heat of lust and wrath punished sinners higher up, but here at the bottom of Hell, it is the cold of hearts which refuse all love that creates the ice imprisoning the traitors. There are four rings of them—traitors to kin, to homeland, to guests, and finally to benefactors. At the center is Satan. In denying the God of love he committed the first act of treason, the primary sin.

from **Canto XXXII**

We stood now in the dark pit of the well,
  far down the slope below the Giant's feet,[1]
  and while I still stared up at the great wall,

I heard a voice cry: "Watch which way you turn:
5 take care you do not trample on the heads
  of the forworn and miserable brethen."

Whereat I turned and saw beneath my feet
  and stretching out ahead, a lake so frozen
  it seemed to be made of glass. So thick a sheet

10 never yet hid the Danube's winter course,
  nor, far away beneath the frigid sky,
  locked the Don up in its frozen source:[2]

for were Tanbernick and the enormous peak
  of Pietrapana[3] to crash down on it,
15 not even the edges would so much as creak.

The way frogs sit to croak, their muzzles leaning
  out of the water, at the time and season[4]
  when the peasant woman dreams of her day's
    gleaning—

Just so the livid dead are sealed in place
20 up to the part at which they blushed for shame,
  and they beat their teeth like storks. Each holds
    his face

bowed toward the ice, each of them testifies
  to the cold with his chattering mouth, to his heart's
    grief
  with tears that flood forever from his eyes.

25 When I had stared about me, I looked down
  and at my feet I saw two clamped together[5]
  so tightly that the hair of their heads had grown

together. "Who are you," I said, "who lie
  so tightly breast to breast?" They strained their
    necks,
30 and when they had raised their heads as if to reply,

the tears their eyes had managed to contain
  up to that time gushed out, and the cold froze them
  between the lids, sealing them shut again

---

1. *Giant's feet.* The giant Antaeus has just lowered Dante and Virgil onto the ice of Cocytus from the ring above.
2. *Danube . . . Don,* great rivers of eastern Europe and western Russia.
3. *Tanbernick . . . Pietrapana,* mountains. Tanbernick is in what is now Yugoslavia; Pietrapana is in northern Italy.
4. *season,* summer.
5. *two clamped together,* two aristocratic brothers who quarrelled over an inheritance and treacherously killed one another.

tighter than any clamp grips wood to wood,
35 and mad with pain, they fell to butting heads
     like billy-goats in a sudden savage mood. . . .

As we approached the center of all weight,[6]
     where I went shivering in eternal shade,
     whether it was my will, or chance, or fate,

40 I cannot say, but as I trailed my Guide
     among those heads, my foot struck violently
     against the face of one. Weeping, it cried:

"Why do you kick me? If you were not sent
     to wreak a further vengeance for Montaperti,[7]
45 why do you add this to my other torment?"

"Master," I said, "grant me a moment's pause
     to rid myself of a doubt concerning this one;
     then you may hurry me at your own pace."

The Master stopped at once, and through the volley
50 of foul abuse the wretch poured out, I said:
     "Who are you who curse others so?" And he:

"And who are *you* who go through the dead larder
     of Antenora[8] kicking the cheeks of others
     so hard, that were you alive, you could not kick
          harder?"

55 "I *am* alive," I said, "and if you seek fame,
     it may be precious to you above all else
     that my notes on this descent include your name."

"Exactly the opposite is my wish and hope,"
     he answered. "Let me be; for it's little you know
60 of how to flatter on this icy slope."

I grabbed the hair of his dog's-ruff and I said:
     "Either you tell me truly who you are,
     or you won't have a hair left on your head."

And he: "Not though you snatch me bald. I swear
65 I will not tell my name nor show my face.
     Not though you rip until my brain lies bare."

I had a good grip on his hair; already
     I had yanked out more than one fistful of it,
     while the wretch yelped, but kept his face turned
          from me;

70 when another said: "Bocca, what is it ails you?
     What the Hell's wrong? Isn't it bad enough
     to hear you bang your jaws? Must you bark too?"

"Now filthy traitor, say no more!" I cried,
     "for to your shame, be sure I shall bear back
75 a true report of you." The wretch replied:

"Say anything you please but go away.
     And if you *do* get back, don't overlook
     that pretty one who had so much to say

just now. Here he laments the Frenchman's price.
80 'I saw Buoso da Duera,'[9] you can report,
     'where the bad salad is kept crisp on ice.' . . .

Leaving him then, I saw two souls[10] together
     in a single hole, and so pinched in by the ice
     that one head made a helmet for the other.

85 As a famished man chews crusts—so the one sinner
     sank his teeth into the other's nape
     at the base of the skull, gnawing his loathsome
          dinner. . . .

"You there," I said, "who show so odiously
     your hatred for that other, tell me why
90 on this condition: that if in what you tell me

you seem to have a reasonable complaint
     against him you devour with such foul relish,
     I, knowing who you are, and his soul's taint,

may speak your cause to living memory,
95 God willing the power of speech be left to me."

---

6. *the center of all weight,* the center of the earth, where
Satan is imprisoned in the ice.
  7. *Montaperti* (mōn´tä per´tē). The speaker here is a Florentine traitor, Bocca degli Abbati, who during the battle
of Montaperti cut off the hand of the Florentine standard
bearer. Without a flag to follow, the troops fled and Florence lost the battle.
  8. *Antenora* (an tə nor´ə), the region of Cocytus in which
the traitors to their countries are punished. It is named
for the Trojan Antenor, who helped betray his city to the
Greeks.
  9. *Buoso da Duera* (bwō´sō dä dwer´ə), who betrayed
his city of Cremona to the French in 1265, by accepting a
bribe to let their army passed unopposed.
10. *two souls,* Count Ugolino (üg ō lē´nō) and Archbishop Ruggieri (rü djer´ē). Together, Ugolino and Ruggieri betrayed Ugolino's grandson, Nino de' Visconti, to
gain power over one of the political factions of Pisa. Then
Ruggieri turned on Ugolino and imprisoned him along with
his sons. After several months their prison was sealed up,
leaving Ugolino and his children to starve. Both Ugolino
and Ruggieri are traitors, but the Archbishop has been
doubly treacherous.

from Canto XXXIII

The sinner raised his mouth from his grim repast
    and wiped it on the hair of the bloody head
    whose nape he had all but eaten away. At last

he began to speak: "You ask me to renew
100   a grief so desperate that the very thought
    of speaking of it tears my heart in two.

But if my words may be a seed that bears
    the fruit of infamy for him I gnaw,
    I shall weep, but tell my story through my tears.

105 Who you may be, and by what powers you reach
    into this underworld, I cannot guess,
    but you seem to me a Florentine by your speech.

I was Count Ugolino, I must explain;
    this reverend grace is the Archbishop Ruggieri:
110   now I will tell you why I gnawed his brain.

That I, who trusted him, had to undergo
    imprisonment and death through his treachery,
    you will know already. What you cannot know—

that is, the lingering inhumanity
115   of the death I suffered—you shall hear in full:
    then judge for yourself if he has injured me.

A narrow window in that coop of stone
    now called the Tower of Hunger for my sake
    (within which others yet must pace alone)

120 had shown me several waning moons already
    between its bars, when I slept the evil sleep[11]
    in which the veil of the future parted for me.

This beast[12] appeared as master of a hunt
    chasing the wolf and his whelps across the mountain
125   that hides Lucca from Pisa. Out in front

of the starved and shrewd and avid pack he had placed
    Gualandi and Sismondi and Lanfranchi[13]
    to point his prey. The father and sons had raced

a brief course only when they failed of breath
130   and seemed to weaken; then I thought I saw
    their flanks ripped open by the hounds' fierce teeth.

Before the dawn, the dream still in my head,
    I woke and heard my sons, who were there with me,
    cry from their troubled sleep, asking for bread.

135 You are cruelty itself if you can keep
    your tears back at the thought of what foreboding
    stirred in my heart; and if you do not weep,

at what are you used to weeping?—The hour when food
    used to be brought, drew near. They were now awake,
140   and each was anxious from his dream's dark mood.

And from the base of that horrible tower I heard
    the sound of hammers nailing up the gates:
    I stared at my sons' faces without a word.

I did not weep: I had turned stone inside.
145   They wept. 'What ails you, Father, you look so strange,'
    my little Anselm, youngest of them, cried.

But I did not speak a word nor shed a tear:
    not all that day nor all that endless night,
    until I saw another sun appear.

150 When a tiny ray leaked into that dark prison
    and I saw staring back from their four faces
    the terror and the wasting of my own,

I bit my hands in helpless grief. And they,
    thinking I chewed myself for hunger, rose
155   suddenly together. I heard them say:

'Father, it would give us much less pain
    if you ate us: it was you who put upon us
    this sorry flesh; now strip it off again.'

I calmed myself to spare them. Ah! hard earth,
160   why did you not yawn open? All that day
    and the next we sat in silence. On the fourth,

Gaddo, the eldest, fell before me and cried,
    stretched at my feet upon that prison floor:
    'Father, why don't you help me?' There he died.

---

11. *evil sleep.* After he had been several months in prison, Ugolino had a prophetic dream in which Ruggieri was a hunter pursuing wolves, who were Ugolino and his sons.
12. *This beast,* Ruggieri.
13. *avid pack . . . Gualandi* (gwä län′dē) *. . . Lanfranchi* (län frän′kē). In Ugolino's dream he sees the aristocrats who sided with Ruggieri as the most ferocious hounds in the pack accompanying the hunter.

165 And just as you see me, I saw them fall
     one by one on the fifth day and the sixth.
     Then, already blind, I began to crawl

     from body to body shaking them frantically.
     Two days I called their names, and they were dead.
170 Then fasting overcame my grief and me."

     His eyes narrowed to slits when he was done,
     and he seized the skull again between his teeth
     grinding it as a mastiff grinds a bone. . . .

Canto XXXIV

     "On march the banners of the King of Hell,"
175 my Master said. "Toward us. Look straight ahead:
     can you make him out at the core of the frozen
         shell?"

     Like a whirling windmill seen afar at twilight,
     or when a mist has risen from the ground—
     just such an engine rose upon my sight

180 stirring up such a wild and bitter wind
     I cowered for shelter at my Master's back,
     there being no other windbreak I could find.

     I stood now where the souls of the last class
     (with fear my verses tell it) were covered wholly;
185 they shone below the ice like straws in glass.

     Some lie stretched out; others are fixed in place
     upright, some on their heads, some on their soles;
     another, like a bow, bends foot to face.

     When we had gone so far across the ice
190 that it pleased my Guide to show me the foul
         creature[14]
     which once had worn the grace of Paradise,

     he made me stop, and, stepping aside, he said:
     "Now see the face of Dis![15] This is the place
     where you must arm your soul against all dread."

195 Do not ask, Reader, how my blood ran cold
     and my voice choked up with fear. I cannot write
         it:
     this is a terror that cannot be told.

     I did not die, and yet I lost life's breath:
     imagine for yourself what I became,
200 deprived at once of both my life and death.

Henry Fuseli, *Dante on the Ice of Cocytus.* c. 1774
British Museum

     The Emperor of the Universe of Pain
     jutted his upper chest above the ice;
     and I am closer in size to the great mountain

     the Titans make around the central pit,
205 than they to his arms. Now, starting from this part,
     imagine the whole that corresponds to it!

     If he was once as beautiful as now
     he is hideous, and still turned on his Maker,
     well may he be the source of every woe!

210 With what a sense of awe I saw his head
     towering above me! for it had three faces:
     one was in front, and it was fiery red;

---

14. *foul creature,* Satan.
15. *Dis,* Satan; Virgil uses the Roman name for Hades, or
Pluto, god of the Underworld in Greek mythology.

Inferno—Canto XXXIV **335**

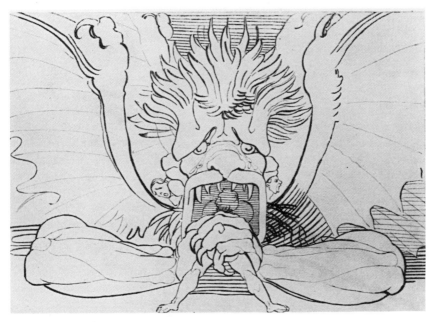

John Flaxman, *Dis.* 1793

the other two, as weirdly wonderful,
    merged with it from the middle of each shoulder
215   to the point where all converged at the top of the
        skull;

the right was something between white and bile;
    the left was about the color that one finds
    on those who live along the banks of the Nile.

Under each head two wings rose terribly,
220   their span proportioned to so gross a bird:
    I never saw such sails upon the sea.

They were not feathers—their texture and their form
    were like a bat's wings—and he beat them so
    that three winds blew from him in one great storm:

225 it is these winds that freeze all Cocytus.
    He wept from his six eyes, and down three chins
    the tears ran mixed with bloody froth and pus.

In every mouth he worked a broken sinner
    between his rake-like teeth. Thus he kept three
230   in eternal pain at his eternal dinner.

For the one in front the biting seemed to play
    no part at all compared to the ripping: at times
    the whole skin of his back was flayed away.

"That soul that suffers most," explained my Guide,
235 "is Judas Iscariot,[16] he who kicks his legs
    on the fiery chin and has his head inside.

Of the other two, who have their heads thrust forward,
    the one who dangles down from the black face
    is Brutus:[17] note how he writhes without a word.

240 And there, with the huge and sinewy arms, is the soul
    of Cassius.—But the night is coming on
    and we must go, for we have seen the whole."

Then, as he bade, I clasped his neck, and he,
    watching for a moment when the wings
245   were opened wide, reached over dexterously

and seized the shaggy coat of the king demon;
    then grappling matted hair and frozen crusts
    from one tuft to another, clambered down.

When we had reached the joint where the great thigh
250   merges into the swelling of the haunch,
    my Guide and Master, straining terribly,

---

16. *Judas Iscariot* (i skar'ē ət), who betrayed Jesus.
17. *Brutus*, along with Cassius (line 241) traitors to their
benefactor, Julius Caesar. The Stoic Brutus suffers silently.

turned his head to where his feet had been[18]
  and began to grip the hair as if he were climbing;
  so that I thought we moved toward Hell again.

255 "Hold fast!" my Guide said, and his breath came shrill
  with labor and exhaustion. "There is no way
  but by such stairs to rise above such evil."

At last he climbed out through an opening
  in the central rock, and he seated me on the rim;
260 then joined me with a nimble backward spring.

I looked up, thinking to see Lucifer
  as I had left him, and I saw instead
  his legs projecting high into the air.

Now let all those whose dull minds are still vexed
265 by failure to understand what point it was
  I had passed through, judge if I was perplexed.

"Get up. Up on your feet," my Master said.
  "The sun already mounts to middle tierce,[19]
  and a long road and hard climbing lie ahead."

270 It was no hall of state we had found there,
  but a natural animal pit hollowed from rock
  with a broken floor and a close and sunless air.

"Before I tear myself from the Abyss,"
  I said when I had risen, "O my Master,
275 explain to me my error in all this:

where is the ice? and Lucifer—how has he
  been turned from top to bottom: and how can the sun
  have gone from night to day so suddenly?"

And he to me: "You imagine you are still
280 on the other side of the center where I grasped
  the shaggy flank of the Great Worm of Evil

which bores through the world—you *were* while I climbed down,
  but when I turned myself about, you passed
  the point to which all gravities are drawn.

285 You are under the other hemisphere where you stand;
  the sky above us is the half opposed
  to that which canopies the great dry land.[20]

Under the mid-point of that other sky[21]
  the Man who was born sinless and who lived
290 beyond all blemish, came to suffer and die.

You have your feet upon a little sphere
  which forms the other face of the Judecca.[22]
  There it is evening when it is morning here.

And this gross Fiend and Image of all Evil
295 who made a stairway for us with his hide
  is pinched and prisoned in the ice-pack still.

On this side he plunged down from heaven's height,
  and the land that spread here once hid in the sea
  and fled North to our hemisphere for fright;

300 and it may be that moved by that same fear,
  the one peak[23] that still rises on this side
  fled upward leaving this great cavern here."

Down there, beginning at the further bound
  of Beelzebub's dim tomb, there is a space
305 not known by sight, but only by the sound

of a little stream[24] descending through the hollow
  it has eroded from the massive stone
  in its endlessly entwining lazy flow.

My Guide and I crossed over and began
310 to mount that little known and lightless road
  to ascend into the shining world again.

He first, I second, without thought of rest
  we climbed the dark until we reached the point
  where a round opening brought in sight the blest

315 and beauteous shining of the Heavenly cars.
  And we walked out once more beneath the Stars.[25]
  1308–1312

---

18. turned his head . . . feet had been. Virgil has reached the exact center of the earth, and to continue on, must reverse his position and begin climbing.
19. middle tierce, around 7:30 A.M.
20. sky above . . . dry land. Dante pictures the northern hemisphere as mostly land, the southern hemisphere as mostly water.
21. mid-point . . . other sky, Jerusalem, where Jesus died on the cross. In medieval cosmology, Jerusalem was held to be the exact middle of the surface of the earth. Dante places the pit of hell directly beneath Jerusalem.
22. Judecca (jü dek′kə), lowest division of the ninth circle of Hell; named for Judas.
23. one peak, the Mount of Purgatory. Dante places it directly above the pit of Hell at the center of the southern hemisphere, as Jerusalem is of the northern.
24. little stream, Lethe (lē′thē), one of the rivers of the Underworld in Classical mythology.
25. Stars. Dante's *Inferno* ends—as do the *Purgatorio* and *Paradiso*—with the beautiful image of starlight, universal symbol of the human aspiration to rise above earthly limits.

THINK AND DISCUSS
Understanding
1. What is Dante's reason for treating Bocca so cruelly?
2. Explain the grudge Ugolino has against Ruggieri.
3. Why does Virgil pivot around as he climbs Satan's haunch?

Analyzing
4. Unlike the other punishments we have seen, the traitors cannot move. Why?
5. Why does Bocca refuse to talk?
6. By contrast, why does Ugolino talk at such length?
7. Why doesn't Satan interfere with them?

Extending
8. Dante puts traitors at the center of Hell. What do you find the most unforgivable sin?

REVIEWING: Symbol
See Handbook of Literary Terms, p. 974.
A **symbol** within a work of literature is a person, place, event, or object which has a meaning in itself, but also suggests other meanings as well.

1. What does the journey Dante takes in the *Inferno* symbolize?
2. How does the poem use the traditional literary symbol, Charon?
3. Explain Dante's use of a historical figure like Bocca to symbolize a particular kind of evil.

THINKING SKILLS
Classifying
To classify is to arrange things according to categories or groups.

1. Classify the imagery of Canto III according to how frequently certain kinds of images appear.
2. Put into two or three categories the similes of Canto XXI.

COMPOSITION
Explaining What Dante Has Learned
Dante must turn away from the Mount of Joy (Canto I, line 75) to take the journey through Hell. Write an essay which will explain to the general reader what he learned in three crucial encounters there: with Francesca, the Navarrese grafter, and Ugolino. Look closely at each scene, defining the specific nature of the damning fault, the character of the punishment, what these people had to say to Dante, and their reasons for talking to him. Use this information in separate paragraphs devoted to each encounter, and then, in a concluding paragraph, define the lessons Dante learned from them all. See "Writing about Theme" in the Writer's Handbook.

Analyzing the Symbolism of Dante's Satan
In the last canto of the *Inferno*, Dante takes forty-two lines (201–242) to describe Satan. Many of the details in his picture are highly symbolic. Write a four-paragraph essay, to be read by your teacher, in which you explain their meaning. Examining the passage closely, look for the way Dante employs size, color, texture, and historical allusions to suggest different kinds of meaning. Use these categories in separate paragraphs and as you explain each, be sure to include brief quotations to illustrate your ideas. See "Writing About Symbolism" in the Writer's Handbook.

ENRICHMENT
Comparing Dante's Illustrators
Dante creates vivid pictures in his poetry, and the *Divine Comedy*—particulary the *Inferno*—has always been a popular subject for artists. Among those who have done illustrations for Dante are Sandro Botticelli (1444?–1510), Henry Fuseli (1742–1825), John Flaxman (1755–1826), William Blake (1757–1827), Eugène Delacroix (1799–1863), Gustave Doré (1833–1883), and Salvador Dali (1904–   ). Find reproductions of some of these illustrations and compare the way various artists have attempted to convey Dante's vision.

Sir Gawain and the Green Knight

Just as writers in Greece kept returning to one story, the Fall of Troy, so that it became a central subject in their literature, so medieval writers, though they wrote about many different times and places, kept coming back to one favorite story, over and over again, as if it held the crucial elements which sparked their imagination, the story of King Arthur and his knights of the round table.

And just like the legend of Troy's fall, Arthurian legend may well spring from a historical figure, a Briton with a Roman name (Artorius) who led his Celtic people in an ultimately futile effort to hold back the Germanic invaders of his homeland, sometime during the first part of the 6th century A.D. When the Anglo-Saxon invaders took over England, Arthur's successors found themselves driven into remote strongholds in Wales, Brittany, and Ireland. There Celtic culture survived, and with it developed legends of an Arthur whose grave had become, as a 9th-century Welsh poem puts it, "The world's enigma . . . ."

When the invasion of the Norman French had made England and western France into a single empire, with French as the language of the aristocrats in power, a revival of interest in these old Celtic tales led to a series of important books. In 1136 a Welshman, Geoffrey of Monmouth, finished a chronicle of the English kings, written in Latin, describing an idealized Arthur, a powerful and brilliant king supported by a splendid court of courageous knights. Imagination had transformed history into something very different from fact. The Norman writer Wace turned Geoffrey's narrative into a long poem, written in French, called *Roman de Brut* (1155) and soon romances about Arthur and his court began appearing in France and Germany as well as in England.

The word *romance* means a tale of knightly adventure and chivalry, with a certain enthusiasm for marvelous and supernatural events. The Arthur legend, with its wide variety of adventure tales about his knights, was the perfect subject for this form, precisely because it dealt with events which were so remote in time and place that the writer's fantasy could go just about wherever it pleased. The audience for this literature was primarily aristocratic, and medieval romances focus upon their concern for achieving knightly perfection through trial and conflict.

Sir Gawain and the Green Knight is the finest Arthurian romance written in English. The identity of its author has been lost. Four of his works, including "Sir Gawain," survive in a single manuscript. He wrote in a provincial dialect which suggests he lived about 150 miles northwest of London. His poem uses an alliterative meter stylish poets, such as his contemporary Geoffrey Chaucer, would probably have thought hopelessly old-fashioned. But the *Gawain*-poet succeeds in evoking the dazzling fantasy of an idealized Arthurian court, in picturing the English countryside as it really looked, in constructing an intricate story which leads to a surprising but convincing conclusion, and in creating in Gawain and his ultimate fault one of the most complex and attractive characters in medieval literature.

from Sir Gawain and the Green Knight

translated by **M. R. Ridley**

Part I

ing Arthur lay at Camelot[1] at Christmas, with many of his lords, great knights, all the noble brotherhood of the Round Table, and they kept high revel with carefree merrymaking. There were many tourneys, with gallant jousting of knights, and after the jousting they rode to the court for song and dance; the festival went on full fifteen days, with all the banqueting and jollity that could be devised.

On New Year's Day there was a great banquet, with double portions, for the whole company. First, Mass was sung in the chapel, with loud chanting of the priests and the rest, and they celebrated the octave of Christmas.[2] When the service came to an end, the King came into the great hall with his knights, and some hurried forward with the New Year's gifts held high above their heads, and there was a busy contest for them; those that won a prize were glad, but even the ladies who won nothing laughed at their failure. So they made merry till it was time for dinner, and then they washed and went to their appointed seats, the noblest, as was right, at the high table. In the center of the dais sat the Queen, Guenevere,[3] with her clear gray eyes, loveliest of ladies, splendidly gowned.

But Arthur would not sit down to eat till all the rest were served. He was so glad in his youth, and boyish in his eagerness, and his young blood ran high and his mind was restless, so that he never could be idle or sit still for long. But there was something else that kept him from his seat, a custom that his high heart had devised, that on a great festival such as this he would eat no meat till he had heard some strange tale of adventure, of the deeds of princes, or feats of arms, some great wonder which he might listen to and believe; or it might be that some strange knight would come, and ask him to name one of his own true knights to joust with him, each staking his life on his skill, and granting the other such advantage as fortune should bring him.

So the tables were set with the choicest fare, and the trumpets sounded a fresh fanfare as a sign that the feast might begin. But the notes had hardly died away when there swung in at the hall door a fearsome warrior, the tallest of all on earth. From the neck to the waist he was so thick-set and squarely built, and he was so long in flank and limb, that one might have thought he was half a giant; but he was in fact a man, as mighty as any horse could bear in saddle, but yet shapely in his mightiness, burly in back and breast, but slender in the waist and with clean-run limbs. They were all amazed at his color, for they saw that he was bright green all over. His clothes were green, too. He wore a plain close-fitting coat of green,

---

1. **Camelot** (kam'ə lot), legendary site of King Arthur's court.
2. **the octave of Christmas.** The observance of major feasts like Christmas occupied a full week, concluding on the eighth day (hence *octave*).
3. **Guenevere,** (gwen'ə vir).

and over that a gay green mantle, lined with close-trimmed white fur. The hood of the mantle was the same, green outside and lined with white fur, and he had thrown it back off his hair so that it lay on his shoulders. His legs were clothed in long green hose, close-fitting, so that you could see the play of the muscles under them. He rode a huge green horse; his mane and his tail, green as the rest of him, were curled and combed and plaited with thread-of-gold and adorned with emeralds.

They all looked at him in wonder, as he sat there on his great horse, flashing and bright as the lightning; and they thought that if it came to fighting there could be no man in the world who could withstand him, so mighty a warrior he seemed. But he wore no armor, no helmet, nor hauberk, nor gorget;[4] he carried no shield, nor lance, nor sword. In one hand he held a bunch of holly, the tree that stays greenest of all when the leaves fall from others in autumn. But in the other hand he grasped his one weapon, and a terrible enough weapon it was, a prodigious battle-ax, with a spike sticking out beyond the head.

The Green Knight rode up the hall, right to the dais, fearless of danger. He greeted no one as he rode, but looked straight before him over their heads, and the first words he spoke were: "Where is the ruler of this company? It is he that I want to see and to have plain speech with him." And with that he let his eyes rove over the company, and scanned each man to see who might seem to be a knight of renown.

Long they gazed at him, astonished what this marvel might mean, the Green Knight on the green horse, greener than grass, both gleaming more like a piece of jewelry, green enamel on gold, than like flesh and blood. They all scanned him, to see what it was that stood there, and walked round him, wondering what his purpose was. They had seen many marvels, but never before such a marvel as this, and they thought he must be some phantom from the land of Faërie.[5] And all were amazed at his words, and some were afraid to answer, and some waited in courtesy for the King to make reply. So they sat still as stones, and there was heavy silence through the great hall, as though they were all asleep.

There was Arthur's adventure for him, plain before his eyes. He stood before the dais, fearless, and gave the stranger a ready salutation. "You are welcome, sir, to this place. I am the master of this house, and my name is Arthur. Light down from your horse, I pray you, and stay and eat with us, and after that let us know what your will is."

But the Green Knight answered him: "Not so; so God help me, who sits throned above the skies, it was none of my errand to wait any while in this dwelling. But your renown, my lord, is spread wide about the world, and the warriors that live in your castle are held to be the best, the stoutest to ride out in their steel-gear, bravest and worthiest of all men on earth, valiant to contend with in all fair contests, and here, I have heard it told, all the true ways of courtesy are known. It is that which has drawn me hither today. You may be sure by this branch which I bear in my hand that I come in peace, seeking no danger. For if I had made my journey with battle in my thoughts, I have a hauberk at home, and a helmet, a shield and a sharp spear, bright-shining, and other weapons too, and I can wield them. But since I look for no war, I wear the softer clothes of a traveler. If you are as bold as all men tell, you will grant me freely the sport that I ask for."

Arthur said, "Sir knight, even if it is just a combat that you crave, we can find a man to fight you."

"No," said he. "I am telling you the truth, it is no fight that I am seeking. All who are sitting around the hall are no more than beardless children, and if I were buckled in my armor, and riding my war charger, there is no man here who could match his feeble might against mine in combat. All I ask in this court is just a Christmas game, seeing that it is the time of Noel and New Year, and here are many young warriors. If there is any man in this hall who counts himself bold enough, hot in blood and rash in brain, stoutly to change stroke for stroke with me, I will give him, as a free gift, this battle-ax. It is heavy enough,

---

4. hauberk (hô′bərk) . . . **gorget** (gôr′jit). A hauberk was a long coat of mail (small metal rings) worn in the twelfth and thirteenth century. A gorget was a piece of armor for the throat.

5. Faërie (fā′ėr ē), fairyland.

and he can wield it as he pleases. I shall abide the first blow, unarmed as I am now. If any man is bold enough to test what I say, let him come swiftly to me and grasp this weapon—I quit-claim[6] it forever, and he can keep it for his own—and I shall stand up to his stroke, steady on the floor of this hall. But you must proclaim my right to have a free blow at him in return, though I will grant him the respite of a year and a day. Now let us see quickly, dares any man speak?"

They had been astonished at first, when he rode into the hall, but they were stiller than ever now, both high and low. The Green Knight turned in his saddle, and his angry eyes roved savagely over the rows of sitting men, and he bent his bristling eyebrows, that flashed green as he moved, and he waved his beard as he sat and waited for someone to rise. And when no one answered to his challenge he coughed scornfully, and gave himself a great stretch with an air of insulting them, and started to speak.

"Well," said he, "is this Arthur's house, of which the renown runs through so many king-doms? What has happened to your conceit and your boasted conquests, the fierceness of your wrath and your high words? All the revels and the renown of the famous Round Table are overturned with one word of one man, for you are all cower-ing for fear, and no one has lifted a finger." And he threw back his head, and laughed loud in their faces. The King felt the insult, and shame made the blood rush to his fair forehead and cheek, as the tempest of his anger rose, and he felt the anger also of his knights rising all round him. And he moved boldly forward, and stood by the Green Knight's stirrup, and spoke.

"Sir, by heaven, what you ask is foolishness. If it is folly that you seek, it is folly you shall rightly find. There is not a man in this hall that is afraid of your big words. Give me your battle-ax, for God's sake, and I will grant you myself the boon you have asked for." He gave him his hand, and the knight got proudly down from the saddle to the floor. Arthur took the ax in his hand, and grasped the helve, and swung it this way and that, trying the weight to see what the feel of it would be when

he struck. The stout warrior stood there before him, towering head and shoulders above any man in the hall. He stood grimly stroking his beard, and not a muscle in his stern face moved as he drew down his coat, no more daunted or dismayed for the stroke that was coming than if someone on the seat beside him had offered him a goblet of wine.

Then Gawain, from where he sat by the Queen's side, leaned forward and spoke to the King. "I pray you, my lord, in plain words, let this combat be mine. Bid me rise from my seat and stand by you, so that without discourtesy to my liege[7] lady the Queen I can leave her side; and I will give you my counsel before all this noble company. In truth it is not seemly, when such a challenge is thrown out in your hall, that you yourself should be so eager to take it up, when there are sitting all round you so many of your knights. There are none in the world firmer of will, or stauncher fighters on a stricken field. I may be the weakest of all of them, and the feeblest of wit; there is nothing about me to praise except that you are my uncle, and all the virtue that is in me is the blood I share with you. But since this business is so foolish, and beneath your dignity as King, and since I have made my request first, grant it to me. Whether I have spo-ken fittingly or not, I leave to this company to decide. Let them speak their minds freely."

So the knights whispered together, and they were all of one mind, that the crowned King should be relieved of the challenge, and Gawain given the game.

Then the King commanded Gawain to rise from his place; and he rose quickly, and came and knelt before the King, and grasped the great ax. And the king let him take it, and lifted up his hand and gave him the blessing of God, and cheerfully bade him be hardy both of heart and hand. "Take care, cousin,"[8] he said, "over your blow; and if you direct it aright I am well sure that you will stand up to the blow that he will deal you later."

---

6. *quit-claim,* transfer of title or right to something.
7. *liege* (lēj), feudal sovereign.
8. *cousin.* This term was loosely used to express close kin-ship.

Gawain went to the Green Knight with the battle-ax in hand, and the Knight waited for him, calm and undismayed, and spoke to Gawain. "Before we go forward with this business, let us say over again our covenant. First, I ask you, sir, tell me truly your name."

"I am called Gawain," he said, "I that am to deal you this buffet, whatever happens later; and a year from today I will come, and no man else with me, and you shall deal me another blow in return, with what weapon you will."

And the Green Knight answered. "Sir Gawain, so may I thrive as I am wondrously eager that you shall let drive at me. By God, sir, I am glad that it is from your hand that I am to get what I asked for here; and you have rehearsed exactly, point by point, all the covenant that I sought of the King, except this—Promise me, on your honor, that at the year's end you yourself will come and seek me out wherever you think I may be found, and take from me the wages for whatever you deal me today before this noble company."

"Where am I to look for you?" said Gawain. "Where do you live? By God who made me, I know nothing of your dwelling, nor from what king's court you come, nor your name. Tell me truly your name, and where you live, and I will use all the skill I have to win my way thither; and that I swear on my troth as a true knight."

"That is enough for New Year," said the Green Knight; "I need no more. If, when you have done me the courtesy of your blow, I tell you my house and my home and my own name, you will know all about me and be able to keep tryst. And if I do not speak, you will be all the better off, for you can stay in your own land, and seek no further. But enough words! Take your grim tool in your hand, and let us see what kind of a man you are with the ax!"

"Gladly, sir knight," said Gawain, and ran his finger along the edge of the ax.

The Green Knight at once took up his stand, with his head a little bent, and his long hair thrown forward over the crown of his head, so that the naked flesh of his neck showed ready for the stroke. Gawain gripped his ax, and put his left

Miniature from the original manuscript of *Sir Gawain and the Green Knight* showing the Green Knight's head magically speaking. c. 1400. British Library

foot forward to get his balance; then he hove up the ax above his head and brought it down swiftly and surely on the bare flesh, so that the sharp steel shore clean through the flesh and the bones and clove his neck in two, and the bright blade drove on and bit into the ground. The fair head fell from the neck and rolled among the feasters, who pushed it away with their feet. The blood spurted from the body and shone bright on the green mantle. The Green Knight did not fall nor even stagger, but strode firmly forward among the knights, and laid hold of his fair head and lifted it up. Then he turned to his horse, gathered the reins, put his foot in the stirrup-iron and swung himself into the saddle. He held his head by the hair, in his hand, and settled himself in his seat as calmly as though nothing had happened to him, though he sat there headless; and he turned himself about, his gruesome bleeding trunk, and many were in dread of him before he had ended what he had to say.

For he held the head in his hand, and turned it so that it faced full at the guests on the high table. And the eyelids lifted, and the eyes gazed at them wide open; and the lips moved, and the head spoke.

"Sir Gawain, be prompt to come as you have promised and seek faithfully till you find me, as you have sworn now in this hall in the hearing of these knights. Make your way to the Green Chapel, I charge you, to receive such a blow as you have just dealt—well you deserve it—to be promptly paid on the morning of next New Year's Day. For men know me as the Knight of the Green Chapel. Seek therefore to find me and fail not, but come, or be called recreant for ever."

With that he gave a roar, and wheeled his horse, and flung out at the hall door with his head in his hand; and the sparks flashed from the flints beneath his horse's hooves. To what land he went no man knew, any more than they had known whence he had come to them. The King and Gawain laughed together at the strangeness of the adventure, but all men there kept it in their hearts for a marvel.

Now take good heed, Sir Gawain, that you do not shrink, but go through to the end with this perilous venture that you have taken upon you.

Part II

Gawain was glad when the venture fell to him in the great hall that New Year's Day, but it seemed a graver thing as the year drew to its end. When the Michaelmas[9] moon was come with its promise of winter, then Gawain began to think of the hard journey that lay before him.

He stayed at Arthur's court till All Saints' Day, and on that day the King held a feast in his honor, with high revel of all the Round Table. And all the courtly knights and the lovely ladies were full of grief for Gawain, but none the less they spoke only of mirth, and made the gay speeches of courtesy with little joy in their hearts. After meat Gawain spoke gravely to his uncle about his journey, and said to him in plain words, "Now, my liege lord, I must ask your leave to depart. You know all about this business that I have on my hands, and I am not going to tell you over again the troubles of it. But I am bound to start on my venture no later than tomorrow morning, to seek out the Green Knight, as God will guide me."

He stayed with them all that day, and the next morning he made himself ready. In full armor he heard the Mass, celebrated at the high altar. Then he came to the King and to his fellow knights of the court, and courteously took his leave of the lords and ladies, and they embraced him and brought him on his way, commending him to Christ. He set spurs to Gringolet,[10] who sprang forward, striking the sparks from the flints with the steel of his hooves. And all who saw the noble knight set out sighed in their hearts.

Many a steep cliff he overpassed as he journeyed, far sundered from his friends, in country where he was a stranger. And at each ford and river passage that he came to, it was seldom that he did not find a foe blocking his path, and one so foul and fell that he must needs fight him. So many wonders the knight met among the hills that it would be hard to tell the tenth part of them. Sometimes he fought with dragons, sometimes with wolves, and then again with trolls of the forest that lived among the crags; with bulls and bears and boars, and ogres that panted after him and pursued him from the high fells. And had he not been a strong fighter and a stubborn, and had not God preserved him, beyond doubt he would many times have been slain and left there dead. But his fights wearied him less than the winter weather, when the cold clear rain fell from the clouds and froze into hail before it reached the faded ground below. More nights than he cared for he slept in his armor among the bare rocks, half dead with the cold and the sleet, while the cold stream came rattling down from the crest high above him, and hung over his head in icicles. So in peril and pain and hardship the knight rode this way and that over the countryside, till the morning of Christmas Eve; and he made

9. **Michaelmas** (mik'əl məs), September 29, a feast in honor of the archangel Michael.
10. **Gringolet,** (gring'gə let).

his prayer to Mary that she would guide him as he rode, and bring him to some dwelling of men.

He had crossed himself but three times when he was aware through the trees of a dwelling circled by a moat, standing on a mound that rose from a piece of meadowland, shut in under the boughs of many great trees that closed in round the moat. It was a castle, the fairest that ever a knight owned, built in a clearing with a park all round it, and round the park a stout palisade of spikes that took in more than two miles of forest land. Gawain looked at the stronghold from that side, and saw it shimmering and shining through the fair oaks, and then he reverently took off his helmet and gave devout thanks to Jesus and St. Julian,[11] gentle Lord and gentle saint, who had thus shown him kindness and heard his prayer. "Now," said he, "grant me good lodging." And with that he touched Gringolet with his golden spurs, and made his way, as chance would have it, to the chief gate, which brought him swiftly to the end of the drawbridge, and he saw the bridge firmly pulled up, and the gates shut fast, and the solid walls that feared no blast of tempest.

Gawain came to a halt on Gringolet by the bank of the deep double ditch that circled the castle. The wall ran down into the water wonderfully deep, and towered up to a huge height above it, wrought of hard hewn stone right up to the cornices, and with bantels[12] of the best under the battlements. There were fair turrets fashioned between, with many loop-holes well devised to shut fast. Gawain had never seen a better barbican.[13] Further in he saw the hall rising high, with towers all about, whose pinnacles rose high aloft, with carven tops cunningly wrought. On the tower roofs his eye picked out many white chimneys that gleamed like chalk cliffs in the sunlight. And there were so many pinnacles, gaily painted, scattered about everywhere and climbing one above another among the embrasures of the castle, that it looked as though it were actually cut out of paper. The knight on his horse thought he would do well if he could contrive to come within the wall and rest pleasantly in that dwelling through the holy season. He called aloud, and soon there came on the wall a courteous porter, who greeted the knight errant, and asked what he desired.

"Good sir," said Gawain, "will you take my message to the lord of the castle, and tell him that I ask for shelter?"

"Yes, by St. Peter,"[14] said the porter; "but I know without asking that you will be welcome, sir knight, to stay here with my master as long as you will."

Then he came down from the wall and came out swiftly, and others with him, to welcome the knight. They let down the great bridge, and came courteously out, and knelt down on the cold ground to give such greeting to the knight as they thought due to him. They gave him passage through the great gate, set full open, and he forthwith told them to rise, and rode in over the bridge. Some came and held his saddle while he got off, and then other willing servants took Gringolet to stable. Then came knights and squires to bring this guest with all joyous welcome into the hall. When he took his helmet from his head, they were ready to take it from his hand in their eagerness to serve him, and they took his sword and his shield. And as they pressed round him, proud men who took pride to honor so princely a guest, he greeted them courteously one by one. Then they brought him, splendid in his armor, into the great hall, where the flames of the fire leapt and gleamed brightly on the hearth. Then the lord of the castle himself came from his own room to give gracious greeting to the knight who stood there. And he said, "You are welcome to all that you can wish. All that is here is yours, to use at your pleasure." "I thank you," said Gawain; "may Christ reward you." And they embraced one another like old friends.

Gawain looked at the host who greeted him so kindly, and thought the owner of the castle looked a valiant warrior. He was a huge man, in the full flower of his age, with a shining beard that covered

---

11. *St. Julian*, patron of hospitality.
12. *bantels*, horizontal courses of masonry jutting out from the wall.
13. *barbican* (bär′bə kən), an outer fortification of a castle or city.
14. *St. Peter*, doorkeeper of heaven; hence patron of porters.

Illuminated capital from the manuscript of a medieval romance showing Sir Gawain. Early 14th century. Pierpont Morgan Library, New York

be a warrior without equal on any stricken field. Gawain washed his hands and sat down to eat. And the quiet well-trained servants served him, with many excellent stews, well seasoned, and doubled portions of them, as was his right, and various kinds of fish, some baked in bread, some grilled on the embers, some boiled and some in well-spiced stews, and all with the subtlest of sauces that tickled his palate.

Then, without pressing him or seeming discourteously inquisitive, they asked him questions about himself, till he told them what court he came from, the court of which Arthur was sole monarch, the great King who was lord of the Round Table, and that he himself who sat in their hall was Gawain, whom fortune had brought to them that Christmas. And when his host knew what knight it was that he was entertaining, he laughed loud in his pleasure. And all in the castle took delight to come as soon as they could into the presence of a knight who was famed above all men in the world for all noble virtues, for prowess in arms and perfection in courtly manners. Each man whispered to his neighbor, "Gawain will give us all a lesson in what knightly manners mean, and anyone who listens to him will have a chance of learning how to talk with the lady that he loves."

By the time that dinner was ended and the noble company rose, it had drawn near to nightfall. The chaplains took their way to the chapel, and rang the bells sweetly, as summons to evensong at that holy season. The lord of the castle went to the chapel, and his lady with him, into their special pew, and Gawain soon gladly followed them. The lord caught him by his robe and led him to his seat, and greeted him warmly, calling him by his name, and said that he was the most welcome to his castle of all knights in the world; and Gawain thanked him heartily and they embraced.

They sat quietly together till the service was ended, and then the lady wished to meet the knight, and she came out of the pew with many fair maidens attending her. She was the fairest of all of them, with her smooth skin, and the lovely color of her cheeks, the grace of her movements and her gracious ways. She was lovelier even than Guenevere, Sir Gawain thought, as he made his way

his chest, the color of beaver's fur. He stood there, stern and stalwart, with his feet firmly planted. His face was fell as fire, and he was forthright in his speech. He was the right man, Gawain thought, to be the lord of the noble company in his halls. He turned back to his room, and gave orders that a man should be assigned to Gawain who would serve him well.

There with gay speeches they unarmed him, took off his plate armor and his bright mail tunic, and the gay raiment below it. Then quickly they brought him all manner of garments, to be his own, so that he could choose which he liked, and have others to change into. When he had made his choice, and arrayed himself in a robe that fitted him well with flowing skirts, through which glowed the gay colors of surcoat and hose, they thought he looked as fresh as the spring, and the handsomest knight that ever had been. Wherever in the world he came from, they thought, he must down the chancel[15] to salute her. She was escorted on her left hand by another lady, older than she, indeed, an ancient dame and held in honor, it seemed, by the knights around her.

Very unlike were the two ladies, for the younger was fresh in her beauty, and her color was clear red in lip and smooth cheek, but the other was yellow and withered, and her cheeks were rough and wrinkled and flabby. She was a worshipful lady, maybe, but not a lovely one. Far sweeter was the other whom she escorted. When Gawain saw that fair lady, that looked kindly at him, he asked leave of the lord and went to meet them. He saluted the elder, bowing low, and he took the other in his arms and gave her the kiss of greeting, and spoke courteously to her.

They desired his better acquaintance, and at once he offered himself as their true servant, if they would have him. They then took him between them and, talking as they went, they brought him to their sitting room, to the hearthside, and ordered the servants to bring spiced wine; and the servants made haste to obey. And the lord often sprang up in high spirits and bade them all make merry. He took his hood off and threw it up and caught it on a spear point, and waved it at them, telling them it was a prize for whoever could devise the merriest sport for Christmastime. "And," said he, "by my faith, I am ready to challenge the best of you before I have to go without my hood; and my friends will help me." So with laughing words the lord made merry, to entertain Gawain with games in the hall that night till he gave order for the lights to be brought. Then Gawain took his leave and went to his bed.

Next day was Christmas Day, when all men remember the time when the Lord God was born on earth to live and die for our salvation, and there is gladness in every dwelling upon earth for His sake. So it was in the lord's castle that day, and they had all manner of dainties, and dishes cunningly cooked that the servants at mealtime brought to the high table. The old ancient lady sat at the head, and the lord took his place beside her. Gawain and the fair lady sat together in the center, in the place of honor, and they were served first, and after them all in the hall, each according to his degree. There was feasting and mirth and much rejoicing, so that it would be hard to tell it all, even if one were to describe it point by point. But it is sure that Gawain and the fair lady took such delight in their companionship, their merry converse with each other and courteous interchange of speech, that no knight and lady ever enjoyed themselves more. All about them was the noise of trumpets and kettledrums, and the shrill music of the pipes, and the buzz of talk; but they had eyes and ears only for each other.

They kept high festival that day and the next day, and the third day after. The third day was St. John's Day,[16] the last of the feast, and as full of gaiety as the rest.

Then the lord asked Gawain straight out what grim task had driven him at that season of festival to ride out so boldly by himself from the King's court, even before the joys of Christmas were wholly over in the dwellings of men.

"Truly," said Gawain, "you are right. It is a great business and a pressing, that has called me out from my own dwelling. I have it laid on me to seek out a place that I do not know whither in the wide world to ride to find it. I would give all the land in Logres,[17] if only, by God's grace, I might come near to it on New Year's morning. Therefore, sir, I ask you now, tell me truly if you have ever heard tell of the Green Chapel, and where in the world it is, and of the Green Knight that dwells there.

Then the lord laughed, and he said, "Stay here with me till New Year's Day, and then rise up and depart. One of my men shall set you on your way, and the Green Chapel is not two miles from here."

Gawain was glad, and laughed merrily. "Now I thank you for this beyond everything else that you have done for me. Since my venture is all but achieved, I will, as you wish, stay with you, and do whatever else you like."

Then the lord took him and set him down and

---

15. chancel (chan'səl), the space around the altar of a church.
16. St. John's Day, December 27, the feast of St. John the Evangelist.
17. Logres (lō'gres), Arthur's kingdom; a name for southern England.

let the ladies be summoned to give him the more pleasure. And they had a merry time, the four of them by themselves. The lord chattered in his delight as though he was almost out of his wits and did not know what he was at. Then he said to the knight, "You are not yet well rested, and you have not had enough of either food or sleep. You shall stay in your room tomorrow, and lie at your ease till Mass time, and come down to your meal when you choose, and my wife shall sit with you and entertain you till I come home again. You will stay here and I will get up early and go hunting."

Gawain bowed to him and granted all he asked.

"Further," said the lord, "we will make a promise between us. Whatever game I kill in the forest, it shall be yours, and whatever good fortune you come by here, give me that in exchange. Let us agree on our honors to make good this exchange, whether it is of trifles or of something better."

"Before God," said Gawain, "I will do it, and it does me good to see you in such a merry mood."

"Let someone bring us wine to drink," said the other, "and the bargain is struck." So he said and they all laughed, and drank their wine and talked gaily together, the two knights and the two ladies. And then they stood up and with elaborate courtesy and many fair words they quietly said good night to one another and kissed, and by the light of many bright torches each was escorted to his soft bed. And just before they parted for the night they reminded each other of their bargain.

Part III

Quite early, before the dawn came, the folk in the castle rose. And the lord of the castle was up as early as any of them, ready dressed for the hunt with many of his knights. He heard Mass, and then ate a hasty breakfast, and was ready with his horn for the hunting field. Before there was even a glimmer of dawn over the land he and his men were mounted, and the kennel men coupled the hounds, and opened the kennel doors, and called the hounds out, blowing clear on the horns the three long notes.

At the first sound of the hunt all the wild creatures trembled, and the deer huddled together in the valley, half mad for fear, and then hastened to the high ground, but they were turned back by the beaters who shouted aloud at them. At each turn in the wood there flashed a shaft, that bit into the brown hides with its broad head, and the deer cried out as they fell bleeding in death along the hillsides. The lord was carried away with joy of the hunting, and now he galloped, and now he dismounted to watch the death of a deer, and he drove hard all day till the night fell.

Meantime, while the lord took his delight in hunting along the woods, the good knight Gawain lay in his soft bed, keeping snug till the light of day gleamed on the walls of his room, with the curtains round him and the gay coverlet over him. And as he lay there dozing he heard a little timid noise at his door, and then heard it quickly open. He brought his head up out of the clothes and lifted a corner of the curtain and took a cautious glance to see what this might be. It was the lady, lovely to look on, that closed the door behind her very softly and quietly, and stole toward the bed.

Gawain did not know what to do, so he lay down again quietly and behaved as though he was still asleep. The lady crept noiselessly over the floor to the bed, and lifted the curtain, came inside and sat down on the edge of the bed, and stayed there a long time, to watch him when he woke. Gawain lay there a long time wondering what this might mean, for it seemed to him very strange; but then he said to himself, "Perhaps it would be better to ask straight out what she desires." So he woke up and stretched himself, turned toward her and opened his eyes, and pretended to be astonished, and crossed himself, to preserve himself from any harm. The lady sat there, with her lovely pink and white cheeks, and her sweet lips, and laughed at him.

"Good morning, Sir Gawain," said she gaily, "you are a careless sleeper, that lets a lady slip thus to your bedside without hearing her. You are Sir Gawain, whom all men hold in honor wherever in the world you ride your ways, and you win great praise among lords and among ladies and among all men that live, for your honor and your courtesy. And now here you are, and we are by our two selves. My lord and his men are hunting afar, the knights in the castle are in their beds and so are my maidens, and the door is shut and close latched. And since I have here in this house the knight that is the honored favorite of all the world, I shall spend my time well while it lasts in talking to him. You are welcome to my person to do with as you please. I am perforce, and must remain, your servant."

"Faith," said Gawain, "that rejoices my heart, even though I am far below what you have said of me. I am unworthy, and I know it, of the honor that you do me."

"Nay," said the lady, "it is far otherwise. Were I the fairest and noblest of all women alive, and had I all the wealth of the world in my hands, so that I could choose as I would from all the men on earth a lover to my liking, there is no man I would choose before you, seeing all that I have found in you of beauty and courtesy and gay spirits, all that I had heard of you before, and now find to be true."

"My noble lady," said Gawain, "You could have chosen far better, but none the less I am very proud that you hold me so high. I am your servant, and I hold you my queen; I offer myself as your true knight, and may Christ reward you for accepting my service."

Thus they spoke of many things till past midmorning, and the lady behaved as though she loved him dearly. But Gawain met her with his perfect courtesy, yet a little distantly, and she thought, "Even if I were the loveliest maiden on earth, he left his love-making behind him when he set out on this journey," for she remembered the grim task that lay before him, and the stroke that might strike him down, which he could not escape. So she spoke of leaving him, and he did not stop her.

She bade him good day, and glanced at him with a laugh, and as she stood by him she surprised him with make-believe severity. "I thank you for my entertainment. But I begin to wonder whether you are Gawain at all."

"Why so?" he asked anxiously, fearing that in some way his words had failed in courtesy.

"Bless you!" she said, "so good and courteous a knight as Gawain is famed to be, the very pattern of knightly manners, could not have talked so long with a lady without asking her for a kiss, even if only by some trifle of a hint at the end of a speech."

"Be it as you wish," said Gawain. "Surely I will kiss you at your bidding. That is no more than your knight's duty; and besides, I should hate to displease you, so you need not ask twice."

Then she came to him, and bent sweetly down, and put her arms round him and kissed him. They commended each other to the keeping of Christ, and she quietly opened the door and went out.

Meantime the lord of the castle was off all day at his hunting, chasing the hinds over heath and through woodland. And by the time that the sun drew down to the west they had killed does and hinds almost beyond counting. Then all the hunters flocked together at the end of the day and made a quarry of all the deer, and cut them up. Each man had his due portion, and on a hide they laid out parts to feed the hounds. Then they blew the kill, and the hounds bayed, and they took up the carcasses, and turned homeward, winding as they rode many clear notes on the horns. And as daylight ended, the whole company was back in the great castle where the knight lived secure. There they found ease, and bright fires kindled. And as the lord came in Gawain met him, and they were glad to greet each other again.

Then the lord commanded all the company to gather in the great hall, and the ladies to come down with their maidens. And then before them all he bade men bring in the venison. And he called laughingly to Gawain and told him the tally of all the swift deer, and showed him what fine condition they had been in. "How does this please you?" said he. "Have I done well? Have I deserved your thanks by my skill in the field?"

"Indeed," said Gawain, "This is the finest kill in a day's hunting that I have seen in seven years in wintertime."

"I hand it over to you," said the knight, "for by our covenant you can claim it for your own."

"True," said Gawain, "and I say the same to you. What I have with honor won in this house I make it over to you with as good will." And he threw his arms round his neck and gave him a kiss as near to the sweetness of the lady's as he could manage. "There are my winnings," he said; "they are all that I can show for my day, but I would hand them over as freely if they were worth more."

"Good," said the other, "and I thank you. Maybe it is the richer prize of the two, if only you would tell me where you were clever enough to win it."

"That was not in the covenant," said Gawain, "so ask me no more; you have been given all that is due you, and do not suspect otherwise." They laughed and made merry, and went to supper, where new delicacies were laid ready for them. Then they said good night, and they all went happily to their beds.

By the third cockcrow the lord was out of his bed, and so were his knights. They heard Mass and took breakfast, and then the company rode out to the woods, before the dawn light came, to hunt the boar. With huntsmen and horns they rode through the flat lands and uncoupled the hounds to draw the thorn brakes.[18]

By the side of the marsh under the crag, where rocks had fallen and lay about in confusion over a knoll, the hounds pressed on to force the boar to break covert, and the men after them. They made casts round the knoll, and the foot of the crag, knowing well that the boar was there, and the first to give tongue was one of the bloodhounds. Then they beat the bushes to rouse him out, and out he swung, bringing disaster to those that stood in his path, a magnificent beast, an old boar that had long ago left the herd, fierce and huge. He was a grim sight, and when he grunted in fury many hearts quailed. At his first rush he hurled three men to the ground, and then without doing more hurt he charged away at full gallop. They hallooed with shouts of "Hi!" and "Hay! Hay!" and put the horns to their lips and blew the recall. There was much merry din of men and of hounds as they sped shouting after the boar. Often he stood at bay, wounding the pack on all sides, and he ripped up many of the hounds with his tusks, and they whined and yelped piteously.

Meantime Gawain lay at ease in his bed in the castle, under the gay coverings, and the lady did not forget to come to say good morning to him. She came early, and was at him to get him to change his mood. She came and drew back the curtain

and peeped in at the knight. Sir Gawain gave her courteous welcome, and she returned his greeting eagerly and sat down beside him quietly, and laughed, and with a loving look she spoke to him. "Sir, if you are indeed Gawain, of all knights the most nobly courteous, it seems strange to me that you know so little of the manners of polite society, and if anyone instructs you in them, forthwith you cast them out of your mind. You have forgotten already the lesson I taught you only yesterday in the plainest words that I could manage."

"What was that?" said Gawain, "for I do not know what you mean, and if it is true, the blame is mine."

"I gave you a lesson in kissing," said the fair lady, "and how to claim a lady's favor when it is plainly there for the asking, as a courteous knight should."

"Dear lady," said he, "take back that speech. I dare not make that request for fear of being refused, since if I were refused I should know that I had been wrong to ask it."

"Faith," said she gaily, "you will certainly not be refused. And even if anyone were so mannerless as to deny you, you are strong enough, surely, to take what you want, consent or none."

"That," said Gawain, "is true enough. But in the land where I come from it brings no luck to use force, or to take any gift that is not given of free will. But I am here at your bidding to kiss or be kissed at your pleasure. You may take my kisses when you like, and cease when you choose."

The lady bent down and kissed him, and they talked long of the griefs and joys of love. "I have wanted to put a question to you," said the lady. "I have heard not one single word from your lips that had anything to do with love. Surely you, that are so courteous and so ready with your vows of knightly service, ought to be eager to instruct a young creature, like me, and give her some notion of the rules and the art of the game of true love. It cannot be that you do not know, for your renown in such things is world-wide. Is it that you think that I am too dull and stupid to understand your

---

18. **draw . . . brakes.** To *draw* in this sense means to force an animal from cover. *Brakes* are thickets.

sweet speeches? Shame on you, Sir Gawain! Here I come all by myself, and sit by your side to learn. Please, give me my lesson while my lord is away."

"Faith," said Gawain, "God reward you for all your kindness. I will do your bidding with all my powers, as I am in duty bound, and always be your faithful servant, so God preserve me!"

Thus the fair lady tested him, and tempted him to wrong, whatever else she wished of him. But he kept her at a distance so skillfully that he failed in neither courtesy nor honor, and there was no sin on either side, and nothing but happiness for both of them. They laughed together and talked long, and then she kissed him, and took her leave and departed.

But the lord rode hard across country after his doomed boar, that rushed over the slopes and broke in his jaws the backs of the best of the hounds whenever he stood at bay, till the bowmen shifted him and made him change his ground in spite of all he could do, such showers of arrows fell on him from the company that gathered round him. At last he was so wearied that he could run no more, but made what haste he could to a hole in a level bank by a rock where the stream ran past. There he got the bank at his back, and began to paw the ground, and the foam dripped from the corners of his mouth as he whetted his white tusks. And the bold men who stood round were by now weary of him and of harassing him from a distance, but there was not a man who dared to close in on him, for he looked as dangerous as ever. He had wounded many of them already, and they shrank from coming within reach of his rending tusks, for he was still fierce and furious and full of fight.

But then came up the lord himself, spurring his horse, and saw the boar standing at bay. He got down from his horse, and left it standing there, and drew his bright sword, and went forward with long strides, passing through the ford to where the grim beast was waiting for him. The boar watched him coming with his weapon in hand, and his bristles rose and he snorted so fiercely that many feared for the knight. The boar made straight at him and the man and the beast fell locked together and the water swirled about them. But the beast

Miniature from the original manuscript of *Sir Gawain and the Green Knight* showing Sir Gawain and the Lady of the Castle. c. 1400. British Library

had the worst of it, for the man watched his mark well at the first charge, and drove the sharp steel firmly into his throat, right up to the hilt, and pierced the heart. The boar snarled and gave up the fight and made away across the stream, but a hundred hounds fell on him, biting furiously, and the men drove him to open ground, where the hounds finished him off.

Then there was loud hallooing, and the blowing of the kill on the loud horns, and the hounds bayed over the boar as their masters bade, they who had been the chief huntsmen in that long chase. Then one who was wise in woodcraft cut up the boar. He cut off the head, and fed the hounds with some of the flesh. Then they slung the carcass on a stout pole, and set off for home. The head was borne before the lord himself, who had slain the beast in the ford by the skill and the strength of his hands.

It seemed a long time before he could see Sir Gawain again, and when they got back to the castle, and came into the hall, he called him, and spoke merrily to him, full of joy. And the ladies were summoned, and all the company. Then he showed them the flesh of the boar, and told them the whole story of the hunt, the huge size and the fierceness of the boar, and the struggle he had with him in the wood to which he had fled. And Gawain praised his prowess and the deed he had achieved, for he had never in his life, he said, seen such a carcass. Then he handled the huge head, and said, by way of praising the lord, that it was a grim sight and he was half afraid of it, even in death.

"Well, Sir Gawain," said the lord, "the prize is your own, as you know, by the sure covenant whereby we bound ourselves."

"True," said Gawain; "and just as faithfully I will now in turn give you my takings." And as he spoke he put his arms round his neck and gave him a kiss, and then at once another, and said, "Now we are quits, and we have both paid all our dues since the time that I came to your castle up till tonight."

"By St. Giles,"[19] said the lord, "you are the best man I know. If you carry on so profitably with this business, you are going to be a wealthy man before you know it."

Gawain lay and slept quietly and sound all night, but the lord, who was full of his hunting, was up and about with the dawn. After they had heard Mass they ate a hasty breakfast, and the lord asked for his horse and went out to meet his knights, who were ready for him, dressed and mounted before the gates of the hall. It was a glorious morning; the hoarfrost sparkled bright on the ground, and the sun rose fiery red against the cloudrack, and his bright rays cut through the mists overhead. The huntsmen uncoupled by the side of a coppice,[20] and the rocks in the wood rang to the notes of the horns. Some of the hounds picked up the scent of the fox where he was lying, and they dashed this way and that across it as they were trained. One of them gave tongue on it, the huntsman called to him, and all the rest made after him, panting in full cry on a high scent. The fox ran before them, and soon they made him break covert, and as soon as they saw him they bayed furiously. He twisted and turned through many a rough patch of undergrowth, and doubled back, and often waited in the bottom of a hedge to listen. So the cunning

fox led them, the lord and his men, all round and about, over hill and dale, till noon.

Meantime Gawain at home slept soundly through the cold morning within the fair curtains. But the lady could not sleep for she was still set in her heart on making love to him. She came in and closed the door behind her. Then she threw open a window, and called to Gawain and mocked him gaily.

"Gawain, Gawain, how can you sleep so sound on so bright a morning?"

Gawain was deep sunk in sleep, but at this he woke and heard her.

He had been deep in gloomy dreams, and muttering as he dreamed, like a man troubled with a throng of dreary thoughts, how that day he had to meet his destiny at the Green Chapel, when he encountered the Green Knight, and had to stand up to his stroke and make no resistance. But when that gracious lady came in he came to his waking senses, and swam up out of his dreams, and made haste to answer her greeting. The lady came to him, laughing sweetly, and bent over him and softly kissed him, and he welcomed her with good cheer. And when he saw her so lovely and so gaily arrayed, with her flawless beauty and her sweet color, joy welled up and warmed his heart. And they smiled gently at each other, and fell into gay talk, and all was joy and happiness and delight between them. It would have been a perilous time for both of them, if Mary had not taken thought for her knight. For that noble princess urged him so, and pressed him so hard to confess himself her lover, that at last he must needs either accept her love or bluntly refuse her. And he was troubled for his courtesy, for fear that he should behave like a churl, but more afraid of a wound to his honor, if he behaved badly to his host, the lord of the castle. And that at any rate, he said to himself, should not happen. So he laughed a little, though kindly, and put aside all the fond loving words that sprang to her lips.

---

19. *St. Giles,* patron of beggars.
20. *coppice* (kop'is), a thicket of small trees, bushes, shrubs, etc.

And she said, "You are to blame, Gawain, if you have no love for the woman that holds you so near her heart, of all women on earth most sorely stricken, unless it is that you already have a lover that pleases you better, and you plighted your troth to her so surely that you will not break faith—and that is what I am coming to believe. Tell me the truth now, for God's sake, and do not hide it, nor make any pretense."

With a kindly smile, said Gawain, "By St. John I have no lover, nor will have one now."

"That," said she, "hurts more than anything else you could say. But I have my answer, and it wounds. Give me one kiss, and I will leave you. There is nothing left for me but sorrow, for I love you dearly." She stooped with a sigh and gave him a sweet kiss, and then she stood up, and said as she stood by him, "Now, my dear, as I go away, do at least this for me; give me some gift, if it is only your glove, that I can have something to remind me of you and lessen my grief."

"I wish I had here," said Gawain, "for your sake, the most precious thing I have in the world. You have deserved ten times over a richer gift of thanks than any I could offer. But to give you a love gift would avail but little, and it is not fitting for your honor to have a glove as a keepsake of Gawain."

"Well," said the lovely lady, "Gawain, noblest of knights, even if I can have nothing of yours, you shall have something of mine." And she held out to him a rich ring of the red gold, with a bright jewel blazing on it that flashed as bright as the sunrays. It was worth a king's ransom, but Gawain refused it.

She said, "If you refuse my ring, because it seems too rich, and you will not be so beholden to me, then I will give you my girdle, which is a cheaper gift." And she took hold of a belt that was fastened round her waist, clasped over her tunic under the bright mantle. It was fashioned of green silk, and trimmed with gold, embroidered only round the edges and adorned with pendants. That she offered to him, and besought him to take it, unworthy gift though it was. But he said that he would accept nothing, neither gold nor keepsake.

"Now are you refusing this silk," said she, "because it seems so cheap a gift? It seems so, I know, a small thing and of little value. But if a man knew the powers that are knit into its fabric, he might hold it at a higher rate. Any man that is girt with this green girdle, when it is close clasped around him, there is no man under heaven that can cut him down, and he cannot be slain by any skill upon earth."

Then Gawain thought about it again, and it came into his head that this was the very thing for the peril that lay before him, when he came to the chapel to meet his doom, and that if he could escape death he would owe much to the charmed girdle. So he was more patient with her as she pressed it on him, and let her speak on. She offered it to him again, and prayed him earnestly to take it, and in the end he consented, and she gave it him eagerly. But she besought him for her sake never to reveal it, but to keep it loyally hidden from her lord. And he promised her that no man should ever know of it, but themselves only. And he thanked her many times and deeply from the bottom of his heart. And she kissed him the third time. Then she took her leave and left him there.

Let us leave him there at his ease, with love all about him, and go back to the lord who was still out in the country at the head of his hunt. By now he had killed the fox that he had hunted all day. As he jumped a hedge to get a view of the rascal, and heard the pack that sped after him, he had seen the fox making his way through a tangled thicket, and all the pack in full cry at his heels. He watched him and waited carefully and drew his bright sword and aimed at him. The fox swerved from the steel, and would have drawn back, but a hound was on him before he could recover, and there right before the horse's hooves they all fell on him and worried[21] him.

The lord dismounted in haste and grasped the fox, snatching him quickly from the hounds' mouths, and held him high over his head and hollaed at the top of his voice, while the hounds

---

21. *worried*, seized with the teeth.

bayed fiercely round him. The huntsmen hurried to his call, and then they skinned the fox, and then turned homeward, for it was near nightfall, blowing great blasts on the horns as they rode. At length the lord got down at his own castle, and found there a fire burning brightly on the hearth, and Gawain beside it.

He met his host in the middle of the hall, and greeted him merrily, and said to him courteously, "Tonight I will be the first to make good our covenant, that we made with so happy an outcome, and sealed it with the draught of wine." Then he embraced the lord and gave him three kisses, as loving and eager as he could make them.

"By God!" said the lord, "you are doing well at your new trade, if you made a cheap bargain."

"No matter for the bargain," said Gawain at once, "so long as I have paid you in full what I owed you."

"Marry," said the other, "mine are poor winnings to set beside yours, for I have hunted all day and I have nothing to show for it but this miserable fox skin—the devil take it!—and that is a poor exchange for the precious things that you have pressed on me, three such warm and loving kisses."

"None the less," said Gawain, "I thank you."

And the lord told him all the tale of the hunt as they stood there. And he appointed one of his men to set Gawain on his way, and bring him over the hills, so that he should have no trouble with his road, and guide him through woodland and brake by the shortest track. Gawain thanked him for his kindness, and then he took his leave of the noble ladies. Then they brought him with lights to his room, and left him to go content to bed. Perhaps he slept less soundly than before, for he had much on his mind for the morrow to keep him awake.

Let him lie there peacefully, for now he is near the goal that he has been seeking. If you will listen, I will tell you how they fared.

Part IV

And New Year's Day drew near, and the night passed, and day drove hard on the heels of the dark. And all the wild weather in the world seemed to be about the castle. There were clouds above that sent their cold breath down to the ground, and there was bitter cold from the north, torturing all ill-clad men. And the snow shivered down bitingly, and pinched all the wild creatures. And the whistling wind swooped down from the heavens and in the dales drove the snow into great drifts.

Sir Gawain listened as he lay in his bed, and for all that he kept his eyes shut it was little he slept. And as each cock crew he knew that his hour was coming nearer. Swiftly he got up, before the dawn, by the dim light of a lamp that gleamed in his room, and he called to his servant, who answered him straightaway, and bade him bring his mail shirt and saddle his horse. The servant rose and brought Gawain his clothes, and dressed him in his full armor. Gawain put this armor on, as gleaming a warrior as any between Britain and the far land of Greece, and he thanked his man, and told him to bring his horse.

And while he put on the glorious clothes—his coat, with the badge clearly worked on velvet, trimmed and set about with precious stones, with embroidered seams, and lined inside with fur—yet he did not leave off the love lace, the lady's gift. That, you may be sure, Gawain for his own sake did not forget. When he had belted on his sword round his hips, then he wound twice round his waist, swiftly and close, the green silken girdle, fit for a fair knight and shining out against the splendid scarlet of the cloth. But it was not for its richness that he wore it, or for pride in its pendants that glittered with the gleam of polished gold, but to save his life, when he had to stand in the face of danger, and, by his covenant, not stir a weapon in his own defense. And now the brave knight was ready to go out to his fate.

There was Gringolet ready waiting for him, his great war-charger. So Gawain rode his way with the one squire who was to guide him on his road to the dolorous place where he was to abide the grim onslaught. They passed by banks where all the boughs were bare, and the icy cold seemed to cling to the cliffs under which they rode. The clouds rode high, but there was ill weather under them.

The mist drizzled on the moor and was heavier on the tops of the hills, so that each had a cap and a cloak of mist about it. The streams swirled and broke about their banks, and foamed white as they came down in spate. It was a hard wandering way they had to find when it lay through woods, till it came to the hour of dawn. Then they were high on a hill, and the white snow lay all round them. And his squire bade Gawain halt.

"Now I have brought you hither, my lord, and you are not far from the place which you have asked for and sought so earnestly. But now I shall tell you the truth, since each day that I have known you the more I have grown to love you; if you would do as I advise, you would fare the better. The place that you press forward to is held full perilous. In that waste land there dwells a man as evil as any on earth. He is stalwart, and grim, and a lover of blows, and mightier than any man on middle-earth, huger than Hector of Troy[22] or any four knights of Arthur's house. And this is what he does at the Green Chapel. There is never a man passes that way, however proud of his prowess in arms, but he smites him down and kills him. He is a violent man, and he knows no mercy in his heart, and I tell you the truth, if once you come there, no matter if you had twenty lives, you are a dead man, if the knight has his will with you. He has dwelt here a long time, and fought many combats, and there is no guard against his grim blows.

"Therefore, for God's sake, sir, leave the man well alone, and go some other way and ride to another country, where Christ may be your speed. And I will turn home again, and I promise you besides that I will keep our secret truly, and never let drop a word that you flinched from meeting any man."

"All the thanks of my heart," said Gawain, slowly, "and good luck to you, who wish me well. I am sure that you would truly keep my secret; but however close you kept it, if I now turned aside, and made haste to flee in the way you tell me to, then I should be a coward knight, and there could be no excuse."

Then he spurred Gringolet, and picked up the track, and made his way along the bank by the side of a shaw,[23] and rode along the rough bank right down to the dale. He reined in Gringolet and halted, and turned on this side and that, looking for the chapel.

He saw nothing like it anywhere, and he thought this strange. Then a little way away over the field he saw a small mound, a smooth swelling knoll, by the waterside where a cascade fell down, and the water of the brook bubbled in the basin as though it were boiling. Gawain gave Gringolet his head and came to the mound, and got down quietly and fastened the reins to the rough bough of a lime tree. Then he walked over to the mound, and strode all round it, wondering what it was. There was a hole in one end, and one on each side, and it was all overgrown with patches of grass; whether it was only an old cave or just a split in a rock, he could not make out.

"Well!" said he, "is this the Green Chapel? This is the kind of place where the devil might say matins[24] at midnight! It is a desolate place, and this chapel, if it is the chapel, is evil looking, all overgrown. It is the right place for the knight in green to perform his devotions after the devil's fashion. I am beginning to think in my heart that it is the fiend that has appointed me this tryst, to destroy me here. It is an unchancy chapel, bad luck to it, the least hallowed church that ever I came into!"

With helm on head and lance in hand he came up to the mound, and then he heard, from a rock high up on a hill beyond the brook, a wondrous loud noise. Hark! it re-echoed on the cliff with the sound of a scythe being whetted on a grindstone. Hark! it whirred and rasped, like water at a mill; it rushed and rang, fearful to hear. Then said Gawain, "By God, this device, I think, is meant to greet me and to sound the challenge for me as I come. God's will be done. To say 'Woe is

---

22. **middle-earth . . . Hector of Troy.** *Middle-earth* is an archaic term for the world. Hector was the greatest Trojan warrior.
23. **shaw,** a small wood or grove.
24. **matins** (mat′nz), morning prayers.

me!' does not help in the least. And though I may have to give up my life, no mere noise is going to scare me."

Then Gawain called aloud, "Who is master here, to keep tryst with me? For now am I, Sir Gawain, walking here and ready. If any man wants aught of me, let him come hither quickly, now or never, to work his will."

"Stay," said a voice from the bank above his head, "and swiftly you shall have all that I once promised you."

Yet the speaker went on for a while with the noise of his whetting before he would come down. Then he made his way down by the side of a crag, and came hurtling out of a crack in the rock with a grim weapon, a new Danish ax, with a massive blade on it, curving by the haft, whetted with a whetstone, and four foot long, measured by the thong that gleamed bright on the haft. There was the Green Knight, appareled as before, the same in his face and his limbs, his locks and his beard, except that this time he strode firmly on his feet, setting the haft to the ground beside him as he walked. And when he came to the water, not wanting to wade it, he used his ax as a jumping pole and leaped over, and came striding lissomely[25] forward, fierce and fell, over the broad stretch of snow that lay all around.

Sir Gawain bent his head no farther than he must for courtesy, and greeted him. The other said, "Sir knight, now men may know that you are one who keeps tryst. Gawain, so God guard me, I tell you you are very welcome to my dwelling, and you have timed your travelings as a true man should. You know the covenants that we made between us. Twelve months ago today you took what chance gave you and I was to give you prompt quittance this New Year's Day. Here we are in this valley by our two selves, and there are no men to part us, however tight we lock swaying in combat. Take your helm off your head, and take your wages, making no more resistance than I made then, when you whipped my head off at one blow."

"Nay," said Gawain, "by the Lord God who gave me life, I shall have no grudge against you, not a grain, for any harm that may fall to me. But keep yourself to the one stroke, and I will stand still, and give you free leave to strike as you will." So he leaned his head down and bared his neck, showing the white skin, making as though he did not care, and giving no sign of fear.

Then the Green Knight got himself quickly ready, took firm hold of his grim tool to smite Gawain, and gathered every ounce of strength in his body together as he rose to the stroke, and drove at him as mightily as though he had a mind to destroy him. And if it had fallen as hard and as true as he seemed to intend, the doughtiest warrior alive would have been dead of the blow. But Gawain glanced sideways at the blade as it came swooping down to strike him to the earth, and he could not help his shoulders shrinking a little from the keen steel. And the Green Knight with a turn of his wrist swerved the blade aside, and then he told Gawain what he thought of him.

"You cannot be Gawain, that is held so good a knight, who never, they say, quailed for any host of men on hill or on dale. And now you flinched like a coward before you felt even a scratch. That is not what I have ever heard of Gawain. I did not flinch nor flee when you aimed your blow at me, and I made no evasions in Arthur's hall. My head fell at my feet, but did I flinch? Not I. And now you quail before any harm comes to you. So I deserve to be called a better knight than you are."

Said Gawain, "I shrank once, but I will not again, even if my head falls on the stones, though I cannot, like you, put it back again on my shoulders if it does! Get ready again, and come to the point. Deal me my doom, and do it out of hand. I will stand up to your stroke, and start away no more till your ax has struck me, and I pledge my troth to that."

"Have at you then," said the other, and hove up the ax, and looked at him as fiercely as though he were mad with anger, and aimed a mighty blow at him; but just as the blade came down he held back before it could wound him. Gawain awaited

---

25. *lissomely*, limberly; supplely

the stroke steadfastly, and flinched this time not the least, but stood still as a stone or the stump of a tree that is anchored with a hundred roots round a rock in the ground.

Then merrily spoke the Green Knight: "Hm! Now that you have got your courage back, it is time to hit you in earnest. Throw back the hood that Arthur gave you, and see whether your neck can stand the blow that is coming."

To which Gawain, now full of wrath, replied in anger, "Drive on, fierce knight; you are too long over your threats. I wonder that you are not scared by your own fierceness."

"Faith," said the Green Knight, "if you are so furious, I will not delay, nor be slow in letting you have what you have come for. Ready!" Then he took his stance for the stroke, and set his lips and knit his brows. It was no wonder that Gawain, with no hope of rescue, little liked the look of him.

He lifted the ax lightly and let it deftly down just by the bare neck. And though he swung at him hard he did him no more hurt than to graze him on one side, so that the very tip of the blade just broke the skin, and the bright blood spurted over his shoulders to the ground. And when Gawain saw the blood red on the snow, he leapt forward more than a spear length, and seized his helm and set it on his head, and gave a twitch with his shoulders to bring his shield round in front of him, and flashed out his bright sword, and spoke fiercely—Never since his mother bore him had he been so gay, now that his trial was over.

"Stop your blows, sir, and deal me no more. I have endured one stroke in this place without making any return; but if you deal me another, be very sure that I will pay it back forthwith, and give you blow for blow again. There is only the one blow due to fall to me here—those were the terms of the covenant made between us in Arthur's hall —so now, good sir, hold your hand."

The Green Knight held off and rested on his ax, the haft on the ground and his arms on the blade, and he watched Gawain standing there, bold and fearless, full armed again, and with never a thought of flinching. And he was glad to see it, and he spoke cheerfully to him in a great voice, so that his words rang clear like bells.

"Good knight, be not so wrathful. No man has here misused you unmannerly, or treated you otherwise than as the covenant allowed, which we made at the King's court. I promised you a stroke, and you have had it and you can count yourself well paid. That blow is full quittance of all that you owe me. Had I wished, I could perhaps have dealt you a buffet more harshly, and done you injury. But, as it was, first I threatened you with a feint, and gave you no wound. That was for the agreement we made the first night at my castle, and for the next day, when you kept troth loyally, and gave me back, like a true man, your gains for the day. And the second feint was for the next day after, when again you had my dear lady's kisses and gave me them again. For those two days I aimed the two strokes at you that were no more than feints and did you no scathe. A true man pays his debts and then need fear no danger. But the third time you failed in your trust, and for that you had to take your third blow and the wound.

"For it is my own green girdle that you are wearing, and it was my own wife that gave it you. I know all about your kisses, and the love-making of my wife, and how you bore yourself, for it was I myself that brought it about. I sent her to make trial of you, and surely I think that you are the most faultless knight that ever trod upon earth. As a pearl for price by the side of a white pea, so, by God's truth, is Gawain beside other gay knights. But just over the girdle, sir, you failed a little, and came short in your loyalty; yet that was not for any intrigue nor for love-making, but just that you loved your life, and I do not blame you for it."

Gawain stood in thought a long while, so overcome with grief that he groaned in his heart, and all the blood in his body seemed to rush to his face as he winced for shame at what the Green Knight said. And the first words that he said were, "Curse upon cowardice and covetousness both; there is evil power in them to destroy a man's virtue." Then he laid his hand to the knot of the girdle, and loosed it, and threw it savagely from him to the Green Knight, and said, "Lo, there is my broken faith, curse on it. I was afraid of your blow, so cowardice taught me to make terms with covetousness, and forget my true nature, the generosity and loyalty that belong to true knights. Now I have shown myself false, I that ever was afraid of any treachery or untruth, and hated them. I make my confesson to you, sir knight, between the two of us. I have behaved very ill. Let me now do what I can to gain your good will; and afterwards I will show that I have learned my lesson."

The Green Knight laughed, and said to him friendlily, "Such harm as I took, I count it wholly cured. You have made such free confession that all your faults are cleansed, and besides you have done your penance at the edge of my blade. I hold you purged of all your offenses and as clean as if you had never failed in virtue since the day you were born. And I give you the gold-hemmed girdle that is green as my gown. Sir Gawain, you will be able to think back on this day's contest when you ride out among great princes. It will be a noble token of the meeting of two chivalrous knights at the Green Chapel. And now, this very New Year's Day, you shall come back with me to my castle, and we will finish off happily the rest of the revel that we left." He pressed him to come, and said, "We must put you on good terms again with my wife, who behaved as your enemy."

"Nay," said Gawain, and took hold of his helm and lifted it from his head, and thanked the Green Knight. "I have stayed too long already. All happiness be yours, and may the great God grant it you, he that brings honor to men. Commend me to your fair and gracious lady, and to that other also, those two whom I honor, who with their devices so cunningly beguiled me. But it is no marvel if a fool goes astray in his wits, and through the wiles of women comes to sorrow.

"But for your girdle—and may God reward you for your kindness—that I will wear with the best will in the world, not for the sake of the splendid gold, nor the silk, nor the pendants that hang from it, nor its costliness, nor the lovely work in it, nor for the honor that I shall get when I am seen wearing it, but as a memorial of my sin. I shall look at it often when I ride out proudly, and I shall

feel remorse in my heart for the fault and frailty of the erring flesh, which is so ready to catch the infection and the stain of ill-doing. So when pride stirs in my heart for my prowess in arms, one glance at the love lace will humble me. But there is one thing I would ask you. Will you tell me your true name that you are called by? Then I will ask no more."

"I will tell you truly," said the other. "Bercilak de Haut-desert[26] I am called in my own land. And it is the might of Morgan la Fay[27] that has brought all this about. She dwells in my house, and she knows all the cunning of magical lore and the crafty ways of it, and has learned the mysteries of Merlin,[28] for once she had dealings in love with that great wizard, who knows all your knights at home. And so Morgan the goddess is her name, and there is never a man so high and proud but she can humble and tame him.

"It was she who sent me to your splendid halls, to make trial of your pride, and to see whether there was truth in the report that runs through the world of the great renown of the Round Table. She sent this marvel to steal your wits away from you, and she hoped to have daunted Guenevere and brought her to death with dismay at that same strange figure that stood like a phantom before the high table, and spoke from the head that he held in his hand. She is that ancient lady whom you saw at my castle, and she is your own aunt, Arthur's half-sister, daughter of that Duchess of Tintagel on whom Uther later begat Arthur, that now is King.[29] So now I ask you, sir knight, come back to my halls and meet your aunt again, and make merry with us. My company all love you, and by my faith I wish you as well as any man on earth for your true loyalty."

---

26. *Bercilak de Haut-desert* (ber′sə läk də ō′dä ser).
27. *Morgan la Fay,* "Morgan the Fairy," a witch who was Arthur's half-sister and continually plotted against him.
28. *Merlin,* a wizard that was Arthur's teacher and counselor.
29. *your own aunt . . . King.* The Duchess of Tintagel was the mother, by her husband the Duke, of Morgan and her sisters, one of whom was Gawain's mother; the Duchess was also the mother, by Uther Pendragon, King of England, of Arthur.

But Gawain still said no, and could not be persuaded. So they embraced and kissed and commended each other to the Prince of Paradise, and parted there in the snow. Gawain mounted and rode off, hasting to the King's castle, and the knight in the bright green went his own way.

And Gawain on Gringolet, with his life given back to him, rode through many wild ways, sometimes with a roof over his head at night, and sometimes sleeping under the stars. He had many adventures by the way, and won many victories. The wound in his neck was healed, and he wore the shining girdle about it, slantwise like a baldric[30] to his other side, and fastened under his left arm in a knot, the token of his fault, to remind him of the stain of it. So he came to the court, sound and whole. And great joy rose in the castle when the great King knew that the good Sir Gawain was come, and rejoiced over it. And the King kissed the knight, and the Queen too, and then many a true knight thronged round him to greet him and ask him how he had fared. He told them all the wonders, all the hardships he had, the adventure at the chapel, and the way the Green Knight dealt with him, the love of the lady, and at last the love lace. And he bared his neck and showed them the wound that he took at the knight's hands as punishment for his failure in troth. When he came to the telling of this part he was tormented, and groaned for grief and sorrow, and the blood rushed to his cheeks with the shame of what he had to confess.

"See, my lord," said Sir Gawain, and laid his hand on the girdle, "this is the band that is sign of my fault, my disgrace, the mark of the cowardice and the covetousness that I yielded to, the token of my broken troth. And I must needs wear it as long as I live. For no man can hide his scar, nor rid himself of it; when once it is fastened upon him it will never depart."

The King comforted the knight, and all the court laughed kindly, and agreed, to cheer him, that all the lords and ladies of the Round Table, everyone of the brotherhood, should wear a slanting baldric of bright green, just like Gawain's. So that became a part of the glory of the Round Table, and ever after a man that wore it was honored. So the ancient books of romance tell us.

And may He that wore the crown of thorns bring us to His bliss.

c. 1375

---

30. *baldric* (bôl'drik), a belt, usually of leather and richly ornamented, hung from one shoulder to the opposite side of the body, to support the wearer's sword, bugle, etc.

Reader's Note

Who Is the Green Knight?

The Green Knight is such a vivid figure that he almost eclipses the hero of the poem in the recollections of some readers. But who is he and what does he represent? The following are some modern scholarly interpretations of the Green Knight.

Coming from outside Arthur's realm of order, [the Green Knight] is a tester; thus he may conceivably represent, though not in any strict allegorical fashion, Nature itself, the phantom or illusion into which every man is introduced at birth and which, to save himself, man must interpret and deal with correctly.

John Gardner

I call the Green Knight "the common enemy man"—Macbeth's periphrasis for the devil. The Hebrew word "Satan" in fact means "adversary" and there is no doubt that the Green Knight is Sir Gawain's adversary. But what sort of enemy? On the whole he seems friendly to Gawain, and cannot be classified as a conventional devil of Christian myth; that is, a damned soul hungering for relief from torment, which he deludedly imagines he can achieve by luring other souls to damnation. The Green Knight is more like the jovial demon of old popular tradition, and also, it seems to me, resembles the kind of devil who tempts within the system and on behalf of God, like Satan in the Book of Job; he knows what good and evil are. But his first appearance is absolutely unequivocal: everything, from Arthur's initial invocation of a "marvel," right through the description of the Green Knight, leads straight to the conclusion of the court that he is a "phantom from Fairyland."

Brian Stone

In folklore and fairy tale the dead not uncommonly carry their heads under their arms to frighten the people they meet. They toss their heads up into the air and play ninepins with their skulls. Pale green, furthermore, is the color of livid corpses: the paintings of the Buddhist art of Tibet, which adhere in their color symbolism to a very definitely prescribed tradition, employ such a green to denote whatever appertains to the kingdom of King Death. We may safely assume that the death-green, towering apparition out of the forlorn valley of the [Green Chapel], carrying an archaic ax over his shoulder instead of a contemporary, chivalric Christian sword and mounted on a steed as remarkable both for color and for size as himself, was the great reaper, Death.

Heinrich Zimmer

THINK AND DISCUSS
Understanding
1. What happens when Gawain strikes the Green Knight with an axe?
2. How is Gawain received in the remote castle he reaches on Christmas Eve?
3. Describe the special characteristic of the gift which Gawain keeps secret from his host.
4. How did the Green Knight survive a beheading?

Analyzing
5. Explain how the rules of chivalry and courtly love govern the way Arthur and Gawain react to the Green Knight's challenge.
6. Describe how **alliteration** intensifies the narration of the axe blow, on page 343.
7. How do the events of Gawain's autumn journey **foreshadow** what lies ahead?
8. What kinds of expectations does the elaborate description of the castle in Part II generate?
9. Explain the difficult problem in courtly good manners which the wife's morning visits pose for Gawain.

10. Why does the narrator shift back and forth between the middle of the hunting scenes and the conversations between Gawain and the lady of the house?
11. How do the warning of the squire who guides Gawain, the appearance of the Green Chapel, and the strange sound Gawain hears constitute the final challenges which he faces before he meets the Green Knight a second time?
12. Explain why Gawain savagely throws away the green girdle.
13. Why does he put it on again?

Extending
14. In your judgment, should Gawain have accepted the challenge in the first place? Arthur calls it "foolishness." Could the whole situation attack the excesses of chivalry?
15. Which point of view do you side with at the end of the story, Gawain, or the people at Arthur's court?
16. To what extent do the *Song of Roland* and "Thorstein the Staff-Struck" also hinge on

Gawain's insistence that "no man can hide his scar"? Explain how those two works explore resolutions that differ from *Sir Gawain and the Green Knight*.

REVIEWING: Setting
See Handbook of Literary Terms, p. 969.

The **setting** of a narrative is the time and place in which the action occurs. The setting can help express the significance of what is happening.

1. In what ways does the appearance of the Green Knight contrast with the setting of the story's first scene?
2. How does the setting for Gawain's second confrontation with the Green Knight help suggest the hero's feelings?

THINKING SKILLS
Synthesizing

To synthesize is to put together parts and elements so as to form a whole, a new pattern or structure not evident before.

1. How does the game which the host and Gawain play in Part III resemble the Green Knight's game in Part I?
2. Explain how, in presenting the game in Part III, the story contrasts the prizes won at the hunt, and the prizes Gawain wins back at the castle.
3. In what ways do the three strokes of the axe in Part IV link with the exchange of prizes in Part III?

VOCABULARY
Context

Use context clues to determine the meaning of the words below. Write the meaning of each word on a separate sheet of paper and then use each in a sentence to indicate that you understand its meaning. Check your work by looking up each word in the Glossary. If you were mistaken about any of the words, write a sec-ond sentence using it correctly. The locater references in parentheses that follow each word indicate first the page on which the word is found; second, the column (*a* = first, *b* = second); third, the paragraph (beginning with the first complete one).

1. *helve* (342a, 3)
2. *buffet* (343a, 2)
3. *troth* (343a, 4)
4. *tryst* (343a, 5)
5. *recreant* (344a, 2)
6. *fells* (344b, 2)
7. *palisade* (345a, 1)
8. *hinds* (349b, 3)
9. *knoll* (350a, 4)
10. *doughtiest* (356b, 1)

COMPOSITION
Describing a Medieval Court

Write a four-paragraph essay, to be read by someone unfamiliar with *Sir Gawain and the Green Knight*, in which you explain what life is like in the medieval court that the poem describes. Devote different paragraphs to clothing, food, manners, and entertainment. As you write your description, include as many specific details from the poem as possible.

Analyzing the Ironic Reversals in *Gawain*

When a plot leads the reader to expect a certain kind of event, and then its opposite occurs, there is an ironic reversal. Write a four-paragraph essay, to be read by your teacher, which analyzes the significance of this phenomenon in *Sir Gawain and the Green Knight*. Examine these three ironic surprises: Sir Gawain thinks he faces death from an axe blow but only gets a slight cut; everyone has considered Gawain a perfect knight but he turns out to be quite imperfect; and yet when Gawain returns to Camelot everyone laughs at his confession of guilt. Determine the significance of these reverses by defining the assumptions implied both by what was expected and by what actually happened. In your essay, after an introductory paragraph explaining the concept of dramatic irony, devote a separate paragraph to your analysis of each of these examples.

The History of Language

The Rise of the Vernacular Languages

The Romans ruled most of western Europe for hundreds of years. When the Roman legions were finally withdrawn in the fourth and fifth centuries A.D., they left behind an enduring legacy—the Latin language. Latin remained the language in which worship and education were conducted throughout the medieval period. The monks who patiently copied their long manuscripts were writing in Latin. This typical picture of the Middle Ages—the monk at his writing desk—points to an essential characteristic of Latin: it was a written language. The common people of Europe, few of whom could read or write, did not use Latin. Instead, they spoke one of a number of vernacular languages, depending on where they lived. The word *vernacular* itself comes from Latin (*vernaculus*, "domestic, native"), and some of the vernacular languages had their origins in Latin, such as those that would eventually be Italian, French, and Spanish. Other vernaculars were based on Celtic or Germanic languages.

While these European vernacular languages were as yet unwritten, they did possess a richly imaginative oral literature. Carrying on ancient traditions of storytelling, the medieval minstrels recited tales of daring and romance in the different vernaculars. They memorized long stories in verse form and kept alive the traditions of Beowulf, Roland, Arthur, and other favorite medieval heroes. The Celtic vernaculars—Irish, Welsh, and Breton—had the richest and earliest development. Poetry in the Irish language survives from as early as the sixth century—the oldest vernacular literature in western Europe. Celtic bards in the centuries that followed created and preserved the huge body of myth and legend from which the great Arthurian romances would eventually come.

But if the vernaculars were the medium of ordinary communication and of traditional storytelling and poetry, Latin continued to be the language of scholarship and all serious writing. For nearly a thousand years, St. Jerome's Latin translation of the Bible was the only version available. The Church had always opposed translating the Latin of the Scriptures into the vernacular languages of Europe, fearing the spread of heresy. The appearance in 1381 of John Wycliffe's English translation of the Bible was therefore an important event in both linguistic and religious history.

An equally important contribution to the development of the European vernaculars came from the independent decisions by major medieval writers like Dante and Chaucer to use them rather than Latin in important works. Dante's decision to compose his *Commedia* in the vernacular was of enormous importance to the development of the Italian language. In an essay, Dante developed the concept of a supreme vernacular form to which the regional dialects of all the Italian cities contribute, but that is not of any one of them. Chaucer, by using the East Midland dialect of London in his *Canterbury Tales* gave literary status to what would eventually become standard English.

Finally, however, it was the invention of printing that completed the linguistic revolution by which the vernacular languages replaced Latin. By the year 1500, tens of thousands of books had been printed in Germany, Italy, France, and England. Many of these books were in Latin, but most of the really popular books, medieval "best sellers" like the Arthurian romances, were in the vernaculars. As time passed, Latin was relegated to the church and the university and Europeans eagerly read and wrote in their own languages.

Themes IN WORLD LITERATURE

THE QUEST

The quest theme is an old and important one in world literature. The word *quest* ultimately comes from a Latin word meaning "to seek." A quest is a seeking, a search. This search can be a literal one, as when the Mesopotamian hero Gilgamesh (page 9) takes a long journey in order to find the secret of immortality. The theme of the quest can also be used as a **symbol**, as in the medieval romances about the Holy Grail, where the search for a sacred object is meant to convey various religious truths. "Whatever is sought for can be caught," says Creon in *Oedipus the King* (page 165) which concerns a search for a guilty man. But in that play the quester and the guilty man turn out to be the same. A German writer observed that a philosopher "must be like Sophocles's Oedipus, who, seeking enlightenment concerning his terrible fate, pursues his indefatigable enquiry, even when he divines that appalling horror awaits him in the answer. But most of us carry in our heart the Jocasta who begs Oedipus for God's sake not to inquire further."

The Quest for Inner Peace

Like Jocasta, many people pursue the quest for peace of mind. T'ao Ch'ien's "Two Poems on Returning to Dwell in the Country" (page 79) concern a return to Nature. But his poem about his cottage (page 79) is more subtle, because in it the poet shows how he can build his home "among the habitations of men" and still find solitude. What personal qualities are required to achieve such solitude in the crowd? The people in "The Peach-Blossom Fountain" (page 80) live a utopian existence, so much so that they make the fisherman spend his life searching again for their ideal country. Apparently both the land and his quest are symbolic.

Another poem about the desire to return is Archilochus's "How Many Times" (page 158), expressing sailors' nostalgia for home. (Our word *nostalgia* comes from the Greek word *nos-*

tos, which means "a return.") Perhaps we are to be reminded of the reunion of Odysseus and Penélopê in the *Odyssey* (page 126).

The medieval Icelandic poem "The Lay of Thrym" (page 305) is about a quest by the god Thor, for the hammer that Thrym, the king of the giants, has stolen from him. To reacquire his weapon, Thor dresses himself as the goddess Freya in a bridal veil. Perhaps this sort of humor is what the original audience sometimes expected from mythic and heroic materials.

The Quest for Virtue

Dante's *Inferno* (page 316) is, of course, Dante's quest to see, describe, and understand Hell. But Dante is on a journey not merely to tour Hell but also to experience the effects of Hell upon himself. As you read the *Inferno*, consider what Dante is learning as he witnesses the punishments of the sinners. The law of punishment in Dante's Hell is that it is symbolic and grimly appropriate: The man who killed by starving others becomes the food of his victim. Some of the dead, who were for neither good nor evil, are not entitled even to a place in Hell, so they remain forever on its borders. It is poetic justice; the punishment fits the crime. But who exactly is a sinner? Since Dante continued to love his Beatrice even after she married another, how does he feel when he hears the story of the adulterous love of Paolo and Francesca? How do you react when Dante becomes sadistic to Bocca the traitor? The answers to such questions show that Dante's *Inferno* thus becomes a challenge for the reader to learn to understand Dante's kind of poetic justice.

Many medieval romances concern a quest, sometimes a search for the Holy Grail believed in the Middle Ages to have survived from the Last Supper. *Sir Gawain and the Green Knight* (page 340) is a literal quest—Sir Gawain's—for the Green Knight's Chapel. But Gawain is also seeking to test his virtues. A more modern

Miniature from a French manuscript showing Sir Lancelot, on the quest of the Holy Grail, confessing his sins to a hermit living in a wicker hut in a tree. c. 1300. Bodleian Library, Oxford

interpreter might say that Gawain is on a quest for integrity, an attempt to maintain his real self in the presence of temptation. This theme is popular in movies, and in Westerns especially. The 1950s classic, *High Noon*, is an example.

The Quest for Experience

In a line from *Song of Myself*, Whitman says, "I am the man; I suffered; I was there." In the poem "There Was a Child Went Forth" (page 654), he might have said, "I was the child; I experienced; I am here." The poem seems to be a quest for self in relationship to the rest of the world—natural, human, and artificial. We are what we experience, the poem says; and it is worth comparing to the line by Wordsworth, "The Child is father of the Man," because of the way the adult learns from the child in both poems.

Two poems by Cavafy, "The Ides of March" (page 773) and "Ithaka" (page 772), treat subjects inspired by antiquity, the assassination of Caesar and the homecoming of Odysseus in the *Odyssey*. The former poem is a warning to the speaker's soul about ambition and how to treat it. The wisest thing to do if one's soul becomes a Caesar is to listen carefully to those who seek

to bring warnings about danger. (Perhaps Artemidoros, bearing the warning, is the quester in this poem.) The other poem, "Ithaka," concerns a homecoming from the sea, a subject also treated in Archilochus's poem. But as a poem about the quest, it says that the joy is in the voyage, not in the arriving. It redefines the theme of the quest by redefining the concepts of experience and destination. Notice that the poet expands the universality of the poem in its last line by referring not to Ithaka (Odysseus's home) but to "these Ithakas" (the homes we all come home to).

Another poet who examines this theme **ironically** is Vosnesensky, whose "Parabolic Ballad" (page 916) is a witty conception about different ways to undertake a quest. Like Cavafy's "Ithaka," the speaker in Vosnesensky's poem is as much interested in the itinerary as in the destination; and like the Greek poem, the Russian poem makes a statement about the role of women waiting at home for their wanderers. But the Russian poem also concludes with ominous political reference that perhaps makes the whole poem ironic. Once you have noticed this reference, you may want to relate the poem to today's headlines about artists in quest of their right to tell the truth as they see it.

364 *The Middle Ages*

THINKING CRITICALLY
ABOUT LITERATURE

UNIT 3   THE MIDDLE AGES

■ CONCEPT REVIEW

Below begins an excerpt from Canto XXVI of the *Inferno*. The eighth circle of Dante's Hell, called *Malebolge* (mä′lā bōl′jā), "the Evil Ditches," is composed of ten concentric trenches in which sinners guilty of various types of fraud are punished. In reading Cantos XXI-XXII (pages 326–331), which describe the fifth of these ditches, you encountered the grafters swimming in a channel of molten tar. The following selection describes the eighth, which is simply a pit in which those guilty of providing evil counsel wander forever with their souls wrapped in giant flames. There Dante and Virgil come upon Odysseus (Dante uses the Latin form of his name, *Ulysses*) and one of the other Greek heroes of the Trojan War, Diomede. They are being punished for advising the other Greeks to employ deceit and theft to win the war. In Book Eleven of the *Odyssey*, when Odysseus visits the Underworld, the soul of the seer Tiresias makes an obscure reference to the hero's "seaborne death." Using that hint, Dante invented his own version of the death of Odysseus.

On the following pages are notes to help you read the excerpt from Canto XXVI and to review some of the literary terms and thinking skills that have appeared in Unit 3. Page numbers in the notes refer to an application or review of literary terms in the unit. A more extensive discussion of these literary terms appears in the Handbook of Literary Terms. On a separate sheet of paper write your answers to the questions that follow this excerpt.

from the Inferno

Dante Alighieri   *translated by* **John Ciardi**

I stood on the bridge, and leaned out from the edge;
   so far, that but for a jut of rock I held to
   I should have been sent hurtling from the ledge

without being pushed. And seeing me so intent,
5 my Guide said: "There are souls within those flames;
   each sinner swathes himself in his own torment."

"Master," I said, "your words make me more sure,
   but I had seen already that it was so
   and meant to ask what spirit must endure

10 the pains of that great flame which splits away
   in two great horns, as if it rose from the pyre
   where Eteocles and Polynices lay?"

He answered me: "Forever round this path
   Ulysses and Diomede move in such dress,
15 united in pain as once they were in wrath;

there they lament the ambush of the Horse
   which was the door through which the noble seed
   of the Romans issued from its holy source;

there they mourn that for Achilles slain
20 sweet Deidamia weeps even in death;
   there they recall the Palladium in their pain."

"Master," I cried, "I pray you and repray
   till my prayer becomes a thousand—if these souls
   can still speak from the fire, oh let me stay

25 until the flame draws near! Do not deny me:
   You see how fervently I long for it!"
   And he to me: "Since what you ask is worthy,

it shall be. But be still and let me speak;
   for I know your mind already, and they perhaps
30 might scorn your manner of speaking, since they were Greek."

And when the flame had come where time and place
   seemed fitting to my Guide, I heard him say
   these words to it: "O you two souls who pace

together in one flame!—if my days above
35 won favor in your eyes, if I have earned
   however much or little of your love

in writing my High Verses, do not pass by,
   but let one of you be pleased to tell where he,
   having disappeared from the known world, went to die."

■ **Symbol** (page 303 and 338): Note that the evil counselors wrap themselves in great tongues of fire.

■ **Eteocles** (ə tē′ə klēz) **and Polynices** (pol ə nī′cēz): sons of Oedipus, and rivals for the throne of Thebes. They killed each other, and when their bodies were being burned in a single funeral pyre, the flames divided in two, driven apart by the mutual hatred of the dead men.
■ **Horse:** the Trojan Horse

■ **Deidamia** (dā′ə däm′-ē ə): Ulysses persuaded Achilles to fight at Troy, and when the hero was killed, Deidamia, who loved him, was heartbroken.
■ **Palladium** (pə lā′dē əm): Ulysses and Diomede stole Troy's sacred image, a statue of Athena called the Palladium that protected the city.
■ **Characterization** (page 312): Note in lines 22–26 Dante's intense interest in meeting the soul of Ulysses.

40 As if it fought the wind, the greater prong
     of the ancient flame began to quiver and hum;
     then moving its tip as if it were the tongue

   that spoke, gave out a voice above the roar.
     "When I left Circe," it said, "who more than a year
45 detained me near Gaëta long before

   Aeneas came and gave the place that name,
     not fondness for my son, nor reverence
     for my aged father, nor Penelope's claim

   to the joys of love, could drive out of my mind
50   the lust to experience the far-flung world
     and the failings and felicities of mankind.

   I put out on the high and open sea
     with a single ship and only those few souls
     who stayed true when the rest deserted me.

55 As far as Morocco and as far as Spain
     I saw both shores; and I saw Sardinia
     and the other islands of the open main.

   I and my men were stiff and slow with age
     when we sailed at last into the narrow pass
60   where, warning all men back from further voyage,

   Hercules' Pillars rose upon our sight.
     Already I had left Ceuta on the left;
     Seville now sank behind me on the right.

   'Shipmates,' I said, 'who through a hundred thousand
65   perils have reached the West, do not deny
     to the brief remaining watch our senses stand

   experience of the world beyond the sun.
     Greeks! You were not born to live like brutes,
     but to press on toward manhood and recognition!'

70 With this brief exhortation I made my crew
     so eager for the voyage I could hardly
     have held them back from it when I was through;

   and turning our stern toward morning, our bow toward night,
     we bore southwest out of the world of man;
75   we made wings of our oars for our fool's flight.

- **Assonance** (page 295): Note the repeated /ĭ/ sound in the short words in line 42.

- **Gaëta** (gä e'tä): Italian coastal town near the island where the witch Circe (sir'sē) imprisoned Ulysses and his men. Later the Trojan hero Aeneas named the town for his nurse.

- **Alliteration** (page 307): Note the repeated consonant sound in lines 50 and 51.

- **Hercules' Pillars:** The Straits of Gibraltar at the western end of the Mediterranean. Passing them, Ulysses and his men enter the unknown waters of the Atlantic Ocean.
- **Ceuta** (sē ü'tä): city on the African side of the Straits

- **Setting** (page 361): Note the contrast between the setting of Ulysses's adventures and that of his punishment in Hell.

- **Evaluating:** Note that the reaction of the Greek sailors illustrates their evaluation of Ulysses' argument.

That night we raised the other pole ahead
 with all its stars, and ours had so declined
 it did not rise out of its ocean bed.

Five times since we had dipped our bending oars
80 beyond the world, the light beneath the moon
 had waxed and waned, when dead upon our course

we sighted, dark in space, a peak so tall
 I doubted any man had seen the like.
 Our cheers were hardly sounded, when a squall

85 broke hard upon our bow from the new land:
 three times it sucked the ship and the sea about
 as it pleased Another to order and command.

At the fourth, the poop rose and the bow went down
 till the sea closed over us and the light was gone."
 1308–1312

■ **peak:** In Dante's geography, the southern hemisphere is all water, except for the island mountain of Purgatory.

■ **Another:** God

THINK AND DISCUSS
Understanding
1. Describe the kind of punishment imposed on the evil counselors.
2. How does Virgil persuade Ulysses to speak?
3. What terminates Ulysses' voyage into the Atlantic?

Analyzing
4. Explain how "the Horse" (line 16) becomes "the door" to Troy's destruction.
5. What motivates Ulysses to leave everything he had once sought?
6. Why would his journey terrify readers in Dante's era?
7. Explain the way lines 80–81 tell how long the ocean voyage took.

Extending
8. Contrast the goal Homer's Odysseus sought, and the goal which Dante's Ulysses pursues.
9. Do you think that Homer's Odysseus belongs in Hell?

REVIEWING LITERARY TERMS
Symbol
1. How do the flames symbolize the sinners' guilty feelings?

Characterization
2. What does the reader learn about Dante from his strong desire to speak with Ulysses?
3. To what extent do Ulysses' desires, expressed in lines 49–51, parallel Dante's?

Assonance
4. What does the repeated vowel sound in line 42 suggest about the movement of the flame?

Alliteration
5. What is the repeated initial consonant sound which dominates lines 50–51?

Setting
6. Why would the setting for Ulysses' punishment especially pain this man?

■ CONTENT REVIEW

THINKING SKILLS

Classifying

1. Explain how prized things in medieval literature help to distinguish between those who are aggressive and those who are passive.
2. Discuss the different ways that medieval writers used either exaggeration or fantasy for expressive purposes.

Generalizing

3. Describe the typical relationship between king or lord and warrior or vassal in medieval literature.
4. What kind of humor usually appears in these works?
5. Dante puts traitors in the lowest circle of Hell. How do other medieval writers judge this fault?

Synthesizing

6. Explain how obtaining justice, even if that means simply getting revenge, recurs in medieval literature.
7. How do medieval writers use the motif of the journey to define life as a test?

Evaluating

8. Do the medieval writers presented here adequately depict the fole which women play in human society?
9. Do medieval writers tend to judge human failings too severely?

■ COMPOSITION REVIEW

Explaining How Medieval Writers Use Animals

Write a four-paragraph essay which will explain to someone unfamiliar with medieval literature the various ways writers of that period use depictions of animals. Start off by listing for yourself all the references to animals you can recall encountering in Unit III. Then, classify them according to whether the animal has a function in the narrative, helps in picturing the scene, or plays a significant symbolic role. Use those categories as the topics for three paragraphs, and then write a conclusion in which you personally evaluate the effectiveness of these references.

Contrasting Medieval Heroes

Both the *Song of Roland* and *Sir Gawain and the Green Knight* depict medieval heroes, but there are significant differences between them. Write a comparison and contrast paper, to be read by your classmates, in which you explain those differences. List for yourself the contrasting characteristics found in these two men. Organize an essay of four paragraphs in which, following an introduction that describes both in general terms, you devote separate paragraphs to their relationships with women, their most important decisions, and how each of them deals with defeat.

Analyzing the Symbolic Use of Landscape

In the *Song of Roland* and Dante's *Divine Comedy* principal characters move through a landscape rich with **symbolic** implications. Write an essay, to be read by your teacher, in which you analyze how landscape structure and detail add meaning to these poems. Taking a piece of scratch paper, sketch first the battlefield at Roncesvalles and how Roland moves through it, especially as he is dying; and then the shape of Dante's Hell, and the route which he and Virgil follow. On these maps, note places where symbols appear. Then plan out your paper, devoting the first paragraph to an explanation of how landscape can serve a symbolic purpose, followed by four paragraphs, one about the general route taken, another about important symbolic elements encountered, in each of these works.

THE RENAISSANCE 1300–1650

1300	1350	1400	1450

HISTORY AND ARTS

- Papacy to Avignon
- Great Plague
- Great Schism begins
- Vatican Library founded
- Fall of Constantinople

PEOPLE

- Dante dies
- Giotto dies
- Petrarch crowned laureate
- Petrarch dies
- Boccaccio dies
- Gutenberg's printing press
- Da Vinci born
- Erasmus born

LITERATURE

- Boccaccio: *Decameron*
- Petrarch: *Canzoniere*

Detail of 14th-century fresco showing plague victims

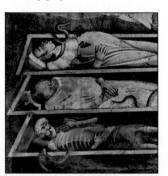

Detail of a leaf from the Gutenberg Bible. c. 1456

Bust of Lorenzo de' Medici by Verrocchio (1435–1488)

1500	1550	1600	1650

Ninety-five Theses •
• Da Vinci: *Mona Lisa*
• Raphael: *School of Athens*
• Michelangelo: Sistine Chapel

• Act of Supremacy
• Calvin's *Institutes*
• Copernican theory
• Vesalius: *On the Structure of the Human Body*
• Council of Trent

• Battle of Lepanto
• Defeat of the Armada
• Jamestown colony

• Columbus to New World
• Da Gama to India
• Lorenzo de' Medici dies

• Magellan's Voyage
• Henry VIII dies
• Elizabeth I becomes queen

• Shakespeare dies

• Machiavelli: *The Prince*
• Rabelais: *Gargantua*
• The Pléiade founded
Globe Theater built •

• Montaigne: *Essays*
• Marlowe: *Dr. Faustus*
• Cervantes: *Don Quixote*
• Shakespeare: *Hamlet*

• Shakespeare: *The Tempest*
• First Folio

Diagram of a helicopter by Da Vinci (1452–1519)

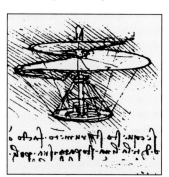

Detail of a late 16th-century view of the Lisbon waterfront

Detail of a view of Jamestown, Virginia. 1607

PREVIEW

UNIT 4   THE RENAISSANCE   1300–1650

Authors
Francesco Petrarch
Giovanni Boccaccio
Niccolò Machiavelli
Pierre de Ronsard
Miguel de Cervantes
William Shakespeare
Christopher Marlowe

Features
Reader's Note: Translating Petrarch
Reading Shakespearean Drama
Comment: Shakespeare and Montaigne
Comment: Shakespeare's Theater—The Globe
The History of Language: The Humanists
   as Translators
Themes in World Literature: The Artist

Application of Literary Terms
sonnet
rhythm
blank verse

Review of Literary Term
plot

Vocabulary Skills
word analogies
archaic words
antonyms

Thinking Skills
generalizing
synthesizing
evaluating

Composition Assignments Include
Writing a Dialogue
Analyzing a Sonnet
Dramatizing a Scene
Writing About Background
Assuming the Role of a Character
Comparing and Contrasting Two Poems
Analyzing a Character's Role
Writing Drama Criticism
Writing an Interior Monologue
Comparing and Contrasting Scenes
Analyzing a Speech
Writing a Thumbnail Biography
Writing a Character Analysis
Analyzing Women's Roles
Writing About Motivation
Discussing a Theme
Writing Persuasively

Enrichment
Researching Petrarch's Sonnets
Readers Theater
Comparing Shakespeare's Illustrators
Listening to Music
Reading Closely
Staging *The Tempest*

Thinking Critically About Literature
Concept Review
Content Review
Composition Review

THE RENAISSANCE   1300–1650

There are many different, sometimes conflicting, definitions of the Renaissance, but for our purpose we can define it as the rebirth of humanity's belief in its potential, based on what was learned from newly discovered or newly available manuscripts from ancient Greece and Rome. It began in Italy during the early years of the fourteenth century and then gradually spread throughout Europe, increasing its impact in new areas as it died down in older ones.

Although we do not know specifically what triggered this cultural rebirth, we do know that a number of factors had been at work near the end of the Middle Ages, and that they prepared the way for the Renaissance and then affected it after it had begun. Among these factors were the return of the Crusaders from the Near East, and the interest resulting from their stories of Islamic culture; the recovery from Islamic sources of the manuscripts of many of Aristotle's works, and the excitement this caused in learned circles; the growth of trade with the Near East and Africa, and the knowledge of other countries that it brought to the leading trading centers, largely in Italy; the accumulation in some of the Italian city-states of great wealth from this trade, which encouraged peasants to leave the land to seek their fortunes in the cities; the periodic plagues and famines that killed twenty percent of Europe's population and left the survivors in an unsettled mood that was ripe for change; and the decline of feudalism, especially in Italy, where it had never had a strong foothold.

THE EARLY RENAISSANCE

It was natural that the Renaissance should have begun in Italy. The Crusaders passed through Italy as they made their way to and from the Near East; their trade with the Near East and Africa made Italians aware of what was going on elsewhere in the world; its major city-states had the wealth to support literary and artistic creativity; and it was not tied to the feudal system. Further, since the Renaissance began with the rediscovery of Greek and Roman literature, it is logical that more Roman manuscripts would be preserved in Italy than elsewhere.

In any event, the Renaissance began early in the fourteenth century in the Italian city-state of Florence. (See the map on page 377.) It began with a renewed interest in the literature of Greece and Rome—particularly that of Rome, since many more Italians knew Latin than knew Greek. For centuries the Catholic Church had preserved this literature in cathedral and monastery libraries. Members of the clergy studied and copied the manuscripts, but there was apparently little or no interest in them outside the Church. The situation changed markedly in the early 1300s as scholars who were not members of the clergy discovered the manuscripts and read them. What they found was a wealth of material—poetry and drama, ideas about government, law, medicine, science—all that had survived of the accumulated wisdom of Greece and Rome. From this they realized what humanity had done in the past and what it was capable of doing, and were encouraged to try to reach, build upon, and surpass the civilization of Greece and Rome. The creative energy that was released expanded over the years into many fields: literature, art, philosophy, government, education, religion, exploration—practically the entire range of human endeavor.

Scholars who took an interest in the literature and life of classical Greece and Rome were known as humanists. Humanism derives its name from Cicero's term *humanitas*, by which he meant the type of education that emphasized the full worth of humanity, specifically the study of literature and philosophy. The early humanists did not forsake religion; indeed, many of them were members of the clergy, but to their religious beliefs they added a belief in humanity itself and in the things humanity was capable of accomplishing.

Francesco Petrarch (1304–1374), an early Florentine scholar, is known as "the first humanist." Probably he did more than anyone else to arouse interest in the ancient manuscripts. He searched for them himself and then either bought or copied them, adding them to his growing library; he even attempted to correct centuries of scribal errors by comparing several manuscripts of the same work. Besides his accomplishments as a scholar, Petrarch developed what is known today as the Italian or Petrarchan sonnet.

During the early years of the Renaissance there was a shortage of scholars who could understand Greek manuscripts and translate them into Latin. Giovanni Boccaccio (1313–1375), a friend of Petrarch and like him a collector of manuscripts, studied Greek and helped to support a Greek scholar at the University of Florence so that Homer could be translated into Latin and made available to those who did not understand Greek.

Interest in ancient manuscripts led to interest in the ruins and artifacts of antiquity, which in turn served as an impetus for the development of Renaissance art. Without wealth to support artists in their work, there could have been no artistic Renaissance. Florence was wealthy, so art flourished there. When the rich Italian city-states were not warring over disputed territory, they competed to see which could produce the best art. During the early Renaissance, this competition led to the great paintings of Giotto, Fra Angelico, and Filippo Lippi, to the sculptures of Donatello, and to the architecture of Brunelleschi.

Italian city-states were nests of intrigue as wealthy and powerful families strove for political dominance. Florence produced the Medici, Milan the Sforzas, Ferrara the Estes, and Rome the Borgias. Technically a republic, Florence actually was ruled by its wealthy merchant class. After 1434 Cosimo de' Medici dominated the government of Florence with the consent of the populace, effectively ending the republic. He ruled until 1464. Like many other Florentines, Cosimo was a humanist. He had studied the classics, and he collected manuscripts from as far away as Alexandria. In fact, he kept forty-five copyists busy transcribing manuscripts. He also managed to find the time and resources to support Florentine artists in their work.

Late in 1347, carried from the East by Genoese ships that docked in Sicily with their stricken crews, the Black Death reached Europe. Plague spread rapidly, killing an estimated one-third to one-half of the population of Europe in the Great Plague of 1348. Petrarch lost the Laura he celebrated in his sonnets to the 1348 plague, and his son to a later one; Boccaccio lost the Fiammetta of his early works to the 1348 plague, but this did not prevent him from using it as the setting for his *Decameron*. While the immediate effect of the plague on Europe was disastrous, in the long run it accelerated the movement of serfs from the land to the cities and larger towns and hastened the end of feudalism.

THE MIDDLE YEARS

The middle period of the Renaissance was characterized by a spirit of adventure and exploration, and the arts continued to flourish, especially in Italy. In fact, Italian culture, which had dominated Europe during the early Renaissance, was to continue to do so, not giving way to the art and literature of France, Spain, and England until later.

During the second half of the fifteenth century the Renaissance reached its height in Italy, but then declined rapidly due to some of the very factors that had helped to establish it there. Italy lacked a strong central government, and its loose structure of independent city-states made it vulnerable to its stronger neighbors. France and Spain used northern Italy for a battleground, fighting four wars there, and in 1527 Rome itself was sacked by an army of mercenaries in the pay of the Holy Roman Emperor. In addition, with the discovery of the New World and a new route to India around Africa, Eur-

Detail of Raphael's fresco *The School of Athens*. 1510–1511. Vatican Palace, Rome
The two figures standing under the arch are Plato (on the left) and Aristotle.

ope's trading centers moved westward, to countries bordering the Atlantic Ocean, and Italy's major source of wealth gradually dried up.

Despite these problems, however, the middle years of the Renaissance produced many artworks recognized today as masterpieces. These include the paintings of Da Vinci, Michelangelo, Titian, and Raphael, and the sculptures of Michelangelo. Machiavelli's *The Prince* (pages 394–400), written in 1513 and based on his observations of politics in the Italian city-states and elsewhere, describes the characteristics a ruler must have to gain and hold power. The middle period of the Renaissance was the golden age of humanism. Because scholarship was international, with Latin as its universal language, news of the discovery of manuscripts spread rapidly, often outstripping other aspects of the Renaissance in moving across Europe.

Many of the rulers of the Italian city-states were humanists. Foremost among them was Lorenzo de' Medici, who ruled Florence from 1469 to 1492 and was known as Lorenzo the Magnificent for his patronage of the arts. Several popes were humanists, such as Nicholas V, who became Pope in 1447 and found one ancient manuscript himself. He sent agents to Constantinople, Germany, and England seeking to buy or copy manuscripts, and kept a corps of translators busy working on them. Eventually his collection contained five thousand volumes and led to the construction of the Vatican Library.

Near the end of the fifteenth century, humanism reached England, making itself felt first in education. Some English humanists traveled to Italy to experience the Renaissance at first hand. The most famous of these scholars, the Oxford Group, introduced the "new learning" (humanism) into Oxford in the 1490s, and just a decade later the greatest humanist of all, Erasmus of Rotterdam, was teaching Greek at Cambridge. Erasmus, a Catholic priest, spent most of his life traveling through Europe, lecturing at various universities and sharing his knowledge of classical studies. He made at least four trips to England and helped to strengthen the Renaissance there.

Without Gutenberg's invention of a method of printing by using movable type, the Renaissance would not have spread so quickly, nor would it have been able to affect so many people. The new printing press meant that manuscripts no longer had to be copied painstakingly by hand; instead, multiple copies could be printed and distributed. To understand the importance of the printing press only a few statistics are needed. In 1450 Gutenberg set up his first press in Mainz. When this was foreclosed, he set up another in 1456. By 1490, just thirty-four years later, there were printers in Germany, France, Italy, Holland, Switzerland, Hungary, Spain, England, Denmark, Sweden, and the Byzantine Empire (Constantinople). People clamored for books. In Germany alone between 1453 and 1500—that is, before the Protestant Reformation—the Vulgate Bible was printed in twenty-six editions.

One of the outgrowths of the Renaissance faith in human potential was an adventurous spirit that led to the Age of Discovery. First came the discovery of the New World by Christopher Columbus in 1492; just five years later, in 1497, Vasco da Gama, sailing from Portugal, found an all-water route to India around the southern tip of Africa, making it no longer necessary to use the long and dangerous overland route. The last major achievement was the circumnavigation of the globe. In 1519 Ferdinand Magellan left Spain with a fleet of ships and nearly three hundred men. In 1522 one ship returned with eighteen men of the original group, and Magellan was not among them—however, one ship *had* completed the journey and it led the way for others.

In 1517, when Martin Luther posted his 95 Theses on a church door in Wittenberg, the Protestant Reformation began. Thirteen years later, in 1530, the Augsburg Confession established Lutheranism as the official Protestant church in most German states. In 1531, by a decree of Parliament, Henry VIII became supreme head of the Church and clergy in England, and Anglicanism became its official religion. The last of the three major Protestant denominations began in 1536, when John Calvin's *Institutes* was published, leading the way to Calvinism.

It took less than twenty years for the three Protestant denominations to break free of the Catholic Church. However, for two centuries before Martin Luther, the Church had been losing power. The move of the papacy from Rome to Avignon in southern France in 1305 was the first step in a long chain of events. Sometimes called the Babylonian Captivity of the Church, this "exile" continued until 1378. Then, from 1378 to 1414, during the Great Schism, there were two popes, one in Avignon and one in Rome. In 1414, with the ascension of Gregory XI to the papacy, there was again only one pope, and he was in Rome. But the papacy had been severely weakened, and the Renaissance belief in the ability of human beings to control their own affairs and their own destiny weakened the Church's power still further. Abuses that had existed within the Church for years worsened. Popes became caught up in Italy's internal wars and in the nationalistic struggles of the day, as one country after another sought to take away the powers of the papacy.

With the coming of the Reformation, the Church attempted to amend its internal affairs. A series of meetings of the Council of Trent from 1545 to 1563 made recommendations, and the Catholic Church launched its own Counter-Reformation.

As might be expected, Renaissance thought led to a new interest in science and medicine, and this interest spread beyond Italy. The English humanist Thomas Linacre translated the medical works of Galen and made them generally available, and in 1543 Andreas Vesalius, a Belgian, published *On the Structure of the Human Body*, complete with 277 woodcuts to supplement its text. The book, which was based on dissection, revised the existing science of anatomy and established the physical basis of modern medicine. Leonardo da Vinci, truly a multi-faceted Renaissance man, was interested in science and invention as well as painting, and anticipated in many ways such later inventions as the airplane. Interestingly, in his own day he was known more as an engineer than as a painter. In 1543 Nicholas Copernicus, a Pole, published *On the Revolutions of the Celestial Orbs*, completely overthrowing the Ptolemaic theory that the earth was the center of the universe.

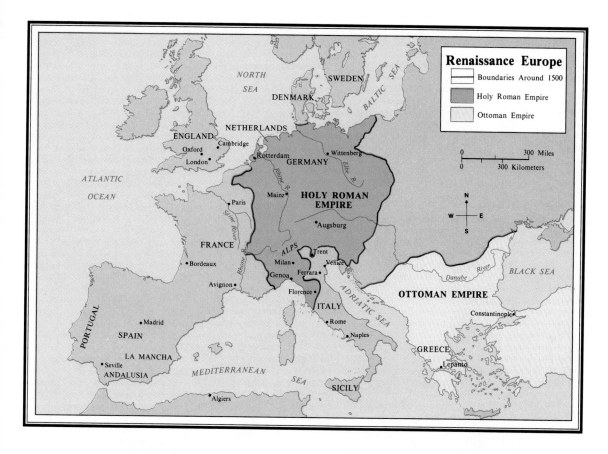

Renaissance Europe

Boundaries Around 1500
Holy Roman Empire
Ottoman Empire

THE LATE RENAISSANCE

By 1550 the Renaissance in Italy had nearly run its course. Its energy had moved westward to France, Spain, and England, countries which were just beginning to feel its effects. Most of Italy was under Spanish control by 1550. In addition, the loss of wealth from its once strong trading centers meant that far less money was available to sponsor artists. Tintoretto and Veronese, the great artists of this period, were both dead by 1600. The late years of the Italian Renaissance also produced the astronomer Galileo (1564–1642). He was the first to employ the telescope, which had been recently invented in the Netherlands, to study the celestial bodies. His first observations, made in late 1609 and early 1610, provided visual proof of the Copernican theory.

The Renaissance was carried back to France by soldiers in the French armies that invaded Italy in the first half of the sixteenth century.

What was disastrous for the Italian Renaissance was thus beneficial to the French Renaissance. In France, however, the original impetus of the Renaissance was toward trade and colonization. The arts flourished later and never reached the level of those of Renaissance Italy. In literature, Ronsard and the other poets who constituted the group known as the *Pléiade* based their work on classical models. In fiction, Rabelais wrote *Gargantua*, a sprawling and irreverent novel. But the major French literary achievement of the period, however, was Montaigne's *Essays*, which introduced a new literary type to the world.

The impact of the Renaissance on Spain was somewhat different. Its early years were marked by voyages to the New World, but parts of the country remained essentially medieval. In literature the Spanish Renaissance produced two great dramatists, Calderon and Lope de Vega; in fiction it produced Miguel de Cervantes, whose

Velázquez, *The Maids of Honor*. 1656. Prado, Madrid. The painting shows the artist in his studio working on a portrait of the members of the Spanish royal family. The princess who has just posed for him is shown among her playmates and maids of honor. The faces of the king and queen can be seen in the mirror on the back wall.

378 *The Renaissance*

Don Quixote is one of the world's great books. Spanish painting too did well in the Renaissance, with such artists as El Greco and Velázquez producing their masterpieces.

The English Renaissance had begun as early as the 1490s, when the Oxford Group of English humanists, aided by their friend Erasmus, brought the Greek language and classical literature to the universities of Oxford and Cambridge. Like the Spanish and French, the English felt the Renaissance desire for adventure and did their own exploring of the New World. In 1588 England's sovereignty on the seas was assured when the English fleet defeated the Spanish Armada. In 1607 the English established their first permanent New World settlement at Jamestown. In the arts, poetry and drama were foremost. The English Renaissance was the age of Shakespeare and Marlowe, of Sidney and Spenser. Even Queen Elizabeth I and her courtiers wrote poetry and considered it one of the accomplishments of educated people.

THE HERITAGE OF THE RENAISSANCE

The Renaissance has left humanity a rich heritage. We who live in America are indebted to its adventurous spirit for discovering and colonizing our homeland. Our art museums contain Renaissance paintings for us to admire, and we can buy reproductions of these paintings for our homes. To the Renaissance too we owe much of our great literature. Shakespeare's plays live on the stage today as they did in the Elizabethan age; the modern novel owes much to both Boccaccio and Cervantes; the modern essay began with Montaigne; and modern politicians still read Machiavelli.

But we are indebted to the Renaissance also for things that we do not see. Our religious freedom came about indirectly from the Reformation, and our American desire for self-realization and personal independence can be traced to Renaissance ideas.

THINKING ABOUT GRAPHIC AIDS
Using the Time Line

The time line on pages 371–372 shows the chronological sequence of the historical and literary events discussed in Unit 4. Use the time line to answer the following questions.

1. Could Gutenberg have printed Machiavelli's *The Prince?*
2. About how many years elapsed between the discovery of America and the founding of the Jamestown colony?
3. Which of the following Florentines died during the Great Plague? (**a**) Petrarch; (**b**) Boccaccio; (**c**) Machiavelli; (**d**) none of them
4. Could a Spanish sailor have served both at Lepanto and with the Armada?
5. When the Globe Theater was built, which of the following plays could have been performed there? (**a**) *Doctor Faustus;* (**b**) *Hamlet;* (**c**) *The Tempest*

Using the Map

The map on page 377 shows Europe and adjacent areas. Use the map to answer the following questions.

1. What does the residence of the popes at Avignon indicate about the dominant political influence on the papacy in the early fourteenth century?
2. Why would northern Italy have been a likely battleground for French and Spanish troops?
3. Which of the following cities was not located within the boundaries of the Holy Roman Empire? (**a**) Wittenberg; (**b**) Bordeaux; (**c**) Mainz
4. Why was the geographical position of Portugal an advantage for voyages around Africa to India in the late fifteenth century?
5. Off the coast of which of the following countries did the battle of Lepanto take place? (**a**) Spain; (**b**) Italy; (**c**) Greece

BIOGRAPHY

Francesco Petrarch
1304–1374

"Father of the Renaissance," "First Humanist," "First Modern Man"— these titles, all applied to Petrarch, give some idea of his importance to his period. That importance has two facets: first, his poetry, chiefly, the sonnets inspired by his love for Laura; second, his interest in the manuscripts of ancient Greece and Rome that made him a leading humanist.

Petrarch was born in Arezzo, where his father had settled temporarily after being banished from Florence for political reasons. Later the family moved to Avignon, where Petrarch's father found a position at the Papal Court. In 1319 Petrarch's father sent him and his brother Gherardo to Montpellier and later to Bologna to study law. Petrarch detested the law, but was able to pursue his interest in the classics, reading Cicero, Seneca, and Virgil, perfecting his writing style, and developing the love of scholarship that never left him.

At the death of their parents in 1326, the brothers returned to Avignon, where Petrarch found employment at the Papal Court. A year later, on April 6, 1327, while attending mass at the Church of St. Clare, Petrarch saw Laura and fell in love with her. The persistence of that love for twenty years, until Laura's death in the Great Plague of 1348, inspired Petrarch to write the sonnets and other poems later collected in his *Cazoniere*—366 poems in all, most of them addressed to Laura. The Laura of Petrarch's sonnets was golden-haired, beautiful, and rich. No one knows for certain who Laura was, but many scholars think that she was Laure de Noves, the wife of Hugues de Sade. Records show that Laure died in the plague. Sometime after first seeing Laura, Petrarch began his travels, often on government business, always in search of old manuscripts. When he was not traveling, Petrarch lived a retired life at Vaucluse, near Avignon, composing his poems to Laura and also writing extensively in Latin. His work bore fruit and he became famous, his love poems circulating in manuscript throughout Italy. In 1341 he was summoned to Rome and crowned with the poet's laurel wreath, the first person to be so honored since ancient times.

In the meantime, Petrarch's interest in classicism, in the literature and life of ancient Greece and Rome, made him the first humanist. Besides searching for lost manuscripts himself, he encouraged his friends to do so. When he found a manuscript he bought it, or if it were not for sale, transcribed it or hired a copyist to transcribe it. Petrarch was traveling in Italy when the news of Laura's death reached him. As might be expected, he went through a spiritual crisis. His brother had become a monk, and for a time Petrarch apparently considered making a similar decision. However, he resumed his life and his travels, and in 1350 met Boccaccio in Florence. Sharing similar interests, the two became lifelong friends. In 1351–1352 Petrarch was back in Vaucluse for the last time. During the next twenty years or so he lived in Milan, Venice, and Padua, finally buying a farm in Arqua, near Padua, where he died in 1374.

See SONNET in the Handbook of Literary Terms, page 971.

It Was the Morning

translated by **Joseph Auslander**

It was the morning of that blessèd day[1]
Whereon the Sun in pity veiled his glare
For the Lord's agony, that, unaware,
I fell a captive, Lady, to the sway

5 Of your swift eyes: that seemed no time to
     stay
The strokes of Love: I stepped into the snare
Secure, with no suspicion: then and there
I found my cue in man's most tragic play.

Love caught me naked[2] to his shaft, his
     sheaf,
10 The entrance for his ambush and surprise
Against the heart wide open through the
     eyes,

The constant gate and fountain of my grief:
How craven so to strike me stricken so,
Yet from you fully armed conceal his bow!

                                    1360

---

1. *that blessèd day,* Good Friday.
2. *naked,* without armor.

Blest Be the Day

translated by **Joseph Auslander**

Blest be the day, and blest the month and
     year,
Season and hour and very moment blest,
The lovely land and place where first
     possessed
By two pure eyes I found me prisoner;

5 And blest the first sweet pain, the first most
     dear,
Which burnt my heart when Love came in
     as guest;
And blest the bow, the shafts which shook
     my breast,
And even the wounds which Love delivered
     there.

Blest be the words and voices which filled
     grove
10 And glen with echoes of my Lady's name;
The sighs, the tears, the fierce despair of
     love;

And blest the sonnet-sources of my fame;
And blest that thought of thoughts which is
     her own,
Of her, her only, of herself alone!

                                    1360

Alas, That Gentle Look

translated by **Morris Bishop**

Alas, that gentle look and that fair face!
Alas for the body's beauty when you wended
your gracious way! Alas, your words that
    mended
the brutal, and taught honor to the base!
5 Alas, that smile of yours, whose wounding
    grace
has come to death, and all my hope is ended!
You'd have been queen of earth, had you
    descended
to a younger world, to a less evil race!

Still I must burn in you, in you respire.
10 I was yours utterly; my stricken heart
can feel no other hurt, after today.
You showered hope upon me and desire
in our last moment, ere we came to part.
And then the wind blew all your words away.

1360

Life Hurries On

translated by **Morris Bishop**

Life hurries on, a frantic refugee,
and death, with great forced marches,
    follows fast,
and all the present leagues with all the past
and all the future to make war on me.
5 Anticipation joins with memory
tearing my soul in torment; and at last,
did not damnation set me so aghast,
I'd put an end to thinking, and be free.

The few glad moments that my heart has
    known
10 return to me; and now I watch in dread
the winds upgathering against my ways,[1]
storm in the harbor, and the pilot prone,
the mast and rigging down; and dark and
    dead
the lovely lights whereon I used to gaze.

1360

---

1. *ways*, timbers on which a ship is built and launched.

The Eyes I Spoke of Once

Translated by **Anthony Mortimer**

The eyes I spoke of once in words that burn,
the arms and hands and feet and lovely face
that took me from myself for such a space
of time and marked me out from other men;

5 the waving hair of unmixed gold that shone,
the smile that flashed with the angelic rays
that used to make this earth a paradise,
are now a little dust, all feeling gone;

and yet I live, grief and disdain to me,
10 left where the light I cherished never shows,
in fragile bark on the tempestuous sea.

Here let my loving song come to a close,
the vein of my accustomed art is dry,
and this, my lyre, turned at last to tears.[1]

1360

---

1. *lyre . . . tears*, a reference to Job 30:31, "My lyre is turned to mourning."

Go, Grieving Rimes of Mine

translated by **Morris Bishop**

Go, grieving rimes of mine, to that hard
    stone
Whereunder lies my darling, lies my dear,
And cry to her to speak from heaven's
    sphere.
Her mortal part with grass is overgrown.

5 Tell her, I'm sick of living; that I'm blown
By winds of grief from the course I ought to
    steer,
That praise of her is all my purpose here
And all my business; that of her alone

Do I go telling, that how she lived and died
10 And lives again in immortality,
All men may know, and love my Laura's
    grace.

Oh, may she deign to stand at my bedside
When I come to die; and may she call to me
And draw me to her in the blessèd place!

                1360

I Keep Lamenting Over Days Gone By

translated by **Anthony Mortimer**

I keep lamenting over days gone by,[1]
the time I spent loving a mortal thing,
with no attempt to soar, although my wing
might give no mean example in the sky.[2]

5 You that my foul unworthy sins descry,
unseen and everlasting, heaven's King,
succor my soul, infirm and wandering,
and what is lacking let your grace supply;

so if I lived in tempest and in war,
10 I die in port and peace; however vain
the stay, at least the parting may be fair.

Now in the little life that still remains
and at my death may your quick hand be
    near:
in others, you well know, my hope is gone.

                1360

---

1. This is Petrarch's last sonnet, and the next-to-last poem
in the *Canzoniere*, which ends with a poem to the Virgin.
2. The humility of the recantation is rendered more poignant by this lingering touch of human pride. Love for the
"mortal thing" has been an obstacle to salvation, but there
is also the explicit regret that it has prevented him from
demonstrating his true worth in the eyes of the world.

Detail of the marginal ornament of an illuminated
manuscript of Petrarch's poems showing a portrait
of Laura. 1470. Bibliothèque Inguimbertine,
Carpentras, France

Reader's Note

Translating Petrarch

On the facing page are four translations of the sonnet by Petrarch that appears in the original Italian below. The first, an early example of the English sonnet, was written by the Earl of Surrey (1517–1547) about two hundred years after Petrarch's original; the last three, demonstrating modern approaches, were written about six hundred years after it. All of the translators, however, faced the same problem. Italian words are easy to rhyme, but English words aren't. It is very difficult to write English poetry in the Italian sonnet format.

Amor, che nel penser mio vive e regna
e 'l suo seggio maggior nel mio cor tene,
talor armato ne la fronte vene;
ivi si loca et ivi pon sua insegna.

5 Quella ch'amare e sofferir ne 'nsegna,
e vol che 'l gran desio, l'accesa spene,
ragion, vergogna e reverenza affrene,
di nostro ardir fra se stessa si sdegna.

Onde Amor paventoso fugge al core,
10 lasciando ogni sua impresa, e piange e trema;
ivi s' asconde e non appar più fore.

Che poss' io far, temendo il mio signore,
se non star seco infin a l' ora estrema?
Ché bel fin fa chi ben amando more.

The four translations show four different approaches to the problem. Surrey uses the English sonnet format, less restrictive because it allows more rhyming words. Armi uses a variation of the Italian sonnet, with only the first four lines in the English mode. Durling follows a totally modern route, using only twelve lines and writing free verse. His poem does have a certain regularity, as most of his lines contain fifteen syllables. Mortimer returns to the Italian sonnet form, but encounters the problem of finding English rhymes to conform to its pat-

tern—and turns this problem to an artistic advantage by having his irregularities occur in the first and last lines of his sonnet: *reigns* should rhyme with *maintain, pain,* and *disdain; right* should rhyme with *out* to complete the *cdecde* rhyme scheme of the sestet.

In Petrarch's original, the thought division occurs at the end of the octave, the first eight lines of the sonnet. Because the translators are following his sense, their thought division occurs in the same place, whether it be the end of the second quatrain of Surrey's English sonnet or the end of the sixth line of Durling's free verse translation. Stated simply, the thought division is the following: the octave ends with the lady's (Laura's) anger or disdain because the poet (Petrarch) has been too ardent in displaying his love; the sestet (the last six lines of the poem) explains the poet's reaction: in fear of her anger, he will hide his love in his heart and keep it there until he dies.

We might expect the Surrey translation to be difficult because it was written four hundred years earlier than the modern translations, but Surrey's approach is also somewhat different. In the sonnets "It Was the Morning" and "Blest Be the Day" (page 381), both written earlier than "Amor, Che Nel Penser Mio Vive e Regna," Petrarch claims to have been wounded by Love. The Surrey translation draws on the earlier sonnets to show that Love and the poet are still at odds. In line 2 he uses "*captive* breast" where all the other translators use "heart." In line 3, all translators show Love as armed or in armor; Surrey alone adds that the armor is that in which Love *fought* the poet. In line 5, all the other translators use the plural to show a close relationship between the poet and Love, but Surrey uses the singular; it is the poet, not Love, that suffers the pain. Only Surrey refers to Love as a coward (line 9), and only Surrey claims to be an innocent sufferer because of Love's guilt (line 12). All four translators have evidently read Petrarch's sonnet sequence; Armi even adds (line 4) the bow and dart referred to in the earlier sonnets.

Henry Howard, Earl of Surrey (1557)

Love, that liveth and reigneth in my
    thought,
That built his seat within my captive breast,
Clad in the arms, wherein with me he fought,
Oft in my face he doth his banner rest.
5 She, that me taught to love, and suffer pain,
My doubtful hope, and eke[1] my hot desire,
With shamefast cloak to shadow and refrain,
Her smiling face converteth straight to ire.
And coward love then to the heart apace
10 Taketh his flight, whereas he lurks, and
    plains[2]
His purpose lost, and dare not show his face.
For my lord's guilt thus faultless bide I
    pains.[3]
Yet from my lord shall not my foot remove.
Sweet is his death, that takes his end by love.

---

1. *eke,* also.
2. *plains,* complains or laments.
3. *bide I pains,* I suffer.

Anna Maria Armi (1946)

Love who within my thought does live and
    reign,
Who keeps his favored seat inside my heart,
Sometimes likes on my forehead to remain,
And there in arms displays his bow and dart.

5 She who taught us to love and suffer pain,
Who demands that desire and ardent hope
Be bound by reason, within worship's scope,
Feels for our daring an inner disdain.

Hence Love in fright again to the heart flies,
10 Abandoning all tasks, and tries to hide,
Trembles and weeps and comes no more
    outside.

What can I do, who fear my master's power,
But stay with him until the final hour?
Because he ends well who well loving dies.

Robert M. Durling (1976)

Love, who lives and reigns in my thought
    and keeps his principal
seat in my heart, sometimes comes forth all
    in armor into my
forehead, there camps, and there sets up his
    banner.

She who teaches us to love and to be patient,
    and wishes my
5 great desire, my kindled hope, to be reined
    in by reason, shame,
and reverence, at our boldness is angry
    within herself.

Wherefore Love flees terrified to my heart,
    abandoning his every
enterprise, and weeps and trembles; there
    he hides and no more appears outside.

10 What can I do, when my lord is afraid,
    except stay with him
until the last hour? For he makes a good end
    who dies loving well.

Anthony Mortimer (1977)

Love, who within my thoughts still lives and
    reigns
and in my heart keeps his chief residence,
sometimes into my brow makes armed
    advance,
to plant his banner and his camp maintain.

5 Then she who teaches us both love and pain,
and wills that burning hope, desire intense,
be checked by reason, shame, and reverence,
receives our ardor with a deep disdain.

So fearful Love turns to the heart in flight,
10 leaving his enterprise, to weep and cower;
and there he hides and dare not venture out.

What can I do, seeing my master's fright,
except stay with him to the final hour?
His death is fair whose love is in the right.

Francesco Petrarch

THINK AND DISCUSS

Understanding

1. Describe the circumstances of Petrarch's first sight of Laura.

Analyzing

2. What can you infer about Laura's character from the descriptions given in the sonnets?
3. Why does Petrarch personify Love as a coward in lines 13–14 of "It Was the Morning"?
4. Explain how "Blest Be the Day" shows greater depth of feeling than does "It Was the Morning."
5. What is the metaphor expressed in line 14 of "Alas, That Gentle Look"? How effective is this line in conveying despair? Explain.
6. "Life Hurries On" is unusually rich in **figurative language,** language that sets up a relationship between essentially unlike things. It includes among other figures of speech **personification** (the assignment of human traits to something that is not human) and **metaphor.** There are seven instances of personification in the octave of "Life Hurries On." What are they? What is the major metaphor of the sestet?
7. "Alas, That Gentle Look," "Life Hurries On," "The Eyes I Spoke of Once," and "Go, Grieving Rimes" all deal with Petrarch's reaction to Laura's death. Trace the development of his grief and mourning in the poems.
8. "I Keep Lamenting" contrasts with the other sonnets written after Laura's death. Explain how this is so.

Extending

9. Do you think that Petrarch was really in love with Laura, or do the sonnets read more like an academic exercise? Explain.

APPLYING: Sonnet H▲
See Handbook of Literary Terms, p. 971.

A **sonnet** is a lyric poem of fourteen lines in iambic pentameter (ten syllables to a line, with the stress on every second syllable). The Italian or Petrarchan sonnet is usually rhymed *abbaabba/cdecde,* with variations possible in the *cdecde* rhyme scheme. Conforming to the division of the rhyme scheme, the first eight lines, or octave, usually state the problem or thought; the last six lines, or sestet, resolve or elaborate on it.

1. What is the rhyme scheme of "Alas, That Gentle Look"?
2. With what problem or thought does the octave deal?
3. How is that problem or thought either resolved or elaborated in the sestet?

COMPOSITION ◄━●
Writing a Dialogue

Imagine that Petrarch is telling you in his own words (prose, not poetry) the story contained in the sonnets you have read. Write this in the form of a dialogue between you and the poet. You ask the questions and make comments, and he responds. Assume that your classmates are the audience for this dialogue. Your dialogue should be about as long as a three-paragraph composition.

Analyzing a Sonnet

Select any sonnet but "Alas, That Gentle Look" and analyze it with regard to rhyme scheme, thought division, artistry, meaning, sincerity, and so forth. Take notes and organize your thoughts into a three- to five-paragraph essay in which you analyze the sonnet. See "Writing About Poetry and Poetic Devices" in the Writer's Handbook.

ENRICHMENT
Researching Petrarch's Sonnets

If you wish to research to learn more about Petrarch's sonnets, you have two choices: (1) read more of them to determine what they add to those you have already read; (2) find several different translations of the same sonnet and compare them. You may use the Reader's Note on pages 384–385 as a guide. In either case, report the results orally to the class.

Like his friend Petrarch, Boccaccio (bō kä′chē ō) was an important figure in the Renaissance. He made valuable contributions through his writing, his scholarship, and his assistance in locating old manuscripts and having them translated. It was he who helped to support a Greek scholar to translate Homer into Latin.

The illegitimate son of a merchant, Boccaccio grew up in Florence. When he was in his early teens his father, intending that he too become a merchant, sent him to Naples to study commerce and law. Boccaccio was dissatisfied with both. Eventually he found his career in writing and scholarship, probably entering into some sort of employment at the court of the King of Naples. While at church, he saw Maria d'Aquino, the illegitimate daughter of the king, and fell in love with her. She became the Fiammetta of several of his works. The similarity to Petrarch's meeting with Laura is obvious; a second similarity is that Maria died in the same plague that killed Laura.

By the time Boccaccio returned to Florence, in 1340 or 1341, his writing career was well launched. He lived in Florence for the rest of his life, representing the Florentine government on missions throughout northern Italy. He also continued to write and to deepen his scholarship. From about 1351 to 1353, Boccaccio worked on *The Decameron,* the book for which he is most famous. In his later years he devoted himself to more serious writing in Latin and to a biography of Dante. In 1373 he was honored by being appointed lecturer on Dante at the University of Florence. He died two years later.

The Decameron, Boccaccio's masterpiece, was an important forerunner of the modern novel. It consisted of a hundred short tales and novellas (works of fiction longer than a short story but shorter than a novel). For his background Boccaccio selected what was probably the most important and disastrous event of the fourteenth century, the Great Plague.

In the frame story, the device that weaves the hundred stories together, Boccaccio has seven young women and three young men, close relatives of some of the women, flee from Florence to escape the plague. Attended by a number of servants, they retire to the country, where they decide to while away some of the time by telling stories, one story apiece for ten days, for a total of a hundred. On eight of the ten days a theme is assigned for the stories—a neat device by Boccaccio to make his book more cohesive. Some of the tales were original, others were in common circulation. What Boccaccio does is to make them remarkably realistic by painting in background detail, providing natural dialogue, and occasionally displaying real insight into character. The ten young people of the frame story are named, characterized, and allowed to enjoy their storytelling.

The story of Federigo's Falcon, which follows, is generally regarded as the best in *The Decameron.* It is told by Filomena, one of the women, on the fifth day, which has for its **theme** stories with a happy ending for lovers who have been through unfortunate experiences.

from The Decameron

Giovanni Boccaccio   *translated by* **Mark Musa** *and* **Peter Bondanella**

Federigo's Falcon

There was once in Florence a young man named Federigo, the son of Messer Filippo Alberighi, renowned above all other men in Tuscany for his prowess in arms and for his courtliness. As often happens to most gentlemen, he fell in love with a lady named Monna[1] Giovanna, in her day considered to be one of the most beautiful and one of the most charming women that ever there was in Florence; and in order to win her love, he participated in jousts and tournaments, organized and gave feasts, and spent his money without restraint; but she, no less virtuous than beautiful, cared little for these things done on her behalf, nor did she care for him who did them. Now, as Federigo was spending far beyond his means and was taking nothing in, as easily happens he lost his wealth and became poor, with nothing but his little farm to his name (from whose revenues he lived very meagerly) and one falcon which was among the best in the world.

More in love than ever, but knowing that he would never be able to live the way he wished to in the city, he went to live at Campi, where his farm was. There he passed his time hawking whenever he could, asked nothing of anyone, and endured his poverty patiently. Now, during the time that Federigo was reduced to dire need, it happened that the husband of Monna Giovanna fell ill, and realizing death was near, he made his last will: he was very rich, and he made his son, who was growing up, his heir, and, since he had loved Monna Giovanna very much, he made her

his heir should his son die without a legitimate heir; and then he died.

Monna Giovanna was now a widow, and as is the custom among our women, she went to the country with her son to spend a year on one of her possessions very close by to Federigo's farm, and it happened that this young boy became friends with Federigo and began to enjoy birds and hunting dogs; and after he had seen Federigo's falcon fly many times, it pleased him so much that he very much wished it were his own, but he did not dare to ask for it, for he could see how dear it was to Federigo. And during this time, it happened that the young boy took ill, and his mother was much grieved, for he was her only child and she loved him enormously; she would spend the entire day by his side, never ceasing to comfort him, and often asking him if there was anything he desired, begging him to tell her what it might be, for if it were possible to obtain it, she would certainly do everything possible to get it. After the young boy had heard her make this offer many times, he said:

"Mother, if you can arrange for me to have Federigo's falcon, I think I would be well very soon."

When the lady heard this, she was taken aback for a moment, and she began to think what she should do. She knew that Federigo had loved her for a long while, in spite of the fact that he never received a single glance from her, and so, she said to herself:

---

1. **Monna**, best translated as "Lady."

"How can I send or go and ask for this falcon of his which is, as I have heard tell, the best that ever flew, and besides this, his only means of support? And how can I be so insensitive as to wish to take away from this gentleman the only pleasure which is left to him?"

And involved in these thoughts, knowing that she was certain to have the bird if she asked for it, but not knowing what to say to her son, she stood there without answering him. Finally the love she bore her son persuaded her that she should make him happy, and no matter what the consequences might be, she would not send for the bird, but rather go herself for it and bring it back to him; so she answered her son:

"My son, take comfort and think only of getting well, for I promise you that the first thing I shall do tomorrow morning is to go for it and bring it back to you."

The child was so happy that he showed some improvement that very day. The following morning, the lady, accompanied by another woman, as if going for a stroll,[2] went to Federigo's modest house and asked for him. Since it was not the season for it, Federigo had not been hawking for some days and was in his orchard, attending to certain tasks; when he heard that Monna Giovanna was asking for him at the door, he was very surprised and happy to run there; as she saw him coming, she greeted him with feminine charm, and once Federigo had welcomed her courteously, she said:

"Greetings, Federigo!" Then she continued: "I have come to compensate you for the harm you have suffered on my account by loving me more than you needed to; and the compensation is this: I, along with this companion of mine, intend to dine with you—a simple meal—this very day."

To this Federigo humbly replied: "Madonna, I never remember having suffered any harm because of you; on the contrary: so much good have I received from you that if ever I have been worth anything, it has been because of your merit and the love I bore for you; and your generous visit is certainly so dear to me that I would spend all over again that which I spent in the past; but you have come to a poor host."

And having said this, he received her into his home humbly, and from there he led her into the garden, and since he had no one there to keep her company, he said:

"My lady, since there is no one else, this good woman here, the wife of this workman, will keep you company while I go to set the table."

Though he was very poor, Federigo, until now, had never before realized to what extent he had wasted his wealth; but this morning, the fact that he found nothing with which he could honor the lady for the love of whom he had once entertained countless men in the past gave him cause to reflect: in great anguish, he cursed himself and his fortune and, like a man beside himself, he started running here and there, but could find neither money nor a pawnable object. The hour was late and his desire to honor the gracious lady was great, but not wishing to turn for help to others (not even to his own workman), he set his eyes upon his good falcon, perched in a small room; and since he had nowhere else to turn, he took the bird, and finding it plump, he decided that it would be a worthy food for such a lady. So, without further thought, he wrung its neck and quickly gave it to his servant girl to pluck, prepare, and place on a spit to be roasted with care; and when he had set the table with the whitest of tablecloths (a few of which he still had left), he returned, with a cheerful face, to the lady in his garden, saying that the meal he was able to prepare for her was ready.

The lady and her companion rose, went to the table together with Federigo, who waited upon them with the greatest devotion, and they ate the good falcon without knowing what it was they were eating. And having left the table and spent some time in pleasant conversation, the lady thought it time now to say what she had come to say, and so she spoke these kind words to Federigo:

"Federigo, if you recall your past life and my virtue, which you perhaps mistook for harshness and cruelty, I do not doubt at all that you will be amazed by my presumption when you hear what

---

2. A young lady of rank would not leave her home without an escort or duenna.

my main reason for coming here is; but if you had children, through whom you might have experienced the power of parental love, it seems certain to me that you would, at least in part, forgive me. But, just as you have no child, I do have one, and I cannot escape the common laws of other mothers; the force of such laws compels me to follow them, against my own will and against good manners and duty, and to ask of you a gift which I know is most precious to you; and it is naturally so, since your extreme condition has left you no other delight, no other pleasure, no other consolation; and this gift is your falcon, which my son is so taken by that if I do not bring it to him, I fear his sickness will grow so much worse that I may lose him. And therefore I beg you, not because of the love that you bear for me, which does not oblige you in the least, but because of your own nobility, which you have shown to be greater than that of all others in practicing courtliness, that you be pleased to give it to me, so that I may say that I have saved the life of my son by means of this gift, and because of it I have placed him in your debt forever."

When he heard what the lady requested and knew that he could not oblige her since he had given her the falcon to eat, Federigo began to weep in her presence, for he could not utter a word in reply. The lady, at first, thought his tears were caused more by the sorrow of having to part with the good falcon than by anything else, and she was on the verge of telling him she no longer wished it, but she held back and waited for Federigo's reply after he stopped weeping. And he said:

"My lady, ever since it pleased God for me to place my love in you, I have felt that Fortune has been hostile to me in many things, and I have complained of her, but all this is nothing compared to what she has just done to me, and I must never be at peace with her again, thinking about how you have come here to my poor home where, while it was rich, you never deigned to come, and you requested a small gift, and Fortune worked to make it impossible for me to give it to you; and why this is so I shall tell you briefly. When I heard that you, out of your kindness, wished to dine with

me, I considered it fitting and right, taking into account your excellence and your worthiness, that I should honor you, according to my possibilities, with a more precious food than that which I usually serve to other people; therefore, remembering the falcon that you requested and its value, I judged it a food worthy of you, and this very day had it roasted and served to you as best I could; but seeing now that you desired it in another way, my sorrow in not being able to serve you is so great that I shall never be able to console myself again."

And after he had said this, he laid the feathers, the feet, and the beak of the bird before her as proof. When the lady heard and saw this, she first reproached him for having killed such a falcon to serve as a meal to a woman; but then to herself she commended the greatness of his spirit, which no poverty was able or would be able to diminish; then, having lost all hope of getting the falcon and, perhaps because of this, of improving the health of her son as well, she thanked Federigo both for the honor paid to her and for his good will, and she left in grief, and returned to her son. To his mother's extreme sorrow, either because of his disappointment that he could not have the falcon, or because his illness must have necessarily led to it, the boy passed from this life only a few days later.

After the period of her mourning and bitterness had passed, the lady was repeatedly urged by her brothers to remarry, since she was very rich and was still young; and although she did not wish to do so, they became so insistent that she remembered the merits of Federigo and his last act of generosity—that is, to have killed such a falcon to do her honor—and she said to her brothers:

"I would prefer to remain a widow, if that would please you; but if you wish me to take a husband, you may rest assured that I shall take no man but Federigo degli Alberighi."

In answer to this, making fun of her, her brothers replied:

"You foolish woman, what are you saying? How can you want him; he hasn't a penny to his name?"

To this she replied: "My brothers, I am well

Manuscript illustration showing an Italian nobleman hunting with a falcon.
c. 1475. New York Public Library

aware of what you say, but I would rather have a man who needs money than money that needs a man."

Her brothers, seeing that she was determined and knowing Federigo to be of noble birth, no matter how poor he was, accepted her wishes and gave her in marriage to him with all her riches; when he found himself the husband of such a great lady, whom he had loved so much and who was so wealthy besides, he managed his financial affairs with more prudence than in the past and lived with her happily the rest of his days.

c. 1351–1353

THINK AND DISCUSS
Understanding
1. How does Federigo lose his fortune?

Analyzing
2. What purpose does Giovanna's husband serve in the story?
3. What purpose does her son serve?
4. Explain what Giovanna means when she says, "I would rather have a man that needs money than money that needs a man."
5. All the characters in this story are well-meaning, and Federigo is the **protagonist** —who or what then is the antagonist, the person or force that works against the protagonist?

Extending
6. How much of this story deals with love and how much with money? Explain.

REVIEWING: Plot H▟
See Handbook of Literary Terms, p. 962.

Plot is a series of events related by the author to bring about the resolution of a conflict or problem. In a strongly plotted story, a conflict or problem is set up; complications arise; a main character takes decisive action, or the situation itself brings about a climax; the conflict is resolved. "Federigo's Falcon" is highly regarded for its plot.

1. What action of Federigo's sets up the original conflict?
2. What complications arise?
3. What decisive action does Giovanna take?
4. How is the conflict resolved?

THINKING SKILLS
Generalizing
To generalize is to draw a general statement from particular information. For example, a historian examines the writings of a particular age and makes a general statement about the values of the culture.

1. What picture of Renaissance manners is suggested by Giovanna's and Federigo's treatment of one another?
2. From Giovanna's discussion with her brothers about her remarriage, what conclusions can you draw about the position of women in Renaissance Italy?

COMPOSITION ◗━━
Dramatizing a Scene
Write in dramatic form the scene in Federigo's dining room where he tells Giovanna she has eaten the falcon. Characters: Federigo, Giovanna, Giovanna's friend, and possibly the servant girl. Assume that you are writing for your classmates. This scene should be about as long as a three-paragraph composition.

Writing About Background
Reread the story, noting those parts that reveal how life was lived in Renaissance Florence—for instance, recreation, inheritance, woman's place, hospitality, chaperones, and so forth. Organize your notes and write a three- to five-paragraph composition describing life at that time and in that place. See "Writing About a Period or Trend" in the Writer's Handbook.

BIOGRAPHY

Niccolò Machiavelli

1469–1527

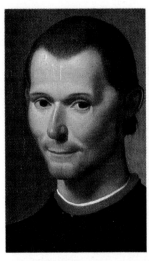

Almost a century passed between Boccaccio's death and the birth of Machiavelli (mäk′ē ə vel′ē). In that time the Renaissance had become firmly entrenched in Florence and throughout Italy. Unlike Petrarch and Boccaccio, whose great literary achievements lay in the realm of poetry and fiction, Machiavelli's major contribution is in nonfiction, a handbook on political power that has application even today.

Born in Florence, the son of a lawyer and small landowner, Machiavelli was learned in the Latin classics, as his writing shows, but no records have survived as to his formal education. His career for a time paralleled that of the Florentine Republic. After serving as a clerk for four years, he was raised to the ranks of officialdom in 1498, and until the fall of the republic in 1512, he held a position that called on him to travel extensively on diplomatic matters and also to concern himself with warfare and the military defense of Florence. On various missions Machiavelli visited Italy, Germany, and France, always close to the sources of power, and apparently also an acute observer of the international and internal politics of the Renaissance.

When the republic finally fell and the Medicis took over direct control of Florence in 1512, Machiavelli, suspected of being involved in a plot to overthrow the Medicis, was dismissed from office, imprisoned, tortured, and finally released under strange terms: he was not permitted to live in the city of Florence, nor could he leave the outlying territory controlled by Florence.

Compelled to retire to his small farm near San Casciano with his wife and five children, Machiavelli began work on *The Prince*, which (hoping for a political position) he dedicated to one of the very Medicis who had been responsible for his downfall. Using his own experience as well as his extensive knowledge of history, he put together a book that purported to show new and aspiring princes how to achieve and retain autocratic power. Machiavelli's other political writing includes a series of *Discourses* on Livy's history of Rome, *The Art of War*, and a history of Florence. However Machiavelli was too much a man of the Renaissance to limit himself to nonfiction. He wrote a novella and several plays, of which one, *The Mandrake*, is regarded as one of the best comedies of the Renaissance. In 1526, when the Medicis collapsed and Florence again became a republic, Machiavelli was, ironically, regarded as a Medici sympathizer and was not offered a place in the new government. He died soon afterward.

The Prince consists of twenty-six chapters, the earlier ones describing various types of principalities, the later ones detailing the personal qualities and attributes a prince should possess. Apparently Machiavelli based his successful prince on Cesare Borgia, whom he had met on his diplomatic travels. The tactics that Machiavelli recommended for the prince were regarded as so ruthless that the adjective *Machiavellian* has come to mean someone using devious methods to gain power.

from The Prince

Niccolò Machiavelli *translated by* **A. Robert Caponigri**

The Things for Which Men and Especially Princes Are Praised and Blamed

It remains now to consider the manner in which a prince should conduct himself toward his subjects and his friends. I know that many writers have treated this topic, so that I am somewhat hesitant in taking it up in my turn lest I appear presumptuous, especially because in what I shall have to say, I shall depart from rules which other writers have laid down. Since it is my intention to write something which may be of real utility to anyone who can comprehend it, it has appeared to me more urgent to penetrate to the effective reality of these matters than to rest content with mere constructions of the imagination. For many writers have constructed imaginary republics and principalities which have never been seen nor known actually to exist. But so wide is the separation between the way men actually live and the way that they ought to live, that anyone who turns his attention from what is actually done to what ought to be done, studies his own ruin rather than his preservation. Any man who wishes to make a profession of goodness in every department of conduct, must inevitably come to ruin among so many men who are not good. Therefore a ruler who wishes to preserve his power must learn to be able not to be good, and to use this knowledge or not use it as necessity may dictate.

Setting aside therefore all vain imaginings about what a prince ought to be and centering our discussion on things as they really are, I submit that all men, and especially princes by their high position, when discussion of their merit arises, are measured according to certain qualities the possession or reputation for which earns them either praise or censure. Thus it is that one is thought liberal, another miserly—using this word in the Tuscan sense, because "avaro" in our language still indicates one who wants to acquire possessions by plunder, while we call one "misero"[1] who abstains too much from the use of what he possesses—another is held to be a benefactor, another a plunderer; one cruel, another compassionate; one faithless to his word, another faithful; one effeminate and lacking in spirit, another full of spirit to the point of rashness; one man is considered courteous, another haughty; one lascivious, another chaste; one, of single intention, another crafty and conniving; one obstinate, another amenable; one grave, another light-hearted; one religious, another unbelieving and so forth. Everyone would of course hold that it would be a most laudable thing in a prince to be possessed of all the favorable qualities enumerated above, but all of these cannot be possessed at once, nor observed in their entirety, for the conditions of human life do not permit this. A prince must therefore be prudent enough to know how to avoid any derogatory reputation for those qualities which might lead him to lose his power, and to be on his guard against those qualities which do carry this danger, in so far as he finds it possible. And if he cannot avoid them, he can tolerate them in himself without too much concern for consequences. Even more, however, he must not draw back from incurring a reputation for those vices without which his position cannot be maintained without difficulty; the reason is that, when the entire matter is considered carefully, certain qualities which appear to be virtues, when practiced will lead to his ruin; while the pursuit of others, which seem to be vices, will insure his own security and the stability of his position.

1. *"avaro"* . . . *"misero."* Machiavelli is exploring the difference between a greedy man and a miser.

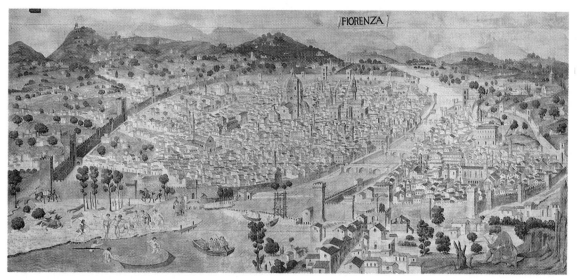

View of Florence. c. 1490. Museo De Firenze Com'era, Florence.

Liberality and Parsimony

I shall begin then with the first of the above mentioned qualities, agreeing that it would indeed be most advantageous to be considered liberal; nevertheless, liberality, if exercised in such a way that you come to be held a free-spending man, may do you harm. This quality, if exercised as a virtue—as it ought to be—will not be obvious, and hence will not prevent your being accused of its contrary. If one wishes to keep up a name for liberality among men, one must not omit any kind of lavish display; however, if he indulges in such display, it will consume all his resources. In the end, he will be forced to place exorbitant burdens upon his people, to resort to excessive taxes and have recourse to such other expedients as may increase revenue in order to maintain this reputation. This mode of conduct will soon begin to earn him the hatred of his subjects, and general contempt when he reaches the point of impoverishment. In addition, his liberality will have benefited few, while offending many. As a consequence, he will be vulnerable at many points and the first real peril will prove a disaster. And, to fill up the measure of this irony, if

the prince, realizing these dangers, tries to withdraw from such a position, he will immediately be marked down as a miser.

Since a prince cannot exercise this virtue of liberality without danger to himself, except by ostentation, he ought not to be concerned about being thought a miser. With the passage of time, he will gradually acquire a reputation for liberality, when it is seen that by cautious expenditure his revenues always are sufficient to his needs, that he is always prepared to repel anyone who attacks him, and that he can carry through his undertakings without imposing exorbitant burdens on his people. All those from whom he takes nothing will deem him liberal, and they will be numerous; all those to whom he gives nothing will think him miserly, but they will be few. In our own days, we have seen that only those who have been thought misers have achieved great things; the others have all exhausted themselves in vain. Pope Julius,[2] though he took advantage of a reputation for lib-

---

2. Pope Julius, Julius II, pope from 1503–1513, a statesman who was responsible for the beautification of Rome.

erality to gain the papacy, on attaining it made no pretense of keeping up that reputation, because he was concerned with being able to carry on his wars. The present king of France[3] wages almost constant warfare without imposing any extraordinary taxes on his country, because his long practice of parsimony had hoarded the means of meeting these added expenditures. The present king of Spain,[4] had he cultivated liberality, would never have been able to achieve as much or carry out successfully so many great undertakings as he had done.

Consequently a prince ought to deem a reputation for miserliness a small thing if it frees him from the necessity of oppressing his subjects, enables him to defend himself, and prevents his becoming poor, despised and rapacious. It is one of those qualities which makes it possible to maintain power. And should someone protest that Caesar rose to imperial power through his reputation for liberality, and many others who enjoyed the reputation for being liberal—and have in fact been so—have risen to the highest positions, I must reply as follows: either you are already a prince or you are in the process of acquiring political power. In the first instance, liberality is a source of danger; in the second instance, however, it is indeed necessary to have a reputation for being liberal. Caesar was one of the competitors for the supreme power in Rome; if, having achieved that power, he had survived but not tempered his vast expenditures, he would have destroyed his position. And if someone else insists: many have been the princes who have had great military success and yet enjoyed the reputation for liberality, I must answer you: the prince expends either his own and his subjects' resources, or those of others. In the first case he is well advised to be frugal; in the second case, he should pass up no opportunity of displaying liberality. The prince who takes the field with his armies and maintains them by raids, by sacking cities and by extortions, is disposing of the resources of others and must display liberality or his soldiers may refuse to follow him. Of that which is not your own or your subjects' you may well be the free dispenser, as were Cyrus,

Caesar, and Alexander;[5] for it does no harm to your reputation but even adds to it. The only thing which brings you harm is to squander your own resources. There is nothing which consumes itself so completely as liberality; even as you exercise it, you lose the power to exercise it. As a result you become either poor and despised or—to escape these consequences—rapacious and hence hated. Contempt and hatred are the two things which above all others a prince must avoid; and liberality will earn you both. Therefore it is wiser to be thought a miser, which brings infamy but not hatred, than, through the desire to be known as a liberal man, to be forced to incur a reputation for rapaciousness, which bring ignominy *and* hatred.

Cruelty and Compassion and Whether It Is Better to Be Loved Than Feared or the Opposite

Coming down now to the other qualities mentioned above, I submit that every prince ought to want to be considered compassionate rather than cruel. At the same time, he must avoid an ill-advised use of compassion. Cesare Borgia[6] was thought cruel; nevertheless, that cruelty of his had restored the Romagna, united it, brought it peace and reduced it to obedience. If one considers the matter carefully, it will be seen that he was in fact much more compassionate than were the Florentines who, in order to avoid being thought cruel, permitted Pistoia to be destroyed.[7] Therefore, a prince ought not to permit a reputation for cruelty to disturb him, if it is the price of keeping his subjects united and obedient. By making examples

---

3. *king of France,* Louis XII, who ruled France from 1498 to 1515.
4. *king of Spain,* Ferdinand of Aragon, who ruled as Ferdinand II from 1479–1516. By his marriage to Isabella of Castile he unified Spain. He drove the Moors from Spain in 1492.
5. *Cyrus, Caesar, and Alexander,* Cyrus (died 529 B.C.), king of Persia and founder of the Persian empire; Alexander (356–323 B.C.), king of Macedonia and conqueror of Greek city-states and much of the Persian empire; Caesar (Julius Caesar) (100–44 B.C.), dictator of Rome from 46 to 44 B.C.
6. *Cesare Borgia* (chä´zä rä bôr´jə), 1475–1507, son of Pope Alexander, said to be model for ruler in *The Prince.*
7. Machiavelli is criticizing the Florentine government for not banishing the leaders of two opposing factions before rioting led to bloodshed.

of a few, he will prove in the end more compassionate than those who, through excess of compassion, permit disorders to arise, which prove in turn the source of murders and violence. For the latter outrages inevitably arouse the entire community, while those few executions which the prince may impose harm only certain persons in particular. Among all princes, it is most nearly impossible for the new prince to avoid a reputation for cruelty, simply because new states are exposed to so many dangers. As Virgil says through the lips of Dido:

Res dura et regni novitas me talia cogunt
Moliri et late fines custode tueri.

Harsh necessity and the newness of my kingdom force me to do such things and to guard my frontiers on every side (*Aeneid* I, 563–4).

Nevertheless, he should be considerate in lending credence and in committing himself to action, nor should he become fearful of his own shadow. He should proceed in a temperate manner, with prudence and humanity, so that over confidence will not make him rash nor will excessive distrustfulness render him unbearable.

From this circumstance, an argument arises: whether it is better to be loved rather than feared, or the opposite. The answer is that one would like to be both one and the other; but since they are difficult to combine, it is more secure to be feared than loved, when one of the two must be surrendered. For it may be said of men in general, that they are ingrates, fickle, deceivers, evaders of danger, desirous of gain. So long as you are doing good for any of them they are all yours, offering you their blood, goods, lives, children, when any real necessity for doing so is remote, but turning away when such need draws near, as I have remarked. The prince who relies wholly on their words, and takes no other precautions, will come to ruin. Friendships gained at a price and not founded on greatness and nobility of soul, are indeed purchased but never possessed; and in times of need cannot be drawn upon. Men are less concerned about giving offense to one who

Detail of an anonymous portrait of Cesare Borgia. c. 1500. Palazzo Venezia, Rome

goes about making himself loved than to one who makes himself feared; love is a bond of obligation which men—sad creatures that they are—break on the first occasion touching their own interests; but fear binds by a threat of punishment which never relaxes. Still, the prince should take care to make himself feared in due measure; though he merits not love, he should avoid being hated. His position is strongest when he is feared but not hated. And he will establish such a relationship if he does not despoil his subjects of their goods and keeps his hands off their women. Even when it is necessary for him to proceed against the blood-kin of anyone, he must make it clear that he does so only for manifest cause and with commensurate justification. Above all, let him keep his hands off others' property, because men forget the death of their own fathers more readily that the loss of their patrimonies. Moreover, pretexts for seizing another's property are never lacking; and one who begins to live by plunder, never fails to find a reason for seizing another's property. Justifications for taking a life, however, present themselves more rarely and are much less convincing.

When the prince is in the field with his armies, directing large numbers of men, it is quite necessary that a reputation for cruelty cause him no concern. Without such a reputation, he can never keep an army united or prevent it from falling into factions. Among Hannibal's[8] most notable achievements must surely be accounted the fact that, though he commanded a very numerous army, drawn from a large diversity of races and led it to battle in foreign lands, no dissension ever arose within its ranks, either between portions of the army or against the commander, either in good or in adverse circumstances. The only thing able to account for this must have been his inhuman cruelty which, together with his inexhaustible resourcefulness, made him an object of terror and veneration to the eyes of his soldiers. The historians who have not analyzed this matter well have given a confused impression of it; on the one hand, admiring his mode of conduct and, on the other, condemning the only quality which could have assured it. To appreciate the fact that none of Hannibal's other qualities could have accounted for this achievement, one need only consider the case of Scipio,[9] whose armies in Spain mutinied against him, a very rare occurrence, not only in his own times, but in the whole of recorded history. The only reason which can account for that mutiny was his excessive compassion, which had led him to grant his soldiers a greater freedom than is consonant with military life. This was the basis of his censure in the Senate by Fabius Maximus,[10] who called him a corrupter of the Roman Army. When one of his legates destroyed Locri[11] without his orders he neither revenged its destruction nor censured the legate, his excessive good nature preventing the one action and the other. A colleague in the Senate recognized this failing when, in Scipio's defense, he pointed out that there are many men who know better how to avoid an error

than how to correct one. This quality of his character would in time have destroyed Scipio's fame and glory, had he conducted himself in this way while exercising the supreme power, the *imperium*. But living as he did under the government of the Senate, this damaging characteristic was not only concealed, but counted as an element of his glory.

Returning to the question of being loved or feared, I conclude that since men give their affection as they please, but yield to fear because the prince inspires it, a wise prince will rest his power on that which is his to control, not on that which lies in the power of others. His only concern must be to avoid being hated, as has been said.

How Princes Should Observe Good Faith

Everyone understands well enough how praiseworthy it is in a prince to keep his word, to live with integrity and not by guile. Nevertheless, the experience of our times teaches us that those princes have achieved great things who have looked upon the keeping of one's word as a matter of little moment and have understood how, by their guile, to twist men's minds; and in the end have surpassed those who have rested their power upon faithfulness.

You ought to understand therefore that there are two ways of fighting, the one by the laws, the other with force. The first is proper to men, the second to beasts; but since in many instances the first is not enough, it is necessary to have recourse to the second. A prince, consequently, must understand how to use the manner proper to the beast as well as that proper to man. This truth has been taught to princes by the writers of ancient times covertly. Thus they described how Achilles and many other

---

8. *Hannibal*, 247–183? B.C., Carthaginian general who crossed the Alps and invaded Italy but was unable to defeat Rome.
9. *Scipio* (sip'ē ō), 234–183 B.C., Roman general who defeated Hannibal at Carthage in 202 B.C. The revolution described here occurred earlier in 206 B.C.
10. *Fabius Maximus*, died 203 B.C., Roman consul and general who used delaying tactics in fighting Hannibal.
11. *Locri* (lō'krī), city in southern Italy captured by Scipio in 205 B.C. He placed it under the government of a legate, or representative, who was brutal to the inhabitants.

of those princes of ancient times were sent to be brought up by the centaur Chiron[12] and educated under his tutelage. To have as teacher a creature half man and half beast means nothing else than that a prince must know how to use the one nature and the other, and that without the one, the other cannot endure.

Since, then, a prince must of necessity know how to use the bestial nature, he should take as his models from among beasts the fox and the lion; for the lion does not defend himself from traps, and the fox does not defend himself from the wolves. One must therefore be a fox to scent out the traps and a lion to ward off the wolves. Those who act simply the lion do not understand the implications of their own actions. A prudent prince cannot—nor ought he—observe faith when such observance may turn against himself, and when the reasons which led him to pledge it have lost their force. If all men were good, this precept would not be valid; but since they are sorry creatures and would not keep faith with you, no obligation binds you to observe it toward them.

Moreover, a prince never lacks legitimate reasons which may impart a convincing color to his nonobservance. One might adduce innumerable modern examples of this truth and show how many treaties of peace, how many promises, have been broken and rendered meaningless through the infidelity of princes. And the one who has known how to act the fox has always come off the better. It is also necessary to know how to lend this vulpine nature an attractive color and to be a great simulator and dissimulator. Men are so simple and so responsive to present necessities that he who would deceive will always find another who will permit himself to be deceived.

There is one recent example which I cannot pass over in silence. [Pope] Alexander VI[13] never acted otherwise, never thought of anything else than to deceive men; and he always found someone on whom he could practice this art. Never was there a man more convincing in his serious statements or in affirming some matter with more impressive oaths, or in observing them less. Nevertheless, his lies always succeeded, just as he intended them to,

Detail of a fresco showing Pope Alexander VI. 1492–1494. Borgia Apartments, the Vatican

because he understood so well this dimension of worldly life.

A prince does not have to possess all of the above named qualities; but he must give the appearance of having them. Even more, I will venture to say that to possess them and to observe them constantly is to create a danger to oneself, but to *seem* to have them is always useful. Thus it is always useful to appear to be compassionate, faithful to one's word, humane, sincere, religious; and the prince should actually cultivate these qualities. But he must keep his mind so disposed that when it is necessary not to exercise them, you may be able

---

12. *Chiron* (kī′ron), a mythological centaur, half horse and half man, who taught Achilles and others.
13. *Pope Alexander VI*, 1431?–1503, a Borgia, father of Cesare, pope from 1492–1503.

and may know how to act in the opposite manner. And this must be understood, that a prince—and especially a new prince—cannot cultivate all those qualities which cause men to be considered good; for he must frequently, in order to maintain his position, act against good faith, against charity, humanity and religion. And still he must have a soul disposed to accommodate itself, as the winds and variations of fortune command. He must, as I have said, not desert the good, if he can abide by it, but must know how to enter upon the ways of evil if he must.

A prince must take care, therefore, that nothing ever issues from his lips which does not appear inspired by the five above mentioned qualities. He must appear, to those who see and hear him, all compassion, all fidelity, all sincerity and integrity, all religion. And nothing is more important than to give an appearance of possessing this last quality. Men, on the whole, judge more by the eye than by the hand; because anyone can see, but it is permitted to few to touch. Everyone sees what you seem to be, few understand what you really are; and those few are not eager to oppose themselves to the opinion of the masses, who have the majesty of the state to defend them. In the actions of all men, and especially of princes, where there is no judge to whom one can appeal, one must look to the result. Let the prince therefore concentrate on winning and maintaining the state. The means he employs will always be judged honorable and be praised by all; for the herd is always taken in by appearances and by results. And in the world, it is only the many who need be considered. The few find a place in the world, only when the many discover reasons for following them; and these reasons will always be the results of events. A certain prince of our own day, whom it is better not to name,[14] never preaches anything but peace and good faith, while being the worst enemy of the one and of the other; and both the one and the other—had he ever observed them—would more than once have stripped him of reputation and power.

1513   1532

---

14. *A certain prince . . . name,* King Ferdinand of Spain (see footnote 4), who had conquered the kingdoms of Naples and Navarre.

THINK AND DISCUSS
Understanding
According to Machiavelli:
1. Why should a prince prefer to be thought miserly rather than liberal?
2. Why should a prince not be disturbed to know he has a reputation for cruelty?
3. Why should a prince take the fox and the lion for his models?

Analyzing
4. What is Machiavelli's opinion of the majority of humanity? Do you agree? Explain.
5. Explain in your own words the meaning of the following quotes.
    a. "But so wide is the separation between the way men actually live and the way that they ought to live, that anyone who turns his attention from what is actually done to

what ought to be done, studies his own ruin rather than his preservation."

b. "A ruler who wishes to preserve his power must learn to be able not to be good, and to use this knowledge or not use it as necessity may dictate."

c. "There are two ways of fighting, the one by the laws, the other by force. The first is proper to man, the second to beasts; but since in many instances the first is not enough, it is necessary to have recourse to the second."

6. Machiavelli uses many **allusions** (references to classical, historical, and mythological figures): Pope Julius, the king of France, the king of Spain, Caesar, Cyrus, Alexander, Cesare Borgia, Virgil, Hannibal, Scipio, Fabius Maximus, Achilles, Chiron, and Pope Alexander VI. What is his purpose?

Extending

7. We may call Machiavelli's tactics dishonorable, but do they work? Explain.
8. "Machiavelli is concerned with what *is*, not with what should be." Explain why you agree or disagree with the statement.
9. Machiavelli's book was available to everyone, not just to princes and aspiring princes. Would this availability affect the tactics he advocated? Explain.
10. Machiavelli says, "Men are less concerned about giving offense to one who goes about making himself loved than to one who makes himself feared." Is this still true today? Explain.

VOCABULARY
Word Analogies

In this exercise you will be dealing with analogies, the sort of vocabulary question that appears on many standardized tests. In answering the questions, you must (1) decide on the relationship that exists between the first set of paired words, and (2) examine the third word and decide which of the three choices can be paired with it to set up a relationship similar to that of the first pair of words. In the example that follows, the colon separating *hot* from *cold* means "is related to." The double colon between *cold* and *tall* means "as." Thus, the example reads "hot is related to cold as tall is related to _____."

> Example: hot : cold :: tall : _____
> (a) high; (b) short; (c) warm.

The correct answer is *b*; *hot* and *cold* are antonyms (opposites), and the antonym of *tall* is *short*. The analogy questions deal with synonyms or antonyms.

Check your Glossary for the meanings of any of the following words that you do not know.

amenable	manifest	rapacious
dissimulator	ostentation	tutelage
frugal	parsimony	
laudable	patrimony	

1. instruction : tutelage :: patrimony : _____
   (a) father; (b) inheritance; (c) coinage.
2. frugal : wasteful :: parsimony : _____
   (a) extravagance; (b) religious; (c) miserly.
3. laudable : praiseworthy :: dissimulator : _____ (a) freak; (b) hypocrite; (c) copier.
4. manifest : obvious :: ostentation : _____
   (a) bone structure; (b) bashfulness; (c) impressive display.
5. rapacious : generous :: amenable : _____
   (a) religious; (b) bad-tempered; (c) agreeable.

Two centuries after the Renaissance began in Italy, it reached France, carried there by the returning French armies that had several times invaded Italy. Ronsard, the greatest French poet of the period, was the son of a man who had served in the Italian campaign and come under the influence of the Renaissance. Young Pierre, whose family belonged to the lesser nobility, was intended for a career as courtier and diplomat. At an early age he became a page at the French court, and in 1537 he traveled to Scotland with Madeleine, the French queen of James V of Scotland. When he was sixteen, however, an illness caused him to lose most of his hearing and ruined his career plans. Instead, Ronsard turned to literature, especially the Greek classics. At the Collège de Coqueret, in Paris, he came under the influence of Jean Dorat, lecturer in Greek literature and an inspiring teacher. Under Dorat's influence, Ronsard and some friends formed a group known as the *Pléiade* (plā'yäd'). They were seven in number, just as seven stars constituted the Pleiades. Their goal was to produce a new French poetry, free from medievalism and modeled on the Greeks. In 1549 Joachim du Bellay, a member of the group, encouraged by Ronsard, published *The Defense and Illustration of the French Language*, which served as the manifesto of the *Pléiade*.

Ronsard's first publication was a collection of odes (1550) modeled on the Greeks. It was recognized as the first great French poetry in that lyric vein. However, Ronsard found other lyric verse forms less restrictive, and adopted the sonnet for much of his poetry. In 1552 he published his first series of sonnets, *Amours de Cassandre*, describing his love for a young lady of his own social class. Three years later he published another collection, written in a less elevated style, to Marie, a peasant girl; and in 1578 yet another collection appeared, *Sonnets pour Hélène*, written several years earlier and addressed to Hélène de Surgères, a maid of honor to the queen. The sonnet "Of His Lady's Old Age" is from this collection and is regarded as Ronsard's best poem.

Besides the sonnets, Ronsard wrote other poetry based on classical models, light verse, patriotic poetry, hymns, part of an epic, and lyrical poems for court entertainments, which he dedicated to Queen Elizabeth of England. Elizabeth responded by sending him a diamond ring. Ronsard was in fact often a part of French court life and maintained a correspondence with both Elizabeth and Mary, Queen of Scots. Ronsard was called the Prince of Poets. The concept of a new French poetry that he and other members of the Pleiades advocated and followed in their own work had a lasting effect on the poetry of France.

"Of His Lady's Old Age" is a close translation of Ronsard's original sonnet. "When You Are Old" is a free adaptation of the Ronsard sonnet. Yeats took the idea of the sonnet and the image of its first four lines, but then developed his poem differently.

Miniature from a French illuminated
manuscript showing a woman painting
a self-portrait. 1402. Bibliothèque
Nationale, Paris

Of His Lady's Old Age

Pierre de Ronsard
translated by **Andrew Lang**

When you are very old, at evening
You'll sit and spin beside the fire, and say,
Humming my songs, "Ah well, ah well-a-
    day!
When I was young, of me did Ronsard sing."
5 None of your maidens that doth hear the
    thing,
Albeit with her weary task foredone,
But wakens at my name, and calls you one
Blest, to be held in long remembering.

I shall be low beneath the earth, and laid
10 On sleep, a phantom in the myrtle shade,
While you beside the fire, a grandame gray;
My love, your pride, remember and regret;
Ah, love me, love! we may be happy yet,
And gather roses, while 'tis called today.
1574   1578

When You Are Old

William Butler Yeats

When you are old and gray and full of sleep,
And nodding by the fire, take down this
    book,
And slowly read, and dream of the soft look
Your eyes had once, and of their shadows
    deep;

5 How many loved your moments of glad
    grace,
And loved your beauty with love false or
    true,
But one man loved the pilgrim soul in you,
And loved the sorrows of your changing face;

And bending down beside the glowing bars,
10 Murmur, a little sadly, how Love fled
And paced upon the mountains overhead
And hid his face amid a crowd of stars.
                            1892

THINK AND DISCUSS

Understanding

1. What **imagery** does Ronsard use in lines 1–4 of "Of His Lady's Old Age" to set a quiet mood?
2. How does the scene Yeats sets in lines 1–4 of "When You Are Old" differ?

Analyzing

3. What is the effect of lines 9–10 on the feelings evoked by "Of His Lady's Old Age"?
4. Line 12 of "Of His Lady's Old Age" is difficult to understand because of its inversion but is pivotal to the meaning of the **sonnet.** What is the lady being asked to remember and regret?
5. At what time in his lady's life do you suppose Ronsard wrote his sonnet? At what time in his lady's life did Yeats write his poem?
6. Both poems deal with the *carpe diem* (seize the day) **theme,** the poets urging their ladies to seize love while they are still young enough to enjoy it. What does Ronsard use to appeal to his lady? What does Yeats use to appeal to his?

Extending

7. Which poem do you think would be more effective in winning the lady, the Ronsard sonnet or the Yeats adaptation? Why?

COMPOSITION

Assuming the Role of a Character

Assume that you are the lady and have just received the poem intended for you, or that you are her father and have accidentally discovered it. What will you be thinking? What will you want to tell the poet? Write a short (2 to 3 paragraphs) note to the poet conveying your feelings. If you wish, you may write your note in the form of a poem.

Comparing and Contrasting Two Poems

Compare and contrast "Of His Lady's Old Age" and "When You Are Old" with regard to structure, character of the lady, sincerity of emotion, and so forth. If you wish, you may express a preference for one of the poems and explain why you prefer it. Your paper should be 3 to 5 paragraphs long.

BIOGRAPHY

Miguel de Cervantes
1547–1616

The Renaissance came late to Spain, and at the time Cervantes (ser-van'tēz') wrote *Don Quixote* enough survived of medievalism and chivalric romances to add timeliness to the other merits of the novel. *Don Quixote* is sometimes called the greatest novel ever written. Its effect on the modern novel cannot even be estimated, and four hundred years after its composition it is still being reinterpreted, a sign that it is very much alive and more of a classic than ever.

Cervantes's father was a surgeon who suffered from deafness and had to travel constantly to make a living. Young Miguel therefore grew up in various Spanish cities and his education was sketchy. In 1569 Cervantes left home and enlisted as a soldier. He fought in the great naval battle of Lepanto (1571), in which the Spanish defeated the Turks. He distinguished himself for bravery, but his left hand was maimed for life, and he received two gunshot wounds in the chest. After further service, while he was en route home in 1575 with his brother, their ship was captured by Barbary pirates and they were sold into slavery in Algiers. Cervantes made four attempts to escape but was recaptured each time. In 1580 he was finally ransomed and returned to Madrid. Although his brother had been released several years earlier, the family's financial situation was worse than ever, as they had gone heavily into debt to raise the money for the ransoms.

Cervantes tried to ease the financial situation by writing, but was not particularly successful. In 1584 he married and then accepted a government post as a roving government representative in Andalusia and La Mancha, becoming well acquainted with the countryside and the people. Part of his responsibility included requisitioning supplies for the Spanish Armada before it sailed for England in 1588. From 1587 to 1602 Cervantes lived in Seville, where he was twice imprisoned, once for debt and once for careless record-keeping. In the prologue to Part One of *Don Quixote*, he says that the Don, "a dry, shriveled, whimsical offspring," was conceived during one of these imprisonments.

Part One of *Don Quixote* was published in 1605 and brought Cervantes immediate fame but little money, as unscrupulous publishers pirated it at once. Cervantes continued to write—novels, poems, plays—and Part Two of *Don Quixote* was published in 1615. A year earlier an author who identified himself as Alonso de Avellaneda had published his own spurious continuation of *Don Quixote*, launching a scorching attack on Cervantes in the preface.

Cervantes has Don Quixote die at the end of Part Two and takes steps to ensure that his character will rest in peace: "And when the priest saw that he had passed away, he bade the notary give him a certificate stating that Alonso Quixano the Good, commonly known as Don Quixote de La Mancha, had died a natural death. This he desired lest any other author should take the opportunity of reviving him from the dead, and presume to write endless histories of his pretended adventures."

from Don Quixote

Miguel de Cervantes   *translated by* **Walter Starkie**

Chapter I

Which tells of the quality and manner of life of the famous gentleman Don Quixote of La Mancha

t a village of La Mancha, whose name I do not wish to remember,[1] there lived a little while ago one of those gentlemen who are wont to keep a lance in the rack, an old buckler, a lean horse, and a swift greyhound. His stew had more beef than mutton in it and most nights he ate a hodgepodge, pickled and cold. Lentil soup on Fridays, "tripe and trouble" on Saturdays,[2] and an occasional pigeon as an extra delicacy on Sundays consumed three quarters of his income. The remainder was spent on a jerkin of fine puce, velvet breeches, and slippers of the same stuff for holidays, and a suit of good, honest homespun for weekdays. His family consisted of a housekeeper about forty, a niece not yet twenty, and a lad who served him both in the field and at home and could saddle the horse or use the pruning knife.

Our gentleman was about fifty years of age, of a sturdy constitution, but wizened and gaunt-featured, an early riser and a devotee of the chase. They say that his surname was Quixada or Quesada (for on this point the authors who have written on this subject differ), but we may reasonably conjecture that his name was Quixana. This, however, has very little to do with our story; enough that in its telling we swerve not a jot from the truth.

You must know that the above-mentioned gentleman in his leisure moments (which was most of the year) gave himself up with so much delight and gusto to reading books of chivalry that he almost entirely neglected the exercise of the chase and even the management of his domestic affairs. Indeed his craze for this kind of literature became so extravagant that he sold many acres of arable land to purchase books of knight-errantry, and he carried off to his house as many as he could possibly find. Above all, he preferred those written by the famous Feliciano de Silva[3] because of the clarity of his writing and his intricate style, which made him value those books more than pearls, especially when he read of those courtships and letters of challenge that knights sent to ladies, often containing expressions such as: "The reason for your unreasonable treatment of my reason so enfeebles my reason that I have reason to complain of your beauty." And again: "The high heavens, which with your divinity divinely fortify you with stars, make you the deserver of the desert that is deserved by your greatness."

These and similar rhapsodies bewildered the poor gentleman's understanding, for he racked his brain day and night to unbowel their meaning, which not even Aristotle himself could have done if he had been raised from the dead for that very purpose. He was not quite convinced of the number of wounds that Don Belianís gave and received in battle, for he considered that however skillful the surgeons that cured him may have been, the worthy knight's face and body must have been bedizened with scars and scabs. Nevertheless he praised the author for concluding his book with the promise of endless adventure, and many times he felt inclined to take up his pen and finish it

---

1. Cervantes did not want any village to be able to claim Don Quixote. La Mancha was one of the areas Cervantes knew well from his duties as a roving government representative.
2. *"tripe and trouble" on Saturdays,* skimpy fare because Saturday was a fast day in memory of the defeat of the Moors in 1212.
3. *Feliciano de Silva,* author of *Don Florisel de Niquea* (1532) and *Amadis of Greece* (1535).

off himself, as it is there promised. He doubtless would have done so, and successfully too, had he not been diverted by other plans and purposes of greater moment.

He often debated with the curate of the village—a man of learning, a graduate of Sigüenza—on the relative merits of Palmerin of England and Amadis of Gaul. But Master Nicholas, the village barber, affirmed that no one could be compared with the Knight of the Sun and that if, indeed, any could be matched with him, it was Don Galaor, the brother of Amadis of Gaul, for he had a nature adapted to every whim of fortune; he was not so namby-pamby and whimpering a knight as his brother, and as for valor, he was in every respect his equal.

In short, he so immersed himself in those romances that he spent whole days and nights over his books; and thus with little sleeping and much reading, his brains dried up to such a degree that he lost the use of his reason. His imagination became filled with a host of fancies he had read in his books—enchantments, quarrels, battles, challenges, wounds, courtships, loves, tortures, and many other absurdities. So true did all this phantasmagoria from books appear to him that in his mind he accounted no history in the world more authentic.

He would say that the Cid Ruiz Díaz was a very gallant knight, but not to be compared with the Knight of the Burning Sword, who with a single thwart blow cleft asunder a brace of hulking, blustering giants. He was better pleased with Bernardo del Carpio, because at Roncesvalles he had slain Roland the Enchanted by availing himself of the stratagem Hercules had employed on Antaeus, the son of the Earth, whom he squeezed to death in his arms. He praised the giant Morgante, for he alone was courteous and well bred among that monstrous brood puffed up with arrogance and insolence. Above all, he admired Rinaldo of Montalbán,[4] especially when he saw him sallying out of his castle to plunder everyone who came his way, and when beyond the seas he made off with the idol of Mohammed which, as history says, was of solid gold. But he would have parted with his housekeeper and his niece into the bargain for the pleasure of rib roasting the traitor Galalón.[5]

At last, having lost his wits completely, he stumbled upon the oddest fancy that ever entered a madman's brain. He believed that it was necessary, both for his own honor and for service of the state, that he should become a knight-errant, roaming through the world with his horse and armor in quest of adventures and practicing all that had been performed by the knights-errant of whom he had read. He would follow their life, redressing all manner of wrongs and exposing himself to continual dangers, and at last, after concluding his enterprises, he would win everlasting honor and renown. The poor gentleman fancied himself already crowned emperor of Trebizond[6] for the valor of his arm. And thus excited by these agreeable delusions, he hastened to put his plans into operation.

The first thing he did was to refurbish some rusty armor that had belonged to his great grandfather and had lain moldering in a corner. He cleaned it and repaired it as best he could, but he found one great defect: instead of a complete helmet there was just the simple morion. This want he ingeniously remedied by making a kind of visor out of pasteboard, and when it was fitted to the morion, it looked like an entire helmet. It is true that in order to test its strength and see if it was swordproof, he drew his sword and gave it two strokes, the first of which instantly destroyed the result of a week's labor. It troubled him to see with what ease he had broken the helmet in pieces, so to protect it from such an accident, he remade it and fenced the inside with a few bars of iron in such a manner that he felt assured of its strength, and without caring to make a second trial, he held it to be a most excellent helmet.

Then he went to see his steed, and although it had more cracks in its hoof than there are quarters

---

4. **Rinaldo of Montalbán,** one of Charlemagne's greatest knights.
5. **Galalón,** also known as Ganelon, one of Charlemagne's soldiers who betrayed Roland at Roncesvalles.
6. **Trebizond,** a medieval empire (1204–1461) in Asia Minor.

in a Spanish real[7] and more faults than Gonella's jade,[8] which was all skin and bone, he thought that neither the Bucephalus of Alexander nor the Cid's Babieca[9] could be compared with it. He spent four days deliberating over what name he would give the horse, for (as he said to himself) it was not right that the horse of so famous a knight should remain without a name. So he endeavored to find one that would express what the animal had been before he had been the mount of a knight-errant, and what he now was. It was indeed reasonable that when the master changed his state, the horse should change his name too and assume one pompous and high-sounding, as suited the new order he was about to profess. So after having devised, erased, and blotted out many other names, he finally decided to call the horse Rozinante—a name, in his opinion, lofty, sonorous, and significant, for it explained that he had been only an ordinary hack before he had been raised to his present status of first of all the hacks in the world.

Now that he had given his horse a name so much to his satisfaction, he resolved to choose one for himself, and after seriously considering the matter for eight whole days, he finally determined to call himself Don Quixote. For that reason the authors who have related this most true story have deduced that his name must undoubtedly have been Quixada and not Quesada, as others would have it. Then, remembering that the valiant Amadis had not been content to call himself simply Amadis, but added thereto the name of his kingdom and native country to render it more illustrious, calling himself Amadis of Gaul, so he, like a good knight, also added the name of his province and called himself Don Quixote of La Mancha. In this way he openly proclaimed his lineage and country, and at the same time he honored it by taking its name.

Now that his armor was scoured, his morion made into a helmet, his horse and himself newly named, he felt that nothing was wanting but a lady of whom to be enamored, for a knight-errant who was loveless was a tree without leaves and fruit, a body without soul. "If," said he, "for my sins or through my good fortune I encounter some giant—a usual occurrence to knights-errant—and bowling him over at the first onset or cleaving him in twain, I finally vanquish and force him to surrender, would not it be better to have some lady to whom I may send him as a trophy? Then, when he comes into her presence, he may kneel before her and humbly say: 'Madam, I am the giant Caraculiambro, Lord of the Island of Malindrania, whom the never-adequately-praised Don Quixote of La Mancha has overcome in single combat. He has commanded me to present myself before you so that your highness may dispose of me as you wish.'" How glad was our knight when he had made these discourses to himself, but chiefly when he had found one whom he might call his lady! It happened that in a neighboring village there lived a good-looking country lass with whom he had been in love, although it is understood that she never knew or was aware of it. She was called Aldonza Lorenzo, and it was to her that he thought fit to entrust the sovereignty of his heart. He sought a name for her that would not vary too much from her own and yet would approach that of a princess or a lady of quality. At last he resolved to call her Dulcinea of El Toboso (she was a native of that town), a name in his opinion musical, uncommon, and expressive, like the others he had devised.

from Chapter VII

Of the second sally of our good knight Don Quixote of La Mancha

. . . During this interval Don Quixote made overtures to a certain laboring man, a neighbor of his and an honest fellow (if such a term can be applied to one who is poor), but with very little wit in his pate. In effect, he said so much to him and made so many promises that the poor wight resolved to set out with him and serve him as squire. Among other things Don Quixote told him that he should be most willing to go with him because some time or another he might meet with an adventure that would earn for him, in the

---

7. *real*, a Spanish coin.
8. *Gonella's jade*. Gonella was a fifteenth-century clown; his jade (a worn-out horse) was the cause of many jokes.
9. *Bucephalus . . . Babieca*, two notable warhorses.

Detail of the title page of an early
English translation of *Don Quixote*.
New York Public Library

twinkling of an eye, some island, and he would
find himself governor of it. With those and other
promises, Sancho Panza (for that was the fellow's
name) left his wife and children and engaged himself as squire to his neighbor. Don Quixote then
set about raising money, and by selling one thing,
pawning another, and throwing away the lot for a
mere song, he gathered a respectable sum. He furnished himself likewise with a buckler borrowed
from a friend, repaired his broken helmet as best
he could, and informed his squire, Sancho, of
the day and hour when he intended to sally forth
so that the latter might supply himself with all
that was needed. He charged him particularly to
carry saddlebags. Sancho said he would do so and
added that he was thinking of bringing an ass with
him, for he had a good one and he was not used
to travel on foot. At the mention of the ass Don
Quixote hesitated a little, racking his brains to
remember any case of a knight-errant who was
attended by a squire mounted on ass-back, but he
could not remember any such case. Nevertheless,
he resolved to let him take his ass, for he intended
to present him with a more dignified mount when
he got the opportunity, by unhorsing the first dis-

courteous knight he came across. He also provided
himself with shirts and other necessities. . . .

After all these preparations had been made,
Don Quixote, without saying farewell to his housekeeper and niece, Panza to his wife and children,
set out one night from the village without being
seen. They traveled so far that night that at daybreak they were sure that no one would find them,
even if they were pursued.

Sancho Panza rode along on his ass like a patriarch, with his saddlebags and wineskin, full of a
huge longing to see himself governor of the island
his master had promised to him. Don Quixote happened to take the same road as on his first journey,
that is, across the Plain of Montiel, which he now
traveled with less discomfort than the last time, for
as it was early in the morning, the rays of the sun
did not beat down directly upon them, but slantwise, and so did not trouble them. Presently Sancho Panza said to his master: "Mind, your worship, sir knight-errant, you don't let slip from your
memory the island you've promised me; I'll be
able to rule it well, no matter how big it is."

To which Don Quixote replied: "I would have
you know, my friend Sancho, that knights-errant

Cervantes 409

of long ago were accustomed to make their squires governors of the islands or kingdoms they won, and I have resolved not to neglect so praiseworthy a custom. Nay, I wish to surpass them in it, for they sometimes, perhaps even on the majority of occasions, waited till their squires were grown old, and then when they were cloyed with service after enduring bad days and worse nights, they conferred upon them some title, such as count or at least marquess, of some valley of more or less account. But if you live and I live, I may, before six days have passed, even conquer a kingdom with a string of dependencies, which would fall in exactly with my plan of crowning you king of one of them. Do not, however, think this strange, for knights-errant of my kind meet with such extraordinary and unexpected chances that I might easily give you still more than I am promising."

"And so," answered Sancho Panza, "by that token, if I became king by one of those miracles you mention, at least my chuck Juana Gutiérrez would become queen and my children princes."

"Who doubts it?" answered Don Quixote.

"I doubt it," replied Sancho Panza, "for I truly believe that even if God were to rain kingdoms down upon earth, none would sit well on the head of Mari Gutiérrez.[10] Believe me, sir, she's not worth two farthings as queen; countess would suit her better, and even then, God help her."

"Leave all in God's hands, Sancho," answered Don Quixote. "He will do what is best for her, but do not humble yourself so far as to be satisfied with anything less than the title of lord-lieutenant."

"I'll not indeed, sir," replied Sancho, "for a famous master like yourself will know what is fit for me and what I can carry."

from **Chapter VIII**

Of the valiant Don Quixote's success in the terrifying and never-before-imagined adventure of the windmills, with other events worthy of happy remembrance

Just then they came in sight of thirty or forty windmills that rise from that plain, and no sooner did Don Quixote see them than he said to his squire: "Fortune is guiding our affairs better than we ourselves could have wished. Do you see over yonder, friend Sancho, thirty or forty hulking giants? I intend to do battle with them and slay them. With their spoils we shall begin to be rich, for this is a righteous war and the removal of so foul a brood from off the face of the earth is a service God will bless."

"What giants?" asked Sancho Panza.

"Those you see over there," replied his master, "with their long arms; some of them have them well-nigh two leagues in length."

"Take care, sir," cried Sancho. "Those over there are not giants but windmills, and those things that seem to be arms are their sails, which when they are whirled around by the wind turn the millstone."

"It is clear," replied Don Quixote, "that you are not experienced in adventures. Those are giants, and if you are afraid, turn aside and pray whilst I enter into fierce and unequal battle with them."

Uttering these words, he clapped spurs to Rozinante, his steed, without heeding the cries of his squire, Sancho, who warned him that he was not going to attack giants but windmills. But so convinced was he that they were giants that he neither heard his squire's shouts nor did he notice what they were, though he was very near them. Instead, he rushed on, shouting in a loud voice: "Fly not, cowards and vile caitiffs; one knight alone attacks you!" At that moment a slight breeze arose and the great sails began to move. When Don Quixote saw this, he shouted again: "Although you flourish more arms than the giant Briareus,[11] you shall pay for it!"

Saying this and commending himself most devoutly to his lady, Dulcinea, whom he begged to help him in this peril, he covered himself with his buckler, couched his lance, charged at Rozi-

---

10. **Mari Gutiérrez**, Sancho's wife, who is also called *Juana*. *Mari* is an abbreviated form of *Maria*, used in compound proper names such as *Mari Gutiérrez*. *Mari* is also used in Spanish to mean *woman* in general; here it means something like, "the woman Gutiérrez."
11. **Briareus**, a mythological giant with a hundred arms and fifty heads, who helped Zeus against the Titans.

nante's full gallop, and rammed the first mill in his way. He ran his lance into the sail, but the wind twisted it with such violence that it shivered the lance in pieces and dragged both rider and horse after it, rolling them over and over on the ground, sorely damaged.

Sancho Panza rushed up to his assistance as fast as his ass could gallop, and when he reached the knight, he found that he was unable to move, such was the blow that Rozinante had given him in the fall.

"God help us!" cried Sancho. "Did I not tell you, sir, to mind what you were doing, for those were only windmills? Nobody could have mistaken them unless he had windmills in his brain."

"Hold your peace, good Sancho," replied Don Quixote. "The affairs of war are, above all others, subject to continual change. Moreover, I am convinced, and that is the truth, that the magician Frestón, the one who robbed me of my study and books,[12] has changed those giants into windmills to deprive me of the glory of victory; such is the enmity he bears against me. But in the end his evil arts will be of little avail against my doughty sword."

"God settle it in His own way," cried Sancho as he helped his master to rise and remount Rozinante, who was well-nigh disjointed by his fall.

They conversed about the recent adventure as they followed the road toward the Pass of Lápice, for there, Don Quixote said, they could not fail to find many and various adventures, seeing that it was a much frequented spot. Nevertheless he was very downcast at the loss of his lance, and in mentioning it to his squire, he said: "I remember having read of a Spanish knight called Diego Pérez de Vargas,[13] who, when he broke his sword in a battle, tore off a huge branch from an oak and with it did such deeds of prowess that day and pounded so many Moors that he earned the surname of Machuca,[14] and so he and his descendants were called from that day onwards Vargas y Machuca. I mention this because I intend to tear from the first oak tree we meet such a branch, with which I am resolved to perform such deeds that you will consider yourself fortunate to wit-

ness, exploits that men will scarcely credit."

"God's will be done," said Sancho. "I'll believe all your worship says; but straighten yourself a bit in the saddle, for you seem to be leaning over on one side, which must be from the bruises you received in your fall."

"That is true," replied Don Quixote, "and if I do not complain, it is because knights-errant must never complain of any wound, even though their guts are protruding from them."

"If that be so, I've no more to say," answered Sancho, "but God knows I'd be glad to hear you complain when anything hurts you. As for myself, I'll never fail to complain at the smallest twinge, unless this business of not complaining applies also to squires."

Don Quixote could not help laughing at the simplicity of his squire and told him that he might complain whenever he pleased and to his heart's content, for he had never read anything to the contrary in the order of chivalry. Sancho then bade his master consider that it was now time to eat, but the latter told him to eat whenever he fancied. As for himself, he had no appetite at the moment. Sancho no sooner had obtained leave than he settled himself as comfortably as he could upon his ass, and taking out of his saddlebags some of the contents, he jogged behind his master, munching deliberately; and every now and then he would take a stiff pull at the wineskin with such gusto that the ruddiest tapster in Málaga would have envied him. While he rode on, swilling away in that manner, he did not remember any promise his master might have made to him, and so far from thinking it a labor, he thought it a life of ease to go roaming in quest of adventures, no matter how perilous they might be.

c.1602–1605   1605

---

12. *Frestón . . . books.* In reality, Don Quixote's niece, housekeeper, and two friends had burned the books and walled up the room in an attempt to bring him to his senses.
13. *Diego Pérez de Vargas,* a Spanish Hercules famous for his exploits.
14. *Machuca.* In Spanish the verb *machucar* means "to pound."

THINK AND DISCUSS
Understanding
1. Where does Don Quixote get the idea of becoming a knight errant?
2. Why does he believe he must take up these duties?
3. How might the windmills look like giants? How might they act like them?
4. Give some examples of how Don Quixote's madness leads him to misinterpret the world around him.

Analyzing
5. In order to go knight-erranting, Don Quixote has to have the armor and other trappings of a knight—most of them makeshift. Explain how the selection parodies each of the following: the knight's steed; his armor; his squire; his lady.
6. Some of the humor in *Don Quixote* is quiet, some is slapstick. What did you find most humorous in the selection?
7. In literature a *foil* is a character whose traits are different from, and thereby show up, the traits of another character. How is Sancho Panza a foil to Don Quixote?

Extending
8. How might Don Quixote exercise his "madness" in today's world?
9. Some scholars claim that Cervantes began by intending to make Don Quixote and Sancho ridiculous but that they took over and changed his whole attitude toward them. Explain why you agree or disagree.
10. *Don Quixote* is regarded as one of the world's greatest books. What do you see in it that might account for this reputation?

VOCABULARY
Archaic Words
Because Don Quixote lived in an earlier world and took as models knights from a still earlier world, some of the words in his adventures (even in translation) may not be familiar to you. The following list contains some of those words, along with several others that are still in common use. Look up in the Glossary the meanings of any words you do not know, then answer the questions on a separate sheet. Not all the words will be used.

arable	jade	real
bedizened	morion	sonorous
buckler	pate	thwart
caitiff	phantasmagoria	wizened
doughty	puce	

1. Don Quixote wore a _____ to protect his head.
2. He carried a _____ to protect his body from blows.
3. He hoped that people would think he was a _____ knight.
4. He did not want people to call him a _____ .
5. He liked having a _____ in his pocket to spend.
6. He would object to having Rozinante called a _____ .
7. He wanted to have a new suit of _____ color.
8. He hoped people would think he had a _____ voice.
9. He would not want his face described as _____ .
10. He would not want the book that collected his adventures described as a _____ .

THINKING SKILLS
Evaluating
To evaluate is to make a judgment based on some sort of standard. For example, a psychiatrist sees a patient and writes an evaluation of that patient based on all the other people he has treated.

1. In your judgment, is Don Quixote a madman or an idealist?
2. How would you evaluate the character of Sancho Panza? Is he a simpleton, a shrewd realist, a buffoon? Explain.

More than two hundred contemporary references to Shakespeare's life have survived, the earliest a record of his baptism in Trinity Church, Stratford-on-Avon, on April 26, 1564. His father, John Shakespeare, a successful glove-maker and merchant, rose through lesser administrative offices to become high bailiff (or mayor) of Stratford. Shakespeare's mother, Mary Arden, came from a well-to-do landowning family.

Probably young William learned Latin and some Greek at the Stratford Grammar School, noted for the excellent education provided by its schoolmasters. In 1582, Shakespeare married Anne Hathaway, who lived in nearby Shottery. The couple had three children—Susanna, born in 1583, and Hamnet and Judith, twins born in 1585. Hamnet, Shakespeare's only son, died at the age of eleven.

There is a gap in the records for the years from 1585 to 1592, but during that time Shakespeare must have been establishing himself as an actor and playwright. In 1592, in a pamphlet titled "A Groatsworth of Wit," Robert Greene called Shakespeare "an upstart crow, beautified with our feathers, that with his tiger's heart wrapped in a player's hide supposes he is as well able to bombast out a blank verse as the rest of you; and being an absolute *Johannes fac totum*, is in his own conceit the only Shake-scene in a country." The reference to blank verse shows that Shakespeare was already writing plays. Greene may have been angry because Shakespeare was taking business away from him and his university-trained friends. The "tiger's heart" refers to a line in Shakespeare's *Henry VI:* "O tiger's heart wrapped in a woman's hide"; "*Johannes fac totum*," meaning Jack-of-all-trades, probably refers to Shakespeare's acting and writing; and "Shake-scene" is an obvious pun on Shakespeare's name.

We find the first records of Shakespeare's association with the theater in 1594, when he is listed as a shareholder in the acting company known as the Lord Chamberlain's Men, later the King's Men. In 1599, when this company built the Globe Theater, he was a shareholder; and when in 1608 the company purchased Blackfriars Theater, he also held a share in that playhouse. In short, his connection with the stage was extremely profitable to him.

During the theatrical season, Shakespeare lived in London but his family remained in Stratford. In 1597 he was wealthy enough to buy New Place, the second largest house in Stratford, and to establish his family there. Probably in 1610 he retired to Stratford, journeying to London as necessary to take care of theatrical business.

Shakespeare died on April 23, 1616, in Stratford and was buried in Trinity Church, where he had been baptized fifty-two years earlier. His plays were collected and published in the First Folio in 1623 by John Hemings and Henry Condell, friends and members of his acting company.

Reading SHAKESPEAREAN DRAMA

By this point in your education, most of you will have studied at least one Shakespearean tragedy—usually *Romeo and Juliet*, *Julius Caesar*, *Macbeth*, or *Hamlet*—but will have had no experience with a comedy. Before you read *The Tempest*, it will be helpful to understand the ways in which it, as a romance (a type of comedy) differs from a Shakespearean tragedy.

The Nature of Comedy Comedy reverses or downplays most of the elements of tragedy. Instead of ending with the death or downfall of the **protagonist,** or leading character, a person of high rank, it ends with a marriage (or a forthcoming marriage) that unites two essentially likeable young people who will presumably assure the continuation of the fabric of society as they produce children of their own. Although the young people may be of high rank, what is stressed about them is not their rank but their youthful high spirits and idealism.

In place of physical violence, comedy uses witty repartee (the rapid exchange of dialogue), often with classical **allusions** and references to people and events that would be familiar to most of the audience if not always to the groundlings. Unfortunately, modern audiences—and sometimes modern scholars—may find these allusions and references difficult to understand.

Like tragedies, comedies make use of soliloquies and asides, in which the characters reveal their thoughts to the audience while alone onstage (soliloquy) or briefly tell the audience, or sometimes one other character and the audience, something that the other characters onstage are not supposed to hear (aside). It is a convention of Elizabethan drama that a character must tell the truth in a soliloquy.

As you read *The Tempest*, try to visualize the scenes as actually taking place before your eyes. Your text contains information about the settings which, combined with stage directions for the actors, should make your task easier. In addition, we have included a diagram of the Globe Theater (page 461) with the various acting areas clearly marked so that you can determine for yourself where the scenes were played and how the actors made their entrances and exits.

Don't let the unrhymed verse in which much of the play is written deter you. Read it as though it were prose, without pausing at the end of a line unless a punctuation mark tells you to. If you come across a word you do not understand, keep reading—the context may help you. Unusual words and difficult passages are explained in sidenotes to make your reading easier. In addition, the side questions will help you to understand what you are reading.

The Sources of *The Tempest* There are several other things about *The Tempest* that you should know before you start reading. Most of Shakespeare's plays have an identifiable source; *The Tempest* does not. We know that he used Montaigne's essay "Of Cannibals" (page 446) for Gonzalo's speech about the ideal commonwealth, and we know that he had been keeping up with travel literature about the New World.

The one element clearly traceable in *The Tempest* is the influence of the Italian *commedia dell' arte*, which made its way to England as part of the interest in things Italian. The *commedia* was improvisational comedy—the actors had a scenario but no written dialogue, making up their lines as they went along. There were a few set lines in **rhyme** that were cues to the end of a scene, and there were set slapstick comedy routines called *lazzi* that the clowns performed. Both elements are present in *The Tempest*. In addition, various *commedia* scenarios contain a shipwreck, a magician, his daughter, a wild man, a disappearing banquet, and a tree in which a character was confined—all of these are present in *The Tempest*.

The Tempest

William Shakespeare

Watercolor sketch by Inigo Jones showing a fiery spirit. This sketch was a costume design for a masque by Thomas Campion that was presented at the English court in 1613 to celebrate the marriage of Elizabeth, the daughter of King James I, to the Elector Palatine. *The Tempest* was also presented as part of the same celebration, and the character of Ariel was probably costumed in a similar fashion. Devonshire Collection, Chatsworth

CHARACTERS

ALONSO, *King of Naples.*
SEBASTIAN, *his brother.*
PROSPERO, *the right Duke of Milan.*
ANTONIO, *his brother, the usurping Duke of Milan.*
FERDINAND, *son to the King of Naples.*
GONZALO, *an honest old Counselor.*
ADRIAN and
FRANCISCO, } *Lords.*
CALIBAN, *a savage and deformed Slave.*
TRINCULO, *a Jester.*
STEPHANO, *a drunken Butler.*
MASTER *of a Ship.*
BOATSWAIN.
MARINERS.

MIRANDA, *daughter to Prospero.*

ARIEL, *an airy Spirit.*
IRIS,
CERES,
JUNO, } *presented by Spirits.*
NYMPHS,
REAPERS,

Other **SPIRITS** *attending on Prospero.*

THE SCENE: *An uninhabited island.*

ACT ONE

SCENE 1.

On a ship at sea. (Played on the Platform Stage and the Tarras, possibly with the use of the Music Gallery above for one of the Mariners, who would thus be at the top of the mast, keeping a lookout for rocks or reefs.) A tempestuous noise of thunder and lightning is heard. Enter from different directions a SHIP-MASTER *and a* BOATSWAIN.

MASTER. Boatswain!

BOATSWAIN. Here, master. What cheer?

MASTER. Good,° speak to th' mariners. Fall to 't, yarely,° or we run ourselves aground. Bestir, bestir. *(Exit. Enter* MARINERS.*)*

5 **BOATSWAIN.** Heigh, my hearts! Cheerly, cheerly, my hearts! Yare, yare! Take in the topsail. Tend° to th' master's whistle.—Blow° till thou burst thy wind, if room enough!° *(Enter* ALONSO, SEBASTIAN, ANTONIO, FERDINAND, GONZALO, *and others.)*

ALONSO. Good boatswain, have care. Where's the master? Play the men.°

10 **BOATSWAIN.** I pray now, keep below.

ANTONIO. Where is the master, bos'n?

BOATSWAIN. Do you not hear him? You mar our labor. Keep your cabins; you do assist the storm.

GONZALO. Nay, good, be patient.

15 **BOATSWAIN.** When the sea is. Hence! What cares these roarers° for the name of king? To cabin! Silence! Trouble us not.

GONZALO. Good, yet remember whom thou hast aboard.

BOATSWAIN. None that I more love than myself. You are a counselor; if you can command these elements to silence, and work the peace of the

20 present, we will not hand° a rope more. Use your authority. If you cannot, give thanks you have lived so long, and make yourself ready in your cabin for the mischance of the hour, if it so hap.—Cheerly, good hearts!—Out of our way, I say. *(Exit.)*

GONZALO. I have great comfort from this fellow. Methinks he hath no

25 drowning mark upon him; his complexion is perfect gallows.° Stand fast, good Fate, to his hanging! Make the rope of his destiny our cable, for our own doth little advantage. If he be not born to be hanged, our case is miserable. *(Exeunt. Enter* BOATSWAIN.*)*

BOATSWAIN. Down with the topmast! Yare! Lower, lower! Bring her to try

30 with main-course. *(A cry within.)* A plague upon this howling! They are

Good, short for "Good boatswain" (see line 9).
yarely, quickly, briskly.

1 Note the instance of synecdoche (the use of a part to represent the whole) in the Boatswain's addressing the mariners as *hearts* in line 5.
Tend, attend.
Blow, addressed to the wind.
if room enough, as long as we have sea room enough.

2 The opening scene of a Shakespeare play should immediately engage the attention of the audience. How does this opening scene accomplish its purpose?
Play the men, get them to work harder.
roarers, waves.
hand, handle.

3 What causes the argument between the Boatswain and the nobles?
complexion . . . gallows, his appearance shows he was born to be hanged and therefore, according to the proverb, in no danger of drowning.

4 What leads Gonzalo to hope that the ship will not sink? Is there any humor in this? Explain.

Frontispiece to Rowe's edition of *The Tempest*. 1709. Folger Shakespeare Library

louder than the weather or our office.° (*Enter* SEBASTIAN, ANTONIO, *and*
GONZALO.) Yet again? What do you here? Shall we give o'er and drown?
Have you a mind to sink?

SEBASTIAN. A pox o' your throat, you bawling, blasphemous, incharitable
35 dog!

BOATSWAIN. Work you then.

ANTONIO. Hang, cur! Hang, you whoreson, insolent noisemaker! We are less
afraid to be drowned than thou art.

40 GONZALO. I'll warrant him for drowning,° though the ship were no stronger
than a nutshell and as leaky as an unstanched wench.

BOATSWAIN. Lay her a-hold, a-hold!° Set her two courses° off to sea again!
Lay her off! (*Enter* MARINERS *wet.*)

MARINERS. All lost! To prayers, to prayers! All lost! (*Exeunt.*)

45 BOATSWAIN. What, must our mouths be cold?°

GONZALO. The King and Prince at prayers! Let's assist them,
For our case is as theirs.

SEBASTIAN.   I am out of patience.

ANTONIO. We are merely cheated of our lives by drunkards.
This wide-chopped° rascal! Would thou mightst lie drowning
The washing of ten tides!°

50 GONZALO.   He'll be hanged yet,
Though every drop of water swear against it
And gape at wid'st to glut him.
(*A confused noise within:*)   "Mercy on us!"—
"We split, we split!"—"Farewell my wife and children!"—
"Farewell, brother!"—"We split, we split, we split!" (*Exit* BOATSWAIN.)

ANTONIO. Let's all sink wi' th' King.

SEBASTIAN. Let's take leave of him   (*Exit with* ANTONIO)

55 GONZALO. Now would I give a thousand furlongs of sea for an acre of barren ground, long hearth, brown furze,° anything. The wills above be
done! But I would fain die a dry death.   (*Exit.*)

SCENE 2.

The island. Before PROSPERO's *cell. (Played on the Platform stage, with one of
the side doors used as* CALIBAN's *cave.) Enter* PROSPERO (*in his magic robe and
carrying his staff*) *and* MIRANDA, *engaged in conversation.*

MIRANDA. If by your art, my dearest father, you have
Put the wild waters in this roar, allay them.
The sky, it seems, would pour down stinking pitch,
But that the sea, mounting to th' welkin's cheek,°
5 Dashes the fire out. O, I have suffered
With those that I saw suffer! A brave° vessel,
Who had, no doubt, some noble creature in her,
Dashed all to pieces. O, the cry did knock

418 *The Renaissance*

---

our office, the noise we
make at our work.

5 What does the
Boatswain mean?

*warrant him for drown-
ing*, guarantee that he will
never be drowned.
a-hold, a-hull, close to the
wind.
courses, sails, that is, fore-
sail as well as mainsail, set
in an attempt to get the
ship back out into open
water.
must . . . cold?, that is,
let us heat up our mouths
with liquor.

wide-chopped, with mouth
wide open.
lie . . . tides, pirates
were hanged on the shore
and left until three tides
had come in.

6 Shakespeare begins
his characterization
immediately. How does
Gonzalo's character thus
far differ from those of
Sebastian and Antonio?
How does it differ from
the Boatswain's?

heath . . . furze, coarse
plants that grow wild.

7 In order to work any
of his white mag-
ic, Prospero must wear
his magic robe. This is
his first appearance in the
play; why might he be
wearing it now? Through-
out the play, note when
he is or is not wearing the
robe as clues to his actions.
welkin's cheek, sky's face.

brave, gallant, splendid.

Against my very heart! Poor souls, they perished.
10 Had I been any god of power, I would
Have sunk the sea within the earth or ere°
It should the good ship so have swallowed and
The fraughting° souls within her.

PROSPERO.   Be collected.°
No more amazement.° Tell your piteous heart
15 There's no harm done.

MIRANDA.   O, woe the day!

PROSPERO.   No harm.
I have done nothing but in care of thee,
Of thee, my dear one, thee, my daughter, who
Art ignorant of what thou art, nought knowing
Of whence I am, nor that I am more better
20 Than Prospero, master of a full° poor cell,
And thy no greater father.

MIRANDA.   More to know
Did never meddle with my thoughts.

PROSPERO.   'Tis time
I should inform thee farther. Lend thy hand,
And pluck my magic garment from me. So,

                    (Lays down his magic robe and staff.)

25 Lie there, my art. Wipe thou thine eyes; have comfort.
The direful spectacle of the wrack, which touched
The very virtue of compassion in thee,
I have with such provision in mine art
So safely ordered that there is no soul—
30 No, not so much perdition° as an hair
Betid° to any creature in the vessel
Which thou heard'st cry, which thou saw'st sink. Sit down;
For thou must now know farther.

MIRANDA.   You have often
Begun to tell me what I am, but stopped
35 And left me to a bootless inquisition,°
Concluding, "Stay, not yet."

PROSPERO.   The hour's now come;
The very minute bids thee ope thine ear.
Obey and be attentive. Canst thou remember
A time before we came unto this cell?
40 I do not think thou canst, for then thou wast not
Out° three years old.

MIRANDA.   Certainly, sir, I can.

PROSPERO. By what? By any other house or person?
Of anything the image, tell me, that
Hath kept with thy remembrance.

MIRANDA.   'Tis far off,
45 And rather like a dream than an assurance

or ere, before.
fraughting, forming the cargo.

[8] What can you infer about Miranda's character from this speech?
collected, calm, composed.
amazement, consternation.

full, very.

[9] In this long dialogue between Prospero and Miranda (lines 22-168), Shakespeare acquaints his audience with the antecedent action, the events that have taken place before the play opens and that will have an effect on what occurs. What should Prospero's removing his magic robe indicate about the information he is about to divulge?

perdition, loss.
Betid, happened.

bootless inquisition, profitless inquiry.

Out, fully.

That my remembrance warrants.° Had I not
Four or five women once that tended me?

PROSPERO. Thou hadst, and more, Miranda. But how is it
That this lives in thy mind? What seest thou else
50   In the dark backward and abysm of time?
If thou rememb'rest aught ere thou cam'st here,
How thou cam'st here thou mayst.

MIRANDA.   But that I do not.

PROSPERO. Twelve year since, Miranda, twelve year since,
Thy father was the Duke of Milan and
55   A prince of power.

MIRANDA.   Sir, are not you my father?

PROSPERO. Thy mother was a piece° of virtue, and
She said thou wast my daughter; and thy father
Was Duke of Milan; and thou his only heir
And princess no worse issued.°

MIRANDA.   O the heavens!
60   What foul play had we, that we came from thence?
Or blessed was 't we did?

PROSPERO.   Both, both, my girl.
By foul play, as thou say'st, we were heaved thence,
But blessedly holp° hither.

MIRANDA.   O, my heart bleeds
To think o' th' teen that I have turned you to,°
65   Which is from° my remembrance! Please you, farther.

PROSPERO. My brother and thy uncle, called Antonio—
I pray thee mark me—that a brother should
Be so perfidious!—he whom next thyself
Of all the world I loved, and to him put
70   The manage of my state, as at that time
Through all the signories° it was the first
And Prospero the prime duke, being so reputed
In dignity, and for the liberal arts
Without a parallel; those being all my study,
75   The government I cast upon my brother
And to my state grew stranger, being transported
And rapt in secret studies. Thy false uncle—
Dost thou attend me?

MIRANDA.   Sir, most heedfully.

PROSPERO. Being once perfected° how to grant suits,
80   How to deny them, who t' advance and who
To trash for overtopping,° new created
The creatures° that were mine, I say, or° changed 'em,
Or else new formed 'em; having both the key°
Of officer and office, set all hearts i' th' state
85   To what tune pleased his ear, that now he was

assurance . . . warrants, certainty that my memory guarantees.

|10| How old is Miranda? How do you know?

piece, masterpiece.

issued, born, descended.

holp, helped.

teen . . . to, pain I have caused you.
is . . . remembrance, I don't remember.

signories, that is, city-states of northern Italy.

|11| From this point on, Prospero repeatedly asks Miranda if she is paying attention to his revelations. Some scholars say this is necessary from the standpoint of practical stagecraft to break up what would otherwise be an overly long speech. What other reason might Shakespeare have for doing this?
perfected, grown skillful.
trash . . . overtopping, restrain from becoming too important or rising too rapidly.
creatures, dependents.
or, either.
key, (1) key for unlocking, (2) tool for tuning stringed instruments.

The ivy which had hid my princely trunk,
And sucked my verdure out on 't. Thou attend'st not.

MIRANDA. O, good sir, I do.

PROSPERO.   I pray thee mark me.
    I, thus neglecting wordly ends, all dedicated
90 To closeness° and the bettering of my mind
    With that which, but by being so retired,
    O'er-prized all popular rate,° in my false brother
    Awaked an evil nature; and my trust,
    Like a good parent,° did beget of him
95 A falsehood in its contrary as great
    As my trust was, which had indeed no limit,
    A confidence sans° bound. He being thus lorded,°
    Not only with what my revenue yielded,
    But what my power might else exact—like one
100 Who having into truth, by telling of it,
    Made such a sinner of his memory
    To credit his own lie°—he did believe
    He was indeed the Duke, out o'° th' substitution,
    And executing th' outward face of royalty,°
105 With all prerogative. Hence his ambition growing—
    Dost thou hear?

MIRANDA.   Your tale, sir, would cure deafness.

PROSPERO. To have no screen between this part he played
    And him° he played it for, he needs will be
    Absolute Milan.° Me, poor man, my library
110 Was dukedom large enough. Of temporal royalties°
    He thinks me now incapable; confederates—°
    So dry he was for sway°—wi' th' King of Naples
    To give him° annual tribute, do him° homage,
    Subject his coronet to his crown,° and bend
115 The dukedom yet unbowed—alas, poor Milan!—
    To most ignoble stooping.

MIRANDA.   O the heavens!

PROSPERO. Mark his condition° and th' event,° then tell me
    If this might be a brother.

MIRANDA.   I should sin
    To think but nobly of my grandmother.
120 Good wombs have borne bad sons.

PROSPERO.   Now the condition.
    This King of Naples, being an enemy
    To me inveterate, hearkens my brother's suit,
    Which was that he, in lieu o' th' premises°
    Of homage and I know not how much tribute,
125 Should presently extirpate° me and mine
    Out of the dukedom and confer fair Milan

12 How has Antonio won over Prospero's former supporters?
closeness, retirement, seclusion.
but . . . rate. Prospero says that the fact that his study was done in private kept ordinary people from forming any notion of its real value.
good parent, alludes to the proverb that good parents often bear bad children.
sans, without.
lorded, raised to lordship, with power and wealth.

like one . . . lie, that is, like someone who has repeated a lie so often that he has corrupted his recollection and come to believe his own lie.
out o', as a result of.
And . . . royalty, and (as a result of) his carrying out all the ceremonial functions of royalty.

13 What does Antonio eventually come to believe about himself?
him, that is, himself.
Absolute Milan, unconditional Duke of Milan.

14 How might Prospero's own actions be in part responsible for the loss of his dukedom?
temporal royalties, rights and duties of a sovereign.
confederates, conspires, allies himself.
dry . . . sway, thirsty for power.
him, that is, the king of Naples.
Subject . . . crown, subject Antonio's coronet to the King of Naples's crown. A *coronet* was the smaller crown worn by rulers of lower rank than a king.
condition, Antonio's pact with the King of Naples.
event, outcome.
in . . . premises, in return for the pledge.
presently extirpate, at once remove.

With all the honors on my brother. Whereon,
A treacherous army levied, one midnight
Fate to th' purpose, did Antonio open
130 The gates of Milan, and, i' th' dead of darkness,
The ministers for th' purpose hurried thence
Me and thy crying self.
MIRANDA.   Alack, for pity!
I, not remem'bring how I cried out then,
Will cry it o'er again. It is a hint°
135 That wrings mine eyes to 't.
PROSPERO.   Hear a little further,
And then I'll bring thee to the present business
Which now's upon 's, without the which this story
Were most impertinent.°
MIRANDA.   Wherefore did they not
That hour destroy us?
PROSPERO.   Well demanded, wench.
140 My tale provokes that question. Dear, they durst not,
So dear the love my people bore me, nor set
A mark so bloody on the business, but
With colors fairer painted their foul ends.
In few,° they hurried us aboard a bark,
145 Bore us some leagues to sea, where they prepared
A rotten carcass of a butt,° not rigged,
Nor tackle, sail, nor mast; the very rats
Instinctively have quit it. There they hoist us,
To cry to th' sea that roared to us, to sigh
150 To th' winds whose pity, sighing back again,
Did us but loving wrong.°
MIRANDA.   Alack, what trouble
Was I then to you!
PROSPERO.   O, a cherubin
Thou wast that did preserve me. Thou didst smile,
Infused with a fortitude from heaven,
155 When I have decked the sea with drops full salt,
Under my burden groaned, which° raised in me
An undergoing stomach,° to bear up
Against what should ensue.
MIRANDA. How came we ashore?
PROSPERO.   By Providence divine.
160 Some food we had, and some fresh water, that
A noble Neapolitan, Gonzalo,
Out of his charity, who being then appointed
Master of this design, did give us, with
Rich garments, linens, stuffs, and necessaries,
165 Which since have steaded much.° So, of his gentleness,

15 How does Antonio obtain the support of the King of Naples?

hint, occasion.

impertinent, irrelevant.

16 Why are Prospero and Miranda not killed by Antonio and his forces?

few, few words.

butt, tub; here, a battered, leaking ship.

loving wrong, that is, the winds pitied Prospero and Miranda though of necessity they blew them from shore.

which, that is, the smile.

undergoing stomach, courage to go on.

steaded much, been of much use.

Knowing I loved my books, he furnished me
From mine own library with volumes that
I prize above my dukedom.

MIRANDA.   Would I might
But ever see that man!

PROSPERO.   Now I arise.   (*Resumes his magic robes.*)

170 Sit still, and hear the last of our sea-sorrow.
Here in this island we arrived; and here
Have I, thy schoolmaster, made thee more profit°
Than other princess'° can that have more time
For vainer hours and tutors not so careful.

175 MIRANDA. Heavens thank you for 't! And now, I pray you, sir,
For still 'tis beating in my mind, your reason
For raising this sea-storm?

PROSPERO.   Know thus far forth.
By accident most strange, bountiful Fortune,
Now my dear lady, hath mine enemies

180 Brought to this shore; and by my prescience
I find my zenith° doth depend upon
A most auspicious star, whose influence°
If now I court not but omit, my fortunes
Will ever after droop. Here cease more questions.

185 Thou art inclined to sleep; 'tis a good dullness,
And give it way. I know thou canst not choose.   (MIRANDA *sleeps.*)
Come away, servant, come! I am ready now.
Approach, my Ariel, come. (*Enter* ARIEL.)

ARIEL. All hail, great master! Grave sir, hail! I come

190 To answer thy best pleasure; be 't to fly,
To swim, to dive into the fire, to ride
On the curled clouds. To thy strong bidding, task°
Ariel and all his quality.°

PROSPERO.   Hast thou, spirit,
Performed to point° the tempest that I bade thee?

195 ARIEL. To every article.
I boarded the King's ship; now on the beak,°
Now in the waist,° the deck, in every cabin,
I flamed amazement.° Sometime I'd divide,
And burn in many places; on the topmast,

200 The yards, and boresprit,° would I flame distinctly,°
Then meet and join. Jove's lightnings, the precursors
O' th' dreadful thunder-claps, more momentary
And sight-outrunning were not; the fire and cracks
Of sulphurous roaring the most mighty Neptune

205 Seem to besiege and make his bold waves tremble,
Yea, his dread trident shake.

PROSPERO.   My brave spirit!

Who was so firm, so constant, that this coil°
Would not infect his reason?

ARIEL.   Not a soul
But felt a fever of the mad° and played
210 Some tricks of desperation. All but mariners
Plunged in the foaming brine and quit the vessel;
Then all afire with me, the King's son, Ferdinand,
With hair up-staring°—then like reeds, not hair—
Was the first man that leapt; cried, "Hell is empty,
215 And all the devils are here."

PROSPERO.   Why, that's my spirit!
But was not this nigh shore?

ARIEL.   Close by, my master.

PROSPERO. But are they, Ariel, safe?

ARIEL.   Not a hair perished.
On their sustaining garments° not a blemish,
But fresher than before; and, as thou bad'st me,
220 In troops I have dispersed them 'bout the isle.
The King's son have I landed by himself,
Whom I left cooling of the air with sighs
In an odd angle° of the isle and sitting,
His arms in this sad knot.°   (Folds his arms.)

PROSPERO.   Of the King's ship,
225 The mariners, say how thou hast disposed,
And all the rest o' th' fleet.

ARIEL.   Safely in harbor
Is the King's ship; in the deep nook, where once
Thou calledst me up at midnight to fetch dew
From the still-vexed Bermoothes,° there she's hid;
230 The mariners all under hatches stowed,
Who, with a charm joined to their suffered labor,°
I have left asleep; and for the rest o' th' fleet,
Which I dispersed, they all have met again
And are upon the Mediterranean flote°
235 Bound sadly home for Naples,
Supposing that they saw the King's ship wracked
And his great person perish.

PROSPERO.   Ariel, thy charge
Exactly is performed. But there's more work.
What is the time o' th' day?

ARIEL.   Past the mid season.°
240 PROSPERO. At least two glasses.° The time 'twixt six and now
Must by us both be spent most preciously.

ARIEL. Is there more toil? Since thou dost give me pains,
Let me remember° thee what thou hast promised,
Which is not yet performed me.

coil, tumult.

of the mad, that is, such as the insane feel.

up-staring, standing on end.

22 What has been Ariel's role in the shipwreck?

sustaining garments, clothes that buoyed them up in the sea.

angle, corner.
arms . . . knot, folded arms are said to be indicative of melancholy.

still-vexed Bermoothes, ever stormy Bermudas.

with . . . labor, by means of a spell added to all the labor they have undergone.
flote, sea.

23 Note that Ariel has separated the ship-wrecked men into several groups. What has become of Ferdinand, the king's son? Of the mariners?

mid season, noon.
glasses, hourglasses.

24 According to Prospero, how many hours remain for him and Ariel to complete their work?
remember, remind.

PROSPERO. How now? Moody?

45   What is 't thou canst demand?

ARIEL. My liberty.

PROSPERO. Before the time be out? No more!

ARIEL. I prithee,

  Remember I have done thee worthy service,

  Told thee no lies, made thee no mistakings, served

  Without or grudge or° grumblings. Thou didst promise

50   To bate° me a full year.

PROSPERO. Dost thou forget

  From what a torment I did free thee?

ARIEL. No.

PROSPERO. Thou dost, and think'st it much to tread the ooze

  Of the salt deep,

  To run upon the sharp wind of the north,

55   To do me business in the veins o' th' earth

  When it is baked with frost.

ARIEL. I do not, sir.

PROSPERO. Thou liest, malignant thing! Hast thou forgot

  The foul witch Sycorax, who with age and envy°

  Was grown into a hoop? Hast thou forgot her?

260 **ARIEL.** No, sir.

PROSPERO. Thou hast. Where was she born? Speak. Tell me.

ARIEL. Sir, in Argier°

PROSPERO. O, was she so? I must

  Once in a month recount what thou hast been,

  Which thou forget'st. This damned witch Syncorax,

265   For mischiefs manifold and sorceries terrible

  To enter human hearing, from Argier,

  Thou know'st, was banished; for one thing she did°

  They would not take her life. Is not this true?

ARIEL. Ay, sir.

270 **PROSPERO.** This blue-eyed° hag was hither brought with child

  And here was left by th' sailors. Thou, my slave,

  As thou report'st thyself, was then her servant;

  And, for° thou wast a spirit too delicate

  To act her earthy and abhorred commands,

275   Refusing her grand hests,° she did confine thee,

  By help of her more potent ministers,

  And in her most unmitigable rage,

  Into a cloven pine, within which rift

  Imprisoned thou didst painfully remain

280   A dozen years; within which space she died

  And left thee there, where thou did'st vent thy groans

  As fast as mill-wheels strike. Then was this island—

  Save for the son that she did litter here,

or grudge or, either grudge or.
bate, remit, deduct.

envy, malice.

25 | What does Ariel ask of Prospero? What is Prospero's reaction?

Argier, Algiers.

one . . . did, perhaps a reference to her pregnancy, for which her life would be spared.
blue-eyed, with dark circles under the eyes.

for, because.

hests, commands.

26 | How does Ariel happen to be on the island?

A freckled whelp hag-born—not honored with
285 A human shape.
ARIEL.   Yes, Caliban her son.
PROSPERO. Dull thing, I say so; he, that Caliban
Whom now I keep in service. Thou best know'st
What torment I did find thee in; thy groans
Did make wolves howl and penetrate the breasts
290 Of ever angry bears. It was a torment
To lay upon the damned, which Sycorax
Could not again undo. It was mine art,
When I arrived and heard thee, that made gape
The pine and let thee out.
ARIEL.   I thank thee, master.
295 PROSPERO. If thou more murmur'st, I will rend an oak
And peg thee in his° knotty entrails till
Thou hast howled away twelve winters.
ARIEL.   Pardon, master;
I will be correspondent° to command
And do my spriting gently.
300 PROSPERO. Do so, and after two days
I will discharge thee.
ARIEL.   That's my noble master!
What shall I do? Say what? What shall I do?
PROSPERO. Go make thyself like a nymph o' th' sea. Be subject
To no sight but thine and mine, invisible
305 To every eyeball else. Go take this shape
And hither come in 't. Go, hence with diligence!   (*Exit* ARIEL.)
Awake, dear heart, awake! Thou hast slept well;
Awake!
MIRANDA. The strangeness of your story put
Heaviness in me.
PROSPERO.   Shake it off. Come on;
310 We'll visit Caliban my slave, who never
Yields us kind answer.
MIRANDA.   'Tis a villain, sir,
I do not love to look on.
PROSPERO.   But, as 'tis,
We cannot miss° him. He does make our fire,
Fetch in our wood, and serves in offices
315 That profit us. What, ho! Slave! Caliban!
Thou earth, thou! Speak.
CALIBAN (*within*).   There's wood enough within.
PROSPERO. Come forth, I say! There's other business for thee.
Come, thou tortoise! When?   (*Enter* ARIEL *like a water-nymph.*)
Fine apparition! My quaint° Ariel,
320 Hark in thine ear.   (*Whispers.*)

426   *The Renaissance*

---

27 This is the first mention by name of Caliban, who will have a major role in the play. From Prospero's description, what do you infer his character will be like?

28 Lines 270–294 provide clues to Ariel's time on the island and to Caliban's age. We have already been told (line 53) that Prospero has been on the island for twelve years. Ariel was confined in the tree for twelve years before Prospero arrived. Assuming that Ariel was confined there immediately after his arrival and released immediately after Prospero arrived, Ariel has been on the island for twenty-four years. Since Sycorax was pregnant when she was exiled there, Caliban must now be twenty-three or twenty-four years old.
his, its.
correspondent, responsive, submissive.
29 What other powers does Ariel have? Some scholars point out that this disguise is unnecessary since Ariel will be invisible to all the characters but Prospero and himself. Shakespeare may, however, have had his audience in mind.

miss, do without.

30 Why does Prospero retain Caliban despite Miranda's dislike for him?

31 Note that Prospero addresses Caliban as "thou earth." How does this contrast with what we know of Ariel's powers?
quaint, ingenious.

ARIEL. My lord, it shall be done. *(Exit.)*

PROSPERO. Thou poisonous slave, got by the devil himself
Upon thy wicked dam, come forth! *(Enter* CALIBAN.*)*

CALIBAN. As wicked° dew as e'er my mother brushed
With raven's feather from unwholesome fen

325 Drop on you both! A south-west° blow on ye
And blister you all o'er!

PROSPERO. For this, be sure, tonight thou shalt have cramps,
Side-stitches that shall pen thy breath up; urchins°
Shall, for that vast° of night that they may work,°

330 All exercise on thee. Thou shalt be pinched
As thick as honeycomb, each pinch more stinging
Than bees that made 'em.

CALIBAN. I must eat my dinner.
This island's mine, by Sycorax my mother,
Which thou tak'st from me. When thou cam'st first,

335 Thou strok'st me and made much of me, wouldst give me
Water with berries in 't, and teach me how
To name the bigger light, and how the less,
That burn by day and night; and then I loved thee
And showed thee all the qualities o' th' isle,

340 The fresh springs, brine-pits, barren place and fertile.
Cursed be I that did so! All the charms
Of Sycorax, toads, beetles, bats, light on you!
For I am all the subjects that you have,
Which first was mine own king; and here you sty me

345 In this hard rock, whiles you do keep from me
The rest o' th' island.

PROSPERO. Thou most lying slave,
Whom stripes° may move, not kindness! I have used thee,
Filth as thou art, with humane care, and lodged thee
In mine own cell, till thou didst seek to violate

350 The honor of my child.

CALIBAN. O ho, O ho! Would 't had been done!
Thou didst prevent me; I had peopled else
This isle with Calibans.

MIRANDA. Abhorred slave,
Which any print of goodness wilt not take,

355 Being capable of all ill! I pitied thee,
Took pains to make thee speak, taught thee each hour
One thing or other. When thou didst not, savage,
Know thine own meaning, but wouldst gabble like
A thing most brutish, I endowed thy purposes

360 With words that made them known. But thy vile race,°
Though thou didst learn, had that in 't which good natures
Could not abide to be with; therefore wast thou

wicked, mischievous, harmful.

south-west, wind thought to bring disease.

32 We have Caliban's first words in line 316 and this speech (lines 323–326). How would you characterize him at this point?

urchins, hedgehogs; here, suggesting goblins in the guise of hedgehogs.

vast, lengthy, desolate time.

that . . . work, evil spirits were thought to be restricted to the hours of darkness.

33 What is Caliban's complaint against Prospero? What connection can you make between this complaint and Ariel's request of Prospero?

stripes, lashes.

race, natural disposition, species, nature.

Deservedly confined into this rock,
Who hadst deserved more than a prison.

365 **CALIBAN.** You taught me language, and my profit on 't
Is, I know how to curse. The red plague rid° you
For learning° me your language!

PROSPERO. Hag-seed,° hence!
Fetch us in fuel; and be quick, thou 'rt best,°
To answer other business. Shrug'st thou, malice?

370 If thou neglect'st or dost unwillingly
What I command, I'll rack thee with old° cramps,
Fill all thy bones with aches,° make thee roar
That beasts shall tremble at thy din.

CALIBAN. No, pray thee.
(*Aside.*) I must obey. His art is of such pow'r,

375 It would control my dam's god, Setebos,
And make a vassal of him.

PROSPERO. So, slave, hence!
(*Exit* CALIBAN. *Enter* FERDINAND; *and* ARIEL, *invisible, playing
and singing.* FERDINAND *does not see* PROSPERO *and* MIRANDA.)

ARIEL (*sings*). *Come unto these yellow sands,*
And then take hands.
Curtsied when you have and kissed,

380 *The wild waves whist,°*
Foot it featly° here and there;
And, sweet sprites, the burden° bear.
Hark, hark!
(Burden, dispersedly° within). *Bow-wow.*

385 *The watch-dogs bark.*
(Burden, dispersedly within.) *Bow-wow.*
Hark, hark! I hear
The strain of strutting chanticleer
Cry, Cock-a-diddle-dow.

390 **FERDINAND.** Where should this music be? I' th' air or th' earth?
It sounds no more; and, sure, it waits upon
Some god o' th' island. Sitting on a bank,
Weeping again the King my father's wrack,
This music crept by me upon the waters,

395 Allaying both their fury and my passion
With its sweet air. Thence I have followed it,
Or it hath drawn me rather. But 'tis gone.
No, it begins again.

ARIEL (*sings*). *Full fathom five thy father lies;*

400 *Of his bones are coral made;*
Those are pearls that were his eyes.
Nothing of him that doth fade

34 What is Miranda's complaint against Caliban? What punishment does she feel he deserved? Some scholars, thinking this speech is too strong for her, attribute it to Prospero.
rid, destroy.
learning, teaching.
35 Comment on Caliban's response. Do you think Shakespeare's audience would have laughed at it? Explain.
Hag-seed, offspring of a female demon.
thou'rt best, you'd be well advised.
old, such as old people suffer; or, plenty of.
aches, pronounced (āch'əs)

36 This is the first of many songs within the play. Like those who attend musical comedies today, Shakespeare's audience enjoyed song and dance. Note the use of onomatopoeia (the sound of a word suggesting the thing it is describing) in lines 384, 386, and 389 (bow-wow, and cock-a-diddle-dow).
whist, being hushed.
featly, nimbly.
burden, refrain.
dispersedly, from all directions.

37 What purpose has Ariel's first song served?

Sir John Everett Millais, *Ferdinand Lured by Ariel*. 1849.
Private Collection

But doth suffer a sea-change
Into something rich and strange.
405 *Sea-nymphs hourly ring his knell:*
    (*Burden within*). *Ding-dong.*
Hark, now I hear them—Ding-dong, bell.

FERDINAND. The ditty does remember° my drowned father.
This is no mortal business, nor no sound
410 That the earth owes.° I hear it now above me.

PROSPERO. The fringed curtains of thine eye advance°
And say what thou seest yond.

MIRANDA.   What is 't? A spirit?
Lord, how it looks about! Believe me, sir,
It carries a brave° form. But 'tis a spirit.

415 PROSPERO. No, wench, it eats and sleeps and hath such senses
As we have, such. This gallant which thou seest
Was in the wrack; and, but he's something stained
With grief, that's beauty's canker,° thou mightst call him
A goodly person. He hath lost his fellows
420 And strays about to find 'em.

MIRANDA.   I might call him
A thing divine, for nothing natural
I ever saw so noble.

PROSPERO (*aside*).   It goes on, I see,
As my soul prompts it. Spirit, fine spirit, I'll free thee
Within two days for this.

FERDINAND (*seeing* MIRANDA). Most sure, the goddess
425 On whom these airs attend!—Vouchsafe° my prayer
May know if you remain° upon this island.
And that you will some good instruction give
How I may bear me° here. My prime° request,
Which I do last pronounce, is, O you wonder!
430 If you be maid or no?

MIRANDA.   No wonder, sir,
But certainly a maid.

FERDINAND.   My language? Heavens!
I am the best° of them that speak this speech,
Were I but where 'tis spoken.

PROSPERO (*coming forward*).   How? The best?
What wert thou, if the King of Naples heard thee?

435 FERDINAND. A single° thing, as I am now, that wonders
To hear thee speak of Naples. He does hear me;
And that he does I weep.° Myself am Naples,°
Who with mine eyes, never since at ebb, beheld
The King my father wracked.

MIRANDA.   Alack, for mercy!

remember, recall.

owes, owns.

38 | What is Ferdinand's reaction to Ariel's song?
advance, raise.

brave, excellent.

but . . . canker, except that he has been weeping, which has marred his good looks.

39 | Compare Miranda's reaction to the sight of Ferdinand with her father's reaction.

40 | This is Prospero's first aside of the play. It lets the audience know something the other characters on stage do not. What is that something?
Vouchsafe, grant.
remain, dwell.
bear me, conduct myself.
prime, chief.

41 | "O you wonder" (line 429) is an example of wordplay. *Miranda* is a Latin name that means "wonderful" or "admirable." What is Ferdinand most interested in learning about Miranda?
best. Ferdinand means that he is now King of Naples.
single, (1) solitary, (2) feeble.
He . . . weep, that is, Ferdinand (who believes he is now the King of Naples) hears himself; and this presumed loss of his father, which he thinks has made him King, also makes him grieve.
Naples, the King of Naples.

440 **FERDINAND.** Yes, faith, and all his lords, the Duke of Milan
　　And his brave son° being twain.

PROSPERO (*aside*).　　　　The Duke of Milan
　　And his more braver daughter could control thee,
　　If now 'twere fit to do 't. At the first sight
　　They have changed eyes.° Delicate Ariel,
445　I'll set thee free for this. (*To* FERDINAND.) A word, good sir.
　　I fear you have done yourself some wrong.° A word!

MIRANDA (*aside*). Why speaks my father so ungently? This
　　Is the third man that e'er I saw, the first
　　That e'er I sighed for. Pity move my father
450　To be inclined my way!

FERDINAND.　　　　O, if a virgin,
　　And your affection not gone forth, I'll make you
　　The Queen of Naples.

PROSPERO.　　　　Soft, sir! One word more.
　　(*Aside*.) They are both in either's pow'rs; but this swift business
　　I must uneasy° make, lest too light winning
455　Make the prize light.° (*To* FERDINAND.) One word more: I charge thee
　　That thou attend me. Thou dost here usurp
　　The name thou ow'st° not, and hast put thyself
　　Upon this island as a spy, to win it
　　From me, the lord on 't.

FERDINAND.　　　　No, as I am a man.
460 **MIRANDA.** There's nothing ill can dwell in such a temple.
　　If the ill spirit have so fair a house,
　　Good things will strive to dwell with 't.

PROSPERO.　　　　　　Follow me.—
　　Speak not you for him; he's a traitor.—Come,
　　I'll manacle thy neck and feet together.
465　Sea-water shalt thou drink; thy food shall be
　　The fresh-brook mussels, withered roots, and husks
　　Wherein the acorn cradled. Follow.

FERDINAND.　　　　No.
　　I will resist such entertainment° till
　　Mine enemy has more pow'r.　(*He draws, and is charmed from moving.*)

MIRANDA.　　　　O dear father,
470　Make not too rash a trial of him, for
　　He's gentle, and not fearful.°

PROSPERO.　　　　What, I say,
　　My foot° my tutor?—Put thy sword up, traitor,
　　Who mak'st a show but dar'st not strike, thy conscience
　　Is so possessed with guilt. Come, from thy ward,°
475　For I can here disarm thee with this stick
　　And make thy weapon drop.　　　　(*Brandishes his staff.*)

brave son. If this refers to Antonio's son, it is the only reference in the play; in Shakespeare's day *brave* could mean "fine," "gallant," or "finely dressed."
changed eyes, exchanged amorous glances.
done . . . wrong, spoken falsely.
42 | What does Prospero mean by this aside?
43 | Is Miranda's reaction understandable? Explain.

uneasy, difficult.
light . . . light, easy . . . cheap.
44 | Explain the meaning of this aside.
ow'st, ownest.

45 | What argument does Miranda give for presuming Ferdinand's goodness?
46 | What excuse does Prospero give for his harsh treatment of Ferdinand? What is his real reason for it?

entertainment, treatment.

gentle . . . fearful, well-born and not cowardly.

foot, subordinate (Miranda, the foot, presumes to instruct Prospero, the head); this may be a Latin-based pun on *ped*, "foot," and *pedagogue*, "tutor."
ward, defensive posture in fencing.

MIRANDA (*trying to hinder him*). Beseech you, father.

PROSPERO. Hence! Hang not on my garments.

MIRANDA.   Sir, have pity!

I'll be his surety.

PROSPERO.   Silence! One word more

Shall make me chide thee, if not hate thee. What,

480   An advocate for an impostor? Hush!

Thou think'st there is no more such shapes as he,

Having seen but him and Caliban. Foolish wench,

To° th' most of men this is a Caliban

And they to him are angels.

MIRANDA.   My affections

485   Are then most humble; I have no ambition

To see a goodlier man.

PROSPERO (*to* FERDINAND). Come on, obey.

Thy nerves° are in their infancy again

And have no vigor in them.

FERDINAND.   So they are

My spirits, as in a dream, are all bound up.

490   My father's loss, the weakness which I feel,

The wrack of all my friends, nor this man's threats

To whom I am subdued, are but light to me,

Might I but through my prison once a day

Behold this maid. All corners else o' th' earth

495   Let liberty make use of; space enough

Have I in such a prison.

PROSPERO (*aside*). It works. (*To* FERDINAND.) Come on.—

Thou hast done well, fine Ariel! (*To* FERDINAND.) Follow me.

(*To Ariel.*) Hark what thou else shalt do me.°

MIRANDA (*to* FERDINAND).   Be of comfort.

My father's of a better nature, sir,

500   Than he appears by speech. This is unwonted

Which now came from him.

PROSPERO (*to* ARIEL).   Thou shalt be as free

As mountain winds; but then exactly do

All points of my command.

ARIEL.   To th' syllable.

PROSPERO (*to* FERDINAND). Come, follow. (*To* MIRANDA.) Speak not for

him.

                                                        (*Exeunt.*)

47 This is a fine illustration of stage directions (instructions to the actors as to what to do onstage) presented within the dialogue of the play. What should the actress (or boy actor) portraying Miranda be doing?

To, compared to.

nerves, sinews.

48 What does Prospero mean?

me, for me.

49 At this point Prospero is involved in several simultaneous activities. We know what is happening with Ferdinand and Miranda, but what may he have been instructing Ariel about?

THINK AND DISCUSS

Understanding

1. How do the mariners and nobles differ in behavior when they know the ship is sinking?
2. In addition to introducing all the major characters, the first act of a Shakespeare drama presents exposition, revealing the events that took place before the play opened but are related to its plot. What antecedent action does Prospero present in his long conversation with Miranda?
3. What antecedent action is presented in his conversation with Ariel?
4. What antecedent action is presented in his conversation with Caliban?

Analyzing

5. In the argument between the nobles and the Boatswain, which side is right? Explain.
6. Compare Miranda's reaction at her first sight of Ferdinand with his reaction to her.
7. Contrast Prospero's behavior toward Ariel with his behavior toward Caliban and account for the difference.
8. Based on what has occurred in Act One, what would you say is Prospero's chief reason for raising the tempest and causing the shipwreck?
9. By now you are aware that Prospero is the **protagonist,** the leading character in the play. What actions has he taken thus far that prove he is the protagonist? The persons opposing the protagonist are called the **antagonists.** Who are they in this play? How do you know?

Extending

10. From what you have read thus far, why do you suppose Shakespeare gave Prospero magic powers?

APPLYING: Rhythm HT
See Handbook of Literary Terms, p. 966.

Rhythm, or meter, in poetry is the arrangement of stressed and unstressed syllables to form a recurring pattern. The most commonly used rhythm is iambic. An iamb, also known as an iambic foot, consists of a single unstressed syllable followed by a single stressed syllable, as in the word *today.* Iambic rhythm is closest to the natural rhythm of English speech; probably this accounts for its extensive use in Shakespeare's plays. Most lines in his plays have five iambic feet; we say that they are written in iambic pentameter.

1. Look at Scene 2, line 11. Miranda is speaking. How many syllables are accented? Which are they? This line is an example of iambic pentameter.
2. Sometimes Shakespeare varies the iambic rhythm for effect. Look at the next line of Miranda's speech (line 12). Do the first two words constitute an iambic foot? Where does the iambic rhythm first vary in this line?
3. Copy this line (line 12) on a separate sheet of paper and indicate the stressed and unstressed syllables.

VOCABULARY

Antonyms

Each word in the first column below has an antonym in the second column. Copy each word in the first column on a separate sheet of paper; then choose a word with the opposite meaning from the second column and write it on the same line. If in doubt, consult your Glossary.

abhorred	desert
allay	effective
bootless	hindsight
diligence	increase
extirpate	nadir
fen	revered
perdition	salvation
perfidious	slothfulness
prescience	spare
zenith	trustworthy

ACT TWO

SCENE 1.

Another part of the island. (Played on the Platform Stage and the Tarras for
ARIEL'S *first appearance.) Enter* ALONSO, SEBASTIAN, ANTONIO, GONZALO,
ADRIAN, FRANCISCO, *and others.*

GONZALO. Beseech you, sir, be merry. You have cause,
    So have we all, of joy, for our escape
    Is much beyond our loss. Our hint of° woe
    Is common; every day some sailor's wife,
5   The masters of some merchant, and the merchant,°
    Have just our theme of woe; but for the miracle,
    I mean our preservation, few in millions
    Can speak like us. Then wisely, good sir, weigh
    Our sorrow with our comfort.

ALONSO.   Prithee, peace.

10 SEBASTIAN (*to* ANTONIO). He receives comfort like cold porridge.°

ANTONIO (*to* SEBASTIAN). The visitor° will not give him o'er° so.

SEBASTIAN. Look, he's winding up the watch of his wit; by and by it will
    strike.

GONZALO. Sir—

15 SEBASTIAN (*to* ANTONIO). One. Tell.°

GONZALO. When every grief is entertained that's offered,
    Comes to th' entertainer—°

SEBASTIAN. A dollar.°

GONZALO. Dolor comes to him, indeed. You have spoken truer than you
20   purposed.

SEBASTIAN. You have taken it wiselier than I meant you should.

GONZALO. Therefore, my lord—

ANTONIO. Fie, what a spendthrift is he of his tongue!

ALONSO. I prithee, spare.

25 GONZALO. Well, I have done. But yet—

SEBASTIAN. He will be talking.

ANTONIO. Which, of he or Adrian, for a good wager, first begins to crow?°

SEBASTIAN. The old cock.°

ANTONIO. The cock'rel.°

30 SEBASTIAN. Done. The wager?

hint of, occasion for.
masters . . . the merchant, officers of some merchant vessel and the merchant himself, the owner.

> **50** How effective is Gonzalo's speech attempting to comfort Alonso, who thinks his son Ferdinand has been drowned? Explain.

porridge, with a pun on *peace* and *pease,* a usual ingredient of porridge.

> **51** Lines 10–166 may be difficult to follow when you read them, but they are clear when the play is acted. Sebastian and Antonio are carrying on a running commentary, sometimes humorous, sometimes sarcastic, on Gonzalo's and Adrian's attempts to comfort and divert Alonso.

visitor, one taking nourishment and comfort to the sick, that is, Gonzalo.
give him o'er, abandon him.
Tell, keep count.
When . . . entertainer, when every sorrow that presents itself is accepted without resistance, there comes to the recipient.
dollar, widely-circulated coin, the German *Thaler* and the Spanish *piece of eight;* Sebastian puns on *entertainer* in the sense of *innkeeper;* to Gonzalo, *dollar* suggests *dolor,* grief.

> **52** Gonzalo has overheard Sebastian's gibe and responds to it. The pun is on *dollar—dolor.*

Which . . . crow, which of the two, Gonzalo or Adrian, do you bet will speak (crow) first.
old cock, that is, Gonzalo.
cock'rel, that is, Adrian.

ANTONIO. A laughter.°

SEBASTIAN. A match!°

ADRIAN. Though this island seem to be desert—

ANTONIO. Ha, ha, ha!

35 SEBASTIAN. So, you're paid.

ADRIAN. Uninhabitable and almost inaccessible—

SEBASTIAN. Yet—

ADRIAN. Yet—

ANTONIO. He could not miss 't.°

40 ADRIAN. It must needs be of subtle, tender, and delicate temperance.°

ANTONIO. Temperance° was a delicate wench.

SEBASTIAN. Ay, and a subtle,° as he most learnedly delivered.°

ADRIAN. The air breathes upon us here most sweetly.

SEBASTIAN. As if it had lungs, and rotten ones.

45 ANTONIO. Or as 'twere perfumed by a fen.

GONZALO. Here is everything advantageous to life.

ANTONIO. True, save means to live.

SEBASTIAN. Of that there's none, or little.

GONZALO. How lush and lusty° the grass looks! How green!

50 ANTONIO. The ground indeed is tawny.°

SEBASTIAN. With an eye° of green in 't.

ANTONIO. He misses not much.

SEBASTIAN. No; he doth but mistake the truth totally.

GONZALO. But the rarity of it is—which is indeed almost beyond credit—

55 SEBASTIAN. As many vouched° rarities are.

GONZALO. That our garments, being, as they were, drenched in the sea, hold notwithstanding their freshness and glosses, being rather new-dyed than stained with salt water.

ANTONIO. If but one of his pockets° could speak, would it not say he lies?

60 SEBASTIAN. Ay, or very falsely pocket up° his report.

GONZALO. Methinks our garments are now as fresh as when we put them on first in Afric, at the marriage of the King's fair daughter Claribel to the King of Tunis.

SEBASTIAN. 'Twas a sweet marriage, and we prosper well in our return.

65 ADRIAN. Tunis was never graced before with such a paragon to° their queen.

GONZALO. Not since widow Dido's° time.

ANTONIO. Widow! A pox o' that! How came that widow in? Widow Dido!

SEBASTIAN. What if he had said "widower Aeneas" too? Good Lord, how you take it!

70 ADRIAN. "Widow Dido" said you? You make me study of that. She was of Carthage, not of Tunis.

GONZALO. This Tunis, sir, was Carthage.

ADRIAN. Carthage?

GONZALO. I assure you, Carthage.

75 ANOTONIO. His word is more than the miraculous harp.°

SEBASTIAN. He hath raised the wall and houses too.

---

laughter, a laugh.

A match, a bargain, agreed.

miss't, (1) avoid saying "Yet"; (2) miss the island.
temperance, climate.
Temperance, a girl's name.
subtle. Here it means *tricky*; in line 40 it means *delicate*.
delivered, uttered (Sebastian joins in the Puritan baiting of Antonio with his use of the pious cant phrase "learnedly delivered").
lusty, healthy.
tawny, dull brown, yellowish.
eye, tinge or spot (perhaps with reference to Gonzalo's eye or judgment).
vouched, certified.
pockets, that is, because they are muddy.
pocket up, conceal or suppress.
to, for.
widow Dido, Queen of Carthage deserted by Aeneas who was in fact a widow when Aeneas, a widower, met her.

53 Gonzalo is geographically inaccurate, to the amusement of Antonio and Sebastian. Tunis is located near (but not at) the site of the ancient city of Carthage. Antonio and Sebastian are amused also at Gonzalo's referring to Dido as "widow" and not as queen or as Aeneas's lover.

miraculous harp, alludes to Amphion's harp with which he raised the walls of Thebes; Gonzalo has exceeded that deed by mistakenly creating a whole city—walls and houses.

ANTONIO. What impossible matter will he make easy next?

SEBASTIAN. I think he will carry this island home in his pocket and give it his son for an apple.

80 ANTONIO. And, sowing the kernels of it in the sea, bring forth more islands.

GONZALO. Ay.°

ANTONIO. Why, in good time.°

GONZALO (to ALONSO). Sir, we were talking that our garments seem now as fresh as when we were at Tunis at the marriage of your daughter, who is

85 now queen.

ANTONIO. And the rarest° that e'er came there.

SEBASTIAN. Bate,° I beseech you, widow Dido.

ANTONIO. O, widow Dido? Ay, widow Dido.

GONZALO. Is not, sir, my doublet as fresh as the first day I wore it? I mean,

90 in a sort.°

ANTONIO. That "sort" was well fished for.

GONZALO. When I wore it at your daughter's marriage?

ALONSO. You cram these words into mine ears against
The stomach° of my sense. Would I had never

95 Married° my daughter there! For, coming thence,
My son is lost and, in my rate,° she too,
Who is so far from Italy removed
I ne'er again shall see her. O thou mine heir
Of Naples and of Milan, what strange fish

100 Hath made his meal on thee?

FRANCISCO.   Sir, he may live.
I saw him beat the surges under him,
And ride upon their backs. He trod the water,
Whose enmity he flung aside, and breasted
The surge most swoll'n that met him. His bold head

105 'Bove the contentious waves he kept, and oared
Himself with his good arms in lusty° stroke
To th' shore, that o'er his wave-worm basis bowed,
As° stooping to relieve him.° I not doubt
He came alive to land.

ALONSO.   No, no, he's gone.

110 SEBASTIAN. Sir, you may thank yourself for this great loss,
That would not bless our Europe with your daughter,
But rather lose her to an African,
Where she at least is banished from your eye,
Who° hath cause to wet the grief on 't.

ALONSO.   Prithee, peace.

115 SEBASTIAN. You were kneeled to and importuned otherwise
By all of us, and the fair soul herself
Weighed between loathness and obedience, at
Which end o' th' beam should bow.° We have lost your son,
I fear, for ever. Milan and Naples have

120 Moe° widows in them of this business' making

Ay. Gonzalo may be reasserting his point about Carthage, or he may be responding ironically to Antonio who in turn answers sarcastically.

in good time, an expression of ironical agreement or amazement; that is, "sure, right away."

rarest, most remarkable, beautiful.

Bate, abate, except, leave out; that is, don't forget Dido, or, let's have no more talk of Dido.

in a sort, in a way.

stomach, appetite.

Married, given in marriage.

rate, estimation, consideration.

54 How effective have been the attempts to comfort and divert Alonso? What may you then infer about his feeling for his son?

lusty, vigorous.

that o'er . . . him. Francisco's image here is of a sea-cliff which waves have hollowed out at its foot. He says the cliff seemed to bend protectively over Ferdinand.

As, as if.

Who, which, that is, the eye.

the fair soul . . . bow, that is, Claribel herself was poised uncertain between unwillingness to marry and obedience to her father as to which end of the scale should sink, which should prevail.

Moe, more.

Than we bring men to comfort them.
The fault's your own.
ALONSO. So is the dear'st° o' th' loss.
GONZALO.   My lord Sebastian,
The truth you speak doth lack some gentleness,
125 And time° to speak it in. You rub the sore,
When you should bring the plaster.
SEBASTIAN.   Very well.
ANTONIO. And most chirurgeonly.°
GONZALO. It is foul weather in us all, good sir,
When you are cloudy.
SEBASTIAN (*to* ANTONIO). Foul weather?
ANTONIO (*to* SEBASTIAN).   Very foul.
130 **GONZALO.** Had I plantation° of this isle, my lord—
ANTONIO. He'd sow 't with nettle-seed.
SEBASTIAN.   Or docks, or mallows.°
GONZALO. And were the king on 't, what would I do?
SEBASTIAN. Scape being drunk for want of wine.
GONZALO. I' th' commonwealth I would by contraries°
135 Execute all things; for no kind of traffic°
Would I admit; no name of magistrate;
Letters° should not be known; riches, poverty,
And use of service,° none; contract, succession,°
Bourn,° bound of land,° tilth,° vineyard, none;
140 No use of metal, corn,° or wine, or oil;
No occupation; all men idle, all,
And women too, but innocent and pure;
No sovereignty—
SEBASTIAN.   Yet he would be king on 't.
ANTONIO. The latter end of his commonwealth forgets the beginning.
145 **GONZALO.** All things in common nature should produce
Without sweat or endeavor. Treason, felony,
Sword, pike, knife, gun, or need of any engine,°
Would I not have; but nature should bring forth,
Of it° own kind, all foison,° all abundance,
150 To feed my innocent people.
SEBASTIAN. No marrying 'mong his subjects?
ANTONIO. None, man; all idle—whores and knaves.
GONZALO. I would with such perfection govern, sir,
T' excel the golden age.
SEBASTIAN.   Save° his Majesty!
155 **ANTONIO.** Long live Gonzalo!
GONZALO.   And—do you mark me, sir?
ALONSO. Prithee, no more. Thou dost talk nothing to me.
GONZALO. I do well believe your Highness, and did it to minister occasion°
to these gentlemen, who are of such sensible° and nimble lungs that they
always use to laugh at nothing.

55 Contrast Sebastian's comments to Alonso with those of Gonzalo and Adrian. What may you infer about Sebastian's character?
dear'st, heaviest, most costly.
time, appropriate time.
chirurgeonly, like a skilled surgeon; Antonio mocks Gonzalo's medical analogy of a plaster applied curatively to a wound.

56 Antonio again mocks Gonzalo's words. What may you infer about his character at this point?
plantation, colonization (with subsequent word-play on the literal meaning).
docks, mallows, various weeds.
by contraries, by what is directly opposite to usual custom.

57 In this speech (lines 134–143) and in his next speech (lines 145–150) Gonzalo is quoting from Montaigne's essay *Of Cannibals* (page 446), much to the further amusement of Sebastian and Antonio.
traffic, trade.
Letters, learning.
use of service, custom of employing servants.
succession, holding of property by right of inheritance.
Bourn, boundaries.
bound of land, landmarks.
tilth, tillage of soil.
corn, grain.
engine, instrument of warfare.
it, its.
foison, plenty.

Save, God save.

minister occasion, furnish opportunity.
sensible, sensitive.
58 Note the wordplay on the word *nothing* in lines 156–162.

160 **ANTONIO.** 'Twas you we laughed at.

GONZALO. Who in this kind of merry fooling am nothing to you; so you may
continue and laugh at nothing still.

ANTONIO. What a blow was there given!

SEBASTIAN. An° it had not fall'n flat-long.

165 **GONZALO.** You are gentlemen of brave mettle; you would lift the moon out
of her sphere, if she would continue in it five weeks without changing.
(Enter ARIEL *invisible playing solemn music.)*

SEBASTIAN. We would so, and then go a-batfowling.

ANTONIO. Nay, good my lord, be not angry.

GONZALO. No, I warrant you, I will not adventure my discretion so weakly.°

170   Will you laugh me asleep? For I am very heavy.°

ANTONIO. Go sleep, and hear us.° *(All sleep except* ALONSO, SEBASTIAN, *and*
ANTONIO.)

ALONSO. What, all so soon asleep? I wish mine eyes
Would, with themselves, shut up my thoughts. I find
They are inclined to do so.

SEBASTIAN.   Please you, sir,

175   Do not omit° the heavy° offer of it.
It seldom visits sorrow; when it doth,
It is a comforter.

ANTONIO.   We two, my lord,
Will guard your person while you take your rest,
And watch your safety.

ALONSO.   Thank you. Wondrous heavy.

(ALONSO sleeps. Exit ARIEL.)

180 **SEBASTIAN.** What a strange drowsiness possesses them!

ANTONIO. It is the quality o' th' climate.

SEBASTIAN.   Why
Doth it not then our eyelids sink? I find not
Myself disposed to sleep.

ANTONIO.   Nor I; my spirits are nimble.
They fell together all, as by consent;

185   They dropped, as by a thunder-stroke. What might,
Worthy Sebastian? O, what might—? No more—
And yet methinks I see it in thy face,
What thou shouldst be. Th' occasion speaks° thee, and
My strong imagination sees a crown

190   Dropping upon thy head.

SEBASTIAN.   What, art thou waking?

ANTONIO. Do you not hear me speak?

SEBASTIAN.   I do; and surely
It is a sleepy language and thou speak'st
Out of thy sleep. What is it thou didst say?
This is a strange repose, to be asleep

195   With eyes wide open—standing, speaking, moving—
And yet so fast asleep.

438 *The Renaissance*

An, if.

59 Sebastian is referring to hunting bats at night, when they are flying; there is a secondary meaning to "batfowling," that of fooling a simpleton. Gonzalo's reaction shows that he is aware of both meanings. Note the stage direction for Gonzalo contained in Antonio's words in line 168.

adventure . . . weakly, risk my reputation for discretion for so trivial a cause (by getting angry at these sarcastic fellows).

heavy, sleepy.

Go . . . us, let our laughing send you to sleep, or, go to sleep and hear us laugh at you.

omit, neglect.

heavy, drowsy.

60 Why might Prospero have used his magic to have everyone sleep except Sebastian and Antonio?

61 As you read lines 185–209, note how cleverly Antonio tempts Sebastian. In lines 190–209, two series of metaphors are used: the first deals with sleeping, the second with the sea. Why might each be appropriate?

speaks, calls upon, pronounces, proclaims (Sebastian as usurper of Alonso's crown.

62 What does Antonio mean?

ANTONIO.   Noble Sebastian,
Thou let'st thy fortune sleep—die, rather; wink'st°
Whiles thou art waking.
SEBASTIAN.   Thou dost snore distinctly;
There's meaning in thy snores.
200 ANTONIO. I am more serious than my custom. You
Must be so too, if heed me; which to do
Trebles thee o'er.°
SEBASTIAN.   Well, I am standing water.°
ANTONIO. I'll teach you how to flow.
SEBASTIAN.   Do so. To ebb
Hereditary sloth° instructs me.
ANTONIO.   O,
205 If you but knew how you the purpose° cherish°
Whiles thus you mock it! How, in stripping it,
You more invest° it! Ebbing men, indeed,
Most often do so near the bottom° run
By their own fear or sloth.
SEBASTIAN.   Prithee say on.
210 The setting° of thine eye and cheek proclaim
A matter° from thee, and a birth indeed
Which throes° thee much to yield.
ANTONIO.   Thus, sir:
Although this lord° of weak remembrance,° this,
Who shall be of as little memory
215 When he is earthed,° hath here almost persuaded—
For he's a spirit of persuasion, only
Professes to persuade°—the King his son's alive,
'Tis as impossible that he's undrowned
As he that sleeps here swims.
SEBASTIAN.   I have no hope
220 That he's undrowned.
ANTONIO.   O, out of that "no hope"
What great hope have you! No hope that way° is
Another way so high a hope that even
Ambition cannot pierce a wink beyond,
But doubt discovery there.° Will you grant with me
225 That Ferdinand is drowned?
SEBASTIAN.   He's gone.
ANTONIO.   Then, tell me,
Who's the next heir of Naples?
SEBASTIAN.   Claribel.
ANTONIO. She that is Queen of Tunis; she that dwells
Ten leagues beyond man's life;° she that from Naples
Can have no note,° unless the sun were post°—
230 The man i' th' moon's too slow—till new-born chins
Be rough and razorable; she that from° whom

wink'st, shut your eyes.

Trebles thee o'er, makes
you three times as great
and rich.
standing water, water
which neither ebbs nor
flows, at a standstill, indecisive.
Hereditary sloth, natural
laziness.
purpose, that is, of being
king.
cherish, that is, make
dear, enrich.
invest, clothe.
the bottom, that is, on
which unadventurous men
may go aground and miss
the tide of fortune.
setting, set expression (of
earnestness).
matter, matter of importance.
throes, causes pain, as in
giving birth.
this lord, that is, Gonzalo.
remembrance, (1) power
of remembering, (2) being
remembered after his
death.
earthed, buried.
only . . . persuade, that
is, whose whole function
(as a privy councilor) is to
persuade.

63 Note how Shake-
speare neatly com-
bines both metaphors
(sleeping and the sea) in
lines 218–219.
that way, that is, in
regard to Ferdinand's
being saved.
Ambition . . . there, ambition itself cannot see any
further than that hope (of
the crown), but is unsure
of itself in seeing even so
far, is dazzled by daring to
think so high.
Ten . . . life, that is, it
would take more than a
lifetime to get there.
note, news, hint.
post, messenger.
from, on our voyage from.

We all were sea-swallowed, though some cast° again,
And by that destiny to perform an act
Whereof what's past is prologue, what to come
235 In yours and my discharge.°

SEBASTIAN. What stuff is this? How say you?
   'Tis true, my brother's daughter's Queen of Tunis;
   So is she heir of Naples; 'twixt which regions
   There is some space.

ANTONIO.   A space whose every cubit
240 Seems to cry out, "How shall that Claribel
   Measure us° back to Naples? Keep in Tunis,
   And let Sebastian wake."° Say this were death
   That now hath seized them; why, they were no worse
   Than now they are. There be that can rule Naples
245 As well as he that sleeps; lords that can prate
   As amply and unnecessarily
   As this Gonzalo; I myself could make
   A chough of as deep chat.° O, that you bore
   The mind that I do! What a sleep were this
250 For your advancement! Do you understand me?

SEBASTIAN. Methinks I do.

ANTONIO.   And how does your content°
   Tender° your own good fortune?

SEBASTIAN.   I remember
   You did supplant your brother Prospero.

ANTONIO.   True.
   And look how well my garments sit upon me,
255 Much feater° than before. My brother's servants
   Were then my fellows; now they are my men.

SEBASTIAN. But, for your conscience?

ANTONIO. Ay, sir, where lies that? If 'twere a kibe,°
   'Twould put me to° my slipper; but I feel not
260 This deity in my bosom. Twenty consciences,
   That stand 'twixt me and Milan,° candied° be they
   And melt ere they molest! Here lies your brother,
   No better than the earth he lies upon,
   If he were that which now he's like—that's dead,
265 Whom I, with this obedient steel, three inches of it,
   Can lay to bed forever; whiles you, doing thus,
   To the perpetual wink° for aye might put
   This ancient morsel, this Sir Prudence, who
   Should not upbraid our course. For all the rest,
270 They'll take suggestion as a cat laps milk;
   They'll tell the clock° to any business that
   We say befits the hour.

SEBASTIAN.   Thy case, dear friend

---

cast, were disgorged (with a pun on casting of parts for a play).

discharge, performance.

64 Do you think Sebastian is as dense as he appears to be? Explain.

Measure us, that is, traverse the cubits, find her way.
wake, that is, to his good fortune.

I . . . chat, I could teach a jackdaw to talk as wisely, or, be such a garrulous talker myself.

content, desire, inclination.
Tender, regard, look after.

feater, more becomingly, fittingly.

kibe, blister on the heel.
put me to, oblige me to wear.
Milan, the dukedom of Milan.
candied, sugared.

65 What is Antonio saying about his conscience?

wink, sleep, closing of eyes.

tell the clock, that is, answer appropriately, chime.

Shall be my precedent. As thou got'st Milan,
I'll come by Naples. Draw thy sword. One stroke
275 Shall free thee from the tribute° which thou payest,
And I the king shall love thee.
ANTONIO.   Draw together;
And when I rear my hand, do you the like,
To fall it on Gonzalo.   (They draw.)
SEBASTIAN.   O, but one word.
          (They talk apart. Enter ARIEL invisible, with music and song.)
ARIEL. My master through his art foresees the danger
280 That you, his friend, are in, and sends me forth—
For else his project dies—to keep them living. (Sings in GONZALO's ear.)
          While you here do snoring lie,
          Open-eyed conspiracy
285   His time° doth take.
          If of life you keep a care,
          Shake off slumber, and beware.
               Awake, awake!
ANTONIO. Then let us both be sudden.
GONZALO (waking). Now, good angels preserve the King!
                                        (The others wake.)
290 ALONSO. Why, how now? ho, awake! Why are you drawn?
          Wherefore this ghastly looking?
GONZALO.   What's the matter?
SEBASTIAN. Whiles we stood here securing° your repose,
          Even now, we heard a hollow burst of bellowing
          Like bulls, or rather lions. Did 't not wake you?
295 It struck mine ear most terribly.
ALONSO.   I heard nothing.
ANTONIO. O, 'twas a din to fright a monster's ear,
          To make an earthquake! Sure it was the roar
          Of a whole herd of lions.
ALONSO. Heard you this, Gonzalo?
300 GONZALO. Upon mine honor sir, I heard a humming
          And that a strange one too, which did awake me.
          I shaked you, sir, and cried. As mine eyes opened,
          I saw their weapons drawn. There was a noise,
          That's verily. 'Tis best we stand upon our guard,
305 Or that we quit this place. Let's draw our weapons.
ALONSO. Lead off this ground, and let's make further search
          For my poor son.
GONZALO.   Heavens keep him from these beasts!
          For he is, sure, i' th' island.
ALONSO.   Lead away.
ARIEL (aside). Prospero my lord shall know what I have done.
310 So, King, go safely on to seek thy son.   (Exeunt severally).

66 In lines 262–269, who is to kill Alonso? Who is to kill Gonzalo? Why are the other nobles to be spared?
tribute, see Act One, Scene 2, lines 113, 124.

67 Why might Prospero be more concerned for Gonzalo than for Alonso?

time, opportunity.

68 Is Gonzalo's reaction in keeping with his character? Explain.

securing, standing guard over.

69 In the second act of a typical Elizabethan drama, the complicating incident occurs; this is an action that cannot be undone, that sets the future course of the play. That action has just occurred in Scene 1. What is it, and why can it not be concealed or undone?

70 Often in Shakespeare's comedies the scene ends neatly on a rhymed couplet, as this scene does.

Detail of Hogarth's *A Scene from* The Tempest, showing Caliban carrying a load of wood. c. 1735. Nostell Priory Collection, Yorkshire

SCENE 2.

Another part of the island. (Played on the Platform Stage.) Enter CALIBAN *with a burden of wood. A noise of thunder heard.*

CALIBAN. All the infections that the sun sucks up
 From bogs, fens, flats, on Prosper fall and make him
 By inch-meal° a disease! His spirits hear me,
 And yet I needs must curse. But they'll nor° pinch,
5 Fright me with urchin-shows,° pitch me i' th' mire,
 Nor lead me, like a firebrand,° in the dark
 Out of my way, unless he bid 'em; but
 For every trifle are they set upon me;
 Sometime like apes that mow° and chatter at me
10 And after bite me, then like hedgehogs which
 Lie tumbling in my barefoot way and mount
 Their pricks at my footfall; sometime am I
 All wound with adders who with cloven tongues
 Do hiss me into madness.   (*Enter* TRINCULO.)
     Lo, now, lo!
15 Here comes a spirit of his, and to torment me
 For bringing wood in slowly. I'll fall flat;
 Perchance he will not mind° me.   (*Lies down.*)
 TRINCULO. Here's neither bush nor shrub, to bear off° any weather at all,
  and another storm brewing; I hear it sing i' th' wind. Yond same black
20 cloud, yond huge one, looks like a foul bombard° that would shed his°
  liquor. If it should thunder as it did before, I know not where to hide my

By inch-meal, inch by inch.
nor, neither.
urchin-shows, apparitions shaped like hedgehogs.
like a firebrand, in the guise of a will-o'-the-wisp.

mow, make faces.

mind, notice.

71 This speech (lines 1–17) is a soliloquy, providing insight into Caliban. Along with the humor of what he has just said, what does it reveal about how Prospero keeps him under control?
bear off, keep off.
foul bombard, dirty leathern bottle.
his, its.

442   *The Renaissance*

head. Yond same cloud cannot choose but fall by pailfuls. (*Sees* CALIBAN.)
What have we here? A man or a fish? Dead or alive? A fish, he smells
like a fish; a very ancient and fish-like smell; a kind of not of the newest
25 Poor-John.° A strange fish! Were I in England now, as once I was, and
had but this fish painted,° not a holiday fool there but would give a piece
of silver. There would this monster make a man;° any strange beast there
makes a man. When they will not give a doit° to relieve a lame beggar, they
will lay out ten to see a dead Indian. Legged like a man! and his fins like
30 arms! Warm, o' my troth! I do now let loose my opinion, hold it no longer:
this is no fish, but an islander, that hath lately suffered by a thunderbolt.
(*Thunder.*) Alas, the storm is come again! My best way is to creep under
his gaberdine;° there is no other shelter hereabout. Misery acquaints a man
with strange bedfellows. I will here shroud° till the dregs° of the storm be
35 past. (*Creeps under* CALIBAN'S *garment. Enter* STEPHANO, *singing, a bottle
in his hand.*)

STEPHANO. *I shall no more to sea, to sea,*
    Here shall I die ashore—
This is a very scurvy tune to sing at a man's funeral. Well, here's my
40 comfort. (*Drinks and sings.*)
    The master, the swabber, the boatswain and I,
      The gunner and his mate
    Loved Mall, Meg, and Marian, and Margery,
      But none of us cared for Kate;
45   *For she had a tongue with a tang.*
    Would cry to a sailor, "Go hang!"
    She loved not the savor of tar nor of pitch,
    Yet a tailor might scratch her where'er she did
      itch.
50   *Then to sea, boys, and let her go hang!*
This is a scurvy tune too; but here's my comfort. (*Drinks.*)

CALIBAN. Do not torment me! Oh!

STEPHANO. What's the matter? Have we devils here? Do you put tricks upon
's with savages and men of Ind,° ha? I have not scaped drowning to be
55 afeard now of your four legs; for it hath been said, "As proper° a man as
ever went on four legs° cannot make him give ground"; and it shall be said
so again while Stephano breathes at'° nostrils.

CALIBAN. This spirit torments me! Oh!

STEPHANO. This is some monster of the isle with four legs, who hath got,
60 as I take it, an ague. Where the devil should he learn our language? I will
give him some relief, if it be but for that.° If I can recover him° and keep
him tame and get to Naples with him, he's a present for any emperor that
ever trod on neat's-leather.°

CALIBAN. Do not torment me, prithee. I'll bring my wood home faster.

65 STEPHANO. He's in his fit now and does not talk after the wisest. He shall
taste of my bottle; if he have never drunk wine afore, it will go near to
remove his fit. If I can recover him and keep him tame, I will not take too
much° for him; he shall pay for him that hath° him, and that soundly.

Poor-John, salted hake,
type of poor fare.
painted, that is, painted
on a sign set up outside of
a booth or tent at a fair.
make a man, make one's
fortune.
doit, small coin.
gaberdine, cloak, loose
upper garment.
shroud, take shelter.
dregs, that is, last
remains.

72 In lines 23–35,
what is Trinculo's
first reaction to Caliban?
Shakespeare is poking fun
at his audience in this
speech; how does he do
it? If we picture Caliban as
wearing a long, shapeless
cloak, how would Trin-
culo's early description of
him fit?

73 With Stephano's en-
trance, the third of
the three low-comic char-
acters has arrived. Shakespeare's audience would
expect further slapstick
and buffoonery, already
begun with Trinculo's
investigation of Caliban.
Ind, India.
proper, handsome.
four legs. The conventional phrase would supply
two legs.
at', at the.

74 The meeting of Cal-
iban with Trinculo
and Stephano in a sense
parodies the meeting of
Miranda with Ferdinand
in the preceding scene.
Explain how this is so.

75 What does Caliban
think is happening?
How should Stephano's
actions bear this out?
for that, that is, for knowing our language.
recover him, cure him.
neat's-leather, cowhide.
I will . . . much, that is,
no sum can be too much.
hath, possesses, receives.

CALIBAN. Thou dost me yet but little hurt;

70   Thou wilt anon, I know it by thy trembling.

Now Prosper works upon thee.

STEPHANO. Come on your ways; open your mouth; here is that which will give language to you, cat. Open your mouth;° this will shake your shaking, I can tell you, and that soundly. (*Gives* CALIBAN *drink.*) You cannot tell

75   who's your friend. Open your chaps° again.

TRINCULO. I should know that voice. It should be—but he is drowned; and these are devils. O defend me!

STEPHANO. Four legs and two voices; a most delicate monster! His forward voice now is to speak well of his friend; his backward voice is to utter foul

80   speeches and to detract. If all the wine in my bottle will recover him, I will help his ague. Come. (*Gives drink.*) Amen! I will pour some in thy other mouth.

TRINCULO. Stephano!

STEPHANO. Doth thy other mouth call me? Mercy, mercy! This is a devil,

85   and no monster. I will leave him; I have no long spoon.°

TRINCULO. Stephano! If thou beest Stephano, touch me and speak to me; for I am Trinculo—be not afeard—thy good friend Trinculo.

STEPHANO. If thou beest Trinculo, come forth. I'll pull thee by the lesser legs. If any be Trinculo's legs, these are they. (*Pulls him out.*) Thou art

90   very Trinculo indeed! How cam'st thou to be the siege° of this mooncalf?° Can he vent° Trinculos?

TRINCULO. I took him to be killed with a thunder-stroke. But art thou not drowned, Stephano? I hope now thou art not drowned. Is the storm overblown? I hid me under the dead moon-calf's gaberdine for fear of

95   the storm. And art thou living, Stephano? O Stephano, two Neapolitans scaped!

STEPHANO. Prithee, do not turn me about; my stomach is not constant.°

CALIBAN. These be fine things, an if° they be not sprites.

That's a brave° god and bears celestial liquor.

100   I will kneel to him.

STEPHANO. How didst thou scape? How cam'st thou hither? Swear by this bottle how thou cam'st hither. I escaped upon a butt of sack° which the sailors heaved o'erboard—by this bottle, which I made of the bark of a tree with mine own hands since I was cast ashore.

105   CALIBAN (*kneeling*). I'll swear upon that bottle to be thy true subject, for the liquor is not earthly.

STEPHANO. Here; swear then how thou escapedst.

TRINCULO. Swum ashore, man, like a duck. I can swim like a duck, I'll be sworn.

110   STEPHANO. Here, kiss the book.° Though thou canst swim like a duck, thou art made like a goose.° (*Gives drink.*)

TRINCULO. O Stephano, hast any more of this?

STEPHANO. The whole butt, man. My cellar is in a rock by the sea-side where my wine is hid. How now, mooncalf? How does thine ague?

cat . . . mouth, allusion to the proverb, "Good liquor will make a cat speak."
chaps, jaws.

> **76** What should Stephano be doing here? How should Caliban react to the drink?

long spoon, allusion to the proverb, "He that sups with the devil has need of a long spoon."

siege, excrement.
mooncalf, monster.
vent, emit.

> **77** Stephano's name means "belly" or "paunch," and he probably was portrayed as fat, with padding if necessary. What evidence is there that Trinculo is thin? Incidentally, Trinculo's name is probably derived from *trinci,* an Italian word referring to the motley (multi-colored) costume of the court jester.

not constant, unsteady.
an if, if.
brave, fine.

> **78** Why does Caliban say he will kneel to Stephano?

butt of sack, barrel of Canary wine.

book, that is, bottle.
made . . . goose, as a fool (jester), Trinculo is not too bright.

115 **CALIBAN**. Hast thou not dropped from heaven?

STEPHANO. Out o' th' moon, I do assure thee. I was the man i' th' moon when time was.°

CALIBAN. I have seen thee in her and I do adore thee. My mistress show'd me thee and thy dog and thy bush.°

120 **STEPHANO**. Come, swear to that; kiss the book. I will furnish it anon with new contents. Swear. *(Gives drink.)*

TRINCULO. By this good light,° this is a very shallow monster! I afeard of him? A very weak monster! The man i' th' moon? A most poor credulous monster! Well drawn,° monster, in good sooth!

125 **CALIBAN**. I'll show thee every fertile inch o' th' island; And I will kiss thy foot. I prithee, be my god.

TRINCULO. By this light, a most perfidious and drunken monster! When 's god's asleep, he'll rob his bottle.

CALIBAN. I'll kiss thy foot. I'll swear myself thy subject.

130 **STEPHANO**. Come on then; down, and swear. *(CALIBAN kneels.)*

TRINCULO. I shall laugh myself to death at this puppy-headed monster. A most scurvy monster! I could find in my heart to beat him—

STEPHANO. Come, kiss.

TRINCULO. But that the poor monster's in drink. An abominable monster!

135 **CALIBAN**. I'll show thee the best springs; I'll pluck thee berries; I'll fish for thee and get thee wood enough. A plague upon the tyrant that I serve! I'll bear him no more sticks, but follow thee, Thou wondrous man.

140 **TRINCULO**. A most ridiculous monster, to make a wonder of a poor drunkard!

CALIBAN. I prithee, let me bring thee where crabs° grow; And I with my long nails will dig thee pig-nuts,° Show thee a jay's nest, and instruct thee how To snare the nimble marmoset.° I'll bring thee

145 To clust'ring filberts,° and sometimes I'll get thee Young scamels° from the rock. Wilt thou go with me?

STEPHANO. I prithee now, lead the way without any more talking. Trinculo, the King and all our company else being drowned, we will inherit° here. Here! Bear my bottle. Fellow Trinculo, we'll fill him by and by again.

150 **CALIBAN** *(sings drunkenly)*. Farewell, master; farewell, farewell!

TRINCULO. A howling monster; a drunken monster!

CALIBAN. *No more dams I'll make for fish,*
      Nor fetch in firing
      At requiring,
155   *Nor scrape trenchering,° nor wash dish.*
      'Ban, 'Ban, Ca–Caliban
      Has a new master, get a new man.
Freedom, high-day!° High-day, freedom! Freedom, high-day, freedom!

160 **STEPHANO**. O brave monster! Lead the way. *(Exeunt.)*

when time was, once upon a time.

dog . . . bush, the man in the moon was popularly imagined to have with him a dog and a bush of thorn.
By . . . light, by God's light, by this good light from heaven.
Well drawn, well pulled (on the bottle).

crabs, crab apples.

pig-nuts, peanuts.

marmoset, small monkey.
filberts, hazelnuts.
scamels, shellfish.

79 We have already been acquainted with Caliban's faults. In what respects does he appear to possess a sort of innocence? Is this understandable? Explain.

inherit, take possession.

80 Stephano would like to rule the island. How many instances have we had thus far of people who desired, rightfully or wrongly, to rule any sort of kingdom?

trenchering, trenchers, wooden plates.
high-day, holiday (?).

81 What is ironic about Caliban's song?

Comment

Shakespeare and Montaigne

Michel de Montaigne (1533–1592) is known as both a philosopher and a writer. His thinking is recorded in his *Essays*, which he reworked and polished until his death. *Essais* is a French word properly translated into modern English as "attempts" or "trials," for Montaigne was developing a type of literature heretofore unheard of. The first two books of essays were published in 1580; a third book was added and the first two expanded in 1588; the whole was reissued after his death in 1595.

We owe to Montaigne the informal structure of the essay, as well as its name. His essays are loosely organized, full of digressions, and written in a conversational style. Four hundred years after they were written, they remain interesting and surprisingly up-to-date.

In 1560, at a court celebration, Montaigne met the cannibals brought back from Brazil by French explorers. The word *cannibal* derives from *Carib*, the name of an Indian tribe of northeastern South America, which also gave its name to the Caribbean Sea. The word *cannibal* was originally used to describe native American Indians and had no connection with the eating of human flesh. Montaigne's essay praises primitive American Indian society, as it was described by French explorers.

Montaigne's essay "Of Cannibals" was read by Shakespeare and is quoted in *The Tempest*. Here is a portion of Montaigne's essay:

"This [Brazil] is a nation . . . in which there is no sort of traffic, no knowledge of letters, no science of numbers, no name for a magistrate or for political superiority, no custom of servitude, no riches or poverty, no contracts, no successions, no partitions, no occupations but leisure ones, no care for any but common kinship, no clothes, no agriculture, no metal, no use of wine or corn. The very words that signify lying, treachery, dissimulation, avarice, envy, belittling, pardon, unheard of."

And here is how Gonzalo describes his ideal commonwealth in *The Tempest*:

"I' th' commonwealth I would by contraries
Execute all things; for no kind of traffic
Would I admit; no name of magistrate;
Letters should not be known; riches, poverty,
And use of service, none; contract, succession,
Bourn, bound of land, tilth, vineyard, none;
No use of metal, corn, or wine, or oil;
No occupation; all men idle, all,
And women too, but innocent and pure;
No sovereignty—. . . .
All things in common nature should produce
Without sweat or endeavor. Treason, felony,
Sword, pike, knife, gun, or need of any
  engine,
Would I not have; but nature should bring
  forth,
Of it own kind, all foison, all abundance,
To feed my innocent people."
  (Act Two, Scene 1, lines 134–43, 145–50)

Portrait of Michel de Montaigne. Late 16th century. Musée Condé, Chantilly

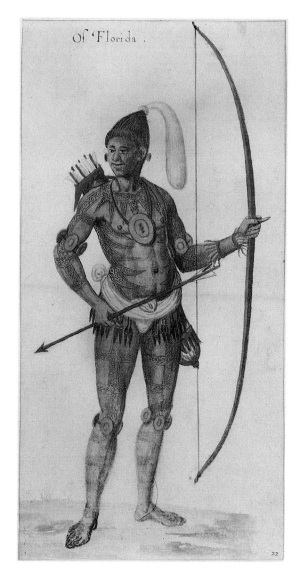

Watercolors by John White showing (left) an Indian warrior from what is now Florida and (right) an Indian village in what is now North Carolina. 1585–1587. British Museum.

In the words of one writer, "Gonzalo's quotation from Montaigne is an invaluable autobiographical touch giving us a clue to one of the creative influences on Shakespeare's own development."

The fact that it is Gonzalo, the "honest old Counselor," who utters this vision of an ideal commonwealth, suggests that this passage is not intended as an unfavorable comment on Montaigne. The meaning of any passage in Shakespeare must be understood in the context of the speaker of the lines; since Gonzalo is kindly and decent, we are probably not meant to interpret his vision of an ideal commonwealth as foolish, although it may be unworldly. But the jeering comments of the wicked lords Sebastian and Antonio serve to point up their own faults rather than the flaws in Gonzalo's generous vision.

THINK AND DISCUSS

Understanding

1. In the low-comedy scene, what does Trinculo at first think Caliban is? Why?
2. What does Caliban think Trinculo is? Why?

Analyzing

3. Contrast Gonzalo's attitude toward the grieving Alonso with the attitudes of Antonio and Sebastian toward him.
4. In Act Two of a Shakespeare play, the **plot** develops through what is sometimes called the complicating incident, in which a character makes a decision from which it is difficult, if not impossible, to turn back. What decision is made by two of the nobles.?
5. What decision is made by Caliban?
6. What do you think of Caliban up to this point in the play? Do you like him, dislike him, or have some other feeling for him? Explain.

Extending

7. Discuss the practicality of Gonzalo's ideal commonwealth (Scene 1, lines 149–169), which Shakespeare bases on Montaigne. (See page 446.)

APPLYING: Blank Verse H⧙

See Handbook of Literary Terms, p. 943.

Blank verse consists of unrhymed lines of iambic pentameter—that is, the lines have ten syllables, and the even-numbered syllables are stressed, as in lines 1–3 of Scene 1, when Gonzalo says:

Bĕseéch / yŏu, sír, / bĕ mér- / rў. Yŏu / hăve caúse,

Sŏ háve / wĕ áll, / ŏf jóy, / fŏr oúr / ĕscápe

Ĭs múch / bĕyónd / oŭr lóss. / Oŭr hínt / ŏf wóe . . .

Marking the unstressed and stressed syllables, as above, is known as scansion. In blank verse the accent is sometimes changed for effect, and occasionally a syllable may be added or deleted. To avoid a singsong monotony, the sense often flows over from line to line, as in lines 2–3 above. We do not pause at the end of a line unless a mark of punctuation tells us to.

1. Locate line 4 of Scene 1; "every" is pronounced as two syllables: "ev-ry." Copy line 4 on a separate sheet of paper and scan it. Is it regular or irregular? Explain.
2. Line 5 is quite irregular. Copy it on a separate sheet of paper and scan it.

COMPOSITION ⊷

Analyzing a Character's Role

Discuss the importance of Ariel's role thus far. Be sure to consider the extent to which his presence and talents are responsible for the action of the play. Your paper should be 3 to 5 paragraphs long. See "Writing About Characters" in the Writer's Handbook.

Writing Drama Criticism

Assume that you are a drama critic and write a three- to five-paragraph review for the local newspaper of the low-comedy scene involving Caliban, Trinculo, and Stephano. You should discuss the actors' appearance, the devices by which they attempt to make the audience laugh, and the audience's reaction to the scene. See "Writing About Drama" in the Writer's Handbook.

ENRICHMENT

Readers Theater

Prepare a Readers Theater presentation of Scene 1. Seven speaking roles are involved: Gonzalo, Alonso, Sebastian, Antonio, Adrian, Francisco, and Ariel. If you prefer a shorter scene, you may stop at line 179. Dramatizing the earlier part of the scene is important, since it will aid in understanding the side conversation taking place between Antonio and Sebastian. If the shorter version is used, Ariel will still be needed but will not have a speaking part.

ACT THREE

SCENE 1.

Before PROSPERO's *cell. (Played on the Platform Stage.) Enter* FERDINAND *bearing a log.*

FERDINAND. There be some sports are painful, and their labor
    Delight in them sets off;° some kinds of baseness
    Are nobly undergone; and most poor matters
    Point to rich ends. This my mean task
5   Would be as heavy to me as odious, but
    The mistress which I serve quickens° what's dead
    And makes my labors pleasures. O, she is
    Ten times more gentle than her father's crabbed,
    And he's composed of harshness. I must remove
10   Some thousands of these logs and pile them up,
    Upon a sore injunction.° My sweet mistress
    Weeps when she sees me work, and says such baseness
    Had never like executor. I forget;
    But these sweet thoughts do even refresh my labors,
15   Most busy lest, when I do it.°

                (Enter MIRANDA; *and* PROSPERO *at a distance, unseen).*

MIRANDA.   Alas, now, pray you,
    Work not so hard. I would the lightning had
    Burnt up those logs that you are enjoined to pile!
    Pray, set it down and rest you. When this burns,
    'Twill weep for having wearied you. My father
20   Is hard at study; pray now, rest yourself.
    He's safe for these three hours.

FERDINAND.   O most dear mistress,
    The sun will set before I shall discharge
    What I must strive to do.

MIRANDA.   If you'll sit down,
    I'll bear your logs the while. Pray give me that.
25   I'll carry it to the pile.

FERDINAND.   No, precious creature,
    I had rather crack my sinews, break my back,
    Than you should such dishonor undergo
    While I sit lazy by.

MIRANDA.   It would become me
    As well as it does you; and I should do it
30   With much more ease, for my good will is to it,
    And yours it is against.

sets off, makes seem greater by contrast.

quickens, gives life to.

sore injunction, severe command.

Most . . . it, that is, when I am working hardest.

82 | Lines 1–15 are a soliloquy by Ferdinand. What do they tell us about his feelings for Miranda?

PROSPERO (*aside*).   Poor worm, thou art infected!
    This visitation° shows it.
MIRANDA.   You look wearily.
FERDINAND. No, noble mistress, 'tis fresh morning with me
    When you are by at night. I do beseech you—
35 Chiefly that I might set it in my prayers—
    What is your name?
MIRANDA.   Miranda.—O my father,
    I have broke your hest° to say so.
FERDINAND.   Admired Miranda!
    Indeed the top of admiration! Worth
    What's dearest to the world! Full many a lady
40 I have eyed with best regard, and many a time
    Th' harmony of their tongues hath into bondage
    Brought my too diligent ear. For several virtues
    Have I liked several women, never any
    With so full soul but some defect in her
45 Did quarrel with the noblest grace she owed°
    And put it to the foil.° But you, O you,
    So perfect and so peerless, are created
    Of every creature's best!
MIRANDA.   I do not know
    One of my sex; no woman's face remember,
50 Save, from my glass, mine own. Nor have I seen
    More that I may call men than you, good friend,
    And my dear father. How features are abroad,
    I am skilless° of; but, by my modesty,
    The jewel in my dower, I would not wish
55 Any companion in the world but you,
    Nor can imagination form a shape,
    Besides yourself, to like of. But I prattle
    Something too wildly, and my father's precepts
    I therein do forget.
FERDINAND.   I am in my condition
60 A prince, Miranda; I do think, a king—
    I would, not so!—and would no more endure
    This wooden slavery than to suffer
    The flesh-fly blow° my mouth. Hear my soul speak:
    The very instant that I saw you, did
65 My heart fly to your service; there resides,
    To make me slave to it; and for your sake
    Am I this patient log-man.
MIRANDA.   Do you love me!
FERDINAND. O heaven, O earth, bear witness to this sound,
    And crown what I profess with kind event°

83 | What does Prospero mean?
visitation, (1) visit, (2) visitation of the plague, that is, infection of love.

hest, command.

84 | More wordplay. Note that "admired" is virtually an anagram of "Miranda."

owed, owned.
put . . . foil, (1) overthrow it (as in wrestling), (2) served as a "foil" or contrast to set it off.

85 | Note that Miranda omits Caliban. Why might she do this?

skilless, ignorant.

blow, befoul with fly eggs.

kind event, favorable outcome.

70 If I speak true! If hollowly, invert
What best is boded me to mischief!° I
Beyond all limit of what else i' th' world
Do love, prize, honor you.

MIRANDA (*weeping*).   I am a fool
To weep at what I am glad of.

PROSPERO (*aside*).   Fair encounter
75 Of two most rare affections! Heavens rain grace
On that which breeds between 'em!

FERDINAND.   Wherefore weep you?

MIRANDA.   At mine unworthiness, that dare not offer
What I desire to give, and much less take
What I shall die to want.° But this is trifling,
80 And all the more it seeks to hide itself
The bigger bulk it shows. Hence, bashful cunning,
And prompt me, plain and holy innocence!
I am your wife, if you will marry me;
If not, I'll die your maid. To be your fellow°
85 You may deny me, but I'll be your servant,
Whether you will or no.

FERDINAND.   My mistress, dearest,
And I thus humble ever.

MIRANDA. My husband, then?

FERDINAND.   Ay, with a heart as willing
As bondage e'er of freedom. Here's my hand.

90 **MIRANDA.** And mine, with my heart in 't. And now farewell
Till half an hour hence.

FERDINAND.   A thousand thousand!°

        (*Exeunt* FERDINAND *and* MIRANDA *severally*).

PROSPERO. So glad of this as they I cannot be,
Who are surprised with all; but my rejoicing
At nothing can be more. I'll to my book,
95 For yet ere supper-time must I perform
Much business appertaining. (*Exit.*)

SCENE 2.

Another part of the island. (Played on the Platform Stage and the Tarras.) Enter
CALIBAN, STEPHANO, *and* TRINCULO.

STEPHANO. Tell not me. When the butt is out,° we will drink water, not a
drop before. Therefore bear up, and board 'em.° Servant-monster, drink
to me.

TRINCULO. Servant-monster? The folly of this island! They say there's but

---

If . . . mischief, if I
speak falsely, change the
best in store for me for
what is worst.

86 What is Prospero's attitude toward the lovers?

want, lack.

fellow, mate, equal.

a thousand thousand, that is, farewells.

87 Why is Prospero not surprised that Miranda and Ferdinand have fallen in love and pledged to marry each other? Why might he rejoice at the betrothal?

88 By this time all three low-comic characters are drunk and staggering over the stage.
out, empty.
bear . . . 'em, Stephano uses the terminology of maneuvering at sea and boarding a vessel under attack as a way of urging an assault on the liquor supply.

5   five upon this isle; we are three of them. If th' other two be brained like
     us, the state totters.

STEPHANO. Drink, servant-monster, when I bid thee. Thy eyes are almost
     set° in thy head.   *(Gives drink.)*

TRINCULO. Where should they be set else? He were a brave° monster indeed
10   if they were set in his tail.

STEPHANO. My man-monster hath drowned his tongue in sack. For my part,
     the sea cannot drown me; I swam, ere I could recover° the shore, five
     and thirty leagues off and on. By this light, thou shalt be my lieutenant,
     monster, or my standard.°

15 TRINCULO. Your lieutenant, if you list;° he's no standard.°

STEPHANO. We'll not run,° Monsieur Monster.

TRINCULO. Nor go° neither, but you'll lie° like dogs and yet say nothing
     neither.

STEPHANO. Moon-calf, speak once in thy life, if thou beest a good moon-
20   calf.

CALIBAN. How does thy honor? Let me lick thy shoe.
     I'll not serve him; he is not valiant.

TRINCULO. Thou liest, most ignorant monster, I am in case to justle° a
     constable. Why, thou deboshed° fish thou, was there ever man a coward
25   that hath drunk so much sack as I today? Wilt thou tell a monstrous lie,
     being but half a fish and half a monster?

CALIBAN. Lo, how he mocks me! Wilt thou let him, my lord?

TRINCULO. "Lord," quoth he? That a monster should be such a natural!°

CALIBAN. Lo, lo, again! Bite him to death, I prithee.

30 STEPHANO. Trinculo, keep a good tongue in your head. If you prove a
     mutineer—the next tree!° The poor monster's my subject and he shall not
     suffer indignity.

CALIBAN. I thank my noble lord. Wilt thou be pleased
     To hearken once again to the suit I made to thee?

35 STEPHANO. Marry,° will I. Kneel and repeat it; I will stand, and so shall
     Trinculo. (CALIBAN *kneels. Enter* ARIEL, *invisible.*)

CALIBAN. As I told thee before, I am subject to a tyrant,
     A sorcerer, that by his cunning hath
     Cheated me of the island.

40 ARIEL. Thou liest.

CALIBAN.   Thou liest, thou jesting monkey, thou!
     I would my valiant master would destroy thee.
     I do not lie.

STEPHANO. Trinculo, if you trouble him any more in 's tale, by this hand,
45   I will supplant some of your teeth.

TRINCULO. Why, I said nothing.

STEPHANO. Mum, then, and no more.—Proceed.

CALIBAN. I say, by sorcery he got this isle;
     From me he got it. If thy greatness will

---

set, fixed in a drunken stare; or sunk, like the sun.

brave, fine, splendid.

recover, arrive at.

standard, standard-bearer, that is, ensign (as distinguished from lieutenant).

list, prefer.

no standard, that is, not able to stand up.

run, retreat.

go, walk.

lie, (1) too drunk to move, they will lie prone on the ground; (2) tell a falsehood.

justle, jostle.

deboshed, debauched.

natural, fool, idiot.

the next tree, that is, you'll hang.

Marry, indeed (originally an oath by the Virgin Mary).

89 Since Ariel is invisible when he speaks, both Caliban and Stephano think Trinculo is speaking, leading to more low-comedy misunderstandings.

50   Revenge it on him—for I know thou dar'st,
      But this thing° dare not—

STEPHANO. That's most certain.

CALIBAN. Thou shalt be lord of it, and I'll serve thee.

STEPHANO. How now shall this be compassed? Canst thou bring me to the
55   party?

CALIBAN. Yea, yea, my lord. I'll yield him thee asleep,
      Where thou mayst knock a nail into his head.

ARIEL. Thou liest; thou canst not.

CALIBAN. What a pied ninny's° this! Thou scurvy patch!°
60   I do beseech thy greatness, give him blows
      And take his bottle from him. When that's gone
      He shall drink nought but brine, for I'll not show him
      Where the quick freshes° are.

STEPHANO. Trinculo, run into no further danger. Interrupt the monster one
65   word further, and, by this hand, I'll turn my mercy out o' doors and make
  a stock-fish° of thee.

TRINCULO. Why, what did I? I did nothing. I'll go farther off.

STEPHANO. Didst thou not say he lied?

ARIEL. Thou liest.

70. STEPHANO. Do I so? Take thou that. (*Beats* TRINCULO.) As you like this,
      give me the lie° another time.

TRINCULO. I did not give the lie. Out o' your wits and hearing too? A pox o'
      your bottle! This can sack and drinking do. A murrain° on your monster,
      and the devil take your fingers!

75 CALIBAN. Ha, ha, ha!

STEPHANO. Now, forward with your tale. (*To* TRINCULO.) Prithee, stand
      further off.

CALIBAN. Beat him enough. After a little time
      I'll beat him too.

80 STEPHANO. Stand farther.—Come, proceed.

CALIBAN. Why, as I told thee, 'tis a custom with him
      I' th' afternoon to sleep. There thou mayst brain him.
      Having first seized his books, or with a log
      Batter his skull, or paunch° him with a stake,
85   Or cut his wezand° with thy knife. Remember
      First to possess his books; for without them
      He's but a sot,° as I am, nor hath not
      One spirit to command. They all do hate him
      As rootedly as I. Burn but his books.
90   He has brave utensils°—for so he calls them—
      Which, when he has a house, he'll deck withal.
      And that most deeply to consider is
      The beauty of his daughter. He himself
      Calls her a nonpareil. I never saw a woman,

---

this thing, Trinculo.

90 This scene, in which Caliban, Stephano, and Trinculo plot against Prospero, parodies the plotting of Antonio and Sebastian in Act Two, Scene 1. Explain how this is so.

pied ninny, fool in motley (the reference is to the jester's suit Trinculo wears). *patch,* fool.

quick freshes, running springs.

stock-fish, dried cod beaten before cooking.

give me the lie, call me a liar to my face.

murrain, plague (literally, a cattle disease.)

paunch, stab in the belly.

wezand, windpipe.

91 Would you characterize Caliban's suggestions of ways to kill Prospero as humorous, vicious, or a combination of the two? Explain. *sot,* fool. *brave utensils,* fine furnishings.

95 But only Sycorax my dam and she;
    But she as far surpasseth Sycorax
    As great'st does least.
STEPHANO. Is it so brave a lass?
CALIBAN. Ay, lord; she will become thy bed, I warrant,
100 And bring thee forth brave brood.
STEPHANO. Monster, I will kill this man. His daughter and I will be king
    and queen—save our Graces!—and Trinculo and thyself shall be viceroys.
    Dost thou like the plot, Trinculo?
TRINCULO. Excellent.
105 STEPHANO. Give me thy hand. I am sorry I beat thee; but, while thou liv'st,
    keep a good tongue in thy head.
CALIBAN. Within this half hour will he be asleep.
    Wilt thou destroy him then?
STEPHANO. Ay, on mine honor.
110 ARIEL (aside). This will I tell my master.
CALIBAN. Thou mak'st me merry; I am full of pleasure.
    Let us be jocund. Will you troll the catch°
    You taught me but while-ere?°
STEPHANO. At thy request, monster, I will do reason, any reason. Come on,
115 Trinculo, let us sing.   (Sings.)
        Flout 'em and scout° 'em
        And scout 'em and flout 'em!
            Thought is free.
CALIBAN. That's not the tune.   (ARIEL plays the tune on a tabor° and pipe.)
120 STEPHANO. What is this same?
TRINCULO. This is the tune of our catch, played by the picture of Nobody.°
STEPHANO. If thou beest a man, show thyself in thy likeness. If thou beest
    a devil, take 't as thou list.°
TRINCULO. O, forgive me my sins!
125 STEPHANO. He that dies pays all debts. I defy thee. Mercy upon us!
CALIBAN. Art thou afeard!
STEPHANO. No, monster, not I.
CALIBAN. Be not afeard. The isle is full of noises,
    Sounds and sweet airs, that give delight and hurt not.
130 Sometimes a thousand twangling instruments
    Will hum about mine ears, and sometime voices
    That, if I then had waked after long sleep,
    Will make me sleep again; and then, in dreaming,
    The clouds methought would open and show riches
135 Ready to drop upon me, that, when I waked,
    I cried to dream again.
STEPHANO. This will prove a brave kingdom to me, where I shall have my
    music for nothing.
CALIBAN. When Prospero is destroyed.

---

92 Remember that Stephano is only a butler, a servant. What he is proposing would be outrageous, as well as amusing, to Shakespeare's audience.

troll the catch, sing the round.
while-ere, a short time ago.

scout, deride.

93 Note the presence in lines 116–117 of internal rhyme, in which a word within the line rhymes with a word at its end.
tabor, small drum.
picture of Nobody, refers to a familiar figure with head, arms, and legs, but no trunk.
take 't . . . list, take my defiance as you please, as best you can.

94 In lines 120–125, Stephano and Trinculo now realize that an invisible being is playing the tune. How do their reactions differ?

95 Contrast Ariel's attitude toward Prospero with Caliban's.

140 **STEPHANO.** That shall be by and by. I remember the story.

TRINCULO. The sound is going away. Let's follow it, and after do our work.

STEPHANO. Lead, monster; we'll follow. I would I could see this taborer; he lays it on.

TRINCULO. Wilt come? I'll follow, Stephano. (*Exeunt following* ARIEL'*s music*).

SCENE 3.

Another part of the island. (Played on the Platform Stage and the Tarras.) Enter ALONSO, SEBASTIAN, ANTONIO, GONZALO, ADRIAN, FRANCISCO, *etc.*

GONZALO. By 'r lakin,° I can go no further, sir;
My old bones aches. Here's a maze trod indeed
Through forth-rights and meanders!° By your patience,
I needs must rest me.

ALONSO.   Old lord, I cannot blame thee,
5 Who am myself attached° with weariness,
To th' dulling of my spirits. Sit down, and rest.
Even here I will put off my hope and keep it
No longer for my flatterer. He is drowned
Whom thus we stray to find, and the sea mocks
10 Our frustrate search on land. Well, let him go.

                    (ALONSO *and* GONZALO *sit.*)

ANTONIO (*aside to* SEBASTIAN). I am right glad that he's so out of hope.
Do not, for° one repulse, forego the purpose
That you resolved t' effect.

SEBASTIAN (*to* ANTONIO).   The next advantage
Will we take throughly.°

ANTONIO (*to* SEBASTIAN). Let it be tonight,
15 For, now they are oppressed with travail, they
Will not, nor cannot, use such vigilance
As when they are fresh.

SEBASTIAN (*to* ANTONIO). I say tonight. No more.

        (*Solemn and strange music; and* PROSPERO *on the top,*° *invisible.*)

ALONSO. What harmony is this? My good friends, hark!

GONZALO. Marvelous sweet music!

(*Enter several strange* SHAPES, *bringing in a banquet,*° *and dance about it with gentle actions of salutations; and, inviting the* KING, *etc., to eat, they depart.*)

20 **ALONSO.** Give us kind keepers,° heavens! What were these?

SEBASTIAN. A living drollery.° Now I will believe
That there are unicorns, that in Arabia
There is one tree, the phoenix' throne, one phoenix
At this hour reigning there.

ANTONIO.   I'll believe both;

By'r lakin, by our Lady-kin, by our lady.
forth-rights and meanders, paths straight and crooked.

attached, seized.

for, because of.
throughly, thoroughly.

[96] Some scholars claim that Prospero wishes those who took part in usurping his throne to realize their sin and to repent. This scene is the climax of that action. As you read, note the different reactions on the part of Gonzalo, who is innocent, and Alonso, Antonio, and Sebastian, who are guilty. As the scene opens, which one of the latter three appears to be about to repent, and why? What of the other two?
on the top, at some high point of the tiring-house or the theater.
banquet, not a large meal as we know it today, but a light meal, probably consisting of nuts and cakes.
kind keepers, guardian angels.
drollery, puppet show.

25 And what does else want credit,° come to me,
And I'll be sworn 'tis true. Travelers ne'er did lie,
Though fools at home condemn 'em.°

GONZALO.   If in Naples
I should report this now, would they believe me
If I should say I saw such islanders?
30 For, certes,° these are people of the island,
Who, though they are of monstrous shape, yet, note,
Their manners are more gentle, kind, than of
Our human generation you shall find
Many, nay, almost any.

PROSPERO (*aside*).   Honest lord,
35 Thou hast said well; for some of you there present
Are worse than devils.

ALONSO.   I cannot too much muse°
Such shapes, such gesture, and such sound, expressing,
Although they want the use of tongue, a kind
Of excellent dumb discourse.

PROSPERO (*aside*).   Praise in departing.°
40 FRANCISCO. They vanished strangely.

SEBASTIAN.   No matter, since
They have left their viands behind; for we have stomachs.
Will 't please you taste of what is here?

ALONSO.   Not I.

GONZALO. Faith, sir, you need not fear. When we were boys,
Who would believe that there were mountaineers
45 Dew-lapped° like bulls, whose throats had hanging at 'em
Wallets of flesh? Or that there were such men
Whose heads stood in their breasts?° Which now we find
Each putter-out of five for one° will bring us
Good warrant of.

ALONSO.   I will stand to° and feed,
50 Although my last—no matter, since I feel
The best is past. Brother, my lord the Duke,
Stand to and do as we.

(*They approach the table. Thunder and lightning. Enter* ARIEL, *like a harpy;°
claps his wings upon the table; and, with a quaint device,° the banquet vanishes.*°)

ARIEL. You are three men of sin, whom Destiny,
That hath to° instrument this lower world
55 And what is in 't, the never-surfeited sea
Hath caused to belch up you, and on this island
Where man doth not inhabit—you 'mongst men
Being most unfit to live. I have made you mad;
And even with such-like valor° men hang and drown
60 Their proper° selves.

want credit, lack credence.
Travelers . . . 'em, a reference to the fantastic stories Renaissance travelers often brought home from abroad (see also lines 44–49).
certes, certainly.

[97] Whom does Prospero mean? Do you agree? Why?

muse, wonder at.
Praise in departing, that is, save your praise until the end of the performance.
Dew-lapped, having a dewlap, or fold of skin hanging from the neck, like cattle; often supposed to refer to people afflicted with goiter.
in their breasts, that is, like the *Anthropophagi* (a mythical tribe) described in *Othello*, act 1, scene 3, l. 146.
putter-out . . . one, one who invests money, or gambles on the risks of travel on the condition that, if he returns safely, he is to receive five times the amount deposited; hence, any traveler.
stand to, fall to, take the risk.
harpy, a fabulous monster with a woman's face and vulture's body, supposed to be a minister of divine vengeance.
quaint device, ingenious stage contrivance.
banquet vanishes, the food vanishes (the table remains until l. 82).

[98] Line 53 obviously does not apply to Gonzalo. What would you have him do while the others approach the table?
to, as its.

such-like valor, the reckless valor derived from madness.
proper, own.

(ALONSO, SEBASTIAN, *and* ANTONIO *draw their swords.*)
          You fools! I and my fellows
Are ministers of Fate. The elements,
Of whom° your swords are tempered, may as well
Wound the loud winds, or with bemocked-at stabs
Kill the still-closing° waters, as diminish
65   One dowle° that's in my plume. My fellow-ministers
Are like° invulnerable. If° you could hurt,
Your swords are now too massy for your strengths
And will not be uplifted. But remember—
For that's my business to you—that you three
70   From Milan did supplant good Prospero;
Exposed unto the sea, which hath requit° it,
Him and his innocent child; for which foul deed
The pow'rs, delaying, not forgetting, have
Incensed the seas and shores, yea, all the creatures,
75   Against your peace. Thee of thy son, Alonso,
They have bereft; and do pronounce by me
Ling'ring perdition, worse than any death
Can be at once, shall step by step attend
You and your ways; whose° wraths to guard you from—
80   Which here, in this most desolate isle, else falls
Upon your heads—is nothing° but heart's sorrow
And a clear° life ensuing.
          (*He vanishes in thunder; then, to soft music, enter the* SHAPES *again, and
                    dance, with mocks and mows,° and carrying out the table.*)
   PROSPERO. Bravely° the figure of this harpy hast thou
Performed, my Ariel; a grace it had devouring.°
85   Of my instruction hast thou nothing bated°
In what thou hadst to say. So, with good life°
And observation strange,° my meaner° ministers
Their several kinds° have done. My high charms work,
And these mine enemies are all knit up
90   In their distractions. They now are in my pow'r;
And in these fits I leave them, while I visit
Young Ferdinand, whom they suppose is drowned,
And his and mine loved darling.   (*Exit above.*)
   GONZALO. I' th' name of something holy, sir, why stand you
95   In this strange stare?
   ALONSO.   O, it° is monstrous, monstrous!
Methought the billows spoke and told me of it;
The winds did sing it to me, and the thunder,
That deep and dreadful organ-pipe, pronounced
The name of Prosper; it did bass my trespass.°
100   Therefore my son i' th' ooze is bedded, and

whom, which.

still-closing, always closing again when parted.
dowle, soft, fine feather.
like, likewise, similarly.
If, even if.
requit, requited, avenged.
whose, refers to the heavenly powers.
is nothing, there is no
way.
clear, unspotted, inno-
cent.

99 This is the first time
in the play that the
three guilty nobles have
been charged with their
crimes to their faces.
According to the Harpy,
how can they escape
the "ling'ring perdition,
worse than any death,"
that is otherwise in store
for them? Which of the
three guilty nobles should
act most affected by this
speech? Why?

mocks and mows, mock-
ing gestures and grimaces.
Bravely, finely, dashingly.
a grace . . . devouring,
that is, you gracefully
caused the banquet to disappear as if you had con-
sumed it.
bated, abated, dimin-
ished.
good life, faithful repro-
duction.
observation strange, exceptional attention to detail.
meaner, subordinate to
Ariel.
several kinds, individual
parts.

100 Has Gonzalo heard
the Harpy's speech?
How do you know?
it, that is, my sin.

bass my trespass, cry out
my trespass like a bass
note in music.

I'll seek him deeper than e'er plummet sounded
And with him there lie mudded.   (*Exit.*)
SEBASTIAN. But one fiend at a time,
I'll fight their legions o'er.°   *o'er*, one after another.
ANTONIO.   I'll be thy second.
                    (*Exeunt* SEBASTIAN *and* ANTONIO).
105 **GONZALO**. All three of them are desperate. Their great guilt,
Like poison given to work a great time after,
Now 'gins to bite the spirits. I do beseech you,
That are of suppler joints, follow them swiftly
And hinder them from what this ecstasy
110 May now provoke them to.
ADRIAN.   Follow, I pray you.   (*Exeunt omnes.*)

THINK AND DISCUSS
Understanding
1. Does Ferdinand ask Miranda to marry him, or vice versa? Quote directly from the play to support your answer.
2. In the low-comedy scene, how does Ariel initiate an argument between Stephano and Trinculo?
3. What happens to the banquet just as the nobles are about to eat it? What reason are they given for this?

Analyzing
4. From Caliban's speech (Scene 2, lines 128–136), what can you infer about his life on the island? Is he happy? Explain.
5. Why is the form of a Harpy appropriate for Ariel to assume in the banquet scene?
6. The **plot** of a Shakespeare drama reaches its structural climax in Act Three. In a comedy, the fortunes of the lovers reach their lowest point and then reverse; in a tragedy, the fortunes of the protagonist reach their highest point and then reverse.

   In *The Tempest*, which is a romance, the main plot deals with Prospero's attempt to have Alonso, Sebastian, and Antonio realize their guilt and repent. One subplot deals with the lovers, Ferdinand and Miranda; another subplot, which is a parody of a tragedy, has Caliban, Stephano, and Trinculo plotting against Prospero. Shakespeare manages to have all three plots reach their structural climax in Act Three. Specifically, where does this climax occur for the guilty nobles?
7. Where does the structural climax occur for Ferdinand and Miranda?
8. Where does the climax occur for Caliban, Stephano, and Trinculo?
9. Do you think that there is any justification for Caliban's plotting against Prospero? To what extent would you condemn his actions, and why?

Extending

10. Which of the three plots described above in question 6 do you think a modern audience would enjoy the most? Why?

COMPOSITION ◀━━●━▶

Analyzing a Character's Role

Discuss the importance of Gonzalo's role thus far. You should go back in time to Prospero's banishment from Milan, then include the scene on the ship and what has happened since the wreck. Your composition should be 3 to 5 paragraphs long. See "Writing About Characters" in the Writer's Handbook.

Writing an Interior Monologue

Put yourself in the mind of Alonzo, Sebastian, or Antonio during Scene 3 and write a first-person interior monologue (what the person is thinking) as the scene takes place. Imagine that your classmates are the audience. Because you are inside the character's mind, your monologue may be disjointed and bring in outside thoughts, such as guilt, besides what is happening. Your monologue should be the equivalent of a three- to five-paragraph composition. Some of you may wish to read your monologue aloud for the rest of the class to enjoy.

ENRICHMENT

Comparing Shakespeare's Illustrators

With its exotic setting and characters, *The Tempest* has been a popular subject for artists. Among those who have done illustrations for the play are William Hogarth (1697–1764), Joseph Wright of Derby (1734–1797), George Romney (1734–1802), Henry Fuseli (1742–1825), James Ward (1769–1855), Sir John Everett Millais (1829–1896), Gustave Doré (1833–1883), and Edmund Dulac (1882–1953). Find reproductions of some of these works (several appear in your text) and compare the various approaches they take to visualizing Shakespeare's fantasy. Two books you might find useful are *Who's Who in Shakespeare* (William Morrow, 1973) by Peter Quennell and Hamish Johnson and *Dulac* (Bantam Books, 1975) edited by David Larkin.

Listening to Music

Composers as well as painters have found inspiration in *The Tempest*. In 1873 the Russian composer Peter Ilich Tchaikovsky (1840–1893) wrote a symphonic fantasia based on Shakespeare's play. The Finnish composer Jean Sibelius (1865–1957) wrote some incidental music for a production of *The Tempest* at the Royal Theatre in Copenhagen in 1926. Both of these compositions are available on CBS recordings. The record number for the Tchaikovsky is CBS IM-39359; that for the Sibelius is CBS M-30390. Obtain a copy of one of these records, or recordings of some other music inspired by *The Tempest*, and examine the composer's response to Shakespeare's play.

Reading Closely

Caliban seems to be regarded differently by the various people he meets. Go back to the beginning of the play and make a list of the different names that people call him. List the act, scene, and line; then the speaker; and then the way Caliban is addressed or referred to. As an example, the first five references follow:

Act	Scene	Line	Speaker	Names
1	2	284	Pros.	freckled whelp hag-born
1	2	315	Pros.	slave
1	2	316	Pros.	thou earth
1	2	318	Pros.	thou tortoise
1	2	321	Pros.	poisonous slave

You will find more than fifty of these references. When you have listed them, see if they follow any pattern. Since this is a lengthy assignment, it may be shared by several students. The results should be reported to the class when they have finished reading the play.

Comment

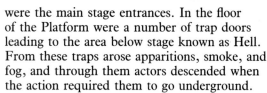

Shakespeare's Theater—The Globe

There was not one Globe Theater, but two. The first, probably completed in 1599, burned to the ground in 1613. A new Globe, promptly erected on the same spot, stood until 1644, when it was torn down, and houses were erected on its site.

We shall probably never know exactly what the Globe looked like. No contemporary pictures of the theater itself have come down to us, and what evidence there is—in the form of maps, carpenters' contracts, verbal descriptions, and the like—is inconclusive. Still, it is possible to reconstruct a theater that has the same spirit, if not the same appearance, as the original. And so Shakespearean theaters around the world have been designed with permanent open stages, and a full-sized replica is currently under construction in London near the original site south of the Thames River.

The Globe Theater was possibly round but more likely many-sided, with an outside diameter, according to the conjectures of scholars, of about 84 feet. Its three tiers of seats, plus an open area for standees, could accommodate about 2000 spectators.

The main acting area, called the Platform, extended out into the audience. At the back was a curtained recess known as the Study that was usually used for interior scenes. At either side were large permanent doors, similar to the street doors of Elizabethan town houses. These were the main stage entrances. In the floor of the Platform were a number of trap doors leading to the area below stage known as Hell. From these traps arose apparitions, smoke, and fog, and through them actors descended when the action required them to go underground.

On the second level there was another curtained recess called the Chamber, generally used for domestic settings. In front of this was a narrow balcony called the Tarras (terrace) connecting two small bay windows or window stages that flanked it. The Tarras was often used in conjunction with the Platform—for example, to represent a hill, battlements, or a gallery from which observers watched action below.

The third level contained a narrow musicians' gallery that could also be used as an acting area. Above it was a canopied roof supported by two large stage posts that rose from the Platform. Sound effects such as thunder or battle "alarums" were produced in the Huts above the Canopy. The Huts also housed a pulley system used for lowering apparitions or objects supposed to appear from midair.

This entire three-story structure, forming the back of the stage and giving the effect of a large Elizabethan town house, was known as the Tiring House. It was the Globe's permanent set. After 1599 Shakespeare probably wrote most of his plays with this set in mind.

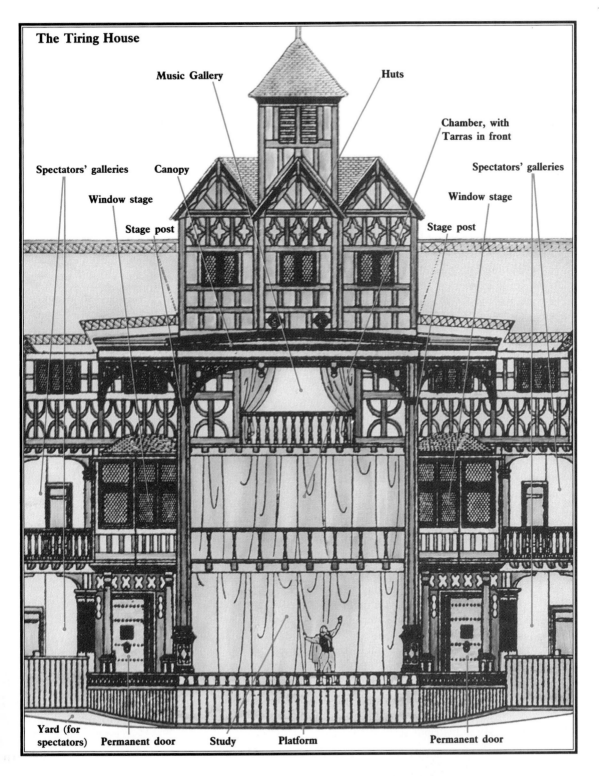

The Tiring House

Music Gallery

Huts

Chamber, with
Tarras in front

Spectators' galleries

Canopy

Spectators' galleries

Window stage

Window stage

Stage post

Stage post

Yard (for
spectators)   Permanent door   Study   Platform   Permanent door

ACT FOUR

SCENE 1.

Before PROSPERO's *cell. (Played on the Platform Stage.) Enter* PROSPERO,
FERDINAND, *and* MIRANDA.

PROSPERO. If I have too austerely punished you,
  Your compensation makes amends, for I
  Have given you here a third° of mine own life,
  Or that for which I live; who once again
5 I tender to thy hand. All thy vexations
  Were but my trials of thy love, and thou
  Hast strangely° stood the test. Here, afore Heaven,
  I ratify this my rich gift. O Ferdinand,
  Do not smile at me that I boast her off,°
10 For thou shalt find she will outstrip all praise
  And make it halt° behind her.
FERDINAND.   I do believe it
  Against an oracle.°
PROSPERO. Then, as my gift and thine own acquisition
  Worthily purchased, take my daughter. But
15 If thou dost break her virgin-knot before
  All sanctimonious° ceremonies may
  With full and holy rite be ministered,
  No sweet aspersion° shall the heavens let fall
  To make this contract grow; but barren hate,
20 Sour-eyed disdain, and discord shall bestrew
  The union of your bed with weeds so loathly
  That you shall hate it both. Therefore take heed,
  As Hymen's° lamps shall light you.
FERDINAND.   As I hope
  For quiet days, fair issue, and long life,
25 With such love as 'tis now, the murkiest den,
  The most opportune place, the strong'st suggestion
  Our worser genius° can, shall never melt
  Mine honor into lust, to take away
  The edge of that day's celebration
30 When I shall think or° Phoebus' steeds are foundered°
  Or Night kept chained below.
PROSPERO.   Fairly spoke.
  Sit then and talk with her; she is thine own.
               (FERDINAND *and* MIRANDA *sit. Enter* ARIEL.)
  What, Ariel! My industrious servant, Ariel!

---

a third, that is, Miranda, into whose education Prospero has put a third of his life, or who represents a large part of what he cares about, along with his dukedom and his learned study.
strangely, extraordinarily.
boast her off, praise her so.
halt, limp.

> **101** Has Prospero's attitude toward Ferdinand really changed? Explain.

Against an oracle, even if an oracle should declare otherwise.
sanctimonious, sacred.

aspersion, dew, shower.

Hymen, the Greek and Roman god of marriage.

worser genius, evil genius, or evil attendant spirit.
or, either.
foundered, broken down, made lame; that is, Ferdinand will wait impatiently for the bridal night.

> **102** In lines 31–32 Prospero clearly signifies his approval of the betrothal of Miranda and Ferdinand.

ARIEL. What would my potent master? Here I am.

35 PROSPERO. Thou and thy meaner fellows your last service
Did worthily perform; and I must use you
In such another trick. Go bring the rabble,°
O'er whom I give thee pow'r, here to this place.
Incite them to quick motion, for I must
40 Bestow upon the eyes of this young couple
Some vanity° of mine art. It is my promise,
And they expect it from me.

ARIEL.   Presently?

PROSPERO. Ay, with a twink.

ARIEL. Before you can say "come" and "go,"
45 And breathe twice and cry "so, so,"
Each one, tripping on his toe,
Will be here with mop and mow.°
Do you love me, master? No?

PROSPERO. Dearly, my delicate Ariel. Do not approach
50 Till thou dost hear me call.

ARIEL.   Well, I conceive.°   (Exit.)

PROSPERO. Look thou be true; do not give dalliance
Too much the rein. The strongest oaths are straw
To th' fire i' th' blood. Be more abstemious,
Or else good night your vow!

FERDINAND.   I warrant you, sir;
55 The white cold virgin snow upon my heart
Abates the ardor of my liver.°

PROSPERO.   Well.
Now come, my Ariel! Bring a corollary,°
Rather than want° a spirit. Appear, and pertly!°
No tongue! All eyes! Be silent.   (Soft music. Enter IRIS.°)

60 IRIS. Ceres,° most bounteous lady, thy rich leas°
Of wheat, rye, barley, vetches,° oats, and pease;
Thy turfy mountains, where live nibbling sheep,
And flat meads thatched with stover,° them to keep;
Thy banks with pioned and twilled° brims,
65 Which spongy April at thy hest betrims,
To make cold nymphs chaste crowns; and thy broom-groves,°
Whose shadow the dismissed bachelor° loves,
Being lass-lorn; thy pole-clipt° vineyard;
And thy sea-marge, sterile and rocky-hard,
70 Where thou thyself dost air—the queen o' th' sky,°
Whose wat'ry arch° and messenger am I,
Bids thee leave these, and with her sovereign grace,
                              (JUNO descends° slowly in her car.)
Here on this grass-plot, in this very place,

rabble, band, the "meaner fellows" of line 35.
vanity, illusion.

103 To celebrate the betrothal, the same spirits who caused the nobles' meal to disappear before their eyes now produce a masque (lines 60–138), an elaborate spectacle popular at court. This masque, however, goes beyond the betrothal of Ferdinand and Miranda, for the play was performed in celebration of a royal betrothal. At court, the lords and ladies (not professional actors) would participate as dancers.

mop and mow, gestures and grimaces.
conceive, understand.
liver, supposedly the seat of the passions.
corollary, surplus, extra supply.
want, lack.
pertly, briskly.
Iris, goddess of the rainbow, and Juno's messenger.
Ceres, goddess of the generative powers of nature.
leas, meadows.
vetches, plants for forage, fodder.
stover, winter fodder for cattle.
pioned and twilled, undercut by the swift current and protected by roots and branches woven into a mat.
broom-groves, clumps of broom, gorse, yellow-flowered shrub.
dismissed bachelor, rejected male lover.
pole-clipt, hedged in with poles; or pruned.
queen o' th' sky, Juno.
wat'ry arch, rainbow.
Juno descends, starts her descent from the "heavens" above the stage.

To come and sport. Her peacocks° fly amain.°

75 Approach, rich Ceres, her to entertain.°   (*Enter* CERES.)

    CERES. Hail, many-colored messenger, that ne'er
Dost disobey the wife of Jupiter,
Who with thy saffron wings upon my flow'rs
Diffusest honey-drops, refreshing show'rs,

80 And with each end of thy blue bow dost crown
My bosky° acres and my unshrubbed down,°
Rich scarf to my proud earth; why hath thy Queen
Summon'd me hither, to this short-grassed green?

    IRIS. A contract of true love to celebrate,

85 And some donation freely to estate°
On the blessed lovers.

    CERES.   Tell me, heavenly bow,
If Venus or her son,° as thou dost know,
Do now attend the Queen? Since they did plot
The means that dusky Dis my daughter got,

90 Her° and her blind boy's scandaled° company
I have forsworn.

    IRIS.   Of her society
Be not afraid. I met her deity°
Cutting the clouds towards Paphos,° and her son
Dove-drawn with her. Here thought they to have done

95 Some wanton charm upon this man and maid,
Whose vows are, that no bed-right shall be paid
Till Hymen's torch be lighted; but in vain;
Mars's hot minion° is returned again;
Her waspish-headed° son has broke his arrows,

100 Swears he will shoot no more, but play with sparrows
And be a boy right out.°   (JUNO *alights.*)

    CERES.   Highest Queen of state,
Great Juno, comes; I know her by her gait.

    JUNO. How does my bounteous sister? Go with me
To bless this twain, that they may prosperous be

105 And honored in their issue.   (*They sing:*)

    JUNO. *Honor, riches, marriage-blessing,*
      Long continuance, and increasing,
      Hourly joys be still upon you!
      Juno sings her blessings on you.

110 CERES. *Earth's increase, foison plenty,°*
      Barns and garners° never empty,
      Vines with clust'ring bunches growing,
      Plants with goodly burden bowing;
      Spring come to you at the farthest

115   *In the very end of harvest!*

peacocks, birds sacred to Juno and used to pull her chariot.
amain, with full speed.
entertain, receive.
bosky, wooded.
down, upland.

[104] If you were producing this entertainment, how would you costume Ceres to represent the goddess of the harvest? How would you costume Iris as the rainbow? In the masque, Shakespeare uses pastoral poetry, a conventional form of lyric poetry that glorifies the rustic life, in the verses of Iris and Ceres.

estate, bestow.
son, that is, Cupid.

[105] This is a reference to the classical myth in which Dis (Pluto) carries off Proserpina (Persephone) to Hades. While in Hades she eats some pomegranate seeds, and therefore must remain underground several months each year. During the period she is underground, her mother Ceres does not bless the fields and the earth must undergo the winter season.

Her, that is, Venus.
scandaled, scandalous.
her deity, Venus.
Paphos, place on the island of Cyprus, sacred to Venus.
Mars's hot minion, that is, Venus, the beloved of Mars.
waspish-headed, fiery, hotheaded, peevish.
right out, outright.
foison plenty, plentiful harvest.
garners, granaries.

[106] What blessings does Juno bestow on the betrothed couple? What blessings does Ceres bestow? How do Ceres's blessings cancel the result of Proserpina's abduction?

Detail of an engraving of a painting by Joseph Wright of Derby (1734–1797).
One of a famous series of paintings commissioned by John Boydell (1719–1804)
to illustrate the works of Shakespeare.

> *Scarcity and want shall shun you;*
> *Ceres' blessing so is on you.*

FERDINAND. This is a most majestic vision, and
　Harmonious charmingly. May I be bold
120　To think these spirits?

PROSPERO.　　　　　Spirits, which by mine art
　I have from their confines called to enact
　My present fancies.

FERDINAND.　　　Let me live here ever;
　So rare a wondered° father and a wise
　Makes this place Paradise.

(JUNO and CERES whisper, and send IRIS on employment.)

PROSPERO.　　　　　Sweet now, silence!
125　Juno and Ceres whisper seriously;
　There's something else to do. Hush and be mute,
　Or else our spell is marred.

IRIS. You nymphs, called Naiads, of the windring° brooks,
　With your sedged crowns and ever-harmless looks,
130　Leave your crisp° channels, and on this green land
　Answer your summons; Juno does command.
　Come, temperate° nymphs, and help to celebrate
　A contract of true love; be not too late.　　　*(Enter certain NYMPHS.)*
　You sunburnt sicklemen, of August weary,
135　Come hither from the furrow and be merry.
　Make holiday; your rye-straw hats put on
　And these fresh nymphs encounter every one
　In country footing.°

　　(Enter certain REAPERS, properly habited. They join with the NYMPHS in a
　　graceful dance, towards the end whereof PROSPERO starts suddenly, and
　　speaks; after which, to a strange, hollow, and confused noise, they heavily°
　　vanish.)

PROSPERO *(aside).*　　I had forgot that foul conspiracy
140　Of the beast Caliban and his confederates
　Against my life. The minute of their plot
　Is almost come. *(To the Spirits.)* Well done! Avoid;° no more!

FERDINAND. This is strange. Your father's in some passion
　That works him strongly.

MIRANDA.　　　　　Never till this day
145　Saw I him touched with anger so distempered.

PROSPERO. You do look, my son, in a moved sort,°
　As if you were dismayed. Be cheerful, sir.
　Our revels° now are ended. These our actors,
　As I foretold you, were all spirits and
150　Are melted into air, into thin air;
　And, like the baseless° fabric of this vision,

wondered, wonder-performing, wondrous.

windring, wandering, winding.

crisp, curled, rippled.

temperate, chaste.

country footing, country dancing.

107 | This is the point at which the lords and ladies of the court would present their dance.
heavily, slowly, dejectedly.

Avoid, depart, withdraw.

moved sort, troubled state, condition.

revels, entertainments, pageants.

baseless, without substance.

The cloud-capped tow'rs, the gorgeous palaces,
The solemn temples, the great globe itself,
Yea, all which it inherit,° shall dissolve
155 And, like this insubstantial pageant faded,
Leave not a rack° behind. We are such stuff
As dreams are made on,° and our little life
Is rounded with a sleep. Sir, I am vexed.
Bear with my weakness; my old brain is troubled.
160 Be not disturbed with my infirmity.
If you be pleased, retire into my cell
And there repose. A turn or two I'll walk
To still my beating mind.
FERDINAND, MIRANDA.   We wish your peace.   (*Exeunt.*)
PROSPERO. Come with a thought!° I thank thee, Ariel. Come.
                                                (*Enter* ARIEL.)
165 ARIEL. Thy thoughts I cleave to. What's thy pleasure?
PROSPERO.   Spirit,
    We must prepare to meet with Caliban.
ARIEL. Ay, my commander. When I presented° Ceres,
    I thought to have told thee of it, but I feared
    Lest I might anger thee.
170 PROSPERO. Say again, where didst thou leave these varlets?
ARIEL. I told you, sir, they were red-hot with drinking,
    So full of valor that they smote the air
    For breathing in their faces; beat the ground
    For kissing of their feet; yet always bending
175 Towards their project. Then I beat my tabor,
    At which, like unbacked° colts, they pricked their ears,
    Advanced° their eyelids, lifted up their noses
    As they smelt music. So I charmed their ears
    That calf-like they my lowing followed through
180 Toothed briers, sharp furzes, pricking goss,° and thorns,
    Which entered their frail shins. At last I left them
    I' th' filthy-mantled° pool beyond your cell,
    There dancing up to th' chins, that the foul lake
    O'erstunk their feet.
PROSPERO.   This was well done, my bird.
185 Thy shape invisible retain thou still.
    The trumpery° in my house, go bring it hither,
    For stale° to catch these thieves.
ARIEL.   I go, I go.   (*Exit.*)
PROSPERO. A devil, a born devil, on whose nature
    Nurture can never stick; on whom my pains,
190 Humanely taken, all, all lost, quite lost!
    And as with age his body uglier grows,

---

which it inherit, who occupy it.

rack, wisp of cloud.

on, of.

108 Prospero's speech (lines 148–158) is often said to represent Shakespeare's own farewell to the stage. What in the speech supports this theory?

with a thought, that is, on the instant, or summoned by my thought, no sooner thought on than here.

presented, acted the part of, or introduced.

unbacked, unbroken, unridden.
Advanced, lifted up.

goss, gorse, a prickly shrub.

filthy-mantled, covered with a slimy coating.

109 How has Ariel been punishing Stephano, Trinculo, and Caliban?

trumpery, cheap goods, the "glistering apparel" mentioned in the following stage directions.
stale, decoy.

So his mind cankers.° I will plague them all,
Even to roaring.   (*Enter* ARIEL, *loaden with glistering apparel, etc.*)
                    Come, hang them on this line.°
(ARIEL *hangs up the showy finery;* PROSPERO *and* ARIEL *remain, invisible.*
                    Enter CALIBAN, STEPHANO, *and* TRINCULO, *all wet.*)

CALIBAN. Pray you, tread softly, that the blind mole may not
195   Hear a foot fall. We now are near his cell.

STEPHANO. Monster, your fairy, which you say is a harmless fairy, has done
      little better than played the Jack with us.°

TRINCULO. Monster, I do smell all horse-piss, at which my nose is in great
      indignation.

200 STEPHANO. So is mine. Do you hear, monster? If I should take a displeasure
      against you, look you—

TRINCULO. Thou wert but a lost monster.

CALIBAN. Good my lord, give me thy favor still.
      Be patient, for the prize I'll bring thee to
205   Shall hoodwink° this mischance. Therefore speak softly.
      All's hushed as midnight yet.

TRINCULO. Ay, but to lose our bottles in the pool—

STEPHANO. There is not only disgrace and dishonor in that, monster, but an
      infinite loss.

210 TRINCULO. That's more to me than my wetting. Yet this is your harmless
      fairy, monster!

STEPHANO. I will fetch off my bottle, though I be o'er ears for my labor.

CALIBAN. Prithee, my King, be quiet. See'st thou here,
      This is the mouth o' th' cell. No noise, and enter.
215   Do that good mischief which may make this island
      Thine own for ever, and I, thy Caliban,
      For aye thy foot-licker.

STEPHANO. Give me thy hand. I do begin to have bloody thoughts.

TRINCULO (*seeing the finery*). O King Stephano! O peer!° O worthy Stephano!
220   Look what a wardrobe here is for thee!

CALIBAN. Let it alone, thou fool! It is but trash.

TRINCULO. O, ho, monster! We know what belongs to a frippery.° O King
      Stephano! (*Takes a gown.*)

STEPHANO. Put off that gown, Trinculo. By this hand, I'll have that gown.

225 TRINCULO. Thy Grace shall have it.

CALIBAN. The dropsy drown this fool! What do you mean
      To dote thus on such luggage?° Let's alone
      And do the murder first. If he awake,
      From toe to crown he'll fill our skins with pinches,
230   Make us strange stuff.

STEPHANO. Be you quiet, monster. Mistress line, is not this my jerkin?° (*Takes
      it down.*) Now is the jerkin under the line.° Now, jerkin, you are like to
      lose your hair and prove a bald jerkin.

---

cankers, festers, grows malignant.

[110] In this brief soliloquy what does Prospero say about his efforts to "civilize" Caliban?

line, lime tree or linden.

played . . . us, made fools of us; tricked us.

hoodwink, cover up, make you not see (a hawking term).

[111] What are Trinculo and Stephano most concerned about?

King . . . peer, alludes to the old ballad beginning, "King Stephen was a worthy peer."
frippery, place where cast-off clothes are sold.
luggage, cumbersome trash.
jerkin, jacket made of leather.
under the line, under the lime tree (with punning sense of being south of the equinoctial line or equator; sailors to the southern regions were popularly supposed to lose their hair from scurvy or other diseases).

TRINCULO. Do, do! We steal by line and level,° an 't like° your Grace.

235 STEPHANO. I thank thee for that jest. Here's a garment for 't. (*Gives a garment.*) Wit shall not go unrewarded while I am king of this country. "Steal by line and level" is an excellent pass of pate.° There's another garment for 't.

TRINCULO. Monster, come, put some lime° upon your fingers, and away with
240 the rest.

CALIBAN. I will have none on 't. We shall lose our time,
And all be turned to barnacles, or to apes
With foreheads villainous low.

STEPHANO. Monster, lay to your fingers. Help to bear this away where my
245 hogshead of wine is, or I'll turn you out of my kingdom. Go to, carry this.

TRINCULO. And this.

STEPHANO. Ay, and this. (*They collect more and more garments. A noise of hunters heard. Enter divers SPIRITS, in shape of dogs and hounds, hunting them about, PROSPERO and ARIEL setting them on.*)

PROSPERO. Hey, Mountain, hey!

ARIEL. Silver! There it goes, Silver!

250 PROSPERO. Fury, Fury! There, Tyrant, there! Hark! Hark!

(CALIBAN, STEPHANO, *and* TRINCULO *are driven out.*)

Go charge my goblins that they grind their joints
With dry convulsions,° shorten up their sinews
With aged° cramps, and more pinch-spotted make them
Then pard° or cat o' mountain.°

ARIEL.   Hark, they roar!

255 PROSPERO. Let them be hunted soundly. At this hour
Lies at my mercy all mine enemies.
Shortly shall all my labors end, and thou
Shalt have the air at freedom. For a little
Follow, and do me service.   (*Exeunt.*)

---

by line and level, by means of plumb-line and carpenter's level, methodically (with pun on *line,* "lime tree," l. 193).
an 't like, if it please.
pass of pate, sally of wit.
lime, birdlime, sticky substance (to give Caliban sticky fingers).

| 112 | Which one of the three shows the most sense? What is ironic about this?

dry convulsions, cramps associated with age and arthritis.
aged, characteristic of old age.
pard, panther or leopard.
cat o' mountain, wildcat.

| 113 | How does Prospero plan to punish the three? How will he reward Ariel?

THINK AND DISCUSS

Understanding

1. What does Prospero instruct Ariel to put out as bait to ruin Caliban's plot to kill him? Who takes the bait? Who does not?

2. Although Act Four consists of a single scene, the action involves two different sets of characters, almost as though there were two scenes. Locate the line number where this break occurs. Which character has remained onstage throughout and thereby prevented the act from having two scenes?

3. Which major group of characters fails to appear at all in Act Four?

4. You have already studied **assonance,** the matching of vowel sounds (but not consonant sounds). Which lines in Ceres's blessing to the betrothed couple (lines 110–117) illustrate assonance?

Analyzing

5. Miranda has only one short speech, and that comes well into the act (lines 144–145). What should Miranda be doing while Ferdinand and Prospero are engaged in their conversation (lines 1–32 and 51–59)? Note what their conversation is about and what the topic may have to do with Miranda's silence.

6. In line 124 Prospero says, "Sweet now, silence." To whom may the line be addressed? Do you think this means that a speech has been omitted, or might it be serving as a stage direction within the dialogue? Explain.

Extending

7. If you were directing a modern version of *The Tempest,* are there any changes that you would make in this act? Explain.

THINKING SKILLS

Synthesizing

To synthesize is to put together parts and elements so as to form a whole, a new pattern or structure not evident before. Synthesis can involve personal experience and imagination. For example, when Shakespeare wrote *The Tempest,* he was synthesizing stories of travel and adventure, Montaigne's essay, elements of myth, romance, comedy, *commedia dell'arte,* and other elements as well, with his own experience and imagination to create a new play.

1. Imagine that Ceres's song (lines 110–117) is a separate poem and create a descriptive title for it.

2. To the modern reader, the Prospero of the end of this act (lines 251–254) may seem merciless and cruel. Explain why this perception is probably incorrect in the context of both the play and the age in general.

COMPOSITION

Comparing and Contrasting Scenes

Compare and contrast the performance of the spirits in the banquet scene with their performance in the betrothal masque. Consider the purpose of each performance and the humans who would be observing it, and also the forms taken by the spirits. You may assume that Ariel played the role of Ceres or of Iris in the betrothal masque. Your paper should be at least three paragraphs long.

Analyzing a Speech

Reread Prospero's speech (lines 148–158) and write a three- to five-paragraph paper in which you discuss the extent to which you think it may—or may not—represent Shakespeare's farewell to the stage. Assume that you are attempting to convince a classmate who does not agree with you. See "Writing to Persuade an Audience" in the Writer's Handbook.

ACT FIVE

SCENE 1.

Before PROSPERO'*s cell. (Played on the Platform Stage and Study.) Enter*
PROSPERO *in his magic robe, with his staff, and* ARIEL.

PROSPERO. Now does my project gather to a head.
My charms crack not, my spirits obey, and Time
Goes upright with his carriage.° How's the day?
ARIEL. On the sixth hour; at which time, my lord,
5   You said our work should cease.
PROSPERO.   I did say so,
When first I raised the tempest. Say, my spirit,
How fares the King and 's followers?
ARIEL.   Confined together
In the same fashion as you gave in charge,
Just as you left them; all prisoners, sir,
10   In the line-grove° which weather-fends° your cell.
They cannot budge till your release.° The King,
His brother, and yours, abide all three distracted,
And the remainder mourning over them,
Brimful of sorrow and dismay; but chiefly
15   Him that you termed, sir, "The good old lord, Gonzalo."
His tears run down his beard like winter's drops
From eaves of reeds.° Your charm so strongly works 'em
That if you now beheld them, your affections
Would become tender.
PROSPERO.   Dost thou think so, spirit?
20   **ARIEL.** Mine would, sir, were I human.
PROSPERO.   And mine shall.
Hast thou, which art but air, a touch, a feeling
Of their afflictions, and shall not myself,
One of their kind, that relish all° as sharply,
Passion° as they, be kindlier moved than thou art?
25   Though with their high wrongs I am struck to th' quick,
Yet with my nobler reason 'gainst my fury
Do I take part. The rarer° action is
In virtue than in vengeance. They being penitent,
The sole drift of my purpose doth extend
30   Not a frown further. Go release them, Ariel.
My charms I'll break, their senses I'll restore,
And they shall be themselves.

---

his carriage, its burden; that is, Time is
unstopped, runs
smoothly.

114 How many hours
have passed since
Prospero's first instruc-
tions to Ariel (see Act
One, Scene 2, lines
239–240)?

line-grove, grove of lime
trees.
weather-fends, protects
from the weather.
your release, you release
them.

eaves of reeds, thatched
roofs.

115 What effects are
Prospero's charms
having on the guilty
nobles? On Gonzalo?

relish all, experience
quite.
Passion, deep feeling.

rarer, nobler.

116 What influences Prospero to break his
charms?

ARIEL.   I'll fetch them, sir.

(*Exit.* PROSPERO *traces a charmed circle with his staff.*)

PROSPERO. Ye elves of hills, brooks, standing lakes, and groves,
And ye that on the sands with printless foot

35   Do chase the ebbing Neptune, and do fly him
When he comes back; you demi-puppets° that
By moonshine do the green sour ringlets° make,
Whereof the ewe not bites; and you whose pastime
Is to make midnight mushrooms, that rejoice

40   To hear the solemn curfew; by whose aid,
Weak masters though ye be, I have bedimmed
The noontide sun, called forth the mutinous winds,
And 'twixt the green sea and the azured vault
Set roaring war; to the dread rattling thunder

45   Have I given fire,° and rifted° Jove's stout oak
With his own bolt; the strong-based promontory
Have I made shake, and by the spurs° plucked up
The pine and cedar; graves at my command
Have waked their sleepers, oped, and let 'em forth

50   By my so potent art.° But this rough magic
I here abjure, and, when I have required°
Some heavenly music, which even now I do,
To work mine end upon their senses that
This airy charm is for, I'll break my staff,

55   Bury it certain fathoms in the earth,
And deeper than did ever plummet sound
I'll drown my book.

(*Solemn music. Here enters* ARIEL *before; then* ALONSO, *with a frantic gesture, attended by* GONZALO; SEBASTIAN *and* ANTONIO *in like manner, attended by* ADRIAN *and* FRANCISCO. *They all enter the circle which* PROSPERO *had made, and there stand charmed; which* PROSPERO *observing, speaks:*)

A solemn air, and° the best comforter
To an unsettled fancy, cure thy brains,

60   Now useless, boiled within thy skull! There stand,
For you are spell-stopped.
Holy Gonzalo, honorable man,
Mine eyes, ev'n sociable° to the show° of thine,
Fall° fellowly drops. The charm dissolves apace,

65   And as the morning steals upon the night,
Melting the darkness, so their rising senses
Begin to chase the ignorant fumes that mantle
Their clearer reason. O good Gonzalo,
My true preserver, and a loyal sir

70   To him thou follow'st! I will pay thy graces°
Home° both in word and deed. Most cruelly

---

demi-puppets, puppets of half-size, that is, elves and fairies.
green sour ringlets, fairy rings, circles in grass (actually produced by mushrooms).

to . . . fire, I have discharged bolts of lightning.
rifted, riven, split.
spurs, roots.

Ye . . . art, this famous passage (lines 33–50) is an embellished paraphrase of Golding's translation of a speech of the witch Medea in Ovid's *Metamorphoses*, Book 7, lines 197–210.
required, requested.

117 Lines 33–57 make up Prospero's final soliloquy. In what way may it be called Shakespeare's farewell to the stage?

and, which is.

sociable, sympathetic.
show, appearance.
Fall, let fall.

pay thy graces, reward your favors.
Home, fully.

Didst thou, Alonso, use me and my daughter.
Thy brother was a furtherer in the act.
Thou art pinched for 't now, Sebastian. Flesh and blood,
75   You, brother mine, that entertained ambition,
Expelled remorse° and nature,° who, with Sebastian,
Whose inward pinches therefore are most strong,
Would here have killed your king, I do forgive thee,
Unnatural though thou art.—Their understanding
80   Begins to swell, and the approaching tide
Will shortly fill the reasonable shore
That now lies foul and muddy. Not one of them
That yet looks on me, or would know me. Ariel,
Fetch me the hat and rapier in my cell.

(*Ariel goes to the cell and returns immediately.*)

85   I will discase° me, and myself present
As I was sometime Milan.° Quickly, spirit;
Thou shalt ere long be free.   (ARIEL *sings and helps to attire him.*)

ARIEL. *Where the bee sucks, there suck I;*
In a cowslip's bell I lie;
90   *There I couch when owls do cry.*
On the bat's back I do fly
After summer merrily.
Merrily, merrily shall I live now
Under the blossom that hangs on the bough.

95   PROSPERO. Why, that's my dainty Ariel! I shall miss thee;
But yet thou shalt have freedom. So, so, so.°
To the King's ship, invisible as thou art!
There shalt thou find the mariners asleep
Under the hatches. The master and the boatswain
100 Being awake, enforce them to this place,
And presently, I prithee.

ARIEL. I drink the air before me, and return
Or ere your pulse twice beat.   (*Exit.*)

GONZALO. All torment, trouble, wonder, and amazement
105 Inhabits here. Some heavenly power guide us
Out of this fearful country!

PROSPERO.   Behold, sir King,
The wronged Duke of Milan, Prospero.
For more assurance that a living prince
Does now speak to thee, I embrace thy body;
110 And to thee and thy company I bid
A hearty welcome.   (*Embraces him.*)

ALONSO.   Whe'er thou be'st he or no,
Or some enchanted trifle° to abuse° me,
As late I have been, I not know. Thy pulse

---

remorse, pity.
nature, natural feeling.

[118] Who is receiving the strongest punishment from Prospero, and why?

discase, disrobe.
As . . . Milan, in my former appearance as Duke of Milan.

[119] Why is Ariel's song appropriate?

So, so, so, expresses approval of Ariel's help as valet.

[120] Why does Gonzalo say this?

trifle, trick of magic.
abuse, deceive.

Beats as of flesh and blood; and, since I saw thee,
115 Th' affliction of my mind amends, with which,
I fear, a madness held me. This must crave,°
An if this be at all,° a most strange story.
Thy dukedom I resign,° and do entreat
Thou pardon me my wrongs. But how should Prospero
120 Be living and be here?

PROSPERO (*to* GONZALO). First, noble friend,
Let me embrace thine age, whose honor cannot
Be measured or confined. *(Embraces him.)*

GONZALO.   Whether this be
Or be not, I'll not swear.

PROSPERO.   You do yet taste
Some subtleties° o' th' isle, that will not let you
125 Believe things certain. Welcome, my friends all!
(Aside to SEBASTIAN *and* ANTONIO.*)* But you, my brace of lords, were I
    so minded,
I here could pluck his Highness' frown upon you
And justify you° traitors. At this time
I will tell no tales.

SEBASTIAN.   The devil speaks in him.

PROSPERO.   No.
130 For you, most wicked sir, whom to call brother
Would even infect my mouth, I do forgive
Thy rankest fault—all of them; and require
My dukedom of thee, which perforce I know
Thou must restore.

ALONSO.   If thou be'st Prospero,
135 Give us particulars of thy preservation,
How thou hast met us here, who three hours since
Were wracked upon this shore; where I have lost—
How sharp the point of this remembrance is!—
My dear son Ferdinand.

PROSPERO.   I am woe° for 't, sir.
140 ALONSO. Irreparable is the loss, and Patience
    Says it is past her cure.

PROSPERO.   I rather think
You have not sought her help, of whose soft grace
For the like loss I have her sovereign aid
And rest myself content.

ALONSO.   You the like loss?
145 PROSPERO. As great to me as late;° and, supportable
    To make the dear loss, have I means much weaker
    Than you may call to comfort you, for I
    Have lost my daughter.

---

crave, require.
An . . . all, if this is actually happening.
Thy . . . resign. Alonso made arrangement with Antonio at the time of Prospero's banishment for Milan to pay tribute to Naples.

121 Has Alonso repented his treachery? Explain.

subtleties, illusions, magical powers.
122 What does Prospero mean by this aside?

justify you, prove you to be.
123 Has Prospero completely forgiven Antonio? Explain.

124 Note that Alonso's estimate of the length of time that has passed supports that established earlier by Prospero for completing the project (act 1, scene 2, lines 239–240).
woe, sorry.

late, recent.
125 What does Prospero mean?

ALONSO. A daughter?

150   O heavens, that they were living both in Naples,
    The king and queen there! That they were, I wish
    Myself were mudded in that oozy bed
    Where my son lies. When did you lose your daughter?

PROSPERO. In this last tempest. I perceive these lords

155   At this encounter do so much admire°
    That they devour their reason and scarce think
    Their eyes do offices of truth, their words
    Are natural breath.° But, howsoev'r you have
    Been justled from your senses, know for certain

160   That I am Prospero and that very duke
    Which was thrust forth of Milan, who most strangely
    Upon this shore, where you were wracked, was landed,
    To be the lord on 't. No more yet of this,
    For 'tis a chronicle of day by day,

165   Not a relation for a breakfast nor
    Befitting this first meeting. Welcome, sir;
    This cell's my court. Here have I few attendants
    And subjects none abroad. Pray you look in.
    My dukedom since you have given me again,

170   I will requite you with as good a thing,
    At least bring forth a wonder, to content ye
    As much as me my dukedom.

       (Here PROSPERO *discovers°* FERDINAND *and* MIRANDA, *playing at chess.)*

MIRANDA. Sweet lord, you play me false.

FERDINAND.   No, my dearest love,

175   I would not for the world.

MIRANDA. Yes, for a score of kingdoms you should wrangle,
    And I would call it fair play.

ALONSO.   If this prove
    A vision of the island, one dear son
    Shall I twice lose.

SEBASTIAN.   A most high miracle!

180 **FERDINAND.** Though the seas threaten, they are merciful;
    I have cursed them without cause.   *(Kneels.)*

ALONSO.   Now all the blessings
    Of a glad father compass thee about!
    Arise, and say how thou cam'st here.

MIRANDA.   O, wonder!
    How many goodly creatures are there here!

185   How beauteous mankind is! O brave° new world,
    That has such people in 't!

PROSPERO.   'Tis new to thee.

ALONSO. What is this maid with whom thou wast at play?

admire, wonder.

scarce . . . breath, scarcely believe that their eyes inform them accurately what they see, or that their words are naturally spoken.

126 The word "wonder" (line 171) represents more word play on Miranda's name. Note too that in line 155 of this speech Shakespeare has Prospero use "admire," a partial anagram of Miranda's name.

discovers, reveals by opening a curtain, presumably rear-stage.

127 Just as Antonio treacherously obtained power over Prospero's dukedom; as Antonio and Sebastian planned to murder Alonso for his kingdom; as Stephano, Trinculo, and Caliban plotted to murder Prospero for the island, so too are Ferdinand and Miranda engaged in a figurative struggle for power in their chess game. How does their brief conversation (lines 173–177) parallel yet differ from the other attempts to gain power?

128 What does Alonso mean in lines 177–179?

brave, splendid, gorgeously appareled, handsome.

129 In what ways are Miranda's comment and Prospero's reply appropriate to their experience with the world? (Note further wordplay as Shakespeare has Miranda begin her speech with "O, wonder.")

Your eld'st° acquaintance cannot be three hours.
Is she the goddess that hath severed us,
190　And brought us thus together?

FERDINAND.　　　　　　　Sir, she is mortal;
But by immortal Providence she's mine.
I chose her when I could not ask my father
For his advice, nor thought I had one. She
195　Is daughter to this famous Duke of Milan,
Of whom so often I have heard renown,
But never saw before; of whom I have
Received a second life; and second father
This lady makes him to me.

ALONSO.　　　　　　　I am hers.
But, O, how oddly will it sound that I
200　Must ask my child forgiveness!

PROSPERO.　　　　　　　There, sir, stop.
Let us not burden our remembrances with
A heaviness that's gone.

GONZALO.　　　　　　　I have inly wept
Or should have spoke ere this. Look down, you gods,
And on this couple drop a blessed crown!
205　For it is you that have chalked forth the way
Which brought us hither.

ALONSO.　　　　　　　I say Amen, Gonzalo!

GONZALO. Was Milan° thrust from Milan, that his issue
Should become kings of Naples? O, rejoice
Beyond a common joy, and set it down
210　With gold on lasting pillars: In one voyage
Did Claribel her husband find at Tunis,
And Ferdinand, her brother, found a wife
Where he himself was lost; Prospero his dukedom
In a poor isle; and all of us ourselves
215　When no man was his own.

ALONSO (to FERDINAND and MIRANDA). Give me your hands.
Let grief and sorrow still° embrace his° heart
That doth not wish you joy!

GONZALO.　　　　　　　Be it so! Amen!
(Enter ARIEL, with the MASTER and BOATSWAIN amazedly following.)
O, look, sir, look, sir! Here is more of us.
I prophesied, if a gallows were on land,
220　This fellow could not drown. Now, blasphemy,
That swear'st grace o'erboard, not an oath on shore?
Hast thou no mouth by land? What is the news?

BOATSWAIN. The best news is that we have safely found
Our King and company; the next, our ship—
225　Which, but three glasses° since, we gave out° split—

476　*The Renaissance*

Is tight and yare° and bravely rigged as when
We first put out to sea.
ARIEL (*aside to* PROSPERO). Sir, all this service
Have I done since I went.
PROSPERO (*aside to* ARIEL). My tricksy spirit!
ALONSO. These are not natural events; they strengthen
230 From strange to stranger. Say, how came you hither?
BOATSWAIN. If I did think, sir, I were well awake,
I'd strive to tell you. We were dead of sleep,
And—how we know not—all clapped under hatches;
Where but even now with strange and several noises
235 Of roaring, shrieking, howling, jingling chains,
And moe diversity of sounds, all horrible,
We were awaked; straightway, at liberty;
Where we, in all her trim, freshly beheld
Our royal, good, and gallant ship, our master
240 Cap'ring to eye° her. On a trice, so please you,
Even in a dream, were we divided from them
And were brought moping° hither.
ARIEL (*aside to* PROSPERO).   Was 't well done?
PROSPERO (*aside to* ARIEL). Bravely, my diligence. Thou shalt be free.
ALONSO. This is as strange a maze as e'er men trod,
245 And there is in this business more than nature
Was ever conduct° of. Some oracle
Must rectify our knowledge.
PROSPERO.   Sir, my liege,
Do not infest° your mind with beating on
The strangeness of this business. At picked° leisure,
250 Which shall be shortly, single° I'll resolve you,
Which to you shall seem probable, of every
These happened accidents;° till when, be cheerful
And think of each thing well. (*Aside to* ARIEL.) Come hither, spirit.
Set Caliban and his companions free;
255 Untie the spell. (*Exit* ARIEL.) How fares my gracious sir?
There are yet missing of your company
Some few odd lads that you remember not.
    (*Enter* ARIEL, *driving in* CALIBAN, STEPHANO, *and* TRINCULO, *in their
    stolen apparel.*)
STEPHANO. Every man shift for all the rest, and let no man take care for
himself; for all is but fortune. Coragio,° bully-monster,° coragio!
260 TRINCULO. If these be true spies which I wear in my head, here's a goodly
sight.
CALIBAN. O Setebos, these be brave spirits indeed!
How fine° my master is! I am afraid
He will chastise me.
265 SEBASTIAN. Ha, ha!

yare, ready.

Cap'ring to eye, dancing for joy to see.

moping, in a daze.

[132] Compare the Boatswain's speeches here with those in Act One, Scene 1. How do you account for the difference?
conduct, guide, leader.

infest, harass, disturb.
picked, chosen, convenient.
single, that is, by my own human powers.
accidents, occurrences.

Coragio, courage.
bully-monster, gallant monster (ironical).

fine, splendidly attired.
[133] What is Caliban's reaction to seeing the nobles? To seeing Prospero?

The Tempest—Act Five, Scene 1 **477**

What things are these, my lord Antonio?
Will money buy 'em?

ANTONIO.   Very like. One of them
Is a plain fish, and no doubt marketable.

PROSPERO. Mark but the badges° of these men, my lords,
270   Then say if they be true.° This misshapen knave,
His mother was a witch, and one so strong
That could control the moon, make flows and ebbs,
And deal in her command without her power.°
These three have robbed me; and this demi-devil—
275   For he's a bastard one—had plotted with them
To take my life. Two of these fellows you
Must know and own;° this thing of darkness I
Acknowledge mine.

CALIBAN.   I shall be pinched to death.

ALONSO. Is not this Stephano, my drunken butler?
280   **SEBASTIAN.** He is drunk now. Where had he wine?

ALONSO. And Trinculo is reeling ripe. Where should they
Find this grand liquor that hath gilded° 'em?
How cam'st thou in this pickle?°

TRINCULO. I have been in such a pickle since I saw you last that, I fear
285   me, will never out of my bones. I shall not fear fly-blowing.°

SEBASTIAN. Why, how now, Stephano?

STEPHANO. O, touch me not! I am not Stephano, but a cramp.

PROSPERO. You'd be king o' the isle, sirrah?°

STEPHANO. I should have been a sore° one then.
290   **ALONSO** (*pointing to* CALIBAN). This is a strange thing as e'er I looked on.

PROSPERO. He is as disproportioned in his manners
As in his shape. Go, sirrah, to my cell;
Take with you your companions. As you look
To have my pardon, trim it handsomely.
295   **CALIBAN.** Ay, that I will; and I'll be wise hereafter
And seek for grace. What a thrice-double ass
Was I to take this drunkard for a god
And worship this dull fool!

PROSPERO.   Go to; away!

ALSONSO. Hence, and bestow your luggage where you found it.
300   **SEBASTIAN.** Or stole it, rather.

                    (*Exeunt* CALIBAN, STEPHANO, *and* TRINCULO.)

PROSPERO. Sir, I invite your Highness and your train
To my poor cell, where you shall take your rest
For this one night; which, part of it, I'll waste°
With such discourse as, I not doubt, shall make it
305   Go quick away—the story of my life,
And the particular accidents° gone by
Since I came to this isle. And in the morn

badges, emblems of cloth or silver worn on the arms of retainers. (Prospero refers here to the stolen clothes as emblems of their villainy.)
true, honest.
deal . . . power, wield the moon's power, either without her authority or beyond her influence.
own, recognize, admit as belonging to you.

gilded, flushed, made drunk.
pickle, (1) fix, predicament, (2) pickling brine.
fly-blowing, that is, being fouled by fly eggs, from which he is saved by being pickled.
sirrah, standard form of address to an inferior.
sore, (1) tyrannical, (2) wracked by pain.

134 These are Caliban's last words in the play. Do you think he has reformed? Explain.

waste, spend.

accidents, occurrences.

I'll bring you to your ship, and so to Naples,
Where I have hope to see the nuptial
310 Of these our dear-beloved solemnized;
And thence retire me to my Milan, where
Every third thought shall be my grave.
ALONSO.   I long
To hear the story of your life, which must
Take° the ear strangely.
PROSPERO.   I'll deliver° all;
315 And promise you calm seas, auspicious gales,
And sail so expeditious that shall catch
Your royal fleet far off. *(Aside to* ARIEL.) My Ariel, chick,
That is thy charge. Then to the elements
Be free, and fare thou well!—Please you, draw near.°

                                                       (Exeunt omnes.)

135 What plans has Prospero for his own future? Lines 311–312 contain what is called a *crux,* a difficult passage that has yet to be satisfactorily explained.
Take, take effect upon, enchant.

deliver, declare, relate.

draw near, that is, enter my cell.

EPILOGUE

Spoken by PROSPERO.

Now my charms are all o'erthrown,
And what strength I have 's mine own,
Which is most faint. Now, 'tis true,
I must be here confined by you,
5 Or sent to Naples. Let me not,
Since I have my dukedom got
And pardoned the deceiver, dwell
In this bare island by your spell,
But release me from my bands°
10 With the help of your good hands.°
Gentle breath of yours my sails
Must fill, or else my project fails,
Which was to please. Now I want°
Spirits to enforce, art to enchant,
15 And my ending is despair,
Unless I be relieved by prayer,°
Which pierces so that it assaults°
Mercy itself and frees° all faults.
As you from crimes° would pardoned be,
20 Let your indulgence set me free.

                                                       (Exit.)

c.1610–1611   1623

bands, bonds.
hands, applause (the noise of which would break the spell of silence).
136 By what action will Prospero be freed from the island?
want, lack.
prayer, Prospero's petition to the audience.
assaults, rightfully gains the attention of.
frees, obtains forgiveness of.
crimes, sins.

137 An epilogue serves to round out the play. How do the last two lines of this epilogue reinforce the theme of *The Tempest?*

THINK AND DISCUSS

Understanding

1. How is Prospero going to end his magical powers?
2. What is to be Ariel's final act before he is set free?
3. What is Caliban's final opinion of Stephano and Trinculo?

Analyzing

4. Account for Antonio's silence (except for lines 267–268) after Prospero has revealed himself to the guilty nobles. How would you have the actor playing the role behave during this time?
5. At the end of the play, the major **plot** and both subplots should be resolved. How does Shakespeare resolve Prospero's attempt to have the guilty nobles realize their sin and repent so that there may be a reconciliation? Is Prospero's attempt completely successful? Explain.
6. How is the comedy subplot (the lovers) resolved?
7. How is the plotting by Caliban, Stephano, and Trinculo resolved? Earlier we mentioned that this plot was virtually a parody of a tragic plot. At the end of a tragedy the **protagonist** dies or suffers greatly. How is this ending parodied in *The Tempest?*

Extending

8. Caliban's future is not provided for in the general reconciliation, other than Prospero's acknowledging him as his own and Caliban's saying that he will seek grace. What do you suppose will happen to him?
9. The **setting** of a play involves both time (historical as well as time of year and of day) and place. How many hours pass between the beginning and end of the play? What evidence does it contain to place it historically in Shakespeare's own era?
10. How does the setting on Prospero's island cater to the Renaissance interest in exploration?

COMPOSITION   ✒

Telling What Happens After the Play

Write an imaginary conversation (or dialogue) in prose between two or more characters that takes place after Act Five and carries the action further. Imagine that your audience is made up of your classmates. Your dialogue should be the length of a three- to five- paragraph composition.

Writing About Poetry

Discuss Ariel's songs and their appropriateness to the play. Consider their content, their applicability, and the artistry of their choice of words, **rhythm,** and other poetic devices. Your composition should be three to five paragraphs long. See "Writing About Poetry and Poetic Devices" in the Writer's Handbook.

ENRICHMENT

Staging *The Tempest*

The best way to appreciate the staging of a Shakespeare play is to imagine how it would have been done in Shakespeare's day. Look again at the diagram of the Globe Theater on page 461 and note all of the acting areas and the various doors and other means of entering and exiting. There are a few rules that must be observed:

1. A scene ends when the stage is empty of actors.
2. Exits and entrances must be carefully arranged so that actors hurrying offstage will not collide with those coming onstage.

Divide your class into five groups, each group being assigned an act for which it will arrange the staging. Do not worry about exit/entrance collisions from the end of one act to the beginning of another. Within your group, discuss and work out all entrances and exits for your act, using the diagram of the Globe Theater. When all groups have finished, each should present its theoretical staging to the rest of the class, again using the Globe Theater diagram.

THE PLAY IN REVIEW
THINK AND DISCUSS
Understanding
1. Throughout the play Prospero uses Ariel to put his thoughts into action. How does he use Ariel to have the nobles shipwrecked on the island?
2. How does he use Ariel to arrange the meeting of Ferdinand and Miranda?
3. How does he use Ariel to avert the killing of Gonzalo and Alonso?
4. How does he use Ariel to spoil the scheming of Caliban, Stephano, and Trinculo?
5. How does he use Ariel to get everyone safely back to Naples?

Analyzing
6. Discuss the appropriateness of the title to the play.
7. What does the role of the Boatswain contribute to the play?
8. What is the purpose of the low-comedy scenes with Caliban, Stephano, and Trinculo?
9. Because *The Tempest* is a romance, it does not require the depth of **characterization** that a tragedy does. Which of its major characters strikes you as being most three-dimensional and believable? Explain.

Extending
10. Explain whether the play could exist without each of the following: Caliban, Ariel, the Ferdinand–Miranda love story.
11. If you were directing the play, how would you have Caliban made up and costumed? Why?
12. Discuss the chances for future and permanent peace between the Kingdom of Naples and the Duchy of Milan.
13. One critic has commented that Prospero has regained his dukedom at the expense of losing his daughter. To what extent do you agree or disagree? Explain.

COMPOSITION
Writing a Thumbnail Biography
Write a thumbnail biography, about three paragraphs in length, of one of the important characters in the play. Assume that you are writing for your local newspaper. If you wish, you may continue the biography beyond the end of the play.

Writing a Character Analysis
Write a detailed, three- to five-paragraph character analysis of one of the major characters in the play. See "Writing About Characters" in the Writer's Handbook.

Analyzing Women's Roles
Write a three- to five-paragraph discussion of the place of women in the action of *The Tempest*. Consider Miranda and also what happened to Claribel.

Writing About Motivation
In a three- to five-paragraph composition, discuss the desire for power (control or mastery) as a motivating factor. Consider what Shakespeare seems to be saying about the right to rule.

Discussing a Theme
Discuss in three paragraphs or more the desire for liberty or personal freedom as a theme of the play. Consider especially Caliban and Ariel. See "Writing About Theme" in the Writer's Handbook.

Writing Persuasively
Modern audiences tend to view Caliban sympathetically. Do you agree or disagree? Write a three- to five-paragraph paper in which you try to persuade your classmates to share your opinion. See "Writing to Persuade an Audience" in the Writer's Handbook.

The Humanists as Translators

The Middle Ages finally came to an end with the Renaissance, the rebirth of art and learning that began in Italy in the fourteenth century and had spread throughout western Europe by the sixteenth century. This was a period of marvelous achievement in all branches of scholarship and the arts.

One of the many changes brought about by the Renaissance was the rise of humanism. The humanists were concerned with human beings and their interests rather than with abstract matters of theology. One of their major accomplishments was the rediscovery of the literature and art of ancient Greece and Rome. Exuberant in their new knowledge of pre-Christian ideas, these scholars regarded themselves as liberators, dispelling the confining conceptions of medieval culture.

The Italian poet Petrarch (born in 1304) is usually considered to have been the father of humanism. His lifelong ambition was to forge links between the ancient cultures of the Greeks and Romans and his own century. Petrarch traveled widely, collecting the old manuscripts in monasteries and cathedral libraries. His contemporary—and close friend—Giovanni Boccaccio established a new literary direction with his *Decameron*, a collection of stories which was the first literary expression of humanistic realism. Boccaccio also discovered important manuscripts in the monastery of Monte Cassino in Italy.

At this time several Italian noblemen became eminent patrons of humanist endeavor. In the tiny principality of Urbino, the prince kept thirty copyists busy for fourteen years, translating Greek and Roman works. Every educated person knew Latin well, but there was a problem finding Greek translators. In the kingdom of Naples, Alfonso the Magnanimous welcomed humanists to court and financed translations. Even the Church sometimes opened her arms to humanism. In the middle 1400s, Pope Nicholas V had a corps of translators busy in Rome. He sent agents to Constantinople, Germany, and England to acquire Greek and Roman manuscripts. In the next century, Pope Leo X supported the teaching of Semitic and Greek languages and continued the search for unpublished works. Many of Leo's cardinals were classical scholars.

The spread of humanism in western Europe was aided by the new printing press and the spread of libraries. These in turn speeded the growth of education. Most of the major universities in Europe were founded during these centuries.

Thomas Linacre was a teacher at Oxford in England. Two of his students were to become celebrated humanists—Desiderius Erasmus and Thomas More. Erasmus translated the ancient writers Euripides, Lucian, and Cicero. Linacre himself translated works on medicine by the Greek physician Galen. His other notable student, Sir Thomas More, combined humanism with a deep religious faith and was executed for the latter.

The humanists were considered the progressives or radicals of their time. It is singular that they reached back a thousand or more years for their progressive ideas.

Miniature from a 16th-century illuminated manuscript showing Petrarch in his study. Biblioteca Morando, Milan

Themes IN WORLD LITERATURE

THE ARTIST

Who is an artist? Surely the composer, the painter, the dancer, and the poet are artists. An architect, who designs a building, is an artist— one Chinese writer compares a well-made poem to a building. But is a magician an artist? Is a mere collector an artist? Is a goldsmith, whose medium is the same as money? What should be the relationship between the artist and money? Between the artist and social change? All these questions, and more, receive attention in our selections about the artist.

The Artist Inspired

The idea that the artist is inspired goes back, in Western culture, to Plato, among others, who maintained that the poet, when he writes a poem, is an instrument through whom a god is speaking. The early Chinese literary critic Lu Chi, in his *Wen Fu*, (page 83), claims that the poet when writing a poem has "his mind a thousand miles away," as he invents new images and even new words, and uses melodies "unplayed for a thousand years or more." "He sees past and present commingle; he sees the whole Four Seas in the single blink of an eye." Lu Chi's poet is both inspired and omniscient; these are more than human powers.

Another poet who boasts of more than human powers is Whitman, who in *Song of Myself*, section 21 (page 653), claims to be inspired (the word means "breathing in") by forces bigger than himself: "The pleasures of heaven are with me and the pains of hell are with me." He is accompanied by the night, "mad naked summer night," and he composes a litany to his lover the earth, in which he prays to the earth to "Smile, for your lover comes." Clearly, this poet "breathes in" the whole universe.

Inspiration is one of the themes of Narayan's "Such Perfection" (page 868). In this story, an artist creates a sculpture of a god that is so realistic that the god becomes the statue and begins to express his awful power. Artistic perfection,

apparently, implies identity, so the artist's fear of his art at the end of the story is a fear not only of his own skills but also of divine inspiration.

The Social Importance of Artists

Alexander the Great, according to Cicero, once stood before the grave of Achilles (the Greek hero of the Trojan War) and said, "You were lucky, young man: You had Homer as the praiser of your manliness." Cicero commented that the statement was true, "for, without the famous *Iliad*, that grave would have buried both his body and his name."

So for at least one authority, the poet is a preserver of noble deeds and names (as in the *Song of Roland*). But for some poets, the future is more important than the past, especially if there is going to be social change and the poet is aware of it early. *The Rubáiyát of Omar Khayyám*, stanza 99 (page 45), depicts the poet as a dreamer of social change. Inspired by love, he wishes to destroy "this sorry Scheme of Things entire" and remold it "nearer to the Heart's Desire."

Rilke is not such an idealist. His poem "Sense of Something Coming" (page 776) is more apprehensive about the impending change. His speaker compares himself to a flag; he can "sense ahead the wind which is coming," but he has to sense it alone, because it has not yet reached those around him. Rilke foresees more than a wind: "I already know the storm, and I am as troubled as the sea."

What troubles Tagore is the subjection of art, which delights the mind, to money, which "keeps men's minds in a turmoil." His story "The Artist" (page 766) concerns a boy with artistic talent and two of the conflicting influences on him: his mother, whose art is her chief amusement, and his guardian uncle, an office manager whose only value in life is to make money. With his mother, the boy creates unorthodox drawings and paintings in childlike

Velázquez, detail of *The Maids of Honor*. 1656.
Prado, Madrid. The entire painting appears on
page 378.

Alice Walker's story, "Everyday Use" (page
922), concerns quilts that are works of folk art.
Dee is outraged that her sister Maggie will, if
given the quilts made by their mother and grandmother, "put them to everyday use" and thereby
ruin them. Dee believes that such art is to be
put on display, but not put to use. The quilts
are given to Maggie, not to Dee, underscoring
the point that the craftsperson's creations can be
both useful and artistic.

Implicit in Tu Fu's poem "Sent to Li Po as a
Gift" (page 87) is an idea of the artist as a maker
or craftsperson. Li Po is described as the type
of the inspired artist, unstable, sporadic in his
work, tempestuous, and Tu Fu questions what
all this turmoil will amount to. Implicit in his
criticism is a very different notion of the role of
the artist—that of the industrious maker working
steadily at his craft.

The Magician as Artist

We can compare the idea of the artist as someone practicing a craft with that of the artist as
a magician, like Shakespeare's Prospero. Both
ideas propose artists who are made, not born:
the craftsperson becomes an artist through hard
work; Prospero becomes an artist through long
study. Neither one is the inspired artist; Prospero instead is a wizard. But he customarily
refers to his magical powers as his "art." We all
know the expression "the magic of poetry"; Prospero is speaking of the poetry of magic. But he is
first of all a magician, not an artist, who, instead
of selling his soul—like Faustus (page 485)—uses
his learning to rule an island by subduing the
spirits he finds there. He is in a sense like the
Wizard of Oz, but with more real power. Prospero's power allows him to control nature; and
we should remember that both magic and art are
a reordering of nature. But he does not control
nature directly; he controls the *spirits* that control nature. And these spirits, such as Ariel (who
may represent Prospero's imagination), reorder
nature in such a way as to make the whole island
enchanted by such art forms as music, poetry,
dance, songs, and a symbolic *masque* (a short
play consisting primarily of music and dance) for
the two young lovers. Indeed, without these arts
that derive from Prospero's magic, there would
be little else in *The Tempest*.

joy; but the uncle claims that such activity will
"ruin" him for the practical world. The conclusion of the story makes clear where Tagore
stands in this age-old debate.

The Artist in the Workshop

A rival theory to that of inspiration is the idea
that the artist is someone who practices a craft
in a studio and dirties the hands in the physical
labor of creation. The sculptor and the cerami-
cist come to mind in this connection; but even
writers have accepted this theory of creativity,
at least as a metaphor. Dante calls an earlier
poet "a better blacksmith of the mother
tongue." Stephen Dedalus, setting out to be a
writer at the end of *A Portrait of the Artist as a
Young Man* (page 778), proclaims, "I go . . . to
forge in the smithy of my soul the uncreated conscience of my race."

THINKING CRITICALLY
ABOUT LITERATURE

UNIT 4   THE RENAISSANCE

■ CONCEPT REVIEW

Below on the left begins the last scene from Christopher Marlowe's
Doctor Faustus, written about 1593. Marlowe, who was born in 1564,
was university-educated and a talented playwright. His tragedies feature a
larger-than-life **protagonist** who controls the action around him until his
fortunes fall apart at the end of the play. Marlowe is also noted for what
the poet Ben Jonson called the "mighty line" of his blank verse. Marlowe's
life ended prematurely in 1593 when he was stabbed in a tavern brawl.
In the following scene, Faustus, a scholar at the University of Wittenberg
in Germany, has sold his soul to the Devil in exchange for twenty-four
years of access to forbidden knowledge—magic and the occult arts. As the
scene opens, his twenty-four years have expired, except for an hour or so;
the Devil is to claim his soul at midnight.

· Below on the right are notes to help you read this scene from *Doctor
Faustus* and to review some of the literary terms and thinking skills that
have appeared in Unit 4. Page numbers in the notes refer to an application
or review of literary terms in the unit. A more extensive discussion of
literary terms is in the Handbook of Literary Terms. On a separate sheet
of paper write your answers to the questions that follow this scene.

from Doctor Faustus

Christopher Marlowe

SCENE 14

Enter FAUSTUS *with the* SCHOLARS.

FAUST. Ah, gentlemen!

FIRST SCHOLAR. What ails Faustus?

FAUST. Ah, my sweet chamber-fellow, had I lived with thee then had I lived
  still, but now I die eternally. Look! comes he not? comes he not?

■ **Rhythm** (page 433): As
you read this selection,
notice where the rhythm
changes.

■ **still:** always

5 **SECOND SCHOLAR.** What means Faustus?

THIRD SCHOLAR. Belike he is grown into some sickness by being over-solitary.

FIRST SCHOLAR. If it be so, we'll have physicians to cure him; 'tis but a surfeit, never fear, man.

FAUST. A surfeit of deadly sin that hath damned both body and soul.

10 **SECOND SCHOLAR.** Yet, Faustus, look up to heaven: remember God's mercies are infinite.

FAUST. But Faustus' offense can ne'er be pardoned; the Serpent that tempted Eve may be saved, but not Faustus. Ah, gentlemen, hear me with patience, and tremble not at my speeches. Though my heart pants and quivers to

15 remember that I have been a student here these thirty years, O would I had never seen Wittenberg, never read book! And what wonders I have done all Germany can witness, yea all the world, for which Faustus hath lost both Germany and the world, yea heaven itself—heaven the seat of God, the throne of the blessed, the kingdom of joy, and must remain in

20 hell forever, hell, ah hell, forever! Sweet friends, what shall become of Faustus, being in hell forever?

THIRD SCHOLAR. Yet, Faustus, call on God.

FAUST. On God, whom Faustus hath abjured? on God, whom Faustus hath blasphemed? Ah, my God, I would weep, but the Devil draws in my tears!

25 Gush forth, blood, instead of tears, yea, life and soul. O he stays my tongue; I would lift up my hands but, see, they hold them, they hold them!

ALL. Who, Faustus?

FAUST. Lucifer and Mephistophilis.

Ah, gentlemen, I gave them my soul for my cunning.

30 **ALL.** God forbid!

FAUST. God forbade it indeed, but Faustus hath done it: for vain pleasure of twenty-four years hath Faustus lost eternal joy and felicity. I writ them a bill with mine own blood, the date is expired, the time will come, and he will fetch me.

35 **FIRST SCHOLAR.** Why did not Faustus tell us of this before, that divines might have prayed for thee?

FAUST. Oft have I thought to have done so, but the Devil threatened to tear me in pieces if I named God, to fetch both body and soul if I once gave ear to divinity; and now 'tis too late. Gentlemen, away, lest you perish

40 with me.

SECOND SCHOLAR. O what shall we do to save Faustus?

FAUST. Talk not of me, but save yourselves and depart.

THIRD SCHOLAR. God will strengthen me: I will stay with Faustus.

FIRST SCHOLAR. Tempt not God, sweet friend, but let us into the next room,

45 and there pray for him.

FAUST. Ay, pray for me, pray for me! And what noise soever ye hear, come not unto me, for nothing can rescue me.

SECOND SCHOLAR. Pray thou, and we will pray that God may have mercy upon thee.

50 **FAUST.** Gentlemen, farewell. If I live till morning I'll visit you; if not, Faustus is gone to hell.

■ **surfeit:** the result of eating too much food

■ **Allusion:** This is a reference to the Bible. Eve also was tempted by the devil.

■ **Wittenberg:** city in Germany, site of university where Faustus taught

■ **read book:** note reference to learning.

■ **Metaphor:** All of these are metaphorical names for heaven.

■ **abjured:** repudiated

■ Note Faustus's increasing despair.

■ **felicity:** state of being happy, especially in a high degree

■ Faustus has signed with his own blood a pact with the devil, selling his soul for 24 years of learning things that are forbidden, and the power that learning brings.

■ **divines:** priests

ALL. Faustus, farewell.

(*Exeunt* SCHOLARS. *The clock strikes eleven.*)

FAUST. Ah, Faustus,
Now hast thou but one bare hour to live
55 And then thou must be damned perpetually!
Stand still, you ever-moving spheres of heaven,
That time may cease and midnight never come;
Fair Nature's eye, rise, rise again, and make
Perpetual day; or let this hour be but
60 A year, a month, a week, a natural day,
That Faustus may repent and save his soul!
O lente lente currite noctis equi.
The stars move still, time runs, the clock will strike,
The Devil will come, and Faustus must be damned.
65 O I'll leap up to my God! Who pulls me down?
See, see, where Christ's blood streams in the firmament!—
One drop would save my soul—half a drop! ah, my Christ!
Ah, rend not my heart for naming of my Christ;
Yet will I call on him—Oh, spare me, Lucifer!
70 Where is it now? 'Tis gone; and see where God
Stretcheth out his arm and bends his ireful brows.
Mountains and hills, come, come and fall on me
And hide me from the heavy wrath of God.
No, no—
75 Then will I headlong run into the earth:
Earth, gape! O no, it will not harbor me.
You stars that reigned at my nativity,
Whose influence hath allotted death and hell,
Now draw up Faustus like a foggy mist
80 Into the entrails of yon laboring cloud
So that my soul may but ascend to heaven.

(*The watch strikes.*)

Ah, half the hour is past;
'Twill all be past anon.
O God,
85 If thou wilt not have mercy on my soul,
Yet for Christ's sake whose blood hath ransomed me
Impose some end to my incessant pain:
Let Faustus live in hell a thousand years,
A hundred thousand, and at last be saved!
90 O, no end is limited to damned souls.
Why wert thou not a creature wanting soul?
Or why is this immortal that thou hast?
Ah, Pythagoras' *metempsychosis*—were that true,
This soul should fly from me, and I be changed
95 Unto some brutish beast.
All beasts are happy, for when they die

■ Faustus has only one hour left to live.

■ **Soliloquy:** Here Faustus lets us see into his heart and the terror he feels as his hour nears.

■ **Blank verse** (page 448): Up to this point this scene has been in prose; from here on it is in blank verse.

■ **spheres of heaven:** a reference to the Ptolemaic system of astronomy, which taught that the universe was composed of moving concentric spheres with the earth at the center.

■ **Metaphor:** "Fair Nature's eye" is a metaphor for the sun.

■ *O lente . . . equi:* "Run slowly, slowly, horses of the night," quoted from Ovid's *Amores*, I. 13.

■ Note how this line is abbreviated for emphasis.

■ **Personification:** The cloud is given entrails.

■ **metempsychosis:** the theory of transmigration of souls; as one living creature dies, its soul is transferred to another.

Their souls are soon dissolved in elements,
But mine must live still to be plagued in hell.
Cursed be the parents that engendered me!
100 No, Faustus, curse thyself, curse Lucifer
That hath deprived thee of the joys of heaven.

(The clock strikes twelve.)

O it strikes, it strikes! Now, body, turn to air
Or Lucifer will bear thee quick to hell.

■ **quick:** alive, lively

(Thunder and lightning.)

O soul, be changed into little water drops
105 And fall into the ocean, ne'er be found.
My God, my God, look not so fierce on me!

(Thunder. Enter Devils.)

Adders and serpents, let me breathe awhile!
Ugly hell, gape not—come not, Lucifer—
I'll burn my books—ah, Mephistophilis!

(Exeunt with him. Enter Chorus.)

110 CHORUS. Cut is the branch that might have grown full straight,
And burned is Apollo's laurel bough
That sometime grew within this learned man.
Faustus is gone: regard his hellish fall,
Whose fiendful fortune may exhort the wise
115 Only to wonder at unlawful things
Whose deepness doth entice such forward wits
To practice more than heavenly power permits.

(Exit.)

Terminat hora diem, terminat author opus.
c.1593

1604

■ Note Faustus's final line; he offers to burn his magic books.
■ **Evaluating:** Note the function of the chorus, which enters this scene for the first time here at the very end of the play.
■ **Apollo's laurel bough:** symbolic of learning
■ **sometime:** formerly

■ *Terminat . . . opus:* As the hour ends the day, the author ends his work.

THINK AND DISCUSS
Understanding
1. What is Faustus's sin?
2. Why is he unable to weep, or call on God, or raise his hands to heaven?

Analyzing
3. What is Faustus's attitude toward the scholars? How loyal are they to him?
4. Does Faustus repent? Why can't he be saved?
5. What is Faustus's tragedy—is it merely his damnation, or is the world the worse for that damnation? Explain.

Extending
6. How does the play show the Renaissance love of learning?
7. How does it show that learning must have limits?

REVIEWING LITERARY TERMS
Rhythm
1. The first section of this scene is written in prose. At what line does the rhythm shift to verse?

Blank Verse
2. The specific kind of verse most of this scene is written in is blank verse. How many syllables are there in a line of blank verse?

3. How many of these syllables are stressed in a typical line of blank verse?
4. What might be Marlowe's purpose in switching to blank verse?

■ CONTENT REVIEW
THINKING SKILLS
Classifying
1. Identify in what language each of the following writers originally wrote: Petrarch; Boccaccio; Machiavelli; Ronsard; Cervantes; Shakespeare.
2. Under the three heads of (1) novel, (2) poetry, and (3) essay, list where each of the following writers made an important contribution: Petrarch; Boccaccio; Ronsard; Montaigne; Cervantes.

Generalizing
3. During the Renaissance there was much concern about the ideal way to govern. Discuss the treatment of this theme by Machiavelli, Montaigne, and Shakespeare.
4. The Renaissance interest in the New World is evident in much of its literature. Discuss the treatment of this in *The Tempest*.

Synthesizing
5. Using the background article and the selections in this unit, describe what it must have been like to live in the Renaissance. What would you fear? How would you occupy your time? What would you talk about?
6. Imagine that you have to come up with a title for this unit other than "The Renaissance." Try to think up a title that would encompass all the selections that you have read in the unit.

Evaluating
7. Compare and contrast the good courtier, as represented by Gonzalo, with the bad, as represented by Antonio in *The Tempest*. Consider which would, by Machiavellian standards, be more successful.
8. Which of the selections you have read would be most interesting to modern readers? Explain.

■ COMPOSITION REVIEW
Analyzing Renaissance Attitudes
From the selections in this unit you have been made aware of various Renaissance attitudes toward women. Discuss these attitudes in a three- to five-paragraph composition. You might consider these questions: Does the country involved affect the attitudes? Are the attitudes vastly different from today's? Which do you find most difficult to understand? To tolerate?

Writing About a Theme
One characteristic of the Renaissance is humanity's belief in its own powers. Write a three- to five-paragraph paper in which you discuss how this attitude is demonstrated in several of the selections you have read.

Comparing Sonnets
Compare Ronsard's **sonnet** with any of Petrarch's sonnets. Consider poetic structure, character of the lady, emotion conveyed, speaker's attitude, and so forth.

Writing About a Theme
Discuss the Renaissance attitude toward sorcery and magic as it is displayed in *The Tempest* and the selection from *Faustus*.

Comparing and Contrasting
From what you have seen of Faustus, write a three- to five-paragraph composition in which you compare and contrast his actions with those Machiavelli recommends in *The Prince* for a man who aspires to be a powerful ruler.

NEOCLASSICISM 1650–1780

1650	1660	1670	1680	1690	1700	1710

HISTORY AND ARTS

- Poussin: *Self-Portrait*
- Rembrandt: *Return of the Prodigal Son*
- Battle of Blenheim
- Greenwich Observatory established
- Restoration of Monarchy
- Comédie Française formed
- Royal Society founded
- Newton: *Principia*
- Fire of London
- Glorious Revolution

PEOPLE

- Descartes dies
- Louis XIV begins Versailles
- La Salle claims Louisiana for France
- Cromwell becomes Lord Protector
- Charles II becomes king
- Peter the Great begins building St. Petersburg
- Molière dies
- William and Mary become joint monarchs
- Milton dies
- Louis XIV dies

LITERATURE

- Molière: *Tartuffe*
- Milton: *Paradise Lost*
- Locke: *Treatise on Civil Government*
- La Fontaine: *Fables*
- Pope: *The Rape of the Lock*

Louis XIV, detail of a painting by Henri Testelin. 1667

A room in the Royal Greenwich Observatory, founded in 1675

Detail of an engraving showing the Battle of Oudenarde. 1708

1720	1730	1740	1750	1760	1770	1780

• Founding of New Orleans

• Bach: *Well-Tempered Clavier*

• Canaletto: *Four Views of Venice*

• Bach: *St. Matthew Passion*

• Hogarth: *The Rake's Progress*

• Handel: *Messiah*

• Tiepolo: *Antony and Cleopatra* frescoes

• Battle of Culloden

• Lisbon earthquake

• Seven Years' War

• Joshua Reynolds: *Georgiana*

• Royal Academy founded

• American Revolution begins

• La Scala opens in Milan

• Leibnitz dies

• George II becomes king

• Newton dies

Benjamin Franklin invents lightning rod •

• Frederick the Great becomes king

• Botanical Garden founded by Linnaeus

• Pope dies

• Swift dies

• Montesquieu dies

• Mozart born

• George III becomes king

• Louis XVI becomes king

• Montesquieu: *Persian Letters*

• Swift: *Gulliver's Travels*

• Swift: *A Modest Proposal*

• Pope: *An Essay on Man*

• Hume: *A Treatise of Human Nature*

• Voltaire: *Zadig*

• Fielding: *Tom Jones*

• Gray: *Elegy Written in a Country Churchyard*

• Diderot: *Encyclopédie*

• Voltaire: *Candide*

• Rousseau: *The Social Contract*

• Smith: *The Wealth of Nations*

• Johnson: *Dictionary of the English Language*

Detail of a portrait of Johann Sebastian Bach (1685–1750)

Detail of Hogarth's painting, *Canvassing for Votes.* 1754

Detail of *Signing of the Declaration of Independence*

PREVIEW

UNIT 5   NEOCLASSICISM   1650–1780

Authors
John Milton
Jean de La Fontaine
Molière
Jonathan Swift
Alexander Pope
Voltaire
Charles de Montesquieu

Features
Comment: Milton's Cosmography
Reader's Note: Translating La Fontaine
Reading a Neoclassic Comedy
Comment: Eighteenth-Century English Gardens
Comment: The Great Chain of Being
The History of Language: Neoclassic
     Regulation of Language
Themes in World Literature: The Social Order

Application of Literary Terms
style
couplet
consonance
epigram

Review of Literary Terms
satire
irony

Vocabulary Skills
context
etymologies
roots

Thinking Skills
evaluating
generalizing
synthesizing

Composition Assignments Include
Writing a Letter
Writing About Characters
Writing a Fable
Writing an Essay
Writing About Writers
Writing to Persuade
Writing a Satire
Writing an Editorial
Writing a Profile
Analyzing a Mock Epic
Writing a Verse Essay
Writing an Epigram
Defining El Dorado
Writing a Personal Essay

Enrichment
Writing a Scenario
Analyzing a Persona
Researching an Epigram

Thinking Critically About Literature
Concept Review
Content Review
Composition Review

NEOCLASSICISM 1650–1780

In Europe in the late seventeenth and eighteenth centuries, there was a general intellectual and literary movement known as the Enlightenment. This movement was characterized by rationalism, that is, by the principle or habit of accepting reason as the supreme authority in matters of opinion, belief, or conduct. Intellectual freedom and relative freedom from prejudice and superstition in religion and politics were ideals typical of the age; as in all ages, behavior often did not match ideals. This movement is also commonly known as the Age of Reason.

FRANCE AND ENGLAND

In the later sixteenth century Spain was the greatest power in Europe; in the seventeenth century France held this position, and in the eighteenth, England. Indeed, the stage of history during the Age of Reason belongs primarily to France and England, who fought each other continually for colonies, trade, and political power but collaborated intellectually to achieve the Enlightenment and the classical ideal of art and literature.

France developed the classical ideal of literary art, and England joined her in expressing it. It was an era of broad intellectual cooperation, when the national traits of Renaissance literature gave way to cosmopolitan standards and international molds. For the first time since the Roman empire, the setting of life in western Europe seemed secure. The triumph of nationalism brought absolute monarchy to almost every country but England, and the increase of wealth from trade and colonies expanded the aristocratic classes. Wealth produced leisure and worldly sophistication, the climate for confident thinking and intellectual discovery. Ideas traveled across national boundaries as freely and persistently as the privileged classes who produced them or embraced them; and nowhere was the traffic of ideas so heavy as across the English Channel.

THE RULE OF THE ANCIENTS

Neoclassicism was a movement in art, music, and literature to revive the principles and practices of ancient Greece and Rome. If the classics of Greece and Rome, long so inspiring to the humanists of the Renaissance, were discredited by the rational speculation of the philosophers and the expanding world of the scientists, they nevertheless reached the climax of their literary influence at this time. The critical pronouncements of Aristotle and Horace hardened into inviolable law, and Euripides, Virgil, and Juvenal became the hallowed models of such important Neoclassic literary figures as the French writer Jean Racine (1639–1699) and the English ones Alexander Pope (1688–1744) and Samuel Johnson (1709–1784).

The reasons for the enormous literary prestige of the ancients are easy to establish. The urbanity of ancient Athens and Rome, and especially the elegant refinement of Roman writers, harmonized with the intellectual sophistication of Neoclassicism. The provincialism and roughness of literature in the centuries between repelled writers in the Age of Reason. The English poet John Dryden (1631–1700) rewrote both Chaucer and Shakespeare to bring them close to the classical ideal of clearness, grace, and regularity. The rational poets reached back over fifteen hundred years to their kindred spirits in antiquity. In Horace, the favorite lyric poet of the new age, they found the literary expression of the Golden Mean. In Ovid they recognized the rational view of love as a society game. In the tragedies of

Sophocles they saw the baleful result in a victory of passion over reason. Into the comedies of Plautus and Terence they read a rational satire of eccentric types of character. In the writings of Cicero and many another they warmed to the rational ideal of stoic conduct. The very range of literary types in antiquity—epic, didactic, lyric, and pastoral poetry, tragedy, comedy, history, essay, criticism, literary letter, epigram, formal satire, even novel—convinced the Neoclassical writers that the ancients had explored just about all the thought and art of which literature could be composed.

As a corollary to this conviction, the Neoclassicists decided that originality of subject matter in art is undesirable, if not impossible. Pope observed, "Nature to all things fixed the limits fit," and those limits were explored by the ancients. To attempt to invent new ideas is to foresake reason and follow the untrustworthy guide of imagination. The business of the rational writer in each new age is rather to restate the ideas of Nature in a new way, more elegant or more appealing to his time. Again it is Pope who phrases it:

True wit is Nature to advantage dressed:
What oft was thought, but ne'er so well expressed.

Hence the Neoclassicists deliberately imitated the literary forms, plots, characters, ideas, and verse of the ancients. Just as Virgil had modeled his *Aeneid* on Homer, the Neoclassical writers would follow them both in their beginnings, their turns of phrase, their episodes and characters. Pope produced close imitations of the satires of Horace, and Dr. Johnson of the satires of Juvenal, carefully adapted to their own place and time. Elegant echoes of phrases from the Roman poets stud the verses of the day. Racine's *Phaedra* retells the tragedy of Euripides' *Hippolytus; The Pot of Gold* of the Roman Plautus reappears in Molière's *Miser*. Yet the Neoclassicists were often more original than they intended to be. As a contemporary critic said of Pope's *Iliad*, "a fine poem, Mr. Pope, but you must not call it Homer." The unmistakable stamp of the Age of Reason is upon all the literature it produced,

and, as it indeed insisted, the method and manner of its writing loom larger than its subject matter.

In both France and England the long century of reason and classicism in literature breaks into two sub-periods around the year 1700. The fifty years that preceded saw the evolution of the rational system and the gradual hardening of the classical ideal. The fifty years that followed saw widespread application of the rational method to all phases of life and the absolute tyranny of the classics in belles lettres. Beyond 1750 forces of revolt emerged, as rationalism and classicism began a half-century of decline. From the social point of view, the aristocracy still dominated the literature of the first period, but the middle-class outlook became increasingly militant in the second.

A powerful influence toward standardizing literature in the classical mold throughout both periods was the conservative French Academy, the body of forty elected "Immortals," chartered by the French statesman Cardinal Richelieu in 1635. (See page 592.) Although it performed a unique service for the French language in compiling its first great dictionary and settling its grammar, it worked against literary experiment in favor of tradition and inflexible rules. Similar academies appeared in Italy, Spain, Holland, and Germany, but none in England. Conformity developed in England under literary dictators in the coffeehouses.

THE RULE OF REASON

Reason became the watchword of the era. The facility for thinking logically which set men and women apart from all other creatures seemed to produce at every turn justification for the new emphasis on mental prowess. The French philosopher René Descartes (1596–1650) determined that of all his studies, only one—mathematics—consisted of infallible truth; thus the laws of mathematics became the basis for the deductive method of reasoning in which one builds from a few simple truths a whole system of inferences. When Descartes applied his method to an examination of the universe, what emerged was a vast machine, operating according to regular and simple laws of nature which

Jean Antoine Watteau (1684–1721), *The French Comedians*. c. 1720.
Metropolitan Museum of Art

moved the atoms of the animate and inanimate worlds in inevitable harmony with each other. The discoveries of the English mathematician and physicist Sir Isaac Newton (1642–1727) reinforced the notion of a rational universe operating according to immutable rules; and both the French philosopher Blaise Pascal (1623–1662) and the German one Gottfried Wilhelm von Leibnitz (1646–1716), who were themselves gifted mathematicians, transferred the mechanistic concept to an explanation of life in general. The universe was governed by laws of harmony and logic. Discover the laws by rational thought; then apply the laws to every aspect of daily existence. Life lived in perfect balance would lead to complete enlightenment of the individual, the state, the world as a whole. Such an assumption was only logical, it seemed; and the assumption evolved into a belief that would drastically alter every aspect of thought and behavior for a hundred years or more.

In religion alone, the effects were far-reaching. A Deity and His creation that were established by laws of reasoning and mathematics differed greatly from the Christian God of love and comfort. A position just short of atheism—known as Deism—was extolled by philosophers and writers like Pope, the Frenchman Voltaire (1694–

1778), and the Americans Benjamin Franklin (1706–1790) and Thomas Jefferson (1743–1826). Though their individual views differed, all maintained a belief in a God that was more rational and intellectual than the God of miracles and divine intervention. Their deity had created the mechanical universe of Descartes and Newton and set it in motion according to mechanical laws. But this god had then retired, leaving the laws of nature to guide the world along its rational course.

Thinkers of the period were far more concerned with human nature than with the divine nature, anyway. Pope himself pronounced the mission of the age in this famous couplet:

Know then thyself; presume not God to scan. The proper study of mankind is man.

Though there were echoes of the Renaissance in this concern with human endeavor, the emphasis was less on the individual than on the species as a whole. How human beings could best live together in society was the topic most often debated in the literary salons and coffeehouses of the day. The 18th-century ideal was an urbane, cosmopolitan, sophisticated individual who sought improvement of society as a whole by achieving a sense of balance in personal spheres of influence. In the Golden Mean of ancient Greece and Rome was to be found the proper code of conduct: a rational, well-tempered life that avoided excesses of emotion and indulgence.

GOVERNMENT

For all the talk of harmony and balance, however, there was little interest in true democracy. The general viewpoint of the period, however sophisticated, remained decidedly aristocratic, and absolute monarchy remained the government of choice. But the rationalists did substitute a new notion of "benevolent despotism" for the older concept of the "divine right" of kings. Rulers "enlightened" by the knowledge of the day would then naturally govern in the best interest of all. In Louis XIV of France, Frederick the Great of Prussia, and Joseph II of Austria can be seen examples of these enlightened yet still absolute rulers.

Only in England was there an obvious exception to the rule, both literally and figuratively. A long battle with the crown over constitutional rights resulted in the Glorious Revolution of 1688—a bloodless uprising in which England's last king of the House of Stuart, James II, was deposed. Parliament offered the crown to James's older daughter Mary, wife of the Dutch ruler, William III of Orange, with the distinct understanding that they would be subject to the will of Parliament. In his *Treatise on Civil Government*, Englishman John Locke (1632–1704) detailed the argument for constitutional government as a reflection of man's natural (and rational) state. His document was a forerunner of louder demands for changes in government that would later destroy the calm so meticulously maintained—at least on the surface—during the age.

ART AND DESIGN

The surface—for the aristocrats and for the middle-class entrepreneurs who with their new wealth sought and bought to emulate the upper class—was indeed a beautiful one. The very names which today epitomize elegance in form and design—names like Wedgwood, Chippendale, Adam, Hepplewhite, Sheraton—are the last names of 18th-century craftsmen. And they represent only a small number of the multiple artisans at work throughout Europe and the Orient during a burgeoning celebration of decoration and adornment. For inspiration the artists of the time looked to ancient Greece and Rome, with an emphasis on formality, balance, and precision. Their variations on classical themes were not only a tribute to man's rationality; they were also an expression of the power and grandeur of human civilization. Neoclassical design even today remains a major influence in architecture and decor.

The buildings and furnishings of the time, however elegant, were but a backdrop for the fashions and manners of the period. In portraits by the Spanish painter Francisco de Goya (1746–1828) and the English one Thomas Gainsborough (1727–1788) are the elaborate trappings of eighteenth-century ladies and gentlemen. Silk knee-breeches, embroidered waistcoats of satin

Richard Wilson (1713–1782), *The Destruction of Niobe's Children.* c. 1759–1760.
Yale Center for British Art

and damask under vivid coats were favored by
men of fashion in their powdered wigs and silk
stockings. Women were even more splendidly
attired in layers of lace and satin covering acres
of hoopskirts. Towering headdresses often completed the look of the day, and a retreat to private
quarters to let down one's hair offered a genuine
sense of release—and relief. Comfort invariably
bowed to style, and what today seems like slavery
to design was then considered a natural pursuit
of the perfection in dress and deportment that
echoed the universal harmony.

ORDER AND HARMONY

That harmony, to the thinkers of the period,
was mathematical in every respect. Every human
concern had a proper place in the system; the
system had specific rules. To follow the rules
was to lead a perfect life. Perhaps the best
example of this systematic approach to daily life
is found in the *Encyclopédie*, a thirty-one volume collaboration by the French writers Denis
Diderot (1713–1784), Voltaire, Charles de Montesquieu (1689–1755), Jean Jacques Rousseau
(1712–1778), and others. In these books was

thought to be contained all the knowledge of man and the universe in ready-reference form. All that could possibly be known was there in carefully alphabetized listings.

Such extreme confidence—or philosophical cockiness, as it appears to the modern thinker—was a trademark of this Age of Enlightenment, in itself a more than boastful declaration of terms. But there were thinkers and writers who saw beyond the glitter of what Leibnitz pronounced as ". . . this best of all possible worlds." In France, the voices (and pens) of Voltaire, Montesquieu, and the playwright Molière (1622–1673) were raised in protest against the artificialities of a perfectly controlled world inhabited by perfectly controlled ladies and gentlemen. Hypocrisy, shallowness, even stupidity, were logical by-products of complacent thinking, an evil of the worst sort, these writers contended. In England, the essayists Joseph Addison (1672–1719) and Richard Steele (1672–1729), the satirist Jonathan Swift (1667–1745), and the poet Pope saw the flaws in the logic, the sins in the smugness. Their protests gave birth to the art of the satire as a prominent literary form.

And there was much to satirize in the Age of Enlightenment, of Reason, of Universal Harmony. In the streets the gilded coaches and brocaded sedan chairs of the rich moved against a background of rags, filth, and stench worse than any modern slum. Poverty was pervasive, and the conditions that would later erupt into violent revolutions festered among the rapidly enlarging ranks of the poor. The Neoclassical Period was, in short, a time of appalling extremes.

THINKING ABOUT GRAPHIC AIDS
Using the Time Line

The time line on pages 490–491 shows the chronological sequence of the historical and literary events discussed in Unit 5. Use the time line to answer the following questions.

1. Which of the following events did *not* take place in 1660? (a) the Restoration of the English monarchy; (b) the founding of the Royal Society; (c) the Fire of London
2. Could Milton have read Montesquieu's *Persian Letters?*
3. Who was the king of England when the American Revolution began? (a) Charles II; (b) Louis XIV; (c) George III
4. Who was born in the same year that the Seven Years' War began?
5. Did Johnson's *Dictionary* appear before the first volumes of the *Encyclopédie?*

BIOGRAPHY

John Milton
1608–1674

Like his most famous characters, Adam and Eve, John Milton knew a lifelong conflict between spiritual idealism and physical reality, between what can be and what instead often is. That he was able to resolve the dichotomies in his own life provides, on a less exalted level, a parallel to his saga of Eden.

Milton was the son of wealthy, cultured parents who, in addition to their love of learning and of the arts, felt a strong interest in the morality and devotion to duty that defined early Puritanism. They provided their son an enviable education with private tutors, followed by studies at St. Paul's School in London and then at Christ's College, Cambridge. Instruction in music, art, poetry—in addition to an impressive background in the classics—marked the young Milton as an inveterate scholar. Even as a child, he knew Greek, Latin, French, Italian, and Hebrew. But when Milton's loving, indulgent parents urged their son to enter the ministry of the Church of England, he refused. A life of intellectual freedom had stimulated the desire for religious freedom. The spiritual idealist had emerged, and though Milton was to remain deeply religious throughout his life, he rejected affiliation with any particular sect.

Retiring to his father's country home in 1632, Milton devoted six years to solitary, intense study of languages, theology, music, science, mathematics. During this period he also occasionally wrote, producing *Comus* (1634), a masque requested by his neighbors; "Lycidas" (1637), a pastoral elegy on the death of a Cambridge classmate; and other poems in Latin and English. Always he affirmed a desire to write a great English epic in the manner of the Greek and Roman writers he had so long revered.

In 1638 Milton embarked on a tour through France, Switzerland, and Italy. He was praised everywhere in his travels for his intelligent, genial manner; but news of impending civil war at home made the self-centered pleasures of his journey intolerable. "For I thought it base," he said, "to be traveling at my ease for intellectual culture while my fellow-countrymen at home were fighting for liberty." He returned home in 1639 to find political turmoil between Charles I and Parliament. Abandoning all thoughts of poetry, Milton turned to writing political tracts with genuine fervor. His pamphlets on the ideals of liberty earned him a position of leadership in the Commonwealth. While Cromwell led England through courageous action, Milton inspired the country through his writing.

In 1642 he married Mary Powell, the young daughter of Royalist sympathizers. She left him a month later; during the three-year period of their separation, Milton issued pamphlets advocating the availability of divorce on grounds of incompatibility. Disturbed enough by the events of their time, English citizens found their spokesman now something of a radical. Though Mary eventually returned and bore him three daughters before her death in 1652, the publicity of this marital crisis damaged his reputation. Only with the publication of his reply to foreign critics of the execution of Charles I, was Milton once again honored as his country's spokesman.

But like the Homer of his childhood studies, Milton was now a blind prophet. He had sacrificed his already failing eyesight to complete a treatise in defense of his country's liberty. Though he continued to serve Cromwell's government, with the aid of a secretary for reading and writing, the events of his life soon all but overwhelmed Milton. His beloved second wife died in childbirth in 1658; and with the Restoration of the monarchy in 1660, the great crusade for political freedom was canceled. His pamphlets were publicly burned; he was imprisoned. Only through the intervention of friends (and a heavy fine along with the loss of most of his property) was his life spared.

Despite the isolation of personal and professional defeat, or perhaps because of it, Milton produced in his final years the masterpieces for which he is most famous. His dream of writing a poem of epic scope and grandeur was realized in *Paradise Lost,* published in 1667. Totally dependent on his daughters for all reading and writing, Milton dictated whole passages at a time, which the girls dutifully, though not always happily, transcribed for hours on end. Considered the greatest epic in the English language, *Paradise Lost* was followed by its sequel, *Paradise Regained,* in 1671 and by the drama *Samson Agonistes* in the same year. Milton's last works mirrored his life. He had known both happiness and despair. Like his characters Adam and Eve and the blind Samson, he had persevered. "Still guides the heavenly vision," he remarked to friends before his death in 1674.

It is the first appearance of that heavenly vision in Genesis which concerns Milton in *Paradise Lost.* In twelve parts or books, each preceded by an argument or summary of the events that follow, Milton chronicles Satan's rebellion against God, Satan's expulsion from Heaven, and his corruption of Adam and Eve. Milton writes in **blank verse** with frequent use of anastrophe, the inversion of the usual order of the parts of a sentence. The result is a distinctive **rhythm** enhanced by vivid visual details. In the selections that follow from Books I, IX, and XII, the storyline is often secondary to the power of Milton's **imagery.**

 See STYLE in the Handbook of Literary Terms, page 973.

from Paradise Lost

John Milton

from **Book I**

Of man's first disobedience, and the fruit
Of that forbidden tree, whose mortal taste
Brought death into the world, and all our woe,
With loss of Eden, till one greater man[1]
5 Restore us, and regain the blissful seat,

Sing heavenly muse,[2] that on the secret top
Of Oreb, or of Sinai, didst inspire

---
1. *greater man,* Christ.
2. *heavenly muse,* the spirit that spoke to Moses on Mount Sinai and Mount Horeb (Oreb) in the wilderness.

That shepherd,[3] who first taught the chosen
   seed,
In the beginning how the heavens and earth
10 Rose out of chaos: Or if Sion hill
Delight thee more, and Siloa's brook[4] that
   flowed
Fast by the oracle of God; I thence
Invoke thy aid to my adventurous song,
That with no middle flight intends to soar
15 Above the Aonian mount,[5] while it pursues
Things unattempted yet in prose or rhyme.
And chiefly thou, O spirit,[6] that dost prefer
Before all temples the upright heart and pure,
Instruct me, for thou knowest; thou from
   the first
20 Wast present, and, with mighty wings outspread
Dove-like satest brooding on the vast abyss
And madest it pregnant: What in me is dark
Illumine, what is low raise and support;
That to the height of this great argument
25 I may assert eternal providence,
And justify the ways of God to men.

The action of *Paradise Lost* begins *in medias
res* (in the midst of things), after Satan's
rebellion and after he and his legions are
driven from Heaven and thrown into Chaos.
The opening episodes show the fallen angels
"rolling in the fiery gulf" until Satan rises
and addresses his companions.

". . . Farewell happy fields
Where joy forever dwells: Hail horrors, hail
Infernal world, and thou profoundest Hell
30 Receive thy new possessor: One who brings
A mind not to be changed by place or time.
The mind is its own place, and in itself
Can make a heaven of Hell, a hell of Heaven.
What matter where, if I be still the same,
35 And what I should be, all but less than[7] he
Whom thunder hath made greater? Here at
   least
We shall be free; the Almighty hath not built
Here for his envy, will not drive us hence:
Here we may reign secure, and in my choice
40 To reign is worth ambition though in Hell:
Better to reign in Hell, than serve in Heaven."

Satan rallies his legions and they build
their kingdom in Hell. Bent on revenge,
Satan searches throughout Chaos to find
the human world. He learns that God has
forbidden Adam and Eve to eat of the fruit
of the Tree of Knowledge, and decides that
he will lure them into disobedience. He
slips into the Garden of Eden, enters the
body of the serpent, and finds Eve alone.
He approaches her, rendering himself
"pleasing" in shape and "lovely," with the
purpose of flattering and thus tricking her.

from **Book IX**
                                   Oft he bowed
His turret crest, and sleek enameled neck,
Fawning, and licked the ground whereon she
   trod.
45 His gentle dumb expression turned at length
The eye of Eve to mark his play; he glad
Of her attention gained, with serpent tongue
Organic, or impulse of vocal air,
His fraudulent temptation thus began.
SATAN:
50 "Wonder not, sovereign mistress, if perhaps
Thou canst, who art sole wonder, much less
   arm
Thy looks, the heaven of mildness, with
   disdain,
Displeased that I approach thee thus, and gaze
Insatiate, I thus single, nor have feared
55 Thy awful brow, more awful thus retired.
Fairest resemblance of thy maker fair,
Thee all things living gaze on, all things thine
By gift, and thy celestial beauty adore
With ravishment beheld, there best beheld
60 Where universally admired; but here
In this enclosure wild, these beasts among,
Beholders rude, and shallow to discern

---

3. *that shepherd,* Moses.
4. *Sion hill . . . Siloa's brook,* sacred places in Jerusalem.
5. *Aonian mount,* Mount Helicon in Greece, home of the
Muses.
6. *spirit,* the Holy Spirit, the third person of the Holy
Trinity, or God.
7. *all but less than,* less only than.

Half what in thee is fair, one man except,
Who sees thee? (and what is one?) who
    shouldst be seen
65 A goddess among gods, adored and served
By angels numberless, thy daily train."
    So glozed[8] the tempter, and his proem[9] tuned;
Into the heart of Eve his words made way,
Though at the voice much marveling; at length
70 Not unamazed she thus in answer spake.

EVE:

"What may this mean? Language of man
    pronounced
By tongue of brute, and human sense
    expressed?
The first at least of these I thought denied
To beasts, whom God on their creation-day
75 Created mute to all articulate sound;
The latter I demur,[10] for in their looks
Much reason, and in their actions oft appears.
Thee, serpent, subtlest beast of all the field
I knew, but not with human voice endued;
80 Redouble then this miracle, and say,
How camest thou speakable of mute, and how
To me so friendly grown above the rest
Of brutal kind, that daily are in sight?
Say, for such wonder claims attention due."
85   To whom the guileful tempter thus replied.

SATAN:

"Empress of this fair world, resplendent Eve,
Easy to me it is to tell thee all
What thou commandest, and right thou
    shouldst be obeyed:
I was at first as other beasts that graze
90 The trodden herb, of abject thoughts and low,
As was my food, nor aught but food discerned
Or sex, and apprehended nothing high:
Till on a day roving the field, I chanced
A goodly tree far distant to behold
95 Laden with fruit of fairest colors mixed,
Ruddy and gold: I nearer drew to gaze;
When from the boughs a savory odor blown,
Grateful to appetite, more pleased my sense
Than smell of sweetest fennel or the teats
100 Of ewe or goat dropping with milk at even,
Unsucked of lamb or kid, that tend their play.
To satisfy the sharp desire I had
Of tasting those fair apples, I resolved

Not to defer; hunger and thirst at once,
105 Powerful persuaders, quickened at the scent
Of that alluring fruit, urged me so keen.
About the mossy trunk I wound me soon,
For high from ground the branches would
    require
Thy utmost reach or Adam's: Round the tree
110 All other beasts that saw, with like desire
Longing and envying stood, but could not
    reach.
Amid the tree now got, where plenty hung
Tempting so nigh, to pluck and eat my fill
I spared not, for such pleasure till that hour
115 At feed or fountain never had I found.
Sated at length, erelong I might perceive
Strange alteration in me, to degree
Of reason in my inward powers, and speech
Wanted not long, though to this shape retained.
120 Thenceforth to speculations high or deep
I turned my thoughts, and with capacious mind
Considered all things visible in heaven,
Or Earth, or Middle,[11] all things fair and good;
But all that fair and good in thy divine
125 Semblance, and in thy beauty's heavenly ray
United I beheld; no fair[12] to thine
Equivalent or second, which compelled
Me thus, though importune perhaps, to come
And gaze, and worship thee of right declared
130 Sovereign of creatures, universal dame."
    So talked the spirited[13] sly snake; and Eve
Yet more amazed unwary thus replied.

EVE:

"Serpent, thy overpraising leaves in doubt
The virtue of that fruit, in thee first proved:
135 But say, where grows the tree, from hence
    how far?
For many are the trees of God that grow
In Paradise, and various, yet unknown
To us, in such abundance lies our choice,
As leaves a greater store of fruit untouched,
140 Still hanging incorruptible, till men

---

8. *glozed,* flattered.
9. *proem,* prologue.
10. *demur,* question; i.e., I doubt that rational sense was denied to animals.
11. *Middle,* the air.
12. *fair,* beauty.
13. *spirited,* possessed by a spirit.

Thomas Cole (1801–
1848), *Expulsion
from the Garden of
Eden.* 1828. Museum
of Fine Arts, Boston

Grow up to their provision, and more hands
Help to disburden nature of her birth."
   To whom the wily adder, blithe and glad.

SATAN:

"Empress, the way is ready, and not long,
145 Beyond a row of myrtles, on a flat
Fast by a fountain, one small thicket past
Of blowing[14] myrrh and balm; if thou accept
My conduct, I can bring thee thither soon."
   "Lead then," said Eve. He leading swiftly
     rolled
150 In tangles, and made intricate seem straight,
To mischief swift. Hope elevates, and joy
Brightens his crest, as when a wandering fire,
Compact of unctuous vapor,[15] which the night
Condenses, and the cold environs round,
155 Kindled through agitation to a flame,
Which oft, they say, some evil spirit attends
Hovering and blazing with delusive light,
Misleads the amazed night-wanderer from his
     way
To bogs and mires, and oft through pond or
     pool,
160 There swallowed up and lost, from succor far.

So glistered the dire snake, and into fraud
Led Eve our credulous mother, to the tree
Of prohibition,[16] root of all our woe;
Which when she saw, thus to her guide she
     spake.

EVE:

165   "Serpent, we might have spared our coming
     hither,
Fruitless to me, though fruit be here to excess,
The credit of whose virtue rest with thee,
Wondrous indeed, if cause of such effects.
But of this tree we may not taste nor touch;
170 God so commanded, and left that command
Sole daughter of his voice:[17] the rest, we live
Law to ourselves, our reason is our law."
   To whom the tempter guilefully replied.

SATAN:

   "Indeed? hath God then said that of the fruit
175 Of all these garden trees ye shall not eat,

---

14. *blowing*, blooming.
15. *Compact . . . vapor,* made of oily mist.
16. *tree/Of prohibition,* forbidden tree.
17. *Sole . . . voice,* his only command.

Milton   **503**

Yet lords declared of all in earth or air?"
To whom thus Eve yet sinless.

EVE:

"Of the fruit
Of each tree in the garden we may eat,
But of the fruit of this fair tree amidst
180 The garden, God hath said, 'Ye shall not eat
Thereof, nor shall ye touch it, lest ye die.' "
She scarce had said, though brief, when now
more bold
The tempter, but with show of zeal and love
To man, and indignation at his wrong,
185 New part puts on,[18] and as to passion moved,
Fluctuates disturbed, yet comely and in act
Raised,[19] as of some great matter to begin.
As when of old some orator renowned
In Athens or free Rome, where eloquence
190 Flourished, since mute, to some great cause
addressed,
Stood in himself collected, while each part,
Motion, each act won audience ere the tongue,
Sometimes in height began, as no delay
Of preface brooking through his zeal of right.[20]
195 So standing, moving, or to height upgrown
The tempter all impassioned thus began.

SATAN:

"O sacred, wise, and wisdom-giving plant,
Mother of science,[21] now I feel thy power
Within me clear, not only to discern
200 Things in their causes, but to trace the ways
Of highest agents, deemed however wise.
Queen of this universe, do not believe
Those rigid threats of death; ye shall not die:
How should ye? by the fruit? it gives you life
205 To knowledge. By the threatener, look on me,
Me who have touched and tasted, yet both live,
And life more perfect have attained than fate
Meant me, by venturing higher than my lot.
Shall that be shut to man, which to the beast
210 Is open? or will God incense his ire
For such a petty trespass, and not praise
Rather your dauntless virtue, whom the pain
Of death denounced,[22] whatever thing death be,
Deterred not from achieving what might lead
215 To happier life, knowledge of good and evil;
Of good, how just? of evil, if what is evil
Be real, why not known, since easier shunned?

God therefore cannot hurt ye, and be just;
Not just, not God;[23] not feared then, nor
obeyed:
220 Your fear itself of death removes the fear.
Why then was this forbid? Why but to awe,
Why but to keep ye low and ignorant,
His worshipers; he knows that in the day
Ye eat thereof, your eyes that seem so clear,
225 Yet are but dim, shall perfectly be then
Opened and cleared, and ye shall be as gods,
Knowing both good and evil as they know.
That ye should be as gods, since I as man,
Internal man,[24] is but proportion meet,
230 I of brute human, ye of human gods.
So ye shall die perhaps, by putting off
Human, to put on gods, death to be wished,
Though threatened, which no worse than this
can bring.
And what are gods that man may not become
235 As they, participating[25] godlike food?
The gods are first, and that advantage use
On our belief, that all from them proceeds;
I question it, for this fair earth I see,
Warmed by the sun, producing every kind,
240 Them nothing: If they all things, who enclosed
Knowledge of good and evil in this tree,
That whoso eats thereof, forthwith attains
Wisdom without their leave? and wherein lies
The offense, that man should thus attain to
know?
245 What can your knowledge hurt him, or this tree
Impart against his will if all be his?
Or is it envy, and can envy dwell
In heavenly breasts? these, these and many more
Causes import[26] your need of this fair fruit.

---

18. *New part puts on,* assumes a new role.
19. *in act/Raised,* poised in stance.
20. *Sometimes in height . . . right.* As if too agitated to begin at the beginning, the speaker bursts into the middle of his speech.
21. *science,* knowledge.
22. *denounced,* threatened.
23. *God therefore . . . God.* The serpent reasons that for God to punish Eve with death would be unjust, and if God were unjust He would not be God.
24. *Internal man,* like man inside (intellectually) but not in appearance.
25. *participating,* sharing.
26. *import,* prove.

250 Goddess humane, reach then, and freely taste."
  He ended, and his words replete with guile
Into her heart too easy entrance won:
Fixed on the fruit she gazed, which to behold
Might tempt alone, and in her ears the sound
255 Yet rung of his persuasive words, impregned[27]
With reason, to her seeming, and with truth;
Meanwhile the hour of noon drew on, and waked
An eager appetite, raised by the smell
So savory of that fruit, which with desire,
260 Inclinable now grown to touch or taste,
Solicited her longing eye; yet first
Pausing a while, thus to herself she mused.

EVE:

  "Great are thy virtues, doubtless, best of
      fruits,
Though kept from man, and worthy to be
      admired,
265 Whose taste, too long forborne, at first assay[28]
Gave elocution to the mute, and taught
The tongue not made for speech to speak thy
      praise:
Thy praise he also who forbids thy use,
Conceals not from us, naming thee the tree
270 Of knowledge, knowledge both of good and evil;
Forbids us then to taste, but his forbidding
Commends thee more, while it infers the good
By thee communicated, and our want:
For good unknown, sure is not had, or had
275 And yet unknown, is as not had at all.
In plain then, what forbids he but to know,
Forbids us good, forbids us to be wise?
Such prohibitions bind not. But if death
Bind us with after-bands, what profits then
280 Our inward freedom? In the day we eat
Of this fair fruit, our doom is, we shall die.
How dies the serpent? he hath eaten and lives,
And knows, and speaks, and reasons, and
      discerns,
Irrational till then. For us alone
285 Was death invented? or to us denied
This intellectual food, for beasts reserved?
For beasts it seems: yet that one beast which
      first
Hath tasted, envies not, but brings with joy
The good befallen him, author unsuspect,[29]
290 Friendly to man, far from deceit or guile.

What fear I then, rather what know to fear
Under this ignorance of good and evil,
Of God or death, of law or penalty?
Here grows the cure of all, this fruit divine,
295 Fair to the eye, inviting to the taste,
Of virtue to make wise: what hinders then
To reach, and feed at once both body and
      mind?"
  So saying, her rash hand in evil hour
Forth reaching to the fruit, she plucked, she eat:
300 Earth felt the wound, and nature from her seat
Sighing through all her works gave signs of
      woe,
That all was lost. Back to the thicket slunk
The guilty serpent, and well might, for Eve
Intent now wholly on her taste, naught else
305 Regarded, such delight till then, as seemed,
In fruit she never tasted, whether true
Or fancied so, through expectation high
Of knowledge, nor was godhead from her
      thought.
Greedily she engorged without restraint,
310 And knew not eating death . . . .

Eve offers the fruit to Adam, who eats out
of love for her. They immediately fall to
accusing each other. Sin and death enter
the world. God orders Adam and Eve
expelled from Eden, and sends the Angel
Michael to execute His will. Michael
shows the future to Adam, and then Adam
goes to wake Eve and depart from Paradise.

from **Book XII**
Descended, Adam to the bower where Eve
Lay sleeping ran before, but found her waked;
And thus with words not sad she him received.
  "Whence thou returnest, and whither
      wentest, I know;
315 For God is also in sleep, and dreams advise,

27. *impregned,* impregnated.
28. *assay,* try.
29. *author unsuspect,* a reliable authority.

Which he hath sent propitious, some great
    good
Presaging, since with sorrow and heart's distress
Wearied I fell asleep: but now lead on;
In me is no delay; with thee to go,
320 Is to stay here; without thee here to stay,
Is to go hence unwilling; thou to me
Art all things under heaven, all places thou,
Who for my willful crime art banished hence.
This further consolation yet secure
325 I carry hence; though all by me is lost,
Such favor I unworthy am vouchsafed,
By me the promised seed shall all restore."

    So spake our mother Eve, and Adam heard
Well pleased, but answered not; for now too
    nigh
330 The archangel stood, and from the other hill
To their fixed station, all in bright array
The cherubim descended; on the ground
Gliding meteorous, as evening mist
Risen from a river o'er the marish[30] glides,
335 And gathers ground fast at the laborer's heel
Homeward returning. High in front advanced,

The brandished sword of God before them
    blazed
Fierce as a comet; which with torrid heat,
And vapor as the Libyan air adust,[31]
340 Began to parch that temperate clime; whereat
In either hand the hastening angel caught
Our lingering parents, and to the eastern gate
Led them direct, and down the cliff as fast
To the subjected plain; then disappeared.
345 They looking back, all the eastern side beheld
Of Paradise, so late their happy seat,
Waved over by that flaming brand, the gate
With dreadful faces thronged and fiery arms:
Some natural tears they dropped, but wiped
    them soon;
350 The world was all before them, where to choose
Their place of rest, and providence their guide:
They hand in hand with wandering steps and
    slow,
Through Eden took their solitary way.

                        1674

---

30. *marish,* marsh.
31. *Libyan air adust,* hot desert winds of Libya.

Milton's Cosmography

    The word *cosmography* comes from the Greek *kosmographia* (*kosmos* world + *graphein* write) meaning "description or view of the world or universe." Milton's cosmography, which is essentially the same as that of the Renaissance and the Middle Ages, is based on a combination of various ancient philosophies which were built around the theory that the earth was the fixed center of the universe. It must be remembered that the systems of Copernicus (1473–1543) and Galileo (1564–1642), which were based on the idea that the sun, not the earth, was at the center of the universe, had not received general acceptance in Milton's time, and that Milton

therefore had some warrant for clinging to the older theories.

    According to the older view, the universe was composed first of Heaven, or the Empyrean. Below Heaven lay Chaos, or infinite space, filled with atoms and warring elements in ceaseless flux. Below or far down in Chaos lay Hell, a vast continent which was cut off from Chaos by walls of enormous thickness. Hanging by a chain from the floor of the Empyrean was the World, or created universe, which was composed of nine concentric spheres through which the planets and fixed stars moved in their courses around the central earth.

THINK AND DISCUSS
Understanding

1. In Book I, Milton declares his purpose for writing *Paradise Lost*. What is this purpose?
2. How does Satan use both flattery and apparent logic to seduce Eve?
3. What is Eve's rationale in finally deciding to eat the fruit?
4. What consolation for her act of disobedience does Eve find in the excerpt from Book XII?

Analyzing

5. What lines support the theory that Milton may have inadvertently made Satan the hero of the poem?
6. What elements of a classical epic are incorporated into *Paradise Lost?*
7. How can the fall of Adam and Eve be seen, paradoxically, as ultimately a fortunate event?
8. How does Milton's version of the story differ from the account in Genesis?

Extending

9. Psychologist Carl Jung saw the psyche as made up of opposite forces, which he called "archetypes." (Literary critics have adopted the term **archetype** to refer to essential images, story-patterns and characters.) These complementary energies have been called yin and yang, right brain and left brain, or masculine and feminine. Jung associated what he viewed as feminine psychological tendencies with the areas of intuitiveness and receptiveness to the unknown or irrational. Assuming the validity of this connection, discuss Satan's choice of Eve as his primary target and the nature of the approach he takes in tempting her.

APPLYING: Style
See Handbook of Literary Terms, p. 973.

Style is the way an author handles language, the choices an author makes with regard to vocabulary and word arrangement. These choices are largely determined by *why* the author is writing in the first place. Just as a person dresses or speaks or behaves to prompt a certain response, so a writer arranges words to elicit a desired reaction from the reader.

1. Compare lines 1–26 from Book I of *Paradise Lost* with lines 340–353 of Book XII. What is Milton's purpose for writing each passage?
2. How does the style of each passage suit the purpose?

THINKING SKILLS
Evaluating

To evaluate is to make a judgment based on some sort of standard.

1. Satan claims that it is "Better to reign in Hell, than serve in Heaven" (line 41). In your judgment, is Satan's ambition perverse or justifiable?
2. Satan claims that he will be free in his new domain. What, in your opinion, is the nature of his freedom, and is it worth the sacrifice it entails?

COMPOSITION
Writing a Letter

Imagine yourself as Eve at the end of her long and eventful life. Write a letter to your great-grandchildren, to be read after your death. Explain in the letter your version of the events in the Garden of Eden.

Writing About Characters

Choose two characters from other literary works you have read (or from your own experience) who have made a "heaven of Hell, a hell of Heaven." In an essay of three or four paragraphs, compare the motivations and justifications for these characters' choices. See "Writing About Characters" in the Writer's Handbook.

Jean de La Fontaine
1621–1695

The "hard core of vital truths"—so La Fontaine described the fables in his first published collection in 1668. But these brief tales in which the characters, usually animals, point out specific truths about life and living existed as a literary form long before La Fontaine's time. Even Aesop, the Greek orator with whom the fable is most usually associated, was only popularizing an established way of indirectly relaying a truth about human behavior. The Bible abounds with fables, although these stories, featuring people rather than animals, are usually referred to as parables. Fables or parables, the intent is the same: to impart wisdom by way of a story, an example, rather than by a directly personal lecture.

Jean de La Fontaine was born at Château-Thierry, France, to successful, cultured parents who planned a life in the Church for their son. When Jean's interests seemed totally unsuited, they insisted on his early marriage to a girl of their choice. But La Fontaine seemed no better suited as a husband than as a cleric; he gradually abandoned his wife and son, not out of dislike but rather out of a persistent immaturity, a chronic inability or unwillingness to conform. Friends supported his wife, just as a succession of patrons supported him while he wrote his poetry. His parents, stymied in two efforts to influence their son's life, achieved an ultimate triumph by their lifelong promotion of the art of poetry. At age twenty-two, La Fontaine heard an ode by the poet Malherbe, and his own obsession with reading and writing emerged.

La Fontaine's verse is simply expressed and often stinging with sarcasm. Yet a definite sense of truth, a genuine validity, pervades his work; and La Fontaine is generally acknowledged as the greatest of the fabulists. In the examples of his work that follow, notice the timelessness of each moral or truth—that is the classic form of the fable. Notice also the cleverness of the phrasing—that instinctive sureness is the legacy of La Fontaine.

The Acorn and the Pumpkin

translated by **Elizur Wright**

God's works are good. This truth to prove
Around the world I need not move;
   I do it by the nearest pumpkin.
"This fruit so large, on vine so small,"
5   Surveying once, exclaimed a bumpkin—
"What could He mean who made us all?
He's left this pumpkin out of place.
If I had ordered in the case,
Upon that oak it should have hung—
10 A noble fruit as ever swung
To grace a tree so firm and strong.
Indeed, it was a great mistake,
   As this discovery teaches,
That I myself did not partake
15 His counsels whom my curate preaches.
All things had then in order come;
   This acorn, for example,
   Not bigger than my thumb,
Had not disgraced a tree so ample.
20 The more I think, the more I wonder
   To see outraged proportion's laws.
   And that without the slightest cause;
God surely made an awkward blunder,"
   With such reflections proudly fraught,
25   Our sage grew tired of mighty thought,
And threw himself on Nature's lap,
Beneath an oak, to take his nap.
Plump on his nose, by lucky hap,
An acorn fell: he waked, and in
30 The matted beard that graced his chin,
He found the cause of such a bruise
As made him different language use.
"O! O!" he cried; "I bleed! I bleed!
And this is what has done the deed!
35 But, truly, what had been my fate,
Had this had half a pumpkin's weight!
I see that God had reasons good,
And all his works well understood."
Thus home he went in humbler mood.

1668

The Lion and the Rat

translated by **Elizur Wright**

To show to all your kindness, it behoves:
There's none so small but you his aid may need.
I quote two fables[1] for this weighty creed,
   Which either of them fully proves.
5   From underneath the sward
      A rat, quite off his guard,
Popped out between a lion's paws.
      The beast of royal bearing
      Showed what a lion was
10   The creature's life by sparing—
      A kindness well repaid;
   For, little as you would have thought
His majesty would ever need his aid,
      It proved full soon
15   A precious boon.
Forth issuing from his forest glen,
   T' explore the haunts of men,
In lion net his majesty was caught,
   From which his strength and rage
20   Served not to disengage.
The rat ran up, with grateful glee,
Gnawed off a rope, and set him free.

By time and toil we sever
What strength and rage could never.

1668

---

1. *two fables.* The second fable, "The Pigeon and the Ant," is not included here.

Translating La Fontaine

Because the regularity and balance of the Neo-classical Age have been replaced by other literary techniques, it is interesting to see what later translators have done with La Fontaine's verse. Appearing below and on the opposite page are four translations of La Fontaine's fable "The Camel and the Floating Sticks." Wright's belongs to the Victorian period; the others are all modern.

La Fontaine's poem can be divided logically into three parts or movements. The first deals with the camel, the second with the floating sticks, and the third with the moral to be drawn from the whole. In the first part we have a fine example of one of the vexing problems faced by all writers, and the four versions show how different translators managed to solve that problem. As common in prose as it is in poetry, the problem is how to avoid using the same word in two nearby constructions when a suitable synonym or substitute cannot be found.

In the case of the La Fontaine poem the word is *camel*, which occurs twice within the first four lines. Wright handles it by using "hump-backed camel" (note the marvelously descriptive adjective), then reverts to Neoclassical inflated diction, calling the beast a "desert wanderer."

Moore, employing modern English, first uses "camel," then refers to the creature as "the curiosity." Her language is simpler than Wright's, but her approach is similar. Displaying an engaging sense of humor, Clark makes the best of a troublesome situation by turning it to her own use and exaggerating it for comic effect. In line 1 she says simply "the camel"; line 2 is colloquially scientific with "new-fangled mammal"; and line 5 manages to have fun with the problem as the stanza ends with an internally-rhyming line, "To throw on the camel a trammel." Unlike the other translators, Ponsot first uses a plural, "camels," then settles for "dromedary," an acceptable synonym.

Probably the most interesting confluence of terms occurs in the second part of the poem, that dealing with the floating sticks. Although we can profitably compare the five sets of terms the translators use to describe the floating sticks, which are first mistaken for a warship and then decline in size and menace as they approach closer, it is in the third term of the series, describing a small boat, that the translators display a fascinating range of terms: Wright uses the very general "boat"; to Moore it is "a wherry"; to Clark "a gig". Ponsot, who employs a somewhat different arrangement of the terms, calls it "a sailboat" and uses "rowboat" where the other employ "bale" or a similar term.

In the third part of the poem, all translators draw basically the same moral, but each expresses it differently; and only Clark extends it from impersonal objects to human beings themselves. The responses range from Wright's "full many *things* on earth," Moore's "how *much* I've seen in the world," and Ponsot's "any *trifle*" to Clark's "the most jaunty of *men* . . . ."

Elizur Wright (1841)

The first who saw the humpbacked camel
    Fled off for life; the next approached with
      care;
    The third with tyrant rope did boldly dare
The desert wanderer to trammel.
5   Such is the power of use to change
    The face of objects new and strange;
    Which grow, by looking at, so tame,
    They do not even seem the same.
And since this theme is up for our attention,
10 A certain watchman I will mention,
    Who, seeing something far
      Away upon the ocean,
      Could not but speak his notion
    That 'twas a ship of war.
15 Some minutes more had past,—
    A bomb-ketch 'twas without a sail,
    And then a boat, and then a bale,
And floating sticks of wood at last!

    Full many things on earth, I wot,
20 Will claim this tale,—and well they may;
    They're something dreadful far away,
    But near at hand—they're not.

Marianne Moore (1954)

A man, encountering a camel,
Fled, shocked by a sight so novel.
Another ventured near. A third then braved
    what they had feared;
The curiosity was snared.
5 We grow accustomed to what at first made us
    afraid,
Though before so alarming we had shivered with
    dread.
    Having seen it, we are prepared
    When we encounter it afterward.
Since I've broached this topic, a word might be
    added
10 About some watchmen who were deluded
By a form at sea. They were so intimidated
    Each of them said he could swear
    That what he saw was a man of war;
Then concluded a fireship was being moored;
15 Then a wherry; then something tied with
    cord,
And then some flotsam that swung and
    swirled.

Ah yes, how much I've seen in the world,
For which these anecdotes account—
Far off, immense; but close at hand to what does
    it amount!

Illustration by Gustave Doré (1833–1883) for an 1867
edition of the La Fontaine's *Fables*

Marie Ponsot (1957)

The first man who saw camels fled;
The second man stopped short, instead,
Then approached them; the third thought it
    ordinary
To bridle a dromedary.
5 Time makes the strange and rare as familiar
    as bread.
What strikes us at first sight as terrible, we
    dread
    Until mere daily ritual
    Has made the sight habitual.
That reminds me: there's a sea-watch I might
    mention.
10 It was kept in times of tension.
Sighting a dim, distant form, vast in
    dimension,
    They cried, "Warships! sound the alarm!"
    And, "Heaven keep our cause from harm!"
Then they looked again, and said they'd seen
    a slow boat . . .
15 No, a sailboat . . . no, a rowboat . . .
What they had sighted was driftwood.
    For some, a suitable gift would
    Be the moral of this story:
Given distance, any trifle takes on glory.

Eunice Clark (1957)
I. THE CAMEL

The first to discover the camel
Fought shy of the new-fangled mammal.
The next was less scared,
And the third fellow dared
5 To throw on the camel a trammel.

II. THE DRIFTWOOD

Some shore watchers raised a great hue,
That a vessel of war was in view.
Then they thought 'twas a sail,
Then a gig, then a bale.
10 At the end only driftwood hove to.

III. ENVOI

Dear reader, the distant or strange
Shrinks fast as it comes within range.
The most jaunty of men,
Heard again and again
15 Will jingle like very small change.

Illustration from an edition of La Fontaine's *Fables*
published in 1776. Bibliothèque des Arts Décoratifs, Paris

The Boy and the Schoolmaster

translated by **Elizur Wright**

Wise counsel is not always wise,
    As this my tale exemplifies.
A boy, that frolicked on the banks of Seine,
Fell in, and would have found a watery grave,
5 Had not that hand that planteth ne'er in vain
A willow planted there, his life to save.
While hanging by its branches as he might,
A certain sage preceptor came in sight;
To whom the urchin cried, "Save, or I'm
        drowned!"
10 The master, turning gravely at the sound,
Thought proper for a while to stand aloof,
And give the boy some seasonable reproof.

"You little wretch! this comes of foolish
        playing,
Commands and precepts disobeying.
15 A naughty rogue, no doubt, you are,
Who thus requite your parents' care.
Alas! their lot I pity much,
Whom fate condemns to watch o'er such."
This having coolly said, and more,
20   He pulled the drowning lad ashore.

This story hits more marks than you suppose.
All critics, pedants, men of endless prose,—
    Three sorts, so richly blessed with progeny.
    The house is blessed that doth not lodge
        any,—
25 May in it see themselves from head to toes.
    No matter what the task,
        Their precious tongues must teach;
    Their help in need you ask,
        You first must hear them preach.

1668

Nothing Too Much

translated by **Elizur Wright**

Look where we will throughout creation,
We look in vain for moderation.
There is a certain golden mean,
Which Nature's sovereign Lord, I ween,
5 Designed the path of all forever.
   Doth one pursue it? Never.
E'en things which by their nature bless,
Are turned to curses by excess.

The grain, best gift of Ceres fair,
10 Green waving in the genial air,
By overgrowth exhausts the soil;
   By superfluity of leaves
   Defrauds the treasure of its sheaves,
And mocks the busy farmer's toil.
15 Not less redundant is the tree,
So sweet a thing is luxury.
The grain within due bounds to keep,
Their Maker licenses the sheep
The leaves excessive to retrench.
20   In troops they spread across the plain,
   And, nibbling down the hapless grain,
Contrive to spoil it, root and branch.
   So, then, with licence from on high,
The wolves are sent on sheep to prey;
25 The whole the greedy gluttons slay;
   Or, if they don't, they try.

Next, men are sent on wolves to take
   The vengeance now condign:
In turn the same abuse they make
30   Of this behest divine.

Of animals, the human kind
Are to excess the most inclined.
On low and high we make the charge,—
Indeed, upon the race at large.
35 There liveth not the soul select
That sinneth not in this respect.
Of "Nought too much," the fact is,
All preach the truth,—none practice.

1668

THINK AND DISCUSS
Understanding
1. What is the specific message or moral of each of these fables?
2. Where is this moral always found?
3. How is **satire** an essential element of fables?

Analyzing
4. Only "The Camel and the Floating Sticks" and "The Lion and the Rat" feature the traditional use of animals as main characters. Do you feel that they are more or less successful as fables than "The Acorn and the Pumpkin" and "The Boy and the Schoolmaster"?
5. In which fables are the personal opinions of the author apparent?

Extending
6. Which fables remind you of experiences you may have had?
7. Elizur Wright happened to see a copy of La Fontaine's fables in a bookshop in New York in 1837, and he immediately decided to translate the stories for his children. Wright's translation was his first and last experience in the world of literature. He went on to become a prominent spokesman in the anti-slavery movement, and later he exposed the corruption rampant in the life-insurance business. He in fact wrote much of the legislation that governs the insurance business today. How is Elizur Wright's life in itself a fable worthy of La Fontaine's pen?

COMPOSITION
Writing a Fable
Write a modern fable on the order of La Fontaine. Use animals as the main characters. Satirize an event or situation that is of current national concern.

Writing an Essay
Carefully review the introduction to this unit. Then, in an essay of several paragraphs, explore the relationship between the overall concerns of Neoclassicism and La Fontaine's message in his fable "Nothing Too Much." See "Writing About a Period or Trend" in the Writer's Handbook.

Molière was born Jean Baptiste Poquelin in Paris in 1622, the son of a successful interior decorator who had achieved the title of upholsterer to the king. Though both his mother and a stepmother had died by the time he was fourteen, Molière's father and grandparents oversaw his extensive studies in the classics, philosophy, and the law. He would, it was assumed, follow his father in the family business; but as a boy, Molière had been taken often to the theater by his grandfather. The second-rate comedies of his youth—with broad farces and stock characters—provided him with ideas and situations for the plays he was later to write. At twenty-one he chose the theater as his profession and adopted Molière as his pen name, perhaps as much to protect his family's name as to establish his separate literary identity. Theater people of the day had no social standing; they were, in fact, often excommunicated by the Church.

An early association with *L'Illustre Theatre* (the Illustrious Theater)—a dramatic troupe of young men and women, like Molière, from established families—led to a tour of the country that lasted twelve years. Though he was twice arrested for debt during the early years with the company, Molière remained a faithful member and eventually began to write plays as well as perform in them. In 1658 Molière achieved the triumph of acting before King Louis XIV and his court. Molière's own farce, *The Love-Sick Doctor*, was on the bill, and a delighted King Louis granted him his own company to be featured regularly at *Le Petit Bourbon*, one of the three most important theaters of the time.

Molière grew bolder with his satiric comedy; and while the King grew more delighted with the performance of each new play, more and more theater-goers saw themselves and their customs ridiculed on Molière's stage. As he continued to write, direct, and perform in over thirty plays, he made many enemies, even though his company was awarded the title of "Troupe to the King." His late marriage to a much younger woman was largely an unhappy one. Two of his three children died in infancy, and his estrangement from his father over his chosen profession was never resolved. An ultimate irony of his life was that he would suffer a fatal hemorrhage while performing the title role of the hypochondriac in his own play, *The Imaginary Invalid*. Priests refused to hear the actor and playwright's final confession; only the intercession of the king, after Molière's widow's pleading, allowed his body, four nights after his death, to be buried in a churchyard.

The Misanthrope, The Would-Be Gentleman, The Doctor in Spite of Himself, and *Tartuffe*—all are among Molière's greatest plays. But it is in *Tartuffe* that the Church's attitude toward Molière's life and death is most clearly echoed. *Tartuffe* is the definitive exposé of a religious hypocrite.

Notice the setting. Neoclassic dramatists devoted themselves to the unities of time and place with a fervor unequaled even by the Greek and Roman playwrights who had served as their inspiration. They believed, for instance, that if an audience happened to be in the theater for a few hours for a performance, then the action of the play should remain within that time span; in exceptional circumstances, the action might extend to a twenty-four-hour period. And since the audience had been in one place throughout the performance, then logically the setting on stage also had to remain constant throughout the play. A single setting, time span, and line of action—these characterized Neoclassic drama.

Notice the playwright's purpose. These predominantly French writers proclaimed truth through entertainment the purpose of drama. Reality and drama were not to be separate entities; one, rather, mirrored the other. Events that did not occur in real life were not therefore suitable subjects for the stage; and while the theater was to be viewed as a place of entertainment, it was to be also a center for moral instruction. The playwright's mission was to demonstrate the timeless morality of a rational and just universe in which, ultimately, good was rewarded and evil was not. A well-ordered play reflected a well-ordered universe.

Neoclassic Staging The theater buildings themselves were anything but well-ordered, however. Most of them had originally been ballrooms or indoor tennis courts. Long, narrow rooms with shallow stages built at one end, and grandstands and galleries arranged around the remaining three walls—these playhouses offered little in the way of acoustical or aesthetic design. The only seats that directly faced the stage were at the far end of the room, and the best view from that vantage point was of the patrons who purchased cheap standing-room-only tickets for the area directly in front of the stage. For many years during the period, patrons could purchase seats directly on the stage itself, but these theater-goers were generally young male aristocrats more interested in showing off their peacock garb than in following the play.

As in the Shakespearean theaters, there was no curtain; players left the stage completely at the end of each scene. Lighting was provided by hundreds of wax candles and small oil lanterns. While the facilities were not much improved from Shakespeare's day, there was one particularly noticeable improvement in the casting policy: the Neoclassical companies included women, who enjoyed both equal rights and equal pay with their male counterparts. An acting troupe generally consisted of some ten to fifteen players; and at the end of a performance, the production costs were deducted from the box office receipts, and the remaining money was then divided among the players. Though most companies received some royal subsidies, an actor's income largely depended on the box office.

Costumes were a vital component in a successful production. Though there eventually evolved a number of conventionalized costumes for certain stock figures like the tragic hero or the buffoon, there was no concern for historical accuracy. Players appeared in the latest elegant fashions of the day: tight knee breeches and low-necked gowns in vivid silks and satins. (See the illustration on page 495.) The expensive wardrobes provided vital decoration for stages with little scenery. The only drawback, at least as far as the players were concerned, was that they had to provide their own costumes.

Tartuffe clearly falls within the traditions of Neoclassic drama. Its action occurs within the span of one day. A table and a closet are the only features required of the single room that serves as the setting, and nearly all of the action is related to the main **theme.** That *Tartuffe* instructs the audience about the evils of religious hypocrisy strengthens the play's connection with the tenets of Neoclassicism; that it simultaneously amuses even the most modern audience marks Molière's comedy as a classic for all time.

Tartuffe

Molière *translated by* **Richard Wilbur**

CHARACTERS

MME. PERNELLE (păr nel′), ORGON's mother
ORGON (ôr gôN′), ELMIRE's husband
ELMIRE (el mēr′), ORGON's wife
DAMIS (dä mēs′), ORGON's son, ELMIRE's stepson
MARIANE (mär yän′), ORGON's daughter, ELMIRE's stepdaughter, in love with VALÈRE
VALÈRE (vä lär′), in love with MARIANE
CLÉANTE (clā änt′), ORGON's brother-in-law
TARTUFFE (tär tüf′), a hypocrite
DORINE (dô rēn′), MARIANE's lady's-maid
M. LOYAL, a bailiff
A POLICE OFFICER
FLIPOTE (flē pōt′), MME PERNELLE's maid

The scene throughout: ORGON's *house in Paris*

Late seventeenth-century painting of various actors who appeared at the Théatre Royal in Paris. Molière is at the far left. Comédie Française, Paris

See COUPLET in the Handbook of Literary Terms, page 946.

ACT ONE

SCENE 1.

MADAME PERNELLE *and* FLIPOTE, *her maid*, ELMIRE, MARIANE, DORINE, DAMIS, CLÉANTE.

MADAME PERNELLE. Come, come, Flipote; it's time I left this place.
ELMIRE. I can't keep up, you walk at such a pace.
MADAME PERNELLE. Don't trouble, child; no need to show me out.
It's not your manners I'm concerned about.
5 **ELMIRE.** We merely pay you the respect we owe.
But, Mother, why this hurry? Must you go?
MADAME PERNELLE. I must. This house appals me. No one in it
Will pay attention for a single minute.
Children, I take my leave much vexed in spirit.
10 I offer good advice, but you won't hear it.
You all break in and chatter on and on.
It's like a madhouse with the keeper gone.
DORINE. If . . .
MADAME PERNELLE. Girl, you talk too much, and I'm afraid
You're far too saucy for a lady's-maid.
15 You push in everywhere and have your say.
DAMIS. But . . .
MADAME PERNELLE. You, boy, grow more foolish every day.
To think my grandson should be such a dunce!
I've said a hundred times, if I've said it once,
That if you keep the course on which you've started,
20 You'll leave your worthy father broken-hearted.
MARIANE. I think . . .
MADAME PERNELLE. And you, his sister, seem so pure,
So shy, so innocent, and so demure.
But you know what they say about still waters.
I pity parents with secretive daughters.

ELMIRE. Now, Mother . . .
25 **MADAME PERNELLE.** And as for you, child, let me add
That your behavior is extremely bad,
And a poor example for these children, too.
Their dear, dead mother did far better than you.
You're much too free with money, and I'm distressed
30 To see you so elaborately dressed.
When it's one's husband that one aims to please,
One has no need of costly fripperies.
CLÉANTE. Oh, Madam, really . . .
MADAME PERNELLE. You are her brother, Sir,
And I respect and love you; yet if I were
35 My son, this lady's good and pious spouse,
I wouldn't make you welcome in my house.
You're full of worldly counsels which, I fear,
Aren't suitable for decent folk to hear.
I've spoken bluntly, Sir; but it behooves us
40 Not to mince words when righteous fervor moves us.
DAMIS. Your man Tartuffe is full of holy speeches . . .
MADAME PERNELLE. And practices precisely what he preaches.
He's a fine man, and should be listened to.
I will not hear him mocked by fools like you.
45 **DAMIS.** Good God! Do you expect me to submit
To the tyranny of that carping hypocrite?
Must we forgo all joys and satisfactions
Because that bigot censures all our actions?
DORINE. To hear him talk—and he talks all the time—
50 There's nothing one can do that's not a crime.
He rails at everything, your dear Tartuffe.
MADAME PERNELLE. Whatever he reproves deserves reproof.

He's out to save your souls, and all of you
Must love him, as my son would have you do.

55 DAMIS. Ah no, Grandmother, I could never take
To such a rascal, even for my father's sake.
That's how I feel, and I shall not dissemble.
His every action makes me seethe and tremble
With helpless anger, and I have no doubt
60 That he and I will shortly have it out.

DORINE. Surely it is a shame and a disgrace
To see this man usurp the master's place—
To see this beggar who, when first he came,
Had not a shoe or shoestring to his name
65 So far forget himself that he behaves
As if the house were his, and we his slaves.

MADAME PERNELLE. Well, mark my words, your
souls would fare far better
If you obeyed his precepts to the letter.

DORINE. You see him as a saint. I'm far less awed;
70 In fact, I see right through him. He's a fraud.

MADAME PERNELLE. Nonsense!

DORINE. His man Laurent's the same, or worse;
I'd not trust either with a penny purse.

MADAME PERNELLE. I can't say what his servant's
morals may be;
His own great goodness I can guarantee.
75 You all regard him with distaste and fear
Because he tells you what you're loath to hear,
Condemns your sins, points out your moral
flaws,
And humbly strives to further Heaven's cause.

DORINE. If sin is all that bothers him, why is it
80 He's so upset when folk drop in to visit?
Is Heaven so outraged by a social call
That he must prophesy against us all?
I'll tell you what I think: if you ask me,
He's jealous of my mistress' company.

85 MADAME PERNELLE. Rubbish! (*To* ELMIRE.) He's
not alone, child, in complaining
Of all your promiscuous entertaining.
Why, the whole neighborhood's upset, I know,
By all these carriages that come and go,
With crowds of guests parading in and out
90 And noisy servants loitering about.
In all of this, I'm sure there's nothing vicious;
But why give people cause to be suspicious?

CLÉANTE. They need no cause; they'll talk in any
case.

Madam, this world would be a joyless place
95 If, fearing what malicious tongues might say,
We locked our doors and turned our friends
away.
And even if one did so dreary a thing,
D'you think those tongues would cease their
chattering?
One can't fight slander; it's a losing battle;
100 Let us instead ignore their tittle-tattle.
Let's strive to live by conscience' clear decrees,
And let the gossips gossip as they please.

DORINE. If there is talk against us, I know the
source:
It's Daphne and her little husband, of course.
105 Those who have greatest cause for guilt and
shame
Are quickest to besmirch a neighbor's name.
When there's a chance for libel, they never
miss it;
When something can be made to seem illicit
They're off at once to spread the joyous news,
110 Adding to fact what fantasies they choose.
By talking up their neighbor's indiscretions
They seek to camouflage their own transgres-
sions,
Hoping that others' innocent affairs
Will lend a hue of innocence to theirs,
115 Or that their own black guilt will come to seem
Part of a general shady color-scheme.

MADAME PERNELLE. All that is quite irrelevant.
I doubt
That anyone's more virtuous and devout
Than dear Orante; and I'm informed that she
120 Condemns your mode of life most vehemently.

DORINE. Oh, yes, she's strict, devout, and has no
taint
Of worldliness; in short, she seems a saint.
But it was time which taught her that disguise;
She's thus because she can't be otherwise.
125 So long as her attractions could enthrall,
She flounced and flirted and enjoyed it all,
But now that they're no longer what they were
She quits a world which fast is quitting her,
And wears a veil of virtue to conceal
130 Her bankrupt beauty and her lost appeal.
That's what becomes of old coquettes today:
Distressed when all their lovers fall away,

Scene from a 1986 production of *Tartuffe* staged at the University of Chicago's Court Theater.

They see no recourse but to play the prude,
And so confer a style on solitude.
135 Thereafter, they're severe with everyone,
Condemning all our actions, pardoning none,
And claiming to be pure, austere, and zealous
When, if the truth were known, they're merely jealous,
And cannot bear to see another know
140 The pleasures time has forced them to forgo.
MADAME PERNELLE (*initially to* ELMIRE). That
    sort of talk is what you like to hear;
Therefore you'd have us all keep still, my dear,
While Madam rattles on the livelong day.
Nevertheless, I mean to have my say.
145 I tell you that you're blest to have Tartuffe
Dwelling, as my son's guest, beneath this roof;
That Heaven has sent him to forestall its wrath
By leading you, once more, to the true path;
That all he reprehends is reprehensible,
150 And that you'd better heed him, and be sensi-
    ble.
These visits, balls, and parties in which you
    revel

Are nothing but inventions of the Devil.
One never hears a word that's edifying:
Nothing but chaff and foolishness and lying,
155 As well as vicious gossip in which one's neighbor
Is cut to bits with épée, foil, and saber.
People of sense are driven half-insane
At such affairs, where noise and folly reign
And reputations perish thick and fast.
160 As a wise preacher said on Sunday last,
Parties are Towers of Babylon,[1] because
The guests all babble on with never a pause;
And then he told a story which, I think . . .
(*To* CLÉANTE.)
    I heard that laugh, Sir, and I saw that wink!
165 Go find your silly friends and laugh some more!
Enough; I'm going; don't show me to the door.
I leave this household much dismayed and
    vexed;

---

1. *Babylon,* a reference to the Biblical story in which God makes the Babylonians speak a number of different languages as punishment for their pride in trying to build a tower to reach heaven. (Genesis 11: 4–9)

I cannot say when I shall see you next.
(*Slapping* FLIPOTE.)
Wake, don't stand there gaping into space!
170　I'll slap some sense into that stupid face.
Move, move, you slut.

SCENE 2.
CLÉANTE, DORINE.

CLÉANTE.　　　　　　　I think I'll stay behind;
I want no further pieces of her mind.
How that old lady . . .
DORINE.　　　　　　Oh, what wouldn't
she say
If she could hear you speak of her that way!
175　She'd thank you for the *lady*, but I'm sure
She'd find the *old* a little premature.
CLÉANTE. My, what a scene she made, and what
a din!
And how this man Tartuffe has taken her in!
DORINE. Yes, but her son is even worse deceived;
180　His folly must be seen to be believed.
In the late troubles, he played an able part
And served his king with wise and loyal heart,[2]
But he's quite lost his senses since he fell
Beneath Tartuffe's infatuating spell.
185　He calls him brother, and loves him as his life,
Preferring him to mother, child, or wife.
In him and him alone will he confide;
He's made him his confessor and his guide;
He pets and pampers him with love more tender
190　Than any pretty mistress could engender,
Gives him the place of honor when they dine,
Delights to see him gorging like a swine.
Stuffs him with dainties till his guts distend,
And when he belches, cries "God bless you,
friend!"
195　In short, he's mad; he worships him; he dotes;
His deeds he marvels at, his words he quotes,
Thinking each act a miracle, each word
Oracular as those that Moses heard.
Tartuffe, much pleased to find so easy a victim,
200　Has in a hundred ways beguiled and tricked
him,
Milked him of money, and with his permission
Established here a sort of Inquisition.

Even Laurent, his lackey, dares to give
Us arrogant advice on how to live;
205　He sermonizes us in thundering tones
And confiscates our ribbons and colognes.
Last week he tore a kerchief into pieces
Because he found it pressed in a *Life of Jesus:*
He said it was a sin to juxtapose
210　Unholy vanities and holy prose.

SCENE 3.
ELMIRE, MARIANE, DAMIS, CLÉANTE, DORINE.

ELMIRE (*to* CLÉANTE). You did well not to follow;
she stood in the door
And said *verbatim* all she'd said before.
I saw my husband coming. I think I'd best
Go upstairs now, and take a little rest.
215　**CLÉANTE.** I'll wait and greet him here; then I
must go.
I've really only time to say hello.
DAMIS. Sound him about my sister's wedding,
please.
I think Tartuffe's against it, and that he's
Been urging Father to withdraw his blessing.
220　As you well know, I'd find that most distressing.
Unless my sister and Valère can marry,
My hopes to wed *his* sister will miscarry,
And I'm determined . . .
DORINE.　　　　　　He's coming.

SCENE 4.
ORGON, CLÉANTE, DORINE.

ORGON.　　　　　　Ah, Brother, good-day.
CLÉANTE. Well, welcome back. I'm sorry I can't
stay.
225　How was the country? Blooming, I trust, and
green?
ORGON. Excuse me, Brother; just one moment.
(*To* DORINE.)
Dorine . . .

---

2. *late troubles . . . heart.* This and later references indicate that there has been civil strife in the kingdom. The king is Louis XIV.

(To CLÉANTE.)

To put my mind at rest, I always learn
The household news the moment I return.

(To DORINE.)

Has all been well, these two days I've been gone?
230 How are the family? What's been going on?

DORINE. Your wife, two days ago, had a bad fever,
And a fierce headache which refused to leave
her.

ORGON. Ah. And Tartuffe?

DORINE.   Tartuffe?
Why, he's round and red,
Bursting with health, and excellently fed.

235 ORGON. Poor fellow!

DORINE.   That night, the mistress was
unable
To take a single bite at the dinner-table.
Her headache-pains, she said, were simply
hellish.

ORGON. Ah. And Tartuffe?

DORINE.   He ate his meal with
relish,
And zealously devoured in her presence
240 A leg of mutton and a brace of pheasants.

ORGON. Poor fellow!

DORINE.   Well, the pains continued
strong,
And so she tossed and tossed the whole night
long,
Now icy-cold, now burning like a flame.
We sat beside her bed till morning came.

245 ORGON. Ah. And Tartuffe?

DORINE.   Why, having eaten,
he rose
And sought his room, already in a doze,
Got into his warm bed, and snored away
In perfect peace until the break of day.

ORGON. Poor fellow!

DORINE.   After much ado, we talked
her
250 Into dispatching someone for the doctor.
He bled her, and the fever quickly fell.

ORGON. Ah. And Tartuffe?

DORINE.   He bore it very well.
To keep his cheerfulness at any cost,
And make up for the blood *Madame* had lost,
255 He drank, at lunch, four beakers full of port.

ORGON. Poor fellow!

DORINE.   Both are doing well, in short.
I'll go and tell *Madame* that you've expressed
Keen sympathy and anxious interest.

SCENE 5.

ORGON, CLÉANTE.

CLÉANTE. That girl was laughing in your face, and
though
260 I've no wish to offend you, even so
I'm bound to say that she had some excuse.
How can you possibly be such a goose?
Are you so dazed by this man's hocus-pocus
That all the world, save him, is out of focus?
265 You've given him clothing, shelter, food, and
care;
Why must you also . . .

ORGON.   Brother, stop right there.
You do not know the man of whom you speak.

CLÉANTE. I grant you that. But my judgment's
not so weak
That I can't tell, by his effect on others . . .

270 ORGON. Ah, when you meet him, you two will be
like brothers!
There's been no loftier soul since time began.
He is a man who . . . a man who . . . an
excellent man.
To keep his precepts is to be reborn.
And view this dunghill of a world with scorn.
275 Yes, thanks to him I'm a changed man indeed.
Under his tutelage my soul's been freed
From earthly loves, and every human tie:
My mother, children, brother, and wife could
die,
And I'd not feel a single moment's pain.

280 CLÉANTE. That's a fine sentiment, Brother; most
humane.

ORGON. Oh, had you seen Tartuffe as I first knew
him,
Your heart, like mine, would have surrendered
to him.
He used to come into our church each day
And humbly kneel nearby, and start to pray.
285 He'd draw the eyes of everybody there
By the deep fervor of his heartfelt prayer:

He'd sigh and weep, and sometimes with a
   sound
Of rapture he would bend and kiss the ground;   330
And when I rose to go, he'd run before
290 To offer me holy-water at the door.
His serving-man, no less devout than he,
Informed me of his master's poverty;
I gave him gifts, but in his humbleness   335
He'd beg me every time to give him less.
295 "Oh, that's too much," he'd cry, "too much by
   twice!
I don't deserve it. The half, Sir, would suffice."
And when I wouldn't take it back, he'd share
Half of it with the poor, right then and there.   340
At length, Heaven prompted me to take him in
300 To dwell with us, and free our souls from sin.
He guides our lives, and to protect our honor
Stays by my wife, and keeps an eye upon her;
He tells me whom she sees, and all she does,   345
And seems more jealous than I ever was!
305 And how austere he is! Why, he can detect
A mortal sin where you would least suspect;
In smallest trifles, he's extremely strict.
Last week, his conscience was severely pricked
Because, while praying, he had caught a flea   350
310 And killed it, so he felt, too wrathfully.
   CLÉANTE. Good God, man! Have you lost your
   common sense—
Or is this all some joke at my expense?
How can you stand there and in all sobriety . . .   355
   ORGON. Brother, your language savors of impiety.
315 Too much free-thinking's made your faith
   unsteady,
And as I've warned you many times already,
'Twill get you into trouble before you're   360
   through.
   CLÉANTE. So I've been told before by dupes like
   you:
Being blind, you'd have all others blind as well;
320 The clear-eyed man you call an infidel,
And he who sees through humbug and pretense
Is charged, by you, with want of reverence.
Spare me your warnings, Brother; I have no fear
Of speaking out, for you and Heaven to hear,
325 Against affected zeal and pious knavery.
There's true and false in piety, as in bravery,
And just as those whose courage shines the most

In battle, are the least inclined to boast,
So those whose hearts are truly pure and lowly
330 Don't make a flashy show of being holy.
There's a vast difference, so it seems to me.
Between true piety and hypocrisy:
How do you fail to see it, may I ask?
Is not a face quite different from a mask?
335 Cannot sincerity and cunning art,
Reality and semblance, be told apart?
Are scarecrows just like men, and do you hold
That a false coin is just as good as gold?
Ah, Brother, man's a strangely fashioned crea-
   ture
340 Who seldom is content to follow Nature,
But recklessly pursues his inclination
Beyond the narrow bounds of moderation,
And often, by transgressing Reason's laws,[3]
Perverts a lofty aim or noble cause.
345 A passing obversation, but it applies.
   ORGON. I see, dear Brother, that you're pro-
   foundly wise;
You harbor all the insight of the age.
You are our one clear mind, our only sage,
The era's oracle, its Cato[4] too.
350 And all mankind are fools compared to you.
   CLÉANTE. Brother, I don't pretend to be a sage,
Nor have I all the wisdom of the age.
There's just one insight I would dare to claim:
I know that true and false are not the same;
355 And just as there is nothing I more revere
Than a soul whose faith is steadfast and sincere,
Nothing that I more cherish and admire
Than honest zeal and true religious fire,
So there is nothing that I find more base
360 Than specious piety's dishonest face—
Than these bold mountebanks, these histrios
Whose impious mummeries and hollow shows
Exploit our love of Heaven, and make a jest
Of all that men think holiest and best;
365 These calculating souls who offer prayers

---

3. *to follow Nature . . . by transgressing Reason's laws.*
These lines reflect the strong belief in the order of the natural world prevalent during the seventeenth and eighteenth
centuries: man could perceive this order through reason
and find virtue and happiness in following it.
4. *Cato*, refers to Marcus Porcius Cato (95–46 B.C.), Roman statesman, soldier, and Stoic philosopher, famous for
his honesty and integrity.

Not to their Maker, but as public wares,
And seek to buy respect and reputation
With lifted eyes and sighs of exaltation;
These charlatans, I say, whose pilgrim souls
Proceed, by way of Heaven, toward earthly
    goals,
Who weep and pray and swindle and extort,
Who preach the monkish life, but haunt the
    court,
Who make their zeal the partner of their vice—
Such men are vengeful, sly, and cold as ice,
And when there is an enemy to defame
They cloak their spite in fair religion's name,
Their private spleen and malice being made
To seem a high and virtuous crusade,
Until, to mankind's reverent applause,
They crucify their foe in Heaven's cause.
Such knaves are all too comon; yet, for the wise,
True piety isn't hard to recognize,
And, happily, these present times provide us
With bright examples to instruct and guide us.
Consider Ariston and Périandre;
Look at Oronte, Alcidamas, Clitandre;
Their virtue is acknowledged; who could
    doubt it?
But you won't hear them beat the drum
    about it.
They're never ostentatious, never vain,
And their religion's moderate and humane;
It's not their way to criticize and chide:
They think censoriousness a mark of pride,
And therefore, letting others preach and rave,
They show, by deeds, how Christians should
    behave.
They think no evil of their fellow man,
But judge of him as kindly as they can.
They don't intrigue and wangle and conspire;
To lead a good life is their one desire;
The sinner wakes no rancorous hate in them;
It is the sin alone which they condemn;
Nor do they try to show a fiercer zeal
For Heaven's cause than Heaven itself could
    feel.
These men I honor, these men I advocate
As models for us all to emulate.
Your man is not their sort at all, I fear:
And, while your praise of him is quite sincere,

I think that you've been dreadfully deluded.
ORGON. Now then, dear Brother, is your speech
    concluded?
CLÉANTE. Why, yes.
ORGON.   Your servant, Sir.
(He turns to go.)
CLÉANTE.   No, Brother; wait.
    There's one more matter. You agreed of late
    That young Valére might have your daughter's
    hand.
ORGON. I did.
CLÉANTE.   And set the date, I understand.
ORGON. Quite so.
CLÉANTE.   You've now postponed it; is that
    true?
ORGON. No doubt.
CLÉANTE.   The match no longer pleases
    you?
ORGON. Who knows?
CLÉANTE.   D'you mean to go back on
    your word?
ORGON. I won't say that.
CLÉANTE.   Has anything occurred
    Which might entitle you to break your pledge?
ORGON. Perhaps.
CLÉANTE.   Why must you hem, and haw,
    and hedge?
    The boy asked me to sound you in this
    affair . . .
ORGON. It's been a pleasure.
CLÉANTE.   But what shall I tell
    Valére?
ORGON. Whatever you like.
CLÉANTE.   But what have you
    decided?
    What are your plans?
ORGON.   I plan, Sir, to be guided
    By Heaven's will.
CLÉANTE.   Come, Brother, don't talk rot.
    You've given Valére your word; will you keep
    it, or not?
ORGON. Good day.
CLÉANTE.   This looks like poor Valére's
    undoing;
    I'll go and warn him that there's trouble brew-
    ing.
                                        CURTAIN

ACT TWO

SCENE 1.

ORGON, MARIANE.

ORGON. Mariane.
MARIANE.   Yes, Father?
ORGON.   A word with you;
     come here.
MARIANE. What are you looking for?
ORGON (*peering into a small closet*).
                         Eavesdroppers, dear.
     I'm making sure we shan't be overheard.
     Someone in there could catch our every word.
5   Ah, good, we're safe. Now, Mariane, my child,
     You're a sweet girl who's tractable and mild,
     Whom I hold dear, and think most highly of.
MARIANE. I'm deeply grateful, Father, for your
     love.
ORGON. That's well said, Daughter; and you can
     repay me
10   If, in all things, you'll cheerfully obey me.
MARIANE. To please you, Sir, is what delights me
     best.
ORGON. Good, good. Now, what d'you think of
     Tartuffe, our guest?
MARIANE. I, Sir?
ORGON.   Yes. Weigh your answer; think it
     through.
MARIANE. Oh, dear. I'll say whatever you wish
     me to.
15 ORGON. That's wisely said, my Daughter. Say of
     him, then,
     That he's the very worthiest of men,
     And that you're fond of him, and would rejoice
     In being his wife, if that should be my choice.
     Well?
MARIANE. What?
ORGON.   What's that?
MARIANE.   I . . .
ORGON.   Well?
MARIANE.   Forgive me, pray.
20 ORGON. Did you not hear me?
MARIANE.   Of *whom*, Sir, must
     I say

That I am fond of him, and would rejoice
In being his wife, if that should be your choice?
ORGON. Why, of Tartuffe.
MARIANE.   But, Father, that's false,
     you know.
Why would you have me say what isn't so?
25 ORGON. Because I am resolved it shall be true.
     That it's my wish should be enough for you.
MARIANE. You can't mean, Father . . .
ORGON.   Yes, Tartuffe shall be
     Allied by marriage to this family,
     And he's to be your husband, is that clear?
     It's a father's privilege . . .

SCENE 2.

DORINE, ORGON, MARIANE.

30 ORGON (*to* DORINE).   What are you doing
     in here?
     Is curiosity so fierce a passion
     With you, that you must eavesdrop in this
     fashion?
DORINE. There's lately been a rumor going
     about—
     Based on some hunch or chance remark, no
     doubt—
35   That you mean Mariane to wed Tartuffe.
     I've laughed it off, of course, as just a spoof.
ORGON. You find it so incredible?
DORINE.   Yes, I do.
     I won't accept that story, even from you.
ORGON. Well, you'll believe it when the thing is
     done.
40 DORINE. Yes, yes, of course. Go on and have your
     fun.
ORGON. I've never been more serious in my life.
DORINE. Ha!
ORGON.   Daughter, I mean it; you're to be his
     wife.
DORINE. No, don't believe your father; it's all a
     hoax.
ORGON. See here, young woman . . .

DORINE.   Come, Sir, no more jokes;
45 You can't fool us.
    ORGON.   How dare you talk that way?
    DORINE. All right, then: we believe you, sad to
        say.
    But how a man like you, who looks so wise
    And wears a moustache of such splendid size,
    Can be so foolish as to . . .
    ORGON.   Silence, please!
50 My girl, you take too many liberties.
    I'm master here, as you must not forget.
    DORINE. Do let's discuss this calmly; don't be
        upset.
    You can't be serious, Sir, about this plan.
    What should that bigot want with Mariane?
55 Praying and fasting ought to keep him busy.
    And then, in terms of wealth and rank, what
        is he?
    Why should a man of property like you
    Pick out a beggar son-in-law?
    ORGON.   That will do.
    Speak of his poverty with reverence.
60 His is a pure and saintly indigence
    Which far transcends all worldly pride and pelf.
    He lost his fortune, as he says himself,
    Because he cared for Heaven alone, and so
    Was careless of his interests here below.
65 I mean to get him out of his present straits
    And help him to recover his estates—
    Which, in his part of the world, have no small
        fame.
    Poor though he is, he's a gentleman just the
        same.
    DORINE. Yes, so he tells us; and, Sir, it seems
        to me
70 Such pride goes very ill with piety.
    A man whose spirit spurns this dungy earth
    Ought not to brag of lands and noble birth;
    Such worldly arrogance will hardly square
    With meek devotion and the life of prayer.
75 . . . But this approach, I see, has drawn a
        blank;
    Let's speak, then, of his person, not his rank.
    Doesn't it seem to you a trifle grim
    To give a girl like her to a man like him?
    When two are so ill-suited, can't you see
80 What the sad consequence is bound to be?

A young girl's virtue is imperilled, Sir,
When such a marriage is imposed on her;
For if one's bridegroom isn't to one's taste,
It's hardly an inducement to be chaste,
85 And many a man with horns[1] upon his brow
Has made his wife the thing that she is now.
It's hard to be a faithful wife, in short,
To certain husbands of a certain sort,
And he who gives his daughter to a man she
    hates
90 Must answer for her sins at Heaven's gates.
Think, Sir, before you play so risky a role.
ORGON. This servant-girl presumes to save my
    soul!
DORINE. You would do well to ponder what I've
    said.
ORGON. Daughter, we'll disregard this dunder-
    head.
95 Just trust your father's judgment. Oh, I'm
    aware
That I once promised you to young Valère;
But now I hear he gambles, which greatly
    shocks me;
What's more, I've doubts about his orthodoxy.
His visits to church, I note, are very few.
100 DORINE. Would you have him go at the same hours
    as you,
And kneel nearby, to be sure of being seen?
ORGON. I can dispense with such remarks,
    Dorine.
(To MARIANE.)
Tartuffe, however, is sure of Heaven's blessing,
And that's the only treasure worth possessing.
105 This match will bring you joys beyond all mea-
    sure;
Your cup will overflow with every pleasure;
You two will interchange your faithful loves
Like two sweet cherubs, or two turtledoves.
No harsh word shall be heard, no frown be seen,
110 And he shall make you happy as a queen.
DORINE. And she'll make him a cuckold, just wait
    and see.
ORGON. What language!
DORINE.   Oh, he's a man of destiny;

---

1. **horns**, a medieval symbol for a husband with an unfaithful wife.

He's *made* for horns, and what the stars demand
Your daughter's virtue surely can't withstand.

115 ORGON. Don't interrupt me further. Why can't you learn

That certain things are none of your concern?

DORINE. It's for your own sake that I interfere.

(*She repeatedly interrupts* ORGON *just as he is turning to speak to his daughter.*)

ORGON. Most kind of you. Now, hold your tongue, d'you hear?

DORINE. If I didn't love you . . .

ORGON.   Spare me your affection.

120 DORINE. I'll love you, Sir, in spite of your objection.

ORGON. Blast!

DORINE.   I can't bear, Sir, for your honor's sake,

To let you make this ludicrous mistake.

ORGON. You mean to go on talking?

DORINE.   If I didn't protest

This sinful marriage, my conscience couldn't rest.

125 ORGON. If you don't hold your tongue, you little shrew . . .

DORINE. What, lost your temper? A pious man like you?

ORGON. Yes! Yes! You talk and talk. I'm maddened by it.

Once and for all, I tell you to be quiet.

DORINE. Well, I'll be quiet. But I'll be thinking hard.

130 ORGON. Think all you like, but you had better guard

That saucy tongue of yours, or I'll . . .

(*Turning back to* MARIANE.)

                         Now, child.

I've weighed this matter fully.

DORINE (*aside*).   It drives me wild

That I can't speak.

(ORGON *turns his head, and she is silent.*)

ORGON.   Tartuffe is no young dandy.

But, still his person . . .

DORINE (*aside*).   Is as sweet as candy.

135 ORGON. Is such that, even if you shouldn't care

For his other merits . . .

(*He turns and stands facing* DORINE, *arms crossed.*)

DORINE (*aside*).   They'll make a lovely pair.

If I were she, no man would marry me

Against my inclination, and go scot-free.

He'd learn, before the wedding-day was over,

140 How readily a wife can find a lover.

ORGON (*to* DORINE). It seems you treat my orders as a joke.

DORINE. Why, what's the matter? 'Twas not to you I spoke.

ORGON. What *were* you doing?

DORINE.   Talking to myself, that's all.

ORGON. Ah! (*Aside.*) One more bit of impudence and gall,

145 And I shall give her a good slap in the face.

(*He puts himself in a position to slap her;* DORINE, *whenever he glances at her, stands immobile and silent.*)

Daughter, you shall accept, and with good grace,

The husband I've selected . . . Your wedding-day . . .

(*To* DORINE.)

Why don't you talk to yourself?

DORINE.   I've nothing to say.

ORGON. Come, just one word.

DORINE.   No thank you, Sir. I pass.

150 ORGON. Come, speak; I'm waiting.

DORINE.   I'd not be such an ass.

ORGON (*turning to* MARIANE). In short, dear Daughter, I mean to be obeyed,

And you must bow to the sound choice I've made.

DORINE (*moving away*). I'd not wed such a monster, even in jest.

(ORGON *attempts to slap her, but misses.*)

ORGON. Daughter, that maid of yours is a thorough pest;

155 She makes me sinfully annoyed and nettled.

I can't speak further; my nerves are too unsettled.

She's so upset me by her insolent talk,

I'll calm myself by going for a walk.

SCENE 3.

DORINE, MARIANE.

DORINE (*returning*). Well, have you lost your
tongue, girl? Must I play
160 Your part, and say the lines you ought to say?
Faced with a fate so hideous and absurd,
Can you not utter one dissenting word?

MARIANE. What good would it do? A father's
power is great.

DORINE. Resist him now, or it will be too late.

165 **MARIANE.** But . . .

DORINE. Tell him one cannot love at a
father's whim;
That you shall marry for yourself, not him;
That since it's you who are to be the bride,
It's you, not he, who must be satisfied;
And that if his Tartuffe is so sublime,
170 He's free to marry him at any time.

MARIANE. I've bowed so long to Father's strict
control,
I couldn't oppose him now, to save my soul.

DORINE. Come, come, Mariane. Do listen to reason, won't you?
Valère has asked your hand. Do you love him,
or don't you?

175 **MARIANE.** Oh, how unjust of you! What can you
mean
By asking such a question, dear Dorine?
You know the depth of my affection for him;
I've told you a hundred times how I adore him.

DORINE. I don't believe in everything I hear;
180 Who knows if your professions were sincere?

MARIANE. They were, Dorine, and you do me
wrong to doubt it;
Heaven knows that I've been all too frank about
it.

DORINE. You love him, then?

MARIANE. Oh, more than I can
express.

DORINE. And he, I take it, cares for you no less?

185 **MARIANE.** I think so.

DORINE. And you both, with equal
fire,
Burn to be married?

MARIANE. That is our one desire.

DORINE. What of Tartuffe, then? What of your
father's plan?

MARIANE. I'll kill myself, if I'm forced to wed that
man.

DORINE. I hadn't thought of that recourse. How
splendid!
190 Just die, and all your troubles will be ended!
A fine solution. Oh, it maddens me
To hear you talk in that self-pitying key.

MARIANE. Dorine, how harsh you are! It's most
unfair.
You have no sympathy for my despair.

195 **DORINE.** I've none at all for people who talk drivel
And, faced with difficulties, whine and snivel.

MARIANE. No doubt I'm timid, but it would be
wrong . . .

DORINE. True love requires a heart that's firm and
strong.

MARIANE. I'm strong in my affection for Valère,
200 But coping with my father is his affair.

DORINE. But if your father's brain has grown so
cracked
Over his dear Tartuffe that he can retract
His blessing, though your wedding-day was
named,
It's surely not Valère who's to be blamed.

205 **MARIANE.** If I defied my father, as you suggest,
Would it not seem unmaidenly, at best?
Shall I defend my love at the expense
Of brazenness and disobedience?
Shall I parade my heart's desires, and
flaunt . . .

210 **DORINE.** No, I ask nothing of you. Clearly you
want
To be Madame Tartuffe, and I feel bound
Not to oppose a wish so very sound.
What right have I to criticize the match?
Indeed, my dear, the man's a brilliant catch.
215 Monsieur Tartuffe! Now, there's a man of
weight!
Yes, yes, Monsieur Tartuffe, I'm bound to
state,
Is quite a person; that's not to be denied;
'Twill be no little thing to be his bride.
The world already rings with his renown;
220 He's a great noble—in his native town;

His ears are red, he has a pink complexion,
And all in all, he'll suit you to perfection.

MARIANE. Dear God!

DORINE.　　　　　　Oh, how triumphant you
　　will feel
At having caught a husband so ideal!

225 MARIANE. Oh, do stop teasing, and use your clev-
　　erness
To get me out of this appalling mess.
Advise me, and I'll do whatever you say.

DORINE. Ah no, a dutiful daughter must obey
Her father, even if he weds her to an ape.

230　You've a bright future; why struggle to escape?
Tartuffe will take you back where his family
　　lives,
To a small town aswarm with relatives—
Uncles and cousins whom you'll be charmed to
　　meet.
You'll be received at once by the elite,

235　Calling upon the bailiff's wife, no less—
Even, perhaps, upon the mayoress,
Who'll sit you down in the *best* kitchen chair.
Then, once a year, you'll dance at the village
　　fair
To the drone of bagpipes—two of them, in
　　fact—

240　And see a puppet-show, or an animal act.
Your husband . . .

MARIANE.　　　　　Oh, you turn my blood to
　　ice!
Stop torturing me, and give me your advice.

DORINE (*threatening to go*). Your servant, Madam.

MARIANE.　　　　　Dorine, I beg of you . . .

DORINE. No, you deserve it; this marriage must
　　go through.

245 MARIANE. Dorine!

DORINE.　　　　No.

MARIANE.　　　　　Not Tartuffe! You know I
　　think him . . .

DORINE. Tartuffe's your cup of tea, and you shall
　　drink him.

MARIANE. I've always told you everything, and
　　relied . . .

DORINE. No. You deserve to be tartuffified.

MARIANE. Well, since you mock me and refuse to
　　care,

250　I'll henceforth seek my solace in despair:

Despair shall be my counsellor and friend,
And help me bring my sorrows to an end.

(*She starts to leave.*)

DORINE. There now, come back; my anger has
　　subsided.
You do deserve some pity, I've decided.

255 MARIANE. Dorine, if Father makes me undergo
This dreadful martyrdom, I'll die, I know.

DORINE. Don't fret; it won't be difficult to dis-
　　cover
Some plan of action . . . But here's Valère,
　　your lover.

SCENE 4.

VALÈRE, MARIANE, DORINE.

VALÈRE. Madam, I've just received some won-
　　drous news

260　Regarding which I'd like to hear your views.

MARIANE. What news?

VALÈRE.　　　　　You're marrying Tartuffe.

MARIANE.　　　　　　　　　　　I find
That Father does have such a match in mind.

VALÈRE. Your father, Madam . . .

MARIANE.　　　　　. . . has just this minute said
That it's Tartuffe he wishes me to wed.

265 VALÈRE. Can he be serious?

MARIANE.　　　　　　Oh, indeed he can;
He's clearly set his heart upon the plan.

VALÈRE. And what position do you propose to
　　take,
Madam?

MARIANE. Why—I don't know.

VALÈRE.　　　　　　For heaven's sake—
You don't know?

MARIANE.　　　No.

VALÈRE.　　　　　Well, well!

MARIANE.　　　　　　　　　Advise me, do.

270 VALÈRE. Marry the man. That's my advice to you.

MARIANE. That's your advice?

VALÈRE.　　　　　　Yes.

MARIANE.　　　　　　　　Truly?

VALÈRE.　　　　　　　　　　Oh, abso-
　　lutely.
You couldn't choose more wisely, more
　　astutely.

Scene from a 1986 production of *Tartuffe* staged at the University of Chicago's Court Theater.

MARIANE. Thanks for this counsel; I'll follow it, of course.

VALÈRE. Do, do; I'm sure 'twill cost you no remorse.

275 MARIANE. To give it didn't cause your heart to break.

VALÈRE. I gave it, Madam, only for your sake.

MARIANE. And it's for your sake that I take it, Sir.

DORINE (*withdrawing to the rear of the stage*). Let's see which fool will prove the stubborner.

VALÈRE. So! I am nothing to you, and it was flat
280 Deception when you . . .

MARIANE.   Please, enough of that.
You've told me plainly that I should agree
To wed the man my father's chosen for me,

And since you've deigned to counsel me so wisely,
I promise, Sir, to do as you advise me.

285 VALÈRE. Ah, no, 'twas not by me that you were swayed.
No, your decision was already made;
Though now, to save appearances, you protest
That you're betraying me at my behest.

MARIANE. Just as you say.

VALÈRE.   Quite so. And I now see
290 That you were never truly in love with me.

MARIANE. Alas, you're free to think so if you choose.

VALÈRE. I choose to think so, and here's a bit of news:

You've spurned my hand, but I know where to
turn
For kinder treatment, as you shall quickly learn.
295 MARIANE. I'm sure you do. Your noble qualities
Inspire affection . . .
VALÈRE.   Forget my qualities,
please.
They don't inspire you overmuch, I find.
But there's another lady I have in mind
Whose sweet and generous nature will not scorn
300 To compensate me for the loss I've borne.
MARIANE. I'm no great loss, and I'm sure that
you'll transfer
Your heart quite painlessly from me to her.
VALÈRE. I'll do my best to take it in my stride.
The pain I feel at being cast aside
305 Time and forgetfulness may put an end to.
Or if I can't forget, I shall pretend to.
No self-respecting person is expected
To go on loving once he's been rejected.
MARIANE. Now, that's a fine, high-minded senti-
ment.
310 VALÈRE. One to which any sane man would assent.
Would you prefer it if I pined away
In hopeless passion till my dying day?
Am I to yield you to a rival's arms
And not console myself with other charms?
315 MARIANE. Go then: console yourself; don't hesi-
tate.
I wish you to; indeed, I cannot wait.
VALÈRE. You wish me to?
MARIANE.   Yes.
VALÈRE.   That's the final straw.
Madame, farewell. Your wish shall be my law.
(He starts to leave, and then returns: this repeatedly.)
MARIANE. Splendid.
VALÈRE (coming back again). This breach, remem-
ber, is of your making;
320 It's you who've driven me to the step I'm taking.
MARIANE. Of course.
VALÈRE (coming back again). Remember, too, that
I am merely
Following your example.
MARIANE.   I see that clearly.
VALÈRE. Enough. I'll go and do your bidding,
then.

MARIANE. Good.
VALÈRE (coming back again). You shall never see
my face again.
325 MARIANE. Excellent.
VALÈRE (walking to the door, then turning about).
Yes?
MARIANE.   What?
VALÈRE.   What's that? What did you say?
MARIANE. Nothing. You're dreaming.
VALÈRE.   Ah. Well, I'm on my way.
Farewell, Madame. (He moves slowly away.)
MARIANE.   Farewell.
DORINE (to MARIANE).   If you ask me,
Both of you are as mad as mad can be.
Do stop this nonsense, now. I've only let you
330 Squabble so long to see where it would get you.
Whoa there, Monsieur Valère!
(She goes and seizes VALÈRE by the arm; he makes
a great show of resistance.)
VALÈRE.   What's this, Dorine?
DORINE. Come here.
VALÈRE.   No, no, my heart's too full of
spleen.
Don't hold me back; her wish must be obeyed.
DORINE. Stop!
VALÈRE.   It's too late now; my decision's
made.
335 DORINE. Oh, pooh!
MARIANE (aside).   He hates the sight of me,
that's plain.
I'll go, and so deliver him from pain.
DORINE (leaving VALÈRE, running after MARIANE).
And now you run away! Come back.
MARIANE.   No, no.
Nothing you say will keep me here. Let go!
VALÈRE (aside). She cannot bear my presence, I
perceive.
340 To spare her further torment, I shall leave.
DORINE (leaving MARIANE, running after VALÈRE).
Again! You'll not escape, Sir; don't you try it.
Come here, you two. Stop fussing and be quiet.
(She takes VALÈRE by the hand, then MARIANE, and
draws them together.)
VALÈRE (to DORINE). What do you want of me?
MARIANE (to DORINE). What is the point of this?
DORINE. We're going to have a little armistice. (To

VALÈRE.)

345   Now, weren't you silly to get so overheated?

VALÈRE. Didn't you see how badly I was treated?

DORINE (*to* MARIANE). Aren't you a simpleton, to have lost your head?

MARIANE. Didn't you hear the hateful things he said?

DORINE (*to* VALÈRE). You're both great fools. Her sole desire, Valère,

350   Is to be yours in marriage. To that I'll swear.

(*To* MARIANE.)

He loves you only, and he wants no wife
But you, Mariane. On that I'll stake my life.

MARIANE (*to* VALÈRE). Then why you advised me so, I cannot see.

VALÈRE (*to* MARIANE). On such a question, why ask advice of *me?*

355 **DORINE.** Oh, you're impossible. Give me your hands, you two.

(*To* VALÈRE.)

Yours first.

VALÈRE (*giving* DORINE *his hand*). But why?

DORINE (*to* MARIANE).   And now a hand from you.

MARIANE (*also giving* DORINE *her hand*). What are you doing?

DORINE.   There: a perfect fit.
You suit each other better than you'll admit.

(VALÈRE *and* MARIANE *hold hands for some time without looking at each other.*)

VALÈRE (*turning toward* MARIANE). Ah, come, don't be so haughty. Give a man

360   A look of kindness, won't you, Mariane?

(MARIANE *turns toward* VALÈRE *and smiles.*)

DORINE. I tell you, lovers are completely mad!

VALÈRE (*to* MARIANE). Now come, confess that you were very bad
To hurt my feelings as you did just now.
I have a just complaint, you must allow.

365 **MARIANE.** *You* must allow that you were most unpleasant . . .

DORINE. Let's table that discussion for the present;
Your father has a plan which must be stopped.

MARIANE. Advise us, then; what means must we adopt?

DORINE. We'll use all manner of means, and all at once.

(*To* MARIANE.)

370   Your father's addled; he's acting like a dunce.
Therefore you'd better humor the old fossil.
Pretend to yield to him, be sweet and docile,
And then postpone, as often as necessary,
The day on which you have agreed to marry.

375   You'll thus gain time, and time will turn the trick.
Sometimes, for instance, you'll be taken sick,
And that will seem good reason for delay;
Or some bad omen will make you change the day—
You'll dream of muddy water, or you'll pass

380   A dead man's hearse, or break a looking-glass.
If all else fails, no man can marry you
Unless you take his ring and say "I do."
But now, let's separate. If they should find
Us talking here, our plot might be divined.

(*To* VALÈRE.)

385   Go to your friends, and tell them what's occurred,
And have them urge her father to keep his word.
Meanwhile, we'll stir her brother into action,
And get Elmire, as well, to join our faction.
Good-bye.

VALÈRE (*to* MARIANE). Though each of us will do his best,

390   It's your true heart on which my hopes shall rest.

MARIANE (*to* VALÈRE). Regardless of what Father may decide,
None but Valère shall claim me as his bride.

VALÈRE. Oh, how those words content me! Come what will . . .

DORINE.   Oh, lovers, lovers! Their tongues are never still.

395   Be off, now.

VALÈRE (*turning to go, then turning back*). One last word . . .

DORINE.   No time to chat:
You leave by this door; and *you* leave by that.

(DORINE *pushes them, by the shoulders, toward opposing doors.*)

                  CURTAIN

ACT THREE

SCENE 1.

DAMIS, DORINE.

DAMIS. May lightning strike me even as I speak,
  May all men call me cowardly and weak,
  If any fear or scruple holds me back
  From settling things, at once, with that great
    quack!
5 **DORINE.** Now, don't give way to violent emotion.
  Your father's merely talked about this notion,
  And words and deeds are far from being one.
  Much that is talked about is left undone.
DAMIS. No, I must stop that scoundrel's machi-
    nations;
10   I'll go and tell him off; I'm out of patience.
DORINE. Do calm down and be practical. I had
    rather
  My mistress dealt with him—and with your
    father.
  She has some influence with Tartuffe, I've
    noted.
  He hangs upon her words, seems most devoted,
15   And may, indeed, be smitten by her charm.
  Pray Heaven it's true! 'Twould do our cause no
    harm.
  She sent for him, just now, to sound him out
  On this affair you're so incensed about;
  She'll find out where he stands, and tell him,
    too,
20   What dreadful strife and trouble will ensue
  If he lends countenance to your father's plan.
  I couldn't get in to see him, but his man
  Says that he's almost finished with his prayers.
  Go, now. I'll catch him when he comes down-
    stairs.
25 **DAMIS.** I want to hear this conference, and I will.
DORINE. No, they must be alone.
DAMIS.   Oh, I'll keep still.
DORINE. Not you. I know your temper. You'd
    start a brawl,
  And shout and stamp your foot and spoil it all.
  Go on.
DAMIS. I won't; I have a perfect right . . .

30 **DORINE.** Lord, you're a nuisance! He's coming;
    get out of sight.
(DAMIS *conceals himself in a closet at the rear of the
stage.*)

SCENE 2.

TARTUFFE, DORINE.

TARTUFFE (*observing* DORINE, *and calling to his
    manservant offstage*).
  Hang up my hair-shirt, put my scourge in place,
  And pray, Laurent, for Heaven's perpetual
    grace.
  I'm going to the prison now, to share
  My last few coins with the poor wretches there.
35 **DORINE** (*aside*). Dear God, what affectation! What
    a fake!
TARTUFFE. You wished to see me?
DORINE.   Yes . . .
TARTUFFE (*taking a handkerchief from his pocket*).
                    For mercy's sake,
  Please take this handkerchief, before you speak.
DORINE. What?
TARTUFFE.   Cover that bosom, girl. The flesh
    is weak.
  And unclean thoughts are difficult to control.
40   Such sights as that can undermine the soul.
DORINE. Your soul, it seems, has very poor de-
    fenses,
  And flesh makes quite an impact on your senses.
  It's strange that you're so easily excited;
  My own desires are not so soon ignited,
45   And if I saw you naked as a beast,
  Not all your hide would tempt me in the least.
TARTUFFE. Girl, speak more modestly; unless
    you do,
  I shall be forced to take my leave of you.
DORINE. Oh, no, it's I who must be on my way;
50   I've just one little message to convey.
  Madame is coming down, and begs you, Sir,
  To wait and have a word or two with her.
TARTUFFE. Gladly.

DORINE (aside).   *That* had a softening effect!
    I think my guess about him was correct.
55 TARTUFFE. Will she be long?
    DORINE.   No: that's her step I hear.
    Ah, here she is, and I shall disappear.

SCENE 3.

ELMIRE, TARTUFFE.

TARTUFFE. May Heaven, whose infinite goodness
    we adore.
    Preserve your body and soul forevermore,
    And bless your days, and answer thus the plea
60 Of one who is its humblest votary.
    ELMIRE. I thank you for that pious wish. But
    please,
    Do take a chair and let's be more at ease.
    (They sit down.)
    TARTUFFE. I trust that you are once more well and
    strong?
    ELMIRE. Oh, yes: the fever didn't last for long.
65 TARTUFFE. My prayers are too unworthy, I am
    sure,
    To have gained from Heaven this most gracious
    cure;
    But lately, Madam, my every supplication
    Has had for object your recuperation.
    ELMIRE. You shouldn't have troubled so. I don't
    deserve it.
70 TARTUFFE. Your health is priceless, Madam, and
    to preserve it
    I'd gladly give my own, in all sincerity.
    ELMIRE. Sir, you outdo us all in Christian charity.
    You've been most kind. I count myself your
    debtor.
    TARTUFFE. 'Twas nothing, Madam. I long to
    serve you better.
75 ELMIRE. There's a private matter I'm anxious to
    discuss.
    I'm glad there's no one here to hinder us.
    TARTUFFE. I too am glad; it floods my heart with
    bliss
    To find myself alone with you like this.
    For just this chance I've prayed with all my
    power—
80 But prayed in vain, until this happy hour.

ELMIRE. This won't take long, Sir, and I hope
    you'll be
    Entirely frank and unconstrained with me.
    TARTUFFE. Indeed, there's nothing I had
    rather do
    Than bare my inmost heart and soul to you.
85 First, let me say that what remarks I've made
    About the constant visits you are paid
    Were prompted not by any mean emotion,
    But rather by a pure and deep devotion,
    A fervent zeal . . .
    ELMIRE.   No need for explanation.
90 Your sole concern, I'm sure, was my salvation.
    TARTUFFE (*taking* ELMIRE's *hand and pressing her
    fingertips*). Quite so; and such great fervor do
    I feel . . .
    ELMIRE. Ooh! Please! You're pinching!
    TARTUFFE.   'Twas from excess of zeal.
    I never meant to cause you pain, I swear.
    I'd rather . . .
    (He places his hand on ELMIRE's *knee.)*
    ELMIRE.   What can your hand be doing there?
95 TARTUFFE. Feeling your gown; what soft, fine-
    woven stuff!
    ELMIRE. Please, I'm extremely ticklish. That's
    enough.
    (She draws her chair away; TARTUFFE *pulls his after
    her.)*
    TARTUFFE (*fondling the lace collar of her gown*).
    My, my, what lovely lacework on your dress!
    The workmanship's miraculous, no less.
    I've not seen anything to equal it.
100 ELMIRE. Yes, quite. But let's talk business for
    a bit.
    They say my husband means to break his word
    And give his daughter to you, Sir. Had you
    heard?
    TARTUFFE. He did once mention it. But I confess
    I dream of quite a different happiness.
105 It's elsewhere, Madam, that my eyes discern
    The promise of that bliss for which I yearn.
    ELMIRE. I see: you care for nothing here below.
    TARTUFFE. Ah, well—my heart's not made of
    stone, you know.
    ELMIRE. All your desires mount heavenward, I'm
    sure,
110 In scorn of all that's earthly and impure.

Scene from a 1986 production of *Tartuffe* staged
at the University of Chicago's Court Theater.

TARTUFFE. A love of heavenly beauty does not
    preclude
    A proper love for earthly pulchritude;
    Our senses are quite rightly captivated
    By perfect works our Maker has created.
115   Some glory clings to all that Heaven has made;
    In you, all Heaven's marvels are displayed.
    On that fair face, such beauties have been lav-
        ished,
    The eyes are dazzled and the heart is ravished;
    How could I look on you, O flawless creature,
120   And not adore the Author of all Nature,
    Feeling a love both passionate and pure
    For you, his triumph of self-portraiture?
    At first, I trembled lest that love should be
    A subtle snare that Hell had laid for me;
125   I vowed to flee the sight of you, eschewing
    A rapture that might prove my soul's undoing;
    But soon, fair being, I became aware
    That my deep passion could be made to square
    With rectitude, and with my bounden duty.
130   I thereupon surrendered to your beauty.
    It is, I know, presumptuous on my part

To bring you this poor offering of my heart,
And it is not my merit, Heaven knows,
But your compassion on which my hopes
    repose.
135   You are my peace, my solace, my salvation;
    On you depends my bliss—or desolation;
    I bide your judgment and, as you think best,
    I shall be either miserable or blest.
       ELMIRE. Your declaration is most gallant, Sir,
140   But don't you think it's out of character?
    You'd have done better to restrain your passion
    And think before you spoke in such a fashion.
    It ill becomes a pious man like you . . .
       TARTUFFE. I may be pious, but I'm human too:
145   With your celestial charms before his eyes,
    A man has not the power to be wise.
    I know such words sound strangely, coming
        from me,
    But I'm no angel, nor was meant to be,
    And if you blame my passion, you must needs
150   Reproach as well the charms on which it feeds.
    Your loveliness I had no sooner seen
    Than you became my soul's unrivalled queen;
    Before your seraph glance, divinely sweet,
    My heart's defenses crumbled in defeat,
155   And nothing fasting, prayer, or tears might do
    Could stay my spirit from adoring you.
    My eyes, my sighs have told you in the past
    What now my lips make bold to say at last,
    And if, in your great goodness, you will deign
160   To look upon your slave, and ease his pain,—
    If, in compassion for my soul's distress,
    You'll stoop to comfort my unworthiness,
    I'll raise to you, in thanks for that sweet manna,
    An endless hymn, an infinite hosanna.
165   With me, of course, there need be no anxiety,
    No fear of scandal or of notoriety.
    These young court gallants, whom all the ladies
        fancy,
    Are vain in speech, in action rash and chancy;
    When they succeed in love, the world soon
        knows it;
170   No favor's granted them but they disclose it
    And by the looseness of their tongues profane
    The very altar where their hearts have lain.
    Men of my sort, however, love discreetly,
    And one may trust our reticence completely.

My keen concern for my good name insures
175 The absolute security of yours;
In short, I offer you, my dear Elmire,
Love without scandal, pleasure without fear.

ELMIRE. I've heard your well-turned speeches to
the end,
180 And what you urge I clearly apprehend.
Aren't you afraid that I may take a notion
To tell my husband of your warm devotion,
And that, supposing he were duly told,
His feelings toward you might grow rather cold?

185 TARTUFFE. I know, dear lady, that your exceed-
ing charity
Will lead your heart to pardon my temerity;
That you'll excuse my violent affection
As human weakness, human imperfection;
And that—O fairest!—you will bear in mind
190 That I'm but flesh and blood, and am not blind.

ELMIRE. Some women might do otherwise, per-
haps,
But I shall be discreet about your lapse:
I'll tell my husband nothing of what's occurred
If, in return, you'll give your solemn word
195 To advocate as forcefully as you can
The marriage of Valère and Mariane,
Renouncing all desire to dispossess
Another of his rightful happiness,
And . . .

SCENE 4.

DAMIS, ELMIRE, TARTUFFE.

DAMIS (emerging from the closet where he has been
hiding). No! We'll not hush up this vile affair;
200 I heard it all inside that closet there,
Where Heaven, in order to confound the pride
Of this great rascal, prompted me to hide.
Ah, now I have my long-awaited chance
To punish his deceit and arrogance,
205 And give my father clear and shocking proof
Of the black character of his dear Tartuffe.

ELMIRE. Ah no, Damis; I'll be content if he
Will study to deserve my leniency.
I've promised silence—don't make me break my
word;
210 To make a scandal would be too absurd.

Good wives laugh off such trifles, and forget
them;
Why should they tell their husbands, and upset
them?

DAMIS. You have your reasons for taking such a
course,
And I have reasons, too, of equal force.
215 To spare him now would be insanely wrong.
I've swallowed my just wrath for far too long
And watched this insolent bigot bringing strife
And bitterness into our family life.
Too long he's meddled in my father's affairs,
220 Thwarting my marriage-hopes, and poor
Valère's.
It's high time that my father was undeceived,
And now I've proof that can't be disbelieved—
Proof that was furnished me by Heaven above.
It's too good not to take advantage of.
225 This is my chance, and I deserve to lose it
If, for one moment, I hesitate to use it.

ELMIRE. Damis . . .

DAMIS.   No, I must do what I think
right.
Madam, my heart is bursting with delight,
And, say whatever you will, I'll not consent
230 To lose the sweet revenge on which I'm bent.
I'll settle matters without more ado;
And here, most opportunely, is my cue.

SCENE 5.

ORGON, DAMIS, TARTUFFE, ELMIRE.

DAMIS. Father, I'm glad you've joined us. Let us
advise you
Of some fresh news which doubtless will sur-
prise you.
235 You've just now been repaid with interest
For all your loving-kindness to our guest.
He's proved his warm and grateful feelings
toward you;
It's with a pair of horns he would reward you.
Yes, I surprised him with your wife, and heard
240 His whole adulterous offer, every word.
She, with her all too gentle disposition,
Would not have told you of his proposition;
But I shall not make terms with brazen lechery,

And feel that not to tell you would be treachery.

245 **ELMIRE.** And I hold that one's husband's peace of mind
Should not be spoilt by tattle of this kind.
One's honor doesn't require it: to be proficient
In keeping men at bay is quite sufficient.
These are my sentiments, and I wish, Damis,
250 That you had heeded me and held your peace.

SCENE 6.

ORGON, DAMIS, TARTUFFE.

ORGON. Can it be true, this dreadful thing I hear?

TARTUFFE. Yes, Brother, I'm a wicked man, I fear:
A wretched sinner, all depraved and twisted,
The greatest villain that has ever existed.
255 My life's one heap of crimes, which grows each minute;
There's naught but foulness and corruption in it;
And I perceive that Heaven, outraged by me,
Has chosen this occasion to mortify me.
Charge me with any deed you wish to name;
260 I'll not defend myself, but take the blame.
Believe what you are told, and drive Tartuffe
Like some base criminal from beneath your roof;
Yes, drive me hence, and with a parting curse:
I shan't protest, for I deserve far worse.

265 **ORGON** (*to* DAMIS). Ah, you deceitful boy, how dare you try
To stain his purity with so foul a lie?

DAMIS. What! Are you taken in by such a bluff?
Did you not hear . . . ?

ORGON. Enough, you rogue, enough!

TARTUFFE. Ah, Brother, let him speak: you're being unjust.
270 Believe his story; the boy deserves your trust.
Why, after all, should you have faith in me?
How can you know what I might do, or be?
Is it on my good actions that you base
Your favor? Do you trust my pious face?
275 Ah, no, don't be deceived by hollow shows;
I'm far, alas, from being what men suppose;

Though the world takes me for a man of worth,
I'm truly the most worthless man on earth.

(*To* DAMIS.)
Yes, my dear son, speak out now: call me the chief
280 Of sinners, a wretch, a murderer, a thief;
Load me with all the names men most abhor;
I'll not complain; I've earned them all, and more;
I'll kneel here while you pour them on my head
As a just punishment for the life I've led.

285 **ORGON** (*to* TARTUFFE). This is too much, dear Brother.

(*To* DAMIS.) Have you no heart?

DAMIS. Are you so hoodwinked by this rascal's art . . . ?

ORGON. Be still, you monster.

(*To* TARTUFFE.)
Brother, I pray you, rise.

(*To* DAMIS.) Villain!

DAMIS. But . . .

ORGON. Silence!

DAMIS. Can't you realize . . . ?

ORGON. Just one word more, and I'll tear you limb from limb.

290 **TARTUFFE.** In God's name, Brother, don't be harsh with him.
I'd rather far be tortured at the stake
Than see him bear one scratch for my poor sake.

ORGON (*To* DAMIS). Ingrate!

TARTUFFE. If I must beg you, on bended knee,
To pardon him . . .

ORGON (*falling to his knees, addressing* TARTUFFE).
Such goodness cannot be!

(*To* DAMIS.)
295 Now, *there's* true charity!

DAMIS. What, you . . . ?

ORGON. Villain, be still!
I know your motives; I know you wish him ill;
Yes, all of you—wife, children, servants, all—
Conspire against him and desire his fall.
Employing every shameful trick you can
300 To alienate me from this saintly man.
Ah, but the more you seek to drive him away,
The more I'll do to keep him. Without delay,

I'll spite this household and confound its pride
By giving him my daughter as his bride.

305 DAMIS. You're going to force her to accept his hand?

ORGON. Yes, and this very night, d'you understand?
I shall defy you all, and make it clear
That I'm the one who gives the orders here.
Come, wretch, kneel down and clasp his blessed feet,
310 And ask his pardon for your black deceit.

DAMIS. I ask that swindler's pardon? Why, I'd rather . . .

ORGON. So! You insult him, and defy your father!
A stick! A stick! (*To* TARTUFFE.) No, no—release me, do.
(*To* DAMIS.)
Out of my house this minute! Be off with you,
315 And never dare set foot in it again.

DAMIS. Well, I shall go, but . . .

ORGON.   Well, go quickly, then.
I disinherit you; an empty purse
Is all you'll get from me—except my curse!

SCENE 7.

ORGON, TARTUFFE.

ORGON. How he blasphemed your goodness! What a son!

320 TARTUFFE. Forgive him, Lord, as I've already done. (*To* ORGON.)
You can't know how it hurts when someone tries
To blacken me in my dear Brother's eyes.

ORGON. Ahh!

TARTUFFE. The mere thought of such ingratitude
Plunges my soul into so dark a mood . . .
325 Such horror grips my heart . . . I gasp for breath,
And cannot speak, and feel myself near death.

ORGON (*he runs, in tears, to the door through which he has just driven his son*). You blackguard!
Why did I spare you? Why did I not
Break you in little pieces on the spot?
Compose yourself, and don't be hurt, dear friend.

330 TARTUFFE. These scenes, these dreadful quar-

rels, have got to end.
I've much upset your household, and I perceive
That the best thing will be for me to leave.

ORGON. What are you saying!

TARTUFFE.   They're all against me here;
They'd have you think me false and insincere.

335 ORGON. Ah, what of that? Have I ceased believing in you?

TARTUFFE. Their adverse talk will certainly continue,
And charges which you now repudiate
You may find credible at a later date.

ORGON. No, Brother, never.

TARTUFFE.   Brother, a wife can sway
340 Her husband's mind in many a subtle way.

ORGON. No, no.

TARTUFFE.   To leave at once is the solution;
Thus only can I end their persecution.

ORGON. No, no, I'll not allow it; you shall remain.

TARTUFFE. Ah, well; 'twill mean much martyrdom and pain,
345 But if you wish it . . .

ORGON.   Ah!

TARTUFFE.   Enough; so be it.
But one thing must be settled, as I see it.
For your dear honor, and for our friendship's sake,
There's one precaution I feel bound to take.
I shall avoid your wife, and keep away . . .

350 ORGON. No, you shall not, whatever they may say.
It pleases me to vex them, and for spite
I'd have them see you with her day and night.
What's more, I'm going to drive them to despair
By making you my only son and heir;
355 This very day, I'll give to you alone
Clear deed and title to everything I own.
A dear, good friend and son-in-law-to-be
Is more than wife, or child, or kin to me.
Will you accept my offer, dearest son?

360 TARTUFFE. In all things, let the will of Heaven be done.

ORGON. Poor fellow! Come, we'll go draw up the deed.
Then let them burst with disappointed greed!

CURTAIN

ACT FOUR

SCENE 1.

CLÉANTE, TARTUFFE.

CLÉANTE. Yes, all the town's discussing it, and truly,
  Their comments do not flatter you unduly.
  I'm glad we've met, Sir, and I'll give my view
  Of this sad matter in a word or two.
5 As for who's guilty, that I shan't discuss;
  Let's say it was Damis who caused the fuss;
  Assuming, then, that you have been ill-used
  By young Damis, and groundlessly accused,
  Ought not a Christian to forgive, and ought
10 He not to stifle every vengeful thought?
  Should you stand by and watch a father make
  His only son an exile for your sake?
  Again I tell you frankly, be advised:
  The whole town, high and low, is scandalized;
15 This quarrel must be mended, and my advice is
  Not to push matters to a further crisis.
  No, sacrifice your wrath to God above,
  And help Damis regain his father's love.
  TARTUFFE. Alas, for my part I should take great joy
20 In doing so. I've nothing against the boy.
  I pardon all, I harbor no resentment;
  To serve him would afford me much contentment.
  But Heaven's interest will not have it so:
  If he comes back, then I shall have to go.
25 After his conduct—so extreme, so vicious—
  Our further intercourse would look suspicious.
  God knows what people would think! Why, they'd describe
  My goodness to him as a sort of bribe;
  They'd say that out of guilt I made pretense
30 Of loving-kindness and benevolence—
  That, fearing my accuser's tongue, I strove
  To buy his silence with a show of love.
  CLÉANTE. Your reasoning is badly warped and stretched.
  And these excuses, Sir, are most far-fetched.

35 Why put yourself in charge of Heaven's cause?
  Does Heaven need our help to enforce its laws?
  Leave vengeance to the Lord, Sir; while we live,
  Our duty's not to punish, but forgive;
  And what the Lord commands, we should obey
40 Without regard to what the world may say.
  What! Shall the fear of being misunderstood
  Prevent our doing what is right and good?
  No, no; let's simply do what Heaven ordains,
  And let no other thoughts perplex our brains.
45 TARTUFFE. Again, Sir, let me say that I've forgiven
  Damis, and thus obeyed the laws of Heaven;
  But I am not commanded by the Bible
  To live with one who smears my name with libel.
  CLÉANTE. Were you commanded, Sir, to indulge the whim
50 Of poor Orgon, and to encourage him
  In suddenly transferring to your name
  A large estate to which you have no claim?
  TARTUFFE. 'Twould never occur to those who know me best
  To think I acted from self-interest.
55 The treasures of this world I quite despise;
  Their specious glitter does not charm my eyes;
  And if I have resigned myself to taking
  The gift which my dear Brother insists on making,
  I do so only, as he well understands,
60 Lest so much wealth fall into wicked hands,
  Lest those to whom it might descend in time
  Turn it to purposes of sin and crime,
  And not, as I shall do, make use of it
  For Heaven's glory and mankind's benefit.
65 CLÉANTE. Forget these trumped-up fears. Your argument
  Is one the rightful heir might well resent;
  It *is* a moral burden to inherit
  Such wealth, but give Damis a chance to bear it.
  And would it not be worse to be accused
70 Of swindling, than to see that wealth misused?
  I'm shocked that you allowed Orgon to broach

This matter, and that you feel no self-reproach;
Does true religion teach that lawful heirs
May freely be deprived of what is theirs?
75 And if the Lord has told you in your heart
That you and young Damis must dwell apart,
Would it not be the decent thing to beat
A generous and honorable retreat,
Rather than let the son of the house be sent,
80 For your convenience, into banishment?
Sir, if you wish to prove the honesty
Of your intentions . . .

TARTUFFE.   Sir, it is half-past
    three.
I've certain pious duties to attend to,
And hope my prompt departure won't offend
    you.
85 CLÉANTE (alone). Damn.

SCENE 2.
ELMIRE, MARIANE, CLÉANTE, DORINE.

DORINE.   Stay, Sir, and help Mar-
    iane, for Heaven's sake!
She's suffering so, I fear her heart will break.
Her father's plan to marry her off tonight
Has put the poor child in a desperate plight.
I hear him coming. Let's stand together, now,
90 And see if we can't change his mind, somehow,
About this match we all deplore and fear.

SCENE 3.
ORGON, ELMIRE, MARIANE, CLÉANTE, DORINE.

ORGON. Hah! Glad to find you all assembled here.
(To MARIANE.)
This contract, child, contains your happiness,
And what it says I think your heart can guess.
95 MARIANE (falling to her knees). Sir, by that Heaven
    which sees me here distressed,
And by whatever else can move your breast,
Do not employ a father's power, I pray you,
To crush my heart and force it to obey you,
Nor by your harsh commands oppress me so
100 That I'll begrudge the duty which I owe—
And do not so embitter and enslave me
That I shall hate the very life you gave me.
If my sweet hopes must perish, if you refuse

To give me to the one I've dared to choose,
105 Spare me at least—I beg you, I implore—
The pain of wedding one whom I abhor;
And do not, by a heartless use of force,
Drive me to contemplate some desperate
    course.
ORGON (feeling himself touched by her). Be firm, my
    soul. No human weakness, now.
110 MARIANE. I don't resent your love for him. Allow
Your heart free rein. Sir; give him your prop-
    erty,
And if that's not enough, take mine from me;
He's welcome to my money; take it, do,
But don't, I pray, include my person too.
115 Spare me, I beg you; and let me end the tale
Of my sad days behind a convent veil.
ORGON. A convent! Hah! When crossed in their
    amours,
All lovesick girls have the same thought as yours.
Get up! The more you loathe the man, and dread
    him,
120 The more ennobling it will be to wed him.
Marry Tartuffe, and mortify your flesh!
Enough; don't start that whimpering afresh.
DORINE. But why . . . ?
ORGON.   Be still, there. Speak
    when you're spoken to.
Not one more bit of impudence out of you.
125 CLÉANTE. If I may offer a word of counsel
    here . . .
ORGON. Brother, in counseling you have no peer;
All your advice is forceful, sound, and clever;
I don't propose to follow it, however.
ELMIRE (to ORGON). I am amazed, and don't know
    what to say;
130 Your blindness simply takes my breath away.
You are indeed bewitched, to take no warning
From our account of what occurred this
    morning.
ORGON. Madam, I know a few plain facts, and one
Is that you're partial to my rascal son;
135 Hence, when he sought to make Tartuffe the
    victim
Of a base lie, you dared not contradict him.
Ah, but you underplayed your part, my pet;
You should have looked more angry, more
    upset.

Scene from a 1986 production of *Tartuffe* staged
at the University of Chicago's Court Theater.

ELMIRE. When men make overtures, must we
    reply
140   With righteous anger and a battle-cry?
    Must we turn back their amorous advances
    With sharp reproaches and with fiery glances?
    Myself, I find such offers merely amusing,
    And make no scenes and fusses in refusing;
145   My taste is for good-natured rectitude,
    And I dislike the savage sort of prude
    Who guards her virtue with her teeth and claws,
    And tears men's eyes out for the slightest cause:
    The Lord preserve me from such honor as that,
150   Which bites and scratches like an alley-cat!
    I've found that a polite and cool rebuff
    Discourages a lover quite enough.
  ORGON. I know the facts, and I shall not be
    shaken.
  ELMIRE. I marvel at your power to be mistaken.
155   Would it, I wonder, carry weight with you
    If I could *show* you that our tale was true?
  ORGON. Show me?
  ELMIRE.   Yes.
  ORGON.   Rot.
  ELMIRE.   Come, what if I found
    a way

To make you see the facts as plain as day?
  ORGON. Nonsense.
  ELMIRE.   Do answer me; don't be
    absurd.
160   I'm not now asking you to trust our word.
    Suppose that from some hiding-place in here
    You learned the whole sad truth by eye and
    ear—
    What would you say of your good friend, after
    that?
  ORGON. Why, I'd say . . . nothing, by Jehosha-
    phat!
165   It can't be true.
  ELMIRE.   You've been too long deceived,
    And I'm quite tired of being disbelieved.
    Come now: let's put my statements to the test,
    And you shall see the truth made manifest.
  ORGON. I'll take that challenge. Now do your
    uttermost.
170   We'll see how you make good your empty boast.
  ELMIRE (*to* DORINE). Send him to me.
  DORINE.   He's crafty; it may be hard
    To catch the cunning scoundrel off his guard.
  ELMIRE. No, amorous men are gullible. Their
    conceit
    So blinds them that they're never hard to cheat.
175   Have him come down. (*To* CLÉANTE *and* MAR-
    IANE.) Please leave us, for a bit.

SCENE 4.

ELMIRE, ORGON.

ELMIRE. Pull up this table, and get under it.
  ORGON. What?
  ELMIRE.   It's essential that you be well-
    hidden.
  ORGON. Why there?
  ELMIRE.   Oh, Heavens! Just do as you
    are bidden.
    I have my plans; we'll soon see how they fare.
180   Under the table, now; and once you're there,
    Take care that you are neither seen nor heard.
  ORGON. Well, I'll indulge you, since I gave my
    word
    To see you through this infantile charade.
  ELMIRE. Once it is over, you'll be glad we played.

(To her husband, who is now under the table.)

185 I'm going to act quite strangely, now, and you
Must not be shocked at anything I do.
Whatever I may say, you must excuse
As part of that deceit I'm forced to use.
I shall employ sweet speeches in the task
190 Of making that imposter drop his mask;
I'll give encouragement to his bold desires,
And furnish fuel to his amorous fires.
Since it's for your sake, and for his destruction,
That I shall seem to yield to his seduction,
195 I'll gladly stop whenever you decide
That all your doubts are fully satisfied.
I'll count on you, as soon as you have seen
What sort of man he is, to intervene,
And not expose me to his odious lust
200 One moment longer than you feel you must.
Remember; you're to save me from my plight
Whenever . . . He's coming! Hush! Keep out
of sight!

SCENE 5.

TARTUFFE, ELMIRE, ORGON.

TARTUFFE. You wish to have a word with me, I'm
told.
ELMIRE. Yes. I've a little secret to unfold.
205 Before I speak, however, it would be wise
To close that door, and look about for spies.
(TARTUFFE goes to the door, closes it, and returns.)
The very last thing that must happen now
Is a repetition of this morning's row.
I've never been so badly caught off guard.
210 Oh, how I feared for you! You saw how hard
I tried to make that troublesome Damis
Control his dreadful temper, and hold his peace.
In my confusion, I didn't have the sense
Simply to contradict his evidence;
215 But as it happened, that was for the best,
And all has worked out in our interest.
This storm has only bettered your position;
My husband doesn't have the least suspicion,
And now, in mockery of those who do,
220 He bids me be continually with you.
And that is why, quite fearless of reproof,

I now can be alone with my Tartuffe,
And why my heart—perhaps too quick to
yield—
Feels free to let its passion be revealed.
225 **TARTUFFE.** Madam, your words confuse me. Not
long ago,
You spoke in quite a different style, you know.
ELMIRE. Ah, Sir, if that refusal made you smart,
It's little that you know of woman's heart,
Or what the heart is trying to convey
230 When it resists in such a feeble way!
Always, at first, our modesty prevents
The frank avowal of tender sentiments;
However high the passion which inflames us,
Still, to confess its power somehow shames us.
235 Thus we reluct, at first, yet in a tone
Which tells you that our heart is overthrown,
That what our lips deny, our pulse confesses,
And that, in time, all noes will turn to yesses.
I fear my words are all too frank and free,
240 And a poor proof of woman's modesty;
But since I'm started, tell me, if you will—
Would I have tried to make Damis be still,
Would I have listened, calm and unoffended,
Until your lengthy offer of love was ended,
245 And been so very mild in my reaction,
Had your sweet words not given me satisfaction?
And when I tried to force you to undo
The marriage-plans my husband has in view,
What did my urgent pleading signify
250 If not that I admired you, and that I
Deplored the thought that someone else might
own
Part of a heart I wished for mine alone?
TARTUFFE. Madam, no happiness is so complete
As when, from lips we love, come words so
sweet;
255 Their nectar floods my every sense, and drains
In honeyed rivulets through all my veins.
To please you is my joy, my only goal;
Your love is the restorer of my soul;
And yet I must beg leave, now, to confess
260 Some lingering doubts as to my happiness.
Might this not be a trick? Might not the catch
Be that you wish me to break off the match
With Mariane, and so have feigned to love me?
I shan't quite trust your fond opinion of me

265 Until the feelings you've expressed so sweetly
Are demonstrated somewhat more concretely,
And you have shown, by certain kind conces-
sions,
That I may put my faith in your professions.

ELMIRE (*she coughs, to warn her husband*). Why be
in such a hurry? Must my heart
270 Exhaust its bounty at the very start?
To make that sweet admission cost me dear,
But you'll not be content, it would appear,
Unless my store of favors is disbursed
To the last farthing, and at the very first.

275 TARTUFFE. The less we merit, the less we dare to
hope,
And with our doubts, mere words can never
cope.
We trust no promised bliss till we receive it;
Not till a joy is ours can we believe it.
I, who so little merit your esteem,
280 Can't credit this fulfillment of my dream,
And shan't believe it, Madam, until I savor
Some palpable assurance of your favor.

ELMIRE. My, how tyrannical your love can be.
And how it flusters and perplexes me!
285 How furiously you take one's heart in hand,
And make your every wish a fierce command!
Come, must you hound and harry me to death?
Will you not give me time to catch my breath?
Can it be right to press me with such force,
290 Give me no quarter, show me no remorse,
And take advantage, by your stern insistence,
Of the fond feelings which weaken my resis-
tance?

TARTUFFE. Well, if you look with favor upon my
love,
Why, then, begrudge me some clear proof
thereof?

295 ELMIRE. But how can I consent without offense
To Heaven, toward which you feel such reverence?

TARTUFFE. If Heaven is all that holds you back,
don't worry.
I can remove that hindrance in a hurry.
Nothing of that sort need obstruct our path.

300 ELMIRE. Must one not be afraid of Heaven's
wrath?

TARTUFFE. Madam, forget such fears, and be my
pupil,
And I shall teach you how to conquer scruple.
Some joys, it's true, are wrong in Heaven's eyes
Yet Heaven is not averse to compromise;
305 There is a science, lately formulated,
Whereby one's conscience may be liberated,
And any wrongful act you care to mention
May be redeemed by purity of intention.
I'll teach you, Madam, the secrets of that sci-
ence;
310 Meanwhile, just place on me your full reliance.
Assuage my keen desires, and feel no dread:
The sin, if any, shall be on my head.

(ELMIRE *coughs, this time more loudly.*)
You've a bad cough.

ELMIRE.   Yes, yes. It's bad indeed.

TARTUFFE (*producing a little paper bag*). A bit of
licorice may be what you need.

315 ELMIRE. No, I've a stubborn cold, it seems. I'm
sure it
Will take much more than licorice to cure it.

TARTUFFE. How aggravating.

ELMIRE.   Oh, more than I can
say.

TARTUFFE. If you're still troubled, think of things
this way:
No one shall know our joys, save us alone,
320 And there's no evil till the act is known;
It's scandal, Madam, which makes it an offense,
And it's no sin to sin in confidence.

ELMIRE (*having coughed once more*).
Well, clearly I must do as you require,
And yield to your importunate desire.
325 It is apparent, now, that nothing less
Will satisfy you, and so I acquiesce.
To go so far is much against my will;
I'm vexed that it should come to this; but still,
Since you are so determined on it, since you
330 Will not allow mere language to convince you,
And since you ask for concrete evidence, I
See nothing for it, now, but to comply.
If this is sinful, if I'm wrong to do it,
So much the worse for him who drove me to it.
335 The fault can surely not be charged to me.

TARTUFFE. Madam, the fault is mine, if fault

there be,
And . . .

ELMIRE. Open the door a little, and peek out;
  I wouldn't want my husband poking about.

TARTUFFE. Why worry about the man? Each day 365
    he grows
340 More gullible; one can lead him by the nose.
  To find us here would fill him with delight,
  And if he saw the worst, he'd doubt his sight.

ELMIRE. Nevertheless, do step out for a minute
  Into the hall, and see that no one's in it.

SCENE 6.

ORGON, ELMIRE.

345 ORGON (*coming out from under the table*). That
    man's a perfect monster, I must admit!
  I'm simply stunned. I can't get over it.

ELMIRE. What, coming out so soon? How prema-
    ture!
  Get back in hiding, and wait until you're sure.
  Stay till the end, and be convinced completely;
350 We mustn't stop till things are proved
    concretely.

ORGON. Hell never harbored anything so vicious!

ELMIRE. Tut, don't be hasty. Try to be judicious.
  Wait, and be certain that there's no mistake.
  No jumping to conclusions, for Heaven's sake!
  (*She places* ORGON *behind her, as* TARTUFFE *re-
  enters.*)

SCENE 7.

TARTUFFE, ELMIRE, ORGON.

355 TARTUFFE (*not seeing* ORGON). Madam, all things
    have worked out to perfection;
  I've given the neighboring rooms a full inspec-
    tion;
  No one's about; and now I may at last . . .

ORGON (*intercepting him*). Hold on, my passionate
    fellow, not so fast!
  I should advise a little more restraint.
360 Well, so you thought you'd fool me, my dear
    saint!

How soon you wearied of the saintly life—
Wedding my daughter, and coveting my wife!
I've long suspected you, and had a feeling
That soon I'd catch you at your double-dealing.
365 Just now, you've given me evidence galore;
  It's quite enough; I have no wish for more.

ELMIRE (*to* TARTUFFE). I'm sorry to have treated
    you so slyly,
  But circumstances forced me to be wily.

TARTUFFE. Brother, you can't think . . .

ORGON.   No more talk from you;
370 Just leave this household, without more ado.

TARTUFFE. What I intended . . .

ORGON.   That seems fairly clear.
  Spare me your falsehoods and get out of here.

TARTUFFE. No, I'm the master, and you're the
    one to go!
  This house belongs to me, I'll have you know,
375 And I shall show you that you can't hurt *me*
  By this contemptible conspiracy,
  That those who cross me know not what
    they do,
  And that I've means to expose and punish you,
  Avenge offended Heaven, and make you grieve
380 That ever you dared order me to leave.

SCENE 8.

ELMIRE, ORGON.

ELMIRE. What was the point of all that angry
    chatter?

ORGON. Dear God, I'm worried. This is no laugh-
    ing matter.

ELMIRE. How so?

ORGON.   I fear I understood his drift.
  I'm much disturbed about that deed of gift.
385 ELMIRE. You gave him . . . ?

ORGON.   Yes, it's all been
    drawn and signed.
  But one thing more is weighing on my mind.

ELMIRE. What's that?

ORGON.   I'll tell you; but first let's see
    if there's
  A certain strong-box in his room upstairs.
                         CURTAIN

ACT FIVE

SCENE 1.

ORGON, CLÉANTE.

CLÉANTE. Where are you going so fast?
ORGON.   God knows!
CLÉANTE.   Then wait;
   Let's have a conference, and deliberate
   On how this situation's to be met.
   ORGON. That strong-box has me utterly upset;
5 This is the worst of many, many shocks.
   CLÉANTE. Is there some fearful mystery in that
    box?
   ORGON. My poor friend Argas brought that box
    to me
   With his own hands, in utmost secrecy;
   'Twas on the very morning of his flight.
10 It's full of papers which, if they came to light,
   Would ruin him—or such is my impression.
   CLÉANTE. Then why did you let it out of your
    possession?
   ORGON. Those papers vexed my conscience, and
    it seemed best
   To ask the counsel of my pious guest.
15 The cunning scoundrel got me to agree
   To leave the strong-box in his custody,
   So that, in case of an investigation,
   I could employ a slight equivocation
   And swear I didn't have it, and thereby,
20 At no expense to conscience, tell a lie.
   CLÉANTE. It looks to me as if you're out on a limb.
   Trusting him with that box, and offering him
   That deed of gift, were actions of a kind
   Which scarcely indicate a prudent mind.
25 With two such weapons, he has the upper hand,
   And since you're vulnerable, as matters stand,
   You erred once more in bringing him to bay.
   You should have acted in some subtler way.
   ORGON. Just think of it: behind that fervent face,
30 A heart so wicked, and a soul so base!
   I took him in, a hungry beggar, and then . . .
   Enough, by God! I'm through with pious men:

Henceforth I'll hate the whole false brother-
   hood,
   And persecute them worse than Satan could.
35 CLÉANTE. Ah, there you go—extravagant as ever!
   Why can you not be rational? You never
   Manage to take the middle course, it seems,
   But jump, instead, between absurd extremes.
   You've recognized your recent grave mistake
40 In falling victim to a pious fake;
   Now, to correct that error, must you embrace
   An even greater error in its place,
   And judge our worthy neighbors as a whole
   By what you've learned of one corrupted soul?
45 Come, just because one rascal made you swallow
   A show of zeal which turned out to be hollow,
   Shall you conclude that all men are deceivers,
   And that, today, there are no true believers?
   Let atheists make that foolish inference;
50 Learn to distinguish virtue from pretense,
   Be cautious in bestowing admiration,
   And cultivate a sober moderation.
   Don't humor fraud, but also don't asperse
   True piety; the latter fault is worse,
55 And it is best to err, if err one must,
   As you have done, upon the side of trust.

SCENE 2.

DAMIS, ORGON, CLÉANTE.

DAMIS. Father, I hear that scoundrel's uttered
   threats
   Against you; that he pridefully forgets
   How, in his need, he was befriended by you,
60 And means to use your gifts to crucify you.
   ORGON. It's true, my boy, I'm too distressed for
    tears.
   DAMIS. Leave it to me, Sir; let me trim his ears.
   Faced with such insolence, we must not waver.
   I shall rejoice in doing you the favor
65 Of cutting short his life, and your distress.

CLÉANTE. What a display of young hotheaded-
ness!

Do learn to moderate your fits of rage.
In this just kingdom, this enlightened age,
One does not settle things by violence.

SCENE 3.

MADAME PERNELLE, MARIANE, ELMIRE, DORINE,
DAMIS, ORGON, CLÉANTE.

70 MADAME PERNELLE. I hear strange tales of very
strange events.

ORGON. Yes, strange events which these two eyes
beheld.

The man's ingratitude is unparalleled.
I save a wretched pauper from starvation,
House him, and treat him like a blood relation,
75 Shower him every day with my largesse,
Give him my daughter, and all that I possess;
And meanwhile the unconscionable knave
Tries to induce my wife to misbehave;
And not content with such extreme rascality,
80 Now threatens me with my own liberality,
And aims, by taking base advantage of
The gifts I gave him out of Christian love,
To drive me from my house, a ruined man,
And make me end a pauper, as he began.

DORINE. Poor fellow!

85 MADAME PERNELLE. No, my son, I'll never bring
Myself to think him guilty of such a thing.

ORGON. How's that?

MADAME PERNELLE. The righteous always were
maligned.

ORGON. Speak clearly, Mother. Say what's on
your mind.

MADAME PERNELLE. I mean that I can smell a rat,
my dear.
90 You know how everybody hates him, here.

ORGON. That has no bearing on the case at all.

MADAME PERNELLE. I told you a hundred times,
when you were small,
That virtue in this world is hated ever;
Malicious men may die, but malice never.

95 ORGON. No doubt that's true, but how does it
apply?

MADAME PERNELLE. They've turned you against
him by a clever lie.

ORGON. I've told you, I was there and saw it done.

MADAME PERNELLE. Ah, slanderers will stop at
nothing, Son.

ORGON. Mother, I'll lose my temper . . . For the
last time,
100 I tell you I was witness to the crime.

MADAME PERNELLE. The tongues of spite are
busy night and noon,
And to their venom no man is immune.

ORGON. You're talking nonsense. Can't you
realize
I saw it; saw it; saw it with my eyes?
105 Saw, do you understand me? Must I shout it
Into your ears before you'll cease to doubt it?

MADAME PERNELLE. Appearances can deceive,
my son. Dear me,
We cannot always judge by what we see.

ORGON. Drat! Drat!

MADAME PERNELLE. One often interprets things
awry;
110 Good can seem evil to a suspicious eye.

ORGON. Was I to see his pawing at Elmire
As an act of charity?

MADAME PERNELLE. Till his guilt is clear,
A man deserves the benefit of the doubt.
You should have waited, to see how things
turned out.

115 ORGON. Great God in Heaven, what more proof
did I need?
Was I to sit there, watching, until he'd . . .
You drive me to the brink of impropriety.

MADAME PERNELLE. No, no, a man of such surpassing piety
Could not do such a thing. You cannot shake
me.
120 I don't believe it, and you shall not make me.

ORGON. You vex me so that, if you weren't my
mother,
I'd say to you . . . some dreadful thing or
other.

DORINE. It's your turn now, Sir, not to be listened
to;
You'd not trust us, and now she won't trust you.

125 CLÉANTE. My friends, we're wasting time which

should be spent
In facing up to our predicament.
I fear that scoundrel's threats weren't made in
sport.
DAMIS. Do you think he'd have the nerve to go to
court?
ELMIRE. I'm sure he won't: they'd find it all too
crude
130 A case of swindling and ingratitude.
 CLÉANTE. Don't be too sure. He won't be at a loss
To give his claims a high and righteous gloss;
And clever rogues with far less valid cause
Have trapped their victims in a web of laws.
135 I say again that to antagonize
A man so strongly armed was most unwise.
 ORGON. I know it; but the man's appalling cheek
Outraged me so, I couldn't control my pique.
 CLÉANTE. I wish to Heaven that we could devise
140 Some truce between you, or some compromise.
 ELMIRE. If I had known what cards he held, I'd
not
Have roused his anger by my little plot.
 ORGON (*to* DORINE, *as* M. LOYAL *enters*).
What is that fellow looking for? Who is he?
Go talk to him—and tell him that I'm busy.

SCENE 4.

MONSIEUR LOYAL, MADAME PERNELLE, ORGON,
DAMIS, MARIANE, DORINE, ELMIRE, CLÉANTE.

145 **MONSIEUR LOYAL.** Good day, dear sister. Kindly
let me see
Your master.
 DORINE. He's involved with company,
And cannot be disturbed just now, I fear.
 MONSIEUR LOYAL. I hate to intrude; but what has
brought me here
Will not disturb your master, in any event.
150 Indeed, my news will make him most content.
 DORINE. Your name?
 MONSIEUR LOYAL. Just say that I bring greet-
ings from
Monsieur Tartuffe, on whose behalf I've come.
 DORINE (*to* ORGON). Sir, he's a very gracious man,
and bears
A message from Tartuffe, which he declares

155 Will make you most content.
 CLÉANTE.   Upon my word.
I think this man had best be seen, and heard.
 ORGON. Perhaps he has some settlement to sug-
gest.
How shall I treat him? What manner would be
best?
 CLÉANTE. Control your anger, and if he should
mention
160 Some fair adjustment, give him your full atten-
tion.
 MONSIEUR LOYAL. Good health to you, good Sir.
May Heaven confound
Your enemies, and may your joys abound.
 ORGON (*aside, to* CLÉANTE). A gentle salutation:
it confirms
My guess that he is here to offer terms.
165 **MONSIEUR LOYAL.** I've always held your family
most dear;
I served your father, Sir, for many a year.
 ORGON. Sir, I must ask your pardon; to my
shame,
I cannot now recall your face or name.
 MONSIEUR LOYAL. Loyal's my name; I come from
Normandy,
170 And I'm a bailiff, in all modesty.
For forty years, praise God, it's been my boast
To serve with honor in that vital post,
And I am here, Sir, if you will permit
The liberty, to serve you with this writ . . .
175 **ORGON.** To—*what?*
 MONSIEUR LOYAL. Now, please, Sir, let us have
no friction:
It's nothing but an order of eviction.
You are to move your goods and family out
And make way for new occupants, without
Deferment or delay, and give the keys . . .
180 **ORGON.** I? Leave this house?
 MONSIEUR LOYAL.   Why yes, Sir, if you
please.
This house, Sir, from the cellar to the roof,
Belongs now to the good Monsieur Tartuffe,
And he is lord and master of your estate
By virtue of a deed of present date,
185 Drawn in due form, with clearest legal
phrasing . . .
 DAMIS. Your insolence is utterly amazing!

Scene from a 1986 production of *Tartuffe* staged at the University of Chicago's Court Theater.

MONSIEUR LOYAL. Young man, my business here is not with you,
    But with your wise and temperate father, who,
    Like every worthy citizen, stands in awe
190   Of justice, and would never obstruct the law.
ORGON. But . . .
MONSIEUR LOYAL. Not for a million, Sir, would you rebel
    Against authority; I know that well.
    You'll not make trouble, Sir, or interfere
    With the execution of my duties here.
195 DAMIS. Someone may execute a smart tattoo
    On that black jacket of yours, before you're through.
MONSIEUR LOYAL. Sir, bid your son be silent. I'd much regret
    Having to mention such a nasty threat
    Of violence, in writing my report.
200 DORINE (*aside*). This man Loyal's a most disloyal sort!
MONSIEUR LOYAL. I love all men of upright character,

And when I agreed to serve these papers, Sir,
It was your feelings that I had in mind.
I couldn't bear to see the case assigned
205   To someone else, who might esteem you less
And so subject you to unpleasantness.
ORGON. What's more unpleasant than telling a man to leave
His house and home?
MONSIEUR LOYAL.   You'd like a short reprieve?
If you desire it, Sir, I shall not press you,
210   But wait until tomorrow to dispossess you.
Splendid. I'll come and spend the night here, then,
Most quietly, with half a score of men.
For form's sake, you might bring me, just before
You go to bed, the keys to the front door.
215   My men, I promise, will be on their best
Behavior, and will not disturb your rest.
But bright and early, Sir, you must be quick
And move out all your furniture, every stick:
The men I've chosen are both young and strong,

Tartuffe—Act Five, Scene 4 **547**

220 And with their help it shouldn't take you long.
In short, I'll make things pleasant and conven-
ient,
And since I'm being so extremely lenient,
Please show me, Sir, a like consideration,
And give me your entire cooperation.
225 **ORGON** (*aside*). I may be all but bankrupt, but I
vow
I'd give a hundred louis,[1] here and now,
Just for the pleasure of landing one good clout
Right on the end of that complacent snout.
CLÉANTE. Careful; don't make things worse.
DAMIS. My bootsole itches
230 To give that beggar a good kick in the breeches.
DORINE. Monsieur Loyal, I'd love to hear the
whack
Of a stout stick across your fine broad back.
MONSIEUR LOYAL. Take care: a woman too may
go to jail if
She uses threatening language to a bailiff.
235 **CLÉANTE.** Enough, enough, Sir. This must not
go on.
Give me that paper, please, and then begone.
MONSIEUR LOYAL. Well, *au revoir*. God give you
all good cheer!
ORGON. May God confound you, and him who
sent you here!

SCENE 5.

ORGON, CLÉANTE, MARIANE, ELMIRE, MADAME
PERNELLE, DORINE, DAMIS.

ORGON. Now, Mother, was I right or not? This
writ
240 Should change your notion of Tartuffe a bit.
Do you perceive his villainy at last?
MADAME PERNELLE. I'm thunderstruck. I'm
utterly aghast.
DORINE. Oh, come, be fair. You mustn't take
offense
At this new proof of his benevolence.
245 He's acting out of selfless love, I know.
Material things enslave the soul, and so
He kindly has arranged your liberation
From all that might endanger your salvation.
ORGON. Will you not ever hold your tongue, you
dunce?

250 **CLÉANTE.** Come, you must take some action, and
at once.
ELMIRE. Go tell the world of the low trick he's
tried.
The deed of gift is surely nullified
By such behavior, and public rage will not
Permit the wretch to carry out his plot.

SCENE 6.

VALÈRE, ORGON, CLÉANTE, ELMIRE, MARIANE,
MADAME PERNELLE, DAMIS, DORINE.

255 **VALÈRE.** Sir, though I hate to bring you more bad
news,
Such is the danger that I cannot choose.
A friend who is extremely close to me
And knows my interest in your family
Has, for my sake, presumed to violate
260 The secrecy that's due to things of state,
And sends me word that you are in a plight
From which your one salvation lies in flight.
That scoundrel who's imposed upon you so
Denounced you to the King an hour ago
265 And, as supporting evidence, displayed
The strong-box of a certain renegade
Whose secret papers, so he testified,
You had disloyally agreed to hide.
I don't know just what charges may be pressed,
270 But there's a warrant out for your arrest;
Tartuffe has been instructed, furthermore,
To guide the arresting officer to your door.
CLÈANTE. He's clearly done this to facilitate
His seizure of your house and your estate.
275 **ORGON.** That man, I must say, is a vicious beast!
VALÈRE. Quick, Sir; you mustn't tarry in the least.
My carriage is outside, to take you hence;
This thousand louis should cover all expense.
Let's lose no time, or you shall be undone;
280 The sole defense, in this case, is to run.
I shall go with you all the way, and place you
In a safe refuge to which they'll never trace you.
ORGON. Alas, dear boy, I wish that I could show
you

---

1. *louis* (lü′i), a gold coin.

My gratitude for everything I owe you.
But now is not the time; I pray the Lord
That I may live to give you your reward.
Farewell, my dears; be careful . . .

CLÉANTE.   Brother, hurry.
We shall take care of things; you needn't worry.

SCENE 7.

THE OFFICER, TARTUFFE, ORGON, VALÈRE, MA-
DAME PERNELLE, ELMIRE, MARIANE, CLÉANTE,
DORINE, DAMIS.

TARTUFFE. Gently, Sir, gently; stay right where
you are.
No need for haste; your lodging isn't far.
You're off to prison, by order of the Prince.

ORGON. This is the crowning blow, you wretch;
and since
It means my total ruin and defeat,
Your villainy is now at last complete.

TARTUFFE. You needn't try to provoke me; it's
no use.
Those who serve Heaven must expect abuse.

CLÉANTE. You are indeed most patient, sweet,
and blameless.

DORINE. How he exploits the name of Heaven! It's
shameless.

TARTUFFE. Your taunts and mockeries are all for
naught;
To do my duty is my only thought.

MARIANE. Your love of duty is most meritorious,
And what you've done is little short of glorious.

TARTUFFE. All deeds are glorious, Madam, which
obey
The sovereign prince who sent me here today.

ORGON. I rescued you when you were destitute;
Have you forgotten that, you thankless brute?

TARTUFFE. No, no, I well remember everything;
But my first duty is to serve my King.
That obligation is so paramount
That other claims, beside it, do not count;
And for it I would sacrifice my wife,
My family, my friend, or my own life.

ELMIRE. Hypocrite!

DORINE.   All that we most revere, he
uses
To cloak his plots and camouflage his ruses.

CLÉANTE. If it is true that you are animated
By pure and loyal zeal, as you have stated,
Why was this zeal not roused until you'd sought
To make Orgon a cuckold, and been caught?
Why weren't you moved to give your evidence
Until your outraged host had driven you hence?
I shan't say that the gift of all his treasure
Ought to have damped your zeal in any mea-
sure;
But if he is a traitor, as you declare,
How could you condescend to be his heir?

TARTUFFE (*to the* OFFICER). Sir, spare me all this
clamor; it's growing shrill.
Please carry out your orders, if you will.

OFFICER. Yes, I've delayed too long, Sir. Thank
you kindly.
You're just the proper person to remind me.
Come, you are off to join the other boarders
In the King's prison, according to his orders.

TARTUFFE. Who? I, Sir?

OFFICER.   Yes.

TARTUFFE.   To prison? This
can't be true!

OFFICER. I owe an explanation, but not to you.
(*To* ORGON.)
Sir, all is well; rest easy, and be grateful.
We serve a Prince to whom all sham is hateful,
A Prince who sees into our inmost hearts,
And can't be fooled by any trickster's arts.
His royal soul, though generous and human,
Views all things with discernment and acumen;
His sovereign reason is not lightly swayed,
And all his judgments are discreetly weighed.
He honors righteous men of every kind,
And yet his zeal for virtue is not blind.
Nor does his love of piety numb his wits
And make him tolerant of hypocrites.
'Twas hardly likely that this man could cozen
A King who's foiled such liars by the dozen.
With one keen glance, the King perceived the
whole
Perverseness and corruption of his soul,
And thus high Heaven's justice was displayed:
Betraying you, the rogue stood self-betrayed.
The King soon recognized Tartuffe as one
Notorious by another name, who'd done
So many vicious crimes that one could fill

Ten volumes with them, and be writing still.
355 But to be brief: our sovereign was appalled
By this man's treachery toward you, which he
        called
The last, worst villainy of a vile career,
And bade me follow the impostor here
To see how gross his impudence could be,
360 And force him to restore your property.
Your private papers, by the King's command,
I hereby seize and give into your hand.
The King, by royal order, invalidates
The deed which gave this rascal your estates,
365 And pardons, furthermore, your grave offense
In harboring an exile's documents.
By these decrees, our Prince rewards you for
Your loyal deeds in the late civil war,
And shows how heartfelt is his satisfaction
370 In recompensing any worthy action.
How much he prizes merit, and how he makes
More of men's virtues than of their mistakes.

DORINE. Heaven be praised!

MADAME PERNELLE.   I breathe again, at last.

ELMIRE. We're safe.

MARIANE.   I can't believe the danger's
        past.

375 ORGON (*to* TARTUFFE). Well, traitor, now you
        see . . .

CLÉANTE.   Ah, Brother, please,
Let's not descend to such indignities.
Leave the poor wretch to his unhappy fate,
And don't say anything to aggravate
His present woes; but rather hope that he
380 Will soon embrace an honest piety,
And mend his ways, and by a true repentance
Move our just King to moderate his sentence.
Meanwhile, go kneel before your sovereign's
        throne
And thank him for the mercies he has shown.

385 ORGON. Well said: let's go at once and, gladly
        kneeling,
Express the gratitude which all are feeling.
Then, when that first great duty has been done,
We'll turn with pleasure to a second one,
And give Valère, whose love has proven so true,
390 The wedded happiness which is his due.

CURTAIN
1664

550 *Neoclassicism*

THINK AND DISCUSS
Understanding
1. How is Act One, Scene 1, vital to the play's exposition?
2. What are Orgon's reasons for allowing Tartuffe to invade his family's home and privacy so completely? Are these reasons valid ones?
3. Tartuffe himself does not appear until the third act. Why does Molière delay his main character's entrance?
4. How does Elmire differ from the stepmother figure often associated with children's fairy tales?
5. How does Tartuffe's background prove a helpful contrivance in the play's resolution?
6. How are Cléante's closing lines in Act Five a confirmation of his admirable qualities?

Analyzing
7. Dorine appears in the play as a socially inferior yet mentally superior character. What lines demonstrate the use of her frankness as a foil for other characters' weaknesses?
8. Trace Orgon's decline from a sincerely pious man to a vindictive zealot. Is his tirade against Damis in Act Three, Scene 6, motivated more by a need to defend Tartuffe or to exert power over his son?
9. If hypocrisy is a major **theme** in *Tartuffe*, then marriage is a secondary one. What aspects of marriage does Molière praise or condemn in the play?

Extending
10. In Book III of *Paradise Lost*, John Milton writes: "For neither man nor angel can discern/Hypocrisy, the only evil that walks/Invisible, except to God alone." Would Molière agree with Milton's contention? Is Tartuffe indeed the visible embodiment of hypocrisy? Or is the hypocrisy of which Milton writes very much like the hypocrisy that Molière addresses in his play—an attitude that remains invisible in its most dangerous form?

APPLYING: Couplet H𝄎
See Handbook of Literary Terms, p. 946.

The simplest definition of a **couplet** is two rhyming lines. Ideally, the lengths of the two lines should be the same, and together they should form a unit of thought with its own grammatical structure. A more specific form is the heroic couplet, a rhymed pair of iambic pentameter lines. The heroic couplet reached its zenith in the Neoclassic period. Alexander Pope (pages 559–573) so popularized the heroic couplet that its influence dominated poetry for many years.

1. Find examples in *Tartuffe* of couplets that seem by modern standards to be artificial and forced.
2. Reread Dorine's comments to Madame Pernelle in Act One, Scene 1, to find examples of well-crafted couplets at their humorous best.

VOCABULARY
Context

Using context as an aid, write the most appropriate definition for each italicized word on a separate sheet of paper.

1. "And you, his sister, seem so pure,/So shy, so innocent, and so *demure*." (a) silly; (b) proper; (c) naughty.
2. "Ah, good, we're safe. Now, Mariane, my child,/You're a sweet girl who's *tractable* and mild." (a) manageable; (b) wild; (c) foolish.
3. "No, I must stop that scoundrel's *machinations*;/I'll go and tell him off; I'm out of patience." (a) inventions; (b) gifts; (c) schemes.
4. "The treasures of this world I quite despise;/Their *specious* glitter does not charm my eyes." (a) precious; (b) false; (c) honest.
5. "Don't humor fraud, but also don't *asperse*/True piety; the latter fault is worse." (a) slander; (b) praise; (c) ignore.

THINKING SKILLS
Generalizing

To generalize is to draw a general conclusion from particular information.

1. Based upon your reading of the play, comment on the following statement: "The theme of *Tartuffe* is that common sense and honesty are always rewarded."
2. Molière's play came into a great deal of criticism during his time. Molière has summarized this criticism: "*Tartuffe*, they say, is a play that offends piety: it is filled with abominations from beginning to end, and nowhere is there a line that does not deserve to be burned." But, he argues, "I have used all the art and skill that I could to distinguish the character of the hypocrite from that of the truly devout man." Elaborate on Molière's defense by citing and explaining some of the ways he makes this distinction in the play.

COMPOSITION
Writing About Writers

Compile a list of writers who, like Molière, have served as effective social critics of their time. Select one from your list. Do some research on the life of this particular writer. Then, in an essay of three to four paragraphs, examine events in the writer's life that led to the role of social critic.

Writing to Persuade

In an essay of three to four paragraphs, with specific references to the text of the play, present a defense of *Tartuffe* against the charge of being offensive to religious teachings. See "Writing to Persuade an Audience" in the Writer's Handbook.

ENRICHMENT
Writing a Scenario

Prepare a scenario, an outline of the expected course of events, for a contemporary version of Molière's *Tartuffe*. As you plan the sequence of happenings for a three- or five-act play, ask yourself these questions: Will any people in the audience recognize themselves in my play? Is my version intended to instruct or to entertain the audience? Is my play a legitimate **satire** or a harmless spoof? Would Molière approve?

Swift's father had died before young Jonathan's birth in Dublin, and his poverty-stricken mother was forced to leave him with an uncle. Though given a fine education, Swift was always distinctly aware of his status as the poor relation. That position continued to embarrass him when, in 1689, he returned to his parents' native England as the secretary (with servant status) to Sir William Temple, a distant kinsman and well-known scholar and essayist. Swift was given the task of tutoring a young ward of Temple's, the eight-year-old Esther Johnson. During the ten years that he supervised her education, Swift grew increasingly fond of the girl. Eventually he took orders in the Anglican church; and some years later when he assumed an Irish pastorate after Sir William's death, Swift brought over Esther and her friend Rebecca Dingley, to live near him. Swift adored Esther until her death in 1728. He called her Stella, the Latin word for star, as Esther meant in Hebrew.

In Ireland, Swift established a literary reputation by publishing two prose satires, *A Tale of a Tub* and *The Battle of the Books*. His prominence led him to become a spokesman for the plight of the Irish clergy, and on several occasions he was sent to England to pursue legislation beneficial to his fellow priests. On his lengthy missions there, Swift became friendly with Addison, Steele, Pope, and other writers. His time in England was intellectually and politically exciting; Swift moved in a world of new ideas and fashions that contrasted sharply with the drabness of Ireland. In 1713, Swift was greatly disappointed to be named Dean of St. Patrick's Cathedral in Dublin; he had hoped instead to receive a church in England, thereby remaining in a society in which he felt more comfortable.

Swift detested his situation in Ireland. All around him he found poverty and despair. But gradually he began to understand that what he saw in Ireland was the result of unjust treatment by English politicians and landlords. Swift the social critic became a spokesman for Irish rights.

His masterpiece, *Gulliver's Travels*, published anonymously in 1726, became an instant best seller. In it he ridiculed the pretensions of the rulers, the scientists, and philosophers of his day. With Stella's death in 1728, Swift's bitterness increased. He had suffered all his life from an inner ear disorder that had caused dizziness and uncontrollable nausea. Now it would cost him his hearing. From this time of suffering, Swift's stinging satire, "A Modest Proposal" (1729), emerged. The contrast between the idle English rich and the starving Irish poor provoked Swift's deepest sense of morality. With his characteristically elegant phrasing, Swift adopts the persona of a philosophical pragmatist who defines a problem and then matter-of-factly offers a solution. That solution stands today as a chilling comment on the horrors of indifference. Around 1740 his health began to fail, and in 1742 he was declared incapable of caring for himself. Before his death in 1745, Swift directed that his savings be used to found a hospital for lunatics and idiots.

A Modest Proposal

Jonathan Swift

For Preventing the Children of
Poor People in Ireland from Being a Burden to
Their Parents or Country, and for Making
Them Beneficial to the Public

t is a melancholy object to those who walk through this great town,[1] or travel in the country, when they see the streets, the roads, and cabin doors crowded with beggars of the female sex, followed by three, four, or six children, all in rags and importuning every passenger for an alms. These mothers, instead of being able to work for their honest livelihood, are forced to employ all their time in strolling to beg sustenance for their helpless infants; who as they grow up either turn thieves, for want of work, or leave their dear native country to fight for the Pretender[2] in Spain, or sell themselves to the Barbados.[3]

I think it is agreed by all parties that this prodigious number of children in the arms, or on the backs, or at the heels of their mothers, and frequently of their fathers, is, in the present deplorable state of the kingdom, a very great additional grievance; and therefore whoever could find out a fair, cheap, and easy method of making these children sound, useful members of the commonwealth would deserve so well of the public as to have his statue set up for a preserver of the nation.

But my intention is very far from being confined to provide only for the children of professed beggars: it is of a much greater extent and shall take in the whole number of infants at a certain age who are born of parents in effect as little able to support them as those who demand our charity in the streets.

As to my own part, having turned my thoughts for many years upon this important subject and maturely weighed the several schemes of other projectors, I have always found them grossly mistaken in their computation. It is true, a child just dropped from its dam may be supported by her milk for a solar year, with little other nourishment: at most not above the value of two shillings, which the mother may certainly get, or the value in scraps, by her lawful occupation of begging; and it is exactly at one year old that I propose to provide for them in such a manner, as, instead of being a charge upon their parents or the parish, or wanting food and raiment for the rest of their lives, they shall, on the contrary, contribute to the feeding and partly to the clothing of many thousands.

There is likewise another great advantage in my scheme, that it will prevent those voluntary abortions and that horrid practice of women murdering their bastard children, alas! too frequent among us, sacrificing the poor innocent babes, I doubt more to avoid the expense than the shame, which would move tears and pity in the most savage and inhuman breast.

---

1. *this great town*, Dublin.
2. *the Pretender*, James Stuart (1688–1766), son of King James II, "pretender" or claimant to the throne which his father had lost in the Revolution of 1688. He was Catholic, and Ireland was loyal to him.
3. *sell . . . Barbados.* Because of extreme poverty, many of the Irish bound or "sold" themselves to obtain passage to the West Indies or other British possessions in North America. They agreed to work for their new masters, usually planters, for a specified number of years.

The number of souls in this kingdom being usually reckoned one million and a half, of these I calculate there may be about two hundred thousand couple whose wives are breeders; from which number I subtract thirty thousand couple, who are able to maintain their own children (although I apprehend there cannot be so many, under the present distresses of the kingdom), but this being granted, there will remain an hundred and seventy thousand breeders. I again subtract fifty thousand for those women who miscarry, or whose children die by accident or disease within the year. There only remain one hundred and twenty thousand children of poor parents annually born. The question therefore is, How this number shall be reared and provided for? which, as I have already said, under the present situation of affairs, is utterly impossible by all the methods hitherto proposed. For we can neither employ them in handicraft or agriculture; we neither build houses (I mean in the country) nor cultivate land: they can very seldom pick up a livelihood by stealing till they arrive at six years old, except where they are of towardly[4] parts; although I confess they learn the rudiments much earlier; during which time they can, however, be properly looked upon only as probationers; as I have been informed by a principal gentleman in the county of Cavan, who protested to me that he never knew above one or two instances under the age of six, even in a part of the kingdom so renowned for the quickest proficiency in that art.

I am assured by our merchants that a boy or a girl before twelve years old is no salable commodity; and even when they come to this age they will not yield above three pounds, or three pounds and half a crown at most, on the exchange; which cannot turn to account either to the parents or kingdom, the charge of nutriment and rags having been at least four times that value.

I shall now therefore humbly propose my own thoughts, which I hope will not be liable to the least objection.

I have been assured by a very knowing American of my acquaintance in London that a young healthy child well nursed is at a year old a most delicious, nourishing, and wholesome food, whether stewed, roasted, baked, or boiled; and I make no doubt that it will equally serve in a fricassee or a ragout.[5]

I do therefore humbly offer it to public consideration that of the hundred and twenty thousand children already computed, twenty thousand may be reserved for breed, whereof only one-fourth part to be males; which is more than we allow to sheep, black cattle, or swine; and my reason is that these children are seldom the fruits of marriage, a circumstance not much regarded by our savages; therefore one male will be sufficient to serve four females. That the remaining hundred thousand may, at a year old, be offered in sale to the persons of quality and fortune through the kingdom; always advising the mother to let them suck plentifully in the last month, so as to render them plump and fat for a good table. A child will make two dishes at an entertainment for friends; and when the family dines alone, the fore or hind quarter will make a reasonable dish, and seasoned with a little pepper or salt will be very good boiled on the fourth day, especially in winter.

I have reckoned upon a medium that a child just born will weigh twelve pounds, and in a solar year, if tolerably nursed, will increase to twenty-eight pounds.

I grant this food will be somewhat dear, and therefore very proper for landlords, who, as they have already devoured most of the parents, seem to have the best title to the children.

Infant's flesh will be in season throughout the year, but more plentifully in March, and a little before and after: for we are told by a grave author, an eminent French physician,[6] that fish being a prolific diet, there are more children born in Roman Catholic countries about nine months after Lent than at any other season; therefore, reckoning a year after Lent, the markets will be more glutted than usual, because the number of popish infants is at least three to one in this kingdom: and therefore it will have one other collateral advantage, by lessening the number of papists among us.

---

4. *towardly*, dutiful; easily managed.
5. *ragout* (ra gü'), a highly seasoned meat stew.
6. *grave author . . . physician*, François Rabelais (c. 1494–1553), who was anything but a "grave author."

I have already computed the charge of nursing a beggar's child (in which list I reckon all cottagers, laborers, and four-fifths of the farmers) to be about two shillings per annum, rags included; and I believe no gentleman would repine to give ten shillings for the carcass of a good fat child, which, as I have said, will make four dishes of excellent nutritive meat, when he has only some particular friend or his own family to dine with him. Thus the squire will learn to be a good landlord and grow popular among his tenants; the mother will have eight shillings net profit and be fit for work till she produces another child.

Those who are more thrifty (as I must confess the times require) may flay the carcass; the skin of which artificially[7] dressed will make admirable gloves for ladies and summer boots for fine gentlemen.

As to our city of Dublin, shambles[8] may be appointed for this purpose in the most convenient parts of it, and butchers we may be assured will not be wanting; although I rather recommend buying the children alive and dressing them hot from the knife as we do roasting pigs.

A very worthy person, a true lover of his country, and whose virtues I highly esteem, was lately pleased, in discoursing on this matter, to offer a refinement upon my scheme. He said that many gentlemen of this kingdom, having of late destroyed their deer, he conceived that the want of venison might be well supplied by the bodies of young lads and maidens, not exceeding fourteen years of age nor under twelve; so great a number of both sexes in every country being now ready to starve for want of work and service; and these to be disposed of by their parents, if alive, or otherwise by their nearest relations. But with due deference to so excellent a friend and so deserving a patriot, I cannot be altogether in his sentiments; for as to the males, my American acquaintance assured me from frequent experience that their flesh was generally tough and lean, like that of our schoolboys, by continual exercise, and their taste disagreeable; and to fatten them would not answer the charge. Then as to the females, it would, I think, with humble submission be a loss to the public, because they soon would become breeders

themselves: and besides, it is not improbable that some scrupulous people might be apt to censure such a practice (although indeed very unjustly), as a little bordering upon cruelty; which, I confess, has always been with me the strongest objection against any project, how well soever intended.

But in order to justify my friend, he confessed that this expedient was put into his head by the famous Psalmanazar,[9] a native of the island Formosa, who came from thence to London above twenty years ago: and in conversation told my friend that in his country when any young person happened to be put to death, the executioner sold the carcass to persons of quality as a prime dainty; and that in his time the body of a plump girl of fifteen, who was crucified for an attempt to poison the emperor, was sold to his imperial majesty's prime minister of state, and other great mandarins of the court, in joints from the gibbet, at four hundred crowns. Neither indeed can I deny that if the same use were made of several plump girls in this town, who, without one single groat to their fortunes, cannot stir abroad without a chair, and appear at a playhouse and assemblies in foreign fineries which they never will pay for, the kingdom would not be the worse.

Some persons of a desponding spirit are in great concern about that vast number of poor people who are aged, diseased, or maimed; and I have been desired to employ my thoughts, what course may be taken to ease the nation of so grievous an encumbrance. But I am not in the least pain upon that matter, because it is very well known that they are every day dying and rotting, by cold and famine, and filth and vermin, as fast as can be reasonably expected. And as to the young laborers, they are now in almost as hopeful a condition: they cannot get work, and consequently pine away for want of nourishment to a degree that if at any time they are accidentally hired to common labor, they have not strength to perform it; and thus the

---

7. *artificially,* artfully; skillfully.
8. *shambles,* slaughterhouses.
9. *Psalmanazar,* the imposter George Psalmanazar (c. 1679–1763), a Frenchman who passed himself off in England as a Formosan, and wrote a totally fictional "true" account of Formosa, in which he described cannibalism.

country and themselves are happily delivered from the evils to come.

I have too long digressed and therefore shall return to my subject. I think the advantages, by the proposal which I have made, are obvious and many, as well as of the highest importance.

For first, as I have already observed, it would greatly lessen the number of papists, with whom we are yearly overrun, being the principal breeders of the nation, as well as our most dangerous enemies; and who stay at home on purpose to deliver the kingdom to the Pretender, hoping to take their advantage by the absence of so many good Protestants, who have chosen rather to leave their country than stay at home and pay tithes against their conscience to an Episcopal curate.[10]

Secondly, the poorer tenants will have something valuable of their own, which by law may be made liable to distress,[11] and help to pay their landlord's rent; their corn and cattle being already seized, and money a thing unknown.

Thirdly, whereas the maintenance of a hundred thousand children, from two years old and upwards, cannot be computed at less than ten shillings a piece per annum, the nation's stock will be thereby increased fifty thousand pounds per annum, beside the profit of a new dish introduced to the tables of all gentlemen of fortune in the kingdom who have any refinement in taste. And the money will circulate among ourselves, the goods being entirely of our own growth and manufacture.

Fourthly, the constant breeders, besides the gain of eight shillings sterling per annum by the sale of their children, will be rid of the charge of maintaining them after the first year.

Fifthly, this food would likewise bring great custom to taverns: where the vintners will certainly be so prudent as to procure the best receipts for dressing it to perfection, and consequently have their houses frequented by all the fine gentlemen, who justly value themselves upon their knowledge in good eating: and a skillful cook, who understands how to oblige his guests, will contrive to make it as expensive as they please.

Sixthly, this would be a great inducement to marriage, which all wise nations have either encouraged by rewards or enforced by laws and penalties. It would increase the care and tenderness of mothers toward their children, when they were sure of a settlement for life to the poor babes, provided in some sort by the public, to their annual profit instead of expense. We should see an honest emulation among the married women, which of them could bring the fattest child to the market. Men would become as fond of their wives during the time of their pregnancy as they are now of their mares in foal, their cows in calf, or sows when they are ready to farrow; nor offer to beat or kick them (as is too frequent a practice) for fear of a miscarriage.

Many other advantages might be enumerated. For instance, the addition of some thousand carcasses in our exportation of barreled beef, the propagation of swine's flesh, and improvement in the art of making good bacon, so much wanted among us by the great destruction of pigs, too frequent at our tables; which are no way comparable in taste or magnificence to a well-grown, fat, yearling child, which roasted whole will make a considerable figure at a lord mayor's feast, or any other public entertainment. But this and many others I omit, being studious of brevity.

Supposing that one thousand families in this city would be constant customers for infants' flesh, besides others who might have it at merry meetings, particularly weddings and christenings, I compute that Dublin would take off annually about twenty thousand carcasses; and the rest of the kingdom (where probably they will be sold somewhat cheaper) the remaining eighty thousand.

I can think of no one objection that will possibly be raised against this proposal, unless it should be urged that the number of people will be thereby much lessened in the kingdom. This I freely own, and it was indeed one principal design in offering it to the world. I desire the reader will observe that I calculate my remedy for this one individual king-

---

10. *Protestants . . . curate.* Swift is here attacking the absentee landlords.
11. *distress,* distraint, the legal seizure of property for payment of debts.

dom of Ireland, and for no other that ever was, is, or, I think, ever can be upon earth. Therefore let no man talk to me of other expedients: of taxing our absentees at five shillings a pound: of using neither clothes nor household furniture, except what is of our own growth and manufacture: of utterly rejecting the materials and instruments that promote foreign luxury: of curing the expensiveness of pride, vanity, idleness, and gaming in our women: of introducing a vein of parsimony, prudence, and temperance: of learning to love our country, in the want of which we differ even from Laplanders and the inhabitants of Topinamboo:[12] of quitting our animosities and factions, nor acting any longer like the Jews, who were murdering one another at the very moment their city was taken:[13] of being a little cautious not to sell our country and conscience for nothing: of teaching landlords to have at least one degree of mercy toward their tenants: lastly, of putting a spirit of honesty, industry, and skill into our shopkeepers; who, if a resolution could now be taken to buy only our native goods, would immediately unite to cheat and exact upon us in the price, the measure, and the goodness, nor could ever yet be brought to make one fair proposal of just dealing, though often and earnestly invited to it.[14]

Therefore, I repeat, let no man talk to me of these and the like expedients, till he has at least some glimpse of hope that there will ever be some hearty and sincere attempt to put them in practice.

But as to myself, having been wearied out for many years with offering vain, idle, visionary thoughts, and at length utterly despairing of success, I fortunately fell upon this proposal; which, as it is wholly new, so it has something solid and real, of no expense and little trouble, full in our own power, and whereby we can incur no danger in disobliging England. For this kind of commodity will not bear exportation, the flesh being of too tender a consistence to admit a long continuance in salt, although perhaps I could name a country which would be glad to eat up our whole nation without it.[15]

After all, I am not so violently bent upon my own opinion as to reject any offer proposed by wise men, which shall be found equally innocent, cheap, easy, and effectual. But before something of that kind shall be advanced in contradiction to my scheme, and offering a better, I desire the author or authors will be pleased maturely to consider two points. First, as things now stand, how they will be able to find food and raiment for an hundred thousand useless mouths and backs. And, secondly, there being a round million of creatures in human figure throughout this kingdom, whose whole subsistence put into a common stock would leave them in debt two millions of pounds sterling, adding those who are beggars by profession to the bulk of farmers, cottagers, and laborers, with their wives and children, who are beggars in effect; I desire those politicians, who dislike my overture, and may perhaps be so bold as to attempt an answer, that they will first ask the parents of these mortals, whether they would not at this day think it a great happiness to have been sold for food at a year old in the manner I prescribe, and thereby have avoided such a perpetual scene of misfortunes as they have since gone through by the oppression of landlords, the impossibility of paying rent without money or trade, the want of common sustenance, with neither house nor clothes to cover them from the inclemencies of the weather, and the most inevitable prospect of entailing the like or greater miseries upon their breed for ever.

I profess, in the sincerity of my heart, that I have not the least personal interest in endeavoring to promote this necessary work, having no other motive than the public good of my country, by advancing our trade, providing for infants, relieving the poor, and giving some pleasure to the rich. I have no children by which I can propose to get a single penny; the youngest being nine years old, and my wife past childbearing.

1729

---

12. *Topinamboo*, a savage area of Brazil.
13. *city was taken*. While the Roman Emperor Titus was besieging Jerusalem, which he took and destroyed in A.D. 70, within the city factions of fanatics were waging bloody warfare.
14. *invited to it*. Swift had already made all these proposals in various pamphlets.
15. *a country . . . without it.* England; this is another way of saying, "The English are devouring the Irish."

THINK AND DISCUSS
Understanding
1. How is Swift's title both misleading and at the same time perfectly appropriate?
2. At what point does Swift's satirical **tone** first become apparent to you?
3. What harsh conditions of life in Ireland are casually revealed in this essay?
4. What specific group does Swift blame for the troubles facing Ireland?

Analyzing
5. Find examples of terms which are usually applied to animals. How does this recurring animal **imagery** contribute to Swift's purpose?
6. How effective is Swift's satire as a medium for reform? Are you emotionally moved by his message, or are you too affected by the details to notice the overall plea for reform?

Extending
7. What are the major targets of this satire? In what ways might the Irish bear some responsibility for their plight?

REVIEWING: Satire H𝟕
See Handbook of Literary Terms, p. 968.
Satire is the technique of ridiculing the vices or follies of people and society, usually for the purpose of producing some change in attitude or action. Although satire may seem negative, it usually implies a positive standard of virtue against which the follies of the age are judged.

1. Look at the list of alternatives on page 557, beginning, "Therefore let no man talk to me of other expedients . . ." and continuing to the end of the paragraph. What function does this list serve in the context of the whole essay?
2. Is the author ridiculing the list of alternatives you have just looked at, or is the object of ridicule something else?

THINKING SKILLS
Synthesizing
To synthesize is to put together parts and elements so as to form a whole, a new pattern or structure not evident before. Synthesis can involve personal experience and imagination.

1. Like Milton's Satan in *Paradise Lost*, Swift was an exile from Paradise, in his case London. Further, like Satan in Hell, Swift became a leader in his place of exile, Dublin. Employing the biographical sketch of Swift on page 552 and the excerpt from *Paradise Lost* (pages 500–506), give some ways in which the character of Satan and the author Swift exhibit a defiance of fate.
2. Swift was a hero to the Irish people in real life; Satan is a villain in *Paradise Lost*. Swift's exile from London was due to political circumstances; Satan's exile from Paradise was due to his actions. From what motives do you think each acted?

COMPOSITION ◄━●
Writing a Satire
Write your own humble solution to a problem affecting society today. Remember to remain sympathetic to your cause even as you satirize the situations surrounding it.

Writing an Editorial
As the editor of your school newspaper, you choose to publish an anonymous letter satirizing the school's administrative staff. You are reprimanded for your decision by the principal. Write an editorial for the next issue of the newspaper. In it, discuss the reasons for your original decision and define your present stance.

ENRICHMENT
Analyzing a Persona
Look up the entry for *persona* in the Glossary of Literary Terms. After reading the entry, look back at "A Modest Proposal" and write a description of the persona in that essay.

BIOGRAPHY

Alexander Pope
1688–1744

In an age that valued beauty and elegance, Alexander Pope was deformed by a childhood struggle with tuberculosis of the spine. In an age when Roman Catholics in England could not vote, hold public office, or even attend the universities, Alexander Pope was a Catholic. In an age when writers enjoyed the patronage of wealthy statesmen, Alexander Pope lived solely on the profits from his writings. Pope became an enormously successful writer, the first, in fact, to show that writing could be a profitable career. He simultaneously evolved into the sharpest of social critics, a man who knew the stings of verbal abuse and showed no hesitancy in striking out at others.

He was born the son of a wealthy London merchant, who retired from business in his son's infancy and settled on a rural property in Windsor Forest. There, young Alexander acquired a lifelong love of natural beauty and gardening. His family nursed his physical infirmities while encouraging his evident artistic interests. In 1709, Pope published his first collection of poetry, the *Pastorals;* and two years later, he was nationally acclaimed for *An Essay on Criticism.* The first work echoed Pope's love of country landscape; it was in many respects an early version of the later Romantic poets' major motif. The second work treats the art of writing well. A didactic poem in the manner of Horace, the *Essay* established Pope at an early age as a skilled satirist.

One of Pope's earliest financial successes had been a translation of Homer's *Iliad.* A reverence for Homer and the other ancient writers was, Pope felt, the basis for any aspiring poet's success. In his *An Essay on Criticism,* Pope defined the three basic rules for a poet: 1) Imitate the poems of Homer and Virgil and Horace; 2) Follow "nature"—write about things that are common to all people at all times; 3) State the general truths about life with greater finesse than any previous writer has been able to do. In this particular essay, Pope perfected the tightly controlled device that would become his trademark as a poet: the heroic couplet, or pair of rhyming iambic pentameter lines. Pope worked and reworked each couplet until it was precisely what he intended it to be.

Pope's insistence on careful phrasing explains in part the fact that, next to Shakespeare, he is the most often quoted English poet. In the selections that follow, from *The Rape of the Lock* and the *Essay on Man,* you will be treated to a display of Pope's intricately executed **couplets**—complete thoughts explored and captured in two lines of poetry. *The Rape of the Lock,* which humorously magnifies the theft of a lock of hair into a catastrophe, is based on an actual incident in society. (See pages 566–567, question 8.) To read it is to witness the birth of the mock epic in English literature. With *The Rape of the Lock* (a shorter version appeared in 1712 and a longer one in 1714), Pope indulged both his love of beauty and his aversion to pretense. The second selection, from *An Essay on Man,* is a look at the state of humanity from the psychological viewpoint of the eighteenth century.

from The Rape of the Lock

Alexander Pope

Canto I

What dire offense from amorous causes springs,
What mighty contests rise from trivial things,
I sing—This verse to Caryll,[1] Muse! is due;
This, even Belinda may vouchsafe to view:
5 Slight is the subject, but not so the praise,
If she inspire, and he approve my lays.
   Say what strange motive, Goddess! could
     compel
A well-bred lord to assault a gentle belle?
O say what stranger cause, yet unexplored,
10 Could make a gentle belle reject a lord?
In tasks so bold, can little men engage,
And in soft bosoms dwells such mighty rage?
   Sol through white curtains shot a timorous
     ray,
And oped those eyes that must eclipse the day;
15 Now lap dogs give themselves the rousing
     shake.
And sleepless lovers, just at twelve, awake:
Thrice rung the bell, the slipper knocked the
     ground,
And the pressed watch returned a silver
     sound.[2]
Belinda still her downy pillow pressed,
20 Her guardian Sylph prolonged the balmy rest.
'Twas he had summoned to her silent bed
The morning dream that hovered o'er her head.
A youth more glittering than a Birth-night
     beau,[3]
(That even in slumber caused her cheek to
     glow)
25 Seemed to her ear his winning lips to lay,
And thus in whispers said, or seemed to
     say. . . .

As Belinda dreams, her guardian
sylph, Ariel, delivers a long speech
explaining the life of the sylphs, and
concludes with a grave warning.

"Of these am I, who thy protection claim,
A watchful sprite, and Ariel is my name.
Late, as I ranged the crystal wilds of air,
30 In the clear mirror of thy ruling star
I saw, alas! some dread event impend,
Ere to the main this morning sun descend,
But heaven reveals not what, or how, or where:
Warned by the Sylph, oh pious maid, beware!
35 This to disclose is all thy guardian can:
Beware of all, but most beware of man!"
   He said; when Shock,[4] who thought she
     slept too long,
Leaped up, and waked his mistress with his
     tongue.
'Twas then, Belinda, if report say true,
40 Thy eyes first opened on a billet-doux;[5]
Wounds, charms, and ardors were no sooner
     read,
But all the vision vanished from thy head.
   And now, unveiled, the toilet[6] stands
     displayed,

---

1. *Caryll*, John Caryll, who suggested that Pope write the poem to heal the breach between the two families.
2. *pressed . . . sound*, a type of watch in which a pressure on the stem would cause the watch to strike the last hour again.
3. *Birth-night beau*, a gentleman dressed in fine clothes for the sovereign's birthday ball.
4. *Shock*, Belinda's dog.
5. *billet-doux*, love letter.
6. *toilet*, dressing table.

Each silver vase in mystic order laid.
45 First, robed in white, the nymph intent adores,
With head uncovered, the cosmetic powers.
A heavenly image in the glass appears,
To that she bends, to that her eye she rears;
The inferior priestess,[7] at her altar's side,
50 Trembling, begins the sacred rites of pride.
Unnumbered treasures ope at once, and here
The various offerings of the world appear;
From each she nicely culls with curious toil,
And decks the goddess with the glittering spoil.
55 This casket India's glowing gems unlocks,
And all Arabia[8] breathes from yonder box.
The tortoise here and elephant unite,
Transformed to combs, the speckled and the
white.
Here files of pins extend their shining rows,
60 Puffs, powders, patches, Bibles, billet-doux.
Now awful[9] Beauty puts on all its arms;
The fair each moment rises in her charms,
Repairs her smiles, awakens every grace,
And calls forth all the wonders of her face;
65 Sees by degrees a purer blush arise,
And keener lightnings quicken in her eyes.
The busy Sylphs surround their darling care;
These set the head, and those divide the hair,
Some fold the sleeve, while others plait the
gown;
70 And Betty's[10] praised for labors not her own.

Canto II

After her elaborate preparations at
the dressing table, Belinda sets out,
"launched on the bosom of the silver
Thames," on her way to Hampton Court,
one of the royal palaces near London, and
the center of her delightful, sophisticated,
and trivial social life.

This nymph, to the destruction of mankind,
Nourished two locks, which graceful
hung behind
In equal curls, and well conspired to deck
With shining ringlets the smooth ivory neck.
75 Love in these labyrinths his slaves detains,

Illustration by Louis du Guernier for *The Rape of the Lock*. 1714. British Library

And mighty hearts are held in slender chains.
With hairy springes[11] we the birds betray,
Slight lines of hair surprise the finny prey,
Fair tresses man's imperial race ensnare,
80 And beauty draws us with a single hair.
The adventurous Baron the bright
locks admired;
He saw, he wished, and to the prize aspired.

---

7. *inferior priestess*, Belinda's maid, Betty.
8. *Arabia*, source of perfumes.
9. *awful*, awesome or awe-inspiring.
10. *Betty*, Belinda's maid.
11. *springes*, nooses to catch birds.

Resolved to win, he meditates the way,
By force to ravish, or by fraud betray;
85 For when success a lover's toils attends,
Few ask, if fraud or force attained his ends.

The sylph Ariel, aware of the threat to
Belinda, summons his fellow sylphs and
sends them to their various stations about
Belinda to guard her every precious possession.

"This day, black omens threat the
    brightest Fair
That ever deserved a watchful spirit's care;
Some dire disaster, or by force, or slight;
90 But what, or where, the Fates have
    wrapped in night.
Whether the nymph shall break Diana's law,[12]
Or some frail china jar receive a flaw;
Or stain her honor, or her new brocade;
Forget her prayers, or miss a masquerade;
95 Or lose her heart, or necklace, at a ball;
Or whether Heaven has doomed that
    Shock must fall.
Haste, then, ye spirits! to your charge repair:
The fluttering fan be Zephyretta's care;
The drops[13] to thee, Brillante, we consign;
100 And, Momentilla, let the watch be thine:
Do thou, Crispissa, tend her favorite lock;
Ariel himself shall be the guard of Shock.
    "To fifty chosen Sylphs, of special note,
We trust the important charge, the petticoat:
105 Oft have we known that sevenfold fence to fail,
Though stiff with hoops, and armed with ribs
    of whale;
Form a strong line about the silver bound,
And guard the wide circumference around.
    "Whatever spirit, careless of his charge,
110 His post neglects, or leaves the fair at large,
Shall feel sharp vengeance soon o'ertake his
    sins,
Be stopped in vials, or tranfixed with pins;
Or plunged in lakes of bitter washes lie,
Or wedged whole ages in a bodkin's[14] eye:
115 Gums and pomatums[15] shall his flight restrain,
While clogged he beats his silken wings in vain;

Or alum styptics[16] with contracting power
Shrink his thin essence like a rivelled flower:
Or, as Ixion[17] fixed, the wretch shall feel
120 The giddy motion of the whirling mill,
In fumes of burning chocolate shall glow,
And tremble at the sea that froths below!"
    He spoke; the spirits from the sails descend;
Some, orb in orb, around the nymph extend,
125 Some thrid[18] the mazy ringlets of her hair,
Some hang upon the pendants of her ear;
With beating hearts the dire event they wait,
Anxious, and trembling for the birth of Fate.

Canto III

Close by those meads, for ever crowned with
    flowers,
130 Where Thames with pride surveys his rising
    towers,
There stands a structure of majestic frame,
Which from the neighboring Hampton takes
    its name.[19]
Here Britain's statesmen oft the fall foredoom
Of foreign tyrants, and of nymphs at home;
135 Here thou, great Anna![20] whom three realms
    obey,
Dost sometimes counsel take—and sometimes
    tea.
    Hither the heroes and the nymphs resort,
To taste awhile the pleasures of a court;
In various talk the instructive hours they
    passed,
140 Who gave the ball, or paid the visit last;
One speaks the glory of the British Queen,
And one describes a charming Indian screen;
A third interprets motions, looks, and eyes;
At every word a reputation dies.

---

12. *Diana's law*, chastity. Diana was the goddess of maid-
enhood.
13. *drops*, pendant earrings.
14. *bodkin*, a large blunt needle with an eye.
15. *pomatums*, perfumed ointments to keep the hair in
place.
16. *alum styptics*, astringents.
17. *Ixion*, in Greek myth, fastened to an endlessly revolving wheel in Hades as punishment for making love to
Juno, queen of the gods.
18. *thrid*, thread; pass through.
19. *name*, Hampton Court, a royal palace near London.
20. *Anna*, Queen Anne (1702-1714).

145 Snuff, or the fan, supply each pause of chat,
    With singing, laughing, ogling, and all that.
       Meanwhile, declining from the noon of day,
    The sun obliquely shoots his burning ray;
    The hungry judges soon the sentence sign,
150 And wretches hang that jurymen may
        dine; . . .

> Belinda joins the pleasure-seekers at
> Hampton Court, and wins at a card game,
> ombre, over the Baron who covets her
> locks. But as the game ends, and they all
> partake of refreshments, the Baron seizes
> his opportunity.

      But when to mischief mortals bend their will,
    How soon they find fit instruments of ill!
    Just then, Clarissa drew with tempting grace
    A two-edged weapon[21] from her shining case;
155 So ladies in romance assist their knight,
    Present the spear, and arm him for the fight.
    He takes the gift with reverence, and extends
    The little engine on his fingers' ends;
    This just behind Belinda's neck he spread,
160 As o'er the fragrant steams she bends her
       head:
    Swift to the lock a thousand sprites repair,
    A thousand wings, by turns, blow back the
       hair;
    And thrice they twitched the diamond in her
       ear;
    Thrice she looked back, and thrice the foe
       drew near.
165 Just in that instant, anxious Ariel sought
    The close recesses of the virgin's thought;
    As on the nosegay in her breast reclined,
    He watched the ideas rising in her mind,
    Sudden he viewed, in spite of all her art,
170 An earthly lover lurking at her heart.
    Amazed, confused, he found his power expired,
    Resigned to fate, and with a sigh retired.
       The peer now spreads the glittering forfex[22]
       wide,
    To inclose the lock; now joins it, to divide.
175 Even then, before the fatal engine closed,
    A wretched Sylph too fondly interposed;

Illustration by Louis du Guernier for *The Rape of the Lock.* 1714. British Library

    Fate urged the shears, and cut the Sylph in
       twain
    (But airy substance soon unites again).
    The meeting points the sacred hair dissever
180 From the fair head, for ever, and for ever!
       Then flashed the living lightning from her
       eyes,
    And screams of horror rend the affrighted skies.
    Not louder shrieks to pitying Heaven are cast,
    When husbands or when lap dogs breathe
       their last;

---

21. *two-edged weapon,* scissors.
22. *forfex,* scissors.

Pope **563**

185 Or when rich China vessels fallen from high,
In glittering dust and painted fragments lie!
   "Let wreaths of triumph now my temples
    twine,"
(The victor cried) "the glorious prize is mine!
While fish in streams, or birds delight in air,
190 Or in a coach and six the British fair,
As long as *Atalantis*[23] shall be read,
Or the small pillow grace a lady's bed,
While visits shall be paid on solemn days,
When numerous wax-lights in bright order
    blaze,
195 While nymphs take treats, or assignations give,
So long my honor, name, and praise shall live!
   What time would spare, from steel receives
    its date,
And monuments, like men, submit to fate!
Steel could the labor of the gods destroy,
200 And strike to dust the imperial towers of Troy;
Steel could the works of mortal pride confound,
And hew triumphal arches to the ground.
What wonder then, fair nymph! thy hairs
    should feel
The conquering force of unresisted steel?"

Canto IV

Confusion and hysteria result from the
Baron's dastardly deed of cutting off
Belinda's lock of hair, and Belinda delivers to the Baron a speech of elevated indignation.

---

205   "For ever cursed be this detested day,
Which snatched my best, my favorite curl
    away!
Happy! ah ten times happy had I been,
If Hampton Court these eyes had never seen!
Yet am not I the first mistaken maid,
210 By love of courts to numerous ills betrayed.
Oh had I rather unadmired remained
In some lone isle, or distant northern land;
Where the gilt chariot never marks the way,
Where none learn ombre, none e'er taste
    bohea![24]

215 There kept my charms concealed from mortal
    eye,
Like roses that in deserts bloom and die.
What moved my mind with youthful lords to
    roam?
Oh had I stayed, and said my prayers at home!
'Twas this, the morning omens seemed to tell:
220 Thrice from my trembling hand the patchbox
    fell;
The tottering china shook without a wind,
Nay, Poll sat mute, and Shock was most
    unkind!
A Sylph too warned me of the threats of fate,
In mystic visions, now believed too late!
225 See the poor remnants of these slighted hairs!
My hands shall rend what ev'n thy rapine
    spares:
These, in two sable ringlets taught to break,
Once gave new beauties to the snowy neck.
The sister-lock now sits uncouth, alone,
230 And in its fellow's fate foresees its own;
Uncurled it hangs, the fatal shears demands;
And tempts, once more, thy sacrilegious hands.
Oh hadst thou, cruel! been content to seize
Hairs less in sight, or any hairs but these!"

Canto V

Such a treacherous deed as the rape of a
lock of lady's hair inevitably results in an
"epic" battle.

---

235 "To arms, to arms!" the fierce virago[25] cries,
And swift as lightning to the combat flies.
All side in parties, and begin the attack;
Fans clap, silks rustle, and tough
    whalebones crack;
Heroes' and heroines' shouts confusedly rise,
240 And bass, and treble voices strike the skies.
No common weapons in their hands are found,
Like gods they fight, nor dread a mortal
    wound.

---

23. *Atalantis,* a popular book of court scandal and gossip.
24. *bohea,* an expensive tea.
25. *virago,* a strong, vigorous woman; amazon.

Belinda attacks the Baron, but to no avail.
They are both deprived of the precious
lock as it rises into the skies. There it is
immortalized and transfigured into a
heavenly body.

See fierce Belinda on the Baron flies,
With more than usual lightning in her eyes;
245 Nor feared the chief the unequal fight to try,
Who sought no more than on his foe to die.
But this bold lord, with manly strength endued,
She with one finger and a thumb subdued:
Just where the breath of life his nostrils drew,
250 A charge of snuff the wily virgin threw;
The Gnomes direct, to every atom just,
The pungent grains of titillating dust.
Sudden, with starting tears each eye o'erflows,
And the high dome re-echoes to his nose.
255 "Now meet thy fate," incensed Belinda cried,
And drew a deadly bodkin[26] from her side.
(The same, his ancient personage to deck,
Her great-great-grandsire wore about his neck
In three seal rings; which after, melted down,
260 Formed a vast buckle for his widow's gown:
Her infant grandame's whistle next it grew,
The bells she jingled, and the whistle blew;
Then in a bodkin graced her mother's hairs,
Which long she wore, and now Belinda wears.)
265 "Boast not my fall" (he cried) "insulting foe!
Thou by some other shalt be laid as low.
Nor think, to die dejects my lofty mind;
All that I dread is leaving you behind!
Rather than so, ah let me still survive,
270 And burn in Cupid's flames—but burn alive."
"Restore the lock!" she cries; and all around
"Restore the lock!" the vaulted roofs rebound.
Not fierce Othello in so loud a strain
Roared for the handkerchief that caused his
pain.[27]
275 But see how oft ambitious aims are crossed,
And chiefs contend till all the prize is lost!
The lock, obtained with guilt, and kept with
pain,
In every place is sought, but sought in vain:
With such a prize no mortal must be blest,

Illustration by Louis du Guernier for *The Rape of
the Lock*. 1714. British Library

280 So Heaven decrees! with Heaven who can
contest?
Some thought it mounted to the lunar sphere,
Since all things lost on earth, are treasured
there.
There heroes' wits are kept in ponderous vases,
And beaux' in snuffboxes and tweezer-cases.

26. *bodkin*, ornamental hairpin shaped like a stiletto.
27. *Othello . . . pain.* In Shakespeare's play, Othello
becomes enraged when his wife Desdemona fails to produce
a highly prized handkerchief and is convinced she has given
it to her supposed lover.

Pope 565

285 There broken vows, and deathbed alms are
        found,
    And lovers' hearts with ends of riband bound;
    The courtier's promises and sick man's prayers,
    The smiles of harlots, and the tears of heirs.
    Cages for gnats, and chains to yoke a flea,
290 Dried butterflies, and tomes of casuistry.[28]
        But trust the Muse—she saw it upward rise,
    Though marked by none but quick poetic eyes:
    (So Rome's great founder to the heavens
        withdrew,
    To Proculus alone confessed in view.)[29]
295 A sudden star, it shot through liquid air,
    And drew behind a radiant trail of hair.
    Not Berenice's lock[30] first rose so bright,
    The heavens bespangling with disheveled light.
    The Sylphs behold it kindling as it flies,
300 And pleased pursue its progress through the
        skies.
        This the beau monde[31] shall from the Mall[32]
        survey,
    And hail with music its propitious ray.
    This, the blest lover shall for Venus take,
    And send up vows from Rosamonda's lake.[33]
305 This Partridge soon shall view in cloudless
        skies,
    When next he looks through Galileo's eyes;

And hence the egregious wizard shall foredoom
The fate of Louis, and the fall of Rome.[34]
    Then cease, bright nymph! to mourn thy
        ravished hair
310 Which adds new glory to the shining sphere!
Not all the tresses that fair head can boast
Shall draw such envy as the lock you lost.
For, after all the murders of your eye,
When, after millions slain, your self shall die;
315 When those fair suns shall set, as set they must,
And all those tresses shall be laid in dust;
This *Lock*, the Muse shall consecrate to fame,
And 'midst the stars inscribe Belinda's name.
1712   1714

---

28. *tomes of casuistry*, books of oversubtle reasoning about conscience and conduct.
29. *So Rome's . . . view.* Proculus, a Roman senator, saw Romulus, the founder of Rome, taken to heaven.
30. *Berenice's lock.* The Egyptian queen Berenice dedicated a lock of her beautiful hair to Venus for the safe return of her husband from war; the hair was turned into a comet. There is a constellation known as *Coma Berenicis*, Berenice's hair.
31. *beau monde*, fashionable society.
32. *Mall*, a promenade in St. James's Park in London.
33. *Rosamonda's lake*, in St. James's Park.
34. *Partridge . . . Rome.* John Partridge (1644–1715) was an astrologer and almanac-maker who annually predicted the downfall of the King of France and of the Pope.

THINK AND DISCUSS
Understanding
1. What details make Belinda's toilette seem more like a religious ceremony than a grooming session?
2. How does the Baron manage to complete his theft despite the presence of the Sylphs? What weapon does the Baron use to achieve his victory?
3. Describe Belinda's plan of reprisal.
4. What ultimately becomes of the precious lock?

Analyzing
5. The Baron's feelings for Belinda are clear, but what are Belinda's feelings for him?
6. Do Belinda's protective Sylphs contribute more to the **plot** of the poem or the atmosphere?
7. Pope's mock epic depends for its effect on the juxtaposition of the serious and the trivial. Find at least five instances.

Extending
8. *The Rape of the Lock* was written to help end a quarrel between the families of Ara-

bella Fermor and Lord Petre. The young lord had in fact cut off a lock of the young lady's hair, and social warfare ensued. Apparently Pope's mock epic was successful in healing the breach, and Arabella ("Belinda") rather enjoyed the attention given her. There was to be no storybook ending to the incident, however, for Arabella and Lord Petre. He married a younger and richer heiress, then died of smallpox within a year. Arabella married another gentleman and later had six children. Pope's poetic comment on this actual incident raises the question of whether his "battle between the sexes" is a legitimate **satire** or a sexist statement. Does Pope seem more prejudiced toward one sex than the other, or does he remain a detached observer? Can you think of other writers who have used a conflict between men and women as a central theme?

APPLYING: Consonance HℤT
See Handbook of Literary Terms, p. 946.

Consonance refers to the repetition of consonant sounds that are preceded by different vowel sounds. It is an effective device for linking sound and meaning. In the following couplet, note how the final word in each line repeats the identical consonant sound preceded by different vowel sounds: "Late, as I ranged the crystal wilds of air,/In the clear mirror of thy ruling star . . ."

1. Identify the end words that illustrate exact rhyme in the following couplets.

   Or alum styptics with contracting power
   Shrink his thin essence like a rivelled flower:
   Or, as Ixion fixed, the wretch shall feel
   The giddy motion of the whirling mill . . .

2. Identify the end words that illustrate consonance in the above couplets.

VOCABULARY
Etymology

Use your Glossary to answer on a separate sheet of paper the following questions about the italicized words.

1. From what language does the word *amorous* derive?
2. What is the meaning of the Old French word *esprit*, from which *sprite* is derived?
3. What is the meaning of the Latin word that is the source of *ardor?*
4. Of what word is *vial* a variant?
5. From what language does *wretch* come, and what was the original meaning of the word?

COMPOSITION ◆━
Writing a Profile

Develop a written profile of Clarissa, a minor though important character in Canto III. Is she the villain of the poem? What are her motives—love or jealousy? Write your profile as a police report on the arrest of an accomplice.

Analyzing a Mock Epic

A mock epic uses the form and **style** of an epic to satirize a trivial subject by making it ridiculous. The traditional epic opens with a statement of its **theme** and includes references to armor and weapons, battles, heroes' boastful speeches, and supernatural elements. Write a comparison of an epic poem and Pope's mock epic.

Eighteenth-Century English Gardens

To build, to plant, whatever you intend,
To rear the column, or the arch to bend,
To swell the terrace, or to sink the grot;
In all, let Nature never be forgot.
But treat the Goddess like a modest fair,
Nor over dress, nor leave her wholly bare;
Let not each beauty everywhere be spied,
Where half the skill is decently to hide.
He gains all points, who pleasingly confounds,
Surprises, varies, and conceals the bounds.
—Alexander Pope, *Epistle to Burlington* (1731)

English gardens of the eighteenth century represented a reaction against the straight lines of precisely spaced trees and avenues of intricately clipped hedges that defined the gardens of Versailles and other great houses of the seventeenth century. "Nature abhors a straight line," declared one designer early on in the century, and his prophetic words signaled a persistent trend toward winding walls and walks, irregularly-shaped pools of water, and broad vistas of "natural" plantings. That the designs were artfully contrived and the landscapes completely altered was only proper. After all, the ideal natural garden of Eden, as described by Milton in his *Paradise Lost*, had been closed on a permanent basis. The only logical choice of the landscape designers who flourished throughout the Age of Reason was to recreate the effect of Eden, with scenery that, according to the writer Sir Horace Walpole (1717–1797), ". . . should differ as much from common nature, as an heroic poem doth from a prose relation."

How best to achieve that effect was a question debated by two opposing schools of landscape design: the simple *vs.* the ornamental. Leading proponent of the first approach was Lancelot "Capability" Brown (1715–83), often considered the king of eighteenth-century gardening. Though his critics considered him too genteel, too serene, his interpretation of the garden as a landscape park forever changed the aesthetics of property design. Brown proposed vast open sweeps of lawn at the front and back of houses spreading out to naturalized lakes with stands of trees on varying levels in the distance. His was a sculptural approach, one that he did not solely invent but one which he perfected above all other designers. At his death, Sir Horace Walpole wrote, ". . . when [Brown] was the happiest man he will be least remembered; so closely did he copy Nature that his works will be mistaken."

The hint of wilderness for which Brown labored grew into wildness in his detractors' landscape plans. It was to be achieved by carving caves out of hillsides, building ruins alongside tortuously winding paths, or pumping rivers to the tops of hills to create cascading waterfalls. Deer roamed freely around the house, in imitation of a wild forest setting, and there were chains across fashionable doorways to keep out the deer (and the cattle as well) when the door was left open for ventilation. Both theories of design celebrated pretense; only in the degree of elaboration were there differences.

Other styles of gardens, needing more labor for upkeep, have vanished over the years, but the concept of the landscape park survives, primarily because many of those same eighteenth-century English gardens themselves survive. Another equally important reason may well be that these gardens—these landscape parks—offer us now, as they did to their original owners, a freedom from clocks and schedules, a reminder of that original garden of Eden we yearn to revisit.

The illustrations on the opposite page were done for *The Landscape* (1794), a didactic poem by Richard Payne Knight (1750–1824) attacking the gardening methods of Capability Brown. The one above shows a typical landscape in Brown's style, displaying a gentle interpretation of nature. The one below shows the same scene as landscaped to show a rougher view of nature. British Library

from An Essay on Man

Alexander Pope

from **Epistle I**

See, through this air, this ocean, and this
    earth,
All matter quick, and bursting into birth.
Above, how high progressive life may go?
Around how wide? how deep extend below?
5 Vast chain of being! which from God began,
Natures ethereal, human, angel, man,
Beast, bird, fish, insect! what no eye can see,
No glass can reach! from infinite to thee!
From thee to nothing!—On superior powers
10 Were we to press inferior might on ours;
Or in the full creation leave a void,
Where one step broken, the great scale's
    destroyed:
From nature's chain whatever link you
    strike,
Tenth, or ten thousandth, breaks the chain
    alike.
15   And if each system in gradation roll,
Alike essential to th' amazing whole;
The least confusion but in one, not all
That system only, but the whole must fall.
Let earth unbalanced from her orbit fly,
20 Planets and suns run lawless through the
    sky;
Let ruling angels from their spheres be
    hurled,
Being on being wrecked, and world on
    world;
Heavens whole foundations to their center
    nod,
And nature trembles to the throne of God.

25 All this dread order break—For whom? For
    thee?
Vile worm!—O madness! pride! impiety!
  What if the foot, ordained the dust to
    tread,
Or hand to toil, aspired to be the head?
What if the head, the eye or ear, repined
30 To serve mere engines to the ruling mind?
Just as absurd, for any part to claim
To be another, in this general frame:
Just as absurd, to mourn the tasks or pains,
The great directing mind of all ordains.
35   All are but parts of one stupendous whole:
Whose body Nature is, and God the soul.
That, changed through all and yet in all the
    same,
Great in the earth as in th' ethereal frame,
Warms in the sun, refreshes in the breeze,
40 Glows in the stars, and blossoms in the trees,
Lives through all life, extends through all
    extent,
Spreads undivided, operates unspent,
Breathes in our soul, informs our mortal part,
As full, as perfect, in a hair, as heart,
45 As full, as perfect, in vile man that mourns,
As the rapt seraph that adores and burns;
To Him no high, no low, no great, no small;
He fills, he bounds, connects, and equals all.
    Cease then, nor Order Imperfection name:
50 Our proper bliss depends on what we blame.
Know thy own Point. This kind, this due
    degree

Of blindness, weakness, Heaven bestows on
　　thee.
Submit—in this, or any other sphere,
Secure to be as blest as thou canst bear.
55 Safe in the hand of one disposing Power,
Or in the natal, or the mortal hour.
All nature is but art, unknown to thee;
All chance, direction which thou canst not
　　see;
All discord, harmony not understood;
60 All partial evil, universal good:
And spite of pride, in erring Reason's
　　spite,
One truth is clear; "Whatever is, is right."

from **Epistle II**
　　Know then thyself, presume not God to
　　　scan;
The proper study of mankind is *man.*
65 Placed on this isthmus of a middle state,
A being darkly wise, and rudely great:
With too much knowledge for the sceptic
　　side,
With too much weakness for the stoic's pride,
He hangs between; in doubt to act, or rest,
70 In doubt to deem himself a god, or beast;
In doubt, his mind or body to prefer,
Born but to die, and reasoning but to err;
Alike in ignorance, his reason such,
Whether he thinks too little, or too much.
75 Chaos of thought and passion, all confused;
Still by himself abused, or disabused;
Created half to rise, and half to fall;
Great lord of all things, yet a prey to all;
Sole judge of truth, in endless error hurled:
80 The glory, jest, and riddle of the world!

from **Epistle IV**
　　God loves from whole to parts: but human
　　　soul
Must rise from individual to the whole.
Self-love but serves the virtuous mind to
　　wake,

As the small pebble stirs the peaceful lake,
85 The center moved, a circle strait succeeds,
Another still, and still another spreads;
Friend, parent, neighbor, first it will
　　embrace,
His country next, and next all human-race,
Wide, and more wide, th' o'erflowings of the
　　mind
90 Take every creature in, of every kind;
Earth smiles around, with boundless bounty
　　blest,
And heav'n beholds its image in his breast.
　　Come then, my friend! my genius come
　　　along,
Oh master of the poet, and the song!
95 And while the muse now stoops, or now
　　ascends,
To man's low passions, or their glorious ends,
Teach me like thee, in various nature wise,
To fall with dignity, with temper rise;
Formed by thy converse, happily to steer
100 From grave to gay, from lively to severe,
Correct with spirit, eloquent with ease,
Intent to reason, or polite to please.
O! while along the stream of time, thy name
Expanded flies, and gathers all its fame,
105 Say, shall my little bark attendant sail,
Pursue the triumph, and partake the gale?
When statesmen, heroes, kings, in dust
　　repose,
Whose sons shall blush their fathers were thy
　　foes,
Shall then this verse to future age pretend
110 Thou wert my guide, philosopher, and
　　friend?
That urged by thee, I turned the tuneful art
From sounds to things, from fancy to the
　　heart;
For wit's false mirror held up nature's light;
Shewed erring pride Whatever is, is right;
115 That reason, passion, answer one great aim;
That true self-love and social are the same;
That virtue only makes our bliss below;
And all our knowledge is, ourselves to know.
1730–32　　　　　　　　　　　　　　**1733–34**

Comment

The Great Chain of Being
by Stephen Jay Gould

Evolution is a satisfying ordering principle and we use it without hesitation today, for evolution both records the pathway of nature and allows us to classify organisms in a coherent manner. But what systems did scientists use before evolution became so popular during the nineteenth century? The "great chain of being," or even gradation of all living things, surely held pride of place among all competitors. Arthur Lovejoy, the celebrated historian of ideas who traced the lineage of this notion in his greatest work, called the chain of being "one of the half-dozen most potent and persistent presuppositions in Western thought. It was, in fact, until not much more than a century ago probably the most widely familiar conception of the general scheme of things, of the constitutive pattern of the universe."

In the great chain of being, each organism forms a definite link in a single sequence leading from the lowest amoeba in a drop of water to ever more complex beings, culminating in, you guessed it, our own exalted selves.

Mark how it mounts to man's imperial race, from the green myriads in the peopled grass . . .

wrote Alexander Pope in his expostulations in heroic couplets from the *Essay on Man.*

Since we tend to confuse evolution with progress, the chain of being has often been misinterpreted as a primitive version of evolutionary theory. Although some nineteenth-century thinkers, in Lovejoy's words, "temporalized" the chain and converted it into a ladder that organisms might climb in their evolutionary advance, the original chain of being was explicitly and vehemently antievolutionary. The chain is a static ordering of unchanging, created entities—a set of creatures placed by God in fixed positions of an ascending hierarchy representing neither time nor history, but the eternal order of things. The static nature of the chain defines its ideological function: Each creature must be satisfied with its assigned place—the serf in his hovel as well as the lord in his castle—for any attempt to rise will disrupt the universe's established order. Again, Alexander Pope:

From Nature's chain whatever link you strike, Tenth, or ten thousandth, breaks the chain alike.

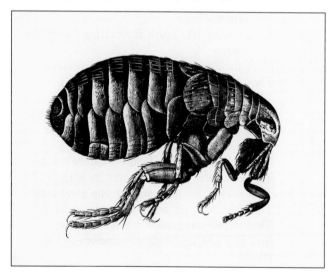

In his *Essay on Man,* Pope reflects on the extremes of the Great Chain of Being, creatures "no eye can see/No glass can reach!" The use of the microscope in the late seventeenth century had begun to reveal the length and complexity of the chain of living things. One of the most influential studies of the microscopic world was Robert Hooke's *Micrographia* (1665), in which appears this illustration of a flea. Hooke wrote that, "The strength and beauty of this small creature, had it no other relation at all to man, would deserve a description. . . ." Houghton Library, Harvard University

THINK AND DISCUSS
Understanding
1. Describe how Pope relates the universe to a giant chain.
2. Explain the reference to "Vile worm!" in line 26.
3. What is the reasoning behind Pope's pronouncement in line 62: "Whatever is, is right"?
4. How is line 78 a contradiction in terms? What point do you think Pope is attempting to make with this contradiction?
5. Summarize the advice Pope gives to his Friend (and to the reader, simultaneously) in lines 93–118.

Analyzing
6. Compare Pope's view of humanity with John Milton's in *Paradise Lost* (pages 500–506).
7. What comparisons does Pope make with inductive and deductive reasoning in lines 81–82?

Extending
8. Do you agree or disagree with Pope's evaluation of humanity?

APPLYING: Epigram H7
See Handbook of Literary Terms, p. 947.
An **epigram** is a short, witty verse or saying, often ending with a wry twist. The heroic couplet as written by Pope lends itself to the expression of paradox in neatly turned epigrams. For example, in speaking of humanity, Pope writes:

> Created half to rise, and half to fall;
> Great lord of all things, yet a prey to all;
> Sole judge of truth, in endless error hurled:
> The glory, jest, and riddle of the world!

1. What two nouns are contrasted in the second line quoted above?
2. What two nouns are contrasted in the third line?
3. What three nouns are contrasted in the last line?
4. What central paradox is being elaborated in these two epigrammatic couplets?

COMPOSITION
Writing a Verse Essay
Write the opening lines of a verse essay on a subject of your choice. "An Essay on School," "An Essay on Television," "An Essay on Vegetarianism," "An Essay on Siblings" are just a few of the possibilities. Try to write the first twenty lines or so of your essay, using the **couplet** form.

Writing an Epigram
Write a couplet that is an epigram. The couplet should be self-contained, witty, and pointed. Think of a title for your epigram, for example, "On a Fast-Food Hot Dog." Then say something about the subject in two lines that rhyme: "Encased in split roll lies smoked sausage treat,/All filler and trimmings, but where's the meat?"

ENRICHMENT
Researching and Analyzing an Epigram
Among the best writers of verse epigrams in English are John Harington, John Heywood, Ben Jonson, John Dryden, Alexander Pope, and Walter Savage Landor. Do some research to discover which of the above is the author of the following epigram:

> Treason doth never prosper. What's the reason?
> For if it prosper, none dare call it treason.

Prepare a brief report to the class on the author of the epigram. Explain the meaning of the poem in terms of the events of the time in which the author lived.

Voltaire was the pen name of François Marie Arouet, the son of a respectable Paris lawyer. Ill health plagued him all during his youth and, in fact, throughout his long life. He began a legal career but abruptly abandoned it, much to his family's chagrin, to pen satirical verses that quickly circulated through the salons of the day. His witty poems earned him an instant celebrity and an almost equally instant banishment from Paris. Authorities eventually sentenced Arouet—who now styled himself Voltaire—to a year in the Bastille. Criticism of the government (and in this case, the monarchy as well) was no petty offense. Yet Voltaire seemed as much inspired as incensed by his punishment.

An incident in 1725 offered Voltaire proof of his precarious position as social critic. He had quickly and wittily returned an insult from the Chevalier de Rohan at an opera performance; several nights later, Voltaire was surprised and savagely beaten by servants of the nobleman. Voltaire's subsequent complaint to the authorities brought him a second period of imprisonment in the Bastille. From then on, he more than sympathized with the rumors of revolution that surfaced with increasing frequency. Voltaire lived away from Paris for most of the rest of his life. Travels to England—and exposure to the theories of Newton and Locke, as well as to the English parliamentary system of government—reinforced his personal and political stand against tyranny in any form. From the relative safety of a chateau in the French countryside, Voltaire spent the next fourteen years in scholarly and scientific research.

At sixty, Voltaire settled near the French/Swiss border, buying an estate on either side so that in case of political persecution, he had only to escape to the neighboring country for asylum. His tactic was a wise one, for throughout the nearly one hundred volumes of his writings—in every form from verse to drama to essay to novel—potentially libelous remarks abounded. In an age which sought to weave a smothering blanket of gentility and placidity, Voltaire made the exposé an art form. In all of his radical activities, Voltaire sounded what was to become his signature cry: "Crush the infamous thing!" His "thing" was synonymous with bigotry, intolerance, and injustice whether in civil or religious matters, personal or public causes.

Of all Voltaire's writings, *Candide* remains the favorite. Alexander Pope had decreed in his *Essay on Man* that "Whatever is, is right"; the German philosopher Leibnitz had similarly envisioned a world in which all forces work for the good of man: "All is for the best in this best of all possible worlds." Voltaire countered that a world of irrational natural forces precluded any glib explanation of daily life. And so with his young hero Candide and the ridiculously rational Dr. Pangloss, Voltaire presented to his readers timeless caricatures of the blind optimists who described truth while refusing to examine it.

from Candide   Voltaire   *translated by* **Tobias Smollett**

Chapter 1
How Candide was brought up in a magnificent castle, and how he was driven from thence.

n the country of Westphalia,[1] in the castle of the most noble Baron of Thunder-ten-tronckh, lived a youth whom nature had endowed with a most sweet disposition. His face was the true index of his mind. He had a solid judgment joined to the most unaffected simplicity; and hence, I presume, he had his name of Candide. The old servants of the house suspected him to have been the son of the Baron's sister, by a mighty good sort of a gentleman of the neighborhood, whom that young lady refused to marry, because he could produce no more than threescore and eleven quarterings[2] in his arms; the rest of the genealogical tree belonging to the family having been lost through the injuries of time.

The Baron was one of the most powerful lords in Westphalia; for his castle had not only a gate, but even windows; and his great hall was hung with tapestry. He used to hunt with his mastiffs and spaniels instead of greyhounds; his groom served him for huntsman; and the parson of the parish officiated as grand almoner. He was called "My Lord" by all his people, and he never told a story but every one laughed at it.

My lady Baroness weighed three hundred and fifty pounds, consequently was a person of no small consideration; and then she did the honors of the house with a dignity that commanded universal respect. Her daughter Cunegund was about seventeen years of age, fresh colored, comely, plump, and desirable. The Baron's son seemed to be a youth in every respect worthy of his father. Pangloss the preceptor was the oracle of the family, and little Candide listened to his instructions with all the simplicity natural to his age and disposition.

Master Pangloss taught the metaphysico-theologo-cosmolo-nigology. He could prove to admiration that there is no effect without a cause; and that, in this best of all possible worlds, the Baron's castle was the most magnificent of all castles, and my lady the best of all possible baronesses.

"It is demonstrable," said he, "that things cannot be otherwise than they are; for as all things have been created for some end, they must necessarily be created for the best end. Observe, for instance, the nose is formed for spectacles, therefore we wear spectacles. The legs are visibly designed for stockings, accordingly we wear stockings. Stones were made to be hewn, and to construct castles, therefore my lord has a magnificent castle; for the greatest baron in the province ought to be the best lodged. Swine were intended to be eaten; therefore we eat pork all the year round: and they who assert that everything is right do not express themselves correctly; they should say, that everything is best."

Candide listened attentively, and believed implicitly; for he thought Miss Cunegund excessively handsome, though he never had the courage to tell her so. He concluded that next to the happiness of being Baron of Thunder-ten-tronckh, the next was that of being Miss Cunegund, the

---

1. **Westphalia,** province of western Germany.
2. **quarterings,** divisions of a family tree.

next that of seeing her every day, and the last that of hearing the doctrine of Master Pangloss, the greatest philosopher of the whole province, and consequently of the whole world.

One day, when Miss Cunegund went to take a walk in a little neighboring wood, which was called a park, she saw, through the bushes, the sage Doctor Pangloss giving a lecture in experimental physics to her mother's chambermaid, a little brown wench, very pretty, and very tractable. As Miss Cunegund had a great disposition for the sciences, she observed with the utmost attention the experiments which were repeated before her eyes; she perfectly well understood the force of the doctor's reasoning upon causes and effects. She retired greatly flurried, quite pensive, and filled with the desire of knowledge, imagining that she might be a sufficing reason for young Candide, and he for her.

On her way back she happened to meet Candide; she blushed, he blushed also: she wished him a good morning in a faltering tone; he returned the salute, without knowing what he said. The next day, as they were rising from dinner, Cunegund and Candide slipped behind the screen; She dropped her handkerchief, the young man picked it up. She innocently took hold of his hand, and he as innocently kissed hers with a warmth, a sensibility, a grace—all very extraordinary; their lips met; their eyes sparkled; their knees trembled; their hands strayed. The Baron of Thunder-ten-tronckh chanced to come by; he beheld the cause and effect, and, without hesitation, saluted Candide with some notable kicks on the breech, and drove him out of doors. Miss Cunegund fainted away, and, as soon as she came to herself, the Baroness boxed her ears. Thus a general consternation was spread over this most magnificent and most agreeable of all possible castles.

Chapter 2
What befell Candide among the Bulgarians.

Candide, thus driven out of this terrestrial paradise, wandered a long time, without knowing where he went; sometimes he raised his eyes, all bedewed with tears, towards heaven, and sometimes he cast a melancholy look towards the magnificent castle where dwelt the fairest of young baronesses. He laid himself down to sleep in a furrow, heartbroken and supperless. The snow fell in great flakes, and, in the morning when he awoke, he was almost frozen to death; however, he made shift to crawl to the next town, which was called Waldberghoff-trarbk-dikdorff, without a penny in his pocket, and half dead with hunger and fatigue. He took up his stand at the door of an inn. He had not been long there, before two men dressed in blue[3] fixed their eyes steadfastly upon him.

"Faith, comrade," said one of them to the other, "yonder is a well-made young fellow, and of the right size."

Thereupon they made up to Candide, and with the greatest civility and politeness invited him to dine with them.

"Gentlemen," replied Candide, with a most engaging modesty, "you do me much honor, but, upon my word, I have no money."

"Money, Sir!" said one of the men in blue to him, "young persons of your appearance and merit never pay anything; why, are not you five feet five inches high?"

"Yes, gentlemen, that is really my size," replied he, with a low bow.

"Come then, Sir, sit down along with us; we will not only pay your reckoning, but will never suffer such a clever young fellow as you to want money. Mankind were born to assist one another."

"You are perfectly right, gentlemen," said Candide; "that is precisely the doctrine of Master Pangloss; and I am convinced that everything is for the best."

His generous companions next entreated him to accept of a few crowns, which he readily complied with, at the same time offering them his note for the payment, which they refused, and sat down to table.

"Have you not a great affection for ——"

"O yes!" he replied, "I have a great affection for the lovely Miss Cunegund."

"May be so," replied one of the men, "but that

---

3. *two . . . blue*, recruiting officers.

is not the question! We are asking you whether you have not a great affection for the King of the Bulgarians?"

"For the King of the Bulgarians?" said Candide. "Not at all. Why, I never saw him in my life."

"Is it possible! Oh, he is a most charming king! Come, we must drink his health."

"With all my heart, gentlemen," Candide said, and he tossed off his glass.

"Bravo!" cried the blues; "you are now the support, the defender, the hero of the Bulgarians; your fortune is made; you are on the high road to glory."

So saying, they put him in irons, and carried him away to the regiment. There he was made to wheel about to the right, to the left, to draw his ramrod, to return his ramrod, to present, to fire, to march, and they gave him thirty blows with a cane; the next day he performed his exercise a little better, and they gave him but twenty; the day following he came off with ten, and was looked upon as a young fellow of surprising genius by all his comrades.

Candide was struck with amazement, and could not for the soul of him conceive how he came to be a hero. One fine spring morning, he took it into his head to take a walk, and he marched straight forward, conceiving it to be a privilege of the human species, as well as of the brute creation, to make use of their legs how and when they pleased. He had not gone above two leagues when he was overtaken by four other heroes, six feet high, who bound him neck and heels, and carried him to a dungeon. A court-martial sat upon him, and he was asked which he liked best, either to run the gauntlet six and thirty times through the whole regiment, or to have his brains blown out with a dozen musket-balls. In vain did he remonstrate to them that the human will is free, and that he chose neither; they obliged him to make a choice, and he determined, in virtue of that divine gift called free will, to run the gauntlet six and thirty times. He had gone through his discipline twice, and the regiment being composed of two thousand men, they composed for him exactly four thousand strokes, which laid bare all his muscles and nerves, from the nape of his neck to his rump. As

they were preparing to make him set out the third time, our young hero, unable to support it any longer, begged as a favor they would be so obliging as to shoot him through the head. The favor being granted, a bandage was tied over his eyes, and he was made to kneel down. At that very instant, his Bulgarian Majesty, happening to pass by, inquired into the delinquent's crime, and being a prince of great penetration, he found, from what he heard of Candide, that he was a young metaphysician, entirely ignorant of the world; and therefore, out of his great clemency, he condescended to pardon him, for which his name will be celebrated in every journal, and in every age. A skillful surgeon made a cure of Candide in three weeks, by means of emollient unguents prescribed by Dioscorides.[4] His sores were now skinned over, and he was able to march, when the King of the Bulgarians gave battle to the King of the Abares.

Candide deserts the army and flees to Holland. A series of extraordinary misadventures follows as he travels around Europe. Finally, with his valet Cacambo he flees to South America. In the following chapter Candide and his servant are about to discover El Dorado, a land of fabulous wealth.

Chapter 17
Candide and his servant arrive in the country of El Dorado. What they saw there.

When they got to the frontiers of the Oreillons, Cacambo said to Candide, "You see, this hemisphere is no better than the other: take my advice, and let us return to Europe by the shortest way possible."

"But how can we get back?" said Candide; "and whither shall we go? To my own country? The Bulgarians and the Abares are laying that waste with fire and sword. Or shall we go to Portugal? There I shall be burnt; and if we abide here, we

---

4. **Dioscorides**, wrote on medical matters in the first century A.D.

are every moment in danger of being spitted. But how can I bring myself to quit that part of the world where Miss Cunegund has her residence?"

"Let us turn towards Cayenne," said Cacambo; "there we shall meet with some Frenchmen; for you know those gentry ramble all over the world; perhaps they will assist us, and God will look with pity on our distress."

It was not so easy to get to Cayenne. They knew pretty nearly whereabouts it lay; but the mountains, rivers, precipices, robbers, savages, were dreadful obstacles in the way. Their horses died with fatigue, and their provisions were at an end. They subsisted a whole month upon wild fruit, till at length they came to a little river bordered with cocoanut palms, the sight of which at once sustained life and hope.

Cacambo, who was always giving as good advice as the old woman[5] herself, said to Candide, "You see there is no holding out any longer; we have travelled enough on foot. I see an empty canoe near the river-side; let us fill it with cocoanuts, get into it, and go down with the stream; a river always leads to some inhabited place. If we do not meet with agreeable things, we shall at least meet with something new."

"Agreed," replied Candide; "let us recommend ourselves to Providence."

They rowed a few leagues down the river, the banks of which were in some places covered with flowers; in others barren; in some parts smooth and level, and in others steep and rugged. The stream widened as they went further on, till at length it passed under one of the frightful rocks whose summits seemed to reach the clouds. Here our two travellers had the courage to commit themselves to the stream beneath this vault, which, contracting in this part, hurried them along with a dreadful noise and rapidity. At the end of four-and-twenty hours, they saw daylight again; but their canoe was dashed to pieces against the rocks. They were obliged to creep along, from rock to rock, for the space of a league, till at last a spacious plain presented itself to their sight, bound by inaccessible mountains. The country appeared cultivated equally for pleasure, and to produce the necessaries of life. The useful and agreeable were here equally blended. The roads were covered, or rather adorned, with carriages formed of glittering materials, in which were men and women of a surprising beauty, drawn with great rapidity by red sheep of a very large size, which far surpassed in speed the finest coursers of Andalusia, Tetuan, or Mequinez.

"Here is a country, however," said Candide, "preferable to Westphalia."

He and Cacambo landed near the first village they saw, at the entrance of which they perceived some children covered with tattered garments of the richest brocade, playing at quoits.[6] Our two inhabitants of the other hemisphere amused themselves greatly with what they saw. The quoits were large round pieces, yellow, red, and green, which cast a most glorious luster. Our travellers picked some of them up, and they proved to be gold, emeralds, rubies, and diamonds, the least of which would have been the greatest ornament to the superb throne of the great Mogul.[7]

"Without doubt," said Cacambo, "those children must be the king's sons, that are playing at quoits."

As he was uttering those words, the schoolmaster of the village appeared, who came to call them to school.

"There," said Candide, "is the preceptor of the royal family."

The little ragamuffins immediately quitted their game, leaving the quoits on the ground with all their other playthings. Candide gathered them up, ran to the schoolmaster, and, with a most respectful bow, presented them to him, giving him to understand by signs that their Royal Highnesses had forgotten their gold and precious stones. The schoolmaster, with a smile, flung them upon the ground, then having examined Candide from head to foot with an air of great surprise, went on his way.

---

5. *the old woman*, Cunegund's companion.
6. *quoits*, game played with iron or rope rings thrown to encircle a peg stuck in the ground.
7. *Mogul*, emperor of India.

Our travellers took care, however, to gather up the gold, the rubies, and the emeralds.

"Where are we?" cried Candide. "The king's children in this country must have an excellent education, since they are taught to show such a contempt for gold and precious stones."

Cacambo was as much surprised as his master.

They at length drew near the first house in the village, which was built after the manner of a European palace. There was a crowd of people round the door, and a still greater number in the house. The sound of the most delightful musical instruments was heard, and the most agreeable smell came from the kitchen. Cacambo went up to the door, and heard those within talking in the Peruvian language, which was his mother tongue; for every one knows that Cacambo was born in a village of Tucuman where no other language is spoken.

"I will be your interpreter here," said he to Candide, "let us go in; this is an eating-house."

Immediately two waiters, and two servant-girls, dressed in cloth of gold, and their hair braided with ribbons of tissue, accosted the strangers, and invited them to sit down to the ordinary. Their dinner consisted of four dishes of different soups, each garnished with two young paroquets,[8] a large dish of bouille[9] that weighed two hundredweight, two roasted monkeys of a delicious flavor, three hundred hummingbirds in one dish, and six hundred fly-birds in another; some excellent ragouts, delicate tarts, and the whole served up in dishes of rock-crystal. Several sorts of liquors, extracted from the sugar-cane, were handed about by the servants who attended.

Most of the company were chapmen and wagoners, all extremely polite: they asked Cacambo a few questions, with the utmost discretion and circumspection; and replied to his in a most obliging and satisfactory manner.

As soon as dinner was over, both Candide and Cacambo thought they would pay very handsomely for their entertainment by laying down two of those large gold pieces which they had picked off the ground; but the landlord and landlady burst into a fit of laughing and held their sides for some

time before they were able to speak.

"Gentlemen," said the landlord, "I plainly perceive you are strangers, and such we are not accustomed to see; pardon us, therefore, for laughing when you offered us the common pebbles of our highways for payment of your reckoning. To be sure, you have none of the coin of this kingdom; but there is no necessity to have any money at all to dine in this house. All the inns, which are established for the convenience of those who carry on the trade of this nation, are maintained by the government. You have found but very indifferent entertainment here, because this is only a poor village; but in almost every other of these public houses you will meet with a reception worthy of persons of your merit."

Cacambo explained the whole of this speech of the landlord to Candide, who listened to it with the same astonishment with which his friend communicated it.

"What sort of a country is this," said the one to the other, "that is unknown to all the world, and in which Nature had everywhere so different an appearance from what she has in ours? Possibly this is that part of the globe where everything is right, for there must certainly be some such place; and, for all that Master Pangloss could say, I often perceived that things went very ill in Westphalia."

Chapter 18
What they saw in the country of El Dorado.

Cacambo vented all his curiosity upon the landlord by a thousand different questions.

The honest man answered him thus: "I am very ignorant, Sir, but I am contented with my ignorance; however, we have in this neighborhood an old man retired from court, who is the most learned and communicative person in the whole kingdom."

He then directed Cacambo to the old man; Candide acted now only a second character, and attended his servant. They entered a quite plain

---

8. *paroquets,* parakeets.
9. *bouille,* boiled beef.

house, for the door was nothing but silver, and the ceiling was only of beaten gold, but wrought in so elegant a taste as to vie with the richest. The antechamber, indeed, was only incrusted with rubies and emeralds; but the order in which everything was disposed made amends for this great simplicity.

The old man received the strangers on a sofa, which was stuffed with hummingbirds' feathers; and ordered his servants to present them with liquors in golden goblets, after which he satisfied their curiosity in the following terms:

"I am now one hundred and seventy-two years old; and I learned of my late father who was equerry to the king the amazing revolutions of Peru, to. which he had been an eye-witness. This kingdom is the ancient patrimony of the Incas, who very imprudently quitted it to conquer another part of the world, and were at length conquered and destroyed themselves by the Spaniards.

"Those princes of their family who remained in their native country acted more wisely. They ordained, with the consent of their whole nation, that none of the inhabitants of our little kingdom should ever quit it; and to this wise ordinance we owe the preservation of our innocence and happiness. The Spaniards had some confused notion of this country, to which they gave the name of El Dorado; and Sir Walter Raleigh, an Englishman, actually came very near it, about a hundred years ago: but the inaccessible rocks and precipices with which our country is surrounded on all sides have hitherto secured us from the rapacious fury of the people of Europe, who have an unaccountable fondness for the pebbles and dirt of our land, for the sake of which they would murder us all to the very last man."

The conversation lasted some time and turned chiefly on the form of government, the customs, the women, the public diversions, and the arts. At length, Candide, who had always had a taste for metaphysics, asked whether the people of that country had any religion.

The old man reddened a little at this question.

"Can you doubt it?" said he. "Do you take us for wretches lost to all sense of gratitude?"

Cacambo asked in a respectful manner what was the established religion of El Dorado. The old man blushed again.

"Can there be two religions then?" he said. "Ours, I apprehend, is the religion of the whole world; we worship God from morning till night."

"Do you worship but one God?" said Cacambo, who still acted as the interpreter of Candide's doubts.

"Certainly," said the old man; "there are not two, nor three, nor four Gods. I must confess the people of your world ask very extraordinary questions."

However, Candide could not refrain from making many more inquiries of the old man; he wanted to know in what manner they prayed to God in El Dorado.

"We do not pray to him at all," said the reverend sage; "we have nothing to ask of him, he has given us all we want, and we give him thanks incessantly."

Candide had a curiosity to see some of their priests, and desired Cacambo to ask the old man where they were.

At this he, smiling, said, "My friends, we are all of us priests; the King and all the heads of families sing solemn hymns of thanksgiving every morning, accompanied by five or six thousand musicians."

"What!" said Cacambo, "have you no monks among you, to dispute, to govern, to intrigue, and to burn people who are not of the same opinion with themselves?"

"Do you take us for fools?" said the old man. "Here we are all of one opinion, and know not what you mean by your monks."

During the whole of this discourse Candide was in raptures, and he said to himself:

"What a prodigious difference is there between this place and Westphalia, and this house and the Baron's castle! If our friend Pangloss had seen El Dorado, he would no longer have said that the castle of Thunder-ten-Tronckh was the finest of all possible edifices: there is nothing like seeing the world, that's certain."

This long conversation being ended, the old man ordered six sheep to be harnessed, and put to the coach, and sent twelve of his servants to escort the travellers to Court.

"Excuse me," said he, "for not waiting on you in person; my age deprives me of that honor. The King will receive you in such a manner that you will have no reason to complain; and doubtless you will make a proper allowance for the customs of the country, if they should not happen altogether to please you."

Candide and Cacambo got into the coach, the six sheep flew, and in less than a quarter of an hour they arrived at the King's palace, which was situated at the further end of the capital. At the entrance was a portal two hundred and twenty feet high, and one hundred wide; but it is impossible for words to express the materials of which it was built. The reader, however, will readily conceive they must have a prodigious superiority over the pebbles and sand which we call gold and precious stones.

Twenty beautiful young virgins-in-waiting received Candide and Cacambo at their alighting from the coach, conducted them to the bath, and clad them in robes woven of the down of hummingbirds; after this they were introduced by the great officers of the crown of both sexes to the King's apartment, between two files of musicians, each file consisting of a thousand, according to the custom of the country. When they drew near to the presence chamber, Cacambo asked one of the officers in what manner they were to pay their obeisance to his Majesty: whether it was the custom to fall upon their knees, or to prostrate themselves upon the ground? whether they were to put their hands upon their heads, or behind their backs? whether they were to lick the dust off the floor? in short, what was the ceremony usual on such occasions?

"The custom," said the great officer, "is to embrace the King, and kiss him on each cheek."

Candide and Cacambo accordingly threw their arms round his Majesty's neck; and he received them in the most gracious manner imaginable, and very politely asked them to sup with him.

While supper was preparing, orders were given to show them the city, where they saw public structures that reared their lofty heads to the clouds; the market-places decorated with a thousand columns; fountains of spring water, besides others of rose water, and of liquors drawn from the sugar-cane, incessantly flowing in the great squares; these were paved with a kind of precious stone that emitted an odor like that of cloves and cinnamon. Candide asked to see the high court of justice, the parliament; but was answered that they have none in that country, being utter strangers to lawsuits. He then inquired, if they had any prisons; they replied, "None." But what gave him at once the greatest surprise and pleasure was the Palace of Sciences, where he saw a gallery two thousand feet long, filled with the various apparatus of mathematics and natural philosophy.

After having spent the whole afternoon in seeing only about the thousandth part of the city, they were brought back to the King's palace. Candide sat down at the table with his Majesty, his servant Cacambo, and several ladies of the Court. Never was entertainment more elegant, nor could any one possibly show more wit than his Majesty displayed while they were at supper. Cacambo explained all the King's *bons mots*[10] to Candide, and although they were translated they still appeared to be *bons mots*. Of all the things that surprised Candide, this was not the least. They spent a whole month in this hospitable place, during which time Candide was continually saying to Cacambo:

"I own, my friend, once more, that the castle where I was born is a mere nothing in comparison with the place where we now are; but still Miss Cunegund is not here, and you yourself have doubtless some mistress in Europe. If we remain here, we shall only be as others are: whereas, if we return to our own world with only a dozen of El Dorado sheep, loaded with the pebbles of this country, we shall be richer than all the kings in Europe . . . and we may easily recover Miss Cunegund."

---

10. *bons mots,* clever sayings or witty remarks.

This speech pleased Cacambo. A fondness for roving, for making a figure in their own country, and for boasting of what they had seen in their travels, was so strong in our two wanderers that they resolved to be no longer happy; and demanded permission of his Majesty to quit the country.

"You are about to do a rash and silly action," said the King; "I am sensible my kingdom is an inconsiderable spot; but when people are tolerably at their ease in any place, I should think it would be their interest to remain there. Most assuredly, I have no right to detain you or any strangers against your wills; this is an act of tyranny to which our manners and our laws are equally repugnant: all men are free; you have an undoubted liberty to depart whenever you please, but you will have many difficulties in passing the frontiers. It is impossible to ascend that rapid river which runs under high and vaulted rocks, and by which you were conveyed hither by a miracle. The mountains by which my kingdom is hemmed in on all sides are ten thousand feet high, and perfectly perpendicular; they are above ten leagues over each, and the descent from them is one continued precipice. However, since you are determined to leave us, I will immediately give orders to the superintendent of machines to cause one to be made that will convey you safely. When they have conducted you to the back of the mountains, nobody can attend you further; for my subjects have made a vow never to quit the kingdom, and they are too prudent to break it. Ask me whatever else you please."

"All we shall ask of your Majesty," said Cacambo, "is a few sheep laden with provisions, pebbles, and the clay of your country."

The King smiled at the request, and said, "I cannot imagine what pleasure you Europeans find in our yellow clay; but take away as much of it as you will, and much good may it do you."

He immediately gave orders to his engineers to make a machine to hoist these two extraordinary men out of the kingdom. Three thousand good mathematicians went to work and finished it in about fifteen days; and it did not cost more than twenty millions sterling of that country's money. Candide and Cacambo were placed on this machine, and they took with them two large red sheep, bridled and saddled, to ride upon when they got on the other side of the mountains; twenty others to serve as pack-horses for carrying provisions; thirty laden with presents of whatever was most curious in the country; and fifty with gold, diamonds, and other precious stones. The King embraced the two wanderers with the greatest cordiality.

It was a curious sight to behold the manner of their setting off, and the ingenious method by which they and their sheep were hoisted to the top of the mountains. The mathematicians and engineers took leave of them as soon as they had conveyed them to a place of safety, and Candide was wholly occupied with the thoughts of presenting his sheep to Miss Cunegund.

"Now," said he, "thanks to heaven, we have more than sufficient to pay the Governor of Buenos Aires for Miss Cunegund, if she is redeemable.[11] Let us make the rest of our way to Cayenne, where we will take ship, and then we may at leisure think of what kingdom we shall purchase."

Chapter 19

What happened to them at Surinam, and how Candide became acquainted with Martin.

Our travellers' first day's journey was very pleasant; they were elated with the prospect of possessing more riches than were to be found in Europe, Asia, and Africa together. Candide, in amorous transports, cut the name of Miss Cunegund on the trees. The second day, two of their sheep sank into a morass, and were swallowed up with their loads; two more died of fatigue some few days afterwards; seven or eight perished with hunger in a desert, and others, at different times, tumbled down precipices; so that, after travelling about a hundred days, they had only two sheep left.

Said Candide to Cacambo, "You see, my dear

---

11. **Cunegund . . . redeemable.** Cunegunde, who arrived in South America with Candide and Cacambo, has been forced to remain in Buenos Aires, where the Governor has fallen in love with her.

friend, how perishable the riches of this world are; there is nothing solid but virtue and the joy of seeing Miss Cunegund again."

"Very true," said Cacambo; "but we have still two sheep remaining, with more treasure than ever the King of Spain will be possessed of; and I espy a town at a distance, which I take to be Surinam, a town belonging to the Dutch. We are now at the end of our troubles, and at the beginning of happiness."

As they drew near the town, they saw a negro stretched on the ground with only one half of his habit, which was a pair of blue cotton drawers; for the poor man had lost his left leg, and his right hand.

"Good God," said Candide in Dutch, "what dost thou here, friend, in this deplorable condition?"

"I am waiting for my master Mynheer Vanderdendur, the famous trader," answered the negro.

"Was it Mynheer Vanderdendur that used you in this cruel manner?"

"Yes, Sir," said the negro; "it is the custom here. They give a pair of cotton drawers twice a year, and that is all our covering. When we labor in the sugar-works, and the mill happens to snatch hold of a finger, they instantly chop off our hand; and when we attempt to run away, they cut off a leg. Both these cases have happened to me, and it is at this expense that you eat sugar in Europe; and yet when my mother sold me for ten pattacoons on the coast of Guinea, she said to me, 'My dear child, bless our fetishes; adore them for ever; they will make thee live happy; thou hast the honor to be a slave to our lords the whites, by which thou wilt make the fortune of us thy parents.' Alas! I know not whether I have made their fortunes; but they have not made mine: dogs, monkeys, and parrots, are a thousand times less wretched than me. The Dutch fetishes[12] who converted me tell me every Sunday that, blacks and whites, we are all children of Adam. As for me, I do not understand any thing of genealogies; but if what these preachers say is true, we are all second cousins; and you must allow, that it is impossible to be worse treated by our relations than we are."

"O Pangloss!" cried out Candide, "such horrid doings never entered thy imagination. Here is an end of the matter; I find myself, after all, obliged to renounce thy Optimism."

"Optimism!" said Cacambo, "what is that?"

"Alas!" replied Candide, "it is the obstinacy of maintaining that everything is best when it is worst": and so saying, he turned his eyes towards the poor negro, and shed a flood of tears; and in this weeping mood he entered the town of Surinam.

Immediately upon their arrival, our travellers inquired if there was any vessel in the harbor which they might send to Buenos Aires. The person they addressed themselves to happened to be the master of a Spanish bark, who offered to agree with them on moderate terms, and appointed them a meeting at a public house. Thither Candide and his faithful Cacambo went to wait for him, taking with them their two sheep.

Candide, who was all frankness and sincerity, made an ingenuous recital of his adventures to the Spaniard, declaring to him at the same time his resolution of carrying off Miss Cunegund.

"In that case," said the shipmaster, "I'll take good care not to take you to Buenos Aires. It would prove a hanging matter to us all. The fair Cunegund is the Governor's favorite mistress."

These words were like a clap of thunder to Candide; he wept bitterly for a long time, and, taking Cacambo aside, he said to him:

"I'll tell you, my dear friend, what you must do. We have each of us in our pockets to the value of five or six millions in diamonds; you are cleverer at these matters than I; you must go to Buenos Aires and bring off Miss Cunegund. If the Governor makes any difficulty, give him a million; if he holds out, give him two. . . . I'll fit out another ship and go to Venice, where I will wait for you: Venice is a free country, where we shall have nothing to fear from Bulgarians, Abares, Jews, or Inquisitors."

Cacambo greatly applauded this wise resolution.

---

12. *fetishes*, medicine men or witch doctors; here, missionary priests.

Engraving by Jean Michel Moreau (1741–1814) from the second edition
of *Candide*. 1785–1787. Bibliothèque Nationale, Paris

584   *Neoclassicism*

He was inconsolable at the thought of parting with so good a master, who treated him more like an intimate friend than a servant; but the pleasure of being able to do him a service soon got the better of his sorrow. They embraced each other with a flood of tears. Candide charged him not to forget the old woman. Cacambo set out the same day. This Cacambo was a very honest fellow.

Candide continued some days longer at Surinam, waiting for any captain to carry him and his two remaining sheep to Italy. He hired domestics and purchased many things necessary for a long voyage; at length, Mynheer Vanderdendur, skipper of a large Dutch vessel, came and offered his service.

"What will you take," said Candide, "to carry me, my servants, my baggage, and these two sheep you see here, direct to Venice?"

The skipper asked ten thousand piastres; and Candide agreed to his demand without hesitation.

"Oh, ho!" said the cunning Vanderdendur to himself, "this stranger must be very rich; he agrees to give me ten thousand piastres without hesitation."

Returning a little while after, he told Candide that upon second consideration he could not undertake the voyage for less than twenty thousand.

"Very well, you shall have them," said Candide.

"Zounds!" said the skipper to himself, "this man agrees to pay twenty thousand piastres with as much ease as ten."

Accordingly he went back again, and told him roundly that he would not carry him to Venice for less than thirty thousand piastres.

"Then you shall have thirty thousand," said Candide.

"Odso!" said the Dutchman once more to himself, "thirty thousand piastres seem a trifle to this man. Those sheep must certainly be laden with an immense treasure. I'll stop here and ask no more; but make him pay down the thirty thousand piastres, and then we shall see."

Candide sold two small diamonds, the least of which was worth more than all the skipper asked. He paid him before-hand, and the two sheep were put on board, and Candide followed in a small boat to join the vessel in the road. The skipper took his opportunity, hoisted his sails, and put out to sea with a favorable wind. Candide, confounded and amazed, soon lost sight of the ship.

"Alas!" said he, "this is a trick like those in our old world!"

He returned back to the shore overwhelmed with grief; and, indeed, he had lost what would have been the fortune of twenty monarchs.

Immediately upon his landing, he applied to the Dutch magistrate: being transported with passion, he thundered at the door; which being opened, he went in, told his case, and talked a little louder than was necessary. The magistrate began with fining him ten thousand piastres for his petulance, and then listened very patiently to what he had to say, promised to examine into the affair at the skipper's return, and ordered him to pay ten thousand piastres more for the fees of the court.

This treatment put Candide out of all patience: it is true, he had suffered misfortunes a thousand times more grievous; but the cool insolence of the judge and of the skipper who robbed him raised his choler and threw him into a deep melancholy. The villainy of mankind presented itself to his mind in all its deformity, and his soul was a prey to the most gloomy ideas. After some time, hearing that the captain of a French ship was ready to set sail for Bordeaux, as he had no more sheep loaded with diamonds to put on board, he hired the cabin at the usual price; and made it known in the town that he would pay the passage and board of any honest man who would give him his company during the voyage; besides making him a present of ten thousand piastres, on condition that such person was the most dissatisfied with his condition and the most unfortunate in the whole province.

Upon this there appeared such a crowd of candidates that a large fleet could not have contained them. Candide, willing to choose from among those who appeared most likely to answer his intention, selected twenty, who seemed to him the most sociable, and who all pretended to merit the preference. He invited them to his inn, and promised to treat them with a supper, on condition that every man should bind himself by an oath to relate his own history. He declared at the same time that he would make choice of that person who should appear to him the most deserving of compassion, and the most justly dissatisfied with his condition of life; and that he would make a present to the rest.

This extraordinary assembly continued sitting till four in the morning. . . . Every story he heard put him in mind of Pangloss.

"My old master," said he, "would be confoundedly put to it to demonstrate his favorite system. Would he were here! Certainly if everything is for the best, it is in El Dorado, and not in the other parts of the world."

At length he determined in favor of a poor scholar who had labored ten years for the booksellers at Amsterdam, being of opinion that no employment could be more detestable.

This scholar, who was in fact a very honest man, had been robbed by his wife, beaten by his son, and forsaken by his daughter, who had run away with a Portuguese. He had been likewise deprived of a small employment on which he subsisted, and he was persecuted by the clergy of Surinam, who took him for a Socinian.[13] It must be acknowledged that the other competitors were, at least, as wretched as he; but Candide was in hopes that the company of a man of letters would relieve the tediousness of the voyage. All the other candidates complained that Candide had done them great injustice; but he stopped their mouths by a present of a hundred piastres to each.

With his traveling companion Martin, Candide undergoes a new series of adventures. They travel to Venice, where Candide is reunited with his valet Cacambo, who tells him that Cunegund is in Constantinople. They travel on to Constantinople, meeting along the way Pangloss and Cunegund's brother, the Baron. As the following scene opens, they are in Turkey and Candide is about to meet Cunegund again for the first time after their long separation.

Chapter 29

In what manner Candide found Cunegund and the old woman again.

While Candide, the Baron, Pangloss, Martin, and Cacambo were relating their several adventures, and reasoning on the contingent or non-contingent events of this world; while they were disputing on causes and effects, on moral and physical evil, on free will and necessity, and on the consolation that may be felt by a person when a slave and chained to an oar in a Turkish galley, they arrived at the house of the Transylvanian prince on the coasts of the Propontis. The first objects they beheld there were Miss Cunegund and the old woman, who were hanging some tablecloths on a line to dry.

The Baron turned pale at the sight. Even the tender Candide, that affectionate lover, upon seeing his fair Cunegund all sun-burned, with blear eyes, a withered neck, wrinkled face and arms, all covered with a red scurf, started back with horror; but, recovering himself, he advanced towards her out of good manners. She embraced Candide and her brother; they embraced the old woman, and Candide ransomed them both.

There was a small farm in the neighborhood, which the old woman proposed to Candide to make a shift with till the company should meet with a more favorable destiny. Cunegund, not knowing that she was grown ugly, as no one had informed her of it, reminded Candide of his promise in so peremptory a manner that the simple lad did not dare to refuse her; he then acquainted the Baron that he was going to marry his sister.

"I will never suffer," said the Baron, "my sister to be guilty of an action so derogatory to her birth and family; nor will I bear this insolence on your part: no, I never will be reproached that my nephews are not qualified for the first ecclesiastical dignities in Germany; nor shall a sister of mine

---

13. **Socinian,** follower of Faustus and Laelius Socinus, Polish theologians who advocated a rational Christianity.

Engraving by Jean Michel Moreau (1741–1814) from the second edition
of *Candide*. 1785–1787. Bibliothèque Nationale, Paris

ever be the wife of any person below the rank of a baron of the Empire."

Cunegund flung herself at her brother's feet, and bedewed them with her tears, but he still continued inflexible.

"Thou foolish fellow," said Candide, "have I not delivered thee from the galleys, paid thy ransom, and thy sister's too who was a scullion, and is very ugly, and yet I condescend to marry her? and shalt thou make claim to oppose the match? If I were to listen only to the dictates of my anger, I should kill thee again."

"Thou mayest kill me again," said the Baron, "but thou shalt not marry my sister while I am living."

Chapter 30
Conclusion.

Candide had, in truth, no great inclination to marry Cunegund; but the extreme impertinence of the baron determined him to conclude the match; and Cunegund pressed him so warmly that he could not recant. He consulted Pangloss, Martin, and the faithful Cacambo. Pangloss composed a fine memorial, by which he proved that the Baron had no right over his sister; and that she might, according to all the laws of the Empire, marry Candide. . . . Martin concluded that they should throw the Baron into the sea: Cacambo decided that he must be delivered to the Turkish captain and sent to the galleys; after which he should be conveyed by the first ship to the Father General at Rome.[14] This advice was found to be very good; the old woman approved of it, and not a syllable was said to his sister; the business was executed for a little money: and they had the pleasure of tricking a Jesuit and punishing the pride of a German baron.

It was altogether natural to imagine that after undergoing so many disasters, Candide married to his mistress, and living with the philosopher Pangloss, the philosopher Martin, the prudent Cacambo, and the old woman, having besides brought home so many diamonds from the country of the ancient Incas, would lead the most agreeable life in the world. But he had been so much cheated by the Jews that he had nothing else left but his little farm; his wife, every day growing more and more ugly, became ill-natured and insupportable; the old woman was infirm, and more bad-tempered yet than Cunegund. Cacambo, who worked in the garden, and carried the produce of it to sell at Constantinople, was past his labor, and cursed his fate. Pangloss despaired of making a figure in any of the German universities. And as to Martin, he was firmly persuaded that a person is equally ill-situated everywhere. He took things with patience. Candide, Martin, and Pangloss disputed sometimes about metaphysics and morality. Boats were often seen passing under the windows of the farm fraught with effendis, pashas, and cadis, that were going into banishment to Lemnos, Mytilene, and Erzeroum. And other cadis, pashas, and effendis were seen coming back to succeed the place of the exiles, and were driven out in their turns. They saw several heads very curiously stuffed with straw, being carried as presents to the Sublime Porte. Such sights gave occasion to frequent dissertations; and when no disputes were carried on, the irksomeness was so excessive that the old woman ventured one day to say to them:

"I would be glad to know which is worst, to be ravished a hundred times by negro pirates, to have one buttock cut off, to run the gauntlet among the Bulgarians, to be whipped and hanged at an *auto-da-fé*, to be dissected, to be chained to an oar in a galley, and in short to experience all the miseries through which every one of us hath passed,—or to remain here doing nothing?"

"This," said Candide, "is a big question."

This discourse gave birth to new reflections, and Martin especially concluded that man was born to live in the convulsions of disquiet, or in the lethargy of idleness. Though Candide did not absolutely agree to this; yet he was sure of nothing. Pangloss avowed that he had undergone dreadful

---

14. *Father General at Rome,* head of the Jesuit order. The Baron had been a member of the Jesuits in South America before being made a galley slave in a Turkish ship.

sufferings; but having once maintained that everything went on as well as possible, he still maintained it, and at the same time believed nothing of it. . . .

In the neighborhood lived a very famous dervish, who passed for the best philosopher in Turkey; him they went to consult: Pangloss, who was their spokesman, addressed him thus:

"Master, we come to intreat you to tell us why so strange an animal as man has been formed?"

"Why do you trouble your head about it?" said the dervish. "Is it any business of yours?"

"But, my Reverend Father," said Candide, "there is a horrible deal of evil on the earth."

"What signifies it," said the dervish, "whether there is evil or good? When his Highness sends a ship to Egypt, does he trouble his head whether the rats in the vessel are at their ease or not?"

"What must then be done?" said Pangloss.

"Be silent," answered the dervish.

"I flattered myself," replied Pangloss, "that we should have the pleasure of arguing with you on causes and effects, on the best of possible worlds, the origin of evil, the nature of the soul, and the pre-established harmony."

At these words the dervish shut the door in their faces.

During this conversation, news was spread abroad that two viziers of the bench and the mufti[15] had just been strangled at Constantinople, and several of their friends impaled. This catastrophe made a great noise for some hours. Pangloss, Candide, and Martin, as they were returning to the little farm, met with a good-looking old man, who was taking the air at his door, under an alcove formed of orange-trees. Pangloss, who was as inquisitive as he was argumentative, asked him what was the name of the mufti who was lately strangled.

"I cannot tell," answered the good old man; "I never knew the name of any mufti or vizier breathing. I am entirely ignorant of the event you speak of; I presume, that in general, such as are concerned in public affairs sometimes come to a miserable end; and that they deserve it: but I never inquire what is happening at Constantinople; I am content with sending thither the produce of the garden which I cultivate."

After saying these words, he invited the strangers to come into his house. His two daughters and two sons presented them with diverse sorts of iced sherbet of their own making; besides *caymac*,[16] heightened with the peel of candied citrons, oranges, lemons, pine-apples, pistachio-nuts, and Mocha coffee unadulterated with the bad coffee of Batavia or the West Indies. After which the two daughters of this good mussulman[17] perfumed the beards of Candide, Pangloss, and Martin.

"You must certainly have a vast estate," said Candide to the Turk.

"I have no more than twenty acres of ground," he replied, "the whole of which I cultivate myself with the help of my children; and our labor keeps off from us three great evils, idleness, vice, and want."

Candide, as he was returning home, made profound reflections on the Turk's discourse.

"This good old man," he said to Pangloss and Martin, "appears to me to have chosen for himself a lot much preferable to that of the six kings with whom we had the honor to sup."

"Human grandeur," said Pangloss, "is very dangerous, if we believe the testimonies of almost all philosophers; for we find Eglon, King of the Moabites, was assassinated by Ehud; Absalom was hanged by the hair of his head, and run through with three darts; King Nadab, son of Jeroboam, was slain by Baasha; King Elah by Zimri; Ahaziah by Jehu; Athaliah by Jehoiada; the Kings Jehoiakim, Jechoniah, and Zedekiah were led into captivity: I need not tell you what was the fate of Crœsus, Astyages, Darius, Dionysius of Syracuse, Pyrrhus, Perseus, Hannibal, Jugurtha, Ariovistus, Cæsar, Pompey, Nero, Otho, Vitellius, Domitian, Richard II of England, Edward II, Henry VI, Richard III, Mary Stuart, Charles I, the three Henrys of France, and the Emperor Henry IV."

---

15. *viziers . . . mufti,* officials of the court of justice.
16. *caymac,* Turkish cream.
17. *mussulman,* Moslem.

"Neither need you tell me," said Candide, "that we must take care of our garden."

"You are in the right," said Pangloss; "for when man was put into the Garden of Eden, it was with an intent to dress it: and this proves that man was not born to be idle."

"Work then without disputing," said Martin; "it is the only way to render life supportable."

The little society, one and all, entered into this laudable design; and set themselves to exert their different talents. The little piece of ground yielded them a plentiful crop. Cunegund indeed was very ugly, but she became an excellent hand at pastry-work; the old woman had the care of the linen.

There was none but did some service. Pangloss used now and then to say to Candide:

"There is a concatenation of all events in the best of possible worlds; for, in short, had you not been kicked out of a fine castle by the backside for the love of Miss Cunegund, had you not been put into the Inquisition, had you not travelled over America on foot, had you not run the Baron through the body, and had you not lost all your sheep which you brought from the good country of El Dorado, you would not have been here to eat preserved citrons and pistachio-nuts."

"Excellently observed," answered Candide; "but let us take care of our garden."

1759

THINK AND DISCUSS
Understanding
1. How is Pangloss's philosophy responsible for Candide's initial misfortune?
2. How is El Dorado one of the most important stops on Candide's itinerary? How is his philosophy affected by what he sees in this special land?
3. How are Candide and Cunegund eventually reunited? Why does Candide decide to go ahead with plans to marry her?
4. How does the closing line of the book reflect Candide's journey toward maturity and philosophical independence from his mentor?

Analyzing
5. A foil is a person who makes another person more clearly visible by contrast. How are Cacambo and Martin effective foils for Candide? What can we learn about Candide from his traveling companions?

6. Who ultimately suffers more—Candide or Cunegund? What comments on the roles of the sexes does Voltaire seem to be making in the novel?
7. Does Candide's final comment reflect a moment of insight—or resignation?

Extending
8. Anatole France, a modern French novelist and essayist, once wrote: "Comedy turns sad as soon as it becomes human. Does not *Don Quixote* sometimes make you grieve? I greatly admire those few books of a serene and smiling desolation, like the incomparable *Don Quixote* or like *Candide*, which are, when properly taken, manuals of indulgence and pity, bibles of benevolence." How is *Candide*, for all its broad humor of **satire**, a compellingly sad work? How does its final scene not only parallel, as France suggests, the saga of *Don Quixote*, but also echo the haunting atmosphere of the closing lines of Milton's *Paradise Lost*?

REVIEWING: Irony H ✏
See Handbook of Literary Terms, p. 955.

Irony is a literary term that describes a contrast between what appears to be and what really is.

1. How does the world appear to Pangloss?
2. How does the world as experienced by Candide differ from the world as described to him by Pangloss?

VOCABULARY
Roots

Use the Glossary to answer the following questions about the structure of the words in the list below. Read each clue, then write on your paper the matching word from the list. You will not use all the words.

dissertation	peremptory
ingenuous	ragout
oracle	remonstrate
pensive	

1. Which word has a root with a meaning that describes a way of speaking?
2. Which word has a root that means something done with a scale?
3. Which word has a root that can mean another word for symbol?
4. Which word has a root that means something done with food?
5. Which word has a root that means something that writers do?

COMPOSITION ✑
Defining El Dorado

Is El Dorado a mythical concept or an attainable reality? In a short essay of two or three paragraphs, define your concept of an El Dorado. Discuss the figurative as well as literal steps you must take to reach it.

Writing a Personal Essay

As you have passed through the many experiences of your high school career, you have undergone a journey as eventful to you as Candide's is to him. Write a personal essay of approximately two pages in which you look back upon your own journey. How were you affected by the perils and surprises of your odyssey? In what ways have you learned to cultivate your own garden, philosophically speaking?

Relating Mood and Tone

Mood is the general atmosphere or prevailing emotion of a work, as created by the choice of words, setting, imagery, and detail. **Tone** is the author's attitude toward the subject matter and the audience. Analyze the tone in *Candide* and then relate this tone to the mood of the selection. See "Writing About Mood or Tone" in the Writer's Handbook.

Neoclassic Regulation of Language

The Latin language had come down to eighteenth-century Europe in a relatively fixed form. Grammar books, dictionaries, and authoritarian schoolmasters had instilled definite conceptions of what was correct usage. None of the vernacular languages that succeeded Latin was so thoroughly regulated until well into the Neoclassic period.

The most astute and able statesmen in seventeeth-century France was Cardinal Richelieu (rish′ə lü), chief minister of the weak King Louis XIII. As one of a number of reforms aimed at strengthening royal power, Richelieu chartered the French Academy in 1635. It was his intention that French literature would contribute to the grandeur of the state. The members of the Academy, limited to forty distinguished literary men (women were excluded), were to maintain standards of literary taste and to establish the correct form of the French language. Their effort, as the members themselves put it, was to "clean up the language and remove the garbage accumulated in the mouths of the common folk or in the magistrate's court or through the abuse of the men in the pulpits who say the right things in the wrong way." In pursuit of this goal, they were to produce a grammar and a dictionary of the French language. Their first dictionary was published in 1694.

There were similar attempts to reform language in England during the Neoclassic period. The Royal Society, founded in 1660 by a group of scientists and other scholars, objected to the unregulated spontaneity that characterized Elizabethan English. Instead, the Society demanded of its members "a close, naked, natural way of speaking; positive expressions, clear senses, a native easiness, bringing all things as near the mathematical plainness as they can." Like the French Academicians, those interested in reforming English tended to disparage what they called "cant" or "low speech," that is, the language of ordinary people. The urge to introduce order into English is evident in hundreds of linguistic projects undertaken during the Neoclassic period, the most celebrated being Samuel Johnson's *Dictionary of the English Language*, published in 1755. Unlike the French Academy's project, Johnson produced his ponderous, two-volume dictionary single-handedly, with the help of six clerks to copy out the quotations that illustrated the proper use of words. Great achievement though it was, Johnson's *Dictionary* offered only a partial solution to the problems of standardizing English, and before the eighteenth century ended there were many other attempts.

Frontispiece of the first edition of the dictionary of the French Academy. 1794. Bibliothèque Nationale. The Academicians are shown presenting the dictionary to King Louis XIV.

THE SOCIAL ORDER

When writers deal with the social order, they may emphasize the idea in the word *social* (that is, people socializing), as Chekhov does in "The Kiss" (page 754); or they may emphasize the idea in the word *order* (that is, a shaping or confining structure), as T'ao Ch'ien does when he speaks of "the Dusty Net" from which he escaped, in the first of the "Two Poems on Returning to Dwell in the Country" (page 79). But whether a writer prefers to observe polite society or escape from it, he or she is dealing with the vital issue of how people manage to live together.

Polite Society

In *The Music Man*, Marian the librarian tells Professor Harold Hill that she was impressed by his show. Hill, a charlatan who is trying to bilk the whole town, says, "Oh, that was nothing." Marian responds, "Oh, yes it *was!*" She does not ordinarily talk this way, saying the opposite of what she means, but she has come under the spell of the Music Man, who is trying to confuse everyone. For Molière in *Tartuffe* (page 514), the issue is similar, but more serious. Molière is afraid that the religious charlatan Tartuffe will have a dangerous effect on all of society because of the influence he has on weak-willed people. Orgon, while under the influence of this impostor, attempts to disinherit his son and to prevent his daughter's marriage. He does not ordinarily think this way, but he has come under the spell of a religious hypocrite, who is trying to confuse everyone. But Tartuffe attempts even greater injustices than these. He tries to marry Orgon's daughter, seduce his wife, usurp his house, and acquire his wealth. And he does all this in the name of religious piety. He is simply an impostor, an outsider who attempts to upset the whole social order.

Chekhov's "The Kiss" also presents a social order near collapse, and the author shows it to us through the eyes of an outsider. Though Ryabovich is the social equal of the other officers invited to an evening with the family of an aris-tocratic general, he is shyer and more sensitive than the others, so that when he is accidentally kissed by an aristocratic young woman in a dark room, the experience inspires him with a rich fantasy life. But because Ryabovich's fantasies deal with the unknown woman who kissed him, Chekhov constantly brings the reader back to his depiction of the artificiality of the general's family. The result is that we learn about aristocrats, officers, and one sensitive soul—three levels of a social order that is close to a fall because of loneliness and lack of communication.

An outsider contemplating a social order is also the subject of "Chu-ch'ēn Village," by Po Chü-i (page 90); but in this poem the social order described is of lower station than the outsider. The speaker is a well-educated man who comes from the world of polite society, "the Realms of Etiquette"—what T'ao Ch'ien, in a similar mood, would call "the Dusty Net." He is a courtier for the prince, but he considers himself temperamentally unsuited for this work. He is envious of the people of remote Chu-ch'ēn, a village that, because of its agricultural simplicity, represents, for him, a higher social order than the court. For the speaker, this village is the ideal society. A hundred miles from their county seat, the villagers have even learned to govern themselves.

Ruling the People

The governing of the people is an ancient problem. Confucius, in the *Analects* (page 75), makes a case for governing by moral force. Instead of recommending that laws and punishments be used on the people, he tells the governor to "keep order among them by ritual"—i.e., by emphasizing participation in the traditional religious rites. What the governor needs is the confidence and trust of the people; so the way to deal with them is to use Confucius's version of the Golden Rule: "Do not do to others what you would not like yourself."

Nero's way of ruling Rome, according to the *Annals* of Tacitus (page 258), could not be further from the Confucian ideal. Tacitus suggests that Rome was destroyed by one man, the Emperor Nero, who burned it to the ground in order to build a new city named after himself. Nero then blamed the Christians for the deed, torturing many of them to death. This, according to Tacitus, was "only to glut the cruelty of one man."

The idea that the cruelty of the leader is justifiable by the worthiness of his goal is one of the main ideas of Machiavelli in *The Prince* (page 394). Of course, the ruler's goal is to retain his office. He may accomplish this goal by keeping the people "united and obedient" in fear of him. Machiavelli is the supreme realist of politics: He asserts that a ruler's reputation for cruelty can be useful in keeping both the people and the army docile. Nero would have agreed.

The Rich and the Poor

An American public official once declared that "the stability of every society that has ever achieved stability has depended on the resignation of its poor to their poverty." In addressing the problem of poverty in Ireland, Swift's "A Modest Proposal" (page 553) puts forth an idea that is intended to fill us with shock and revulsion, because he believes it is the only way to bring the attention of influential readers to the calamitous state of affairs. But whom does Swift blame for that state of affairs? England is the governor, the country responsible for depriving Ireland of its freedoms. The Irish, too, have contributed to their own problem by not buying Irish products. But it is hard to see where the Irish would obtain the money with which to buy them. Swift's proposal intends to inform us of that fact in the most vivid way.

Heine's poem "The Silesian Weavers" (page 619) presents the poor themselves as speaking. Their words condemn the religious establishment, the king, and the country that sanction their poverty. The king is described as "the rich man's king." When "The Silesian Weavers" was written, it provided a topical comment on the harsh working conditions endured by the weavers, and the indifference of the affluent to the suffering of the poor. Implicit in the poem is the idea that social upheaval is necessary to remedy injustice.

Alice Walker's "Everyday Use" (page 922)

Conspiracy, a lithograph done in 1898 by Käthe Kollwitz (1867–1945), one of a series on the theme of the Silesian weavers. National Gallery of Art, Washington

portrays the interaction of a poor woman and one of her daughters with a second daughter who has left home, become prosperous, and returns to her old home on a visit. The story depicts the dignity of poor people and the importance of values other than those of worldly success.

Tolstoy's fable "How Much Land Does a Man Need?" (page 669) is a cautionary tale about temptation and greed—greed for the very thing that peasants seldom have, their own land. The main character, a peasant, has a desire to acquire more and more land. But the title informs us of Tolstoy's values and prepares us for the ending, in which the peasant literally kills himself by trying to encompass too much land. The very thing he lusts after is the cause of his death.

THINKING CRITICALLY
ABOUT LITERATURE

UNIT 5   NEOCLASSICISM   1650–1780

■ CONCEPT REVIEW

Below on the left is one of the *Persian Letters* (1721) by Charles de Montesquieu (1689–1755), French lawyer, philosopher, and writer. His *Persian Letters* is made up of a series of fictional letters satirizing French life. The letters are supposed to have passed between two Persian travelers in Europe, the outgoing Rica and the more thoughtful Usbek. Their frankness and openness allow the reader to accept them as neutral observers of all that they encounter. Through his characters Montesquieu comments on the social and political events of the day, and also on the manners and morals of the society in which he lived.

Below on the right are notes to help you read and to review some of the literary terms and thinking skills that have appeared in Unit 5. Page numbers in the notes refer to an application or review of a literary term in the unit. A more extensive discussion of these terms is in the Handbook of Literary Terms. On a separate sheet of paper write your answers to the questions that follow this excerpt.

from the Persian Letters

Charles de Montesquieu   *translated by* **J. Robert Loy**

Letter 54

Rica to Usbek in ——

This morning I was in my room, which, as you know, is separated from the others only by a very thin partition with openings in several places so that all that gets said in the next room can be heard. A man who was striding back and forth was saying to another: "I don't know how to explain it, but everything is turning against me. For over three days I have said nothing to my honor, and I have embarked pell-mell into every conversation without anyone's paying the slightest attention to me or addressing me twice. I had prepared several witticisms with which to spice my conversation; no one would ever let me work them in. I had a very pretty tale to tell but every time just as I wanted to get to it, people would escape it as if on purpose. I have several puns that have been aging in my head for four days without my getting the slightest use

■ **Style** (page 507): Note the easy, conversational style employed in this selection.

■ **Satire** (page 558): As you read, note what is being satirized in this letter.

■ **Epigram** (page 573): Note throughout this letter the concern the two men show with acquiring a reputation for uttering short, witty sayings with a sharp point.

from them. If this continues I believe I shall finish up a booby. Such would seem to be my unlucky star, and I can't seem to free myself. Yesterday I had hoped to sparkle with three or four old ladies, who certainly never get the better of me, and I was planning to say the prettiest things in the world. I spent more than a quarter of an hour directing my conversation, but they never kept to the same subject, and they cut off, like some fatal Parcae, the thread of all my talk. Do you want me to tell you something? The reputation of being a wit costs a lot to uphold. I don't know how you managed it."

"An idea just came to me," continued the other. "Let's work together to build up our wit; let's co-operate. Every day we will tell each other what we should talk about, and we shall help each other so well that if someone comes to interrupt us in the middle of our ideas, we shall drag him along ourselves, and if he does not come along willingly, we shall use violence. We shall agree on the places where we must approve, those where we must smile, others where we must laugh outright and resoundingly. You will see that we shall set the tone for all conversations and that people will admire the vivacity of our minds and the pertinence of our repartee. We shall protect each other with mutual nods. Today you will sparkle; tomorrow you will be my second. I shall enter into a house with you and cry as I point you out: 'I must tell you a very clever reply monsieur just made to a man we found in the street.' And I shall turn toward you and say: 'He didn't expect to at all, he was quite astonished.' Then I shall recite some of my verses and you will say: 'I was there when he composed them; it was during a supper party and he didn't take time off to reflect one minute.' Often we shall mock each other and people will say: "See how well they attack! How well they defend themselves! They don't spare each other. Let's just see how he'll get out of that one. Marvelous! What presence of mind! Why, it's a regular battle!' But by evening they will not find it possible to believe that we had skirmished earlier. We shall have to buy certain books—witticisms collected for those without wit who would like to counterfeit it. Everything depends on having good models. After six months, I should like us to be able to hold a full hour's conversation completely filled with witticisms. But we must be careful about one thing, and that is to be sure our witticisms make their way. It's not enough to say them; they must be spread and strewn everywhere. If not, it's so much lost, and I must confess that there is nothing so discouraging as to see a charming thing one has said die in the ear of some fool who hears it. True, there is often a compensation, for we are also capable of saying stupidities which get by *incognito*, and that's our sole consolation in such situations. There, my dear fellow, is the method we must follow. Do as I say and I promise you a chair in the Academy before six months have gone by. Which means that our working days will not be long. For, by that time, you can forget your technique; you will be a witty man no matter what you do. It can be noted that in France, as soon as a man makes his appearance in a particular company, he takes on from the start what is called the *esprit de corps*. You will do the same, and I fear for you only an excess of applause."

From Paris, the 6th of the
Moon of Zilcade, 1714.

■ **booby**: a dull, stupid person; a fool.

■ **Parcae** (pär′sē): the three cruel Fates (in Roman myths) who arbitrariiy control everyone's life and destiny. The name comes from the Latin word *pars*, which means "lot" in the sense of destiny.

■ **Irony** (page 591): Note the irony of working "together to build up our wit."

■ **Evaluating**: Satire that is smiling and gentle in tone is sometimes called Horatian (after the Roman poet Horace); satire that is angry and bitter is sometimes called Juvenalian (after the Roman poet Juvenal). Which of these two terms best describes Montesquieu's satire in this letter?

■ **incognito** (in kog nē′tō): concealed, disguised, unknown.

■ **Academy**: the French Academy, chartered by Cardinal Richelieu in 1635 (see page 592).

■ **esprit de corps** (e sprē′- də kôr′): group spirit, comradeship.

THINK AND DISCUSS

Understanding

1. Who is supposed to be writing this letter, who is the recipient of it, and where do they come from?
2. Whose conversation is overheard and reported in the letter?

Analyzing

3. What reputation do the two Europeans wish to acquire?
4. How do they plan to acquire this reputation?

Extending

5. How do you think this quest for reputation appears to Rica and Usbek?
6. What do you think the gentlemen's quest for reputation tells you about their society?

REVIEWING LITERARY TERMS

Style

1. Why is an easy, conversational style appropriate to this selection?

Satire

2. Would you describe the satire in this selection as smiling or angry?

Epigram

3. Coleridge wrote of the epigram: "What is an epigram? A dwarfish whole,/Its body brevity, and wit its soul." Why is wit the "soul" of an epigram?

Irony

4. What is ironic about working hard to appear witty?

■ CONTENT REVIEW

THINKING SKILLS

Classifying

1. Satire employs wit to ridicule and reform. Which of the works in this unit are not satirical?

Generalizing

2. Based on your reading of the selection from *Candide,* what is Voltaire's view of the philosophy of Dr. Pangloss?

Synthesizing

3. If you could create your own paradise, what elements from the Garden of Eden in *Paradise Lost* and El Dorado in *Candide* might you combine?

Evaluating

4. Do you think Swift's protest against conditions in Ireland might have been more effectively expressed in straightforward prose, or do you think his use of a satiric and ironic prose is more effective? Explain.

■ COMPOSITION REVIEW

Writing About Tone

Pope's *Rape of the Lock* and *Essay on Man* are very different in intention and purpose. One is a satire, the other an argument in verse. In a brief essay contrast the **tone** in Pope's two poems, and explain why the different tone is appropriate to each.

Comparing and Contrasting

The selection from Pope's *Essay on Man* articulates an optimistic philosophy of "Whatever is, is right." The selections from Voltaire's *Candide* satirize optimism. Compare and contrast the two selections in their interpretation of evil and suffering in the world.

ROMANTICISM AND REALISM

1780	1790	1800	1810	1820	1830

HISTORY AND ARTS

- Battle of Yorktown
- Peace of Versailles
- Mozart: *Don Giovanni*
- U.S. Constitution ratified
- French Revolution begins
- Washington, D.C. founded
- David: *The Death of Marat*
- Rosetta stone found
- Louisiana Purchase
- War of 1812
- Battle of Waterloo
- Goya: *Disasters of War*
- Erie Canal finished •
- Delacroix: *Liberty Leading the People* •
- Beethoven: *Ninth Symphony*
- Decembrist Revolt

PEOPLE

- Napoleon invades Russia
- Franklin dies •
- Louis XVI executed
- Napoleon becomes emperor
- Washington becomes President
- Napoleon abdicates •
- Mozart dies
- Jefferson becomes President
- Keats dies
- Byron dies
- Victoria born

LITERATURE

- Rousseau: *Confessions*
- Wordsworth and Coleridge: *Lyrical Ballads*
- Boswell: *Life of Johnson*
- Paine: *The Rights of Man*
- Mary Shelley: *Frankenstein* •
- Jacob and Wilhelm Grimm: *Fairy Tales*
- Byron: *Childe Harold's Pilgrimage*
- Goethe: *Faust*, Part I
- Pushkin: *Eugene Onegin*
- Heine: • *Book of Songs*

Detail of David's painting, *The Death of Marat.* 1793

Detail of a portrait of Ludwig van Beethoven (1770–1827)

Detail of a portrait of Darwin at the age of thirty. 1840

1840	1850	1860	1870	1880

Darwin: *On the Origin of Species* • Marx: *Capital* •

• Brooklyn Bridge opened

• Voyage of the *Beagle* begins • Revolutions of 1848 • Suez Canal begun

• First Impressionist exhibition

• First Reform Bill • Marx and Engels: *Communist Manifesto*

• Battle of Gettysburg

• Emancipation Proclamation

• Crystal Palace built • Transatlantic cable completed

Crimean War begins • • Indian Mutiny • Franco-Prussian War

Neanderthal Man discovered •

• Goethe dies

Nobel invents dynamite • • Schliemann excavates Troy

• Victoria becomes queen • Heine dies • Victoria becomes Empress of India

• Pushkin dies • Lincoln becomes President

Lincoln assassinated • Flaubert dies •

• Emerson: *Nature* • Hawthorne: *The Scarlet Letter*

• Poe: *The Fall of the House of Usher* • Melville: *Moby Dick* • Hugo: *Les Misérables*

• Turgenev: *A Sportsman's Sketches* • Tolstoy: *War and Peace*

• Gogol: *Dead Souls* • Dostoevski: *Crime and Punishment*

• Whitman: *Leaves of Grass*

Detail of a portrait of
Karl Marx (1818–1883)

Colored print showing the
Crystal Palace. 1851

Detail of a cyclorama showing
Pickett's Charge, July 3, 1863

PREVIEW

UNIT 6   ROMANTICISM AND REALISM   1780–1880

Authors

Johann Wolfgang von Goethe
Heinrich Heine
Alexander Pushkin
Victor Hugo
Nikolai Gogol
Walt Whitman

Gustave Flaubert
Leo Tolstoy
Emily Dickinson
Mark Twain
Guy de Maupassant
William Wordsworth

Features
Comment: The Faust Legend
Reader's Note: Translating "The Loreley"
The History of Language: The Study of
    Comparative Language
Themes in World Literature: The Outsider

Application of Literary Terms
point of view
free verse
stereotype

Review of Literary Terms
inference
point of view

Vocabulary Skills
context, dictionary
dictionary and etymology
antonyms

Thinking Skills
synthesizing
evaluating
generalizing

Composition Assignments Include
Writing to Describe
Writing to Compare and Contrast
Writing a Protest
Writing About Point of View
Writing About Personal Experience
Writing a Poem
Writing About Imagery
Writing About Theme
Writing a Folk Tale
Writing Metaphorically
Defending a Poet's Style
Writing a Speech
Writing a Newspaper Report
Extending the Story
Writing About Satire

Enrichment
Preparing a Radio Script
Combining Music and Literature
Speaking and Listening
Examining Advertising
Comparing Stories

Thinking Critically About Literature
Concept Review
Content Review
Composition Review

ROMANTICISM AND REALISM 1780–1880

ROMANTICISM

A difficult term to define simply, *Romanticism* refers to a broad intellectual and cultural movement, rather than to a particular school of writers. In many ways a reaction against the Enlightenment, this movement also reflected new springs of feeling and thought derived from contemporary events, particularly the political turbulence of the period 1780–1830. The effects of Romanticism did not appear at the same time or in the same way throughout Europe and America. However, the Romantics did share a common outlook as they turned from a reliance on society's values to a belief in the ultimate truth of individual experience; from an emphasis on rationalism to an acceptance of the importance of feelings; from a conception of the world as a machine to a glorification of nature.

THE AGE OF REVOLUTION

The French writer Jean Jacques Rousseau (1712–1778) is considered the chief prophet of Romanticism. His writings in the early 1750s proclaimed his belief in the innate goodness of natural man uncorrupted by civilization. In 1762, building on the political thought of the English philosopher John Locke, Rousseau published his famous treatise, *The Social Contract*, in which he advocated the common people's right to revolt against social and political inequities. It began with a savage indictment: "Man is born free; and everywhere he is in chains." Expressed in their writings, the democratic ideas of Rousseau and other thinkers who supported the rights of the people over those of kings, did much to break those chains. The individuals who created the American and French Revolutions embraced these political ideas eagerly.

The American Revolution (1775–1783) severed all political ties between Britain and the newly established United States, whose Declaration of Independence proposed a society based on the premise that "all men are created equal." Throughout Europe, political unrest grew as liberals and their middle-class supporters attacked the concept of absolute monarchy and the oppression of the common people.

France experienced a political upheaval in 1789 when the severe financial problems of Louis XVI's decadent government resulted in the formation of a new legislative body, the National Assembly. This date marks the beginning of the French Revolution. Rioting and disorder spread, and the rallying cry of "Liberty, Equality, Fraternity" ignited the fervor of the revolutionaries. The storming of the Bastille, an old fortress in Paris where a few political prisoners were being held, symbolized the battle between the common citizen and the authority of the monarchy, aristocracy, and church. In August, 1789, the National Assembly adopted the Declaration of the Rights of Man and Citizen, making all citizens equal under the law. In 1791, a constitutional monarchy was established, but demands of the radicals for a republic turned the moderate revolution into a bloodbath, beginning with the execution of Louis XVI in 1793 and continuing through a Reign of Terror in which more than 25,000 people died.

At this same period, France's internal problems were further complicated by war with a number of European nations, whose monarchs saw the restoration of the French king as necessary to their own survival. After suffering some initial defeats, the French citizen-armies carried out a series of remarkably successful campaigns between 1793 and 1795. However, continuing war with Austria and Great Britain and severe internal conflicts paved the way for a successful young general, Napoleon Bonaparte, to lead a coup d'état which made him the ruler of France in 1799. He was elected first consul for life in 1802 and made himself emperor in 1804.

Napoleon's military genius, swift rise to power, and grandiose plans captured the people's admiration and the writers' imagination. This "son of the French Revolution," as he called himself, conquered most of Europe in the name of liberty before a disastrous retreat from Russia in 1812, vividly described in Victor Hugo's "Russia 1812" (page 629). The armies of England, Russia, Prussia, and Austria combined to defeat the French in the "Battle of Nations" at Leipzig in 1813, and the allied invasion of Paris in 1814 forced Napoleon to abdicate his throne and live in exile on the island of Elba. A second attempt at seizing power in 1815 failed when his army was defeated at Waterloo. Napoleon's accomplishments of instituting domestic reform, particularly the codification of French law, and of spreading the ideals of the French Revolution and stimulating nationalism throughout Europe—which later contributed to his downfall—must be weighed against the suffering and death caused by his wars. Napoleon's defeat and the resulting Congress of Vienna (1815) restored the French monarchy and suppressed liberalism and democracy wherever possible. Throughout Europe the forces of conservatism, led by the Austrian statesman Metternich, clashed with those of liberalism, nationalism, and democracy, leading to more revolutions.

ROMANTIC LITERATURE

Political revolt and artistic rebellion went hand-in-hand. As the people forced reform and toppled governments, artists abandoned the restrictions of Neoclassicism and gave free reign to the imagination. Johann Wolfgang von Goethe, Germany's greatest poet, was a leader of the Storm and Stress movement in Germany, a precursor of Romanticism. This literary movement emphasized individualism and emotion and rejected the Neoclassic concern with order and reason. In Goethe's *Faust* (page 609), the **protagonist's** focus on self-realization causes him to strive for the infinite, making him the **archetypal** Romantic hero.

The appearance in 1798 of *Lyrical Ballads*, by William Wordsworth and Samuel Taylor Coleridge, signaled the beginning of the English Romantic movement. In the Preface to the second edition, Wordsworth defined poetry as "the spontaneous overflow of powerful feelings" and formulated the theory that poetry should be about humble life and written in a "language really used by men" as opposed to "poetic diction." Victor Hugo called Romanticism "liberalism in literature." In his Preface to his verse play *Cromwell* in 1827, he denounced Neoclassic literary conventions, asserting that "there are no rules other than the general laws of nature."

In America, Walt Whitman, in the Preface to the 1855 edition of his verse collection *Leaves of Grass*, proclaimed the poet's role as seer, announced his belief that the "common people," not the upper class, provide the best "poetic material," and echoed Rousseau's concept of the innate goodness of humanity. He introduced his revolutionary theory of versification which abandoned traditional metrical forms, as was clearly demonstrated in the poems in *Leaves of Grass*. Another American poet, Emily Dickinson, also cast aside certain conventions in her verse. Both of these poets were influenced by the American writer Ralph Waldo Emerson. Emerson had encountered German philosophy through writers he met while traveling abroad. He incorporated its Romantic idealism with his ideas of self-reliance and free-thinking into Transcendentalism, the dominant American philosophy of the nineteenth century. This mystical philosophy expresses the belief that within human beings there is an insight or intuition which transcends sensory experience and logic and makes it possible to recognize universal truths. This possibility is the subject of Dickinson's poem "Tell All the Truth But Tell It Slant" (page 680). The theme of individualism so prominent in Emerson's writing is also expressed in Whitman's "Song of Myself" (page 652.)

This Romantic individualism was tied to nationalism, as many writers looked to their countries' pasts to examine the heritage that contributed to a nation's uniqueness. According to the poet Heinrich Heine, the interest in the Middle Ages was particularly significant in German Romanticism. Studies of folk customs and folk literature were stimulated by Bishop Percy's col-

Fall of the Bastille: 14 July 1789 By Claude Cholat, an amateur painter who
was one of those attacking the prison. 1789. Musée Carnavalet, Paris

lection of ballads, *Reliques of Ancient English
Poetry* (1765), which was translated into German and other languages. Jacob and Wilhelm
Grimm gathered folk tales from German peasants and published them in their famous collection (1812). Heine's fascination with German
folklore led him to use the simple language and
form of the folk ballad for his well-known poem
"The Loreley" (page 619). The Russian poet
Pushkin transformed folk stories into narrative
poetry, such as "The Bridegroom" (page 624).
The eighteenth century had despised the Middle Ages as a period of "Gothic" barbarism,
but now literature set in remote periods and
describing strange and exotic events became
very popular. These "Gothic tales" were
designed to evoke terror. Coleridge's principal
contribution to *Lyrical Ballads*, "The Rime of

the Ancient Mariner," with a voyage to mysterious polar regions and supernatural happenings,
represents this new Romantic fascination with
the macabre and grotesque.

The central subject of the Romantic writers,
however, was nature. The Romantics viewed
nature with reverence and awe. Goethe describes
nature's glory—the world at sunset, "all of its
peaks on fire, all of its vales becalmed."
Coleridge, in "The Rime of the Ancient Mariner," evokes nature's rejuvenating power—"water-snakes . . . Blue, glossy green, and velvet black . . . happy living things"—breaking
the spell of a deadman's curse. Dickinson alludes to nature as a source of knowledge—
"The simple news that Nature told,/With tender majesty." Wordsworth, the pre-eminent Romantic poet of nature, speaks of it as divine—

"something far more deeply interfused,/Whose dwelling is the light of setting suns,/And the round ocean and the living air,/And the blue sky and the mind of man;/A motion and a spirit . . . ."

Overall, Romanticism reflected the optimistic spirit of the age, the belief that humanity could shape its destiny. While the Romantic movement declined after a brief resurgence in the 1830s, its emphasis on individualism lives on as part of our modern outlook.

REALISM

Realism, a nineteenth-century movement countering Romanticism, was defined by the American writer William Dean Howells as "nothing more or less than the truthful treatment of material." Centering mainly on prose fiction, the Realists' aim was verisimilitude, the appearance of reality in a literary work, not to be confused with the accuracy of journalistic writing. The subjects were usually ordinary people undergoing plausible, everyday experiences. With this movement, Romantic idealism gave way to prosaic reality, subjectivity to objectivity, fascination with the remote past to concern with the present. Events of the period influenced the Realists greatly as they set about imitating life in their writing. *Madame Bovary* (page 661), by French writer Gustave Flaubert, has been cited as the masterpiece of realistic fiction due to the author's dispassionate, detached manner and the precise details he used to portray the dreary lives of ordinary middle-class people.

THE INDUSTRIAL REVOLUTION

Scientific advancements and related technological discoveries, increasing mechanization, and materialism contributed to the decline of the Romantic movement as industrialization transformed the economy and society of nineteenth-century Western Europe and the United States.

The industrial revolution had begun in late eighteenth-century Britain. James Watt's invention of the first practical steam engine (patented in 1769), advances in textile production, and other technological innovations resulted in the first urban factories, improved transportation systems, and expansion of the iron and steel industry. The English poet Alfred Tennyson expressed one impact of nineteenth-century industrialization in "Locksley Hall," where the speaker exults "in the steamship, in the railway, in the thoughts that shake mankind." Increased industrial productivity in the 1830s and 1840s earned Great Britain the title of the "workshop of the world." England dominated world markets, becoming the first nation to obtain its major income from manufacturing. But with the spread of industrialism came severe problems: a shift in population from rural agricultural areas to urban industrial centers ill-equipped to handle the increased numbers; inhumane working conditions in factories; grinding poverty in slums; and inefficiency and corruption in government. Social ills became the subject of Realistic literary works in place of the Romantics' favorite topic, nature. The plight of men, women, and even children working long hours under harsh and often dangerous conditions was portrayed in English fiction by novelists such as Charles Dickens.

The years 1830–1870 saw the spread of industrialization to the rest of northern Europe and the United States. Not all literature about technological progress focused on its negative effects. In America, Walt Whitman in "Song of Myself" and other poems, such as "To a Locomotive in Winter" (page 657), praised the powerful new machines and the workers who ran them. Mark Twain's "love affair" with the steamboat started when he was a boy and is delightfully chronicled in *Life on the Mississippi* (page 684). Protest literature in the United States at mid-century tended to center on the evils of slavery and later on the Civil War (1861–1865), rather than the problems resulting from industrialization.

POLITICAL UNREST

In Europe, writers protested the abuses of the factory system, the unresponsive or repressive government, and the widening gap between the rich and the poor. Heinrich Heine vividly portrayed the workers' reactions to these problems in his poem "The Silesian Weavers" (page 619). Heine's empathy for the workers' problems had attracted him to Saint-Simonianism, a socialist movement centered in Paris. The

Abbey in an Oak Forest by Caspar David Friedrich. 1809–1810.
Staatliche Museen, Berlin

French philosopher and social reformer Saint-Simon (1760–1825) proposed a planned economy run by a benevolent group of industrialists and scientists who would protect the laboring class. By the 1830s, socialism was spreading quickly as a response to the evils of industrialism. In 1848 German socialists Karl Marx and Friedrich Engels wrote one of the most influential docu- ments in modern history, the *Communist Mani- festo*. Marx and Engels perceived the history of society as a class struggle. They depicted the opposing forces in the nineteenth century as the capitalists, the class who owned the means of production, and the proletariat, the wage-laborers "enslaved by the machine." The *Com- munist Manifesto* closed with a famous exhorta-

A Bar at the Folies-Bergère by Édouard Manet. 1881–1882.
Courtauld Institute Galleries, London

tion: "The workers have nothing to lose but
their chains. They have a world to gain. Workers of the world, unite!" The Communists' aim
was to end the dominance of the middle class,
thereby abolishing the class system and ending private property rights. Leo Tolstoy's story
"How Much Land Does a Man Need?" (page
669) reflects a similar belief that private ownership of land encourages greed.

During the 1840s and 1850s, the economic
and political situation in Europe worsened, causing a new series of revolts. Crop failures that
resulted in severe food shortages led to food riots
in 1847. Unemployment, the alliance between
impoverished workers and political liberals who
wanted reforms, and the continuing influence
of nationalism all contributed to the revolutions

that convulsed the continent in 1848. Many
writers became embroiled in the upheavels. In
France, King Louis Philippe abdicated after the
revolution of 1848. The Second Republic was
then formed. Poet and novelist Victor Hugo,
who was elected deputy to the National Assembly, supported the new President, Louis
Napoleon, the nephew of Napoleon Bonaparte.
However, when Louis Napoleon seized power in
1851 and proclaimed himself emperor in 1852,
Hugo helped organize resistance to his tyrannical
policies, and the writer was forced to flee France.
This Second Empire was relatively short-lived,
ending in 1870 when Napoleon III was deposed
during the Franco-Prussian War and the Third
Republic was established amid the violent class
conflict of the Paris Commune.

The quest for national unity in areas disunited or under alien rule, such as Italy and Germany, grew strong under the leadership of cunning statesmen. Count Camillo di Cavour, the prime minister of Sardinia from 1852 to 1861, used diplomacy and foreign wars in his successful efforts to unite the individual Italian states into one kingdom. The Prussian statesman Otto von Bismarck employed power politics to unite a number of principalities into a German Empire. Bismarck declared that "the great questions of the day will not be decided by speeches and majority decision, but by blood and iron."

Britain's liberal posture allowed its government to escape the wave of revolutions. A series of reform bills addressed many of the country's internal problems. Under Queen Victoria, British rule spread over large areas of Africa and Asia, making England the largest and most powerful empire in the world. Economic and scientific advancement and a sense of moral purpose coexisted with an emphasis on middle-class respectability throughout the Victorian Age.

In Russia, the tyranny of the czarist state continued. Intellectuals who criticized the government were attacked. Author Nikolai Gogol left the country in 1836 after his play satirizing Russian officialdom, *The Inspector General*, angered government officials. Gogol's short story "The Overcoat" (page 632) also targeted the bureaucracy. Its portrayal of a shy, nondescript, poverty-stricken clerk introduced the concept of the "little man" in fiction—the person of low social and economic position living in an impersonal and inhumane society, pushed around by powerful people.

The ideals of nationalism had become the reality of power politics and imperialism, subverting the promise of the French Revolution that had inspired Wordsworth in 1791 to write: "Bliss was it in that dawn to be alive." Idealism was derided. The underlying pessimism of French author Guy de Maupassant's story "The False Gems" (page 689) reflects the materialism and disillusionment of the period. The theory of evolution put forth by Charles Darwin in his revolutionary book *Origin of Species* (1859) spoke of natural selection and survival of the fittest. Some people used this theory to justify economic and political struggles among nations that would lead

to the supremacy of the "favored races." Darwin's theory also influenced a group of writers called Naturalists to use a scientific, objective approach to literature, and to depict people as victims of their heredity and environment.

Revolt and change, action and reaction, characterized the political climate and the literary movements that dominated the nineteenth century. Romantic writers rebelled against the strictures of Neoclassicism; Realists rejected the idealism and subjectivity of the Romanticists. However, literary movements always retain some aspects of the movements that they replace. Romantic and Realistic elements live on, blended together in the immense scope of the world's contemporary literature.

THINKING ABOUT GRAPHIC AIDS
Using the Time Line

The time line on pages 598–599 shows the chronological sequence of the historical and literary events discussed in Unit 6. Use the time line to answer the following questions.

1. Who was the President of the United States at the time of the French Revolution?
2. How long was Napoleon emperor of France? (a) five years; (b) ten years; (c) fifteen years
3. Which of the following events did *not* occur in 1837? (a) the death of Pushkin; (b) the passage of the First Reform Bill; (c) the coronation of Queen Victoria
4. Could Darwin's *Origin of Species* have influenced Marx and Engels's *Communist Manifesto?*
5. Could Flaubert have attended the first Impressionist exhibition?

Considered Germany's greatest poet, Johann Wolfgang von Goethe (gėr′tə) has been ranked with Homer, Dante, and Shakespeare for creative genius. Poet, dramatist, novelist, philosopher, and scientist, he was born in the German town of Frankfurt-am-Main, on August 28, 1749. His father, a wealthy lawyer, directed the education of his son and daughter at home through private tutors. At the age of sixteen Goethe began his study of law at the University of Leipzig, where he found falling in love and composing verses more interesting than his academic pursuits. A serious illness interrupted his schooling, but in 1770, after his recovery, he went to Strassburg to study law and medicine. There he met the literary critic Johann Gottfried von Herder who greatly influenced his thinking and prompted his involvement as a leader in the *Sturm und Drang* ("Storm and Stress") movement. This German literary movement, a Romantic reaction against Neoclassicism, valued individualism and emotion more than formalism and reason. Receiving a law degree in 1771, Goethe returned to Frankfurt and then spent four months as a lawyer in Wetzlar. While there, his traumatic involvement in a love triangle and the suicide of a friend caused him great anguish. This experience is reflected in his autobiographical novel *The Sorrows of Young Werther*, his first international success.

In 1775 the celebrated author accepted an invitation from Duke Karl August to visit Weimar where he soon became the Duke's close friend and a prominent government official. Many years of combining writing with political and social duties proved burdensome, so he secretly planned a trip to Italy in 1786. While in Italy, Goethe immersed himself in the study of classical antiquity. On his return to Weimar two years later, he began living with Christiane Vulpius, who bore him a son. They eventually married. Goethe accepted the position of director of the court theater and also became increasingly involved in scientific studies of anatomy, botany, optics, meteorology, and mineralogy. In 1795–96 he published *Wilhelm Meister's Apprenticeship*, the definitive example of the *Bildungsroman* ("novel of education"), which describes the development of a young person. This novel greatly influenced later German fiction.

Goethe's restless nature drove him to produce an amazing number and variety of works: poetry, drama, novels, satire, scientific writing, and autobiography. His masterpiece, the poetic drama *Faust*, was composed over a sixty-year timespan and reflects the comprehensiveness of his learning and experience. Goethe shared his plans and initial drafts with his friend and colleague Friedrich von Schiller who urged the great poet to complete the play. Referring to the *Fragment* published in 1790, Schiller wrote, "there reigns in those scenes the power and the fullness of genius which unmistakably reveals the first master." Part I of *Faust* was finished in 1808 and Part II in 1831, a year before Goethe's death.

Faust, more than 12,000 lines in length, was intended to be read rather than performed. In the Prologue, the introduction to the drama in which the heavenly host accompanies the Lord, three archangels step forward to sing praises of the Lord and his creation. The devil, in the form of Mephistopheles, then arrives from earth and comments on the condition of humankind. The scenes from Part I that follow the Prologue serve to introduce the character of Faust and his quest for all knowledge and experience, the focus of the rest of the poem.

from Faust

Johann Wolfgang von Goethe   *translated by* **Louis MacNeice**

from the PROLOGUE

MEPHISTOPHELES. Since you, O Lord, once more approach and ask
If business down with us be light or heavy—
And in the past you've usually welcomed me—
That's why you see me also at your levee.[1]
5 Excuse me, I can't manage lofty words—
Not though your whole court jeer and find me low;
My pathos certainly would make you laugh
Had you not left off laughing long ago.
Your suns and worlds mean nothing much to me;
10 How men torment themselves, that's all I see.
The little god of the world,[2] one can't reshape, reshade him;
He is as strange today as that first day you made him.
His life would be not so bad, not quite,
Had you not granted him a gleam of Heaven's light;
15 He calls it Reason, uses it not the least
Except to be more beastly than any beast.
He seems to me—if your Honor does not mind—
Like a grasshopper—the long-legged kind—
That's always in flight and leaps as it flies along
20 And then in the grass strikes up its same old song.
I could only wish he confined himself to the grass!
He thrusts his nose into every filth, alas.
  LORD. Mephistopheles, have you no other news?
Do you always come here to accuse?
25 Is nothing ever right in your eyes on earth?

MEPHISTOPHELES. No, Lord! I find things there as downright bad as ever.
I am sorry for men's days of dread and dearth;
Poor things, *my* wish to plague 'em isn't fervent.
LORD. Do you know Faust?
MEPHISTOPHELES.   The Doctor?
LORD.   Aye, my servant.
30 **MEPHISTOPHELES.** Indeed! He serves you oddly enough, I think.
The fool has no earthly habits in meat and drink.
The ferment in him drives him wide and far,
That he is mad he too has almost guessed;
He demands of heaven each fairest star
35 And of earth each highest joy and best,
And all that is new and all that is far
Can bring no calm to the deep-sea swell of his breast.
LORD. Now he may serve me only gropingly,
Soon I shall lead him into the light.
40 The gardener knows when the sapling first turns green
That flowers and fruit will make the future bright.
MEPHISTOPHELES. What do you wager? You will lose him yet,
Provided *you* give *me* permission
To steer him gently the course I set.

---

1. *levee,* a formal reception in the morning; French kings used to hold levees in the morning while they were getting up and dressing.
2. *little . . . world.* Humankind, made in God's image, was given rule over all creatures.

45 **LORD.** So long as he walks the earth alive,
   So long you may try what enters your head;
   Men make mistakes as long as they strive.[3]
   MEPHISTOPHELES. I thank you for that; as regards
      the dead,
   The dead have never taken my fancy.
50 I favor cheeks that are full and rosy-red;
   No corpse is welcome to my house;
   I work as the cat does with the mouse.
   LORD. Very well; you have my full permission.
   Divert this soul from its primal source
55 And carry it, if you can seize it,
   Down with you upon your course—
   And stand ashamed when you must needs admit:
   A good man with his groping intuitions
   Still knows the path that is true and fit.
60 **MEPHISTOPHELES.** All right—but it won't last for
      long.
   I'm not afraid my bet will turn out wrong.
   And, if my aim prove true and strong,
   Allow me to triumph wholeheartedly.
   Dust shall he eat—and greedily—
65 Like my cousin the Snake[4] renowned in tale and
      song.
   LORD. That too you are free to give a trial;
   I have never hated the likes of you.
   Of all the spirits of denial
   The joker is the last that I eschew.
70 Man finds relaxation too attractive—
   Too fond too soon of unconditional rest;
   Which is why I am pleased to give him a
      companion
   Who lures and thrusts and must, as devil,
      be active.
   But ye, true sons of Heaven, it is your duty
75 To take your joy in the living wealth of beauty.
   The changing Essence which ever works and lives
   Wall you around with love, serene, secure!
   And that which floats in flickering appearance
   Fix ye it firm in thoughts that must endure.
80 **CHOIR OF ANGELS.** Thine aspect cheers the Hosts
      of Heaven
   Though what Thine essence none can say,
   And all Thy loftiest creations
   Keep the high state of their first day.
                                    (*Heaven closes.*)

MEPHISTOPHELES (*alone*). I like to see the Old One
   now and then
85 And try to keep relations on the level.
   It's really decent of so great a person
   To talk so humanely even to the Devil. . . .

from PART I

(*In a high-vaulted narrow Gothic room*[5] FAUST, *restless,
in a chair at his desk*)

FAUST. Here stand I, ach, Philosophy
   Behind me and Law and Medicine too
90 And, to my cost, Theology—
   All these I have sweated through and through
   And now you see me a poor fool
   As wise as when I entered school!
   They call me Master, they call me Doctor,
95 Ten years now I have dragged my college[6]
   Along by the nose through zig and zag
   Through up and down and round and round
   And this is all that I have found—
   The impossibility of knowledge!
100 It is this that burns away my heart;
   Of course I am cleverer than the quacks,
   Than master and doctor, than clerk and priest,
   I suffer no scruple or doubt in the least,
   I have no qualms about devil or burning,
105 Which is just why all joy is torn from me,
   I cannot presume to make use of my learning,
   I cannot presume I could open my mind
   To proselytize and improve mankind.
   Besides, I have neither goods nor gold,
110 Neither reputation nor rank in the world;
   No dog would choose to continue so!
   Which is why I have given myself to Magic
   To see if the Spirit may grant me to know
   Through its force and its voice full many a secret,
115 May spare the sour sweat that I used to pour out
   In talking of what I know nothing about,

---

3. **Men . . . strive.** This speech carries the major idea of
the poem, which is completed in the concluding lines of
the Lord's next speech.
4. **Snake,** Satan, in the guise of a serpent, who tempted
Eve in the Garden of Eden.
5. **Gothic room.** The general setting of the poem is Germany in the late Middle Ages.
6. **college,** students.

May grant me to learn what it is that girds
The world together in its inmost being,
That the seeing its whole germination, the seeing
120 Its workings, may end my traffic in words.

Easter Holiday

In previous scenes, Faust, frustrated in
his search for ultimate knowledge by the
limitations of human reason, resorts to
magic, conjuring up the Earth Spirit who
rejects his pleas for help. In a state of
despair, he contemplates suicide and prepares a goblet of poison, but the tolling of
the church bells and singing of the Easter
choruses celebrating Christ's resurrection
renew his desire to live. His assistant,
Wagner, arrives, and they take a walk
in the countryside. The beauty of spring
and the warmth and simple contentment
of common folk rejuvenate Faust. In the
following speech, he turns from his frus-
tration at human limitations to a celebration of nature, projecting his infinite aspirations through the **metaphor** of winged
flight that would enable him to follow a
deified setting sun.

FAUST. Happy the man who swamped in this sea of
Error
Still hopes to struggle up through the watery wall;
What we don't know is exactly what we need
And what we know fulfills no need at all.
125 But let us not with such sad thoughts
Make this good hour an hour undone!
Look how the cottages on the green
Shine in the glow of the evening sun!
He[7] backs away, gives way, the day is overspent,
130 He hurries off to foster life elsewhere.
Would I could press on his trail, on his trail for
ever—
Alas that I have no wings to raise me into the air!
Then I should see in an everlasting sunset
The quiet world before my feet unfold,
135 All of its peaks on fire, all of its vales becalmed,
And the silver brook dispersed in streams of gold.
Not the wild peaks with all their chasms
Could interrupt my godlike flight;

140 Already the bays of the sea that the sun has warmed
Unfurl upon my marvelling sight.
But in the end the sungod seems to sink away,
Yet the new impulse sets me again in motion,
I hasten on to drink his eternal light,
145 With night behind me and before me day,
Above me heaven and below me ocean.
A beautiful dream—yet the sun leaves me behind.
Alas, it is not so easy for earthly wing
To fly on level terms with the wings of the mind.
150 Yet born with each of us is the instinct
That struggles upwards and away
When over our heads, lost in the blue,
The lark pours out her vibrant lay;
When over rugged pine-clad ranges
155 The eagle hangs on outspread wings
And over lake and over plain
We see the homeward-struggling crane.

The Pact with the Devil

Returning to his study, Faust's feelings of
contentment ebb away, and Mephistopheles attempts to take advantage of his despondency. The scholar initially resists the
devil's ploys, but in this scene, a second
visit by the demon results in a wager
between the two.

(*The same room. Later.*)

FAUST. Who's knocking? Come in! *Now* who wants
to annoy me?
MEPHISTOPHELES (*outside door*). It's I.
FAUST. Come in!
MEPHISTOPHELES (*outside door*). You must say
"Come in" three times.
FAUST. Come in then!
MEPHISTOPHELES (*entering*). Thank you; you over-
joy me.
160 We two, I hope, we shall be good friends;
To chase those megrims[8] of yours away
I am here like a fine young squire today,
In a suit of scarlet trimmed with gold
And a little cape of stiff brocade,

---

7. *He.* The sun is personified as a god.
8. *megrims* (mē′grimz), morbid low spirits.

165 With a cock's feather in my hat
And at my side a long sharp blade,[9]
And the most succinct advice I can give
Is that you dress up just like me,
So that uninhibited and free
170 You may find out what it means to live.

FAUST. The pain of earth's constricted life, I fancy,
Will pierce me still, whatever my attire;
I am too old for mere amusement,
Too young to be without desire.
175 How can the world dispel my doubt?
You must do without, you must do without!
That is the everlasting song
Which rings in every ear, which rings,
And which to us our whole life long
180 Every hour hoarsely sings.
I wake in the morning only to feel appalled,
My eyes with bitter tears could run
To see the day which in its course
Will not fulfil a wish for me, not one;
185 The day which whittles away with obstinate carping
All pleasures—even those of anticipation,
Which makes a thousand grimaces to obstruct
My heart when it is stirring in creation.
And again, when night comes down, in anguish
190 I must stretch out upon my bed
And again no rest is granted me,
For wild dreams fill my mind with dread.
The God who dwells within my bosom
Can make my inmost soul react;
195 The God who sways my every power
Is powerless with external fact.
And so existence weighs upon my breast
And I long for death and life—life I detest.

MEPHISTOPHELES. Yet death is never a wholly welcome guest.

200 FAUST. O happy is he whom death in the dazzle of victory
Crowns with the bloody laurel in the battling swirl!
Or he whom after the mad and breakneck dance
He comes upon in the arms of a girl!
O to have sunk away, delighted, deleted,
205 Before the Spirit of the Earth, before his might!

MEPHISTOPHELES. Yet I know someone who failed to drink
A brown juice[10] on a certain night.

FAUST. Your hobby is espionage—is it not?

MEPHISTOPHELES. Oh I'm not omniscient—but I know a lot.

210 FAUST. Whereas that tumult in my soul
Was stilled by sweet familiar chimes
Which cozened the child that yet was in me
With echoes of more happy times,
I now curse all things that encompass
215 The soul with lures and jugglery
And bind it in this dungeon of grief
With trickery and flattery.
Cursed in advance be the high opinion
That serves our spirit for a cloak!
220 Cursed be the dazzle of appearance
Which bows our senses to its yoke!
Cursed be the lying dreams of glory,
The illusion that our name survives!
Cursed be the flattering things we own,
225 Servants and ploughs, children and wives!
Cursed be Mammon[11] when with his treasures
He makes us play the adventurous man
Or when for our luxurious pleasures
He duly spreads the soft divan!
230 A curse on the balsam of the grape!
A curse on the love that rides for a fall!
A curse on hope! A curse on faith!
And a curse on patience most of all! . . .

MEPHISTOPHELES. Stop playing with your grief which battens[12]
235 Like a vulture on your life, your mind!
The worst of company would make you feel
That you are a man among mankind.
Not that it's really my proposition
To shove you among the common men;
240 Though I'm not one of the Upper Ten,[13]
If you would like a coalition
With me for your career through life,
I am quite ready to fit in,
I'm yours before you can say knife.
245 I am your comrade;

---

9. In a suit . . . blade, theatrical costume of a typical Spanish cavalier.
10. A brown juice, the poison Faust almost drank when in the depths of despair.
11. Mammon, material wealth.
12. battens, grows fat.
13. Upper Ten. Mephistopheles is one of the devils, but he is not in the Upper Ten in the medieval arrangement of the diabolical hierarchy.

Faust and Mephistopheles by Eugène Delacroix. 1826–1827. The Wallace Collection, London

If you so crave,
I am your servant, I am your slave.
FAUST. And what have I to undertake in return?
MEPHISTOPHELES. Oh it's early days[14] to discuss
 what that is.
250 **FAUST.** No, no, the devil is an egoist
 And ready to do nothing gratis
 Which is to benefit a stranger.
 Tell me your terms and don't prevaricate!
255 A servant like you in the house is a danger.
 MEPHISTOPHELES. I will bind myself to your service
 in this world,
 To be at your beck[15] and never rest nor slack;
 When we meet again on the other side,
 In the same coin you shall pay me back.
260 **FAUST.** The other side gives me little trouble;
 First batter this present world to rubble,
 Then the other may rise—if that's the plan.
 This earth is where my springs of joy have started,

And this sun shines on me when broken-hearted;
265 If I can first from them be parted,
 Then let happen what will and can!
 I wish to hear no more about it—
 Whether there too men hate and love
 Or whether in those spheres too, in the future,
270 There is a Below or an Above.
 MEPHISTOPHELES. With such an outlook you can
 risk it.
 Sign on the line! In these next days you will get
 Ravishing samples of my arts;
 I am giving you what never man saw yet.
275 **FAUST.** Poor devil, can *you* give anything ever?
 Was a human spirit in its high endeavor
 Even once understood by one of your breed?

---

14. *early days,* too soon.
15. *beck,* motion of the head or hand meant as a call or command.

Have you got food which fails to feed?
Or red gold which, never at rest,
280 Like mercury runs away through the hand?
A game at which one never wins?
A girl who, even when on my breast,
Pledges herself to my neighbor with her eyes?
The divine and lovely delight of honor
285 Which falls like a falling star and dies?
Show me the fruits which, before they are plucked,
decay
And the trees which day after day renew their green!

MEPHISTOPHELES. Such a commission doesn't
alarm me,
I have such treasures to purvey.
290 But, my good friend, the time draws on when we
Should be glad to feast at our ease on something
good.

FAUST. If ever I stretch myself on a bed of ease,
Then I am finished! Is that understood?
If ever your flatteries can coax me
295 To be pleased with myself, if ever you cast
A spell of pleasure that can hoax me—
Then let *that* day be my last!
That's my wager!

MEPHISTOPHELES. Done!

FAUST. Let's shake!
If ever I say to the passing moment
300 "Linger a while! Thou art so fair!"
Then you may cast me into fetters,
I will gladly perish then and there!
Then you may set the death-bell tolling,
Then from my service you are free,
305 The clock may stop, its hand may fall,
And that be the end of time for me!

MEPHISTOPHELES. Think what you're saying, we
shall not forget it.

FAUST. And you are fully within your rights;
I have made no mad or outrageous claim.
310 If I stay as I am, I am a slave—
Whether yours or another's, it's all the same.

MEPHISTOPHELES. I shall this very day at the College Banquet[16]
Enter your service with no more ado,
But just one point—As a life-and-death insurance
315 I must trouble you for a line or two.

FAUST. So you, you pedant, you too like things in
writing?

Have you never known a man? Or a man's word?
Never?
Is it not enough that my word of mouth
Puts all my days in bond for ever?
320 Does not the world rage on in all its streams
And shall a promise hamper *me*?
Yet this illusion reigns within our hearts
And from it who would be gladly free?
Happy the man who can inwardly keep his word;
325 Whatever the cost, he will not be loath to pay!
But a parchment, duly inscribed and sealed,
Is a bogey[17] from which all wince away.
The word dies on the tip of the pen
And wax and leather lord it then.
330 What do you, evil spirit, require?
Bronze, marble, parchment, paper?
Quill or chisel or pencil of slate?
You may choose whichever you desire.

MEPHISTOPHELES. How can you so exaggerate
335 With such a hectic rhetoric?
Any little snippet is quite good—
And you sign it with one little drop of blood.

FAUST. If that is enough and is some use,
One may as well pander to your fad.

340 **MEPHISTOPHELES.** Blood is a very special juice.

FAUST. Only do not fear that I shall break this con-
tract.
What I promise is nothing more
Than what all my powers are striving for.
345 I have puffed myself up too much, it is only
Your sort that really fits my case.
The great Earth Spirit has despised me
And Nature shuts the door in my face.
The thread of thought is snapped asunder,
350 I have long loathed knowledge in all its fashions.
In the depths of sensuality
Let us now quench our glowing passions!
And at once make ready every wonder
Of unpenetrated sorcery!
355 Let us cast ourselves into the torrent of time,
Into the whirl of eventfulness,
Where disappointment and success,

---

16. *College Banquet*, ceremonial dinner following award-
ing of doctoral degrees.
17. *bogey*, person or thing, usually imaginary, that is
feared without reason.

Pleasure and pain may chop and change
As chop and change they will and can;
360   It is restless action makes the man.
    MEPHISTOPHELES. No limit is fixed for you, no
        bound;
    If you'd like to nibble at everything
    Or to seize upon something flying round—
    Well, may you have a run for your money!
365   But seize your chance and don't be funny!
    FAUST. I've told you, it is no question of happiness.
    The most painful joy, enamored hate, enlivening
    Disgust—I devote myself to all excess.
    My breast, now cured of its appetite for
        knowledge,
370   From now is open to all and every smart,
    And what is allotted to the whole of mankind
    That will I sample in my inmost heart,
    Grasping the highest and lowest with my spirit,
    Piling men's weal and woe upon my neck,
375   To extend myself to embrace all human selves
    And to founder in the end, like them, a wreck.
    MEPHISTOPHELES. O believe *me*, who have been
        chewing
    These iron rations many a thousand year,
    No human being can digest
380   This stuff, from the cradle to the bier.
    This universe—believe a devil—
    Was made for no one but a god!
    He exists in eternal light
    But *us* he has brought into the darkness
385   While *your* sole portion is day and night.
    FAUST. I will all the same!
    MEPHISTOPHELES. That's very nice.
    There's only one thing I find wrong;
    Time is short, art is long.
    You could do with a little artistic advice.
390   Confederate with one of the poets
    And let him flog his imagination
    To heap all virtues on your head,
    A head with such a reputation:
    Lion's bravery,
395   Stag's velocity,
    Fire of Italy,
    Northern tenacity.
    Let *him* find out the secret art
    Of combining craft with a noble heart
400   And of being in love like a young man,

Hotly, but working to a plan.
    Such a person—*I'd* like to meet him;
    "Mr. Microcosm"[18] is how I'd greet him.
    FAUST. What am I then if fate must bar
405   My efforts to reach that crown of humanity
    After which all my senses strive?
    MEPHISTOPHELES. You are in the end . . . what
        you are.
    You can put on full-bottomed wigs with a million
        locks,
    You can put on stilts[19] instead of your socks,
410   You remain for ever what you are.
    FAUST. I feel my endeavors have not been worth
        a pin
    When I raked together the treasures of the human
        mind,
    If at the end I but sit down to find
    No new force welling up within.
415   I have not a hair's breadth more of height,
    I am no nearer the Infinite.
    MEPHISTOPHELES. My very good sir, you look at
        things
    Just in the way that people do;
    We must be cleverer than that
420   Or the joys of life will escape from you.
    Hell! You have surely hands and feet,
    Also a head and you-know-what;
    The pleasures I gather on the wing,
    Are they less mine? Of course they're not!
425   Suppose I can afford six stallions,
    I can add that horse-power to my score
    And dash along and be a proper man
    As if my legs were twenty-four.
    So good-bye to thinking! On your toes!
430   The world's before us. Quick! Here goes!
    I tell you, a chap who's intellectual
    Is like a beast on a blasted heath
    Driven in circles by a demon
    While a fine green meadow lies round beneath.
435 **FAUST.** How do we start?
    MEPHISTOPHELES. We just say go—and skip.

---

18. *Mr. Microcosm,* a person or thing thought of as a
miniature representation of the universe; used here to indicate a person who would unite all of the qualities listed by
Mephistopheles in this speech.
19. *stilts,* high-heeled shoes or boots used by seventeenth-
century actors.

But please get ready for this pleasure trip.
                          (Exit Faust)

Only look down on knowledge and reason,
The highest gifts that men can prize,
Only allow the spirit of lies

440 To confirm you in magic and illusion,
And then I have you body and soul.
Fate has given this man a spirit
Which is always pressing onwards, beyond control,
And whose mad striving overleaps

445 All joys of the earth between pole and pole.
Him shall I drag through the wilds of life
And through the flats of meaninglessness,
I shall make him flounder and gape and stick
And to tease his insatiableness

450 Hang meat and drink in the air before his watering lips;
In vain he will pray to slake his inner thirst,
And even had he not sold himself to the devil
He would be equally accursed.

1808

Comment

The Faust Legend

The motif of a person making a pact with the devil abounds in folklore and literature. In the early sixteenth century in Germany, tales about a man named Faustus who was associated with the black arts of magic circulated among the common folk. Two actual historical figures have been cited as possible sources for the name: Georg Faust, a German magician whose success was attributed to his great mystical powers, and Dr. Johannes Faustus, who received a doctor of divinity degree at Heidelberg University in 1509. The Faustian legend first appeared in print in 1587 in a work of German popular literature called *The History of Dr. Johann Faustus*. Later translated into English, it furnished Christopher Marlowe with the basis for his play, *Doctor Faustus* (page 485).

Goethe encountered the Faust legend as a youth through popular literature and puppet plays. Heinrich Heine, a contemporary of Goethe, describes the *History* mentioned above being hawked at annual fairs: "A grey book, poorly printed on blotting paper and decorated with rough woodcuts . . . in which you may read in great detail how the arch-magician Johannes Faustus, a learned doctor who had studied all sciences, in the end threw away his books and formed an alliance with the devil,

whereby he was able to enjoy all sensual pleasures on earth, but in exchange has to give his soul over to infernal perdition." Marlowe's *Doctor Faustus* follows the folk tradition, ending with devils dragging Faust off to hell, but in Goethe's play Mephistopheles is unable to prevent the ultimate ascension of Faust's soul into heaven. The great German poet transforms the old tale with its pointed moral lesson into a tribute to the aspirations of the human spirit. Faust's striving toward the infinite marks him a Romantic hero.

Since Goethe's time, the Faust **theme** has continued to be popular with artists. Charles Gounod's opera *Faust* (1859) and Thomas Mann's novel *Doktor Faustus* (1947) are famous examples. The Faust legend has frequently been pictured, ranging from drawings and paintings by the French painter Eugène Delacroix (1798?–1863) to illustrations on matchbook covers and breadboxes. The concept of the Faustian drive has even influenced modern language usage. Today the term *Faustian* is used to characterize any insatiable hunger for knowledge or experience; and the price some people pay for success, the sacrifice of their moral or ethical principles, is called a Faustian bargain.

THINK AND DISCUSS
Understanding
1. What is Mephistopheles's view of the earth's inhabitants, particularly Faust?
2. How does Mephistopheles challenge the Lord with his wager? Why does the Lord agree to this proposal?
3. What values does Faust curse in lines 210–233?
4. What are the stipulations of the wager between Faust and the devil?
5. What plans for Faust does Mephistopheles reveal in his final monologue (lines 437–453)?

Analyzing
6. In the Prologue, Mephistopheles uses a **simile** comparing man to a grasshopper. In the sunset speech (lines 121–156), Faust symbolizes his aspirations through a **metaphor** of winged flight. Explain why these figures of speech are appropriate.
7. Why is Faust dissatisfied with his life?

Extending
8. What elements of Romanticism can be found in these scenes from *Faust*? Cite specific evidence.
9. In what ways does Mephistopheles's temptation of Faust parallel Satan's temptation of Eve in John Milton's *Paradise Lost?* (See pages 501–505.)

VOCABULARY
Context, Dictionary
Using context as an aid, write the most appropriate definition for each italicized word on a separate sheet of paper. Use your glossary to check your answer.
1. "I cannot presume to make use of my learning,/I cannot presume I could open my mind/To *proselytize* and improve mankind." (a) investigate; (b) prosecute; (c) convert.
2. "Whereas that tumult in my soul/Was stilled by sweet familiar chimes/Which *cozened* the child that yet was in me/With echoes of more happy times . . ." (a) caressed; (b) beguiled; (c) startled.

3. "Tell me your terms and don't *prevaricate!*/ A servant like you in the house is a danger." (a) procrastinate; (b) complain; (c) lie.
4. "I shall make him flounder and gape and stick/And to tease his insatiableness/Hang meat and drink in the air before his watering lips;/In vain he will pray to *slake* his inner thirst." (a) slow; (b) satisfy; (c) increase.

COMPOSITION
Writing to Describe
Look at the description of Mephistopheles (lines 162–166) in which he wears the costume of a Spanish cavalier to give the feeling of uninhibited freedom. What type of clothes would he be portrayed as wearing today to achieve the same effect? Write a prose description of today's costume and explain your reasons for choosing this type of dress.

Writing to Compare and Contrast
Reread the lines concerning the two separate but related wagers that take place between the Lord and Mephistopheles in the Prologue and between Faust and Mephistopheles in the Pact scene. Make a list of the terms stipulated by each participant. Write a 3–5 paragraph paper comparing and contrasting the two wagers. Include an introduction about the contest for Faust's soul. In your conclusion explain how these pacts relate to **characterization** or theme.

ENRICHMENT
Preparing a Radio Script
The Louis MacNeice translation of *Faust* was originally commissioned by the British Broadcast Corporation for a series of radio programs. As a class project, prepare a radio script of the scenes presented here. Be sure to include an introduction and appropriate sound effects, especially the musical background. Assemble a cast and tape your performance. Share this production with other students.

Heinrich Heine (hī′nə), celebrated as a poet, satirist, and journalist, was a Romantic who used his sharp wit to attack Romanticism in his late work, a German who spent his last thirty years in France. Born to middle-class Jewish parents in an anti-Semitic Germany, he received some Hebrew training, but also attended a Catholic school. Heine moved to Hamburg, where his wealthy uncle Salomon Heine sponsored his unsuccessful entry into the business world. He became infatuated with his uncle's daughter, Amalie. His unrequited love for his cousin was to furnish the ironical tone of his love lyrics. In 1819, again supported by his uncle, he began to study law, exploring history and literature also. He received his law degree in 1825. At this time, he went through the formality of converting to Lutheranism, a step designed to help him in his new profession. He then traveled throughout Germany, England, and Italy, chronicling his experiences in *Pictures of Travel*. In 1827 Heine's *Book of Songs*, a collection of his sentimental and satirical lyrics, was published to great popular acclaim and established him as a Romantic poet. Many of these poems were set to music by well-known composers, including Mendelssohn, Schubert, and Schumann.

His failure to obtain a coveted professorship in Munich and his dislike of Prussia's repressive politics resulted in his emigration to Paris, in his view a haven of political and social freedom. He was also attracted to Saint-Simonianism, a socialist movement centered there that advocated a classless utopian society. Received as a celebrity, he moved in a social circle of famous writers, artists, musicians, and politicians. He continued writing, attempting in many of his works to foster a better relationship between the Germans and French. Nevertheless, in 1835 a Prussian edict banned Heine's works because of his association with a group of liberal writers known as Young Germany. In 1841 he married an uneducated French woman who soon became his nurse, as his health rapidly deteriorated due to a progressive disease of the spine. By 1848, he was paralyzed. He lived in great pain on his "mattress-grave" for eight more years, still composing verse. Although he wished to be buried in Paris, his love for his native country is shown by his suggestion for a simple epitaph: "Here lies a German poet."

Two of the following selections, "My Songs, You Say" and "The Loreley," reflect his cynical attitude toward love. For the passionate Heine, a heartless beauty has destructive powers, much like those of the legendary siren whose song lured sailors to their death in his ballad. The name "Loreley" derives from the word *lurelei*, meaning "elfin rock," a cliff near treacherous reefs in the Rhine River. In addition to love poems, Heine wrote about contemporary subjects in works such as "The Silesian Weavers," which depicts the plight of the weavers who in 1844 revolted against unbelievably harsh labor conditions. Although they realized their rebellion would be doomed to failure, the workers proceeded with it as a sign of protest.

My Songs, You Say

translated by **Louis Untermeyer**

My songs, you say are poisoned.
    How else, love, could it be?
You have, with deadly magic,
    Poured poison into me.

5 My songs, you say, are poisoned.
    And well I know it, too.
I carry a thousand serpents
    And, love, among them—you.

1823   1824

The Loreley

translated by **Aaron Kramer**

I cannot explain the sadness
That's fallen on my breast.
An old, old fable haunts me,
And will not let me rest.

5 The air grows cool in the twilight,
And softly the Rhine flows on;
The peak of a mountain sparkles
Beneath the setting sun.

More lovely than a vision,
10 A girl sits high up there;
Her golden jewelry glistens,
She combs her golden hair.

With a comb of gold she combs it,
And sings an evensong;
15 The wonderful melody reaches
A boat, as it sails along.

The boatman hears, with an anguish
More wild than was ever known;
He's blind to the rocks around him;
20 His eyes are for her alone.

—At last the waves devoured
The boat, and the boatman's cry;
And this she did with her singing,
The golden Loreley.

1823   1824

Detail of *Weaver's March*, an etching by Käthe Kollwitz. 1897. Staatliche Museen, Berlin

The Silesian Weavers

translated by **Aaron Kramer**

In gloomy eyes there wells no tear.
Grinding their teeth, they are sitting here:
"Germany, your shroud's on our loom;
And in it we weave the threefold doom.
5   We weave; we weave.

"Doomed be the God who was deaf to our prayer
In Winter's cold and hunger's despair.
All in vain we hoped and bided;
He only mocked us, hoaxed, derided—
10   We weave; we weave.

"Doomed be the king, the rich man's king,
Who would not be moved by our suffering,
Who tore the last coin out of our hands,
And let us be shot by his blood-thirsty bands—
15   We weave; we weave.

"Doomed be the fatherland, false name,
Where nothing thrives but disgrace and shame,
Where flowers are crushed before they unfold,
Where the worm is quickened by rot and mold—
20   We weave; we weave.

"The loom is creaking, the shuttle flies;
Not night nor day do we close our eyes.
Old Germany, your shroud's on our loom
And in it we weave the threefold doom;
25   We weave; we weave."

1844   *Heine* **619**

Reader's Note

Translating "The Loreley"

"Poetry hardly bears the process of exportation. To be rightly esteemed it needs to be enjoyed in the land of its birth, like certain tropical fruits."

—Heinrich Heine

Like many other poets of the Romantic period in Germany, Heine was inspired by folk literature—the traditional stories and songs of the common people—especially the simplicity of form and language of the ballads. Heine cast "The Loreley" in the traditional four-line stanza of the folk ballad. Here are the first two stanzas of Heine's poem in the original German:

Ich weiss nicht, was soll es bedeuten,
Dass ich so traurig bin,
Ein Märchen aus alten Zeiten,
Das kommt mir nicht aus dem Sinn.

Die Luft ist kühl und es dunkelt,
Und ruhig fliesst der Rhein;
Der Gipfel des Berges funkelt
Im Abendsonnenschein.

Both Aaron Kramer's translation on the previous page and the translations on the opposite page by Louis Untermeyer, Hal Draper, and Alexander Macmillan use the traditional ballad stanza.

The musical quality of Heine's verse is enhanced by its strong **rhythm.** Meter in German is determined by stressed and unstressed syllables, as it is in English. Each line of the original poem contains three stressed syllables, with the number of unstressed syllables varying from line to line. The meter is called trimeter (three feet) because of the three accented syllables. All four translators have also used trimeter.

Translators often lament the "tyranny" of meter and especially **rhyme** because the words that convey the most precise meaning in the second language rarely fit the required meter or rhyme pattern of the original. The marvelous German noun *Abendsonnenschein* in line eight of Heine's original demonstrates the problem. *Abend* means "evening" or "night"; *sonnen,* "sun"; and *schein,* "shine." Since this noun cannot be translated by one English word, the terms replacing it cannot have the same metrical emphasis as the original noun.

Unlike English, the German language contains multiple endings for most words, and therefore feminine (two-syllable) rhymes found in the odd-numbered lines of Heine's original, such as *dunkelt* (line 5) and *funkelt* (line 7), are common in German verse. Due to the relatively small quantity of such rhymes available in English, the translator must decide whether their musical effect is worth the restriction of possible word choices. Three of the featured translators duplicated the feminine rhymes. For the rhymes in lines 5 and 7, for example, Untermeyer substitutes "darkles/sparkles"; Macmillan, "dimmer/shimmer"; and Draper, "darkling/sparkling."

A significant feature of the ballads is the simplicity of the diction, the language used in these poems. Louis Untermeyer notes that Heine, in his effort to achieve the folksong quality in his verses, would "rewrite a quatrain as many as six or seven times, simplifying it with each new version." Heine's "Loreley" is written in the words of everyday speech, as are the translations. Macmillan's Scottish version with its archaic spelling of some words may be difficult for modern readers, but it reflects the simple language of the Scottish folk.

In most literary ballads, patterned after folk ballads, the **tone** is objective with little or no sense of a narrator or author's presence. Heine's interjection of the pronoun "I" in the first and last stanza of "The Loreley" makes the tone more personal, the emotional impact more poignant. All four translators begin their poems with the first person, but only Draper follows the original by returning to the subjective point of view in the last stanza.

Louis Untermeyer (1923)

I do not know why this confronts me,
  This sadness, this echo of pain;
A curious legend still haunts me,
  Still haunts and obsesses my brain:

5 The air is cool and it darkles;
  Softly the Rhine flows by.
The mountain peak still sparkles
  In the fading flush of the sky.

And on one peak, half-dreaming
10   She sits, enthroned and fair;
Like a goddess, dazzling and gleaming,
  She combs her golden hair.

With a golden comb she is combing
  Her hair as she sings a song—
15 A song that, heard through the gloaming,
  Is magically sweet and strong.

The boatman has heard; it has bound him
  In the throes of a strange, wild love.
He is blind to the reefs that surround him;
20   He sees but the vision above.

And lo, the wild waters are springing—
  The boat and the boatman are gone . . .
And this, with her poignant singing,
  The Loreley has done.

Hal Draper (1982)

I do not know what it means that
I am so sadly inclined;
There is an old tale and its scenes that
Will not depart from my mind.

5 The air is cool and darkling,
And peaceful flows the Rhine;
The mountain top is sparkling,
The setting sunbeams shine.

The fairest maid is reclining
10 In wondrous beauty there;
Her golden jewels are shining,
She combs her golden hair.

With a golden comb she is combing,
And sings a song so free,
15 It casts a spell on the gloaming,
A magical melody.

The boatman listens, and o'er him
Wild-aching passions roll;
He sees but the maiden before him,
20 He sees not reef or shoal.

I think, at last the wave swallows
The boat and the boatman's cry;
And this is the fate that follows
The song of the Lorelei.

Alexander Macmillan (19th century)

I canna tell what has come ower° me   *over*
  That I am sae eerie° and wae;°   *so frightened/ woeful*
An auld-warld° tale comes before me,   *old-world*
  It haunts me by nicht° and by day.   *night*

5 From the cool lift° the gloamin' draps°   *sky/twilight drops*
    dimmer,
  And the Rhine slips saftly by;
The taps° of the mountains shimmer   *tops*
  I' the lowe° o' the sunset sky.   *blaze*

Up there, in a glamor entrancin',
10   Sits a maiden wondrous fair;
Her gowden° adornments are glancing,   *golden*
  She is kaimin'° her gowden hair.   *combing*

As she kaims it the gowd kaim glistens,
  The while she is singin' a song
15 That hauds° the rapt soul that listens,   *holds*
  With its melody sweet and strong.

The boy, floating by in vague wonder,
  Is seized with a wild weird love;
He sees na° the black rocks under,—   *not*
20   He sees but the vision above.

The waters their waves are flingin'
  Ower boatie and boatman anon;°   *at once*
And this, with her airtful singin',
  The Waterwitch Lurley hath done.

Heinrich Heine

THINK AND DISCUSS
Understanding
1. What is the relationship between the speaker and the woman he is addressing in "My Songs, You Say"?
2. In "The Silesian Weavers," list the elements of the "threefold doom" the workers are weaving into Germany's shroud. What are their complaints against each of these elements?

Analyzing
3. "The Loreley" is often regarded as one of Heine's most Romantic poems. What elements of Romanticism do you see in this ballad?
4. What does the repetition of the description about the siren's combing her golden hair accomplish in "The Loreley"?
5. Heine has been praised for his bold **metaphors**. In "The Loreley," what does the magical song represent? Why is the serpent an effective **image** in "My Songs, You Say"? How is weaving a shroud an appropriate metaphor in "The Silesian Weavers"?
6. What emotional effect is created by the refrain that ends each stanza of "The Silesian Weavers"?

Extending
7. The **theme** of the beautiful singer who lures boatmen to their destruction is a recurrent one in literature. What examples are you familiar with?
8. Does "The Silesian Weavers," which was written in response to a specific event in 1844, have meaning for today's reader or do we read it for purely historical and lyrical reasons?

THINKING SKILLS
Synthesizing
To synthesize is to put together parts and elements so as to form a whole, a new pattern or structure not evident before.

1. Imagine that "My Songs, You Say" is spoken by the Loreley in response to the poet's depiction of her in "The Loreley." Create a new title for "My Songs, You Say" based on this situation.
2. Imagine that the Loreley poems you have read personify Germany as the destructive water nymph. What then might the poet Heine be saying about his relationship with his native land?

COMPOSITION
Writing a Protest
Write a short poem or prose piece in which you assume the role of an oppressed person or group reacting to a specific event that has occurred during your lifetime, perhaps something that has happened to you. Express the hostile feelings generated by this oppression. Be specific in your complaints, concrete in your imagery, and impassioned in your **tone**.

Writing to Compare and Contrast
Reread the four translations of "The Loreley." Determine which you think is the best translation. Make a list of the reasons you prefer that version. Write a five-paragraph essay in which you explain your choice. Elements to be considered are word choice, imagery, **rhyme, rhythm,** and tone.

ENRICHMENT
Combining Music and Literature
Locate the sheet music for "The Loreley." If possible, have someone play the tune on the piano. As a group, sing the song in English. Ask someone who knows German to recite or sing this ballad in its original language, either as a performance for the class or as a recording on tape to be shared with the class.

BIOGRAPHY

Alexander Pushkin
1799–1837

Recognized as Russia's greatest poet, Alexander Pushkin was also a dramatist, novelist, and short-story writer. He was born in Moscow in 1799. His parents' busy social life as members of the Russian nobility left them little time for their children, particularly the difficult "Sasha," as Alexander was called. He was left in the care of his nurse, Arina Rodinovna, who entertained him with wonderful stories from Russian folklore that he later transformed so well into the narrative poem "Ruslan and Ludmilla," and other outstanding poetry and prose tales. Educated at an elite school, he was upon graduation appointed to government service in Petersburg. His writing and dissolute life provided distractions for him from the official duties that he resented. Pushkin's poetry was well-received, but his general insubordination, his friendship with political rebels, and the liberal writings in which he attacked serfdom and autocratic rule made him politically suspect. The young writer became the target of government surveillance that continued for the rest of his life. He was transferred to remote posts, an unofficial exile, until he was dismissed from the civil service in 1824. Banished to his family's estate near Pskov, Pushkin suffered from his isolation, but continued producing fine poetry.

Favorably impressed by Pushkin's writing, the new czar, Nicholas I, invited him to Moscow in 1826. Even though the Czar admired Pushkin's writing, he forced the author to submit to censorship that Nicholas personally oversaw. In 1831 Pushkin married Natalya Goncharova, a beautiful, but frivolous, young woman. Unappreciative of her husband's literary genius, she insisted on their becoming increasingly involved in the social life of the Imperial Court. In 1837, attentions paid to his wife by a Frenchman serving in the Russian army resulted in a duel. Pushkin, badly wounded, died two days later.

The difficulty of translating the power and clarity of Pushkin's writing has limited his influence on literature outside of Russia, but in his own country his importance is clearly paramount. His novel in verse, *Eugene Onegin*, is considered the most influential work in all Russian literature. His poetry has been set to music in songs and operas by distinguished composers. Tchaikovsky said that Pushkin's lyrics "sang themselves." In *Eugene Onegin*, the poet attributes "the fruits of . . . [his] imaginings" to his "ancient nurse" whose folk stories had fascinated him so. The following selection, "The Bridegroom," echoes these ancient tales. In "The Prophet" (page 627) Pushkin uses biblical language and **allusions** as he defines the role of the poet as a prophet.

The Bridegroom

Alexander Pushkin   *translated by* **D. M. Thomas**

For three days Natasha,
The merchant's daughter,
Was missing. The third night,
She ran in, distraught.
5 Her father and mother
Plied her with questions.
She did not hear them,
She could hardly breathe.

Stricken with foreboding
10 They pleaded, got angry,
But still she was silent;
At last they gave up.
Natasha's cheeks regained
Their rosy color.
15 And cheerfully again
She sat with her sisters.

Once at the shingle-gate
She sat with her friends
—And a swift troika[1]
20 Flashed by before them;
A handsome young man
Stood driving the horses;
Snow and mud went flying,
Splashing the girls.

25 He gazed as he flew past,
And Natasha gazed.
He flew on. Natasha froze.
Headlong she ran home.
"It was he! It was he!"
30 She cried. "I know it!

I recognized him! Papa,
Mama, save me from him!"

Full of grief and fear,
They shake their heads, sighing.
35 Her father says: "My child,
Tell me everything.
If someone has harmed you,
Tell us . . . even a hint."
She weeps again and
40 Her lips remain sealed.

The next morning, the old
Matchmaking woman
Unexpectedly calls and
Sings the girl's praises;
45 Says to the father: "You
Have the goods and I
A buyer for them:
A handsome young man.

"He bows low to no one,
50 He lives like a lord
With no debts nor worries;
He's rich and he's generous,
Says he will give his bride,
On their wedding-day,
55 A fox-fur coat, a pearl,
Gold rings, brocaded dresses.

---

1. *troika,* a Russian carriage or sleigh pulled by three horses harnessed abreast.

"Yesterday, out driving,
He saw your Natasha;
Shall we shake hands
60 And get her to church?"
The woman starts to eat
A pie, and talks in riddles,
While the poor girl
Does not know where to look.

65 "Agreed," says her father;
"Go in happiness
To the altar, Natasha;
It's dull for you here;
A swallow should not spend
70 All its time singing,
It's time for you to build
A nest for your children."

Natasha leaned against
The wall and tried
75 To speak—but found herself
Sobbing; she was shuddering
And laughing. The matchmaker
Poured out a cup of water,
Gave her some to drink,
80 Splashed some in her face.

Her parents are distressed.
Then Natasha recovered,
And calmly she said:
"Your will be done. Call
85 My bridegroom to the feast,
Bake loaves for the whole world,
Brew sweet mead and call
The law to the feast."

"Of course, Natasha, angel!
90 You know we'd give our lives
To make you happy!"
They bake and they brew;
The worthy guests come,
The bride is led to the feast,
95 Her maids sing and weep;
Then horses and a sledge

Girl in a Checkered Shawl, a drawing by Boris Kustodiev.
1919. State Russian Museum, Leningrad

With the groom—and all sit.
The glasses ring and clatter,
The toasting-cup is passed
100 From hand to hand in tumult,
The guests are drunk.

BRIDEGROOM
"Friends, why is my fair bride
Sad, why is she not
Feasting and serving?"

105 The bride answers the groom:
"I will tell you why
As best I can. My soul
Knows no rest, day and night
I weep; an evil dream
110 Oppresses me." Her father

Says: "My dear child, tell us
What your dream is."

"I dreamed," she says, "that I
Went into a forest,
115 It was late and dark;
The moon was faintly
Shining behind a cloud;
I strayed from the path;
Nothing stirred except
120 The tops of the pine-trees.

"And suddenly, as if
I was awake, I saw
A hut. I approach the hut
And knock at the door
125 —Silence. A prayer on my lips
I open the door and enter.
A candle burns. All
Is silver and gold."

BRIDEGROOM
"What is bad about that?
130 It promises wealth."

BRIDE
"Wait, sir, I've not finished.
Silently I gazed
On the silver and gold,
The cloths, the rugs, the silks
135 From Novgorod, and I
Was lost in wonder.

"Then I heard a shout
And a clatter of hoofs . . .
Someone has driven up
140 To the porch. Quickly
I slammed the door and hid
Behind the stove. Now
I hear many voices . . .
Twelve young men come in,

145 "And with them is a girl,
Pure and beautiful.
They've taken no notice
Of the ikons,[2] they sit
To the table without

150 Praying or taking off
Their hats. At the head,
The eldest brother,

At his right, the youngest;
At his left, the girl.
155 Shouts, laughs, drunken clamor . . ."

BRIDEGROOM
"That betokens merriment."

BRIDE
"Wait, sir, I've not finished.
The drunken din goes on
And grows louder still.
160 Only the girl is sad.

"She sits silent, neither
Eating nor drinking;
But sheds tears in plenty;
The eldest brother
165 Takes his knife and, whistling,
Sharpens it; seizing her by
The hair he kills her
And cuts off her right hand."

"Why," says the groom, "this
170 Is nonsense! Believe me,
My love, your dream is not evil."
She looks him in the eyes.
"And from whose hand
Does this ring come?"
175 The bride said. The whole throng
Rose in the silence.

With a clatter the ring
Falls, and rolls along
The floor. The groom blanches,
180 Trembles. Confusion . . .
"Seize him!" the law commands.
He's bound, judged, put to death.
Natasha is famous!
Our song at an end.

1825

---

2. *ikons*, icons—pictures or images of Christ, an angel, or
a saint, usually painted on wood or ivory, and venerated
as sacred in the Eastern Orthodox Church.

The Prophet

Alexander Pushkin
translated by **Babette Deutsch**

Athirst in spirit, through the gloom
Of an unpeopled waste I blundered,
And saw a six-winged Seraph[1] loom
Where the two pathways met and sundered.
5 He set his fingers on my eyes:
His touch lay soft as slumber lies—
And like an eagle's, scared and shaken,
Did my prophetic eyes awaken.
He touched my ears, and lo! they rang
10 With a reverberating clang:
I heard the spheres revolving, chiming,
The angels in their roaring sweep,
The monsters moving in the deep,
The vines low in the valley climbing.
15 And from my mouth the Seraph wrung
Forth by its roots my sinful tongue,
The idle tongue that slyly babbled,
The vain, malicious, the unchaste,
And the wise serpent's sting he placed
20 In my numb mouth with hand blood-
      dabbled;
And with a sword he clove my breast,
Drew forth the heart that shook with dread
And in my gaping bosom pressed
A glowing coal of fire[2] instead.

25 Upon the wastes, a lifeless clod,
I lay, and heard the voice of God:
"Arise, O prophet, look and ponder:
Arise, charged with my will, and spurred!
As over roads and seas you wander,
30 Kindle men's hearts with this, my Word."
1826   1826

---

1. *Seraph*, one of the celestial beings surrounding the throne of God and acting as messengers.
2. *glowing coal of fire*. The reference is to the story of the prophet Isaiah, whose lips were cleansed by God with a burning coal to prepare him for his prophetic mission. (Isaiah 6:1–8)

THINK AND DISCUSS

Understanding
1. In "The Bridegroom," what is the pattern of the dialogue between Natasha and the groom at the wedding feast?
2. In "The Prophet," what are the changes the seraph makes to the speaker's body?

Analyzing
3. In "The Bridegroom," why does the father agree to the wedding plans so quickly?
4. In "The Prophet," how does each change improve the body, making the person more fit for the role of prophet?

Extending
5. Why is Natasha famous at the end of "The Bridegroom"?
6. Many Romantics believed that the poet was a mystically inspired prophet. Why do you think Pushkin used the biblical **allusion** to Isaiah in "The Prophet"?

REVIEWING: Inference H7
See Handbook of Literary Terms, p. 954.

When you reach a conclusion about a character or situation based upon what the author implies through a limited amount of information, you are making an **inference**. The following questions are not answered directly in "The Bridegroom," but by making inferences you can answer them.

1. Why did Natasha refuse to answer her parents' questions about her three-day absence and about her reaction to the handsome young man who drove by in the troika?
2. Why does Natasha become hysterical when the plans are being made?

BIOGRAPHY

Victor Hugo
1802–1885

The titles "Supreme Poet of French Romanticism" and "Prince of Poets" were given by the French to their countryman Victor Hugo. He gained recognition for his poetic gifts at an early age, receiving an award from the prestigious French Academy when he was only fifteen. Hugo published his first volume of poetry in 1822, the same year he married Adele Foucher, his childhood sweetheart. In 1832 Hugo fell in love with a beautiful young actress, Juliette Drouet, who became his mistress, a liaison that lasted fifty years. Many of his lyrics express his intense feelings for her.

In his early career, he wrote intimate **lyric** poetry and plays and was recognized as the leader of the young French Romantics. He announced his doctrine of Romanticism in the famous Preface to his verse play *Cromwell* in 1827. Rejecting the strict rules and emphasis on unity of **tone** in Neoclassical drama, he advocated a new poetry that would reconcile contrasts, mixing "the grotesque with the sublime . . . the bestial with the spiritual." In 1831 he published his famous novel *The Hunchback of Notre Dame* and one of his best collections of poems, *The Autumn Leaves*. This volume and later works, with their richly musical verse and vivid imagery, explore the past.

Public recognition of his genius also brought political rewards. The official poet of France for fifteen years, he was a peer under the monarchy of Louis Philippe and, after Louis's fall, was elected deputy to the national assembly. Hugo initially supported President Louis Napoleon's government, but later helped organize resistance to him when he seized power in 1851 and became emperor as Napoleon III in 1852. Forced to flee France because of his defense of liberty, Hugo spent nineteen years in exile on the British Channel Islands of Jersey and Guernsey, continuing to produce magnificent poetry and fiction, including *Les Misérables* (1862), one of many novels expressing his humanitarian concerns. Upon his return to France when the Republic was restored, he re-entered the political world briefly and then turned his efforts solely to writing. At his death in 1885, two million people lined the streets to honor him as his coffin was placed in the Pantheon in Paris.

The following selection is excerpted from a longer poem "The Expiation," the best known piece in his 1853 collection *The Chastisements*. These lines refer to the daring invasion of Russia by Napoleon Bonaparte and his Grand Army. (Hugo's father, General Joseph Hugo, had once served under Napoleon, whose courage the poet admired.) In 1812 Napoleon and his troops entered Moscow "triumphantly," only to find the city abandoned and in flames. Unable to procure food and shelter and suffering from the bitter cold, the army began a costly retreat westward across the frozen plains. Two-thirds of the Grand Army died in the retreat.

Russia 1812

Victor Hugo
translated by **Robert Lowell**

The snow fell, and its power was multiplied.
For the first time the Eagle[1] bowed its head—
dark days! Slowly the Emperor returned—
behind him Moscow! Its onion domes[2] still
    burned.
5 The snow rained down in blizzards—rained
    and froze.
Past each white waste a further white waste
    rose.
None recognized the captains or the flags.
Yesterday the Grand Army, today its dregs!
No one could tell the vanguard from the
    flanks.
10 The snow! The hurt men struggled from the
    ranks,
hid in the bellies of dead horses, in stacks
of shattered caissons.[3] By the bivouacs,[4]
one saw the picket dying at his post,
still standing in his saddle, white with frost,
15 the stone lips frozen to the bugle's mouth!
Bullets and grapeshot mingled with the snow,
that hailed . . . The Guard, surprised at
    shivering, march
in a dream now; ice rimes[5] the gray mustache.
The snow falls, always snow! The driving mire
20 submerges; men, trapped in that white
    empire,
have no more bread and march on barefoot
    —gaps!
They were no longer living men and troops,
but a dream drifting in a fog, a mystery,
mourners parading under the black sky.
25 The solitude, vast, terrible to the eye,
was like a mute avenger everywhere,
as snowfall, floating through the quiet air,
buried the huge army in a huge shroud.
Could anyone leave this kingdom? A crowd—
30 each man, obsessed with dying, was alone.
Men slept—and died! The beaten mob
    sludged on,

Detail of *Episode in the Retreat from Russia*
by Joseph-Ferdinand Boissard de Boisdenier. 1835
Musée des Beaux-Arts, Rouen

ditching the guns to burn their carriages.
Two foes. The North, the Czar. The North
    was worse.
In hollows where the snow was piling up,
35 one saw whole regiments fallen asleep.
Attila's dawn, Cannaes of Hannibal![6]
The army marching to its funeral!

---

1. *Eagle*, Napoleon's nickname; also the emblem of his armies.
2. *onion domes*, onion-shaped spires of Russian buildings.
3. *caissons*, boxes for ammunition.
4. *bivouacs*, temporary outdoor camps
5. *rimes*, covers with frost
6. *Attila's dawn, Cannaes of Hannibal*, victories leading to eventual defeats. Attila, leader of the Huns in their invasions of Europe, was finally defeated by the Romans and Goths in A.D. 451. Hannibal, a Carthaginian general, crushed the Roman army at Cannae in 216 B.C., but it was his last significant victory in a campaign that resulted in his ultimate defeat.

Litters, wounded, the dead, deserters—swarm,
crushing the bridges down to cross a stream.
40 They went to sleep ten thousand, woke up four.
Ney,[7] bringing up the former army's rear,
hacked his horse loose from three disputing
    Cossacks . . .[8]
All night, the *qui vive?*[9] The alert! Attacks;
retreats! White ghosts would wrench away
    our guns,
45 or we would see dim, terrible squadrons,
circles of steel, whirlpools of savages,
rush sabering through the camp like
    dervishes.
And in this way, whole armies died at night.

The Emperor was there, standing—he saw.
50 This oak already trembling from the axe,
watched his glories drop from him branch by
    branch:
chiefs, soldiers. Each one had his turn and
    chance—
they died! Some lived. These still believed
    his star,
and kept their watch. They loved the man of
    war,
55 this small man with his hands behind his back,
whose shadow, moving to and fro, was black
behind the lighted tent. Still believing, they
accused their destiny of *lèse-majesté.*[10]
His misfortune had mounted on their back.
60 The man of glory shook. Cold stupefied
him, then suddenly he felt terrified.
Being without belief, he turned to God:
"God of armies, is this the end?" he cried.
And then at last the expiation came,
65 as he heard some one call him by his name,
some one half-lost in shadow, who said, "No,
Napoleon." Napoleon understood,
restless, bareheaded, leaden, as he stood
before his butchered legions in the snow.
1852   1853

---

7. *Ney,* (nā), Michel Ney (1769–1815), general commanding the rear guard of the French army.
8. *Cossacks,* Russians skilled in horsemanship.
9. *qui vive?,* "who goes there?," used as a challenge by
the sentry.
10. *lèse-majesté,* high treason; literally "injured majesty."

THINK AND DISCUSS
Understanding
1. Who are the French troops' two enemies?
Which is the worse?
2. How many men does line 40 claim died in
a single night?
3. What does the terrified Napoleon ask in line
63?

Analyzing
4. Hugo is noted for his intense **images.** Pick
out three that you think most vividly portray the plight of the troops.
5. Hugo characteristically uses multiple
metaphors. Explain the three metaphors he
uses for Napoleon.
6. How does the repetition of the word *snow*
work as an organizing device and as a means
of conveying feeling?
7. What other white images reinforce the stark-
ness of the white snow?
8. In line 43 and the first word of line 44, how
do the syntax and punctuation aid in the
emotional impact?

Extending
9. Look up the meaning of the word *expiation* (line 64). Why do you think the answer
Napoleon receives (lines 66–67) is an expiation?
10. Compare "Russia 1812" to Li Po's "Fighting South of the Ramparts" (page 85).
Discuss other war poems that you have read.
Do they glorify war or paint a realistic picture?

ENRICHMENT
Speaking and Listening
Divide the class into two or three groups.
Assign an equal number of lines to each student in a group. Practice reading the poem
aloud, working together on interpretation of
lines, emphasis upon individual words, and
modulation of tone of voice. Share your group's
recitation of the poem with the class.

Nikolai Gogol (ni ko lī′ gō′gol), Russian novelist, dramatist, and short-story writer, has been labeled both a Realist and a Romantic. His work is difficult to categorize. Born in 1809, the son of a landowner, Nikolai attended a provincial school where he faced "ingratitude, injustice, and icy contempt," as he stated in a letter to his mother. Feeling isolated, he turned to writing while a student. Leaving school in 1828, he journeyed to St. Petersburg, hoping to find an exciting life and literary fame. An epic poem that he published himself was ridiculed by the critics, and Gogol destroyed all the copies he could find. He took a government post, but continued writing and was encouraged in his efforts by a new friend, the great Russian poet Alexander Pushkin. His two-volume collection of stories about Ukrainian life, *Evenings on a Farm Near Dikanka*, published in 1831–1832, was well-received.

Finding the civil service boring, Gogol next became a history teacher in a young women's school and then a lecturer in history at the University of St. Petersburg. It soon became clear that he was not qualified for a professorship, and he resigned in less than a year. At that time writing became his primary focus.

His satirical comedy, *The Inspector General*, first performed in 1836, pleased the liberals in the audience but angered the bureaucrats, the target of his **satire**. *The Inspector General* brought Gogol fame, but the play created such controversy that he became ill. Gogol left Russia two months later and spent most of the next twelve years in Western Europe, traveling and writing. In 1842, he published his masterful novel, *Dead Souls*, in a four-volume edition of his works that also included his most famous short story, "The Overcoat."

As his mental and physical health deteriorated, religion became an obsession. In 1848, he made a pilgrimage to Jerusalem. When he returned to Russia, he continued his work on a sequel to his *Dead Souls*. Suffering from severe depression, he burned the unfinished manuscript and other writing shortly before he died in 1852. Gogol's influence upon Russian fiction is considerable. "The Overcoat," with its grimly accurate depiction of lower-class life in Russia, is cited as the beginning of literary Realism there. The famous remark, "We have all come out from under Gogol's 'Overcoat,'" attributed to Dostoevsky, captures the significance of the work to other Russian writers. However, not all readers agree upon categorizing "The Overcoat" as Realism, a label that would seem to ignore the comedy and fantasy present in the story. Perhaps the best way to approach this question of classification is to see "The Overcoat" as a stage in Gogol's movement toward Realism.

The Overcoat

Nikolai Gogol   *translated by* **Andrew R. MacAndrew**

nce, in a department . . . but better not mention which department. There is nothing touchier than departments, regiments, bureaus, in fact, any caste of officials. Things have reached the point where every individual takes an insult to himself as a slur on society as a whole. It seems that not long ago a complaint was lodged by the police inspector of I forget which town, in which he stated clearly that government institutions had been imperiled and his own sacred name taken in vain. In evidence he produced a huge volume, practically a novel, in which, every ten pages, a police inspector appears, and what's more, at times completely drunk. So, to stay out of trouble, let us refer to it just as *a department*.

And so, once, in *a department*, there worked a clerk. This clerk was nothing much to speak of: he was small, somewhat pockmarked, his hair was somewhat reddish and he even looked somewhat blind. Moreover, he was getting thin on top, had wrinkled cheeks and a complexion that might be aptly described as hemorrhoidal. But that's the Petersburg climate for you.

As to his civil-service category (for first a man's standing should be established), he was what is called an eternal pen-pusher, a lowly ninth-class clerk, the usual butt of the jeers and jokes of those writers who have the congenial habit of biting those who cannot bite back.

The clerk's name was Shoenik. There is no doubt that this name derives from shoe but we know nothing of how, why, or when. His father,

his grandfather, and even his brother-in-law wore boots, having new soles put on them not more than three times a year.

His first name was Akaky, like his father's, which made him Akaky Akakievich.[1] This may sound somewhat strange and contrived but it is not contrived at all, and, in view of the circumstances, any other name was unthinkable. If I am not mistaken, Akaky Akakievich was born on the night between the 22nd and the 23rd of March. His late mother, an excellent woman and the wife of a clerk, had made all the arrangements for the child's christening, and, while she was still confined to her bed, the godparents arrived: the worthy Ivan Yeroshkin, head clerk in the Senate, and Arina Whitetumkin, the wife of a police captain, a woman of rare virtue.

The new mother was given her pick of the following three names for her son: Mochius, Sossius, and that of the martyr, Hotzazat. "That won't do," Akaky's late mother thought. "Those names are . . . how shall I put it . . ." To please her, the godparents opened the calendar at another page and again three names came out: Strifilius, Dulius, and Varachasius.

"We're in a mess," the old woman said. "Who ever heard of such names? If it was something like Varadat or Varuch, I wouldn't object . . . but Strifilius and Varachasius . . ."

So they turned to yet another page and out came Pavsicachius and Vachtisius.

"Well, that's that," the mother said. "That set-

---

1. **Akaky Akakievich,** (ä kä kē′ ä kä kē′ye vich).

tles it. He'll just have to be Akaky like his father."

So that's how Akaky Akekievich originated.

And when they christened the child it cried and twisted its features into a sour expression as though it had a foreboding that it would become a ninth-class clerk.

Well, that's how it all happened and it has been reported here just to show that the child couldn't have been called anything but Akaky.

No one remembers who helped him get his appointment to the department or when he started working there. Directors and all sorts of chiefs came and went but he was always to be found at the same place, in the same position, and in the same capacity, that of copying clerk. Until, after a while, people began to believe that he must have been born just as he was, shabby frock coat, bald patch, and all.

In the office, not the slightest respect was shown him. The porters didn't get up when he passed. In fact, they didn't even raise their eyes, as if nothing but an ordinary fly had passed through the reception room. His chiefs were cold and despotic with him. Some head clerks would just thrust a paper under his nose without even saying, "Copy this," or "Here's a nice interesting little job for you," or some such pleasant remark as is current in well-bred offices. And Akaky Akakievich would take the paper without glancing up to see who had put it under his nose or whether the person was entitled to do so. And right away he would set about copying it.

The young clerks laughed at him and played tricks on him to the limit of their clerkish wit. They made up stories about him and told them in front of him. They said that his seventy-year-old landlady beat him and asked him when the wedding would be. They scattered scraps of paper which they said was snow over his head. But with all this going on, Akaky Akakievich never said a word and even acted as though no one were there. It didn't even affect his work and in spite of their loud badgering he made no mistakes in his copying. Only when they tormented him unbearably, when they jogged his elbow and prevented him from getting on with his work, would he say:

"Let me be. Why do you do this to me? . . ."

And his words and the way he said them sounded strange. There was something touching about them. Once a young man who was new to the office started to tease him, following the crowd. Suddenly he stopped as if awakened from a trance and, after that, he couldn't stand the others, whom at first he had deemed decent people. And for a long time to come, during his gayest moments, he would suddenly see in his mind's eye the little, balding clerk and he would hear the words, "Let me be. Why do you do this to me?" and within those words rang the phrase, "I am your brother." And the young man would cover his face with his hands. Later in life, he often shuddered, musing about the wickedness of man toward man and all the cruelty and vulgarity which are concealed under refined manners. And this, he decided, was also true of men who were considered upright and honorable.

It would be hard to find a man who so lived for his job. It would not be enough to say that he worked conscientiously—he worked with love. There, in his copying, he found an interesting, pleasant world for himself and his delight was reflected in his face. He had his favorites among the letters of the alphabet and, when he came to them, he would chuckle, wink and help them along with his lips so that they could almost be read on his face as they were formed by his pen.

Had he been rewarded in proportion with his zeal, he would, perhaps to his own surprise, have been promoted to fifth-class clerk. But all he got out of it was, as his witty colleagues put it, a pin for his buttonhole and hemorrhoids to sit on.

Still, it would be unfair to say that no attention had ever been paid him. One of the successive directors, a kindly man, who thought Akaky Akakievich should be rewarded for his long service, suggested that he be given something more interesting than ordinary copying. So he was asked to prepare an already drawn-up document for referral to another department. Actually, all he had to do was to give it a new heading and change some of the verbs from the first to the third person. But Akaky Akakievich found this work so complicated that he broke into a sweat and finally, mopping his brow, he said:

"Oh no, I would rather have something to copy instead."

After that they left him to his copying forever. And aside from it, it seemed, nothing existed for him.

He never gave a thought to his clothes. His frock coat, which was supposed to be green, had turned a sort of mealy reddish. Its collar was very low and very narrow so that his neck, which was really quite ordinary, looked incredibly long—like the spring necks of the head-shaking plaster kittens which foreign peddlers carry around on their heads on trays. And, somehow, there was always something stuck to Akaky Akakievich's frock coat, a wisp of hay, a little thread. Then too, he had a knack of passing under windows just when refuse happened to be thrown out and as a result was forever carrying around on his hat melon rinds and other such rubbish.

Never did he pay any attention to what was going on around him in the street. In this he was very different from the other members of the pen-pushing brotherhood, who are so keen-eyed and observant that they'll notice an undone strap on the bottom of someone's trousers, an observation that unfailingly molds their features into a sly sneer. But even when Akaky Akakievich's eyes were resting on something, he saw superimposed on it his own well-formed, neat handwriting. Perhaps it was only when, out of nowhere, a horse rested its head on his shoulder and sent a blast of wind down his cheek that he'd realized he was not in the middle of a line but in the middle of a street.

When he got home he would sit straight down to the table and quickly gulp his cabbage soup, followed by beef and onions. He never noticed the taste and ate it with flies and whatever else God happened to send along. When his stomach began to feel bloated, he would get up from the table, take out his inkwell, and copy papers he had brought with him from the office. And if there weren't any papers to copy for the office, he would make a copy for his own pleasure, especially if the document were unusual. Unusual, not for the beauty of its style, but because it was addressed to some new or important personage.

Even during those hours when light has completely disappeared from the gray Petersburg sky and the pen-pushing brotherhood have filled themselves with dinner of one sort or another, each as best he can according to his income and his preference; when everyone has rested from the scraping of pens in the office, from running around on their own and others' errands; when the restless human being has relaxed after the tasks, sometimes unnecessary, he sets himself; and the clerks hasten to give over the remaining hours to pleasure—the more enterprising among them rushes to the theater, another walks in the streets, allotting his time to the inspection of ladies' hats; another spends his evening paying compliments to some prettyish damsel, the queen of a small circle of clerks; another, the most frequent case, goes to visit a brother clerk, who lives somewhere on the third or fourth floor, in two small rooms with a hall of a kitchen and some little pretensions to fashion, a lamp or some other article bought at great sacrifice, such as going without dinner or outside pleasures—in brief, at the time when all clerks have dispersed among the lodgings of their friends to play a little game of whist, sipping tea from glasses and nibbling biscuits, inhaling the smoke from their long pipes, relaying, while the cards are dealt, some bit of gossip that has trickled down from high society, a thing which a Russian cannot do without whatever his circumstances, and even, when there's nothing else to talk about, telling once again the ancient joke about the commandant to whom it was reported that someone had hacked the tail off the horse of the monument to Peter the First—in a word, when everyone else was trying to have a good time, Akaky Akakievich was not even thinking of diverting himself.

No one had ever seen him at a party in the evening. Having written to his heart's content, he would go to bed, smiling in anticipation of the morrow, of what God would send him to copy.

Thus flowed the life of a man who, on a yearly salary of four hundred rubles, was content with his lot. And perhaps it would have flowed on to old age if it hadn't been for the various disasters which are scattered along life's paths, not only for ninth-class clerks, but even for eighth-, seventh-, sixth-class clerks and all the way up to State Councilors, Privy Councilors, and even to those who counsel no one, not even themselves.

In Petersburg, there's a formidable enemy for all those who receive a salary in the neighborhood of four hundred rubles a year. The enemy is none other than our northern cold, although they say it's very healthy.

Between eight and nine in the morning, at just the time when the streets are filled with people walking to their offices, the cold starts to mete out indiscriminately such hard, stinging flicks on noses that the wretched clerks don't know where to put them. And when the cold pinches the brows and brings tears to the eyes of those in high positions, ninth-class clerks are completely defenseless. They can only wrap themselves in their threadbare overcoats and run as fast as they can the five or six blocks to the office. Once arrived, they have to stamp their feet in the vestibule until their abilities and talents, which have been frozen on the way, thaw out once again.

Akaky Akakievich had noticed that for some time the cold had been attacking his back and shoulders quite viciously, try as he might to sprint the prescribed distance. He finally began to wonder whether the fault did not lie with his overcoat. When he gave it a good looking-over in his room, he discovered that in two or three places—the shoulders and back—it had become very much like gauze. The cloth was worn so thin that it let the draft in, and, to make things worse, the lining had disintegrated.

It must be noted that Akaky Akakievich's overcoat had also been a butt of the clerks' jokes. They had even deprived it of its respectable name, referring to it as the old dressing gown. And, as far as that goes, it did have a strange shape. Its collar shrank with every year, since it was used to patch other areas. And the patching, which did not flatter the tailor, made the overcoat baggy and ugly.

Having located the trouble, Akaky Akakievich decided to take the cloak to Petrovich, a tailor who lived somewhere in the fourth floor, up a back stairs, and who, one-eyed and pockmarked as he was, was still quite good at repairing clerks' and other such people's trousers and frock coats, provided he happened to be sober and hadn't other things on his mind.

We shouldn't, of course, waste too many words on the tailor, but since it has become the fashion to give a thorough description of every character figuring in a story, there's nothing to be done but to give you Petrovich.

At first he was called just Grigory and was the serf of some gentleman or other. He began to call himself Petrovich when he received his freedom and took to drinking rather heavily on all holidays, on the big ones at first and then, without distinction, on all church holidays—on any day marked by a little cross on the calendar. In this he was true to the traditions of his forefathers, and, when his wife nagged him about it, he called her impious and a German. Now that we've mentioned his wife, we'd better say a word or two about her, too. But unfortunately very little is known about her, except that Petrovich had a wife who wore a bonnet instead of a kerchief, but was apparently no beauty, since, on meeting her, it occurred to no one but an occasional soldier to peek under that bonnet of hers, twitching his mustache and making gurgling sounds.

Going up the stairs leading to Petrovich's place, which, to be honest about it, were saturated with water and slops and exuded that ammonia smell which burns your eyes and which you'll always find on the back stairs of all Petersburg houses—going up those stairs, Akaky Akakievich was already conjecturing how much Petrovich would ask and making up his mind not to pay more than two rubles.[2]

The door stood open because Petrovich's wife was cooking some fish or other and had made so much smoke in the kitchen that you couldn't even see the cockroaches. Akaky

---

2. *rubles*. A ruble is the monetary unit of Russia, a coin or note equal to 100 kopeks.

Akaky Akakievich at Petrovich's, a drawing by Boris Kustodiev for an unpublished
edition of Gogol's works. 1905. State Russian Museum, Leningrad

Akakievich went through the kitchen without even
seeing Mrs. Petrovich and finally reached the other
room, where he saw Petrovich sitting on a wide,
unpainted wooden table, with his legs crossed
under him like a Turkish pasha.

He was barefoot, as tailors at work usually are,
and the first thing Akaky Akakievich saw was
Petrovich's big toe, with its twisted nail, thick
and hard like a tortoise shell. A skein of silk and
cotton thread hung around Petrovich's neck. On
his knees there was some old garment. For the
past three minutes he had been trying to thread
his needle, very irritated at the darkness of the
room and even with the thread itself, muttering under his breath: "It won't go through, the
pig, it's killing me, the bitch!" Akaky Akakievich
was unhappy to find Petrovich so irritated. He
preferred to negotiate when the tailor was a little under the weather, or, as his wife put it,
"when the one-eyed buzzard had a load on." When
caught in such a state, Petrovich usually gave way
very readily on the price and would even thank
Akaky Akakievich with respectful bows and all
that. True, afterwards, his wife would come whining that her husband had charged too little because
he was drunk; but all you had to do was add ten
kopeks and it was a deal.

This time, however, Perovich seemed to be
sober and therefore curt, intractable, and likely
to charge an outrageous price. Akaky Akakievich
realized this and would have liked to beat a hasty
retreat, but the die was cast. Petrovich had fixed
his one eye on him and Akaky Akakievich involuntarily came out with:

"Hello, Petrovich."

"Wish you good day, sir," said Petrovich and

bent his eye toward Akaky Akakievich's hands to see what kind of spoil he had brought him.

"Well, Petrovich, I've come . . . see . . . the thing is . . . to . . ."

It should be realized that Akaky Akakievich used all sorts of prepositions, adverbs and all those meaningless little parts of speech when he spoke. Moreover, if the matter were very involved, he generally didn't finish his sentences and opened them with the words: "This, really, is absolutely, I mean to say . . ." and then nothing more—he had forgotten that he hadn't said what he wanted to.

"What is it then?" Petrovich asked, looking over Akaky Akakievich's frock coat with his one eye, the collar, the sleeves, the back, the tails, the buttonholes, all of which he was already acquainted with, since, repairs and all, it was his own work. That's just what tailors do as soon as they see you.

"Well, it's like this, Petrovich . . . my cloak, well, the material . . . look, you can see, everywhere else it's very strong, well, it's a bit dusty and it looks rather shabby, but it's not really . . . look, it's just in one place it's a little . . . on the back here, and here too . . . it's a little worn . . . and here on this shoulder too, a little—and that's all. There's not much work . . ."

Petrovich took Akaky Akakievich's old dressing gown, as his colleagues called it, spread it out on the table and looked it over at length. Then he shook his head and, stretching out his hand, took from the window sill a snuffbox embellished with the portrait of a general, though just what general it was impossible to tell since right where his face used to be there was now a dent glued over with a piece of paper. Taking some snuff, Petrovich spread the overcoat out on his hands, held it up against the light and again shook his head. Then he turned the overcoat inside out, with the lining up, and shook his head again. Then, once more, he removed the snuffbox lid with its general under the piece of paper and, stuffing snuff into his nose, closed the box, put it away, and finally said:

"No. It can't be mended. It's no use."

At these words, Akaky Akakievich's heart turned over.

"But why can't it be, Petrovich?" he said in the imploring voice of a child. "Look, the only trouble is that it's worn around the shoulders. I'm sure you have some scraps of cloth . . ."

"As for scraps, I suppose I could find them," Petrovich said, "but I couldn't sew them on. The whole thing is rotten. It'd go to pieces the moment you touched it with a needle."

"Well, if it starts to go, you'll catch it with a patch . . ."

"But there's nothing for patches to hold to. It's too far gone. It's only cloth in name—a puff of wind and it'll disintegrate."

"Still, I'm sure you can make them hold just the same. Otherwise, really, Petrovich, see what I mean . . ."

"No," Petrovich said with finality, "nothing can be done with it. It's just no good. You'd better make yourself some bands out of it to wrap round your legs when it's cold and socks aren't enough to keep you warm. The Germans thought up those things to make money for themselves."—Petrovich liked to take a dig at the Germans whenever there was a chance.—"As to the overcoat, it looks as if you'll have to have a new one made."

At the word "new" Akaky Akakievich's vision became foggy and the whole room began to sway. The only thing he saw clearly was the general with the paper-covered face on the lid of Petrovich's snuffbox.

"What do you mean a *new* one?" he said, talking as if in a dream. "I haven't even got the money . . ."

"A new one," Petrovich repeated with savage calm.

"Well, but if I really had to have a new one, how would it be that . . ."

"That is, what will it cost?"

"Yes."

"Well, it will be over one hundred and fifty rubles," Petrovich said, pursing his lips meaningfully. He liked strong effects, he liked to perplex someone suddenly and then observe the grimace that his words produced.

"A hundred and fifty rubles for an overcoat!" shrieked the poor Akaky Akakievich, shrieked perhaps for the first time in his life, since he was always noted for his quietness.

"Yes, sir," said Petrovich, "but what an overcoat! And if it is to have marten on the collar and a silk-lined hood, that'll bring it up to two hundred."

"Please, Petrovich, please," Akaky Akakievich said beseechingly, not taking in Petrovich's words or noticing his dramatic effects, "mend it somehow, just enough to make it last a little longer."

"No sir, it won't work. It would be a waste of labor and money."

Akaky Akakievich left completely crushed. And when he left, Petrovich, instead of going back to his work, remained for a long time immobile, his lips pursed meaningfully. He was pleased with himself for having upheld his own honor as well as that of the entire tailoring profession.

Akaky Akakievich emerged into the street feeling as if he were in a dream. "So that's it," he repeated to himself. "I never suspected it would turn out this way . . ." and then, after a brief pause, he went on: "So that's it! Here's how it turns out in the end, and I, really, simply couldn't have forseen it." After another, longer pause, he added: "And so here we are! Here's how things stand. I in no way expected . . . but this is impossible . . . what a business!" Muttering thus, instead of going home, he went in the opposite direction, without having the slightest idea of what was going on.

As he was walking, a chimney sweep brushed his dirty side against him and blackened his whole shoulder; a whole bucketful of lime was showered over him from the top of a house under construction. But he noticed nothing and only when he bumped into a watchman who, resting his halberd near him, was shaking some snuff out of a horn into his calloused palm, did he come to a little and that only because the watchman said:

"Ya hafta knock my head off? Ya got the whole sidewalk, ain'tcha?"

This caused him to look about him and turn back toward home. Only then did he start to collect his thoughts and to see his real position clearly. He began to talk to himself, not in bits of phrases now but sensibly, as to a wise friend in whom he could confide.

"Oh no," he said, "that wasn't the moment to speak to Petrovich. Right now he's sort of . . . his wife obviously has given him a beating . . . that sort of thing. It'd be better if I went and saw him Sunday morning. After Saturday night, his one eye will be wandering and he'll be tired and in need of another drink, and his wife won't give him the money. So I'll slip him a quarter and that will make him more reasonable and so, for the overcoat . . ." Thus Akaky Akakievich tried to reassure himself, and persuaded himself to wait for Sunday.

When that day came, he waited at a distance until he saw Petrovich's wife leave the house and then went up. After his Saturday night libations, Petrovich's eye certainly was wandering. He hung his head and looked terribly sleepy. But, despite all that, as soon as he learned what Akaky Akakievich had come about, it was as if the devil had poked him.

"It can't be done," he said. "You must order a new one."

Here Akaky Akakievich pressed the quarter on him.

"Thank you," Petrovich said. "I'll drink a short one to you, sir. And as to the overcoat, you can stop worrying. It's worthless. But I'll make you a first-rate new one. That I'll see to."

Akaky Akakievich tried once more to bring the conversation around to mending, but Petrovich, instead of listening, said:

"I'll make you a new one, sir, and you can count on me to do my best. I may even make the collar fastened with silver-plated clasps for you."

At this point Akaky Akakievich saw that he'd have to have a new overcoat and he became utterly depressed. Where was he going to get the money? There was of course the next holiday bonus. But the sum involved had long ago been allotted to other needs. He had to order new trousers, to pay the cobbler for replacing the tops of his boots. He owed the seamstress for three shirts and simply had to have two items of underwear which one cannot refer to in print. In fact, all the money, to the last kopek, was owed, and even if the director made an unexpectedly generous gesture and allotted him, instead of forty rubles, a whole forty-five or even fifty, the difference would be a drop in the ocean in the overcoat outlay.

It is true Akaky Akakievich knew that, on occasions, Petrovich slapped on heaven knows what exorbitant price, so that even his wife couldn't refrain from exclaiming:

"Have you gone mad, you fool! One day he accepts work for nothing, and the next, something gets into him and makes him ask for more than he's worth himself."

But he also knew that Petrovich would agree to make him a new overcoat for eighty rubles. Even so, where was he to find the eighty? He could perhaps scrape together half that sum. Even a little more. But where would he get the other half? . . . Let us, however, start with the first half and see where it was to come from.

Akaky Akakievich had a rule: whenever he spent one ruble, he slipped a copper into a little box with a slot in its side. Every six months, he counted the coppers and changed them for silver. He'd been doing this for a long time and, after all these years, had accumulated more than forty rubles. So this came to one half. But what about the remaining forty rubles?

Akaky Akakievich thought and thought and decided that he would have to reduce his regular expenses for an entire year at least. It would mean going without his evening tea; not burning candles at night, and, if he absolutely had to have light, going to his landlady's room and working by her candle. It would mean, when walking in the street, stepping as carefully as possible over the cobbles and paving stones, almost tiptoeing, so as not to wear out the soles of his boots too rapidly, and giving out his laundry as seldom as possible, and, so that it shouldn't get too soiled, undressing as soon as he got home and staying in just his thin cotton dressing gown, which, if time hadn't taken pity on it, would itself have collapsed long ago.

It must be admitted that, at first, he suffered somewhat from these restrictions. But then he became accustomed to them somehow and things went smoothly again. He even got used to going hungry in the evenings, but then he was able to feed himself spiritually, carrying within him the eternal idea of his overcoat-to-be. It was as if his existence had become somehow fuller, as if he had married and another human being were there with him, as if he were no longer alone on life's road but walking by the side of a delightful companion. And that companion was none other than the overcoat itself, with its thick padding and strong lining that would last forever. In some way, he became more alive, even stronger-minded, like a man who has determined his ultimate goal in life.

From his face and actions all the marks of vacillation and indecision vanished.

At times, there was even a fire in his eyes and the boldest, wildest notions flashed through his head—perhaps he should really consider having marten put on the collar? The intensity of these thoughts almost distracted his attention from his work. Once he almost made a mistake, which caused him to exclaim—true, very softly— "Oof!" and to cross himself.

At least once each month he looked in on Petrovich to discuss the overcoat—the best place to buy the material, its color, its price . . . Then, on the way home, a little worried but always pleased, he mused about how, finally, all this buying would be over and the coat would be made.

Things went ahead faster than he had expected. Beyond all expectations, the director granted Akaky Akakievich not forty, nor forty-five, but a whole sixty rubles. Could he have had a premonition that Akaky Akakievich needed a new overcoat, or had it just happened by itself? Whatever it was, Akaky Akakievich wound up with an extra twenty rubles. This circumstance speeded matters up. Another two or three months of moderate hunger and he had almost all of the eighty rubles he needed. His heartbeat, generally very quiet, grew faster.

As soon as he could, he set out for the store with Petrovich. They bought excellent material, which is not surprising since they had been planning the move for all of six months, and a month had seldom gone by without Akaky Akakievich dropping into the shop to work out prices. Petrovich himself said that there was no better material to be had.

For the lining they chose calico, but so good and thick that, Petrovich said, it even looked better and glossier than silk. They did not buy marten because it was too expensive. Instead they got cat, the best available—cat which at a distance could always be taken for marten. Petrovich spent two full weeks on the overcoat because of all the quilting he had to do. He charged twelve rubles for his work—it was impossible to take less; it had been sewn with silk, with fine double seams, and Petrovich had gone over each seam again afterwards with his own teeth, squeezing out different patterns with them.

It was—well, it's hard to say exactly which day it was, but it was probably the most solemn day in Akaky Akakievich's life, the day Petrovich finally brought him the overcoat. He brought it in the morning, just before it was time to go to the office. There couldn't have been a better moment for the coat to arrive, because cold spells had been creeping in and threatened to become even more severe. Petrovich appeared with the coat, as befits a good tailor. He had an expression of importance on his face that Akaky Akakievich had never seen before. He looked very much aware of having performed an important act, an act that carries tailors over the chasm which separates those who merely put in linings and do repairs from those who create.

He took the overcoat out of the gigantic handkerchief—just fresh from the wash—in which he had wrapped it to deliver it. The hankerchief he folded neatly and put in his pocket, ready for use. Then he took the coat, looked at it with great pride and, holding it in both hands threw it quite deftly around Akaky Akakievich's shoulders. He pulled and smoothed it down at the back, wrapped it around Akaky Akakievich, leaving it a little open at the front. Akaky Akakievich, a down-to-earth sort of man, wanted to try out the sleeves. Petrovich helped him to pull his arms through and it turned out that with the sleeves too it was good. In a word, it was clear that the coat fitted perfectly.

Petrovich didn't fail to take advantage of the occasion to remark that it was only because he did without a signboard, lived in a small side street, and had known Akaky Akakievich for a long time that he had charged him so little. On Nevsky Avenue, nowadays, he said, they'd have taken seventy-five rubles for the work alone. Akaky Akakievich had no desire to debate the point with Petrovich—he was always rather awed by the big sums which Petrovich liked to mention to impress people. He paid up, thanked Petrovich, and left for the office wearing his new overcoat.

Petrovich followed him and stood for a long time in the street, gazing at the overcoat from a distance. Then he plunged into a curving side street, took a short cut, and reemerged on the street ahead of Akaky Akakievich, so that he could have another look at the coat from another angle.

Meanwhile, Akaky Akakievich walked on, bubbling with good spirits. Every second of every minute he felt the new overcoat on his shoulders and several times he even let out a little chuckle of inward pleasure. Indeed, the overcoat presented him with a double advantage: it was warm and it was good. He didn't notice his trip at all and suddenly found himself before the office building. In the porter's lodge, he slipped off the overcoat, inspected it, and entrusted it to the porter's special care.

No one knows how, but it suddenly became general knowledge in the office that Akaky Akakievich had a new overcoat and that the old dressing gown no longer existed. Elbowing one another, they all rushed to the cloakroom to see the new coat. Then they proceeded to congratulate him. He smiled at first, but then the congratulations became too exuberant, and he felt embarrassed. And when they surrounded him and started trying to persuade him that the very least he could do was to invite them over one evening to drink to the coat, Akaky Akakievich felt completely at a loss, didn't know what to do with himself, what to say or how to talk himself out of it. And a few minutes later, all red in the face, he was trying rather naively to convince them that it wasn't a new overcoat at all, that it wasn't much, that it was an old one.

In the end, a clerk, no lesser person than an assistant to the head clerk, probably wanting to show that he wasn't too proud to mingle with those beneath him, said:

"All right then, I'll do it instead of Akaky Akakievich. I invite you all over for a party. Come over to my place tonight. Incidentally, it happens to be my birthday today."

Naturally the clerks now congratulated the head clerk's assistant and happily accepted his invitation. Akaky Akakievich started to excuse himself, but he was told that it would be rude on his part, a disgrace, so he had to give way in the end. And later he was even rather pleased that he had accepted, since it would give him an opportunity to wear the new coat in the evening too.

Akaky Akakievich felt as if it were a holiday. He arrived home in the happiest frame of mind, took off the overcoat, hung it up very carefully on the wall, gave the material and the lining one more admiring inspection. Then he took out that ragged item known as the old dressing gown and put it next to the new overcoat, looked at it and began to laugh, so great was the difference between the two. And long after that, while eating his dinner, he snorted every time he thought of the dressing gown. He felt very gay during his dinner, and afterwards he did no copying whatsoever. Instead he wallowed in luxury for a while, lying on his bed until dark. Then, without further dallying, he dressed, pulled on his new overcoat and went out.

It is, alas, impossible to say just where the party-giving clerk lived. My memory is beginning to fail me badly and everything in Petersburg, streets and houses, has become so mixed up in my head that it's very difficult to extract anything from it and to present it in an orderly fashion. Be that as it may, it is a fact that the clerk in question lived in a better district of the city, which means not too close to Akaky Akakievich.

To start with, Akaky Akakievich had to pass through a maze of deserted, dimly lit streets, but, toward the clerk's house, the streets became lighter and livelier. More pedestrians began flashing by more often; there were some well-dressed ladies and men with beaver collars. And, instead of the drivers with their wooden, fretworked sledges studded with gilt nails, he came across smart coachmen in crimson velvet caps, in lacquered sledges, with bearskin lap rugs. He even saw some carriages darting past with decorated boxes, their wheels squeaking on the snow.

Akaky Akakievich gazed around him. For several years now he hadn't been out in the evening. He stopped before the small, lighted window of a shop, staring curiously at a picture of a pretty woman kicking off her shoe and thereby showing her whole leg, which was not bad at all; in the background, some man or other with side whiskers and a handsome Spanish goatee was sticking his head through a door leading to another room. Akaky Akakievich shook his head, snorted, smiled and walked on. Why did he snort? Was it because he had come across something that, although completely strange to him, still aroused in him, as it would in anyone, a certain instinct —or did he think, as many clerks do, along the following lines: "Well, really, the French! If they are after something . . . that sort of thing . . . then, really! . . ." Maybe he didn't even think that. After all, one can't just creep into a man's soul and find out everything he's thinking.

At last he reached the house in which the head clerk's assistant lived. And he lived in style, on the second floor, with the staircase lighted by a lantern. In the hall, Akaky Akakievich found several rows of galoshes. Amidst the galoshes, a samovar was hissing and puffing steam. All around the walls hung overcoats and cloaks, some with beaver collars and others with velvet lapels. The noise and talk that could be heard through the partition became suddenly clear and resounding when the door opened and a servant came out with a tray of empty glasses, a cream jug, and a basket of cookies. It was clear that the clerks had arrived long before and had already drunk their first round of tea.

Akaky Akakievich hung his coat up and went in. In a flash, he took in the candles, the clerks, the pipes, the card tables, while his ears were filled with the hubbub of voices rising all around him and the banging of chairs being moved. Awkwardly, he paused in the middle of the room, trying to think what to do. But he had been noticed and his arrival was greeted with a huge yell. Immediately everybody rushed out into the hall to have another look at his new overcoat. Akaky Akakievich felt a bit confused, but, being an uncomplicated man, he was rather pleased when everyone agreed that it was a good overcoat.

Soon, however, they abandoned him and his overcoat and turned their attention, as was to be expected, to the card tables.

The din, the voices, the presence of so many people—all this was unreal to Akaky Akakievich. He had no idea how to behave, where to put his hands, his feet, or, for that matter, his whole body. He sat down near a card table, stared at the cards and peeked in turn into the faces of the players. In a little while he got bored and began to yawn, feeling rather sleepy—it was long past his usual bedtime. He wanted to take leave of the host, but they wouldn't let him go. He really had to toast his new overcoat with champagne, they insisted. They made Akaky Akakievich drink two glasses of champagne, after which he felt that the party was becoming gayer, but nevertheless he was quite unable to forget that it was now midnight and that he should have gone home long ago.

In spite of everything his host could think up to keep him, he went quietly out into the hall, found his overcoat, which to his annoyance was lying on the floor, shook it, carefully removed every speck he could find on it, put it on and walked down the stairs and out into the street.

The street was still lighted. Some little stores, those meeting places for servants and people of every sort, were open, while others, although closed, still showed a long streak of light under their doors, which indicated that the company had not yet dispersed and that the menservants and maids were finishing up their gossip and their conversations, leaving their masters perplexed as to their whereabouts.

Akaky Akakievich walked along in such a gay mood that, who knows why, he almost darted after a lady who flashed by him like a streak of light-ning, every part of her body astir with independent, fascinating motion. Still, he restrained himself immediately, went back to walking slowly and even wondered where that compulsion to gallop had come from.

Soon there stretched out before him those deserted streets which, even in the daytime, are not so gay, and, now that it was night, looked even more desolate. Fewer street lamps were lit—obviously a smaller oil allowance was given out in this district. Then came wooden houses and fences; not a soul around, nothing but glistening snow and the black silhouettes of the low, sleeping hovels with their shuttered windows. He came to the spot where the street cut through a square so immense that the houses opposite were hardly visible beyond its sinister emptiness.

God knows where, far away on the edge of the world, he could see the glow of a brazier by a watchman's hut.

Akaky Akakievich's gay mood definitely waned. He could not suppress a shiver as he stepped out into the square, a foreboding of evil in his heart. He glanced behind him and to either side—it was like being in the middle of the sea. "No, it's better not to look," he thought, and walked on with his eyes shut. And when he opened them again to see if the other side of the square was close, he saw instead, standing there, almost in front of his nose, people with mustaches, although he couldn't make out, exactly who or what. Then his vision became foggy and there was a beating in his chest.

"Why, here's my overcoat," one of the people thundered, grabbing him by the collar.

Akaky Akakievich was just going to shout out "Help!" when another brought a fist about the size of a clerk's head up to his very mouth, and said:

"You just try and yell . . ."

Akaky Akakievich felt them pull off his coat, then he received a knee in the groin. He went down on his back and after that he lay in the snow and felt nothing more.

When he came to a few minues later and scrambled to his feet, there was no one around. He felt cold and, when he realized that the overcoat was gone, desperate. He let out a yell. But his voice

Akaky Akakievich Returns from the Party, a drawing by Boris Kustodiev for an unpublished edition of Gogol's works. 1905. State Russian Museum, Leningrad.

didn't come close to reaching the other side of the square.

Frantic, he hollered all the way across the square as he scrambled straight toward the watchman's hut. The watchman was standing beside it, leaning on his halberd, and gazing out across the square, wondering who it could be running toward him and shouting. At last Akaky Akakievich reached him. Gasping for breath, he began shouting at him—what sort of a watchman did he think he was, hadn't he seen anything, and why the devil had he allowed them to rob a man? The watchman said he had seen no one except the two men who had stopped Akaky Akakievich in the middle of the square, who he had thought were friends of his, and that instead of hollering at the watchman, he'd better go and see the police inspector tomorrow and the inspector would find out who had taken the overcoat.

Akaky Akakievich hurried home; he was in a terrible state. The little hair he had left, on his temples and on the back of his head, was completely disheveled, there was snow all down one side of him and on his chest and all over his trousers. His old landlady, hearing his impatient banging on the door, jumped out of bed and, with only one shoe on, ran to open up, clutching her nightgown at the neck, probably out of modesty. When she saw the state Akaky Akakievich was in, she stepped back.

When he told her what had happened, she threw up her hands and said that he should go straight to the borough Police Commissioner, that the local police inspector could not be trusted, that he'd just make promises and give him the runaround. So it was best, she said, to go straight to the borough Commissioner. In fact, she even knew him because Anna, her former Finnish cook, had now got a job as a nanny at his house. And the landlady herself often saw him driving past their house.

Moreover, she knew he went to church every Sunday and prayed and at the same time looked cheerful and was obviously a good man. Having heard her advice, Akaky Akakievich trudged off sadly to his room and somehow got through the night, though exactly how must be imagined by those who know how to put themselves in another man's place.

Early the next morning, he went to the borough Commissioner's. But it turned out that he was still asleep. He returned at ten and again was told he was asleep. He went back at eleven and was told that the Commissioner was not home. He tried again during the dinner hour but the secretaries in the reception room would not let him in and wanted to know what business had brought him. For once in his life Akaky Akakievich decided to show some character and told them curtly that he must see the Commissioner personally, that they'd better let him in since he was on official government business, that he would lodge a complaint against them and that then they would see.

The secretaries didn't dare say anything to that and one of them went to call the Commissioner. The Commissioner reacted very strangely to Akaky Akakievich's story of the robbery. Instead of concentrating on the main point, he asked Akaky Akakievich what he had been doing out so late, whether he had stopped off somewhere on his way, hadn't he been to a house of ill repute. Akaky Akakievich became very confused and when he left he wasn't sure whether something would be done about his overcoat or not.

That day he did not go to his office for the first time in his life. The next day he appeared, looking very pale and wearing his old dressing gown, which now seemed shabbier than ever. His account of the theft of his overcoat touched many of the clerks, although, even now, there were some who poked fun at him. They decided on the spot to take up a collection for him but they collected next to nothing because the department employees had already had to donate money for a portrait of the Director and to subscribe to some book or other, on the suggestion of the section chief, who

was a friend of the author's. So the sum turned out to be the merest trifle.

Someone, moved by compassion, decided to help Akaky Akakievich by giving him good advice. He told him that he had better not go to his local inspector because, even supposing the inspector wanted to impress his superiors and managed to recover the coat, Akaky Akakievich would still find it difficult to obtain it at the police station unless he could present irrefutable proof of ownership. The best thing was to go through a certain important personage who, by writing and contacting the right people, would set things moving faster. So Akaky Akakievich decided to seek an audience with the important personage.

Even to this day, it is not known exactly what position the important personage held or what his duties consisted of. All we need to know is that this important personage had become important quite recently and that formerly he had been an unimportant person. And even his present position was unimportant compared with other, more inportant ones. But there is always a category of people for whom somebody who is unimportant to others is an important personage. And the personage in question used various devices to play up his importance: for instance, he made the civil servants of lower categories come out to meet him on the stairs before he'd even reached his office; and a subordinate could not approach him directly but had to go through proper channels. That's the way things are in Holy Russia—everyone tries to ape his superior.

They say that one ninth-class clerk, when he was named section chief in a small office, immediately had a partition put up to make a separate room, which he called the conference room. He stationed an usher at the door who had to open it for all those who came in, although the conference room had hardly enough space for a writing table, even without visitors. The audiences and the manner of our important personage were impressive and stately, but quite uncomplicated. The key to his system was severity. He liked to say: "Severity, severity, severity," and as he uttered the word for the third time, he usually looked very meaningfully into the face of the person he was talking to. True, it was not too clear what need there was for all this severity since the ten-odd employees who made up the whole administrative apparatus of his office were quite frightened enough as it was. Seeing him coming, they would leave their work and stand to attention until he had crossed the room. His usual communication with his inferiors was full of severity and consisted almost entirely of three phrases: "How dare you!" "Who do you think you're talking to?" and "Do you appreciate who I am?" Actually, he was a kindly man, a good friend and obliging, but promotion to a high rank had gone to his head, knocked him completely off balance, and he just didn't know how to act. When he happened to be with equals, he was still a decent fellow, and, in a way, by no means stupid. But whenever he found himself among those who were below him—even a single rank—he became impossible. He fell silent and was quite pitiable, because even he himself realized that he could have been having a much better time. Sometimes he was obviously longing to join some group in a lively conversation, but he would be stopped by the thought that he would be going too far, putting himself on familiar terms and thereby losing face. And so he remained eternally in silent, aloof isolation, only occasionally uttering some monosyllabic sounds, and, as a result, he acquired a reputation as a deadly bore.

It was to this important personage that Akaky Akakievich presented himself, and at a most unpropitious moment to boot. That is, very unpropitious for him, although quite suitable for the important personage. The latter was in his office talking gaily to a childhood friend who had recently come to Petersburg and whom he hadn't seen for many years. This was the moment when they announced that there was a man named Shoenik to see him.

"Who's he?" the personage wanted to know.

"Some clerk," they told him.

"I see. Let him wait. I am not available now."

Here it should be noted that the important personage was greatly exaggerating. He was available.

He and his friend had talked over everything imaginable. For some time now the conversation had been interlaced with lengthy silences, and they weren't doing much more than slapping each other on the thigh and saying:

"So that's how it is, Ivan Abramovich."

"Yes, indeed, Stepan Varlamovich!"

Still Akaky Akakievich had to wait, so that his friend, who had left the government service long ago and now lived in the country, could see what a long time employees had to wait in his reception room.

At last, when they had talked and had sat silent facing each other for as long as they could stand it, when they had smoked a cigar reclining in comfortable armchairs with sloping backs, the important personage, as if he had just recalled it, said to his secretary who was standing at the door with papers for a report:

"Wait a minute. Wasn't there a clerk waiting? Tell him to come in."

Seeing Akaky Akakievich's humble appearance and his wretched old frock coat, he turned abruptly to face him and said: "What do you want?"

He spoke in the hard, sharp voice which he had deliberately developed by practicing at home before a mirror an entire week before he had taken over his present exalted position.

Akaky Akakievich, who had felt properly subdued even before this, felt decidedly embarrased. He did his best, as far as he could control his tongue, to explain what had happened. Of course, he added even more than his usual share of phrases like "that is to say" and "so to speak." The overcoat, he explained, was completely new and had been cruelly taken away from him and he had turned to the important personage, that is to say, come to him, in the hope that he would, so to speak, intercede for him somehow, that is to say, write to the Superintendent of Police or, so to speak, to someone, and find the overcoat.

For some unimaginable reason the important personage found his manner too familiar.

"My dear sir," he answered sharply, "don't you

know the proper channels? Do you realize whom you're addressing and what the proper procedure should be? You should first have handed in a petition to the office. It would have gone to the head clerk. From him it would have reached the section head, who would have approached my secretary and only then would the secretary have presented it to me. . . ."

"But, Your Excellency," said Akaky Akakievich, trying to gather what little composure he had and feeling at the same time that he was sweating terribly, "I, Your Excellency, ventured to trouble you because secretaries, that is to say . . . are, so to speak, an unreliable lot. . . ."

"What, what, what?" demanded the important personage. "Where did you pick up such an attitude? Where did you get such ideas? What is this insubordination that is spreading among young people against their chiefs and superiors?"

The important personage, apparently, had not noticed that Akaky Akakievich was well over fifty. Thus, surely, if he could be called young at all it would only be relatively, that is, to someone of seventy.

"Do you realize to whom you are talking? Do you appreciate who I am? Do you really realize, do you, I'm asking you?"

Here he stamped his foot and raised his voice to such a pitch that there was no need to be an Akaky Akakievich to be frightened.

And Akaky Akakievich froze completely. He staggered, his whole body shook, and he was quite unable to keep his feet. If a messenger hadn't rushed over and supported him, he would have collapsed onto the floor. They carried him out almost unconscious.

And the important personage, pleased to see that his dramatic effect had exceeded his expectations, and completely delighted with the idea that a word from him could knock a man unconscious, glanced at his friend to see what he thought of it all and was pleased to see that the friend looked somewhat at a loss and that fear had extended to him too.

Akaky Akakievich remembered nothing about getting downstairs and out into the street. He could feel neither hand nor foot. In all his life he had never been so severely reprimanded by a high official, and not a direct chief of his at that. He walked open-mouthed through a blizzard, again and again stumbling off the sidewalk. The wind, according to Petersburg custom, blew at him from all four sides at once, out of every side street. In no time it had blown him a sore throat and he got himself home at last quite unable to say a word. His throat was swollen and he went straight to bed. That's how severe the effects of an adequate reprimand can be.

The next day he was found to have a high fever. Thanks to the generous assistance of the Petersburg climate, the illness progressed beyond all expectations. A doctor came, felt his pulse, found there was nothing he could do and prescribed a poultice. That was done so that the patient would not be deprived of the beneficial aid of medicine. The doctor added, however, that, by the way, the patient had another day and a half to go, after which he would be what is called kaput. Then, turning to the landlady, the doctor said:

"And you, my good woman, I'd not waste my time if I were you. I'd order him the coffin right away. A pine one. The oak ones, I imagine, would be too expensive for him."

Whether Akaky Akakievich heard what for him were fateful words, and, if he heard, whether they had a shattering effect on him and whether he was sorry to lose his wretched life, are matters of conjecture. He was feverish and delirious the whole time. Apparitions, each stranger than the last, kept crowding before him. He saw Petrovich and ordered an overcoat containing some sort of concealed traps to catch the thieves who were hiding under his bed, so that every minute he kept calling his landlady to come and pull out the one who had even slipped under his blanket. Next, he would ask why his old dressing gown was hanging there in front of him when he had a new overcoat. Then he would find himself standing before the important personage, listening to the reprimand and repeating over and over: "I am sorry, Your Excellency, I am sorry."

Then he began to swear, using the most frightful words, which caused his old landlady to cross herself in horror; never in her life had she heard anything like it from him, and what made it even worse was that they came pouring out on the heels of the phrase, "Your Excellency." After that he talked complete nonsense and it was impossible to make out anything he was saying, except that his disconnected words kept groping for that lost overcoat of his. Then, at last, poor Akaky Akakievich gave up the ghost.

They did not bother to seal his room or his belongings because there were no heirs and, moreover, very little to inherit—namely, a bundle of goose quills, a quire of white government paper, three pairs of socks, a few buttons that had come off his trousers, and the old dressing-gown coat already mentioned. God knows whom they went to; even the reporter of this story did not care enough to find out.

They took Akaky Akakievich away and buried him. And Petersburg went on without him exactly as if he had never existed. A creature had vanished, disappeared. He had had no one to protect him. No one had ever paid him the slightest attention. Not even that which a naturalist pays to a common fly which he mounts on a pin and looks at through his microscope. True, this creature, who had meekly borne the office jokes and gone quietly to his grave, had had, toward the end of his life, a cherished visitor—the overcoat, which for a brief moment had brightened his wretched existence. Then a crushing blow had finished everything, a blow such as befalls the powerful of the earth. . . .

A few days after his death, a messenger from his office was sent to his lodgings with an order summoning him to report immediately; the chief was asking for him. But the messenger had to return alone and to report that Akaky Akakievich could not come.

"Why not?" he was asked.

"Because," the messenger said, "he died. They buried him four days ago."

That is how the department found out about Akaky Akakievich's death, and the next day a new clerk sat in his place: he was much taller and his handwriting was not as straight. In fact, his letters slanted considerably.

But who would have imagined that that was not the end of Akaky Akakievich, that he was fated to live on and make his presence felt for a few days after his death as if in compensation for having spent his life unnoticed by anyone? But that's the way it happened and our little story gains an unexpectedly fantastic ending. Rumors suddenly started to fly around Petersburg that a ghost was haunting the streets at night in the vicinity of the Kalinkin Bridge. The ghost, which looked like a little clerk, was purportedly searching for a stolen overcoat and used this pretext to pull the coats off the shoulders of everyone he met without regard for rank or title. And it made no difference what kind of coat it was—cat, beaver, fox, bearskin, in fact any of the furs and skins people have thought up to cover their own skins with.

One of the department employees saw the ghost with his own eyes and instantly recognized Akaky Akakievich. However, he was so terrified that he dashed off as fast as his legs would carry him and so didn't get a good look; he only saw from a distance that the ghost was shaking his finger at him. Complaints kept pouring in, and not only from petty employees, which would have been understandable. One and all, even Privy Councilors, were catching chills in their backs and shoulders from having their overcoats peeled off. The police were ordered to catch the ghost at any cost, dead or alive, and to punish him with due severity as a warning to others. And what's more, they nearly succeeded.

To be precise, a watchman caught the ghost redhanded, grabbed it by the collar, in Kiryushkin Alley, as it was trying to pull the coat off a retired musician who, in his day, used to tootle on the flute. Grabbing it, he called for help from two colleagues of his and asked them to hold on to it for just a minute. He had, he said, to get his snuffbox out of his boot so that he could bring some feeling back to his nose, which had been frostbitten six times in his life. But it was evidently snuff that even a ghost couldn't stand. The man, closing his right nostril with his finger, had hardly sniffed up half a fistful into the left when the ghost sneezed so violently that the three watchmen were blinded by the resulting shower. They all raised their fists to wipe their eyes and, when they could see again, the ghost had vanished. They even wondered whether they had really held him at all. After that, watchmen were so afraid of the ghost that they felt reluctant to interfere with live robbers and contented themselves with shouting from a distance: "Hey you! On your way!"

And the clerk's ghost began to haunt the streets well beyond the Kalinkin Bridge, spreading terror among the meek.

However, we have completely neglected the important personage, who really, in a sense, was the cause of the fantastic direction that this story—which, by the way, is completely true—has taken. First of all, it is only fair to say that, shortly after poor Akaky Akakievich, reduced to a pulp, had left his office, the important personage felt a twinge of regret. Compassion was not foreign to him—many good impulses stirred his heart, although his position usually prevented them from coming to the surface. As soon as his visiting friend had left the office, his thoughts returned to Akaky Akakievich. And after that, almost every day, he saw in his mind's eye the bloodless face of the little clerk who had been unable to take a proper reprimand. This thought was so disturbing that a week later he went so far as to send a clerk from his office to see how Akaky Akakievich was doing and to find out whether, in fact, there was any way to help him. And when he heard the news that Akaky Akakievich had died suddenly of a fever, it was almost a blow to him, even made him feel guilty and spoiled his mood for the whole day.

Trying to rid himself of these thoughts, to forget the whole unpleasant business, he went to a party at a friend's house. There he found himself in respectable company and, what's more, among people nearly all of whom were of the same standing so that there was absolutely nothing to oppress him. A great change came over him. He let himself go, chatted pleasantly, was amiable, in a word, spent a very pleasant evening. At supper, he drank a couple of glasses of champagne, a well-recommended prescription for inducing good spirits. The champagne gave him an inclination for something special and so he decided not to go home but instead to pay a little visit to a certain well-known lady named Karolina Ivanovna, a lady, it seems, of German extraction, toward whom he felt very friendly. It should be said that the important personage was no longer a young man, that he was a good husband, the respected father of a family. His two sons, one of whom already had a civil-service post, and his sweet-faced sixteen-year-old daughter, who had a slightly hooked but nevertheless pretty little nose, greeted him every day with a "Bon jour, Papa." His wife, a youngish woman and not unattractive at that, gave him her hand to kiss and then kissed his. But although the important personage was quite content with these displays of family affection, he considered it the proper thing to do to have, for friendship's sake, a lady friend in another part of the city. This lady friend was not a bit prettier or younger than his wife, but the world is full of such puzzling things and it is not our business to judge them.

So the important personage came down the steps, stepped into his sledge, and said to the coachman:

"To Karolina Ivanovna's."

Wrapping his warm luxurious fur coat around him, he sat back in his seat. He was in that state so cherished by Russians, in which, without your having to make any effort, thoughts, each one pleasanter than the last, slip into your head by themselves.

Perfectly content, he went over all the most pleasant moments at the party, over the clever retorts that had caused that select gathering to laugh. He even repeated many of them under his breath and, still finding them funny, laughed heartily at them all over again, which was natural enough. However, he kept being bothered by gusts of wind which would suddenly blow, God knows from where or for what reasons, cutting his face, throwing lumps of snow into it, filling the cape of his coat like a sail and throwing it over his head, so that he had to extricate himself from it again and again.

Suddenly the important personage felt someone grab him violently from behind. He turned around and saw a small man in a worn-out frock coat. Terrified, he recognized Akaky Akakievich, his face as white as the snow and looking altogether very ghostly indeed. Fear took over completely when the important personage saw the ghost's mouth twist and, sending a whiff of the grave into his face, utter the following words:

"I've caught you at last. I've got you by the collar now! It's the coat I need. You did nothing about mine and hollered at me to boot. Now I'll take yours!"

The poor important personage almost died. He may have displayed force of character in the office and, in general, toward his inferiors, so that after one glance at his strong face and manly figure, people would say: "Quite a man," but now, like many other mighty-looking people, he was so frightened that he began to think, and not without reason, that he was about to have an attack of something or other. He was even very helpful in peeling off his coat, after which he shouted to the coachman in a ferocious tone:

"Home! As fast as you can!"

The coachman, hearing the ferocious tone which the important personage used in critical moments and which was sometimes accompanied with something even more drastic, instinctively ducked his head and cracked his whip, so that they tore away like a streak. In a little over six minutes the important personage was in front of his house. Instead of being at Karolina Ivanovna's, he was somehow staggering to his room, pale, terrified, and coatless. There he spent such a restless night

that the next morning, at breakfast, his daughter said:

"You look terribly pale this morning, Papa."

But Papa was silent, and he didn't say a word to anyone about what had happened to him, or where he had been or where he had intended to go. This incident made a deep impression upon him. From then on his subordinates heard far less often: "How dare you!" and "Do you know whom you're talking to?" And even when he did use these expressions it was after listening to what others had to say.

But even more remarkable—after that night, Akaky Akakievich's ghost was never seen again. The important personage's overcoat must have fitted him snugly. At any rate, one no longer heard of coats being torn from people's shoulders. However, many busybodies wouldn't let the matter rest there and maintained that the ghost was still haunting certain distant parts of the city. And, sure enough, a watchman in the Kolomna district caught a glimpse of the ghost behind a house. But he was rather a frail watchman. (Once an ordinary, but mature, piglet, rushing out of a private house, knocked him off his feet to the huge delight of a bunch of cabbies, whom he fined two kopeks each for their lack of respect—then he spent the proceeds on tobacco.) So, being rather frail, the watchman didn't dare to arrest the ghost. Instead he followed it in the darkness until at last it stopped suddenly, turned to face him, and asked:

"You looking for trouble?"

And it shook a huge fist at him, much larger than any you'll find among the living.

"No," the watchman said, turning away.

This ghost, however, was a much taller one and wore an enormous mustache. It walked off, it seems, in the direction of the Obukhov Bridge and soon dissolved into the gloom of night.

1839–1841   1842

THINK AND DISCUSS
Understanding
1. "The Overcoat" is said to have made prominent the "little man" in fiction: the humble person living in an inhumane society, pushed around by powerful people. What are some of the ways Gogol indicates Akaky Akakievich's status as a "little man"?

Analyzing
2. Gogol often **satirized** government bureaucracy. What does the author imply about the state of government efficiency in this work? Explain your answer.
3. The new overcoat assumes a great importance to Akaky. Trace the developing significance of the coat in his mind and discuss what it eventually comes to **symbolize** for him.
4. Reread the last paragraphs describing the theft of the important personage's coat (page 649); then go back and reread the paragraphs dealing with the theft of Akaky's overcoat (page 642). What similarities do you find? Why is the important personage better able to handle the loss than Akaky?
5. What prevents this story from being tragic?

Extending
6. What reasons might Gogol have had for introducing the element of fantasy after Akaky's death? Would the story have been more or less appealing to you without it?
7. Do you see any parallels between the actions of Akaky's ghost and Prospero's use of magic in Shakespeare's *The Tempest* (page 415)?

APPLYING: Point of View   H𝖅
See Handbook of Literary Terms, p. 963.

The vantage point from which an author presents the actions and characters in a story is called **point of view.** The story may be related by a character (*first-person* point of view) or by a narrator who does not participate in the action (*third-person* point of view). Further, the third-person narrator may be *omniscient* (able to see into the minds of all characters) or *limited* (confined to a single character's perceptions). Sometimes a third-person narrator may take on a *persona*, the characteristics of a character in the story.

1. What is the point of view in "The Overcoat"?
2. The narrator here has a persona with distinctive qualities that make him seem almost like a character. In what way does the narrator himself resemble his main character, Akaky?
3. In the first paragraph, how does the narrator create the illusion that the story is true?

COMPOSITION   ⟨━○
Writing About Point of View
Write an essay describing the probable effect upon the story if Akaky had been the narrator. Use the answers to the point-of-view questions to help you in your prewriting. In your conclusion, point out the way the mood of the story, the overall atmosphere or prevailing emotional aura of the work, would be altered by this change of narrators. See "Writing About Point of View" in the Writer's Handbook.

Writing About Personal Experience
Write a paragraph about the way the desire for a material possession can become overwhelming. Describe the feelings evoked by the contemplation of buying the product and the emotional response to owning it. Use concrete details from your own experiences or those of others.

ENRICHMENT
Examining Advertising
Look through newspapers and magazines for advertisements for products that imply or promise benefits not related directly to the product, such as becoming popular by driving a certain car. Share these with the class and discuss the effects of these claims upon the prospective buyer.

The poetry of Walt Whitman, considered today one of America's most important poets, drew mixed reactions from his contemporaries. A leading critic of the time called Whitman's verse a "gathering of muck." But the philosopher and essayist Ralph Waldo Emerson congratulated Whitman on the first edition of *Leaves of Grass* in 1855. He wrote, "I find it the most extraordinary piece of wit and wisdom that America has yet contributed." Whitman's significant influence upon modern poetry validates Emerson's view.

Walt Whitman was born on Long Island, New York, one of nine children. The Whitmans moved to Brooklyn in 1823. Because of the family's economic problems, he attended school only until the age of ten, but compensated for his inadequate formal education by voracious reading. A series of jobs followed—office boy, printer's helper, country school teacher, editor, and writer for various papers and magazines. His first literary efforts resulted in conventional poetry and didactic fiction. In 1848, during a trip to New Orleans, the country's grandeur and diversity impressed the author greatly. Upon his return to Brooklyn, he again held a series of jobs while undergoing his extraordinary metamorphosis into a revolutionary poet. In 1855, he published a slim volume of his collected poems, *Leaves of Grass*. In the preface, he announced the role of the poet as a seer and his view of a dynamic America as "the greatest poem." In eight subsequent editions he greatly revised and expanded this body of poetry.

Although too old to enlist, Whitman, an admirer of Lincoln, was greatly affected by the Civil War, as many of his poems attest. After visiting his wounded brother in Virginia, he spent several years in Washington, holding various government jobs and visiting and helping hospitalized soldiers.

In 1873, Whitman suffered a stroke which partially paralyzed him. However, he recovered sufficiently to do some traveling in the United States and Canada. In 1886, he purchased a home in Camden, New Jersey, where many well-known writers visited him. The early image of the bearded, robust, hot-tempered "poet of the people" changed to that of the "good gray poet," physically incapacitated but still brilliant. This prophet of American democracy, honored in his old age, continued to be revered after his death in 1892.

The unconventional diction, sharply focused images, and surging rhythm of his innovative free verse, his poetic signature, are seen in the following poems. The excerpts from "Song of Myself" were untitled and unnumbered in the original text, but have since been numbered for reference purposes.

Walt Whitman

 See FREE VERSE in the Handbook of Literary Terms, page 951.

from Song of Myself

6

A child said *What is the grass?* fetching it to me with full hands,
How could I answer the child? I do not know what it is any more than he.

I guess it must be the flag of my disposition, out of hopeful green stuff woven.

Or I guess it is the handkerchief of the Lord,
5 A scented gift and remembrancer designedly dropped,
Bearing the owner's name someway in the corners, that we may see and remark, and say *Whose?*

Or I guess the grass is itself a child, the produced babe of the vegetation.

Or I guess it is a uniform hieroglyphic,
And it means, Sprouting alike in broad zones and narrow zones,
10 Growing among black folks as among white.
Canuck, Tuckahoe, Congressman, Cuff,[1] I give them the same, I receive them the same.

And now it seems to me the beautiful uncut hair of graves.

Tenderly will I use you curling grass,
It may be you transpire from the breasts of young men,
15 It may be if I had known them I would have loved them,
It may be you are from old people, or from offspring taken soon out of their mothers' laps,
And here you are the mothers' laps.

This grass is very dark to be from the white heads of old mothers,
Darker than the colorless beards of old men,
20 Dark to come from under the faint red roofs of mouths.

O I perceive after all so many uttering tongues,
And I perceive they do not come from the roofs of mouths for nothing.

I wish I could translate the hints about the dead young men and women,
And the hints about old men and mothers, and the offspring taken soon out of their laps.

25 What do you think has become of the young and old men?
And what do you think has become of the women and children?

---

1. *Canuck . . . Cuff.* Canuck (ke nuk') is slang for a Canadian. Tuckahoe (tuk'ə hō)
is a nickname for an inhabitant of eastern Virginia. Cuff, from the African word *cuffee*
meaning "a black person," is slang for a black American.

The Lackawanna Valley by George Inness. 1855. National Gallery of Art, Washington

They are alive and well somewhere,
The smallest sprout shows there is really no death,
And if ever there was it led forward life, and does not wait at the end to arrest it,
30 And ceased the moment life appeared.

All goes onward and outward, nothing collapses,
And to die is different from what anyone supposed, and luckier.

17
These are really the thoughts of all men in all ages and lands, they are not original with me,
35 If they are not yours as much as mine they are nothing, or next to nothing,
If they are not the riddle and the untying of the riddle they are nothing,
If they are not just as close as they are distant they are nothing.
This is the grass that grows wherever the land is and the water is,
This is the common air that bathes the globe.

21
40 I am the poet of the Body and I am the poet of the Soul,
The pleasures of heaven are with me and the pains of hell are with me,
The first I graft and increase upon myself, the latter I translate into a new tongue.

I am the poet of the woman the same as the man,
And I say it is as great to be a woman as to be a man,
45 And I say there is nothing greater than the mother of men.

I chant the chant of dilation or pride,
We have had ducking and deprecating about enough,
I show that size is only development.

Have you outstript the rest? are you the President?
50 It is a trifle, they will more than arrive there every one, and still pass on.

I am he that walks with the tender and growing night,
I call to the earth and sea half-held by the night.

Press close bare-bosom'd night—press close magnetic nourishing night!
Night of south winds—night of the large few stars!
55 Still nodding night—mad naked summer night.

Smile O voluptuous cool-breath'd earth!
Earth of the slumbering and liquid trees!
Earth of departed sunset—earth of the mountains misty-topt!
Earth of the vitreous pour of the full moon just tinged with blue!
60 Earth of shine and dark mottling the tide of the river!
Earth of the limpid gray of clouds brighter and clearer for my sake!
Far-swooping elbow'd earth—rich apple-blossom'd earth!
Smile, for your lover comes.

Prodigal, you have given me love—therefore I to you give love!
65 O unspeakable passionate love.

1855

There Was a Child Went Forth

There was a child went forth every day,
And the first object he look'd upon, that object he became, B And that object became part of him for the day or a certain part of the day,
Or for many years or stretching cycles of years.

5 The early lilacs became part of this child,
And grass and white and red morning-glories, and white and red clover, and the song of the phoebe-bird,

And the Third-month[1] lambs and the sow's pink-faint litter, and the mare's foal and the cow's
    calf,
And the noisy brood of the barnyard or by the mire of the pond-side,

And the fish suspending themselves so curiously below there, and the beautiful curious liquid,
10 And the water-plants with their graceful flat heads, all became part of him.

The field-sprouts of Fourth-month and Fifth-month became part of him,
Winter-grain sprouts and those of the light-yellow corn, and the esculent roots of the garden,
And the apple-trees cover'd with blossoms and the fruit afterward, and woodberries, and the commonest
    weeds by the road,
And the old drunkard staggering home from the outhouse of the tavern whence he had lately
    risen,
15 And the schoolmistress that pass'd on her way to the school,
And the friendly boys that pass'd, and the quarrelsome boys,
And the tidy and fresh-cheek'd girls, and the barefoot Negro boy and girl,
And all the changes of city and country wherever he went.

His own parents, he that had father'd him and she that had conceiv'd him in her womb and
    birth'd him
20 They gave this child more of themselves than that,
They gave him afterward every day, they became part of him.

The mother at home quietly placing the dishes on the supper-table,
The mother with mild words, clean her cap and gown, a wholesome odor falling off her person
    and clothes as she walks by,
The father, strong, self-sufficient, manly, mean, anger'd, unjust,
25 The blow, the quick loud word, the tight bargain, the crafty lure,
The family usages, the language, the company, the furniture, the yearning and swelling heart,
Affection that will not be gainsay'd, the sense of what is real, the thought if after all it should
    prove unreal,
The doubts of day-time and the doubts of night-time, the curious whether and how,
Whether that which appears so is so, or is it all flashes and specks?
30 Men and women crowding fast in the streets, if they are not flashes and specks what are they?
The streets themselves and the facades of houses, and goods in the windows,
Vehicles, teams, the heavy-plank'd wharves, the huge crossing at the ferries,
The village on the highland seen from afar at sunset, the river between,
Shadows, aureola and mist, the light falling on roofs and gables of white or brown two
    miles off,

---

1. **Third-month,** March. Whitman used the Quaker method of designating months by
number. His maternal grandmother was a Quaker.

35 The schooner near by sleepily dropping down the tide, the little boat slack-tow'd astern,
The hurrying tumbling waves, quick-broken crests, slapping,
The strata of color'd clouds, the long bar of maroon-tint away solitary by itself, the spread of
    purity it lies motionless in,
The horizon's edge, the flying sea-crow, the fragrance of salt marsh and shore mud,
These become part of that child who went forth every day, and who now goes, and will always
    go forth every day.

1855

When I Heard the Learn'd Astronomer

When I heard the learn'd astronomer,
When the proofs, the figures, were ranged in columns before me,
When I was shown the charts and diagrams, to add, divide, and measure them,
When I sitting heard the astronomer where he lectured with much applause in the
    lecture-room,
5 How soon unaccountable I became tired and sick,
Till rising and gliding out I wander'd off by myself,
In the mystical moist night-air, and from time to time,
Look'd up in perfect silence at the stars.

1865

A Noiseless Patient Spider

A noiseless patient spider,
I mark'd where on a little promontory it stood isolated,
Mark'd how to explore the vacant vast surrounding,
It launch'd forth filament, filament, filament, out of itself,
5 Ever unreeling them, ever tirelessly speeding them.

And you O my soul where you stand,
Surrounded, detached, in measureless oceans of space,
Ceaselessly musing, venturing, throwing, seeking the spheres to connect them,
Till the bridge you will need be form'd, till the ductile anchor hold,
10 Till the gossamer thread you fling catch somewhere, O my soul.

1868   1881

To a Locomotive in Winter

Thee for my recitative,[1]
Thee in the driving storm even as now, the snow, the winter-day declining,
Thee in thy panoply, thy measur'd dual throbbing and thy beat convulsive,
Thy black cylindric body, golden brass and silvery steel,
5 Thy ponderous side-bars, parallel and connecting rods, gyrating, shuttling at thy sides,
Thy metrical, now swelling pant and roar, now tapering in the distance,
Thy great protruding head-light fix'd in front,
Thy long, pale, floating vapor-pennants, tinged with delicate purple,
The dense and murky clouds out-belching from thy smoke-stack,
10 Thy knitted frame, thy springs and valves, the tremulous twinkle of thy wheels,
Thy train of cars behind, obedient, merrily following,
Through gale or calm, now swift, now slack, yet steadily careering:
Type of the modern—emblem of motion and power—pulse of the continent.
For once come serve the Muse[2] and merge in verse, even as here I see thee,
15 With storm and buffeting gusts of wind and falling snow,
By day thy warning ringing bell to sound its notes,
By night thy silent signal lamps to swing.

Fierce-throated beauty!
Roll through my chant with all thy lawless music, thy swinging lamps at night,
20 Thy madly-whistled laughter, echoing, rumbling like an earthquake, rousing all,
Law of thyself complete, thine own track firmly holding,
(No sweetness debonair of tearful harp or glib piano thine,)
Thy trills of shrieks by rocks and hills return'd,
Launch'd o'er the prairies wide, across the lakes,
25 To the free skies unpent and glad and strong.

1881

---

1. *recitative,* passage, part, or piece of music with rhythm and phrasing of ordinary speech.
Operas, which Whitman frequently attended, often contain long recitatives.
2. *Muse,* (from Greek mythology) one of the nine goddesses of the fine arts and sciences;
the spirit that inspires a poet or composer.

Walt Whitman

THINK AND DISCUSS
Understanding

1. Grass, as a central **image,** is a unifying motif in "Song of Myself." The noted Whitman scholar, Gay Wilson Allen, states that "the **protagonist** 'I' is searching for the meaning of life in the cycle of birth, death, and rebirth: a search that begins with 'observing a spear of summer grass.' " What lines in section 6 capture this birth/death/rebirth cycle?

2. What is the time of day and season of the year at the beginning and at the end of "There Was a Child Went Forth"?

3. What do the descriptions of the father and mother in "There Was a Child Went Forth" reveal about the speaker's attitude toward them?

4. In "When I Heard the Learn'd Astronomer," what effect does the astronomy lesson have upon the speaker? How does the speaker react to the stars in their natural **setting?**

5. Explain the basic **analogy** in "A Noiseless Patient Spider."

6. Whitman is famous for his cataloging technique, his enumeration of images or abstractions. What is being cataloged in "To a Locomotive in Winter"? What keeps this listing from being tedious?

Analyzing

7. "Song of Myself" has been considered the first American epic, celebrating the individual rather than an ancient hero. Who is the "I" in this poem?

8. In the first eleven lines of section 6 of "Song of Myself," Whitman calls the grass a flag woven "out of hopeful green stuff," "the handkerchief of the Lord," "a child," and "a uniform hieroglyphic." What does each of these comparisons suggest about the **symbolic** meaning of the grass? Considered as a whole, do these symbols suggest positive or negative associations with the grass? Explain.

9. In "There Was a Child Went Forth," the objects the child observes become part of him. What method does Whitman use to indicate the child's increased perception, his expansion of awareness?

10. In "When I Heard the Learn'd Astronomer," Whitman does not use colorful imagery in his description of the astronomy lesson. Why not?

11. Discuss the isolation imagery in "A Noiseless Patient Spider."

Extending

12. Read aloud some of the lines from Pope's *Essay on Man* (page 570). Then read some lines from "Song of Myself." Compare the **rhythm** of the two poems.

See Handbook of Literary Terms, p. 951.

Walt Whitman was the first American poet to make extensive use of **free verse**, a type of poetry that differs from conventional verse forms in being "free" from a fixed pattern of meter and rhyme, but using rhythm and other poetic devices. The rhythm in his poetry grew out of the ebb and flow of thought and action in his verse, rather than a prescribed scheme. In his 1855 Preface to *Leaves of Grass*, Whitman wrote: "The rhyme and uniformity of perfect poems show the free growth of metrical laws and bud from them as unerringly and loosely as lilacs or roses on a bush." His innovative style pioneered the way for future poets to flee the restrictions of set meter and rhyme schemes.

1. Because writers of free verse do not rely on rhyme or conventional meter to hold lines or stanzas together, they often use grammatical units, such as phrases or clauses, or poetic devices, such as **apostrophe** or significant repetition, to accomplish this purpose. In section 21 of "Song of Myself," what is the principal grammatical unit of (**a**) each line in the first three stanzas and (**b**) of lines 57–61?
2. What literary devices are used in lines 56 and 63 to help unify the stanza? What mark of punctuation ends all but one line of this stanza?
3. Copy line 53 on a separate sheet of paper. Mark the stressed and unstressed syllables. Does the line follow a regular meter?

VOCABULARY
Dictionary and Etymology

Use your Glossary to answer the questions about each italicized word from Whitman's poems. Write the answers on your paper, and be sure you can spell and pronounce each word.

1. What is an example of an *esculent* root?
2. What is the meaning of the Latin root *esca*?
3. Give two different meanings of the word *facade*.
4. Could Whitman have been thinking of the two meanings of *facade* in line 31 of "There Was a Child Went Forth"?
5. What does the Latin root *facies* mean?
6. What is the definition of *aureola* as it is used in line 34 of "There Was a Child Went Forth"?
7. What is the meaning of the Latin root *aurum*?
8. From what Latin root does *limpid* come? What is the meaning of the root?
9. From what language does the word *hieroglyphic* come?
10. What do the root words *hieros* and *glyphē* mean?

COMPOSITION
Writing a Poem

Using free verse, write a serious poem or a parody (a humorous imitation of a serious writing) in which you catalog the experiences that have become a part of your being as you have matured. Emulate Whitman's sharply focused images and parallel grammatical structure. Although Whitman used both positive and negative images, overall he tended to idealize America. You may wish to emphasize the pleasant events in your life. In a parody, you might name only the mundane aspects of growing up in America.

Writing About Imagery

Whitman found the sounds of America fascinating. Write an essay discussing the aural **imagery** in "To a Locomotive in Winter." In your prewriting, make a list of the sounds described. Show how this imagery relates to the first line of the poem and to the locomotive as an "emblem of motion and power." See "Writing About Poetry and Poetic Devices" in the Writer's Handbook.

Le mot juste, "the precise word," was the goal of Flaubert (flō ber′) as the novelist and short-story writer labored to perfect his prose style. He wrote to a friend, describing the process that took six weeks to produce twenty-five pages: "I have worked on them, recopied them, changed them, recast them." Because of his brilliant style, realistic fictional detail, and authorial detachment, he is credited with creating the form of the modern novel.

Gustave Flaubert was born in Rouen, France, where his father was an eminent surgeon. The young Flaubert enjoyed reading Romantic authors —Hugo was one of his favorites—and writing letters and plays which he performed. Upon finishing his schooling, he followed his father's urging and went to Paris to study law. However, in 1844 his lack of real interest in the legal profession and the first of many attacks due to a nervous disorder caused him to return to the family home. Flaubert met and fell in love with the poet Louise Colet in 1846, and their stormy relationship lasted until 1855, despite many bitter quarrels. For years the author carefully worked on his masterpiece *Madame Bovary*. First published as a magazine serial in 1856, its subject matter, the life of a young married woman who seeks to fulfill her romantic fantasies through love affairs, shocked many readers. Flaubert was officially charged with offenses "against public morality and religion." His defense was that rather than making adultery seem attractive as he was accused of doing, his portrayal of the tragic results of his heroine's tawdry affairs was an object lesson in morality. He was exonerated, and the notoriety of the trial assured the novel's success with the public. Flaubert became a celebrity, moving in the best circles in Paris. Among his friends were members of the imperial court and famous writers, such as George Sand and Guy de Maupassant. Although he published five more books, including the fine *Sentimental Education* (1869), none was as well received as *Madame Bovary*. His fictional subjects were French middle-class society (which he ridiculed) and exotic history, like that of ancient Carthage, the setting of his novel *Salammbô* (1862). His work greatly influenced a group of young French writers calling themselves "realists," and such famous authors as Henry James and Joseph Conrad. Flaubert lost much of his fortune in his later years when he attempted to alleviate his niece's severe financial difficulties. He died at Croisset in 1880.

The excerpt from *Madame Bovary* presented here takes place at Vaubyessard, a chateau belonging to the Marquis d'Andervilliers. Emma Bovary, a beautiful young woman, stirred by reading romantic novels, envisions an ideal love. She feels imprisoned by her boring middle-class life with her tedious husband, Charles, a country doctor. An unexpected invitation to a ball at Vaubyessard enflames her desire to be part of a more glamorous, affluent world.

from Madame Bovary

Gustave Flaubert   *translated by* **Mildred Marmur**

Chapter 8

he château, of modern construction, in the Italian style, had two projecting wings and three front entrances. It was spread out at the back of an immense lawn on which several cows were grazing between clumps of large, evenly spaced trees while groups of shrubs, rhododendron, syringa, and snowballs projected their unequal tufts of foliage along the winding sandy road. A stream passed under a bridge. Through the haze could be seen the thatch-roofed buildings scattered across the meadow. This latter was set in between the gentle slopes of two tree-covered hills. In the groves behind the house, set on two parallel lines, were the coach houses and stables, sole remains of the old, demolished château.

Charles's carriage arrived at the middle flight of steps; servants appeared; the marquis came forward, and offering his arm to the doctor's wife, he led her into the foyer.

It was high ceilinged and paved with marble tiles, and the combined noise of steps and voices echoed in it as in a church. A staircase faced it, and to the left a gallery overlooking the garden led to a billiard room, from which you could hear the ivory balls clicking as soon as you approached the door.

As she was crossing it to get to the drawing room, Emma noticed the serious-faced men, chins set over cravats folded high and all wearing decorations, standing around the table. They would smile silently as they hit with their cues. On the dark wood panels were large gilded frames with names written in black letters on their lower borders. She read: "Jean-Antoine d'Andervilliers d'Yverbonville, Count de la Vaubyessard, and Baron de la Fresnaye, killed in the battle of Coutras, October 20, 1587." And on another: "Jean-Antoine-Henri-Guy d'Andervilliers de la Vaubyessard, Admiral of France and Knight of the Order of St. Michael, wounded in the battle of La Hougue-Saint-Vaast, May 29, 1692, died at La Vaubyessard, January 23, 1693." Those that followed could barely be made out because the light from the lamps, directed on the green cloth of the billard table, left the rest of the room in shadow. It turned the hanging canvases brown and highlighted only the cracks in the varnish; and from all the large gilt-edged black squares only some lighter part of the painting would emerge here and there—a pale forehead, two eyes staring at you, wigs unfurling over the powdered shoulders, red suits, or perhaps the buckle of a garter at the top of a fleshy calf.

The marquis opened the drawing-room door; one of the women arose (the marquise herself), came forward to meet Emma, and sat her down beside her on a small settee, where she began to chat amiably, as if she had known her a long time. She was a woman of about forty, with handsome shoulders, an aquiline nose, and a drawling voice; she wore a simple lace shawl that fell back in a point over her chestnut hair. A fair-haired young woman was sitting beside her in a high-backed chair, and gentlemen with tiny flowers in their lapels were talking to the ladies gathered around the fireplace.

Dinner was served at seven. The men, who outnumbered the ladies, sat down at the first table, in the hall, and the women were placed at the second, in the dining room with the marquis and the marquise.

As she entered, Emma felt herself enveloped in a warm atmosphere, a mixture of flower scent and the aroma of fine linens, of well-seasoned meat and truffles. The candles in the candelabra played their elongated flames over the silver platter covers; crystal pieces misted over reflected each other with pale glimmers. There were bunches of flowers set in a line along the entire table, and in the wide-bordered dishes napkins folded in the shape of bishop's miters held small oval-shaped rolls.

The red claws of the lobsters hung over the dishes; huge pieces of fruit were piled on each other in openwork baskets; the quails still bore their plumage; clouds of steam kept rising; and the butler, in silk stockings, knee breeches, white cravat, and frilled shirt, solemn as a judge, passing the already carved platters between the guests' shoulders, would make the piece you selected jump with one flick of the knife. On the large porcelain stove with its copper fittings, a statue of a woman draped to the chin stared steadily at the roomful of people.

Madame Bovary noticed that several of the women had not put their gloves in their wineglasses.

At the upper end of the table, alone among all the women, there was one old man eating, bending over his well-filled platter with his napkin knotted in back like a child, drops of sauce dribbling from his mouth. His eyes were bloodshot and he wore a small pigtail tied with a black ribbon. It was the marquis' father-in-law, the old Duke of Laverdière, once favorite of the Count d'Artois in the days of the Marquis de Conflans's hunting parties in Vaudreuil; it was said he had been Marie-Antoinette's lover between Messieurs de Coigny and de Lauzun. He had led a thoroughly debauched life, filled with duels, wagers, and abductions, had run through his fortune and been the terror of his entire family. A servant behind his chair was shouting into his ear the names of dishes that the old man would point to with his finger, mumbling. Emma could not keep herself from staring at the slack-mouthed old man as on someone extraordinary and august. He had lived at Court and slept in the bed of queens!

Iced champagne was served. Emma shivered all over at the prickly sensation in her mouth. She had never seen pomegranates before nor eaten pineapple. Even the granulated sugar seemed to her whiter and finer than elsewhere.

After dinner the ladies went up to their rooms to get ready for the ball.

Emma dressed with the meticulous care of an actress making her debut. She arranged her hair as the hairdresser had suggested and pulled on the *barège* dress that had been spread out on the bed. Charles's pants were too tight around the stomach.

"The shoe straps are going to be in my way when I dance," he said.

"Dance?" she asked.

"Yes."

"You're out of your mind! They'll laugh at you. Stay in your place. Besides, it's more suitable for a doctor," she added.

Charles said no more. He paced up and down the room waiting for Emma to finish dressing.

Her back was turned to him, and he looked at her reflection in the mirror between the two candles. Her black eyes seemed even blacker. Her hair, gently puffed toward the ears, gleamed with a bluish luster; a rose in her chignon was trembling on its fragile stem. It had artificial dewdrops at the tips of its leaves. She wore a pale saffron-colored dress, set off by three bunches of pompon roses mingled with greenery.

Charles went over to kiss her on the shoulder.

"Let go of me!" she said. "You'll wrinkle my dress!"

A violin flourish and the sounds of a horn could be heard. She descended the staircase, restraining herself from running.

The quadrilles had begun. More people were arriving, jostling each other. She stationed herself on a settee near the door.

When the quadrille was over, the floor remained free. Groups of men stood and chatted while the liveried servants brought in large trays. Along the row of seated women, painted fans were fluttering, bouquets half concealed smiling faces, and gold-stoppered perfume bottles were being turned in half-opened hands whose tight white gloves revealed the shape of the fingernails and hugged the wrists. Lace trimmings, diamond brooches, and bracelets with lockets trembled on bodices, sparkled on breasts, jingled on bare arms. The hairdos, securely arranged and twisted at the napes, were crowned with clusters or bunches of forget-me-nots, jasmine, pomegranate blossoms, wheat ears, or cornflowers. The mothers, sitting quietly in their places, wore red turbans and frowning expressions.

Emma's heart was beating a bit faster when, her partner holding her by the tips of his fingers, she took her place in line and awaited the fiddler's stroke to begin. But the emotion soon disappeared, and swaying to the rhythm of the orchestra, she glided forward, moving her neck lightly. A smile came to her lips at certain delicate strains of the violin during its solo moments; you could hear the clinking of gold coins dropping onto the card tables in the next room; then everything began at once, the cornet emitted a loud blast, feet fell in measure, skirts swirled out and rustled against each other, hands joined, then separated; the same eyes that lowered before you looked up again at yours.

Several men (about fifteen) between twenty-five and forty years of age, scattered among the dancers or chatting at the entrances, distinguished themselves from the crowd by their family resemblance despite the differences in their ages, dress, and facial features.

Their clothes, better made, seemed of a finer cloth, and their hair, made to gleam by more refined pomades, was brought forward in curls toward the temples. They had the complexion of wealth, that whiteness that is accentuated by the pallor of porcelain, the sheen of watered satin, the varnish of fine furniture, and that is nurtured by a diet of exquisitely prepared food. Their necks turned in relaxed manner over low-folded cravats, their long sideburns fell over turned-down collars; they wiped their lips with elegantly scented handkerchiefs embroidered with large monograms. Those who were beginning to age looked young, and a certain maturity lay over the faces of the young ones. The calm of daily satisfied passions showed in their indifferent glances, but their gentle manners did not completely mask that special brutality that stems from their relatively easy conquests, the handling of thoroughbred horses and

Portrait of a young woman of the period of Flaubert's Emma Bovary. 1835. Musée Monétaire, Paris

the company of fallen women, in which the muscles are flexed and vanity sated.

A few feet from Emma a gentleman in a blue coat was talking about Italy with a pale young woman wearing a pearl necklace. They were praising the size of the pillars at St. Peter's, Tivoli, Vesuvius, Castellamare, and the Cascine; the roses of Genoa; the Colosseum in the moonlight. Emma listened with her other ear to a conversation full of words she did not understand. In the center of a group was a very young man who had beaten Miss Arabelle and Romulus the week before and won two thousand louis by jumping a ditch in England. One man was complaining that his racers were getting fat; another, about the way a printing error had garbled his horse's name.

The air in the ballroom grew heavy; the lights were fading. People began moving toward the billiard room. A servant climbing on a chair broke two windowpanes; at the noise of the shattered glass, Madame Bovary looked round and saw some peasants, their faces pressed to the window, staring at her from the garden. Then the memory of Les Bertaux came back to her. She saw the farm again, the muddy pond, her father in a smock under the apple trees, and she saw once more herself in the dairy skimming the cream from the milk cans with her finger. But in the splendor of the present hour, her past life, so clear until now, was disappearing completely, and she almost doubted that she had lived it. She was here, and outside the ballroom there was merely shadow cast over all the rest. She ate a maraschino-flavored ice, which she held in her left hand in a silver-gilt shell, and half closed her eyes, the spoon between her teeth.

A woman near her dropped her fan as a man danced by. "Would you be so kind, Monsieur," the woman said, "and pick my fan up from under the sofa?"

The gentleman kneeled down, and as he reached out, Emma saw the young woman's hand throw something white, folded into a triangle, into his hat. The gentleman picked up the fan and held it out to the woman respectfully; she thanked him with a nod and began to sniff her bouquet.

After supper, at which many Spanish and Rhine wines were served, along with bisque and cream-of-almond soups, Trafalgar puddings, and all sorts of cold meats, surrounded by jellied molds, quivering on the plates, the carriages began going off, one after the other. By pulling the muslin curtain away from the corner one could see the light of their lanterns gliding through the night. The settees began to empty; there were still some card players; the musicians moistened the tips of their fingers on their tongues; Charles was leaning against a door, half asleep.

The cotillion began at three in the morning. Emma did not know how to waltz. Everyone was waltzing, even Mademoiselle d'Andervilliers and the marquise; there remained now only the château guests, about a dozen people.

One of the dancers, familiarly addressed as viscount, whose extremely low-cut waistcoat seemed molded on his chest, came a second time to invite Madame Bovary, assuring her that he would lead her and that she would manage well.

They began slowly, then moved more rapidly. Everything was turning around them, the lights, furniture, paneling, and the floor, like a disk on a pivot. Passing near the doors, the hem of Emma's dress flared out against her partner's trousers; their legs intertwined; he looked down at her, she raised her eyes to him; a numbness overcame her, she stopped. They started again and the viscount, with a more rapid movement, swept her away, disappeared with her to the end of the gallery, where, out of breath, she almost fell and for one moment leaned her head on his chest. And then, still turning, but more gently now, he led her back to her place; she leaned back against the wall and put her hand before her eyes.

When she opened them again, there was a woman seated on a stool in the middle of the floor with three dancers on their knees before her. She chose the viscount and the violin struck up again.

They were stared at. Up and down they went, she with her body held rigid, chin down, and he always in the same pose, holding himself erect, elbow rounded, face jutting forward. How she could waltz! They continued for a long time and tired out the others.

People chatted a while and after the "good nights," or rather "good mornings," the house guests went to sleep.

Charles dragged himself upstairs, clinging to the banister; his legs "couldn't stand up another minute." He had spent five solid hours standing near the tables watching the whist games without understanding a thing about them. And so he heaved a great sigh of relief when his boots were finally removed.

Emma wrapped a shawl around her shoulders, opened the window, and leaned out.

The night was black. A few drops of rain were falling. She breathed in the humid breeze that was refreshing her eyelids. With the ball music still humming in her ears, she was trying to stay awake in order to prolong the illusion of this luxurious life that she would have to abandon in a short while.

Family Reunion by Jean-Frédéric Bazille. 1867. Musée d'Orsay, Paris

Day broke. She looked at the château windows for a long time, trying to guess which were the bedrooms of the various people she had noticed the night before. She would have liked to know about their lives, to enter into them, to become involved with them.

But she was shivering with cold. She undressed and snuggled between the sheets against Charles, who was asleep.

There were a lot of people at breakfast; the doctor was amazed that no liquor was served. Later Mademoiselle d'Andervilliers picked up what was left of the rolls in a basket to carry them to the swans on the lake, and they went for a walk in the hothouses, where exotic plants bristling with hairy leaves rose in pyramids beneath hanging vases, which, like over-crowded serpents' nests, dropped long, twisted green tendrils over their edges. The orangery at the far end led via a covered passage to the outhouses. The marquis took Emma to the stable to amuse her. Above the basket-shaped racks, porcelain plaques bore the horses' names in black. When they passed by, each animal stirred in its stall and clicked its tongue. The floor of the saddle room glistened like a drawing-room floor. Coach harnesses were set in the middle on two revolving columns and the bits, whips, stirrups, and curbs were all lined up along the wall.

Meanwhile, Charles went to ask a servant to ready his buggy. They brought it around to the front, and when all their luggage had been packed in, the Bovarys took leave of the marquis and marquise and headed back to Tostes.

Emma said nothing and watched the wheels turn. Charles, seated on the edge of the seat, was driving with his arms outstretched, and the small horse ambled along between its oversized shafts. The slack reins hitting its crupper grew moist with its lather, and the box roped on behind kept making loud, steady thuds against the body.

They were on the heights of Thibourville when suddenly some horsemen passed before them, laughing, with cigars in their mouths. Emma thought she recognized the viscount; she turned around and saw nothing on the horizon but heads moving up and down in rhythm with the uneven cadence of the trot and gallop.

Half a mile later they had to stop to tie a cord around the breech band, which had broken. As Charles took one last look at the harness, he saw something on the ground between the horse's legs; and he picked up a cigar case edged with green silk and emblazoned with a coat of arms in the center as on a coach door.

"There are still two cigars inside," he said. "They'll be for tonight after dinner."

"You smoke?" she asked.

"Sometimes, when I have the chance."

He put his find in his pocket and whipped the horse.

Dinner was not ready when they arrived home. Madame became furious. Nastasie answered with insolence.

"Get out!" Emma said. "You brazen creature! I'm sending you away!"

For dinner there was onion soup with a bit of veal cooked in sorrel. Facing Emma, Charles said, rubbing his hands together with a contented look: "It feels good to be home again!"

They could hear Nastasie crying. He was rather fond of the poor girl. In the old days when he had been a widower, she had kept him company on many an empty evening. She was his first patient, his oldest acquaintance in the district.

"Have you sent her away for good?" he said finally.

"Yes. Who's stopping me?" she answered.

They warmed themselves in the kitchen while their bedroom was being readied. Charles began to smoke. He smoked with his lips puckered, spitting every minute, recoiling at each puff.

"You'll make yourself sick," she said disdainfully.

He put his cigar down and ran off to gulp down a glass of cold water from the pump. Emma, seizing the cigar case, threw it hastily into the bottom of the cupboard.

The next day was long. She walked about in her garden, passing back and forth over the same paths, stopping in front of the flower beds, the fruit-tree trellises, the plaster curé, staring with bewilderment at all these once familiar things. How far away the ball already seemed! Why should there be such a distance between yesterday morning and tonight? Her trip to Vaubyessard had made a gap in her life like one of those great crevices that a storm sometimes carves out in the mountains in a single night. She resigned herself, however; reverently she packed away in the chest of drawers her lovely dress and even her satin slippers, whose soles had yellowed from the floor wax. Her heart was like them; the wealth had rubbed off on her, something that would never be erased.

And so the memory of the ball became a preoccupation for Emma. Every Wednesday she would say to herself on awaking: "Ah! A week ago today —two weeks ago—three weeks ago, I was there." Little by little the faces blurred in her memory; she forgot the quadrille tunes; she no longer saw the livery and the rooms so clearly; some of the details faded away, but the regret remained.

1851–1856   1857

THINK AND DISCUSS

Understanding

1. Describe the life at Vaubyessard.
2. How does Flaubert indicate the disparity between the glittering scene at the ball and Emma's background?
3. The reactions of Emma and Charles at the end of the dance illustrate the divergence in their perspectives. Describe their thoughts and actions.

Analyzing

4. One of the **themes** of the novel is stupidity: the inability to perceive reality and to adjust to it. How does Emma's reaction to the marquis's father-in-law and the actual description of the old man at the dinner party illustrate this theme?
5. Reread the conversation between Emma and Charles that takes place as they dress for the ball and the dialogue following their return home. What do the couple's words reveal about their relationship?
6. Flaubert uses the device of a recurring image in his fiction, for example the elegant cigar case Charles finds on the way home from the ball. How does Charles react to it? What does the case symbolize to Emma?
7. What is the specific situation that causes Emma to fire Nastasie? Is there another reason for her rash action?

Extending

8. Find the **simile** that describes the effect of the trip to Vaubyessard upon Emma. How do you think it will ultimately affect her marriage?
9. In Cervantes's *Don Quixote*, pages 406–411, the **protagonist** gets his romantic ideas from reading books about chivalry, just as Emma bases her visions of ideal love upon sentimental novels. Their illusions blind them both to reality. What are the principal ways they differ?
10. To some contemporary readers, the essence of this novel is the plight of women trapped by narrow circumstances and restricted opportunities. Although the movement for women's rights has helped to correct these problems, in what ways are some women restricted even today?
11. What similarities do you see between Emma's view of marriage and that of the speaker of "When I Make Myself Imagine" from *The Pillow Book*, page 94?

THINKING SKILLS

Evaluating

To evaluate is to make a judgment based on some sort of standard.

1. A snob is someone who cares too much for rank, wealth, and position, and too little for real achievement or merit. In your judgment, is Emma Bovary a snob?
2. Another definition of a snob is a person who tries too hard to please superiors and who ignores inferiors. Is Emma a snob in this sense?

COMPOSITION

Writing About Personal Experience

Emma is so affected by the excitement of the ball that long after it is over she has visions about "circling in the waltz . . . on the viscount's arm." Describe a special experience that continued to affect you for some time after the event.

Writing About Theme

Write a composition showing how Flaubert demonstrates the theme of illusion and reality in this chapter. Use your answers from the questions on this topic to help you in your prewriting. Be sure to show the reality of Emma's situation, Emma's inability to see the truth due to her romantic illusions, and the damage that results. See "Writing About Theme" in the Writer's Handbook.

Russian novelist and short-story writer, Count Leo Tolstoy, author of one of the most important novels in world literature, *War and Peace*, was also a noted moral philosopher. Born into the aristocracy, Tolstoy and his three brothers were educated on the family estate of Yasnaya Polyana by private tutors. Tolstoy's mother died when he was two, and seven years later his father died. The children then lived with relatives.

In 1844, Tolstoy began studying Oriental languages at Kazan University and a year later transferred to the Faculty of Law, but failed to apply himself in either field. In 1847, he left the university to return to Yasnaya Polyana, which he had just inherited. His attempts to help the serfs through reforms on his estate went badly, and he often escaped to Moscow where he led a libertine life. In 1851, he joined his brother Nicholas to serve in the military. His transfer from the Caucasus to Sevastopol during the Crimean War resulted in his writing the *Sevastopol Sketches*. The critical acclaim given his realistic account of the war gained him entrance into the literary circles of Petersburg after he left the army. In 1857–1859, Tolstoy made two European tours. He also established an experimental school for the peasant children on his estate, addressing the needs of individual students and rejecting traditional disciplinary methods and grading systems. In 1862, he married Sofya Andreyevna Bers, a well-educated, pretty woman who helped him with his teaching, bore him thirteen children, and managed the household, freeing Tolstoy for his writing which she admired. Tolstoy began his monumental work, *War and Peace*, in 1861, and it was published in 1865–1869. This realistic historical novel condemns war and vividly presents a vast panorama of Russian society. His second great novel, *Anna Karenina*, a tragic story of adulterous love, was published in 1875–1877.

At the beginning of the 1880s, Tolstoy underwent a spiritual crisis that had a profound effect upon his personal and professional life. He became a moral reformer, rejecting established religion and civil authority. Severe conflicts with his wife arose when he wished to give away all of his property in addition to renouncing the rights to everything written by him after 1881. Most of his writing became centered on moral and ethical issues. His followers formed Tolstoyan societies that embraced his belief in universal love, social justice, non-violence, and passive resistance to evil. At the age of 82, the author's desire to practice his beliefs more fully prompted him to leave his estate on a pilgrimage. He died while on the journey.

After his religious conversion, Tolstoy often used old folk tales as a basis for his short fiction to illustrate his moral teachings. The following story exemplifies his beliefs concerning private ownership of land.

How Much Land Does a Man Need?

Leo Tolstoy *translated by* **Louise and Aylmer Maude**

1

An elder sister came to visit her younger sister in the country. The elder was married to a shopkeeper in town, the younger to a peasant in the village. As the sisters sat over their tea talking, the elder began to boast of the advantages of town life, saying how comfortably they lived there, how well they dressed, what fine clothes her children wore, what good things they ate and drank, and how she went to the theater, promenades, and entertainments.

The younger sister was piqued, and in turn disparaged the life of a shopkeeper, and stood up for that of a peasant.

"I wouldn't change my way of life for yours," said she. "We may live roughly, but at least we're free from worry. You live in better style than we do, but though you often earn more than you need, you're very likely to lose all you have. You know the proverb, 'Loss and gain are brothers twain.' It often happens that people who're wealthy one day are begging their bread the next. Our way is safer. Though a peasant's life is not a rich one, it's long. We'll never grow rich, but we'll always have enough to eat."

The elder sister said sneeringly:

"Enough? Yes, if you like to share with the pigs and the calves! What do you know of elegance or manners! However much your good man may slave, you'll die as you live—in a dung heap—and your children the same."

"Well, what of that?" replied the younger sister. "Of course our work is rough and hard. But on the other hand, it's sure, and we need not bow to anyone. But you, in your towns, are surrounded by temptations; today all may be right, but tomorrow the Evil One may tempt your husband with cards, wine, or women, and all will go to ruin. Don't such things happen often enough?"

Pahom, the master of the house, was lying on the top of the stove and he listened to the women's chatter.

"It is perfectly true," thought he. "Busy as we are from childhood tilling mother earth, we peasants have no time to let any nonsense settle in our heads. Our only trouble is that we haven't land enough. If I had plenty of land I shouldn't fear the Devil himself!"

The women finished their tea, chatted a while about dress, and then cleared away the tea things and lay down to sleep.

But the Devil had been sitting behind the stove and had heard all that had been said. He was pleased that the peasant's wife had led her husband into boasting and that he had said that if he had plenty of land he would not fear the Devil himself.

"All right," thought the Devil. "We'll have a tussle. I'll give you land enough; and by means of the land I'll get you into my power."

2

Close to the village there lived a lady, a small landowner who had an estate of about three hundred acres. She had always lived on good terms with the peasants until she engaged as her manager an old soldier, who took to burdening the people with fines. However careful Pahom tried to be, it happened again and again that now a horse of his got among the lady's oats, now a cow strayed into her garden, now his calves found their way into her meadows—and he always had to pay a fine.

Pahom paid up, but grumbled, and, going home in a temper, was rough with his family. All through that summer Pahom had much trouble because of this manager, and he was actually glad when winter came and the cattle had to be stabled. Though he grudged the fodder when they could no longer graze on the pasture land, at least he was free from anxiety about them.

In the winter the news got about that the lady was going to sell her land and that the keeper of the inn on the high road was bargaining for it. When the peasants heard this they were very much alarmed.

"Well," thought they, "if the innkeeper gets the land, he'll worry us with fines worse than the lady's manager. We all depend on that estate."

So the peasants went on behalf of their village council and asked the lady not to sell the land to the innkeeper, offering her a better price for it themselves. The lady agreed to let them have it. Then the peasants tried to arrange for the village council to buy the whole estate, so that it might be held by them all in common. They met twice to discuss it, but could not settle the matter; the Evil One sowed discord among them and they could not agree. So they decided to buy the land individually, each according to his means; and the lady agreed to this plan as she had to the other.

Presently Pahom heard that a neighbor of his was buying fifty acres, and that the lady had consented to accept one half in cash and to wait a year for the other half. Pahom felt envious.

"Look at that," thought he, "the land is all being sold, and I'll get none of it." So he spoke to his wife.

"Other people are buying," said he, "and we must also buy twenty acres or so. Life is becoming impossible. That manager is simply crushing us with his fines."

So they put their heads together and considered how they could manage to buy it. They had one hundred rubles laid by. They sold a colt and one half of their bees, hired out one of their sons as a farm hand and took his wages in advance, borrowed the rest from a brother-in-law, and so scraped together half the purchase money.

Having done this, Pahom chose a farm of forty acres, some of it wooded, and went to the lady to bargain for it. They came to an agreement, and he shook hands with her upon it and paid her a deposit in advance. Then they went to town and signed the deeds, he paying half the price down, and undertaking to pay the remainder within two years.

So now Pahom had land of his own. He borrowed seed and sowed it on the land he had bought. The harvest was a good one, and within a year he had managed to pay off his debts both to the lady and to his brother-in-law. So he became a landowner, plowing and sowing his own land, making hay on his own land, cutting his own trees, and feeding his cattle on his own pasture. When he went out to plow his fields, or to look at his growing corn, or at his grass meadows, his heart would fill with joy. The grass that grew and the flowers that bloomed there seemed to him unlike any that grew elsewhere. Formerly, when he had passed by that land, it had appeared the same as any other land, but now it seemed quite different.

3

So Pahom was well contented, and everything would have been right if the neighboring peasants would only not have trespassed on his wheatfields and meadows. He appealed to them most civilly, but they still went on: now the herdsmen would let the village cows stray into his meadows, then horses from the night pasture would get among his corn. Pahom turned them out again and again, and forgave their owners, and for a long time he forbore to prosecute anyone. But at last he lost patience and complained to the District Court. He knew it was the peasants' want of land, and no evil intent on their part, that caused the trouble, but he thought:

"I can't go on overlooking it, or they'll destroy all I have. They must be taught a lesson."

So he had them up, gave them one lesson, and then another, and two or three of the peasants were fined. After a time Pahom's neighbors began to bear him a grudge for this, and would now and then let their cattle on to his land on purpose. One peasant even got into Pahom's wood at night and cut down five young lime trees for their bark. Pahom, passing through the wood one day, noticed something white. He came nearer

The Mowers by Grigory Miasoyedov. 1887. State Russian Museum, Leningrad

and saw the stripped trunks lying on the ground, and close by stood the stumps where the trees had been. Pahom was furious.

"If he'd only cut one here and there it would have been bad enough," thought Pahom, "but the rascal has actually cut down a whole clump. If I could only find out who did this, I'd get even with him."

He racked his brains as to who it could be. Finally he decided: "It must be Simon—no one else could have done it." So he went to Simon's homestead to have a look around, but he found nothing and only had an angry scene. However, he now felt more certain than ever that Simon had done it, and he lodged a complaint. Simon was summoned. The case was tried, and retried, and at the end of it all Simon was acquitted, there being no evidence against him. Pahom felt still more aggrieved, and let his anger loose upon the Elders and the Judges.

"You let thieves grease your palms," said he. "If you were honest folk yourselves you wouldn't let a thief go free."

So Pahom quarreled with the judges and with his neighbors. Threats to burn his hut began to be uttered. So though Pahom had more land, his place in the community was much worse than before.

About this time a rumor got about that many people were moving to new parts.

"There's no need for me to leave my land," thought Pahom. "But some of the others may leave our village and then there'd be more room for us. I'd take over their land myself and make my estates somewhat bigger. I could then live more at ease. As it is, I'm still too cramped to be comfortable."

One day Pahom was sitting at home when a peasant, passing through the village, happened to drop in. He was allowed to stay the night, and supper was given him. Pahom had a talk with this peasant and asked him where he came from. The stranger answered that he came from beyond the Volga,[1] where he had been working. One word

---

1. *Volga,* river located in European Russia.

led to another, and the man went on to say that many people were settling in those parts. He told how some people from his village had settled there. They had joined the community there and had had twenty-five acres per man granted them. The land was so good, he said, that the rye sown on it grew as high as a horse, and so thick that five cuts of a sickle made a sheaf. One peasant, he said, had brought nothing with him but his bare hands, and now he had six horses and two cows of his own.

Pahom's heart kindled with desire.

"Why should I suffer in this narrow hole if one can live so well elsewhere?" he thought. "I'll sell my land and my homestead here, and with the money I'll start afresh over there and get everything new. In this crowded place one is always having trouble. But I must first go and find out all about it myself."

Toward summer he got ready and started out. He went down the Volga on a steamer to Samara, then walked another three hundred miles on foot, and at last reached the place. It was just as the stranger had said. The peasants had plenty of land: every man had twenty-five acres of communal land given him for his use and anyone who had money could buy, besides, at a ruble and a half an acre, as much good freehold land as he wanted.

Having found out all he wished to know, Pahom returned home as autumn came on, and began selling off his belongings. He sold his land at a profit, sold his homestead and all his cattle, and withdrew from membership in the village. He only waited till the spring, and then started with his family for the new settlement.

4

As soon as Pahom and his family reached their new abode, he applied for admission into the council of a large village. He stood treat to the Elders and obtained the necessary documents. Five shares of communal land were given him for his own and his sons' use: that is to say—125 acres (not all together, but in different fields) besides the use of the communal pasture. Pahom put up the buildings he needed and bought cattle. Of the communal land alone he had three times as much as at his former home, and the land was good wheat

land. He was ten times better off than he had been. He had plenty of arable land and pasturage, and could keep as many head of cattle as he liked.

At first, in the bustle of building and settling down, Pahom was pleased with it all, but when he got used to it he began to think that even here he hadn't enough land. The first year he sowed wheat on his share of the communal land and had a good crop. He wanted to go on sowing wheat, but had not enough communal land for the purpose, and what he had already used was not available, for in those parts wheat is sown only on virgin soil or on fallow land. It is sown for one or two years, and then the land lies fallow till it is again overgrown with steppe grass. There were many who wanted such land, and there was not enough for all, so that people quarreled about it. Those who were better off wanted it for growing wheat, and those who were poor wanted it to let to dealers, so that they might raise money to pay their taxes. Pahom wanted to sow more wheat, so he rented land from a dealer for a year. He sowed much wheat and had a fine crop, but the land was too far from the village—the wheat had to be carted more than ten miles. After a time Pahom noticed that some peasant dealers were living on separate farms and were growing wealthy, and he thought:

"If I were to buy some freehold land and have a homestead on it, it would be a different thing altogether. Then it would all be fine and close together."

The question of buying freehold land recurred to him again and again.

He went on in the same way for three years, renting land and sowing wheat. The seasons turned out well and the crops were good, so that he began to lay by money. He might have gone on living contentedly, but he grew tired of having to rent other people's land every year and having to scramble for it. Wherever there was good land to be had, the peasants would rush for it and it was taken up at once, so that unless you were sharp about it, you got none. It happened in the third year that he and a dealer together rented a piece of pasture land from some peasants, and they had already plowed it up, when there was some dispute and the peasants went to law about it, and things fell out so that the labor was all lost.

"If it were my own land," thought Pahom, "I should be independent, and there wouldn't be all this unpleasantness."

So Pahom began looking out for land which he could buy, and he came across a peasant who had bought thirteen hundred acres, but having got into difficulties was willing to sell again cheap. Pahom bargained and haggled with him, and at last they settled the price at fifteen hundred rubles, part in cash and part to be paid later. They had all but clinched the matter when a passing dealer happened to stop at Pahom's one day to get feed for his horses. He drank tea with Pahom, and they had a talk. The dealer said that he was just returning from the land of the Bashkirs,[2] far away, where he had bought thirteen thousand acres of land, all for a thousand rubles. Pahom questioned him further, and the dealer said:

"All one has to do is to make friends with the chiefs. I gave away about one hundred rubles' worth of silk robes and carpets, besides a case of tea, and I gave wine to those who would drink it; and I got the land for less than three kopecks an acre." And he showed Pahom the title deed, saying:

"The land lies near a river, and the whole steppe[3] is virgin soil."

Pahom plied him with questions, and the dealer said:

"There's more land there than you could cover if you walked a year, and it all belongs to the Bashkirs. They're as simple as sheep, and land can be got almost for nothing."

"There, now," thought Pahom, "with my one thousand rubles, why should I get only thirteen hundred acres, and saddle myself with a debt besides? If I take it out there, I can get more than ten times as much for my money.

5

Pahom inquired how to get to the place, and as soon as the grain dealer had left him, he prepared to go there himself. He left his wife to look after the homestead, and started on his journey, taking his hired man with him. They stopped at a town on their way and bought a case of tea, some wine, and other presents, as the grain dealer had advised.

On and on they went until they had gone more than three hundred miles, and on the seventh day they came to a place where the Bashkirs had pitched their round tents. It was all just as the dealer had said. The people lived on the steppe, by a river, in felt-covered tents. They neither tilled the ground nor ate bread. Their cattle and horses grazed in herds on the steppe. The colts were tethered behind the tents, and the mares were driven to them twice a day. The mares were milked, and from the milk kumiss[4] was made. It was the women who prepared the kumiss, and they also made cheese. As far as the men were concerned, drinking kumiss and tea, eating mutton, and playing on their pipes was all they cared about. They were all stout and merry, and all the summer long they never thought of doing any work. They were quite ignorant, and knew no Russian, but were good-natured enough.

As soon as they saw Pahom, they came out of their tents and gathered around the visitor. An interpreter was found, and Pahom told them he had come about some land. The Bashkirs seemed very glad; they took Pahom and led him into one of the best tents, where they made him sit on some down cushions placed on a carpet, while they sat around him. They gave him some tea and kumiss, and had a sheep killed, and gave him mutton to eat. Pahom took presents out of his cart and distributed them among the Bashkirs, and divided the tea amongst them. The Bashkirs were delighted. They talked a great deal among themselves and then told the interpreter what to say.

"They wish to tell you," said the interpreter, "that they like you and that it's our custom to do all we can to please a guest and to repay him for his gifts. You have given us presents, now tell us which of the things we possess please you best, that we may present them to you."

---

2. **Bashkirs,** Asiatic nomads living on the Russian plains. Tolstoy admired their simplicity. He visited their encampments frequently to share in their primitive life style and partake of the kumiss (a fermented drink), considered a tonic.
3. **steppe,** vast treeless plain in Russia.
4. **kumiss,** fermented mare's milk.

"What pleases me best here," answered Pahom, "is your land. Our land is crowded and the soil is worn out, but you have plenty of land, and it is good land. I never saw the likes of it."

The interpreter told the Bashkirs what Pahom had said. They talked among themselves for a while. Pahom could not understand what they were saying, but saw that they were much amused and heard them shout and laugh. Then they were silent and looked at Pahom while the interpreter said:

"They wish me to tell you that in return for your presents they will gladly give you as much land as you want. You have only to point it out with your hand and it is yours."

The Bashkirs talked again for a while and began to dispute. Pahom asked what they were disputing about, and the interpreter told him that some of them thought they ought to ask their chief about the land and not act in his absence, while others thought there was no need to wait for his return.

6

While the Bashkirs were disputing, a man in a large fox-fur cap appeared on the scene. They all became silent and rose to their feet. The interpreter said: "This is our chief himself."

Pahom immediately fetched the best dressing gown and five pounds of tea, and offered these to the chief. The chief accepted them and seated himself in the place of honor. The Bashkirs at once began telling him something. The chief listened for a while, then made a sign with his head for them to be silent, and addressing himself to Pahom, said in Russian:

"Well, so be it. Choose whatever piece of land you like; we have plenty of it."

"How can I take as much as I like?" thought Pahom. "I must get a deed to make it secure, or else they may say: 'It is yours,' and afterward may take it away again."

"Thank you for your kind words," he said aloud. "You have much land, and I only want a little. But I should like to be sure which portion is mine. Could it not be measured and made over to me? Life and death are in God's hands. You good people give it to me, but your children might wish to take it back again."

"You are quite right," said the chief. "We will make it over to you."

"I heard that a dealer had been here," continued Pahom, "and that you gave him a little land, too, and signed title deeds to that effect. I should like to have it done in the same way."

The chief understood.

"Yes," replied he, "that can be done quite easily. We have a scribe, and we will go to town with you and have the deed properly sealed."

"And what will be the price?" asked Pahom.

"Our price is always the same: one thousand rubles a day."

Pahom did not understand.

"A day? What measure is that? How many acres would that be?"

"We do not know how to reckon it out," said the chief. "We sell it by the day. As much as you can go around on your feet in a day is yours, and the price is one thousand rubles a day."

Pahom was surprised.

"But in a day you can get around a large tract of land," he said.

The chief laughed.

"It will all be yours!" said he. "But there is one condition: If you don't return on the same day to the spot whence you started, your money is lost."

"But how am I to mark the way that I have gone?"

"Why, we shall go to any spot you like and stay there. You must start from that spot and make your round, taking a spade with you. Wherever you think necessary, make a mark. At every turning, dig a hole and pile up the turf; then afterward we will go around with a plow from hole to hole. You may make as large a circuit as you please, but before the sun sets you must return to the place you started from. All the land you cover will be yours."

Pahom was delighted. It was decided to start early next morning. They talked a while, and after drinking some more kumiss and eating some more mutton, they had tea again, and then the night came on. They gave Pahom a feather bed to sleep on, and the Bashkirs dispersed for the night, promising to assemble the next morning at day-

The Steppe in the Afternoon by Aleksei Kondratievich Savrasov. 1852 State Russian Museum, Leningrad

break and ride out before sunrise to the appointed spot.

7

Pahom lay on the feather bed, but could not sleep. He kept thinking about the land.

"What a large tract I'll mark off!" thought he, "I can easily do thirty-five miles in a day. The days are long now, and within a circuit of thirty-five miles what a lot of land there will be! I'll sell the poorer land or let it to peasants, but I'll pick out the best and farm it myself. I'll buy two ox teams and hire two more laborers. About a hundred and fifty acres shall be plowland, and I'll pasture cattle on the rest."

Pahom lay awake all night and dozed off only just before dawn. Hardly were his eyes closed when he had a dream. He thought he was lying in that same tent and heard somebody chuckling outside. He wondered who it could be, and rose and went out, and he saw the Bashkir chief sitting in front of the tent holding his sides and rolling about with laughter. Going nearer to the chief, Pahom asked, "What are you laughing at?" But he saw that it was no longer the chief but the grain dealer who had recently stopped at his house and had told him about the land. Just as Pahom was going to ask: "Have you been here long?" he saw that it was not the dealer, but the peasant who had come up from the Volga long ago to Pahom's old home. Then he saw that it was not the peasant either, but the Devil himself with hoofs and horns, sitting there and chuckling, and before him lay a man, prostrate on the ground, barefooted, with only trousers and a shirt on. And Pahom dreamed that he looked more attentively to see what sort of man it was lying there, and he saw that the man was dead, and that it was himself. Horror-struck, he awoke.

"What things one dreams about!" thought he.

Looking around he saw through the open door that the dawn was breaking.

"It's time to wake them up," thought he. "We ought to be starting."

He got up, roused his man (who was sleeping in his cart), bade him harness, and went to call the Bashkirs.

"It's time to go to the steppe to measure the land," he said.

The Bashkirs rose and assembled, and the chief

came, too. Then they began drinking kumiss again, and offered Pahom some tea, but he would not wait.

"If we are to go, let's go. It's high time," said he.

8

The Bashkirs got ready and they all started: some mounted on horses and some in carts. Pahom drove in his own small cart with his servant and took a spade with him. When they reached the steppe, the red dawn was beginning to kindle. They ascended a hillock (called by the Bashkirs a *shikhan*) and, dismounting from their carts and their horses, gathered in one spot. The chief came to Pahom and, stretching out his arm toward the plain:

"See," said he, "all this, as far as your eye can reach, is ours. You may have any part of it you like."

Pahom's eyes glistened; it was all virgin soil, as flat as the palm of your hand, as black as the seed of a poppy, and in the hollows different kinds of grasses grew breast-high.

The chief took off his fox-fur cap, placed it on the ground, and said:

"This will be the mark. Start from here, and return here again. All the land you go around shall be yours."

Pahom took out his money and put it on the cap. Then he took off his outer coat, remaining in his sleeveless undercoat. He unfastened his girdle and tied it tight below his stomach, put a little bag of bread into the breast of his coat, and, tying a flask of water to his girdle, he drew up the tops of his boots, took the spade from his man, and stood ready to start. He considered for some moments which way he had better go—it was tempting everywhere.

"No matter," he concluded, "I'll go toward the rising sun."

He turned his face to the east, stretched himself, and waited for the sun to appear above the rim.

"I must lose no time," he thought, "and it's easier walking while it's still cool."

The sun's rays had hardly flashed above the horizon when Pahom, carrying the spade over his shoulder, went down into the steppe.

Pahom started walking neither slowly nor quickly. After having gone a thousand yards he stopped, dug a hole, and placed pieces of turf one on another to make it more visible. Then he went on; and now that he had walked off his stiffness he quickened his pace. After a while he dug another hole.

Pahom looked back. The hillock could be distinctly seen in the sunlight, with the people on it, and the glittering iron rims of the cartwheels. At a rough guess Pahom concluded that he had walked three miles. It was growing warmer; he took off his undercoat, slung it across his shoulder, and went on again. It had grown quite warm now; he looked at the sun—it was time to think of breakfast.

"The first shift is done, but there are four in a day, and it's too soon yet to turn. But I'll just take off my boots," said he to himself.

He sat down, took off his boots, stuck them into his girdle, and went on. It was easy walking now.

"I'll go on for another three miles," thought he, "and then turn to the left. This spot is so fine that it would be a pity to lose it. The further one goes, the better the land seems."

He went straight on for a while, and when he looked around, the hillock was scarcely visible and the people on it looked like black ants, and he could just see something glistening there in the sun.

"Ah," thought Pahom, "I have gone far enough in this direction; it's time to turn. Besides, I'm in a regular sweat, and very thirsty."

He stopped, dug a large hole, and heaped up pieces of turf. Next he untied his flask, had a drink, and then turned sharply to the left. He went on and on; the grass was high, and it was very hot.

Pahom began to grow tired; he looked at the sun and saw that it was noon.

"Well," he thought, "I must have a rest."

He sat down, and ate some bread and drank some water; but he did not lie down, thinking that if he did he might fall asleep. After sitting a little while, he went on again. At first he walked easily; the food had strengthened him; but it had become terribly hot and he felt sleepy. Still he went on, thinking: "An hour to suffer, a lifetime to live."

He went a long way in this direction also, and was about to turn to the left again, when he perceived a damp hollow; "It would be a pity to leave that out," he thought. "Flax would do well there." So he went on past the hollow and dug a hole on the other side of it before he made a sharp turn. Pahom looked toward the hillock. The heat made the air hazy; it seemed to be quivering, and through the haze the people on the hillock could scarcely be seen.

"Ah," thought Pahom, "I have made the sides too long; I must make this one shorter." And he went along the third side, stepping faster. He looked at the sun: it was nearly halfway to the horizon, and he had not yet done two miles of the third side of the square. He was still ten miles from the goal.

"No," he thought, "though it will make my land lopsided, I must hurry back in a straight line now. I might go too far, and as it is I have a great deal of land."

So Pahom hurriedly dug a hole and turned straight toward the hillock.

9

Pahom went straight toward the hillock, but he now walked with difficulty. He was exhausted from the heat, his bare feet were cut and bruised, and his legs began to fail. He longed to rest, but it was impossible if he meant to get back before sunset. The sun waits for no man, and it was sinking lower and lower.

"Oh, Lord," he thought, "If only I have not blundered trying for too much! What if I am too late?"

He looked toward the hillock and at the sun. He was still far from his goal, and the sun was already near the rim of the sky.

Pahom walked on and on; it was very hard walking, but he went quicker and quicker. He pressed on, but was still far from the place. He began running, threw away his coat, his boots, his flask, and his cap, and kept only the spade which he used as a support.

"What am I to do?" he thought again. "I've grasped too much and ruined the whole affair. I can't get there before the sun sets."

And this fear made him still more breathless. Pahom kept on running; his soaking shirt and trousers stuck to him, and his mouth was parched. His breast was working like a blacksmith's bellows, his heart was beating like a hammer, and his legs were giving way as if they did not belong to him. Pahom was seized with terror lest he should die of the strain.

Though afraid of death, he could not stop. "After having run all that way they will call me a fool if I stop now," thought he.

And he ran on and on, and drew near and heard the Bashkirs yelling and shouting to him, and their cries inflamed his heart still more. He gathered his last strength and ran on.

The sun was close to the rim of the sky and, cloaked in mist, looked large, and red as blood. Now, yes, now, it was about to set! The sun was quite low, but he was also quite near his goal. Pahom could already see the people on the hillock waving their arms to make him hurry. He could see the fox-fur cap on the ground and the money in it, and the chief sitting on the ground holding his sides. And Pahom remembered his dream.

"There's plenty of land," thought he, "but will God let me live on it? I have lost my life, I have lost my life! Never will I reach that spot!"

Pahom looked at the sun, which had reached the earth: one side of it had already disappeared. With all his remaining strength he rushed on, bending his body forward so that his legs could hardly follow fast enough to keep him from falling. Just as he reached the hillock it suddenly grew dark. He looked up—the sun had already set!

He gave a cry: "All my labor has been in vain," thought he, and was about to stop, but he heard the Bashkirs still shouting and remembered that though to him, from below, the sun seemed to have set, they on the hillock could still see it. He took a long breath and ran up the hillock. It was still light there. He reached the top and saw the cap. Before it sat the chief, laughing and holding his sides. Again Pahom remembered his dream, and he uttered a cry: his legs gave way beneath him, he fell forward and reached the cap with his hands.

"Ah, that's a fine fellow!" exclaimed the chief.

"He has gained much land!"

Pahom's servant came running up and tried to raise him, but he saw that blood was flowing from his mouth. Pahom was dead.

The Bashkirs clicked their tongues to show their pity.

His servant picked up the spade and dug a grave long enough for Pahom to lie in, and buried him in it.

Six feet from his head to his heels was all he needed.

1886

THINK AND DISCUSS
Understanding
1. What contrast is presented at the opening of the story?
2. How does Pahom enter into the pact with the Devil?
3. What is the effect of Pahom's first purchase of land?
4. What does the Bashkir chief mean when he says the price of the land is one thousand rubles *a day?*
5. What is the moral of the story?

Analyzing
6. Why does Pahom keep moving to new land?
7. Tolstoy advocated the abolishment of private property rights. Who in this story represents this view? How does Tolstoy convey the benefits of such a stand?
8. Now that you have read the entire story, look again at the opening scene and first speech by Pahom's wife. In retrospect, how is her description of the advantages of life in the country ironical and how does it tie into the title and the final sentence of the story?

Extending
9. As you have seen in this unit, pacts with the Devil are a common motif in world literature. Compare and contrast the ways in which Tolstoy in this story and Goethe in *Faust* portray such pacts. Has Pahom made a "Faustian bargain"? (See pages 611–616.)
10. How does the conclusion of this folktale contrast with the ending of Pushkin's "The Bridegroom" (page 624)? Why do you think Tolstoy chose this type of ending?

11. Discuss how owning something can stimulate your desire for more, with the result that your purchases far exceed your actual need or even use for the product.

THINKING SKILLS
Generalizing
To generalize is to draw a general conclusion from particular information.

1. What evidence does the elder sister draw upon in reaching her conclusion that life in town is superior to life in the country?
2. Upon what information does the younger sister base her belief that country life is better?

COMPOSITION
Writing a Folk Tale
Write a "modern" folk tale or rewrite an old folk story in which you exemplify a moral teaching. Use the conventions of traditional folk tales, such as supernatural happenings and strong narrative emphasis rather than extensive character development.

Writing About Theme
Write an essay tracing Tolstoy's use of the folk motif of the pact with the Devil. Be sure to discuss the terms of the pact, the "Evil One's" influence on the peasants' negotiations for communal land to be bought by the village council, and Pahom's dream in which the devil appears in various guises. Your conclusion should explain the thematic significance of Pahom's dream in relation to his death. See "Writing About Theme" in the Writer's Handbook.

678 *Romanticism and Realism*

A recluse in a white dress, wandering through her family's flower garden or shut away in her room, refusing to see her visitors; this is the romanticized view of the American poet Emily Dickinson. But it is the originality and power of her verse that ranks her as an outstanding nineteenth-century writer. Emily Dickinson was born in Amherst, Massachusetts, and lived and died there, rarely leaving her home after age thirty. Her stern father, a lawyer, congressman, and treasurer of Amherst College, dominated the family. Many biographers stress his influence upon Emily, whose description of him says much: "His heart was pure and terrible."

Dickinson attended Amherst Academy from 1840 to 1847 and then Mt. Holyoke Female Seminary. Although she was religious, she did not accept the doctrine of the New England church. Attempts by the headmistress of the seminary to convert her and a period of illness led to Dickinson's withdrawal after one year. After her formal education ended, frail health and personal choice led her to a secluded life. However, she did keep in touch with friends, mainly through letters, and she maintained close ties with her family. Much speculation has been made about a mysterious love in Dickinson's life since many of her poems are addressed to an unidentified but obviously beloved "Master." Most of the conjecture has centered on Rev. Charles Wadsworth, a clergyman with whom she corresponded and who visited her twice in Amherst. However, as one biographer notes, "Emily Dickinson's understanding of the human heart is not to be explained in terms of any one person."

Dickinson's verse became her "letter to the world," but only a few of her poems were published during her lifetime. Writing in virtual isolation, she turned for advice to literary critic Thomas Wentworth Higginson in 1862, sending him four poems and asking him, "Are you too deeply occupied to say if my verse is alive?" Higginson encouraged her through a correspondence that continued for the rest of her life.

Dickinson wrote 1,775 poems, noted for their aphoristic style, slant rhymes, and eccentric grammar. She shared some of them with friends and relatives, but her secretive nature kept even her immediate family from realizing the extent of her writing. Initial drafts were scribbled on scraps of paper, and later most of them were copied in ink on sheets of stationery which she assembled into packets. It was such packets, containing some seven hundred poems, that so surprised her beloved sister Lavinia when she found them locked in a box after Emily's death in 1886. Dickinson's complete works were not published until 1955.

This Is My Letter to the World

This is my letter to the World
That never wrote to Me—
The simple News that Nature told—
With tender Majesty

5 Her Message is committed
To Hands I cannot see—
For love of Her—Sweet—countrymen—
Judge tenderly—of Me

c. 1862   1890

"Hope" Is the Thing with Feathers

"Hope" is the thing with feathers—
That perches in the soul—
And sings the tune without the words—
And never stops—at all—

5 And sweetest—in the Gale—is heard—
And sore must be the storm—
That could abash the little Bird
That kept so many warm—

10 I've heard it in the chillest land—
And on the strangest Sea—
Yet, never, in Extremity,
It asked a crumb—of Me.

c. 1861   1891

Tell All the Truth But Tell It Slant

Tell all the Truth but tell it slant—
Success in Circuit lies
Too bright for our infirm Delight
The Truth's superb surprise
5 As Lightning to the Children eased
With explanation kind
The Truth must dazzle gradually
Or every man be blind—

c. 1865   1945

I Like to See It Lap the Miles

I like to see it lap the Miles—
And lick the Valleys up—
And stop to feed itself at Tanks—
And then—prodigious step

5 Around a Pile of Mountains—
And supercilious peer
In Shanties—by the sides of Roads—
And then a Quarry pare

To fit its Ribs
10 And crawl between
Complaining all the while
In horrid—hooting stanza—
Then chase itself down Hill—

And neigh like Boanerges[1]—
15 Then—punctual as a Star
Stop—docile and omnipotent
At its own stable door—

c. 1862   1891

---

1. **Boanerges** (bō′ə nėr′jĕz), a loud preacher or orator.

Because I Could Not Stop for Death

Because I could not stop for Death—
He kindly stopped for me—
The Carriage held but just Ourselves—
And Immortality.

5 We slowly drove—He knew no haste
And I had put away
My labor and my leisure too,
For His Civility—

We passed the School, where Children strove
10 At Recess—in the Ring—
We passed the Fields of Gazing Grain—
We passed the Setting Sun—

Or rather—He passed Us—
The Dews drew quivering and chill—
15 For only Gossamer, my Gown—
My Tippet—only Tulle—

We paused before a House that seemed
A Swelling of the Ground—
The Roof was scarcely visible—
20 The Cornice—in the Ground—

Since then—'tis Centuries—and yet
Feels shorter than the Day
I first surmised the Horses' Heads
Were toward Eternity—

c. 1863   1890

Meditation by George Newell Bowers. 1889.
Museum of Fine Arts, Springfield, Massachusetts

Emily Dickinson

THINK AND DISCUSS
Understanding
1. In "Tell All the Truth But Tell It Slant," what reason does Dickinson give for her lack of directness?
2. What things are being compared in the extended **metaphor** of "I Like to See It Lap the Miles"?
3. In "Because I Could Not Stop for Death," how is death presented?

Analyzing
4. One of Dickinson's favorite techniques is the use of the extended metaphor. In " 'Hope' Is the Thing with Feathers," (**a**) what is the basic metaphor in lines 1 and 2? (**b**) Why is the song without words? (**c**) What do the gale and storm represent? (**d**) How strong is hope? (**e**) Why is the word *crumb* in the last line appropriate?
5. In Dickinson's poetry, a common **rhythm** is alternating iambic tetrameter (four foot) and trimeter (three foot) lines. An iambic foot consists of an unaccented syllable followed by an accented one. In "I Like to See It Lap the Miles," with its fairly regular meter, what does she achieve by varying the accent pattern with the initial word of the next to the last line ("Stop")?
6. Dickinson often used slant **rhyme,** frequently found in hymns and folk poetry. This rhyme scheme employs **consonance** for sound similarity in words at the end of lines. The vowel sounds of the words are not quite identical, but they are followed by the same consonant sound: for example, "soul/all." Which poem has this rhyming pattern for the words ending its even numbered lines in *all* its quatrains (stanzas with four lines)?

Extending
7. Compare the treatment of a nineteenth-century **symbol** of modern technology in Dickinson's "I Like to See It Lap the Miles" with Whitman's "To a Locomotive in Winter."

VOCABULARY
Antonyms
Each numbered item consists of a word in capital letters, followed by four words designated by letters. Choose the word that is most nearly opposite in meaning to the word in capital letters. Write the letter and word on a separate sheet of paper.

1. ABASH: (**a**) hit; (**b**) halt; (**c**) encourage; (**d**) thrill.
2. PRODIGIOUS: (**a**) small; (**b**) pitiful; (**c**) immense; (**d**) profitable.
3. SUPERCILIOUS: (**a**) proud; (**b**) disconcerting; (**c**) silly; (**d**) humble.
4. DOCILE: (**a**) delicate; (**b**) dumb; (**c**) disobedient; (**d**) delirious.
5. OMNIPOTENT: (**a**) oppressive; (**b**) powerless; (**c**) insignificant; (**d**) lethargic.

COMPOSITION
Writing Metaphorically
Write a short poem or a paragraph in which you use an indirect approach to your topic through a metaphor. In other words, make your reader solve the riddle as Dickinson does in much of her poetry.

Defending a Poet's Style
Emily Dickinson's **style,** with its eccentric grammar and irregular form, was too innovative for some readers. Even her friend Thomas Wentworth Higginson initially suggested that she make revisions that would result in a more conventional style. The young poet politely ignored these suggestions. However, since only a few poems were published before her death and she left no instructions concerning the rest, editors felt free to correct her work. Individual words, punctuation, and rhyme were changed to produce "more polished" verse, changes that actually marred the power of her poetry. Write a letter defending Dickinson's style to those people who chose to revise her poems. See "Writing to Persuade an Audience" in the Writer's Handbook.

Samuel Langhorne Clemens, who used the pseudonym Mark Twain, has been called the "Lincoln of American literature." Ernest Hemingway went so far as to say that "all modern American literature comes from one book by Mark Twain called *Huckleberry Finn*." This great humorist, journalist, lecturer, and novelist was the first American writer to successfully employ the vernacular (everyday, informal speech) as the narrative medium in an important literary work.

Shortly after Twain's birth, the family moved to Hannibal, Missouri, on the banks of the Mississippi River. His schooling ended at age twelve when his father died. Twain became a printer's apprentice and worked for his brother Orion who was the editor of a local newspaper. He later worked for newspapers in the East, but returned to Missouri in 1857. At that time he fulfilled the dream of his youth: he became a riverboat pilot on the Mississippi River. His pen name is taken from a cry meaning "two fathoms deep" used in river navigation. When the Civil War closed all commercial traffic on the river, Twain joined the Confederate Army with some friends, but managed to get himself discharged in two weeks. He followed his brother to Nevada, where he tried prospecting for a brief time and then continued his journalism.

Moving farther west, Twain arrived in San Francisco in 1865. While there, he wrote "The Celebrated Jumping Frog of Calaveras County," a humorous story that won him national fame. Hired by newspapers to be a travel correspondent, he used his Western humor to enliven accounts of his trips to Hawaii, Europe, and the Holy Land. These travels provided materials for his lecture tours and for the very popular work *The Innocents Abroad* (1869). By 1870, when he married Olivia Langdon, he was editor of the Buffalo *Express*. They moved to Hartford in 1871 where Twain produced the famous *The Adventures of Tom Sawyer* (1876), *Life on the Mississippi* (1883), and *The Adventures of Huckleberry Finn* (1884). Twain's business affairs were less successful. He was involved in two financial ventures that promised great fortune, but which resulted in bankruptcy: an impractical typesetting machine and a publishing company. In order to pay back his debts, Twain made a world lecture tour.

Always quick to satirize humanity's foibles, Twain became more pessimistic about life after a series of personal tragedies, the deaths of his wife and two daughters. Although he continued to travel and write until his death, his late works are quite bitter in tone.

In 1875, Twain's articles on the "old Mississippi days of steamboating glory and grandeur" appeared in the *Atlantic Monthly*. He later expanded these autobiographical pieces into a book, *Life on the Mississippi*. The following excerpt demonstrates his characteristic frontier humor.

from Life on the Mississippi

Mark Twain

hen I was a boy, there was but one permanent ambition among my comrades in our village on the west bank of the Mississippi River. That was, to be a steamboatman. We had transient ambitions of other sorts, but they were only transient. When a circus came and went, it left us all burning to become clowns; the first Negro minstrel show that ever came to our section left us all suffering to try that kind of life; now and then we had a hope that if we lived and were good, God would permit us to be pirates. These ambitions faded out, each in its turn; but the ambition to be a steamboatman always remained.

Once a day a cheap, gaudy packet[1] arrived upward from St. Louis, and another downward from Keokuk.[2] Before these events, the day was glorious with expectancy; after them, the day was a dead and empty thing. Not only the boys, but the whole village, felt this. After all these years I can picture that old time to myself now, just as it was then: the white town drowsing in the sunshine of a summer's morning; the streets empty, or pretty nearly so; one or two clerks sitting in front of the Water Street stores, with their splint-bottomed chairs[3] tilted back against the walls, chins on breasts, hats slouched over their faces, asleep—with shingle-shavings enough around to show what broke them down; a sow, and a litter of pigs loafing along the sidewalk, doing a good business in watermelon rinds and seeds; two or three lonely little freight piles scattered about the levee; a pile of skids[4] on the slope of the stone-paved wharf, and the fragrant town drunkard asleep in the shadow of them; two or three wood flats[5] at

the head of the wharf, but nobody to listen to the peaceful lapping of the wavelets against them; the great Mississippi, the majestic, the magnificent Mississippi, rolling its mile-wide tide along, shining in the sun; the dense forest away on the other side; the point above the town, and the point below, bounding the river-glimpse and turning it into a sort of sea, and withal a very still and brilliant and lonely one. Presently a film of dark smoke appears above one of those remote points: instantly a Negro drayman,[6] famous for his quick eye and prodigious voice, lifts up the cry, "S-t-e-a-m-boat a-comin'!" and the scene changes! The town drunkard stirs, the clerks wake up, a furious clatter of drays follows, every house and store pours out a human contribution, and all in a twinkling the dead town is alive and moving. Drays, carts, men, boys, all go hurrying from many quarters to a common center, the wharf. Assembled there, the people fasten their eyes upon the coming boat as upon a wonder they are seeing for the first time. And the boat *is* rather a handsome sight, too. She is long and sharp and trim and pretty; she has two tall, fancy-topped chimneys, with a gilded device of some kind swung between

---

1. *packet,* a boat that carries mail, passengers, and goods regularly on a fixed route.
2. *Keokuk,* a Mississippi River town in the southeastern corner of Iowa, about fifty miles above Hannibal.
3. *splint-bottomed chairs,* chairs with seats woven of thin strips (splints) of wood.
4. *skids,* timber, frame, etc., on which something rests, or on which something heavy may slide.
5. *wood flats,* small flat-bottomed boats.
6. *drayman,* person who drives a dray, a cart or wagon for carrying heavy loads.

The Mississippi in Time of Peace, a lithograph by Fanny Palmer published by
Currier & Ives. 1865. Museum of the City of New York

them; a fanciful pilot house, all glass and ginger-bread, perched on top of the texas deck[7] behind them; the paddle boxes[8] are gorgeous with a picture or with gilded rays above the boat's name; the boiler deck, the hurricane deck,[9] and the texas deck are fenced and ornamented with clean white railings; there is a flag gallantly flying from the jack staff;[10] the furnace doors are open and the fires glaring bravely; the upper decks are black with passengers; the captain stands by the big bell, calm, imposing, the envy of all; great volumes of the blackest smoke are rolling and tumbling out of the chimneys—a husbanded grandeur created with a bit of pitch pine just before arriving at a town; the crew are grouped on the forecastle; the broad stage[11] is run far-out over the port bow, and a deck hand stands picturesquely on the end of it

with a coil of rope in his hand; the pent steam is screaming through the gauge cocks; the captain lifts his hand, a bell rings, the wheels stop; then they turn back, churning the water to foam, and the steamer is at rest. Then such a scramble as

---

7. texas deck. The texas is a range of staterooms adjacent to the pilot house reserved for officers. The texas deck adjoins these living quarters.

8. paddle boxes, the wooden coverings built over the upper part of the paddle wheels which propelled the steamer.

9. the boiler deck, the hurricane deck, the boiler deck is that part of the upper deck immediately over the boilers; the hurricane deck is the topmost deck.

10. jack staff, a short pole erected at the front of the vessel.

11. forecastle . . . stage. The forecastle is an upper deck at the forward part of the ship; the stage is a stage-plank or gangplank.

there is to get aboard, and to get ashore, and to take in freight and to discharge freight, all at one and the same time; and such a yelling and cursing as the mates facilitate it all with! Ten minutes later the steamer is under way again, with no flag on the jack staff and no black smoke issuing from the chimneys. After ten more minutes the town is dead again, and the town drunkard asleep by the skids once more.

My father was a justice of the peace, and I supposed he possessed the power of life and death over all men, and could hang anybody that offended him. This was distinction enough for me as a general thing; but the desire to be a steamboatman kept intruding, nevertheless. I first wanted to be a cabin boy, so that I could come out with a white apron on and shake a tablecloth over the side, where all my old comrades could see me; later I thought I would rather be the deckhand who stood on the end of the stage-plank with the coil of rope in his hand, because he was particularly conspicuous. But these were only daydreams —they were too heavenly to be contemplated as real possibilities.

By and by one of our boys went away. He was not heard of for a long time. At last he turned up as apprentice engineer or "striker" on a steamboat. This thing shook the bottom out of all my Sunday-school teachings. That boy had been notoriously worldly, and I just the reverse; yet he was exalted to this eminence, and I left in obscurity and misery. There was nothing generous about this fellow in his greatness. He would always manage to have a rusty bolt to scrub while his boat tarried at our town, and he would sit on the inside guard[12] and scrub it, where we all could see him and envy him and loathe him. And whenever his boat was laid up he would come home and swell around the town in his blackest and greasiest clothes, so that nobody could help remembering that he was a steamboatman; and he used all sorts of steamboat technicalities in his talk, as if he were so used to them that he forgot common people could not understand them. He would speak of the "labboard"[13] side of a horse in an easy, natural way that would make one wish he was dead. And he was always talking about "St. Looy" like an old

citizen; he would refer casually to occasions when he was "coming down Fourth Street," or when he was "Passing by the Planter's House," or when there was a fire and he took a turn on the brakes of "the old Big Missouri"; and then he would go on and lie about how many towns the size of ours were burned down there that day. Two or three of the boys had long been persons of consideration among us because they had been to St. Louis once and had a vague general knowledge of its wonders, but the day of their glory was over now. They lapsed into a humble silence, and learned to disappear when the ruthless cub engineer approached. This fellow had money, too, and hair oil. Also an ignorant silver watch and a showy brass watch chain. He wore a leather belt and used no suspenders. If ever a youth was cordially admired and hated by his comrades, this one was. No girl could withstand his charms. He "cut out" every boy in the village. When his boat blew up at last, it diffused a tranquil contentment among us such as we had not known for months. But when he came home the next week, alive, renowned, and appeared in church all battered up and bandaged, a shining hero, stared at and wondered over by everybody, it seemed to us that the partiality of Providence for an undeserving reptile had reached a point where it was open to criticism.

This creature's career could produce but one result, and it speedily followed. Boy after boy managed to get on the river. The minister's son became an engineer. The doctor's and the postmaster's sons became mud clerks;[14] the wholesale liquor dealer's son became a barkeeper on a boat; four sons of the chief merchant, and two sons of the county judge, became pilots. Pilot was the grandest position of all. The pilot, even in those days of trivial wages, had a princely salary—from a hundred and fifty to two hundred and fifty dollars a month, and no board to pay. Two months of his wages would pay a preacher's salary for a

12. *inside guard,* part of the steamboat's deck which curves out over the paddle wheel.
13. *"lab-board,"* larboard, the left or port side of a ship.
14. *mud clerks,* second clerks on river steamers, whose duty it was to go ashore at unimportant stops, often mere mudbanks, to receive or check off freight.

year. Now some of us were left disconsolate. We could not get on the river—at least our parents would not let us.

So, by and by, I ran away. I said I would never come home again till I was a pilot and could come in glory. But somehow I could not manage it. I went meekly aboard a few of the boats that lay packed together like sardines at the long St. Louis wharf, and humbly inquired for the pilots, but got only a cold shoulder and short words from mates and clerks. I had to make the best of this sort of treatment for the time being, but I had comforting daydreams of a future when I should be a great and honored pilot, with plenty of money, and could kill some of these mates and clerks and pay for them.

1874   1875

THINK AND DISCUSS
Understanding
1. Why was being a steamboat pilot the ambition of all the boys in the village?
2. How does the picture of the village before the boat's arrival contrast with the scene immediately following its appearance?
3. Describe the narrator as a youth.

Analyzing
4. What makes the description of the village and river in the second paragraph so effective?
5. Why is the steamboat described in such detail?
6. A typical characteristic of Western humor is exaggeration. Find two examples of Twain's use of this device.
7. Cite two humorous examples each of (a) colloquial language (everyday or conversational speech) and (b) inflated diction (formal language used in an informal context).

Extending
8. In Whitman's "There Was a Child Went Forth" (page 654), he says that an object the child sees becomes part of him. If Whitman had written about the young boy depicted in this excerpt, what elements would he have enumerated as making a permanent impression upon the youth?

REVIEWING: Point of View H𝟸
See Handbook of Literary Terms, p. 963.

Point of view is the perspective from which a story is told. The narration may be omniscient or limited; first person or third person. First-person point of view is necessarily limited in that the narrator relates the story through the eyes of one person. Twain often used the distorted perceptions of a limited narrator to create humor.

1. Who is the narrator of this selection?
2. How does the author convey the feelings of a young adolescent without speaking directly in the boy's voice (as he does in *Huckleberry Finn*)?
3. Give two examples of distorted perceptions that make this piece humorous.

COMPOSITION
Writing a Speech
Twain received an honorary degree from Oxford University in England. (He was so delighted that he even wore his hooded robe later at his daughter's wedding.) Assume his identity and write a short speech accepting the degree. Keep in mind your youthful ambitions, limited formal schooling, fame as a humorous speaker, and your audience.

Writing a Newspaper Report
Write a straight newspaper report about the explosion of the steamboat. Name the local young man who was hurt and describe his position on the crew and the extent of his injuries. While you will have to use your imagination to supply some of these details, be objective in **tone** and relate only what a reporter would be able to ascertain through interviews or eyewitness accounts.

Maupassant (mō′pə sänt), nineteenth-century French Realist and master of the short story, was born and spent his early life in Normandy. His parents separated when he was eleven, and he lived with his very cultured mother who tutored him until he was thirteen. Following three years at a seminary near Rouen (he was expelled), he attended public school. After graduation, he served in the Franco-Prussian War and later became a civil servant, but his ambition was to become a writer. The famous author Gustave Flaubert, a friend of Madame de Maupassant, became the young Maupassant's mentor. With Flaubert's strict guidance, Maupassant underwent a rigorous regimen, developing his literary talents for nearly seven years while earning a living by working in various government ministries. In 1875, he began associating socially with Emile Zola and some other Naturalistic authors. They published a volume of short stories in 1880 in which a Maupassant story first appeared. Its great success established the author as an outstanding writer, and his many subsequent works (including some three hundred short stories, six novels, and a great deal of journalism) sustained this reputation.

Maupassant's literary work made him a rich man. He enjoyed his affluent life, but he suffered from ill health, including eye problems, migraine headaches, and hallucinations. Fearing that he was going insane as his brother had, he traveled extensively, seeking relief and medical help. His efforts were futile, and when his worst fears were realized, he tried to commit suicide. He spent the last eighteen months of his life in an insane asylum where he died.

Maupassant's early life in Normandy, his experiences in the Franco-Prussian War, and his long stint as a government worker provided the subjects for his writing. The best-known features of his **style** in short fiction are the underlying pessimism, ironic **tone,** and surprise endings, which have influenced many modern short-story authors.

See STEREOTYPE in the Handbook of Literary Terms, page 972.

The False Gems

Guy de Maupassant *translated by* **M. Walter Dunne**

. Lantin had met the young woman at a *soirée*, at the home of the assistant chief of his bureau, and at first sight had fallen madly in love with her.

She was the daughter of a country physician who had died some months previously. She had come to live in Paris, with her mother, who visited much among her acquaintances, in the hope of making a favorable marriage for her daughter. They were poor and honest, quiet and unaffected.

The young girl was a perfect type of the virtuous woman whom every sensible young man dreams of one day winning for life. Her simple beauty had the charm of angelic modesty, and the imperceptible smile which constantly hovered about her lips seemed to be the reflection of a pure and lovely soul. Her praises resounded on every side. People never tired of saying: "Happy the man who wins her love! He could not find a better wife."

Now M. Lantin enjoyed a snug little income of $700, and, thinking he could safely assume the responsibilities of matrimony, proposed to this model young girl and was accepted.

He was unspeakably happy with her; she governed his household so cleverly and economically that they seemed to live in luxury. She lavished the most delicate attentions on her husband, coaxed and fondled him, and the charm of her presence was so great that six years after their marriage M. Lantin discovered that he loved his wife even more than during the first days of their honeymoon.

He only felt inclined to blame her for two things: her love of the theater, and a taste for false jewelry. Her friends (she was acquainted with some officers' wives) frequently procured for her a box at the theater, often for the first representations of the new plays; and her husband was obliged to accompany her, whether he willed or not, to these amusements, though they bored him excessively after a day's labor at the office.

After a time, M. Lantin begged his wife to get some lady of her acquaintance to accompany her. She was at first opposed to such an arrangement; but, after much persuasion on his part, she finally consented—to the infinite delight of her husband.

Now, with her love for the theater came also the desire to adorn her person. True, her costumes remained as before, simple, and in the most correct taste; but she soon began to ornament her ears with huge rhinestones which glittered and sparkled like real diamonds. Around her neck she wore strings of false pearls, and on her arms bracelets of imitation gold.

Her husband frequently remonstrated with her, saying:

"My dear, as you cannot afford to buy real diamonds, you ought to appear adorned with your beauty and modesty alone, which are the rarest ornaments of your sex."

But she would smile sweetly, and say:

"What can I do? I am so fond of jewelry. It is my only weakness. We cannot change our natures."

Then she would roll the pearl necklaces around her fingers, and hold up the bright gems for her husband's admiration, gently coaxing him:

"Look! are they not lovely? One would swear they were real."

M. Lantin would then answer, smilingly:

Interrupted Reading by Jean-Baptiste Camille Corot. c. 1870. The Art Institute of Chicago

"You have Bohemian tastes, my dear."

Often of an evening, when they were enjoying a tête-à-tête by the fireside, she would place on the tea table the leather box containing the "trash," as M. Lantin called it. She would examine the false gems with a passionate attention as though they were in some way connected with a deep and secret joy, and she often insisted on passing a necklace around her husband's neck, and laughing heartily would exclaim: "How droll you look!" Then she would throw herself into his arms and kiss him affectionately.

One evening in the winter she attended the opera, and on her return was chilled through and through. The next morning she coughed, and eight days later she died of inflammation of the lungs.

M. Lantin's despair was so great that his hair became white in one month. He wept unceasingly; his heart was torn with grief, and his mind was haunted by the remembrance, the smile, the voice—by every charm of his beautiful, dead wife.

Time, the healer, did not assuage his grief. Often during office hours, while his colleagues were discussing the topics of the day, his eyes would suddenly fill with tears, and he would give vent to his grief in heartrending sobs. Everything in his wife's room remained as before her decease; and here he was wont to seclude himself daily and think of her who had been his treasure—the joy of his existence.

But life soon became a struggle. His income, which in the hands of his wife had covered all household expenses, was now no longer sufficient for his own immediate wants; and he wondered how she could have managed to buy such excellent wines, and such rare delicacies, things which he could no longer procure with his modest resources.

He incurred some debts and was soon reduced to absolute poverty. One morning, finding himself without a cent in his pocket, he resolved to sell something, and, immediately, the thought occurred to him of disposing of his wife's paste jewels. He cherished in his heart a sort of rancor against the false gems. They had always irritated him in the past, and the very sight of them spoiled somewhat the memory of his lost darling.

To the last days of her life, she had continued to make purchases; bringing home new gems almost every evening. He decided to sell the heavy necklace which she seemed to prefer, and which, he thought, ought to be worth about six or seven francs; for although paste it was, nevertheless, of very fine workmanship.

He put it in his pocket and started out in search of a jeweler's shop. He entered the first one he saw; feeling a little ashamed to expose his misery, and also to offer such a worthless article for sale.

"Sir," said he to the merchant, "I would like to know what this is worth."

The man took the necklace, examined it, called his clerk and made some remarks in an undertone; then he put the ornament back on the counter, and looked at it from a distance to judge of the effect.

M. Lantin was annoyed by all this detail and was on the point of saying: "Oh! I know well enough it is not worth anything," when the jeweler said: "Sir, that necklace is worth from twelve to fifteen thousand francs; but I could not buy it unless you tell me now whence it comes."

The widower opened his eyes wide and remained gaping, not comprehending the merchant's meaning. Finally he stammered: "You say —are you sure?" The other replied dryly: "You can search elsewhere and see if anyone will offer you more. I consider it worth fifteen thousand at the most. Come back here if you cannot do better."

M. Lantin, beside himself with astonishment, took up the necklace and left the store. He wished time for reflection.

Once outside, he felt inclined to laugh, and said

to himself: "The fool! Had I only taken him at his word! That jeweler cannot distinguish real diamonds from paste."

A few minutes after, he entered another store in the Rue de la Paix. As soon as the proprietor glanced at the necklace, he cried out:

"Ah, *parbleu!* I know it well; it was bought here."

M. Lantin was disturbed, and asked:

"How much is it worth?"

"Well, I sold it for twenty thousand francs. I am willing to take it back for eighteen thousand when you inform me, according to our legal formality, how it comes to be in your possession."

This time M. Lantin was dumbfounded. He replied:

"But—but—examine it well. Until this moment I was under the impression that it was paste."

Said the jeweler:

"What is your name, sir?"

"Lantin—I am in the employ of the Minister of the Interior. I live at No. 16 Rue des Martyrs."

The merchant looked through his books, found the entry, and said: "That necklace was sent to Mme. Lantin's address, 16 Rue des Martyrs, July 20, 1876."

The two men looked into each other's eyes—the widower speechless with astonishment, the jeweler scenting a thief. The latter broke the silence by saying:

"Will you leave this necklace here for twenty-four hours? I will give you a receipt."

"Certainly," answered M. Lantin, hastily. Then, putting the ticket in his pocket, he left the store.

He wandered aimlessly through the streets, his mind in a state of dreadful confusion. He tried to reason, to understand. His wife could not afford to purchase such a costly ornament. Certainly not. But, then, it must have been a present!—a present!—a present from whom? Why was it given her?

He stopped and remained standing in the middle of the street. A horrible doubt entered his mind—she? Then all the other gems must have been presents, too! The earth seemed to tremble beneath him—the tree before him was falling

—throwing up his arms, he fell to the ground, unconscious. He recovered his senses in a pharmacy into which the passers-by had taken him, and was then taken to his home. When he arrived he shut himself up in his room and wept until nightfall. Finally, overcome with fatigue, he threw himself on the bed, where he passed an uneasy, restless night.

The following morning he arose and prepared to go to the office. It was hard to work after such a shock. He sent a letter to his employer requesting to be excused. Then he remembered that he had to return to the jeweler's. He did not like the idea; but he could not leave the necklace with that man. So he dressed and went out.

It was a lovely day; a clear blue sky smiled on the busy city below, and men of leisure were strolling about with their hands in their pockets.

Observing them, M. Lantin said to himself: "The rich, indeed, are happy. With money it is possible to forget even the deepest sorrow. One can go where one pleases, and in travel find that distraction which is the surest cure for grief. Oh! if I were only rich!"

He began to feel hungry, but his pocket was empty. He again remembered the necklace. Eighteen thousand francs! Eighteen thousand francs! What a sum!

He soon arrived in the Rue de la Paix, opposite the jeweler's. Eighteen thousand francs! Twenty times he resolved to go in, but shame kept him back. He was hungry, however—very hungry, and had not a cent in his pocket. He decided quickly, ran across the street in order not to have time for reflection, and entered the store.

The proprietor immediately came forward and politely offered him a chair; the clerks glanced at him knowingly.

"I have made inquiries, M. Lantin," said the jeweler, "and if you are still resolved to dispose of the gems, I am ready to pay you the price I offered."

"Certainly, sir" stammered M. Lantin.

Whereupon the proprietor took from a drawer eighteen large bills, counted and handed them to M. Lantin, who signed a receipt and with a trembling hand put the money into his pocket.

As he was about to leave the store, he turned toward the merchant, who still wore the same knowing smile, and lowering his eyes, said:

"I have—I have other gems which I have received from the same source. Will you buy them also?"

The merchant bowed: "Certainly, sir."

M. Lantin said gravely: "I will bring them to you." An hour later he returned with the gems.

The large diamond earrings were worth twenty thousand francs; the bracelets thirty-five thousand; the rings, sixteen thousand; a set of emeralds and sapphires, fourteen thousand; a gold chain with solitaire pendant, forty thousand—making the sum of one hundred and forty-three thousand francs.

The jeweler remarked, jokingly:

"There was a person who invested all her earnings in precious stones."

M. Lantin replied, seriously:

"It is only another way of investing one's money."

That day he lunched at Voisin's and drank wine worth twenty francs a bottle. Then he hired a carriage and made a tour of the Bois, and as he scanned the various turn-outs with a contemptuous air he could hardly refrain from crying out to the occupants:

"I, too, am rich!—I am worth two hundred thousand francs."

Suddenly he thought of his employer. He drove up to the office, and entered gaily, saying:

"Sir, I have come to resign my position. I have just inherited three hundred thousand francs."

He shook hands with his former colleagues and confided to them some of his projects for the future; then he went off to dine at the Café Anglais.

He seated himself beside a gentleman of aristocratic bearing, and during the meal informed the latter confidentially that he had just inherited a fortune of four hundred thousand francs.

For the first time in his life he was not bored at the theater, and spent the remainder of the night in a gay frolic.

Six months afterward he married again. His second wife was a very virtuous woman, with a violent temper. She caused him much sorrow.

THINK AND DISCUSS

Understanding

1. What is the relationship between Lantin and his wife?
2. The schemes of women form a recurrent **theme** in Maupassant's work. What hints are given that things are not what the husband believes them to be?
3. Why does Lantin sell his wife's jewels?

Analyzing

4. Why is Monsieur Lantin's wife not named in the story?
5. How deep is the husband's grief? What kind of comment is Maupassant making about human nature through this point?
6. What is Lantin's reaction to his newfound fortune?
7. Explain Maupassant's use of **irony** in the concluding paragraph.

Extending

8. Maupassant was Flaubert's apprentice. Do you see any similarity in the ways that character is revealed in this story and the excerpt from *Madame Bovary* on pages 661–666?

APPLYING: Stereotype HZ
See Handbook of Literary Terms, p. 972.

A **stereotype** is a fixed, generalized image of a character, setting, or plot. The mad scientist, the haunted house, the rags-to-riches story are all examples of familiar stereotypical elements in fiction. While bad writers may employ stereotypes through indifference or simple lack of talent, good writers may use them intentionally, to serve, for example, as foils to more fully developed characters or for satirical purposes.

1. What stereotype is presented in the beginning of "The False Gems"?
2. What purpose does Maupassant have in employing this stereotype?

COMPOSITION ◄●▬

Extending the Story

Write an expanded version of this story or a sequel to it in which you describe the future of Lantin's second marriage. Keep in mind Lantin's view of an ideal wife found in the first part of the story and the description of the second wife given in the last paragraph. You may wish to give your version an ironic twist.

Writing About Satire

One of the basic features of Maupassant's fiction is his **satire** of the behavior and attitudes of the French middle class. "The False Gems," for example, ridicules the middle-class vision of the ideal wife. In a paper of three or four paragraphs, examine Maupassant's satirical approach in this story, discussing his use of irony and the **tone** of his satirical portrait of Mme. Lantin. See "Writing About Irony and Satire" in the Writer's Handbook.

ENRICHMENT

Comparing Stories

Locate and read Maupassant's "The Necklace" which was written after "The False Gems." Note the way jewelry is used in each story. Then locate and read Henry James's tale "Paste." James commented that he created his own story by "transposing the terms" of Maupassant's "The Necklace." Compare and contrast the two stories by Maupassant with "Paste."

The Study of Comparative Language

Latin, Greek, and Hebrew were the ancient languages studied by Medieval, Renaissance, and Neoclassical scholars. It was not until near the end of the eighteenth century that another significant ancient language was discovered by Europeans.

Comparative linguists at this time noted that some languages were so closely related to others that it could not be mere chance or coincidence. The linguists concluded that these languages must have descended from a common original.

In the 1780s, when the English had been in India only a few decades, British scholars began studying Sanskrit, the classical language of ancient India. The similarities of some of its basic words to Greek and Latin were so striking that a new theory of comparative language came about. This theory proposed that Sanskrit and the European languages comprised a single "family" of languages. This new linguistic grouping was called the "Indo-European" languages.

The writer who popularized this theory was a German, Friedrich von Schlegel. In 1808 he published *The Language and Wisdom of the Hindus*, in which he claimed that Greek and Latin and virtually all the European languages were descended from Sanskrit. Schlegel's book provided a tremendous impetus to language study. It prompted another German, twenty-five-year-old Franz Bopp, to found the new science of comparative grammar with his 1816 book *On the Conjugational System of the Sanskrit Language in Comparison with the Greek, Latin, Persian, and Germanic Languages*.

A third German, Jacob Grimm, endorsed Schlegel's idea in his *German Grammar*, published in four volumes between 1819 and 1837. In the twentieth century, however, not many students of comparative language accept Sanskrit as the ancestor of European languages. Instead, current scholarship usually contends that Sanskrit and the European languages are descended from Proto-Indo-European, a prehistoric language. It was probably first spoken in the area northeast of the Black Sea, on the south Russian steppe.

Jacob Grimm became interested in comparative language study through his extensive work in the field of folklore. With his younger brother Wilhelm, he collected hundreds of German folk tales and published them in their famous collection in 1812. Both brothers had a thorough knowledge of most of the Indo-European languages, including Sanskrit. They were among the first scholars to point out the similarities in folk tales of various cultures.

The importance of the Grimm brothers' contribution to language study can hardly be exaggerated. They worked together for fifty years in all branches of philology, or language study. Jacob was especially influential, producing a classic study tracing the historical development of all the Germanic languages.

Detail of a photograph of Jacob (left) and Wilhelm Grimm. c. 1850

THE OUTSIDER

There are many kinds of outsiders in literature, and many ways in which characters become outsiders. The most literal sort of "outsider" is the stranger, the person who comes from outside the community, like the author of Psalm 137 (page 35), one of the Jews in exile in Babylon, who mourns, "How shall we sing the Lord's song in a strange land?" The outsider can also be a person who, for one reason or another, feels alienated within the community to which he belongs. This can be because the individual cannot or will not meet the standards of that community, like Caliban in *The Tempest* (page 415). When Miranda points out the care she has taken to educate him, he bitterly retorts, "You taught me language; and my profit on't/Is, I know how to curse." Or the outsider can be someone who is responding to a higher standard. Pushkin's prophet (page 627) has a mystical experience in which he becomes illuminated and awakened. He thus also becomes homeless—a wandering spokesman for God. In this century, the outsider has acquired respectability. One writer has even declared that civilization is "the creation of its outlaws."

The Isolation of the Outsider

The speaker's isolation in the Egyptian **lyric** "A Dialogue of a Man With His Soul" (page 17) is that of the just man in an unjust society. The injustice the speaker sees makes him hunger and thirst for righteousness, and affects him so severely that he praises death in lyrical terms. Finally, however, he can say, like Job, "I know that my redeemer liveth." His dream of justice is not just a dream.

Two works in this text deal with the way a character's dreams or fantasies relate to his or her isolation. The works are Flaubert's *Madame Bovary* and Gogol's "The Overcoat."

In the chapter of *Madame Bovary* reprinted here (page 661), Charles and Emma Bovary travel to the chateau of a marquis to attend an all-night dinner and dance. The opulent and aristocratic atmosphere of the party is far removed from the reality of Charles's rural medical practice, but is ironically close to the dreams of the unhappy Emma, whose fantasies include some of the very things she sees and does at the dance. It becomes clear at the party, in the way she treats her husband, that Emma's dreams isolate her from other people. And after she returns to their humdrum home, it becomes even clearer that the more her nostalgia for the romantic wealthy life remains with her, the more isolated she is going to be.

In "The Overcoat" (page 632), the dreams and fantasies of the downtrodden Akaky Akakievich also have a relationship to his isolation. This pauper's dream of an elegant new overcoat makes his isolation more tolerable. When he finally receives his new overcoat, he is in a state of bliss, so that we feel happy for him. And when he loses his coat, we feel sorry for him, especially because of the indifference of the public officials. But we may have forgotten that there was a time, before he started dreaming of a new overcoat, when Akaky was delighted just to be an impoverished copyist with a coat that was threadbare. And we may also have forgotten that a coat is just a coat—it is not an answer to the problem of isolation.

The question of our attitude toward Akaky's isolation is related to the question of just which people Gogol is **satirizing.** At the beginning of the story, the way Akaky's superiors treat him makes us think the story is satirizing the class system in Czarist Russia. Akaky, however, is happy under this system, so perhaps Gogol does not intend to satirize the system only. Perhaps he is also making fun of Akaky, a man who prefers copying to thinking. Indeed, at key points in the story we realize that Akaky is both pathetic and comic.

"The Little Bouilloux Girl" (page 833) by Colette, concerns the isolation of the prettiest girl in town, an isolation that can be acute if she is grooming herself, as is Nana Bouilloux, to marry well. Often, in literary works, such a girl does succeed in her plan. Nana Bouilloux, however, has another fate in store for her, one that she invites upon herself by setting her standards too high.

Women, often considered isolated in modern society, have been outsiders in other societies, too. The Book of Ruth, from the Old Testament (page 27), tells the story of a woman of Moab named Ruth, who marries a man from Judah whose family is living in Moab. When her husband dies, Ruth chooses to move to Judah with her mother-in-law, where she thus is an outsider by choice, and, as a woman, is also powerless. But she remains loyal to her adopted family, people, and land.

Artists as Outsiders

Other writers have created unsuccessful or isolated artists. Psalm 137 creates the idea of a whole nation of artists who are outsiders: they are in captivity, far from home, and are required to sing their songs for their hated captors. In protest, they hang their harps upon the willow trees and pray for revenge. Unlike the psalmist, the Chinese poet T'ao Ch'ien presents a serene view of the outsider as artist, a view that emphasizes detachment, not alienation. In his poem "I Built My Cottage Among the Habitations of Men" (page 79), he speaks of his special capacity to abstract himself from the human bustle of his surroundings: "A heart that is distant creates its own solitude." However, T'ao Ch'ien has also experienced alienation from society. In the first of his "Two Poems on Returning to Dwell in the Country" (page 79), he speaks of the unhappiness of his years spent in "the Dusty Net" of Chinese officialdom. A later Chinese poet, Po Chü-i, expresses similar feelings of alienation from polite society. In his poem, "Chu-ch'ēn Village" (page 90), he speaks of the bitterness of his early years: "I was born in the Realms of Etiquette;/In early years, unprotected and poor./Alone, I learnt to distinguish between Evil and Good;/Untutored, I toiled at bitter tasks./The World's Law honors Learning and Fame;/Scholars prize marriages and Caps./With these fetters I gyved my own hands;/Truly I became a much-deceived man."

Emily Dickinson's poem "This Is My Letter to the World" (page 680) seems to say that though the world has no message for her, she has a message for the world, and that it comes from Nature, and therefore tells the truth. The message, however, goes to an audience from which she is isolated, so she ends the poem with a plea for the good will of the future.

In the section of Joyce's *A Portrait of the Artist as a Young Man* reprinted here (page 778), Stephen Dedalus makes his decision to become an artist. How successful an artist will he be? At one point he quotes a line from his collection of quotations and then analyzes it in such a way as to make his appreciation of it more important than the line itself. Is not Stephen somewhat wrapped up in himself? The climax of this chapter is Stephen's encounter with the birdlike girl in the water. Joyce's description of the girl is written in breathtaking prose. But does it not also show that Stephen is still too isolated by his worship of beautiful language for its own sake, too caught up in himself to create other characters the way a writer must?

Chalk sketch of Cosette by Emile Bayard for 1904 edition of *Les Misérables*
Musée Victor Hugo, Paris

THINKING CRITICALLY ABOUT LITERATURE

UNIT 6   ROMANTICISM AND REALISM

■ CONCEPT REVIEW

Below on the left are the stanzas of William Wordsworth's poem "Resolution and Independence." The poem centers upon the speaker's personal crisis and the manner in which he is rescued from his despondency.

On the right are notes to help you read this poem and to review some of the literary terms and thinking skills covered in Unit 6. Page numbers in the notes refer to an application or review of literary terms earlier in the unit. These concepts are also discussed in the Handbook of Literary Terms. On a separate sheet of paper write your answers to the questions following the poem.

Resolution and Independence

William Wordsworth

There was a roaring in the wind all night;
The rain came heavily and fell in floods;
But now the sun is rising calm and bright;
The birds are singing in the distant woods:
5 Over his own sweet voice the stock-dove broods;
The jay makes answer as the magpie chatters:
And all the air is filled with pleasant noise of waters.

All things that love the sun are out of doors;
The sky rejoices in the morning's birth;
10 The grass is bright with raindrops;—on the moors
The hare is running races in her mirth;
And with her feet she from the plashy earth
Raises a mist, that, glittering in the sun,
Runs with her all the way wherever she doth run.

15 I was a traveler then upon the moor;
I saw the hare that raced about with joy;
I heard the woods and distant waters roar,
Or heard them not, as happy as a boy:
The pleasant season did my heart employ:

■ **Setting:** Note the atmosphere evoked by the setting, with its details of weather, place, and sounds.
■ **moors:** open wastelands.

■ **plashy:** splashy.

■ **Point of View** (pages 650 and 687): Note how the use of a first-person narrator directs the reader's attention to the emotional effect of the experience.

20 My old remembrances went from me wholly;
And all the ways of men so vain and melancholy.

But, as it sometimes chanceth, from the might
Of joy in minds that can no further go,
As high as we have mounted in delight
25 In our dejection do we sink as low,
To me that morning did it happen so;
And fears, and fancies, thick upon me came;
Dim sadness—and blind thoughts, I knew not, nor could name.

I heard the skylark warbling in the sky;
30 And I bethought me of the playful hare;
Even such a happy child of earth am I;
Even as these blissful creatures do I fare;
Far from the world I walk, and from all care;
But there may come another day to me—
35 Solitude, pain of heart, distress, and poverty.

My whole life I have lived in pleasant thought.
As if life's business were a summer mood;
As if all needful things would come unsought
To genial faith, still rich in genial good:
40 But how can He expect that others should
Build for him, sow for him, and at his call
Love him, who for himself will take no heed at all?

I thought of Chatterton, the marvelous boy,
The sleepless soul that perished in his pride;
45 Of Him who walked in glory and in joy
Following his plow, along the mountain side:
By our own spirits are we deified:
We poets in our youth begin in gladness;
But thereof come in the end despondency and madness.

50 Now, whether it were by peculiar grace,
A leading from above, a something given,
Yet it befell, that, in this lonely place,
When I with these untoward thoughts had striven,
Beside a pool bare to the eye of heaven
55 I saw a man before me unawares:
The oldest man he seemed that ever wore gray hairs.

As a huge stone is sometimes seen to lie
Couched on the bald top of an eminence;
Wonder to all who do the same espy,
60 By what means it could thither come, and whence;
So that it seems a thing endued with sense;
Like a sea-beast crawled forth, that on a shelf
Of rock or sand reposeth, there to sun itself:

■ **He:** Coleridge, who was brilliant but weak and impractical.
■ **Chatterton:** English poet who committed suicide at age 17.
■ **Him:** Robert Burns, Scottish poet who was born into poverty and who suffered from ill health as an adult.

■ **Inference** (p. 627): Note what is being implied about the reason the speaker sees this old man at this particular time.

■ **Simile:** Note the simile in this stanza and how the two elements, the huge stone and the sea beast, are fused and related to the man through the first line of the next stanza.

Such seemed this man, not all alive nor dead.
65 Nor all asleep—in his extreme old age:
His body was bent double, feet and head
Coming together in life's pilgrimage:
As if some dire constraint of pain, or rage
Of sickness felt by him in times long past,
70 A more than human weight upon his frame had cast.

Himself he propped, limbs, body, and pale face.
Upon a long gray staff of shaven wood:
And, still as I drew near with gentle pace.
Upon the margin of that moorish flood
75 Motionless as a cloud the old man stood;
That heareth not the loud winds when they call,
And moveth altogether, if it move at all.

At length, himself unsettling, he the pond
Stirred with his staff and fixedly did look
80 Upon the muddy water, which he conned,
As if he had been reading in a book:
And now a stranger's privilege I took;
And, drawing to his side, to him did say,
"This morning gives us promise of a glorious day."

85 A gentle answer did the old man make,
In courteous speech which forth he slowly drew:
And him with further words I thus bespake:
"What occupation do you there pursue?
This is a lonesome place for one like you."
90 Ere he replied, a flash of mild surprise
Broke from the sable orbs of his yet vivid eyes.

His words came feebly, from a feeble chest,
But each in solemn order followed each,
With something of a lofty utterance dressed;
95 Choice word, and measured phrase, above the reach
Of ordinary men; a stately speech;
Such as grave Livers do in Scotland use.
Religious men, who give to God and man their dues.

He told, that to these waters he had come
100 To gather leeches, being old and poor:
Employment hazardous and wearisome!
And he had many hardships to endure:
From pond to pond he roamed, from moor to moor;
Housing, with God's good help, by choice or chance;
105 And in this way he gained an honest maintenance.

The old man still stood talking by my side;
But now his voice to me was like a stream

■ **Rhyme:** The rhyme scheme is rhyme royal, a seven-line iambic pentameter stanza rhyming *ababbcc*.

■ **moorish:** on a moor

■ **Diction:** Note the description of the aged man's speech.

■ **leeches:** bloodsucking worms that live chiefly in freshwater ponds and streams; formerly frequently used medically for bloodletting.

Scarce heard; nor word from word could I divide:
And the whole body of the man did seem
110 Like one whom I had met with in a dream;
Or like a man from some far region sent,
To give me human strength, by apt admonishment.

My former thoughts returned: the fear that kills:
And hope that is unwilling to be fed;
115 Cold, pain and labor, and all fleshly ills;
And mighty poets in their misery dead.
Perplexed, and longing to be comforted,
My question eagerly did I renew,
"How is it that you live, and what is it you do?"

120 He with a smile did then his words repeat;
And said that, gathering leeches, far and wide
He traveled; stirring thus about his feet
The waters of the pools where they abide.
"Once I could meet with them on every side;
125 But they have dwindled long by slow decay;
Yet still I persevere, and find them where I may."

While he was talking thus, the lonely place,
The old man's shape, and speech, all troubled me:
In my mind's eye I seemed to see him pace
130 About the weary moors continually,
Wandering about alone and silently.
While I these thoughts within myself pursued,
He, having made a pause, the same discourse renewed.

And soon with this he other matter blended,
135 Cheerfully uttered, with demeanor kind,
But stately in the main; and when he ended,
I could have laughed myself to scorn to find
In that decrepit man so firm a mind.
"God," said I, "be my help and stay secure;
140 I'll think of the leech-gatherer on the lonely moor!"
1802   1807

THINK AND DISCUSS
Understanding
1. Who is the speaker?
2. Why are other poets mentioned?

Analyzing
3. What is the purpose of the **similes** in lines 57–77?
4. What does the old man's speech indicate about him?
5. What does the leech-gatherer **symbolize**?

Extending

6. Rhyme royal is usually associated with narration about lofty topics. Why do you think Wordsworth used it in this poem about a decrepit old man who has such a lowly trade?

REVIEWING LITERARY TERMS
Point of View

1. Is the speaker immediately experiencing his meeting with the leech-gatherer or recollecting an event from the past? What effect does this have on the emotion conveyed by the poem?

Inference

2. What do you infer from lines 50–56 as to the reason the speaker encounters the leech-gatherer at this particular time?

■ CONTENT REVIEW
THINKING SKILLS
Classifying

1. Designate each of the following authors as Romanticist or Realist: (**a**) Whitman; (**b**) Flaubert; (**c**) Pushkin; (**d**) Twain; (**e**) Maupassant; (**f**) Gogol; (**g**) Hugo; (**h**) Goethe; (**i**) Tolstoy.

2. In which of the following selections is a folk tale or legend central to the work? (**a**) "The False Gems"; (**b**) *Faust;* (**c**) "How Much Land Does a Man Need?"; (**d**) "The Loreley"; (**e**) "The Overcoat"; (**f**) "Russia 1812"; (**g**) "The Bridegroom"; (**h**) "My Songs, You Say."

Generalizing

3. Write a brief definition of Romanticism and Realism derived from your study of the works in this unit.

4. Describe the Romantics' view of the poet's role as depicted in Pushkin's "The Prophet," Whitman's "Song of Myself" and "A Noiseless Patient Spider," and Dickinson's "Tell All the Truth But Tell It Slant" and "This Is My Letter to the World."

5. The Romantics placed great emphasis upon nature in their writing. Briefly describe the treatment of the natural world in the excerpt from *Faust*, "The Loreley," and "When I Heard the Learn'd Astronomer."

Synthesizing

6. Compare and contrast the depiction of the life for the lower class in Russian society in Gogol's "The Overcoat" and Tolstoy's "How Much Land Does a Man Need?" Does either of these stories present a picture of oppression similar to that found in Heine's poem "The Silesian Weavers"?

7. Realists frequently explore the **theme** of illusion and reality. Compare and contrast the treatment of this theme in the selection from Flaubert's *Madame Bovary* and Maupassant's short story, "The False Gems."

Evaluating

8. The **protagonist** of a Romantic work is often depicted as striving toward the infinite or undergoing a mystical experience, while the leading character in a Realistic work is usually shown as an ordinary person leading an unextraordinary life, an existence circumscribed by human limitations. Which type of literature most appeals to you? Explain your answer, using examples from this unit and other appropriate works that you have read.

9. What is distinctive about the versification of the two American poets presented in this unit?

■ COMPOSITION REVIEW
Understanding Symbolism

In much verse, comprehending the poem's full significance involves understanding the **symbolism.** Write an essay explaining the meaning of the major nature symbols in two of the following poems: Wordsworth's "Resolution and Independence," Hugo's "Russia 1812," excerpts from Whitman's "Song of Myself," and Dickinson's "Because I Could Not Stop for Death."

Analyzing Point of View

Write an essay explaining how first person **point of view** shapes the way the reader perceives either characterization or theme in Gogol's "The Overcoat" and the excerpt from Twain's *Life on the Mississippi*. In your conclusion, evaluate each author's choice of narrator.

ODERNISM 1880–1940

1880	1890	1900	1910

HISTORY AND ARTS
- X-rays discovered
- First airplane flight
- Monet: *Haystacks at Giverny*
- Cezanne: *Mont Sainte-Victoire*
- Germany annexes Tanganyika
- First motion picture
- Einstein's relativity theory
- Leopold II acquires Congo
- Spanish-American War
- Wright: Robie House
- First automobile
- Radium discovered
- First steel-frame building
- Boxer rebellion
- Suffragette • demonstrations
- Debussy: *Afternoon of a Faun* •
- Planck's quantum theory
- British Labour Party formed •
- Stravinsky: *The Rite of Spring* •

PEOPLE
- Victoria's Diamond Jubilee •
- Zola dies
- Ibsen dies
- George V becomes king
- Flaubert dies
- Edward VII becomes king •
- Peary to North Pole •
- Nihilists assassinate Alexander II
- William II becomes kaiser
- Tagore wins Nobel Prize •
- Dreyfus convicted
- Wilson becomes President •

LITERATURE
- Nobel prizes established
- Tagore: *Gitanjali* •
- Ibsen: *A Doll House*
- Ibsen: *Hedda Gabler*
- Conrad: *Heart of Darkness*
- Zola: *Nana*
- Freud: *The Interpretation of Dreams* •
- Chekhov: *Three Sisters*
- Twain: *Huckleberry Finn*
- Shaw: *Man and Superman* •
- Shaw: *Pygmalion* •
- First volume of *The Oxford English Dictionary*
- Chekhov: *The Cherry Orchard*

Detail of a photograph showing the Wright Brothers. 1903

Detail of a photograph of Albert Einstein. c. 1905

Robie House, designed by Frank Lloyd Wright. 1909

1920	1930	1940

- World War I begins
- Griffith: *Birth of a Nation*
- Russian Revolution
- World War I ends
- Treaty of Versailles
- Bauhaus founded
- 19th Amendment
- First radio broadcasts

- Gershwin: *Rhapsody in Blue*
- Eisenstein: *Potemkin*
- Scopes trial
- First Five-Year Plan begins
- Great Depression starts

- Picasso: *Guernica*
- Moore: *Reclining Figure*
- World War II starts
- Chaplin: *Modern Times*
- Spanish Civil War begins

Lindbergh flies Atlantic •
- Nicholas II executed
- Mussolini comes to power
- Lenin dies
- Kafka dies

- Roosevelt becomes President
- Hitler becomes chancellor
- George VI becomes king
- Freud dies

Churchill becomes prime minister •

- Akhmatova: *Beads*
- Kafka: *The Metamorphosis*
- Joyce: *A Portrait of the Artist as a Young Man*

- Joyce: *Ulysses*
- T. S. Eliot: *The Waste Land*
- Rilke: *Duino Elegies*
- Kafka: *The Trial*
- Kafka: *The Castle*

- Dinesen: *Seven Gothic Tales*
- Dinesen: *Out of Africa*
- Joyce: *Finnegans Wake*

Detail of John Nash's painting *Over the Top*. c. 1918

Lenin (1870–1924), detail of a painting by Vladimir Serov

Charlie Chaplin in a scene from the film *Modern Times*. 1936

PREVIEW

UNIT 7　　　MODERNISM　1880–1940

Authors
Henrik Ibsen
Anton Chekhov
Rabindranath Tagore
C. P. Cavafy
Rainer Maria Rilke
James Joyce
Franz Kafka
Isak Dinesen
Anna Akhmatova
Gabriela Mistral
Colette

Features
Reading a Realistic Drama
Comment: *Kafkaesque*
Reader's Note: Translating "Meciendo"
The History of Language: *The Oxford
    English Dictionary*
Themes in World Literature: Men and
    Women

Application of Literary Terms
connotation/denotation
mood

Review of Literary Terms
characterization
tone
simile

Vocabulary Skills
pronunciation key
synonyms
dictionary/glossary

Thinking Skills
classifying
generalizing
evaluating

Composition Assignments Include
Writing to Persuade
Writing About a Period
Writing About a Personal Experience
Comparing Literary Characters
Writing a Dialogue
Stating a Preference
Writing to the Author
Analyzing and Relating Poems
Writing About a Picture
Writing About a Poem
Being a Character in a Story
Analyzing a Character
Assuming the Point of View of a Character
Analyzing Descriptive Style
Imagining a Situation
Relating Two Poems

Enrichment
Trying Nora for Desertion
Speaking/Listening
Imagining Gregor's Metamorphosis

Thinking Critically About Literature
Concept Review
Content Review
Composition Review

BACKGROUND

MODERNISM   1880–1940

The modern world began on 29 May 1919
when photographs of a solar eclipse, taken on
the island of Principe off West Africa and at
Sobral in Brazil, confirmed the truth of a new
theory of the universe.

Paul Johnson, Modern Times

Everyone has heard phrases like "modern art"
or "modern times" and has some sense of the
significant characteristics of twentieth-century
culture and history that they convey. But when
exactly does the "modern" period begin? What
event or trend can serve as a benchmark separating the world of the nineteenth century from
that in which we live? Historian Paul Johnson
sees the confirmation of Einstein's Theory of
Relativity in 1919 as inaugurating the modern
world. Another recent historian used 1916, when
new technology raised the destructiveness of the
battles of World War I to unprecedented levels,
as the watershed. Both these dates reflect a concern with science and technology. Literary historians tend to date the advent of modernism
far earlier, to the last decades of the nineteenth
century, when many of the great writers of
that period, like Flaubert and Dostoevsky, had
died, and the characteristic literary figures of
the new period, like Ibsen and Chekhov, were
writing their first important works. Employing
1880—the year of Flaubert's death—as a starting point, several significant characteristics of
the Modern Period can be identified.

THE GROWTH OF IMPERIALISM

Imperialism can be defined as the policy of
extending the rule, authority, or influence of
one country over other countries or colonies.
Throughout most of the nineteenth century,
colonial expansion by the nations of Europe
had been relatively small. Economists of the

period had argued that colonies held no economic advantages and were too costly to defend.
But the last quarter of the century saw a dramatic turnabout as the major European powers—followed eventually by the United States—engaged
in a scramble to obtain millions of square miles
of Asia, Africa, and Oceania. By 1914 they controlled some 80 percent of the earth's surface.
Very different attitudes were expressed toward
the impact of this new growth of imperialism. In
a celebrated poem Rudyard Kipling instructed
the Americans in the Philippines to "Take up
the White Man's burden—/The savage wars
of peace—/Fill full the mouth of Famine/And
bid the sickness cease . . ." But in the same
year (1899), Joseph Conrad described imperialist
adventurers in Africa far differently in his novella
Heart of Darkness: "To tear treasure out of the
bowels of the land was their desire, with no more
moral purpose at the back of it than there is in
burglars breaking into a safe."

What was behind the growth of imperialism was the fierce economic competition that
developed during the latter half of the nineteenth century between England and her new
industrial and commercial rivals, Germany and
the United States. England, the first modern
industrial state, had been "the Workshop of the
World," but now its factories were aging, and
former customers were becoming competitors.
Germany, fresh from its victory in the Franco-
Prussian War (1870), and the United States,
recovered from its own Civil War (1861–1865),
now became serious threats to English economic
predominance.

A SCIENTIFIC REVOLUTION

This increased economic competition was propelled by rapid developments in science and
technology. The period of the end of the nine-

Queen Victoria arriving at St. Paul's Cathedral for Diamond Jubilee service in 1897.
Detail of a painting by Andrew Carrick Gow (1848–1920). Guildhall Art Gallery

teenth century and the beginning of the twentieth was unprecedented in inventiveness: it transformed technology from a steam-and-iron basis to one of electricity, the internal combustion engine, steel, and alloys. It pioneered the telephone, the automobile, and the radio. It witnessed the beginnings of aviation and laid the groundwork for the nuclear age that would

follow. During the late 1880s and the 1890s, a series of inventions by the American Thomas A. Edison and others created a characteristically modern fusion of technology, art, and mass entertainment—motion pictures. The application of scientific techniques to industry developed new materials, such as synthetic chemicals, and new processes, like mass production of consumer goods. The impact of science, however, went far beyond a mere catering to mass comforts or gadgetry. It effected a revolution in the most fundamental beliefs that human beings had about the universe and themselves.

Charles Darwin's theory of evolution, expressed in his book *On the Origin of Species by Means of Natural Selection* (1859), seemed to destroy old assumptions about human nature and destiny, leaving people uncertain about themselves and their future. The English novelist H. G. Wells, himself a spokesman of the new science, described well the dismay it produced: "Science is a match that man has just got alight. He thought he was in a room—in moments of devotion, a temple—and that his light would be reflected from and display walls inscribed with wonderful secrets. . . . It is a curious sensation, now that the preliminary splutter is over and the flame burns up clear, to see . . . in place of all that human comfort and beauty he anticipated—darkness still."

While Darwin's writings transformed biology, the work of such scientists as Ernest Rutherford (1871–1937), Max Planck (1879–1947), and particularly Albert Einstein (1879–1955) was revolutionizing physics. In 1905 Einstein published a paper in which he put forward a new vision of the cosmos. Einstein's Special Theory of Relativity overturned the conception of a three-dimensional universe that had been dominant in physics since it had been put forward by Isaac Newton over two hundred years earlier. Einstein's theory of relativity has changed our attitude toward the structure and mechanics of the universe, and its implications have permeated not only modern science, but twentieth-century philosophical, moral, and even esthetic concepts as well.

Even more important in its cultural implications than physics or biology, was the development of modern psychology, the science of human behavior. The Russian scientist Ivan Pavlov (1849–1936) did important research on the influence of physical stimuli on an involuntary process. Far less mechanistic than Pavlov's psychology of "conditioned reflexes" were the theories of the Austrian Sigmund Freud (1856–1939). Placing far greater emphasis than any of his predecessors on the element of

the unconscious in human nature, Freud pioneered the technique of psychoanalysis in the 1890s.

SOCIAL DARWINISM

As they gained acceptance, Darwin's theories were applied to economics as well as biology. One Victorian scientist had summed up the theory of evolution as "survival of the fittest." Some late nineteenth-century industrialists saw this as justifying cutthroat competition and other commercial abuses. This outlook is often described as "social Darwinism." In destroying his economic rivals, one railroad magnate argued that "the fortunes of the railroad companies are determined by the law of the survival of the fittest"; another expressed his philosophy of social Darwinism more succinctly: "The public be damned."

The enemies of capitalism also saw Darwin's work as supporting their position. The social philosopher Karl Marx (1818–1883), whose writings form the theoretical basis of communism, wrote to his colleague Friedrich Engels (1820–1895) about *On the Origin of Species*: "Darwin's book is very important and serves me as a basis in natural science for the class struggle in history." During the latter part of the nineteenth century a variety of radical political movements developed throughout Europe and the United States. In their proposed solutions to the problems of poverty and social injustice, these radicals differed from each other nearly as much as they did from their capitalist foes. At one extreme were radical anarchists, like the Nihilists in Russia, who conducted a terrorist movement in the late 1870s, climaxing in the assassination of Tsar Alexander II in 1881. At the other extreme were the Fabian Socialists in England, who advocated working within the capitalist system to achieve peaceful social change. Fabian Socialism led the way to the creation of the British Labour Party in 1900. The decades after 1900 were also a time of new militancy in the women's suffrage movement. Suffragettes in England besieged the Houses of Parliament and assaulted politicians unsympathetic to their cause. The first European country to allow women to vote was Norway in 1907, but only after World War I were women allowed to vote in Great Britain and the United States.

Weakened by World War I, the three-hundred-year-old tsarist monarchy was overthrown in Russia early in 1917. Moderates formed a provisional government, but radical Marxists, led by V. I. Lenin (1870–1924), seized power in November. During the 1920s and 1930s, Lenin and his successor, Joseph Stalin (1879–1953), succeeded in establishing communism in Russia, developing in the process the apparatus of the modern totalitarian state—secret police, political trials, and concentration camps. Anna Akhmatova's poem *Requiem 1935–1940* (page 820) recalls the victims of Stalinist terror. Right-wing dictatorships employing many of the same methods were established by Fascist leader Benito Mussolini (1883–1945) in Italy and by Nazi leader Adolf Hitler (1889–1945) in Germany.

The Spanish Civil War (1936–1939), between the Loyalist supporters of the left-wing government, and the right-wing followers of General Francisco Franco (1892–1975), anticipated the alliances of World War II (1939–1945). The Soviet Union aided the Loyalist side, while Germany and Italy aided Franco. The aerial bombardment of Spanish cities, like the Basque town of Guernica (see page 709), also gave a foretaste of the destructiveness of World War II.

MODERN LITERATURE

In a lecture on modern writing that she delivered in 1924, the English novelist Virginia Woolf made a famous pronouncement that "in or about December, 1910, human character changed." She admitted that her choice of an exact date was arbitrary. (It was apparently prompted by her recollection of the impact of a famous exhibit of modern art that had taken place in London in November, 1910.) But she felt that it was undeniable that an enormous cultural change had taken place since the end of the nineteenth century. "All human relations have shifted—those between masters and servants, husbands and wives, parents and children. And when human relations change there is at the same time a change in religion, conduct, politics, and literature."

During the final decades of the nineteenth century, literature came to be dominated by two new movements, naturalism

and symbolism. Developing out of realism and strongly influenced by the thinking of Darwin and other nineteenth-century scientists, naturalism depicted people's lives as rigidly determined by forces of heredity and environment. Naturalist writers rejected faith, revelation, authority, tradition, and intuition as legitimate sources of truth. In their view meaning comes only from experience, and literature should reflect the application of scientific methods of observation. The great theorist of naturalism was the French writer Émile Zola (1840–1902). Between 1871 and 1893 he wrote about family life in twenty novels that resemble a doctor's casebook of patients. In its rejection of Romantic optimism, naturalism tended toward the bleak and sordid in its subject matter. When it existed, love was not a sublime and ennobling emotion, but mere chemistry operating between people. The universe was indifferent to the hopes and struggles of individuals.

With its source in romanticism's emphasis on the power of the imagination, the symbolist movement arose as a reaction to realism and naturalism. The symbolist writers did not examine the world with a scientist's eye, but instead searched for symbols that would serve to express imaginative truths. To the symbolists the sounds of words were as important as their meanings, and images were sought that would appeal simultaneously to different senses. As literary movements, both naturalism and symbolism were at their height in the last two decades of the nineteenth century. But many modern writers whose works appeared later, like James Joyce (1882–1941), exhibit both naturalist and symbolist influences.

Modern drama begins with the plays of the Norwegian writer Henrik Ibsen (1829–1906). In the early part of his career, Ibsen employed the historical or poetic subjects favored by Romantic dramatists like Goethe. In the 1870s, however, Ibsen began to turn his attention to contemporary problems of social injustice in his homeland. In plays such as *A Doll House* (1879), *An Enemy of the People* (1882), and *Hedda Gabler* (1890), Ibsen examines the relationships of his characters against a background of social tensions. The most striking dramatist to follow Ibsen's path was the Irish playwright Bernard Shaw (1856–1950). In his "comedies of ideas," like

Pablo Picasso (1881–1973), *Guernica*. 1937. Casón del Buen Retiro, Madrid

Man and Superman (1903), *Pygmalion* (1913), and *Heartbreak House* (1919), Shaw's characters served as vehicles for his satirical attacks on social conventions.

MODERN ART

The modern movements in painting, like those in literature, grew out of nineteenth-century romanticism and realism. The French realist painter Gustave Courbet (1819–1877) once stated that he did not paint angels because he had never seen one. Courbet stirred other painters to begin a movement later known as impressionism. The impressionists ignored such traditional subjects as Biblical, historical, or mythological stories to focus on the ordinary details of middle-class life. They abandoned the studio and attempted to capture natural scenes in all their variations of light and shadow. Among the important impressionist painters were Claude Monet (1840–1926), Edgar Degas (1834–1917), and Auguste Renoir (1841–1919). Other painters, however, turned away from impressionism. The experiments of Paul Cézanne (1839–1906), in which natural objects like a bowl of fruit or a landscape were depicted more and more in terms of their abstract forms, would eventually lead to the cubist paintings of Pablo Picasso (1881–1973).

THINKING ABOUT GRAPHIC AIDS
Using the Time Line

The time line on pages 702–703 shows the chronological sequence of the historical and literary events discussed in Unit 7. Use the time line to answer the following questions.

1. Which of the following writers could *not* have been considered for the Nobel Prize?
   (a) Flaubert; (b) Zola; (c) Kafka
2. Who was king of England during World War I? (a) Edward VII; (b) George V; (c) George VI
3. Could Americans have received the news of the end of World War I on their radios?
4. Which of the following works by Kafka were published after his death? (a) "The Metamorphosis"; (b) *The Trial;* (c) *The Castle*
5. Does Picasso's painting *Guernica* commemorate an episode from the Spanish Civil War or World War II?

In April, 1850, a twenty-two-year-old Norwegian journeyed to his nation's capital to take entrance exams for medical school. He failed sections in mathematics and Greek, and so his country was denied a doctor but given its most famous literary figure, a man who has been called the father of modern drama.

Henrik Ibsen was the oldest of five surviving children born to well-to-do parents in a tiny coastal town in Norway. When Ibsen was seven, his father suffered financial ruin, and the family had to move to an isolated farm. Friends who had feasted at the generous table of the Ibsens during the years of prosperity now shunned the family. The young Ibsen was disgusted by the snobbery and provincialism of local society and became an introvert—reading, painting, drawing, and staging puppet shows.

At fifteen he became a druggist's apprentice, and in his spare time he wrote poetry, some of which was published. After six years in the unfriendly atmosphere of the small town, he had saved enough money to go to Christiania (now Oslo), only to be rejected by the university. However, his first play, *Catiline*, had just been published and before long he was invited to be a stage manager and playwright for the National Theater in Bergen and later director of the Norwegian Theater in Christiania.

In 1864 he left Norway and began a twenty-seven-year period of voluntary exile which was to produce his finest work. The play *Brand* (1866) established Ibsen as the pioneer of revolt against dead thought and outmoded traditions. He followed it with *Peer Gynt* (1867), which was based on Norwegian folklore, and *Emperor and Galilean* (1873), a complex study of the struggle between paganism and early Christianity.

By this time Ibsen was well known and financially comfortable. In his subsequent plays he abandoned historical subjects and began to address contemporary social problems. Not only political reform interested him, but also technological advances, the new psychology of the subconscious mind, and the social ramifications of Darwin's theory of evolution. *Pillars of Society* (1877) deals with a wealthy and hypocritical businessman. In this play Ibsen's subtlety of characterization, psychological insight, and ability to strip the masks from respected people and institutions were a revelation to his contemporaries.

On December 4, 1879, *A Doll House* was published in Copenhagen. Its success was sensational. The first printing was sold out within a month, as were the second and third, an event without precedent for a play in Scandinavia. No drama had ever been so widely discussed and debated by both habitual playgoers and people not normally interested in the theater. Ten more plays followed *A Doll House*, the best known being *Ghosts* (1881), *An Enemy of the People* (1882), *The Wild Duck* (1884), *Hedda Gabler* (1890), and *The Master Builder* (1892). After a series of debilitating strokes, Ibsen died in Oslo in 1906.

Reading A REALISTIC DRAMA

A Doll House has often been called the beginning of modern drama. Its subject matter is realistic and—when the play first appeared—shocking. There is no slight detail or line of dialogue that does not make a contribution to the total effect.

Notice the stage directions. The stage directions serve an imaginative function. Those that begin Act One inform you that you are in a comfortable middle-class home and that it is Christmastime. When Act Two begins the stage directions indicate that the Christmas celebration is over. The tree (moved to the center of the stage at the end of Act One) is now stripped of ornament except for burnt-down candles and has been pushed aside. In Act Three the tree is gone and a table and chairs dominate the center of the stage. At this table Krogstad and Mrs. Linde will hammer out a new life for themselves, and the life of the Helmers will disintegrate after their first real conversation in eight years of marriage. Changes in lighting are obvious to the playgoer, but the reader must note them in the stage directions and see the **symbolism** of the darkness and the lighted lamp that Nora eventually calls for. The most famous line of the play is the concluding stage direction: "From below, the sound of a door slamming shut."

Notice psychological realism. Another aspect of *A Doll House* that marks it as modern and realistic is the relative absence of classical dramatic conventions such as asides to the audience or the use of one basic set to represent many different places. Ibsen does, however, employ the soliloquy, in which characters speak aloud the thoughts that in real life would remain unspoken.

In the early words and actions of the play,

Nora eats forbidden macaroons and Torvald addresses her with extravagant pet names. Never having had a real mother, Nora has been doted on first by her father and now by her husband. The gifts that she buys for her children underscore her acceptance of traditional Victorian sex-roles: clothes and a sword for Ivar, a horse and a trumpet for Bob, "and a doll and a doll's bed here for Emmy."

Notice dramatic structure. But Nora is more than just a petted creature. Unbeknownst to Torvald, she has saved his life by borrowing money for a needed trip, a transaction that also necessitated a forgery. In these and other acts of deception we see the beginnings of conflict. Torvald is opposed to being in debt and has an exaggerated concern for appearances. Nora doesn't understand that when he says he would like the opportunity to make a supreme sacrifice for her, he is only mouthing the words and thinking of the heroic figure he would cut. The rising action of the **plot** builds as the **theme** of disease and heredity are illustrated in the figures of Dr. Rank and Krogstad and in what we learn of Nora's father and the father of Dr. Rank.

The climax of the play comes when Torvald reads Krogstad's letter and reacts in a manner different from what Nora had anticipated. "I'm beginning to understand everything now," she says. The resolution, or denouement (meaning "untying"), is Nora's pained but determined decision to untie the knot of their marriage by desertion. Mrs. Linde and Krogstad, survivors of life's hardships, will presumably forge a strong marriage based on mutual respect and understanding. The future of Nora and Torvald is at best uncertain—requiring a "miracle" before they can be reunited.

A Doll House

Henrik Ibsen   *translated by* **Rolf Fjelde**

THE CHARACTERS
TORVALD HELMER, *a lawyer*
NORA, *his wife*
DR. RANK
MRS. LINDE
NILS KROGSTAD, *a bank clerk*
THE HELMERS' THREE SMALL CHILDREN
ANNE-MARIE, *their nurse*
HELENE, *a maid*
A DELIVERY BOY
The action takes place in HELMER's *residence.*

ACT ONE

A comfortable room, tastefully but not expensively furnished. A door to the right in the back wall leads to the entryway; another to the left leads to HELMER's *study. Between these doors, a piano. Midway in the left-hand wall a door, and farther back a window. Near the window a round table with an armchair and a small sofa. In the right-hand wall, toward the rear, a door, and nearer the foreground a porcelain stove with two armchairs and a rocking chair beside it. Between the stove and the side door, a small table. Engravings on the walls. An* étagère *with china figures and other small art objects; a small bookcase with richly bound books; the floor carpeted; a fire burning in the stove. It is a winter day.*

A bell rings in the entryway; shortly after we hear the door being unlocked. NORA *comes into the room, humming happily to herself; she is wearing street clothes and carries an armload of packages, which she puts down on the table to the right. She has left the hall door open; and through it a* DELIVERY BOY *is seen, holding a Christmas tree and a basket, which he gives to the* MAID *who let them in.*

NORA. Hide the tree well, Helene. The children mustn't get a glimpse of it till this evening, after it's trimmed. (*To the* DELIVERY BOY, *taking out her purse.*) How much?
DELIVERY BOY. Fifty, ma'am.
NORA. There's a crown. No, keep the change. (*The* BOY *thanks her and leaves.* NORA *shuts the door. She laughs softly to herself while taking off her street things. Drawing a bag of macaroons from her pocket, she eats a couple, then steals over and listens at her husband's study door.*) Yes, he's home. (*Hums again as she moves to the table right.*)
HELMER (*from the study*). Is that my little lark twittering out there?
NORA (*busy opening some packages*). Yes, it is.
HELMER. Is that my squirrel rummaging around?
NORA. Yes!
HELMER. When did my squirrel get in?
NORA. Just now. (*Putting the macaroon bag in her pocket and wiping her mouth.*) Do come in, Torvald, and see what I've bought.
HELMER. Can't be disturbed. (*After a moment he*

Scene from the 1973 film of *A Doll House* showing Claire Bloom as Nora and Anthony Hopkins as Helmer.

opens the door and peers in, pen in hand.) Bought, you say? All that there? Has the little spendthrift been out throwing money around again?

NORA. Oh, but Torvald, this year we really should let ourselves go a bit. It's the first Christmas we haven't had to economize.

HELMER. But you know we can't go squandering.

NORA. Oh yes, Torvald, we can squander a little now. Can't we? Just a tiny, wee bit. Now that you've got a big salary and are going to make piles and piles of money.

HELMER. Yes—starting New Year's. But then it's a full three months till the raise comes through.

NORA. Pooh! We can borrow that long.

HELMER. Nora! *(Goes over and playfully takes her by the ear.)* Are your scatterbrains off again? What if today I borrowed a thousand crowns, and you squandered them over Christmas week, and then on New Year's Eve a roof tile fell on my head, and I lay there—

NORA *(putting her hand on his mouth)*. Oh! Don't say such things!

HELMER. Yes, but what if it happened—then what?

NORA. If anything so awful happened, then it just wouldn't matter if I had debts or not.

HELMER. Well, but the people I'd borrowed from?

NORA. Them? Who cares about them! They're strangers.

HELMER. Nora, Nora, how like a woman! No,

but seriously, Nora, you know what I think about that. No debts! Never borrow! Something of freedom's lost—and something of beauty, too—from a home that's founded on borrowing and debt. We've made a brave stand up to now, the two of us; and we'll go right on like that the little while we have to.

NORA *(going toward the stove)*. Yes, whatever you say, Torvald.

HELMER *(following her)*. Now, now, the little lark's wings mustn't droop. Come on, don't be a sulky squirrel. *(Taking out his wallet.)* Nora, guess what I have here.

NORA *(turning quickly)*. Money!

HELMER. There, see. *(Hands her some notes.)* Good grief, I know how costs go up in a house at Christmastime.

NORA. Ten—twenty—thirty—forty. Oh, thank you, Torvald; I can manage no end on this.

HELMER. You really will have to.

NORA. Oh yes, I promise I will! But come here so I can show you everything I bought. And so cheap! Look, new clothes for Ivar here—and a sword. Here a horse and a trumpet for Bob. And a doll and a doll's bed here for Emmy; they're nothing much, but she'll tear them to bits in no time anyway. And here I have dress material and handkerchiefs for the maids. Old Anne-Marie really deserves something more.

HELMER. And what's in that package there?

NORA *(with a cry)*. Torvald, no! You can't see that till tonight!

HELMER. I see. But tell me now, you little prodigal, what have you thought of for yourself?

NORA. For myself? Oh, I don't want anything at all.

HELMER. Of course you do. Tell me just what—within reason—you'd most like to have.

NORA. I honestly don't know. Oh, listen, Torvald—

HELMER. Well?

NORA *(fumbling at his coat buttons, without looking at him)*. If you want to give me something, then maybe you could—you could—

HELMER. Come on, out with it.

NORA *(hurriedly)*. You could give me money, Torvald. No more than you think you can spare; then one of these days I'll buy something with it.

HELMER. But Nora—

NORA. Oh, please, Torvald darling, do that! I beg you, please. Then I could hang the bills in pretty gilt paper on the Christmas tree. Wouldn't that be fun?

HELMER. What are those little birds called that always fly through their fortunes?

NORA. Oh yes, spendthrifts; I know all that. But let's do as I say, Torvald; then I'll have time to decide what I really need most. That's very sensible, isn't it?

HELMER *(smiling)*. Yes, very—that is, if you actually hung onto the money I give you, and you actually used it to buy yourself something. But it goes for the house and for all sorts of foolish things, and then I only have to lay out some more.

NORA. Oh, but Torvald—

HELMER. Don't deny it, my dear little Nora. *(Putting his arm around her waist.)* Spendthrifts are sweet, but they use up a frightful amount of money. It's incredible what it costs a man to feed such birds.

NORA. Oh, how can you say that! Really, I save everything I can.

HELMER *(laughing)*. Yes, that's the truth. Everything you can. But that's nothing at all.

NORA *(humming, with a smile of quiet satisfaction)*. Hm, if you only knew what expenses we larks and squirrels have, Torvald.

HELMER. You're an odd little one. Exactly the way your father was. You're never at a loss for scaring up money; but the moment you have it, it runs right out through your fingers; you never know what you've done with it. Well, one takes you as you are. It's deep in your blood. Yes, these things are hereditary, Nora.

NORA. Ah, I could wish I'd inherited many of Papa's qualities.

HELMER. And I couldn't wish you anything but just what you are, my sweet little lark. But wait; it seems to me you have a very—what should I call it?—a very suspicious look today—

NORA. I do?

HELMER. You certainly do. Look me straight in the eye.

NORA (*looking at him*). Well?

HELMER (*shaking an admonitory finger*). Surely my sweet tooth hasn't been running riot in town today, has she?

NORA. No. Why do you imagine that?

HELMER. My sweet tooth really didn't make a little detour through the confectioner's?

NORA. No, I assure you, Torvald—

HELMER. Hasn't nibbled some pastry?

NORA. No, not at all.

HELMER. Not even munched a macaroon or two?

NORA. No, Torvald, I assure you, really—

HELMER. There, there now. Of course I'm only joking.

NORA (*going to the table, right*). You know I could never think of going against you.

HELMER. No, I understand that; and you *have* given me your word. (*Going over to her.*) Well, you keep your little Christmas secrets to yourself, Nora darling. I expect they'll come to light this evening, when the tree is lit.

NORA. Did you remember to ask Dr. Rank?

HELMER. No. But there's no need for that; it's assumed he'll be dining with us. All the same, I'll ask him when he stops by here this morning. I've ordered some fine wine. Nora, you can't imagine how I'm looking forward to this evening.

NORA. So am I. And what fun for the children, Torvald!

HELMER. Ah, it's so gratifying to know that one's gotten a safe, secure job, and with a comfortable salary. It's a great satisfaction, isn't it?

NORA. Oh, it's wonderful!

HELMER. Remember last Christmas? Three whole weeks before, you shut yourself in every evening till long after midnight, making flowers for the Christmas tree, and all the other decorations to surprise us. Ugh, that was the dullest time I've ever lived through.

NORA. It wasn't at all dull for me.

HELMER (*smiling*). But the outcome *was* pretty sorry, Nora.

NORA. Oh, don't tease me with that again. How could I help it that the cat came in and tore everything to shreds.

HELMER. No, poor thing, you certainly couldn't. You wanted so much to please us all, and that's what counts. But it's just as well that the hard times are past.

NORA. Yes, it's really wonderful.

HELMER. Now I don't have to sit here alone, boring myself, and you don't have to tire your precious eyes and your fair little delicate hands—

NORA (*clapping her hands*). No, is it really true, Torvald, I don't have to? Oh, how wonderfully lovely to hear! (*Taking his arm.*) Now I'll tell you just how I've thought we should plan things. Right after Christmas—(*The doorbell rings.*) Oh, the bell. (*Straightening the room up a bit.*) Somebody would have to come. What a bore!

HELMER. I'm not at home to visitors, don't forget.

MAID (*from the hall doorway*). Ma'am, a lady to see you—

NORA. All right, let her come in.

MAID (*to* HELMER). And the doctor's just come too.

HELMER. Did he go right to my study?

MAID. Yes, he did. (HELMER *goes into his room. The* MAID *shows in* MRS. LINDE, *dressed in traveling clothes, and shuts the door after her.*)

MRS. LINDE (*in a dispirited and somewhat hesitant voice*). Hello, Nora.

NORA (*uncertain*). Hello—

MRS. LINDE. You don't recognize me.

NORA. No, I don't know—but wait, I think— (*Exclaiming.*) What! Kristine! Is it really you?

MRS. LINDE. Yes, it's me.

NORA. Kristine! To think I didn't recognize you. But then, how could I? (*More quietly.*) How you've changed, Kristine!

MRS. LINDE. Yes, no doubt I have. In nine—ten long years.

NORA. Is it so long since we met! Yes, it's all of that. Oh, these last eight years have been a happy time, believe me. And so now you've come in to town, too. Made the long trip in the winter. That took courage.

MRS. LINDE. I just got here by ship this morning.

NORA. To enjoy yourself over Christmas, of course. Oh, how lovely! Yes, enjoy ourselves, we'll do that. But take your coat off. You're not still cold? *(Helping her.)* There now, let's get cozy here by the stove. No, the easy chair there! I'll take the rocker here. *(Seizing her hands.)* Yes, now you have your old look again; it was only in that first moment. You're a bit more pale, Kristine—and maybe a bit thinner.

MRS. LINDE. And much, much older, Nora.

NORA. Yes, perhaps a bit older; a tiny, tiny bit; not much at all. *(Stopping short; suddenly serious.)* Oh, but thoughtless me, to sit here, chattering away. Sweet, good Kristine, can you forgive me?

MRS. LINDE. What do you mean, Nora?

NORA *(softly)*. Poor Kristine, you've become a widow.

MRS. LINDE. Yes, three years ago.

NORA. Oh, I knew it, of course; I read it in the papers. Oh, Kristine, you must believe me; I often thought of writing you then, but I kept postponing it, and something always interfered.

MRS. LINDE. Nora dear, I understand completely.

NORA. No, it was awful of me, Kristine. You poor thing, how much you must have gone through. And he left you nothing?

MRS. LINDE. No.

NORA. And no children?

MRS. LINDE. No.

NORA. Nothing at all, then?

MRS. LINDE. Not even a sense of loss to feed on.

NORA *(looking incredulously at her)*. But Kristine, how could that be?

MRS. LINDE *(smiling wearily and smoothing her hair)*. Oh, sometimes it happens, Nora.

NORA. So completely alone. How terribly hard that must be for you. I have three lovely children. You can't see them now; they're out with the maid. But now you must tell me everything—

MRS. LINDE. No, no, no, tell me about yourself.

NORA. No, you begin. Today I don't want to be selfish. I want to think only of you today. But there *is* something I must tell you. Did you hear of the wonderful luck we had recently?

MRS. LINDE. No, what's that?

NORA. My husband's been made manager in the bank, just think!

MRS. LINDE. Your husband? How marvelous!

NORA. Isn't it? Being a lawyer is such an uncertain living, you know, especially if one won't touch any cases that aren't clean and decent. And of course Torvald would never do that, and I'm with him completely there. Oh, we're simply delighted, believe me! He'll join the bank right after New Year's and start getting a huge salary and lots of commissions. From now on we can live quite differently—just as we want. Oh, Kristine, I feel so light and happy! Won't it be lovely to have stacks of money and not a care in the world?

MRS. LINDE. Well, anyway, it would be lovely to have enough for necessities.

NORA. No, not just for necessities, but stacks and stacks of money!

MRS. LINDE *(smiling)*. Nora, Nora, aren't you sensible yet? Back in school you were such a free spender.

NORA *(with a quiet laugh)*. Yes, that's what Torvald still says. *(Shaking her finger.)* But "Nora, Nora" isn't as silly as you all think. Really, we've been in no position for me to go squandering. We've had to work, both of us.

MRS. LINDE. You too?

NORA. Yes, at odd jobs—needlework, crocheting, embroidery, and such—*(Casually.)* and other things too. You remember that Torvald left the department when we were married? There was no chance of promotion in his office, and of course he needed to earn more money. But that first year he drove himself terribly. He took on all kinds of extra work that kept him going morning and night. It wore him down, and then he fell deathly ill. The doctors said it was essential for him to travel south.

MRS. LINDE. Yes, didn't you spend a whole year in Italy?

NORA. That's right. It wasn't easy to get away, you know. Ivar had just been born. But of course we had to go. Oh, that was a beautiful trip, and it saved Torvald's life. But it cost a frightful sum, Kristine.

MRS. LINDE. I can well imagine.

NORA. Four thousand, eight hundred crowns it cost. That's really a lot of money.

MRS. LINDE. But it's lucky you had it when you needed it.

NORA. Well, as it was, we got it from Papa.

MRS. LINDE. I see. It was just about the time your father died.

NORA. Yes, just about then. And, you know, I couldn't make that trip out to nurse him. I had to stay here, expecting Ivar any moment, and with my poor sick Torvald to care for. Dearest Papa, I never saw him again, Kristine. Oh, that was the worst time I've known in all my marriage.

MRS. LINDE. I know how you loved him. And then you went off to Italy?

NORA. Yes. We had the means now, and the doctors urged us. So we left a month after.

MRS. LINDE. And your husband came back completely cured?

NORA. Sound as a drum!

MRS. LINDE. But—the doctor?

NORA. Who?

MRS. LINDE. I thought the maid said he was a doctor, the man who came in with me.

NORA. Yes, that was Dr. Rank—but he's not making a sick call. He's our closest friend, and he stops by at least once a day. No, Torvald hasn't had a sick moment since, and the children are fit and strong, and I am, too. (*Jumping up and clapping her hands.*) Oh, dear God, Kristine, what a lovely thing to live and be happy! But how disgusting of me—I'm talking of nothing but my own affairs. (*Sits on a stool close by* KRIS-TINE, *arms resting across her knees.*) Oh, don't be angry with me! Tell me, is it really true that you weren't in love with your husband? Why did you marry him, then?

MRS. LINDE. My mother was still alive, but bedridden and helpless—and I had my two younger brothers to look after. In all conscience, I didn't think I could turn him down.

NORA. No, you were right there. But was he rich at the time?

MRS. LINDE. He was very well off, I'd say. But the business was shaky, Nora. When he died, it all fell apart, and nothing was left.

NORA. And then—?

MRS. LINDE. Yes, so I had to scrape up a living with a little shop and a little teaching and whatever else I could find. The last three years have been like one endless workday without a rest for me. Now it's over, Nora. My poor mother doesn't need me, for she's passed on. Nor the boys, either; they're working now and can take care of themselves.

NORA. How free you must feel—

MRS. LINDE. No—only unspeakably empty. Nothing to live for now. (*Standing up anxiously.*) That's why I couldn't take it any longer out in that desolate hole. Maybe here it'll be easier to find something to do and keep my mind occupied. If I could only be lucky enough to get a steady job, some office work—

NORA. Oh, but Kristine, that's so dreadfully tiring, and you already look so tired. It would be much better for you if you could go off to a bathing resort.

MRS. LINDE (*going toward the window*). I have no father to give me travel money, Nora.

NORA (*rising*). Oh, don't be angry with me.

MRS. LINDE (*going to her*). Nora dear, don't you be angry with me. The worst of my kind of situation is all the bitterness that's stored away. No one to work for, and yet you're always having to snap up your opportunities. You have to live; and so you grow selfish. When you told me the happy change in your lot, do you know I was delighted less for your sakes than for mine?

NORA. How so? Oh, I see. You think maybe Torvald could do something for you.

MRS. LINDE. Yes, that's what I thought.

NORA. And he will, Kristine! Just leave it to me; I'll bring it up so delicately—find something attractive to humor him with. Oh, I'm so eager to help you.

MRS. LINDE. How very kind of you, Nora, to be so concerned over me—double kind, considering you really know so little of life's burdens yourself.

NORA. I—? I know so little—?

MRS. LINDE (*smiling*). Well, my heavens—a little needlework and such—Nora, you're just a child.

NORA (*tossing her head and pacing the floor*). You don't have to act so superior.

MRS. LINDE. Oh?

NORA. You're just like the others. You all think I'm incapable of anything serious.

MRS. LINDE. Come now—

NORA. That I've never had to face the raw world.

MRS. LINDE. Nora dear, you've just been telling me all your troubles.

NORA. Hm! Trivia! (*Quietly.*) I haven't told you the big thing.

MRS. LINDE. Big thing? What do you mean?

NORA. You look down on me so, Kristine, but you shouldn't. You're proud that you worked so long and hard for your mother.

MRS. LINDE. I don't look down on a soul. But it *is* true: I'm proud—and happy, too—to think it was given to me to make my mother's last days almost free of care.

NORA. And you're also proud thinking of what you've done for your brothers.

MRS. LINDE. I feel I've a right to be.

NORA. I agree. But listen to this, Kristine—I've also got something to be proud and happy for.

MRS. LINDE. I don't doubt it. But whatever do you mean?

NORA. Not so loud. What if Torvald heard! He mustn't, not for anything in the world. Nobody must know, Kristine. No one but you.

MRS. LINDE. But what is it, then?

NORA. Come here. (*Drawing her down beside her on the sofa.*) It's true—I've also got something to be proud and happy for. I'm the one who saved Torvald's life.

MRS. LINDE. Saved—? Saved how?

NORA. I told you about the trip to Italy. Torvald never would have lived if he hadn't gone south—

MRS. LINDE. Of course; your father gave you the means—

NORA (*smiling*). That's what Torvald and all the rest think, but—

MRS. LINDE. But—?

NORA. Papa didn't give us a pin. I was the one who raised the money.

MRS. LINDE. You? That whole amount?

NORA. Four thousand, eight hundred crowns. What do you say to that?

MRS. LINDE. But Nora, how was it possible? Did you win the lottery?

NORA (*disdainfully*). The lottery? Pooh! No art to that.

MRS. LINDE. But where did you get it from then?

NORA (*humming, with a mysterious smile*). Hmm, tra-la-la-la.

MRS. LINDE. Because you couldn't have borrowed it.

NORA. No? Why not?

MRS. LINDE. A wife can't borrow without her husband's consent.

NORA (*tossing her head*). Oh, but a wife with a little business sense, a wife who knows how to manage—

MRS. LINDE. Nora, I simply don't understand—

NORA. You don't have to. Whoever said I *borrowed* the money? I could have gotten it other ways. (*Throwing herself back on the sofa.*) I could have gotten it from some admirer or other. After all, a girl with my ravishing appeal—

MRS. LINDE. You lunatic.

NORA. I'll bet you're eaten up with curiosity, Kristine.

MRS. LINDE. Now listen here, Nora—you haven't done something indiscreet?

NORA (*sitting up again*). Is it indiscreet to save your husband's life?

MRS. LINDE. I think it's indiscreet that without his knowledge you—

NORA. But that's the point: he mustn't know! My Lord, can't you understand? He mustn't ever know the close call he had. It was to *me* the doctors came to say his life was in danger—that nothing could save him but a stay in the south. Didn't I try strategy then! I began talking about how lovely it would be for me to travel abroad like other young wives; I begged and I cried; I told him please to remember my condition, to be kind and indulge me; and then I dropped a hint that he could easily take out a loan. But at that, Kristine, he nearly exploded. He said I was frivolous, and it was his duty as man of the house not to indulge me in whims and fancies—as I think he called them. Aha, I thought, now you'll just have to be saved—and that's when I saw my chance.

Scene from the 1973 film version of *A Doll House* showing Anna Massey as Mrs. Linde and Claire Bloom as Nora.

MRS. LINDE. And your father never told Torvald the money wasn't from him?

NORA. No, never. Papa died right about then. I'd considered bringing him into my secret and begging him never to tell. But he was too sick at the time—and then, sadly, it didn't matter.

MRS. LINDE. And you've never confided in your husband since?

NORA. For heaven's sake, no! Are you serious? He's so strict on that subject. Besides—Torvald, with all his masculine pride—how painfully humiliating for him if he ever found out he was in debt to me. That would just ruin our relationship. Our beautiful, happy home would never be the same.

MRS. LINDE. Won't you ever tell him?

NORA (*thoughtfully, half smiling*). Yes—maybe sometime, years from now, when I'm no longer so attractive. Don't laugh! I only mean when Torvald loves me less than now, when he stops enjoying my dancing and dressing up and reciting for him. Then it might be wise to have something in reserve—(*Breaking off.*) How ridiculous! That'll never happen—Well, Kristine, what do you think of my big secret? I'm capable of something too, hm? You can imagine, of course, how this thing hangs over me. It really hasn't been easy meeting the payments on time. In the business world there's what they call quarterly interest and what they call amortization, and these are always so terribly hard to manage. I've had to skimp a little here and there, wherever I could, you know. I could hardly spare anything from my house allowance, because Torvald has to live well. I couldn't let the children go poorly dressed; whatever I got for them, I felt I had to use up completely—the darlings!

MRS. LINDE. Poor Nora, so it had to come out of your own budget, then?

NORA. Yes, of course. But I was the one most responsible, too. Every time Torvald gave me money for new clothes and such, I never used more than half; always bought the simplest, cheapest outfits. It was a godsend that everything looks so well on me that Torvald never noticed. But it did weigh me down at times, Kristine. It *is* such a joy to wear fine things. You understand.

MRS. LINDE. Oh, of course.

NORA. And then I found other ways of making money. Last winter I was lucky enough to get a lot of copying to do. I locked myself in and sat writing every evening till late in the night. Ah, I was tired so often, dead tired. But still it was wonderful fun, sitting and working like that, earning money. It was almost like being a man.

MRS. LINDE. But how much have you paid off this way so far?

NORA. That's hard to say, exactly. These accounts, you know, aren't easy to figure. I only know that I've paid out all I could scrape together. Time and again I haven't known where to turn. (*Smiling.*) Then I'd sit here dreaming of a rich old gentleman who had fallen in love with me—

MRS. LINDE. What! Who is he?

NORA. Oh, really! And that he'd died, and when his will was opened, there in big letters it said, "All my fortune shall be paid over in cash, immediately, to that enchanting Mrs. Nora Helmer."

MRS. LINDE. But Nora dear—who *was* this gentleman?

NORA. Good grief, can't you understand? The old man never existed; that was only something I'd dream up time and again whenever I was at my wits' end for money. But it makes no difference now; the old fossil can go where he pleases for all I care; I don't need him or his will—because now I'm free. (*Jumping up.*) Oh, how lovely to think of that, Kristine! Carefree! To know you're carefree, utterly carefree; to be able to romp and play with the children, and to keep up a beautiful, charming home—every-thing just the way Torvald likes it! And think, spring is coming, with big blue skies. Maybe we can travel a little then. Maybe I'll see the ocean again. Oh yes, it *is* so marvelous to live and be happy! (*The front doorbell rings.*)

MRS. LINDE (*rising*). There's the bell. It's probably best that I go.

NORA. No, stay. No one's expected. It must be for Torvald.

MAID (*from the hall doorway*). Excuse me, ma'am—there's a gentleman here to see Mr. Helmer, but I didn't know—since the doctor's with him—

NORA. Who is the gentleman?

KROGSTAD (*from the doorway*). It's me, Mrs. Helmer. (MRS. LINDE *starts and turns away toward the window.*)

NORA (*stepping toward him, tense, her voice a whisper*). You? What is it? Why do you want to speak to my husband?

KROGSTAD. Bank business—after a fashion. I have a small job in the investment bank, and I hear now your husband is going to be our chief—

NORA. In other words, it's—

KROGSTAD. Just dry business, Mrs. Helmer. Nothing but that.

NORA. Yes, then please be good enough to step into the study. (*She nods indifferently as she sees him out by the hall door, then returns and begins stirring up the stove.*)

MRS. LINDE. Nora—who was that man?

NORA. That was a Mr. Krogstad—a lawyer.

MRS. LINDE. Then it really was him.

NORA. Do you know that person?

MRS. LINDE. I did once—many years ago. For a time he was a law clerk in our town.

NORA. Yes, he's been that.

MRS. LINDE. How he's changed.

NORA. I understand he had a very unhappy marriage.

MRS. LINDE. He's a widower now.

NORA. With a number of children. There now, it's burning. (*She closes the stove door and moves the rocker a bit to one side.*)

MRS. LINDE. They say he has a hand in all kinds of business.

NORA. Oh? That may be true; I wouldn't know. But let's not think about business. It's so dull. (DR. RANK *enters from* HELMER'*s study.*)

RANK (*still in the doorway*). No, no, really—I don't want to intrude, I'd just as soon talk a little while with your wife. (*Shuts the door, then notices* MRS. LINDE.) Oh, beg pardon. I'm intruding here too.

NORA. No, not at all. (*Introducing him.*) Dr. Rank, Mrs. Linde.

RANK. Well now, that's a name much heard in this house. I believe I passed the lady on the stairs as I came.

MRS. LINDE. Yes, I take the stairs very slowly. They're rather hard on me.

RANK. Uh-hm, some touch of internal weakness?

MRS. LINDE. More overexertion, I'd say.

RANK. Nothing else? Then you're probably here in town to rest up in a round of parties?

MRS. LINDE. I'm here to look for work.

RANK. Is that the best cure for overexertion?

MRS. LINDE. One has to live, Doctor.

RANK. Yes, there's a common prejudice to that effect.

NORA. Oh, come on, Dr. Rank—you really do want to live yourself.

RANK. Yes, I really do. Wretched as I am, I'll gladly prolong my torment indefinitely. All my patients feel like that. And it's quite the same, too, with the morally sick. Right at this moment there's one of those moral invalids in there with Helmer—

MRS. LINDE (*softly*). Ah!

NORA. Who do you mean?

RANK. Oh, it's a lawyer, Krogstad, a type you wouldn't know. His character is rotten to the root—but even he began chattering all-importantly about how he had to *live.*

NORA. Oh? What did he want to talk to Torvald about?

RANK. I really don't know. I only heard something about the bank.

NORA. I didn't know that Krog—that this man Krogstad had anything to do with the bank.

RANK. Yes, he's gotten some kind of berth down there. (*To* MRS. LINDE.) I don't know if you also have, in your neck of the woods, a type of per-son who scuttles about breathlessly, sniffing out hints of moral corruption, and then maneuvers his victim into some sort of key position where he can keep an eye on him. It's the healthy these days that are out in the cold.

MRS. LINDE. All the same, it's the sick who most need to be taken in.

RANK (*with a shrug*). Yes, there we have it. That's the concept that's turning society into a sanatorium. (NORA, *lost in her thoughts, breaks out into quiet laughter and claps her hands.*)

RANK. Why do you laugh at that? Do you have any real idea of what society is?

NORA. What do I care about dreary old society? I was laughing at something quite different— something terribly funny. Tell me, Doctor—is everyone who works in the bank dependent now on Torvald?

RANK. Is that what you find so terribly funny?

NORA (*smiling and humming*). Never mind, never mind! (*Pacing the floor.*) Yes, that's really immensely amusing: that we—that Torvald has so much power now over all those people. (*Taking the bag out of her pocket.*) Dr. Rank, a little macaroon on that?

RANK. See here, macaroons! I thought they were contraband here.

NORA. Yes, but these are some that Kristine gave me.

MRS. LINDE. What? I—?

NORA. Now, now, don't be afraid. You couldn't possibly know that Torvald had forbidden them. You see, he's worried they'll ruin my teeth. But hmp! Just this once! Isn't that so, Dr. Rank? Help yourself! (*Puts a macaroon in his mouth.*) And you too, Kristine. And I'll also have one, only a little one—or two, at the most. (*Walking about again.*) Now I'm really tremendously happy. Now there's just one last thing in the world that I have an enormous desire to do.

RANK. Well! And what's that?

NORA. It's something I have such a consuming desire to say so Torvald could hear.

RANK. And why can't you say it?

NORA. I don't dare. It's quite shocking.

MRS. LINDE. Shocking?

RANK. Well, then it isn't advisable. But in front of us you certainly can. What do you have such a desire to say so Torvald could hear?

NORA. I have such a huge desire to say—to hell and be damned!

RANK. Are you crazy?

MRS. LINDE. My goodness, Nora!

RANK. Go on, say it. Here he is.

NORA (hiding the macaroon bag). Shh, shh, shh! (HELMER comes in from his study, hat in hand, overcoat over his arm.)

NORA (going toward him). Well, Torvald dear, are you through with him?

HELMER. Yes, he just left.

NORA. Let me introduce you—this is Kristine, who's arrived here in town.

HELMER. Kristine—? I'm sorry, but I don't know—

NORA. Mrs. Linde, Torvald dear. Mrs. Kristine Linde.

HELMER. Of course. A childhood friend of my wife's, no doubt?

MRS. LINDE. Yes, we knew each other in those days.

NORA. And just think, she made the long trip down here in order to talk with you.

HELMER. What's this?

MRS. LINDE. Well, not exactly—

NORA. You see, Kristine is remarkably clever in office work, and so she's terribly eager to come under a capable man's supervision and add more to what she already knows—

HELMER. Very wise, Mrs. Linde.

NORA. And then when she heard that you'd become a bank manager—the story was wired out to the papers—then she came in as fast as she could and— Really, Torvald, for my sake you can do a little something for Kristine, can't you?

HELMER. Yes, it's not at all impossible. Mrs. Linde, I suppose you're a widow?

MRS. LINDE. Yes.

HELMER. Any experience in office work?

MRS. LINDE. Yes, a good deal.

HELMER. Well, it's quite likely that I can make an opening for you—

NORA (clapping her hands). You see, you see!

HELMER. You've come at a lucky moment, Mrs. Linde.

MRS. LINDE. Oh, how can I thank you?

HELMER. Not necessary. (Putting his overcoat on.) But today you'll have to excuse me—

RANK. Wait, I'll go with you. (He fetches his coat from the hall and warms it at the stove.)

NORA. Don't stay out long, dear.

HELMER. An hour; no more.

NORA. Are you going too, Kristine?

MRS. LINDE (putting on her winter garments). Yes, I have to see about a room now.

HELMER. Then perhaps we can all walk together.

NORA (helping her). What a shame we're so cramped here, but it's quite impossible for us to—

MRS. LINDE. Oh, don't even think of it! Good-bye, Nora dear, and thanks for everything.

NORA. Good-bye for now. Of course you'll be back this evening. And you too, Dr. Rank. What? If you're well enough? Oh, you've got to be! Wrap up tight now. (In a ripple of small talk the company moves out into the hall; children's voices are heard outside on the steps.)

NORA. There they are! There they are! (She runs to open the door. The children come in with their nurse, ANNE-MARIE.) Come in, come in! (Bends down and kisses them.) Oh, you darlings—! Look at them, Kristine. Aren't they lovely!

RANK. No loitering in the draft here.

HELMER. Come, Mrs. Linde—this place is unbearable now for anyone but mothers. (DR. RANK, HELMER, and MRS. LINDE go down the stairs. ANNE-MARIE goes into the living room with the children. NORA follows, after closing the hall door.)

NORA. How fresh and strong you look. Oh, such red cheeks you have! Like apples and roses. (The children interrupt her throughout the following.) And it was so much fun? That's wonderful. Really? You pulled both Emmy and Bob on the sled? Imagine, all together! Yes, you're a clever boy, Ivar. Oh, let me hold her a bit, Anne-Marie. My sweet little doll baby! (Takes the smallest from the nurse and dances with her.)

Yes, yes, Mama will dance with Bob as well. What? Did you throw snowballs? Oh, if I'd only been there! No, don't bother, Anne-Marie—I'll undress them myself. Oh yes, let me. It's such fun. Go in and rest; you look half frozen. There's hot coffee waiting for you on the stove. (*The nurse goes into the room to the left.* NORA *takes the children's winter things off, throwing them about, while the children talk to her all at once.*) Is that so? A big dog chased you? But it didn't bite? No, dogs never bite little, lovely doll babies. Don't peek in the packages, Ivar! What is it? Yes, wouldn't you like to know. No, no, it's an ugly something. Well? Shall we play? What shall we play? Hide-and-seek? Yes, let's play hide-and-seek. Bob must hide first. I must? Yes, let me hide first. (*Laughing and shouting, she and the children play in and out of the living room and the adjoining room to the right. At last* NORA *hides under the table. The children come storming in, search, but cannot find her, then hear her muffled laughter, dash over to the table, lift the cloth up and find her. Wild shouting. She creeps forward as if to scare them. More shouts. Meanwhile, a knock at the hall door; no one has noticed it. Now the door half opens, and* KROGSTAD *appears. He waits a moment; the game goes on.*)

KROGSTAD. Beg pardon, Mrs. Helmer—

NORA (*with a strangled cry, turning and scrambling to her knees*). Oh! What do you want?

KROGSTAD. Excuse me. The outer door was ajar; it must be someone forgot to shut it—

NORA (*rising*). My husband isn't home, Mr. Krogstad.

KROGSTAD. I know that.

NORA. Yes—then what do you want here?

KROGSTAD. A word with you.

NORA. With—? (*To the children, quietly.*) Go in to Anne-Marie. What? No, the strange man won't hurt Mama. When he's gone, we'll play some more. (*She leads the children into the room to the left and shuts the door after them. Then, tense and nervous:*) You want to speak to me?

KROGSTAD. Yes, I want to.

NORA. Today? But it's not yet the first of the month—

KROGSTAD. No, it's Christmas Eve. It's going to be up to you how merry a Christmas you have.

NORA. What is it you want? Today I absolutely can't—

KROGSTAD. We won't talk about that till later. This is something else. You do have a moment to spare, I suppose?

NORA. Oh yes, of course—I do, except—

KROGSTAD. Good. I was sitting over at Olsen's Restaurant when I saw your husband go down the street—

NORA. Yes?

KROGSTAD. With a lady.

NORA. Yes. So?

KROGSTAD. If you'll pardon my asking: wasn't that lady a Mrs. Linde?

NORA. Yes.

KROGSTAD. Just now come into town?

NORA. Yes, today.

KROGSTAD. She's a good friend of yours?

NORA. Yes, she is. But I don't see—

KROGSTAD. I also knew her once.

NORA. I'm aware of that.

KROGSTAD. Oh? You know all about it. I thought so. Well, then let me ask you short and sweet: is Mrs. Linde getting a job in the bank?

NORA. What makes you think you can cross-examine me, Mr. Krogstad—you, one of my husband's employees? But since you ask, you might as well know—yes, Mrs. Linde's going to be taken on at the bank. And I'm the one who spoke for her, Mr. Krogstad. Now you know.

KROGSTAD. So I guessed right.

NORA (*pacing up and down*). Oh, one does have a tiny bit of influence, I should hope. Just because I am a woman, don't think it means that— When one has a subordinate position, Mr. Krogstad, one really ought to be careful about pushing somebody who—hm—

KROGSTAD. Who has influence?

NORA. That's right.

KROGSTAD (*in a different tone*). Mrs. Helmer, would you be good enough to use your influence on my behalf?

NORA. What? What do you mean?

KROGSTAD. Would you please make sure that I

keep my subordinate position in the bank.

NORA. What does that mean? Who's thinking of taking away your position?

KROGSTAD. Oh, don't play the innocent with me. I'm quite aware that your friend would hardly relish the chance of running into me again; and I'm also aware now whom I can thank for being turned out.

NORA. But I promise you—

KROGSTAD. Yes, yes, yes, to the point: there's still time, and I'm advising you to use your influence to prevent it.

NORA. But Mr. Krogstad, I have absolutely no influence.

KROGSTAD. You haven't? I thought you were just saying—

NORA. You shouldn't take me so literally. I! How can you believe that I have any such influence over my husband?

KROGSTAD. Oh, I've known your husband from our student days. I don't think the great bank manager's more steadfast than any other married man.

NORA. You speak insolently about my husband, and I'll show you the door.

KROGSTAD. The lady has spirit.

NORA. I'm not afraid of you any longer. After New Year's, I'll soon be done with the whole business.

KROGSTAD (restraining himself). Now listen to me, Mrs. Helmer. If necessary, I'll fight for my little job in the bank as if it were life itself.

NORA. Yes, so it seems.

KROGSTAD. It's not just a matter of income; that's the least of it. It's something else— All right, out with it! Look, this is the thing. You know, just like all the others, of course, that once, a good many years ago, I did something rather rash.

NORA. I've heard rumors to that effect.

KROGSTAD. The case never got into court; but all the same, every door was closed in my face from then on. So I took up those various activities you know about. I had to grab hold somewhere; and I dare say I haven't been among the worst. But now I want to drop all that. My boys are growing up. For their sakes, I'll have to win back as much respect as possible here in town. That job in the bank was like the first rung in my ladder. And now your husband wants to kick me right back down in the mud again.

NORA. But for heaven's sake, Mr. Krogstad, it's simply not in my power to help you.

KROGSTAD. That's because you haven't the will to—but I have the means to make you.

NORA. You certainly won't tell my husband that I owe you money?

KROGSTAD. Hm—what if I told him that?

NORA. That would be shameful of you. (Nearly in tears.) This secret—my joy and my pride—that he should learn it in such a crude and disgusting way—learn it from you. You'd expose me to the most horrible unpleasantness—

KROGSTAD. Only unpleasantness?

NORA (vehemently). But go on and try. It'll turn out the worse for you, because then my husband will really see what a crook you are, and then you'll never be able to hold your job.

KROGSTAD. I asked if it was just domestic unpleasantness you were afraid of?

NORA. If my husband finds out, then of course he'll pay what I owe at once, and then we'd be through with you for good.

KROGSTAD (a step closer). Listen, Mrs. Helmer—you've either got a very bad memory, or else no head at all for business. I'd better put you a little more in touch with the facts.

NORA. What do you mean?

KROGSTAD. When your husband was sick, you came to me for a loan of four thousand, eight hundred crowns.

NORA. Where else could I go?

KROGSTAD. I promised to get you that sum—

NORA. And you got it.

KROGSTAD. I promised to get you that sum, on certain conditions. You were so involved in your husband's illness, and so eager to finance your trip, that I guess you didn't think out all the details. It might just be a good idea to remind you. I promised you the money on the strength of a note I drew up.

NORA. Yes, and that I signed.

KROGSTAD. Right. But at the bottom I added some lines for your father to guarantee the loan. He was supposed to sign down there.

NORA. Supposed to? He did sign.

KROGSTAD. I left the date blank. In other words, your father would have dated his signature himself. Do you remember that?

NORA. Yes, I think—

KROGSTAD. Then I gave you the note for you to mail to your father. Isn't that so?

NORA. Yes.

KROGSTAD. And naturally you sent it at once—because only some five, six days later you brought me the note, properly signed. And with that, the money was yours.

NORA. Well, then; I've made my payments regularly, haven't I?

KROGSTAD. More or less. But—getting back to the point—those were hard times for you then, Mrs. Helmer.

NORA. Yes, they were.

KROGSTAD. Your father was very ill, I believe.

NORA. He was near the end.

KROGSTAD. He died soon after?

NORA. Yes.

KROGSTAD. Tell me, Mrs. Helmer, do you happen to recall the date of your father's death? The day of the month, I mean.

NORA. Papa died the twenty-ninth of September.

KROGSTAD. That's quite correct; I've already looked into that. And now we come to a curious thing—(Taking out a paper.) which I simply cannot comprehend.

NORA. Curious thing? I don't know—

KROGSTAD. This is the curious thing: that your father co-signed the note for your loan three days after his death.

NORA. How—? I don't understand.

KROGSTAD. Your father died the twenty-ninth of September. But look. Here your father dated his signature October second. Isn't that curious, Mrs. Helmer? (NORA is silent.) Can you explain it to me? (NORA remains silent.) It's also remarkable that the words "October second" and the year aren't written in your father's hand, but rather in one that I think I know. Well, it's easy

to understand. Your father forgot perhaps to date his signature, and then someone or other added it, a bit sloppily, before anyone knew of his death. There's nothing wrong in that. It all comes down to the signature. And there's no question about *that*, Mrs. Helmer. It really *was* your father who signed his own name here, wasn't it?

NORA (*after a short silence, throwing her head back and looking squarely at him*). No, it wasn't. *I* signed Papa's name.

KROGSTAD. Wait, now—are you fully aware that this is a dangerous confession?

NORA. Why? You'll soon get your money.

KROGSTAD. Let me ask you a question—why didn't you send the paper to your father?

NORA. That was impossible. Papa was so sick. If I'd asked him for his signature, I also would have had to tell him what the money was for. But I couldn't tell him, sick as he was, that my husband's life was in danger. That was just impossible.

KROGSTAD. Then it would have been better if you'd given up the trip abroad.

NORA. I couldn't possibly. The trip was to save my husband's life. I couldn't give that up.

KROGSTAD. But didn't you ever consider that this was a fraud against me?

NORA. I couldn't let myself be bothered by that. You weren't any concern of mine. I couldn't stand you, with all those cold complications you made, even though you knew how badly off my husband was.

KROGSTAD. Mrs. Helmer, obviously you haven't the vaguest idea of what you've involved yourself in. But I can tell you this: it was nothing more and nothing worse that I once did—and it wrecked my whole reputation.

NORA. You? Do you expect me to believe that you ever acted bravely to save your wife's life?

KROGSTAD. Laws don't inquire into motives.

NORA. Then they must be very poor laws.

KROGSTAD. Poor or not—if I introduce this paper in court, you'll be judged according to law.

NORA. This I refuse to believe. A daughter hasn't a right to protect her dying father from anxi-

Scene from the 1973 film version of *A Doll House* showing Claire Bloom as Nora.

ety and care? A wife hasn't a right to save her husband's life? I don't know much about laws, but I'm sure that somewhere in the books these things are allowed. And you don't know anything about it—you who practice the law? You must be an awful lawyer, Mr. Krogstad.

KROGSTAD. Could be. But business—the kind of business we two are mixed up in—don't you think I know about that? All right. Do what

you want now. But I'm telling you *this*: if I get shoved down a second time, you're going to keep me company. (*He bows and goes out through the hall.*)

NORA (*pensive for a moment, then tossing her head*). Oh, really! Trying to frighten me! I'm not so silly as all that. (*Begins gathering up the children's clothes, but soon stops.*) But—? No, but that's impossible! I did it out of love.

THE CHILDREN (*in the doorway, left*). Mama, that strange man's gone out the door.

NORA. Yes, yes, I know it. But don't tell anyone about the strange man. Do you hear? Not even Papa!

THE CHILDREN. No, Mama. But now will you play again?

NORA. No, not now.

THE CHILDREN. Oh, but Mama, you promised.

NORA. Yes, but I can't now. Go inside; I have too much to do. Go in, go in, my sweet darlings. (*She herds them gently back in the room and shuts the door after them. Settling on the sofa, she takes up a piece of embroidery and makes some stitches, but soon stops abruptly.*) No! (*Throws the work aside, rises, goes to the hall door and calls out.*) Helene! Let me have the tree in here. (*Goes to the table, left, opens the table drawer, and stops again.*) No, but that's utterly impossible!

MAID (*with the Christmas tree*). Where should I put it, ma'am?

NORA. There. The middle of the floor.

MAID. Should I bring anything else?

NORA. No, thanks. I have what I need. (*The* MAID, *who has set the tree down, goes out.*)

NORA (*absorbed in trimming the tree*). Candles here—and flowers here. That terrible creature! Talk, talk, talk! There's nothing to it at all. The tree's going to be lovely. I'll do anything to please you, Torvald. I'll sing for you, dance for you—(HELMER *comes in from the hall, with a sheaf of papers under his arm.*)

NORA. Oh! You're back so soon?

HELMER. Yes. Has anyone been here?

NORA. Here? No.

HELMER. That's odd. I saw Krogstad leaving the front door.

NORA. So? Oh yes, that's true. Krogstad was here a moment.

HELMER. Nora, I can see by your face that he's been here, begging you to put in a good word for him.

NORA. Yes.

HELMER. And it was supposed to seem like your own idea? You were to hide it from me that he'd been here. He asked you that, too, didn't he?

NORA. Yes, Torvald, but—

HELMER. Nora, Nora, and you could fall for that? Talk with that sort of person and promise him anything? And then in the bargain, tell me an untruth.

NORA. An untruth—?

HELMER. Didn't you say that no one had been here? (*Wagging his finger.*) My little songbird must never do that again. A songbird needs a clean beak to warble with. No false notes. (*Putting his arm about her waist.*) That's the way it should be, isn't it? Yes, I'm sure of it. (*Releasing her.*) And so, enough of that. (*Sitting by the stove.*) Ah, how snug and cozy it is here. (*Leafing among his papers.*)

NORA (*busy with the tree, after a short pause*). Torvald!

HELMER. Yes.

NORA. I'm so much looking forward to the Stenborgs' costume party, day after tomorrow.

HELMER. And I can't wait to see what you'll surprise me with.

NORA. Oh, that stupid business!

HELMER. What?

NORA. I can't find anything that's right. Everything seems so ridiculous, so inane.

HELMER. So my little Nora's come to *that* recognition?

NORA (*going behind his chair, her arms resting on its back*). Are you very busy, Torvald?

HELMER. Oh—

NORA. What papers are those?

HELMER. Bank matters.

NORA. Already?

HELMER. I've gotten full authority from the retiring management to make all necessary changes in personnel and procedure. I'll need Christmas week for that. I want to have everything in order by New Year's.

NORA. So that was the reason this poor Krogstad—

HELMER. Hm.

NORA (*still leaning on the chair and slowly stroking the nape of his neck*). If you weren't so very busy, I would have asked you an enormous favor, Torvald.

HELMER. Let's hear. What is it?

NORA. You know, there isn't anyone who has your good taste—and I want so much to look well at the costume party. Torvald, couldn't you take over and decide what I should be and plan my costume?

HELMER. Ah, is my stubborn little creature calling for a lifeguard?

NORA. Yes, Torvald, I can't get anywhere without your help.

HELMER. All right—I'll think it over. We'll hit on something.

NORA. Oh, how sweet of you. (*Goes to the tree again. Pause.*) Aren't the red flowers pretty—? But tell me, was it really such a crime that this Krogstad committed?

HELMER. Forgery. Do you have any idea what that means?

NORA. Couldn't he have done it out of need?

HELMER. Yes, or thoughtlessness, like so many others. I'm not so heartless that I'd condemn a man categorically for just one mistake.

NORA. No, of course not, Torvald!

HELMER. Plenty of men have redeemed themselves by openly confessing their crimes and taking their punishment.

NORA. Punishment—?

HELMER. But now Krogstad didn't go that way. He got himself out by sharp practices, and that's the real cause of his moral breakdown.

NORA. Do you really think that would—?

HELMER. Just imagine how a man with that sort of guilt in him has to lie and cheat and deceive on all sides, has to wear a mask even with the nearest and dearest he has, even with his own wife and children. And with the children, Nora—that's where it's most horrible.

NORA. Why?

HELMER. Because that kind of atmosphere of lies infects the whole life of a home. Every breath the children take in is filled with the germs of something degenerate.

NORA (coming closer behind him). Are you sure of that?

HELMER. Oh, I've seen it often enough as a lawyer. Almost everyone who goes bad early in life has a mother who's a chronic liar.

NORA. Why just—the mother?

HELMER. It's usually the mother's influence that's dominant, but the father's works in the same way, of course. Every lawyer is quite familiar with it. And still this Krogstad's been going home year in, year out, poisoning his own children with lies and pretense; that's why I call him morally lost. (Reaching his hands out toward her.) So my sweet little Nora must promise me never to plead his cause. Your hand on it. Come, come, what's this? Give me your hand. There, now. All settled. I can tell you it'd be impossible for me to work alongside of him. I literally feel physically revolted when I'm anywhere near such a person.

NORA (withdraws her hand and goes to the other side of the Christmas tree). How hot it is here! And I've got so much to do.

HELMER (getting up and gathering his papers). Yes, and I have to think about getting some of these read through before dinner. I'll think about your costume, too. And something to hang on the tree in gilt paper, I may even see about that. (Putting his hand on her head.) Oh you, my darling little songbird. (He goes into his study and closes the door after him.)

NORA (softly, after a silence). Oh, really! it isn't so. It's impossible. It must be impossible.

ANNE-MARIE (in the doorway, left). The children are begging so hard to come in to Mama.

NORA. No, no, no, don't let them in to me! You stay with them, Anne-Marie.

ANNE-MARIE. Of course, ma'am. (Closes the door.)

NORA (pale with terror). Hurt my children—! Poison my home? (A moment's pause; then she tosses her head.) That's not true. Never in all the world.

ACT TWO

Same room. Beside the piano the Christmas tree now stands stripped of ornament, burned-down candle stubs on its ragged branches. NORA's *street clothes lie on the sofa.* NORA, *alone in the room, moves restlessly about; at last she stops at the sofa and picks up her coat.*

NORA (dropping the coat again). Someone's coming! (Goes toward the door, listens.) No—there's no one. Of course—nobody's coming today, Christmas Day—or tomorrow, either. But maybe—(Opens the door and looks out.) No, nothing in the mailbox. Quite empty. (Coming forward.) What nonsense! He won't do anything serious. Nothing terrible could happen. It's impossible. Why, I have three small children. (ANNE-MARIE, with a large carton, comes in from the room to the left.)

ANNE-MARIE. Well, at last I found the box with the masquerade clothes.

NORA. Thanks. Put it on the table.

ANNE-MARIE (does so). But they're all pretty much of a mess.

NORA. Ahh! I'd love to rip them in a million pieces!

ANNE-MARIE. Oh, mercy, they can be fixed right up. Just a little patience.

NORA. Yes, I'll go get Mrs. Linde to help me.

ANNE-MARIE. Out again now? In this nasty weather? Miss Nora will catch cold—get sick.

NORA. Oh, worse things could happen— How are the children?

ANNE-MARIE. The poor mites are playing with their Christmas presents, but—

NORA. Do they ask for me much?

ANNE-MARIE. They're so used to having Mama around, you know.

NORA. Yes. but Anne-Marie, I *can't* be together with them as much as I was.

ANNE-MARIE. Well, small children get used to anything.

NORA. You think so? Do you think they'd forget their mother if she was gone for good?

ANNE-MARIE. Oh, mercy—gone for good!

NORA. Wait, tell me, Anne-Marie—I've wondered

so often—how could you ever have the heart to give your child over to strangers?

ANNE-MARIE. But I had to, you know, to become little Nora's nurse.

NORA. Yes, but how could you *do* it?

ANNE-MARIE. When I could get such a good place? A girl who's poor and who's gotten in trouble is glad enough for that. Because that slippery fish, he didn't do a thing for me, you know.

NORA. But your daughter's surely forgotten you.

ANNE-MARIE. Oh, she certainly has not. She's written to me, both when she was confirmed and when she was married.

NORA (*clasping her about the neck*). You old Anne-Marie, you were a good mother for me when I was little.

ANNE-MARIE. Poor little Nora, with no other mother but me.

NORA. And if the babies didn't have one, then I know that you'd— What silly talk! (*Opening the carton.*) Go in to them. Now I'll have to— Tomorrow you can see how lovely I'll look.

ANNE-MARIE. Oh, there won't be anyone at the party as lovely as Miss Nora. (*She goes off into the room, left.*)

NORA (*begins unpacking the box, but soon throws it aside*). Oh, if I dared to go out. If only nobody would come. If only nothing would happen here while I'm out. What craziness—nobody's coming. Just don't think. This muff —needs a brushing. Beautiful gloves, beautiful gloves. Let it go. Let it go! One, two, three, four, five, six— (*With a cry.*) Oh, there they are! (*Poises to move toward the door, but remains irresolutely standing.* MRS. LINDE *enters from the hall, where she has removed her street clothes.*)

NORA. Oh, it's you, Kristine. There's no one else out there? How good that you've come.

MRS. LINDE. I hear you were up asking for me.

NORA. Yes, I just stopped by. There's something you really can help me with. Let's get settled on the sofa. Look, there's going to be a costume party tomorrow evening at the Stenborgs' right above us, and now Torvald wants me to go as a Neapolitan peasant girl and dance the tarantella that I learned in Capri.

Scene from the 1973 film version of *A Doll House* showing Dame Edith Evans as Anne-Marie and Claire Bloom as Nora.

MRS. LINDE. Really, are you giving a whole performance?

NORA. Torvald says yes, I should. See, here's the dress. Torvald had it made for me down there; but now it's all so tattered that I just don't know—

MRS. LINDE. Oh, we'll fix that up in no time. It's nothing more than the trimmings—they're a bit loose here and there. Needle and thread? Good, now we have what we need.

NORA. Oh, how sweet of you!

MRS. LINDE (*sewing*). So you'll be in disguise tomorrow, Nora. You know what? I'll stop by then for a moment and have a look at you all dressed up. But listen, I've absolutely forgotten to thank you for that pleasant evening yesterday.

NORA (*getting up and walking about*). I don't think it was as pleasant as usual yesterday. You should have come to town a bit sooner, Kristine— Yes, Torvald really knows how to give a home elegance and charm.

MRS. LINDE. And you do, too, if you ask me. You're not your father's daughter for nothing. But tell me, is Dr. Rank always so down in the mouth as yesterday?

NORA. No, that was quite an exception. But he goes around critically ill all the time—tuberculosis of the spine, poor man. You know, his father was a disgusting thing who kept mistresses and so on—and that's why the son's been sickly from birth.

MRS. LINDE (*lets her sewing fall to her lap*). But my dearest Nora, how do you know about such things?

NORA (*walking more jauntily*). Hmp! When you've had three children, then you've had a few visits from—from women who know something of medicine, and they tell you this and that.

MRS. LINDE (*resumes sewing; a short pause*). Does Dr. Rank come here every day?

NORA. Every blessed day. He's Torvald's best friend from childhood, and *my* good friend, too. Dr. Rank almost belongs to this house.

MRS. LINDE. But tell me—is he quite sincere? I mean, doesn't he rather enjoy flattering people?

NORA. Just the opposite. Why do you think that?

MRS. LINDE. When you introduced us yesterday, he was proclaiming that he'd often heard my name in this house; but later I noticed that your husband hadn't the slightest idea who I really was. So how could Dr. Rank—?

NORA. But it's all true, Kristine. You see, Torvald loves me beyond words, and, as he puts it, he'd like to keep me all to himself. For a long time he'd almost be jealous if I even mentioned any of my old friends back home. So of course I dropped that. But with Dr. Rank I talk a lot about such things, because he likes hearing about them.

MRS. LINDE. Now listen, Nora; in many ways you're still like a child. I'm a good deal older than you, with a little more experience. I'll tell you something: you ought to put an end to all this with Dr. Rank.

NORA. What should I put an end to?

MRS. LINDE. Both parts of it, I think. Yesterday you said something about a rich admirer who'd provide you with money—

NORA. Yes, one who doesn't exist—worse luck. So?

MRS. LINDE. Is Dr. Rank well off?

NORA. Yes, he is.

MRS. LINDE. With no dependents?

NORA. No, no one. But—

MRS. LINDE. And he's over here every day?

NORA. Yes, I told you that.

MRS. LINDE. How can a man of such refinement be so grasping?

NORA. I don't follow you at all.

MRS. LINDE. Now don't try to hide it, Nora. You think I can't guess who loaned you the forty-eight hundred crowns?

NORA. Are you out of your mind? How could you think such a thing! A friend of ours, who comes here every single day. What an intolerable situation that would have been!

MRS. LINDE. Then it really wasn't him.

NORA. No, absolutely not. It never even crossed my mind for a moment— And he had nothing to lend in those days; his inheritance came later.

MRS. LINDE. Well, I think that was a stroke of luck for you, Nora dear.

NORA. No, it never would have occurred to me to ask Dr. Rank— Still, I'm quite sure that if I had asked him—

MRS. LINDE. Which you won't, of course.

NORA. No, of course not. I can't see that I'd ever need to. But I'm quite positive that if I talked to Dr. Rank—

MRS. LINDE. Behind your husband's back?

NORA. I've got to clear up this other thing; *that's* also behind his back. I've *got* to clear it all up.

MRS. LINDE. Yes, I was saying that yesterday, but—

NORA (*pacing up and down*). A man handles these problems so much better than a woman—

MRS. LINDE. One's husband does, yes.

NORA. Nonsense. (*Stopping.*) When you pay everything you owe, then you get your note back, right?

MRS. LINDE. Yes, naturally.

NORA. And can rip it into a million pieces and burn

it up—that filthy scrap of paper!

MRS. LINDE (*looking hard at her, laying her sewing aside, and rising slowly*). Nora, you're hiding something from me.

NORA. You can see it in my face?

MRS. LINDE. Something's happened to you since yesterday morning. Nora, what is it?

NORA (*hurrying toward her*). Kristine! (*Listening.*) Shh! Torvald's home. Look, go in with the children a while. Torvald can't bear all this snipping and stitching. Let Anne-Marie help you.

MRS. LINDE (*gathering up some of the things*). All right, but I'm not leaving here until we've talked this out. (*She disappears into the room, left, as* TORVALD *enters from the hall.*)

NORA. Oh, how I've been waiting for you, Torvald dear.

HELMER. Was that the dressmaker?

NORA. No, that was Kristine. She's helping me fix up my costume. You know, it's going to be quite attractive.

HELMER. Yes, wasn't that a bright idea I had?

NORA. Brilliant! But then wasn't I good as well to give in to you?

HELMER. Good—because you give in to your husband's judgment? All right, you little goose, I know you didn't mean it like that. But I won't disturb you. You'll want to have a fitting, I suppose.

NORA. And you'll be working?

HELMER. Yes. (*Indicating a bundle of papers.*) See. I've been down to the bank. (*Starts toward his study.*)

NORA. Torvald.

HELMER (*stops*). Yes.

NORA. If your little squirrel begged you, with all her heart and soul, for something—?

HELMER. What's that?

NORA. Then would you do it?

HELMER. First, naturally, I'd have to know what it was.

NORA. Your squirrel would scamper about and do tricks, if you'd only be sweet and give in.

HELMER. Out with it.

NORA. Your lark would be singing high and low in every room—

HELMER. Come on, she does that anyway.

NORA. I'd be a wood nymph and dance for you in the moonlight.

HELMER. Nora—don't tell me it's that same business from this morning?

NORA (*coming closer*). Yes, Torvald, I beg you, please!

HELMER. And you actually have the nerve to drag that up again?

NORA. Yes, yes, you've got to give in to me; you *have* to let Krogstad keep his job in the bank.

HELMER. My dear Nora, I've slated his job for Mrs. Linde.

NORA. That's awfully kind of you. But you could just fire another clerk instead of Krogstad.

HELMER. This is the most incredible stubbornness! Because you go and give an impulsive promise to speak up for him, I'm expected to—

NORA. That's not the reason, Torvald. It's for your own sake. That man does writing for the worst papers; you said it yourself. He could do you any amount of harm. I'm scared to death of him—

HELMER. Ah, I understand. It's the old memories haunting you.

NORA. What do you mean by that?

HELMER. Of course, you're thinking about your father.

NORA. Yes, all right. Just remember how those nasty gossips wrote in the papers about Papa and slandered him so cruelly. I think they'd have had him dismissed if the department hadn't sent you up to investigate, and if you hadn't been so kind and open-minded toward him.

HELMER. My dear Nora, there's a notable difference between your father and me. Your father's official career was hardly above reproach. But mine is; and I hope it'll stay that way as long as I hold my position.

NORA. Oh, who can ever tell what vicious minds can invent? We could be so snug and happy now in our quiet, carefree home—you and I and the children, Torvald! That's why I'm pleading with you so—

HELMER. And just by pleading for him you make it impossible for me to keep him on. It's already known at the bank that I'm firing Krogstad. What if it's rumored around now that the new bank manager was vetoed by his wife—

NORA. Yes, what then—?

HELMER. Oh yes—as long as our little bundle of stubbornness gets her way—! I should go and make myself ridiculous in front of the whole office—give people the idea I can be swayed by all kinds of outside pressure. Oh, you can bet I'd feel the effects of that soon enough! Besides—there's something that rules Krogstad right out at the bank as long as I'm the manager.

NORA. What's that?

HELMER. His moral failings I could maybe overlook if I had to—

NORA. Yes, Torvald, why not?

HELMER. And I hear he's quite efficient on the job. But he was a crony of mine back in my teens—one of those rash friendships that crop up again and again to embarrass you later in life. Well, I might as well say it straight out: we're on a first-name basis. And that tactless fool makes no effort at all to hide it in front of others. Quite the contrary—he thinks that entitles him to take a familiar air around me, and so every other second he comes booming out with his "Yes, Torvald!" and "Sure thing, Torvald!" I tell you, it's been excruciating for me. He's out to make my place in the bank unbearable.

NORA. Torvald, you can't be serious about all this.

HELMER. Oh no? Why not?

NORA. Because these are such petty considerations.

HELMER. What are you saying? Petty? You think I'm petty!

NORA. No, just the opposite, Torvald dear. That's exactly why—

HELMER. Never mind. You call my motives petty; then I might as well be just that. Petty! All right! We'll put a stop to this for good. (*Goes to the hall door and calls.*) Helene!

NORA. What do you want?

HELMER. (*searching among his papers*). A decision. (*The* MAID *comes in.*) Look here; take this letter; go out with it at once. Get hold of a messenger and have him deliver it. Quick now. It's already addressed. Wait, here's some money.

MAID. Yes, sir. (*She leaves with the letter.*)

HELMER. (*straightening his papers*). There, now, little Miss Willful.

NORA. (*breathlessly*). Torvald, what was that letter?

HELMER. Krogstad's notice.

NORA. Call it back, Torvald! There's still time. Oh, Torvald, call it back! Do it for my sake—for your sake, for the children's sake! Do you hear, Torvald; do it! You don't know how this can harm us.

HELMER. Too late.

NORA. Yes, too late.

HELMER. Nora dear, I can forgive you this panic, even though basically you're insulting me. Yes, you are! Or isn't it an insult to think that *I* should be afraid of a courtroom hack's revenge? But I forgive you anyway, because this shows so beautifully how much you love me. (*Takes her in his arms.*) This is the way it should be, my darling Nora. Whatever comes, you'll see: when it really counts, I have strength and courage enough as a man to take on the whole weight myself.

NORA. (*terrified*). What do you mean by that?

HELMER. The whole weight, I said.

NORA. (*resolutely*). No, never in all the world.

HELMER. Good. So we'll share it, Nora, as man and wife. That's as it should be. (*Fondling her.*) Are you happy now? There, there, there—not these frightened dove's eyes. It's nothing at all but empty fantasies— Now you should run through your tarantella and practice your tambourine. I'll go to the inner office and shut both doors, so I won't hear a thing; you can make all the noise you like. (*Turning in the doorway.*) And when Rank comes, just tell him where he can find me. (*He nods to her and goes with his papers into the study, closing the door.*)

NORA. (*standing as though rooted, dazed with fright, in a whisper*). He really could do it. He will do it. He'll do it in spite of everything. No, not that, never, never! Anything but that! Escape! A way out— (*The doorbell rings.*) Dr. Rank! Anything but that! *Anything*, whatever it is! (*Her hands pass over her face, smoothing it; she pulls herself together, goes over and opens the hall door.* DR. RANK *stands outside, hanging his fur coat up. During the following scene, it begins getting dark.*)

NORA. Hello, Dr. Rank. I recognized your ring.

But you mustn't go in to Torvald yet; I believe he's working.

RANK. And you?

NORA. For you, I always have an hour to spare—you know that. *(He has entered, and she shuts the door after him.)*

RANK. Many thanks. I'll make use of these hours while I can.

NORA. What do you mean by that? While you can?

RANK. Does that disturb you?

NORA. Well, it's such an odd phrase. Is anything going to happen?

RANK. What's going to happen is what I've been expecting so long—but I honestly didn't think it would come so soon.

NORA *(gripping his arm)*. What is it you've found out? Dr. Rank, you have to tell me!

RANK *(sitting by the stove)*. It's all over with me. There's nothing to be done about it.

NORA *(breathing easier)*. Is it you—then—?

RANK. Who else? There's no point in lying to one's self. I'm the most miserable of all my patients, Mrs. Helmer. These past few days I've been auditing my internal accounts. Bankrupt! Within a month I'll probably be laid out and rotting in the churchyard.

NORA. Oh, what a horrible thing to say.

RANK. The thing itself is horrible. But the worst of it is all the other horror before it's over. There's only one final examination left; when I'm finished with that, I'll know about when my disintegration will begin. There's something I want to say. Helmer with his sensitivity has such a sharp distaste for anything ugly. I don't want him near my sickroom.

NORA. Oh, but Dr. Rank—

RANK. I won't have him in there. Under no condition. I'll lock my door to him— As soon as I'm completely sure of the worst, I'll send you my calling card marked with a black cross, and you'll know then the wreck has started to come apart.

NORA. No, today you're completely unreasonable. And I wanted you so much to be in a really good humor.

RANK. With death up my sleeve? And then to suffer this way for somebody else's sins. Is there any justice in that? And in every single family, in some way or another, this inevitable retribution of nature goes on—

NORA *(her hands pressed over her ears)*. Oh, stuff! Cheer up! Please—be gay!

RANK. Yes, I'd just as soon laugh at it all. My poor, innocent spine, serving time for my father's gay army days.

NORA *(by the table, left)*. He was so infatuated with asparagus tips and *pâté de foie gras*, wasn't that it?

RANK. Yes—and with truffles.

NORA. Truffles, yes. And then with oysters, I suppose?

RANK. Yes, tons of oysters, naturally.

NORA. And then the port and champagne to go with it. It's so sad that all these delectable things have to strike at our bones.

RANK. Especially when they strike at the unhappy bones that never shared in the fun.

NORA. Ah, that's the saddest of all.

RANK *(looks searchingly at her)*. Hm.

NORA *(after a moment)*. Why did you smile?

RANK. No, it was you who laughed.

NORA. No, it was you who smiled, Dr. Rank!

RANK *(getting up)*. You're even a bigger tease than I'd thought.

NORA. I'm full of wild ideas today.

RANK. That's obvious.

NORA *(putting both hands on his shoulders)*. Dear, dear Dr. Rank, you'll never die for Torvald and me.

RANK. Oh, that loss you'll easily get over. Those who go away are soon forgotten.

NORA *(looks fearfully at him)*. You believe that?

RANK. One makes new connections, and then—

NORA. Who makes new connections?

RANK. Both you and Torvald will when I'm gone. I'd say you're well under way already. What was that Mrs. Linde doing here last evening?

NORA. Oh, come—you can't be jealous of poor Kristine?

RANK. Oh yes, I am. She'll be my successor here in the house. When I'm down under, that woman will probably—

NORA. Shh! Not so loud. She's right in there.

RANK. Today as well. So you see.

NORA. Only to sew on my dress. Good gracious, how unreasonable you are. (Sitting on the sofa.) Be nice now, Dr. Rank. Tomorrow you'll see how beautifully I'll dance; and you can imagine then that I'm dancing only for you—yes, and of course for Torvald, too—that's understood. (Takes various items out of the carton.) Dr. Rank, sit over here and I'll show you something.

RANK (sitting). What's that?

NORA. Look here. Look.

RANK. Silk stockings.

NORA. Flesh-colored. Aren't they lovely? Now it's so dark here, but tomorrow— No, no, no, just look at the feet. Oh well, you might as well look at the rest.

RANK. Hm—

NORA. Why do you look so critical? Don't you believe they'll fit?

RANK. I've never had any chance to form an opinion on that.

NORA (glancing at him a moment). Shame on you. (Hits him lightly on the ear with the stockings.) That's for you. (Puts them away again.)

RANK. And what other splendors am I going to see now?

NORA. Not the least bit more, because you've been naughty. (She hums a little and rummages among her things.)

RANK (after a short silence). When I sit here together with you like this, completely easy and open, then I don't know—I simply can't imagine—whatever would have become of me if I'd never come into this house.

NORA (smiling). Yes, I really think you feel completely at ease with us.

RANK (more quietly, staring straight ahead). And then to have to go away from it all—

NORA. Nonsense, you're not going away.

RANK (his voice unchanged). —and not even be able to leave some poor show of gratitude behind, scarcely a fleeting regret—no more than a vacant place that anyone can fill.

NORA. And if I asked you now for—? No—

RANK. For what?

NORA. For a great proof of your friendship—

RANK. Yes, yes?

NORA. No, I mean—for an exceptionally big favor—

RANK. Would you really, for once, make me so happy?

NORA. Oh, you haven't the vaguest idea what it is.

RANK. All right, then tell me.

NORA. No, but I can't, Dr. Rank—it's all out of reason. It's advice and help, too—and a favor—

RANK. So much the better. I can't fathom what you're hinting at. Just speak out. Don't you trust me?

NORA. Of course. More than anyone else. You're my best and truest friend, I'm sure. That's why I want to talk to you. All right, then, Dr. Rank: there's something you can help me prevent. You know how deeply, how inexpressibly dearly Torvald loves me; he'd never hesitate a second to give up his life for me.

RANK (leaning close to her). Nora—do you think he's the only one—

NORA (with a slight start). Who—?

RANK. Who'd gladly give up his life for you.

NORA (heavily). I see.

RANK. I swore to myself you should know this before I'm gone. I'll never find a better chance. Yes, Nora, now you know. And also you know now that you can trust me beyond anyone else.

NORA (rising, natural and calm). Let me by.

RANK (making room for her, but still sitting). Nora—

NORA (in the hall doorway). Helene, bring the lamp in. (Goes over to the stove.) Ah, dear Dr. Rank, that was really mean of you.

RANK (getting up). That I've loved you just as deeply as somebody else? Was that mean?

NORA. No, but that you came out and told me. That was quite unnecessary—

RANK. What do you mean? Have you known—?

(The MAID comes in with the lamp, sets it on the table, and goes out again.)

RANK. Nora—Mrs. Helmer—I'm asking you: have you known about it?

NORA. Oh, how can I tell what I know or don't know? Really, I don't know what to say— Why did you have to be so clumsy, Dr. Rank! Everything was so good.

RANK. Well, in any case, you now have the knowledge that my body and soul are at your command. So won't you speak out?

NORA (*looking at him*). After that?

RANK. Please, just let me know what it is.

NORA. You can't know anything now.

RANK. I have to. You mustn't punish me like this. Give me the chance to do whatever is humanly possible for you.

NORA. Now there's nothing you can do for me. Besides, actually, I don't need any help. You'll see—it's only my fantasies. That's what it is. Of course! (*Sits in the rocker, looks at him, and smiles.*) What a nice one you are, Dr. Rank. Aren't you a little bit ashamed, now that the lamp is here?

RANK. No, not exactly. But perhaps I'd better go—for good?

NORA. No, you certainly can't do that. You must come here just as you always have. You know Torvald can't do without you.

RANK. Yes, but *you*?

NORA. You know how much I enjoy it when you're here.

RANK. That's precisely what threw me off. You're a mystery to me. So many times I've felt you'd almost rather be with me than with Helmer.

NORA. Yes—you see, there are some people that one loves most and other people that one would almost prefer being with.

RANK. Yes, there's something to that.

NORA. When I was back home, of course I loved Papa most. But I always thought it was so much fun when I could sneak down to the maids' quarters, because they never tried to improve me, and it was always so amusing, the way they talked to each other.

RANK. Aha, so it's *their* place that I've filled.

NORA (*jumping up and going to him*). Oh, dear, sweet Dr. Rank, that's not what I meant at all. But you can understand that with Torvald it's just the same as with Papa— (*The* MAID *enters from the hall.*)

MAID. Ma'am—please! (*She whispers to* NORA *and hands her a calling card.*)

NORA (*glancing at the card*). Ah! (*Slips it into her pocket.*)

RANK. Anything wrong?

NORA. No, no, not at all. It's only some—it's my new dress——

RANK. Really? But—there's your dress.

NORA. Oh, that. But this is another one—I ordered it—Torvald mustn't know—

RANK. Ah, now we have the big secret.

NORA. That's right. Just go in with him—he's back in the inner study. Keep him there as long as—

RANK. Don't worry. He won't get away. (*Goes into the study.*)

NORA (*to the* MAID). And he's standing waiting in the kitchen?

MAID. Yes, he came up by the back stairs.

NORA. But didn't you tell him somebody was here?

MAID. Yes, but that didn't do any good.

NORA. He won't leave?

MAID. No, he won't go till he's talked with you, ma'am.

NORA. Let him come in, then—but quietly. Helene, don't breathe a word about this. It's a surprise for my husband.

MAID. Yes, yes, I understand— (*Goes out.*)

NORA. This horror—it's going to happen. No, no, no, it can't happen, it mustn't. (*She goes and bolts* HELMER's *door. The* MAID *opens the hall door for* KROGSTAD *and shuts it behind him. He is dressed for travel in a fur coat, boots, and a fur cap.*)

NORA (*going toward him*). Talk softly. My husband's home.

KROGSTAD. Well, good for him.

NORA. What do you want?

KROGSTAD. Some information.

NORA. Hurry up, then. What is it?

KROGSTAD. You know, of course, that I got my notice.

NORA. I couldn't prevent it, Mr. Krogstad. I fought for you to the bitter end, but nothing worked.

KROGSTAD. Does your husband's love for you run so thin? He knows everything I can expose you to, and all the same he dares to—

NORA. How can you imagine he knows anything about this?

KROGSTAD. Ah, no—I can't imagine it either, now. It's not at all like my fine Torvald Helmer to have so much guts—

NORA. Mr. Krogstad, I demand respect for my

husband!

KROGSTAD. Why, of course—all due respect. But since the lady's keeping it so carefully hidden, may I presume to ask if you're also a bit better informed than yesterday about what you've actually done?

NORA. More than you ever could teach me.

KROGSTAD. Yes, I *am* such an awful lawyer.

NORA. What is it you want from me?

KROGSTAD. Just a glimpse of how you are, Mrs. Helmer. I've been thinking about you all day long. A cashier, a night-court scribbler, a—well, a type like me also has a little of what they call a heart, you know.

NORA. Then show it. Think of my children.

KROGSTAD. Did you or your husband ever think of mine? But never mind. I simply wanted to tell you that you don't need to take this thing too seriously. For the present, I'm not proceeding with any action.

NORA. Oh no, really! Well—I knew that.

KROGSTAD. Everything can be settled in a friendly spirit. It doesn't have to get around town at all; it can stay just among us three.

NORA. My husband must never know anything of this.

KROGSTAD. How can you manage that? Perhaps you can pay me the balance?

NORA. No, not right now.

KROGSTAD. Or you know some way of raising the money in a day or two?

NORA. No way that I'm willing to use.

KROGSTAD. Well, it wouldn't have done you any good, anyway. If you stood in front of me with a fistful of bills, you still couldn't buy your signature back.

NORA. Then tell me what you're going to do with it.

KROGSTAD. I'll just hold onto it—keep it on file. There's no outsider who'll even get wind of it. So if you've been thinking of taking some desperate step—

NORA. I have.

KROGSTAD. Been thinking of running away from home—

NORA. I have!

KROGSTAD. Or even of something worse—

NORA. How could you guess that?

KROGSTAD. You can drop those thoughts.

NORA. How could you guess I was thinking of *that*?

KROGSTAD. Most of us think about *that* at first. I thought about it too, but I discovered I hadn't the courage—

NORA (*lifelessly*). I don't either.

KROGSTAD (*relieved*). That's true, you haven't the courage? You too?

NORA. I don't have it—I don't have it.

KROGSTAD. It would be terribly stupid, anyway. After that first storm at home blows out, why, then— I have here in my pocket a letter for your husband—

NORA. Telling everything?

KROGSTAD. As charitably as possible.

NORA (*quickly*). He mustn't ever get that letter. Tear it up. I'll find some way to get money.

KROGSTAD. Beg pardon, Mrs. Helmer, but I think I just told you—

NORA. Oh, I don't mean the money I owe you. Let me know how much you want from my husband, and I'll manage it.

KROGSTAD. I don't want any money from your husband.

NORA. What do you want, then?

KROGSTAD. I'll tell you what. I want to recoup, Mrs. Helmer; I want to get on in the world—and there's where your husband can help me. For a year and a half I've kept myself clean of anything disreputable—all that time struggling with the worst conditions; but I was satisfied, working my way up step by step. Now I've been written right off, and I'm just not in the mood to come crawling back. I tell you, I want to move on. I want to get back in the bank—in a better position. Your husband can set up a job for me—

NORA. He'll never do that!

KROGSTAD. He'll do it. I know him. He won't dare breathe a word of protest. And once I'm in there together with him, you just wait and see! Inside of a year, I'll be the manager's right-hand man. It'll be Nils Krogstad, not Torvald Helmer, who runs the bank.

NORA. You'll never see the day!

KROGSTAD. Maybe you think you can—

NORA. I have the courage now—for *that.*

KROGSTAD. Oh, you don't scare me. A smart, spoiled lady like you—

NORA. You'll see; you'll see!

KROGSTAD. Under the ice, maybe? Down in the freezing, coal-black water? There, till you float up in the spring, ugly, unrecognizable, with your hair falling out—

NORA. You don't frighten me.

KROGSTAD. Nor do you frighten me. One doesn't do these things, Mrs. Helmer. Besides, what good would it be? I'd still have him safe in my pocket.

NORA. Afterwards? When I'm no longer—?

KROGSTAD. Are you forgetting that *I'll* be in control then over your final reputation? (NORA *stands speechless, staring at him.*) Good; now I've warned you. Don't do anything stupid. When Helmer's read my letter, I'll be waiting for his reply. And bear in mind that it's your husband himself who's forced me back to my old ways. I'll never forgive him for that. Good-bye, Mrs. Helmer. *(He goes out through the hall.)*

NORA *(goes to the hall door, opens it a crack, and listens).* He's gone. Didn't leave the letter. Oh no, no, that's impossible too! *(Opening the door more and more.)* What's that? He's standing outside—not going downstairs. He's thinking it over? Maybe he'll—? (*A letter falls in the mailbox; then* KROGSTAD's *footsteps are heard, dying away down a flight of stairs.* NORA *gives a muffled cry and runs over toward the sofa table. A short pause.)* In the mailbox. *(Slips warily over to the hall door.)* It's lying there. Torvald, Torvald—now we're lost!

MRS. LINDE *(entering with the costume from the room, left).* There now, I can't see anything else to mend. Perhaps you'd like to try—

NORA *(in a hoarse whisper).* Kristine, come here.

MRS. LINDE *(tossing the dress on the sofa).* What's wrong? You look upset.

NORA. Come here. See that letter? *There!* Look—through the glass in the mailbox.

MRS. LINDE. Yes, yes, I see it.

NORA. That letter's from Krogstad—

MRS. LINDE. Nora—it's Krogstad who loaned you the money!

NORA. Yes, and now Torvald will find out everything.

MRS. LINDE. Believe me, Nora, it's best for both of you.

NORA. There's more you don't know. I forged a name.

MRS. LINDE. But for heaven's sake—?

NORA. I only want to tell you that, Kristine, so that you can be my witness.

MRS. LINDE. Witness? Why should I—?

NORA. If I should go out of my mind—it could easily happen—

MRS. LINDE. Nora!

NORA. Or anything else occurred—so I couldn't be present here—

MRS. LINDE. Nora, Nora, you aren't yourself at all!

NORA. And someone should try to take on the whole weight, all of the guilt, you follow me—

MRS. LINDE. Yes, of course, but why do you think—?

NORA. Then you're my witness that it isn't true, Kristine. I'm very much myself; my mind right now is perfectly clear; and I'm telling you: nobody else has known about this; I alone did everything. Remember that.

MRS. LINDE. I will. But I don't understand all this.

NORA. Oh, how could you ever understand it? It's the miracle now that's going to take place.

MRS. LINDE. The miracle?

NORA. Yes, the miracle. But it's so awful, Kristine. It mustn't take place, not for anything in the world.

MRS. LINDE. I'm going right over and talk with Krogstad.

NORA. Don't go near him; he'll do you some terrible harm!

MRS. LINDE. There was a time once when he'd gladly have done anything for me.

NORA. He?

MRS. LINDE. Where does he live?

NORA. Oh, how do I know? Yes. (*Searches in her pocket.*) Here's his card. But the letter, the letter—!

HELMER *(from the study, knocking on the door).* Nora!

NORA *(with a cry of fear).* Oh! What is it? What

do you want?

HELMER. Now, now, don't be so frightened. We're not coming in. You locked the door—are you trying on the dress?

NORA. Yes, I'm trying it. I'll look just beautiful, Torvald.

MRS. LINDE (*who has read the card*). He's living right around the corner.

NORA. Yes, but what's the use? We're lost. The letter's in the box.

MRS. LINDE. And your husband has the key?

NORA. Yes, always.

MRS. LINDE. Krogstad can ask for his letter back unread; he can find some excuse—

NORA. But it's just this time that Torvald usually—

MRS. LINDE. Stall him. Keep him in there. I'll be back as quick as I can. (*She hurries out through the hall entrance.*)

NORA (*goes to* HELMER'*s door, opens it, and peers in*). Torvald!

HELMER (*from the inner study*). Well—does one dare set foot in one's own living room at last? Come on, Rank, now we'll get a look— (*In the doorway.*) But what's this?

NORA. What, Torvald dear?

HELMER. Rank had me expecting some grand masquerade.

RANK (*in the doorway*). That was my impression, but I must have been wrong.

NORA. No one can admire me in my splendor—not till tomorrow.

HELMER. But Nora, dear, you look so exhausted. Have you practiced too hard?

NORA. No, I haven't practiced at all yet.

HELMER. You know, it's necessary—

NORA. Oh, it's absolutely necessary, Torvald. But I can't get anywhere without your help. I've forgotten the whole thing completely.

HELMER. Ah, we'll soon take care of that.

NORA. Yes, take care of me, Torvald, please! Promise me that? Oh, I'm so nervous. That big party— You must give up everything this evening for me. No business—don't even touch your pen. Yes? Dear Torvald, promise?

HELMER. It's a promise. Tonight I'm totally at your service—you little helpless thing. Hm—but first there's one thing I want to—

(*Goes toward the hall door.*)

NORA. What are you looking for?

HELMER. Just to see if there's any mail.

NORA. No, no, don't do that, Torvald!

HELMER. Now what?

NORA. Torvald, please. There isn't any.

HELMER. Let me look, though. (*Starts out.* NORA, *at the piano, strikes the first notes of the tarantella.* HELMER, *at the door, stops.*) Aha!

NORA. I can't dance tomorrow if I don't practice with you.

HELMER (*going over to her*). Nora dear, are you really so frightened?

NORA. Yes, so terribly frightened. Let me practice right now; there's still time before dinner. Oh, sit down and play for me, Torvald. Direct me. Teach me, the way you always have.

HELMER. Gladly, if it's what you want. (*Sits at the piano.*)

NORA (*snatches the tambourine up from the box, then a long, varicolored shawl, which she throws around herself, whereupon she springs forward and cries out:*) Play for me now! Now I'll dance! (HELMER *plays and* NORA *dances.* RANK *stands behind* HELMER *at the piano and looks on.*)

HELMER (*as he plays*). Slower. Slow down.

NORA. Can't change it.

HELMER. Not so violent, Nora!

NORA. Has to be just like this.

HELMER (*stopping*). No, no, that won't do at all.

NORA (*laughing and swinging her tambourine*). Isn't that what I told you?

RANK. Let me play for her.

HELMER (*getting up*). Yes, go on. I can teach her more easily then. (RANK *sits at the piano and plays;* NORA *dances more and more wildly.* HELMER *has stationed himself by the stove and repeatedly gives her directions; she seems not to hear them; her hair loosens and falls over her shoulders; she does not notice, but goes on dancing.* MRS. LINDE *enters.*)

MRS. LINDE (*standing dumbfounded at the door*). Ah—!

NORA (*still dancing*). See what fun, Kristine!

HELMER. But Nora darling, you dance as if your life were at stake.

NORA. And it is.

HELMER. Rank, stop! This is pure madness. Stop it, I say! (RANK *breaks off playing, and* NORA *halts abruptly.*)

HELMER (*going over to her*). I never would have believed it. You've forgotten everything I taught you.

NORA (*throwing away the tambourine*). You see for yourself.

HELMER. Well, there's certainly room for instruction here.

NORA. Yes, you see how important it is. You've got to teach me to the very last minute. Promise me that, Torvald?

HELMER. You can bet on it.

NORA. You mustn't, either today or tomorrow, think about anything else but me; you mustn't open any letters—or the mailbox—

HELMER. Ah, it's still the fear of that man—

NORA. Oh yes, yes, that too.

HELMER. Nora, it's written all over you—there's already a letter from him out there.

NORA. I don't know. I guess so. But you mustn't read such things now; there mustn't be anything ugly between us before it's all over.

RANK (*quietly to* HELMER). You shouldn't deny her.

HELMER (*putting his arm around her*). The child can have her way. But tomorrow night, after you've danced—

NORA. Then you'll be free.

MAID (*in the doorway, right*). Ma'am, dinner is served.

NORA. We'll be wanting champagne, Helene.

MAID. Very good, ma'am. (*Goes out.*)

HELMER. So—a regular banquet, hm?

NORA. Yes, a banquet—champagne till daybreak! (*Calling out.*) And some macaroons, Helene. Heaps of them—just this once.

HELMER (*taking her hands*). Now, now, now—no hysterics. Be my own little lark again.

NORA. Oh, I will soon enough. But go on in—and you, Dr. Rank. Kristine, help me put up my hair.

RANK (*whispering, as they go*). There's nothing wrong—really wrong, is there?

HELMER. Oh, of course not. It's nothing more than this childish anxiety I was telling you

Scene from the 1973 film version of *A Doll House* showing Claire Bloom as Nora.

about. (*They go out, right.*)

NORA. Well?

MRS. LINDE. Left town.

NORA. I could see by your face.

MRS. LINDE. He'll be home tomorrow evening. I wrote him a note.

NORA. You shouldn't have. Don't try to stop anything now. After all, it's a wonderful joy, this waiting here for the miracle.

MRS. LINDE. What is it you're waiting for?

NORA. Oh, you can't understand that. Go in to them; I'll be along in a moment. (MRS. LINDE *goes into the dining room.* NORA *stands a short while as if composing herself; then she looks at her watch.*)

NORA. Five. Seven hours to midnight. Twenty-four hours to the midnight after, and then the tarantella's done. Seven and twenty-four? Thirty-one hours to live.

HELMER (*in the doorway, right*). What's become of the little lark?

NORA (*going toward him with open arms*). Here's your lark!

ACT THREE

Same scene. The table, with chairs around it, has been moved to the center of the room. A lamp on the table is lit. The hall door stands open. Dance music drifts down from the floor above. MRS. LINDE *sits at the table, absently paging through a book, trying to read, but apparently unable to focus her thoughts. Once or twice she pauses, tensely listening for a sound at the outer entrance.*

MRS. LINDE (*glancing at her watch*). Not yet—and there's hardly any time left. If only he's not—(*Listening again.*) Ah, there he is. (*She goes out in the hall and cautiously opens the outer door. Quiet footsteps are heard on the stairs. She whispers:*) Come in. Nobody's here.

KROGSTAD (*in the doorway*). I found a note from you at home. What's back of all this?

MRS. LINDE. I just *had* to talk to you.

KROGSTAD. Oh? And it just *had* to be here in this house?

MRS. LINDE. At my place it was impossible; my room hasn't a private entrance. Come in; we're all alone. The maid's asleep, and the Helmers are at the dance upstairs.

KROGSTAD (*entering the room*). Well, well, the Helmers are dancing tonight? Really?

MRS. LINDE. Why not?

KROGSTAD. How true—why not?

MRS. LINDE. All right, Krogstad, let's talk.

KROGSTAD. Do we two have anything more to talk about?

MRS. LINDE. We have a great deal to talk about.

KROGSTAD. I wouldn't have thought so.

MRS. LINDE. No, because you've never understood me, really.

KROGSTAD. Was there anything more to understand—except what's all too common in life? A calculating woman throws over a man the moment a better catch comes by.

MRS. LINDE. You think I'm so thoroughly calculating? You think I broke it off lightly?

KROGSTAD. Didn't you?

MRS. LINDE. Nils—is that what you really thought?

KROGSTAD. If you cared, then why did you write me the way you did?

MRS. LINDE. What else could I do? If I had to break off with you, then it was my job as well to root out everything you felt for me.

KROGSTAD (*wringing his hands*). So that was it. And this—all this, simply for money!

MRS. LINDE. Don't forget I had a helpless mother and two small brothers. We couldn't wait for you, Nils; you had such a long road ahead of you then.

KROGSTAD. That may be; but you still hadn't the right to abandon me for somebody else's sake.

MRS. LINDE. Yes—I don't know. So many, many times I've asked myself if I did have that right.

KROGSTAD (*more softly*). When I lost you, it was as if all the solid ground dissolved from under my feet. Look at me; I'm a half-drowned man now, hanging onto a wreck.

MRS. LINDE. Help may be near.

KROGSTAD. It was near—but then you came and blocked it off.

MRS. LINDE. Without my knowing it, Nils. Today for the first time I learned that it's you I'm replacing at the bank.

KROGSTAD. All right—I believe you. But now that you know, will you step aside?

MRS. LINDE. No, because that wouldn't benefit you in the slightest.

KROGSTAD. Not "benefit" me, hm! I'd step aside anyway.

MRS. LINDE. I've learned to be realistic. Life and hard, bitter necessity have taught me that.

KROGSTAD. And life's taught me never to trust fine phrases.

MRS. LINDE. Then life's taught you a very sound thing. But you do have to trust in actions, don't you?

KROGSTAD. What does that mean?

MRS. LINDE. You said you were hanging on like a half-drowned man to a wreck.

KROGSTAD. I've good reason to say that.

MRS. LINDE. I'm also like a half-drowned woman on a wreck. No one to suffer with; no one to care for.

KROGSTAD. You made your choice.

MRS. LINDE. There wasn't any choice then.

KROGSTAD. So—what of it?

MRS. LINDE. Nils, if only we two shipwrecked people could reach across to each other.

KROGSTAD. What are you saying?

MRS. LINDE. Two on one wreck are at least better off than each on his own.

KROGSTAD. Kristine!

MRS. LINDE. Why do you think I came into town?

KROGSTAD. Did you really have some thought of me?

MRS. LINDE. I have to work to go on living. All my born days, as long as I can remember, I've worked, and it's been my best and my only joy. But now I'm completely alone in the world; it frightens me to be so empty and lost. To work for yourself—there's no joy in that. Nils, give me something—someone to work for.

KROGSTAD. I don't believe all this. It's just some hysterical feminine urge to go out and make a noble sacrifice.

MRS. LINDE. Have you ever found me to be hysterical?

KROGSTAD. Can you honestly mean this? Tell me—do you know everything about my past?

MRS. LINDE. Yes.

KROGSTAD. And you know what they think I'm worth around here.

MRS. LINDE. From what you were saying before, it would seem that with me you could have been another person.

KROGSTAD. I'm positive of that.

MRS. LINDE. Couldn't it happen still?

KROGSTAD. Kristine—you're saying this in all seriousness? Yes, you are! I can see it in you. And do you really have the courage, then—?

MRS. LINDE. I need to have someone to care for; and your children need a mother. We both need each other. Nils, I have faith that you're good at heart—I'll risk everything together with you.

KROGSTAD (gripping her hands). Kristine, thank you, thank you— Now I know I can win back a place in their eyes. Yes—but I forgot—

MRS. LINDE (listening). Shh! The tarantella. Go now! Go on!

KROGSTAD. Why? What is it?

MRS. LINDE. Hear the dance up there? When that's over, they'll be coming down.

KROGSTAD. Oh, then I'll go. But—it's all pointless. Of course, you don't know the move I made against the Helmers.

MRS. LINDE. Yes, Nils, I know.

KROGSTAD. And all the same, you have the courage to—?

MRS. LINDE. I know how far despair can drive a man like you.

KROGSTAD. Oh, if I only could take it all back.

MRS. LINDE. You easily could—your letter's still lying in the mailbox.

KROGSTAD. Are you sure of that?

MRS. LINDE. Positive. But—

KROGSTAD (looks at her searchingly). Is that the meaning of it, then? You'll save your friend at any price. Tell me straight out. Is that it?

MRS. LINDE. Nils—anyone who's sold herself for somebody else once isn't going to do it again.

KROGSTAD. I'll demand my letter back.

MRS. LINDE. No, no.

KROGSTAD. Yes, of course. I'll stay here till Helmer comes down; I'll tell him to give me my letter again—that it only involves my dismissal—that he shouldn't read it—

MRS. LINDE. No, Nils, don't call the letter back.

KROGSTAD. But wasn't that exactly why you wrote me to come here?

MRS. LINDE. Yes, in that first panic. But it's been a whole day and night since then, and in that time I've seen such incredible things in this house. Helmer's got to learn everything; this dreadful secret has to be aired; those two have to come to a full understanding; all these lies and evasions can't go on.

KROGSTAD. Well, then, if you want to chance it. But at least there's one thing I can do, and do right away—

MRS. LINDE (listening). Go now, go, quick! The dance is over. We're not safe another second.

KROGSTAD. I'll wait for you downstairs.

MRS. LINDE. Yes, please do; take me home.

KROGSTAD. I can't believe it; I've never been so happy. (*He leaves by way of the outer door; the door between the room and the hall stays open.*)

MRS. LINDE (*straightening up a bit and getting together her street clothes*). How different now! How different! Someone to work for, to live for—a home to build. Well, it is worth the try! Oh, if they'd only come! (*Listening.*) Ah, there they are. Bundle up. (*She picks up her hat and coat.* NORA's *and* HELMER's *voices can be heard outside; a key turns in the lock, and* HELMER *brings* NORA *into the hall almost by force. She is wearing the Italian costume with a large black shawl about her; he has on evening dress, with a black domino open over it.*)

NORA (*struggling in the doorway*). No, no, no, not inside! I'm going up again. I don't want to leave so soon.

HELMER. But Nora dear—

NORA. Oh, I beg you, please, Torvald. From the bottom of my heart, *please*—only an hour more!

HELMER. Not a single minute, Nora darling. You know our agreement. Come on, in we go; you'll catch cold out here. (*In spite of her resistance, he gently draws her into the room.*)

MRS. LINDE. Good evening.

NORA. Kristine!

HELMER. Why, Mrs. Linde—are you here so late?

MRS. LINDE. Yes, I'm sorry, but I did want to see Nora in costume.

NORA. Have you been sitting here, waiting for me?

MRS. LINDE. Yes. I didn't come early enough; you were all upstairs; and then I thought I really couldn't leave without seeing you.

HELMER (*removing* NORA's *shawl*). Yes, take a good look. She's worth looking at, I can tell you that, Mrs. Linde. Isn't she lovely?

MRS. LINDE. Yes, I should say—

HELMER. A dream of loveliness, isn't she? That's what everyone thought at the party, too. But she's horribly stubborn—this sweet little thing. What's to be done with her? Can you imagine, I almost had to use force to pry her away.

NORA. Oh, Torvald, you're going to regret you didn't indulge me, even for just a half hour more.

HELMER. There, you see. She danced her tarantella and got a tumultuous hand—which was well earned, although the performance may have been a bit too naturalistic—I mean it rather overstepped the proprieties of art. But never mind—what's important is, she made a success, an overwhelming success. You think I could let her stay on after that and spoil the effect? Oh no; I took my lovely little Capri girl—my capricious little Capri girl, I should say—took her under my arm; one quick tour of the ballroom, a curtsy to every side, and then—as they say in novels—the beautiful vision disappeared. An exit should always be effective, Mrs. Linde, but that's what I can't get Nora to grasp. Phew, its hot in here. (*Flings the domino on a chair and opens the door to his room.*) Why's it dark in here? Oh yes, of course. Excuse me. (*He goes in and lights a couple of candles.*)

NORA (*in a sharp, breathless whisper*). So?

MRS. LINDE (*quietly*). I talked with him.

NORA. And—?

MRS. LINDE. Nora—you must tell your husband everything.

NORA (*dully*). I knew it.

MRS. LINDE. You've got nothing to fear from Krogstad, but you have to speak out.

NORA. I won't tell.

MRS. LINDE. Then the letter will.

NORA. Thanks, Kristine. I know now what's to be done. Shh!

HELMER (*reentering*). Well, then, Mrs. Linde—have you admired her?

MRS. LINDE. Yes, and now I'll say good night.

HELMER. Oh, come, so soon? Is this yours, this knitting?

MRS. LINDE. Yes, thanks. I nearly forgot it.

HELMER. Do you knit, then?

MRS. LINDE. Oh yes.

HELMER. You know what? You should embroider instead.

MRS. LINDE. Really? Why?

HELMER. Yes, because it's a lot prettier. See here, one holds the embroidery so, in the left hand, and then one guides the needle with the right— so—in an easy, sweeping curve—right?

MRS. LINDE. Yes, I guess that's—

HELMER. But, on the other hand, knitting—it can never be anything but ugly. Look, see here, the arms tucked in, the knitting needles going up and down—there's something Chinese about it. Ah, that was really a glorious champagne they served.

MRS. LINDE. Yes, goodnight, Nora, and don't be stubborn anymore.

HELMER. Well put, Mrs. Linde!

MRS. LINDE. Good night, Mr. Helmer.

HELMER (accompanying her to the door). Good night, good night. I hope you get home all right. I'd be very happy to—but you don't have far to go. Good night, good night. (She leaves. He shuts the door after her and returns.) There, now, at last we got her out the door. She's a deadly bore, that creature.

NORA. Aren't you pretty tired, Torvald?

HELMER. No, not a bit.

NORA. You're not sleepy?

HELMER. Not at all. On the contrary, I'm feeling quite exhilarated. But you? Yes, you really look tired and sleepy.

NORA. Yes, I'm very tired. Soon now I'll sleep.

HELMER. See! You see! I was right all along that we shouldn't stay longer.

NORA. Whatever you do is always right.

HELMER (kissing her brow). Now my little lark talks sense. Say, did you notice what a time Rank was having tonight?

NORA. Oh, was he? I didn't get to speak with him.

HELMER. I scarcely did either, but it's a long time since I've seen him in such high spirits. (Gazes at her a moment, then comes nearer her.) Hm—it's marvelous, though, to be back home again—to be completely alone with you. Oh, you bewitchingly lovely young woman.

NORA. Torvald, don't look at me like that!

HELMER. Can't I look at my richest treasure? At all that beauty that's mine, mine alone—completely and utterly.

NORA (moving around to the other side of the table). You mustn't talk to me that way tonight.

HELMER (following her). The tarantella is still in your blood, I can see—and it makes you even more enticing. Listen. The guests are beginning to go. (Dropping his voice.) Nora—it'll soon be quiet through this whole house.

NORA. Yes, I hope so.

HELMER. You do, don't you, my love? Do you realize—when I'm out at a party like this with you—do you know why I talk to you so little, and keep such a distance away; just send you a stolen look now and then—you know why I do it? It's because I'm imagining then that you're my secret darling, my secret young bride-to-be, and that no one suspects there's anything between us.

NORA. Yes, yes; oh, yes, I know you're always thinking of me.

HELMER. And then when we leave and I place the shawl over those fine young rounded shoulders—over that wonderful curving neck—then I pretend that you're my young bride, that we're just coming from the wedding, that for the first time I'm bringing you into my house—that for the first time I'm alone with you—completely alone with you, your trembling young beauty! All this evening I've longed for nothing but you. When I saw you turn and sway in the tarantella—my blood was pounding till I couldn't stand it—that's why I brought you down here so early—

NORA. Go away, Torvald! Leave me alone. I don't want all this.

HELMER. What do you mean? Nora, you're teasing me. You will, won't you? Aren't I your husband—? (A knock at the outside door.)

NORA (startled). What's that?

HELMER (going toward the hall). Who is it?

RANK (outside). It's me. May I come in a moment?

HELMER (with quiet irritation). Oh, what does he want now? (Aloud.) Hold on. (Goes and opens the door.) Oh, how nice that you didn't just pass us by!

RANK. I thought I heard your voice, and then I wanted so badly to have a look in. (Lightly glancing about.) Ah, me, these old familiar haunts. You have it snug and cozy in here, you two.

HELMER. You seemed to be having it pretty cozy upstairs, too.

RANK. Absolutely. Why shouldn't I? Why not take in everything in life? As much as you can, anyway, and as long as you can. The wine was superb—

HELMER. The champagne especially.

RANK. You noticed that too? It's amazing how much I could guzzle down.

NORA. Torvald also drank a lot of champagne this evening.

RANK. Oh?

NORA. Yes, and that always makes him so entertaining.

RANK. Well, why shouldn't one have a pleasant evening after a well-spent day?

HELMER. Well spent? I'm afraid I can't claim that.

RANK (*slapping him on the back*). But I can, you see!

NORA. Dr. Rank, you must have done some scientific research today.

RANK. Quite so.

HELMER. Come now—little Nora talking about scientific research!

NORA. And can I congratulate you on the results?

RANK. Indeed you may.

NORA. Then they were good?

RANK. The best possible for both doctor and patient—certainty.

NORA (*quickly and searchingly*). Certainty?

RANK. Complete certainty. So don't I owe myself a gay evening afterwards?

NORA. Yes, you're right, Dr. Rank.

HELMER. I'm with you—just so long as you don't have to suffer for it in the morning.

RANK. Well, one never gets something for nothing in life.

NORA. Dr. Rank—are you very fond of masquerade parties?

RANK. Yes, if there's a good array of odd disguises—

NORA. Tell me, what should we two go as at the next masquerade?

HELMER. You little featherhead—already thinking of the next!

RANK. We two? I'll tell you what: you must go as Charmed Life—

HELMER. Yes, but find a costume for *that!*

RANK. Your wife can appear just as she looks every day.

HELMER. That was nicely put. But don't you know what you're going to be?

RANK. Yes, Helmer, I've made up my mind.

HELMER. Well?

RANK. At the next masquerade I'm going to be invisible.

HELMER. That's a funny idea.

RANK. They say there's a hat—black, huge—have you never heard of the hat that makes you invisible? You put it on, and then no one on earth can see you.

HELMER (*suppressing a smile*). Ah, of course.

RANK. But I'm quite forgetting what I came for. Helmer, give me a cigar, one of the dark Havanas.

HELMER. With the greatest pleasure. (*Holds out his case.*)

RANK. Thanks. (*Takes one and cuts off the tip.*)

NORA (*striking a match*). Let me give you a light.

RANK. Thank you. (*She holds the match for him; he lights the cigar.*) And now good-bye.

HELMER. Good-bye, good-bye, old friend.

NORA. Sleep well, Doctor.

RANK. Thanks for that wish.

NORA. Wish me the same.

RANK. You? All right, if you like— Sleep well. And thanks for the light. (*He nods to them both and leaves.*)

HELMER (*his voice subdued*). He's been drinking heavily.

NORA (*absently*). Could be. (HELMER *takes his keys from his pocket and goes out in the hall.*) Torvald—what are you after?

HELMER. Got to empty the mailbox; it's nearly full. There won't be room for the morning papers.

NORA. Are you working tonight?

HELMER. You know I'm not. Why—what's this? Someone's been at the lock.

NORA. At the lock—?

HELMER. Yes, I'm positive. What do you suppose—? I can't imagine one of the maids—? Here's a broken hairpin. Nora, it's yours—

NORA (*quickly*). Then it must be the children.

HELMER. You'd better break them of that. Hm, hm—well, opened it after all. (*Takes the contents out and calls into the kitchen.*) Helene! Helene, would you put out the lamp in the hall. (*He returns to the room, shutting the hall door, then displays the handful of mail.*) Look how it's piled up. (*Sorting through them.*) Now what's this?

NORA (*at the window*). The letter! Oh, Torvald, no!

HELMER. Two calling cards—from Rank.

NORA. From Dr. Rank?

HELMER (*examining them*). "Dr. Rank, Consulting Physician." They were on top. He must have dropped them in as he left.

NORA. Is there anything on them?

HELMER. There's a black cross over the name. See? That's a gruesome notion. He could almost be announcing his own death.

NORA. That's just what he's doing.

HELMER. What! You've heard something? Something he's told you?

NORA. Yes. That when those cards came, he'd be taking his leave of us. He'll shut himself in now and die.

HELMER. Ah, my poor friend! Of course I knew he wouldn't be here much longer. But so soon— And then to hide himself away like a wounded animal.

NORA. If it has to happen, then it's best it happens in silence—don't you think so, Torvald?

HELMER (*pacing up and down*). He'd grown right into our lives. I simply can't imagine him gone. He with his suffering and loneliness—like a dark cloud setting off our sunlit happiness. Well, maybe it's best this way. For him, at least. (*Standing still.*) And maybe for us too, Nora. Now we're thrown back on each other completely. (*Embracing her.*) Oh you, my darling wife, how can I hold you close enough? You know what, Nora—time and again I've wished you were in some terrible danger, just so I could stake my life and soul and everything for your sake.

NORA (*tearing herself away, her voice firm and decisive*). Now you must read your mail, Torvald.

HELMER. No, no, not tonight. I want to stay with you, dearest.

NORA. With a dying friend on your mind?

HELMER. You're right. We've both had a shock. There's ugliness between us—these thoughts of death and corruption. We'll have to get free of them first. Until then—we'll stay apart.

NORA (*clinging about his neck*). Torvald—good night! Good night!

HELMER (*kissing her on the cheek*). Good night, little songbird. Sleep well, Nora. I'll be reading my mail now. (*He takes the letters into his room and shuts the door after him.*)

NORA (*with bewildered glances, groping about, seizing* HELMER's *domino, throwing it around her, and speaking in short, hoarse, broken whispers*). Never see him again. Never, never. (*Putting her shawl over her head.*) Never see the children either—them, too. Never, never. Oh, the freezing black water! The depths—down— Oh, I wish it were over— He has it now; he's reading it—now. Oh no, no, not yet. Torvald, good-bye, you and the children— (*She starts for the hall; as she does,* HELMER *throws open his door and stands with an open letter in his hand.*)

HELMER. Nora!

NORA (*screams*). Oh—!

HELMER. What is this? You know what's in this letter?

NORA. Yes, I know. Let me go! Let me out!

HELMER (*holding her back*). Where are you going?

NORA (*struggling to break loose*). You can't save me, Torvald!

HELMER (*slumping back*). True! Then it's true what he writes? How horrible! No, no, it's impossible—it can't be true.

NORA. It *is* true. I've loved you more than all this world.

HELMER. Ah, none of your slippery tricks.

NORA (*taking one step toward him*). Torvald—!

HELMER. What *is* this you've blundered into!

NORA. Just let me loose. You're not going to suffer for my sake. You're not going to take on my guilt.

HELMER. No more playacting. (*Locks the hall door.*) You stay right here and give me a reckoning. You understand what you've done? Answer! You understand?

NORA (*looking squarely at him, her face hardening*). Yes. I'm beginning to understand everything now.

HELMER (*striding about*). Oh, what an awful awakening! In all these eight years—she who was my pride and joy—a hypocrite, a liar—worse,

worse—a criminal! How infinitely disgusting it all is! The shame! (NORA *says nothing and goes on looking straight at him. He stops in front of her.*) I should have suspected something of the kind. I should have known. All your father's flimsy values— Be still! All your father's flimsy values have come out in you. No religion, no morals, no sense of duty— Oh, how I'm punished for letting him off! I did it for your sake, and you repay me like this.

NORA. Yes, like this.

HELMER. Now you've wrecked all my happiness—ruined my whole future. Oh, it's awful to think of. I'm in a cheap little grafter's hands; he can do anything he wants with me, ask for anything, play with me like a puppet—and I can't breathe a word. I'll be swept down miserably into the depths on account of a featherbrained woman.

NORA. When I'm gone from this world, you'll be free.

HELMER. Oh, quit posing. Your father had a mess of those speeches too. What good would that ever do me if you were gone from this world, as you say? Not the slightest. He can still make the whole thing known; and if he does, I could be falsely suspected as your accomplice. They might even think that I was behind it—that I put you up to it. And all that I can thank you for—you that I've coddled the whole of our marriage. Can you see now what you've done to me?

NORA (*icily calm*). Yes.

HELMER. It's so incredible, I just can't grasp it. But we'll have to patch up whatever we can. Take off the shawl. I said, take it off! I've got to appease him somehow or other. The thing has to be hushed up at any cost. And as for you and me, it's got to seem like everything between us is just as it was—to the outside world, that is. You'll go right on living in this house, of course. But you can't be allowed to bring up the children; I don't dare trust you with them— Oh, to have to say this to someone I've loved so much! Well, that's done with. From now on happiness doesn't matter; all that matters is saving the bits and pieces, the appearance— (*The doorbell rings.* HELMER *starts.*) What's that? And so late. Maybe the worst—? You think he'd—? Hide, Nora! Say you're sick. (NORA *remains standing motionless.* HELMER *goes and opens the door.*)

MAID (*half dressed, in the hall*). A letter for Mrs. Helmer.

HELMER. I'll take it. (*Snatches the letter and shuts the door.*) Yes, it's from him. You don't get it; I'm reading it myself.

NORA. Then read it.

HELMER (*by the lamp*). I hardly dare. We may be ruined, you and I. But—I've got to know. (*Rips open the letter, skims through a few lines, glances at an enclosure, then cries out joyfully.*) Nora! (NORA *looks inquiringly at him.*) Nora! Wait— better check it again— Yes, yes, it's true. I'm saved. Nora, I'm saved!

NORA. And I?

HELMER. You too, of course. We're both saved, both of us. Look. He's sent back your note. He says he's sorry and ashamed—that a happy development in his life—oh, who cares what he says! Nora, we're saved! No one can hurt you. Oh, Nora, Nora—but first, this ugliness all has to go. Let me see— (*Takes a look at the note.*) No, I don't want to see it; I want the whole thing to fade like a dream. (*Tears the note and both letters to pieces, throws them into the stove and watches them burn.*) There—now there's nothing left— He wrote that since Christmas Eve you— Oh, they must have been three terrible days for you, Nora.

NORA. I fought a hard fight.

HELMER. And suffered pain and saw no escape but— No, we're not going to dwell on anything unpleasant. We'll just be grateful and keep on repeating: it's over now, it's over! You hear me, Nora? You don't seem to realize—it's over. What's it mean—that frozen look? Oh, poor little Nora, I understand. You can't believe I've forgiven you. But I have, Nora; I swear I have. I know that what you did, you did out of love for me.

NORA. That's true.

HELMER. You loved me the way a wife ought to love her husband. It's simply the means that you couldn't judge. But you think I love you any the less for not knowing how to handle your affairs? No, no—just lean on me; I'll guide you and teach you. I wouldn't be a man if this feminine helplessness didn't make you twice as attractive to me. You mustn't mind those sharp words I said—that was all in the first confusion of thinking my world had collapsed. I've forgiven you, Nora; I swear I've forgiven you.

NORA. My thanks for your forgiveness. (*She goes out through the door, right.*)

HELMER. No, wait— (*Peers in.*) What are you doing in there?

NORA (*inside*). Getting out of my costume.

HELMER (*by the open door*). Yes, do that. Try to calm yourself and collect your thoughts again, my frightened little songbird. You can rest easy now; I've got wide wings to shelter you with. (*Walking about close by the door.*) How snug and nice our home is, Nora. You're safe here; I'll keep you like a hunted dove I've rescued out of a hawk's claws. I'll bring peace to your poor, shuddering heart. Gradually it'll happen, Nora; you'll see. Tomorrow all this will look different to you; then everything will be as it was. I won't have to go on repeating I forgive you; you'll feel it for yourself. How can you imagine I'd ever conceivably want to disown you—or even blame you in any way? Ah, you don't know a man's heart, Nora. For a man there's something indescribably sweet and satisfying in knowing he's forgiven his wife—and forgiven her out of a full and open heart. It's as if she belongs to him in two ways now: in a sense he's given her fresh into the world again, and she's become his wife and his child as well. From now on that's what you'll be to me—you little, bewildered, helpless thing. Don't be afraid of anything, Nora; just open your heart to me, and I'll be conscience and will to you both—(NORA *enters in her regular clothes.*) What's this? Not in bed? You've changed your dress?

NORA. Yes, Torvald, I've changed my dress.

HELMER. But why now, so late?

NORA. Tonight I'm not sleeping.

HELMER. But Nora dear—

NORA (*looking at her watch*). It's still not so very late. Sit down, Torvald; we have a lot to talk over. (*She sits at one side of the table.*)

HELMER. Nora—what is this? That hard expression—

NORA. Sit down. This'll take some time. I have a lot to say.

HELMER (*sitting at the table directly opposite her*). You worry me, Nora. And I don't understand you.

NORA. No, that's exactly it. You don't understand me. And I've never understood you either—until tonight. No, don't interrupt. You can just listen to what I say. We're closing out accounts, Torvald.

HELMER. How do you mean that?

NORA (*after a short pause*). Doesn't anything strike you about our sitting here like this?

HELMER. What's that?

NORA. We've been married now eight years. Doesn't it occur to you that this is the first time we two, you and I, man and wife, have ever talked seriously together?

HELMER. What do you mean—seriously?

NORA. In eight whole years—longer even—right from our first acquaintance, we've never exchanged a serious word on any serious thing.

HELMER. You mean I should constantly go and involve you in problems you couldn't possibly help me with?

NORA. I'm not talking of problems. I'm saying that we've never sat down seriously together and tried to get to the bottom of anything.

HELMER. But dearest, what good would that ever do you?

NORA. That's the point right there: you've never understood me. I've been wronged greatly, Torvald—first by Papa, and then by you.

HELMER. What! By us—the two people who've loved you more than anyone else?

NORA (*shaking her head*). You never loved me. You've thought it fun to be in love with me, that's all.

HELMER. Nora, what a thing to say!

NORA. Yes, it's true now, Torvald. When I lived at home with Papa, he told me all his opinions, so I had the same ones too; or if they were different I hid them, since he wouldn't have cared for that. He used to call me his doll-child, and he played with me the way I played with my dolls. Then I came into your house—

HELMER. How can you speak of our marriage like that?

NORA (*unperturbed*). I mean, then I went from Papa's hands into yours. You arranged everything to your own taste, and so I got the same taste as you—or I pretended to; I can't remember. I guess a little of both, first one, then the other. Now when I look back, it seems as if I'd lived here like a beggar—just from hand to mouth. I've lived by doing tricks for you, Torvald. But that's the way you wanted it. It's a great sin what you and Papa did to me. You're to blame that nothing's become of me.

HELMER. Nora, how unfair and ungrateful you are! Haven't you been happy here?

NORA. No, never. I thought so—but I never have.

HELMER. Not—not happy!

NORA. No, only lighthearted. And you've always been so kind to me. But our home's been nothing but a playpen. I've been your doll-wife here, just as at home I was Papa's doll-child. And in turn the children have been my dolls. I thought it was fun when you played with me, just as they thought it fun when I played with them. That's been our marriage, Torvald.

HELMER. There's some truth in what you're saying—under all the raving exaggeration. But it'll all be different after this. Playtime's over; now for the schooling.

NORA. Whose schooling—mine or the children's?

HELMER. Both yours and the children's, dearest.

NORA. Oh, Torvald, you're not the man to teach me to be a good wife to you.

HELMER. And you can say that?

NORA. And I—how am I equipped to bring up children?

HELMER. Nora!

NORA. Didn't you say a moment ago that that was no job to trust me with?

HELMER. In a flare of temper! Why fasten on that?

NORA. Yes, but you were so very right. I'm not up to the job. There's another job I have to do first. I have to try to educate myself. You can't help me with that. I've got to do it alone. And that's why I'm leaving you now.

HELMER (*jumping up*). What's that?

NORA. I have to stand completely alone, if I'm ever going to discover myself and the world out there. So I can't go on living with you.

HELMER. Nora, Nora!

NORA. I want to leave right away. Kristine should put me up for the night—

HELMER. You're insane! You've no right! I forbid you!

NORA. From here on, there's no use forbidding me anything. I'll take with me whatever is mine. I don't want a thing from you, either now or later.

HELMER. What kind of madness is this!

NORA. Tomorrow I'm going home—I mean, home where I came from. It'll be easier up there to find something to do.

HELMER. Oh, you blind, incompetent child!

NORA. I must learn to be competent, Torvald.

HELMER. Abandon your home, your husband, your children! And you're not even thinking what people will say.

NORA. I can't be concerned about that. I only know how essential this is.

HELMER. Oh, it's outrageous. So you'll run out like this on your most sacred vows.

NORA. What do you think are my most sacred vows?

HELMER. And I have to tell you that! Aren't they your duties to your husband and children?

NORA. I have other duties equally sacred.

HELMER. That isn't true. What duties are they?

NORA. Duties to myself.

HELMER. Before all else, you're a wife and a mother.

NORA. I don't believe in that anymore. I believe that, before all else, I'm a human being, no less than you—or anyway, I ought to try to become one. I know the majority thinks you're right, Torvald, and plenty of books agree with you, too. But I can't go on believing what the majority says, or what's written in books. I have to think over these things myself and try to understand them.

HELMER. Why can't you understand your place in your own home? On a point like that, isn't there one everlasting guide you can turn to? Where's your religion?

NORA. Oh, Torvald, I'm really not sure what religion is.

HELMER. What—?

NORA. I only know what the minister said when I was confirmed. He told me religion was this thing and that. When I get clear and away by myself, I'll go into that problem too. I'll see if what the minister said was right, or, in any case, if it's right for me.

HELMER. A young woman your age shouldn't talk like that. If religion can't move you, I can try to rouse your conscience. You do have some moral feeling? Or, tell me—has that gone too?

NORA. It's not easy to answer that, Torvald. I simply don't know. I'm all confused about these things. I just know I see them so differently from you. I find out, for one thing, that the law's not at all what I'd thought—but I can't get it through my head that the law is fair. A woman hasn't a right to protect her dying father or save her husband's life! I can't believe that.

HELMER. You talk like a child. You don't know anything of the world you live in.

NORA. No, I don't. But now I'll begin to learn for myself. I'll try to discover who's right, the world or I.

HELMER. Nora, you're sick; you've got a fever. I almost think you're out of your head.

NORA. I've never felt more clearheaded and sure in my life.

HELMER. And—clearheaded and sure—you're leaving your husband and children?

NORA. Yes.

HELMER. Then there's only one possible reason.

NORA. What?

HELMER. You no longer love me.

NORA. No. That's exactly it.

HELMER. Nora! You can't be serious!

NORA. Oh, this is so hard, Torvald—you've been so kind to me always. But I can't help it. I don't love you anymore.

HELMER (struggling for composure). Are you also clearheaded and sure about that?

NORA. Yes, completely. That's why I can't go on staying here.

HELMER. Can you tell me what I did to lose your love?

NORA. Yes, I can tell you. It was this evening when the miraculous thing didn't come—then I knew you weren't the man I'd imagined.

HELMER. Be more explicit; I don't follow you.

NORA. I've waited now so patiently eight long years—for, my Lord, I know miracles don't come every day. Then this crisis broke over me, and such a certainty filled me: *now* the miraculous event would occur. While Krogstad's letter was lying out there, I never for an instant dreamed that you could give in to his terms. I was so utterly sure you'd say to him: go on, tell your tale to the whole wide world. And when he'd done that—

HELMER. Yes, what then? When I'd delivered my own wife into shame and disgrace—!

NORA. When he'd done that, I was so utterly sure that you'd step forward, take the blame on yourself and say: I am the guilty one.

HELMER. Nora—!

NORA. You're thinking I'd never accept such a sacrifice from you? No, of course not. But what good would my protests be against you? That was the miracle I was waiting for, in terror and hope. And to stave that off, I would have taken my life.

HELMER. I'd gladly work for you day and night, Nora—and take on pain and deprivation. But there's no one who gives up honor for love.

NORA. Millions of women have done just that.

HELMER. Oh, you think and talk like a silly child.

NORA. Perhaps. But you neither think nor talk like the man I could join myself to. When your big fright was over—and it wasn't from any threat against me, only for what might damage you—when all the danger was past, for you it was just as if nothing had happened. I was exactly the same, your little lark, your doll, that you'd have to handle with double care now that

I'd turned out so brittle and frail. (*Gets up.*) Torvald—in that instant it dawned on me that for eight years I've been living here with a stranger, and that I'd even conceived three children—oh, I can't stand the thought of it! I could tear myself to bits.

HELMER (*heavily*). I see. There's a gulf that's opened between us—that's clear. Oh, but Nora, can't we bridge it somehow?

NORA. The way I am now, I'm no wife for you.

HELMER. I have the strength to make myself over.

NORA. Maybe—if your doll gets taken away.

HELMER. But to part! To part from you! No, Nora, no—I can't imagine it.

NORA (*going out, right*). All the more reason why it has to be. (*She reenters with her coat and a small overnight bag, which she puts on a chair by the table.*)

HELMER. Nora, Nora, not now! Wait till tomorrow.

NORA. I can't spend the night in a strange man's room.

HELMER. But couldn't we live here like brother and sister—

NORA. You know very well how long that would last. (*Throws her shawl about her.*) Good-bye, Torvald. I won't look in on the children. I know they're in better hands than mine. The way I am now, I'm no use to them.

HELMER. But someday, Nora—someday—?

NORA. How can I tell? I haven't the least idea what'll become of me.

HELMER. But you're my wife, now and wherever you go.

NORA. Listen, Torvald—I've heard that when a wife deserts her husband's house just as I'm doing, then the law frees him from all responsibility. In any case, I'm freeing you from being responsible. Don't feel yourself bound, any more than I will. There has to be absolute freedom for us both. Here, take your ring back. Give me mine.

HELMER. That too?

NORA. That too.

HELMER. There it is.

NORA. Good. Well, now it's all over. I'm putting the keys here. The maids know all about keeping up the house—better than I do. Tomorrow, after I've left town, Kristine will stop by to pack up everything that's mine from home. I'd like those things shipped up to me.

HELMER. Over! All over! Nora, won't you ever think about me?

NORA. I'm sure I'll think of you often, and about the children and the house here.

HELMER. May I write you?

NORA. No—never. You're not to do that.

HELMER. Oh, but let me send you—

NORA. Nothing. Nothing.

HELMER. Or help you if you need it.

NORA. No. I accept nothing from strangers.

HELMER. Nora—can I never be more than a stranger to you?

NORA (*picking up the overnight bag*). Ah, Torvald—it would take the greatest miracle of all—

HELMER. Tell me the greatest miracle!

NORA. You and I both would have to transform ourselves to the point that— Oh, Torvald, I've stopped believing in miracles.

HELMER. But I'll believe. Tell me! Transform ourselves to the point that—?

NORA. That our living together could be a true marriage. (*She goes out down the hall.*)

HELMER (*sinks down on a chair by the door, face buried in his hands*). Nora! Nora! (*Looking about and rising.*) Empty. She's gone. (*A sudden hope leaps in him.*) The greatest miracle—? (*From below, the sound of a door slamming shut.*)

1879

THINK AND DISCUSS

ACT ONE

Understanding

1. What activity has Nora engaged in prior to her entrance at the beginning of the play?
2. What gifts has Nora purchased for the children?
3. What is Torvald's feeling about assuming debt?
4. What trait does Torvald say that Nora has inherited from her father?

Analyzing

5. What does the business of the macaroons tell you about Nora?
6. Describe the way Torvald treats Nora in Act One.
7. Contrast Nora and Mrs. Linde in age, mood, and attitude toward life.
8. Why has it been necessary for Nora to borrow money from Krogstad? How has she been managing her payments?

Extending

9. What evidence is there that Krogstad's visit worries Nora? Why do you suppose the playwright has her stoke the fire in the stove after he arrives?
10. In what ways does Dr. Rank's visit dampen the pleasant "doll-house" atmosphere of the Helmer home? What qualification does he place on his acceptance of Nora's invitation to return in the evening?
11. What impression of Nora and the family situation do you get from the romp with the children? What event destroys the gaiety of the moment?
12. This play demonstrates the late nineteenth-century movement known as naturalism. (See Glossary of Literary Terms, page 1018.) What evidence is there that Torvald has been influenced by the current belief that heredity and environment determine the nature of the individual?
13. To what extent has Nora changed in the course of Act One?

ACT TWO

Understanding

1. What is different about the location and condition of the Christmas tree as Act Two begins?
2. What do we learn about the nurse and her daughter?
3. Who does Mrs. Linde think has loaned Nora the money?
4. What is the nature of Dr. Rank's disease?
5. What does Mrs. Linde suspect about Dr. Rank's frequent visits to the Helmer household?
6. What "petty considerations" lie behind Torvald's insistence on firing Krogstad?

Analyzing

7. What **inference** can you make about what Nora is planning to do, based on her conversation with the nurse, Anne-Marie?
8. What request does Nora make of Helmer on page 731, and how does she approach the subject?
9. How does the theme of "disease" link Dr. Rank to Krogstad and Nora?
10. How does Nora tease Rank as she is preparing to ask him the big favor? What similar tactics has she used before?
11. Why does Nora put her hands over her ears when Rank speaks of suffering for the sins of his father?
12. What is the miracle that Nora keeps referring to?

Extending

13. Why is Mrs. Linde surprised that Nora knows so much about Dr. Rank's disease?
14. Why does Ibsen have it begin to get dark during the conversation between Dr. Rank and Nora? What might explain the stage business of having the maid bring in a lamp (page 734)?
15. Look up "tarantella" in your Glossary. How is the tarantella an appropriate dance for Nora to be performing at the coming party?
16. Why does Nora decide not to ask Rank for money? Does her logic seem sensible today,

or does it seem like outmoded Victorian morality?

ACT THREE
Understanding
1. Where are Nora and Torvald when Act Three opens?
2. Why does Krogstad come to the Helmers' home?
3. Why did Mrs. Linde choose the man she did instead of Krogstad?

Analyzing
4. On page 741 Krogstad asks, "Is that the meaning of it, then? You'll save your friend at any price. Tell me straight out. Is that it?" What suspicion lies behind this question?
5. Why does Mrs. Linde tell Krogstad not to demand his letter back?
6. Why is Nora so reluctant to leave the party?
7. What is the real reason that Dr. Rank drops in at the Helmers' after he leaves the masquerade party?
8. On page 745 Nora says, "I'm beginning to understand everything now." What new realization is she coming to?

Extending
9. The audience that saw the premiere of this play in 1879 were shocked by the ending. Is Nora's decision still shocking today?
10. The famous slamming door that ends this play has been called "the closing of the door of the 19th century." Why?

COMPOSITION
Writing to Persuade
Write a composition in which you argue either for or against the proposition, "A woman's highest obligation is to herself, not to her husband and family." Use Nora Helmer to illustrate your point. Be prepared to share your paper with other class members. See "Writing to Persuade an Audience" in the Writer's Handbook.

Writing About a Period
Using *A Doll House* as your source of information, write an essay about middle-class life in Norway in the 1870s. Describe the values held by the various characters, the role of money, social taboos, women's place in society, and any other ideas that occurred to you as you read the play. See "Writing About a Period or Trend" in the Writer's Handbook.

ENRICHMENT
Trying Nora for Desertion
Nora Helmer is on trial. Select class members to take the parts of the characters in the play. Find volunteers to be judge, prosecuting attorney, and defense attorney. You may wish also to select a bailiff and court reporter. All class members not assigned a part will become the jury. The charge against Nora is desertion.

The two attorneys should take care in preparing opening and closing statements and questions they intend to ask of the witnesses they will call. Students portraying the various members of the play should review their characters and respond to attorneys' questions appropriately. (Dr. Rank is ill but not too feeble to testify.) The student taking the role of judge should be prepared to sustain or overrule attorney objections and to instruct the jury. He or she might be given the task of assigning the penalty or punishment in the event that Nora is found guilty. The classroom can be rearranged to simulate a courtroom.

BIOGRAPHY

Anton Chekhov

1860–1904

Anton Chekhov was born at Taganrog, Russia, where his father was a grocer. His grandfather had been a serf, liberated by imperial edict a year after Anton was born. The boy received his early formal education at the local secondary school and in 1879 entered the University of Moscow where he studied medicine. To help pay his educational expenses, Chekhov began writing slight, amusing stories. These early works are generally brief sketches with little depth. His later works show an increasing concern for people and society, but an undertow of the early humor always remains.

Chekhov received his M.D. degree in 1884 and worked briefly in a hospital in a small town outside of Moscow. Most of his time, however, he devoted to writing. The influence of his professional study upon the subject matter and expression of some of his stories is quite obvious.

By 1886 Chekhov had written more than 300 short stories. The collection in which "The Kiss" (page 754) first appeared was published in 1888. It also contained such little masterpieces as "Happiness" and a famous descriptive story, "The Steppe," which won him the Pushkin Prize.

In 1890 Chekhov made a grim journey to the island of Sakhalin, off the coast of Siberia, on which there was a penal colony. He spent the summer there making a detailed study of convict life. The resulting book was instrumental in effecting at least some measure of reform in the Russian penal system.

The works of Chekhov's later period, especially such plays as *The Sea Gull* (1896), *Uncle Vanya* (1897), *Three Sisters* (1901), and *The Cherry Orchard* (1904), attempt to depict the tragedy that lies behind much of everyday living. The plays were baffling to many of his contemporaries. Leo Tolstoy admitted his own confusion, and yet could still perceive Chekhov's genius. He said: "I have as yet no clear picture of Chekhov's plays. But it is possible that in the future, perhaps a hundred years hence, people will be amazed at what they find in Chekhov about the inner workings of the human soul."

Never a robust man, Chekhov had contracted pulmonary tuberculosis in the winter of 1883. Seeking a warmer climate he spent the winter of 1897 in Nice, France, where he became interested in the trial of the French Jew Alfred Dreyfus, an army officer unjustly accused of treason, whom Chekhov staunchly defended. He then spent three years living in Yalta, where his health gradually degenerated. He died in Germany at a health resort to which his doctors had sent him. A master of the short story and a superbly subtle dramatist, Chekhov always managed his effects within a minimum number of pages. All his finest work reflects his dictum: "Conciseness is the sister of talent."

The Kiss

Anton Chekhov   *translated by* **R. E. C. Long**

n the evening of the twentieth of May, at eight o'clock, all six batteries of the N Artillery Brigade on their way to camp arrived at the village of Miestechky with the intention of spending the night.

The confusion was at its worst—some officers fussed about the guns, others in the church square arranged with the quartermaster—when from behind the church rode a civilian upon a most remarkable mount. The small, short-tailed bay with well-shaped neck progressed with a wobbly motion, all the time making dance-like movements with its legs as if some one were switching its hoofs. When he had drawn rein level with the officers the rider doffed his cap and said ceremoniously—

"His Excellency, General von Rabbek, whose house is close by, requests the honor of the officers' company at tea. . . ."

The horse shook its head, danced, and wobbled to the rear; its rider again took off his cap, and, turning his strange steed, disappeared behind the church.

"The devil take it!" was the general exclamation as the officers dispersed to their quarters. "We can hardly keep our eyes open, yet along comes this von Rabbek with his tea! I know that tea!"

The officers of the six batteries had lively memories of a past invitation. During recent maneuvers they had been asked, together with their Cossack comrades, to tea at the house of a local country gentleman, an officer in retirement, by title a Count; and this hearty, hospitable Count overwhelmed them with attentions, fed them to satiety, poured vodka down their throats, and made them stay the night. All this, of course, they enjoyed. The trouble was that the old soldier entertained his guests too well. He kept them up till daybreak while he poured forth tales of past adventures; he dragged them from room to room to point out valuable paintings, old engravings, and rare arms; he read them holograph letters from celebrated men. And the weary officers, bored to death, listened, gaped, yearned for their beds, and yawned cautiously in their sleeves, until at last when their host released them it was too late for sleep.

Was von Rabbek another old Count? It might easily be. But there was no neglecting his invitation. The officers washed and dressed, and set out for von Rabbek's house. At the church square they learnt that they must descend the hill to the river, and follow the bank till they reached the general's gardens, where they would find a path direct to the house. Or, if they chose to go up hill, they would reach the general's barns half a verst from Miestetchky. It was this route they chose.

"But who is this von Rabbek?" asked one. "The man who commanded the N Cavalry Division at Plevna?"

"No, that was not von Rabbek, but simply Rabbe—without the von."

"What glorious weather!"

At the first barn they came to, two roads diverged; one ran straight forward and faded in the dusk; the other turning to the right led to the general's house. As the officers drew near they talked less loudly. To right and left stretched rows of red-roofed brick barns, in aspect heavy and morose as the barracks of provincial towns. In front gleamed the lighted windows of von Rabbek's house.

"A good omen, gentlemen!" cried a young officer. "Our setter runs in advance. There is game ahead!"

On the face of Lieutenant Lobytko, the tall stout officer referred to, there was not one trace of hair though he was twenty-five years old. He was famed among comrades for the instinct which told him of the presence of women in the neighborhood. On hearing his comrade's remark, he turned his head and said—

"Yes. There are women there. My instinct tells me."

A handsome, well-preserved man of sixty, in mufti,[1] came to the hall door to greet his guests. It was von Rabbek. As he pressed their hands, he explained that though he was delighted to see them, he must beg pardon for not asking them to spend the night; as guests he already had his two sisters, their children, his brother, and several neighbors—in fact, he had not one spare room. And though he shook their hands and apologized and smiled, it was plain that he was not half as glad to see them as was last year's Count, and that he had invited them merely because good manners demanded it. The officers climbing the soft-carpeted steps and listening to their host understood this perfectly well; and realized that they carried into the house an atmosphere of intrusion and alarm. Would any man—they asked themselves—who had gathered his two sisters and their children, his brother and his neighbors, to celebrate, no doubt, some family festival, find pleasure in the invasion of nineteen officers whom he had never seen before?

A tall, elderly lady, with a good figure, and a long face with black eyebrows, who resembled closely the ex-Empress Eugenie,[2] greeted them at the drawing-room door. Smiling courteously and with dignity, she affirmed that she was delighted to see the officers, and only regretted that she could not ask them to stay the night. But the courteous, dignified smile disappeared when she turned away, and it was quite plain that she had seen many officers in her day, that they caused not the slight-

est interest, and that she had invited them merely because an invitation was dictated by good breeding and by her position in the world.

In a big dining-room seated at a big table sat ten men and women, drinking tea. Behind them, veiled in cigar-smoke, stood several young men, among them one, red-whiskered and extremely thin, who spoke English loudly with a lisp. Through an open door the officers saw into a brightly lighted room with blue wall-paper.

"You are too many to introduce singly, gentlemen!" said the general loudly, with affected joviality. "Make one another's acquaintance, please—without formalities!"

The visitors, some with serious, even severe faces, some smiling constrainedly, all with a feeling of awkwardness, bowed, and took their seats at the table. Most awkward of all felt Staff-Captain Riabovich, a short, round-shouldered, spectacled officer, whiskered like a lynx. While his brother officers looked serious or smiled constrainedly, his face, his lynx whiskers, and his spectacles seemed to explain: "I am the most timid, modest, undistinguished officer in the whole brigade." For some time after he took his seat at the table he could not fix his attention on any single thing. Faces, dresses, the cut-glass cognac bottles, the steaming tumblers, the molded cornices—all merged in a single, overwhelming sentiment which caused him intense fright and made him wish to hide his head. Like an inexperienced lecturer he saw everything before him, but could distinguish nothing, and was in fact the victim of what men of science diagnose as "psychical blindness."

But slowly conquering his diffidence, Riabovich began to distinguish and observe. As became a man both timid and unsocial, he remarked first of all the amazing temerity of his new friends. Von Rabbek, his wife, two elderly ladies, a girl in lilac, and the red-whiskered youth who, it appeared, was a young von Rabbek, sat down among the officers as unconcernedly as if they had held rehearsals, and at once plunged into various heated

---

1. *mufti,* civilian clothes when worn by a military person.
2. *ex-Empress Eugenie,* empress of the French (1853–70), wife of Napoleon III.

arguments in which they soon involved their guests. That artillerists have a much better time than cavalrymen or infantrymen was proved conclusively by the lilac girl, while von Rabbek and the elderly ladies affirmed the converse. The conversation became desultory. Riabovich listened to the lilac girl fiercely debating themes she knew nothing about and took no interest in, and watched the insincere smiles which appeared on and disappeared from her face.

While the von Rabbek family with amazing strategy inveigled their guests into the dispute, they kept their eyes on every glass and mouth. Had every one tea, was it sweet enough, why didn't one eat biscuits, was another fond of cognac? And the longer Riabovich listened and looked, the more pleased he was with this disingenuous, disciplined family.

After tea the guests repaired to the drawing-room. Instinct had not cheated Lobytko. The room was packed with young women and girls, and ere a minute had passed the setter-lieutenant stood beside a very young, fair-haired girl in black, and, bending down as if resting on an invisible sword, shrugged his shoulders coquettishly. He was uttering, no doubt, most unentertaining nonsense, for the fair girl looked indulgently at his sated face, and exclaimed indifferently, "Indeed!" And this indifferent "Indeed!" might have quickly convinced the setter that he was on a wrong scent.

Music began. As the notes of a mournful waltz throbbed out of the open window, through the heads of all flashed the feeling that outside that window it was spring-time, a night of May. The air was odorous of young poplar leaves, of roses and lilacs—and the waltz and the spring were sincere. Riabovich, with waltz and cognac mingling tipsily in his head, gazed at the window with a smile; then began to follow the movements of the women; and it seemed that the smell of roses, poplars, and lilacs came not from the gardens outside, but from the women's faces and dresses.

They began to dance. Young von Rabbek waltzed twice round the room with a very thin girl; and Lobytko, slipping on the parquetted floor, went up to the girl in lilac, and was granted a dance. But Riabovich stood near the door with the wall-flowers, and looked silently on. Amazed at the daring of men who in sight of a crowd could take unknown women by the waist, he tried in vain to picture himself doing the same. A time had been when he envied his comrades their courage and dash, suffered from painful heart-searchings, and was hurt by the knowledge that he was timid, round-shouldered, and undistinguished, that he had lynx whiskers, and that his waist was much too long. But with years he had grown reconciled to his own insignificance, and now looking at the dancers and loud talkers, he felt no envy, but only mournful emotions.

At the first quadrille von Rabbek junior approached and invited two non-dancing officers to a game of billiards. The three left the room; and Riabovich who stood idle, and felt impelled to join in the general movement, followed. They passed the dining-room, traversed a narrow glazed corridor, and a room where three sleepy footmen jumped from a sofa with a start; and after walking, it seemed, through a whole houseful of rooms, entered a small billiard-room.

Von Rabbek and the two officers began their game. Riabovich, whose only game was cards, stood near the table and looked indifferently on, as the players, with unbuttoned coats, wielded their cues, moved about, joked, and shouted obscure technical terms. Riabovich was ignored, save when one of the players jostled him or caught his cue, and turning towards him said briefly, "Pardon!" so that before the game was over he was thoroughly bored, and impressed by a sense of his superfluity, resolved to return to the drawing-room, and turned away.

It was on the way back that his adventure took place. Before he had gone far he saw that he had missed the way. He remembered distinctly the room with the three sleepy footmen; and after passing through five or six rooms entirely vacant, he saw his mistake. Retracing his steps, he turned to the left, and found himself in an almost dark room which he had not seen before; and after hesitating a minute, he boldly opened the first door he saw, and found himself in complete darkness. Through a chink of the door in front peered a bright light; from afar throbbed the dulled music

of a mournful mazurka. Here, as in the drawing-room, the windows were open wide, and the smell of poplars, lilacs, and roses flooded the air.

Riabovich paused in irresolution. For a moment all was still. Then came the sound of hasty footsteps; then, without any warning of what was to come, a dress rustled, a woman's breathless voice whispered "At last!" and two soft, scented, unmistakably womanly arms met round his neck, a warm cheek impinged on his, and he received a sounding kiss. But hardly had the kiss echoed through the silence when the unknown shrieked loudly, and fled away—as it seemed to Riabovich—in disgust. Riabovich himself nearly screamed, and rushed headlong towards the bright beam in the door-chink.

As he entered the drawing-room his heart beat violently, and his hands trembled so perceptibly that he clasped them behind his back. His first emotion was shame, as if every one in the room already knew that he had just been embraced and kissed. He retired into his shell, and looked fearfully around. But finding that hosts and guests were calmly dancing or talking, he regained courage, and surrendered himself to sensations experienced for the first time in life. The unexampled had happened. His neck, fresh from the embrace of two soft, scented arms, seemed anointed with oil; near his left moustache, where the kiss had fallen, trembled a slight, delightful chill, as from peppermint drops; and from head to foot he was soaked in new and extraordinary sensations, which continued to grow and grow.

He felt that he must dance, talk, run into the garden, laugh unrestrainedly. He forgot altogether that he was round-shouldered, undistinguished, lynx-whiskered, that he had an "indefinite exterior"—a description from the lips of a woman he had happened to overhear. As Madame von Rabbek passed him he smiled so broadly and graciously that she came up and looked at him questioningly.

"What a charming house you have!" he said, straightening his spectacles.

And Madame von Rabbek smiled back, said that the house still belonged to her father, and asked were his parents alive, how long he had been in the Army, and why he was so thin. After hearing his answers she departed. But though the conversation was over, he continued to smile benevolently, and think what charming people were his new acquaintances.

At supper Riabovich ate and drank mechanically what was put before him, heard not a word of the conversation, and devoted all his powers to the unravelling of his mysterious, romantic adventure. What was the explanation? It was plain that one of the girls, he reasoned, had arranged a meeting in the dark room, and after waiting some time in vain had, in her nervous tension, mistaken Riabovich for her hero. The mistake was likely enough, for on entering the dark room Riabovich had stopped irresolutely as if he, too, were waiting for some one. So far the mystery was explained.

"But which of them was it?" he asked, searching the women's faces. She certainly was young, for old women do not indulge in such romances. Secondly, she was not a servant. That was proved unmistakably by the rustle of her dress, the scent, the voice . . .

When at first he looked at the girl in lilac she pleased him; she had pretty shoulders and arms, a clever face, a charming voice. Riabovich piously prayed that it was she. But, smiling insincerely, she wrinkled her long nose, and that at once gave her an elderly air. So Riabovich turned his eyes on the blonde in black. The blonde was younger, simpler, sincerer; she had charming kiss-curls, and drank from her tumbler with inexpressible grace. Riabovich hoped it was she—but soon he noticed that her face was flat, and bent his eyes on her neighbor.

"It is a hopeless puzzle," he reflected. "If you take the arms and shoulders of the lilac girl, add the blonde's curls, and the eyes of the girl on Lobytko's left, then——"

He composed a portrait of all these charms, and had a clear vision of the girl who had kissed him.

But she was nowhere to be seen.

Supper over, the visitors, sated and tipsy, bade their entertainers good-bye. Both host and hostess again apologized for not asking them to spend the night.

"I am very glad, very glad, gentlemen!" said the general, and this time seemed to speak sincerely, no doubt because speeding the parting guest is a kindlier office than welcoming him unwelcomed. "I am very glad indeed! I hope you will visit me on your way back. Without ceremony, please! Which way will you go? Up the hill? No, go down the hill and through the garden. That way is shorter."

The officers took his advice. After the noise and glaring illumination within doors, the garden seemed dark and still. Until they reached the wicket-gate all kept silence. Merry, half tipsy, and content, as they were, the night's obscurity and stillness inspired pensive thoughts. Through their brains, as through Riabovich's, sped probably the same question: "Will the time ever come when I, like von Rabbek, shall have a big house, a family, a garden, the chance of being gracious—even insincerely—to others, of making them sated, tipsy, and content?"

But once the garden lay behind them, all spoke at once, and burst into causeless laughter. The path they followed led straight to the river, and then ran beside it, winding around bushes, ravines, and over-hanging willow-trees. The track was barely visible; the other bank was lost entirely in gloom. Sometimes the black water imaged stars, and this was the only indication of the river's speed. From beyond it sighed a drowsy snipe, and beside them in a bush, heedless of the crowd, a nightingale chanted loudly. The officers gathered in a group, and swayed the bush, but the nightingale continued his song.

"I like his cheek!" they echoed admiringly. "He doesn't care a kopeck! The old rogue!"

Near their journey's end the path turned up the hill, and joined the road not far from the church enclosure; and there the officers, breathless from climbing, sat on the grass and smoked. Across the river gleamed a dull red light, and for want of a subject they argued the problem, whether it was a bonfire, a window-light, or something else.

Riabovich looked also at the light, and felt that it smiled and winked at him as if it knew about the kiss.

On reaching home, he undressed without delay, and lay upon his bed. He shared the cabin with Lobytko and a Lieutenant Merzliakov, a staid, silent little man, by repute highly cultivated, who took with him everywhere *The Messenger of Europe*,[3] and read it eternally. Lobytko undressed, tramped impatiently from corner to corner, and sent his servant for beer. Merzliakov lay down, balanced the candle on his pillow, and hid his head behind *The Messenger of Europe*.

"Where is she now?" muttered Riabovich, looking at the soot-blacked ceiling.

His neck still seemed anointed with oil, near his mouth still trembled the speck of peppermint chill. Through his brain twinkled successively the shoulders and arms of the lilac girl, the kiss-curls and honest eyes of the girl in black, the waists, dresses, brooches. But though he tried his best to fix these vagrant images, they glimmered, winked, and dissolved; and as they faded finally into the vast black curtain which hangs before the closed eyes of all men, he began to hear hurried footsteps, the rustle of petticoats, the sound of a kiss. A strong, causeless joy possessed him. But as he surrendered himself to this joy, Lobytko's servant returned with the news that no beer was obtainable. The lieutenant resumed his impatient march up and down the room.

"The fellow's an idiot," he exclaimed, stopping first near Riabovich and then near Merzliakov. "Only the worst numbskull and blockhead can't get beer! *Canaille!*"[4]

"Every one knows there's no beer here," said Merzliakov, without lifting his eyes from *The Messenger of Europe*.

"You believe that!" exclaimed Lobytko. "Lord in heaven, drop me on the moon, and in five minutes I'll find both beer and women! I will find them myself! Call me a rascal if I don't!"

He dressed slowly, silently lighted a cigarette, and went out.

"Rabbek, Grabbek, Labbek," he muttered, stopping in the hall. "I won't go alone, devil take me! Riabovich, come for a walk! What?"

As he got no answer, he returned, undressed slowly, and lay down. Merzliakov sighed, dropped *The Messenger of Europe*, and put out the light. "Well?" muttered Lobytko, puffing his cigarette in the dark.

Riabovich pulled the bed-clothes up to his chin, curled himself into a roll, and strained his imagination to join the twinkling images into one coherent whole. But the vision fled him. He soon fell asleep, and his last impression was that he had been caressed and gladdened, that into his life had crept something strange, and indeed ridiculous, but uncommonly good and radiant. And this thought did not forsake him even in his dreams.

When he awoke the feeling of anointment and peppermint chill were gone. But joy, as on the night before, filled every vein. He looked entranced at the window-panes gilded by the rising sun, and listened to the noises outside. Some one spoke loudly under the very window. It was Lebedetzky, commander of his battery, who had just overtaken the brigade. He was talking to the sergeant-major, loudly, owing to lack of practice in soft speech.

"And what next?" he roared.

"During yesterday's shoeing, your honor, *Golubtchik*[5] was pricked. The *feldscher*[6] ordered clay and vinegar. And last night, your honor, mechanic Artemieff was drunk, and the lieutenant ordered him to be put on the limber[7] of the reserve gun-carriage."

The sergeant-major added that Karpov had forgotten the tent-pegs and the new lanyards for the friction-tubes, and that the officers had spent the evening at General von Rabbek's. But here at the window appeared Lebedetzky's red-bearded face. He blinked his short-sighted eyes at the drowsy men in bed, and greeted them.

"Is everything all right?"

---

3. **The Messenger of Europe,** a Russian periodical favored by the intelligentsia.
4. *Canaille* (ka nī′), a French word meaning "rabble" or "riffraff."
5. **Golubtchik.** The horse's name means "little pigeon."
6. **feldscher,** assistant regimental doctor.
7. *limber,* the detachable front part of the carriage of a field gun.

"The saddle wheeler galled his withers with the new yoke," answered Lobytko.

The commander sighed, mused a moment, and shouted—

"I am thinking of calling on Alexandra Yegorovna. I want to see her. Good-bye! I will catch you up before night."

Fifteen minutes later the brigade resumed its march. As he passed von Rabbek's barns Riabovich turned his head and looked at the house. The Venetian blinds were down; evidently all still slept. And among them slept she—she who had kissed him but a few hours before. He tried to visualize her asleep. He projected the bedroom window opened wide with green branches peering in, the freshness of the morning air, the smell of poplars, lilacs, and roses, the bed, a chair, the dress which rustled last night, a pair of tiny slippers, a ticking watch on the table—all these came to him clearly with every detail. But the features, the kind, sleepy smile—all, in short, that was essential and characteristic—fled his imagination as quicksilver flees the hand. When he had covered half a verst he again turned back. The yellow church, the house, gardens, and river were bathed in light. Imaging an azure sky, the green-banked river specked with silver sunshine flakes was inexpressibly fair; and, looking at Miestechky for the last time, Riabovich felt sad, as if parting for ever with something very near and dear.

By the road before him stretched familiar, uninteresting scenes; to the right and left, fields of young rye and buckwheat with hopping rooks; in front, dust and the napes of human necks; behind, the same dust and faces. Ahead of the column marched four soldiers with swords—that was the advance guard. Next came the bandsmen. Advance guard and bandsmen, like mutes in a funeral procession, ignored the regulation intervals and marched too far ahead. Riabovich, with the first gun of Battery No. 5, could see four batteries ahead.

To a layman, the long, lumbering march of an artillery brigade is novel, interesting, inexplicable. It is hard to understand why a single gun needs so many men; why so many, such strangely harnessed horses are needed to drag it. But to

Riabovich, a master of all these things, it was profoundly dull. He had learned years ago why a solid sergeant-major rides beside the officer in front of each battery; why the sergeant-major is called the *unosni*, and why the drivers of leaders and wheelers ride behind him. Riabovich knew why the near horses are called saddle-horses, and why the off horses are called led-horses—and all of this was interesting beyond words. On one of the wheelers rode a soldier still covered with yesterday's dust, and with a cumbersome, ridiculous guard on his right leg. But Riabovich, knowing the use of this leg-guard, found it in no way ridiculous. The drivers, mechanically and with occasional cries, flourished their whips. The guns in themselves were impressive. The limbers were packed with tarpaulin-covered sacks of oats; and the guns themselves, hung around with teapots and satchels, looked like harmless animals, guarded for some obscure reason by men and horses. In the lee of the gun tramped six gunners, swinging their arms; and behind each gun came more *unosniye*, leaders, wheelers; and yet more guns, each as ugly and uninspiring as the one in front. And as every one of the six batteries in the brigade had four guns, the procession stretched along the road at least half a verst. It ended with a wagon train, with which, its head bent in thought, walked the donkey Magar, brought from Turkey by a battery commander.

Dead to his surroundings, Riabovich marched onward, looking at the napes ahead or at the faces behind. Had it not been for last night's event, he would have been half asleep. But now he was absorbed in novel, entrancing thoughts. When the brigade set out that morning he had tried to argue that the kiss had no significance save as a trivial though mysterious adventure; that it was without real import; and that to think of it seriously was to behave himself absurdly. But logic soon flew away and surrendered him to his vivid imaginings. At times he saw himself in von Rabbek's dining-room, *tête-à-tête*[8] with a composite being, formed of the girl in lilac and the blonde in black. At

---

8. **tête-à-tête**, in intimate conversation.

times he closed his eyes, and pictured himself with a different, this time quite an unknown, girl of cloudy feature; he spoke to her, caressed her, bent over her shoulder; he imagined war and parting . . . then reunion, the first supper together, children. . . .

"To the brakes!" rang the command as they topped the brow of each hill.

Riabovich also cried "To the brakes!" and each time dreaded that the cry would break the magic spell, and recall him to realities.

They passed a big country house. Riabovich looked across the fence into the garden, and saw a long path, straight as a ruler, carpeted with yellow sand, and shaded by young birches. In an ecstasy of enchantment, he pictured little feminine feet treading the yellow sand; and, in a flash, imagination restored the woman who had kissed him, the woman he had visualized after supper the night before. The image settled in his brain and never afterwards forsook him.

The spell reigned until midday, when a loud command came from the rear of the column.

"Attention! Eyes right! Officers!"

In a *calèche*[9] drawn by a pair of white horses appeared the general of brigade. He stopped at the second battery, and called out something which no one understood. Up galloped several officers, among them Riabovich.

"Well, how goes it?" The general blinked his red eyes, and continued, "Are there any sick?"

Hearing the answer, the little skinny general mused a moment, turned to an officer, and said—

"The driver of your third-gun wheeler has taken off his leg-guard and hung it on the limber. *Canaille!* Punish him!"

Then raising his eyes to Riabovich, he added—

"And in your battery, I think, the harness is too loose."

Having made several other equally tiresome remarks, he looked at Lobytko, and laughed.

"Why do you look so downcast, Lieutenant Lobytko? You are sighing for Madame Lopukhov, eh? Gentlemen, he is pining for Madame Lopukhov!"

Madame Lopukhov was a tall, stout lady, long past forty. Being partial to big women, regardless of age, the general ascribed the same taste to his subordinates. The officers smiled respectfully; and the general, pleased that he had said something caustic and laughable, touched the coachman's back and saluted. The *calèche* whirled away.

"All this, though it seems to me impossible and unearthly, is in reality very commonplace," thought Riabovich, watching the clouds of dust raised by the general's carriage. "It is an everyday event, and within every one's experience. . . . This old general, for instance, must have loved in his day; he is married now, and his wife loves him, though he has an ugly red neck and no waist. . . . Salmanoff is coarse, and a typical Tartar, but he has had a romance ending in marriage. . . . I, like the rest, must go through it all sooner or later."

And the thought that he was an ordinary man, and that his life was ordinary, rejoiced and consoled him. He boldly visualized *her* and his happiness, and let his imagination run mad.

Towards evening the brigade ended its march. While the other officers sprawled in their tents, Riabovich, Merzliakov, and Lobytko sat around a packing-case and supped. Merzliakov ate slowly, and, resting *The Messenger of Europe* on his knees, read on steadily. Lobytko, chattering without cease, poured beer into his glass. But Riabovich, whose head was dizzy from uninterrupted daydreams, ate in silence. When he had drunk three glasses he felt tipsy and weak; and an overmastering impulse forced him to relate his adventure to his comrades.

"A most extraordinary thing happened to me at von Rabbek's," he began, doing his best to speak in an indifferent, ironical tone. "I was on my way, you understand, from the billiard-room. . . ."

And he attempted to give a very detailed history of the kiss. But in a minute he had told the whole story. In that minute he had exhausted every detail; and it seemed to him terrible that the story required such a short time. It ought, he felt, to have lasted all the night. As he finished, Lobytko,

---

9. calèche (ka'lesh'), a convertible carriage with two banks of seats that face each other and a separate compartment for the driver.

who as a liar himself believed in no one, laughed incredulously. Merzliakov frowned, and, with his eyes still glued to *The Messenger of Europe,* said indifferently—

"God knows who it was! She threw herself on your neck, you say, and didn't cry out! Some lunatic, I expect!"

"It must have been a lunatic," agreed Riabovich.

"I, too, have had adventures of that kind," began Lobytko, making a frightened face. "I was on my way to Kovno. I travelled second class. The carriage was packed, and I couldn't sleep. So I gave the guard a ruble, and he took my bag, and put me in a *coupé.* I lay down, and pulled my rug over me. It was pitch dark, you understand. Suddenly I felt some one tapping my shoulder and breathing in my face. I stretched out my hand, and felt an elbow. Then I opened my eyes. Imagine! A woman! Coal-black eyes, lips red as good coral, nostrils breathing passion, breasts—buffers!"

"Draw it mild!" interrupted Merzliakov in his quiet voice. "I can believe about the breasts, but if it was pitch dark how could you see the lips?"

By laughing at Merzliakov's lack of understanding, Lobytko tried to shuffle out of the dilemma. The story annoyed Riabovich. He rose from the box, lay on his bed, and swore that he would never again take any one into his confidence.

Life in camp passed without event. The days flew by, each like the one before. But on every one of these days Riabovich felt, thought, and acted as a man in love. When at daybreak his servant brought him cold water, and poured it over his head, it flashed at once into his half-awakened brain that something good and warm and caressing had crept into his life.

At night when his comrades talked of love and of women, he drew in his chair, and his face was the face of an old soldier who talks of battles in which he has taken part. And when the rowdy officers, led by setter Lobytko, made Don Juanesque raids upon the neighboring "suburb," Riabovich, though he accompanied them, was morose and conscience-struck, and mentally asked *her* forgiveness. In free hours and sleepless nights, when his brain was obsessed by memories of childhood, of his father, his mother, of everything akin and dear, he remembered always Miestechky, the dancing horse, von Rabbek, von Rabbek's wife, so like the ex-Empress Eugenie, the dark room, the chink in the door.

On the thirty-first of August he left camp, this time not with the whole brigade but with only two batteries. As an exile returning to his native land, he was agitated and enthralled by day-dreams. He longed passionately for the queer-looking horse, the church, the insincere von Rabbeks, the dark room; and that internal voice which cheats so often the love-lorn whispered an assurance that he should see *her* again. But doubt tortured him. How should he meet her? What must he say? Would she have forgotten the kiss? If it came to the worse—he consoled himself—if he never saw her again, he might walk once more through the dark room, and remember. . . .

Towards evening the white barns and well-known church rose on the horizon. Riabovich's heart beat wildly. He ignored the remark of an officer who rode by, he forgot the whole world, and he gazed greedily at the river glimmering afar, at the green roofs, at the dove-cote, over which fluttered birds, dyed golden by the setting sun.

As he rode towards the church, and heard again the quartermaster's raucous voice, he expected every second a horseman to appear from behind the fence and invite the officers to tea. . . . But the quartermaster ended his harangue, the officers hastened to the village, and no horseman appeared.

"When Rabbek hears from the peasants that we are back he will send for us," thought Riabovich. And so assured was he of this, that when he entered the hut he failed to understand why his comrades had lighted a candle, and why the servants were preparing the samovar.

A painful agitation oppressed him. He lay on his bed. A moment later he rose to look for the horseman. But no horseman was in sight. Again he lay down; again he rose; and this time, impelled by restlessness, went into the street, and walked towards the church. The square was dark and deserted. On the hill stood three silent soldiers. When they saw Riabovich they started and saluted, and he, returning their salute, began to descend the well-remembered path.

Beyond the stream, in a sky stained with purple, the moon slowly rose. Two chattering peasant women walked in a kitchen garden and pulled cabbage leaves; behind them their log cabins stood out black against the sky. The river bank was as it had been in May; the bushes were the same; things differed only in that the nightingale no longer sang, that it smelt no longer of poplars and young grass.

When he reached von Rabbek's garden Riabovich peered through the wicket-gate. Silence and darkness reigned. Save only the white birch trunks and patches of pathway, the whole garden merged in a black, impenetrable shade. Riabovich listened greedily, and gazed intent. For a quarter of an hour he loitered; then hearing no sound, and seeing no light, he walked wearily towards home.

He went down to the river. In front rose the general's bathing box; and white towels hung on the rail of the bridge. He climbed on to the bridge and stood still; then, for no reason whatever, touched a towel. It was clammy and cold. He looked down at the river which sped past swiftly, murmuring almost inaudibly against the bathing-box piles. Near the left bank glowed the moon's ruddy reflection, overrun by ripples which stretched it, tore it in two, and, it seemed, would sweep it away as twigs and shavings are swept.

"How stupid! How stupid!" thought Riabovich, watching the hurrying ripples. "How stupid everything is!"

Now that hope was dead, the history of the kiss, his impatience, his ardor, his vague aspirations and disillusion appeared in a clear light. It no longer seemed strange that the general's horseman had not come, and that he would never again see *her* who had kissed him by accident instead of another. On the contrary, he felt, it would be strange if he did ever see her again. . . .

The water flew past him, whither and why no one knew. It had flown past in May; it had sped a stream into a great river; a river, into the sea; it had floated on high in mist and fallen again in rain; it might be, the water of May was again speeding past under Riabovich's eyes. For what purpose? Why?

And the whole world—life itself seemed to Riabovich an inscrutable, aimless mystification. . . . Raising his eyes from the stream and gazing at the sky, he recalled how Fate in the shape of an unknown woman had once caressed him; he recalled his summer fantasies and images—and his whole life seemed to him unnaturally thin and colorless and wretched. . . .

When he reached the cabin his comrades had disappeared. His servant informed him that all had set out to visit "General Fonrabbkin," who had sent a horseman to bring them. . . . For a moment Riabovich's heart thrilled with joy. But that joy he extinguished. He cast himself upon his bed, and wroth with his evil fate, as if he wished to spite it, ignored the invitation.

1888

THINK AND DISCUSS
Understanding
1. Why are the officers distressed at being invited to tea at General von Rabbek's house?
2. Why is Lobytko known as "the setter"?
3. When you first meet him in the story, how is Riabovich described? What does his appearance seem to say about him?
4. Describe Riabovich's "adventure."

Analyzing
5. By what means does Riabovich relieve the boredom and routine of an artillery brigade on the march?
6. Why does the thought of being an "ordinary man" (page 761) please Riabovich?
7. What surprises Riabovich when he describes the incident of the kiss to his comrades? Why

is he annoyed after Lobytko tells of a similar incident?

8. Riabovich twice visits the riverbank near the von Rabbeks' garden, once in May and again in August. What is missing from the scene during the autumn visit? What does that difference symbolize?

Extending

9. Riabovich, Lobytko, and Merzliakov are recognizable types whom one might meet today in any military unit or other place where men are brought together in the absence of women. Describe each man and the stereotype he represents.

REVIEWING: Characterization HZ
See Handbook of Literary Terms, p. 944.

Characterization is the method an author uses to acquaint the reader with his or her characters. A character's physical traits and personality may be described *directly* by the author or by another character in the story. Ordinarily, however, such direct characterization must be supported by indirect characterization; that is, the character must act and speak in a manner that supports what we have been directly told about him or her.

1. How is the direct characterization of Riabovich reinforced by what he says and does?
2. How does the author make the minor character von Rabbek and his family into foils for the main character, Riabovich?

VOCABULARY
Pronunciation Key

Use the Pronunciation Key in the Glossary to answer the following questions. Write your answers on a separate sheet of paper. Be sure you understand the meaning of each word.

1. How many syllables are there in *satiety?*
2. Is the *o* in the first syllable of *holograph* long or short?
3. Is *morose* accented on the first or second syllable?
4. Does the second syllable of *cornice* rhyme with the second syllable of *office* or of *suffice?*
5. The word *inveigle* can be pronounced in two ways. What are they?

COMPOSITION
Writing About a Personal Experience

Write about a social situation in which you have felt uncomfortably out-of-place or superfluous. Be sure to tell the time, the place, the other people involved, and what it was about them that made you feel out of place. Describe what you did to overcome your uncomfortableness or to make yourself inconspicuous. You might conclude your composition with a paragraph about people or social situations that you intend to avoid in the future, or about how you have managed to overcome the feelings of insecurity that beset you in that earlier time. Your audience is your teacher.

Comparing Literary Characters

Write a composition in which you compare and contrast Riabovich with a similar character or characters you have read about in other short stories, novels, or plays. Think of characters who, like Riabovich, find an escape in their fantasies from the drab realities of their actual selves. You might consider James Thurber's title character from the famous short story, "The Secret Life of Walter Mitty," among others. See "Writing About Characters" in the Writer's Handbook.

BIOGRAPHY

Rabindranath Tagore

1861–1941

Rabindranath Tagore was born in Bengal, a province of British India, into a wealthy family that was well known for intellectual accomplishments. In his immediate family were a financier, a founder of a religious reform movement, painters, a philosopher, musicians, and India's first woman novelist. In his youth he traveled widely in his own land as well as abroad and did advanced study in England. He began to write in Bengali while still quite young, trying his hand at stories, lyrics, dramas, and poetry. As a mature man he branched out into literary criticism, sociology, and philosophy both in his native language and in English.

He interrupted his activities to live the life of a contemplative hermit floating in a boat on the waters of one of the tributaries of the sacred Ganges River. When he eventually resumed his professional life, he was respected as a man of refined wisdom and great piety. He established an open-air school in western Bengal, and under the spreading branches of the mango trees, he discussed his ideas of religion, philosophy, and art with his youthful disciples. He was knighted by the British crown in 1915 but repudiated the title four years later in protest of the Amritsar Massacre, in which British troops fired on a crowd of Indians demonstrating against the government.

Tagore is best known for *Gitanjali* (Song Offerings), a collection of religious poems that he himself translated into English and published with an admiring introduction written by his friend, the Irish poet William Butler Yeats. However, the volume represents only one facet of a many-sided talent. It leaves out the humor and the intellectual rigor of which he is capable. His short stories range from broad comedy and subtle satire to philosophy and mysticism. He is also a writer and singer of songs that remain popular wherever Bengali is spoken. His dramas are often marked by complex social commentary. Tagore was awarded the Nobel Prize for Literature in 1913, winning out over such other candidates as Thomas Hardy, Anatole France, and Pierre Loti.

The Artist

Rabindranath Tagore
translated by **Mary Lago, Tarum Gupta,** *and* **Amiya Chakravarty**

Govinda came to Calcutta after graduation from high school in Mymensingh. His widowed mother's savings were meager, but his own unwavering determination was his greatest resource. "I *will* make money," he vowed, "even if I have to give my whole life to it." In his terminology, wealth was always referred to as *pice*.[1] In other words he had in mind a very concrete image of something that could be seen, touched, and smelled; he was not greatly fascinated with fame, only with the very ordinary *pice*, eroded by circulation from market to market, from hand to hand, the tarnished *pice*, the *pice* that smells of copper, the original form of Kuvera,[2] who assumes the assorted guises of silver, gold, securities, and wills, and keeps men's minds in a turmoil.

After traveling many tortuous roads and getting muddied repeatedly in the process, Govinda had now arrived upon the solidly paved embankment of his wide and free-flowing stream of money. He was firmly seated in the manager's chair at the MacDougal Gunnysack Company. Everyone called him MacDulal.[3]

When Govinda's lawyer-brother, Mukunda, died, he left behind a wife, a four-year-old son, a house in Calcutta, and some cash savings. In addition to this property there was some debt; therefore, provision for his family's needs depended upon frugality. Thus his son, Chunilal, was brought up in circumstances that were undistinguished in comparison with those of the neighbors.

Mukunda's will gave Govinda entire responsibility for this family. Ever since Chunilal was a baby, Govinda had bestowed spiritual initiation upon his nephew with the sacred words: "Make money."

The main obstacle to the boy's initiation was his mother, Satyabati. She said nothing outright; her opposition showed in her behavior. Art had always been her hobby. There was no limit to her enthusiasm for creating all sorts of original and decorative things from flowers, fruits and leaves, even foodstuffs, from paper and cloth cutouts, from clay and flour, from berry juices and the juices of other fruits, from *jaba-* and *shiuli*-flower stems. This activity brought her considerable grief, because anything unessential or irrational has the character of flash floods in July: it has considerable mobility, but in relation to the utilitarian concerns of life it is like a stalled ferry. Sometimes there were invitations to visit relatives; Satyabati forgot them and spent the time in her bedroom with the door shut, kneading a lump of clay. The relatives said, "She's terribly stuck-up." There was no satisfactory reply to this. Mukunda had known, even on the basis of his bookish knowledge, that value judgments can be made about art too. He had been thrilled by the noble connotations of the word "art," but he could not conceive of its having any connection with the work of his own wife.

This man's nature had been very equable. When his wife squandered time on unessential whims, he had smiled at it with affectionate delight. If anyone in the household made a slighting remark, he had protested immediately. There had been a singular self-contradiction in Mukunda's makeup; he had been an expert in the practice of law, but it must be conceded that he had had no worldly wisdom with regard to his household affairs. Plenty of money had passed through his hands, but since it had not preoccupied his thoughts, it had left his mind free.

---

1. *pice*, a coin.
2. *Kuvera*, (sometimes spelled Kubera) the Hindu god of wealth.
3. *MacDulal*, a play on *dulal*, which means darling or spoiled child.

Nor could he have tyrannized over his dependents in order to get his own way. His living habits had been very simple; he had never made any unreasonable demands for the attention or services of his relatives.

Mukunda had immediately silenced anyone in the household who cast an aspersion upon Satyabati's disinterest in housework. Now and then, on his way home from court, he would stop at Radhabazar to buy some paints, some colored silk and colored pencils, and stealthily he would go and arrange them on the wooden chest in his wife's bedroom. Sometimes, picking up one of Satyabati's drawings, he would say, "Well, this one is certainly very beautiful."

One day he had held up a picture of a man, and since he had it upside down, he had decided that the legs must be a bird's head. He had said, "Satu, this should be framed—what a marvelous picture of a stork!" Mukunda had gotten a certain delight out of thinking of his wife's art work as child's play, and the wife had taken a similar pleasure in her husband's judgment of art. Satyabati had known perfectly well that she could not hope for so much patience, so much indulgence, from any other family in Bengal. No other family would have made way so lovingly for her overpowering devotion to art. So, whenever her husband had made extravagant remarks about her painting, Satyabati could scarcely restrain her tears.

One day Satyabati lost even this rare good fortune. Before his death her husband had realized one thing quite clearly: the responsibility for his debt-ridden property must be left in the hands of someone astute enough to skillfully steer even a leaky boat to the other shore. This is how Satyabati and her son came to be placed completely under Govinda's care. From the very first day Govinda made it plain to her that the *pice* was the first and foremost thing in life. There was such profound degradation in his advice that Satyabati would shrink with shame.

Nevertheless, the worship of money continued in diverse forms in their daily life. If there had been some modesty about it, instead of such constant discussion, it wouldn't have been so bad. Satyabati knew in her heart that all of this lowered her son's

Santi Devi, *Water Goddess*. Collection Betty LaDuke

standard of values, but there was nothing to do but endure it. Since those delicate emotions endowed with uncommon dignity are the most vulnerable, they are very easily hurt or ridiculed by rude or insensitive people.

The study of art requires all sorts of supplies. Satyabati had received these for so long without even asking that she had felt no reticence with regard to them. Amid the new circumstances in the family she felt terribly ashamed to charge all these unessential items to the housekeeping budget. So she would save money by economizing on her own food and have the supplies purchased and brought in secretly. Whatever work she did was done furtively, behind closed doors. She was not afraid of a scolding, but the stares of insensitive observers embarrassed her.

Now Chuni was the only spectator and critic of her artistic activity. Gradually he became a participant. He began to feel its intoxication. The child's offense could not be concealed, since it overflowed the pages of his notebook onto the walls of the house. There were stains on his face, on his hands, on the cuffs of his shirt. Indra, the king of the gods, does not spare even the soul of a little boy in the effort to tempt him away from the worship of money.

On the one hand the restraint increased, on the other hand the mother collaborated in the violations. Occasionally the head of the company would take his office manager, Govinda, along on business trips out of town. Then the mother and son would get together in unrestrained joy. This was the absolute extreme of childishness! They drew pictures of animals that God has yet to create. The likeness of the dog would get mixed up with that of the cat. It was difficult to distinguish between fish and fowl. There was no way to preserve all these creations; their traces had to be thoroughly obliterated before the head of the house returned. Only Brahma, the Creator, and Rudra, the Destroyer, witnessed the creative delight of these two persons; Vishnu, the heavenly Preserver, never arrived.

The compulsion for artistic creation ran strong in Satyabati's family. There was an older nephew, Rangalal, who rose overnight to fame as an artist. That is to say, the connoisseurs of the land roared with laughter at the unorthodoxy of his art. Since their stamp of imagination did not coincide with his, they had a violent scorn for his talent. But curiously enough, his reputation thrived upon disdain and flourished in this atmosphere of opposition and mockery. Those who imitated him most took it upon themselves to prove that the man was a hoax as an artist, that there were obvious defects even in his technique.

This much-maligned artist came to his aunt's home one day, at a time when the office manager was absent. After persistent knocking and shoving at the door he finally got inside and found that there was nowhere to set foot on the floor. The cat was out of the bag.

"It is obvious," said Rangalal, "that the image of creation has emerged anew from the soul of the artist; this is not random scribbling. He and that god who creates form are the same age. Get out all the drawings and show them to me."

Where should they get the drawings? That artist who draws pictures all over the sky in myriad colors, in light and shadow, calmly discards his mists and mirages. Their creations had gone the same way. With an oath Rangalal said to his aunt, "From now on, I'll come and get whatever you make."

There came another day when the office manager had not returned. Since morning the sky had brooded in the shadows of July; it was raining. No one monitored the hands of the clock and no one wanted to know about them. Today Chuni began to draw a picture of a sailing boat while his mother was in the prayer room. The waves of the river looked like a flock of hungry seals just on the point of swallowing the boat. The clouds seemed to cheer them on and float their shawls overhead, but the seals were not conventional seals, and it would be no exaggeration to say of the clouds: "Light and mist merge in the watery waste." In the interests of truth it must be said that if boats were built like this one, insurance companies would never assume such risks. Thus the painting continued; the sky-artist drew fanciful pictures, and inside the room the wide-eyed boy did the same.

No one realized that the door was open. The office manager appeared. He roared in a thunderous voice, "What's going on?"

The boy's heart jumped and his face grew pale. Now Govinda perceived the real reason for Chunilal's examination errors in historical dates. Meanwhile the crime became all the more evident as Chunilal tried unsuccessfully to hide the drawing under his shirt. As Govinda snatched the picture away, the design he saw on it further astonished him. Errors in historical dates would be preferable to this. He tore the picture to pieces. Chunilal burst out crying.

From the prayer room Satyabati heard the boy's weeping and she came running. Both Chunilal and the torn pieces of the picture were on the floor. Govinda went on enumerating the reasons for his nephew's failure in the history examination and suggesting dire remedies.

Satyabati had never said a word about Govinda's behavior toward them. She had quietly endured everything, remembering that this was the person on whom her husband had relied. Now her eyes were wet with tears, and shaking with anger, she said hoarsely, "Why did you tear up Chuni's picture?"

Govinda said, "Doesn't he have to study? What will become of him in the future?"

"Even if he becomes a beggar in the street," answered Satyabati, "he'll be better off in the future. But I hope he'll never be like you. May his pride in his God-given talent be more than your pride in *pices*. This is my blessing for him, a mother's blessing."

"I can't neglect my responsibility," said Govinda. "I will not tolerate this. Tomorrow I'll send him to a boarding school; otherwise, you'll ruin him."

The office manager returned to the office. The rain fell in torrents and the streets flowed with water.

Holding her son's hand, Satyabati said, "Let's go, dear."

Chuni said, "Go where, Mother?"

"Let's get out of this place."

The water was knee-deep at Rangalal's door. Satyabati came in with Chunilal. She said, "My dear boy, you take charge of him. Keep him from the worship of money."

1929

THINK AND DISCUSS
Understanding
1. Explain how the following characters are related: Govinda, Mukunda, Satyabati, Chunilal, and Rangalal.
2. What pinnacle of business success has Govinda reached?
3. Why does Govinda assume control of the raising of Chunilal?

Analyzing
4. Explain how Satyabati's art work is like "flash floods in July" (page 766).
5. Why do Satyabati's relatives consider her "stuck-up"?
6. Describe Mukunda's attitude toward his wife's art work. How well can he appreciate it?
7. How is Satyabati's practice of art affected after the death of Mukunda?
8. What is **ironic** about Rangalal's rise to fame as an artist?
9. Who is the sky-artist? How is the sky-artist's painting like that of Chunilal?

Extending
10. In the implied controversy between materialism and art, where do the author's sympathies lie?
11. How does the author generate humor in the story?

COMPOSITION
Writing a Dialogue
Imagine a telephone call from Govinda to Rangalal after Govinda learns where Chunilal has gone. Write a dialogue in which you reflect the two men's different ideas about the importance of money.

Stating a Preference
What kind of art or music do you like most and what kind do you dislike? For instance, do you prefer classical art and dislike modern art, or do you prefer the music of the 1960s to modern rock? Write a composition in which you first defend your preference and then strongly condemn what you dislike. Be sure to refer to specific artists and specific pieces of work, whether it is music or painting.

BIOGRAPHY

C. P. Cavafy
1863–1933

Although he was born and spent most of his life in Alexandria, Egypt, Constantine Peter Cavafy was a Greek poet who wrote in an artful combination of literary Greek and the spoken Greek of his day. His subject matter usually has a classical or Byzantine setting. Often he achieves irony by superimposing these ancient situations on modern events. He published only one slim volume of poems during his lifetime. Many of his poems were merely distributed among friends who, recognizing their literary excellence, gathered and published them after the poet's death. Cavafy is the unnamed poet who appears repeatedly in the *Alexandria Quartet*, written by Lawrence Durrell. He first became known to the English-speaking world in E. M. Forster's *Pharos and Pharillon* (1923), a collection of essays about Alexandria. *The Complete Poems of Cavafy* was published in 1961 with an introduction by W. H. Auden.

Cavafy's poems are characterized by a straightforward, unembellished style and an unsentimental, ironic tone. Today he is recognized as one of the finest modern Greek poets.

 Review **TONE** in the Handbook of Literary Terms, page 976.

Waiting for the Barbarians

translated by **Edmund Keeley** *and* **Philip Sherrard**

What are we waiting for, assembled in the forum?

　The barbarians are due here today.

Why isn't anything going on in the senate?
Why are the senators sitting there without legislating?

5   Because the barbarians are coming today.
What's the point of senators making laws now?
Once the barbarians are here, they'll do the legislating.

Why did our emperor get up so early,
and why is he sitting enthroned at the city's main gate,
10 in state, wearing the crown?

    Because the barbarians are coming today
    and the emperor's waiting to receive their leader.
    He's even got a scroll to give him,
    loaded with titles, with imposing names.

15 Why have our two consuls and praetors[1] come out today
wearing their embroidered, their scarlet togas?
Why have they put on bracelets with so many amethysts,
rings sparkling with magnificent emeralds?
Why are they carrying elegant canes
20 beautifully worked in silver and gold?

    Because the barbarians are coming today
    and things like that dazzle the barbarians.

Why don't our distinguished orators turn up as usual
to make their speeches, say what they have to say?

25   Because the barbarians are coming today
    and they're bored by rhetoric and public speaking.

Why this sudden bewilderment, this confusion?
(How serious people's faces have become.)
Why are the streets and squares emptying so rapidly,
30 everyone going home lost in thought?

    Because night has fallen and the barbarians haven't come.
    And some of our men just in from the border say
    there are no barbarians any longer.

Now what's going to happen to us without barbarians?
35 Those people were a kind of solution.

1898   **1904**

---

1. *praetors*, magistrates in ancient Rome.

Ithaka

translated by **Edmund Keeley** *and* **Philip Sherrard**

As you set out for Ithaka[1]
hope your road is a long one,
full of adventure, full of discovery.
Laistrygonians, Cyclops,
5 angry Poseidon[1]—don't be afraid of them:
you'll never find things like that on your way
as long as you keep your thoughts raised high,
as long as a rare excitement
stirs your spirit and your body.
10 Laistrygonians, Cyclops,
wild Poseidon—you won't encounter them
unless you bring them along inside your soul,
unless your soul sets them up in front of you.

Hope your road is a long one.
15 May there be many summer mornings when,
with what pleasure, what joy,
you enter harbors you're seeing for the first
time;
may you stop at Phoenician trading stations
to buy fine things,
20 mother of pearl and coral, amber and ebony,
sensual perfume of every kind—
as many sensual perfumes as you can;
and may you visit many Egyptian cities
to learn and go on learning from their scholars.

25 Keep Ithaka always in your mind.
Arriving there is what you're destined for.
But don't hurry the journey at all.
Better if it lasts for years,
so you're old by the time you reach the island,
30 wealthy with all you've gained on the way,
not expecting Ithaka to make you rich.
Ithaka gave you the marvelous journey.
Without her you wouldn't have set out.
She has nothing left to give you now.

35 And if you find her poor, Ithaka won't have
fooled you.
Wise as you will have become, so full of
experience,
you'll have understood by then what these
Ithakas mean.

1910   1911

---

1. *Ithaka,* the island kingdom ruled by Odysseus (Ulysses)
to which Odysseus attempts to return after the Trojan War.
His journey is lengthened by numerous adventures.
2. *Laistrygonians . . . Cyclops . . . Poseidon.* The
Laistrygonians are cannibal giants who destroy eleven of
Odysseus's twelve ships; Cyclops is the one-eyed giant whom
Odysseus blinds; Poseidon, father of Polyphemus and lord
of the sea, raises a storm to shipwreck Odysseus.

The Ides of March

translated by **Edmund Keeley** *and*
Philip Sherrard

My soul, guard against pomp and glory.
And if you can't curb your ambitions,
at least pursue them hesitantly, cautiously.
And the higher you go,
5 the more searching and careful you need to be.

And when you reach your summit, Caesar
 at last—
when you assume the role of someone that
 famous—
then be specially careful as you go out into
 the street,
a conspicuous man of power with your retinue;
10 and should a certain Artemidoros[1]
come up to you out of the crowd, bringing
 a letter,
and say hurriedly: "Read this right away.
There are important things in it concerning
 you,"
be sure to stop; be sure to postpone
15 all talk or business; be sure to brush off
all those who salute and bow to you
(they can be seen later); let even
the Senate itself wait—and find out at once
what important message Artemidoros has for
 you.

1906   **1910**

---

1. Artemidoros. In Shakespeare's Julius Caesar, Artemidoros is a teacher of rhetoric who tries to warn Caesar of
the plot against him. Caesar, however, does not read the
note Artemidoros passes to him.

An Old Man

translated by **Edmund Keeley** *and*
Philip Sherrard

At the noisy end of the café, head bent
over the table, an old man sits alone,
a newspaper in front of him.

And in the miserable banality of old age
5 he thinks how little he enjoyed the years
when he had strength, and wit, and looks.

He knows he's very old now: sees it, feels it.
Yet it seems he was young just yesterday.
The time's gone by so quickly, gone by so
 quickly.

10 And he thinks how Discretion fooled him,
how he always believed, so stupidly,
that cheat who said: "Tomorrow. You have
 plenty of time."

He remembers impulses bridled, the joy
he sacrificed. Every chance he lost
15 now mocks his brainless prudence.

But so much thinking, so much remembering
makes the old man dizzy. He falls asleep,
his head resting on the café table.

1894   **1897**

THINK AND DISCUSS
Understanding
1. How many speakers are there in "Waiting for the Barbarians"?
2. In "Waiting for the Barbarians," what things impress the barbarians, according to the speaker answering the questions? What things do not impress them?
3. What does the speaker of the poem "Ithaka" tell the reader to ask for?
4. In "Ithaka," what is necessary in order to be safe from the Laistrygonians, the Cyclops, and Poseidon?
5. To whom or what is "The Ides of March" addressed?
6. In "An Old Man," where is the old man and what is he doing? What has happened to him at the end of the poem?

Analyzing
7. Why have the people been waiting so expectantly in "Waiting for the Barbarians"? To what problem might the barbarians have been "a kind of solution"?
8. In "Ithaka" what do Ithaka and the journey there **symbolize?**
9. What is the significance of the title of "The Ides of March"?
10. What sort of warning is being given in "The Ides of March"?
11. What example(s) of **personification** do you find in "An Old Man"?
12. In "An Old Man," what mistake has he made in living his life as he did?

Extending
13. What indications in "Waiting for the Barbarians" suggest that the setting (like that of "The Ides of March") is ancient Rome? What role did the barbarians play in the history of the Roman Empire?
14. Does the message of "Ithaka" seem compatible with the message of "The Ides of March"? Explain.
15. What approach to life is suggested by "The Ides of March"?

16. Does the theme of "An Old Man" seem closer to that of "The Ides of March" or of "Ithaka"? Explain.
17. Look up the term *carpe diem* in the Glossary of Literary Terms, page 1013. Is "An Old Man" an example of *carpe diem*? Explain.

REVIEWING: Tone H
See Handbook of Literary Terms, p. 976.
Tone is the author's attitude toward the subject and toward the audience.

1. What is the tone of "Waiting for the Barbarians"?
2. By what means is the tone of the poem generated?

COMPOSITION
Writing to the Author
Imagine that Cavafy is still alive. Write him a letter in which you describe your reactions to the poems of his that you have just read. You may choose to congratulate him, to take issue with his ideas, to complain of "mixed messages," or to ask for explanations of his meaning. Be sure to observe proper letter-writing form.

Analyzing and Relating Poems
Taken together, the four poems of Cavafy present a broad view of life. Write an essay in which you use Cavafy's poems to illustrate his world view. Your audience will be your teacher.

ENRICHMENT
Speaking/Listening
Locate copies of the poems "Ulysses," by Alfred Lord Tennyson, and "Do Not Go Gentle Into That Good Night," by Dylan Thomas. Practice reading the poems aloud, and then read them to the class. Compare and contrast Tennyson's use of antiquity with that of Cavafy and the ideas about old age developed by Cavafy, Tennyson, and Thomas.

Rilke, who ranks with the great German poets, was born in Prague, Czechoslovakia, of German parents. He studied at universities in Prague, Munich, and Berlin. In 1899 and again in 1900 Rilke visited Russia, where he met Tolstoy and was much impressed by the vast country and its people. Between these visits he wrote in seven successive nights *Stories of God* (1904), a collection of tales that convey his impressions of the Russian landscape and its inhabitants.

In 1902 he met the sculptor Auguste Rodin and accepted employment as his private secretary. From Rodin he learned to observe objects with meticulous accuracy and to select details that would convey the impression he wished to create. He also learned from the sculptor that perfection can be achieved by hard work even in the absence of inspiration.

In 1906, after leaving Rodin, Rilke brought out a novel that had considerable popularity, *The Tale of the Love and Death of Cornet Christopher Rilke*. *New Poems* (1907–8) is considered by many his masterpiece. In it he formulates the idea that perfect form and movement convey the presence of God. Rilke's other best-known collections are *Duino Elegies* (1923), on which he labored for ten years, and *Sonnets to Orpheus* (1923), written while he was completing the elegies.

 Review SIMILE in the Handbook of Literary Terms, page 970.

The Cadet Picture of My Father

translated by **Robert Lowell**

There's absence in the eyes. The brow's in
    touch
with something far. Now distant boyishness
and seduction shadow his enormous lips,
the slender aristocratic uniform
5 with its Franz Josef[1] braid; both the hands
    bulge
like gloves upon the saber's basket hilt.
The hands are quiet, they reach out toward
    nothing—
I hardly see them now, as if they were

the first to grasp distance and disappear,
10 and all the rest lies curtained in itself,
and so withdrawn, I cannot understand
my father as he bleaches on this page—

Oh quickly disappearing photograph
in my more slowly disappearing hand!

---

1. *Franz Josef* (1830–1916), emperor of Austria and king of Hungary.

Sense of Something Coming

translated by **Robert Bly**

I am like a flag in the center of open space.
I sense ahead the wind which is coming, and must live it through,
while the things of the world still do not move:
the doors still close softly, and the chimneys are full of silence,
5 the windows do not rattle yet, and the dust still lies down.

I already know the storm, and I am as troubled as the sea.
I leap out, and fall back,
and throw myself out, and am absolutely alone
in the great storm.

THINK AND DISCUSS
Understanding
1. Which of Rilke's two poems is a **sonnet**?

Analyzing
2. What does the author mean by the phrase "distant boyishness" in line 2 of "The Cadet Picture of My Father"?
3. Explain the final two lines of "The Cadet Picture of My Father."
4. For what is the coming wind and storm a **metaphor** in "Sense of Something Coming"?

Extending
5. In the two selections by Rilke, what examples of well-chosen details and effective **images** do you find and what are their various effects?

REVIEWING: Simile HT
See Handbook of Literary Terms, p. 970.
  A **simile** is a figure of speech involving a direct comparison, usually with the words *like* or *as*, between basically unlike things that have something in common.

1. What are the two similes in "Sense of Something Coming"?
2. What do you learn about the speaker of the poem from the two similes with which he describes himself?

COMPOSITION
Writing About a Picture
  Select an old picture of one of your parents or other relatives from a family album or photo collection. Write about the contrast between the younger person in the picture and the way that person looks today. Try to express the emotions you feel when looking at the picture. For instance, has the person's appearance improved or deteriorated with age? Does the clothing seem dated. If the picture is of a parent, do you see something of yourself in it? You may wish to do the assignment in prose or as a poem.

Writing About a Poem
  What is the "something coming" to which the speaker refers? Write an essay of three to five paragraphs in which you consider the various possibilities that the poem suggests.

On the basis of a few poems, a play, and four works of fiction—*Dubliners*, *A Portrait of the Artist as a Young Man*, *Ulysses*, and *Finnegans Wake*—James Joyce has come to be regarded as one of the most original and influential writers of the twentieth century. He was born in Dublin, the eldest of a family of ten children. His father was a civil servant, continually in financial difficulties; his mother was mild-mannered and pious. Educated in Jesuit schools, he later attended University College, Dublin, where he was a brilliant scholar, accomplished in Latin, French, Italian, and Norwegian (the last to enable him to read the plays of Henrik Ibsen, whom he intensely admired). Disillusionment with Catholicism and the cultural climate of Dublin caused him to leave Ireland for a self-imposed exile in the Italian city of Trieste, and later in Paris and Zurich. Joyce's life during these years was a continual struggle against poverty, eye diseases, and the hostility of censors. During his later years, however, he began to enjoy an international reputation as a modern literary master. He was at work on a sequel to *Finnegans Wake* when he died in Zurich in 1941.

Joyce's writing marks a sharp break with the fiction of the nineteenth century. He locates the center of the action in the minds of his characters. Incident and plot are subordinated to psychological revelation. Each word and detail has a calculated purpose, and the meaning of the story is presented as an *epiphany*—a moment of heightened awareness that can occur as a result of a trivial encounter, object, or event. *A Portrait of the Artist as a Young Man* (1916), Joyce's artistic and spiritual autobiography, displays the culmination of this narrative technique. *Ulysses* (1922), perhaps this century's most famous novel, is a dazzlingly original attempt to tell the story of a group of Dubliners on a single day and at the same time present a symbolic view of human history. *Finnegans Wake* (1939) carries the strenuous stylistic experimentation of *Ulysses* even further, expressing the nightlong dream of a Dublin tavern-keeper in a complex synthetic language created from the many languages Joyce knew.

What follows is an excerpt from Chapter Four of *A Portrait of the Artist as a Young Man*. In the passage given here, Stephen has just decided to be an artist and to reject the narrow and confining world of his family, his religion, and his nationality. It is important to remember the closeness of Stephen's last name to that of the mythological artisan Daedalus, who made wings of wax and feathers with which he and his son Icarus escaped from imprisonment on the island of Crete. Heedless of his father's warning, Icarus flew too close to the sun and the wings melted, plunging him into the sea. At times in the book Stephen identifies with the fabulous inventor and at other times with the tragic-heroic son. Watch for the references to bulls, birds, flying, and water in what follows, and note the interplay of Christian and classical elements.

from A Portrait of the Artist as a Young Man

James Joyce

He could wait no longer.

From the door of Byron's publichouse to the gate of Clontarf[1] Chapel, from the gate of Clontarf Chapel to the door of Byron's publichouse, and then back again to the chapel and then back again to the publichouse he had paced slowly at first, planting his steps scrupulously in the spaces of the patchwork of the footpath, then timing their fall to the fall of verses. A full hour had passed since his father had gone in with Dan Crosby, the tutor, to find out for him something about the university. For a full hour he had paced up and down, waiting: but he could wait no longer.

He set off abruptly for the Bull,[2] walking rapidly lest his father's shrill whistle might call him back; and in a few moments he had rounded the curve at the police barrack and was safe.

Yes, his mother was hostile to the idea, as he had read from her listless silence. Yet her mistrust pricked him more keenly than his father's pride and he thought coldly how he had watched the faith which was fading down in his soul aging and strengthening in her eyes. A dim antagonism gathered force within him and darkened his mind as a cloud against her disloyalty: and when it passed, cloudlike, leaving his mind serene and dutiful towards her again, he was made aware dimly and without regret of a first noiseless sundering of their lives.

The university! So he had passed beyond the challenge of the sentries who had stood as guardians of his boyhood and had sought to keep him among them that he might be subject to them and serve their ends. Pride after satisfaction uplifted him like long slow waves. The end he had been born to serve yet did not see had led him to escape by an unseen path: and now it beckoned to him once more and a new adventure was about to be opened to him. It seemed to him that he heard notes of fitful music leaping upwards a tone and downwards a diminished fourth, upwards a tone and downwards a major third, like triple-branching flames leaping fitfully, flame after flame, out of a midnight wood. It was an elfin prelude, endless and formless; and, as it grew wilder and faster, the flames leaping out of time, he seemed to hear from under the boughs and grasses wild creatures racing, their feet pattering like rain upon the leaves. Their feet passed in pattering tumult over his mind, the feet of hares and rabbits, the feet of harts and hinds and antelopes, until he heard them no more and remembered only a proud cadence from Newman:[3]—

1. *Clontarf,* an Irish place name meaning "bull's meadow."
2. *the Bull.* In Clontarf at the mouth of the Liffey River there is a seawall called the Bull that extends into Dublin Bay creating a harbor. At the end of the seawall stands North Bull Lighthouse. Nearby is Bull Island.
3. *a proud cadence from Newman,* John Henry Newman (1801–1890), an English churchman, Roman Catholic cardinal, and author.

—Whose feet are as the feet of harts and underneath the everlasting arms.[4]

The pride of that dim image brought back to his mind the dignity of the office he had refused.[5] All through his boyhood he had mused upon that which he had so often thought to be his destiny and when the moment had come for him to obey the call he had turned aside, obeying a wayward instinct. Now time lay between: the oils of ordination[6] would never anoint his body. He had refused. Why?

He turned seaward from the road at Dollymount and as he passed on to the thin wooden bridge he felt the planks shaking with the tramp of heavily shod feet. A squad of Christian Brothers[7] was on its way back from the Bull and had begun to pass, two by two, across the bridge. Soon the whole bridge was trembling and resounding. The uncouth faces passed him two by two, stained yellow or red or livid by the sea, and as he strove to look at them with ease and indifference, a faint stain of personal shame and commiseration rose to his own face. Angry with himself he tried to hide his face from their eyes by gazing down sideways into the shallow swirling water under the bridge but he still saw a reflection therein of their topheavy silk hats, and humble tapelike collars and loosely hanging clerical clothes.

—Brother Hickey.

Brother Quaid.

Brother MacArdle.

Brother Keogh.

Their piety would be like their names, like their faces, like their clothes; and it was idle for him to tell himself that their humble and contrite hearts, it might be, paid a far richer tribute of devotion than his had ever been, a gift tenfold more acceptable than his elaborate adoration. It was idle for him to move himself to be generous towards them, to tell himself that if he ever came to their gates, stripped of his pride, beaten and in beggar's weeds, that they would be generous towards him, loving him as themselves. Idle and embittering, finally, to argue, against his own dispassionate certitude, that the commandment of love[8] bade us not to love our neighbor as ourselves with the same amount and intensity of love but to love him as ourselves with the same kind of love.

He drew forth a phrase from his treasure and spoke it softly to himself:

—A day of dappled seaborne clouds.—[9]

The phrase and the day and the scene harmonized in a chord. Words. Was it their colors? He allowed them to glow and fade, hue after hue: sunrise gold, the russet and green of apple orchards, azure of waves, the gray-fringed fleece of clouds. No, it was not their colors: it was the poise and balance of the period itself. Did he then love the rhythmic rise and fall of words better than their associations of legend and color? Or was it that, being as weak of sight as he was shy of mind, he drew less pleasure from the reflection of the glowing sensible world through the prism of a language many-colored and richly storied than from the contemplation of an inner world of individual emotions mirrored perfectly in a lucid supple periodic prose?

He passed from the trembling bridge on to firm land again. At that instant, as it seemed to him, the air was chilled; and looking askance towards the water he saw a flying squall darkening and crisping suddenly the tide. A faint click at his heart, a faint throb in his throat told him once more of how his flesh dreaded the cold infrahuman odor of the sea: yet he did not strike across the downs on his left but held straight on along the spine of rocks that pointed against the river's mouth.

A veiled sunlight lit up faintly the gray sheet of water where the river was embayed. In the

---

4. *"Whose feet . . . arms,"* a quote from Newman's *The Idea of a University Defined and Illustrated.*
5. *office he had refused.* Stephen has decided not to study for the priesthood.
6. *oils of ordination.* The sacrament of Holy Orders, the ceremony in which priests are ordained, involves anointing with oils.
7. *Christian Brothers,* an order of Catholic men, the male counterpart of nuns.
8. *the commandment of love.* In Matthew 22:39 Jesus states, "And the second [commandment] is like to this: Thou shalt love thy neighbor as thyself."
9. *A day . . . clouds,* from *The Testimony of the Rocks; or Geology in Its Bearings on the Two Theologies, Natural and Revealed* by Hugh Miller; Stephen remembers the quote imperfectly.

distance along the course of the slowflowing Liffey slender masts flecked the sky and, more distant still, the dim fabric of the city lay prone in haze. Like a scene on some vague arras, old as man's weariness, the image of the seventh city of christendom[10] was visible to him across the timeless air, no older nor more weary nor less patient of subjection than in the days of the thingmote.[11]

Disheartened, he raised his eyes towards the slow-drifting clouds, dappled and seaborne. They were voyaging across the deserts of the sky, a host of nomads on the march, voyaging high over Ireland, westward bound. The Europe they had come from lay out there beyond the Irish Sea, Europe of strange tongues and valleyed and woodbegirt and citadelled and of entrenched and marshalled races. He heard a confused music within him as of memories and names which he was almost conscious of but could not capture even for an instant; then the music seemed to recede, to recede, to recede: and from each receding trail of nebulous music there fell always one long-drawn calling note, piercing like a star the dusk of silence. Again! Again! Again! A voice from beyond the world was calling.

—Hello, Stephanos![12]

—Here comes The Dedalus!

—Ao! . . . Eh, give it over, Dwyer, I'm telling you or I'll give you a stuff in the kisser for yourself. . . . Ao!

—Good man, Towser! Duck him!

—Come along, Dedalus! Bous Stephanoumenos! Bous Stephaneforos![13]

—Duck him! Guzzle him now, Towser!

—Help! Help! . . . Ao!

He recognized their speech collectively before he distinguished their faces. The mere sight of that medley of wet nakedness chilled him to the bone. Their bodies, corpsewhite or suffused with a pallid golden light or rawly tanned by the suns, gleamed with the wet of the sea. Their divingstone, poised on its rude supports and rocking under their plunges, and the rough-hewn stones of the sloping breakwater over which they scrambled in their horseplay, gleamed with cold wet luster. The towels with which they smacked their bodies were heavy with cold seawater: and drenched with cold brine was their matted hair.

He stood still in deference to their calls and parried their banter with easy words. How characterless they looked: Shuley without his deep unbuttoned collar, Ennis without his scarlet belt with the snaky clasp, and Connolly without his Norfolk coat with the flapless sidepockets! It was a pain to see them and a sword-like pain to see the signs of adolescence that made repellent their pitiable nakedness. Perhaps they had taken refuge in number and noise from the secret dread in their souls. But he, apart from them and in silence, remembered in what dread he stood of the mystery of his own body.

—Stephanos Dedalos! Bous Stephanoumenos! Bous Stephaneforos!

Their banter was not new to him and now it flattered his mild proud sovereignty. Now, as never before, his strange name seemed to him a prophecy. So timeless seemed the gray warm air, so fluid and impersonal his own mood, that all ages were as one to him. A moment before the ghost of the ancient kingdom of the Danes had looked forth through the vesture of the haze-wrapped city. Now, at the name of the fabulous artificer,[14] he seemed to hear the noise of dim waves and to see a winged form flying above the waves and slowly climbing the air. What did it mean? Was it a quaint device opening a page of some medieval book of prophecies and symbols, a hawklike man flying sunward above the sea, a prophecy of the end he had been born to serve and had been following through the mists of childhood and boyhood, a symbol of the artist forging anew in his workshop out of the sluggish matter of the earth a new soaring impalpable imperishable being?

---

10. *seventh city of christendom,* Dublin.
11. *thingmote,* under the rule of the Danes, the place of the council of law.
12. *Stephanos,* the Greek form of Stephen, meaning "crown" or "garland."
13. *Bous Stephanoumenos! Bous Stephaneforos. Bous* can mean either bull or ox in Greek. Bous Stephanoumenos would mean the bull or ox that is crowned or garlanded as for sacrifice. Stephaneforos means "wreath-bearing" but suggests not sacrifice but exaltation and glory.
14. *the fabulous artificer,* Daedalus, in Greek mythology the cunning artisan who built the Labyrinth and who made wings of feathers and wax for himself and his son; Stephen's namesake.

His heart trembled; his breath came faster and a wild spirit passed over his limbs as though he were soaring sunward. His heart trembled in an ecstasy of fear and his soul was in flight. His soul was soaring in an air beyond the world and the body he knew was purified in a breath and delivered of incertitude and made radiant and commingled with the element of the spirit. An ecstasy of flight made radiant his eyes and wild his breath and tremulous and wild and radiant his wind-swept limbs.

—One! Two! . . . Look out!

—O, Cripes, I'm drownded!

—One! Two! Three and away!

—The next! The next!

—One! . . . Uk!

—Stephaneforos!

His throat ached with a desire to cry aloud, the cry of a hawk or eagle on high, to cry piercingly of his deliverance to the winds. This was the call of life to his soul not the dull gross voice of the world of duties and despair, not the inhuman voice that had called him to the pale service of the altar. An instant of wild flight had delivered him and the cry of triumph which his lips withheld cleft his brain.

—Stephaneforos!

What were they now but the cerements shaken from the body of death—the fear he had walked in night and day, the incertitude that had ringed him round, the shame that had abased him within and without—cerements, the linens of the grave?

His soul had arisen from the grave of boyhood, spurning her graveclothes. Yes! Yes! Yes! He would create proudly out of the freedom and power of his soul, as the great artificer whose name he bore, a living thing, new and soaring and beautiful, impalpable, imperishable.

He started up nervously from the stoneblock for he could no longer quench the flame in his blood. He felt his cheeks aflame and his throat throbbing with song. There was a lust of wandering in his feet that burned to set out for the ends of the earth. On! On! his heart seemed to cry. Evening would deepen above the sea, night fall upon the plains, dawn glimmer before the wanderer and show him strange fields and hills and faces. Where?

He looked northward towards Howth.[15] The sea had fallen below the line of seawrack on the shallow side of the breakwater and already the tide was running out fast along the foreshore. Already one long oval bank of sand lay warm and dry amid the wavelets. Here and there warm isles of sand gleamed above the shallow tides and about the isles and around the long bank and amid the shallow currents of the beach were lightclad figures, wading and delving.

In a few moments he was barefoot, his stockings folded in his pockets, and his canvas shoes dangling by their knotted laces over his shoulders and, picking a pointed salteaten stick out of the jetsam among the rocks, he clambered down the slope of the breakwater.

There was a long rivulet in the strand and, as he waded slowly up its course, he wondered at the endless drift of seaweed. Emerald and black and russet and olive, it moved beneath the current, swaying and turning. The water of the rivulet was dark with endless drift and mirrored the high-drifting clouds. The clouds were drifting above him silently and silently the sea-tangle was drifting below him; and the gray warm air was still: and a new wild life was singing in his veins.

Where was his boyhood now? Where was the soul that had hung back from her destiny, to brood alone upon the shame of her wounds and in her house of squalor and subterfuge to queen it in faded cerements and in wreaths that withered at the touch? Or where was he?

He was alone. He was unheeded, happy, and near to the wild heart of life. He was alone and young and wilful and wildhearted, alone amid a waste of wild air and brackish waters and the sea-harvest of shells and tangle and veiled gray sunlight and gayclad lightclad figures of children and girls and voices childish and girlish in the air.

A girl stood before him in midstream, alone and still, gazing out to sea. She seemed like one whom magic had changed into the likeness of a strange and beautiful seabird. Her long slender bare legs were delicate as a crane's and pure save where

15. **Howth,** the northeast headland of Dublin Bay.

an emerald trail of seaweed had fashioned itself as a sign upon the flesh. Her thighs, fuller and softhued as ivory, were bared almost to the hips where the white fringes of her drawers were like feathering of soft white down. Her slateblue skirts were kilted boldly about her waist and dovetailed behind her. Her bosom was as a bird's, soft and slight, slight and soft as the breast of some dark-plumaged dove. But her long fair hair was girlish: and girlish, and touched with the wonder of mortal beauty, her face.

She was alone and still, gazing out to sea; and when she felt his presence and the worship of his eyes her eyes turned to him in quiet sufferance of his gaze, without shame or wantonness. Long, long she suffered his gaze and then quietly withdrew her eyes from his and bent them towards the stream, gently stirring the water with her foot hither and thither. The first faint noise of gently moving water broke the silence, low and faint and whispering, faint as the bells of sleep; hither and thither, hither and thither: and a faint flame trembled on her cheek.

—Heavenly God! cried Stephen's soul, in an outburst of profane joy.

He turned away from her suddenly and set off across the strand. His cheeks were aflame; his body was aglow; his limbs were trembling. On and on and on and on he strode, far out over the sands, singing wildly to the sea, crying to greet the advent of the life that had cried to him.

Her image had passed into his soul for ever and no word had broken the holy silence of his ecstasy. Her eyes had called him and his soul had leaped at the call. To live, to err, to fall, to triumph, to recreate life out of life! A wild angel had appeared to him, the angel of mortal youth and beauty, an envoy from the fair courts of life, to throw open before him in an instant of ecstasy the gates of all the ways of error and glory. On and on and on and on!

He halted suddenly and heard his heart in the silence. How far had he walked? What hour was it?

There was no human figure near him nor any sound borne to him over the air. But the tide was near the turn and already the day was on the wane. He turned landward and ran towards the shore and, running up the sloping beach, reckless of the sharp shingle, found a sandy nook amid a ring of tufted sandknolls and lay down there that the peace and silence of the evening might still the riot of his blood.

He felt above him the vast indifferent dome and the calm processes of the heavenly bodies; and the earth beneath him, the earth that had borne him, had taken him to her breast.

He closed his eyes in the languor of sleep. His eyelids trembled as if they felt the vast cyclic movement of the earth and her watchers, trembled as if they felt the strange light of some new world. His soul was swooning into some new world, fantastic, dim, uncertain as under sea, traversed by cloudy shapes and beings. A world, a glimmer, or a flower? Glimmering and trembling, trembling and unfolding, a breaking light, an opening flower, it spread in endless succession to itself, breaking in full crimson and unfolding and fading to palest rose, leaf by leaf and wave of light by wave of light, flooding all the heavens with its soft flushes, every flush deeper than other.[16]

Evening had fallen when he woke and the sand and arid grasses of his bed glowed no longer. He rose slowly and, recalling the rapture of his sleep, sighed at its joy.

He climbed at the crest of the sandhill and gazed about him. Evening had fallen. A rim of the young moon cleft the pale waste of skyline, the rim of a silver hoop embedded in gray sand; and the tide was flowing in fast to the land with a low whisper of her waves, islanding a few last figures in distant pools.

1916

---

16. *Glimmering . . . other*, a reference to Dante's *Il Paradiso* in which God is seen in a vision as a rose of light.

THINK AND DISCUSS
Understanding
1. For whom is Stephen waiting at the beginning of the excerpt?
2. How did he pass his hour of waiting before he set off for the Bull?
3. What question is Stephen asking himself as he walks toward the bridge?
4. Describe Stephen's actions once he arrives at the water.

Analyzing
5. In earlier portions of the story Stephen is often teased and bullied by the other students. How does he react to their banter and their manipulation of his name?
6. What is Stephen's opinion of the group of young men who pass on the bridge?
7. Having his name variously rendered in Greek causes Stephen to go backward in time to the Greece of ancient myth. With which mythological character does he identify? Describe his mood at that moment.
8. To what does Stephen **metaphorically** compare his former fear, incertitude, and shame?

Extending
9. Critics often say that a baptism takes place during this episode of the novel. Explain.
10. An *epiphany* is a sudden manifestation or perception of the essential nature or meaning of something. Joyce himself coined the term in its literary usage, defining it as a moment in which "the soul of the commonest object . . . seems to us radiant . . . its soul, its whatness leaps to us from the vestment of its appearance." Describe the epiphany experienced by Stephen.

APPLYING: Connotation/Denotation H7
See Handbook of Literary Terms, p. 945.

Connotation refers to the associations and added meanings surrounding a word that are not part of its literal dictionary meaning, or **denotation.** Examine the following passage from *A*

Portrait of the Artist as a Young Man: "A faint click at his heart, a faint throb in his throat told him once more of how his flesh dreaded the cold infrahuman odor of the sea."

1. What denotation do *infrahuman* and *bestial* share?
2. How do their connotations differ?

VOCABULARY
Synonyms
The list at the left contains words from the selection. The list at the right contains synonyms. On your paper write each numbered word and its synonym.

1. sundering   **a.** quivering
2. tremulous   **b.** splitting
3. strand   **c.** deception
4. clamber   **d.** shore
5. subterfuge **e.** scramble

THINKING SKILLS
Classifying
To classify is to arrange similar ideas or things into groups or categories. In coming to an understanding of a challenging work of literature, it is often helpful to make lists of related items.

Reread the excerpt beginning at "Their banter was not new to him . . ." (page 780) and continuing to ". . . and a faint flame trembled on her cheek" (page 782). List words and phrases that would fit in the following categories: *Birds and Flying, Classical Allusions, Water.*

COMPOSITION
Being a Character in a Story
Pretend that you were the girl bathing in the rivulet. Write a diary entry about the episode and your encounter with the young man.

Analyzing a Character
In a brief essay (two or three paragraphs), discuss what qualities of the mythological characters Daedalus and Icarus are revealed by Stephen in the excerpt you have read.

Guilt and alienation are pervasive themes in the work of Franz Kafka, generally considered along with Thomas Mann to be the leading writer in German of the twentieth century. His most important works are the short stories "The Metamorphosis," "The Judgment," "In the Penal Colony," and "The Hunger Artist," and three unfinished novels—*The Trial, The Castle,* and *Amerika,* these last three published after his death.

He was born in Prague, Czechoslovakia, a provincial capital of the Austro-Hungarian Empire, at a time when Austria-Hungary was on the point of dividing into its constituent nationalities. Although he spent most of his life in that city, it was not until midlife that he learned the Czech language. His father, a well-to-do Jewish merchant, sent him to German-speaking schools with the intention of making him more acceptable to the city's cultural and professional elite. Thus he was separated from the Czech majority as a German and from the Germans as a Jew. He also could not find any sense of belonging among the orthodox Jews, since he did not practice Judaism and only studied it late in life. Probably the greatest cause of estrangement came from his ambivalent feelings toward his father, from whom he never sensed affection but only implacable hostility which Franz, both as a boy and as a man, felt he deserved. In 1906 Kafka was awarded the degree of Doctor of Jurisprudence but never practiced law. Instead he settled into a tedious position with the civil service. A lonely and contemplative person, he seems to have found relief and a degree of satisfaction in writing.

The agonized relationship with his father appears to have been more a product of Franz's sensitivity than of his parent's harshness. Hermann Kafka rarely used physical punishment, but the mere threat affected the boy more severely than an actual beating and left him with the guilty feeling that even though he was forgiven he actually deserved punishment. The elder Kafka fiercely imposed table manners on the children and proceeded to ignore them himself. Like the father in "The Metamorphosis," Hermann Kafka was a powerful, bull-necked man whose physical strength intimidated the frail, tubercular Franz. Late in life Kafka wrote a lengthy letter to his father in which he set out the whole father-son relationship and simultaneously condemned and exonerated his parent. Characteristically, he never sent the letter. Similarly, his three engagements (two to the same woman) never ended in marriage. To complete the pattern, he instructed a friend, Max Brod, to destroy all his unpublished manuscripts and not to allow further printing of what he had published during his lifetime. Kafka was probably aware that his instructions would not be followed. Brod preserved for humanity some of the most fascinating and enigmatic literature of all time.

The Metamorphosis

Franz Kafka
translated by **Willa** *and* **Edwin Muir**

I

AS GREGOR Samsa awoke one morning from uneasy dreams he found himself transformed in his bed into a gigantic insect. He was lying on his hard, as it were armor-plated, back and when he lifted his head a little he could see his domelike brown belly divided into stiff arched segments on top of which the bed quilt could hardly keep in position and was about to slide off completely. His numerous legs, which were pitifully thin compared to the rest of his bulk, waved helplessly before his eyes.

What has happened to me? he thought. It was no dream. His room, a regular human bedroom, only rather too small, lay quiet between the four familiar walls. Above the table on which a collection of cloth samples was unpacked and spread out—Samsa was a commercial traveler—hung the picture which he had recently cut out of an illustrated magazine and put into a pretty gilt frame. It showed a lady, with a fur cap on and a fur stole, sitting upright and holding out to the spectator a huge fur muff into which the whole of her forearm had vanished!

Gregor's eyes turned next to the window, and the overcast sky—one could hear raindrops beating on the window gutter—made him quite melancholy. What about sleeping a little longer and forgetting all this nonsense, he thought, but it could not be done, for he was accustomed to sleep on his right side and in his present condition he could not turn himself over. However violently he forced himself toward his right side he always rolled onto his back again. He tried it at least a hundred times, shutting his eyes to keep from seeing his struggling legs, and only desisted when he began to feel in his side a faint dull ache he had never experienced before.

Oh God, he thought, what an exhausting job I've picked on! Traveling about day in, day out. It's much more irritating work than doing the actual business in the office; and on top of that there's the trouble of constant traveling, of worrying about train connections, the bad and irregular meals, casual acquaintances that are always new and never become intimate friends. The devil take it all! He felt a slight itching up on his belly; slowly pushed himself on his back nearer to the top of the bed so that he could lift his head more easily; identified the itching place which was surrounded by many small white spots the nature of which he could not understand and made to touch it with a leg, but drew the leg back immediately, for the contact made a cold shiver run through him.

He slid down again into his former position. This getting up early, he thought, makes one quite stupid. A man needs his sleep. Other commercials live like harem women. For instance, when I come back to the hotel of a morning to write up the orders I've got, these others are only sitting down to the breakfast. Let me just try that with my chief; I'd be sacked on the spot. Anyhow, that might be quite a good thing for me, who can tell? If I didn't have to hold my hand because of my parents I'd have given notice long ago, I'd have gone to the chief and told him exactly what I think of him. That would knock him endways from his desk! It's a queer way of doing, too, this sitting on high at a desk and talking down to employees, especially when they have to come quite near because the chief is hard of hearing. Well, there's still hope; once I've saved enough money to pay back my parents' debts to him—that should take another five or six years—I'll do it without fail. I'll cut myself completely loose then. For the moment, though, I'd better get up, since my train goes at five.

He looked at the alarm clock ticking on the chest. Heavenly Father! he thought. It was half-past six o'clock and the hands were quietly moving on, it was even past the half-hour, it was getting on toward a quarter to seven. Had the alarm clock not gone off? From the bed one could see that it had been properly set for four o'clock; of course it must have gone off. Yes, but was it possible to sleep quietly through that ear-splitting noise? Well, he had not slept quietly, yet apparently all the more soundly for that. But what was he to do now? The next train went at seven o'clock; to catch that he would need to hurry like mad and his samples weren't even packed up, and he himself wasn't feeling particularly fresh and active. And even if he did catch the train he wouldn't avoid a row with the chief, since the firm's porter would have been waiting for the five o'clock train and would have long since reported his failure to turn up. The porter was a creature of the chief's, spineless and stupid. Well, supposing he were to say he was sick? But that would be most unpleas- ant and would look suspicious, since during his five years' employment he had not been ill once. The chief himself would be sure to come with the sick-insurance doctor, would reproach his parents with their son's laziness, and would cut all excuses short by referring to the insurance doctor, who of course regarded all mankind as perfectly healthy malingerers. And would he be so far wrong on this occasion? Gregor really felt quite well, apart from a drowsiness that was utterly superfluous after such a long sleep, and he was even unusually hungry.

As all this was running through his mind at top speed without his being able to decide to leave

his bed—the alarm clock had just struck a quarter to seven—there came a cautious tap at the door behind the head of his bed. "Gregor," said a voice—it was his mother's—"it's a quarter to seven. Hadn't you a train to catch?" That gentle voice! Gregor had a shock as he heard his own voice answering hers, unmistakably his own voice, it was true, but with a persistent horrible twittering squeak behind it like an undertone, which left the words in their clear shape only for the first moment and then rose up reverberating around them to destroy their sense, so that one could not be sure one had heard them rightly. Gregor wanted to answer at length and explain everything, but in the circumstances he confined himself to say- ing: "Yes, yes, thank you, Mother, I'm getting up now." The wooden door between them must have kept the change in his voice from being notice- able outside, for his mother contented herself with this statement and shuffled away. Yet this brief exchange of words had made the other members of the family aware that Gregor was still in the house, as they had not expected, and at one of the side doors his father was already knocking, gent- ly, yet with his fist. "Gregor, Gregor," he called, "What's the matter with you?" And after a little while he called again in a deeper voice: "Gregor! Gregor!" At the other side door his sister was say- ing in a low, plaintive tone: "Gregor? Aren't you well? Are you needing anything?" He answered them both at once: "I'm just ready," and did his best to make his voice sound as normal as possible by enunciating the words very clearly and leaving long pauses between them. So his father went back to his breakfast, but his sister whispered: "Gregor, open the door, do." However, he was not thinking of opening the door, and felt thankful for the pru- dent habit he had acquired in traveling of locking all doors during the night, even at home.

His immediate intention was to get up quietly without being disturbed, to put on his clothes and above all eat his breakfast, and only then consider what else was to be done, since in bed, he was well aware, his meditations would come to no sensible conclusion. He remembered that often enough in bed he had felt small aches and pains, probably caused by awkward postures, which had proved purely imaginary once he got up, and he looked forward eagerly to seeing this morning's delusions gradually fall away. That the change in his voice was nothing but the precursor of a severe chill, a standing ailment of commercial travelers, he had not the least possible doubt.

To get rid of the quilt was quite easy; he had only to inflate himself a little and it fell off by itself. But the next move was difficult, especially because he was so uncommonly broad. He would have needed arms and hands to hoist himself up; instead he had only the numerous little legs which never stopped waving in all directions and which he could not control in the least. When he tried to bend one of them it was the first to stretch itself straight; and did he succeed at last in making it do what he wanted, all the other legs meanwhile waved the more wildly in a high degree of unpleasant agitation. "But what's the use of lying idle in bed," said Gregor to himself.

He thought that he might get out of bed with the lower part of his body first, but this lower part, which he had not yet seen and of which he could form no clear conception, proved too difficult to move; it shifted so slowly; and when finally, almost wild with annoyance, he gathered his forces together and thrust out recklessly, he had miscalculated the direction and bumped heavily against the lower end of the bed, and the stinging pain he felt informed him that precisely this lower part of his body was at the moment probably the most sensitive.

So he tried to get the top part of himself out first, and cautiously moved his head toward the edge of the bed. That proved easy enough, and despite its breadth and mass the bulk of his body at last slowly followed the movement of his head. Still, when he finally got his head free over the edge of the bed he felt too scared to go on advancing, for after all if he let himself fall in this way it would take a miracle to keep his head from being injured. And at all costs he must not lose consciousness now, precisely now; he would rather stay in bed.

But when after a repetition of the same efforts he lay in his former position again, sighing, and watched his little legs struggling against each other more wildly than ever, if that were possible, and saw no way of bringing any order into this arbitrary confusion, he told himself again that it was impossible to stay in bed and that the most sensible course was to risk everything for the smallest hope of getting away from it. At the same time he did not forget to remind himself occasionally that cool reflection, the coolest possible, was much better than desperate resolves. In such moments he focused his eyes as sharply as possible on the window, but, unfortunately, the prospect of the morning fog, which muffled even the other side of the narrow street, brought him little encouragement and comfort. "Seven o'clock already," he said to himself when the alarm clock chimed again, "seven o'clock already and still such a thick fog." And for a little while he lay quiet, breathing lightly, as if perhaps expecting such complete repose to restore all things to their real and normal condition.

But then he said to himself: "Before it strikes a quarter past seven I must be quite out of this bed, without fail. Anyhow, by that time someone will have come from the office to ask for me, since it opens before seven." And he set himself to rocking his whole body at once in a regular rhythm, with the idea of swinging it out of the bed. If he tipped himself out in that way he could keep his head from injury by lifting it at an acute angle when he fell. His back seemed to be hard and was not likely to suffer from a fall on the carpet. His biggest worry was the loud crash he would not be able to help making, which would probably cause anxiety, if not terror, behind all the doors. Still, he must take the risk.

When he was already half out of the bed—the new method was more a game than an effort, for he needed only to hitch himself across by rocking to and fro—it struck him how simple it would be if he could get help. Two strong people—he thought of his father and the servant girl—would be amply sufficient; they would only have to thrust their arms under his convex back, lever him out of the bed, bend down with their burden, and then be patient enough to let him turn himself right over onto the floor, where it was to be hoped his legs would then find their proper function. Well, ignoring the fact that the doors were all locked, ought he really to call for help? In spite of his misery he could not suppress a smile at the very idea of it.

He had got so far that he could barely keep his equilibrium when he rocked himself strongly, and he would have to nerve himself very soon for the final decision since in five minutes' time it would be quarter past seven—when the front doorbell rang. "That's someone from the office," he said to himself, and grew almost rigid, while his little legs only jigged about all the faster. For a moment everything stayed quiet. "They're not going to open the door," said Gregor to himself, catching at some kind of irrational hope. But then of course the servant girl went as usual to the door with her heavy tread and opened it. Gregor needed only to hear the first good morning of the visitor to know immediately who it was—the chief clerk himself. What a fate, to be condemned to work for a firm where the smallest omission at once gave rise to the gravest suspicion! Were all employees in a body nothing but scoundrels, was there not among them one single loyal devoted man who, had he wasted only an hour or so of the firm's time in a morning, was so tormented by conscience as to be driven out of his mind and actually incapable of leaving his bed? Wouldn't it really have been sufficient to send an apprentice to inquire—if any inquiry were necessary at all—did the chief clerk himself have to come and thus indicate to the entire family, an innocent family, that this suspicious circumstance could be investigated by no one less versed in affairs than himself? And more through the agitation caused by these reflections than through any act of will Gregor swung himself out of bed with all his strength. There was a loud thump, but it was not really a crash. His fall was broken to some extent by the carpet, his back, too, was less stiff than he thought, and so there was merely a dull thud, not so very startling. Only he had not lifted his head carefully enough and had hit it; he turned it and rubbed it on the carpet in pain and irritation.

"That was something falling down in there," said the chief clerk in the next room to the left. Gregor tried to suppose to himself that something like what had happened to him today might some-day happen to the chief clerk; one really could not deny that it was possible. But as if in brusque reply to this supposition the chief clerk took a couple of firm steps in the next-door room and his patent leather boots creaked. From the right-hand room his sister was whispering to inform him of the situation: "Gregor, the chief clerk's here." "I know," muttered Gregor to himself; but he didn't dare to make his voice loud enough for his sister to hear it.

"Gregor," said his father now from the left-hand room, "the chief clerk has come and wants to know why you didn't catch the early train. We don't know what to say to him. Besides, he wants to talk to you in person. So open the door, please. He will be good enough to excuse the untidiness of your room." "Good morning, Mr. Samsa," the chief clerk was calling amiably meanwhile. "He's not well," said his mother to the visitor, while his father was still speaking through the door, "he's not well, sir, believe me. What else would make him miss a train! The boy thinks about nothing but his work. It makes me almost cross the way he never goes out in the evenings; he's been here the last eight days and has stayed at home every single evening. He just sits there quietly at the table reading a newspaper or looking through railway timetables. The only amusement he gets is doing fretwork. For instance, he spent two or three evenings cutting out a little picture frame; you would be surprised to see how pretty it is; it's hanging in his room; you'll see it in a minute when Gregor opens the door. I must say I'm glad you've come, sir; we should never have got him to unlock the door by ourselves; he's so obstinate; and I'm sure he's unwell, though he wouldn't have it to be so this morning." "I'm just coming," said Gregor slowly and carefully, not moving an inch for fear of losing one word of the conversation. "I can't think of any other explanation, madame," said the chief clerk, "I hope it's nothing serious. Although on the other hand I must say that we men of business—fortunately or unfortunately—very often simply have to ignore any slight indisposition, since business must be attended to." "Well, can the chief clerk come in now?" asked Gregor's father impatiently, again knocking on the door. "No," said Gregor. In the left-hand room a painful silence followed this refusal, in the right-hand room his sister began to sob.

Why didn't his sister join the others? She was probably newly out of bed and hadn't even begun to put on her clothes yet. Well, why was she crying? Because he wouldn't get up and let the chief clerk in, because he was in danger of losing his job, and because the chief would begin dunning his parents again for the old debts? Surely these were things one didn't need to worry about for the present. Gregor was still at home and not in the least thinking of deserting the family. At the moment, true, he was lying on the carpet and no one who knew the condition he was in could seriously expect him to admit the chief clerk. But for such a small discourtesy, which could plausibly be explained away somehow later on, Gregor could hardly be dismissed on the spot. And it seemed to Gregor that it would be much more sensible to leave him in peace for the present than to trouble him with tears and entreaties. Still, of course, their uncertainty bewildered them all and excused their behavior.

"Mr. Samsa," the chief clerk called now in a louder voice, "what's the matter with you? Here you are, barricading yourself in your room, giving only 'yes' and 'no' for answers, causing your parents a lot of unnecessary trouble and neglecting—I mention this only in passing—neglecting your business duties in an incredible fashion. I am speaking here in the name of your parents and of your chief, and I beg you quite seriously to give me an immediate and precise explanation. You amaze me, you amaze me. I thought you were a quiet, dependable person, and now all at once you seem bent on making a disgraceful exhibition of yourself. The chief did hint to me early this morning a possible explanation for your disappearance—with reference to the cash payments that were entrusted to you recently—but I almost pledged my solemn word of honor that this could not be so. But now that I see how incredibly obstinate you are, I no longer have the slightest desire to take your part at all. And your position in the firm is not so unassailable. I came with the intention of telling you all this in private, but since you are wasting my time so needlessly I don't see why your parents shouldn't hear it too. For some time past your work has been most unsatisfactory; this is not the season of the year for a business boom, of course, we admit that, but a season of the year for doing no business at all, that does not exist, Mr. Samsa, must not exist."

"But, sir," cried Gregor, beside himself and in his agitation forgetting everything else, "I'm just going to open the door this very minute. A slight illness, an attack of giddiness, has kept me from getting up. I'm still lying in bed. But I feel all right again. I'm getting out of bed now. Just give me a moment or two longer! I'm not quite so well as I thought. But I'm all right, really. How a thing like that can suddenly strike one down! Only last night I was quite well, my parents can tell you, or rather I did have a slight presentiment. I must have showed some sign of it. Why didn't I report it at the office! But one always thinks that an indisposition can be got over without staying in the house. Oh sir, do spare my parents! All that you're reproaching me with now has no foundation; no one has ever said a word to me about it. Perhaps you haven't looked at the last orders I sent in. Anyhow, I can still catch the eight o'clock train, I'm much the better for my few hours' rest. Don't let me detain you here, sir; I'll be attending to business very soon, and do be good enough to tell the chief so and to make my excuses to him!"

And while all this was tumbling out pell-mell and Gregor hardly knew what he was saying, he had reached the chest quite easily, perhaps because of the practice he had had in bed, and was now trying to lever himself upright by means of it. He meant actually to open the door, actually to show himself and speak to the chief clerk; he was eager to find out what the others, after all their insistence, would say at the sight of him. If they were horrified then the responsibility was no longer his and he could stay quiet. But if they took it calmly, then he had no reason either to be upset, and could really get to the station for the eight o'clock train if he hurried. At first he slipped down a few times from the polished surface of the chest, but at length with a last heave he stood upright; he paid no more attention to the pains in the lower part of his body, however they smarted. Then he let himself fall against the back of a nearby chair, and clung with his little legs to the edge of it. That brought him into control of himself again and he stopped speaking, for now he could listen to what the chief clerk was saying.

"Did you understand a word of it?" the chief clerk was asking; "surely he can't be trying to make fools of us?" "Oh dear," cried his mother, in tears, "perhaps he's terribly ill and we're tormenting him. Grete! Grete!" she called out then. "Yes Mother?" called his sister from the other side. They were calling to each other across Gregor's room. "You must go this minute for the doctor. Gregor is ill. Go for the doctor, quick. Did you hear how he was speaking?" "That was no human voice," said the chief clerk in a voice noticeably low beside the shrillness of the mother's. "Anna! Anna!" his father was calling through the hall to the kitchen, clapping his hands, "get a locksmith at once!" And the two girls were already running through the hall with a swish of skirts—how could his sister have got dressed so quickly?—and were tearing the front door open. There was no sound of its closing again; they had evidently left it open, as one does in houses where some great misfortune has happened.

But Gregor was now much calmer. The words he uttered were no longer understandable, apparently, although they seemed clear enough to him, even clearer than before, perhaps because his ear had grown accustomed to the sound of them. Yet at any rate people now believed that something was wrong with him, and were ready to help him. The positive certainty with which these first measures had been taken comforted him. He felt himself drawn once more into the human circle and hoped for great and remarkable results from both the doctor and the locksmith, without really distinguishing precisely between them. To make his voice as clear as possible for the decisive conversation that was now imminent he coughed a little, as quietly as he could, of course, since this noise too might not sound like a human cough for all he was able to judge. In the next room meanwhile there was complete silence. Perhaps his parents were sitting at the table with the chief clerk, whispering, perhaps they were all leaning against the door and listening.

Slowly Gregor pushed the chair toward the door, then let go of it, caught hold of the door for support—the soles at the end of his little legs were somewhat sticky—and rested against it for a moment after his efforts. Then he set himself to turning the key in the lock with his mouth. It seemed, unhappily, that he hadn't really any teeth—what could he grip the key with?—but on the other hand his jaws were certainly very strong; with their help he did manage to set the key in motion, heedless of the fact that he was undoubtedly damaging them somewhere, since a brown fluid issued from his mouth, flowed over the key, and dripped on the floor. "Just listen to that," said the chief clerk next door; "he's turning the key." That was a great encouragement to Gregor; but they should all have shouted encouragement to him, his father and mother too: "Go on, Gregor," they should have called out, "keep going, hold on to that key!" And in the belief that they were all following his efforts intently, he clenched his jaws recklessly on the key with all the force at his command. As the turning of the key progressed he circled around the lock, holding on now only with his mouth, pushing on the key, as required, or pulling it down again with all the weight of his body. The louder click of the finally yielding lock literally quickened Gregor. With a deep breath of relief he said to himself: "So I didn't need the locksmith," and laid his head on the handle to open the door wide.

Since he had to pull the door toward him, he was still invisible when it was really wide open. He had to edge himself slowly around the near half of the double door, and to do it very carefully if he was not to fall plump upon his back just on the threshold. He was still carrying out this difficult maneuver, with no time to observe anything else, when he heard the chief clerk utter a loud "Oh!"—it sounded like a gust of wind—and now he could see the man, standing as he was nearest to the door, clapping one hand before his open mouth and slowly backing away as if driven by some invisible steady pressure. His mother—in spite of the chief clerk's being there her hair was still undone and sticking up in all directions—first clasped her hands and looked at his father, then took two steps toward Gregor and fell on the floor among her outspread skirts, her face quite hidden on her breast. His father knotted his fist with a fierce expression on his face as if he meant to knock Gregor back into his room, then looked uncertainly around the living room, covered his eyes with his hands, and wept till his great chest heaved.

Gregor did not go now into the living room, but leaned against the inside of the firmly shut wing of the door, so that only half his body was visible and his head above it bending sideways to look at the others. The light had meanwhile strengthened; on the other side of the street one could see clearly a section of the endlessly long, dark gray building opposite—it was a hospital—abruptly punctuated by its row of regular windows; the rain was still falling, but only in large singly discernible and literally singly splashing drops. The breakfast dishes were set out on the table lavishly, for breakfast was the most important meal of the day to Gregor's father, who lingered it out for hours over various newspapers. Right opposite Gregor on the wall hung a photograph of himself in military service, as a lieutenant, hand on sword, a carefree smile on his face, inviting one to respect his uniform and military bearing. The door leading to the hall was open, and one could see that the front door stood open too, showing the landing beyond and the beginning of the stairs going down.

"Well," said Gregor, knowing perfectly that he was the only one who had retained any composure, "I'll put my clothes on at once, pack up my samples, and start off. Will you only let me go? You see, sir, I'm not obstinate, and I'm willing to work; traveling is a hard life, but I couldn't live without it. Where are you going, sir? To the office? Yes? Will you give a true account of all this? One can be temporarily incapacitated, but that's just the moment for remembering former services and bearing in mind that later on, when the incapacity has been got over, one will certainly work with all the more industry and concentration. I'm loyally bound to serve the chief, you know that very well. Besides, I have to provide for my parents and my sister. I'm in great difficulties, but I'll get

Lithograph by Ottomar Starke done as cover illustration for "The Metamorphosis," published in November, 1915, as a two-number volume (22/23) in the *Newest Day* series.

out of them again. Don't make things any worse for me than they are. Stand up for me in the firm. Travelers are not popular there, I know. People think they earn sacks of money and just have a good time. A prejudice there's no particular reason for revising. But you, sir, have a more comprehensive view of affairs than the rest of the staff, yes, let me tell you in confidence, a more comprehensive view than the chief himself, who, being the owner, lets his judgment easily be swayed against one of his employees. And you know very well that the traveler, who is never seen in the office almost the whole year around, can so easily fall a victim to gossip and ill luck and unfounded complaints, which he mostly knows nothing about, except when he comes back exhausted from his rounds, and only then suffers in person from their evil consequences, which he can no longer trace back to the original causes. Sir, sir, don't go away without a word to me to show that you think me in the right at least to some extent!"

But at Gregor's very first words the chief clerk had already backed away and only stared at him with parted lips over one twitching shoulder. And while Gregor was speaking he did not stand still one moment but stole away toward the door, without taking his eyes off Gregor, yet only an inch at a time, as if obeying some secret injunction to leave the room. He was already at the hall, and the suddenness with which he took his last step out of the living room would have made one believe he had burned the sole of his foot. Once in the hall he stretched his right arm before him toward the staircase, as if some supernatural power were waiting there to deliver him.

Gregor perceived that the chief clerk must on no account be allowed to go away in this frame of mind if his position in the firm were not to be endangered to the utmost. His parents did not understand this so well; they had convinced themselves in the course of years that Gregor was settled for life in this firm, and besides they were so preoccupied with their immediate troubles that all foresight had forsaken them. Yet Gregor had this foresight. The chief clerk must be detained, soothed, persuaded, and finally won over; the whole future of Gregor and his family depended on it! If only his sister had been there! She was intelligent; she had begun to cry while Gregor was still lying quietly on his back. And no doubt the chief clerk, so partial to ladies, would have been guided by her; she would have shut the door of the flat and in the hall talked him out of his horror. But she was not there, and Gregor would have to handle the situation himself. And without remembering that he was still unaware what powers of movement he possessed, without even remembering that his words in all possibility, indeed in all likelihood, would again be unintelligible, he let go the wing of the door, pushed himself through the opening, started to walk toward the chief clerk, who was already ridiculously clinging with both hands to the railing on the landing; but immediately, as he was feeling for a support, he fell down with a little cry upon all his numerous legs. Hardly was he down when he experienced for the first time this morning a sense of physical comfort; his legs had firm ground under them; they were completely obedient, as he noted with joy; they even strove to carry him forward in whatever direction he chose; and he was inclined to believe that a final relief from all his sufferings was at hand. But in the same moment as he found himself on the floor, rocking with suppressed eagerness to move, not far from his mother, indeed just in front of her, she, who had seemed so completely crushed, sprang all at once to her feet, her arms and fingers outspread, cried: "Help, for God's sake, help!" bent her head down as if to see Gregor better, yet on the contrary kept backing senselessly away; had quite forgotten that the laden table stood behind her; sat upon it hastily, as if in absence of mind, when she bumped into it; and seemed altogether unaware that the big coffeepot beside her was upset and pouring coffee in a flood over the carpet.

"Mother, Mother," said Gregor in a low voice, and looked up at her. The chief clerk, for the moment, had quite slipped from his mind; instead, he could not resist snapping his jaws together at the sight of the streaming coffee. That made his mother scream again, she fled from the table and fell into the arms of his father, who hastened to catch her. But Gregor had now no time to spare for his parents; the chief clerk was already on the stairs; with his chin on the banisters he was taking one last backward look. Gregor made a spring, to be as sure as possible of overtaking him; the chief clerk must have divined his intention, for he leaped down several steps and vanished; he was still yelling "Ugh!" and it echoed through the whole staircase.

Unfortunately, the flight of the chief clerk seemed completely to upset Gregor's father, who had remained relatively calm until now, for instead of running after the man himself, or at least not hindering Gregor in his pursuit, he seized in his right hand the walking stick that the chief clerk had left behind on a chair, together with a hat and greatcoat, snatched in his left hand a large newspaper from the table, and began stamping his feet and flourishing the stick and the newspaper to drive Gregor back into his room. No entreaty of Gregor's availed, indeed no entreaty was even understood; however humbly he bent his head his father only stamped on the floor the more loudly. Behind his father his mother had torn open a window, despite the cold weather, and was leaning far out of it with her face in her hands. A strong draught set in from the street to the staircase, the window curtains blew in, the newspapers on the table fluttered, stray pages whisked over the floor. Pitilessly Gregor's father drove him back, hissing and crying "Shoo!" like a savage. But Gregor was quite unpracticed in walking backwards, it really was a slow business. If he only had a chance to turn around he could get back to his room at once, but he was afraid of exasperating his father by the slowness of such a rotation and at any moment the stick in his father's hand might hit him a fatal blow on the back or on the head. In the end, however, nothing else was left for him to do since to his horror he observed that in moving backwards he could not even control the direction he took; and so, keeping an anxious eye on his father all the time over his shoulder, he began to turn around as quickly as he could, which was in reality very slowly. Perhaps his father noted his good intentions, for he did not interfere except every now and then to help him in the maneuver from a distance with the point of the stick. If only he would have stopped making that unbearable hissing noise! It made Gregor quite lose his head. He had turned almost completely around when the hissing noise so distracted him that he even turned a little the wrong way again. But when at last his head was fortunately right in front of the doorway, it appeared that his body was too broad simply to get through the opening. His father, of course, in his present mood was far from thinking of such a thing as opening the other half of the door, to let Gregor have enough space. He had merely the fixed idea of driving Gregor back into his room as quickly as possible. He would never have suffered Gregor to make the circumstantial preparations for standing up on end and perhaps slipping his way through

the door. Maybe he was now making more noise than ever to urge Gregor forward, as if no obstacle impeded him; to Gregor, anyhow, the noise in his rear sounded no longer like the voice of one single father; this was really no joke, and Gregor thrust himself—come what might—into the doorway. One side of his body rose up, he was tilted at an angle in the doorway, his flank was quite bruised, horrid blotches stained the white door, soon he was stuck fast and, left to himself, could not have moved at all, his legs on one side fluttered trembling in the air, those on the other were crushed painfully to the floor—when from behind his father gave him a strong push which was literally a deliverance and he flew far into the room, bleeding freely. The door was slammed behind him with the stick, and then at last there was silence.

II

Not until it was twilight did Gregor awake out of a deep sleep, more like a swoon than a sleep. He would certainly have waked up of his own accord not much later, for he felt himself sufficiently rested and well slept, but it seemed to him as if a fleeting step and a cautious shutting of the door leading into the hall had aroused him. The electric lights in the street cast a pale sheen here and there on the ceiling and the upper surfaces of the furniture, but down below, where he lay, it was dark. Slowly, awkwardly trying out his feelers, which he now first learned to appreciate, he pushed his way to the door to see what had been happening there. His left side felt like one single long, unpleasantly tense scar, and he had actually to limp on his two rows of legs. One little leg, moreover, had been severely damaged in the course of that morning's events—it was almost a miracle that only one had been damaged—and trailed uselessly behind him.

He had reached the door before he discovered what had really drawn him to it: the smell of food. For there stood a basin filled with fresh milk in which floated little sops of white bread. He could almost have laughed with joy, since he was now still hungrier than in the morning, and he dipped his head almost over the eyes straight into the milk. But soon in disappointment he withdrew it again; not only did he find it difficult to feed because of his tender left side—and he could only feed with the palpitating collaboration of his whole body—he did not like the milk either, although milk had been his favorite drink and that was certainly why his sister had set it there for him, indeed it was almost with repulsion that he turned away from the basin and crawled back to the middle of the room.

He could see through the crack of the door that the gas was turned on in the living room, but while usually at this time his father made a habit of reading the afternoon newspaper in a loud voice to his mother and occasionally to his sister as well, not a sound was now to be heard. Well, perhaps his father had recently given up this habit of reading aloud, which his sister had mentioned so often in conversation and in her letters. But there was the same silence all around, although the flat was certainly not empty of occupants. "What a quiet life our family has been leading," said Gregor to himself, and as he sat there motionless staring into the darkness he felt great pride in the fact that he had been able to provide such a life for his parents and sister in such a fine flat. But what if all the quiet, the comfort, the contentment were now to end in horror? To keep himself from being lost in such thoughts Gregor took refuge in movement and crawled up and down the room.

Once during the long evening one of the side doors was opened a little and quickly shut again, later the other side door too; someone had apparently wanted to come in and then thought better of it. Gregor now stationed himself immediately before the living-room door, determined to persuade any hesitating visitor to come in or at least to discover who it might be; but the door was not opened again and he waited in vain. In the early morning, when the doors were locked, they had all wanted to come in, now that he had opened one door and the other had apparently been opened during the day, no one came in and even the keys were on the other side of the doors.

It was late at night before the gas went out in the living room, and Gregor could easily tell that his parents and his sister had all stayed awake until then, for he could clearly hear the three of them stealing away on tiptoe. No one was likely to visit him, not until the morning, that was certain; so he had plenty of time to meditate at his leisure on how he was to arrange his life afresh. But the lofty, empty room in which he had to lie flat on the floor filled him with an apprehension he could not account for, since it had been his very own room for the past five years—and with a half-unconscious action, not without a slight feeling of shame, he scuttled under the sofa, where he felt comfortable at once, although his back was a little cramped and he could not lift his head up, and his only regret was that his body was too broad to get the whole of it under the sofa.

He stayed there all night, spending the time partly in a light slumber, from which his hunger kept waking him up with a start, and partly in worrying and sketching vague hopes, which all led to the same conclusion, that he must lie low for the present and, by exercising patience and the utmost consideration, help the family to bear the inconvenience he was bound to cause them in his present condition.

Very early in the morning, it was still almost night, Gregor had the chance to test the strength of his new resolutions, for his sister, nearly fully dressed, opened the door from the hall and peered in. She did not see him at once, yet when she caught sight of him under the sofa—well, he had to be somewhere, he couldn't have flown away, could he?—she was so startled that without being able to help it she slammed the door shut again. But as if regretting her behavior she opened the door again immediately and came in on tiptoe, as if she were visiting an invalid or even a stranger. Gregor had pushed his head forward to the very edge of the sofa and watched her. Would she notice that he had left the milk standing, and not for lack of hunger, and would she bring in some other kind of food more to his taste? If she did not do it of her own accord, he would rather starve than draw her attention to the fact, although he felt a wild impulse to dart out from under the sofa, throw himself at her feet, and beg her for something to eat. But his sister at once noticed, with surprise, that the basin was still full, except for a little milk that had been spilled all around it, she lifted it immediately, not with her bare hands, true, but with a cloth and carried it away. Gregor was wildly curious to know what she would bring instead, and made various speculations about it. Yet what she actually did next, in the goodness of her heart, he could never have guessed at. To find out what he liked she brought him a whole selection of food, all set out on an old newspaper. There were old, half-decayed vegetables, bones from last night's supper covered with a white sauce that had thickened; some raisins and almonds; a piece of cheese that Gregor would have called uneatable two days ago; a dry roll of bread, a buttered roll, and a roll both buttered and salted. Besides all that, she set down again the same basin, into which she had poured some water, and which was apparently to be reserved for his exclusive use. And with fine tact, knowing that Gregor would not eat in her presence, she withdrew quickly and even turned the key, to let him understand that he could take his ease as much as he liked. Gregor's legs all whizzed toward the food. His wounds must have healed completely, moreover, for he felt no disability, which amazed him and made him reflect how more than a month ago he had cut one finger a little with a knife and had still suffered pain from the wound only the day before yesterday. Am I less sensitive now? he thought, and sucked greedily at the cheese, which above all the other edibles attracted him at once and strongly. One after another and with tears of satisfaction in his eyes he quickly devoured the cheese, the vegetables, and the sauce; the fresh food, on the other hand, had no charms for him, he could not even stand the smell of it and actually dragged away to some little distance the things he could eat. He had long finished his meal and was only lying lazily on the same spot when his sister turned the key slowly as a sign for him to retreat. That roused him at once, although he was nearly asleep, and he hurried under the sofa again. But it took considerable self-control for him to stay under the sofa, even for the short time his sister was in the room, since the large meal had swollen his body somewhat and he was so cramped he could hardly breathe. Slight attacks of breathlessness afflicted him and his eyes were starting a little out of his head as he watched his unsuspecting sister sweeping together with a broom not only the remains of what he had eaten but even the things he had not touched, as if these were now of no use to anyone, and hastily shoveling it all into a bucket, which she covered with a wooden lid and carried away. Hardly had she turned her back when Gregor came from under the sofa and stretched and puffed himself out.

In this manner Gregor was fed, once in the early morning while his parents and the servant girl were still asleep, and a second time after they had all had their midday dinner, for then his parents took a short nap and the servant girl could be sent out on some errand or other by his sister. Not that they would have wanted him to starve, of course, but perhaps they could not have borne to know more about his feeding than from hearsay, perhaps too his sister wanted to spare them such little anxieties wherever possible, since they had quite enough to bear as it was.

Under what pretext the doctor and the locksmith had been got rid of on that first morning Gregor could not discover, for since what he said was not understood by the others it never struck any of them, not even his sister, that he could understand what they said, and so whenever his sister came into his room he had to content himself with hearing her utter only a sigh now and then and an occasional appeal to the saints. Later on, when she had got a little used to the situation—of course she could never get completely used to it—she sometimes threw out a remark which was kindly meant or could be so interpreted. "Well, he liked his dinner today," she would say when Gregor had made a good clearance of his food; and when he had not eaten, which gradually happened more and more often, she would say almost sadly: "Everything's been left standing again."

But although Gregor could get no news directly, he overheard a lot from the neighboring rooms, and as soon as voices were audible, he would run to the door of the room concerned and press his whole body against it. In the first few days especially there was no conversation that did not refer to him somehow, even if only indirectly. For two whole days there were family consultations at every mealtime about what should be done; but also between meals the same subject was discussed, for there were always at least two members of the family at home, since no one wanted to be alone in the flat and to leave it quite empty was unthinkable. And on the very first of these days the household cook—it was not quite clear what and how much she knew of the situation—went down on her knees to his mother and begged leave to go, and when she departed, a quarter of an hour later, gave thanks for her dismissal with tears in her eyes as if for the greatest benefit that could have been conferred on her, and without any prompting swore a solemn oath that she would never say a single word to anyone about what had happened.

Now Gregor's sister had to cook too, helping her mother; true, the cooking did not amount to much, for they ate scarcely anything. Gregor was always hearing one of the family vainly urging another to eat and getting no answer but: "Thanks, I've had all I want," or something similar. Perhaps they drank nothing either. Time and again his sister kept asking his father if he wouldn't like some beer and offered kindly to go and fetch it herself, and when he made no answer suggested that she could ask the concierge to fetch it, so that he need feel no sense of obligation, but then a round "No" came from his father and no more was said about it.

In the course of that very first day Gregor's father explained the family's financial position and prospects to both his mother and his sister. Now and then he rose from the table to get some voucher or memorandum out of the small safe he had rescued from the collapse of his business five years earlier. One could hear him opening the complicated lock and rustling papers out and shutting it again. This statement made by his father was the first cheerful information Gregor had heard since his imprisonment. He had been of the opinion that nothing at all was left over from his father's business, at least his father had never said anything to the contrary, and of course he had not asked him directly. At that time Gregor's sole desire was to do his utmost to help the family to forget as soon as possible the catastrophe that had overwhelmed the business and thrown them all

into a state of complete despair. And so he had set to work with unusual ardor and almost overnight had become a commercial traveler instead of a little clerk, with of course much greater chances of earning money, and his success was immediately translated into good round coin which he could lay on the table for his amazed and happy family. These had been fine times, and they had never recurred, at least not with the same sense of glory, although later on Gregor had earned so much money that he was able to meet the expenses of the whole household and did so. They had simply got used to it, both the family and Gregor; the money was gratefully accepted and gladly given, but there was no special uprush of warm feeling. With his sister alone had he remained intimate, and it was a secret plan of his that she, who loved music, unlike himself, and could play movingly on the violin, should be sent next year to study at the Conservatorium, despite the great expense that would entail, which must be made up in some other way. During his brief visits home the Conservatorium was often mentioned in the talks he had with his sister, but always merely as a beautiful dream which could never come true, and his parents discouraged even these innocent references to it; yet Gregor had made up his mind firmly about it and meant to announce the fact with due solemnity on Christmas Day.

Such were the thoughts, completely futile in his present condition, that went through his head as he stood clinging upright to the door and listening. Sometimes out of sheer weariness he had to give up listening and let his head fall negligently against the door, but he always had to pull himself together again at once, for even the slight sound his head made was audible next door and brought all conversation to a stop. "What can he be doing now?" his father would say after a while, obviously turning toward the door, and only then would the interrupted conversation gradually be set going again.

Gregor was now informed as amply as he could wish—for his father tended to repeat himself in his explanations, partly because it was a long time since he had handled such matters and partly because his mother could not always grasp things at once—that a certain amount of investments, a very small amount it was true, had survived the wreck of their fortunes and had even increased a little because the dividends had not been touched meanwhile. And besides that, the money Gregor brought home every month—he had kept only a few dollars for himself—had never been quite used up and now amounted to a small capital sum. Behind the door Gregor nodded his head eagerly, rejoiced at this evidence of unexpected thrift and foresight. True, he could really have paid off some more of his father's debts to the chief with this extra money, and so brought much nearer the day on which he could quit his job, but doubtless it was better the way his father had arranged it.

Yet this capital was by no means sufficient to let the family live on the interest of it; for one year, perhaps, or at the most two, they could live on the principal, that was all. It was simply a sum that ought not to be touched and should be kept for a rainy day; money for living expenses would have to be earned. Now his father was still hale enough but an old man, and he had done no work for the past five years and could not be expected to do much; during these five years, the first years of leisure in his laborious though unsuccessful life, he had grown rather fat and become sluggish. And Gregor's old mother, how was she to earn a living with her asthma, which troubled her even when she walked through the flat and kept her lying on a sofa every other day panting for breath beside an open window? And was his sister to earn her bread, she who was still a child of seventeen and whose life hitherto had been so pleasant, consisting as it did in dressing herself nicely, sleeping long, helping in the housekeeping, going out to a few modest entertainments, and above all playing the violin? At first whenever the need for earning money was mentioned Gregor let go his hold on the door and threw himself down on the cool leather sofa beside it, he felt so hot with shame and grief.

Often he just lay there the long nights through without sleeping at all, scrabbling for hours on the leather. Or he nerved himself to the great effort of pushing an armchair to the window, then crawled up over the window sill and, braced against the chair, leaned against the windowpanes, obviously in some recollection of the sense of freedom that looking out of a window always used to give him. For in reality day by day things that were even a little way off were growing dimmer to his sight; the hospital across the street, which he used to execrate for being all too often before his eyes, was now quite beyond his range of vision, and if he had not known that he lived in Charlotte Street, a quiet street but still a city street, he might have believed that his window gave on a desert waste where gray sky and gray land blended indistinguishably into each other. His quick-witted sister only needed to observe twice that the armchair stood by the window; after that whenever she had tidied the room she always pushed the chair back to the same place at the window and even left the inner casements open.

If he could have spoken to her and thanked her for all she had to do for him, he could have borne her ministrations better; as it was, they oppressed him. She certainly tried to make as light as possible of whatever was disagreeable in her task, and as time went on she succeeded, of course, more and more, but time brought more enlightenment to Gregor too. The very way she came in distressed him. Hardly was she in the room when she rushed to the window, without even taking time to shut the door, careful as she was usually to shield the sight of Gregor's room from the others, and as if she were almost suffocating tore the casements open with hasty fingers, standing then in the open draught for a while even in the bitterest cold and drawing deep breaths. This noisy scurry of hers upset Gregor twice a day; he would crouch trembling under the sofa all the time, knowing quite well that she would certainly have spared him such a disturbance had she found it at all possible to stay in his presence without opening the window.

On one occasion, about a month after Gregor's metamorphosis, when there was surely no reason for her to be still startled at his appearance, she came a little earlier than usual and found him gazing out of the window, quite motionless, and thus well placed to look like a bogey. Gregor would not have been surprised had she not come in at all, for she could not immediately open the window while he was there, but not only did she retreat, she jumped back as if in alarm and banged the door shut; a stranger might well have thought that he had been lying in wait for her there meaning to bite her. Of course he hid himself under the sofa at once, but he had to wait until midday before she came again, and she seemed more ill at ease than usual. This made him realize how repulsive the sight of him still was to her, and it was bound to go on being repulsive, and what an effort it must cost her not to run away even from the sight of the small portion of his body that stuck out from under the sofa. In order to spare her that, therefore, one day he carried a sheet on his back to the sofa—it cost him four hours' labor—and arranged it there in such a way as to hide him completely, so that even if she were to bend down she could not see him. Had she considered the sheet unnecessary, she would certainly have stripped it off the sofa again, for it was clear enough that this curtaining and confining of himself was not likely to conduce to Gregor's comfort, but she left it where it was, and Gregor even fancied that he caught a thankful glance from her eye when he lifted the sheet carefully a very little with his head to see how she was taking the new arrangement.

For the first fortnight his parents could not bring themselves to the point of entering his room, and he often heard them expressing their appreciation of his sister's activities, whereas formerly they had frequently scolded her for being as they thought a somewhat useless daughter. But now, both of them often waited outside the door, his father and his mother, while his sister tidied his room, and as soon as she came out she had to tell them exactly how things were in the room, what Gregor had eaten, how he had conducted himself this time, and whether there was not perhaps some slight improvement in his condition. His mother, moreover, began relatively soon to want to visit him, but his father and sister dissuaded her at first with arguments which Gregor listened to very attentively and altogether approved. Later, however, she had to be held back by main force, and when she cried out: "Do let me in to Gregor, he is my unfortunate son! Can't you understand that I must go to him?" Gregor thought that it might be

well to have her come in, not every day, of course, but perhaps once a week; she understood things, after all, much better than his sister, who was only a child despite the efforts she was making and had perhaps taken on so difficult a task merely out of childish thoughtlessness.

Gregor's desire to see his mother was soon fulfilled. During the daytime he did not want to show himself at the window, out of consideration for his parents, but he could not crawl very far around the few square yards of floor space he had, nor could he bear lying quietly at rest all during the night, while he was fast losing any interest he had ever taken in food, so that for mere recreation he had formed the habit of crawling crisscross over the walls and ceiling. He especially enjoyed hanging suspended from the ceiling; it was much better than lying on the floor; one could breathe more freely; one's body swung and rocked lightly; and in the almost blissful absorption induced by this suspension it could happen to his own surprise that he let go and fell plump on the floor. Yet he now had his body much better under control than formerly, and even such a big fall did him no harm. His sister at once remarked the new distraction Gregor had found for himself—he left traces behind him of the sticky stuff on his soles wherever he crawled—and she got the idea in her head of giving him as wide a field as possible to crawl in and of removing the pieces of furniture that hindered him, above all the chest of drawers and the writing desk. But that was more than she could manage all by herself; she did not dare ask her father to help her; and as for the servant girl, a young creature of sixteen who had had the courage to stay on after the cook's departure, she could not be asked to help, for she had begged as a special favor that she might keep the kitchen door locked and open it only on a definite summons; so there was nothing left but to apply to her mother at an hour when her father was out. And the old lady did come, with exclamations of joyful eagerness, which, however, died away at the door of Gregor's room. Gregor's sister, of course, went in first, to see that everything was in order before letting his mother enter. In great haste Gregor pulled the sheet lower and rucked it more in folds so that it really looked as if it had been thrown accidentally over the sofa. And this time he did not peer out from under it; he renounced the pleasure of seeing his mother on this occasion and was only glad that she had come at all. "Come in, he's out of sight," said his sister, obviously leading her mother in by the hand. Gregor could now hear the two women struggling to shift the heavy old chest from its place, and his sister claiming the greater part of the labor for herself, without listening to the admonitions of her mother, who feared she might overstrain herself. It took a long time. After at least a quarter of an hour's tugging his mother objected that the chest had better be left where it was, for in the first place it was too heavy and could never be got out before his father came home, and standing in the middle of the room like that it would only hamper Gregor's movements, while in the second place it was not at all certain that removing the furniture would be doing a service to Gregor. She was inclined to think to the contrary; the sight of the naked walls made her own heart heavy, and why shouldn't Gregor have the same feeling, considering that he had been used to his furniture for so long and might feel forlorn without it. "And doesn't it look," she concluded in a low voice—in fact she had been almost whispering all the time as if to avoid letting Gregor, whose exact whereabouts she did not know, hear even the tones of her voice, for she was convinced that he could not understand her words—"doesn't it look as if we were showing him, by taking away his furniture, that we have given up hope of his ever getting better and are just leaving him coldly to himself? I think it would be best to keep his room exactly as it has always been, so that when he comes back to us he will find everything unchanged and be able all the more easily to forget what has happened in between."

On hearing these words from his mother Gregor realized that the lack of all direct human speech for the past two months together with the monotony of family life must have confused his mind, otherwise he could not account for the fact that he had quite earnestly looked forward to having his room emptied of furnishing. Did he really want his warm room, so comfortably fitted with old family furniture, to be turned into a naked den in which he would certainly be able to crawl unhampered in all directions but at the price of shedding simultaneously all recollection of his human background? He had indeed been so near the brink of forgetfulness that only the voice of his mother, which he had not heard for so long, had drawn him back from it. Nothing should be taken out of his room; everything must stay as it was; he could not dispense with the good influence of the furniture on his state of mind; and even if the furniture did hamper him in his senseless crawling around and around, that was no drawback but a great advantage.

Unfortunately his sister was of the contrary opinion; she had grown accustomed, and not without reason, to consider herself an expert in Gregor's affairs as against her parents, and so her mother's advice was now enough to make her determined on the removal not only of the chest and the writing desk, which had been her first intention, but of all the furniture except the indispensable sofa. This determination was not, of course, merely the outcome of childish recalcitrance and of the self-confidence she had recently developed so unexpectedly and at such cost; she had in fact perceived that Gregor needed a lot of space to crawl about in, while on the other hand he never used the furniture at all, so far as could be seen. Another factor might also have been the enthusiastic temperament of an adolescent girl, which seeks to indulge itself on every opportunity and which now tempted Grete to exaggerate the horror of her brother's circumstances in order that she might do all the more for him. In a room where Gregor lorded it all alone over empty walls no one save herself was likely ever to set foot.

And so she was not to be moved from her resolve by her mother, who seemed moreover to be ill at ease in Gregor's room and therefore unsure of herself, was soon reduced to silence, and helped her daughter as best she could to push the chest outside. Now, Gregor could do without the chest, if need be, but the writing desk he must retain. As soon as the two women had got the chest out of his room, groaning as they pushed it, Gregor stuck his head out from under the sofa to see how he might intervene as kindly and cautiously as possible. But as bad luck would have it, his mother was the first to return, leaving Grete clasping the chest in the room next door where she was trying to shift it all by herself, without of course moving it from the spot. His mother however was not accustomed to the sight of him, it might sicken her and so in alarm Gregor backed quickly to the other end of the sofa, yet could not prevent the sheet from swaying a little in front. That was enough to put her on the alert. She paused, stood still for a moment, and then went back to Grete.

Although Gregor kept reassuring himself that nothing out of the way was happening, but only a few bits of furniture were being changed around, he soon had to admit that all this trotting to and fro of the two women, their little ejaculations, and the scraping of furniture along the floor affected him like a vast disturbance coming from all sides at once, and however much he tucked in his head and legs and cowered to the very floor he was bound to confess that he would not be able to stand it for long. They were clearing his room out; taking away everything he loved; the chest in which he kept his fret saw and other tools was already dragged off; they were now loosening the writing desk which had almost sunk into the floor, the desk at which he had done all his homework when he was at the commercial academy, at the grammar school before that, and, yes, even at the primary school—he had no more time to waste in weighing the good intentions of the two women, whose existence he had by now almost forgotten, for they were so exhausted that they were laboring in silence and nothing could be heard but the heavy scuffling of their feet.

And so he rushed out—the women were just leaning against the writing desk in the next room to give themselves a breather—and four times changed his direction, since he really did not know what to rescue first, then on the wall opposite, which was already otherwise cleared, he was struck by the picture of the lady muffled in so much fur and quickly crawled up to it and pressed himself to the glass, which was a good surface to hold on to and comforted his hot belly. This picture at least, which was entirely hidden beneath him, was going to be removed by nobody. He turned his head toward the door of the living room so as to observe the women when they came back.

They had not allowed themselves much of a rest and were already coming; Grete had twined her arm around her mother and was almost supporting her. "Well, what shall we take now?" said Grete, looking around. Her eyes met Gregor's from the wall. She kept her composure, presumably because of her mother, bent her head down to her mother, to keep her from looking up, and said, although in a fluttering, unpremeditated voice: "Come, hadn't we better go back to the living room for a moment?" Her intentions were clear enough to Gregor, she wanted to bestow her mother in safety and then chase him down from the wall. Well, just let her try it! He clung to his picture and would not give it up. He would rather fly in Grete's face.

But Grete's words had succeeded in disquieting her mother, who took a step to one side, caught sight of the huge brown mass on the flowered wallpaper, and before she was really conscious that what she saw was Gregor, screamed in a loud, hoarse voice: "Oh God, oh God!" fell with outspread arms over the sofa as if giving up, and did not move. "Gregor!" cried his sister, shaking her fist and glaring at him. This was the first time she had directly addressed him since his metamorphosis. She ran into the next room for some aromatic essence with which to rouse her mother from her fainting fit. Gregor wanted to help too—there was still time to rescue the picture—but he was stuck fast to the glass and had to tear himself loose; he then ran after his sister into the next room as if he could advise her, as he used to do; but then had to stand helplessly behind her; she meanwhile searched among various small bottles and when she turned around started in alarm at the sight of him; one bottle fell on the floor and broke; a splinter of glass cut Gregor's face and some kind of corrosive medicine splashed him;

without pausing a moment longer Grete gathered up all the bottles she could carry and ran to her mother with them; she banged the door shut with her foot. Gregor was now cut off from his mother, who was perhaps nearly dying because of him; he dared not open the door for fear of frightening away his sister, who had to stay with her mother; there was nothing he could do but wait; and harassed by self-reproach and worry he began now to crawl to and fro, over everything, walls, furniture, and ceiling, and finally in his despair, when the whole room seemed to be reeling around him, fell down onto the middle of the big table.

A little while elapsed. Gregor was still lying there feebly and all around was quiet, perhaps that was a good omen. Then the doorbell rang. The servant girl was of course locked in her kitchen, and Grete would have to open the door. It was his father. "What's been happening?" were his first words; Grete's face must have told him everything. Grete answered in a muffled voice, apparently hiding her head on his breast: "Mother has been fainting, but she's better now. Gregor's broken loose." "Just what I expected," said his father, "just what I've been telling you, but you women would never listen." It was clear to Gregor that his father had taken the worst interpretation of Grete's all too brief statement and was assuming that Gregor had been guilty of some violent act. Therefore Gregor must now try to propitiate his father, since he had neither time nor means for an explanation. And so he fled to the door of his own room and crouched against it, to let his father see as soon as he came in from the hall that his son had the good intention of getting back into his room immediately and that it was not necessary to drive him there, but that if only the door were opened he would disappear at once.

Yet his father was not in the mood to perceive such fine distinctions. "Ah!" he cried as soon as he appeared, in a tone that sounded at once angry and exultant. Gregor drew his head back from the door and lifted it to look at his father. Truly, this was not the father he had imagined to himself; admittedly he had been too absorbed of late in his new recreation of crawling over the ceiling to take the same interest as before in what was happening elsewhere in the flat, and he ought really to be prepared for some changes. And yet, and yet, could that be his father? The man who used to lie wearily sunk in bed whenever Gregor set out on a business journey; who welcomed him back of an evening lying in a long chair in a dressing gown; who could not really rise to his feet but only lifted his arms in greeting, and on the rare occasions when he did go out with his family, on one or two Sundays a year and on highest holidays, walked between Gregor and his mother, who were slow walkers anyhow, even more slowly than they did, muffled in his old greatcoat, shuffling laboriously forward with the help of his crook-handled stick which he set down most cautiously at every step and, whenever he wanted to say anything, nearly always came to a full stop and gathered his escort around him? Now he was standing there in fine shape; dressed in a smart blue uniform with gold buttons, such as bank messengers wear; his strong double chin bulged over the stiff high collar of his jacket; from under his bushy eyebrows his black eyes darted fresh and penetrating glances; his onetime tangled white hair had been combed flat on either side of a shining and carefully exact parting. He pitched his cap, which bore a gold monogram, probably the badge of some bank, in a wide sweep across the whole room onto a sofa and with the tail-ends of his jacket thrown back, his hands in his trouser pockets, advanced with a grim visage toward Gregor. Likely enough he did not himself know what he meant to do; at any rate he lifted his feet uncommonly high, and Gregor was dumbfounded at the enormous size of his shoe soles. But Gregor could not risk standing up to him, aware as he had been from the very first day of his new life that his father believed only the severest measures suitable for dealing with him. And so he ran before his father, stopping when he stopped and scuttling forward again when his father made any kind of move. In this way they circled the room several times without anything decisive happening, indeed the whole operation did not even look like a pursuit because it was carried out so slowly. And so Gregor did not leave the floor, for he feared that his father might take as a piece of peculiar wickedness any excursion of his over the walls or the ceiling. All the same, he could not stay this course much longer, for while his father took one step he had to carry out a whole series of movements. He was already beginning to feel breathless, just as in his former life his lungs had not been very dependable. As he was staggering along, trying to concentrate his energy on running, hardly keeping his eyes open; in his dazed state never even thinking of any other escape than simply going forward; and having almost forgotten that the walls were free to him, which in this room were well provided with finely carved pieces of furniture full of knobs and crevices—suddenly something lightly flung landed close behind him and rolled before him. It was an apple; a second apple followed immediately; Gregor came to a stop in alarm; there was no point in running on, for his father was determined to bombard him. He had filled his pockets with fruit from the dish on the sideboard and was now shying apple after apple, without taking particularly good aim for the moment. The small red apples rolled about the floor as if magnetized and cannoned into each other. An apple thrown without much force grazed Gregor's back and glanced off harmlessly. But another following immediately landed right on his back and sank in; Gregor wanted to drag himself forward, as if this startling, incredible pain could be left behind him; but he felt as if nailed to the spot and flattened himself out in a complete derangement of all his senses. With his last conscious look he saw the door of his room being torn open and his mother rushing out ahead of his screaming sister, in her underbodice, for her daughter had loosened her clothing to let her breathe more freely and recover from her swoon, he saw his mother rushing toward his father, leaving one after another behind her on the floor her loosened petticoats, stumbling over her petticoats straight to his father and embracing him, in complete union with him—but here Gregor's sight began to fail—with her hands clasped around his father's neck as she begged for her son's life.

Comment

Kafkaesque

A sure sign of an established writer is that his name has been made into an adjective, the meaning of which is clear to all educated people. We speak of Sophoclean irony, Aeschylean tragedy, and Homeric epithets. A person may be a Shakespearean scholar. A passage of stirring, epic poetry or a vision of Hell or Paradise might be described as *Miltonic*. Wry humor like that of George Bernard Shaw is often called *Shavian*.

The characteristic senselessness of the situations in which so many of Franz Kafka's fictional characters find themselves has given rise to the term *Kafkaesque*. In 1947 a writer in the *New Yorker* referred to a "Kafka-esque nightmare of blind alleys." In 1954, Austrian novelist Arthur Koestler, in *Invisible Writing*, mentioned "that weird, Kafka-esque pattern" of the Moscow purges. The hyphen disappeared in the 1958 issue of the *Spectator* that contained the phrase, "An authentic Kafkaesque atmosphere of despair and horror." Mystery writer Nicholas Freeling needed no suffix when he wrote in 1971, "So little of what one did made any sense. One lived in a Kafka world." The earliest such usage recorded in *The Oxford English Dictionary* dates back to 1936, when in a letter Malcolm Lowry wrote of a "Kafka" situation. Other adjectival variations include *Kafkaish*, *Kafkan* and *Kafkian*, but the word most commonly chosen by contemporary writers seeking to describe something horrible, mindless, and beyond the restraints of logic is *Kafkaesque*.

III

The serious injury done to Gregor, which disabled him for more than a month—the apple went on sticking in his body as a visible reminder, since no one ventured to remove it—seemed to have made even his father recollect that Gregor was a member of the family, despite his present unfortunate and repulsive shape, and ought not to be treated as an enemy, that, on the contrary, family duty required the suppression of disgust and the exercise of patience, nothing but patience.

And although his injury had impaired, probably forever, his powers of movement, and for the time being it took him long, long minutes to creep across his room like an old invalid—there was no question now of crawling up the wall—yet in his own opinion he was sufficiently compensated for this worsening of his condition by the fact that toward evening the living-room door, which he used to watch intently for an hour or two beforehand, was always thrown open, so that lying in the darkness of his room, invisible to the family, he could see them all at the lamp-lit table and listen to their talk, by general consent as it were, very different from his earlier eavesdropping.

True, their intercourse lacked the lively character of former times, which he had always called to mind with a certain wistfulness in the small hotel bedrooms where he had been wont to throw himself down, tired out, on damp bedding. They were now mostly very silent. Soon after supper his father would fall asleep in his armchair; his mother and sister would admonish each other to be silent; his mother, bending low over the lamp, stitched at fine sewing for an underwear firm; his sister, who had taken a job as a salesgirl, was learning shorthand and French in the evenings on the chance of bettering herself. Sometimes his father woke up, and as if quite unaware that he had been sleeping said to his mother: "What a lot of sewing you're doing today!" and at once fell asleep again, while the two women exchanged a tired smile.

With a kind of mulishness his father persisted in keeping his uniform on even in the house; his dressing gown hung uselessly on its peg and he slept fully dressed where he sat, as if he were ready for service at any moment and even here only at the beck and call of his superior. As a result, his uniform, which was not brand-new to start with, began to look dirty, despite all the loving care of the mother and sister to keep it clean, and Gregor often spent whole evenings gazing at the many greasy spots on the garment, gleaming with gold buttons always in a high state of polish, in which the old man sat sleeping in extreme discomfort and yet quite peacefully.

As soon as the clock struck ten his mother tried to rouse his father with gentle words and to persuade him after that to get into bed, for sitting there he could not have a proper sleep and that was what he needed most, since he had to go on duty at six. But with the mulishness that had obsessed him since he became a bank messenger he always insisted on staying longer at the table, although he regularly fell asleep again and in the end only with the greatest trouble could be got out of his armchair and into his bed. However insistently Gregor's mother and sister kept urging him with gentle reminders, he would go on slowly shaking his head for a quarter of an hour, keeping his eyes shut, and refuse to get to his feet. The mother plucked at his sleeve, whispering endearments in his ear, the sister left her lessons to come to her mother's help, but Gregor's father was not to be caught. He would only sink down deeper in his chair. Not until the two women hoisted him up by the armpits did he open his eyes and look at them both, one after the other, usually with the remark: "This is a life. This is the peace and quiet of my old age." And leaning on the two of them he would heave himself up, with difficulty, as if he were a great burden to himself, suffer them to lead him as far as the door and then wave them off and go on alone, while the mother abandoned her needlework and the sister her pen in order to run after him and help him farther.

Who could find time, in this overworked and tired-out family, to bother about Gregor more than was absolutely needful? The household was reduced more and more; the servant girl was turned off; a gigantic bony charwoman with white hair flying around her head came in morning and evening to do the rough work; everything else was done by Gregor's mother, as well as great piles of sewing. Even various family ornaments, which his mother and sister used to wear with pride at parties and celebrations, had to be sold, as Gregor discovered of an evening from hearing them all discuss the prices obtained. But what they lamented most was the fact that they could not leave the flat which was much too big for their present circumstances, because they could not think of any way to shift Gregor. Yet Gregor saw well enough that consideration for him was not the main difficulty preventing the removal, for they could have easily shifted him in some suitable box with a few air holes in it; what really kept them from moving into another flat was rather their own complete hopelessness and the belief that they had been singled out for a misfortune such as had never happened to any of their relations or acquaintances. They fulfilled to the uttermost all that the world demands of poor people, the father fetched breakfast for the small clerks in the bank, the mother devoted her energy to making underwear for strangers, the sister trotted to and fro behind the counter at the behest of customers, but more than this they had not the strength to do. And the wound in Gregor's back began to nag at him afresh when his mother and sister, after getting his father into bed, came back again, left their work lying, drew close to each other, and sat cheek by cheek; when his mother, pointing toward his room, said: "Shut that door now, Grete," and he was left again in darkness, while next door the women mingled their tears or perhaps sat dry-eyed staring at the table.

Gregor hardly slept at all by night or by day. He was often haunted by the idea that next time the door opened he would take the family's affairs in hand again just as he used to do; once more, after this long interval, there appeared in his thoughts the figures of the chief and the chief clerk, the commercial travelers and the apprentices, the porter who was so dull-witted, two or three friends in other firms, a chambermaid in one of the rural hotels, a sweet and fleeting memory, a cashier in a milliner's shop, whom he had wooed earnestly but too slowly—they all appeared, together with strangers or people he had quite forgotten, but instead of helping him and his family they were one and all unapproachable and he was glad when they vanished. At other times he would not be in the mood to bother about his family, he was only filled with rage at the way they were neglecting him, and although he had no clear idea of what he might care to eat he would make plans for getting into the larder to take the food that was after all his due, even if he were not hungry. His sister no longer took thought to bring him what might especially please him, but in the morning and at noon before she went to business hurriedly pushed into his room with her foot any food that was available, and in the evening cleared it out again with one sweep of the broom, heedless of whether it had been merely tasted, or—as most frequently happened—left untouched. The cleaning of his room, which she now did always in the evenings, could not have been more hastily done. Streaks of dirt stretched along the walls, here and there lay balls of dust and filth. At first Gregor used to station himself in some particularly filthy corner when his sister arrived, in order to reproach her with it, so to speak. But he could have sat there for weeks without getting her to make any improvement; she could see the dirt as well as he did, but she had simply made up her mind to leave it alone. And yet, with a touchiness that was new to her, which seemed anyhow to have infected the whole family, she jealously guarded her claim to be the soul caretaker of Gregor's room. His mother once subjected his room to a thorough cleaning, which was achieved only by means of several buckets of water—all this dampness of course upset Gregor too and he lay widespread, sulky, and motionless on the sofa—but she was well punished for it. Hardly had his sister noticed the changed aspect of his room that evening than she rushed in high dudgeon into the living room and, despite the imploringly raised hands of her mother, burst into a storm of weeping, while her parents—her father had of course been startled out of his chair—looked on at first in helpless amazement; then they too began to go into action; the father reproached the mother on his right for not having left the cleaning of Gregor's room to his sister; shrieked at the sister on his left that never again was she to be allowed to clean Gregor's room; while the mother tried to pull the father into his bedroom, since he was beyond himself with agitation; the sister, shaken with sobs, then beat upon the table with her small fists; and Gregor hissed loudly with rage because not one of them thought of shutting the door to spare him such a spectacle and so much noise.

Still, even if the sister, exhausted by her daily work, had grown tired of looking after Gregor as she did formerly, there was no need for his mother's intervention or for Gregor's being neglected at all. The charwoman was there. This old widow, whose strong bony frame had enabled her to survive the worst a long life could offer, by no means recoiled from Gregor. Without being in the least curious she had once by chance opened the door of his room and at the sight of Gregor, who, taken by surprise, began to rush to and fro although no one was chasing him, merely stood there with her arms folded. From that time she never failed to open his door a little for a moment, morning and evening, to have a look at him. At first she even used to call him to her, with words which apparently she took to be friendly, such as: "Come along, then, you old dung beetle!" or "Look at the old dung beetle, then!" To such allocutions Gregor made no answer, but stayed motionless where he was, as if the door had never been opened. Instead of being allowed to disturb him so senselessly whenever the whim took her, she should rather have been ordered to clean out his room daily, that charwoman! Once, early in the morning—heavy rain was lashing on the windowpanes, perhaps a sign that spring was on the way—Gregor was so exasperated when she began addressing him again that he ran at her, as if to attack her, although slowly and feebly enough. But the charwoman instead of showing fright merely lifted high a chair that happened to be beside the door, and as she stood there with her mouth wide open it was clear that she meant to shut it only when she brought the chair down on Gregor's back. "So you're not coming any nearer?" she asked, as Gregor turned away again,

and quietly put the chair back into the corner.

Gregor was now eating hardly anything. Only when he happened to pass the food laid out for him did he take a bit of something in his mouth as a pastime, kept it there for an hour at a time, and usually spat it out again. At first he thought it was chagrin over the state of his room that prevented him from eating, yet he soon got used to the various changes in his room. It had become a habit in the family to push into his room things there was no room for elsewhere, and there were plenty of these now, since one of the rooms had been let to three lodgers. These serious gentlemen—all three of them with full beards, as Gregor once observed through a crack in the door—had a passion for order, not only in their own room but, since they were now members of the household, in all its arrangements, especially in the kitchen. Superfluous, not to say dirty, objects they could not bear. Besides, they had brought with them most of the furnishings they needed. For this reason many things could be dispensed with that it was no use trying to sell but that should not be thrown away either. All of them found their way into Gregor's room. The ash can likewise and the kitchen garbage can. Anything that was not needed for the moment was simply flung into Gregor's room by the charwoman, who did everything in a hurry; fortunately Gregor usually saw only the object, whatever it was, and the hand that held it. Perhaps she intended to take the things away again as time and opportunity offered, or to collect them until she could throw them all out in a heap, but in fact they just lay wherever she happened to throw them, except when Gregor pushed his way through the junk heap and shifted it somewhat, at first out of necessity, because he had not room enough to crawl, but later with increasing enjoyment, although after such excursions, being sad and weary to death, he would lie motionless for hours. And since the lodgers often ate their supper at home in the common living room, the living-room door stayed shut many an evening, yet Gregor reconciled himself quite easily to the shutting of the door, for often enough on evenings when it was opened he had disregarded it entirely and lain in the darkest corner of his room, quite unnoticed by the family. But on one occasion the charwoman left the door open a little and it stayed ajar even when the lodgers came in for supper and the lamp was lit. They set themselves at the top end of the table where formerly Gregor and his father and mother had eaten their meals, unfolded their napkins, and took knife and fork in hand. At once his mother appeared in the other doorway with a dish of meat and close behind her his sister with a dish of potatoes piled high. The food steamed with a thick vapor. The lodgers bent over the food set before them as if to scrutinize it before eating, in fact the man in the middle, who seemed to pass for an authority with the other two, cut a piece of meat as it lay on the dish, obviously to discover if it were tender or should be sent back to the kitchen. He showed satisfaction, and Gregor's mother and sister, who had been watching anxiously, breathed freely and began to smile.

The family itself took its meals in the kitchen. Nonetheless, Gregor's father came into the living room before going into the kitchen and with one prolonged bow, cap in hand, made a round of the table. The lodgers all stood up and murmured something in their beards. When they were alone again they ate their food in almost complete silence. It seemed remarkable to Gregor that among the various noises coming from the table he could always distinguish the sound of their masticating teeth, as if this were a sign to Gregor that one needed teeth in order to eat, and that with toothless jaws even of the finest make one could do nothing. "I'm hungry enough," said Gregor sadly to himself, "but not for that kind of food. How these lodgers are stuffing themselves, and here am I dying of starvation."

On that very evening—during the whole of his time there Gregor could not remember ever having heard the violin—the sound of violin-playing came from the kitchen. The lodgers had already finished their supper, the one in the middle had brought out a newspaper and given the other two a page apiece, and now they were leaning back at ease reading and smoking. When the violin began to play they pricked up their ears, got to their feet, and went on tiptoe to the hall door where they stood huddled together. Their movements must have been heard in the kitchen, for Gregor's father called out: "Is the violin-playing disturbing you, gentlemen? It can be stopped at once." "On the contrary," said the middle lodger, "could not Fräulein Samsa come and play in this room, beside us, where it is much more convenient and comfortable?" "Oh certainly," cried Gregor's father, as if he were the violin-player. The lodgers came back into the living room and waited. Presently Gregor's father arrived with the music stand, his mother carrying the music and his sister with the violin. His sister quietly made everything ready to start playing; his parents, who had never let rooms before and so had an exaggerated idea of the courtesy due to lodgers, did not venture to sit down on their own chairs; his father leaned against the door, the right hand thrust between two buttons of his livery coat, which was formally buttoned up; but his mother was offered a chair by one of the lodgers and, since she left the chair just where he had happened to put it, sat down in a corner to one side.

Gregor's sister began to play; the father and mother, from either side, intently watched the movements of her hands. Gregor, attracted by the playing, ventured to move forward a little until his head was actually inside the living room. He felt hardly any surprise at his growing lack of consideration for the others; there had been a time when he prided himself on being considerate. And yet just on this occasion he had more reason than ever to hide himself, since, owing to the amount of dust that lay thick in his room and rose into the air at the slightest movement, he too was covered with dust; fluff and hair and remnants of food trailed with him, caught on his back and along his sides; his indifference to everything was much too great for him to turn on his back and scrape himself clean on the carpet, as once he had done several times a day. And in spite of his condition, no shame deterred him from advancing a little over the spotless floor of the living room.

To be sure, no one was aware of him. The family was entirely absorbed in the violin-playing;

the lodgers, however, who first of all had stationed themselves, hands in pockets, much too close behind the music stand so that they could all have read the music, which must have bothered his sister, had soon retreated to the window, half whispering with downbent heads, and stayed there while his father turned an anxious eye on them. Indeed, they were making it more than obvious that they had been disappointed in their expectation of hearing good or enjoyable violin-playing, that they had had more than enough of the performance and only out of courtesy suffered a continued disturbance of their peace. From the way they all kept blowing the smoke of their cigars high in the air through nose and mouth one could divine their irritation. And yet Gregor's sister was playing so beautifully. Her face leaned sideways, intently and sadly her eyes followed the notes of music. Gregor crawled a little farther forward and lowered his head to the ground so that it might be possible for his eyes to meet hers. Was he an animal, that music had such an effect upon him? He felt as if the way were opening before him to the unknown nourishment he craved. He was determined to push forward till he reached his sister, to pull at her skirt and so let her know that she was to come into his room with her violin, for no one here appreciated her playing as he would appreciate it. He would never let her out of his room, at least, not so long as he lived; his frightful appearance would become, for the first time, useful to him; he would watch all the doors of his room at once and spit at intruders; but his sister should need no constraint, she should stay with him of her own free will; she should sit beside him on the sofa, bend down her ear to him, and hear him confide that he had had the firm intention of sending her to the Conservatorium, and that, but for his mishap, last Christmas—surely Christmas was long past?—he would have announced it to everybody without allowing a single objection. After this confession his sister would be so touched that she would burst into tears, and Gregor would then raise himself to her shoulder and kiss her on the neck, which, now that she went to business, she kept free of any ribbon or collar.

"Mr. Samsa!" cried the middle lodger to Gregor's father, and pointed, without wasting any more words, at Gregor, now working himself slowly forward. The violin fell silent, the middle lodger first smiled to his friends with a shake of the head and then looked at Gregor again. Instead of driving Gregor out, his father seemed to think it more needful to begin by soothing down the lodgers, although they were not at all agitated and apparently found Gregor more entertaining than the violin-playing. He hurried toward them and, spreading out his arms, tried to urge them back into their own room and at the same time to block their view of Gregor. They now began to be really a little angry, one could not tell whether because of the old man's behavior or because it had just dawned on them that all unwittingly they had such a neighbor as Gregor next door. They demanded explanations of his father, they waved their arms like him, tugged uneasily at their beards, and only with reluctance backed toward their room. Meanwhile Gregor's sister, who stood there as if lost when her playing was so abruptly broken off, came to life again, pulled herself together all at once after standing for a while holding violin and bow in nervelessly hanging hands and staring at her music, pushed her violin into the lap of her mother, who was still sitting in her chair fighting asthmatically for breath, and ran into the lodgers' room to which they were now being shepherded by her father rather more quickly than before. One could see the pillows and blankets on the beds flying under her accustomed fingers and being laid in order. Before the lodgers had actually reached their room she had finished making the beds and slipped out.

The old man seemed once more to be so possessed by his mulish self-assertiveness that he was forgetting all the respect he should show to his lodgers. He kept driving them on and driving them on until in the very door of the bedroom the middle lodger stamped his foot loudly on the floor and so brought him to a halt. "I beg to announce," said the lodger, lifting one hand and looking also at Gregor's mother and sister, "that because of the disgusting conditions prevailing in this household and family"—here he spat on the floor with emphatic brevity—"I give you notice on the spot. Naturally I won't pay you a penny for the days I have lived here, on the contrary I shall consider bringing an action for damages against you, based on claims—believe me—that will be easily susceptible of proof." He ceased and stared straight in front of him, as if he expected something. In fact his two friends at once rushed into the breach with these words: "And we too give notice on the spot." On that he seized the door handle and shut the door with a slam.

Gregor's father, groping with his hands, staggered forward and fell into his chair; it looked as if he were stretching himself there for his ordinary evening nap, but the marked jerkings of his head, which were as if uncontrollable, showed that he was far from asleep. Gregor had simply stayed quietly all the time on the spot where the lodgers had espied him. Disappointment at the failure of his plan, perhaps also the weakness arising from extreme hunger, made it impossible for him to move. He feared, with a fair degree of certainty, that at any moment the general tension would discharge itself in a combined attack upon him, and he lay waiting. He did not react even to the noise made by the violin as it fell off his mother's lap from under her trembling fingers and gave out a resonant note.

"My dear parents," said his sister, slapping her hand on the table by way of introduction, "things can't go on like this. Perhaps you don't realize that, but I do. I won't utter my brother's name in the presence of this creature, and so all I say is: we must try to get rid of it. We've tried to look after it and to put up with it as far as is humanly possible, and I don't think anyone could reproach us in the slightest."

"She is more than right," said Gregor's father to himself. His mother, who was still choking for lack of breath, began to cough hollowly into her hand with a wild look in her eyes.

His sister rushed over to her and held her forehead. His father's thoughts seemed to have lost their vagueness at Grete's words, he sat more upright, fingering his service cap that lay among the plates still lying on the table from the lodgers' supper, and from time to time looked at the still form of Gregor.

"We must try to get rid of it," his sister now said explicitly to her father, since her mother was coughing too much to hear a word, "it will be the death of both of you, I can see that coming. When one has to work as hard as we do, all of us, one can't stand this continual torment at home on top of it. At least I can't stand it any longer." And she burst into such a passion of sobbing that her tears dropped on her mother's face, where she wiped them off mechanically.

"My dear," said the old man sympathetically, and with evident understanding, "but what can we do?"

Gregor's sister merely shrugged her shoulders to indicate the feeling of helplessness that had now overmastered her during her weeping fit, in contrast to her former confidence.

"If he could understand us," said her father, half questioningly; Grete, still sobbing, vehemently waved a hand to show how unthinkable that was.

"If he could understand us," repeated the old man, shutting his eyes to consider his daughter's conviction that understanding was impossible, "then perhaps we might come to some agreement with him. But as it is—"

"He must go," cried Gregor's sister, "that's the only solution, Father. You must just try to get rid of the idea that this is Gregor. The fact that we've believed it for so long is the root of all our trouble. But how can it be Gregor? If this were Gregor, he would have realized long ago that human beings can't live with such a creature, and he'd have gone away on his own accord. Then we wouldn't have any brother, but we'd be able to go on living and keep his memory in honor. As it is, this creature persecutes us, drives away our lodgers, obviously wants the whole apartment to himself, and would have us all sleep in the gutter. Just look, Father," she shrieked all at once, "he's at it again!" And in an access of panic that was quite incomprehensible to Gregor she even quitted her mother, literally thrusting the chair from her as if she would rather sacrifice her mother than stay so near to Gregor, and rushed behind her father, who also rose up, being simply upset by her agitation, and half spread his arms out as if to protect her.

Yet Gregor had not the slightest intention of frightening anyone, far less his sister. He had only begun to turn around in order to crawl back to his room, but it was certainly a startling operation to watch, since because of his disabled condition he could not execute the difficult turning movements except by lifting his head and then bracing it against the floor over and over again. He paused and looked around. His good intentions seemed to have been recognized; the alarm had only been momentary. Now they were all watching him in melancholy silence. His mother lay in her chair, her legs stiffly outstretched and pressed together, her eyes almost closing for sheer weariness; his father and his sister were sitting beside each other, his sister's arm around the old man's neck.

Perhaps I can go on turning around now, thought Gregor, and began his labors again. He could not stop himself from panting with the effort, and had to pause now and then to take breath. Nor did anyone harass him, he was left entirely to himself. When he had completed the turn-around he began at once to crawl straight back. He was amazed at the distance separating him from his room and could not understand how in his weak state he had managed to accomplish the same journey so recently, almost without remarking it. Intent on crawling as fast as possible, he barely noticed that not a single word, not an ejaculation from his family, interfered with his progress. Only when he was already in the doorway did he turn his head around, not completely, for his neck muscles were getting stiff, but enough to see that nothing had changed behind him except that his sister had risen to her feet. His last glance fell on his mother, who was not quite overcome by sleep.

Hardly was he well inside his room when the door was hastily pushed shut, bolted, and locked. The sudden noise in his rear startled him so much that his little legs gave beneath him. It was his sister who had shown such haste. She had been stand-ing ready waiting and had made a light spring forward, Gregor had not even heard her coming, and she cried "At last!" to her parents as she turned the key in the lock.

"And what now?" said Gregor to himself, looking around in the darkness. Soon he made the discovery that he was now unable to stir a limb. This did not surprise him, rather it seemed unnatural that he should ever actually have been able to move on these feeble little legs. Otherwise he felt relatively comfortable. True, his whole body was aching, but it seemed that the pain was gradually growing less and would finally pass away. The rotting apple in his back and the inflamed area around it, all covered with soft dust, already hardly troubled him. He thought of his family with tenderness and love. The decision that he must disappear was one that he held to even more strongly than his sister, if that were possible. In this state of vacant and peaceful meditation he remained until the tower clock struck three in the morning. The first broadening of light in the world outside the window entered his consciousness once more. Then his head sank to the floor of its own accord and from his nostrils came the last faint flicker of his breath.

When the charwoman arrived early in the morning—what between her strength and her impatience she slammed all the doors so loudly, never mind how often she had been begged not to do so, that no one in the whole apartment could enjoy any quiet sleep after her arrival—she noticed nothing unusual as she took her customary peep into Gregor's room. She thought he was lying motionless on purpose, pretending to be in the sulks; she credited him with every kind of intelligence. Since she happened to have the long-handled broom in her hand she tried to tickle him up with it from the doorway. When that too produced no reaction she felt provoked and poked at him a little harder, and only when she had pushed him along the floor without meeting any resistance was her attention aroused. It did not take her long to establish the truth of the matter, and her eyes widened, she let out a whistle, yet did not waste much time over it but tore open the door of the Samsas' bedroom and yelled into the darkness at the top of her voice: "Just look at this, it's dead; it's lying here dead and done for!"

Mr. and Mrs. Samsa started up in their double bed and before they realized the nature of the charwoman's announcement had some difficulty in overcoming the shock of it. But then they got out of bed quickly, one on either side, Mr. Samsa throwing a blanket over his shoulders, Mrs. Samsa in nothing but her nightgown; in this array they entered Gregor's room. Meanwhile the door of the living room opened, too, where Grete had been sleeping since the advent of the lodgers; she was completely dressed as if she had not been to bed, which seemed to be confirmed also by the paleness of her face. "Dead?" said Mrs. Samsa, looking questioningly at the charwoman, although she would have investigated for herself, and the fact was obvious enough without investigation. "I should say so," said the charwoman, proving her words by pushing Gregor's corpse a long way to one side with her broomstick. Mrs. Samsa made a movement as if to stop her, but checked it. "Well," said Mr. Samsa, "now thanks be to God." He crossed himself, and the three women followed his example. Grete, whose eyes never left the corpse, said: "Just see how thin he was. It's such a long time since he's eaten anything. The food came out again just as it went in." Indeed, Gregor's body was completely flat and dry, as could only now be seen when it was no longer supported by the legs and nothing prevented one from looking closely at it.

"Come in beside us, Grete, for a little while," said Mrs. Samsa with a tremulous smile, and Grete, not without looking back at the corpse, followed her parents into their bedroom. The charwoman shut the door and opened the window wide. Although it was so early in the morning a certain softness was perceptible in the fresh air. After all, it was already the end of March.

The three lodgers emerged from their room and were surprised to see no breakfast; they had been forgotten. "Where's our breakfast?" said the middle lodger peevishly to the charwoman. But she put her finger to her lips and hastily, without a word, indicated by gestures that they should go into Gregor's room. They did so and stood, their hands in the pockets of their somewhat shabby coats, around Gregor's corpse in the room where it was now fully light.

At that the door of the Samsas' bedroom opened and Mr. Samsa appeared in his uniform, his wife on one arm, his daughter on the other. They all looked a little as if they had been crying; from time to time Grete hid her face on her father's arm.

"Leave my house at once!" said Mr. Samsa, and pointed to the door without disengaging himself from the women. "What do you mean by that?" said the middle lodger, taken somewhat aback, with a feeble smile. The two others put their hands behind them and kept rubbing them together, as if in gleeful expectation of a fine set-to in which they were bound to come off the winners. "I mean just what I say," answered Mr. Samsa, and advanced in a straight line with his two companions toward the lodger. He stood his ground at first quietly, looking at the floor as if his thoughts were taking a new pattern in his head. "Then let us go, by all means," he said, and looked up at Mr. Samsa as if in a sudden access of humility he were expecting some renewed sanction for this decision. Mr. Samsa merely nodded briefly once or twice with meaning eyes. Upon that the lodger really did go with long strides into the hall, his two friends had been listening and had quite stopped rubbing their hands for some moments and now went scuttling after him as if afraid that Mr. Samsa might get into the hall before them and cut them off from their leader. In the hall they all three took their hats from the rack, their sticks from the umbrella stand, bowed in silence, and quitted the apartment. With a suspiciousness that proved quite unfounded Mr. Samsa and the two women followed them out to the landing; leaning over the banister they watched the three figures slowly but surely going down the long stairs, vanishing from sight at a certain turn of the staircase on every floor and coming into view again after a moment or so; the more they dwindled, the more the Samsa family's interest in them dwindled, and when a butcher's boy met them and passed them on the stairs coming up proudly with a tray on his head, Mr. Samsa and the two women soon left the landing and as if a burden had been lifted from them went back into their apartment.

They decided to spend this day in resting and going for a stroll; they had not only deserved such a respite from work, but absolutely needed it. And so they sat down at the table and wrote three notes of excuse, Mr. Samsa to his board of management, Mrs. Samsa to her employer, and Grete to the head of her firm. While they were writing, the charwoman came in to say that she was going now, since her morning's work was finished. At first they only nodded without looking up, but as she kept hovering there they eyed her irritably. "Well?" said Mr. Samsa. The charwoman stood grinning in the doorway as if she had good news to impart to the family but meant not to say a word unless properly questioned. The small ostrich feather standing upright on her hat, which had annoyed Mr. Samsa ever since she was engaged, was waving gaily in all directions. "Well, what is it then?" asked Mrs. Samsa, who obtained more respect from the charwoman than the others. "Oh," said the charwoman, giggling so amiably that she could not at once continue, "just this, you don't need to bother about how to get rid of the thing next door. It's been seen to already." Mrs. Samsa and Grete bent over their letters again, as if preoccupied; Mr. Samsa, who perceived that she was eager to begin describing it all in detail, stopped her with a decisive hand. But since she was not allowed to tell her story, she remembered the great hurry she was in, obviously deeply huffed: "Bye, everybody," she said, whirling off violently, and departed with a frightful slamming of doors.

"She'll be given notice tonight," said Mr. Samsa, but neither from his wife nor his daughter did he get any answer, for the charwoman seemed to have shattered again the composure they had barely achieved. They rose, went to the window and stayed there, clasping each other tight. Mr. Samsa turned in his chair to look at them and quietly observed them for a little. Then he called out: "Come along, now, do. Let bygones be bygones. And you might have some consideration for me." The two of them complied at once, hastened to him, caressed him, and quickly finished their letters.

Then they all three left the apartment together, which was more than they had done for months, and went by tram into the open country outside the town. The tram, in which they were the only passengers, was filled with warm sunshine. Leaning comfortably back in their seats they canvassed their prospects for the future, and it appeared on closer inspection that these were not at all bad, for the jobs they had got, which so far they had never really discussed with each other, were all three admirable and likely to lead to better things later on. The greatest immediate improvement in their condition would of course arise from moving to another house; they wanted to take a smaller and cheaper but also better situated and more easily run apartment than the one they had, which Gregor had selected. While they were thus conversing, it struck both Mr. and Mrs. Samsa, almost at the same moment, as they became aware of their daughter's increasing vivacity, that in spite of all the sorrow of recent times, which had made her cheeks pale, she had bloomed into a pretty girl with a good figure. They grew quieter and half unconsciously exchanged glances of complete agreement, having come to the conclusion that it would soon be time to find a good husband for her. And it was like a confirmation of their new dreams and excellent intentions that at the end of their journey their daughter sprang to her feet first and stretched her young body.

1915

THINK AND DISCUSS
Understanding
1. What transformation has taken place in Gregor as the story opens?
2. Describe Gregor's job.
3. How well is Gregor able to communicate verbally in his new condition?
4. What are the reactions of Gregor's mother and father to Gregor's appearance in Section One of the story?

Analyzing
5. Describe Gregor's relationship with his chief, or boss. (Don't confuse the chief with the chief clerk.) Why doesn't Gregor quit his job? Describe Gregor's reaction to his predicament.
6. Is it possible that Gregor is happier as an insect than he was as a person? Explain.

Extending
7. Review the material in the biographical sketch of Kafka on page 784. To what extent does Kafka seem to be portraying his own situation in this story? For instance, how is the name Samsa similar to Kafka?
8. What elements of humor do you find in the story, if any?
9. Writers of the Modernist period are similar in that they show the influences of then recent scientific studies and philosophies. How does this story support Darwin's doctrine of the survival of the fittest? Is the ending happy or sad?

VOCABULARY
Dictionary/Glossary
Read the appropriate Glossary entry in order to answer the following questions. Be prepared to pronounce each of the italicized words.

1. What is the plural form of *metamorphosis?*
2. Write a word that rhymes with the word *row*, meaning "a noisy quarrel or disturbance."
3. What Glossary entry includes the word *dunning?* What does the entry word mean?
4. What is the common American spelling of the word *draught?*
5. A person who uses a *pretext* may be accused of "weaving a story" to use as a "cover-up." How does the etymology of *pretext* support this figurative accusation?
6. What does a *malingerer* do?
7. What are the meanings of *ardor* and *ardere*, the Latin verb from which *ardor* is derived?
8. How long is a *fortnight?* Why can we say the word contains a number?

ENRICHMENT
Imagining Gregor's Metamorphosis
When Kafka learned that his publisher planned a cover illustration for "The Metamorphosis," he wrote "The insect itself must not be illustrated by a drawing. It cannot be shown at all, not even from a distance." He apparently wanted each reader to imagine Gregor's transformation unassisted. Using any medium you prefer, create your own image of the creature into which Gregor changes.

BIOGRAPHY

Isak Dinesen
1885–1962

"I belong to an ancient, idle, wild, and useless tribe, perhaps I am even one of the last members of it, who, for many thousands of years, in all countries and parts of the world, has, now and again, stayed for a time among the hard-working honest people in real life, and sometimes has thus been fortunate enough to create another sort of reality for them, which in some way or another, has satisfied them. I am a storyteller." This self-description by Isak Dinesen is true only up to a point. A storyteller she most definitely is, but she is neither idle nor useless nor a stranger to hard work, as any reader of her autobiographical *Out of Africa* (or viewer of the movie based on that book) will attest.

Born Karen Blixen in Denmark, she studied painting in Copenhagen, Paris, and Rome after taking a degree in English at Oxford University. She married a cousin, Baron Bror Blixen, and lived from 1914 to 1931 on a coffee plantation in British East Africa, now Kenya. *Out of Africa* was published simultaneously (under her pen name, Isak Dinesen) in Danish and English in 1937. The book, telling of her life on the African farm, her affection for the natives, and her relationship with an English airman, Denys Finch-Hatton, made her an international literary success. Her other important books are *Seven Gothic Tales* (1934) and *Winter's Tales* (1942) in which she displays her delicate subtlety in characterization and description and a distinctive mood of mystery and mysticism.

During World War II, after the coffee plantation had failed and Dinesen had returned to Denmark, she helped many Jews escape the Nazis by opening the family home as a runaway station. "There were Jews in the kitchen and Nazis in the garden. The hair-raising problem was to keep them from meeting."

Strikingly beautiful as a young woman, Dinesen had to undergo several spinal operations and spent many of her last years in pain, unable to eat properly. Though extremely fragile, her weight never exceeding eighty-five pounds, her lined face became more fascinating than the beautiful face of her girlhood and she was a popular subject for the most notable photographers and artists.

from Out of Africa

Isak Dinesen

o Denys Finch-Hatton I owe what was, I think, the greatest, the most transporting pleasure of my life on the farm: I flew with him over Africa. There, where there are few or no roads and where you can land on the plains, flying becomes a thing of real and vital importance in your life, it opens up a world. Denys had brought out his Moth machine; it could land on my plain on the farm only a few minutes from the house, and we were up nearly every day.

You have tremendous views as you get up above the African highlands, surprising combinations and changes of light and coloring, the rainbow on the green sunlit land, the gigantic upright clouds and big wild black storms, all swing round you in a race and a dance. The lashing hard showers of rain whiten the air askance. The language is short of words for the experiences of flying, and will have to invent new words with time. When you have flown over the Rift Valley and the volcanoes of Suswa and Longonot, you have travelled far and have been to the lands on the other side of the moon. You may at other times fly low enough to see the animals on the plains and to feel towards them as God did when he had just created them, and before he commissioned Adam to give them names.

But it is not the visions but the activity which makes you happy, and the joy and glory of the flyer is the flight itself. It is a sad hardship and slavery to people who live in towns, that in all their movements they know of one dimension only; they walk along the line as if they were led on a string. The transition from the line to the plane into the two dimensions, when you wander across a field or through a wood, is a splendid liberation to the slaves, like the French Revolution. But in the air you are taken into the full freedom of the three dimensions; after long ages of exile and dreams the homesick heart throws itself into the arms of space. The laws of gravitation and time,

> ". . . in life's green grove,
> Sport like tame beasts, none knew how
> gentle they could be!"

Every time that I have gone up in an airplane and looking down have realized that I was free of the ground, I have had the consciousness of a great new discovery. "I see:" I have thought, "This was the idea. And now I understand everything."

One day Denys and I flew to Lake Natron, ninety miles southeast of the farm, and more than four thousand feet lower, two thousand feet above sea level. Lake Natron is the place from where they take soda. The bottom of the lake and the shores are like some sort of whitish concrete, with a strong, sour, and salt smell.

The sky was blue, but as we flew from the plains in over the stony and bare lower country, all color seemed to be scorched out of it. The whole landscape below us looked like delicately marked tortoise-shell. Suddenly, in the midst of it was the lake. The white bottom, shining through the water, gives it, when seen from the air, a striking, an unbelievable azure-color, so clear that for a moment you shut your eyes at it; the expanse of water lies in the bleak tawny land like a big bright aquamarine. We had been flying high, now we went down, and as we sank our own shade, dark-blue, floated under us upon the light-blue lake. Here live thousands of flamingoes, although I do not know how they exist in the brackish water—surely there are no fish here. At our approach they spread out in large circles and fans, like the rays of a setting sun, like an artful Chinese pattern on

Aerial photograph of
Dinesen's farm in Kenya

silk or porcelain, forming itself and changing, as we looked at it.

We landed on the white shore, that was white-hot as an oven, and lunched there, taking shelter against the sun under the wing of the airplane. If you stretched out your hand from the shade, the sun was so hot that it hurt you. Our bottles of beer when they first arrived with us, straight out of the ether, were pleasantly cold, but before we had finished them, in a quarter of an hour, they became as hot as a cup of tea.

While we were lunching, a party of Masai warriors appeared on the horizon, and approached quickly. They must have spied the airplane landing from a distance, and resolved to have a close look at it, and a walk of any length, even in a country like this, means nothing to a Masai. They came along, the one in front of the other, naked, tall and narrow, their weapons glinting; dark like peat on the yellow grey sand. At the feet of each of them lay and marched a small pool of shadow, these were, besides our own, the only shadows in the country as far as the eye reached. When they came up to us they fell in line, there were five of

them. They stuck their heads together and began to talk to one another about the airplane and us. A generation ago they would have been fatal to us to meet. After a time one of them advanced and spoke to us. As they could only speak Masai and we understood but little of the language, the conversation soon slackened, he stepped back to his fellows and a few minutes later they all turned their back upon us, and walked away, in single file, with the wide white burning salt-plain before them.

"Would you care," said Denys, "to fly to Naivasha? But the country lying between is very rough, we could not possibly land anywhere on the way. So we shall have to go up high and keep up at twelve thousand feet."

The flight from Lake Natron to Naivasha was *Das Ding an sich*.[1] We took a bee-line, and kept

---

1. ***Das Ding an sich.*** In his *Critique of Pure Reason*, German philosopher Immanuel Kant maintained that all sense experience must be inherently rational, and therefore, that rational knowledge about experience is possible. But although reason can understand a thing considered as an object of experience, reason cannot understand "the thing-in-itself" (*Ding an sich*).

at twelve thousand feet all the way, which is so high that there is nothing to look down for. At Lake Natron I had taken off my lambskin-lined cap, now up here the air squeezed my forehead, as cold as iced water; all my hair flew backwards as if my head was being pulled off. This path, in fact, was the same as was, in the opposite direction, every evening taken by the Roc,[2] when, with an elephant for her young in each talon, she swished from Uganda home to Arabia. Where you are sitting in front of your pilot, with nothing but space before you, you feel that he is carrying you upon the outstretched palms of his hands, as the Djinn carried Prince Ali[3] through the air, and that the wings that bear you onward are his. We landed at the farm of our friends at Naivasha; the mad diminutive houses, and the very small trees surrounding them, all threw themselves flat upon their backs as they saw us descending.

When Denys and I had not time for long journeys we went out for a short flight over the Ngong Hills, generally about sunset. These hills, which are amongst the most beautiful in the world, are perhaps at their loveliest seen from the air, when the ridges, bare towards the four peaks, mount, and run side by side with the airplane, or suddenly sink down and flatten out into a small lawn.

Here in the hills there were buffaloes. I had even, in my very young days—when I could not live till I had killed a specimen of each kind of African game—shot a bull out here. Later on, when I was not so keen to shoot as to watch the wild animals, I had been out to see them again. I had camped in the hills by a spring half way to the top, bringing my servants, tents, and provisions with me, and Farah[4] and I had been up in the dark, ice cold mornings to creep and crawl through bush and long grass, in the hope of catching a glimpse of the herd; but twice I had had to go back without success. That the herd lived there, neighbors of mine to the West, was still a value in the life on the farm, but they were serious-minded, self-sufficient neighbors, the old nobility of the hills, now somehow reduced; they did not receive much.

But one afternoon as I was having tea with some friends of mine from up-country, outside the house, Denys came flying from Nairobi and went over our heads out westwards; a little while after he turned and came back and landed on the farm. Lady Delamere and I drove down to the plain to fetch him up, but he would not get out of his airplane.

"The buffalo are out feeding in the hills," he said, "come out and have a look at them."

"I cannot come," I said, "I have got a tea-party up at the house."

"But we will go and see them and be back in a quarter of an hour," said he.

This sounded to me like the propositions which people make to you in a dream. Lady Delamere would not fly, so I went up with him. We flew in the sun, but the hillside lay in a transparent brown shade, which soon we got into. It did not take us long to spy the buffalo from the air. Upon one of the long rounded green ridges which run, like folds of a cloth gathered together at each peak, down the side of the Ngong mountain, a herd of twenty-seven buffalo were grazing. First we saw them a long way below us, like mice moving gently on a floor, but we dived down, circling over and along their ridge, a hundred and fifty feet above them and well within shooting distance; we counted them as they peacefully blended and separated. There was one very old big black bull in the herd, one or two younger bulls, and a number of calves. The open stretch of sward upon which they walked was closed in by bush; had a stranger approached on the ground they would have heard or scented him at once, but they were not prepared for advance from the air. We had to keep moving above them all the time. They heard the noise of our machine and stopped grazing, but they did not seem to have it in them to look up. In the end they realized that something very strange was

---

2. *the Roc*, an enormous bird in the *Arabian Nights*, notably in the story of "Sinbad the Sailor."
3. *the Djinn . . . Ali.* The Djinn (Jinn or Genie) is a supernatural power who aids Prince Ali in "Ali Baba and the Forty Thieves" from the *Arabian Nights*.
4. *Farah.* Farah Aden was a Somali tribesman who served Dinesen all the time she was in Africa.

about; the old bull first walked out in front of the herd, raising his hundredweight horns, braving the unseen enemy, his four feet planted on the ground—suddenly he began to trot down the ridge and after a moment he broke into a canter. The whole clan now followed him, stampeding head-long down, and as they switched and plunged into the bush, dust and loose stones rose in their wake. In the thicket they stopped and kept close togeth-er, it looked as if a small glade in the hill had been paved with dark grey stones. Here they believed themselves to be covered to the view, and so they were to anything moving along the ground, but they could not hide themselves from the eyes of the bird of the air. We flew up and away. It was like having been taken into the heart of the Ngong Hills by a secret unknown road.

When I came back to my tea-party, the teapot on the stone table was still so hot that I burned my fingers on it. The Prophet[5] had the same experi-ence when he upset a jug of water, and the Arch-angel Gabriel took him, and flew with him through the seven heavens, and when he returned, the water had not yet run out of the jug.

In the Ngong Hills there also lived a pair of eagles. Denys in the afternoons used to say: "Let us go and visit the eagles." I have once seen one of them sitting on a stone near the top of the moun-tain, and getting up from it, but otherwise they spent their life up in the air. Many times we have chased one of these eagles, careening and throwing ourselves on to one wing and then to the other, and I believe that the sharp-sighted bird played with us. Once, when we were running side by side, Denys stopped his engine in mid air, and as he did so I heard the eagle screech.

The Natives liked the airplane, and for a time it was the fashion on the farm to portray her, so that I would find sheets of paper in the kitchen, or the kitchen wall itself, covered with drawings of her, with the letters ABAK carefully copied out. But they did not really take any interest in her or in our flying.

Natives dislike speed, as we dislike noise, it is to them, at the best, hard to bear. They are also on friendly terms with time, and the plan of beguiling or killing it does not come into their heads. In fact the more time you can give them, the happier they are, and if you commission a Kikuyu to hold your horse while you make a visit, you can see by his face that he hopes you will be a long, long time about it. He does not try to pass the time then, but sits down and lives.

Neither do the natives have much sympathy with any kind of machinery or mechanics. A group of the young generation have been carried away by the enthusiasm of the European for the motor-car, but an old Kikuyu said to me of them that they would die young, and it is likely that he was right, for renegades come of a weak line of the nation. Amongst the inventions of civiliza-tion which the natives admire and appreciate are matches, a bicycle, and a rifle, still they will drop these the moment there is any talk of a cow.

Frank Greswolde-Williams, of the Kedong Val-ley, took a Masai with him to England as a sice,[6] and told me that a week after his arrival he rode his horses in Hyde Park as if he had been born in London. I asked this man when he came back to Africa what he found very good in England. He thought my question over with a grave face and after a long time courteously said that the white men had got very fine bridges.

I have never seen an old native who, for things which moved by themselves without apparent interference by man or by the forces of nature, expressed anything but distrust and a certain feel-ing of shame. The human mind turns away its eye from witchcraft as from something unseemly. It may be forced to take an interest in the effects of it, but it will have nothing to do with the inside working, and no one has ever tried to squeeze out of a witch the exact recipe for her brew.

Once, when Denys and I had been up, and were landing on the plain of the farm, a very old Kikuyu came up and talked to us:

"You were up very high to-day," he said, "we could not see you, only hear the airplane sing like a bee."

---

5. **The Prophet,** Mohammed, the founder of Islam.
6. *sice* (sīs), a groom or attendant.

I agreed that we had been up high.

"Did you see God?" he asked.

"No, Ndwetti," I said, "we did not see God."

"Aha, then you were not up high enough," he said, "but now tell me: do you think that you will be able to get up high enough to see him?"

"I do not know, Ndwetti," I said.

"And you, Bedâr," he said, turning to Denys, "what do you think? Will you get up high enough in your airplane to see God?"

"Really I do not know," said Denys.

"Then," said Ndwetti, "I do not know at all why you two go on flying."

1937

THINK AND DISCUSS
Understanding
1. What does the author refer to as "the most transporting pleasure of my life on the farm"?
2. What does Isak Dinesen find notable about her flight to Lake Natron?
3. At the time of the narration, how have Dinesen's feelings about Africa's wild animals, especially the buffaloes, changed from when she was young?

Analyzing
4. Based on what he says and does in this excerpt, what is your impression of Denys Finch-Hatton? Explain.
5. Why do you think the herd of buffaloes behave as they do when the plane is flying overhead?
6. How does the author explain the natives' lack of interest in flying?
7. Which inventions of civilization impress the natives? What do they value most and why?

Extending
8. Reread the passage on page 817 where Dinesen talks about commissioning a Kikuyu to "hold your horse while you make a visit." What is the Kikuyu's hope and expectation about this chore? Would yours be the same?
9. What generalization can you make about the African natives' reaction to "civilization" based on the remarks of the Masai who visited England and the "very old Kikuyu" who questioned Denys and Isak about their airplane ride?

COMPOSITION
Assuming the Point of View of a Character
Imagine that you are either the leader of the Masai group who come to the plane at Lake Natron or the "very old Kikuyu" who speaks to Denys and Isak at the conclusion of the excerpt. You are talking to the children of your settlement about white people and their ways. Try to capture what you think would be their feeling about what we consider "civilization" and modern living. What things, if any, would impress you? What things might you be scornful of or unimpressed by? Review the selection for clues to what the Africans think about whites and their machines.

Analyzing Descriptive Style
Isak Dinesen is famed for her ability to describe **settings** and situations. Choose two or three of the situations that you found most memorable in this excerpt. Then try to put your finger on what made the writing come alive for you. Was it the selection of adjectives, the use of similes, allusions, connotative language? Be sure to refer to specific phrasing and tell what effect it had upon you as reader. You should write four or five paragraphs. See "Writing About Nonfiction" in the Writer's Handbook.

Anna Gorenko was born on the Black Sea coast not far from Odessa. Before she was a year old, her family moved north to Tsarskoe Selo ("the Tsar's Village"), which is now renamed after the great Russian author Alexander Pushkin, who spent his youth there. Because her father did not want the shame of a woman poet using his name, she chose the pen name Akhmatova, the name of the last Tartar princess of the Golden Horde and also of a Tartar great-grandmother.

In 1910 she finally agreed to marry the poet Nikolai Gumilyev, who had attempted suicide after she rejected one of his earlier marriage proposals. Two years later her first collection, *Evening*, appeared. She and her husband were founders of the poetic school known as Acmeism, which preached the need for classical form and clarity in the face of Symbolist mistiness and ideological preoccupations. The marriage was not a happy one. Several of her poems, such as "Hands Clenched Under My Shawl" (page 820), reflect their marital discord. Gumilyev was shot by the Bolsheviks in 1921 as an alleged counter-revolutionary. Even though Akhmatova and he had been divorced for three years, she never could escape the taint of having been associated with Gumilyev. At the beginning of the Stalinist Terror in the 1930s, her son, Lev Gumilyev, was arrested, released, rearrested, and sent to the labor camps. Also arrested at this time was Nikolai Punin, an art critic and historian with whom she had been living. The latter arrest is referred to in her poem "Requiem" (page 820). That poem was composed over the course of five years, except for the prologue and "Instead of a Foreword," which were added much later. For at least seventeen years it existed only in the memories of the poet and a few trusted friends, for to have a written manuscript fall into the hands of the authorities would have meant an immediate death sentence.

Akhmatova could have fled the Soviet Union to a safer country that was more congenial to an artist. However, she felt an obligation to remain with her countrymen. Her poetry provides a link with Russian poetry of the past while still being modern in language and content. Huge crowds came to her funeral in Leningrad to express their gratitude for the endurance which allowed her to outlive her enemies.

See MOOD in the Handbook of Literary Terms, page 958.

Hands Clenched Under My Shawl

translated by **Robert Tracy**

Hands clenched under my shawl . . .
"You are pale today, I think?"
—He was drunk, for I had poured him
A bitter grief to drink.

5 No forgetting his stagger away,
His mouth twisted in pain . . .
I ran after, but couldn't catch up,
I ran to the gate on the lane.

I panted, "Only a joke,
10 That's all. Leave and you'll kill
Me." His smile terrible, calm.
He said, "Don't stand in the chill."

Lot's Wife

translated by **Richard Wilbur**

The just man followed then his angel guide
Where he strode on the black highway,
    hulking and bright;
But a wild grief in his wife's bosom cried,
Look back, it is not too late for a last sight

5 *Of the red towers of your native Sodom, the square*
Where once you sang, the gardens you shall mourn,
And the tall house with empty windows where
You loved your husband and your babes were born.

She turned, and looking on the bitter view
10 Her eyes were welded shut by mortal pain;
Into transparent salt her body grew,
And her quick feet were rooted in the plain.

Who would waste tears upon her? Is she not
The least of our losses, this unhappy wife?
15 Yet in my heart she will not be forgot
Who, for a single glance, gave up her life.

Requiem 1935–1940

translated by **Richard McKane**

No, not under the vault of another sky,
not under the shelter of other wings.
I was with my people then,
there where my people were doomed to be.

1961

Instead of a Foreword
During the terrible years of Yezhovshchina[1] I
spent seventeen months in the prison queues
in Leningrad. One day someone recognized me.
Then a woman with lips blue with cold who was
standing behind me, and of course had never heard
of my name, came out of the numbness which
affected us all and whispered in my ear—(we all
spoke in whispers there):
    "Can you describe this?"
    I said, "I can!"
    Then something resembling a smile slipped over
what had once been her face.

1 April 1957 Leningrad

1. *Yezhovshchina*, head of Stalin's secret police in the late
1930s who was himself purged.

Dedication

The mountains bend before this grief,
the great river does not flow,
but the prison locks are strong
and behind them the convicts' holes
5 and a deathly sadness.
For someone the fresh wind blows,
for someone the sunset basks . . .
We don't know, we are the same everywhere;
we only hear the repellent clank of keys,
10 the heavy steps of the soldiers.
We rose as though to early mass,
and went through the savage capital,
and we used to meet there, more lifeless than
    the dead,
the sun lower, the Neva[2] mistier,
15 but in the distance hope still sings.
Condemned . . . Immediately the tears start,
one woman, already isolated from everyone else,
as though her life had been wrenched from
    her heart,
as though she had been smashed flat on
    her back,
20 still, she walks on . . . staggers . . . alone . . .
Where now are the chance friends
of my two hellish years?
What do they see in the Siberian blizzard,
what comes to them in the moon's circle?
25 I send them my farewell greeting.

March 1940

Introduction

It was a time when only the dead
smiled, happy in their peace.
And Leningrad dangled like a useless pendant
at the side of its prisons.
5 A time when, tortured out of their minds,
the convicted walked in regiments,
and the steam whistles sang
their short parting song.
Stars of death stood over us,
10 and innocent Russia squirmed
under the bloody boots,
under wheels of black Marias.[3]

1

They took you away at dawn,
I walked after you as though you were being
    borne out,
the children were crying in the dark room,
the candle swam by the ikon-stand.
5 The cold of the ikon on your lips.
Death sweat on your brow . . . Do not forget!
I will howl by the Kremlin towers
like the wives of the Streltsy.[4]

1935

2

The quiet Don[5] flows quietly,
the yellow moon goes into the house,

goes in with its cap askew,
the yellow moon sees the shadow.

5 This woman is sick,
this woman is alone,

husband in the grave, son in prison,
pray for me.

3

No, this is not me—someone else suffers.
I couldn't stand this: let black drapes
cover what happened,
and let them take away the street lights . . .
    Night.

4

If I could show you, the mocker,
everybody's favorite,
happy sinner of Tsarskoe Selo,[6]
how your life will turn out:
5 you will stand at Kresty[7]

---

2. *Neva*, a great river that flows through Leningrad.
3. *black Marias*, the patrol cars that transported prisoners to jail.
4. *Streltsy.* The Streltsy were a body of soldiers organized about 1550 by Ivan the Terrible. In 1698 Peter the Great defeated them outside Moscow, executed 800 of them, and disbanded the others.
5. *The quiet Don*, another great river of Russia.
6. *Tsarskoe Selo*, Russian village where Akhmatova had lived in her youth.
7. *Kresty*, literally "crosses"; it is a prison in Leningrad, the name referring to the layout of the building.

three hundredth in the line with your prison
    parcel,
and set fire to the new year ice
with your hot tears.
There the prison poplar sways,
10 silence—and how many
innocent lives are ending there . . .

5

For seventeen months I have been screaming,
calling you home.
I flung myself at the executioner's feet.
You are my son and my terror.
5 Everything is confused for ever,
and I can no longer tell
beast from man,
and how long I must wait for the execution.
Only the dusty flowers,
10 the clank of censers, and tracks
leading from somewhere to nowhere.
An enormous star
looks me straight in the eye
and threatens swift destruction.

1939

6

Weightless weeks fly by,
I will never grasp what happened.
How the white nights[8] looked
at you, my son, in prison,
5 how they look again
with the burning eye of the hawk,
they speak of your tall cross,
they speak of death.

1939

7

Verdict

The stone word fell
on my still living breast.
Never mind, I was prepared,
somehow I'll come to terms with it.

5 Today I have much work to do:
I must finally kill my memory,

I must, so my soul can turn to stone,
I must learn to live again.

Or else . . . The hot summer rustle,
10 like holiday time outside my window.
I have felt this coming for a long time,
this bright day and the empty house.

Summer 1939

8

To Death

You will come anyway—so why not now?
I am waiting for you—it's very difficult for me.
I have put out the light and opened the door
to you, so simple and wonderful.
5 Assume any shape you like,
burst in as a poison gas shell,
or creep up like a burglar with a heavy weight,
or poison me with typhus vapors.
Or come with a denunciation thought up by you
10 and known *ad nauseam* to everyone,
so that I may see over the blue cap[9]
the janitor's fear-whitened face.
I don't care now. The Yenisey rolls on,[10]
the Pole star shines.
15 And the blue luster of loving eyes
conceals the final horror.

19 August 1939

9

Already madness has covered
half my soul with its wing,
and gives me strong liquor to drink,
and lures me to the black valley.

5 I realized that I must
hand victory to it,
as I listened to my delirium,
already alien to me.

It will not allow me to take
10 anything away with me
(however I beseech it,
however I pester it with prayer):

---

8. *white nights.* In Leningrad because it is so far north the sun never totally sets during certain seasons.
9. *the blue cap,* a policeman.
10. *Yenisey,* great river of Siberia.

not the terrible eyes of my son,
the rock-like suffering,
15 not the day when the storm came,
not the prison visiting hour,

nor the sweet coolness of hands,
nor the uproar of the lime trees' shadows,
nor the distant, light sound—
20 the comfort of last words.

4 May 1940

10
Crucifixion

"Weep not for Me, Mother,
in the grave I have life."

I

The choir of angels glorified the great hour,
the heavens melted in flames.
He said to His Father: "Why hast Thou
    forsaken Me?"
and to His Mother: "Oh, weep not for Me . . ."

II

5 Mary Magdalene smote her breast and wept,
the disciple whom He loved turned to stone,
but where the Mother stood in silence
nobody even dared look.

1940

Epilogue

I

I found out how faces droop,
how terror looks out from under the eyelids,
how suffering carves on cheeks
hard pages of cuneiform,
5 how curls ash-blonde and black
turn silver overnight,
a smile fades on submissive lips,
fear trembles in a dry laugh.
I pray not for myself alone,
10 but for everyone who stood with me,
in the cruel cold, in the July heat,
under the blind, red wall.

II

The hour of remembrance has drawn close again.
I see you, hear you, feel you.

15 The one they hardly dragged to the window,
the one who no longer treads this earth,

the one who shook her beautiful head,
and said: "Coming here is like coming home."

I would like to call them all by name,
20 but the list was taken away and I can't
    remember.

For them I have woven a wide shroud
from the humble words I heard among them.

I remember them always, everywhere,
I will never forget them, whatever comes.

25 And if they gag my tormented mouth
with which one hundred million people cry,

then let them also remember me
on the eve of my remembrance day.

If they ever think of building
30 a memorial to me in this country,

I solemnly give my consent,
only with this condition: not to build it

near the sea where I was born;
my last tie with the sea is broken;

35 nor in Tsarsky Sad[11] by the hallowed stump
where an inconsolable shadow seeks me,

but here, where I stood three hundred hours,
and they never unbolted the door for me.

Since even in blessed death I am terrified
40 that I will forget the thundering of the Black
    Marias,

forget how the hateful door slammed,
how an old woman howled like a wounded beast.

And let the melting snow stream
like tears from my motionless, bronze eyelids,

45 let the prison dove call in the distance
and the boats go quietly on the Neva.

March 1940

---

11. *Tsarsky Sad*, a place name; literally, "the Tsar's Garden."

THINK AND DISCUSS

Understanding

1. Describe the situation involving the speaker and the man she addresses in "Hands Clenched Under My Shawl."
2. What happened to Lot's wife, and what did she do to bring about her fate?
3. Describe in your own words what the author of "Requiem" is asked to do in "Instead of a Foreword."
4. In "Requiem," what do we learn has happened to the speaker's husband and son?

Analyzing

5. What emotion is the speaker expressing in "Hands Clenched Under My Shawl"?
6. What is the usual opinion about Lot's wife? How does the speaker of Akhmatova's poem respond to the old Bible story?
7. In section 4 of "Requiem," the speaker contrasts her carefree early life with her present situation. Describe that contrast. What do you think the "prison parcel" is?
8. There are numerous references to crosses in "Requiem." Where are they and what meanings do the references give to the poem?
9. To whom is "Requiem" dedicated?
10. The four-line poem at the beginning of "Requiem" was written in 1961. Why do you think Akhmatova added it at that time? Refer to the biographical sketch before you answer.

Extending

11. What purpose do you feel is served by a poem such as "Requiem"? How would you respond to a person who complained that the subject matter is unpleasant and depressing?

APPLYING: Mood　H⫯

See Handbook of Literary Terms, p. 958.

The **mood** of a piece of literature is the overall atmosphere or feeling that it generates. It is the end product of the interplay of connotation, imagery, irony, rhyme, and a number of other elements of literature.

1. What single word do you think best describes the mood of the Akhmatova poems you have just read?
2. Choose one of the first two poems ("Hands Clenched Under My Shawl" or "Lot's Wife") or one section of "Requiem" and describe the mood and the words, images, and any other factors that you think generate that mood.

THINKING SKILLS

Generalizing

To generalize is to draw a general conclusion from particular information. For example, you can make some broad observations about an author's philosophy and style by studying his or her works.

1. Make a general statement about life in the Soviet Union based on the poems of Akhmatova.
2. What general view about the different values of men and women is suggested by "Lot's Wife"?

COMPOSITION　◀━▪

Imagining a Situation

"Hands Clenched Under My Shawl" describes the aftermath of a situation in which a woman (perhaps a wife) has behaved badly and driven her loved one (perhaps a husband) from her. Write a brief story or dialogue in which you portray such a situation.

Relating Two Poems

Write a composition of five or six paragraphs to be shared with the class on how the basic **theme** of "Lot's Wife" is illustrated and particularized in "Requiem." For instance you might show how Leningrad is like Sodom and how Akhmatova is like Lot's wife.

BIOGRAPHY

Gabriela Mistral
1889–1957

Jeronimo Godoy was a light-hearted schoolteacher in the Elqui River Valley region of northern Chile and something of a poet. He married a widow, Doña Petronila Alcayaga, also a teacher, and they settled in the small town of Vicuña, where on April 7, 1889, Doña Petronila gave birth to Lucila Godoy Alcayaga, who was to become famous in South American literature as Gabriela Mistral. Her father, who was out of work at the time of the birth, wrote a poem celebrating the event and simultaneously lamenting the fate of the new arrival. Three years later he left home one day and was never heard from again.

Mistral's life story is so well known in South America that it has taken on the quality of legend. Her mother claims to have found her daughter escaping loneliness by having intimate conversations with the birds and flowers of the garden that her father had made for her before he departed. Another story says that she was expelled from school because she was considered too stupid to learn. Still she became educated enough to find a job as a schoolteacher, and at the age of twenty she fell in love with a railroad employee. Numerous versions of the love affair have become popular. One fact that is definite is that after a period of angry estrangement, the young man shot himself in the head and died. The experience inspired some of her most impassioned poems.

Her pen name is generally assumed to be a combination of the names of two great poets, Gabriele D'Annunzio of Italy and Frédéric Mistral of France, but it is surely no accident that the surname is also the name given to a cold, dry wind that blows in the Mediterranean area. The name was first widely heard in 1914 when she won a poetry prize at the Floral Games in Santiago de Chile with some poems dedicated to a dead man. Her other favorite themes are religion, love of the land, and love of children. Mistral received from the hands of the King of Sweden the Nobel Prize for Literature in 1945, the first Latin American writer so honored.

The Stable

translated by **Langston Hughes**

When midnight came
and the Child's first cry arose,
a hundred beasts awakened
and the stable became alive.

5 And drawing near they came
reaching out toward the Child
a hundred eager necks
like a forest swaying.

An ox whose eyes were as tender
10 as though filled with dew,
lowered its head to breathe
quietly in His face.

Against Him rubbed a lamb
with the softest of soft fleece,
15 and two baby goats squatted,
licking His hands.

The walls of the stable
unnoticed were covered
with pheasants and with geese
20 and cocks and with blackbirds.

The pheasants flew down
and swept over the Child
tails of many colors;
while the geese with wide bills
25 smoothed His pallet of straw;
and a swarm of blackbirds
became a veil rising and falling
above the new born.

The Virgin, confused among such horns
30 and whiteness of breathing,
fluttered hither and yon
unable to pick up her Child.

And Joseph arrived laughing
to help her in her confusion,
35 and the upset stable was like
a forest in the wind.

1957

Fear

translated by **Langston Hughes**

I do not want them to turn
my child into a swallow;
she might fly away into the sky
and never come down again to my doormat;
5 or nest in the eaves where my hands
could not comb her hair.
I do not want them to turn
my child into a swallow.

I do not want them to make
10 my child into a princess.
In tiny golden slippers how could
she play in the field?
And when night came, no longer
would she lie by my side.
15 I do not want them to make
my child into a princess.

And I would like even less
that one day they crown her queen.
They would raise her to a throne
20 where my feet could not climb.
I could not rock her to sleep
when nighttime came.
I do not want them to make
my child into a queen.

1957

To My Husband

translated by **Langston Hughes**

Husband, do not embrace me. You caused
    it to rise from the
depths of me like a water lily. Let me be like
    still water.

Love me, love me now a little more! I, so
    small, will
duplicate you on all the highways. I, so poor,
    will give
5 you other eyes, other lips, through which
    you may enjoy the
world; I, so frail, will split myself asunder
    for love's
sake like a broken jar, that the wine of life
    might flow.

Forgive me! I walk so clumsily, so clumsily
    serve your
glass; but you filled me like this and gave me
    this strangeness
10 with which I move among things.

Treat me more than ever kindly. Do not
    roughly stir my
blood; do not disturb my breathing.

Now I am nothing but a veil; all my body is
    a veil beneath
which a child sleeps.

1957

THINK AND DISCUSS
Understanding
1. Who is the Child in "The Stable"? How do you know?
2. What fears are expressed by the speaker of "Fear"?

Analyzing
3. What new additions to the famous story does the poet insert in "The Stable"? What is their effect?
4. Why does the speaker of "To My Husband" tell her husband not to embrace her? What is her condition?

Extending
5. The biographical sketch of Gabriela Mistral informs you that she had a tragic love affair early in life. She never married or bore any children. Judging from the selections presented here, what is her attitude toward motherhood and children? Refer to specifics in the poems in your answer.

THINKING SKILLS
Evaluating
To evaluate is to make a judgment based on some kind of standard. For example, a critic reads a novel and writes a review that includes judgments about how well written, humorous, suspenseful, true-to-life, or interesting it is compared to other books he or she has read.

1. Read the four translations of Mistral's poem "Meciendo" on pages 828–829. Imagine that you are an editor faced with the task of selecting one of the four translations that you feel is superior. Explain the reasons for your choice.
2. Religion, motherhood, and meditations on death are themes that unify the writing of Gabriela Mistral. Show how these themes mingle in her poems.

Translating "Meciendo"

The translator of Mistral's "Meciendo" must capture the beautiful simplicity of the original phrasing and its gentle "rocking" rhythm—an example of sound reinforcing sense.

In the original there is an alternation of trimeter and dimeter lines. The dimeter lines also have at least approximate rhymes. The final line of each stanza is the same. Translator Doris Dana places the verb of the first sentence of stanza one in the first line, whereas in the original the verb appears in line two. This necessitates a change of the adverb "divino" to an adjective: "The sea is divine." The second stanza is very close to the original, the only departure being the rendering of "en la noche" as "by night" instead of the more direct "in the night." The final stanza contains a verb shift from line two to line one—the same as took place in the opening stanza. She is unable to avoid a minor metrical irregularity in that line. In English the phrase "God, the Father" contains equal stressed accents on the first and third syllables; however, in Spanish "Dios Padre" has a strong accent on the second syllable and only a secondary accent

on the first syllable. Thus her translation of this line contains four accented syllables whereas the original contained only three.

Muriel Kittel manages a uniform trimeter rhythm which is pleasing albeit different from that of Mistral. The most scrupulously accurate translation is that of Seymour Resnick. His only departure is to change the noun series "los mares amantes" and "los vientos amantes" to participle-noun combinations "loving seas" and "loving winds." All four translators did something similar in order to avoid "seas-lovers" and "winds-lovers," which sound clumsy in English.

Langston Hughes has made the loosest translation of the four in order to maintain the *abcb* rhyme scheme in each stanza. Also, in the title and in each stanza he substitutes "cradle" for the harsh monosyllable of "rock," with its multiple meanings. In the last three lines of the poem an anapestic rhythm lends a sense of closure at the expense of the refrain-like exact repetition of each stanza's fourth line, which is present in the original and in all the other translations.

Meciendo ("Rocking")

by Gabriela Mistral

Langston Hughes (1957)

El mar sus millares de olas
mece, divino.
Oyendo a los mares amantes,
mezo a mi niño.

The sea cradles
its millions of stars divine.
Listening to the seas in love,
I cradle the one who is mine.

5 El viento errabundo en la noche
mece a los trigos.
Oyendo a los vientos amantes,
mezo a mi niño.

5 The errant wind in the night
cradles the wheat.
Listening to the winds in love,
I cradle my sweet.

Dios Padre sus miles de mundos
10 mece sin ruido.
Sintiendo su mano en la sombra,
mezo a mi niño.

God Our Father cradles
10 His thousands of worlds without sound.
Feeling His hand in the darkness,
I cradle the babe I have found.

Muriel Kittel (1961)

With divine rhythm the ocean
rocks its myriad waves.
Listening to the waters' love,
I rock this child of mine.

5 The night-wandering wind
rocks the fields of wheat.
Listening to the winds' love,
I rock this child of mine.

Silently God the Father
10 rocks his numerous worlds.
Feeling his hand in the darkness,
I rock this child of mine.

Seymour Resnick (1964)

The sea its thousands of waves
Divinely rocks.
Listening to the loving seas
I rock my child.

5 The wind wandering in the night
Rocks the fields of wheat.
Listening to the loving winds
I rock my child.

God in Heaven His thousands of worlds
10 Rocks without noise.
Feeling His hand in the dark
I rock my child.

Doris Dana (1961)

The sea rocks her thousands of waves.
The sea is divine.
Hearing the loving sea
I rock my son.

5 The wind wandering by night
rocks the wheat.
Hearing the loving wind
I rock my son.

God, the Father, soundlessly rocks
10 His thousands of worlds.
Feeling His hand in the shadow
I rock my son.

Pablo Picasso, *The Mother*. 1901.
St. Louis Art Museum

The Oxford English Dictionary

In 1879 Dr. James Augustus Henry Murray (1837–1915), the President of the Philological Society, began work on the Society's monumental dictionary project. The Philological Society had been organized in 1842. Beginning with some 200 members, the Society's purpose was to investigate the history and structure of language. Up to this time, no English dictionary had included organized and detailed information on the history of words. To correct this deficiency, the Society resolved in January, 1858, to prepare a new dictionary that would display the entire history of every word that was or had been in the English language.

For the next twenty years, first under the editorship of Herbert Coleridge (great-nephew of Samuel Taylor Coleridge), and later of F. J. Furnivall, materials toward the new dictionary were gathered by a large number of volunteer readers, who scoured English literature in search of quotations displaying the meanings of words at different historical periods. (There were a number of American volunteers, and Coleridge at one point suggested that they confine themselves to the literature of the eighteenth century, but his proposal was not closely followed.)

One basic question Murray had to consider during his early years as editor was "What is the English language?" He saw it not as a vocabulary defined by the speech habits of a single class or ethnic group, but rather like a grouping in botany or zoology, its typical species related to other species in which the features characteristic of the group become less and less distinct. The organic grouping that formed the English language he saw as composed of a central core of thousands of words constituting the common vocabulary of the language and linked on every side to more specialized vocabularies. He illustrated this with a diagram:

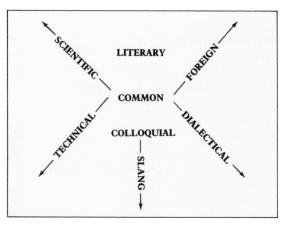

Under Murray, who was the first full-time editor the Society was able to employ, the dictionary project went forward far more swiftly. By April 19, 1882, the first copy was ready for the printer, and by November, 1883, the first volume, A–B, was out. Nevertheless, Murray did not live to see the completion of the project. He died in July, 1915 (shortly after completing work on the section *Trink–Turndown*). It was not until June 6, 1928, seventy years since the Philological Society had begun work on its new dictionary "on historical principles," that a banquet was held to celebrate the completion of the project, now known as *The Oxford English Dictionary*.

James A. H. Murray (1837–1915), editor of *The Oxford English Dictionary*.

MEN AND WOMEN

Poets, playwrights, tale-tellers, artists, and composers have devoted much time to the theme of love. This most human of emotions, at once mysterious, complex, maddening, and satisfying, has been explored, redefined, analyzed, denigrated, and glorified by anyone who has ever felt it and by a few who have not. Being in love inspires as many to creative highs as being out of love. Not only does the course of true love seldom run smooth, it sometimes seems the rockiest of journeys. Love begins in desire, perhaps, and ends in acceptance, ideally.

Love as Desire

"If that Shirazi Turk will take my heart in her hand/I will give up for her Bokhara and Samarqand." In these opening lines to his most famous poem (page 54), the Persian writer Hafiz expresses the idea that desire can make a lover feel as powerful as a king. But in some of the bittersweet songs in the Indian drama *Shakuntala* (page 62), a real king tells how powerless love makes him feel—paralyzed by desire and beauty and regret. As these examples suggest, the theme of love as desire can be treated in a variety of ways. The Roman poet Horace takes a genial approach, and in his ode beginning "You shy from me, Chloe, like a fawn" (page 238), he displays a sweet understanding of a young girl's uncertainty about men, acknowledging not only the girl's fears but even those of her mother. Where Horace is sympathetic, another Roman poet, Catullus, is urgent. In his poem beginning "Lesbia, let us live and love" (page 234), he points to the brevity of human life as an argument for the prompt enjoyment of love. This poem is a famous expression of the *carpe diem* (kär′pe dē′em) theme. *Carpe diem* is a Latin phrase meaning "enjoy the present day." When poets accuse their loved ones of being too coy, they often use the *carpe diem* argument.

In Boccaccio's story "Federigo's Falcon" (page 388), a lover finally wins his lady simply because of the excess of his devotion. Throughout his courtship of her, Monna Giovanna never gives Federigo "a single glance." Yet Federigo says to her, "If ever I have been worth anything, it has been because of the love I bore for you." Their relationship reflects the tradition of *courtly love* so common in medieval romances, in which the extravagantly gallant behavior of the lover receives more emphasis than the beauty and grace of the beloved. You may be reminded of popular songs in which the singer complains of being his girl's "fool" or "clown" while receiving no attention in return.

Star-crossed Lovers

The disapproval of young love by adults is a common literary theme. In the Egyptian poem beginning "I think I'll go home and lie very still" (page 20), the speaker plans a deception to enable him to see his beloved without arousing anyone's suspicions. The feeling in this poem is light-hearted, but the theme of lovers thwarted by disapproving parents is generally a tragic one. The most famous of these unfortunate couples are Shakespeare's "star-crossed lovers," Romeo and Juliet. An earlier example of this theme is the classical story of "Pyramus and Thisbe" (page 254), retold by the Roman poet Ovid. Ovid dwells on the pathos of the young lovers' deaths and the repentance of their parents. In Ovid's story, the deaths are largely the result of simple bad luck and misunderstanding. Apparently poets sometimes let their young lovers die even when the lovers seem justified in their rebellion against the status quo. The film *West Side Story* provides a good example of such an ending.

The Ambivalence of Love

Not only do different literary works reflect varying attitudes toward love, but often a single work will express conflicting feelings toward the beloved. "I hate and love," says Catullus in another of his poems (page 235). Hafiz in his poem "The Crier" (page 54) expresses a similar ambivalence in his feelings. After admitting that his lost beloved is "a wastrel, a wanton, shame-abandoned," he nevertheless pleads that she be sent back to him promptly. Women are also troubled by conflicting feelings toward those they love. In the Egyptian poem beginning "I was simply off to see Nefrus my friend" (page 20), the speaker, a young woman, both desires and fears the attentions of the young man she loves. The speaker in Li Po's "The River-Merchant's Wife: A Letter" (page 84), another young woman, has also experienced such conflicting feelings, largely because of her husband's desertion of her. The speaker in the poem beginning "Hands clenched under my shawl" (page 820), by the Russian poet Anna Akhmatova, expresses a harsh and unresolved ambivalence toward her lover. Akhmatova's poem "Lot's Wife" (page 820) pictures another unhappy, self-divided woman, one who both loses and triumphs by breaking her husband's rules.

Walter Richard Sickert (1860–1942), *Ennui.* c. 1914. Tate Gallery, London

The War Between Men and Women

A comic treatment of the war between men and women is Pope's *The Rape of the Lock* (page 560). Pope's version of this theme is in the form of an epic, but one in which a trivial quarrel between a young man and a young woman is treated with mock seriousness, as if it were a duel between heroes.

The appearance of Ibsen's play *A Doll House* (page 712) is often viewed as signaling the beginning of a new phase in the conflict between men and women. When a young woman finds that her seemingly ideal marriage is an illusion, she leaves home, slamming the door behind her. In the words of one critic, ". . . that slammed door reverberated across the roof of the world." *A Doll House* unhesitatingly addressed the question of the proper role of women, and of marriage, in society. To her husband's assertion that "Before all else you're a wife and a mother," Nora responds, "I don't believe that anymore. I believe that, before all else, I'm a human being, no less than you—or anyway, I ought to try to become one." Such words will sound familiar to those who watch contemporary movies and television, where the war between the sexes has recently become more serious.

For a truce in the war between the sexes, read the story of Odysseus and Penelope (page 126) and the conclusion of Book XII of *Paradise Lost* (page 505). In both works, husband and wife are reunited happily.

THINKING CRITICALLY ABOUT LITERATURE

UNIT 7 MODERNISM

■ CONCEPT REVIEW

Below on the left is a short story by the French writer Colette (1873–1954). On the right are notes to help you read and to review some of the literary terms and thinking skills that have appeared in Unit 7. Page numbers in the notes refer to an application or review of literary terms in the unit. A more extensive discussion of these terms is in the Handbook of Literary Terms. On a separate sheet of paper write your answers to the questions that follow this excerpt.

The Little Bouilloux Girl

Colette *translated by* **Enid Mcleod** *and* **Una Troubridge**

■ **Bouilloux** (bwē yü′).

The little Bouilloux girl was so lovely that even we children noticed it. It is unusual for small girls to recognize beauty in one of themselves and pay homage to it. But there could be no disputing such undeniable loveliness as hers. Whenever my mother met the little Bouilloux girl in the street, she would stop her and bend over her as she was wont to bend over her yellow tea rose, her red flowering cactus or her Azure Blue butterfly trustfully asleep on the scaly bark of the pine tree. She would stroke her curly hair, golden as a half-ripe chestnut, and her delicately tinted cheeks, and watch the incredible lashes flutter over her great dark eyes. She would observe the glimmer of the perfect teeth in her peerless mouth, and when, at last, she let the child go on her way, she would look after her, murmuring, "It's prodigious!"

Several years passed, bringing yet further graces to the little Bouilloux girl. There were certain occasions recorded by our admiration: a prize giving at which, shyly murmuring an unintelligible recitation, she glowed through her tears like a peach under a summer shower. The little Bouilloux girl's first communion caused a scandal: the same evening, after vespers, she was seen drinking a half pint at the *Café du Commerce*, with her father, the sawyer, and that night she danced, already feminine and flirtatious, a little unsteady in her white slippers, at the public ball.

■ **Simile** (page 776): Note the effectiveness of the simile describing the girl's hair color.

■ **sawyer:** one who saws wood in a sawmill.

With an arrogance to which she had accustomed us, she informed us later, at school, that she was to be apprenticed.

"Oh! Who to?"

"To Madame Adolphe."

"Oh! And are you to get wages at once?"

"No. I'm only thirteen, I shall start earning next year."

She left us without emotion, and coldly we let her go. Already her beauty isolated her and she had no friends at school, where she learned very little. Her Sundays and her Thursdays brought no intimacy with us; they were spent with a family that was considered "unsuitable," with girl cousins of eighteen well known for their brazen behavior, and with brothers, cartwright apprentices, who sported ties at fourteen and smoked when they escorted their sister to the Parisian shooting gallery at the fair or to the cheerful bar that the widow Pimolle had made so popular.

The very next morning on my way to school I met the little Bouilloux girl setting out for the dressmaker's workrooms, and I remained motionless, thunderstruck with jealous admiration, at the corner of the Rue des Soeurs, watching Nana Bouilloux's retreating form.

She had exchanged her black pinafore and short childish frock for a long skirt and a pleated blouse of pink sateen. She wore a black alpaca apron and her exuberant locks, disciplined and twisted into a "figure of eight," lay close as a helmet about the charming new shape of a round imperious head that retained nothing childish except its freshness and the not yet calculated impudence of a little village adventuress.

That morning the upper forms hummed like a hive.

"I've seen Nana Bouilloux! In a long dress, my dear, would you believe it? And her hair in a chignon! She had a pair of scissors hanging from her belt too!"

At noon I flew home to announce breathlessly:

"Mother! I met Nana Bouilloux in the street! She was passing our door. And she had on a long dress! Mother, just imagine, a long dress! And her hair in a chignon! And she had high heels and a pair of . . ."

"Eat, Minet-Chéri, eat, your cutlet will be cold."

"And an apron, mother, such a lovely alpaca apron that looked like silk! Couldn't I possibly . . ."

"No, Minet-Chéri, you certainly couldn't."

"But if Nana Bouilloux can . . ."

"Yes, Nana Bouilloux, at thirteen, can, in fact she should, wear a chignon, a short apron and a long skirt—it's the uniform of all little Bouilloux girls throughout the world, at thirteen—more's the pity."

"But . . ."

"Yes, I know you would like to wear the complete uniform of a little Bouilloux girl. It includes all that you've seen, and a bit more besides: a letter safely hidden in the apron pocket, an admirer who smells of wine and of cheap cigars; two admirers, three admirers and a little later on plenty of tears . . . and a sickly child hidden away, a child that has lain for months crushed by constricting stays. There it is, Minet-Chéri, the entire uniform

■ **Simile:** Another comparison that generates a vivid image.

■ **cartwright apprentices:** workers apprenticed to cartmakers.

■ **chignon** (shē′nyon): a large rolled arrangement of the hair, worn at the back of the head by women.

■ **Minet-Chéri** (mē ne-shā rē′): a term of endearment.

■ **Characterization** (page 764): Note the details of clothing which stereotype the little girl.

■ **Mood** (p. 824): Note how this description of imagined details of the Bouilloux girl's life contributes to the overall atmosphere and feeling of the story.

of the little Bouilloux girls. Do you still want it?"

"Of course not, mother, I only wanted to see if a chignon . . ."

But my mother shook her head, mocking but serious.

"No, no! You can't have the chignon without the apron, the apron without the letter, the letter without the high-heeled slippers, or the slippers without . . . all the rest of it! It's just a matter of choice!"

My envy was soon exhausted. The resplendent little Bouilloux girl became no more than a daily passer-by whom I scarcely noticed. Bareheaded in winter and summer, her gaily colored blouses varied from week to week, and in very cold weather she swathed her elegant shoulders in a useless little scarf. Erect, radiant as a thorny rose, her eyelashes sweeping her cheeks or half revealing her dark and dewy eyes, she grew daily more worthy of queening it over crowds, of being gazed at, adorned and bedecked with jewels. The severely smoothed crinkliness of her chestnut hair could still be discerned in little waves that caught the light in the golden mist at the nape of her neck and round her ears. She always looked vaguely offended with her small, velvety nostrils reminding one of a doe.

She was fifteen or sixteen now—and so was I. Except that she laughed too freely on Sundays, in order to show her white teeth, as she hung on the arms of her brothers or her girl cousins, Nana Bouilloux was behaving fairly well.

"For a little Bouilloux girl, very well indeed!" was the public verdict.

She was seventeen, then eighteen; her complexion was like a peach on a south wall, no eyes could meet the challenge of hers and she had the bearing of a goddess. She began to take the floor at fetes and fairs, to dance with abandon, to stay out very late at night, wandering in the lanes with a man's arm round her waist. Always unkind, but full of laughter, provoking boldness in those who would have been content merely to love her.

Then came a St. John's Eve when she appeared on the dance floor that was laid down on the *Place du Grand-Jeu* under the melancholy light of malodorous oil lamps. Hobnailed boots kicked up the dust between the planks of the "floor." All the young men, as was customary, kept their hats on while dancing. Blonde girls became claret-colored in their tight bodices, while the dark ones, sunburned from their work in the fields, looked black. But there, among a band of haughty workgirls, Nana Bouilloux, in a summer dress sprigged with little flowers, was drinking lemonade laced with red wine when the Parisians arrived on the scene.

They were two Parisians such as one sees in the country in summer, friends of a neighboring landowner, and supremely bored; Parisians in tussore and white serge, come for a moment to mock at a village midsummer fete. They stopped laughing when they saw Nana Bouilloux and sat down near the bar in order to see her better. In low voices they exchanged comments which she pretended not to hear, since her pride as a beautiful creature would not let her turn her eyes in their direction and giggle like her companions. She heard the words: "A swan among geese! A Greuze! A crime to let such a wonder bury herself here. . . ." When the young man in the white suit asked the little Bouilloux girl for a waltz she got up without surprise and danced with him gravely, in silence. From time to time her eyelashes, more beautiful than

■ **Simile:** The comparison to a thorny rose suggests not only her beauty but also her capacity to inflict pain.

■ **Simile:** Yet another comparison to a peach.

■ **St. John's Eve:** The feast of St. John the Baptist is celebrated as a holiday in France on June 24.

■ **tussore** (tus'ôr): a tan silk.

■ **Greuze** (groez): Nana Bouilloux is likened to a portrait by the French painter Jean Baptiste Greuze (1725–1805).

■ **Evaluating:** What judgments about small-town life are implicit in the Parisian's comments?

a glance, brushed against her partner's fair moustache.

After the waltz the two Parisians went away, and Nana Bouilloux sat down by the bar, fanning herself. There she was soon approached by young Leriche, by Houette, even by Honce the chemist, and even by Possy the cabinetmaker, who was aging, but none the less a good dancer. To all of them she replied, "Thank you, but I'm tired," and she left the ball at half-past ten o'clock.

And after that, nothing more ever happened to the little Bouilloux girl. The Parisians did not return, neither they, nor others like them. Houette, Honce, young Leriche, the commercial travelers with their gold watch chains, soldiers on leave and sheriff's clerks vainly climbed our steep street at the hours when the beautifully coiffed sempstress, on her way down it, passed them by stiffly with a distant nod. They looked out for her at dances, where she sat drinking lemonade with an air of distinction and answered their importunities with "Thank you very much, but I'm not dancing, I'm tired." Taking offense, they soon began to snigger: "Tired! Her kind of tiredness lasts for thirty-six weeks!" and they kept a sharp watch on her figure. But nothing happened to the little Bouilloux girl, neither that nor anything else. She was simply waiting, possessed by an arrogant faith, conscious of the debt owed by the hazard that had armed her too well. She was awaiting . . . not the return of the Parisian in white serge, but a stranger, a ravisher. Her proud anticipation kept her silent and pure; with a little smile of surprise, she rejected Honce, who would have raised her to the rank of chemist's lawful wife, and she would have nothing to say to the sheriff's chief clerk. With never another lapse, taking back, once and for all, the smiles, the glances, the glowing bloom of her cheeks, the red young lips, the shadowy blue cleft of her breasts which she had so prodigally lavished on mere rustics, she awaited her kingdom and the prince without a name.

Years later, when I passed through my native village, I could not find the shade of her who had so lovingly refused me what she called "The uniform of little Bouilloux girls." But as the car bore me slowly, though not slowly enough—never slowly enough—up a street where I have now no reason to stop, a woman drew back to avoid the wheel. A slender woman, her hair well dressed in a bygone fashion, dressmaker's scissors hanging from a steel "châtelaine" on her black apron. Large, vindictive eyes, a tight mouth sealed by long silence, the sallow cheeks and temples of those who work by lamplight; a woman of forty-five or . . . Not at all; a woman of thirty-eight, a woman of my own age, of exactly my age, there was no room for doubt. As soon as the car allowed her room to pass, "the little Bouilloux girl" went on her way down the street, erect and indifferent, after one anxious, bitter glance had told her that the car did not contain the long-awaited ravisher.   **1922**

■ **Tone** (page 774): The tone of these remarks is bitterly sarcastic.

■ **châtelaine** (sha tlen'): a hooklike clasp worn at a woman's waist.

THINK AND DISCUSS
Understanding
1. What specific physical features are mentioned in the opening paragraph that contribute to the little Bouilloux girl's beauty?

2. What is the public's opinion of the Bouilloux girl and her family?

3. In the final paragraph, what had the narrator been seeking in her native village?

Analyzing

4. Why won't the narrator's mother allow the narrator to dress and wear her hair in the manner of Nana Bouilloux?
5. Describe the effect on Nana of her encounter with the two Parisians.

Extending

6. Do you feel that Nana deserves her fate? Explain.
7. What do you learn from this story about a small provincial French town—about its gossip, morals, schools, festivities?

REVIEWING LITERARY TERMS
Simile

1. In the first paragraph of her story, Colette writes: "Whenever my mother met the little Bouilloux girl in the street, she would stop her and bend over her as she was wont to bend over her yellow tea rose, her red flowering cactus or her Azure Blue butterfly trustfully asleep on the scaly bark of the pine tree." Does the comparison in this statement constitute a simile? Why or why not?

Characterization

2. In telling the story of the Bouilloux girl, the narrator reveals her own character as it develops from childhood to adulthood. Trace the changes in her character.

Tone

3. Describe the author's attitude toward "little Bouilloux girls throughout the world," toward the Parisians, and toward the villagers.

■ CONTENT REVIEW
THINKING SKILLS
Classifying

1. The following selections contain one or more important allusions: "The Ides of March," "Ithaka," from *A Portrait of the Artist As a Young Man*, "Lot's Wife," and "The Stable." Make a chart with the selections listed down the side and the following heads across the top: *Literary, Biblical, Historical, Mytholog-*

ical. For each selection place a check mark under each head that describes the allusion or allusions contained in the title. (There may be more than one check for a given selection.) Be prepared to identify the allusions that you are classifying.

Generalizing

2. Describe the role of women in the various societies depicted in *A Doll House*, "The Metamorphosis," and "The Artist."

Synthesizing

3. During the period spanned by this unit, great fortunes were made by colonialists and industrialists, and there was an accompanying decline in religion and spirituality brought about by Darwin's theories and scientific and technological advancements. What comment on materialism is made by the selections you have read? Be sure to refer to specific titles in your answer.

Evaluating

4. A fantasy is a story that goes beyond the boundaries of known reality. "The Metamorphosis" is a good example of a fantasy. In your judgment, how is fantasy employed by Kafka to make a serious comment on reality?

■ COMPOSITION REVIEW
Contrasting Cultures

Tagore's "The Artist" and the biographical sketch of Tagore provide glimpses of Indian life and culture. *A Doll House* is a study of middle-class Norway at about the same time period. In a three-paragraph paper contrast the two cultures. Be sure to use specific examples when making your points.

Writing About Mood

Choose one of the following poets—Cavafy, Rilke, Akhmatova, Mistral—and write about the **mood** or atmosphere of his or her poems. Write a thesis statement about the range of mood in the various poems. Then devote one paragraph to each individual poem focusing on the details of setting, imagery, subject matter, and language that generate the mood.

RECENT LITERATURE 1940–

1940	1945	1950	1955	1960	1965

HISTORY AND ARTS
• Xerography process invented
• World War II begins • First atom bombs exploded • DNA described • Rachel Carson: *Silent Spring*
• Fall of France • World War II ends • Korean War begins
• Lascaux cave paintings discovered • People's Republic of China established
Civil-rights march • on Washington
• Welles: *Citizen Kane* • Dead Sea scrolls discovered • *Sputnik I* launched
• First computer developed • Israel established • Mau-Mau uprisings
Chinese Cultural • Revolution begins
UN established • • India becomes independent

PEOPLE
• Mistral wins Nobel Prize • Einstein dies • Khrushchev becomes premier
Mussolini executed • • Hitler dies • Stalin dies • John XXIII becomes pope
• Joyce dies • Roosevelt dies De Gaulle becomes president •
King wins • Nobel Prize
• Fermi splits atom • Gandhi assassinated Kennedy becomes President •
Hillary and Tenzing climb Mt. Everest • Kennedy assassinated •

LITERATURE
• Laye: *The African Child*
• Anouilh: *Antigone* • Orwell: *Nineteen Eighty-Four* • Singer: *Gimpel the Fool*
• Camus: *The Stranger* • Miller: *Death of a Salesman* • Narayan: *The Guide*
• Borges: *Fictions* • Narayan: *The Financial Expert*
The Diary of Anne Frank • • Ellison: *Invisible Man*
Auden: *The Age of Anxiety* • • Osborne: *Look Back in Anger*

Orson Welles in a scene from the film *Citizen Kane*. 1941

Nuclear Energy, a sculpture by Henry Moore.

Communist forces entering Peking, detail of a Chinese poster. 1949

1970	1975	1980	1985	1990

- Six-Day War
  - Russia invades Czechoslovakia
  - Tet Offensive
    - *Apollo XI* mission
      - Arab oil embargo
      - Watergate hearings

- Civil war begins in Lebanon
  - U.S. celebrates bicentennial
    - Camp David Accords
      - Sandinistas overthrow Somoza
        - Iran-Iraq War begins
      - *Solidarity* formed in Poland
        - Israel invades Lebanon

- Falklands War
  - Bhopal disaster
  - Chernobyl disaster
  - Palestinian uprising begins

- King assassinated
  - Nixon visits China
    - Mao Zedong dies
    - Martinson wins Nobel Prize
  - Nixon resigns

- Singer wins Nobel Prize
  - Shah flees Iran
  - Sadat assassinated

- Indira Gandhi assassinated
- Alfonsin becomes president
  - Gorbachev becomes premier
    - Soyinka wins Nobel Prize

- Voznesensky: *Antiworlds*
- Márquez: *One Hundred Years of Solitude*
  - Walker: *In Search of Our Mother's Gardens*

- Grass: *The Flounder*
  - Golding: *Rites of Passage*
  - Gordimer: *July's People*
  - Eco: *The Name of the Rose*
  - Fuentes: *The Old Gringo* •

- Atwood: *The Handmaid's Tale*
  - Márquez: *Love in the Time of Cholera*

Martin Luther King, Jr., in Washington, D.C., August 1963

Apollo XI astronaut on the moon, July 20, 1969

The signing of the Camp David Accords, March 26, 1979

PREVIEW

UNIT 8   RECENT LITERATURE   1940–

Authors
Jorge Luis Borges
Salvatore Quasimodo
Isaac Bashevis Singer
Harry Martinson
R. K. Narayan
Jean Anouilh
Camara Laye
Andrei Voznesensky
Alice Walker
Albert Camus

Features
Reader's Note: "The Circular Ruins"
Comment: The Messina Earthquake
Comment: Nataraja
Reader's Note: *Antigone*
Reader's Note: Translating "Goya"
The History of Language: English—A
    World Language
Themes in World Literature: Past and
    Present

Review of Literary Terms
imagery
setting
theme
characterization

Vocabulary Skills
context
synonyms and dictionary

Thinking Skills
generalizing
evaluating

Composition Assignments Include
Writing a Feature Story
Analyzing Borges's Style
Writing About Quasimodo's Nobel Citation
Analyzing a Character
Analyzing Singer's Style
Discussing Allegory
Writing Diary Entries
Discussing Vignettes
Writing a Newspaper Account
Analyzing Narayan's Technique
Seeing the Tragedy Through Ismene's Eyes
Analyzing Antigone's Character
Analyzing Creon's Character
Following Creon's Logic
Writing a Short Short Story
Analyzing the Poem
Comparing and Contrasting Characters
Analyzing the Narrator

Enrichment
Readers Theater
Reading Sophocles' *Antigone*
Debating the Issues in *Antigone*

Thinking Critically About Literature
Concept Review
Content Review
Composition Review

RECENT LITERATURE   1940–

The years covered in this unit begin in the agony of World War II, which added new terrors—the Holocaust and the atom bomb—to the familiar horrors of past conflicts. The postwar period has added anxiety to agony, with the continuing threat of global nuclear warfare, as well as the enormous destructiveness caused by the many minor wars—a number of them still in progress—that have occurred. Yet, as in any era, the picture is not all bad. The many evils of the recent past have co-existed with tremendous advances in science, including the eradication of some epidemic diseases and the first steps in the exploration of space. As always, people throughout the world are hoping for an age of peace and understanding. As always, the realization of this hope will depend on whether human wisdom and compassion outweigh human folly and selfishness.

WORLD WAR II

In 1933 Adolf Hitler came to power in Germany. His goal was to expand the power of Germany until he controlled all of Europe. In 1938 he annexed Austria and Czechoslovakia. In 1939, after signing a non-aggression pact with Russia, Hitler attacked Poland. England and France, who had guaranteed Polish independence, declared war on Germany. Italy, ruled by Hitler's fascist ally Mussolini, joined Germany, as did Japan, forming the Axis powers. At first the Axis triumphed. In 1940 the Germans overran Denmark, Norway, the Low Countries, and France. In 1941 German armies invaded Russia, seizing a vast amount of territory and killing or capturing millions of Soviet troops. On December 7, 1941, Japan attacked the American naval base at Pearl Harbor in Hawaii, destroying much of the American Pacific fleet. The Japanese also attacked the Philippines, British Malaya, and other places in Asia. By 1942 the war between the Allies—the United States, Britain, Russia, and twenty-three other nations—and the Axis had become worldwide.

In 1942 the tide of war began to shift in favor of the Allies. After several victories in sea battles in the South Pacific, the Americans began to retake the islands seized by the Japanese. The German invasion of Russia was eventually halted by their defeat at the battle of Stalingrad. From that time on, Soviet troops took the offensive in eastern Europe, and Germany steadily retreated. In 1944, the Allies opened a second front by invading the northwest coast of France. Italy had already surrendered to the Allies in 1943. Germany surrendered in May, 1945. Early in August, 1945, after two atomic bombs had largely destroyed the cities of Hiroshima and Nagasaki, the Japanese surrendered.

The liberation of Europe revealed the full horror of the Nazi regime. Millions of people—Poles, Russians, Czechs, Yugoslavs, Gypsies, and others—had perished in German concentration camps in eastern Europe. Worst of all was the Nazi program of genocide carried out against Europe's Jews. By the end of the war, the Nazis had murdered nearly six million Jews. Jewish community life in Europe, which had existed since Roman times, was almost totally destroyed, an event which has come to be known as "the Holocaust."

THE POSTWAR WORLD

As World War II was ending, the leaders of the Allied powers planned a new international organization dedicated to world peace. In June, 1945, representatives of fifty-one countries signed the charter of the new organization, which was called the United Nations. A less hopeful sign was the development of what became known as the "Cold War," the increasingly hostile relations between the United States and its former ally, the Soviet Union, the two "superpowers" who now dominated world politics. The presence of these two superpowers served to polarize international relations in the postwar period. Each tended to regard the other as a rival, at times as a dangerous enemy. This rivalry led to enormous military spending for both conventional and nuclear weapons by the two countries, a situation referred to as "the arms race." With certain brief periods of improved relations between the United States and the Soviet Union, both the Cold War and the arms race continue up to the present.

As the Cold War developed in the West, great political changes took place in Asia. One of the most important of these was the success of the communist revolutionaries in China. In October, 1949, the Communists, led by Mao Zedong (mä′ō dzù′dùng′), proclaimed the birth of the People's Republic of China. Mao was determined to transform Chinese society by collectivizing agriculture and building up China's industrial and military strength. In 1957 he launched the "Great Leap Forward," a program aimed at increasing food and industrial production at the same time. Although this first program was a failure, by the mid-1960s most Chinese had somewhat better living conditions than before the communist revolution. Food was rationed, but few people starved, and health conditions had improved. In the face of these modest improvements, Mao feared that the Chinese people were losing their revolutionary spirit. To counteract this, in 1966 Mao began the "Great Proletarian Cultural Revolution," a purge of intellectuals who he felt were lukewarm in their devotion to true communism. Soon the Cultural Revolution got out of hand. Anyone with an education was attacked. Eventually Mao was forced to use the army to restore order. By the time Mao Zedong died in 1976, China had made some progress in recovering from the disastrous effects of the cultural revolution.

Profound changes took place in India, Africa, the Middle East, and Latin America as well. The impact of World War II led to the crumbling of the British Empire in India. In 1947 the Indian subcontinent was divided into two countries—India, where the population was mostly Hindu, and Pakistan, where it was mostly Moslem. (See the map inside the back cover.) Religious fanatics on both sides rioted, and at least 500,000 people died. In 1948, when Indian leader Mohandas K. Gandhi tried to make peace between the Hindus and Moslems, he was assassinated by a Hindu fanatic. Although India has made considerable progress in both industrialization and food production, the country continues to be troubled by sectarian violence. In 1984 Prime Minister Indira Gandhi was assassinated by two of her bodyguards. The assassins were Sikhs, members of another of India's religious minorities.

Before World War II, almost all of Africa south of the Sahara was composed of British, French, Portuguese, or Belgian colonies. During the postwar period, independence movements swept through this region with amazing speed. In 1950 only four states on the entire African continent were independent. By 1980, there were over fifty independent African states, a third of the total membership of the United Nations. Although these nations had freed themselves from European colonialism, they continued to face persistent problems, including drought, famine, disease, illiteracy, lack of industrial development, civil war, and the fluctuations of the world economy. Military coups and dictatorships, rather than democratically elected governments, remain the rule in Africa up to the present.

In 1947, the United Nations voted to partition the former British mandate of Palestine into a Jewish and an Arab state, but the Arabs did not accept partition. When Israel declared its independence in 1948, the surrounding Arab states attacked it. Many Palestinian Arabs became refugees. After three decades marked by periodic wars, Israel and Egypt signed the Camp David Accords in 1979, by which Egypt became the first Arab country to formally recognize Israel's existence. Islamic unity was further weakened in 1980 by the outbreak of war between Iran and Iraq.

Like the Middle East, Latin America has had a turbulent history in the postwar period. In 1959, a revolution led by Fidel Castro overthrew a

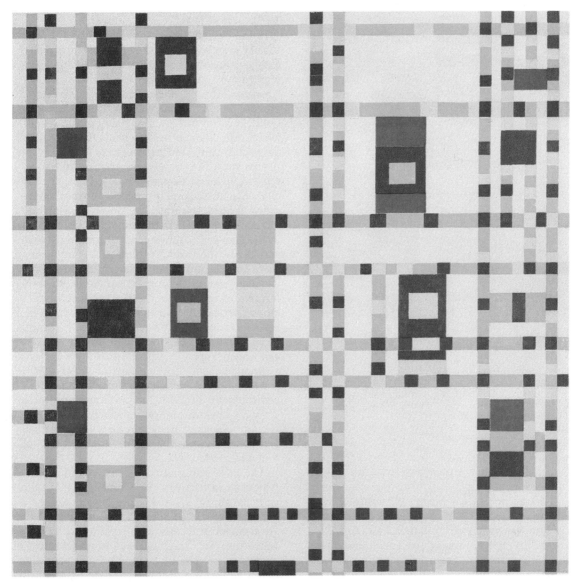

Piet Mondrian (1872–1944), *Broadway Boogie Woogie.* 1942–1943.
Museum of Modern Art, New York

corrupt dictatorship in Cuba. Although Castro's revolution led to improvements in public housing, health, and education, it was at the price of turning Cuba into a communist dictatorship. In 1961, with the help of the United States, Cuban refugees made an unsuccessful attempt to invade Cuba. In October, 1962, the discovery of Soviet missile bases on the island led to the Cuban missile crisis. In a tense showdown, President Kennedy made it clear that the United States would not let the missiles remain. After a week of frightening suspense, Soviet Premier Khrushchev withdrew the missiles in exchange for a pledge that the United States would not invade Cuba.

Richard Estes (1936–), *Drugstore*. 1970.
Art Institute of Chicago

Cuban-American relations have remained hostile to the present.

The recent political history of most of Latin America, like that of Africa, has been marked by brutal dictatorships and military coups. In Argentina, for example, a succession of authoritarian governments, civilian and military, followed one another as economic conditions grew steadily worse. Between 1976 and 1983, the military junta ruling the country conducted a reign of terror in which thousands of people were kidnapped, tortured, and murdered. But in 1982 Argentina was defeated by Britain in its attempt to seize the Falkland Islands. (See the map inside the back cover.) As a result of this humiliating military disaster, civilian control of the government returned to Argentina. Free elections were held in late 1983, and Raul Alfonsin (äl fon sēn′) was elected president.

THE UNITED STATES

In the United States, the aftermath of World War II saw the growth of social reform movements, especially those dedicated to ending racial segregation and protecting the civil rights of American women, blacks, and other minority groups. One milestone was the 1954 Supreme Court decision in *Brown v. Board of Education*, which ruled that separate schools for black students and white students were unconstitutional. A year later, the successful boycott of the segregated buses in Montgomery, Alabama, by the city's black residents, propelled a twenty-seven-year-old black minister, the Reverend Martin Luther King, Jr., into a position of leadership in the civil-rights movement. During the 1960s and 1970s, the various groups that composed the women's movement strongly attacked traditional views of the role of women in American society. While they had some success in ending sex-based discrimination, they failed in their most highly publicized goal, the passage of an Equal Rights Amendment to the American Constitution.

Another focus for the efforts of social reformers in the recent period has been the natural environment. In 1962, the publication of Rachel Carson's book *Silent Spring*, which describes the harmful effects of pesticides on wildlife, helped launch the movement to control environmental pollution.

The most politically divisive event in recent American history was the Vietnam War. In the early 1960s, the United States began sending American troops to South Vietnam, to assist the government in its war with communist rebels, called the Viet Cong, and later with the forces of communist North Vietnam. By 1968, more than half a million Americans were fighting there. In that year during Tet, the Vietnamese New Year season, the Viet Cong and North Vietnamese launched a massive offensive that overran most of the major South Vietnamese cities. Though ultimately unsuccessful militarily, the Tet Offensive helped turn the tide of American public opinion against the war in Vietnam. A long process of American withdrawal began. Peace treaties were finally signed in 1973. Without American support, South Vietnam fell to communist armies in 1975.

RECENT LITERATURE

During World War I and the years immediately following appeared some of the most characteristic and influential literature of the twentieth century—the classics of modernism, including works by Thomas Mann, Franz Kafka, D. H. Lawrence, Jaroslav Hašek, James Joyce, T. S. Eliot, Ernest Hemingway, and F. Scott Fitzgerald. There is a perception that the period of World War II was a less "literary" one, less productive of important writing. But this generalization, while perhaps reflecting some truth about the relative cultural richness of the two periods, also unfairly depreciates the literature of the 1940s. During this period appeared the greatest works of a number of important writers of the recent past, including Albert Camus, Bertolt Brecht, George Orwell, Richard Wright, Hermann Hesse, Arthur Koestler, Harry Martinson, Jean Anouilh, Arthur Miller, Alberto Moravia, Jorge Luis Borges, and Jean-Paul Sartre.

Many of these works reflected the conditions of World War II and the immediate postwar period. Anouilh's play *Antigone* (page 874) was first performed in 1942, while the Germans were still occupying France. While Anouilh used Sophocles' tragedy *Antigone* as the basis for his own play, its wartime audiences saw in Anouilh's *Antigone* a character who, like members of the French Resistance movement, was willing to sacrifice her life for her ideals; in Creon they saw an image of the Vichy government that was collaborating with the Nazis. The war also figures in works written long after it was over. "Goya" (page 918), by the Russian poet Andrei Voznesensky, was written in 1959, but recalls his childhood memories of the German invasion of the Soviet Union in 1941. The bleakness of the postwar period in England, where food and clothing continued to be rationed for several years, was well reflected in George Orwell's famous anti-utopian novel, *Nineteen Eighty-Four*.

The end of colonialism and the rise of nationalist movements in many parts of Asia, Africa, and Latin America, created interest in the new literature coming out of these areas. The first of these new writers to become known tended to be those who wrote in one of the languages of the former colonial empires. For example, the Indian writer R. K. Narayan, who writes in English, is probably better known in the West than the writers using any of the subcontinent's many native languages and dialects. In stories like "Such Perfection" (page 868), Narayan pictures life in the small towns and villages of South India. The Guinean writer Camara Laye, who wrote in French, described in his autobiography, *The African Child* (page 905), what it was like to grow up in an African tribal society just emerging into the modern world. Although born in Buenos Aires, Jorge Luis Borges was culturally as European as he was Argentinian. Written in Spanish, his poetry and short stories, like "The Circular Ruins" (page 847), reflect both his Latin-American background and his curiosity about other cultures.

Paralleling the emergence of the literatures of the Third World into a new prominence was the rapid development of black literature in the United States. Stimulated by the growth of the civil-rights movement, literature by black writers such as Ralph Ellison, James Baldwin, Lorraine Hansberry, LeRoi Jones, Alice Walker, Toni Morrison, and others found a new recognition. Alice Walker's short story, "Everyday Use" (page 922), presents a brilliantly observed picture of this period of cultural transition for American blacks.

THINKING ABOUT GRAPHIC AIDS
Using the Time Line

The time line on pages 838–839 shows the chronological sequence of the historical and literary events discussed in Unit 8. Use the time line to answer the following questions.

1. During what war were the Lascaux cave paintings discovered?
2. Did President Nixon visit China before or after the death of Mao Zedong?
3. Was Anouilh's *Antigone* written before or after the Fall of France?
4. Which of the following world leaders was *not* assassinated? (a) Gandhi (b) Stalin (c) Kennedy (d) King (e) Sadat
5. When was Orwell's *Nineteen Eighty-Four* published? (a) 1947; (b) 1949; (c) 1951

One of the most original and influential authors of the twentieth century, Borges (bôr'hās) was a profoundly learned man who often built his stories around philosophical principles or incorporated abstruse lore in them, sometimes with a bit of ironic humor. Borges was born in Buenos Aires, Argentina. His father, trained as a lawyer, was also a linguist, psychologist, teacher, translator, and the author of one unsuccessful novel; his mother was the translator of a number of English and American writers, including Nathaniel Hawthorne and Herman Melville. Borges had an English governess and an English grandmother; the family library contained a large number of books in English; and as a child Borges would sit on his grandmother's lap while she read him children's stories in English. It is therefore not surprising that he learned to read English before he learned to read Spanish; but he learned both at an unusually early age.

Borges was a precocious child who by the age of six had written a short story in Spanish; by the time he was nine, he had read the *Cid*, Cervantes, Dickens, Kipling, Twain, Poe, H. G. Wells, *The Arabian Nights*, and assorted mythologies. While the Borges family was traveling in Europe in 1914, World War I broke out, and they took refuge in Switzerland. Borges and his sister Norah attended school in Geneva, and developed an even more international outlook than they already possessed. From 1919 to 1921, Borges was in Spain, where his first poems were published and he became involved in Ultraism, a literary movement that aspired to reform Spanish poetry. In 1921, his education completed, Borges returned to Buenos Aires with high hopes of introducing South American poets to Ultraism. During the next few years he wrote poetry and founded or collaborated on several literary periodicals. Gradually he lost his interest in Ultraism.

In 1939, after his father's death, Borges took the first of his full-time positions, becoming Municipal Librarian of Buenos Aires. Later he served as Director of the National Library, remaining there until 1973, except for the period 1946–1955. In 1946, the Argentine dictator, Juan Perón, angered that Borges did not actively support him and his policies, and had even signed a petition against him, demoted him from librarian to chicken inspector in the Buenos Aires public markets—an action deliberately designed to hurt and insult. Borges did the only thing he could do—he resigned from the civil service. In 1955, after the fall of Perón, he was reinstated. In the interim Borges continued to write and to lecture at various universities. He taught in the United States at Harvard University, the University of Oklahoma, and the University of Texas.

In addition to poetry and short stories, Borges wrote essays and movie scenarios and translated works into Spanish from a number of different languages. From the volume of his work, it is difficult to believe that in 1927 he began a series of operations to save his eyesight. They slowed the progress of his hereditary blindness but could not stop it altogether. Borges referred to its onset as a "slow, summer twilight" but did not allow it to impede his work. Borges's fame will probably rest on his short stories, but he did not begin writing them until after he was injured in a freak accident. Climbing the stairs of his home, he hit his head on a window casement. The injury and its consequences kept him hospitalized for three weeks, and he claims (with Borgesian humor) that he began writing short stories as an experiment to see whether his brain had been damaged. In one of the best known of his stories, "The Circular Ruins," Borges has combined elements of the ancient Zoroastrian religion with ideas derived from Berkeley's philosophy of Idealism, which maintains that the world does not exist outside the mind of the divinity or the beholder.

The Circular Ruins

Jorge Luis Borges *translated by* **James E. Irby**

And if he left off dreaming about you . . .
Through the Looking Glass, IV[1]

o one saw him disembark in the unanimous[2] night, no one saw the bamboo canoe sink into the sacred mud, but in a few days there was no one who did not know that the taciturn man came from the South and that his home had been one of those numberless villages upstream in the deeply cleft side of the mountain, where the Zend language[3] has not been contaminated by Greek and where leprosy is infrequent. What is certain is that the gray man kissed the mud, climbed up the bank without pushing aside (probably, without feeling) the blades which were lacerating his flesh, and crawled, nauseated and bloodstained, up to the circular enclosure crowned with a stone tiger or horse, which sometimes was the color of flame and now was that of ashes. This circle was a temple which had been devoured by ancient fires, profaned by the miasmal jungle, and whose god no longer received the homage of men. The stranger stretched himself out beneath the pedestal. He was awakened by the sun high overhead. He was not astonished to find that his wounds had healed; he closed his pallid eyes and slept, not through weakness of flesh but through determination of will. He

---

1. Through the Looking Glass, IV, a reference to the book by Lewis Carroll, a sequel to his *Alice's Adventures in Wonderland.* In Chapter IV, Alice, in the company of the identical schoolboy twins Tweedledum and Tweedledee, comes upon the Red King, who is sleeping under a tree. The context in which the quoted line appears is as follows:
"He's dreaming now," said Tweedledee: "and what do you think he's dreaming about?"
Alice said, "Nobody can guess that."
"Why, about *you!*" Tweedledee exclaimed, clapping his hands triumphantly. "And if he left off dreaming about you, where do you suppose you'd be?"
"Where I am now, of course," said Alice.
"Not you!" Tweedledee retorted contemptuously. "You'd be nowhere. Why, you're only a sort of thing in his dream!"
2. unanimous, here used to mean "complete, total."
3. Zend language, the language of the Zend-Avesta, the sacred scriptures of the seventh-century B.C. Persian teacher, Zarathustra. He is more widely known as Zoroaster, the Greek transliteration of the name. The followers of Zoroaster's teachings are still numerous in parts of Asia.

knew that this temple was the place required for his invincible intent; he knew that the incessant trees had not succeeded in strangling the ruins of another propitious temple downstream which had once belonged to gods now burned and dead; he knew that his immediate obligation was to dream. Toward midnight he was awakened by the inconsolable shriek of a bird. Tracks of bare feet, some figs and a jug warned him that the men of the region had been spying respectfully on his sleep, soliciting his protection or afraid of his magic. He felt a chill of fear, and sought out a sepulchral niche in the dilapidated wall where he concealed himself among unfamiliar leaves.

The purpose which guided him was not impossible, though supernatural. He wanted to dream a man; he wanted to dream him in minute entirety and impose him on reality. This magic project had exhausted the entire expanse of his mind; if some one had asked him his name or to relate some event of his former life, he would not have been able to give an answer. This uninhabited, ruined temple suited him, for it contained a minimum of visible world; the proximity of the workmen also suited him, for they took it upon themselves to provide for his frugal needs. The rice and fruit they brought him were nourishment enough for his body, which was consecrated to the sole task of sleeping and dreaming.

At first, his dreams were chaotic; then in a short while they became dialectic[4] in nature. The stranger dreamed that he was in the center of a circular amphitheater which was more or less the burnt temple; clouds of taciturn students filled the tiers of seats; the faces of the farthest ones hung at a distance of many centuries and as high as the stars, but their features were completely precise. The man lectured his pupils on anatomy, cosmography,[5] and magic: the faces listened anxiously and tried to answer understandingly, as if they guessed the importance of that examination which would redeem one of them from his condition of empty illusion and interpolate him into the real world. Asleep or awake, the man thought over the answers of his phantoms, did not allow himself to be deceived by impostors, and in certain perplexities he sensed a growing intelligence.

He was seeking a soul worthy of participating in the universe.

After nine or ten nights he understood with a certain bitterness that he could expect nothing from those pupils who accepted his doctrine passively, but that he could expect something from those who occasionally dared to oppose him. The former group, although worthy of love and affection, could not ascend to the level of individuals; the latter preexisted to a slightly greater degree. One afternoon (now afternoons were also given over to sleep, now he was only awake for a couple of hours at daybreak) he dismissed the vast illusory student body for good and kept only one pupil. He was a taciturn, sallow boy, at times intractable, and whose sharp features resembled those of his dreamer. The brusque elimination of his fellow students did not disconcert him for long; after a few private lessons, his progress was enough to astound the teacher. Nevertheless, a catastrophe took place. One day, the man emerged from his sleep as if from a viscous desert, looked at the useless afternoon light which he immediately confused with the dawn, and understood that he had not dreamed. All that night and all day long, the intolerable lucidity of insomnia fell upon him. He tried exploring the forest, to lose his strength; among the hemlock[6] he barely succeeded in experiencing several short snatches of sleep, veined with fleeting, rudimentary visions that were useless. He tried to assemble the student body but scarcely had he articulated a few brief words of exhortation when it became deformed and was then erased. In his almost perpetual vigil, tears of anger burned his old eyes.

He understood that modeling the incoherent and vertiginous matter of which dreams are composed was the most difficult task that a man could undertake, even though he should penetrate all the enigmas of a superior and inferior order; much more difficult than weaving a rope out of sand or coining the faceless wind. He swore he would for-

---

4. *dialectic*, here used to mean "concerned with the process of discussion or argument."
5. *cosmography*, science that deals with the general appearance and structure of the universe.
6. *hemlock*, an evergreen tree.

Max Ernst (1891–1976), *The Whole City.*
1935–1936. Kunsthaus Zurich

get the enormous hallucination which had thrown him off at first, and he sought another method of work. Before putting it into execution, he spent a month recovering his strength, which had been squandered by his delirium. He abandoned all premeditation of dreaming and almost immediately succeeded in sleeping a reasonable part of each day. The few times that he had dreams during this period, he paid no attention to them. Before resuming his task, he waited until the moon's disk was perfect. Then, in the afternoon, he purified himself in the waters of the river, worshiped the planetary gods, pronounced the prescribed syllables of a mighty name, and went to sleep. He dreamed almost immediately, with his heart throbbing.

He dreamed that it was warm, secret, about the size of a clenched fist, and of a garnet color within the penumbra of a human body as yet without face or sex; during fourteen lucid nights he dreamt of it with meticulous love. Every night he perceived it more clearly. He did not touch it; he only permitted himself to witness it, to observe it, and occasionally to rectify it with a glance. He perceived it and lived it from all angles and distances. On the fourteenth night he lightly touched the pulmonary artery with his index finger, then the whole heart, outside and inside. He was satisfied with the examination. He deliberately did not

dream for a night; he then took up the heart again, invoked the name of a planet, and undertook the vision of another of the principal organs. Within a year he had come to the skeleton and the eyelids. The innumerable hair was perhaps the most difficult task. He dreamed an entire man—a young man, but who did not sit up or talk, who was unable to open his eyes. Night after night, the man dreamt him asleep.

In the Gnostic cosmogonies, demiurges fashion a red Adam who cannot stand;[7] as clumsy, crude and elemental as this Adam of dust was the Adam of dreams forged by the wizard's nights. One afternoon, the man almost destroyed his entire work, but then changed his mind. (It would have been better had he destroyed it.) When he had exhausted all supplications to the deities of the

---

7. ***In the Gnostic cosmogonies, demiurges fashion a red Adam who cannot stand.*** A cosmogony is a theory or story which explains the origin of the universe. Gnosticism was a religious cult, mixing Persian, Syrian, Egyptian, and Greek influences, which flourished in the first centuries A.D. In the Gnostic myth of man's creation, the demiurge was a minor deity who had trespassed against one of the seven supreme deities and was thus banished from their circle. He roamed the universe and, through either arrogance or ignorance, took himself to be the supreme being. As such, he fashioned out of clay a man in his own image. He had not, however, the power to give life to his model. At the critical moment in his project, the seven supreme deities intervened and completed the creation of man, in the hope that man would recognize through knowledge (from the Greek, *gnosis*) the true nature of the universe.

earth, he threw himself at the feet of the effigy which was perhaps a tiger or perhaps a colt and implored its unknown help. That evening, at twilight, he dreamt of the statue. He dreamt it was alive, tremulous: it was not an atrocious bastard of a tiger and a colt, but at the same time these two fiery creatures and also a bull, a rose, and a storm. This multiple god revealed to him that his earthly name was Fire, and that in this circular temple (and in others like it) people had once made sacrifices to him and worshiped him, and that he would magically animate the dreamed phantom, in such a way that all creatures, except Fire itself and the dreamer, would believe it to be a man of flesh and blood. He commanded that once this man had been instructed in all the rites, he should be sent to the other ruined temple whose pyramids were still standing downstream, so that some voice would glorify him in that deserted edifice. In the dream of the man that dreamed, the dreamed one awoke.

The wizard carried out the orders he had been given. He devoted a certain length of time (which finally proved to be two years) to instructing him in the mysteries of the universe and the cult of fire. Secretly, he was pained at the idea of being separated from him. On the pretext of pedagogical necessity, each day he increased the number of hours dedicated to dreaming. He also remade the right shoulder, which was somewhat defective. At times, he was disturbed by the impression that all this had already happened. . . . In general, his days were happy; when he closed his eyes, he thought: *Now I will be with my son.* Or, more rarely: *The son I have engendered is waiting for me and will not exist if I do not go to him.*

Gradually, he began accustoming him to reality. Once he ordered him to place a flag on a faraway peak. The next day the flag was fluttering on the peak. He tried other analogous experiments, each time more audacious. With a certain bitterness, he understood that his son was ready to be born—and perhaps impatient. That night he kissed him for the first time and sent him off to the other temple whose remains were turning white downstream, across many miles of inextricable jungle and marshes. Before doing this (and

so that his son should never know that he was a phantom, so that he should think himself a man like any other) he destroyed in him all memory of his years of apprenticeship.

His victory and peace became blurred with boredom. In the twilight times of dusk and dawn, he would prostrate himself before the stone figure, perhaps imagining his unreal son carrying out identical rites in other circular ruins downstream; at night he no longer dreamed, or dreamed as any man does. His perceptions of the sounds and forms of the universe became somewhat pallid: his absent son was being nourished by these diminutions of his soul. The purpose of his life had been fulfilled; the man remained in a kind of ecstasy. After a certain time, which some chroniclers prefer to compute in years and others in decades, two oarsmen awoke him at midnight; he could not see their faces, but they spoke to him of a charmed man in a temple of the North, capable of walking on fire without burning himself. The wizard suddenly remembered the words of the god. He remembered that of all the creatures that people the earth, Fire was the only one who knew his son to be a phantom. This memory, which at first calmed him, ended by tormenting him. He feared lest his son should meditate on this abnormal privilege and by some means find out he was a mere simulacrum. Not to be a man, to be a projection of another man's dreams—what an incomparable humiliation, what madness! Any father is interested in the sons he has procreated (or permitted) out of the mere confusion of happiness; it was natural that the wizard should fear for the future of that son whom he had thought out entrail by entrail, feature by feature, in a thousand and one secret nights.

His misgivings ended abruptly, but not without certain forewarnings. First (after a long drought) a remote cloud, as light as a bird, appeared on a hill; then, toward the South, the sky took on the rose color of leopard's gums; then came clouds of smoke which rusted the metal of the nights; afterwards came the panic-stricken flight of wild animals. For what had happened many centuries before was repeating itself. The ruins of the sanctuary of the god of Fire was destroyed by fire.

In a dawn without birds, the wizard saw the concentric[8] fire licking the walls. For a moment, he thought of taking refuge in the water, but then he understood that death was coming to crown his old age and absolve him from his labors. He walked toward the sheets of flame. They did not bite his flesh, they caressed him and flooded him without heat or combustion. With relief, with humiliation, with terror, he understood that he also was an illusion, that someone else was dreaming him.

1944

---

8. *concentric*, here used to mean "encircling."

Reader's Note

"The Circular Ruins"

Like most Borges stories, "The Circular Ruins" can be interpreted in a number of ways, but analyzing the clues Borges provides is probably the best way to arrive at the interpretation he intends. Analysis begins with the title, which is also the **setting.** Moving from the title to the story itself, we find that the circular ruins are located in Persia (modern Iran), probably many years in the past. The clue here is the Zend language, which was the language of Zoroastrianism, an ancient religion traceable to at least the seventh century B.C. With the rise of Islam in the seventh century A.D., the Zoroastrians fled to either India or the remote regions of Persia —where, because of the mountainous terrain, there are rivers that flow from south to north, as does the river described in the story.

Zoroastrianism is itself entwined in the plot of the story. The chief symbol of the religion is fire, which is regarded as a sign of divine power and as a purifying agent. Ordinarily Zoroastrian fire-temples are not used for congregational worship, but as shrines where the priest says prayers for individuals and maintains the sacred flame. In the Borges story, the wizard is a later-generation priest who observes some of the rituals of Zoroastrianism.

The next Borges clue, an obvious one, is the epigraph from Lewis Carroll's fantasy, *Through the Looking Glass,* the sequel to *Alice in Wonderland.* In this book Carroll plays with the concept of the dreamer and the dreamed—the person who is told, or who realizes—that he or she is only a phantom of someone else's dream. If we follow Borges's clue and actually read all of Chapter IV, we will see that early in the chapter

Tweedledee and Tweedledum engage in a sort of chop-logic with Alice. At one point Tweedledee says, ". . . if it was so, it might be; if it were so, it would be; but as it isn't, it ain't. That's logic." Obviously here Carroll is satirizing logic and its applications. In Borges this is paralleled by the wizard's first attempt to dream a son. His dream begins with dialectics (argument) and continues with his lectures and questions and answers —his attempt to use logic to select his son. Elsewhere, in speaking of his writing, Borges says he will "dream the plot" of a story; and in an essay on Shakespeare he has a voice from the whirlwind (a biblical reference) say to Shakespeare, "I dreamed the world the way you dreamed your work, my Shakespeare: one of the forms of my dream was you, who, like me, are many and no one." The wizard's second attempt at dreaming a son is successful, because it involves dreaming a physical creation. The intervention of the fire-god to awaken the creation and provide duties for it reverts to Zoroastrianism. Still later, the destruction of the jungle and the temple (but not entirely, for it will be used again) is the purifying act of fire to prevent the vegetation from overwhelming the temple.

Through the Looking Glass ends with a poem, the last stanza of which reads as follows:

Ever drifting down the stream—
Lingering in a golden gleam—
Life, what is it but a dream?

Here the concept of the dreamer and dreamed person is expanded to claim that life itself is a dream. This is a theory that Borges subscribed to because of his acceptance of the idealistic philosophy of Bishop George Berkeley (1685–1753), who claimed that the world does not exist beyond the mind of the divinity or of the beholder.

Finally, in an essay called "A New Refutation of Time," Borges mentions Berkeley and ends with the following: "Time is the substance from which I am made. Time is a river which sweeps me along, but I am the river; it is a tiger which mangles me, but I am the tiger; it is a fire which consumes me, but I am the fire. Unfortunately, the world is real; I, unfortunately, am Borges."

Note the Zoroastrian symbols from "The Circular Ruins": the river, the tiger, and the fire.

Having followed Borges's clues, we are able to read and appreciate "The Circular Ruins" on three levels. The simplest is the straight plot without consideration of any clues; the second is as an application of Berkeley's philosophy, neatly set in a remote area where fire-temples could exist; and the third is as a fictional description of the relationship between the author and the characters he or she "dreams" and who often seem to the author to take on a life of their own.

THINK AND DISCUSS

Understanding

1. What hints are there early in the story that the protagonist is not a man of flesh and blood?

Analyzing

2. Why does the wizard choose to lecture on anatomy, cosmography, and magic?
3. Why does the wizard's second project of organic creation seem to work better than his first?
4. Why might the Fire God periodically destroy his own temples?
5. Is there any significance to the fact that all the movement of the story is downstream, rather than upstream? Explain.
6. Would the wizard have welcomed death more than the knowledge of his true nature? Explain.

Extending

7. Do you think Borges was wise in choosing a very primitive setting for a story as intellectually sophisticated as this? Why or why not?
8. What elements can you find in the relationship of the wizard to his son that have relevance to real family situations?
9. The wizard's problems in creating a son suggest some of the difficulties authors have in creating convincing fictional characters. Try to equate these problems. What pitfalls or limitations might an author face if he, like the wizard, relied solely upon either dialogue or physical description in creating his characters?
10. Using the **style** of the story as your criterion, what reasons might you offer to explain why Borges has never written anything longer than a short story?

COMPOSITION

Writing a Feature Story

Assume that rumors of the wizard's story have reached modern America and that you, as a journalist, have been sent to the area where he lived to write a feature story about him. You are to examine the ruined temples, interview the natives and anyone else you meet (if you wish, you may add characters), and then write your story, which should be four or five paragraphs long.

Analyzing Borges's Style

Reread the selection, noting the things that make Borges's style unique. Pay special attention to his descriptions—what is *not* described or is merely outlined, as well as what is fully described. Consider also the questions he leaves unanswered, as well as those he does answer. Take notes and write a five-paragraph composition in which you analyze Borges's style. Assume that it will be read by your classmates. See "Writing to Analyze an Author's Style" in the Writer's Handbook.

The Italian poet Quasimodo was born in Syracuse, on the island of Sicily, and it is Sicily that lies at the heart of his poetry. From an early age he was affected by the harsh but beautiful countryside and the ancient ruins that were a part of the landscape. He himself calls Sicily his horizon: ". . . the land of ancient civilizations, of cities of the dead, of prison quarries, of caryatids rising out of the grass . . ." Of his poems, Quasimodo says that the images always take shape in his native Sicilian dialect.

When Quasimodo was seven, he accompanied his father, who was a railway worker, to Messina in the wake of an earthquake that devastated the area. He never forgot this first encounter with death and destruction and the sound of shooting as looters were summarily executed. In the poem "To My Father" (page 854) he describes these early experiences in Messina.

Although Quasimodo wrote verse from the time he was fifteen until he was twenty, he wanted to be an engineer and attended technical schools and later the Polytechnic Institute in Rome. Upon graduation he accepted a position in the State Civil Engineers Bureau (1926) that took him to Reggio Calabria, in the southern part of Italy. He was just a ferry-boat ride away from Messina, and the return to familiar scenes stimulated him to begin writing poetry again. "And Suddenly It's Evening" (page 855), a product of this period, was included in *Waters and Lands: 1920–1929*, his first poetry collection.

Deciding that he wanted to devote his life to poetry, Quasimodo left engineering in 1929 to work as an editor and critic, first for a publishing house and then for a magazine. In 1941 he became a professor of Italian Literature at the Giuseppe Verdi Conservatory in Milan, remaining there until 1964. More than twenty volumes of his poems have been published in Italian. In addition, he has edited poetry collections and translated more than thirty works into Italian, among them Shakespeare's *Romeo and Juliet*, *Macbeth*, *Richard III*, *The Tempest*, *Othello*, and *Antony and Cleopatra*.

When he received notification of his Nobel Prize award, Quasimodo commented that the honor "relates in particular to the grave problem of the anxiety of modern man, which is at the heart of all my work." Soon a controversy arose over his poem "To the New Moon" (page 855), which had prompted a telegram from the president of the Professional Writers' Association of the Soviet Union congratulating Quasimodo for his "vigorous poems which had won many readers in the Soviet Union, where it is not forgotten that you were one of the first writers to devote a poem to our *Sputnik*." To those who criticized what they saw as his pro-Soviet position, Quasimodo replied that he had not wanted to glorify the *Sputnik* but rather "this new moon created by the genius of men, with God's help."

Review IMAGERY in the Handbook of Literary Terms, page 953.

To My Father

translated by **Allen Mandelbaum**

Where Messina lay
violet upon the waters, among the mangled
    wires
and rubble, you walk along the rails
and switches in your islander's
5 cock-of-the-walk beret. For three days now,
the earthquake boils, it's hurricane December
and a poisoned sea. Our nights fall
into the freight cars; we, young livestock,
count our dusty dreams with the dead
10 crushed by iron, munching almonds
and apples dried in garlands. The science
of pain put truth and blades into our games
on the lowlands of yellow malaria
and tertian fever[1] swollen with mud.

15 Your patience, sad and delicate,
robbed us of fear,
a lesson of days linked to the death
we had betrayed, to the scorn of the thieves
seized among the debris, and executed in the
    dark
20 by the firing squads of the landing parties, a
    tally
of low numbers adding up exact
concentric, a scale of future life.

Back and forth your sun cap moved
in the little space they always left you.
25 For me, too, everything was measured
and I have borne your name
a little beyond the hatred and the envy.
That red on your cap was a mitre;
a crown with eagle's wings.
30 And now in the eagle of your ninety years
I wanted to speak to you—your parting
signals colored by the night-time lantern—
to speak to you from this imperfect
wheel of the world,
35 within a flood of crowded walls,
far from the Arabian jasmine
where you are still, to tell you
what once I could not—difficult
affinity of thoughts—to tell you (not only
40 the marshland locust, the mastic tree can hear)
as the watchman of the fields tells his master:
"I kiss your hands." This, nothing else.
Life is darkly strong.

---

1. **tertian fever**, fever, such as malaria, that recurs every
other day.

Comment

The Messina Earthquake

On December 28, 1908, a massive earthquake devastated southern Italy and eastern Sicily, completely destroying the cities of Regio and Messina, and many villages, and killing 150,000 people. In the following account of his childhood, Quasimodo describes his experience of this disaster:

"I was born in Syracuse on August 20, 1901. My father was a railway worker. When the crossing bell announced the passage of one of the very rare trains through this sulphur-mining country, its tinkling seemed to last forever. . . . I first went to school in Gela, where I felt the shock of the Messina earthquake. Three days later my father was sent into the desolated city. This was my first encounter with death. Looters were being shot. We were locked into the railway cars, and as new tremors occurred we were dispatched from one disaster to another. The nearest villages were Megara Iblea and Sferro: they made one think of Greece and her lush landscapes. I was baptized in Roccalumera, a few miles from Taormina. My grandmother was a true Greek, a native of Patras. I learned early to read and write, and I became acquainted with the poets. I did not yet understand them, but they left an indelible impression on me."

And Suddenly It's Evening

translated by **A. Michael de Luca**

Each of us stands alone upon the heart of the
    earth
transfixed by a beam of sunlight:
and suddenly it's evening.

                 1930

To the New Moon

translated by **Allen Mandelbaum**

In the beginning God created the heaven
and the earth; then in His exact
day He set the lights in heaven,
and on the seventh day He rested.

5 After millions of years, man,
made in His image and likeness,
never resting, with his
secular intelligence,
without fear, in the serene sky
10 of an October night,[1]
set other luminaries like
those that turned
from the creation of the world. Amen.

---

1. *October night*. On October 4, 1957, *Sputnik*, the first artificial satellite, was launched by the U.S.S.R.

THINK AND DISCUSS

Understanding

1. In "To My Father," what detail of his father's dress does Quasimodo emphasize? Why might he have noticed this?
2. What impression of Messina is conveyed by the first stanza?
3. In "And Suddenly It's Evening," what is being compared to evening?
4. In "To the New Moon," what is the "new moon"?

Analyzing

5. In "To My Father," what is meant by "the death/we had betrayed" (lines 17–18)?
6. What is Quasimodo's attitude toward his father?
7. What does Quasimodo want to tell his father—and does tell him in the poem?
8. Explain the meaning of the last line of the poem, "Life is darkly strong."
9. Why does the speaker in "And Suddenly It's Evening" say, "Each of us stands alone"?
10. The first stanza of "To the New Moon" is based on the first chapter of Genesis (see page 21). Why would Quasimodo use this passage to open his poem?
11. This poem ends with the word "Amen," meaning "So be it." What does this suggest about the poet's attitude toward "the new moon"?
12. What is the mood of this poem—melancholy, amazed, resigned, wondering, or something else?

Extending

13. Would you say that "To My Father" supports the old adage, "Like father, like son"? Explain.
14. Judging from Quasimodo's choice of words and images in "And Suddenly It's Evening," what do you think might be his attitude toward existence and its end?
15. More than thirty years have passed since Quasimodo wrote "To the New Moon." Do you think it is dated? Explain.

REVIEWING: Imagery   H7
See Handbook of Literary Terms, p. 953.

Imagery means the concrete words or details that appeal to the senses of sight, sound, touch, smell, and taste, or to internal feelings. "To My Father" is an excellent example of the use of imagery in a poem, for it begins with sensory images and then moves to images suggesting Quasimodo's internal feelings.

1. In stanza 1, what concrete details does Quasimodo use to suggest the damage done by the earthquake?
2. Throughout the poem, Quasimodo uses concrete details that suggest his father's work on the railroad. What are they?
3. In the last stanza, what concrete details does Quasimodo use to suggest his love for his father?

COMPOSITION

Writing About Quasimodo's Nobel Citation

When the Nobel Prize for Literature was awarded to Quasimodo in 1959, the accompanying citation explained that the award was "For his lyrical poetry, which with classical fire expresses the tragic experience of life in our own times." In a composition of four or five paragraphs to be read by your teacher, explain the extent to which the citation applies to these three poems.

Analyzing a Character

Based on what you have learned about Quasimodo and his thoughts from these three poems, write a composition of four or five paragraphs in which you analyze his character. Consider what you have found out about his childhood, his feeling for his father, his attitude toward science, his feelings about life itself. Expect that you will be asked to share your paper with your classmates.

BIOGRAPHY

Isaac Bashevis Singer

1904–

Although he lives in the United States and received his Nobel Prize in 1978 as an American, Singer was born in Poland and still writes in Yiddish. In 1935 he emigrated to the United States, where his brother, the novelist Israel Joshua Singer (1893–1944), author of *The Brothers Ashkenazi,* was already a recognized writer. Both brothers eventually became naturalized American citizens. Singer's father was a Hassidic rabbi, both grandfathers were rabbis, and Singer himself spent seven years at a rabbinical seminary in Poland. From this background comes his understanding of Judaism and of the people of Poland's Jewish *shtetls* (villages).

When Singer began writing at age fifteen, he used Hebrew but then switched to Yiddish because he thought Hebrew was a dying language. Ironically, the establishment of the state of Israel, where the official language is Hebrew, has resulted in a revitalization of Hebrew literature, while the Holocaust destroyed the *shtetls* where Yiddish was spoken. The destruction of the Jewish world which Singer knew and of which he writes may mean that sometime in the future its way of life will be preserved only in works of literature like his. Before the Holocaust, Yiddish was spoken by eleven million people in the *shtetls;* by the end of World War II that number had been reduced to four million, and it continues to decline. Today Singer is known as the foremost living writer of Yiddish literature.

Singer's fiction is marked by the inclusion of a wealth of specific detail, so that his readers feel they are actually seeing, hearing, smelling, feeling, even tasting the things he describes. Of his fictional technique, Singer has said, "When I tell a story, I tell a story. I don't try to discuss, criticize, or analyze my characters," and "Whenever a writer tries to be more than a storyteller, he becomes less." Typically he writes about people who lived in the Polish *shtetls* in the late nineteenth and early part of the twentieth century. "The Old Man" is an example of how he is able to bring this age and place to life for later generations. When Singer was awarded the Nobel Prize in 1978, his citation read "for his impassioned narrative art which, with roots in a Polish-Jewish cultural tradition, brings universal human conditions to life."

The Old Man

Isaac Bashevis Singer
translated by **Norbert Guterman and Elaine Gottlieb**

1

t the beginning of the great war,[1] Chaim Sachar[2] of Krochmalna Street in Warsaw[3] was a rich man. Having put aside dowries of a thousand rubles each for his daughters, he was about to rent a new apartment, large enough to include a Torah-studying son-in-law.[4] There would also have to be additional room for his ninety-year-old father, Reb Moshe Ber, a Turisk hassid,[5] who had recently come to live with him in Warsaw.

But two years later, Chaim Sachar's apartment was almost empty. No one knew where his two sons, young giants, who had been sent to the front, had been buried. His wife and two daughters had died of typhus. He had accompanied their bodies to the cemetery, reciting the memorial prayer for the three of them, pre-empting the most desirable place at the prayer stand in the synagogue,[6] and inviting the enmity of other mourners, who accused him of taking unfair advantage of his multiple bereavement.

After the German occupation of Warsaw, Chaim Sachar, a tall, broad man of sixty who traded in live geese, locked his store. He sold his furniture by the piece, in order to buy frozen potatoes and moldy dried peas, and prepared gritty blackish noodles for himself and his father, who had survived the grandchildren.

Although Chaim Sachar had not for many months been near a live fowl, his large caftan was still covered with goose down, his great broad-brimmed hat glistened with fat, and his heavy, snub-toed boots were stained with slaughter-house

blood. Two small eyes, starved and frightened, peered from beneath his disheveled eyebrows; the red rims about his eyes were reminiscent of the time when he could wash down a dish of fried liver and hard-boiled eggs with a pint of vodka every morning after prayer. Now, all day long, he wandered through the marketplace, inhaling butcher-shop odors and those from restaurants, sniffing like a dog, and occasionally napping on porters' carts. With the refuse he had collected in a basket, he fed his kitchen stove at night; then, rolling the sleeves over his hairy arms, he would grate turnips on a grater. His father, meanwhile, sat warming himself at the open kitchen door, even though it was midsummer. An open Mishna[7] treatise lay across his knees, and he complained constantly of hunger.

As though it were all his son's fault, the old man would mutter angrily, "I can't stand it much longer . . . this gnawing. . . ."

Without looking up from his book, a treatise on impurity, he would indicate the pit of his stomach and resume his mumbling in which the word

---

1. *the great war,* World War I.
2. *Chaim Sachar,* (Hī'm säH'ər).
3. *Warsaw,* capital and chief city of Poland.
4. *Torah-studying son-in-law.* The Torah (tôr'ə) is the entire body of Jewish law and tradition.
5. *Reb . . . hassid,* (has'id). *Reb* is the title given to the head of a Hassidic community. The Hassids are a Jewish sect founded in the 1700s in Poland. Turisk (tü rěsk') is a town in the Ukraine.
6. *synagogue* (sin'ə gôg), a building used by Jews for religious worship and instruction. The "Houses of Study" mentioned in the story are synagogues.
7. *Mishna* (mish'nə), a collection of Jewish laws and traditions based on Mosaic law, codified in A.D. 210.

"impure" recurred like a refrain. Although his eyes were a murky blue, like the eyes of a blind man, he needed no glasses, still retained some of his teeth, yellow and crooked as rusty nails, and awoke each day on the side on which he had fallen asleep. He was disturbed only by his rupture, which nevertheless, did not keep him from plodding through the streets of Warsaw with the help of his pointed stick, his "horse," as he called it. At every synagogue he would tell stories about wars, about evil spirits, and of the old days of cheap and abundant living when people dried sheepskins in cellars and drank spirits directly from the barrel through a straw. In return, Reb Moshe Ber was treated to raw carrots, slices of radish, and turnips. Finishing them in no time, he would then, with a trembling hand, pluck each crumb from his thinning beard—still not white—and speak of Hungary, where more than seventy years before, he had lived in his father-in-law's house. "Right after prayer, we were served a large decanter of wine and a side of veal. And with the soup there were hard-boiled eggs and crunchy noodles."

Hollow-cheeked men in rags, with ropes about their loins, stood about him, bent forward, mouths watering, digesting each of his words, the whites of their eyes greedily showing, as if the old man actually sat there eating. Young yeshiva[8] students, faces emaciated from fasts, eyes shifty and restless as those of madmen, nervously twisted their long earlocks[9] around their fingers, grimacing, as though to suppress stomach-aches, repeating ecstatically, "That was the time. A man had his share of heaven and earth. But now we have nothing."

For many months Reb Moshe Ber shuffled about searching for a bit of food; then, one night in late summer, on returning home, he found Chaim Sachar, his first-born, lying in bed, sick, barefoot, and without his caftan. Chaim Sachar's face was as red as though he had been to a steam bath, and his beard was crumpled in a knot. A neighbor woman came in, touched his forehead, and chanted, "Woe is me, it's that sickness. He must go to the hospital."

Next morning the black ambulance reappeared in the courtyard. Chaim Sachar was taken to the hospital; his apartment was sprayed with carbolic acid;[10] and his father was led to the disinfection center, where they gave him a long white robe and shoes with wooden soles. The guards, who knew him well, gave him double portions of bread under the table and treated him to cigarettes. The Sukkoth[11] holiday had passed by the time the old man, his shaven chin concealed[12] beneath a kerchief, was allowed to leave the disinfection center. His son had died long before, and Reb Moshe Ber said the memorial prayer, *kaddish*,[13] for him. Now alone in the apartment, he had to feed his stove with paper and wood shavings from garbage cans. In the ashes he baked rotten potatoes, which he carried in his scarf, and in an iron pot, he brewed chicory.[14] He kept house, made his own candles by kneading bits of wax and suet around wicks, laundered his shirt beneath the kitchen faucet, and hung it to dry on a piece of string. He set the mousetraps each night and drowned the mice each morning. When he went out he never forgot to fasten the heavy padlock on the door. No one had to pay rent in Warsaw at that time. Moreover, he wore his son's boots and trousers. His old acquaintances in the House of Study envied him. "He lives like a king!" they said, "He has inherited his son's fortune!"

The winter was difficult. There was no coal, and since several tiles were missing from the stove, the apartment was filled with thick black smoke each time the old man made a fire. A crust of blue ice and snow covered the window panes by November, making the rooms constantly dark or dusky. Overnight, the water on his night table froze in the pot. No matter how many clothes he piled over him in bed, he never felt warm; his feet

---

8. *yeshiva* (yə shē′və), a Jewish school for higher studies, often a rabbinical seminary.
9. *earlocks,* long sidelocks worn by Orthodox Jewish males.
10. *carbolic acid,* a chemical used as a disinfectant.
11. *Sukkoth* (sùk′əs), a Jewish harvest festival of either eight or nine days celebrated in September or October.
12. *chin concealed.* His beard had been shaved because it might harbor infection. He concealed its absence because Orthodox Jewish males did not cut their beards.
13. *kaddish* (kä′dish), a Hebrew prayer recited by a person mourning for a deceased relative.
14. *chicory,* the root of a wildflower, roasted and used as a substitute for coffee.

Roman Vishniac (1897–1990), photograph of
an old Jew in Warsaw. 1938

tables, nondescript fellows with long matted hair
and rags over their swollen feet—men who, having lost all they had in the war, were half-naked
or covered only with torn clothes, bags slung
over their shoulders. All day long, while orphans
recited *kaddish*, women stood in throngs around
the Holy Ark,[15] loudly praying for the sick, and
filling his ears with their moans and lamentations.
The room, dim and stuffy, smelled like a mortuary
chamber from the numerous anniversary candles[16]
that were burning. Every time Reb Moshe Ber,
his head hanging down, fell asleep, he would burn
himself on the stove. He had to be escorted home
at night, for his shoes were hobnailed, and he was
afraid he might slip on the ice. The other tenants
in his house had given him up for dead. "Poor
thing—he's gone to pieces."

One December day, Reb Moshe Ber actually did
slip, receiving a hard blow on his right arm. The
young man escorting him, hoisted Reb Moshe Ber
on his back, and carried him home. Placing the
old man on his bed without undressing him, the
young man ran away as though he had committed a burglary. For two days the old man groaned,
called for help, wept, but no one appeared. Several
times each day he said his Confession of Sins, praying for death to come quickly, pounding his chest
with his left hand. It was quiet outside in the daytime, as though everyone had died; a hazy green
twilight came through the windows. At night he
heard scratching noises as though a cat were trying to climb the walls; a hollow roar seemed to
come repeatedly from underground. In the darkness the old man fancied that his bed stood in the
middle of the room and all the windows were open.
After sunset on the second day he thought he saw
the door open suddenly, admitting a horse with
a black sheet on its back. It had a head as long
as a donkey's and innumerable eyes. The old man
knew at once that this was the Angel of Death.
Terrified, he fell from his bed, making such a
racket that two neighbors heard it. There was a

---

15. Holy Ark, cabinet in a synagogue for housing the
scrolls of the Torah. Torah in this sense means the Pentateuch, the first five books of the Bible.
16. anniversary candles, memorial candles burned from
sunset to sunset on the anniversary of a death.

remained stiff, and as soon as he began to doze,
the entire pile of clothes would fall off, and he
would have to climb out naked to make his bed
once more. There was no kerosene; even matches
were at a premium. Although he recited chapter upon chapter of the Psalms, he could not fall
asleep. The wind, freely roaming about the rooms,
banged the doors; even the mice left. When he
hung up his shirt to dry, it would grow brittle
and break, like glass. He stopped washing himself; his face became coal black. All day long he
would sit in the House of Study, near the red-hot
iron stove. On the shelves, the old books lay like
piles of rags; tramps stood around the tin-topped

commotion in the courtyard; a crowd gathered, and an ambulance was summoned. When he came to his senses, Reb Moshe Ber found himself in a dark box, bandaged and covered up. He was sure this was his hearse, and it worried him that he had no heirs to say *kaddish*, and that therefore the peace of his grave would be disturbed. Suddenly he recalled the verses he would have to say to Duma, the Prosecuting Angel,[17] and his bruised, swollen face twisted into a corpselike smile:

What man is he that liveth and shall not see death?
Shall he deliver his soul from the grave?

2

After Passover,[18] Reb Moshe Ber was discharged from the hospital. Completely recovered, he once more had a great appetite but nothing to eat. All his possessions had been stolen; in the apartment only the peeling walls remained. He remembered Jozefow, a little village near the border of Galicia,[19] where for fifty years he had lived and enjoyed great authority in the Turisk hassidic circle, because he had personally known the old rabbi. He inquired about the possibilities of getting there, but those he questioned merely shrugged their shoulders, and each said something different. Some assured him Jozefow had been burned to the ground, wiped out. A wandering beggar, on the other hand, who had visited the region, said that Jozefow was more prosperous than ever, that its inhabitants ate the Sabbath white bread even on week days. But Jozefow was on the Austrian side of the border, and whenever Reb Moshe Ber broached the subject of his trip, men smiled mockingly in their beards and waved their hands. "Don't be foolish, Reb Moshe Ber. Even a young man couldn't do it."

But Reb Moshe Ber was hungry. All the turnips, carrots, and watery soups he had eaten in public kitchens had left him with a hollow sensation in his abdomen. All night he would dream of Jozefow knishes[20] stuffed with ground meat and onions, of tasty concoctions of tripe and calf's feet, chicken fat and lean beef. The moment he closed his eyes he would find himself at some wedding or circumcision feast. Large brown rolls were piled up on the long table, and Turisk hassidim in silken caftans with high velvet hats over their skull caps, danced, glasses of brandy in their hands, singing:

What's a poor man
Cooking for his dinner?
Borscht and potatoes!
Borscht and potatoes!
Faster, faster, hop-hop-hop!

He was the chief organizer of all those parties; he quarreled with the caterers, scolded the musicians, supervised every detail, and having no time to eat anything, had to postpone it all for later. His mouth watering, he awoke each morning, bitter that not even in his dream had he tasted those wonderful dishes. His heart pounded; his body was covered with a cold perspiration. The light outside seemed brighter every day, and in the morning, rectangular patterns of sunlight would waver on the peeling wall, swirling, as though they mirrored the rushing waves of a river close by. Around the bare hook for a chandelier on the crumbling ceiling, flies hummed. The cool golden glow of dawn illumined the window panes, and the distorted image of a bird in flight was always reflected in them. Beggars and cripples sang their songs in the courtyard below, playing their fiddles and blowing little brass trumpets. In his shirt, Reb Moshe Ber would crawl down from the one remaining bed, to warm his feet and stomach and to gaze at the barefoot girls in short petticoats who were beating red comforters. In all directions feathers flew, like white blossoms, and there were familiar scents of rotten straw and tar. The old man, straightening his crooked fingers, pricking up his long hairy ears as though to hear distant noises, thought for the thousandth time that if he didn't get out of here

---

17. **Duma, the Prosecuting Angel.** In the cabala, the system of Jewish mysticism that developed during the Middle Ages, Duma was the prince of Gehinnom, the abode of sinners.
18. **Passover**, an annual Jewish holiday commemorating the escape of the Hebrews from Egypt, where they had been slaves. It occurs in March or April and lasts eight days.
19. **Galicia** (gə lish′ə), a region in central Europe, now divided between Poland and the Soviet Union.
20. **knishes**, pastry made of dough, wrapped around a stuffing of potato, cheese, etc.

this very summer, he never would.

"God will help me," he would tell himself. "If he wills it, I'll be eating in a holiday arbor[21] at Jozefow."

He wasted a lot of time at first by listening to people who told him to get a passport and apply for a visa. After being photographed, he was given a yellow card, and then he had to stand with hordes of others for weeks outside the Austrian consulate on a crooked little street somewhere near the Vistula.[22] They were constantly being cursed in German and punched with the butts of guns by bearded, pipe-smoking soldiers. Women with infants in their arms wept and fainted. It was rumored that visas were granted only to prostitutes and to men who paid in gold. Reb Moshe Ber, going there every day at sunrise, sat on the ground and nodded over his Beni Issachar treatise, nourishing himself with grated turnips and moldy red radishes. But since the crowd continued to increase, he decided one day to give it all up. Selling his cotton-padded caftan to a peddler, he bought a loaf of bread, and a bag in which he placed his prayer shawl and phylacteries,[23] as well as a few books for good luck; and planning to cross the border illegally, he set out on foot.

It took him five weeks to get to Ivangorod. During the day, while it was warm, he walked barefoot across the fields, his boots slung over his shoulders, peasant fashion. He fed on unripened grain and slept in barns. German military police often stopped him, scrutinized his Russian passport[24] for a long time, searched him to see that he was not carrying contraband, and then let him go. At various times, as he walked, his intestines popped out of place; he lay on the ground and pushed them back with his hands. In a village near Ivangorod he found a group of Turisk hassidim, most of them young. When they heard where he was going and that he intended to enter Galicia, they gaped at him, blinking, then, after whispering among themselves, they warned him, "You're taking a chance in times like these. They'll send you to the gallows on the slightest pretext."

Afraid to converse with him, lest the authorities grow suspicious, they gave him a few marks[25] and got rid of him. A few days later, in that vil-

lage, people spoke in hushed voices of an old Jew who had been arrested somewhere on the road and shot by a firing squad. But not only was Reb Moshe alive by then; he was already on the Austrian side of the border. For a few marks, a peasant had taken him across, hidden in a cart under a load of straw. The old man started immediately for Rajowiec. He fell ill with dysentery there and lay in the poorhouse for several days. Everyone thought he was dying, but he recovered gradually.

Now there was no shortage of food. Housewives treated Reb Moshe Ber to brown buckwheat with milk, and on Saturdays he even ate cold calf's foot jelly and drank a glass of brandy. The moment his strength returned, he was off again. The roads were familiar here. In this region, the peasants still wore the white linen coats and quadrangular caps with tassels that they had worn fifty years ago; they had beards and spoke Ukrainian. In Zamosc the old man was arrested and thrown into jail with two young peasants. The police confiscated his bag. He refused gentile[26] food and accepted only bread and water. Every other day he was summoned by the commandant who, as though Reb Moshe Ber were deaf, screamed directly into his ear in a throaty language. Comprehending nothing, Reb Moshe Ber simply nodded his head and tried to throw himself at the commandant's feet. This went on until after Rosh Hashanah;[27] only then did the Zamosc Jews learn that an old man from abroad was being held in jail. The rabbi and the head of the community obtained his release by paying the commandant a ransom.

Reb Moshe Ber was invited to stay in Zamosc until after Yom Kippur,[28] but he would not con-

---

21. *arbor,* one of the booths constructed of branches and decorated with flowers and fruit that are used in celebrating Sukkoth.
22. *Vistula* (vis′chə lə), a river in Poland flowing from the Carpathian Mountains to the Baltic Sea.
23. *phylacteries* (fə lak′tər ēz), small leather cases containing texts from the Jewish law, worn by Orthodox Jewish males during weekday morning prayers.
24. *Russian passport.* At the time at which Singer's story takes place, Poland was a part of the Russian empire.
25. *marks,* German coins.
26. *gentile* (jen′til), not Jewish.
27. *Rosh Hashanah* (rosh′ hə shä′nə), the Jewish New Year, usually occurring in September.
28. *Yom Kippur,* (yom kip′ər), a Jewish fast day of atonement for sins. It occurs ten days after Rosh Hashanah.

sider it. He spent the night there, took some bread, and set out on foot for Bilgorai at daybreak. Trudging across harvested fields, digging turnips for food, he refreshed himself in the thick pinewoods with whitish berries, large, sour and watery, which grow in damp places and are called Valakhi in the local dialect. A cart gave him a lift for a mile or so. A few miles from Bilgorai, he was thrown to the ground by some shepherds who pulled off his boots and ran away with them.

Reb Moshe Ber continued barefoot, and for this reason did not reach Bilgorai until late at night. A few tramps, spending the night in the House of Study, refused to let him in, and he had to sit on the steps, his weary head on his knees. The autumnal night was clear and cold; against the dark yellow, dull glow of the starry sky, a flock of goats, silently absorbed, peeled bark from the wood that had been piled in the synagogue courtyard for winter. As though complaining of an unforgettable sorrow, an owl lamented in a womanish voice, falling silent and then beginning again, over and over. People with wooden lanterns in their hands came at daybreak to say the *Selichoth* prayers. Bringing the old man inside, they placed him near the stove and covered him with discarded prayer shawls from the chest. Later in the morning they brought him a heavy pair of hobnailed, coarse-leathered military boots. The boots pinched the old man's feet badly, but Reb Moshe Ber was determined to observe the Yom Kippur fast at Jozefow, and Yom Kippur was only one day off.

He left early. There were no more than about four miles to travel, but he wanted to arrive at dawn, in time for the *Selichoth* prayers. The moment he had left town, however, his stiff boots began to cause him such pain, that he couldn't take a step. He had to pull them off and go barefoot. Then there was a downpour with thunder and lightning. He sank knee deep in puddles, kept stumbling, and became smeared with clay and mud. His feet swelled and bled. He spent the night on a haystack under the open sky, and it was so cold that he couldn't sleep. In the neighboring villages, dogs kept barking, and the rain went on forever. Reb Mosher Ber was sure his end had

come. He prayed God to spare him until the *Nilah* prayer, so that he might reach heaven purified of all sin. Later, when on the eastern horizon, the edges of clouds began to glow, while the fog grew milky white, Reb Moshe Ber was infused with new strength and once again set off for Jozefow.

He reached the Turisk circle at the very moment when the hassidim had assembled in the customary way, to take brandy and cake. A few recognized the new arrival at once, and there was great rejoicing for he had long been thought dead. They brought him hot tea. He said his prayers quickly, ate a slice of white bread with honey, gefilte fish made of fresh carp, and kreplach,[29] and took a few glasses of brandy. Then he was led to the steam bath. Two respectable citizens accompanied him to the seventh shelf and personally whipped him with two bundles of new twigs, while the old man wept for joy.

Several times during Yom Kippur, he was at the point of fainting, but he observed the fast until it ended. Next morning the Turisk hassidim gave him new clothes and told him to study the Torah. All of them had plenty of money, since they traded with Bosnian and Hungarian soldiers, and sent flour to what had been Galicia in exchange for smuggled tobacco. It was no hardship for them to support Reb Moshe Ber. The Turisk hassidim knew who he was—a hassid who had sat at the table of no less a man than Reb Motele of Chernobel! He had actually been a guest at the famous wonder-rabbi's home!

A few weeks later, the Turisk hassidim, timber merchants, just to shame their sworn enemies, the Sandzer hassidim, collected wood and built a house for Reb Moshe Ber and married him to a spinster, a deaf and dumb village girl of about forty.

Exactly nine months later she gave birth to a son—now he had someone to say *kaddish* for him. As though it were a wedding, musicians played at the circumcision ceremony. Well-to-do house-

---

29. *gefilte* (gə fil'tə) *fish* . . . *kreplach* (krep'laH). Gefilte fish are cooked fish minced with bread crumbs, eggs, etc., and served in the form of balls or cakes. A kreplach is a triangular or square dumpling that contains chopped meat or cheese and is usually served in soup.

wives baked cakes and looked after the mother. The place where the banquet was held, the assembly room of the Turisk circle, smelled of cinnamon, saffron, and the women's best Sabbath dresses. Reb Moshe Ber wore a new satin caftan and high velvet hat. He danced on the table, and for the first time, mentioned his age:

"And Abraham was a hundred years old," he recited, "when his son Isaac was born unto him. And Sarah said: God hath made me laugh so that all who hear will laugh with me."

He named the boy Isaac.[30]   **1957**

---

30. *Isaac.* The name Isaac means "laughter."

THINK AND DISCUSS
Understanding
1. As the story opens, Chaim Sachar is a wealthy man with a thriving family. What effect does the war have on the family group?
2. How does Reb Moshe Ber manage to survive after his son's death?

Analyzing
3. What purpose do Chaim Sachar and his family serve in the story?
4. How does Singer convey the impression of the slow starvation of the Jewish people of Warsaw?
5. What sustains Reb Moshe Ber physically on his long journey to Jozefow? What sustains him spiritually?
6. What causes Reb Moshe Ber to name his son Isaac?
7. Although all of this story takes place during the war, Singer seems to mention it only in passing. Why?

Extending
8. Is it feasible that a man in his nineties could survive the journey from Warsaw to Jozefow? Could he father a child? If you do not believe this, how do you explain the story?
9. One reader has commented that Singer has provided such detailed descriptions of people and background that it would be easy to make a movie from this selection. Explain why you agree or disagree.

REVIEWING: Setting HₜZ
See Handbook of Literary Terms, p. 969.

Setting is the time and place in which the events of a narrative occur. We know that the opening of "The Old Man" is set in Warsaw during the early years of World War I.

1. Approximately how much time passes from the opening of the story to its end? (You will have to compute this from details in the story.) If Reb Moshe Ber was ninety when the story opened, how old is he when it ends?
2. Contrast the Warsaw setting with that of Jozefow after Reb Moshe Ber has arrived.

COMPOSITION
Analyzing Singer's Style
One of the elements that gives Singer's writing a highly individual style is the wealth of realistic detail he provides. Write a composition of four to five paragraphs to be shared with your classmates in which you discuss his style and point out specific instances of his use of realistic detail. Consider such things as his descriptions of characters and settings, as well as his descriptions of hunger and intense cold. See "Writing to Analyze an Author's Style" in the Writer's Handbook.

Discussing Allegory
Consider the possibility that this selection is an allegory of the ability of the Jewish people to survive despite extraordinary hardships. In a composition of four to five paragraphs to be shared with your classmates discuss this theory, using evidence from the story to support the points you are making.

Swedish writer Harry Martinson successfully employed many literary types—poetry, novels, travel books, radio plays, dramas—even an epic poem about space flight, *Aniara*, that was turned into an opera. Unfortunately, only a small portion of his output has been translated into English. Martinson was born in a small town in southern Sweden, the son of a sea captain. However, he was orphaned when he was six, and his childhood years were unhappy. Since at that time no social legislation protected orphaned children, he was passed around from household to household in the community. When he was fifteen, after a number of unsuccessful attempts, he finally managed to run away to sea and became a cabin boy on a small ship. Working as a stoker and seaman, Martinson traveled throughout the world. During his years at sea, Martinson also educated himself. In 1927 he published his first book of poems, *Ghost-ship*, and thereafter was a full-time writer. Many of his works, among them "Cable Ship" (page 866), reflect his travels and his experiences at sea.

The vignettes on which both "The Cable Ship" and "March Evening" (page 866) are based are also a part of Martinson's novel *The Road* (1948), his most highly praised work. An account of a tramp's adventures, it obviously owes a debt to the author's early experiences. Martinson's space epic *Aniara: A Review of Man in Time and Space* (1956) consists of 103 cantos. It tells the story of a giant spaceship filled with refugees from the doomed planet Earth on an irreversible, equally doomed journey into space. The poem is notable for its science-based symbolism and its attention to the individual destinies of many of the travelers.

In 1949 Martinson was honored by becoming the first self-educated person to be elected to the Swedish Academy. When he received the 1974 Nobel Prize, his citation read, "For writings that catch the dewdrop and reflect the cosmos."

Cable Ship

translated by **Richard Vowles**

We fished up the Atlantic cable between
    Barbados and Tortuga
Held up our lanterns
And plastered new rubber on the wound in its
    back
Latitude fifteen north, longitude sixty-one west.
5 When we set our ear to the gnawed place
We heard a humming in the cable.
—It's millionaires in Montreal and St. John
    discussing
The price of Cuban sugar and the lowering
Of our wages, said one of us.

10 We stood there long and thought, in a circle
    of lanterns,
We patient cable fishermen,
Then lowered the mended cable
To its place in the sea.

1926

March Evening

translated by **Robert Bly**

Winterspring, nightfall, thawing.
Boys have lit a candle in a snowball house.
For the man in the evening train that rattles
    past,
it is a red memory surrounded by gray time,
5 calling, calling, out of stark woods just
    waking up.
And the man who was traveling never got home,
his life stayed behind, held by that lantern and
    that hour.

1934

THINK AND DISCUSS
Understanding
1. In "Cable Ship," what message does one of the crewmen say he hears in the humming of the cable?
2. "March Evening" is a *vignette,* a brief incident or scene. What takes place in the poem?

Analyzing
3. What might have been going through the minds of the crewmen of the cable ship as they "stood there long and thought, in a circle of lanterns" (line 10)?
4. Explain in what sense "the man who was traveling never got home" (line 6) in "March Evening."

Extending
5. "March Evening" describes a kind of *epiphany,* a moment of heightened awareness that can occur as a result of a trivial encounter, object, or event. Can you recall such an incident from your own life? If you wish, you and your classmates might discuss such moments and what they reveal.

THINKING SKILLS
Generalizing
To generalize is to draw a general conclusion from specific information.
What generalization about the sailors' attitudes can be drawn from "Cable Ship"?

COMPOSITION
Writing Diary Entries
Write several diary entries for either the speaker of "Cable Ship" or the man on the train in "March Evening." Have the diary entries provide insight into what occurs in the poem, why it occurs, and what the result is insofar as the diarist is concerned.

Discussing Vignettes
Using these two poems as your examples, write a paper of three to five paragraphs to be read by your teacher in which you discuss Martinson's ability to create vignettes that probe the human soul and raise more questions than they answer.

BIOGRAPHY

R. K. Narayan

1907–

The subcontinent of India has a great number of languages. R. K. Narayan is the best-known Indian author using one of these many languages, English. In a tribute to him, the novelist Graham Greene calls him "one of the glories of English literature." Narayan's works have been translated into all the European languages and into Hebrew. A native of southern India, Narayan was born in Madras, and grew up in Mysore, where he lives today. Mysore gave him the inspiration for Malgudi, the fictional town he created and populated with characters from his novels and short stories. Because of his ability to create, sustain, and expand his imaginary community, Narayan is often compared to William Faulkner, who has done something similar in his fictional Yoknapatawpha County. However, Narayan's touch is lighter and more comical than Faulkner's, and his prose style is far simpler. Ordinarily he maintains a slightly detached, slightly humorous attitude toward his characters, whom he never fails to treat sympathetically. This attitude is evident in his depiction of Soma, the sculptor who is the protagonist of "Such Perfection" (page 868).

Critics have commented on Narayan's success in combining the English language with the Indian settings of his fiction. In a BBC radio interview with Narayan, William Walsh claimed that Narayan's English takes on an Indian flavor by avoiding "the American purr of the combustion engine . . . [and] the thick marmalade quality of British English." Narayan himself says, "English is a very adaptable language. And it's so transparent it can take on the tint of any country." Despite their localized backgrounds, Narayan's novels and stories of Malgudi become universal because they deal with human experiences and emotions that are universal. In "Such Perfection" Soma is torn between the desire to have his beautiful statue of Nataraja installed in a temple for all to worship, and doing what he must to achieve that end—mutilate the statue in some way, for it is too perfect to be viewed by humans. Here is one facet of the age-old conflict between the artist and religion, or the conflict between the individual and the demands of tradition. As do most Narayan characters, Soma grows from his experience, and the short story, which could have had a tragic ending, concludes happily. Narayan's Malgudi novels include *Swami and Friends* (1935), *The Bachelor of Arts* (1937), *The Dark Room* (1938), *The English Teacher* (1945), *Mr. Sampath* (1949), *The Financial Expert* (1952), *The Guide* (1958), *The Man-Eater of Malgudi* (1962), and *The Vendor of Sweets* (1967). Some of his best short stories are included in *Malgudi Days* (1982). Narayan has also written essays, sketches, and memoirs, and has translated versions of the Indian epics, the *Mahabharata* and the *Ramayana*, into English.

Such Perfection

R. K. Narayan

 sense of great relief filled Soma as he realized that his five years of labor were coming to an end. He had turned out scores of images in his lifetime, but he had never done any work to equal this. He often said to himself that long after the Deluge had swept the earth this Nataraja[1] would still be standing on His pedestal.

No other human being had seen the image yet. Soma shut himself in and bolted all the doors and windows and plied his chisel by the still flame of a mud lamp, even when there was a bright sun outside. It made him perspire unbearably, but he did not mind it so long as it helped him to keep out prying eyes. He worked with a fierce concentration and never encouraged anyone to talk about it.

After all, his labors had come to an end. He sat back, wiped the perspiration off his face and surveyed his handiwork with great satisfaction. As he looked on he was overwhelmed by the majesty of this image. He fell prostrate before it, praying, "I have taken five years to make you. May you reside in our temple and bless all human beings!" The dim mud flame cast subtle shadows on the image and gave it an undertone of rippling life. The sculptor stood lost in this vision. A voice said, "My friend, never take this image out of this room. It is too perfect. . . ." Soma trembled with fear. He looked round. He saw a figure crouching in a dark corner of the room—it was a man. Soma dashed forward and clutched him by the throat. "Why did you come here?" The other writhed under the grip and replied, "Out of admiration for you. I have always loved your work. I have waited for five years. . . ."

"How did you come in?"

"With another key while you were eating inside. . . ."

Soma gnashed his teeth. "Shall I strangle you before this God and offer you as sacrifice?" "By all means," replied the other, "if it will help you in any way . . . but I doubt it. Even with a sacrifice you cannot take it out. It is too perfect. Such perfection is not for mortals." The sculptor wept. "Oh, do not say that. I worked in secrecy only for this perfection. It is for our people. It is a God coming into their midst. Don't deny them that." The other prostrated before the image and prayed aloud, "God give us the strength to bear your presence. . . ."

This man spoke to people and the great secret was out. A kind of dread seized the people of the village. On an auspicious day, Soma went to the temple priest and asked, "At the coming full moon my Nataraja must be consecrated. Have you made a place for him in the temple?" The priest answered, "Let me see the image first. . . ." He went over to the sculptor's house, gazed on the image and said, "This perfection, this God, is not for mortal eyes. He will blind us. At the first chant of prayer before him, he will dance . . . and we shall be wiped out. . . ." The sculptor looked so unhappy that the priest added, "Take your chisel and break a little toe or some other part of the image, and it will be safe. . . ." The sculptor replied that he would sooner crack the skull of his visitor. The leading citizens of the village came

---

1. **Deluge . . . Nataraja.** According to Hindu mythology, mankind is destroyed in a vast flood and then recreated every 4,320,000 years. This has occurred seven times in the past, and will occur seven more times in the future. Nataraja (nä´tä rä´jä), "the Lord of the Dance," is one of the forms of the Hindu god Shiva. See page 870.

over and said, "Don't mistake us. We cannot give your image a place in our temple. Don't be angry with us. We have to think of the safety of all the people in the village. . . . Even now if you are prepared to break a small finger . . ."

"Get out, all of you," Soma shouted. "I don't care to bring this Nataraja to your temple. I will make a temple for him where he is. You will see that it becomes the greatest temple on earth. . . ." Next day he pulled down a portion of the wall of the room and constructed a large doorway opening on the street. He called Rama, the tom-tom beater, and said, "I will give you a silver coin for your trouble. Go and proclaim in all nearby villages that this Nataraja will be consecrated at the full moon. If a large crowd turns up, I will present you with a lace shawl."

At the full moon, men, women and children poured in from the surrounding villages. There was hardly an inch of space vacant anywhere. The streets were crammed with people. Vendors of sweets and toys and flowers shouted their wares, moving about in the crowd. Pipers and drummers, groups of persons chanting hymns, children shouting in joy, men greeting each other—all this created a mighty din. Fragrance of flowers and incense hung over the place. Presiding over all this there was the brightest moon that ever shone on earth.

The screen which had covered the image parted. A great flame of camphor was waved in front of the image, and bronze bells rang. A silence fell upon the crowd. Every eye was fixed upon the image. In the flame of the circling camphor Nataraja's eyes lit up. His limbs moved, his anklets jingled. The crowd was awe-stricken. The God pressed one foot on earth and raised the other in dance. He destroyed the universe under his heel, and smeared the ashes over his body, and the same God rattled the drum in his hand and by its rhythm set life in motion again. . . . Creation, Dissolution and God attained a meaning now; this image brought it out . . . the bells rang louder every second. The crowd stood stunned by this vision vouchsafed to them.

At this moment a wind blew from the east. The moon's disc gradually dimmed. The wind gath-

Bronze statue of Shiva Nataraja. 13th century.
The Nelson-Atkins Museum of Art, Kansas City, Missouri

ered force, clouds blotted out the moon; people looked up and saw only pitchlike darkness above. Lightning flashed, thunder roared and fire poured down from the sky. It was a thunderbolt striking a haystack and setting it ablaze. Its glare illuminated the whole village. People ran about in panic, searching for shelter. The population of ten villages crammed in that village. Another thunderbolt hit a house. Women and children shrieked and wailed. The fires descended with a tremendous hiss as a mighty rain came down. It rained as it had never rained before. The two lakes, over which the village road ran, filled, swelled and joined over the road. Water flowed along the streets. The wind screamed and shook the trees and the homes. "This is the end of the world!" wailed the people through the storm.

The whole of the next day it was still drizzling. Soma sat before the image, with his head bowed in thought. Trays and flowers and offerings lay scattered under the image, dampened by rain. Some of his friends came wading in water, stood before him and asked, "Are you satisfied?" They stood over him like executioners and repeated the question and added, "Do you want to know how many lives have been lost, how many homes washed out and how many were crushed by the storm?"

"No, no, I don't want to know anything," Soma replied. "Go away. Don't stand here and talk."

"God has shown us only a slight sign of his power. Don't tempt Him again. Do something. Our lives are in your hands. Save us, the image is too perfect."

After they were gone he sat for hours in the same position, ruminating. Their words still troubled him. "Our lives are in your hands." He knew what they meant. Tears gathered in his eyes. "How can I mutilate this image? Let the whole world burn, I don't care. I can't touch this image." He lit a lamp before the God and sat watching. Far off the sky rumbled. "It is starting again. Poor human beings, they will all perish this time." He looked at the toe of the image. "Just one neat stroke with the chisel, and all troubles will end." He watched the toe, his hands trembled. "How can I?" Outside, the wind began to howl. People were gathering in front of his house and were appealing to him for help.

Soma prostrated before the God and went out. He stood looking at the road over which the two lakes had joined. Over the eastern horizon a dark mass of cloud was rolling up. "When that cloud comes over, it will wash out the world. Nataraja! I cannot mutilate your figure, but I can offer myself as a sacrifice if it will be any use. . . ." He shut his eyes and decided to jump into the lake. He checked himself. "I must take a last look at the God before I die." He battled his way through the oncoming storm. The wind shrieked. Trees shook and trembled. Men and cattle ran about in panic.

He was back just in time to see a tree crash on the roof of his house. "My home," he cried, and ran in. He picked up his Nataraja from amidst splintered tiles and rafters. The image was unhurt except for a little toe which was found a couple of yards off, severed by a falling splinter.

"God himself has done this to save us!" people cried.

The image was installed with due ceremonies at the temple on the next full moon. Wealth and honors were showered on Soma. He lived to be ninety-five, but he never touched his mallet and chisel again.

1947

Comment

Nataraja

Nataraja ("The Lord of the Dance") is a form or manifestation of Shiva, one of the three great gods of Hinduism—the others are Brahma (the Creator) and Vishnu (the Preserver). Their worship goes back to at least 1200 B.C. Shiva, who has 1,008 names, is often called the Destroyer because his worshipers believe he is able to destroy the universe by setting in motion the fire and flood of doomsday. One of Nataraja's dances initiates this destruction. As Lord of the Dance, Nataraja can perform 108 different dances. They are divided into two groups, the gentle and the fierce. Of the fierce dances, the tandāva, or cosmic doomsday dance, is the most dangerous. It is a vision of this dance that the villagers in Narayan's story "Such Perfection" see after the statue of Nataraja has been consecrated. Typically Nataraja is depicted in the act of dancing, with a halo of flames around his body, one foot raised, and holding fire and a drum in his upper hands to signify both his destructive power and his rhythmic creativity. In "Such Perfection" he cancels his doomsday destruction when he sounds his drum and the rhythm recreates the universe.

THINK AND DISCUSS
Understanding
1. Why is Soma unable to break off a finger or toe of his statue?
2. Before the storm, Soma is warned three times. Who warns him, and with what results?
3. When Soma attempts to consecrate the statue, how does one of these warnings come true?

Analyzing
4. Why might Soma have been so secretive about his Nataraja all the while he was creating it?
5. Why do none of the people attempt to mutilate the statue?
6. Is Soma's attitude toward his creation typical of the feeling of the artist for something beautiful he has created? Explain.
7. Is this story more about religion or art? Explain.

Extending
8. The ancient Greeks believed that *hubris* (excessive pride) was sometimes responsible for human tragedy. How does their concept apply here—or does it?

REVIEWING: Theme Hᛚ
See Handbook of Literary Terms, p. 975.
   The **theme** is the underlying meaning of a literary work. A theme may be directly stated, but more often it is implied.

1. Why are the gods angry at Soma's creation?
2. How does he attempt to appease them? With what result?
3. What then is the implied theme?
4. Which of the warnings Soma receives before he attempts to consecrate the statue comes closest to expressing the theme?

VOCABULARY
Context
   Use the context provided in each numbered sentence below (and your Glossary if necessary) to select the correct adjective from the following list to fill in the blank. Use a separate sheet of paper for your answers.

disheveled	propitious	taciturn
intractable	rudimentary	tremulous
meticulous	ruminating	
nondescript	secular	

1. They did not know even the _____ facts about the game.
2. With _____ care, the artist put the final brushstrokes to the miniature.
3. His appearance was so _____ that people had trouble remembering him.
4. A birthday party is a _____ occasion, not a religious one.
5. When the _____ man finally did say something, everyone listened to him.
6. The medics had to use a straitjacket on the _____ man.
7. After the ride in the convertible, we all looked somewhat _____.
8. They waited for the _____ moment to launch the new ship.
9. She showed her fear of speaking in front of an audience by her _____ voice.
10. A _____ person is digesting what he or she is reading.

COMPOSITION
Writing a Newspaper Account
   Write an eyewitness newspaper account of the storm. You will have to invent the casualties and the amount of damage it caused. Include the information about Soma and his statue, but write the story from the viewpoint either of someone who believes the storm was caused by the perfection of the statue or of someone who is skeptical.

Analyzing Narayan's Technique
   "Such Perfection" has something of the two-dimensional quality of folk literature. Reread the story, noting the details that Narayan provides to create this effect. Among other things, consider his use of color, his descriptions of the statue itself, and his physical descriptions of the characters. Consider the story's elements of myth or folk tale. Write a five-paragraph essay for your classmates in which you describe Narayan's technique.

BIOGRAPHY

Jean Anouilh
1910–1987

So prolific was the French dramatist Jean Anouilh (ä nü′ē) that before his death he had written more than forty plays (not counting translations), a ballet, and a number of filmscripts. He is widely regarded as one of the greatest playwrights of the twentieth century, and his works have been translated into twenty-seven different languages. *Antigone* (page 874), his updating of Sophocles' classical tragedy, is among his best-known works.

Anouilh was born near the city of Bordeaux in southwestern France. His father was a tailor, his mother a pianist in a theater orchestra. As a child, he was taken to see the dramas for which his mother played, but because he was so young had to be taken home at intermission without seeing how they ended. He claimed, seriously or otherwise, that not seeing the endings and having to complete the plays in his own mind helped him become a dramatist. By the time Anouilh was nine, he was trying to write plays in imitation of the French dramatist Edmond Rostand (1868–1918), author of *Cyrano de Bergerac*. At sixteen he wrote his first long play—which was never produced or published.

After receiving most of his education in Bordeaux, Anouilh studied law for a brief period at the University of Paris. Then he began working for an advertising agency, where his writing ran the gamut from advertising copy to gags for movies. In 1931 he became secretary to the Comédie des Champs Élysées, and in 1932 his first play, *The Ermine*, was produced. At this point, Anouilh decided to devote himself entirely to writing, a career he followed until his death. Anouilh created a division of his dramatic works into several categories. Chief among these are the *pièces noires*, the "black plays," which are tragic in content, and *pièces roses*, the "pink plays," which are happier and more romantic.

Anouilh often presents in his dramas the problems of characters who no longer have a solid foundation of tradition and religion on which to base their decisions. In *Antigone*, King Creon displays this skeptical attitude in his debate with Antigone, who is determined to follow religious tradition and give her brother's body a ritual burial so his soul will not roam the earth. Sartre's comment about Anouilh's plays in general is especially applicable to *Antigone*. He says that the plays are "violent and brief, centered on one single event; there are few players and the story is compressed within a short space of time, sometimes only a few hours . . . A single set, a few entrances, a few exits, intense arguments among the characters who defend their individual rights with passion."

The production of *Antigone* in 1942, while Paris was occupied by the Germans, assured Anouilh's reputation with the French. They saw in Antigone a character who, like members of the Resistance movement, was willing to sacrifice herself for her beliefs, in Creon a representation of the collaborationists. So universal is Anouilh's play, however, that modern American audiences have become more interested in Creon, the problems he faces, and the decisions he makes.

Reader's Note

Antigone

Most of Anouilh's plays can be considered under one of two general headings: *pièces roses* or *pièces noires*. *Antigone*, based on Sophocles' tragedy of the same name, belongs to the category of the *pièces noires*.

Anouilh's *Antigone* was first produced in February, 1942, during the Nazi occupation of France. Since all plays had to be approved by the Germans before production, Anouilh's play had to pass their censors. Perhaps its classical title was misleading, or perhaps the censors failed to read it closely enough, or perhaps they overlooked the way in which Antigone's role paralleled the activities of members of the French Resistance who faced danger and death in fighting against tyranny for a cause that they believed was right—in any event, the play was an immediate success and established Anouilh's reputation in his country.

Although the play is based on Sophocles' *Antigone*, and although Anouilh carefully followed the basic **plot**, he used the mythological story to comment on France during the German Occupation, and he did this largely through his **characterization** of Antigone and the extended debate she has with Creon midway through the play.

The staging of *Antigone* is stark. Its scenery is sparse, its props minimal—a single **setting**, staged before a semicircular gray cloth cyclorama, with three semicircular steps, two archways, one at either end of the stage, a table, two chairs, and a stool. The action is continuous and takes place in this single setting. Anouilh uses lighting to establish the time of day and the mood, and sometimes also to signal the end of a scene, a momentary blackout serving that purpose. Attention is thus focused on the actors and what they are saying.

Anouilh pays little attention to such dramatic conventions as the traditional act and scene divisions, soliloquies, and asides. Instead, he adheres to the unities of time and place of the classical theater: the events occur over a period of about twelve hours, and within a single setting. Although the play is generally tragic, some humor is introduced through the roles of the three Guards.

Anouilh also follows Greek tragedy in employing a Chorus to describe the action and on occasion to speak to one of the characters. However, his Chorus is used largely to philosophize on the nature of tragedy and how it operates in this particular play. In addition, Anouilh introduces deliberate anachronisms—such as cigarettes and fast motor cars—into the texture of the play. Through this device, he is able to keep his audience disoriented in time, at one level watching the working out of a familiar tragedy, at another seeing the events against the modern backdrop of German-occupied France.

The play opens with a prologue in which all the characters are onstage at once, carrying out their ordinary activities as though this were a normal day and they were unaware of the impending tragedy. The Chorus introduces them one by one, comments on them, and describes the fate of those doomed to die that day. Thus the audience knows immediately what is to happen and can concentrate on *why* the tragedy occurs and *how* Anouilh manages to bring it about.

Following this, the rising action begins as Antigone is seen with, in turn, her Nurse, her sister, Ismene, and her fiancé, Haemon. The conflict is established almost at once as we learn that Antigone is determined to bury the corpse of her brother Polynices despite the decree by Creon, ruler of Thebes, forbidding such burial under pain of death. Ismene emerges as more practical and self-serving than Antigone, and Haemon as a well-intentioned lover who is not let into Antigone's secret.

When Antigone is apprehended by three Guards as she makes a second attempt to bury her brother's body, Creon dismisses the Guards and he and Antigone engage in a lengthy and heated debate, each advancing arguments and rebutting or ignoring those of the other. The climax of the play occurs when Antigone refuses to accept Creon's arguments and decides to die rather than leave her brother unburied. From that point the falling action moves rapidly to the denouement, which finds Antigone, Haemon, and Creon's wife Eurydice dead, and Creon preparing to go on with the business of ruling by attending a five-o'clock cabinet meeting. Only the people of Thebes appear to have benefited from the tragedy, since they are now assured of internal peace. The play ends with a brief epilogue in which the Chorus comments upon what has occurred.

Antigone

Jean Anouilh   *translated by* **Lewis Galantière**

CHARACTERS

CHORUS
ANTIGONE (an tig′ə nē)
NURSE
ISMENE (is mē′nē)
HAEMON (hē′mən)
CREON (krē′on)

FIRST GUARD, *Jonas*
SECOND GUARD, *a corporal*
THIRD GUARD
MESSENGER
PAGE
EURYDICE (yŭ rid′ə sē)

Opening scene of the 1947 production of *Antigone* showing set design featuring cyclorama.

A gray cloth cyclorama, semicircular, hangs at the back of the set. At the bottom of the cyclorama, a stair, of three steps, sweeps in a semicircle. Downstage, right and left, two archways. The curtains part in the center for entrance and exit. A table stands left of center-stage, with matching chairs set at either end. A small stool is placed right of the chair at the right of the table. ANTIGONE, her hands clasped round her knees, sits on the top step. The THREE GUARDS sit on the steps, in a small group, playing cards. CHORUS stands on the top step. EURYDICE sits on the top step, just left of center, knitting. The NURSE sits on the second step, left of EURYDICE. ISMENE stands in front of arch, left, facing HAEMON, who stands left of her. CREON sits in the chair at right end of the table, his arm over the shoulder of his Page, who sits on the stool beside his chair. The MESSENGER is leaning against the downstage portal of the right arch. The curtain rises slowly; then CHORUS turns and moves downstage.

CHORUS. Well, here we are.

These people are about to act out for you the story of Antigone.

That thin little creature sitting by herself, staring straight ahead, seeing nothing, is Antigone. She is thinking. She is thinking that the instant I finish telling you who's who and what's what in this play, she will burst forth as the tense, sallow, willful girl whose family would never take her seriously and who is about to rise up alone against Creon, her uncle, the King.

Another thing that she is thinking is this: she is going to die. Antigone is young. She would much rather live than die. But there is no help for it. When your name is Antigone, there is only one part you can play; and she will have to play hers through to the end.

From the moment the curtain went up, she began to feel that inhuman forces were whirling her out of this world, snatching her away from her sister Ismene, whom you see smiling and chatting with that young man; from all of us who sit or stand here, looking at her, not in the least upset ourselves—for we are not doomed to die tonight.

The young man talking to Ismene (*turning and indicating* HAEMON) to the gay and beautiful Ismene—is Haemon. He is the King's son, Creon's son. Antigone and he are engaged to be married. You wouldn't have thought she was his type. He likes dancing, sports, competition; he likes women, too. Now look at Ismene again. She is certainly more beautiful than Antigone. She is the girl you'd think he'd go for. Well . . .

There was a ball one night. Ismene wore a new evening frock. She was radiant. Haemon danced every dance with her. And yet, that same night, before the dance was over, suddenly he went in search of Antigone, found her sitting alone—like that, with her arms clasped round her knees—and asked her to marry him. We still don't know how it happened. It didn't seem to surprise Antigone in the least. She looked up at him out of those solemn eyes of hers, smiled sort of sadly and said "yes." That was all. The band struck up another dance. Ismene, surrounded by a group of young men, laughed out loud. And . . . well, here is Haemon expecting to marry Antigone. He won't, of course. He didn't know, when he asked her, that the earth wasn't meant to hold a husband of Antigone, and that this princely distinction was to earn him no more than the right to die sooner than he might otherwise have done.

(*Turning toward* CREON.)

That gray-haired, powerfully built man sitting lost in thought, with his little page at his side, is Creon, the King. His face is lined. He is tired. He practices the difficult art of a leader of men. When he was younger, when Oedipus[1] was King and Creon was no more than the King's brother-in-law, he was different. He loved music, bought rare manuscripts, was a kind of art patron. He would while away whole afternoons in the antique shops of this city of Thebes. But Oedipus died. Oedipus's sons died. Creon had to roll up his sleeves and take over the kingdom. Now and then, when he goes to bed

---

1. **Oedipus** (ĕd′ə pəs). For the story of Oedipus, see page 163.

weary with the day's work, he wonders whether this business of being a leader of men is worth the trouble. But when he wakes up, the problems are there to be solved; and like a conscientious workman, he does his job.

Creon has a wife, a Queen. Her name is Eurydice.[2] There she sits, the old lady with the knitting, next to the Nurse who brought up the two girls. She will go on knitting all through the play, till the time comes for her to go to her room and die. She is a good woman, a worthy, loving soul. But she is no help to her husband. Creon has to face the music alone. Alone with his page, who is too young to be of any help. The others? Well, let's see.

(*He points toward the* MESSENGER.)

That pale young man leaning against the wall is the Messenger. Later on he will come running in to announce that Haemon is dead. He has a premonition of catastrophe. That's what he is brooding over. That's why he won't mingle with the others.

As for those three red-faced card players—they are not a bad lot. They have wives they are afraid of, kids who are afraid of them; they're bothered by the little day-to-day worries that beset us all. At the same time—they are guards. One smells of garlic, another of beer; but they're policemen: eternally innocent, no matter what crimes are committed; eternally indifferent, for nothing that happens can matter to them. They are quite prepared to arrest anybody at all, including Creon himself, should the order be given by a new leader.

That's the lot. Now for the play.

Oedipus, who was the father of the two girls, Antigone and Ismene, had also two sons, Eteocles and Polynices.[3] After Oedipus died, it was agreed that the two sons should share his throne, each to reign over Thebes in alternate years.

(*Gradually, the lights on the stage have been dimmed.*)

But when Eteocles, the elder son, had reigned a full year, and time had come for him to step down, he refused to yield up the throne to his younger brother. There was civil war. Polynices brought up allies—six foreign princes; and in the course of the war he and his foreigners were defeated, each in front of one of the seven gates of the city. The two brothers fought, and they killed one another in single combat just outside the city walls. Now Creon is King.

(CHORUS *is leaning, at this point, against the left proscenium arch.[4] By now the stage is dark, with only the cyclorama bathed in dark blue. A single spot lights up the face of* CHORUS.)

Creon has issued a solemn edict that Eteocles, with whom he had sided, is to be buried with pomp and honors, and that Polynices is to be left to rot. The vultures and the dogs are to bloat themselves on his carcass. Nobody is to go into mourning for him. No gravestone is to be set up in his memory. And above all, any person who attempts to give him religious burial will himself be put to death. (*While* CHORUS *has been speaking the characters have gone out one by one.* CHORUS *disappears through the left arch.*)

It is dawn, gray and ashen, in a house asleep. ANTIGONE *steals in from out of doors, through the arch, right. She is carrying her sandals in her hand. She pauses, looking off through the arch, taut, listening, then turns and moves across downstage. As she reaches the table, she sees the* NURSE *approaching through the arch, left. She runs quickly toward the exit. As she reaches the steps, the* NURSE *enters through arch and stands still when she sees* ANTIGONE.

NURSE. Where have you been?
ANTIGONE. Nowhere. It was beautiful. The whole world was gray when I went out. And now—you wouldn't recognize it. It's like a post card: all pink, and green, and yellow. You'll have to get up earlier, Nurse, if you want to see a world without color.

---

2. *Eurydice* (yu̇ rid′ə sē′).
3. *Eteocles* (i tē′ə klēz) . . . *Polynices* (pol′i nī′sēz).
4. *proscenium arch,* the section of a theater that frames the stage and supports the curtain.

NURSE. It was still pitch black when I got up. I went to your room, for I thought you might have flung off your blanket in the night. You weren't there.

ANTIGONE (*comes down the steps*). The garden was lovely. It was still asleep. Have you ever thought how lovely a garden is when it is not yet thinking of men?

NURSE. You hadn't slept in your bed. I couldn't find you. I went to the back door. You'd left it open.

ANTIGONE. The fields were wet. They were waiting for something to happen. The whole world was breathless, waiting. I can't tell you what a roaring noise I seemed to make alone on the road. It bothered me that whatever was waiting wasn't waiting for me. I took off my sandals and slipped into a field. (*She moves down to the stool and sits.*)

NURSE (*kneels at* ANTIGONE's *feet to chafe them and put on the sandals*). You'll do well to wash your feet before you go back to bed, Miss.

ANTIGONE. I'm not going back to bed.

NURSE. Don't be a fool! You get some sleep! And me, getting up to see if she hasn't flung off her blanket; and I find her bed cold and nobody in it!

ANTIGONE. Do you think that if a person got up every morning like this, it would be just as thrilling every morning to be the first girl out of doors?

(NURSE *puts* ANTIGONE's *left foot down, lifts her other foot and chafes it.*)

NURSE. Morning my grandmother! It was night. It still is. And now, my girl, you'll stop trying to squirm out of this and tell me what you were up to. Where've you been?

ANTIGONE. That's true. It was still night. There wasn't a soul out of doors but me, who thought that it was morning. Don't you think it's marvelous—to be the first person who is aware that it is morning?

NURSE. Oh, my little flibbertigibbet! Just can't imagine what I'm talking about, can she? Go on with you! I know that game. Where have you been, wicked girl?

ANTIGONE (*soberly*). No. Not wicked.

Scene from the 1978 production of *Antigone* by The Acting Company.

NURSE. You went out to meet someone, didn't you? Deny it if you can.

ANTIGONE. Yes. I went out to meet someone.

NURSE. A lover?

ANTIGONE. Yes, Nurse. Yes, the poor dear. I have a lover.

NURSE (*stands up, bursting out*). Ah, that's very nice now, isn't it? Such goings-on! You, the daughter of a king, running out to meet lovers. And we work our fingers to the bone for you, we slave to bring you up like young ladies! (*She sits on chair, right of table.*) You're all alike, all of you. Even you—who never used to stop to primp in front of a looking glass, or smear your mouth with rouge, or dindle and dandle to make the boys ogle you, and you ogle back. How many times I'd say to myself, "Now that one, now: I wish she was a little more of a coquette—always wearing the same dress, her hair tumbling round her face. One thing's sure," I'd say to myself, "none of the boys will look at her while Ismene's about, all curled and cute and tidy and trim. I'll have this one on my hands for the rest of my life." And now, you see? Just like your sister, after all. Only worse: a hypocrite. Who is the lad? Some little scamp, eh? Somebody you can't bring home and show to your family, and say, "Well, this is him, and I mean to marry him and no other." That's how it is, is it? Answer me!

ANTIGONE (*smiling faintly*). That's how it is. Yes, Nurse.

NURSE. Yes, says she! God save us! I took her when she wasn't that high. I promised her poor mother I'd make a lady of her. And look at her! But don't you go thinking this is the end of this, my young 'un. I'm only your nurse and you can play deaf and dumb with me; I don't count. But your Uncle Creon will hear of this! That, I promise you.

ANTIGONE (*a little weary*). Yes, Creon will hear of this.

NURSE. And we'll hear what he has to say when he finds out that you go wandering alone o' nights. Not to mention Haemon. For the girl's engaged! Going to be married! Going to be married, and she hops out of bed at four in the morning to meet somebody else in a field. Do you know what I ought to do to you? Take you over my knee the way I used to do when you were little.

ANTIGONE. Please, Nurse, I want to be alone.

NURSE. And if you so much as speak of it, she says she wants to be alone!

ANTIGONE. Nanny, you shouldn't scold, dear. This isn't a day when you should be losing your temper.

NURSE. Not scold, indeed! Along with the rest of it, I'm to like it. Didn't I promise your mother? What would she say if she was here? "Old Stupid!" That's what she'd call me. "Old Stupid. Not to know how to keep my little girl pure! Spend your life making them behave, watching over them like a mother hen, running after them with mufflers and sweaters to keep them warm, and eggnogs to make them strong; and then at four o'clock in the morning, you who always complained you never could sleep a wink, snoring in your bed and letting them slip out into the bushes." That's what she'd say, your mother. And I'd stand there, dying of shame if I wasn't dead already. And all I could

do would be not to dare look her in the face; and "That's true," I'd say. "That's all true what you say, Your Majesty."

ANTIGONE. Nanny, dear. Dear Nanny. Don't cry. You'll be able to look Mamma in the face when it's your time to see her. And she'll say, "Good morning, Nanny. Thank you for my little Antigone. You did look after her so well." She knows why I went out this morning.

NURSE. Not to meet a lover?

ANTIGONE. No. Not to meet a lover.

NURSE. Well, you've a queer way of teasing me, I must say! Not to know when she's teasing me! (*Rises to stand behind* ANTIGONE.) I must be getting awfully old, that's what it is. But if you loved me, you'd tell me the truth. You'd tell me why your bed was empty when I went along to tuck you in. Wouldn't you?

ANTIGONE. Please, Nanny, don't cry any more. (ANTIGONE *turns partly toward* NURSE, *puts an arm up to* NURSE's *shoulder. With her other hand,* ANTIGONE *caresses* NURSE's *face.*) There now, my sweet red apple. Do you remember how I used to rub your cheeks to make them shine? My dear, wrinkled red apple! I didn't do anything tonight that was worth sending tears down the little gullies of your dear face. I am pure, and I swear that I have no other lover than Haemon. If you like, I'll swear that I shall never have any other lover than Haemon. Save your tears, Nanny, save them, Nanny dear; you may still need them. When you cry like that, I become a little girl again; and I mustn't be a little girl today.

(ANTIGONE *rises and moves upstage.* ISMENE *enters through arch, left. She pauses in front of arch.*)

ISMENE. Antigone! What are you doing up at this hour? I've just been to your room.

NURSE. The two of you, now! You're both going mad, to be up before the kitchen fire has been started. Do you like running about without a mouthful of breakfast? Do you think it's decent for the daughters of a king? (*She turns to* ISMENE.) And look at you, with nothing on, and the sun not up! I'll have you both on my hands with colds before I know it.

ANTIGONE. Nanny dear, go away now. It's not

chilly, really. Summer's here. Go and make us some coffee. Please, Nanny, I'd love some coffee. It would do me so much good.

NURSE. My poor baby! Her head's swimming, what with nothing on her stomach, and me standing here like an idiot when I could be getting her something hot to drink. (*Exit* NURSE.) (*A pause.*)

ISMENE. Aren't you well?

ANTIGONE. Of course I am. Just a little tired. I got up too early. (ANTIGONE *sits on a chair, suddenly tired.*)

ISMENE. I couldn't sleep, either.

ANTIGONE. Ismene, you ought not to go without your beauty sleep.

ISMENE. Don't make fun of me.

ANTIGONE. I'm not, Ismene, truly. This particular morning, seeing how beautiful you are makes everything easier for me. Wasn't I a miserable little beast when we were small? I used to fling mud at you, and put worms down your neck. I remember tying you to a tree and cutting off your hair. Your beautiful hair! How easy it must be never to be unreasonable with all that smooth silken hair so beautifully set round your head.

ISMENE (*abruptly*). Why do you insist upon talking about other things?

ANTIGONE (*gently*). I am not talking about other things.

ISMENE. Antigone, I've thought about it a lot.

ANTIGONE. Have you?

ISMENE. I thought about it all night long. Antigone, you're mad.

ANTIGONE. Am I?

ISMENE. We cannot do it.

ANTIGONE. Why not?

ISMENE. Creon will have us put to death.

ANTIGONE. Of course he will. That's what he's here for. He will do what he has to do, and we will do what we have to do. He is bound to put us to death. We are bound to go out and bury our brother. That's the way it is. What do you think we can do to change it?

ISMENE (*releases* ANTIGONE's *hand; draws back a step*). I don't want to die.

ANTIGONE. I'd prefer not to die, myself.

ISMENE. Listen to me, Antigone. I thought about it all night. I'm older than you are. I always think things over, and you don't. You are impulsive. You get a notion in your head and you jump up and do the thing straight off. And if it's silly, well, so much the worse for you. Whereas, *I* think things out.

ANTIGONE. Sometimes it is better not to think too much.

ISMENE. I don't agree with you! (ANTIGONE *looks at* ISMENE, *then turns and moves to chair behind table.* ISMENE *leans on end of table top, toward* ANTIGONE.) Oh, I know it's horrible. And I pity Polynices just as much as you do. But all the same, I sort of see what Uncle Creon means.

ANTIGONE. I don't want to "sort of see" anything.

ISMENE. Uncle Creon is the king. He has to set an example!

ANTIGONE. But I am not the king; and I don't have to set people examples. Little Antigone gets a notion in her head—the nasty brat, the willful, wicked girl; and they put her in a corner all day, or they lock her up in the cellar. And she deserves it. She shouldn't have disobeyed!

ISMENE. There you go, frowning, glowering, wanting your own stubborn way in everything. Listen to me. I'm right oftener than you are.

ANTIGONE. I don't want to be right!

ISMENE. At least you can try to understand.

ANTIGONE. Understand! The first word I ever heard out of any of you was that word "understand." Why didn't I "understand" that I must not play with water—cold, black, beautiful flowing water—because I'd spill it on the palace tiles. Or with earth, because earth dirties a little girl's frock. Why didn't I "understand" that nice children don't eat out of every dish at once; or give everything in their pockets to beggars; or run in the wind so fast that they fall down; or ask for a drink when they're perspiring; or want to go swimming when it's either too early or too late, merely because they happen to feel like swimming. Understand! I don't want to understand. There'll be time enough to understand when I'm old. . . . If I ever *am* old. But not now.

ISMENE. He is stronger than we are, Antigone. He is the king. And the whole city is with him.

Scene from the 1978 production of *Antigone*
by The Acting Company.

Thousands and thousands of them, swarming
through all the streets of Thebes.

ANTIGONE. I am not listening to you.

ISMENE. His mob will come running, howling as
it runs. A thousand arms will seize our arms.
A thousand breaths will breathe into our faces.
Like one single pair of eyes, a thousand eyes will
stare at us. We'll be driven in a tumbrel through
their hatred, through the smell of them and their
cruel, roaring laughter. We'll be dragged to the
scaffold for torture, surrounded by guards with
their idiot faces all bloated, their animal hands
clean-washed for the sacrifice, their beefy eyes
squinting as they stare at us. And we'll know
that no shrieking and no begging will make them
understand that we want to live, for they are
like slaves who do exactly as they've been told,
without caring about right or wrong. And we
shall suffer, we shall feel pain rising in us until
it becomes so unbearable that we *know* it must
stop. But it won't stop; it will go on rising and
rising, like a screaming voice. Oh, I can't, I
can't, Antigone!

(*A pause.*)

ANTIGONE. How well have you thought it all out?

ISMENE. I thought of it all night long. Didn't you?

ANTIGONE. Oh, yes.

ISMENE. I'm an awful coward, Antigone.

ANTIGONE. So am I. But what has that to do with
it?

ISMENE. But, Antigone! Don't you want to go on
living?

ANTIGONE. Go on living! Who was it that was
always the first out of bed because she loved the
touch of the cold morning air on her bare skin?
Who was always the last to bed because nothing
less than infinite wearinesss could wean her from
the lingering night? Who wept when she was
little because there were too many grasses in the
meadow, too many creatures in the field, for her
to know and touch them all?

ISMENE (*clasps* ANTIGONE's *hands, in a sudden rush
of tenderness*). Darling little sister!

ANTIGONE (*repulsing her*). No! For heaven's
sake! Don't paw me! And don't let us start
sniveling! You say you've thought it all out.
The howling mob—the torture—the fear of
death. . . . They've made up your mind for
you. Is that it?

ISMENE. Yes.

ANTIGONE. All right. They're as good excuses as
any.

ISMENE. Antigone, be sensible. It's all very well
for men to believe in ideas and die for them.
But you are a girl!

ANTIGONE. Don't I know I'm a girl? Haven't I
spent my life cursing the fact that I was a girl?

ISMENE (*with spirit*). Antigone! You have everything in the world to make you happy. All
you have to do is reach out for it. You are
going to be married; you are young; you are
beautiful. . . .

ANTIGONE. I am not beautiful.

ISMENE. Yes, you are! Not the way other girls are.
But it's always you that the little boys turn to
look back at when they pass us in the street.
And when you go by, the little girls stop talking.
They stare and stare at you, until we've turned
a corner.

ANTIGONE (*a faint smile*). "Little boys—little girls."

ISMENE (*challenging*). And what about Haemon? (*A pause.*)

ANTIGONE. I shall see Haemon this morning. I'll take care of Haemon. You always said I was mad; and it didn't matter how little I was or what I wanted to do. Go back to bed now, Ismene. The sun is coming up, and, as you see, there is nothing I can do today. Our brother Polynices is as well guarded as if he had won the war and were sitting on his throne. Go along. You are pale with weariness.

ISMENE. What are you going to do?

NURSE (*calls from offstage*). Come along, my dove. Come to breakfast.

ANTIGONE. I don't feel like going to bed. However, if you like, I'll promise not to leave the house till you wake up. Nurse is getting me breakfast. Go and get some sleep. The sun is just up. Look at you: you can't keep your eyes open. Go.

ISMENE. And you will listen to reason, won't you? You'll let me talk to you about this again? Promise?

ANTIGONE. I promise. I'll let you talk. I'll let all of you talk. Go to bed, now. (ISMENE *goes to arch; exit.*) Poor Ismene!

NURSE (*enters through arch, speaking as she enters*). Come along, my dove. I've made you some coffee and toast and jam. (*She turns toward arch as if to go out.*)

ANTIGONE. I'm not really hungry, Nurse.

(NURSE *stops, looks at* ANTIGONE, *then moves behind her.*)

NURSE (*very tenderly*). Where is your pain?

ANTIGONE. Nowhere, Nanny dear. But you must keep me warm and safe, the way you used to do when I was little. Nanny! Stronger than all fever, stronger than any nightmare, stronger than the shadow of the cupboard that used to snarl at me and turn into a dragon on the bedroom wall. Stronger than the thousand insects gnawing and nibbling in the silence of the night. Stronger than the night itself, with the weird hooting of the night birds that frightened me even when I couldn't hear them. Nanny, stronger than death. Give me your hand, Nanny, as if I were ill in bed, and you sitting beside me.

NURSE. My sparrow, my lamb! What is it that's eating your heart out?

ANTIGONE. Oh, it's just that I'm a little young still for what I have to go through. But nobody but you must know that.

NURSE (*places her other arm around* ANTIGONE's *shoulder*). A little young for what, my kitten?

ANTIGONE. Nothing in particular, Nanny. Just—all this. Oh, it's so good that you are here. I can hold your calloused hand, your hand that is so prompt to ward off evil. You are very powerful, Nanny.

NURSE. What is it you want me to do for you, my baby?

ANTIGONE. There isn't anything to do, except put your hand like this against my cheek. (*She places the* NURSE's *hand against her cheek. A pause, then, as* ANTIGONE *leans back, her eyes shut*). There! I'm not afraid any more. Not afraid of the wicked ogre, nor of the sandman, nor of the dwarf who steals little children. (*A pause.* ANTIGONE *resumes on another note.*) Nanny. . . .

NURSE. Yes?

ANTIGONE. My dog, Puff. . . .

NURSE (*straightens up, draws her hand away*). Well?

ANTIGONE. Promise me that you will never scold her again.

NURSE. Dogs that dirty up a house with their filthy paws deserve to be scolded.

ANTIGONE. I know. Just the same, promise me.

NURSE. You mean you want me to let her make a mess all over the place and not say a thing?

ANTIGONE. Yes, Nanny.

NURSE. You're asking a lot. The next time she wets my living-room carpet, I'll. . . .

ANTIGONE. Please, Nanny, I beg of you!

NURSE. It isn't fair to take me on my weak side, just because you look a little peaked today. . . . Well, have it your own way. We'll mop up and keep our mouth shut. You're making a fool of me, though.

ANTIGONE. And promise me that you will talk to her. That you will talk to her often.

NURSE (*turns and looks at* ANTIGONE). Me, talk to a dog!

ANTIGONE. Yes. But mind you: you are not to talk to her the way people usually talk to dogs. You're to talk to her the way I talk to her.

NURSE. I don't see why both of us have to make fools of ourselves. So long as you're here, one ought to be enough.

ANTIGONE. But if there was a reason why I couldn't go on talking to her. . . .

NURSE (*interrupting*). Couldn't go on talking to her! And why couldn't you go on talking to her? What kind of poppycock . . . ?

ANTIGONE. And if she got too unhappy, if she moaned and moaned, waiting for me with her nose under the door as she does when I'm out all day, then the best thing, Nanny, might be to have her mercifully put to sleep.

NURSE. Now what *has* got into you this morning? (HAEMON *enters through arch.*) Running around in the darkness, won't sleep, won't eat (ANTIGONE *sees* HAEMON)—and now it's her dog she wants killed. I never.

ANTIGONE (*interrupting*). Nanny! Haemon is here. Go inside, please. And don't forget that you've promised me. (NURSE *goes to arch; exit.* ANTIGONE *rises.*) Haemon, Haemon! Forgive me for quarreling with you last night. (*She crosses quickly to* HAEMON *and they embrace.*) Forgive me for everything. It was all my fault. I beg you to forgive me.

HAEMON. You know that I've forgiven you. You had hardly slammed the door, your perfume still hung in the room, when I had already forgiven you. (*He holds her in his arms and smiles at her. Then draws slightly back.*) You stole that perfume. From whom?

ANTIGONE. Ismene.

HAEMON. And the rouge? and the face powder? and the frock? Whom did you steal them from?

ANTIGONE. Ismene.

HAEMON. And in whose honor did you get yourself up so elegantly?

ANTIGONE. I'll tell you everything. (*She draws him closer.*) Oh, darling, what a fool I was! To waste a whole evening! A whole, beautiful evening!

HAEMON. We'll have other evenings, my sweet.

ANTIGONE. Perhaps we won't.

HAEMON. And other quarrels, too. A happy love is full of quarrels, you know.

ANTIGONE. A happy love, yes. Haemon, listen to me.

HAEMON. Yes?

ANTIGONE. Don't laugh at me this morning. Be serious.

HAEMON. I am serious.

ANTIGONE. And hold me tight. Tighter than you have ever held me. I want all your strength to flow into me.

HAEMON. There! With all my strength. (*A pause.*)

ANTIGONE (*breathless*). That's good. (*They stand for a moment, silent and motionless.*) Haemon! I wanted to tell you. You know—the little boy we were going to have when we were married?

HAEMON. Yes?

ANTIGONE. I'd have protected him against everything in the world.

HAEMON. Yes, dearest.

ANTIGONE. Oh, you don't know how I should have held him in my arms and given him my strength. He wouldn't have been afraid of anything, I swear he wouldn't. Not of the falling night, nor of the terrible noonday sun, nor of all the shadows, or all the walls in the world. Our little boy, Haemon! His mother wouldn't have been very imposing: her hair wouldn't always have been brushed; but she would have been strong where he was concerned, so much stronger than all those real mothers with their real bosoms and their aprons around their middle. You believe that, don't you, Haemon?

HAEMON (*soothingly*). Yes, yes, my darling.

ANTIGONE. And you believe me when I say that you would have had a real wife?

HAEMON. Darling, you are my real wife.

ANTIGONE (*pressing against him and crying out*). Haemon, you loved me! You did love me that night, didn't you? You're sure of it!

HAEMON (*rocking her gently*). What night, my sweet?

ANTIGONE. And you are very sure, aren't you, that that night, at the dance, when you came to the corner where I was sitting, there was no mistake? It was me you were looking for? It wasn't another girl? And you're sure that never, not in your most secret heart of hearts, have you said to yourself that it was Ismene you ought to have asked to marry you?

HAEMON (*reproachfully*). Antigone, you are idiotic. You might give me credit for knowing my own mind. It's you I love, and no one else.

ANTIGONE. But you love me as a woman—as a woman wants to be loved, don't you? Your arms around me aren't lying, are they? Your hands, so warm against my back—they're not lying? This warmth that's in me; this confidence, this sense that I am safe, secure, that flows through me as I stand here with my cheek in the hollow of your shoulder: they are not lies, are they?

HAEMON. Antigone, darling, I love you exactly as you love me. With all of myself. (*They kiss.*)

ANTIGONE. I'm sallow, and I'm scrawny. Ismene is pink and golden. She's like a fruit.

HAEMON. Look here, Antigone. . . .

ANTIGONE. Ah, dearest, I am ashamed of myself. But this morning, this special morning, I must know. Tell me the truth! I beg you to tell me the truth! When you think about me, when it strikes you suddenly that I am going to belong to you—do you have the feeling that—that a great empty space is being hollowed out inside you, that there is something inside you that is just—dying?

HAEMON. Yes, I do, I do.

(*A pause.*)

ANTIGONE. That's the way I feel. And another thing. I wanted you to know that I should have been very proud to be your wife—the woman whose shoulder you would put your hand on as you sat down to table, absentmindedly, as upon a thing that belonged to you. (*After a moment, draws away from him. Her tone changes.*) There! Now I have two things more to tell you. And when I have told them to you, you must go away instantly, without asking any questions. However strange they may seem to you. However much they may hurt you. Swear that you will!

HAEMON (*beginning to be troubled*). What are these

Scene from the 1978 production of *Antigone* by The Acting Company.

things that you are going to tell me?

ANTIGONE. Swear, first, that you will go away without one word. Without so much as looking at me. (*She looks at him, wretchedness in her face.*) You hear me, Haemon. Swear it, please. This is the last mad wish that you will ever have to grant me.

(*A pause.*)

HAEMON. I swear it, since you insist. But I must tell you that I don't like this at all.

ANTIGONE. Please, Haemon. It's very serious. You must listen to me and do as I ask. First, about last night, when I came to your house. You asked me a moment ago why I wore Ismene's dress and rouge. It was because I was stupid. I wasn't very sure that you loved me as a woman; and I did it—because I wanted you to want me. I was trying to be more like other girls.

HAEMON. Was *that* the reason? My poor. . . .

ANTIGONE. Yes. And you laughed at me. And we quarreled; and my awful temper got the better of me and I flung out of the house. . . . The real reason was that I wanted you to take me; I wanted to be your wife before. . . .

HAEMON. Oh, my darling. . . .

ANTIGONE (*shuts him off*). You swore you wouldn't ask any questions. You swore, Haemon. (*Turns her face away and goes on in a hard voice.*) As a matter of fact, I'll tell you why. I wanted to be your wife last night because I love you that way very—very strongly. And also because—Oh, my darling, my darling, forgive me; I'm going to cause you quite a lot of pain. (*She draws away from him.*) I wanted it also because I shall never, never be able to marry you, never! (HAEMON *is stupefied and mute; then he moves a step toward her.*) Haemon! You took a solemn oath! You swore! Leave me quickly! Tomorrow the whole thing will be clear to you. Even before tomorrow: this afternoon. If you please, Haemon, go now. It is the only thing left that you can do for me if you still love me.

(*A pause as* HAEMON *stares at her. Then he turns and goes out through the arch.* ANTIGONE *stands motionless, then moves to a chair at end of table and lets herself gently down on it.*)

ANTIGONE (*in a mild voice, as of calm after storm.*) Well, it's over for Haemon, Antigone.

(ISMENE *enters through arch, pauses for a moment in front of it when she sees* ANTIGONE, *then crosses behind table.*)

ISMENE. I can't sleep, I'm terrified. I'm so afraid that, even though it is daylight, you'll still try to bury Polynices. Antigone, little sister, we all want to make you happy—Haemon, and Nurse, and I, and Puff whom you love. We love you, we are alive, we need you. And you remember what Polynices was like. He was our brother, of course. But he's dead; and he never loved you. He was a bad brother. He was like an enemy in the house. He never thought of you. Why should you think of him? What if his soul does have to wander through endless time without rest or peace? Don't try something that is beyond your strength. You are always defying the world, but you're only a girl, after all. Stay at home tonight. Don't try to do it, I beg you. It's Creon's doing, not ours.

ANTIGONE. You are too late, Ismene. When you first saw me this morning, I had just come in from burying him. (*Exit* ANTIGONE *through arch.*)

(*The lighting, which by this time has reached a point of early morning sun, is quickly dimmed out, leaving the stage bathed in a light blue color.* ISMENE *runs out after* ANTIGONE. *On* ISMENE's *exit the lights are brought up suddenly to suggest a later period of the day.* CREON *and* PAGE *enter through curtain upstage.* CREON *stands on the top step; his* PAGE *stands at his right side.*)

CREON. A private of the guards, you say? One of those standing watch over the body? Show him in.

(*The* PAGE *crosses to arch; exit.* CREON *moves down to end of table.* PAGE *reenters, preceded by the* FIRST GUARD, *livid with fear.* PAGE *remains on upstage side of arch.* GUARD *salutes.*)

GUARD. Private Jonas, Second Battalion.

CREON. What are you doing here?

GUARD. It's like this, sir. Soon as it happened, we said: "Got to tell the chief about this before anybody else spills it. He'll want to know right away." So we tossed a coin to see which one would come up and tell you about it. You see, sir, we thought only one man had better come, because, after all, you don't want to leave the body without a guard. Right? I mean, there's three of us on duty, guarding the body.

CREON. What's wrong about the body?

GUARD. Sir, I've been seventeen years in the service. Volunteer. Wounded three times. Two mentions. My record's clean. I know my business and I know my place. I carry out orders. Sir, ask any officer in the battalion; they'll tell you. "Leave it to Jonas. Give him an order: he'll carry it out." That's what they'll tell you, sir. Jonas, that's me—that's my name.

CREON. What's the matter with you, man? What are you shaking for?

GUARD. By rights it's the corporal's job, sir. I've been recommended for a corporal, but they haven't put it through yet. June, it was supposed to go through.

CREON (*interrupts*). Stop chattering and tell me

why you are here. If anything has gone wrong, I'll break all three of you.

GUARD. Nobody can say we didn't keep our eye on that body. We had the two-o'clock watch—the tough one. You know how it is, sir. It's nearly the end of the night. Your eyes are like lead. You've got a crick in the back of your neck. There's shadows, and the fog is beginning to roll in. A fine watch they give us! And me, seventeen years in the service. But we was doing our duty all right. On our feet, all of us. Anybody says we were sleeping is a liar. First place, it was too cold. Second place——(CREON *makes a gesture of impatience.*) Yes, sir. Well, I turned around and looked at the body. We wasn't only ten feet away from it, but that's how I am. I was keeping my eye on it. (*Shouts.*) Listen, sir, I was the first man to see it! Me! They'll tell you. I was the one let out that yell!

CREON. What for? What was the matter?

GUARD. Sir, the body! Somebody had been there and buried it. (CREON *comes down a step on the stair. The* GUARD *becomes more frightened.*) It wasn't much, you understand. With us three there, it couldn't have been. Just covered over with a little dirt, that's all. But enough to hide it from the buzzards.

CREON. By God, I'll——(*He looks intently at the* GUARD.) You are sure that it couldn't have been a dog, scratching up the earth?

GUARD. Not a chance, sir. That's kind of what we hoped it was. But the earth was scattered over the body just like the priests tell you you should do it. Whoever did that job knew what he was doing, all right.

CREON. Who could have dared? (*He turns and looks at the* GUARD.) Was there anything to indicate who might have done it?

GUARD. Not a thing, sir. Maybe we heard a footstep—I can't swear to it. Of course we started right into search, and the corporal found a shovel, a kid's shovel no bigger than that, all rusty and everything. Corporal's got the shovel for you. We thought maybe a kid did it.

CREON (*to himself*). A kid! (*He looks away from the* GUARD.) I broke the back of the rebellion; but like a snake, it is coming together again. Polynices' friends, with their gold, blocked by my orders in the banks of Thebes. The leaders of the mob, stinking of garlic and allied to envious princes. And the temple priests, always ready for a bit of fishing in troubled waters. A kid! I can imagine what he is like, their kid: a baby-faced killer, creeping in the night with a toy shovel under his jacket. (*He looks at his* PAGE.) Though why shouldn't they have corrupted a real child? Very touching! Very useful to the party, an innocent child. A martyr. A real white-faced baby of fourteen who will spit with contempt at the guards who kill him. A free gift to their cause: the precious, innocent blood of a child on my hands. (*He turns to the* GUARD.) They must have accomplices in the Guard itself. Look here, you. Who knows about this?

GUARD. Only us three, sir. We flipped a coin, and I came right over.

CREON. Right. Listen, now. You will continue on duty. When the relief squad comes up, you will tell them to return to barracks. You will uncover the body. If another attempt is made to bury it, I shall expect you to make an arrest and bring the person straight to me. And you will keep your mouths shut. Not one word of this to a human soul. You are all guilty of neglect of duty, and you will be punished; but if the rumor spreads through Thebes that the body received burial, you will be shot—all three of you.

GUARD (*excitedly*). Sir, we never told nobody, I swear we didn't. Anyhow, I've been up here. Suppose my pals spilled it to the relief; I couldn't have been with them and here too. That wouldn't be my fault if they talked. Sir, I've got two kids. You're my witness, sir, it couldn't have been me. I was here with you. I've got a witness! If anybody talked, it couldn't have been me! I was. . . .

CREON (*interrupting*). Clear out! If the story doesn't get around, you won't be shot.

(*The* GUARD *salutes, turns, and exits at the double.* CREON *turns and paces upstage, then comes down to the end of the table.*)

CREON. A child! (*He looks at* PAGE.) Come along,

my lad. Since we can't hope to keep this to ourselves, we shall have to be the first to give out the news. And after that, we shall have to clean up the mess. (*PAGE crosses to side of* CREON. *CREON puts his hand on* PAGE's *shoulder.*) Would you be willing to die for me? Would you defy the Guard with your little shovel? (*PAGE looks up at* CREON.) Of course you would. You would do it, too. (*A pause.* CREON *looks away from* PAGE *and murmurs.*) A child! (CREON *and* PAGE *go slowly upstage center to top step.* PAGE *draws aside the curtain, through which exit* CREON *with* PAGE *behind him.*)

(*As soon as* CREON *and* PAGE *have disappeared,* CHORUS *enters and leans against the upstage portal or arch, left. The lighting is brought up to its brightest point to suggest mid-afternoon.* CHORUS *allows a pause to indicate that a crucial moment has been reached in the play, then moves slowly downstage, center. He stands for a moment silent, reflecting, and then smiles faintly.*)

CHORUS. The spring is wound up tight. It will uncoil of itself. That is what is so convenient in tragedy. The least little turn of the wrist will do the job. Anything will set it going: a glance at a girl who happens to be lifting her arms to her hair as you go by; a feeling when you wake up on a fine morning that you'd like a little respect paid to you today, as if it were as easy to order as a second cup of coffee; one question too many, idly thrown out over a friendly drink—and the tragedy is on.

The rest is automatic. You don't need to lift a finger. The machine is in perfect order; it has been oiled ever since time began, and it runs without friction. Death, treason, and sorrow are on the march; and they move in the wake of storm, of tears, of stillness. Every kind of stillness. The hush when the executioner's ax goes up at the end of the last act. The unbreathable silence when, at the beginning of the play, the two lovers, their hearts bared, their bodies naked, stand for the first time face to face in the darkened room, afraid to stir. The silence inside you when the roaring crowd acclaims the winner—so that you think of a film without a sound track, mouths agape and no sound coming out of them, a clamor that is no more than a picture; and you, the victor, already vanquished, alone in the desert of your silence. That is tragedy.

Tragedy is clean, it is restful, it is flawless. It has nothing to do with melodrama—with wicked villains, persecuted maidens, avengers, sudden revelations, and eleventh-hour repentances. Death, in a melodrama, is really horrible because it is never inevitable. The dear old father might so easily have been saved; the honest young man might so easily have brought in the police five minutes earlier.

In a tragedy, nothing is in doubt and everyone's destiny is known. That makes for tranquility. There is a sort of fellow-feeling among characters in a tragedy: he who kills is as innocent as he who gets killed; it's all a matter of what part you are playing. Tragedy is restful; and the reason is that hope, that foul, deceitful thing, has no part in it. There isn't any hope. You're trapped. The whole sky has fallen on you, and all you can do about it is to shout.

Don't mistake me: I said "shout"; I did not say groan, whimper, complain. That you cannot do. But you can shout aloud; you can get all those things said that you never thought you'd be able to say—or never even knew you had it in you to say. And you don't say these things because it will do any good to say them; you know better than that. You say them for their own sake; you say them because you learn a lot from them.

In melodrama you argue and struggle in the hope of escape. That is vulgar; it's practical. But in tragedy, where there is no temptation to try to escape, argument is gratuitous: it's kingly.

(*Voices of the* GUARDS *and scuffling sound heard through the archway.* CHORUS *looks in that direction.*)

CHORUS (*in a changed tone*). The play is on. Antigone has been caught. For the first time in her life, little Antigone is going to be able to be herself. (*Exit* CHORUS *through arch.*)

(*A pause, while the offstage voices rise in volume, then the* FIRST GUARD *enters, followed by* SECOND *and* THIRD GUARDS, *holding the arms of* ANTIGONE

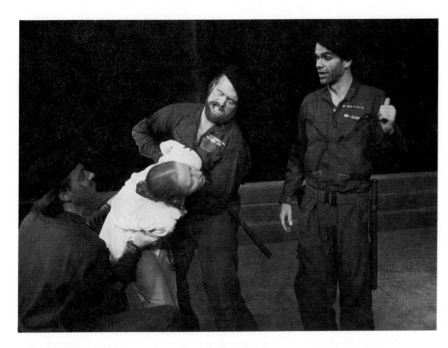

Scene from the 1978 production of *Antigone* by The Acting Company.

and dragging her along. The FIRST GUARD, *speaking as he enters, crosses swiftly to end of the table. The* TWO GUARDS *and* ANTIGONE *stop downstage.*)

FIRST GUARD (*recovered from his fright*). Come on, now, Miss, give it a rest. The chief will be here in a minute and you can tell him about it. All I know is my orders. I don't want to know what you were doing there. People always have excuses; but I can't afford to listen to them, see. Why, if we had to listen to all the people who want to tell us what's the matter with this country, we'd never get our work done. (*To the* GUARDS) You keep hold of her and I'll see that she keeps her face shut.

ANTIGONE. They are hurting me. Tell them to take their dirty hands off me.

FIRST GUARD. Dirty hands, eh? The least you can do is try to be polite, Miss. Look at me: I'm polite.

ANTIGONE. Tell them to let me go. I shan't run away. My father was King Oedipus. I am Antigone.

FIRST GUARD. King Oedipus' little girl! Well, well, well! Listen, Miss, the night watch never picks up a lady but they say, you better be careful: I'm sleeping with the police commissioner.

(*The* GUARDS *laugh.*)

ANTIGONE. I don't mind being killed, but I don't want them to touch me.

FIRST GUARD. And what about stiffs, and dirt, and such like? You wasn't afraid to touch them, was you? "Their dirty hands!" Take a look at your own hands. (ANTIGONE, *handcuffed, smiles despite herself as she looks down at her hands. They are grubby.*) You must have lost your shovel, didn't you? Had to go at it with your fingernails the second time, I'll bet. By God, I never saw such nerve! I turn my back for about five seconds; I ask a pal for a chew; I say "thanks"; I get the tobacco stowed away in my cheek—the whole thing don't take ten seconds; and there she is, clawing away like a hyena. Right out in broad daylight! And did she scratch and kick when I grabbed her! Straight for my eyes with them nails she went. And yelling something fierce about, "I haven't finished yet; let me finish!" She ain't got all her marbles! . . . Listen, we're going to get a bonus out of this. What do you say we throw a party, the three of us?

SECOND GUARD. At the old woman's? Behind Market Street?

Anouilh **887**

THIRD GUARD. Suits me. Sunday would be a good day. We're off duty Sunday. What do you say we bring our wives?

FIRST GUARD. No. Let's have some fun this time. Bring your wife, there's always something goes wrong. First place, what do you do with the kids? Bring them, they always want to go to the can just when you're right in the middle of a game of cards or something. Listen, who would have thought an hour ago that us three would be talking about throwing a party now? The way I felt when the old man was interrogating me, we'd be lucky if we got off with being docked a month's pay. I want to tell you, I was scared.

SECOND GUARD. You sure we're going to get a bonus?

FIRST GUARD. Yes. Something tells me this is big stuff.

THIRD GUARD (to SECOND GUARD). What's-his-name, you know—in the Third Battalion? He got an extra month's pay for catching a firebug.

SECOND GUARD. If we get an extra month's pay, I vote we throw the party at the Arabian's.

FIRST GUARD. You're crazy! He charges twice as much for liquor as anybody else in town. Unless you want to go upstairs, of course. Can't do that at the old woman's.

THIRD GUARD. Well, we can't keep this from our wives, no matter how you work it out. You get an extra month's pay, and what happens? Everybody in the battalion knows it, and your wife knows it too. They might even line up the battalion and give it to you in front of everybody, so how could you keep your wife from finding out?

FIRST GUARD. Well, we'll see about that. If they do the job out in the barrack yard—of course that means women, kids, everything.

ANTIGONE. I should like to sit down, if you please.

(A pause, as the FIRST GUARD thinks it over.)

FIRST GUARD. Let her sit down. But keep hold of her.

(The TWO GUARDS start to lead her toward the chair at end of table. The curtain upstage opens, and CREON enters, followed by his PAGE. FIRST GUARD turns and moves upstage a few steps. Seeing CREON, he calls out, " 'Tenshun!" The THREE GUARDS salute.

CREON, seeing ANTIGONE handcuffed to THIRD GUARD, stops on the top step, astonished.)

CREON. Antigone! (To the FIRST GUARD) Take off those handcuffs!

(FIRST GUARD crosses above table to left of ANTIGONE.)

CREON. What is this? (CREON and his PAGE come down off the steps.)

(FIRST GUARD takes key from his pocket and unlocks the cuff on ANTIGONE's hand. ANTIGONE rubs her wrist as she crosses below table toward chair at end of table. SECOND and THIRD GUARDS step back to front of arch. FIRST GUARD turns upstage toward CREON.)

FIRST GUARD. The watch, sir. We all came this time.

CREON. Who is guarding the body?

FIRST GUARD. We sent for the relief.

(CREON comes down.)

CREON. But I gave orders that the relief was to go back to barracks and stay there! (ANTIGONE sits on chair at left of table.) I told you not to open your mouth about this!

FIRST GUARD. Nobody's said anything, sir. We made this arrest, and brought the party in, the way you said we should.

CREON (to ANTIGONE). Where did these men find you?

FIRST GUARD. Right by the body.

CREON. What were you doing near your brother's body? You knew what my orders were.

FIRST GUARD. What was she doing? Sir, that's why we brought her in. She as digging up the dirt with her nails. She was trying to cover up the body all over again.

CREON. Do you realize what you are saying?

FIRST GUARD. Sir, ask these men here. After I reported to you, I went back, and first thing we did, we uncovered the body. The sun was coming up and it was beginning to smell, so we moved it up on a little rise to get him in the wind. Of course, you wouldn't expect any trouble in broad daylight. But just the same, we decided one of us had better keep his eye peeled all the time. About noon, what with the sun and the smell, and as the wind dropped and I wasn't feeling none too good, I went over to my pal to get a chew. I just had time to say "thanks" and stick it in my mouth, when I turned round and there she was, clawing away at the dirt with both hands. Right out in broad daylight! Wouldn't you think when she saw me come running she'd stop and leg it out of there? Not her! She went right on digging as fast as she could, as if I wasn't there at all. And when I grabbed her, she scratched and bit and yelled to leave her alone, she hadn't finished yet, the body wasn't all covered yet, and the like of that.

CREON (*to* ANTIGONE). Is this true?

ANTIGONE. Yes, it is true.

FIRST GUARD. We scraped the dirt off as fast as we could, then we sent for the relief and we posted them. But we didn't tell them a thing, sir. And we brought in the party so's you could see her. And that's the truth, so help me God.

CREON (*to* ANTIGONE). And was it you who covered the body the first time? In the night?

ANTIGONE. Yes, it was. With a toy shovel we used to take to the seashore when we were children. It was Polynices' own shovel; he had cut his name in the handle. That was why I left it with him. But these men took it away; so the next time, I had to do it with my hands.

FIRST GUARD. Sir, she was clawing away like a wild animal. Matter of fact, first minute we saw her, what with the heat haze and everything, my pal says, "That must be a dog," he says. "Dog!" I says, "that's a girl, that is!" And it was.

CREON. Very well! (*Turns to the* PAGE.) Show these men to the anteroom. (*The* PAGE *crosses to the arch, stands there, waiting.* CREON *moves behind the table. To the* FIRST GUARD) You three men will wait outside. I may want a report from you later.

FIRST GUARD. Do I put the cuffs back on her, sir?

CREON. No.

(*The* THREE GUARDS *salute, do an about-turn, and exeunt through arch, right.* PAGE *follows them out. A pause.*)

CREON. Had you told anybody what you meant to do?

ANTIGONE. No.

CREON. Did you meet anyone on your way—coming or going?

ANTIGONE. No, nobody.

CREON. Sure of that, are you?

ANTIGONE. Perfectly sure.

CREON. Very well. Now listen to me. You will go straight to your room. When you get there, you will go to bed. You will say that you are not well and that you have not been out since yesterday. Your nurse will tell the same story. (*He looks toward arch, through which the* GUARDS *have gone out.*) And I'll get rid of those three men.

ANTIGONE. Uncle Creon, you are going to a lot of trouble for no good reason. You must know that I'll do it all over again tonight.

(*A pause. They look one another in the eye.*)

CREON. Why did you try to bury your brother?

ANTIGONE. I owed it to him.

CREON. I had forbidden it.

ANTIGONE. I owed it to him. Those who are not buried wander eternally and find no rest. If my brother were alive, and he came home weary after a long day's hunting, I should kneel down and unlace his boots, I should fetch him food and drink, I should see that his bed was ready for him. Polynices is home from the hunt. I owe it to him to unlock the house of the dead in which my father and my mother are waiting to welcome him. Polynices has earned his rest.

CREON. Polynices was a rebel and a traitor, and you know it.

ANTIGONE. He was my brother.

CREON. You heard my edict. It was proclaimed throughout Thebes. You read my edict. It was posted up on the city walls.

ANTIGONE. Of course I did.

CREON. You knew the punishment I decreed for any person who attempted to give him burial.

ANTIGONE. Yes, I knew the punishment.

CREON. Did you by any chance act on the assumption that a daughter of Oedipus, a daughter of Oedipus's stubborn pride, was above the law?

ANTIGONE. No, I did not act on that assumption.

CREON. Because if you had acted on that assumption, Antigone, you would have been deeply wrong. Nobody has a more sacred obligation to obey the law than those who make the law. You are a daughter of lawmakers, a daughter of kings, Antigone. You must observe the law.

ANTIGONE. Had I been a scullery maid washing my dishes when that law was read aloud to me, I should have scrubbed the greasy water from my arms and gone out in my apron to bury my brother.

CREON. What nonsense! If you had been a scullery maid, there would have been no doubt in your mind about the seriousness of that edict. You would have known that it meant death; and you would have been satisfied to weep for your brother in your kitchen. But you! You thought that because you come of the royal line, because you were my niece and were going to marry my son, I shouldn't dare have you killed.

ANTIGONE. You are mistaken. Quite the contrary. I never doubted for an instant that you would have me put to death.

(A pause, as CREON *stares fixedly at her.)*

CREON. The pride of Oedipus! Oedipus and his headstrong pride all over again. I can see your father in you—and I believe you. Of course you thought that I should have you killed! Proud as you are, it seemed to you a natural climax in your existence. Your father was like that. For him as for you human happiness was meaning-less; and mere human misery was not enough to satisfy his passion for torment. *(He sits on stool behind the table.)* You come of people for whom the human vestment is a kind of strait jacket: it cracks at the seams. You spend your lives wriggling to get out of it. Nothing less than a cosy tea party with death and destiny will quench your thirst. The happiest hour of your father's life came when he listened greedily to the story of how, unknown to himself, he had killed his own father and dishonored the bed of his own mother. Drop by drop, word by word, he drank in the dark story that the gods had destined him first to live and then to hear. How avidly men and women drink the brew of such a tale when their names are Oedipus—and Antigone! And it is so simple, afterwards, to do what your father did, to put out one's eyes and take one's daughter begging on the highways.

Let me tell you, Antigone: those days are over for Thebes. Thebes has a right to a king without a past. My name, thank God, is only Creon. I stand here with both feet firm on the ground: with both hands in my pockets; and I have decided that so long as I am king—being less ambitious than your father was—I shall merely devote myself to introducing a little order into this absurd kingdom; if that is possible.

Don't think that being a king seems to me romantic. It is my trade; a trade a man has to work at every day; and like every other trade, it isn't all beer and skittles. But since it is my trade, I take it seriously. And if, tomorrow, some wild and bearded messenger walks in from some wild and distant valley—which is what happened to your dad—and tells me that he's not quite sure who my parents were, but thinks that my wife Eurydice is actually my mother, I shall ask him to do me the kindness to go back where he came from; and I shan't let a little matter like that persuade me to order my wife to take a blood test and the police to let me know whether or not my birth certificate was forged. Kings, my girl, have other things to do than to surrender themselves to their private feelings. *(He looks at her and smiles.)* Hand *you* over to be killed! *(He rises, moves to end of table and sits on the top of table.)* I have other plans for you. You're going to marry Haemon; and I want you to fatten up a bit so that you can give him a sturdy boy. Let me assure you that Thebes needs that boy a good deal more than it needs your death. You will go to your room, now, and do as you have been told; and you won't say a word about this to anybody. Don't fret about the guards: I'll see that their mouths are shut. And don't annihilate me with those eyes. I know that you think I am a brute, and I'm sure you must consider me very prosaic. But the fact is, I have always been fond of you, stubborn though you always were. Don't forget that the first doll you ever had came from me.

(A pause. ANTIGONE *says nothing, rises, and crosses slowly below the table toward the arch.* CREON *turns and watches her.)*

CREON. Where are you going?

ANTIGONE *(stops downstage; without any show of rebellion)*. You know very well where I am going.

CREON (*after a pause*). What sort of game are you playing?

ANTIGONE. I am not playing games.

CREON. Antigone, do you realize that if, apart from those three guards, a single soul finds out what you have tried to do, it will be impossible for me to avoid putting you to death? There is still a chance that I can save you; but only if you keep this to yourself and give up your crazy purpose. Five minutes more, and it will be too late. You understand that?

ANTIGONE. I must go and bury my brother. Those men uncovered him.

CREON. What good will it do? You know that there are other men standing guard over Polynices. And even if you did cover him over with earth again, the earth would again be removed.

ANTIGONE. I know all that. I know it. But that much, at least, I can do. And what a person can do, a person ought to do.

(*A pause.*)

CREON. Tell me, Antigone, do you believe all that flummery about religious burial? Do you really believe that a so-called shade of your brother is condemned to wander forever homeless if a little earth is not flung on his corpse to the accompaniment of some priestly abracadabra? Have you ever listened to the priests of Thebes when they were mumbling their formula? Have you ever watched those dreary bureaucrats while they were preparing the dead for burial—skipping half the gestures required by the ritual, swallowing half their words, hustling the dead into their graves out of fear that they might be late for lunch?

ANTIGONE. Yes, I have seen all that.

CREON. And did you never say to yourself, as you watched them, that if someone you really loved lay dead under the shuffling, mumbling ministrations of the priests, you would scream aloud and beg the priests to leave the dead in peace?

ANTIGONE. Yes, I've thought all that.

CREON. And you still insist upon being put to death—merely because I refuse to let your brother go out with that grotesque passport; because I refuse his body the wretched consolation of that mass-production jibber-jabber,

which you would have been the first to be embarrassed by if I had allowed it. The whole thing is absurd!

ANTIGONE. Yes, it's absurd.

CREON. Then why, Antigone, why? For whose sake? For the sake of them that believe in it? To raise them against me?

ANTIGONE. No.

CREON. For whom then if not for them and not for Polynices either?

ANTIGONE. For nobody. For myself.

(*A pause as they stand looking at one another.*)

CREON. You must want very much to die. You look like a trapped animal.

ANTIGONE. Stop feeling sorry for me. Do as I do. Do your job. But if you are a human being, do it quickly. That is all I ask of you. I'm not going to be able to hold out for ever.

CREON (*takes a step toward her*). I want to save you, Antigone.

ANTIGONE. You are the king, and you are all-powerful. But that you cannot do.

CREON. You think not?

ANTIGONE. Neither save me nor stop me.

CREON. Prideful Antigone! Little Oedipus!

ANTIGONE. Only this can you do: have me put to death.

CREON. Have you tortured, perhaps?

ANTIGONE. Why would you do that? To see me cry? To hear me beg for mercy? Or swear whatever you wish, and then begin over again?

(*A pause.*)

CREON. You listen to me. You have cast me for the villain in this little play of yours, and yourself for the heroine. And you know it, you damned little mischiefmaker! But don't you drive me too far! If I were one of your preposterous little tyrants that Greece is full of, you would be lying in a ditch this minute with your tongue pulled out and your body drawn and quartered.[5] But you can see something in my face that makes me hesitate to send for the guards and turn you over

---

5. **drawn and quartered**, ancient method of execution for treason. The condemned person's intestines were pulled out (*drawn*) and the body chopped into four parts.

to them. Instead, I let you go on arguing; and you taunt me, you take the offensive. (*He grasps her left wrist.*) What are you driving at, you she-devil?

ANTIGONE. Let me go. You are hurting my arm.

CREON (*gripping her tighter*). I will not let you go.

ANTIGONE (*moans*). Oh!

CREON. I was a fool to waste words. I should have done this from the beginning. (*He looks at her.*) I may be your uncle—but we are not a particularly affectionate family. Are we, eh? (*Through his teeth, as he twists.*) Are we? (CREON *propels* ANTIGONE *round below him to his side.*) What fun for you, eh? To be able to spit in the face of a king who has all the power in the world; a man who has done his own killing in his day; who has killed people just as pitiable as you are—and who is still soft enough to go to all this trouble in order to keep you from being killed.

(*A pause.*)

ANTIGONE. Now you are squeezing my arm too tightly. It doesn't hurt any more.

(CREON *stares at her, then drops her arm.*)

CREON. I shall save you yet. (*He goes below the table to the chair at end of table, takes off his coat, and places it on the chair.*) God knows, I have things enough to do today without wasting my time on an insect like you. There's plenty to do, I assure you, when you've just put down a revolution. But urgent things can wait. I am not going to let politics be the cause of your death. For it is a fact that this whole business is nothing but politics: the mournful shade of Polynices, the decomposing corpse, the sentimental weeping, and the hysteria that you mistake for heroism—nothing but politics.

Look here. I may not be soft, but I'm fastidious. I like things clean, shipshape, well-scrubbed. Don't think that I am not just as offended as you are by the thought of that meat rotting in the sun. In the evening, when the breeze comes in off the sea, you can smell it in the palace, and it nauseates me. But I refuse even to shut my window. It's vile; and I can tell you what I wouldn't tell anybody else: it's stupid, monstrously stupid. But the people of Thebes have got to have their noses rubbed into it a little

longer. My God! If it was up to me, I should have had them bury your brother long ago as a mere matter of public hygiene. I admit that what I am doing is childish. But if the feather-headed rabble I govern are to understand what's what, that stench has got to fill the town for a month!

ANTIGONE (*turns to him*). You are a loathsome man!

CREON. I agree. My trade forces me to be. We could argue whether I ought or ought not to follow my trade; but once I take on the job, I must do it properly.

ANTIGONE. Why do you do it at all?

CREON. My dear, I woke up one morning and found myself King of Thebes. God knows, there were other things I loved in life more than power.

ANTIGONE. Then you should have said "no."

CREON. Yes, I could have done that. Only, I felt that it would have been cowardly. I should have been like a workman who turns down a job that has to be done. So I said "yes."

ANTIGONE. So much the worse for you, then. I didn't say "yes." I can say "no" to anything I think vile, and I don't have to count the cost. But because you said "yes," all that you can do, for all your crown and your trappings, and your guards—all that you can do is to have me killed.

CREON. Listen to me.

ANTIGONE. If I want to. I don't have to listen to you if I don't want to. You've said your "yes." There is nothing more you can tell me that I don't know. You stand there, drinking in my words. (*She moves behind chair.*) Why is it that you don't call your guards? I'll tell you why. You want to hear me out to the end; that's why.

CREON. You amuse me.

ANTIGONE. Oh, no, I don't. I frighten you. That is why you talk about saving me. Everything would be so much easier if you had a docile, tongue-tied little Antigone living in the palace. I'll tell you something, Uncle Creon: I'll give you back one of your own words. You are too fastidious to make a good tyrant. But you are going to have to put me to death today, and you know it. And that's what frightens you. God! Is there anything uglier than a frightened man!

CREON. Very well. I am afraid, then. Does that satisfy you? I am afraid that if you insist upon it, I shall have to have you killed. And I don't want to.

ANTIGONE. I don't have to do things that I think are wrong. If it comes to that, you didn't really want to leave my brother's body unburied, did you? Say it! Admit that you didn't.

CREON. I have said it already.

ANTIGONE. But you did it just the same. And now, though you don't want to do it, you are going to have me killed. And you call that being a king!

CREON. Yes, I call that being a king.

ANTIGONE. Poor Creon! My nails are broken, my fingers are bleeding, my arms are covered with the welts left by the paws of your guards—but I am a queen!

CREON. Then why not have pity on me, and live? Isn't your brother's corpse, rotting there under my windows, payment enough for peace and order in Thebes? My son loves you. Don't make me add your life to the payment. I've paid enough.

ANTIGONE. No, Creon! You said "yes," and made yourself king. Now you will never stop paying.

CREON. But God in heaven! Won't you try to understand me! I'm trying hard enough to understand you! There had to be one man who said "yes." Somebody had to agree to captain the ship. She had sprung a hundred leaks; she was loaded to the water line with crime, ignorance, poverty. The wheel was swinging with the wind. The crew refused to work and were looting the cargo. The officers were building a raft, ready to slip overboard and desert the ship. The mast was splitting, the wind was howling, the sails were beginning to rip. Every man jack on board was about to drown—and only because the only thing they thought of was their own skins and their cheap little day-to-day traffic. Was that a time, do you think, for playing with words like "yes" and "no"? Was that a time for a man to be weighing the pros and cons, wondering if he wasn't going to pay too dearly later on; if he wasn't going to lose his life, or his family, or his touch with other men? You grab the wheel, you right the ship in the face of a mountain of water. You shout an order, and if one man refuses to obey, you shoot straight into the mob. Into the mob, I say! The beast as nameless as the wave that crashes down upon your deck; as nameless as the whipping wind. The thing that drops when you shoot may be someone who poured you a drink the night before; but it has no name. And you, braced at the wheel, you have no name, either. Nothing has a name—except the ship, and the storm. (A pause as he looks at her.) Now do you understand?

ANTIGONE. I am not here to understand. That's all very well for you. I am here to say "no" to you, and die.

CREON. It is easy to say "no."

ANTIGONE. Not always.

CREON. It is easy to say "no." To say "yes," you have to sweat and roll up your sleeves and plunge both hands into life up to the elbows. It is easy to say "no," even if saying "no" means death. All you have to do is to sit still and wait. Wait to go on living; wait to be killed. That is the coward's part. "No" is one of your man-made words. Can you imagine a world in which trees say "no" to the sap? In which beasts say "no" to hunger or to propagation? Animals are good, simple, tough. They move in droves, nudging one another onwards, all traveling the same road. Some of them keel over, but the rest go on; and no matter how many may fall by the wayside, there are always those few left that go on bringing their young into the world, traveling the same road with the same obstinate will, unchanged from those who sent before.

ANTIGONE. Animals, eh, Creon! What a king you could be if only men were animals!

(A pause. CREON turns and looks at her.)

CREON. You despise me, don't you? (ANTIGONE is silent. CREON goes on, as if to himself.) Strange. Again and again, I have imagined myself holding this conversation with a pale young man I have never seen in the flesh. He would have come to assassinate me, and would have failed. I would be trying to find out from him why he wanted to kill me. But with all my logic and all my powers of debate, the only thing I could get out of him would be that he despised me. Who would have thought that the white-faced boy would turn out to be you? And that the debate would arise out of something so meaningless as the burial of your brother?

ANTIGONE (*repeats contemptuously*). Meaningless!

CREON (*earnestly, almost desperately*). And yet, you must hear me out. My part is not an heroic one, but I shall play my part. I shall have you put to death. Only, before I do, I want to make one last appeal. I want to be sure that you know what you are doing as well as I know what I am doing. Antigone, do you know what you are dying for? Do you know the sordid story to which you are going to sign your name in blood, for all time to come?

ANTIGONE. What story?

CREON. The story of Eteocles and Polynices, the story of your brothers. You think you know it, but you don't. Nobody in Thebes knows that story but me. And it seems to me, this afternoon, that you have a right to know it too.

(*A pause.* ANTIGONE *moves to chair and sits.*)

CREON. It's not a pretty story. (*He turns, gets stool from behind the table and places it between the table and the chair.*) You'll see. (*He looks at her for a moment.*) Tell me, first. What do you remember about your brothers? They were older than you, so they must have looked down on you. And I imagine that they tormented you—pulled your pigtails, broke your dolls, whispered secrets to each other to put you in a rage.

ANTIGONE. They were big and I was little.

CREON. And later on, when they came home wearing evening clothes, smoking cigarettes, they would have nothing to do with you; and you thought they were wonderful.

ANTIGONE. They were boys and I was a girl.

CREON. You didn't know why, exactly, but you knew that they were making your mother unhappy. You saw her in tears over them; and your father would fly into a rage because of them. You heard them come in, slamming doors, laughing noisily in the corridors—insolent, spineless, unruly, smelling of drink.

ANTIGONE (*staring outward*). Once, it was very early and we had just got up. I saw them coming home, and hid behind a door. Polynices was very pale and his eyes were shining. He was so handsome in his evening clothes. He saw me, and said: "Here, this is for you"; and he gave me a big paper flower that he had brought home from his night out.

CREON. And of course you still have that flower. Last night, before you crept out, you opened a drawer and looked at it for a time, to give yourself courage.

ANTIGONE. Who told you so?

CREON. Poor Antigone! With her night-club flower. Do you know what your brother was?

ANTIGONE. Whatever he was, I know that you will say vile things about him.

CREON. A cheap, idiotic bounder, that is what he was. A cruel, vicious little voluptuary. A little beast with just wit enough to drive a car faster and throw more money away than any of his pals. I was with your father one day when Polynices, having lost a lot of money gambling, asked him to settle the debt; and when your father refused, the boy raised his hand against him and called him a vile name.

ANTIGONE. That's a lie!

CREON. He struck your father in the face with his fist. It was pitiful. Your father sat at his desk with his head in his hands. His nose was bleeding. He was weeping with anguish. And in a corner of your father's study, Polynices stood sneering and lighting a cigarette.

ANTIGONE. That's a lie.

(*A pause.*)

CREON. When did you last see Polynices alive? When you were twelve years old. *That's* true, isn't it?

ANTIGONE. Yes, that's true.

CREON. Now you know why. Oedipus was too chicken-hearted to have the boy locked up. Polynices was allowed to go off and join the Argive[6] army. And as soon as he reached Argos, the attempts upon your father's life began—upon the life of an old man who could-

---

6. *Argive* (är′jīv, är′gīv), of Argos. In ancient times Argos was one of the principal city-states of the Peloponessus, the southern part of Greece.

n't make up his mind to die, couldn't bear to be parted from his kingship. One after another, men slipped into Thebes from Argos for the purpose of assassinating him, and every killer we caught always ended by confessing who had put him up to it, who had paid him to try it. And it wasn't only Polynices. That is really what I am trying to tell you. I want you to know what went on in the back room, in the kitchen of politics; I want you to know what took place in the wings of this drama in which you are burning to play a part.

Yesterday, I gave Eteocles a State funeral, with pomp and honors. Today, Eteocles is a saint and a hero in the eyes of all Thebes. The whole city turned out to bury him. The schoolchildren emptied their saving boxes to buy wreaths for him. Old men, orating in quavering, hypocritical voices, glorified the virtues of the great-hearted brother, the devoted son, the loyal prince. I made a speech myself; and every temple priest was present with an appropriate show of sorrow and solemnity in his stupid face. And military honors were accorded the dead hero.

Well, what else could I have done? People had taken sides in the civil war. Both sides couldn't be wrong; that would be too much. I couldn't have made them swallow the truth. Two gangsters was more of a luxury than I could afford. (*He pauses for a moment.*) And this is the whole point of my story. Eteocles, that virtuous brother, was just as rotten as Polynices. That greathearted son had done his best, too, to procure the assassination of his father. That loyal prince had also offered to sell out Thebes to the highest bidder.

Funny, isn't it? Polynices lies rotting in the sun while Eteocles is given a hero's funeral and will be housed in a marble vault. Yet I have absolute proof that everything that Polynices did, Eteocles had plotted to do. They were a pair of blackguards—both engaged in selling out Thebes, and both engaged in selling out each other; and they died like the cheap gangsters they were, over a division of the spoils.

But, as I told you a moment ago, I had to make a martyr of one of them. I sent out to the holocaust for their bodies; they were found clasped in one another's arms—for the first time in their lives, I imagine. Each had been spitted on the other's sword, and the Argive cavalry had trampled them down. They were mashed to a pulp, Antigone. I had the prettier of the two carcasses brought in and gave it a State funeral; and I left the other to rot. I don't know which was which. And I assure you, I don't care.

(*Long silence, neither looking at the other.*)

ANTIGONE (*in a mild voice*). Why do you tell me all this?

CREON. Would it have been better to let you die a victim to that obscene story?

ANTIGONE. It might have been. I had my faith.

CREON. What are you going to do now?

ANTIGONE (*rises to her feet in a daze*). I shall go up to my room.

CREON. Don't stay alone. Go and find Haemon. And get married quickly.

ANTIGONE (*in a whisper*). Yes.

CREON. All this is really beside the point. You have your whole life ahead of you—and life is a treasure.

ANTIGONE. Yes.

CREON. And you were about to throw it away. Don't think me fatuous if I say that I understand you; and that at your age I should have done the same thing. A moment ago, when we were quarreling, you said I was drinking in your words. I was. But it wasn't you I was listening to; it was a lad named Creon who lived here in Thebes many years ago. He was thin and pale, as you are. His mind, too, was filled with thoughts of self-sacrifice. Go and find Haemon. And get married quickly, Antigone. Be happy. Life flows like water, and you young people let it run away through your fingers. Shut your hands; hold on to it, Antigone. Life is not what you think it is. Life is a child playing around your feet, a tool you hold firmly in your grip, a bench you sit down upon in the evening, in your garden. People will tell you that that's not life, that life is something else. They will tell you that because they need your strength and your fire, and they will want to make use of you. Don't listen to them. Believe me, the only poor consolation that we have in our old age is to discover that what I have just said to you is true. Life is nothing more than the happiness that you get out of it.

ANTIGONE (*murmurs, lost in thought*). Happiness. . . .

CREON (*suddenly a little self-conscious*). Not much of a word, is it?

ANTIGONE (*quietly*). What kind of happiness do you foresee for me? Paint me the picture of your happy Antigone. What are the unimportant little sins that I shall have to commit before I am allowed to sink my teeth into life and tear happiness from it? Tell me: to whom shall I have to lie? Upon whom shall I have to fawn? To whom must I sell myself? Whom do you want me to leave dying, while I turn away my eyes?

CREON. Antigone, be quiet.

ANTIGONE. Why do you tell me to be quiet when all I want to know is what I have to do to be happy? This minute; since it is this very minute that I must make my choice. You tell me that life is so wonderful. I want to know what I have to do in order to be able to say that myself.

CREON. Do you love Haemon?

ANTIGONE. Yes, I love Haemon. The Haemon I love is hard and young, faithful and difficult to satisfy, just as I am. But if what I love in Haemon is to be worn away like a stone step by the tread of the thing you called life, the thing you call happiness, if Haemon reaches the point where he stops growing pale with fear when I grow pale, stops thinking that I must have been killed in an accident when I am five minutes late, stops feeling that he is alone on earth when I laugh and he doesn't know why—if he too has to learn to say "yes" to everything—why, no, then, no! I do not love Haemon!

CREON. You don't know what you are talking about!

ANTIGONE. I do know what I am talking about! Now it is you who have stopped understanding. I am too far away from you now, talking to you from a kingdom you can't get into, with your quick tongue and your hollow heart. (*Laughs.*) I laugh, Creon, because I see you suddenly as you must have been at fifteen: the same look

of impotence in your face and the same inner conviction that there was nothing you couldn't do. What has life added to you, except those lines in your face, and that fat on your stomach?

CREON. Be quiet, I tell you!

ANTIGONE. Why do you want me to be quiet? Because you know that I am right? Do you think I can't see in your face that what I am saying is true? You can't admit it, of course; you have to go on growling and defending the bone you call happiness.

CREON. It is your happiness, too, you little fool!

ANTIGONE. I spit on your happiness! I spit on your idea of life—that life that must go on, come what may. You are all like dogs that lick everything they smell. You with your promise of a humdrum happiness—provided a person doesn't ask too much of life. I want everything of life, I do; and I want it now! I want it total, complete: otherwise I reject it! I will *not* be moderate. I will *not* be satisfied with the bit of cake you offer me if I promise to be a good little girl. I want to be sure of everything this very day; sure that everything will be as beautiful as when I was a little girl. If not, I want to die!

CREON. Scream on, daughter of Oedipus! Scream on, in your father's own voice!

ANTIGONE. In my father's own voice, yes! We are of the tribe that asks questions, and we ask them to the bitter end. Until no tiniest chance of hope remains to be strangled by our hands. We are of the tribe that hates your filthy hope, your docile, female hope; hope, your whore. . . .

CREON (*grasps her by her arms*). Shut up! If you could see how ugly you are, shrieking those words!

ANTIGONE. Yes, I am ugly! Father was ugly, too. (CREON *releases her arms, turns and moves away. Stands with his back to* ANTIGONE.)

ANTIGONE. But Father became beautiful. And do you know when? (*She follows him to behind the table.*) At the very end. When all his questions had been answered. When he could no longer doubt that he *had* killed his own father; that he *had* gone to bed with his own mother. When all hope was gone, stamped out like a beetle. When it was absolutely certain that nothing,

nothing could save him. Then he was at peace; then he could smile, almost; then he became beautiful. . . . Whereas you! Ah, those faces of yours, you candidates for election to happiness! It's you who are the ugly ones, even the handsomest of you—with the ugly glint in the corner of your eyes, that ugly crease at the corner of your mouths. Creon, you spoke the word a moment ago: the kitchen of politics. You look it and you smell of it.

CREON (*struggles to put his hand over her mouth*). I order you to shut up! Do you hear me?

ANTIGONE. *You* order me? Cook! Do you really believe that you can give me orders?

CREON. Antigone! The anteroom is full of people! Do you want them to hear you?

ANTIGONE. Open the doors! Let us make sure that they can hear me!

CREON. By God! You shut up, I tell you!

(ISMENE *enters through arch.*)

ISMENE (*distraught*). Antigone!

ANTIGONE (*turns to* ISMENE). You, too? What do you want?

ISMENE. Oh, forgive me, Antigone. I've come back. I'll be brave. I'll go with you now.

ANTIGONE. Where will you go with me?

ISMENE (*to* CREON). Creon! If you kill her, you'll have to kill me too.

ANTIGONE. Oh, no, Ismene. Not a bit of it. I die alone. You don't think I'm going to let you die with me after what I've been through? You don't deserve it.

ISMENE. If you die, I don't want to live. I don't want to be left behind, alone.

ANTIGONE. You chose life and I chose death. Now stop blubbering. You had your chance to come with me in the black night, creeping on your hands and knees. You had your chance to claw up the earth with your nails, as I did; to get yourself caught like a thief, as I did. And you refused it.

ISMENE. Not any more. I'll do it alone tonight.

ANTIGONE (*turns round toward* CREON). You hear that, Creon? The thing is catching! Who knows but that lots of people will catch the disease from me! What are you waiting for? Call in your guards! Come on, Creon! Show a little courage!

Scene from the 1978 production of *Antigone* by The Acting Company.

It only hurts for a minute! Come on, cook!

CREON (*turns toward arch and calls*). Guard!

(GUARDS *enter through arch.*)

ANTIGONE (*in a great cry of relief*). At last, Creon!

(CHORUS *enters through left arch.*)

CREON (*to the* GUARDS). Take her away! (CREON *goes up on top step.*)

(GUARDS *grasp* ANTIGONE *by her arms, turn and hustle her toward the arch, right, and exeunt.* ISMENE *mimes horror, backs away toward the arch, left, then turns and runs out through the arch. A long pause as* CREON *moves slowly downstage.*)

CHORUS (*behind* CREON; *speaks in a deliberate voice*). You are out of your mind, Creon. What have you done?

CREON (*his back to* CHORUS). She had to die.

CHORUS. You must not let Antigone die. We shall carry the scar of her death for centuries.

CREON. She insisted. No man on earth was strong

enough to dissuade her. Death was her purpose, whether she knew it or not. Polynices was a mere pretext. When she had to give up that pretext, she found another one—that life and happiness were tawdry things and not worth possessing. She was bent upon only one thing: to reject life and to die.

CHORUS. She is a mere child, Creon.

CREON. What do you want me to do for her? Condemn her to live?

HAEMON (*calls from offstage*). Father!

(HAEMON *enters through arch, right.* CREON *turns toward him.*)

CREON. Haemon, forget Antigone. Forget her, my dearest boy.

HAEMON. How can you talk like that?

CREON (*grasps* HAEMON *by the hands*). I did everything I could to save her, Haemon. I used every argument. I swear I did. The girl doesn't love you. She could have gone on living for you; but she refused. She wanted it this way; she wanted to die.

HAEMON. Father! The guards are dragging Antigone away! You've got to stop them! (*He breaks away from* CREON.)

CREON (*looks away from* HAEMON). I can't stop them. It's too late. Antigone has spoken. The story is all over Thebes. I cannot save her now.

CHORUS. Creon, you must find a way. Lock her up. Say that she has gone out of her mind.

CREON. Everybody will know it isn't so. The nation will say that I am making an exception of her because my son loves her. I cannot.

CHORUS. You can still gain time, and get her out of Thebes.

CREON. The mob already knows the truth. It is howling for her blood. I can do nothing.

HAEMON. But, Father, you are master in Thebes!

CREON. I am master under the law. Not above the law.

HAEMON. You cannot let Antigone be taken from me. I am your son!

CREON. I cannot do anything else, my poor boy. She must die and you must live.

HAEMON. Live, you say! Live a life without Antigone? A life in which I am to go on admiring you as you busy yourself about your kingdom,

make your persuasive speeches, strike your attitudes? Not without Antigone. I love Antigone. I will not live without Antigone!

CREON. Haemon—you will have to resign yourself to life without Antigone. (*He moves to left of* HAEMON.) Sooner or later there comes a day of sorrow in each man's life when he must cease to be a child and take up the burden of manhood. That day has come for you.

HAEMON (*backs away a step*). That giant strength, that courage. That massive god who used to pick me up in his arms and shelter me from shadows and monsters—was that you, Father? Was it of you I stood in awe? Was that man you?

CREON. For God's sake, Haemon, do not judge me! Not you, too!

HAEMON (*pleading now*). This is all a bad dream, Father. You are not yourself. It isn't true that we have been backed up against a wall, forced to surrender. We don't have to say "yes" to this terrible thing. You are still king. You are still the father I revered. You have no right to desert me, to shrink into nothingness. The world will be too bare, I shall be too alone in the world, if you force me to disown you.

CREON. The world *is* bare, Haemon, and you *are* alone. You must cease to think your father all-powerful. Look straight at me. See your father as he is. That is what it means to grow up and be a man.

HAEMON (*stares at* CREON *for a moment*). I tell you that I will not live without Antigone. (*Turns and goes quickly out through arch.*)

CHORUS. Creon, the boy will go mad.

CREON. Poor boy! He loves her.

CHORUS. Creon, the boy is wounded to death.

CREON. We are all wounded to death.

(FIRST GUARD *enters through arch, right, followed by* SECOND *and* THIRD GUARDS *pulling* ANTIGONE *along with them.*)

FIRST GUARD. Sir, the people are crowding into the palace!

ANTIGONE. Creon, I don't want to see their faces. I don't want to hear them howl. You are going to kill me; let that be enough. I want to be alone until it is over.

CREON. Empty the palace! Guards at the gates!

(CREON *quickly crosses toward the arch; exit.*)
(TWO GUARDS *release* ANTIGONE; *exeunt behind* CREON. CHORUS *goes out through arch, left. The lighting dims so that only the area about the table is lighted. The cyclorama is covered with a dark blue color. The scene is intended to suggest a prison cell, filled with shadows and dimly lit.* ANTIGONE *moves to stool and sits. The* FIRST GUARD *stands upstage. He watches* ANTIGONE, *and as she sits, he begins pacing slowly downstage, then upstage. A pause.*)

ANTIGONE (*turns and looks at the* GUARD). It's you, is it?

GUARD. What do you mean, me?

ANTIGONE. The last human face that I shall see. (*A pause as they look at each other, then* GUARD *paces upstage, turns, and crosses behind table.*) Was it you that arrested me this morning?

GUARD. Yes, that was me.

ANTIGONE. You hurt me. There was no need for you to hurt me. Did I act as if I was trying to escape?

GUARD. Come on now, Miss. It was my business to bring you in. I did it. (*A pause. He paces to and fro upstage. Only the sound of his boots is heard.*)

ANTIGONE. How old are you?

GUARD. Thirty-nine.

ANTIGONE. Have you any children?

GUARD. Yes. Two.

ANTIGONE. Do you love your children?

GUARD. What's that got to do with you? (*A pause. He paces upstage and downstage.*)

ANTIGONE. How long have you been in the Guard?

GUARD. Since the war. I was in the army. Sergeant. Then I joined the Guard.

ANTIGONE. Does one have to have been an army sergeant to get into the Guard?

GUARD. Supposed to be. Either that or on special detail. But when they make you a guard, you lose your stripes.

ANTIGONE (*murmurs*). I see.

GUARD. Yes. Of course, if you're a guard, everybody knows you're something special; they know you're an old N.C.O.[7] Take pay, for instance. When you're a guard you get your pay, and on top of that you get six months' extra pay, to make sure you don't lose anything by not being a sergeant any more. And of course

you do better than that. You get a house, coal, rations, extras for the wife and kids. If you've got two kids, like me, you draw better than a sergeant.

ANTIGONE (*barely audible*). I see.

GUARD. That's why sergeants, now, they don't like guards. Maybe you noticed they try to make out they're better than us? Promotion, that's what it is. In the army, anybody can get promoted. All you need is good conduct. Now in the Guard, it's slow, and you have to know your business—like how to make out a report and the like of that. But when you're an N.C.O. in the Guard, you've got something that even a sergeant-major ain't got. For instance. . . .

ANTIGONE (*breaking him off*). Listen.

GUARD. Yes, Miss.

ANTIGONE. I'm going to die soon.

(*The* GUARD *looks at her for a moment, then turns and moves away.*)

GUARD. For instance, people have a lot of respect for guards, they have. A guard may be a soldier, but he's kind of in the civil service, too.

ANTIGONE. Do you think it hurts to die?

GUARD. How would I know? Of course, if somebody sticks a saber in your guts and turns it round, it hurts.

ANTIGONE. How are they going to put me to death?

GUARD. Well, I'll tell you. I heard the proclamation all right. Wait a minute. How did it go now? (*He stares into space and recites from memory.*) "In order that our fair city shall not be pol-luted with her sinful blood, she shall be im-mured—immured." That means, they shove you in a cave and wall up the cave.

ANTIGONE. Alive?

GUARD. Yes. . . . (*He moves away a few steps.*)

ANTIGONE (*murmurs*). O tomb! O bridal bed! Alone! (ANTIGONE *sits there, a tiny figure in the middle of the stage. You would say she felt a little chilly. She wraps her arms round herself.*)

GUARD. Yes! Outside the southeast gate of the town. In the Cave of Hades. In broad daylight.

---

7. *N.C.O.*, a noncommissioned officer, such as a corporal or sergeant.

Some detail, eh, for them that's on the job! First they thought maybe it was a job for the army. Now it looks like it's going to be the Guard. There's an outfit for you! Nothing the Guard can't do. No wonder the army's jealous.

ANTIGONE. A pair of animals.

GUARD. What do you mean, a pair of animals?

ANTIGONE. When the winds blow cold, all they need do is to press close against one another. I am all alone.

GUARD. Is there anything you want? I can send out for it, you know.

ANTIGONE. You are very kind. (*A pause.* ANTIGONE *looks up at the* GUARD.) Yes, there is something I want. I want you to give someone a letter from me, when I am dead.

GUARD. How's that again? A letter?

ANTIGONE. Yes, I want to write a letter; and I want you to give it to someone for me.

GUARD (*straightens up*). Now, wait a minute. Take it easy. It's as much as my job is worth to go handing out letters from prisoners.

ANTIGONE (*removes a ring from her finger and holds it out toward him*). I'll give you this ring if you will do it.

GUARD. Is it gold? (*He takes the ring from her.*)

ANTIGONE. Yes, it is gold.

GUARD (*shakes his head*). Uh-uh. No can do. Suppose they go through my pockets. I might get six months for a thing like that. (*He stares at the ring, then glances off right to make sure that he is not being watched.*) Listen, tell you what I'll do. You tell me what you want to say, and I'll write it down in my book. Then, afterwards, I'll tear out the pages and give them to the party, see? If it's in my handwriting, it's all right.

ANTIGONE (*winces*). In your handwriting? (*She shudders slightly.*) No. That would be awful. The poor darling! In your handwriting.

GUARD (*offers back the ring*). O.K. It's no skin off my nose.

ANTIGONE (*quickly*). Of course, of course. No, keep the ring. But hurry. Time is getting short. Where is your notebook?

(*The* GUARD *pockets the ring, takes his notebook and pencil from his pocket, puts his foot up on chair, and rests the notebook on his knee, licks his pencil.*)

ANTIGONE. Ready? (*He nods.*) Write now. "My darling. . . ."

GUARD (*writes as he mutters*). The boy friend, eh?

ANTIGONE. "My darling. I wanted to die, and perhaps you will not love me any more. . . ."

GUARD (*mutters as he writes*). ". . . will not love me any more."

ANTIGONE. "Creon was right. It is terrible to die."

GUARD (*repeats as he writes*). ". . . terrible to die."

ANTIGONE. "And I don't even know what I am dying for. I am afraid. . . ."

GUARD (*looks at her*). Wait a minute! How fast do you think I can write?

ANTIGONE (*takes hold of herself*). Where are you?

GUARD (*reads from his notebook*). "And I don't even know what I am dying for."

ANTIGONE. No. Scratch that out. Nobody must know that. They have no right to know. It's as if they saw me naked and touched me, after I was dead. Scratch it all out. Just write: "Forgive me."

GUARD (*looks at* ANTIGONE). I cut out everything you said there at the end, and I put down, "Forgive me"?

ANTIGONE. Yes. "Forgive me, my darling. You would all have been so happy except for Antigone. I love you."

GUARD (*finishes the letter*). ". . . I love you." (*He looks at her.*) Is that all?

ANTIGONE. That's all.

GUARD (*straightens up, looks at notebook*). Damn funny letter.

ANTIGONE. I know.

GUARD (*looks at her*). Who is it to?

(*A sudden roll of drums begins and continues until after* ANTIGONE's *exit. The* FIRST GUARD *pockets the notebook.*)

FIRST GUARD (*shouts at* ANTIGONE). O.K. That's enough out of you! Come on!

(SECOND *and* THIRD GUARDS *enter through arch.* ANTIGONE *rises.* GUARDS *seize her and exeunt with her. The lighting moves up to suggest late afternoon.* CHORUS *enters.*)

CHORUS. And now it is Creon's turn.

(MESSENGER *runs through the arch, right.*)

MESSENGER. The Queen . . . the Queen! Where is the Queen?

CHORUS. What do you want with the Queen? What have you to tell the Queen?

MESSENGER. News to break her heart. Antigone had just been thrust into the cave. They hadn't finished heaving the last block of stone into place when Creon and the rest heard a sudden moaning from the tomb. A hush fell over us all, for it was not the voice of Antigone. It was Haemon's voice that came forth from the tomb. Everybody looked at Creon; and he howled like a man demented: "Take away the stones! Take away the stones!" The slaves leaped at the wall of stones, and Creon worked with them, sweating and tearing at the blocks with his bleeding hands. Finally a narrow opening was forced, and into it slipped the smallest guard.

Antigone had hanged herself by the cord of her robe, by the red and golden twisted cord of her robe. The cord was round her neck like a child's collar. Haemon was on his knees, holding her in his arms and moaning, his face buried in her robe. More stones were removed, and Creon went into the tomb. He tried to raise Haemon to his feet. I could hear him begging Haemon to rise to his feet. Haemon was deaf to his father's voice, till suddenly he stood up of his own accord, his eyes dark and burning. Anguish was in his face, but it was the face of a little boy. He stared at his father. Then suddenly struck him—hard; and he drew his sword. Creon leaped out of range. Haemon went on staring at him, his eyes full of contempt—a glance that was like a knife, and that Creon couldn't escape. The King stood trembling in the far corner of the tomb, and Haemon kept on staring. Then, without a word, he stabbed himself and lay down beside Antigone, embracing her in a great pool of blood.

(*A pause as* CREON *and* PAGE *enter through arch on the* MESSENGER'*s last words.* CHORUS *and the* MESSENGER *both turn to look at* CREON; *then exit the* MESSENGER *through curtain.*)

CREON. I have had them laid out side by side. They are together at last, and at peace. Two lovers on the morrow of their bridal. Their work is done.

CHORUS. But not yours, Creon. You have still one thing to learn. Eurydice, the Queen, your wife. . . .

CREON. A good woman. Always busy with her garden, her preserves, her sweaters—those sweaters she never stopped knitting for the poor. Strange, how the poor never stop needing sweaters. One would almost think that was all they needed.

CHORUS. The poor in Thebes are going to be cold this winter, Creon. When the Queen was told of her son's death, she waited carefully until she had finished her row, then put down her knitting calmly—as she did everything. She went up to her room, her lavender-scented room, with its embroidered doilies and its pictures framed in plush; and there, Creon, she cut her throat. She is laid out now in one of those two old-fashioned twin beds, exactly where you went to her one night when she was still a maiden. Her smile is still the same, scarcely a shade more melancholy. And if it were not for that great red blot on the bed linen by her neck, one might think she was asleep.

CREON (*in a dull voice*). She, too. They are all asleep. (*Pause.*) It must be good to sleep.

CHORUS. And now you are alone, Creon.

CREON. Yes, all alone. (*To* PAGE) My lad.

PAGE. Sir?

CREON. Listen to me. They don't know it, but the truth is the work is there to be done, and a man can't fold his arms and refuse to do it. They say it's dirty work. But if we didn't do it, who would?

PAGE. I don't know, sir.

CREON. Of course you don't. You'll be lucky if you never find out. In a hurry to grow up, aren't you?

PAGE. Oh, yes, sir.

CREON. I shouldn't be if I were you. Never grow up if you can help it. (*He is lost in thought as the hour chimes.*) What time is it?

PAGE. Five o'clock, sir.

CREON. What have we on at five o'clock?

PAGE. Cabinet meeting, sir.

CREON. Cabinet meeting. Then we had better go along to it.

(*Exeunt* CREON *and* PAGE *slowly through arch, left.*)

(CHORUS *moves downstage.*)

CHORUS. And there we are. It is quite true that if it had not been for Antigone they would all have been at peace. But that is over now. And they are all at peace. All those who were meant to die have died: those who believed one thing, those who believed the contrary thing, and even those who believed nothing at all, yet were caught up in the web without knowing why. All dead: stiff, useless, rotting. And those who have survived will now begin quietly to forget the dead: they won't remember who was who or which was which. It is all over. Antigone is calm tonight, and we shall never know the name of the fever that consumed her. She has played her part.

(THREE GUARDS *enter, resume their places on steps as at the rise of the curtain, and begin to play cards.*)

CHORUS. A great melancholy wave of peace now settles down upon Thebes, upon the empty palace, upon Creon, who can now begin to wait for his own death.

Only the guards are left, and none of this matters to them. It's no skin off their noses. They go on playing cards. (CHORUS *walks toward the arch, left, as the curtain falls.*)

1942

THINK AND DISCUSS
Understanding

1. What does Antigone do in violation of Creon's express command?
2. If we consider that the play is set in ancient Thebes, it contains many anachronisms. List a few.

Analyzing

3. How old should Antigone be to fit her role in the play? Justify your answer.
4. Is Creon fair in supporting Eteocles' claim to the throne rather than that of Polynices? Explain.
5. What is the irony in Creon's statement that he took the less disfigured of the two corpses and said it was the body of Eteocles?
6. Who wins the Antigone/Creon debate? Explain.
7. How essential to the play is the Chorus? Explain.
8. How is Ismene a foil to Antigone?
9. Do Antigone and Creon have tragic flaws? If so, explain what they are.

Extending

10. One reader has said that the tragedy here is that both Antigone and Creon are right, and therefore neither can win their debate or their struggle. Comment on this.
11. Traditionally this play has been performed in modern evening dress. What effect do you think this has on the performance? Would other costumes be more effective? Explain.
12. In what ways does the play reflect on Hitler's occupation of France?
13. Some modern American critics think that Creon, not Antigone, is the hero of the play. Explain why you agree or disagree.

VOCABULARY
Context

Some of the words that you have encountered in *Antigone* are italicized in the following questions. The locater references in parentheses that follow each word indicate first the page on which the word is found; second, the column (*a* = first, *b* = second); third, the line. Answer the questions on a separate piece of paper. If you need help, consult the Glossary. Be prepared to give reasons for your answers.

1. Where would you be most likely to find a *coquette* (877b, 18): in a barnyard, at a dance, or in a bureau drawer?

2. If someone is *glowering* (879b, 24) at you, is he more likely to be happy or angry?

3. Is a *prosaic* (890b, 38) piece of writing more likely to be interesting or dull?

4. If someone *fawns* (896a, 15) on you, is that person angry at you or trying to get a favor from you?

5. Is a *tawdry* (898a, 5) dress more likely to be worn by a rich woman or a poor woman?

6. Would a *willful* (875a, 28) child be stubborn or easy-going?

7. What would a *tumbrel* (880a, 8) be most likely to contain: dirty clothes, acrobats, or condemned criminals?

8. Is a *gratuitous* (886b, 36) compliment more likely to be solicited or unsolicited?

9. What would you be most likely to find in a *scullery* (890a, 1): books, tools, or dishes?

10. Would you be most likely to find *blackguards* (895a, 43) in a prison, in the army, or in a deck of playing cards?

COMPOSITION

Seeing the Tragedy Through Ismene's Eyes

Assume that Ismene kept a diary in which she recorded the important events in her life and her reactions to them. Write entries covering the events of the play. Begin with the battle between Eteocles and Polynices and end with Creon's going to the five o'clock cabinet meeting.

Analyzing Antigone's Character

In a five-paragraph composition to be shared with your classmates, analyze Antigone's character. Reread the play to answer the following questions and to find other information that might be helpful: Is Antigone heroic? Selfish? Immature? Proud? Stubborn? Neurotic? An innocent victim? Use your first paragraph for an overall statement, your next three paragraphs to discuss aspects of Antigone's character, and your last to summarize your findings. See "Writing About Characters" in the Writer's Handbook.

Analyzing Creon's Character

In a five-paragraph composition to be shared with your classmates, analyze Creon's character. Reread the play to answer the following ques-

tions and to find other information that might be helpful: Is Creon cruel? Weak? Arrogant? Patriotic? Victimized? Overly concerned with politics? Over-hasty in making decisions? Unable to see all sides of a problem? Use your first paragraph for an overall statement, your next three paragraphs to discuss aspects of Creon's character, and your last to summarize your findings.

Following Creon's Logic

Creon prides himself on his logic and mistakenly assumes he will have no problem in convincing Antigone to give up her project of burying her brother regardless of the consequences. Reread the debate scene, following his logic and Antigone's rebuttals of it. Take notes and use them as the basis for a five-paragraph composition to be shared with your classmates in which you discuss Creon's logic and why it failed.

ENRICHMENT
Readers Theater

Mount a readers theater presentation of the play. If facilities are available, you might wish to videotape this for presentation to other classes. You will need a director and twelve students for the performance. The roles of Antigone, the Nurse, Ismene, and Eurydice should be played by girls; those of Creon, Haemon, the Page, and the Three Guards by boys; and those of the Chorus and Messenger by either girls or boys. You might also consider using additional students to pantomime some of the off-stage events as they are described by the Guard and the Messenger.

Reading Sophocles' *Antigone*

Read Sophocles' *Antigone* and take notes for a report (oral or written) in which you compare and contrast the two versions, Sophocles' and Anouilh's. Consider characters added or deleted by Anouilh, changes in Anouilh's plot, and the emotional level of the play itself.

Debating the Issues in *Antigone*

Have students form two groups, one of which sees everything from Creon's side, the other from Antigone's side. Students not participating in the activity are to judge which group presents the stronger arguments.

Of all the authors represented in this unit, only Camara Laye has had first-hand experience with both traditional and modern society—with his tribal village in the West African nation of Guinea and with Western Europe. Laye details many of these experiences in *The African Child* (page 905), an autobiographical novel based on his boyhood in what was then French Guinea. After his early schooling in Kouroussa, Laye attended high school in Conakry, the capital of Guinea; then he received a scholarship to study engineering near Paris, where he obtained his professional certificate. He remained in France for nearly six years.

While in Paris, perhaps because of loneliness, perhaps to retain memories of a lifestyle he knew was changing, Laye began to write down reminiscences of his childhood. They grew into *The African Child*, published in French as *l'Enfant noir* in 1953 and translated into English a year later. In 1954 he published his second novel, *The Radiance of the King*, which is generally regarded as his finest work.

On his return to Guinea in 1956, Laye worked as an engineer for the French. Then, in 1958, when Guinea became independent, he served the new government as a diplomat in Ghana, Liberia, and other African countries. Eventually he was named director of the Center of Research and Studies in Conakry. By 1960, however, Laye was trying to be released from government service, and his writings, critical of the new regime, got him into trouble with President Sekou Toure. He encountered severe censorship when he was told he had to soften the text of his latest work, *Dramouss* (translated as *A Dream of Africa*), or face exile. Laye chose another alternative, self-exile, and with his wife and children escaped to Senegal. The book, published without censorship in 1966, contains much that is critical of President Toure and his government. At one point in the novel Laye has Fatoman, his protagonist, warn a political meeting: "Someone must say that though colonialism . . . was an evil thing for our country, the regime you are now introducing will be a catastrophe whose evil consequences will be felt for decades. Someone must speak out and say that a regime built on spilt blood through the actions of incendiaries of huts and houses is nothing but a regime of anarchy and dictatorship, a regime based on violence."

Laye died in Senegal in 1980. In *The African Child*, he describes a generally happy childhood, surrounded by love, during which he regarded with wonder and devotion his father's achievements as a master coppersmith and forger of gold trinkets. The book details folk superstitions that Laye, though writing in Paris, seems sincerely to believe. Without sentiment, he describes his inner conflict between wanting to follow in his father's footsteps and wanting to go on with his education. *The African Child* is honestly written, describing the joys and pains of growing up that are universal, regardless of where the child lives and grows.

from The African Child

Camara Laye   *translated by* **James Kirkup**

I

was a little boy playing round my father's hut. How old would I have been at that time? I cannot remember exactly. I still must have been very young: five, maybe six years old. My mother was in the workshop with my father, and I could just hear their familiar voices above the noise of the anvil and the conversation of the customers.

Suddenly I stopped playing, my whole attention fixed on a snake that was creeping round the hut. He really seemed to be "taking a turn" round the hut. After a moment I went over to him. I had taken in my hand a reed that was lying in the yard—there were always some lying around; they used to get broken off the fence of plaited reeds that marked the boundary of our compound—and I thrust this reed into the reptile's mouth. The snake did not try to get away: he was beginning to enjoy our little game; he was slowly swallowing the reed; he was devouring it, I thought, as if it were some delicious prey, his eyes glittering with voluptuous bliss; and inch by inch his head was drawing nearer to my hand. At last the reed was almost entirely swallowed up, and the snake's jaws were terribly close to my fingers.

I was laughing, I had not the slightest fear, and now I know that the snake would not have hesitated much longer before burying his fangs in my fingers if, at that moment, Damany, one of the apprentices, had not come out of the workshop. The apprentice shouted to my father, and almost at once I felt myself lifted off my feet: I was safe in the arms of one of my father's friends!

There was a terrific commotion going on all round me; my mother was shouting harder than anyone; and she gave me a few sharp slaps. I began to weep, more upset by the sudden uproar than by the blows I had received. A little later, when I had calmed down a little and the shouting had died down around me, my mother solemnly warned me never to play such a game again; and I promised, although I could not really see where the danger in it lay.

My father's hut was near the workshop, and I would often play there beneath the veranda that ran round the outside. It was my father's private hut. It was built like all our huts, of mud that had been pounded and molded into bricks with water; it was round, and proudly helmeted with thatch. It was entered by a rectangular doorway. Inside, a tiny window let in a thin shaft of daylight. On the right there was the bed, made of beaten earth like the bricks, spread with a simple wicker-work mat on which was a pillow stuffed with kapok.[1] At the rear of the hut, right under the window where the light was strongest, were the toolboxes. On the left were the *boubous* and the prayer-rugs.[2] Finally, at the head of the bed, hanging over the pillow and watching over my father's slumber, there was a series of pots that contained extracts from plants and the bark of trees. These pots all had metal lids and they were profusely and curiously garlanded with chaplets of cowrie shells;[3] it did not take me long to discover that they were the most important things in the hut: they contained the magic charms, those mysterious liquids that keep evil spirits at bay, and, smeared on the body, make it invulnerable to black magic, to all kinds of black magic. My father, before he went to bed, never failed to smear his body with a little of each liquid, first one, then another, for each charm had its own

---

1. *kapok* (kā'pok), the silky fibers around the seeds of a tropical silk-cotton tree.
2. **boubous** (bü'büz) . . . *prayer-rugs. Boubous* are loose cotton garments, draping the whole figure. A prayer rug is a small Oriental carpet used by Moslems to kneel on when praying.
3. *cowrie shells*, the brightly colored, smooth shells of any of several tropical mollusks, used as money in some parts of Africa and Asia.

particular property: but exactly *what* property I do not know: I left my father's house too soon.

From the veranda under which I played I could keep an eye on the workshop opposite, and they for their part could keep an eye on me. This workshop was the main building in our compound. That is where my father was generally to be found, supervising the work, forging the most important items himself, or repairing delicate mechanisms; here it was that he received his friends and his customers, so that the place resounded with noise from morning to night. Moreover, everyone entering or leaving our compound had to pass through the workshop, so that there was a perpetual coming and going, though no one ever seemed to be in a hurry: each one would pause to have a word with my father and spend a few moments watching the work in hand. Sometimes I would draw near the door, but I rarely went in, for everyone used to frighten me there, and I would run away as soon as anyone tried to lay hands on me. It was not until very much later that I got into the habit of crouching in a corner of the workshop and watching the fire blazing in the forge.

My private domain at that time consisted of the veranda that ran round the outside of my father's hut; and the orange tree that grew in the middle of the compound.

As soon as you had crossed the workshop and gone through the door at the back, you could see the orange tree. If I compare it with the giants of our native forests, the tree was not very big, but its mass of glossy leaves used to cast a dense shadow that was a cool refuge from the blazing sun. When it was in flower, a heady perfume was wafted over the entire compound. When the fruit appeared, we were allowed only to look: we had to possess our souls in patience until they were ripe. Then my father, who, as head of the family—a family of innumerable members—governed the compound, would give the order to pick them. The men who did the picking brought their baskets one by one to my father, who shared them out among the inhabitants of the compound, his neighbors and his customers; after that we were permitted to help ourselves from the baskets, as much as we liked! My father was an open-handed and, in fact,

a lavish giver; no matter who turned up, he would share our meals; and as I could never keep up with the speed at which such guests used to eat, I might have remained everlastingly hungry if my mother had not taken the precaution of putting my share on one side.

"Sit here," she would say, "and eat, for your father's crazy."

She did not look upon such guests with too kindly an eye; there were too many of them for her liking, all bent on filling their bellies at her expense. My father, for his part, ate very sparingly: he was a very abstemious man.

We lived near the railway track. The trains travelled along outside the fence of plaited reeds which marked the confines of our compound; in fact they ran so close to it that sparks from the engines would sometimes set fire to the palisade, and we all would have to rush to put it out at once, if we did not want to see the whole thing go up in flames. These alarums, rather frightening, but rather exciting too, made me watch every train that went by; and even when there was not a train in sight—for at that time the traffic on the railroad depended entirely on the river traffic, which was very irregular—I would go and spend long periods just looking at the gleaming metal rails. They always glittered cruelly under the fierce sun, for at this point there was no foliage to diminish its intensity. Baked by the sun from early morning, the ballast of red stone was burningly hot: so hot in fact that the oil which fell from the engines was immediately evaporated, leaving not the slightest trace. Was it this oven-like warmth or the oil, the inescapable smell of the oil, which attracted the snakes? I do not know. The fact is that I often came across snakes crawling over the sun-baked ballast; and inevitably the snakes used to creep into the compound.

Ever since the day I had been forbidden to play with snakes, I would run to my mother as soon as I saw one.

"There's a snake!" I would cry.

"What, another?" my mother would shout.

And she would come running out to see what sort of a snake it was. If it was just a snake like any other snake—actually, they were all quite different!—she would beat it to death at once; and, like all the women of our country, she would work herself up into a frenzy, beating the snake to a pulp, whereas the men would content themselves with a single hard blow, neatly struck.

One day, however, I noticed a little black snake with a strikingly marked body that was proceeding leisurely in the direction of the workshop. I ran to warn my mother, as usual. But as soon as my mother saw the black snake she said to me gravely: "My son, this one must not be killed: he is not as other snakes, and he will not harm you; you must never interfere with him."

Everyone in our compound knew that this snake must not be killed; excepting myself, and, I suppose, my little playmates, who were still just ignorant children.

"This snake," my mother added, "is your father's guiding spirit."

I gazed dumbfounded at the little snake. He was proceeding calmly towards the workshop; he was moving gracefully, very sure of himself, and almost as if conscious of his immunity; his body, black and brilliant, glittered in the harsh light of the sun. When he reached the workshop, I noticed for the first time, cut out level with the ground, a small hole in the wall. The snake disappeared through this hole.

"Look," said my mother, "the serpent is going to pay your father a visit."

Although I was familiar with the supernatural, this sight filled me with such astonishment that I was struck dumb. What business would a snake have with my father? And why this particular snake? No one had to kill him, because he was my father's guiding spirit! At any rate, that was the explanation my mother had given me. But what exactly *was* a "guiding spirit"? What were these guiding spirits that I encountered almost everywhere, forbidding one thing, commanding another to be done? I could not understand it at all, though their presences were around me as I grew to manhood. There were good spirits, and there were evil ones; and more evil than good ones, it seemed to me. And how was I to know that this snake was harmless? It looked the same as any other snake; it was, of course, a *black* snake, and

certainly there was something unusual about it; but after all, it *was* only a snake! I was absolutely baffled, but I did not ask my mother about it: I felt I would have to ask my father himself about it, almost as if this mystery was something in which women could have no part; it was a mysterious affair that could only be discussed with men. I decided to wait until nightfall.

Immediately after the evening meal, when the palavers were over, my father bade his friends farewell and went to sit under the veranda of his hut; I went and sat near him. I began by questioning him in a roundabout manner, as all children do, and on every subject under the sun. Finally, unable to restrain myself any longer, I asked: "My father, what is that little snake that comes to visit you?"

"What snake do you mean?"

"Why, the little black snake that my mother forbids us to kill."

"Ah!" he said.

He gazed at me for a long while. He seemed to be considering whether to answer or not. Perhaps he was thinking about how old I was, perhaps he was wondering if it was not a little too soon to confide such a secret to a twelve-year-old boy. Then suddenly he made up his mind.

"That snake," he said, "is the guiding spirit of our race. Can you understand that?"

"Yes," I answered, although I did not understand very well.

"The snake," he went on, "has always been with us; he has always made himself known to one of us. In our time, it is to me that he has made himself known."

"That is true," I said.

And I said it with all my heart, for it seemed obvious to me that the snake could have made himself known to no one but my father. Was not my father the head man in our compound? Was it not my father who had authority over all the blacksmiths in our district? Was he not the most skilled? Was he not, after all, my father?

"How did he make himself known?" I asked.

"First of all, he made himself known in the semblance of a dream. He appeared to me several times in slumber, and he told me the day on which he would appear to me in reality: he gave me the precise time and place. But when I really saw him for the first time, I was filled with fear. I took him for a snake like any other snake, and I had to keep myself in control, or I would have tried to kill him. When he saw that I did not receive him kindly, he turned away and departed the way he had come. And there I stood, watching him depart, and wondering all the time if I should not simply have killed him there and then; but a power greater than myself stayed my hand and prevented me from pursuing him. I stood watching him disappear. And even then, at that very moment, I could easily have overtaken him; a few swift strides would have been enough; but I was struck motionless by a kind of paralysis. Such was my first encounter with the little black snake."

He was silent a moment, then went on: "The following night, I saw the snake again in my dream. 'I came as I foretold,' he said, 'but thou didst not receive me kindly; nay, rather I did perceive that thou didst intend to receive me unkindly: I did read it thus in thine eyes. Wherefore dost thou reject me? Lo, I am the guiding spirit of thy race, and it is even as the guiding spirit of thy race that I make myself known to thee, as to the most worthy. Therefore forbear to look with fear upon me, and beware that thou dost not reject me, for behold, I bring thee good fortune.' After that, I received the serpent kindly when he made himself known to me a second time; I received him without fear, I received him with loving kindness, and he has brought me nothing but good."

My father again was silent for a moment, then he said: "You can see for yourself that I am not more gifted than any other man, that I have nothing which other men have not also, and even that I have less than others, since I give everything away, and would even give away the last thing I had, the shirt on my back. Nevertheless, I am better known than other men, and my name is on everyone's tongue, and it is I who have authority over all the blacksmiths in the five cantons.[4] If these things are so, it is by virtue of this snake alone, who is the guiding spirit of our race. It is to this snake that I owe everything, and it is he likewise who gives me warning of all that is to happen. Thus I

am never surprised, when I awake, to see this or that person waiting for me outside my workshop: I already know that he or she will be there. No more am I surprised when this or that motor bicycle or bicycle breaks down, or when an accident happens to a clock: because I had foreknowledge of what would come to pass. Everything is transmitted to me in the course of the night, together with an account of all the work I shall have to perform, so that from the start, without having to cast about in my mind, I know how to repair whatever is brought to me; and it is these things that have established my renown as a craftsman. But all this—let it never be forgotten—I owe to the snake, I owe it to the guiding spirit of our race."

He was silent; and then I understood why, when my father used to come back from a walk, he could enter the workshop and say to the apprentices: "During my absence, this or that person has been here, he was dressed in such and such a way, he came from such and such a place and he brought with him such and such a piece of work to be done." And all marvelled at this curious knowledge. Now I understood how my father obtained his information. When I raised my eyes, I saw that my father was watching me.

"I have told you all these things, little one, because you are my son, the eldest of my sons, and because I have nothing to hide from you. There is a certain form of behavior to observe, and certain ways of acting in order that the guiding spirit of our race may approach you also. I, your father, was observing that form of behavior which persuades our guiding spirit to visit us. Oh, perhaps not consciously. But nevertheless it is true that if you desire the guiding spirit of our race to visit you one day, if you desire to inherit it in your turn, you will have to conduct yourself in the selfsame manner; from now on, it will be necessary for you to be more and more in my company."

He gazed at me with burning eyes, then suddenly he heaved a sigh.

"I fear, I very much fear, little one, that you are not often enough in my company. You are all day at school, and one day you shall depart from

---

4. *cantons*, small parts or political divisions of a country.

that school for a greater one. You will leave me, little one. . . ."

And again he heaved a sigh. I saw that his heart was heavy within him. The hurricane lamp hanging on the veranda cast a harsh glare on his face. He suddenly seemed to me like an old man.

"Father!" I cried.

"Son . . ." he whispered.

And I was no longer sure whether I ought to continue to attend the school or whether I ought to remain in the workshop: I felt unutterably confused.

"Go now," said my father.

I got up and went to my mother's hut. The night was full of sparkling stars; an owl was hooting nearby. Ah, what was the right path for me? Did I know yet where that path lay? My perplexity was boundless as the sky, and mine was a sky, alas, without any stars. . . . I entered my mother's hut, which at that time was mine also, and went to bed at once. But sleep evaded me, and I tossed restlessly on my bed.

"What's the matter with you?" asked my mother.

"Nothing."

No, I couldn't find anything to say.

"Why don't you go to sleep?" went on my mother.

"I don't know."

"Go to sleep!" she said.

"Yes," I said.

"Sleep . . . Nothing can resist sleep," she said sadly.

Why did she, too, appear so sad? Had she divined my distress? Anything that concerned me she sensed very deeply. I was trying to sleep, but I shut my eyes and lay still in vain: the image of my father under the storm-lantern would not leave me. He had suddenly seemed so old, he who was so youthful, so active, more youthful and more active than any of us and who in the running of races never let himself be outstripped by anyone, whose limbs were swifter than the limbs of all our young men. . . . "Father! . . . Father! . . ." I kept repeating it. "Father, what must I do, what is the right thing to do?" And I wept quietly, and weeping I fell asleep.

After that, we never mentioned the little black snake again: my father had spoken to me about him for the first and the last time. But from that time forth, as soon as I saw the little snake, I would run and sit in the workshop. I would watch him glide through the little hole in the wall. As if informed of his presence, my father at that instant would turn his eyes to the hole and give a smile. The snake would proceed straight towards him, opening his jaws. When he was within reach, my father would stroke him with his hand, and the snake would accept the caress with a quivering of his whole body: never did I see the little snake attempt to do the slightest harm to my father. That caress, and the answering tremor—but I ought to say: that appealing caress and that answering tremor—threw me each time into an inexpressible confusion: I would imagine I know not what mysterious conversation . . . the hand inquired, and the tremor replied. . . .

Yes, it was like a conversation. Would I, too, converse like that one day? No: I was still attending the school. Yet I should have liked so much to place my hand, my own hand, on the snake, and to understand and listen to that tremor too; but I did not know how the snake would have taken my hand, and I felt now, that he would have nothing to tell me; I was afraid that he would never have anything to tell me. . . .

When my father felt that he had stroked the snake enough, he left him alone; then the snake would coil himself under the edge of one of the sheepskins on which my father was seated, facing his anvil.

II

Of all the different kinds of work my father performed, none fascinated me so much as his skill with gold. No other occupation was so noble, no other needed such a delicate touch; and, moreover, this sort of work was always a kind of festival: it was a real festival that broke the monotony of ordinary working days.

So if a woman, accompanied by a go-between, crossed the threshold of the workshop, I would follow her in at once. I knew what she wanted: she had brought some gold and wanted to ask my father to transform it into a trinket. The woman would have collected the gold in the placers of Siguiri, where, for months on end, she would have crouched over the river, washing the mud and patiently extracting from it the grains of gold. These women never came alone: they were well aware that my father had other things to do than to make trinkets for all and sundry; and even if the making of jewellery had been his main occupation, they would have realized that they were not his first or his only customers, and that their wants could not be immediately attended to.

Generally these women required the trinket for a certain date, either for the festival of Ramadan or for the Tabaski;[5] or for some other family festivity, or for a dance ceremony.

Thereupon, to better their chance of being quickly served, and the more easily to persuade my father to interrupt the work he had in hand, they would request the services of an official praise-singer, a go-between, and would arrange with him in advance what fee they would pay for his good offices.

The praise-singer would install himself in the workshop, tune up his cora, which is our harp, and would begin to sing my father's praises. This was always a great event for me. I would hear recalled the lofty deeds of my father's ancestors, and the names of these ancestors from the earliest times; as the couplets were reeled off, it was like watching the growth of a great genealogical tree that spread its branches far and wide and flourished its boughs and twigs before my mind's eye. The harp played an accompaniment to this vast utterance of names, expanding it and punctuating it with notes that were now soft, now shrill. Where did the praise-singer get his information from? He must certainly have developed a very retentive memory stored with facts handed down to him by his predecessors, for this is the basis of all our oral traditions. Did he embellish the truth? It is very likely: flattery is the praise-singer's stock-in-trade! Nevertheless, he was not allowed to take too many liberties with tradition, for it is part of the praise-singer's task to preserve it. But in those days such considerations did not enter my head, which I would hold high and proud; for I used

to feel quite drunk with so much praise, which seemed to reflect some of its effulgence upon my own small person.

I could tell that my father's vanity was being inflamed, and I already knew that after having sipped this milk-and-honey he would lend a favorable ear to the woman's request. But I was not alone in my knowledge; the woman also had seen my father's eyes gleaming with contented pride; and she would hold out her grains of gold as if the whole thing was settled: my father, taking up his scales, would weigh the gold.

"What sort of trinket do you desire?" he would ask.

"I want . . ." And often it would happen that the woman did not know really what she wanted, because she would be so torn by desire, because she would have liked to have many, many trinkets, all out of the same small quantity of gold: but she would have had to have much more than she had brought with her to satisfy such a desire, and eventually she would have to content herself with some more modest wish.

"When do you want it for?" my father would ask.

And she would always want it at once.

"Why are you in such a hurry? How do you expect me to find the time?"

"It's very urgent, I can assure you," the woman would reply.

"That's what all women say, when they want an ornament. Well, I'll see what I can do. Now are you happy?"

Then he would take the clay pot that was kept specially for the smelting of gold and pour in the grains; thereupon he would cover the gold with powdered charcoal, a charcoal which he obtained by the use of plant juices of exceptional purity; finally he would place a large lump of the same kind of charcoal over the whole thing.

Then, having seen the work duly undertaken, the woman, by now quite satisfied, would go back to her household tasks, leaving her go-between to

5. **Ramadan** (ram′ə dän′) . . . **Tabaski** (tä bäs′kē). Ramadan is the ninth month of the Moslem year, during which fasting is rigidly practiced daily from dawn until sunset. The Tabaski is a Guinean festival.

carry on with the praise-singing which had already proved so advantageous to her.

On a sign from my father, the apprentices would start working the two pairs of sheepskin bellows which were placed on the ground at each side of the forge and linked to it by earthen pipes. These apprentices remained seated all the time, with crossed legs, in front of the bellows; at least the younger did, for the elder would sometimes be allowed to take part in the craftsmen's work and the younger—in those days it was Sidafa—only had to work the bellows and watch the proceedings while awaiting his turn to be elevated to less rudimentary tasks. For a whole hour they would both be working the levers of the bellows till the fire in the forge leapt into flame, becoming a living thing, a lively and merciless spirit.

Then my father, using long pincers, would lift the clay pot and place it on the flames.

Immediately all work would more or less stop in the workshop: actually while the gold is being melted and while it is cooling all work with copper or aluminum is supposed to stop, for fear that some fraction of these less noble metals might fall among the gold. It is only steel that can still be worked at such times. But workmen who had some piece of steel work in hand would either hasten to finish it or would openly stop work to join the other apprentices gathered round the forge. In fact, there were often so many of them at these times pressing round my father that I, the smallest, would have to get up and push my way in among them, so as not to miss any of the operation.

It might happen that, feeling he had too little room to work in, my father would make his apprentices stand well away from him. He would merely raise his hand in a simple gesture: at that particular moment he would never utter a word, and no one else would, no one was allowed to utter a word, even the go-between's voice would no longer be raised in song; the silence would be broken only by the panting of the bellows and by the faint hissing of the gold. But if my father never used to utter actual words at this time, I know that he was uttering them in his mind; I could see it by his lips that kept working while he bent over

the pot and kept stirring the gold and the charcoal with a bit of wood that would keep bursting into flame, and so had to be constantly replaced by a fresh bit.

What were the words my father's lips were forming? I do not know; I do not know for certain: I was never told what they were. But what else could they have been, if not magical incantations? Were they not the spirits of fire and gold, of fire and air, air breathed through the earthen pipes, of fire born of air, of gold married with fire—were not these the spirits he was invoking? Was it not their help and their friendship he was calling upon in this marriage of elemental things? Yes, it was almost certainly those spirits he was calling upon, for they are the most elemental of all spirits, and their presence is essential at the melting of gold.

The operation that was going on before my eyes was simply the smelting of gold; but it was something more than that: a magical operation that the guiding spirits could look upon with favor or disfavor; and that is why there would be all round my father that absolute silence and that anxious expectancy. I could understand, though I was just a child, that there was no craft greater than the goldsmith's. I expected a ceremony, I had come to be present at a ceremony, and it really was one, though very protracted. I was still too young to be able to understand why it was so protracted; nevertheless, I had an inkling, beholding the almost religious concentration of all those present as they watched the mixing process.

When finally the gold began to melt, I used to feel like shouting, and perhaps we would all have shouted if we had not been forbidden to make a sound: I would be trembling, and certainly everyone else would be trembling as we sat watching my father stirring the mixture, still a heavy paste in which the charcoal was gradually being consumed. The next stage followed swiftly; the gold now had the fluidity of water. The guiding spirits had smiled on the operation!

"Bring me the brick!" my father would say, thus lifting the ban that until then had kept us all silent.

The brick, which an apprentice would place beside the fire, was hollowed out, generously greased with Galam butter. My father would take the pot off the fire, tilt it carefully, and I would watch the gold flowing into the brick, flowing like liquid fire. True, it was only a very sparse trickle of fire, but oh, how vivid, how brilliant! As the gold flowed into the brick, the grease would splutter and flame and give off a thick smoke that caught in the throat and stung the eyes, leaving us all weeping and coughing.

It occurred to me later on that my father could easily have relinquished all the work of smelting the gold to one or other of his assistants: they were not without experience in these matters; they had taken part hundreds of times in the same preparations and they would certainly have brought the work to a successful conclusion. But as I have told you, my father kept moving his lips! We could not hear those words, those secret words, those incantations which he addressed to powers that we should not, that we could not hear or see: this was essential. Only my father was versed in the science of conjuring the spirits of fire, air and gold, and conjuring evil spirits, and that is why he alone conducted the whole operation.

By now the gold would have cooled in the hollow of the brick, and my father would begin to hammer and stretch it. This was the moment when his work as a goldsmith really began. I noticed that before embarking on it he never failed to stroke stealthily the little snake coiled up under the sheepskin; one can only assume that this was his way of gathering strength for what remained to be done, and which was the most difficult.

But was it not extraordinary, was it not miraculous that on these occasions the little black serpent always coiled up under the sheepskin? He was not always there, he did not visit my father every day, but he was always present whenever there was gold to be worked.

Moreover, it is our custom to keep apart from the working of gold all influences outside those of the jeweller himself. And indeed it is not precisely because the jeweller alone possesses the secret of his incantations; but also because the working of gold, besides being a task of the greatest skill, is a matter of confidence, of conscience, a task which is not undertaken excepting after due reflection and experiment. Finally, I do not think that any jeweller would renounce the opportunity of performing such a task—I ought to say, such a spectacle!—in which he can display his abilities with a virtuosity that his work as a blacksmith or a mechanic or even as a sculptor is never invested with; even though in these more humble tasks his skill is no less wonderful, even though the statues which he carves in wood with his adze are not insignificant works!

The snake's presence came as no surprise to me; ever since that evening when my father had talked to me about the guiding spirit of our race, it had ceased to surprise me; it was quite natural that the snake should be there: he had knowledge of the future. Did he impart any of that knowledge to my father? It seemed to me quite obvious that he did: did he not always warn him of what was going to happen? But I had another reason for believing implicitly in the powers of the little snake.

The craftsman who works in gold must first of all purify himself, that is, he must wash himself all over and, of course, abstain from all sexual relationships during the whole time. Great respecter of ceremony as he was, it would have been impossible for my father to ignore these rules. Now I never saw him make these preparations; I would see him address himself to his work without any apparent preliminaries. But from that moment it was obvious that, forewarned by his black guiding spirit in a dream of the task that would await him in the morning, my father must have prepared for it as soon as he arose, and had entered his workshop in a state of purity, his body smeared with the magical substances hidden in his numerous pots full of secret potions. So I believe my father never entered his workshop except in a state of ritual purity; and that is not because I want to make him out as being better than he is—he is a man like any other, and has a man's weaknesses—but always when it was a matter of ritual he was uncompromisingly strict.

The woman for whom the trinket was being made, and who would often have looked in to see how the work was getting on, would come for the final time, not wanting to miss anything of the marvellous sight as the gold wire, which my father had succeeded in spinning, was transformed into a trinket. She was here now, devouring with her eyes the fragile golden wire, following its tranquil and inevitable spirals round the little metal cone which gave the trinket its shape. My father would be watching her out of the corner of his eye, and sometimes I would see the corners of his mouth twitch into a smile: the woman's avid attentiveness amused him.

"Are you trembling?" he would say to her.

"*Am* I trembling?" she would ask.

And we would all burst out laughing at her. For she *was* trembling! She was trembling with covetousness for the spiral pyramid in which my father was inserting, among the convolutions, tiny grains of gold. When finally he terminated the work by placing at the summit the largest grain of gold, the woman would jump excitedly to her feet.

Then, while my father was slowly turning the trinket round in his fingers, smoothing it into perfect shape, no one could have displayed such utter happiness as the native woman, not even the praise-singer, whose trade it was to do so, and who, during the whole process of transformation, had kept on singing his praises, accelerating his rhythm, increasing his flatteries as the trinket took shape, and praising my father's talents to the skies.

Indeed, the praise-singer participated in a curious—I was going to say direct, effective—way in the work. He, too, was intoxicated with the joy of creation; he declaimed his rapture, and plucked his harp like a man inspired; he warmed to the task as if he had been the craftsman himself, as if the trinket had been made by his own hands. He was no longer a paid thurifer;[6] he was no longer just the man whose services each and anyone could hire; he had become a man who creates his song under the influence of some very personal, interior necessity.

When my father, after having soldered the large grain of gold that crowned the summit, held out his work to be admired, the go-between would no longer be able to contain himself, and would intone the douga—the great chant which is only sung for celebrated men, and which is danced to only for them.

But the douga is a tremendous chant, a provocative chant, a chant that the go-between would not

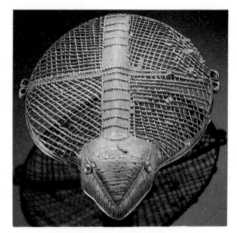

Ashanti gold emblem in the form of a turtle. Metropolitan Museum of Art

venture to sing, and that the man for whom it is sung would not venture to dance to, without certain precautions.

My father, forewarned in a dream, had been able to take these precautions as soon as he got up; the praise-singer had taken them as a matter of course when he had made his bargain with the woman. Just as my father had done, he had smeared his body with magic lotions and so had rendered himself invulnerable to the bad spirits which the douga would undoubtedly stir into activity, invulnerable also even to his fellow praise-singers who, jealous perhaps, were only waiting to hear the chant, the note of exaltation and the loss of control which that exaltation entails, to cast their evil spells upon him.

At the first notes of the douga, my father would rise and utter a cry in which happiness and triumph were equally mingled; and brandishing in his right hand the hammer that was the symbol of his profession, and in his left a ram's horn filled with magic substances, he would dance the glorious dance.

No sooner had he finished than workmen and apprentices, friends and customers in their turn,

---

6. thurifer (thĕr′ə fĕr). A thurifer is a person who carries a censer, the container in which incense is burned during religious ceremonies; here the word thurifer is applied metaphorically to the praise-singer.

not forgetting the woman for whom the trinket had been created, would flock round him, congratulating him, showering praises on him, and complimenting at the same time the go-between, who found himself laden with gifts, gifts that are almost the only resources he has in his wandering life, that he leads after the fashion of the troubadours of old. Beaming, aglow with dancing and the praises he had received, my father would offer kola nuts,[7] that small change of Guinean civility.

All that now remained to be done was to redden the trinket in a little water mixed with chlorine and sea salt. I could go now: the ceremony was over! But often, as I was leaving the workshop, my mother, who might be in the yard pounding millet[8] or rice, would call me.

"Where have you been?" she would ask, although she knew very well where I had been.

"In the workshop."

"Oh, yes, your father was making something out of gold. Gold! It's always gold!"

And she would pound furiously the helpless bowl of rice or millet. "Your father's ruining his health! You see what he's doing."

"He's been dancing the douga," I would reply.

"The douga! The douga won't stop him ruining his eyesight! And you would be better off playing here in the yard instead of going and breathing the dust and smoke in the workshop!"

My mother did not like my father to work with gold. She knew how harmful the soldering of gold can be: a jeweller can wear his lungs out, puffing at his blowpipe, and his eyes suffer by being so close to the intense heat of the forge; and even more perhaps from the microscopic delicacy of the work. But even if there had been no danger in it, my mother still would have disliked this sort of work: she held it in suspicion, for you cannot solder gold without the help of other metals, and my mother used to think that it was not strictly honest to keep the gold which was saved by its alloys, although this was the accepted thing; and she, too, was quite prepared, whenever she took cotton to be woven, to receive in return a piece of cloth of only half the original weight.

1953

---

7. *kola nuts,* the seeds of an African evergreen.
8. *millet,* a cereal grass.

THINK AND DISCUSS
Understanding
1. Laye talks about the snake that has attached itself to his father and is the guiding spirit of their race. How does the snake aid his father?
2. What is the role of the go-between in the making of a gold trinket?
3. Why does Laye's mother not like his father to smelt gold?

Analyzing
4. After Laye's father has told him of the snake, Laye faces a conflict. What is it?
5. Why is the role of the praise-singer vital to the tribal society?
6. What seems to be Laye's attitude toward the smelting of the gold and the making of the trinket?

7. Besides the making of the gold trinket, what other evidence is there of trade?

Extending
8. Which of the elements of tribal culture that Laye talks about do you, as a student in modern America, have difficulty understanding or accepting?

THINKING SKILLS
Evaluating
To evaluate is to make a judgment based on some sort of standard.

1. How effective is this selection in presenting a picture of a society in transition from tribal ways to modern civilization?
2. How effective is it in conveying the universal delights and pains of growing up?

One of Russia's great modern poets, Voznesensky speaks for the people of Russia in ways that have occasionally led to difficulties with Soviet authorities. He was born in Moscow to a father who was an engineer and professor and a mother who was a teacher. Early in Voznesensky's life his mother introduced him to the works of the Russian writers Feodor Dostoevski (1821–1881), Alexandr Blok (1880–1921), and Boris Pasternak (1890–1960). She read poetry aloud so he could hear its **rhythms** and appreciate its sounds. Voznesensky himself claims that Pasternak influenced him most. As a teenager, he sent some of his poems to the older poet, who responded by inviting Voznesensky to visit him. Naturally, those early poems were written in Pasternak's style. Years later, when Voznesensky sent samples of his mature poetry, Pasternak commented, "Yes, this is no longer Pasternak—this is Voznesensky, a poet in his own right."

As Voznesensky grew up, he turned away from poetry and became interested in drawing and painting. He received a degree in architecture from the Moscow Educational Institute but then reverted to his first love and became a poet.

There can be no doubt that Voznesensky loves his country and its people. He refers to poetry as Russia's national art, and his books of poems are so popular that hundreds of thousands of Russians want copies, with the result that an edition sells out a few hours after it has reached the booksellers. Audiences at his poetry readings average about seventeen thousand, a figure that is amazing to Americans. Voznesensky sees the poet's task as presenting questions, not answering them, of encouraging people to think and to develop their individualism. During the 1960s, he was often accused of being obscure, and in 1969 his poems were no longer published in literary journals. In 1967 he was scheduled to do a poetry reading in New York City, but two days before the reading he sent a terse telegram: "Can't come." Shortly after that he wrote a letter to *Pravda* criticizing the Writers' Union. It was not published in Russia but sometime later did appear in *The New York Times*. It read in part: "Clearly the leadership of the union does not regard writers as human beings. This lying, prevarication, and knocking people's heads together is standard practice."

The two Voznesensky poems included in this unit show the wide range of his background and poetic style. In "Goya" (page 918), he expresses strong anti-war feelings through assuming the *persona* of the Spanish artist Goya and describing scenes of the German invasion of Russia in 1941 as though they were part of a series of etchings done by Goya during the Napoleonic Wars. In "Parabolic Ballad" (page 916) Voznesensky's **tone** is lighter as he describes the odd paths taken by people in reaching their goals. Again he deals with an artist—this time the French painter Gauguin—but uses that portion of his poem as the introduction to more serious thoughts that come at the end, thoughts he himself might have had more than once as he wondered whether his outspokenness might lead to his own exile in Siberia.

Parabolic Ballad

Andrei Voznesensky   *translated by* **W. H. Auden**

Along a parabola life like a rocket flies,
Mainly in darkness, now and then on a rainbow.
Red-headed bohemian Gauguin[1] the painter
Started out life as a prosperous stockbroker.
5 In order to get to the Louvre[2] from
    Montmartre[3]
He made a detour all through Java, Sumatra,
Tahiti, the Isles of Marquesas.[4]

                    With levity
He took off in flight from the madness of
    money,
The cackle of women, the frowst of academies,
10 Overpowered the force of terrestrial gravity.

The high priests drank their porter[5] and kept
    up their jabbering:
"Straight lines are shorter, less steep than
    parabolas.
It's more proper to copy the heavenly
    mansions."

He rose like a howling rocket, insulting them
15 With a gale that tore off the tails of their frock
    coats.

So he didn't steal into the Louvre by the front
    door
But on a parabola smashed through the ceiling.
In finding their truths lives vary in daring:
Worms come through holes and bold men on
    parabolas.

20 There once was a girl who lived in my
    neighborhood.
We went to one school, took exams
    simultaneously.
But I took off with a bang,
                  I went whizzing

Through the prosperous double-faced stars of
    Tiflis.[6]
Forgive me for this idiotic parabola.
25 Cold shoulders in a pitch-dark vestibule . . .
Rigid, erect as a radio antenna rod
Sending its call sign out through the freezing
Dark of the universe, how you rang out to me
An undoubtable signal, an earthly stand-by
30 From whom I might get my flight bearings to
    land by.
The parabola doesn't come to us easily.

Laughing at law with its warnings and
    paragraphs
Art, love, and history race along recklessly
Over a parabolic trajectory.

35 He is leaving tonight for Siberia.
                    Perhaps
A straight line after all is the shortest one
    actually.

                            1960

---

1. *Gauguin* (gō gaN'), Paul (1848–1903), French painter who left France and went to the South Seas where island peoples and scenes became subjects for his work.
2. *Louvre* (lüv'rə), an art museum in Paris, originally a palace of the French kings.
3. *Montmartre* (môN mär'trə), a district in the northern part of Paris, famous as an artists' neighborhood in the latter part of the nineteenth century.
4. *Java, . . . Marquesas,* islands in the Pacific visited by Gauguin.
5. *porter,* a heavy, dark-brown beer.
6. *Tiflis,* or Tblisi, a city in the southwestern part of the Soviet Union, capital of the Georgian S.S.R.

THINK AND DISCUSS

Understanding

1. According to the speaker, what constitutes a parabolic life?
2. What in Gauguin's life leads the speaker to describe it as a parabola?

Analyzing

3. Who might the frock-coated priests of stanzas 2 and 3 be? Apply their "jabbering" to Gauguin's life and art.
4. What is parabolic about the speaker's love affair? Is the girl necessary to his present life? How do you know?
5. What is the situation of the man described in lines 35–36? Who or what might he represent? What question does his situation raise?

Extending

6. Why do you think Voznesensky allots the smallest number of lines to his example from history—might his own position in Russia have anything to do with that? Explain.

COMPOSITION

Writing a Short Short Story

Lines 20–31 outline the speaker's love affair with a girl. Add enough details to permit you to write a story of no more than five paragraphs about that love affair. You may assign whatever names you wish to your characters, or you may leave them nameless. Expect that your classmates will read your story.

Analyzing the Poem

Reread the poem, noting the lines that do not refer directly to Gauguin, the speaker, or the unidentified "he." Based on these lines (and considering the three examples mentioned above as illustrations of the point Voznesensky is making), analyze the organization of the poem and its content. Then write a composition of three to five paragraphs for your teacher in which you report the results of your analysis. As an alternative, analyze the imagery and pace of the poem and any other devices you find that add to its impression on you. Take notes, and write a composition of three to five paragraphs for your teacher in which you report your findings.

Reader's Note

Translating "Goya"

During World War II, Voznesensky and his mother lived as refugees in a small village in the Ural Mountains. Once when his father came home on leave from Leningrad, he brought a book of etchings by the Spanish artist Goya depicting the horrors of Napoleon's invasion of Spain. (See the illustration on page 919.) Although Voznesensky was only nine at the time, the impact of these images stayed with him. Goya became for him a universal symbol of war. "Even today," the poet said in a 1963 interview, "he reminds me of the partisans shot by the Germans, of wolves, of our neighbor who was mourning her dead son, of the sirens during the bombardments of Moscow." Written in 1959, "Goya" is perhaps Voznesensky's most famous poem. In it he adopts the persona of the Spanish artist to describe the horrors of the German invasion of the Soviet Union in 1941.

On page 918 is the poem as it appears in the Cyrillic script. On pages 918–919 are four English translations. In the original, Voznesensky uses exclamation points, dashes, and divided lines to create a sense of breathlessness. Of the four translators, Herbert Marshall comes the closest to the original in this respect.

Voznesensky's original poem contains four stanzas. Only the Kunitz translation adheres strictly to the stanzaic arrangement of the original. The other translators employ five or more stanzas. Perhaps the most striking image in the poem occurs in the third stanza, which describes a hanged woman whose body is compared to a tolling bell. In Voznesensky's original she is an "old woman." Of the four translators, only Anselm Hollo imitates the Russian poet here. In the Deutsch and Kunitz translations, she is simply a "woman"; in the Marshall translation, she is a "girl."

In the final stanza of Voznesensky's original, he speaks of "grapes of retaliation." Three of the four translators have chosen to render this by the familiar phrase the "grapes of wrath." Deutsch misses the Biblical resonance of this phrase, but is closer to Voznesensky with her "grapes of retribution." The fourth stanza is difficult to interpret. Kunitz applies logic and has the speaker hurl westward "the ashes of the uninvited guest." In the other translations the speaker identifies himself with the ashes. In translating the last lines of the poem, all four translators agree in presenting the speaker as hammering the stars into the sky like nails—the nails possibly meant to evoke an image of Christ's crucifixion and thus heighten the poem's expression of innocent suffering.

Russian is a difficult language to translate, and in translation nearly all the effects of the sounds of the Russian words are lost. In "Goya" Voznesensky makes a striking use of both **alliteration** and **assonance**: "*Ya Góya . . . nagóye . . . ya górye . . . ya gólos . . . góda . . . ya gólod . . . ya górlo . . . ya góloi . . .*" The four translators, especially Deutsch and Marshall, have some success in imitating Voznesensky's repeated initial *g* sounds. But the effect of his assonance is largely lost.

ГОЙЯ

Я — Гойя!
Глазницы воронок мне выклевал ворог,
          слетая на поле нагое.

Я — горе.

Я — голос.
Войны, городов головни
          на снегу сорок первого года.

Я — голод.

Я — горло
Повешенной бабы, чье тело, как колокол,
          било над площадью голой...

Я — Гойя!

О грозди
Возмездья! Взвил залпом на Запад —
          я пепел незваного гостя!
И в мемориальное небо вбил крепкие звезды —
Как гвозди.

Я — Гойя.

Anselm Hollo (1962)

I am Goya: my eyes are destroyed
by enemy beaks.
    Shell-holes stare from the naked field.

I am misery,

5   the Voice of War
the voice of charred cities' timber
on the snow of the year
    Forty-one.

I am the old woman's throat
10 who was hung, whose body sang like a bell
over the naked townsquare. . . .

I am Goya
Grapes of Wrath! Dust
I am, raised by the barrage in the West.
15   Dust of the intruder . . .

And bright stars

were hammered in the memorial sky

like nails.

Yes, I
20   am Goya.

Herbert Marshall (1966)

I—am Goya!
The foe gouged my eyes' craters
      flying over the naked field.
I—am grief.

I—am the grim voice
5 Of war, the cinders of cities
      on the snow fields of '41.
I—am hunger.

I—am the gullet
Of the girl garrotted, whose body tolled like a bell,
      over the naked square . . .
I—am Goya!

10 O grapes
Of wrath! In salvoes I soared to the West—
    I am the ashes of the uninvited guest.
And with strong stars the memorial skies I impaled—
Like nails.

I—am Goya.

Francisco Goya
(1746–1828),
etching from the
series *Disasters
of War*. 1810–1815.
Metropolitan
Museum of Art

Stanley Kunitz (1966)

I am Goya
of the bare field, by the enemy's beak gouged
till the craters of my eyes gape
I am grief

5 I am the tongue
of war, the embers of cities
on the snows of the year 1941
I am hunger

I am the gullet
10 of a woman hanged whose body like a bell
tolled over a blank square
I am Goya

O grapes of wrath!
I have hurled westward
                      the ashes of the uninvited guest!
15 and hammered stars into the unforgetting sky—like nails
I am Goya

Babette Deutsch (1965)

I'm Goya!
The enemy, gliding down upon naked fields,
                   has pecked out my sockets: blindly the craters gaze.

I am grief.
5 I'm the groan
Of war, the embers of cities glowing
                     black on the snow of the year forty-one.

I'm hunger.
I'm the closed gullet
10   of the woman who hangs there, her body a bell
                     tolling over the bare square.

I'm Goya!
O grapes
               of retribution! I soared like a shot going west,
                 I, the ashes of an unbidden guest!

15 Into the memorial sky I hammered strong stars—
Like nails.
I'm Goya!

BIOGRAPHY

Alice Walker

1944–

At present Alice Walker is undoubtedly best known for her epistolary novel *The Color Purple* (1982) and the motion picture that was made from it. However, in addition to being a novelist, she is a recognized poet, a biographer, an essayist, and an accomplished short-story writer. Her works deal largely with the experiences of black women in a world where they must overcome both sexual and racial prejudice. Many of Walker's short stories on this theme have been collected in *In Love and Trouble: Stories of Black Women* (1973), which includes "Everyday Use" (page 922).

Walker was born in Eatonton, Georgia, where her father farmed as a sharecropper and her mother worked alongside him. Alice was the youngest of the eight children born to the couple. She attended Spelman College in Atlanta and Sarah Lawrence College in New York, from which she graduated in 1965. Since that time she has been active on *Ms.* Magazine, becoming an editor in 1974, and has taught writing and literature at a number of colleges and universities.

Once, Walker's first collection of verse, published in 1968, was an outgrowth of her civil-rights work and dealt with that work as well as with her experiences during a trip to Africa. In her next volume of poetry, *Revolutionary Petunias* (1973), she describes the Georgia she knew during her childhood. Also published in 1973 was *Langston Hughes,* Walker's full-length biography of the black poet and leader of the Harlem Renaissance. Walker showed herself to be a capable editor and anthologist with the publication in 1979 of *I Love Myself When I Am Laughing,* a collection of the writings of black writer Zora Neale Hurston (1901–1960), whose talent is only being recognized many years after her death. In her essay collection *In Search of Our Mothers' Gardens* (1983), Walker provides insights into the lives of such black women as Coretta Scott King, the widow of Dr. Martin Luther King, and also gives a partial portrait of her own development as a writer.

In "Everyday Use" Walker deals with a simple episode—the one-day visit to her family home in the rural South of a bright, college-educated young black woman now living in the North.

Everyday Use

Alice Walker

for your grandmama

will wait for her in the yard that Maggie and I made so clean and wavy yesterday afternoon. A yard like this is more comfortable than most people know. It is not just a yard. It is like an extended living room. When the hard clay is swept clean as a floor and the fine sand around the edges lined with tiny, irregular grooves, anyone can come and sit and look up into the elm tree and wait for the breezes that never come inside the house.

Maggie will be nervous until after her sister goes: she will stand hopelessly in corners, homely and ashamed of the burn scars down her arms and legs, eying her sister with a mixture of envy and awe. She thinks her sister has held life always in the palm of one hand, that "no" is a word the world never learned to say to her.

You've no doubt seen those TV shows where the child who has "made it" is confronted, as a surprise, by her own mother and father, tottering in weakly from backstage.[1] (A pleasant surprise, of course: What would they do if parent and child came on the show only to curse out and insult each other?) On TV mother and child embrace and smile into each other's faces. Sometimes the mother and father weep, the child wraps them in her arms and leans across the table to tell how she would not have made it without their help. I have seen these programs.

Sometimes I dream a dream in which Dee and I are suddenly brought together on a TV program of this sort. Out of a dark and softseated limousine I am ushered into a bright room filled with many people. There I meet a smiling, gray, sporty man like Johnny Carson who shakes my hand and tells me what a fine girl I have. Then we are on the stage and Dee is embracing me with tears in her eyes. She pins on my dress a large orchid, even though she has told me once that she thinks orchids are tacky flowers.

In real life I am a large, big-boned woman with rough, man-working hands. In the winter I wear flannel nightgowns to bed and overalls during the day. I can kill and clean a hog as mercilessly as a man. My fat keeps me hot in zero weather. I can work outside all day, breaking ice to get water for washing; I can eat pork liver cooked over the open fire minutes after it comes steaming from the hog. One winter I knocked a bull calf straight in the brain between the eyes with a sledge hammer and had the meat hung up to chill before nightfall. But of course all this does not show on television. I am the way my daughter would want me to be: a hundred pounds lighter, my skin like an uncooked barley pancake. My hair glistens in the hot bright lights. Johnny Carson has much to do to keep up with my quick and witty tongue.

But that is a mistake. I know even before I wake up. Who ever knew a Johnson with a quick tongue? Who can even imagine me looking a strange white man in the eye? It seems to me I have talked to them always with one foot raised in flight, with my head turned in whichever way is farthest from them. Dee, though. She would

---

1. *You've no doubt . . . backstage,* a reference to television shows such as *This Is Your Life,* popular in the 1950s.

always look anyone in the eye. Hesitation was no part of her nature.

"How do I look, Mama?" Maggie says, showing just enough of her thin body enveloped in pink skirt and red blouse for me to know she's there, almost hidden by the door.

"Come out into the yard," I say.

Have you ever seen a lame animal, perhaps a dog run over by some careless person rich enough to own a car, sidle up to someone who is ignorant enough to be kind to him? That is the way my Maggie walks. She has been like this, chin on chest, eyes on ground, feet in shuffle, ever since the fire that burned the other house to the ground.

Dee is lighter than Maggie, with nicer hair and a fuller figure. She's a woman now, though sometimes I forget. How long ago was it that the other house burned? Ten, twelve years? Sometimes I can still hear the flames and feel Maggie's arms sticking to me, her hair smoking and her dress falling off her in little black papery flakes. Her eyes seemed stretched open, blazed open by the flames reflected in them. And Dee. I see her standing off under the sweet gum tree she used to dig gum out of; a look of concentration on her face as she watched the last dingy gray board of the house fall in toward the red-hot brick chimney. Why don't you do a dance around the ashes? I'd wanted to ask her. She had hated the house that much.

I used to think she hated Maggie, too. But that was before we raised the money, the church and me, to send her to Augusta[2] to school. She used to read to us without pity; forcing words, lies, other folks' habits, whole lives upon us two, sitting trapped and ignorant underneath her voice. She washed us in the river of make-believe, burned us with a lot of knowledge we didn't necessarily need to know. Pressed us to her with the serious way she read, to shove us away at just the moment, like dimwits, we seemed about to understand.

Dee wanted nice things. A yellow organdy dress to wear to her graduation from high school; black pumps to match a green suit she'd made from an old suit somebody gave me. She was determined to stare down any disaster in her efforts. Her eyelids would not flicker for minutes at a time. Often I fought off the temptation to shake her. At sixteen she had a style of her own: and knew what style was.

I never had an education myself. After second grade the school was closed down. Don't ask me why: in 1927 colored asked fewer questions than they do now. Sometimes Maggie reads to me. She stumbles along good-naturedly but can't see well. She knows she is not bright. Like good looks and money, quickness passed her by. She will marry John Thomas (who has mossy teeth in an earnest face) and then I'll be free to sit here and I guess just sing church songs to myself. Although I never was a good singer. Never could carry a tune. I was always better at a man's job. I used to love to milk till I was hooked in the side[3] in '49. Cows are soothing and slow and don't bother you, unless you try to milk them the wrong way.

I have deliberately turned my back on the house. It is three rooms, just like the one that burned, except the roof is tin; they don't make shingle roofs any more. There are no real windows, just some holes cut in the sides, like the portholes in a ship, but not round and not square, with rawhide holding the shutters up on the outside. This house is in a pasture, too, like the other one. No doubt when Dee sees it she will want to tear it down. She wrote me once that no matter where we "choose" to live, she will manage to come see us. But she will never bring her friends. Maggie and I thought about this and Maggie asked me, "Mama, when did Dee ever *have* any friends?"

She had a few. Furtive boys in pink shirts hanging about on washday after school. Nervous girls who never laughed. Impressed with her they worshiped the well-turned phrase, the cute shape, the scalding humor that erupted like bubbles in lye. She read to them.

When she was courting Jimmy T she didn't have much time to pay to us, but turned all her fault-finding power on him. He *flew* to marry a cheap

---

2. **Augusta**, city in Georgia.
3. **hooked in the side**, hit in the side by a cow's horn.

city girl from a family of ignorant flashy people. She hardly had time to recompose herself.

When she comes I will meet—but there they are!

Maggie attempts to make a dash for the house, in her shuffling way, but I stay her with my hand. "Come back here," I say. And she stops and tries to dig a well in the sand with her toe.

It is hard to see them clearly through the strong sun. But even the first glimpse of leg out of the car tells me it is Dee. Her feet were always neat-looking, as if God himself had shaped them with a certain style. From the other side of the car comes a short, stocky man. Hair is all over his head a foot long and hanging from his chin like a kinky mule tail. I hear Maggie suck in her breath. "Uhnnnh," is what it sounds like. Like when you see the wriggling end of a snake just in front of your foot on the road. "Uhnnnh."

Dee next. A dress down to the ground, in this hot weather. A dress so loud it hurts my eyes. There are yellows and oranges enough to throw back the light of the sun. I feel my whole face warming from the heat waves it throws out. Earrings gold, too, and hanging down to her shoulders. Bracelets dangling and making noises when she moves her arm up to shake the folds of the dress out of her armpits. The dress is loose and flows, and as she walks closer, I like it. I hear Maggie go "Uhnnnh" again. It is her sister's hair. It stands straight up like the wool on a sheep. It is black as night and around the edges are two long pigtails that rope about like small lizards disappearing behind her ears.

"Wa-su-zo-Tean-o!"[4] she says, coming on in that gliding way the dress makes her move. The short stocky fellow with the hair to his navel is all grinning and he follows up with "Asalamalakim,[5] my mother and sister!" He moves to hug Maggie but she falls back, right up against the back of my chair. I feel her trembling there and when I look up I see the perspiration falling off her chin.

"Don't get up," says Dee. Since I am stout it takes something of a push. You can see me trying to move a second or two before I make it. She turns, showing white heels through her sandals,

and goes back to the car. Out she peeks next with a Polaroid. She stoops down quickly and lines up picture after picture of me sitting there in front of the house with Maggie cowering behind me. She never takes a shot without making sure the house is included. When a cow comes nibbling around the edge of the yard she snaps it and me and Maggie *and* the house. Then she puts the Polaroid in the back seat of the car, and comes up and kisses me on the forehead.

Meanwhile Asalamalakim is going through motions with Maggie's hand. Maggie's hand is as limp as a fish, and probably as cold, despite the sweat, and she keeps trying to pull it back. It looks like Asalamalakim wants to shake hands but wants to do it fancy. Or maybe he don't know how people shake hands. Anyhow, he soon gives up on Maggie.

"Well," I say. "Dee."

"No, Mama," she says. "Not 'Dee,' Wangero Leewanika Kemanjo!"

"What happened to 'Dee'?" I wanted to know.

"She's dead," Wangero said. "I couldn't bear it any longer, being named after the people who oppress me."

"You know as well as me you was named after your aunt Dicie," I said. Dicie is my sister. She named Dee. We called her "Big Dee" after Dee was born.

"But who was *she* named after?" asked Wangero.

"I guess after Grandma Dee," I said.

"And who was she named after?" asked Wangero.

"Her mother," I said, and saw Wangero was getting tired. "That's about as far back as I can trace it," I said. Though, in fact, I probably could have carried it back beyond the Civil War through the branches.

"Well," said Asalamalakim, "there you are."

"Uhnnnh," I heard Maggie say.

"There I was not," I said, "before 'Dicie'

---

4. *"Wa-su-zo-Tean-o!"*, a greeting in one of the several Bantu languages of central and southern Africa.
5. *"Asalamalakim"* (ə säˈləmˈä leˈkum), Peace be with you. [Arabic]

cropped up in our family, so why should I try to trace it that far back?"

He just stood there grinning, looking down on me like somebody inspecting a Model A car.[6] Every once in a while he and Wangero sent eye signals over my head.

"How do you pronounce this name?" I asked.

"You don't have to call me by it if you don't want to," said Wangero.

"Why shouldn't I?" I asked. "If that's what you want us to call you, we'll call you."

"I know it might sound awkward at first," said Wangero.

"I'll get used to it," I said. "Ream it out again."

Well, soon we got the name out of the way. Asalamalakim had a name twice as long and three times as hard. After I tripped over it two or three times he told me to just call him Hakim-a-barber. I wanted to ask him was he a barber, but I didn't really think he was, so I didn't ask.

"You must belong to those beef-cattle peoples down the road," I said. They said "Asalamalakim" when they met you, too, but they didn't shake hands. Always too busy: feeding the cattle, fixing the fences, putting up salt-lick shelters,[7] throwing down hay. When the white folks poisoned some of the herd the men stayed up all night with rifles in their hands. I walked a mile and a half just to see the sight.

Hakim-a-barber said, "I accept some of their doctrines, but farming and raising cattle is not my style." (They didn't tell me, and I didn't ask, whether Wangero (Dee) had really gone and married him.)

We sat down to eat and right away he said he didn't eat collards and pork was unclean.[8] Wangero, though, went on through the chitlins and corn bread, the greens and everything else. She talked a blue streak over the sweet potatoes. Everything delighted her. Even the fact that we still used the benches her daddy made for the table when we couldn't afford to buy chairs.

"Oh, Mama!" she cried. Then turned to Hakim-a-barber. "I never knew how lovely these benches are. You can feel the rump prints," she said, running her hands underneath her and along the bench. Then she gave a sigh and her hand closed over Grandma Dee's butter dish. "That's it!" she said. "I knew there was something I wanted to ask you if I could have." She jumped up from the table and went over in the corner where the churn stood, the milk in it clabber[9] by now. She looked at the churn and looked at it.

"This churn top is what I need," she said. "Didn't Uncle Buddy whittle it out of a tree you all used to have?"

"Yes," I said.

"Uh huh," she said happily. "And I want the dasher,[10] too,"

"Uncle Buddy whittle that, too?" asked the barber.

Dee (Wangero) looked up at me.

"Aunt Dee's first husband whittled the dash," said Maggie so low you almost couldn't hear her. "His name was Henry, but they called him Stash."

"Maggie's brain is like an elephant's," Wangero said, laughing. "I can use the churn top as a centerpiece for the alcove table," she said, sliding a plate over the churn, "and I'll think of something artistic to do with the dasher."

When she finished wrapping the dasher the handle stuck out. I took it for a moment in my hands. You didn't even have to look close to see where hands pushing the dasher up and down to make butter had left a kind of sink in the wood. In fact, there were a lot of small sinks; you could see where thumbs and fingers had sunk into the wood. It was beautiful light yellow wood, from a tree that grew in the yard where Big Dee and Stash had lived.

After dinner Dee (Wangero) went to the trunk at the foot of my bed and started rifling through it. Maggie hung back in the kitchen over the dishpan. Out came Wangero with two quilts. They had been pieced by Grandma Dee and then Big Dee and me had hung them on the quilt frames on the front porch and quilted them. One was in the Lone

---

6. **Model A car,** a Ford automobile that replaced the Model T in 1928.

7. **salt-lick shelters,** block of salt set in a shelter, especially in a pasture, for the cattle to lick.

8. **unclean.** Moslems are forbidden by their religion to eat pork.

9. **clabber,** thick, sour milk.

10. **dasher,** device for stirring the cream in a churn.

American quilt in "Lone Star" pattern. c. 1850. National Museum of American History, Washington, D.C.

Star pattern. The other was Walk Around the Mountain. In both of them were scraps of dresses Grandma Dee had worn fifty and more years ago. Bits and pieces of Grandpa Jarrell's Paisley shirts. And one teeny faded blue piece, about the size of a penny matchbox, that was from Great Grandpa Ezra's uniform that he wore in the Civil War.

"Mama," Wangero said sweet as a bird. "Can I have these old quilts?"

I heard something fall in the kitchen, and a minute later the kitchen door slammed.

"Why don't you take one or two of the others?" I asked. "These old things was just done by me and Big Dee from some tops your grandma pieced before she died."

"No," said Wangero. "I don't want those. They are stitched around the borders by machine."

"That'll make them last better," I said.

"That's not the point," said Wangero. "These are all pieces of dresses Grandma used to wear. She did all this stitching by hand. Imagine!" She held the quilts securely in her arms, stroking them.

"Some of the pieces, like those lavender ones, come from old clothes her mother handed down to her," I said, moving up to touch the quilts. Dee (Wangero) moved back just enough so that I couldn't reach the quilts. They already belonged to her.

"Imagine!" she breathed again, clutching them closely to her bosom.

"The truth is," I said, "I promised to give them quilts to Maggie, for when she marries John Thomas."

She gasped like a bee had stung her.

"Maggie can't appreciate these quilts!" she said. "She'd probably be backward enough to put them to everyday use."

"I reckon she would," I said. "God knows I been saving 'em for long enough with nobody using 'em. I hope she will!" I didn't want to bring up how I had offered Dee (Wangero) a quilt when she went away to college. Then she had told me they were old-fashioned, out of style.

"But they're *priceless*!" she was saying now, furiously; for she has a temper. "Maggie would put them on the bed and in five years they'd be in rags. Less than that!"

"She can always make some more," I said. "Maggie knows how to quilt."

Dee (Wangero) looked at me with hatred. "You just will not understand. The point is these quilts, *these* quilts!"

"Well," I said, stumped. "What would *you* do with them?"

"Hang them," she said. As if that was the only thing you *could* do with quilts.

Maggie by now was standing in the door. I could almost hear the sound her feet made as they scraped over each other.

"She can have them, Mama," she said, like somebody used to never winning anything, or having anything reserved for her. "I can 'member Grandma Dee without the quilts."

I looked at her hard. She had filled her bottom lip with checkerberry snuff[11] and it gave her face a kind of dopey, hangdog look. It was Grandma Dee and Big Dee who taught her how to quilt herself. She stood there with her scarred hands hidden in the folds of her skirt. She looked at her sister with something like fear but she wasn't mad at her. This was Maggie's portion. This was the way she knew God to work.

When I looked at her like that something hit me in the top of my head and ran down to the soles of my feet. Just like when I'm in church and the spirit of God touches me and I get happy and shout. I did something I never had done before: hugged Maggie to me, then dragged her on into the room, snatched the quilts out of Miss Wangero's hands and dumped them into Maggie's lap. Maggie just sat there on my bed with her mouth open.

"Take one or two of the others," I said to Dee.

But she turned without a word and went out to Hakim-a-barber.

"You just don't understand," she said, as Maggie and I came out to the car.

"What don't I understand?" I wanted to know.

"Your heritage," she said. And then she turned to Maggie, kissed her, and said, "You ought to try to make something of yourself, too, Maggie. It's really a new day for us. But from the way you and Mama still live you'd never know it."

She put on some sunglasses that hid everything above the tip of her nose and her chin.

Maggie smiled; maybe at the sunglasses. But a real smile, not scared. After we watched the car dust settle I asked Maggie to bring me a dip of snuff. And then the two of us sat there just enjoying, until it was time to go in the house and go to bed.   1973

---

11. *checkerberry snuff,* powdered tobacco taken into the nose or mouth, made from the bright-red berry of the wintergreen plant.

THINK AND DISCUSS
Understanding
1. How do the narrator and Maggie prepare for Dee's visit?
2. Why does Dee want the churn parts and the quilts? Does she show any love for them?
3. How do the narrator and Maggie react after the visit is over?

Analyzing
4. What is Dee's real reason for visiting her mother and sister?

5. What do Dee's and Hakim's appearances immediately tell about them?
6. Why does Dee take so many Polaroid pictures of her mother, her sister, and the house? Why does she keep exchanging glances with Hakim over her mother's head?
7. What do the quilts mean to Dee? To Maggie? Why then does Maggie offer to give them up?
8. What leads the narrator to take the quilts away from Dee and put them in Maggie's lap?

9. What is the irony in Dee's telling her mother and sister they don't understand their heritage?
10. In gaining all her sophistication, what has Dee lost?
11. What is the basic conflict in this story? Is it between the narrator and Dee, Maggie and Dee, or old ways and new ways? Explain.
12. Explain the significance of the title.

Extending
13. One reader has said that Dee treats her family, their home, and their belongings more like quaint curiosities than a tourist would. Comment on this statement.

REVIEWING: Characterization
See Handbook of Literary Terms, p. 944.

Characterization consists of the methods an author uses to develop the personality of a character in a literary work. These include describing the character's physical appearance, actions, and inner thoughts or revealing attitudes and reactions of other characters.

1. What in Maggie's physical appearance has led to her shyness and her feeling of being inferior to her sister?
2. When Maggie offers to give up her quilts to Dee, what is revealed of her character?
3. What does Dee think of Maggie's character? How do you know?
4. How does the narrator's refusal to allow Dee to take the quilts from Maggie affect Maggie's character? How do you know?

VOCABULARY
Synonyms and Dictionary
The list at the left contains words from selections in this unit. The list at the right contains synonyms or brief definitions of the words. On your paper write each numbered word and the letter of its synonym or definition. You may use the Glossary to check meanings.

1. abstemious		a. brilliance
2. semblance		b. prolonged
3. effulgence		c. artistic skill
4. unutterably		d. eager
5. protracted		e. unspeakably
6. virtuosity		f. appearance
7. levity		g. move sideways
8. avid		h. stealthy
9. furtive		i. lack of seriousness
10. sidle		j. sparing in eating or drinking; moderate

COMPOSITION
Comparing and Contrasting Characters
In a five-paragraph composition for your classmates, compare and contrast the characters of Maggie and Dee. Consider their early years, the fire, Dee's going off to college while Maggie remains at home, their different attitudes toward life, etc.

Analyzing the Narrator
One of the joys of reading this story is to see the narrator's character reveal itself bit by bit. Reread the story, noting the instances where what she thinks, says, or does reveals something about her. Assemble your notes and use them as the basis for a five-paragraph composition to be read by your teacher.

ENRICHMENT
Readers Theater
This is an unusually good selection for a readers theater dramatization. You will need four students to represent the characters: the narrator, Maggie, Dee, and Hakim. Since the narrator's role is so long, two or more students may be designated to share it. The students should keep in mind the characterization of those they represent—Dee's feeling of superiority; Maggie's of inferiority; the narrator's insight, wisdom, and fairness; and Hakim's willingness to follow Dee's lead in everything.

English—a World Language?

In the summer of 1987, seven thousand people from sixty countries gathered in Warsaw to commemorate the hundredth anniversary of Esperanto (es′pə rän′tō), the "universal language" invented in 1887 by a Polish eye-doctor, Ludovic Zamenhof (zä′men hōf). Zamenof had observed how the Polish, Russian, and German inhabitants of Warsaw constantly quarreled. He attributed this to their inability to understand each other's speech, and decided that if everyone spoke a common language, national differences would end. In the next hundred years, his simple artificial language achieved support in many countries and is currently taught at a number of American colleges. But although perhaps as many as ten million people throughout the world use Esperanto today, neither it nor any of the other artificial languages, such as Interlingua and Novial, are the speech of any real community. As a recent history of English puts it, "They remain a slightly stilted monument to late-Victorian scientific rationalism."

Compare the ten million speakers of Esperanto with the estimated billion people who speak the English language. The worldwide acceptance of English has been perhaps the most striking phenomenon in the recent history of language. There are at least three reasons for the extraordinary popularity of English. One is linguistic—English is more adaptable and grammatically simpler than most languages (except artificial ones like Esperanto). The other two reasons are political. The first is the worldwide influence of the British Empire in the eighteenth, nineteenth, and twentieth centuries. The second is the emergence of the English-speaking United States as a superpower following World War II.

English has the largest and richest vocabulary of any of the world's languages—over 600,000 words—many of them specialized or technical terms that have entered the language in this century. Two world wars provided such terms as *zeppelin*, *U-boat*, *blitzkrieg*, *jeep*, *concentration camp*, and *A-bomb*; from the sciences came *neu-rosis*, *antibiotic*, *radio*, *television*, *transistor*, and *laser;* from the arts came *montage*, *surrealism*, and *absurdist*. The enormous number of English words, and the linguistic flexibility and omniverousness that have created this huge vocabulary, make English particularly suited to be the international language of science and culture.

The worldwide influence of English is evident in the use of hybrid English words by the speakers of many other languages. The French use words like *le drugstore* and *le weekend;* the Japanese describe an apartment as a *man-shon* (mansion) and talk of eating *aisu-kurimu* (ice cream). Though some foreign governments try to officially discourage these linguistic imports, the tendency they reflect will probably continue in the future.

Street sign in Budapest, Hungary, with its message in Hungarian, English, German, and Russian.

Themes IN WORLD LITERATURE

PAST AND PRESENT

. . . what's past is prologue . . . ."
Shakespeare, *The Tempest*

A constant theme in literature is the relationship between the present and the past. Storytelling presupposes the passage of time, and the passage of time brings the present into contact with the past. At the opening of *The Tempest* (page 415), the magician Prospero delivers an account to his daughter Miranda of how they came to dwell on their island. He begins by urging her to try to look into "the dark backward and abysm of time," to see herself as she once was, a princess. He concludes by associating this account of their past with "the present business/Which now's upon's; without the which this story/Were most impertinent." In other words, the present, without the past, is unintelligible; the past, without the present, is unimportant. Several ways in which the present and the past interact in literature are considered in the following article.

Memory

Memory, a way of bringing the past into present awareness, is often introduced into lyric poetry. In his poignant poem, "Remembering Golden Bells" (page 83), Po Chü-i describes how his grief for his daughter, who died in infancy, is brought back to him by the sight of her former nurse. "And when I remember," he says, "how just at the time she died/She lisped strange sounds, beginning to learn to talk,/Then I know that the ties of flesh and blood/Only bind us to a load of grief and sorrow." Psalm 137 (page 33) also speaks of the pain brought by memory. "By the rivers of Babylon, there we sat down,/Yea, we wept, when we remembered Zion." But the Psalmist sees these painful recollections as a sacred duty. "If I forget thee, O Jerusalem,/Let my right hand forget her cunning./If I do not remember thee,/Let my tongue cleave to the roof of my mouth."

Memory can also be a bringer of consolation. Petrarch's sonnets often describe the pain he experienced because of his love for Laura. In the sonnet "Life Hurries On" (page 382), this pain, or some other, has brought him to the point of death: "All the present leagues with the past/and all the future to make war on me." But much as a dying person is said to see his whole life passing before his eyes, Petrarch calls up his memory of the "few glad moments" he has known. And these few glad memories are the only positive note in the poem. Sappho, in her poem "Someone, I Tell You" (page 155), derives consolation by anticipating other people's future memories of her: "Someone, I tell you,/will remember us./We are oppressed by/fears of oblivion/yet are always saved/by judgment of good men."

Sometimes the emotions generated by memory are neither positive nor negative, but somewhere in between, as in Camus's lyrical essay "Between Yes and No" (page 932). The essay is a reverie describing his memories during an hour in which he sits in a cafe, an hour in which he recalls "not a moment of past happiness but a feeling of strangeness." In this meditation, Camus remembers events from his childhood and contemplates the meaning of happiness, of life, of death, of old age. His recollection of his life with his mother, "the tender and despairing image of two people's loneliness together," generates a mood in him that is finally neither happy nor sad. Another lyric poem that deals with the power of memory is Martinson's "March Evening" (page 866). It briefly describes the experience of a man on a train who observes that some boys outside have "lit a candle in a snowball house." For the traveler, it is "a red memory surrounded by gray time," and it so arrests him that he "never got home,/his life stayed behind, held by that/lantern and that hour." In this poem, memory becomes more powerful than consciousness. As William Faulkner observed, "Memory believes before knowing remembers."

History

One of the most obvious ways in which the past and present interact is in the writing of history. Edward Gibbon described history as "little more than the register of the crimes, follies, and misfortunes of mankind." This bleak estimate would certainly apply to much of the work of the classical historian Gibbon most admired, Tacitus, whose masterpiece, the *Annals* (page 251) is an account of the reigns of the Roman emperors from Tiberius through Nero. What relationship do historians see between the past and the present? Thucydides, author of *The Peloponnesian War* (page 214), indicated his view in the course of a remark on the value he felt his work could have for his readers: "If those who will wish to study the clear record of what happened in the past and what will, in due course, tend to be repeated with some degree of similarity (as is the way of human events), judge this work to be of help to them, it will content me."

The historical past also appears in literature in the form of allusion. In *A Modest Proposal* (page 553), Swift at one point criticizes his fellow Irish for their "animosities and factions." In doing this he makes an allusion to the capture of Jerusalem by the Romans in A.D. 70, when the members of different sects among the Jewish defenders "were murdering one another at the moment their city was taken." Both Machiavelli in his study of ruling, *The Prince* (page 394), and Cicero in his epistle "On Friendship" (page 230) make frequent use of historical allusion in developing their arguments. For these authors and the educated audiences for which they wrote, the historical past was vividly present, a great storehouse of example and illustration.

Sometimes an author uses an allusion not to the real past, but to an imagined past. Anouilh wrote his play *Antigone* (page 874) while France was being occupied by German troops during World War II. The play's first audiences in 1944 saw in Antigone a character who, like members of the French Resistance movement, was willing to sacrifice her life for her ideals; in Creon they saw an image of the Vichy government that was collaborating with the Germans.

The Past in the Present

Coming from the South, the region of the United States in the most intimate contact with its history, Faulkner felt that "The past isn't dead. It isn't even past." Like the South, the Soviet Union is a place deeply involved with its history. The Russian poet Akhmatova, in her "Requiem 1935–1940" (page 820), recalls the victims of Stalin's purges, herself among them. Her poem is a grim depiction of sickness, isolation, hysteria, and defeat—a commemoration of one of the darkest hours in Russian history. Yet the poem's "Epilogue" expresses her imaginative triumph, a triumph of memory over terror. Another Russian poet, Voznesensky, describes some of the horrors of the German invasion of the Soviet Union during World War II in "Goya" (page 918). In his poem Voznesensky assumes the persona of the great Spanish artist Goya, whose etchings of Napoleon's invasion of Spain vividly picture the cruelty of war. By having his Goya describe Hitler's invasion of Russia, Voznesensky achieves a complex imaginative layering of past and present.

Alice Walker is a Southerner, like Faulkner. In her short story "Everyday Use" (page 922), she evokes the past of black Southerners. Like Akhmatova, she celebrates the triumph of memory over adversity. The past, she seems to say, should not be turned into some kind of museum exhibit. It should continue to interact with and sustain people in the present. It should be for "everyday use."

Scene from the 1947 production of *Antigone*.

THINKING CRITICALLY
ABOUT LITERATURE

UNIT 8   RECENT LITERATURE   1940–

■ CONCEPT REVIEW

Below on the left is an excerpt from "Between Yes and No," an auto-biographical essay by the French writer Albert Camus (kä mY′), winner of the 1957 Nobel Prize for literature. Camus was born in 1913 in Algeria, the setting of his most famous novel, *The Stranger*, and of the recollection contained in the following excerpt.

Below on the right are notes to help you read this excerpt and to review some of the literary terms and thinking skills that have appeared in Unit 8. Page numbers in the notes refer to an application or review. A more extensive discussion of these terms is in the Handbook of Literary terms. On a separate sheet of paper write your answers to the questions following the excerpt.

from Between Yes and No

Albert Camus
translated by **Ellen Conroy Kennedy**

In this Moorish café, at the far end of the Arab town, I recall not a moment of past happiness but a feeling of strangeness. It is already night. On the walls, canary-yellow lions pursue green-clad sheiks among five-branched palm trees. In a corner of the café, an acetylene lamp gives a flickering light. The real light comes from the fire, at the bottom of a small stove adorned with yellow and green enamel. The flames light up the middle of the room, and I can feel them reflected on my face. I sit facing the doorway and the bay. Crouched in a corner, the café owner seems to be looking at my glass, which stands there empty with a mint leaf at the bottom. There is no one in the main room, noises rise from the town opposite, while further off in the bay lights shine. I hear the Arab breathe heavily, and his eyes glow in the dusk. Is that the sound of the sea far off? The world sighs toward me in a long rhythm, and brings me the peace and indifference of immortal things. Tall red shadows

■ **Arab town:** the Arab quarter of Algiers

■ **Setting** (page 864): Note the specific details that enrich the setting.

■ **Imagery** (page 856): As you read, be aware of Camus's use of imagery to create vivid pictures of what is occurring.

make the lions on the walls sway with a wavelike motion. The air grows cool. A foghorn sounds at sea. The beams from the lighthouse begin to turn: one green, one red, and one white. And still the world sighs its long sigh. A kind of secret song is born of this indifference. And I am home again. I think of a child living in a poor district. That neighborhood, that house! There were only two floors, and the stairs were unlit. Even now, long years later, he could go back there on the darkest night. He knows that he could climb the stairs without stumbling once. His very body is impregnated with this house. His legs retain the exact height of the steps; his hand, the instinctive, never-conquered horror of the bannister. Because of the cockroaches.

■ Here Camus goes back in reverie to a scene from his childhood.

On summer evenings, the workingmen sit on their balconies. In his apartment, there was only one tiny window. So they would bring the chairs down, put them in front of the house, and enjoy the evening air. There was the street, the ice-cream vendor next door, the cafés across the way, and the noise of children running from door to door. But above all, through the wide fig trees there was the sky. There is a solitude in poverty, but a solitude that gives everything back its value. At a certain level of wealth, the heavens themselves and the star-filled night are nature's riches. But seen from the very bottom of the ladder, the sky recovers its full meaning: a priceless grace. Summer nights mysterious with crackling stars! Behind the child was a stinking corridor, and his little chair, splitting across the bottom, sank a little beneath his weight. But, eyes raised, he drank in the pure night. Sometimes a large tram would rattle swiftly past. A drunk would stand singing at a street corner, without disturbing the silence.

The child's mother sat as silently. Sometimes, people would ask her: "What are you thinking about?" And she would answer: "Nothing." And it was quite true. Everything was there, so she thought about nothing. Her life, her interests, her children were simply there, with a presence too natural to be felt. She was frail, had difficulty in thinking. She had a harsh and domineering mother who sacrificed everything to a touchy animal pride and had long held sway over her weak-minded daughter. Emancipated by her marriage, the daughter came home obediently when her husband died. He died a soldier's death, as they say. One could see his gold-framed military medal and *croix de guerre* in a place of honor. The hospital sent the widow the small shell splinter found in his body. She kept it. Her grief has long since disappeared. She has forgotten her husband, but still speaks of her children's father. To support these children, she goes out to work and gives her wages to her mother, who brings them up with a whip. When she hits them too hard, the daughter tells her: "Don't hit them on the head." Because they are her children she is very fond of them. She loves them with a hidden and impartial love. Sometimes, on those evenings he's remembering, she would come back from her exhausting work (as a cleaning woman) to find the house empty, the old woman out shopping, the children still at school. She would huddle in a chair, gazing in front of her, wandering off in the dizzy pursuit of a crack along the floor. As the night thickened around her, her muteness would seem irredeemably desolate. If the child came in, he would see her

■ **Characterization** (page 928): With this sentence, Camus begins his characterization of his mother. As you read, note the various devices he uses to reveal her character.

■ **croix de guerre** (krwä də ger′): literally, "cross of war," a French military award for heroism in combat

thin shape and bony shoulders, and stop, afraid. He is beginning to feel a lot of things. He is scarcely aware of his own existence, but this animal silence makes him want to cry with pain. He feels sorry for his mother; is this the same as loving her? She has never hugged or kissed him, for she wouldn't know how. He stands a long time watching her. Feeling separate from her, he becomes conscious of her suffering. She does not hear him, for she is deaf. In a few moments, the old woman will come back, life will start up again: the round light cast by the kerosene lamp, the oilcloth on the table, the shouting, the swearing. Meanwhile, the silence marks a pause, an immensely long moment. Vaguely aware of this, the child thinks the surge of feeling in him is love for his mother. And it must be, because after all she is his mother.

■ Note the confusion in the child's mind about his mother.

She is thinking of nothing. Outside, the light, the noises; here, silence in the night. The child will grow, will learn. They are bringing him up and will ask him to be grateful, as if they were sparing him pain. His mother will always have these silences. He will suffer as he grows. To be a man is what counts. His grandmother will die, then his mother, then he.

His mother has given a sudden start. Something has frightened her. He looks stupid standing there gazing at her. He ought to go and do his homework. The child has done his homework. Today he is in a sordid café. Now he is a man. Isn't that what counts? Surely not, since doing homework and accepting manhood leads to nothing but old age.

Still crouching in his corner, the Arab sits with his hands clasped round his feet. The scent of roasting coffee rises from the terraces and mingles with the excited chatter of young voices. The hooting of a tugboat adds its grave and tender note. The world is ending here as it does each day, and all its measureless torments now give rise to nothing but this promise of peace. The indifference of this strange mother! Only the immense solitude of the world can be the measure of it. One evening, they had called her son—he was already quite grown up—to his mother's side. A fright had brought on a serious mental shock. She was in the habit of going out on the balcony at the end of the day. She would take a chair and lean her mouth against the cold and salty iron of the railing. Then she would watch the people going past. Behind her, the night would gradually thicken. In front of her, the shops would suddenly light up. The street would fill with people and lights. She would gaze emptily out until she forgot where she was. On this particular evening, a man had loomed up behind her, dragged her backward, knocked her about, and run away when he heard a noise. She had seen nothing, and fainted. She was in bed when her son arrived. He decided, on the doctor's advice, to spend the night with her. He stretched out on the bed, by her side, lying on the top of the blankets. It was summer. The fear left by the recent drama hung in the air of the overheated room. Footsteps were rustling and doors creaked. The smell of the vinegar used to cool his mother's brow floated in the heavy air. She moved restlessly about, whimpering, sometimes giving a sudden start, which would shake him from his brief snatches of sleep. He would wake drenched in sweat, ready to act—only to fall back heavily after glancing at his watch on which the night light threw dancing

■ At this point Camus ends his first reverie and returns to the present.

■ Here Camus begins his second reverie.

shadows. It was only later that he realized how much they had been alone that night. Alone against the others. The "others" were asleep, while they both breathed the same fever. Everything in the old house seemed empty. With the last midnight trams all human hope seemed drained away, all the certainties of city noises gone. The house was still humming with their passage; then little by little everything died away. All that remained was a great garden of silence interrupted now and then by the sick woman's frightened moans. He had never felt so lost. The world had melted away, taking with it the illusion that life begins again each morning. Nothing was left, his studies, ambitions, things he might choose in a restaurant, favorite colors. Nothing but the sickness and death he felt surrounded by. . . . And yet, at the very moment that the world was crumbling, he was alive. Finally he fell asleep, but not without taking with him the tender and despairing image of two people's loneliness together. Later, much later, he would remember this mingled scent of sweat and vinegar, this moment when he had felt the ties attaching him to his mother. As if she were the immense pity he felt spread out around him, made flesh, diligently, without pretense, playing the part of a poor old woman whose fate moves men to tears.

1937

■ At this point Camus begins to understand his feelings for his mother.

■ **Theme** (page 871): Note that Camus's theme is implied rather than stated.

THINK AND DISCUSS
Understanding
1. What "happens" in this excerpt?
2. What were some of the difficulties experienced by Camus's mother?

Analyzing
3. What does the atmosphere of the cafe contribute to the mood of this essay?
4. What does Camus mean when he writes, "There is a solitude in poverty, but it is a solitude that gives everything back its value"?
5. What is the emotional relationship between Camus and his mother?

Extending
6. The title of the essay, "Between Yes and No," signifies the choice between accepting and rejecting life. Based on the portion of the essay you have read, what response does Camus make to this choice?

REVIEWING LITERARY TERMS
Setting
1. What is the actual setting of the selection?
2. What is the setting of Camus's first reverie? of his second?

Imagery
3. In the opening sentence, Camus mentions "a feeling of strangeness." How does the imagery of the first paragraph help convey that feeling?
4. In Camus's first reverie, how does the imagery emphasize the poverty of his family?

Characterization
5. What physical handicap does Camus's mother have?
6. How does this handicap affect her communication with others?
7. In writing about his mother, what does Camus reveal about his own personality?

Theme
8. How does the last sentence of this excerpt relate to Camus's theme in "Between Yes and No"?

■ CONTENT REVIEW
THINKING SKILLS
Classifying
1. Some of the selections in Unit 8 picture traditional (i.e., pre-industrial) societies; others picture societies essentially modern. Classify

each of the following selections under the heading "traditional" or "modern." (a) "An Old Man"; (b) "To the New Moon"; (c) "March Evening"; (d) "Such Perfection"; (e) *The African Child*.

Generalizing

2. A significant theme in recent literature has been the past. Using the selections by Borges, Anouilh, and Voznesensky, make several generalizations about the manner in which contemporary writers have employed the past as a theme.

Synthesizing

3. Unit 8 is a chronological grouping. Employing one of the themes that have been discussed earlier in the book, such as The Quest, The Artist, The Social Order, or The Outsider, create a thematic grouping of some of the Unit 8 selections, explaining in a paragraph how each selection you have chosen embodies this theme.

Evaluating

4. Both *The African Child* and "Everyday Use" picture societies in transition. Selecting one or both of these selections, discuss and react to the cultural values expressed.

■ COMPOSITION REVIEW

Writing a Letter

A major reason for studying world literature is to gain an understanding of people who come from cultures other than our own. Write a letter to one of the editors of this book in which you discuss what you have learned about these people from this unit and evaluate the unit in terms of what you have learned. Be sure to refer specifically to the selections that you consider to be especially important.

Discussing Family Relationships

A number of the selections in this unit deal with family relationships: "The Old Man," "The Circular Ruins," "To My Father," *Antigone*, *The African Child*, "Everyday Use," and "Between Yes and No." Write a five-paragraph composition for your teacher in which you discuss the importance of family relationships and

explain how they are treated in any three of these selections. Use your first paragraph for a general introduction, then allot one paragraph apiece to the selections you are using, and use your final paragraph to summarize the points you have been making.

Discussing Background Detail

Some of the selections in this unit are rich in background detail. In a five-paragraph composition for your teacher, discuss the purpose of this detail and its effectiveness in any three of the following: "The Old Man," "Everyday Use," "Between Yes and No," and *The African Child*. As an alternative, compare and contrast one of these selections with one in which the use of background detail is sparse, such as "The Circular Ruins" or "Such Perfection."

Comparing and Contrasting Short Stories

This unit contains four short stories that vary in setting and other elements: "The Old Man," "The Circular Ruins," "Such Perfection," and "Everyday Use." Select any two of them and write a five-paragraph composition for your classmates in which you compare and contrast them with regard to whichever of the following elements of the short story seem most appropriate: plot, setting, characterization, point of view, theme, and style. Probably you will not use all of these elements, and possibly you will find other points of comparison. As an alternative, do an in-depth comparison of the styles of any two of these short-story authors.

Writing Literary Criticism

One of the purposes of literature is to cast light on the human condition, to deepen our understanding of ourselves and others. Select two or three of the selections in this unit that you think are especially effective in carrying out this purpose, and write a five-paragraph composition for your classmates in which you explain why you have chosen them. Make your first paragraph general in nature, your next three specific with regard to your selections, and your last a conclusion that sums up your findings/reasons. You might wish to join with other students writing on this topic to do a tabulation to see which selections are mentioned most frequently.

Édouard Manet (1832–1883), *Portrait of Émile Zola* (detail). 1868. Musée d'Orsay, Paris

HANDBOOK OF LITERARY TERMS

■ ALLITERATION

"Loki, Loki, listen well.
Unmarked by men, unmarked by gods,
Someone has stolen my sacred Hammer."

These lines are spoken by Thor at the beginning of "The Lay of Thrym" (page 305). What consonant sound is repeated in the first line? the second? the third? The repetition of sounds, usually consonants, at the beginning of words or accented syllables is called **alliteration.** Alliteration, which may appear in one line or run throughout several lines, can serve to unify thoughts, to reinforce meaning, or simply to create a musical effect. Norse poetry, such as "The Lay of Thrym," relies heavily on alliteration to establish its meter and convey its mood.

Note the sounds alliterated in the following lines that describe the bold knight Sir Lancelot:

His broad clear brow in sunlight glowed;
On burnished hooves his war-horse trode;
From underneath his helmet flowed
His coal-black curls as on he rode,
    As he rode down to Camelot.

Alfred, Lord Tennyson
from **"The Lady of Shalott"**

1. What initial consonant sounds are alliterated within a line or between lines?
2. What impressions about Lancelot do the sounds in the descriptions "broad brow" and "coal-black curls" convey? Consider, for example, what would be lost if "wide forehead" and "dark, wavy hair" were substituted for the original phrases.

■ ALLITERATION

The repetition of sounds, usually consonants, at the beginning of words or accented syllables.

■ Apply to **"The Lay of Thrym,"** page 305.

■ ALLUSION

As you read the following poem, recall the biblical story of Ruth (page 27).

Ruth

They would waken
face to face, the windshield
crystalled, the car
so cold they had to get out.
5 Beyond the apple orchard
they saw where the dawn sun
fell among plowed fields
in little mounds of shadow
and a small stream ran black below
10 where the rocks slept.
Her wrists pounding
against it, she rubbed
the water into eyes
and temples, the iron taste
15 faint on her tongue.
And they'd get going, stopping
for Cokes and gas
and cold candy bars all
through Ohio,
20 and when the sun failed
north of Toledo,
they were almost there,
the night sky burning
up ahead at River Rouge[1]
25 like another day.

Another day.
Now he was gone, the children
grown up and gone,
and she back home,
30 or whatever you could call it,
West Virginia,
A wafer of sunlight
on the pillow, and she rose
and heard the mice startled
35 beneath the floorboards. Washed
in the sink, lit the stove,
and waited. Another day
falling into the fields, tufted
like a child's quilt.

1. **River Rouge,** a manufacturing town near Detroit.

40 Beyond the empty yard,
   a wall of poplars stared back,
   their far sides
   still darkness, and beyond,
   its teeth dulled with rust,
45 the harrow tilted
   on one frozen wheel, sliding
   back to earth.

Philip Levine

1. What is the setting of the first stanza? the
   second?
2. What time period elapses before the events
   in the second stanza?
3. In what sense has the woman in the poem
   undergone both a physical and an emotional
   journey?

Apart from the title, this poem can be read as
a narrative about a woman who travels with her
family from West Virginia to Michigan, then
returns home years later. Yet the poem's meaning is enhanced if one is familiar with the biblical story of Ruth. There are similarities between
the title character of this poem and the Moabite
Ruth of the Old Testament. The biblical Ruth,
a young childless widow, faithfully follows her
mother-in-law to her native land, Bethlehem in
Judea. What similarities can you find between
these two Ruths? How are they different?

Although these Ruths live in far different
times and places, they have both followed a
loved one to an unfamiliar place. Levine's poem
has special significance for readers who recognize why the title character is named Ruth. Such
a reference to something outside the work itself
is called an **allusion.** An **allusion** is a brief reference to a person, event, or place, real or fictional, or to a work of art.

Allusions may draw on literature (referring to
an impractical, foolish person as a *Don Quixote*),
history (the term *Watergate* as used to indicate
a political scandal), the Bible (labeling an ideal
place an *Eden*), mythology (referring to a handsome man as an *Adonis*), or any aspect of ancient
or modern society or culture (references to the
second half of the twentieth century as the
atomic age). *The Prince* by Machiavelli (page
394) is full of historical, literary, and mythological allusions.

"I think it's high time you had a holiday, Miss Fraser."

Recognizing allusions, which can serve to
establish character, mood, setting, or tone, in
a work, adds substantially to a reader's enjoyment and understanding. Sometimes, comprehending an allusion is essential to a reader's
basic understanding of a work. For example,
you must understand the biblical allusion in the
title of "Lot's Wife" (page 820) to fully comprehend the poem. In such cases, you must rely on
your own knowledge; refer to footnotes, if they
are provided; or do research.

The cartoon above is humorous only to someone familiar with the mythological Medusa, a
hideous creature with snakes for hair, whose
gaze turned people to stone.

■ ALLUSION

**A reference to a person, thing, event,
situation, or aspect of culture, real or
fictional. Art, mythology, religion, literature,
history, or any aspect of culture may be a
source of allusion. Allusion may contribute to
the vividness of a work or be central to its very
meaning.**

■ Apply to **On Friendship**, page 230.

Allusion 939

■ ANALOGY

The Arrow and the Song

I shot an arrow into the air,
It fell to earth, I knew not where;
For, so swiftly it flew, the sight
Could not follow it in its flight.

5 I breathed a song into the air,
It fell to earth, I knew not where;
For who has sight so keen and strong
That it can follow the flight of song?

Long, long afterward, in an oak
10 I found the arrow, still unbroke;
And the song, from beginning to end,
I found again in the heart of a friend.

Henry Wadsworth Longfellow

1. What acts does the speaker perform in the first two stanzas of the poem?
2. What are the effects of these acts, according to the final stanza?

Longfellow describes the far-reaching effects of a kind word or act by making a comparison. This kind of detailed comparison between two objects, events, situations, or ideas that are basically unlike but share something in common is called an **analogy.** Frequently a complex or unfamiliar object or idea is compared to a simpler or familiar one in order to explain the first. An arrow shot and found much later solidly wedged in a tree memorably conveys the influence of a kind word or act toward a friend. Analogies are often stated like this: a kind act (or word) is to a friend as an arrow is to a tree; or, more briefly, *kindness : friend :: arrow : tree.*

Note the detailed comparison developed in the following description.

The face of the water, in time, became a wonderful book—a book that was a dead language to the uneducated passenger, but which told its mind to me without reserve, delivering its most cherished secrets as clearly as if it uttered them with a voice. And it was not a book to be read once and thrown aside, for it had a new story to tell every day. Throughout the long twelve hundred miles there was never a page that was void of interest, never one that you could leave unread without loss, never one that you would want to skip, thinking you could find higher enjoyment in some other thing. There never was so wonderful a book written by man; never one whose interest was so absorbing; so unflagging, so sparklingly renewed with every reperusal. The passenger who could not read it was charmed with a peculiar sort of faint dimple on its surface (on the rare occasions when he did not overlook it altogether); but to the pilot that was an *italicized* passage; indeed, it was more than that, it was a legend of the largest capitals, with a string of shouting exclamation points at the end of it, for it meant that a wreck or a rock was buried there that could tear the life out of the strongest vessel that ever floated. It is the faintest and simplest expression the water ever makes, and the most hideous to a pilot's eye. In truth, the passenger who could not read this book saw nothing but all manner of pretty pictures in it, painted by the sun and shaded by the clouds, whereas to the trained eye these were not pictures at all, but the grimmest and most dead earnest of reading matter.

Mark Twain
from *Life on the Mississippi*

1. What are three similarities between the water (the Mississippi River) and a book?
2. In what sense might a buried rock be "a legend of the largest capitals, with a string of shouting exclamation points at the end"?
3. According to this analogy, what is the "most dead earnest of reading matter"?

■ ANALOGY

A rather fully developed comparison between two things or ideas that are basically unlike although they share something in common. Frequently, something unfamiliar or complex will be described in terms of something familiar or simple.

■ Apply to the **Apology,** page 221.

■ APOSTROPHE

In Ovid's *Metamorphoses* (page 254), Pyramus and Thisbe address the wall that separates them in this way:

. . . "You envious barrier,
Why get in our way? Would it be too much to ask you
To open wide for an embrace, or even
Permit us room to kiss in? Still, we are grateful,
5 We owe you something, we admit; at least
You let us talk together."

This kind of direct address of an inanimate object, a person not present or living, or an abstract quality is called an **apostrophe**. The use of apostrophe can serve to heighten mood, intensify thought, or even to provide humor. In Milton's *Paradise Lost* (page 500), Satan lures Eve to the fruit of the forbidden tree by apostrophizing it thus:

"O sacred, wise, and wisdom-giving plant,
Mother of science, now I feel thy power
Within me clear, not only to discern
Things in their causes, but to trace the ways
Of highest agents, deemed however wise.

In Marlowe's *Doctor Faustus* (page 485), Faustus, who is about to be carried away to Hell, pleads with the universe to stop moving and allow him to live longer:

"Stand still, you ever-moving spheres of heaven,
That time may cease and midnight never come."

Various poems have apostrophized the sun, the moon, sleep, different features of the face, historical figures, and emotions ranging from love to despair. Many poems begin with an invocation, or apostrophe, to a muse—the spirit that inspires a poet, composer, or writer.

■ APOSTROPHE

A figure of speech in which an absent or dead person, an abstract concept, or an inanimate object is directly addressed.

■ Apply to **"The River-Merchant's Wife: A Letter,"** page 84.

■ ARCHETYPE

Most Americans and many people outside of the United States would recognize the wandering hero known as the Lone Ranger. Although this character is a product of the American Old West, he is a direct descendant of ancient wanderers from other countries such as Odysseus (page 126) and Don Quixote (page 406). A recognizable character, symbol, plot, or theme that appears in a variety of myths, folklore, and literature from many cultures is called an **archetype**.

Both *The Tempest* (page 415) and *Paradise Lost* (page 500) portray an archetypal character who has fallen from good fortune or grace and is banished. Other archetypal characters in literature include the young initiate, the comical sidekick, and the fatal woman. Which of these archetypes can you find in selections in this book?

Some archetypal themes include those of love, guilt, redemption, and death. Plot structures can also be archetypes. One such plot pattern, based on the hero's descent into the underworld, appears in Dante's *Inferno* (page 316). Another archetypal plot involves the process of death and rebirth, as described in the *Bhagavad Gita* (page 60): "As a man leaves an old garment and puts on one that is new, the Spirit leaves his mortal body and wanders on to one that is new." Another archetypal plot structure involves an attempted flight in which one meets the very thing he is fleeing from. This pattern of ironic flight appears in "The Man Who Fled from Azrael" (page 48) and *Oedipus the King* (page 165).

Some works are archetypal in more ways than one. Among the many archetypal characters in *The Tempest* are the banished hero, the innocent young woman, and the kindly old counselor. Both the sea voyage and the enchanted island provide archetypal settings, while the theme of estrangement from and reconciliation with a family member is a fundamental plot pattern.

As you read, you will recognize repeated universal patterns that are appealing on basic and unconscious levels, as myths and dreams are. Such patterns evoke in readers a strong emotional response. For example, readers of

The Tempest find the reconciliation of Prospero and Antonio especially stirring because it fulfills expectations and completes a pattern.

■ ARCHETYPE

A character, symbol, plot, or theme that recurs often enough in literary works to have universal significance. Archetypes appeal to readers on a fundamental level, as dreams and myths do.

■ Apply to **The Epic of Gilgamesh**, page 12.

The Prodigal Son, a wood engraving by Albrecht Dürer (1471–1528)

■ ASSONANCE

Here, where the world is quiet;
  Here, where all trouble seems
Dead winds' and spent waves' riot
  In doubtful dreams of dreams;
5 I watch the green field growing
For reaping folk and sowing,
For harvest-time and mowing,
  A sleepy world of streams.

Algernon Charles Swinburne
from **"The Garden of Proserpine"**

How would you describe the mood of the passage above? What word is repeated in line 4? What other words in this passage echo the long *e* sound in *dreams*?

The recurring long *e* sound in these lines is an example of **assonance**—identical vowel sounds followed by different consonant sounds (green/ field/ sleepy/ streams). Assonance differs from rhyme, in which both the vowel sounds and the consonant sounds that follow them are identical (green/ seen; field/ shield). The use of assonance can enhance musical quality, reinforce meaning, and establish mood in a work. In the preceding passage by Swinburne, assonance establishes a peaceful mood and serves to unify the stanza.

Determine where assonance occurs in the following lines.

Thou still unravished bride of quietness,
Thou foster-child of silence and slow time, . . .

John Keats
from **"Ode on a Grecian Urn"**

And the Raven, never flitting, still is sitting, *still* is sitting
On the pallid bust of Pallas just above my chamber door.

Edgar Allan Poe
from **"The Raven"**

■ ASSONANCE

The repetition of identical vowel sounds followed by different consonant sounds.

■ Apply to the **Song of Roland**, page 284.

■ BLANK VERSE

The passage below describes Satan, who is banished by God for his rebellion. As you read the lines softly to yourself, note their rhythm.

Nine times the space that measure day and night
To mortal men, he, with his horrid crew,
Lay vanquished, rolling in the fiery gulf,
Confounded, though immortal. But his doom
5 Reserved him to more wrath; for now the thought
Both of lost happiness and lasting pain
Torments him: round he throws his baleful eyes,
That witnessed huge affliction and dismay,
Mixed with obdurate pride and steadfast hate.
10 At once, as far as Angels ken, he views
The dismal situation waste and wild.
A dungeon horrible, on all sides round,
As one great furnace flamed; yet from those flames
No light; but rather darkness visible
15 Served only to discover sights of woe,
Regions of sorrow, doleful shades, where peace
And rest can never dwell, hope never comes. . . .

John Milton
from **Paradise Lost**

What is the predominant rhythm of these lines? Are the lines rhymed or unrhymed: *Paradise Lost* is written in **blank verse**— unrhymed iambic pentameter. A line of iambic pentameter has five units or feet, each with an unaccented syllable followed by an accented one (‿ ´). The rhythm of the first line can be indicated as follows.

Nine times the space that measure day and night.

Popularized in the sixteenth century by English poets, blank verse reflects the natural, conversational rhythms of English speech. Occasionally, lines in a blank-verse passage may vary from a strict iambic pentameter pattern. Such departures can lend variety and reinforce meaning. For example, line 9 in the preceding passage from *Paradise Lost,* which contains feet that are not iambic, highlights the intense emotions of Satan.

Read the following excerpts and determine which use blank verse.

"My father loved injustice, and lived long;
Crowned with gray hairs he died, and full of sway.
I loved the good he scorned, and hated wrong—
The gods declare my recompense today. . . ."

Matthew Arnold
from **"Mycerinus"**

Beat! beat! beat!—blow! bugles! blow!
Through the windows—through doors—burst like a
  ruthless force,
Into the solemn church, and scatter the congregation,
Into the school where the scholar is studying . . .

Walt Whitman
from **"Beat! Beat! Drums!"**

But do not let us quarrel any more.
No, my Lucrezia; bear with me for once:
Sit down and all shall happen as you wish.
You turn your face, but does it bring your heart?

Robert Browning
from **"Andrea Del Sarto"**

■ BLANK VERSE

Unrhymed poetry in iambic pentameter—lines of five feet, each foot with an unstressed syllable followed by a stressed one. Blank verse reflects the natural rhythms of the English language.

■ Apply to **The Tempest**, page 434.

■ CHARACTERIZATION

In the following novel excerpt, Aleksei Vronsky, a young Russian officer, is described by another character.

"Vronsky is one of the sons of Count Kirill Ivanovitch Vronsky, and one of the finest specimens of the gilded youth of Petersburg. I made his acquaintance in Tver when I was there on official business, and he came there for the levy of recruits. Fearfully rich, handsome, great connections, an aide-de-camp, and with all that a very nice, good-natured fellow. But he's more than simply a good-natured fellow, as I've found out here—he's a cultivated man, too, and very intelligent; he's a man who'll make his mark."

Leo Tolstoy
from **Anna Karenina**

1. What do you learn about Vronsky's background and personality in this passage?
2. What details provided in the passage seem to indicate that Vronsky will "make his mark"?

The means by which an author introduces and develops a character is called **characterization.** Writers may create lifelike characters by describing their physical appearance, personality, behavior, thoughts, feelings, or speech.

The character of Vronsky is further developed in the paragraph below.

". . . I traveled yesterday with Vronsky's mother," she went on; "and his mother talked without a pause of him, he's her favorite. I know mothers are partial, but . . . "

"What did his mother tell you?"

"Oh, a great deal! And I know that he's her favorite; still one can see how chivalrous he is . . . Well, for instance, she told me that he had wanted to give up all his property to his brother, that he had done something extraordinary when he was quite a child, saved a woman out of the water. He's a hero, in fact," said Anna. . . .

1. What details indicate that Vronsky is "more than simply a good-natured fellow"?
2. Do you think that this passage presents a character who is too heroic? If so, read the

following passage, which describes Vronsky.

If Vronsky had indeed on previous occasions struck and impressed people who did not know him by his air of unhesitating composure, he seemed now more haughty and self-possessed than ever. He looked at people as if they were things. A nervous young man, a clerk in a law-court, sitting opposite him, hated him for that look. . . .

Vronsky saw nothing and no one. He felt himself a king, not because he believed that he had made an impression on Anna—he did not yet believe that,—but because the impressions she had made on him gave him happiness and pride.

What would come of it all he did not know, he did not even think. He felt that all his forces, hitherto dissipated, wasted, were centered on one thing. . . .

What additional information about Vronsky is revealed in this passage?

Vronsky is a *round* character—that is, he is fully developed and acts according to complex and believable patterns of emotion, motivation, and behavior. The title character in *Madame Bovary* (page 661) is a round character, as is Nora Helmer in *A Doll House* (page 712).

Flat characters, on the other hand, are one-dimensional and lacking in complexity. Flat characters who behave in predictable patterns or present a fixed, generalized view about people or groups of people are called *stereotypes*.

Another way to classify characters is *dynamic* versus *static*. Dynamic characters develop and grow in response to events or motives, while static ones remain the same throughout the course of the narrative, untouched by events and people they encounter.

■ CHARACTERIZATION

The means an author uses to develop the personality of a character in a literary work. Authors can describe a character's physical appearance, personality, thoughts, behavior, feelings, and speech. Characters may be *round* or *flat*—as in a *stereotype*—and *dynamic* or *static*.

■ Apply to **The Odyssey**, page 143.

■ CONNOTATION/ DENOTATION

In the excerpt from *Don Quixote* (page 406), the protagonist, whose old horse has more faults than a clown's "jade, which was all skin and bone," names his nag Rozinante and raises him "to his present status of first of all the hacks in the world." Then Don Quixote and his steed venture out into the world.

1. How many synonyms for *horse* can you find in the preceding paragraph?
2. Which of these words has favorable associations? unfavorable associations?

Many words have a double significance— strict dictionary definitions, or **denotations**, and emotional associations that are personal or universal, called **connotations**. *Jade* (an inferior or worn-out horse), *hack* (a work horse), *nag*, and *steed* are all synonyms for horse. Yet the first three words, whether used to describe a horse or a human, conjure up unfavorable associations. The word *steed*, on the other hand, suggests a noble animal, worthy of a knight-errant, as Don Quixote fancies himself. To understand a work of literature, one must recognize not only the denotations of words, but also their connotations, which enhance the overall meaning.

What associations do you have for the word *sunrise*? Beginnings? an early morning jog? the sound of an alarm clock? How do these personal associations differ from the following dictionary definition?

sun rise (sun′rīz′), *n.* **1** the first appearance of the sun above the horizon at the beginning of day. **2** the time when the sun first appears; the beginning of day. **3** the display of light or color in the sky at this time.

The following lines express the connotations that sunrise has for Romeo.

ROMEO.
  (Catching sight of JULIET *at her dimly lighted window.)*
  But soft, what light through yonder window
    breaks?
  It is the east, and Juliet is the sun.
  Arise, fair sun, and kill the envious moon,

5 Who is already sick and pale with grief,
  That thou her maid art far more fair than she.

William Shakespeare
from **Romeo and Juliet**

1. To what does Romeo compare the sunrise?
2. Are these connotations favorable or unfavorable?
3. Why would the moon be envious of Juliet?

As you read the following passage, determine what connotations the word *sunrise* has for Kate Clephane.

No more sunrises for Kate Clephane. They were associated with too many lost joys—coming home from balls where one had danced one's self to tatters, or from suppers where one had lingered, counting one's winnings (it was wonderful, in the old days, how often she had won, or friends had won for her, staking a *louis* just for fun, and cramming her hands with thousand franc bills); associated, too, with the scramble up hill through the whitening gray of the garden, flicked by scented shrubs, caught on perfidious prickles, up to the shuttered villa askew on its heat-soaked rock—and then, at the door, in the laurustinus-shade that smelt of honey, that unexpected kiss. . . .

Edith Wharton
from **The Mother's Recompense**

1. With what does Kate Clephane associate sunrise?
2. Are her associations pleasant or unpleasant?

■ CONNOTATION

The emotional or cultural associations surrounding a word, as opposed to its strict, literal dictionary meaning.

■ DENOTATION

The strict dictionary meaning of a word, presented objectively, without emotional associations.

■ Apply to **A Portrait of the Artist as a Young Man**, page 778.

■ CONSONANCE

Arms and the Boy

Let the boy try along this bayonet-blade
How cold steel is, and keen with hunger of blood;
Blue with all malice, like a madman's flash;
And thinly drawn with famishing for flesh.

5 Lend him to stroke these blind, blunt bullet-leads
Which long to nuzzle in the hearts of lads,
Or give him cartridges of fine zinc teeth,
Sharp with the sharpness of grief and death.

For his teeth seem for laughing round an apple,
10 There lurk no claws behind his fingers supple;
And God will grow no talons at his heels,
Nor antlers through the thickness of his curls.

Wilfred Owen

1. Do the final words in each pair of lines produce exact rhymes?
2. What is similar about the sounds in word pairs such as *leads/lads, teeth/death*? *apple/supple* and *heels/curls*?

Although there are no exact rhymes in the final words in each pair of lines, these words share common sounds. Such repetition of identical consonant sounds that are preceded by different vowel sounds is called **consonance**. Like any sound device, consonance contributes to the musical effects of a poem. In addition, it reinforces meaning by suggesting associations between word pairs such as *blade* and *blood*.

■ CONSONANCE

The repetition of identical consonant sounds that are preceded by different vowel sounds.

■ Apply to **The Rape of the Lock**, page 560.

■ COUPLET

Why has not Man a microscopic eye?
For this plain reason, Man is not a Fly.

Alexander Pope
from **An Essay on Man**

A thing of beauty is a joy forever;
Its loveliness increases; it will never
Pass into nothingness; but still will keep
A bower quiet for us, and a sleep . . .

John Keats
from "**Endymion**"

What is the rhyme scheme of each of the above excerpts? Is the rhythm of each rhyming pair the same or different?

In poetry, two consecutive rhymed lines having the same meter are called a **couplet**. *Tartuffe* is written entirely in couplets. A couplet may contain a complete thought, or the thought may continue beyond the end of the two lines. When a couplet contains a complete thought and is written in iambic pentameter, it is called a *heroic couplet*. The term comes from the notion that this meter aptly expresses the serious subjects that characterize epic or "heroic" verse.

Neoclassical writers of the eighteenth century in England found the heroic couplet well suited to their verse. Often such verse conveyed brief, witty observations called *epigrams*. (See page 947.)

1. Which of the poetic excerpts above contains a couplet that expresses a complete thought?
2. Which of the examples is a heroic couplet?

■ COUPLET

A pair of rhyming lines with identical meter. A heroic couplet is a pair of rhymed verse lines in iambic pentameter that contains a complete thought.

■ Apply to **Tartuffe**, page 517.

■ EPIGRAM

The heart that is distant creates its own solitude.

T'ao Ch'ien
from **"I Built My Cottage . . ."**

Thy praise or dispraise is to me alike;
One doth not stroke me, nor the other strike.

Ben Jonson
from **Epigrams**

Happy families are all alike; every unhappy family
    is unhappy in its own way.

Leo Tolstoy
from **Anna Karenina**

Know then thyself, presume not God to scan;
The proper study of mankind is *man*.

Alexander Pope
from **An Essay on Man**

Each of the preceding statements is a short, witty statement called an **epigram**. Originally, in Greece, epigrams were inscriptions on tombs. As such, they had to be brief, witty and insightful. Today, the term refers to a short poem or saying that expresses a truth or a bit of wisdom and often ends with a clever twist.

"The Soul of Goodness in Things Evil" (page 49) consists of a series of epigrams. Pope's *Essay on Man* (page 570) contains many epigrams in heroic couplet form, such as the one above. When a brief saying includes a moral, as the preceding observation about mankind by Pope does, it is called an *aphorism*. Closely related to epigrams and aphorisms are *proverbs*—brief traditional sayings known to many people that express popular wisdom: "Haste makes waste."

■ EPIGRAM

A short, witty saying, often ending with a clever twist.

■ Apply to **An Essay on Man**, page 570.

■ FIGURATIVE LANGUAGE

There Is a Garden in Her Face

There is a garden in her face
    Where roses and white lilies grow;
A heavenly paradise is that place,
    Wherein all pleasant fruits do flow:
5   There cherries grow which none may buy
        Till "Cherry-ripe" themselves do cry.
Those cherries fairly do enclose
    Of orient pearl a double row,
Which when her lovely laughter shows,
10   They look like rosebuds filled with snow;
        Yet them nor peer nor prince can buy
        Till "Cherry-ripe" themselves do cry.
Her eyes like angels watch them still;
    Her brows like bended bows do stand,
15 Threatening with piercing frowns to kill
    All that attempt, with eye or hand,
        Those sacred cherries to come nigh
        Till "Cherry-ripe" themselves do cry.

Thomas Campion

1. In what ways might a pretty face resemble a garden?
2. What are the two predominant colors mentioned in the poem, as suggested by lilies and pearls versus roses and cherries?
3. What parts of the beloved's face resemble cherries and pearls (lines 7–9)?
4. To what are the lover's brows compared (line 14)? Given this comparison, what do the "piercing frowns" represent?

The poet has used words in an imaginative way to describe a fair face. This description is not to be taken literally; that is, no one's face contains flowers or fruit. Yet these images serve to convey the color and vitality of a beautiful face.

Language that goes beyond the literal, matter-of-fact meanings of words is called **figurative language**. Such language, which provides vividness, conciseness, and force, helps readers see things in new ways. The various devices of figurative language are called *figures of speech*. The most common figures of speech are *sim-*

ile, *metaphor, personification, hyperbole, apostrophe, synecdoche,* and *metonymy.*

Simile

A **simile** is a direct comparison, indicated by the words *like, as, appears, than,* or *seems,* between two basically dissimilar things that nonetheless share something in common. In the preceding poem, Thomas Campion compares a beloved's lips to rosebuds, her eyes to angels, and her brows to bended bows.

A simile may be elaborate and extended over many lines. Common in epics, this type of simile is called an *epic simile.* Here is an epic simile from the *Odyssey* (page 126) describing the reunion of Odysseus and Penelope.

Now from his breast into his eyes the ache
of longing mounted, and he wept at last,
his dear wife, clear and faithful, in his arms,
longed for as the sunwarmed earth is longed for
    by a swimmer
5 spent in rough water where his ship went down
under Poseidon's blows, gale winds and tons
    of sea.
Few men can keep alive through a big surf
to crawl, clotted with brine, on kindly beaches
in joy, in joy, knowing the abyss behind . . . .

Metaphor

Like a simile, a **metaphor** compares two basically unlike things that have something in common. However, there is no connective such as *like* or *as* in a metaphor. Metaphors can be directly stated. (She is a volcano) or implied (She erupted, spewing out hot words of anger). Note that in line 15 of "There Is a Garden in Her Face" Campion implies, rather than directly states, that the woman's frowns are arrows, with the phrase "piercing frowns."

A metaphor that is developed at length throughout an entire work or part of it is called an *extended metaphor.* In "I Like to See It Lap the Miles" (page 680), Dickinson develops an extended metaphor comparing a train to a horse; "Hope Is the Thing with Feathers" (page 680) expresses at some length a comparison between hope and a bird.

Personification

Personification is a figure of speech in which human qualities are attributed to abstractions, ideas, animals, or inanimate objects. In "Because I Could Not Stop for Death" (page 681), Dickinson endows death with human qualities, portraying it as a gentleman caller who transports the speaker in his carriage. Milton, in *Paradise Lost* (page 500), uses personification in the following description of Eve's eating of the forbidden fruit: ". . . she plucked, she eat:/Earth felt the wound, and nature from her seat/Sighing through all her works gave tales of woe . . . ."

Hyperbole

A figure of speech that uses extreme exaggeration for effect is called **hyperbole.** References to "a mountain of food on a plate" or "eyes that shine brighter than the sun" are examples of hyperbole. Used chiefly for emphasis, hyperbole can achieve either a comic or a serious effect. The love poems of Catullus (pages 234–235), who claims that he loves "More than any man/Can ever love" and promises kisses "hundred thousands by the score," are hyperbolic.

Apostrophe

A figure of speech in which an inanimate object, a person not present or living, or an abstract quality is directly addressed is called an **apostrophe.** In "Soul, Soul" (page 157), Archilochus commands his soul: "Throw forward your chest . . ./But never crow in victory." "Akhenaton's Hymn to the Sun" (page 18) is one of many poems that addresses a celestial body. Many epics, such as *Paradise Lost* (page 500), begin with an apostrophe to a muse, or spirit of inspiration.

Synecdoche

Synecdoche is a figure of speech in which a part stands for the whole or the whole stands for a part. In the expression "All hands on deck," *hands* stands for laborers (part for whole). Referring to a policeman as "the law" is an example of using the whole to represent a part. Other examples of synecdoche are *sail* for boat, *motor* for automobile, *head* for person or animal, and *Broadway* for the commercial theater in general.

Metonymy

Metonymy is a figure of speech in which one term naming an object is substituted for another word with which it is closely associated. Thus money may be referred to as *bread* (which it buys) or *green* (its color), the President is represented as *the White House*, and pen is used to indicate the act of writing.

What figure of speech is illustrated in the cartoon below?

■ FIGURATIVE LANGUAGE

Language used in a nonliteral way to express a suitable relationship between essentially unlike things. Such use of language invests it with vitality and conciseness. The more common figures of speech are simile, metaphor, personification, hyperbole, apostrophe, synecdoche, and metonymy.

■ Apply to **The Epic of Gilgamesh**, page 9.

"It didn't tug at my heart."

■ FORESHADOWING

The following words are spoken by Oedipus in an effect to discover and avenge the death of King Laius.

Now my curse on the murderer. Whoever he is,
a lone man unknown in his crime
or one among many, let that man drag out
his life in agony, step by painful step—
5   I curse myself as well . . . if by any chance
he proves to be an intimate of our house,
here at my hearth, with my full knowledge,
may the curse I just called down on him strike me!

Sophocles
from **Oedipus the King**

Sophocles gives readers many hints of what is to happen in this play. The technique of providing clues about future events in a story is called **foreshadowing**. Oedipus does not realize that he is foreshadowing his own fate. But the audience, many of whom are familiar with the pattern of the plot, recognize the irony in Oedipus's prediction.

The following passage describes the reactions of a middle-class heroine to a brief encounter with wealth at a fancy ball.

. . . How far away the ball already seemed! Why should there be such a distance between yesterday morning and tonight? Her trip to Vaubyessard had made a gap in her life like one of those great crevices that a storm sometimes carves out in the mountains in a single night. She resigned herself, however; reverently she packed away in the chest of drawers her lovely dress and even her satin slippers, whose soles had yellowed from the floor wax. Her heart was like them; the wealth had rubbed off on her, something that would never be erased.

And so the memory of the ball became a preoccupation for Emma. . . .

Gustave Flaubert
from **Madame Bovary**

1. What do you think the author means by "the wealth had rubbed off on her"?
2. What future goals might this description foreshadow?

What example of foreshadowing do you find in the words that Romeo, about to marry Juliet, says to Friar Lawrence?

. . . But come what sorrow can,
It cannot countervail the exchange of joy
That one short minute gives me in her sight.
Do thou but close our hands with holy words,
Then love-devouring death do what he dare;
It is enough I may but call her mine.

William Shakespeare
from **Romeo and Juliet**

■ FORESHADOWING

The providing of clues about what is going to happen in the plot. Often, in drama, it is a source of irony, since the audience knows more about the outcome than the characters do.

■ Apply to the **Odyssey**, page 135.

"You won't get away with this!"

© Harley Schwadron

■ FREE VERSE

There Was Crimson Clash of War

There was crimson clash of war.
Lands turned black and bare;
Women wept;
Babes ran, wondering.
5 There came one who understood not these things.
He said: "Why is this?"
Whereupon a million strove to answer him.
There was such intricate clamor of tongues,
That still the reason was not.

Stephen Crane

Examine the line length and the rhythm of the poem above.

1. Are the lines of equal length?
2. Is the rhythm regular or irregular?
3. Do the lines rhyme?

Some poems lack regular rhythm and a definite rhyme scheme. Poems such as the preceding one by Crane are written in free verse—verse that is "free" from fixed patterns of rhythm, rhyme, and line length. Instead, free verse relies on poetic devices such as imagery, figurative language, and often some form of stanzaic organization to link ideas and provide unity. Most importantly, free verse achieves its music with sound devices such as repetition, assonance, consonance, and alliteration to achieve rhythmic effects. In the preceding poem, note the use of alliteration (crimson/clash, black/bare, women/wept/wondering); assonance (clash/lands/black); and consonance (war/bare).

As you read the following poem, look for patterns of rhythm and sound.

Good Night

Many ways to spell good night.

Fireworks at a pier on the Fourth of July
   spell it with red wheels and yellow spokes.
They fizz in the air, touch the water and quit.
Rockets make a trajectory of gold-and-blue
   and then go out.

5 Railroad trains at night spell with a smokestack
   mushrooming a white pillar.

Steamboats run a curve in the Mississippi
   crying in a baritone that crosses lowland
   cottonfields to a razorback hill.

It is easy to spell good night.
       Many ways to spell good night.

Carl Sandburg

1. What words and phrases are repeated in this poem?
2. What vowel sound is repeated in the words *red*, *spell*, and *yellow* in line 2? in the words *fizz*, *in*, and *quit* in line 3?
3. What initial consonant sound is alliterated in four words in line 6?

Imagine that Sandburg had chosen to use a consistent line length, regular rhythm, and end rhyme in a poem that began thus:

There are many ways to spell good night.
One such way is through fireworks bright—
Reds and yellows fizz, then fade,
Rockets that disappear in a parade.

What has been lost in this new version?

■ FREE VERSE

Verse that has no fixed patterns of rhyme, rhythm, or line length. Although "free" from the demands of regular rhythm and rhyme, free verse achieves its effects with sound devices and subtle patterns of rhythm.

■ Apply to "**Song of Myself**," page 652.

■ HYPERBOLE

A Red, Red Rose

O my luve is like a red, red rose,
  That's newly sprung in June;
O my luve is like the melodie
  That's sweetly played in tune.

5 As fair art thou, my bonnie lass,
  So deep in luve am I;
And I will luve thee still, my dear,
  Till a' the seas gang dry.

Till a' the seas gang dry, my dear,
10 And the rocks melt wi' the sun;
And I will luve thee still, my dear,
  While the sands o' life shall run.

And fare thee weel, my only luve,
  And fare thee weel a while!
And I will come agin, my luve,
  Tho' it were ten thousand mile!

              Robert Burns

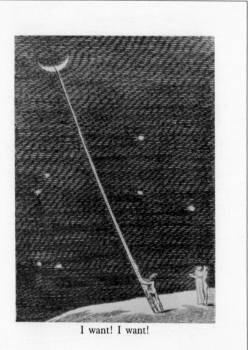

I want! I want!

William Blake (1757–1827), metal engraving for
The Gates of Paradise, 1793

1. What example of exaggeration can you find in stanza 2? stanza 3?
2. The poet might have chosen to say simply "I love you very much." Why do you think he chose to exaggerate?

Hyperbole is the use of exaggeration for effect. This effect might be comic, satiric, or sentimental, depending on the tone of the work. Which of these words would you choose to describe Burns's poem? Not confined to poetry, hyperbole is frequently found in legends such as the American tales of Paul Bunyan, and in yarns, such as the story about the day it was so cold that you couldn't find heat anywhere, not even in the dictionary. Many memorable quotations, such as this one by Gene Fowler, derive their wit from hyperbole: "Writing is easy; all you do is sit staring at a blank sheet of paper until the drops of blood form on your forehead."

In each of the following, what effect is achieved by the use of hyperbole?

Give place, ye lovers, here before
That spent your boasts and brags in vain;
My lady's beauty passeth more
5 The best of yours, I dare well sayn,
Than doth the sun the candle light,
Or brightest day the darkest night.

    Henry Howard, Earl of Surrey
    from "In Praise of His Love . . ."

The King's Epitaph

Here lies a great and mighty King,
  Whose promise none relies on;
He never said a foolish thing,
  Nor ever did a wise one.

    John Wilmot, Earl of Rochester

■ HYPERBOLE

The use of exaggeration for effect.

■ Apply to "**If That Shirazi Turk,**" page 54.

■ IMAGERY

When Father Came Home For Lunch

I listen to my parents' language,
watch my father eat his separate meal,
the railroad motor car
cooling off and waiting
5 on the siding by the section house.
He sits with his back to the burning woodstove
in a captain's chair
and eats the family left-overs,
a bowl of rice balanced in his hand,
10 chopsticks flicking
around to the bowls & dishes
arranged in front of him.

Mother adds fried onions, a fried egg
and potatoes to his main bowl.
15 He adds catsup, shoyu
and mixes it with the white radish,
egg plant and cold chicken.
He works around to the mustard-caked bowl
before each mouth of rice,
20 sauce hanging from his moustache.
Hot coffee, heavy with sugar & cream,
steams from a china mug.
Half-an-hour of noisy manners
and he's gone, back to work
25 in oily bib overalls.
I can still smell sweat
soaking his long-sleeved workshirt.

James Masao Mitsui

1. To which senses does this poem appeal?
2. What do you learn about the father?
3. Is the scene vague or vivid? Explain.

The poet uses word pictures that appeal to
the senses to add clarity and immediacy to his
description. Sensory details in a literary work
are called **imagery.** By describing experiences
known through the senses, imagery evokes in
readers a complex of emotional associations.

An image may appeal to any of these senses: sight, hearing, smell, taste, touch, internal feelings, or the motor sense that is related
to motion or muscle activity. Although Mitsui's
poem makes its primary appeal to the senses
of taste and sight, there are images that evoke

the senses of hearing (chopsticks flicking, noisy
manners) and smell (burning woodstove, oily
bib overalls, and sweat-soaked workshirt).

An image may be a simple, literal representation with no underlying meaning other
than the sights, sounds, or feelings described.
Most of the images in the preceding poem are
literal. Images may also be figurative, based on
unexpected associations or figures of speech. As
you read the following passage, find examples
of literal and figurative imagery.

. . . Someone pushed open the street door at two
in the afternoon in the mortal silence of the heat and
the braces in the foundation shook with such force
that Amaranta and her friends sewing on the porch,
Rebeca sucking her finger in her bedroom, Úrsula in
the kitchen, Aureliano in the workshop, and even José
Arcadio Buendía under the solitary chestnut tree had
the impression that an earthquake was breaking up the
house. A huge man had arrived. His square shoulders
barely fitted through the doorways. He was wearing a
medal of Our Lady of Help around his bison neck,
his arms and chest were completely covered with cryp-
tic tattooing, and on his right wrist was the tight copper bracelet of the *niños-en-cruz* amulet. His skin was
tanned by the salt of the open air, his hair was short
and straight like the mane of a mule, his jaws were of
iron, and he wore a sad smile. He had a belt on that
was twice as thick as the cinch of a horse, boots with
leggings and spurs and iron on the heels, and his presence gave the quaking impression of a seismic tremor.
He went through the parlor and the living room, carrying some half-worn saddlebags in his hand, and he
appeared like a thunderclap on the porch with the bego-
nias where Amaranta and her friends were paralyzed,
their needles in the air.

Gabriel García Márquez
from One Hundred Years of Solitude

■ IMAGERY

**Sensory details that provide vividness and
immediacy in a literary work by arousing in
readers a complex of emotional associations.**

■ Apply to **"A Dialogue of a Man with His Soul,"** page 17.

Imagery 953

■ INFERENCE

The following account is narrated by a young protagonist named David Copperfield.

. . . The garden bell rang. We went out to the door; and there was my mother, looking even unusually pretty, I thought, and with her a gentleman with beautiful black hair and whiskers, who had walked home with us from church last Sunday. . . .

He patted me on the head; but somehow, I didn't like him or his deep voice, and I was jealous that his hand should touch my mother's in touching me—which it did. I put it away, as roughly as I could.

"Oh Davy!" remonstrated my mother.

"Dear boy!" said the gentleman. "I cannot wonder at his devotion!"

I never saw such a beautiful color on my mother's face before. She gently chid me for being rude; and, keeping me close to her shawl, turned to thank the gentleman for taking so much trouble as to bring her home. She put out her hand to him as she spoke, and, as he met it with his own, she glanced, I thought, at me.

"Let us say 'good night,' my fine boy," said the gentleman, when he had bent his head—*I* saw him!—over my mother's little glove.

"Good night!" said I.

"Come! Let us be the best friends in the world!" said the gentleman, laughing. "Shake hands!"

My right hand was in my mother's left, so I gave him the other.

"Why that's the wrong hand, Davy!" laughed the gentleman.

My mother drew my right hand forward, but I was resolved, for my former reason, not to give it to him, and I did not. I gave him the other, and he shook it heartily, and said I was a brave fellow, and went away.

At this minute I see him turn round in the garden, and give us a last look with his ill-omened black eyes, before the door was shut.

Charles Dickens
from **David Copperfield**

1. What feelings does David have toward the gentleman? Can you find any indications that David's initial impressions are justified?
2. Why does David refuse to shake hands with his right hand?

3. Why do you think David's mother blushes at the gentleman's comment about David's devotion?
4. What indications are there that she is anxious David and the gentleman will become friends?

In answering these questions, you have made **inferences**—reasonable conclusions drawn from the information provided. In order to understand and appreciate literature, you must draw inferences from the information the author has included about the behavior of characters and the meaning of events. Dickens has provided clues in this passage by which you can infer that David's mother and the gentleman are romantically involved, that David is jealous, and that his mother is anxious for the males in her life to accept one another. Further, mention of the gentleman's "ill-omened black eyes" foreshadows his future mistreatment of David.

What inferences can you make about the cartoon below? On what have you based your inferences?

■ INFERENCE

A reasonable conclusion about characters or events based on the limited information provided by an author.

■ Apply to **Oedipus the King**, page 181.

BEWARE OF DOG!

■ IRONY

Why is this cartoon humorous? Your answer will probably touch on the fact that imminent disaster is about to befall the man as he takes great precautions to ensure his safety. A contrast between what is said and what is meant, between what is expected and what actually happens, or between what appears to be and what really is, is called **irony.**

Many comic one-liners derive their humor from irony. What is ironic about each of the following?

I love being a writer. What I can't stand is the paperwork. (Peter De Vries)

It took me fifteen years to discover I had no talent for writing, but I couldn't give it up because by that time I was too famous. (Robert Benchley)

There are three types of irony. In *verbal irony,* the surface meaning of words is opposite to the intended, underlying meaning. To detect verbal irony, readers must consider an author's tone. The following poem relies for its effect on verbal irony.

Does It Matter?

Does it matter?—losing your legs? . . .
For people will always be kind.
And you need not show that you mind
When the others come in after hunting
5 To gobble their muffins and eggs.

Does it matter?—losing your sight? . . .
There's such splendid work for the blind;
And people will always be kind.
As you sit on the terrace remembering
10 And turning your face to the light.

Do they matter?—those dreams from the pit? . . .
You can drink and forget and be glad,
And people won't say that you're mad;
For they'll know you've fought for your country
15 And no one will worry a bit.

Siegfried Sassoon

1. How would you answer the question posed in the title?

Drawing by Chas. Addams; © 1979 The New Yorker Magazine, Inc.

2. Read line 7 aloud as you think the poet intended it to be read. How would you describe your tone?

Irony of situation is a contrast between what is expected or intended and what actually happens. The cartoon on this page illustrates irony of situation, as do several selections in this book. The Moslem in "The Man Who Fled from Azrael" (page 48) encounters death, the very thing from which he flees.

Dramatic irony occurs when the reader or viewer knows more about the actual situation than the speaker or characters do. In *Oedipus the King* (page 165), the protagonist is unaware that he himself is the criminal he seeks, although the audience knows this.

■ IRONY

A contrast between what seems to be and what actually is. Verbal irony occurs when what is said is the opposite of what is meant. Irony of situation occurs when what actually happens is the opposite of what is expected; dramatic irony occurs when the audience or reader knows more than the characters do.

■ Apply to "The Padshah and the Slave," page 52.

■ LYRIC

Blow, Blow, Thou Winter Wind

Blow, blow, thou winter wind!
Thou art not so unkind
   As man's ingratitude;
Thy tooth is not so keen,
5 Because thou art not seen,
   Although thy breath be rude.
Heigh ho! sing, heigh ho! unto the green holly:
Most friendship is feigning, most loving mere folly:
10   Then, heigh ho, the holly!
   This life is most jolly.

   Freeze, freeze, thou bitter sky!
That dost not bite so nigh
   As benefits forgot;
15   Though thou the waters warp,
Thy sting is not so sharp
   As friend remembered not.
Heigh ho! sing, heigh ho!

William Shakespeare

1. What human faults does the wind remind the speaker of?
2. What basic emotions does the winter wind evoke for the speaker?
3. Why do you think the speaker addresses the winter wind rather than a spring breeze?

"Blow, Blow, Thou Winter Wind" is an example of a **lyric** poem—a short poem, personal in tone, in which a speaker expresses a state of mind or feeling rather than tells a story. To the Greeks, a lyric was a poem sung to the accompaniment of a lyre, a harplike instrument. A lyric can express any one of a wide range of emotions, from despair to exultation. In "Miserable with Desire" (page 156), for example, Archilochus communicates passionate desire, while "How Many Times" (page 158) expresses nostalgia.

During the English Renaissance, the lyric flourished. Many of Shakespeare's plays include lyrics, such as the preceding one from *As You*

Like It. The lyric has survived in modern poetry, retaining its musical qualities, personal tone, and sustained emotion. Some examples are "Sense of Something Coming" (page 776), "Hands Clenched Under My Shawl" (page 820), and "To My Husband" (page 829).

The structure of a lyric may be formal, as in odes and sonnets, or irregular, such as with free verse. In order to achieve a sustained emotional quality, lyric poetry relies heavily on sound devices and mood to convey its ideas.

Here is another lyric from a Shakespearean play. What emotion is evoked?

O Mistress Mine

O mistress mine, where are you roaming?
O stay and hear; your true love's coming,
   That can sing both high and low:
5 Trip no further, pretty sweeting;
Journeys end in lovers meeting,
   Every wise man's son doth know.
What is love? 't is not hereafter;
Present mirth hath present laughter;
   What's to come is still unsure:
10 In delay there lies no plenty;
Then come kiss me, sweet and twenty;
   Youth's a stuff will not endure.

William Shakespeare
from **Twelfth Night**

■ LYRIC

A brief, highly personal poem in which a speaker expresses a feeling or state of mind, such as love, anguish, or regret.

■ Apply to the poetry of Sappho, pages 159–160.

■ METAPHOR

The following description appears at the beginning of a short story. As you read it, look for comparisons the author makes in order to describe this character.

Besides the neutral expression that she wore when she was alone, Mrs. Freeman had two others, forward and reverse, that she used for all her human dealings. Her forward expression was steady and driving like the advance of a heavy truck. Her eyes never swerved to left or right but turned as the story turned as if they followed a yellow line down the center of it . . . .

Flannery O'Connor
from **"Good Country People"**

1. To what is the author comparing Mrs. Freeman?
2. What words indicate this comparison?
3. Judging from this description, what kind of person is Mrs. Freeman?

This description of Mrs. Freeman in terms of a car or truck relies on a figure of speech called a metaphor. Like a simile, a **metaphor** makes a comparison between two basically unlike things that nonetheless have something in common. Unlike a simile, a metaphor uses no connective such as *like* or *as*. "She is very protective of her children" is a literal statement. "She is a mother hen" restates the same idea as a metaphor. A metaphor may be implied rather than directly stated: "She clucks over her brood of children."

Metaphors must be both appropriate and consistent. An inconsistent metaphor such as the following is called a *mixed metaphor*: "Unless you can iron out your difficulties, you'll be all washed up." Like all figurative language, metaphors force associations that provide fresh insights.

A figurative comparison that is developed throughout an entire work or a large part of it is called an *extended metaphor*. Note how two things are compared at length and in several ways in the following poem.

My Sheep Are Thoughts

My sheep are thoughts, which I both guide
   and serve;
Their pasture is fair hills of fruitless love;
On barren sweets they feed, and feeding sterve![1]
I wail their lot, but will not other prove;
5 My sheep-hook is wan hope, which all upholds;
My weeds,[2] desire, cut out in endless folds;
What wool my sheep shall bear, whilst thus
   they live,
In you it is, you must the judgment give.

Sir Philip Sidney
from **Arcadia**

---

1. *sterve,* starve.
2. *weeds,* clothes.

---

1. What kind of work does the speaker do?
2. Does the speaker's love appear to be returned or not? What words or phrases indicate this?
3. What will determine whether or not the sheep will bear wool, according to lines 7 and 8?

According to this poem, the shepherd is the victim of barren, fruitless love. All hope of fruitfulness (bearing wool) depends on the judgment (decision) of the lover.

■ METAPHOR

A figurative comparison between two basically unlike things without using connectives such as *like* or *as*.

■ Apply to the Psalms, page 33.

■ MOOD

The cold passed reluctantly from the earth, and the retiring fogs revealed an army stretched out on the hills, resting. As the landscape changed from brown to green, the army awakened, and began to tremble with eagerness at the noise of rumors. It cast its eyes upon the roads, which were growing from long troughs of liquid mud to proper thoroughfares. A river, amber-tinted in the shadow of its banks, purled at the army's feet; and at night, when the stream had become of a sorrowful blackness, one could see across it the red, eyelike gleam of hostile campfires set in the low brows of distant hills.

Stephen Crane
from **The Red Badge of Courage**

1. How would you describe the atmosphere of this passage?
2. What words and phrases create this atmosphere?
3. To what sense does the description mainly appeal?

Crane has used phrases ("tremble with eager-ness," "noise of rumors") and images of color ("brown to green," "red, eyelike gleam of hos-tile campfires") to create an atmosphere of ten-sion and expectancy. The atmosphere and feel-ing that writers create in a work through their choice of words, images, setting, and details is called **mood**. Words that describe mood can range from *peaceful* and *joyful* to *foreboding* and *eerie*.

In some works, the mood that is established at the beginning is generally sustained through-out. For example, Shakespeare uses the witches in the opening scene of Macbeth to establish a prevailing atmosphere of evil and the super-natural. Often the mood of a written work will shift, thus providing a dramatic change of pace. For example, the drowsy peacefulness in *Life on the Mississippi* (page 684) gives way to bustling excitement once the steamboat arrives.

Note the mood in the following passage from *A Portrait of the Artist as a Young Man* (page 778).

He was alone. He was unheeded, happy and near to the wild heart of life. He was alone and young and willful and wild-hearted, alone amid a waste of wild air and brackish waters and the sea-harvest of shells and tangle and veiled grey sunlight and gayclad lightclad figures of children and girls and voices childish and girlish in the air.

1. How would you describe this mood?
2. What words and phrases help create this atmosphere?

Not confined to literature, mood is an impor-tant quality in works of art and music. How would you describe the mood established in the picture below?

■ MOOD

The general atmosphere or prevailing emotion of a work, as created by the choice of words, setting, images, and details.

■ Apply to "**Hands Clenched Under My Shawl**," page 820.

Douglass Percy Bliss, *The Fall of the House of Usher*. 1938

■ NARRATIVE POETRY

The following poem narrates a story found in the Bible (II Kings 19:35). In the eighth century B.C., King Sennacherib of Assyria led his army against Jerusalem. But the night before the attack, a plague destroyed the army. According to the Bible, the God of Israel directly intervened on the part of the Jews, sending the Angel of Death to assist them.

The Destruction of Sennacherib

The Assyrian came down like the wolf on the fold,
And his cohorts were gleaming in purple and gold;
And the sheen of their spears was like stars on the sea,
When the blue wave rolls nightly on deep Galilee.

5   Like the leaves of the forest when Summer is green,
That host with their banners at sunset were seen:
Like the leaves of the forest when Autumn hath blown,
That host on the morrow lay withered and strown.

For the Angel of Death spread his wings on the blast,
10 And breathed in the face of the foe as he passed;
And the eyes of the sleepers waxed deadly and chill,
And their hearts but once heaved, and for ever grew
        still!

And there lay the steed with his nostril all wide,
But through it there rolled not the breath of his pride;
15 And the foam of his gasing lay white on the turf,
And cold as the spray of the rock-beating surf.

And there lay the rider distorted and pale,
With the dew on his brow, and the rust on his mail:
And the tents were all silent, the banners alone,
20 The lances unlifted, the trumpet unblown.

And the widows of Ashur[1] are loud in their wail,
And the idols are broke in the temple of Baal[2];
And the might of the Gentile,[3] unsmote by the sword,
Hath melted like snow in the glance of the Lord!

George Gordon, Lord Byron

---

1. *Ashur*, Assyria.
2. *Baal*, an ancient Near Eastern god.
3. *Gentile*, non-Jewish; here, the Assyrians.

1. What story does this poem tell?
2. Who are the victors in this battle? What enables them to win?

"The Destruction of Sennacherib" is a **narrative poem**—a poem that tells a story or relates a pattern of events leading up to a climax. Narrative poetry relies on the compressed, figurative language that marks all poetry. Note, for example, the figurative details that depict the Assyrians as they prepare for battle. In shorter narrative poems, details are telescoped so that the story moves quickly. In many narrative poems, characterization is developed and motivation is apparent. Unlike a lyric, which develops a basic emotion rather than a story, a narrative poem concentrates on events rather than sustained emotion.

One type of narrative poem is the *ballad*, which is arranged into four-line stanzas with a particular iambic measure and a fixed rhyme scheme. "The Lorely" (page 619) is a ballad. Another kind of narrative poem is the *epic*, which is characterized by extreme length, a dignified tone, and heroic characters and events. Epics represented in this book are the *Odyssey* (page 126), the *Aeneid* (page 242), and *Paradise Lost* (page 500).

■ NARRATIVE POETRY

Poetry that relates a story or a series of events.

■ Apply to the **Odyssey**, page 126.

■ PARADOX

'Tis the love of right/Lures men to wrong.

Rumi
from **"The Soul of Goodness in Things Evil"**

A man does not appreciate the value of immunity
from a misfortune until it has befallen him.

Sadi
from **"The Padshah and the Slave"**

Prepare for war with peace in thy soul.

from the **Bhagavad Gita**

Whoever comes to the gates of death, knows the
value of life.

from the **Babur-nama**

Although these statements appear to be contradictory, each is in some respect true. In
what sense might one make preparations for war
by keeping peace in mind? Choose one other
of these seemingly self-contradictory statements
and explain how it makes sense.

Each of these statements contains a
paradox—an apparent contradiction that is nevertheless true. The blind seer Tiresias in *Oedipus the King* (page 165) is a paradoxical figure—a
sightless character who possesses tremendous
insight. In "On Friendship" (page 230), Cicero
explains the paradoxical nature of real friendship: ". . . friends are together when they are
separated, they are rich when they are poor,
strong when they are weak, and . . . they live
on after they have died." In the poem "Love
and Hate" (page 235), Catullus notes the paradoxical coexistence of these conflicting emotions.

Emily Dickinson explores paradoxes in two
of her poems, titled "Success Is Counted Sweetest" and "Much Madness is Divinest Sense."
Can you guess from these titles how each of her
observations might be true?

■ PARADOX

**A statement, character, or situation that
appears to be contradictory but that is
nonetheless true.**

■ Apply to **"The Man Who Fled from Azrael,"** page 48.

This image of two dragons
swallowing one another, from
an 18th-century alchemical
work, suggests the mutually
contradictory nature of the
terms of a paradox.

■ PERSONIFICATION

All day the gusty north wind bore
The loosening drift its breath before;
Low circling round its southern zone,
The sun through dazzling snow-mist shone.
5 No church bell lent its Christian tone
To the savage air, no social smoke
Curled over woods of snow-hung oak.
A solitude made more intense
By dreary voicéd elements,
10 The shrieking of the mindless wind
The moaning tree boughs swaying blind,
And on the glass the unmeaning beat
Of ghostly fingertips of sleet.

John Greenleaf Whittier
***from* Snowbound**

1. What qualities of the wind seem human?
2. What human attributes are ascribed to the tree boughs (line 11) and the sleet (line 13)?

Whittier has created a memorable description of a snowstorm by making the winter elements seem vivid and humanlike. Described as "shrieking" and "mindless," the wind *breathes*, rather than *blows*. The sounds of the winter elements become "dreary voices," the tree boughs are "moaning" and "swaying blind," and the sleet beats down with "ghostly fingertips." This type of figurative language that attributes human characteristics to nonhuman things, events, or abstractions is called **personification**.

What human qualities are ascribed to books in the following passage?

Books are a delightful society. If you go into a room filled with books, even without taking them down from their shelves, they seem to speak to you, to welcome you.

William Ewart Gladstone

In "Because I Could Not Stop for Death" (page 681), Dickinson personifies death as a gentleman caller. In "Life Hurries On" (page 382), life is portrayed as "a frantic refugee."

We use personification in our daily speech when we speak of a shy violet, a laughing brook, or a scolding bluejay. Sometimes life, but not necessarily human life, is attributed to ideas or inanimate objects. For example, you might say that love is blind or that the sea raged and lunged.

Poets recognize the ability of personification to enliven objects and abstractions. But personification is not confined to poetry. Notice how personification is achieved, particularly through adjectives, in the following description.

Then there lay stretched out before us, to the right, confused heaps of buildings, with here and there a spire or steeple, looking down upon the herd below; and here and there, again, a cloud of lazy smoke, and in the foreground a forest of ships' masts, cheery with flapping sails and waving flags. Crossing from among them to the opposite shore, were steam ferry boats laden with people, coaches, horses, wagons, baskets, boxes: crossed and recrossed by other ferry boats: all traveling to and fro: and never idle. Stately among these restless Insects, were two or three large ships, moving with slow majestic pace, as creatures of a prouder kind, disdainful of their puny journeys, and making for the broad sea.

Charles Dickens
***from* American Notes**

■ PERSONIFICATION

The attributing of human qualities to nonhuman or nonliving things—abstractions, ideas, animals, or objects.

■ Apply to "Night," page 58.

HANDBOOK OF LITERARY TERMS

■ PLOT

The succession of interrelated events in a story, which lead to and resolve a conflict, is called its **plot**. Events in a carefully constructed plot are linked in a cause-effect relationship, with one incident leading to the next. A successful plot makes us wonder what is going to happen next and how things will turn out at the end. Some people even read the last page of a novel first, then backtrack to see how events have led to that end. Even authors such as O. Henry, who is noted for surprise endings, plant subtle clues that hint of the outcome.

Note how the highlights in the following plot summary of *Madame Bovary* (page 661) are interrelated.

Emma wanted to be swept off her feet by a romantic hero. But her inexperience led her to marry a dull country doctor named Charles. After they had been married for a few months—frustrating months for Emma—they went to a family dinner-dance at the home of a marquis. The event rekindled Emma's romantic dreams and aroused her contempt for Charles. Later, when she met a local squire, she entered into a liaison with him. But her dreams were shattered when he abandoned her. . . .

The first part of the plot, called *exposition*, introduces the main characters, establishes the setting, and provides background information. Often details that seem irrelevant in the exposition become significant as the story unfolds. At times, details in the exposition are revealed through *flashbacks*—scenes or events presented out of chronological order. Flashbacks interrupt the story in order to provide important background information.

The *climax* is the decisive point in the plot at which the problem must be resolved in some way. At this turning point, the action usually changes course. Sometimes it is hard to pinpoint the main turning point in a story, since the climax may be subtle—perhaps a moment

of truth or insight. One could make a case that the climax of "The False Gems" (page 689) is either the point at which M. Lantin initially decides to sell his deceased wife's necklace or the apocalyptic moment when he becomes aware of her infidelity.

The *rising action*, or *complication*, is the mounting of tension or developing of the struggle between conflicting characters or forces. It precedes the climax. Events that follow the climax and serve to resolve the conflict are called the *falling action*.

The *denouement*, a word derived from a French word that means "the untying," refers to the *resolution* of the plot. In the resolution, readers learn what finally happens to the main characters. In "The False Gems," the denouement occurs when M. Lantin decides to use his new-found wealth to enjoy life.

The structure of a plot can be indicated in this way.

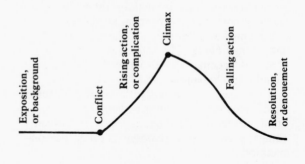

■ PLOT

The pattern of interrelated events in a story that present and resolve a conflict

■ Apply to *Oedipus the King*, page 200.

■ POINT OF VIEW

1. What kind of cuisine would diners expect who entered each of the four doors?
2. What do you know about the chef?
3. How does your bird's-eye view provide you with more information than the diners have?

© Punch/Rothco

Most events, pictures, and stories can be presented from more than one perspective, or **point of view.** In the cartoon to the right, your vantage point allows you to know something the diners don't—that the same chef is cooking food for all four restaurants.

Because every story can be told from a number of perspectives, an author must decide on a particular point of view from which to present the narrative. To this end, the author chooses a narrator who shapes the way the characters, actions, settings, and events are perceived by the reader.

The narrator may be a character within the work who uses pronouns such as *I* or *we* and presents information according to what that character knows, experiences, or infers. Such stories are said to be told from the *first-person* point of view. *Life on the Mississippi* (page 684) is told by a first-person narrator.

A story related by a narrator who is not a character in the story is said to be told from the *third-person* point of view. The narrator uses pronouns such as *he, she,* and *they.* If a third-person narrator knows and relates the thoughts of one particular character in the story, the point of view is said to be *third-person limited.* "Portrait of the Artist as a Young Man" (page 778) is told by a third-person narrator who presents thoughts and perception from Stephen Dedalus's point of view.

Another type of third-person narrator is able to relate the thoughts, feelings, and perceptions of any or all characters. Such an all-knowing narrator as appears in "How Much Land Does a Man Need?" (page 669) is said to present a story from an *omniscient* point of view.

Decide from which point of view—first-person, third-person limited, or third-person omniscient—each of the following is told.

In a certain reign there was a lady not of the first rank whom the emperor loved more than any of the others. The grand ladies with high ambitions thought her a presumptuous upstart, and lesser ladies were still more resentful. Everything she did offended someone. Probably aware of what was happening, she fell seriously ill and came to spend more time at home than at court. The emperor's pity and affection quite passed bounds. No longer caring what his ladies and courtiers might say, he behaved as if intent upon stirring gossip.

Lady Murasaki
from **The Tale of Genji**

In those days I was not the man I am today. That is, I *was* the same Tevye, and yet not exactly the same. The same old woman, as they say, but in a different bonnet. How so? I was as poor as a man could be, completely penniless. If you want to know the truth I'm not a rich man now either, but compared with what I was then I can now really call myself a man of wealth. I have a horse and wagon of my own, a couple of cows that give milk, and a third that is about to calve. We can't complain. We have cheese and butter and fresh cream all the time. We make it ourselves; that is, our family does. We all work. No one is idle. My wife milks the cows; the children carry pitchers and pails, churn the butter. And I myself, as you see, drive to market every morning . . . .

Sholom Aleichem
from "Tevye Wins a Fortune"

Frederick left; descended the stairs (how prodigiously long ago he had climbed them!); went through the streets to his home, the little earthen figure in his hand, perplexed and sick of heart. In front of his house he stopped, shook the fist fiercely for a moment in which he was clutching the figurine, and felt a great urge to smash the ridiculous thing to the ground. He did not do so; he bit his lip and entered the house. Never before had he been so agitated, so tormented by conflicting emotions.

Herman Hesse
from "Within and Without"

There is yet another third-person point of view in which the narrator describes only what can be seen, recording events like a newspaper reporter or a camera. This is called a *third-person objective* (or *dramatic*) point of view.

■ POINT OF VIEW

The vantage point from which an author presents the actions and characters in a story. The story may be related by a character (*first-person* point of view) or by a narrator who does not participate in the action (*third-person* point of view). Further, the third-person narrator may be *omniscient*—able to see into the minds of all characters; *limited*—confined to a single character's perceptions; or *objective*—describing only what can be seen.

■ Apply to **"The Overcoat,"** page 632.

■ PROTAGONIST/ ANTAGONIST

The main character in a short story, play, or novel is called the **protagonist**. The protagonist (which originally referred to an actor playing the lead in a Greek drama), who may or may not be the narrator, is always involved in the main action of the plot.

Usually the protagonist is in conflict against an opponent, or **antagonist**. Satan is the antagonist in *Paradise Lost* (page 500); the Green Knight in *Sir Gawain and the Green Knight* (page 340). In some stories, the protagonist may be opposed, not by another character, but by external forces. In "The Old Man" (page 858), the protagonist grapples with the forces of winter, old age, illness, and hunger.

When a character possesses traits that provide a contrast to the protagonist's, he or she is called a *foil*. In "The Artist" (page 766), the impractical, artistic Satyabati provides a foil to the materialistic Govinda.

"At this point, the action shifts to a luxurious office in Threadneedle Street, where our hero . . ."

■ PROTAGONIST

The central character in a literary work.

■ ANTAGONIST

A character or force opposing the protagonist.

■ Apply to **Oedipus the King**, page 165.

■ RHYME

It is a beauteous evening, calm and free,	*a*
The holy time is quiet as a Nun	*b*
Breathless with adoration; the broad sun	*b*
Is sinking down in its tranquillity;	*a*
5 The gentleness of heaven broods o'er the Sea:	*a*
Listen! the mighty Being[1] is awake,	*c*
And doth with his eternal motion make	*c*
A sound like thunder—everlastingly.	*a*

William Wordsworth
from "It Is a Beauteous Evening"

---

1. *Being,* the ocean.

Rhyme—the repetition of similar or identical sounds in stressed syllables—can please the ear, provide unity in a work, create mood, and provide emphasis. Rhyme can serve to establish the rhythms in a line or to unify an entire stanza or poem. Like all sound devices, rhyme should reinforce meaning and tone and contribute toward the total effect of a work.

The most common types of rhyme are end rhyme, internal rhyme, slant rhyme, and feminine rhyme. Poets often combine several of these types of rhyme to create mood and musical effect.

End rhyme is the rhyming of words at the end of lines of poetry. The *rhyme scheme,* or pattern of rhyme, can be charted. The rhyme scheme of the lines above by Wordsworth have been indicated by italicized letters on the right. The first rhyme is labeled *a* (and all similar end rhymes); the second rhyme, *b*; the third rhyme, *c*.

Internal rhyme is the rhyming of words or accented syllables within a line. This kind of rhyme can be used to achieve emphasis or variety in a line, as in the following example:

For the moon never beams without bringing me dreams
 Of the beautiful Annabel Lee;
And the stars never rise but I see the bright eyes
 Of the beautiful Annabel Lee . . .

Edgar Allan Poe
from "Annabel Lee"

Another kind of rhyme, called *slant rhyme* (or half rhyme) occurs when the sounds of words are similar but not identical (*sat/ met; board/ bed*). This kind of rhyme appears in many of Emily Dickinson's poems. The italicized word pair in the following lines contains slant rhymes.

Strong Son of God, immortal *Love,*
 Whom we, that have not seen thy face,
 By faith, and faith alone, embrace,
Believing where we cannot *prove* . . .

Alfred, Lord Tennyson
from In Memoriam

A rhyme scheme may occur in words of more than one syllable such as *never/ clever, history/ mystery.* This kind of rhyme, in which stressed rhyming syllables are followed by identical unstressed syllables, is called *feminine rhyme.* Note the following example:

The cock is crowing,
The steam is flowing,
The small birds twitter,
The lake doth glitter . . .

William Wordsworth
from "Written in March"

Some critics consider any sound technique such as alliteration or assonance a form of rhyme. But all critics agree that poets should avoid rhyme that is forced or contrived (*ring/ wondering*) or trite (*love/ above*). Rhyme is most effective when it reinforces the mood and meaning of a work. Find one poem that rhymes in this book and examine how rhyme contributes to the overall effect of the work.

■ RHYME

The repetition of similar or identical sounds in accented words or syllables. Common types of rhyme include *end rhyme*, *internal rhyme*, *slant rhyme*, and *feminine rhyme*.

■ Apply to **The Rubáiyát of Omar Khayyám**, page 45.

■ RHYTHM

As you listen to everyday conversation, you'll notice that certain words and syllables receive more emphasis than others. Just as ordinary speech has stressed and unstressed sounds, poetry has patterns of accented and unaccented syllables that form a beat, or **rhythm.** Although poems may or may not use rhyme, all poetry—even free verse, to some extent—has rhythm that is regular or irregular. An identifiable pattern of stressed and unstressed sounds in poetry is called *meter*.

In order to determine the meter, or rhythm, of a poetic passage, you can mark stressed syllables with the symbol ´, and unstressed syllables with the symbol ˘. In addition, each line can be divided into smaller units, each with an accented syllable and one or more unaccented syllables. Such units of measure, called *feet*, are divided by a slash. Determining the metrical pattern in poetry is called *scansion*. Notice how the rhythm of the first few lines from *Tartuffe* can be indicated.

A man / whose spir- / it spurns / this dun- / gy earth

Ought not / to brag / of lands / and no- / ble birth;

Such world- / ly ar- / rogance / will hard- / ly square

With meek / devo- / tion and / the life / of prayer.

Determining the metrical pattern in poetry is called *scansion*. Notice how small patterns of accent repeat themselves within a line in *Tartuffe*. The number of these patterns or feet within a line may range from one to eight. The preceding passage has five feet per line. The following terms are used to represent the number of feet that occupy a line of poetry.

FEET

one foot:	*monometer*
two feet:	*dimeter*
three feet:	*trimeter*
four feet:	*tetrameter*
five feet:	*pentameter*
six feet:	*hexameter*
seven feet:	*heptameter*
eight feet:	*octameter*

Pentameter, tetrameter, and trimeter are probably the most common line lengths in regular English verse.

In determining the metrical pattern of each foot, one must examine the pattern of stressed and unstressed syllables that make up each foot. For example, the feet in the preceding passage from *Tartuffe* consist of units that contain an unstressed syllable followed by a stressed one. Such a pattern is called an iamb or iambic foot. Thus, the metrical pattern of *Tartuffe* can be described as *iambic pentameter*.

The four basic kinds of feet are illustrated by the following words, according to their accented patterns: *refer, whisper, recommend, fortify*. The major accent or stress patterns can be indicated this way:

STRESS PATTERN

˘ ´ refer: iamb or iambus
´ ˘ whisper: trochee
˘ ˘ ´ recommend: anapest
´ ˘ ˘ fortify: dactyl

IAMB: This meter, reflected in the word *refer*, is the measure most commonly used in verse written in the English language. Notice how the accents fall in the following lines;

Excuse / me, I / can't man- / age loft- / y words—

Not though / your whole / court jeer / and find / me

low;

My path- / os cer- / tainly / would make / you laugh

Had you / not left / off laugh- / ing long / ago.

Johann Wolfgang von Goethe
from Faust

TROCHEE: This two-syllabled metrical foot, with its accent on the first syllable as in the word *whisper*, is the opposite of the iamb. Examine the following passage.

Téll me / nót, in / mournful / númbers,

Lífe is / bút an / émpty / dréam!

Fór the / soul is / déad that / slúmbers,

And things / áre not / whát they / seém.

Henry Wadsworth Longfellow
from "A Psalm of Life"

ANAPEST: This three-syllabled measure consists of two unaccented syllables followed by one accented one, as in the word *recommend*. Although this meter is seldom used throughout an entire poem, it can be combined with other meters to achieve variety, emphasis, and music. Note how the following anapest lines are introduced by an iambic foot.

Then hére's / to our bóy- / hood, its góld / and its gráy!

The stárs / of its wín- / ter, the déws / of its Máy!

And whén / we have dóne / with our lífe- / lasting tóys,

Dear Fá- / ther, take cáre / of thy chíl- / dren, THE

BÓYS!

Oliver Wendell Holmes
from "The Boys"

DACTYL: The dactyl is a foot of three syllables, which consists of an accented syllable followed by two unaccented ones, as in the word *fortify*. Longfellow sometimes used this meter, usually with variations, as in the following passage.

This is the / fórest pri- / méval; but / where áre

the / héarts that be- / neáth it

Léaped like the / róe, when he / héars in the /

wóodland the / vóice of the / húntsman?

Whére is the / thátch-roofed / víllage, the / hóme

of A- / cádian / fármers,—

Mén whose lives / glíded / on like / rívers that /

wáter the / wóodlands . . .

Henry Wadsworth Longfellow
from Evangeline

Occasionally, a poetic foot may be composed of two accented syllables, as in the words *thatch-roofed* in line 3 of the previous passage from *Evangeline* by Longfellow. A foot made up of two stressed syllables is called a *spondee*. Spondees serve occasionally as substitute feet to vary the meter in a line. Locate the spondee in the following line:

The sun exhaled its warm breath on the earth.

Scan the following poem by determining the kind and number of feet in the lines. Note that there are some variations in the dominant meter of the poem.

The sea gives her shells to the shingle,
   The earth gives her streams to the sea;
They are many, but my gift is single,
   My verses, the first fruits of me.
5 Let the wind take the green and the gray leaf,
   Cast forth without fruit upon air;
Take rose-leaf and vine-leaf and bay-leaf
   Blown loose from the hair.

Algernon Charles Swinburne
from "Dedication" to Poems and Ballads

■ RHYTHM

The arrangement of stressed and unstressed syllables in speech or writing. Rhythm, or meter, may be regular, or it may vary within a line or work. The four most common meters are iamb, trochee, anapest, and dactyl.

■ Apply to **The Tempest**, page 415.

■ SATIRE

1. What do you think the cartoonist is making fun of in the drawing below?
2. What is ironic about using billboards to make America beautiful?
3. Would you consider this cartoon humorous or deeply critical?

This cartoon relies on **satire**—a technique that ridicules people or institutions in order to reveal their foolishness or vice. Surely, using billboards that obliterate natural scenery is not an effective way to keep a country beautiful. Satire serves variously to entertain, to criticize, or to instruct. Occasionally, it is designed to produce action or reform. Ranging in intensity from good-natured observation to savage ridicule, satire may include exaggeration, wit, humor, or irony.

Swift's "A Modest Proposal" (page 553) is a bitter piece of satire used to highlight the problem of poverty in Ireland. What word would you use to describe the tone of the following satiric comment?

A Frenchman can humiliate an Englishman just as readily as an Englishman can humiliate an American, and an American a Canadian. One of Canada's most serious literary needs is some lesser nation to domineer over and shame by displays of superior taste.

Robertson Davies

Parody, a humorous imitation of the style, characters, or subject matter of serious writing, is a form of satire. Parody is designed to ridicule a work or to point up or exaggerate its characteristics.

What is being satirized in the following poem?

Procrastination

Tomorrow you will live, you always cry;
In what far country does this morrow lie,
That 'tis so mighty long ere it arrive?
Beyond the Indies does this morrow live?
'Tis so far fetched, this morrow, that I fear
'Twill be both very old and very dear.
Tomorrow I will live, the fool does say;
Today itself's too late: the wise lived yesterday.

Martial

■ SATIRE

A technique that exposes human weaknesses or social evils. Satire may use exaggeration, wit, irony, or humor to make its point. The satirist may adopt a tone ranging from good-natured humor to biting ridicule or scorn. Satire may serve to entertain, to instruct, or to reform or bring about action.

■ Apply to "**The Red Cockatoo**," page 88.

■ SETTING

The early autumn day was warm and charming, and our stroll through the bright-colored, busy streets of the old French seaport was sufficiently entertaining. We walked along the sunny, noisy quays and then turned into a wide, pleasant street which lay half in sun and half in shade—a French provincial street, that looked like an old water-color drawing; tall, gray, steep-roofed, red-gabled, many-storied houses; green shutters on windows and old scrollwork above them; flower pots in balconies and white-capped women in doorways. We walked in the shade; all this stretched away on the sunny side of the street and made a picture.

Henry James
from **Four Meetings**

1. What is the time of year and the place of the preceding passage?
2. What mood is conveyed in this description?

Setting is the time and place in which the action of a narrative occurs. Setting can be general (somewhere in Germany during the 1940s) or specific (a gymnasium in Greenwich Village). James has chosen a picturesque street in a French seaport in August as the backdrop for his narrative. Setting, which can be revealed through dialogue, action, or imagery, contributes to the mood of a work and can develop characterization.

Later in this story, the narrator visits the main character in a New England town called Grimwater. Note how this setting contrasts with that of the French seaport.

I found Miss Spencer's residence without difficulty. The Baptist church was easily identified, and the small dwelling near it, of a rusty white, with a large central chimney stack and a Virginia creeper, seemed naturally and properly the abode of a frugal old maid with a taste for the picturesque. As I approached, I slackened my pace, for I had heard that someone was always sitting in the front yard, and I wished to reconnoiter. I looked cautiously over the low white fence which separated the small garden space from the unpaved street; but I descried nothing in the shape of a Countess. A small straight path led up to the crooked doorstep, and on either side of it was a little grass plot, fringed with currant bushes. In the middle of the grass, on either side, was a large quince tree, full of antiquity and contortions, and beneath one of the quince trees were placed a small table and a couple of chairs. On the table lay a piece of unfinished embroidery and two or three books in bright-colored paper covers. I went in at the gate and paused halfway along the path, scanning the place for some farther token of its occupant, before whom—I could hardly have said why—I hesitated abruptly to present myself. Then I saw that the poor little house was very shabby. I felt a sudden doubt of my right to intrude; for curiosity had been my motive, and curiosity here seemed singularly indelicate.

1. How does this physical setting differ from the previous one?
2. How does the mood change?

Along with time and place, setting may also convey social climate. For example, the second passage from "Four Meetings" suggests that Miss Spencer's social status is one of shabby gentility. In *The Metamorphosis* (page 785), the Samsa family is revealed as lower-middle class and urban—struggling, declining, and materialistic. *Madame Bovary* (page 661), set in nineteenth-century France in the region of Rouen, reveals characters that are middle class but provincial. In *A Doll House* (page 712), Ibsen never identifies the city in which the Helmers live. Perhaps he is highlighting what he considers a universal, not a national, problem by focusing on what could be any nineteenth-century middle-class home. The main setting in a work may change, as it does in "Ruth" (page 27) when the main character moves from Moab to Judah.

■ SETTING

The time and place in which the action of a narrative occurs. Setting, which helps establish mood and reveal character, can also reveal social climate. It may directly affect the development of the plot and provide important clues about events and motivation.

■ Apply to the **Babur-nama**, page 64.

HANDBOOK OF LITERARY TERMS

■ SIMILE

What things are being compared in each of the examples below?

A room without books is like a body without a soul.

Cicero

For a dyed-in-the-wool author nothing is as dead as a book once it is written . . . . She is rather like a cat whose kittens have grown-up. While they were a-growing she was passionately interested in them but now they seem hardly to belong to her—and probably she is involved with another batch of kittens as I am involved with other writing.

Rumer Godden

1. What similarities do a room without books and a soulless body have?
2. Under what circumstances might an author resemble a cat?

A stated comparison between two basically unlike things, usually indicated by the words *like, as, appears, seems,* or *than,* is called a **simile.** A simile is a kind of figurative language; therefore, the things compared must be essentially unlike, although they have something in common. "Sam's eyes shone like his father's" is not a simile; "Sam's eyes shone like bright gems" is a simile. Like any figurative language, similes should provide a novel insight or a fresh way of viewing something.

Occasionally, a simile may be elaborate and involved. Such similes, which appear in the *Odyssey* (page 126) and *Paradise Lost* (page 500), are called *epic* or *Homeric similes.* (See page 948.)

Note how the following poem is developed through various similes.

Symphony in Yellow

An omnibus across the bridge
   Crawls like a yellow butterfly,
   And, here and there, a passer-by
Shows like a little restless midge.

5 Big barges full of yellow hay
   Are moved against the shadowy wharf,
   And, like a yellow silken scarf,
The thick fog hangs along the quay.

10 The yellow leaves begin to fade
   And flutter from the Temple elms,
   And at my feet the pale green Thames
Lies like a rod of rippled jade.

Oscar Wilde

1. To what is the bus compared? the passer-by? the fog? the Thames?
2. What connecting word is used in each case to indicate the comparison?

The following cartoon relies on simile for its humorous effect.

"We say 'guilty,' your honor, guilty as a weasel in a henhouse."

© Punch/Rothco

■ SIMILE

A figure of speech that involves a direct comparison between two unlike things, usually with the words *like* or *as*.

■ Apply to "**Sent to Li Po as a Gift,**" page 87.

■ SONNET

A **sonnet** is a lyric poem of fourteen lines, usually iambic pentameter, and with one of several fixed rhyme schemes. Note the rhyme scheme of the following sonnet.

September 3, 1802

Earth has not anything to show more fair:
  Dull would he be of soul who could pass by
  A sight so touching in its majesty:
This City now doth, like a garment, wear
5 The beauty of the morning; silent, bare,
  Ships, towers, domes, theaters, and temples lie
  Open unto the fields, and to the sky;
All bright and glittering in the smokeless air.

Never did sun more beautifully steep
10 In his first splendor, valley, rock, or hill;
Ne'er saw I, never felt, a calm so deep!
  The river glideth at his own sweet will:
Dear God! the very houses seem asleep;
  And all that mighty heart is lying still!

William Wordsworth

1. What is the rhyme scheme of Wordsworth's sonnet?
2. Into which two parts does the poem fall?
3. What is the predominant meter?

A sonnet that can be divided into eight opening lines rhyming *abba abba* and six concluding lines rhyming *cde cde* or *cd cd cd* is called an *Italian* or *Petrarchan* sonnet (after the Italian poet Petrarch, page 380). The eight-line stanza or *octave* usually presents a proposition, dilemma, or question, while the six-line stanza or *sestet* provides a comment, application, or solution. The octave of Wordsworth's sonnet is devoted mainly to the beauty of this morning city scene. The sestet expresses the speaker's response to the scene. The predominant meter is iambic pentameter, although in certain cases both meter and rhyme scheme may depart from the norm.

The following is a different type of sonnet. Can you determine in what ways it differs from the Italian sonnet?

Sonnet 71

No longer mourn for me when I am dead
  Than you shall hear the surly sullen bell
Give warning to the world that I am fled
  From this vile world, with vilest worms to dwell:

5 Nay, if you read this line, remember not
  The hand that writ it; for I love you so,
That I in your sweet thoughts would be forgot,
  If thinking on me then should make you woe.

O! if, I say, you look upon this verse,
10 When I perhaps compounded am with clay,
Do not so much as my poor name rehearse,
  But let your love even with my life decay;

Lest the wise world should look into your moan,
And mock you with me after I am gone.

William Shakespeare

1. What is the rhyme scheme of Shakespeare's sonnet?
2. Into what four parts does the poem fall?

Shakespeare's sonnet falls into a classification that characteristically embodies four divisions: three groups of four lines each, called *quatrains*, and two concluding rhymed lines called a *couplet*. The concluding couplet usually provides a comment or a mental twist to the preceding train of thought. Note the shift in thought in the last two lines of Shakespeare's sonnet. A sonnet such as Shakespeare's that can be divided into three quatrains and a concluding couplet (rhyme scheme: abab cdcd efef gg) is called an *Elizabethan* (English) or Shakespearean sonnet.

■ SONNET

A lyric poem of fourteen lines, usually iambic pentameter, and having a fixed rhyme scheme. Depending upon the patterns of rhyme and organization of thought, the sonnet may be classified as Shakespearean (English; Elizabethan) or Petrarchan (Italian).

■ Apply to "**It Was the Morning**," page 381.

■ STEREOTYPE

Drawing by Ed Fisher; © 1984 The New Yorker Magazine, Inc.

"I'm an old-fashioned private eye, Miss Jones. If this little mystery of yours has anything to do with computers, forget it."

What kind of picture do you conjure up when you hear the term *private eye*? Your mental image is probably one of a hard-boiled, heavy drinking, cigarette-smoking gumshoe, dressed in a trenchcoat. Such fixed, generalized ideas about a character or situation are called **stereotypes.** Stereotyped characters, also called stock characters, are broadly drawn with no individualizing qualities. Stereotypical characters conform to standardized mental pictures and behave in predictable patterns.

In real life, stereotypes such as the mousy librarian, the nagging mother-in-law, the tight-fisted Scot, the conniving lawyer, and the gullible country boy are usually unjustified and can often be dangerous. When they appear in literature, stereotypes are often used by authors to provide quickly and easily recognizable types. In addition, they can function as effective contrasts, or *foils*, for main characters who are more fully portrayed. It is up to the reader to recognize stereotypes in literature, and to determine what, if any, purpose they are intended to accomplish.

Certain recognizable plots may be developed according to a formula: the young orphan who is later revealed to be of noble birth, the star-crossed lovers who perish, and the banished hero who is finally reunited with loved ones. Even settings may be stereotypical—the haunted estate, the decadent European city, and the sleepy Western locale. Experienced moviegoers often claim that they can predict the outcome of a Western after the first five minutes by observing early clues that point toward one of the several plot patterns.

The cartoon on this page suggests several stereotypes other than the private eye himself. There is the attractive young woman who requires the services of a detective, along with the possibility that a romance might develop between the two.

■ STEREOTYPE

A fixed, generalized image of a character, setting, or plot. Although hack writers may unwittingly create stereotypes, skillful writers use stereotypes for a purpose—to serve as immediately recognizable types or as foils to more fully developed characters.

■ Apply to "**The False Gems**," page 689.

■ STYLE

As you read the following love poems, think about ways in which they differ.

Behold, thou art fair, my love; behold, thou art fair; thou hast doves' eyes within thy locks: thy hair is as a flock of goats, that appear from mount Gilead.

2 Thy teeth are like a flock of sheep that are even shorn, which came up from the washing; whereof every one bear twins, and none is barren among them.

3 Thy lips are like a thread of scarlet, and thy speech is comely: thy temples are like a piece of a pomegranate within thy locks.

4 Thy neck is like the tower of David builded for an armory, whereon there hang a thousand bucklers, all shields of mighty men.

5 Thy two breasts are like two young roes that are twins, which feed among the lilies.

6 Until the day break, and the shadows flee away, I will get me to the mountain of myrrh, and to the hill of frankincense.

7 Thou art all fair, my love; there is no spot in thee.

8 Come with me from Lebanon, my spouse, with me from Lebanon: look from the top of Amana, from the top of Shenir and Hermon, from the lions' dens, from the mountains of the leopards.

9 Thou hast ravished my heart, my sister, my spouse; thou hast ravished my heart with one of thine eyes, with one chain of thy neck.

from **The Song of Solomon 4**
The King James Translation

Sonnet 130

My mistress' eyes are nothing like the sun;
Coral is far more red than her lips' red;
If snow be white, why then her breasts are dun;
If hairs be wires, black wires grow on her head.
5 I have seen roses damasked, red and white,
But no such roses see I in her cheeks;
And in some perfumes is there more delight
Than in the breath that from my mistress reeks.
I love to hear her speak, yet well I know
10 That music hath a far more pleasing sound;
I grant I never saw a goddess go;
My mistress, when she walks, treads on the ground:
    And yet, by heaven, I think my love as rare
    As any she belied with false compare.

William Shakespeare

1. How would you describe the tone of each poem?
2. Which poem uses regular rhythm and rhyme?
3. In which work is the beloved directly addressed?
4. Which poem do you prefer? Why?

These two poems, both focusing on different aspects of the beloved, are written according to two very different styles. **Style** is the manner in which writers use language to express their ideas. Structure, word choice and arrangement, tone, sound effects, and use of imagery and figurative language determine style.

In each case, the writer has chosen a form, or structure, that suits the ideas expressed. The exuberant free-verse lines of "The Song of Solomon" convey a passionate, idealistic view of love, while the controlled quatrains and wry twist of the concluding couplet of Shakespeare's sonnet present a more reasoned treatment of love. In addition, Shakespeare's poem mocks the popular sonnets of his day that heaped praise on each feature of a loved one. Although free from regular rhyme and rhythm, the biblical poem achieves a cadence through repetition of phrases and the accumulation of similes.

The biblical poem, which directly addresses a lover, is intensely personal, while the tone of Shakespeare's poem is ironic. In analyzing the diction, or word choice, in a work, try to determine whether it is conversational, formal, informal, ornate, simple, or quaint. Note, for example, that "The Song of Solomon" uses archaic words such as *thou, thine, thy,* and *thee.* Both poems rely on imagery and figurative language, although "The Song of Solomon" develops these comparisons more fully and draws heavily on sensuous, pastoral images.

■ STYLE

The means by which writers use language to express their ideas. Style is determined by an author's choice of structure, selection and arrangement of words, tone, and degree of reliance on sound effects, imagery, and figurative language.

■ Apply to **Paradise Lost**, page 500.

■ SYMBOL

The Ox

I love thee, pious ox; a gentle feeling
Of vigor and of peace thou giv'st my heart.
How solemn, like a monument, thou art!
Over wide fertile fields thy calm gaze stealing,

Unto the yoke with grave contentment kneeling,
To man's quick work thou dost thy strength impart.
He shouts and goads, and answering thy smart,
Thou turn'st on him thy patient eyes appealing.

From thy broad nostrils, black and wet, arise
10 Thy breath's soft fumes; and on the still air swells,
Like happy hymn, thy lowing's mellow strain.

In the grave sweetness of thy tranquil eyes
Of emerald, broad and still reflected dwells
All the divine green silence of the plain.

Giosuè Carducci

1. What words would you use to describe a
   beast of burden such as an ox?
2. What words does the writer use to describe
   the ox in this poem?
3. What is the mood of this poem?
4. How would you describe the attitude toward
   life expressed in this poem?

In this poem, the ox serves as a **symbol**—an
object or event that stands for something other
than itself, often an abstract idea or concept.
The poet addresses the ox, using descriptive
words such as *patient, tranquil,* and *mellow* to
characterize it. Clearly it is not its strength, but
the gentle, peaceful nature of this animal that
the poet finds appealing. Words such as *pious,*

hymn, and *divine* indicate that the ox also has
spiritual significance. From the final line of the
poem, readers can infer that this animal represents the sacredness and peace of unspoiled
nature.

A symbol may form the basis of an entire
poem. In "Two Poems on Returning to Dwell
in the Country" (page 79), images of the
country are developed throughout to represent
the peaceful simplicity of unspoiled nature.
Frequently, however, a symbol may appear only
briefly in a work. Note, for example, the serpent, traditionally symbolic of evil or temptation, who appears in *The Epic of Gilgamesh*
(page 9), "Genesis" (page 23), and *Paradise Lost*
(page 500).

Symbols that appear in many different cultures, such as the dove representing peace and
a set of scales representing justice, are called
universal. In the *Inferno* (page 316), for example, the little hill that Dante must climb, the
dark woods he encounters, and the gate on
the threshold of hell symbolize, respectively,
human aspiration, life's difficulties, and an
entrance into a new phase of life. Throughout
literature, physical journeys such as Dante's
symbolize a progression through life in quest of
some goal. Some symbols, however, have special significance within the context of a given
work, as the quilt does in "Everyday Use" (page
922). What does this quilt symbolize?

■ SYMBOL

**A concrete image used to represent something
abstract, such as a concept or idea.**

■ Apply to **"The Lay of the Werewolf,"** page 297.

Great seal of the
United States

Gorgon, Greek
symbol for terror

Ankh, Egyptian
symbol of life.

Peace symbol

Victory laurel

■ THEME

A Poison Tree

I was angry with my friend:
I told my wrath, my wrath did end.
I was angry with my foe:
I told it not, my wrath did grow.

5 And I watered it in fears,
Night and morning with my tears;
And I sunnéd it with smiles,
And with soft deceitful wiles.

And it grew both day and night,
10 Till it bore an apple bright;
And my foe beheld it shine,
And he knew that it was mine.

And into my garden stole
When the night had veiled the pole:
15 In the morning glad I see
My foe outstretched beneath the tree.

William Blake

1. What does the speaker do when he becomes angry with a friend?
2. How does the speaker react differently when he becomes angry with a foe?
3. What effect does the "fruit" of his anger have?
4. What statement does this poem appear to be making about the results of uncontrolled anger?

This poem is not about a tree, but about anger that is allowed to grow. The message of the poem can be summarized thus: Anger that is nourished can be devastating to both parties involved.

The deeper, underlying meaning of a work is its **theme**. Although a theme may be directly stated, it is more often implied through characterization, images, or tone.

The selections from Rumi included in this book have as their theme the limitations of knowledge. The underlying meaning of "The Acorn and the Pumpkin" (page 509) is that humans should not question the Divine plan that directs the universe, although such a plan may seem incomprehensible. Pope directly states this theme in couplet form in *An Essay on Man* (page 570): "Know then thyself, presume not God to scan;/The proper study of mankind is man." State the themes of two other works that are included in this book.

Some works, especially those written purely for entertainment, have no theme. Other works have several themes. Among the themes in the Book of Ruth (page 27) are the need for tolerance and the rewards of loyalty.

Do not confuse the subject of a work with its theme. While the subject of "A Noiseless Patient Spider" (page 656) is the insect mentioned in the title, the theme of this poem is the human yearning for close relationships (symbolized by the connecting filaments of the web).

What is the theme of the following poem?

On His Blindness

When I consider how my light is spent,
Ere half my days, in this dark world and wide,
And that one talent which is death to hide
Lodged with me useless, though my soul more bent
5 To serve therewith my Maker, and present
My true account, lest He, returning, chide;
"Doth God exact day-labor, light denied?"
I fondly ask. But Patience, to prevent
That murmur, soon replies: "God doth not need
10 Either man's work or His own gifts; who best
Bear His mild yoke, they serve Him best. His state
Is kingly: thousands at His bidding speed,
And post o'er land and ocean without rest:
They also serve who only stand and wait."

John Milton

■ THEME

The underlying meaning of a literary work. A theme may be directly stated but is more often implied. Theme differs from the subject of a literary work in that it usually makes an observation about the subject. Some literary works have no theme; others have more than one.

■ Apply to **Ruth**, page 27.

■ TONE

Surprise

My heart went fluttering with fear
Lest you should go, and leave me here
To beat my breast and rock my head
And stretch me sleepless on my bed.
5 Ah, clear they see and true they say
That one shall weep, and one shall stray
For such is Love's unvarying law. . . .
I never thought, I never saw
That I should be the first to go;
10 How pleasant that it happened so!

Dorothy Parker

1. What are the speaker's initial fears about love, as expressed in the first seven lines?
2. What is the "surprise" mentioned in the title?
3. What adjective best describes Parker's final attitude toward her subject: *affectionate, angry, amused, bitter*?

Parker's poem differs from conventional love poems such as "Miserable with Desire" (page 156) and "Blest Be the Day" (page 381) because she views the anguish and the fleeting nature of love with amusement. Through her choice of words, images, and surprise ending, she conveys her attitude toward love—an attitude that is lighter and more humorous than that of most poets.

Parker's attitude is revealed through **tone**—the author's relationship to his or her material, to the audience, or to both. Readers must recognize tone in order to determine whether a writer views a subject with disdain, formality, nostalgia, or admiration. Occasionally a writer's tone will reflect several attitudes, or it may change within a single work, as it does in "Surprise."

Words used to describe the tone of a work include *objective* or *subjective, formal* or *informal, playful* or *somber, admiring* or *critical,* and *sincere* or *ironic.* Decide which of these words (or choose your own) you would use to describe the tone of the following works: "A Modest Proposal" (page 553), "At His Brother's Grave" (page 235), *Don Quixote* (page 406), "The Silesian Weavers" (page 619).

Several words may be used to describe the tone of a given work. For example, Parker's tone is both amused and ironic, with an unexpected turn at the end of the poem.

Although tone and mood are related, they should not be confused. Mood is the overall effect that a work has on a reader, while tone involves the voice and attitudes of the writer. The mood in "The Silesian Weavers" is one of sadness and doom, but the tone is one of protest.

It is particularly important in determining the mood of a work to recognize whether or not it contains irony, hyperbole, understatement, or satire. Unless you recognize such techniques, a work may seem puzzling or ridiculous. Readers who fail to identify Swift's ironic and satiric tone will misread "A Modest Proposal."

Note how the following love poem differs dramatically from Parker's work in tone. Observe how Browning's style suits her tone.

Sonnet 22

When our two souls stand up erect and strong,
Face to face, silent, drawing nigh and nigher,
Until the lengthening wings break into fire
At either curvéd point—what bitter wrong
5 Can the earth do to us, that we should not long
Be here contented? Think. In mounting higher,
The angels would press on us and aspire
To drop some golden orb of perfect song
Into our deep, dear silence. Let us stay
10 Rather on earth, Belovéd—where the unfit
Contrarious moods of men recoil away
And isolate pure spirits, and permit
A place to stand and love in for a day,
With darkness and the death-hour rounding it.

Elizabeth Barrett Browning

■ TONE

An author's attitude toward his or her subject matter and audience. Tone, which can be stated or implied, should not be confused with mood.

■ Apply to **The Pillow Book**, page 94.

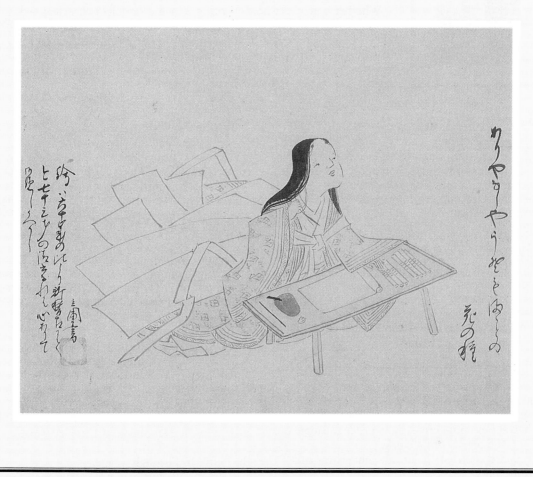

Ryūho (1595–1669), *Was It True or Not True?* 1667. Ryūho's painting pictures the young Lady Murasaki beginning to write *The Tale of Genji*.

WRITER'S HANDBOOK

WRITER'S HANDBOOK

The Writing Process

Whether you are at home writing a long essay or in class responding to an essay test question, the strategy for writing about literature is the same. The most important thing is to read the assignment carefully and be sure you do what is asked. This article will give you specific tips on how to apply three steps of the **writing process**—prewriting, writing, and revising—to assignments on writing about literature.

PREWRITING

Strange as it may seem, getting ready to write often takes more time than the actual writing. Yet going carefully and thoroughly through the preliminary thinking and planning stage not only makes the writing itself both easier and faster, but it helps insure that you will produce a better paper.

Sample Assignment

Like all epic poems, Virgil's *Aeneid* is distinguished by elevated language, created, in part, by the use of particular figures of speech. Analyze the use of figurative language in the *Aeneid* to show how it contributes to the overall effect of the poem.

1. Identify the Task

Assignments to write about literature tend to repeat the same set of verbs. It is essential that you understand the differences among them.

Analyze: examine critically in order to single out the components of a work.

Compare/contrast: point out similarities and differences.

Convince: persuade by argument or proof.

Create: produce from your own thought or imagination.

Defend: write in favor of an opinion.

Describe: give a picture or account of something.

Discuss: consider all sides of a question.

Explain: make something understandable.

Illustrate: make clear by examples, comparisons, quotations, or other textual evidence.

Imagine: form an idea or image; put yourself or a character into a hypothetical situation.

Interpret: explain or come to understand.

Support: prove ideas, claims, or opinions.

In addition, look for and underline key words in the assignment and identify the intended audience. Your audience will determine the amount of background you need to supply, and also the sophistication of your style and vocabulary. If no other audience is mentioned in the assignment, assume that you are writing for your teacher.

2. Begin by Reading Carefully

Reading carefully often means reading more than once, perhaps the entire selection or perhaps just parts of it. Check meanings of words and passages you don't at first understand. Acquaint yourself with the literary devices the author uses and pay attention to structure, relationships, and the progression of events or ideas. Careful reading often involves asking yourself questions and making notes as you read. Since the sample assignment specifically mentions figurative language, you may want to review that article in the Handbook of Literary Terms.

3. Think It Through

Class discussions may give you some ideas to help you get started, but you should do some careful thinking on your own. Consider your purpose in writing, and ask yourself questions about the selection. Try to achieve an understanding not only of *what* it means but *how*; that is, how the author presents ideas and information and what literary devices are used to make those ideas or information comprehensible.

Try *brainstorming* by yourself or with classmates. Jot down your random thoughts and see if some patterns emerge. Making charts or cluster diagrams can also be helpful in this stage.

4. Take Notes

Some note-taking you may do casually as you first read; at other times, you needn't start taking notes until you begin work on a specific assignment. Then, the assignment may direct you to the kind of information you will need. As you reread the *Aeneid*, take notes on the types of figurative language you find and note the best examples of each of them. A next step would be to generalize what sort of effect this figurative language produces in context. (See "Writing Notes and Summaries" in the Writer's Handbook, page 986.)

5. Make a Working Plan

Your assignment may contain hints about the best way to organize your notes. The sample assignment asks you to show how figurative language contributes to the overall effect. This immediately suggests that you should describe the effect in your first paragraph and then devote each subsequent paragraph to one or more figures of speech. You can use one of the following methods, but keep in mind that this is a *working* plan that you can change as needed.

Write a purpose statement. A simple statement of your purpose will help you organize your ideas. You may be able to use this statement as the basis for your thesis statement.

Construct an outline. Make it as simple or as complex as necessary for your purpose. Refer to it as you write to make sure you stay on the right track, and after writing, use it again to check your work. (See the model outline on page 980.)

Diagram ideas and details. Charts and cluster diagrams are often helpful in the preliminary phase of getting your ideas on paper.

6. Write a Thesis Statement

Assignments that ask for a single paragraph response can be developed around a topic sentence stating the main point of the paragraph. Longer papers, however, are nearly always founded on a thesis statement, generally placed in the opening paragraph, that explains your subject and the aspects of it that you will be covering in the paragraphs that follow.

Often the wording of the assignment will supply much of the wording of your thesis statement. Note how this model thesis statement responds to the sample assignment:

> To achieve an elevated, heroic style, Virgil makes extensive use of various types of figurative language, among them simile, metaphor, hyperbole, personification, and apostrophe.

WRITING

Write your first draft quickly, getting your ideas down before you lose them. Don't worry about grammar, spelling, or correctness at this stage. Just put your notes into rough sentence and paragraph form.

Write an introductory paragraph. The main purpose of your first paragraph is to present your thesis statement. If your teacher is your audience, you can get to the point quickly; however, sometimes you will need to sketch in background material in order for the thesis statement to make sense.

Develop your points in body paragraphs. In the following paragraphs, present the substance of your explanation or argument. Generally, each main point you wish to make will be presented in a separate paragraph.

Come to a conclusion. The concluding paragraph ordinarily restates the thesis statement with certain amplifications, or it can summarize or make a final comment. It should *not* be identical to the introduction.

Write a title. The best titles are simple and brief and give an indication of what your essay is about. For example, "Irony of Situation in 'The Kiss,'" or "Dramatic Conventions in *Oedipus the King*."

REVISING

If you can, put your first draft aside for a few hours or days. When you come back to it, you may come up with new ideas or spot contradictions and flaws in logic. Often it is helpful to get the opinion of a friend or reading group. Reading the paper aloud will help you locate clumsy phrasing. You can use these questions as a checklist:

Content and Organization
- Is there a strong thesis statement that effectively expresses the topic?
- Is each point made in the thesis statement developed in a separate paragraph?
- Are general statements supported by specific references and examples from the text?
- Does each sentence in a paragraph relate to the topic of that paragraph?
- Is there logic in the ordering of the ideas in a paragraph and in the ordering of the paragraphs?
- Are there transitional words within and between paragraphs?
- Is the information sufficient, or should more be added?
- Does the concluding paragraph give a sense of closure?

Style
- Is the language used simple and direct?
- Is there wordiness and clutter that can be eliminated?
- Are tone and point of view consistent?
- Is there variety in the length and type of sentences?
- Has proper subordination been used in combining sentences?
- Is tense consistent? (Using the present tense throughout will help you avoid awkward tense shifts.)
- Are there needless repetitions or too many ideas joined with *and*?
- Have you used active verbs rather than passive or linking verbs wherever possible?
- Have you avoided clichés and slang?
- Do all pronouns have clear antecedents?

Mechanics
- Is each paragraph indented?
- Have you used correct spelling, capitalization, and punctuation throughout?
- Are there fragments or run-on sentences?
- Have you put the titles of short stories, poems, and essays in quotation marks and used underlining (italics) for longer works?

The model outline and essay shown here and on the next page were written to fulfill the sample assignment on page 978.

You will find this article helpful in completing the assignment on page 21 and most of the other composition assignments in this book.

OUTLINE

I. Introduction
  A. Elevated language
    1. Appropriate to epic
    2. Virgil's "beauty of language and style"
  B. Thesis statement
II. Simile & metaphor
  A. Much metaphorical language
    1. Direct (stated) (ll. 225–7)
    2. Implied (ll. 16, 563–4)
  B. Simile
    1. Special form of metaphor (li. 360)
    2. Extended simile regular feature (ll. 335–7)
      a. Comparison appropriate
      b. Adds "texture"
III. Hyperbole
  A. Great deeds imply exaggeration (li. 3)
  B. Meant literally in heroic age? (ll. 318, 180–4)
IV. Personification & apostrophe
  A. Simple literary device
    1. Personification (li. 283)
    2. Apostrophe (ll. 216–7)
  B. Literal call upon deity
    1. Pleas for help
    2. Prayers & invocations (ll. 113, 127–30)
    3. Understandable in age of Roman gods
V. Conclusion

Figurative Language in the <u>Aeneid</u>

We would expect Virgil's <u>Aeneid</u> to contain elevated language appropriate to its epic content, but it has furthermore been described as having a "beauty of language and style rarely equaled in world literature." To achieve this elevated, heroic style, Virgil makes extensive use of various types of figurative language, among them simile, metaphor, hyperbole, personification, and apostrophe.

To begin with, much of the language of the <u>Aeneid</u> is metaphorical. Some metaphors, like "darkness/Came from the ocean, the great shade covering earth/And heaven" (lines 225–227), are direct. Far more frequent, however, are implied metaphors, such as "Shaking off grief" (line 16) and "the rain of weapons/And the cloud of massing Greeks" (lines 563–564). Similes, a special form of metaphor, appear so often as to be a regular feature of this epic. Some are brief and simple; for example, Hecuba and her daughters are described in line 360, "Like doves by a black storm driven." It is the extended simile that most calls attention to itself, though; for example:

Like wolves, marauders in black mist, whom hunger
Drives blindly on, whose whelps, abandoned, wait them
Dry-jawed, so we went on . . . (lines 335–337)

The comparison of ravaging soldiers to wolves is completely appropriate. Such extended similes add immeasurably to the texture of thought and imagery of the poem.

An epic concerns itself with great deeds, and wherever great deeds are mentioned, some amount of exaggeration is to be expected. Virgil does indeed use hyperbole in a number of places, as in "a horse as big as a mountain" (line 3). But how is one to interpret such phrases as "the clamor and confusion, reaching heaven" (line 318) and such descriptions as the serpents "With monstrous coils . . . . Looping in giant spirals" (lines 180–184)? In a narrative context in which the gods interfere directly in the actions of humans and in which such things as monstrous sea serpents are commonplace, perhaps many such descriptions are meant to be taken literally.

Personification and apostrophe also figure prominently in the poem. There are examples of simple personification, such as "the happy crops" (line 283), and of simple apostrophe, such as "O motherland! O Ilium, home of gods,/O walls of Troy!" (lines 216–217). But when Aeneas exclaims, "oh, by the gods above" (line 113), or when Sinon invokes, "Eternal fires,/Inviolable godhead, be my witness, /You altars, you accursed swords, you fillets/Which I as victim wore . . ." (lines 127–130), we are not dealing so much with literary devices as with direct addresses to a pantheon of gods that both Virgil and his audience believed in.

Through the use of this figurative language, Virgil creates an elevated, heroic, and beautiful style well suited to the larger-than-life actions of men and gods with which he illustrates his epic canvas.

WRITER'S HANDBOOK

Developing Your Style

In literature, **style** generally refers to the stamp of a writer's distinctive personality. An author can write in different styles, however, to suit different purposes, and you can develop your own style to make whatever statement you choose about yourself and your writing. To do this, you must be willing to plan carefully and to revise extensively—sometimes even to start afresh. You can examine the works of famous writers to see what makes their style effective, but it is more important to present your own ideas in your own way.

1. Find Your Own Voice

"An author can have nothing truly his own but his style" said Isaac D'Israeli in *Literary Miscellanies*. A natural phase of young writers is to imitate the way their favorite authors write. Some search a thesaurus to find words that sound impressive. Both of these exercises can help you become a good writer, but they are merely stages in developing your own style.

Use words and sentence constructions that feel natural to you. Your main purpose is to communicate ideas clearly. To ornament your writing for the sake of ornament may confuse or even annoy your reader. Don't show off.

2. Consider Your Audience

When you discuss literature in class, you naturally use a different vocabulary and different sentence structures than when you tell a bedtime story to your little brother or sister. In your writing as well, your style in writing an editorial for the student newspaper will be different from the one you use in writing a postcard to your best friend. To consider your audience means to take into account the background and educational level of those who may read your work. Some assignments in writing about literature will specify an audience for you; for assignments that do not, you will have to decide how much you need to explain. Generally speaking, in writing about literature, you are safe in assuming that your audience is familiar with the literature you are writing about.

3. Be Honest

It's always easier to write about what you truly believe. Although when you write class assignments there is a natural tendency to write what you think your teacher wants to hear, you'll find that an honest expression of your own strongly held convictions will be better received than a mere parroting of someone else's notions.

Sometimes you will need to write about something that seems at first not particularly interesting to you. In this case, use some of your prewriting time to find your own angle, a particular slant that you do find interesting—or at least that will enable you to write convincingly.

4. Be Direct

Write clearly and forcefully and resist the temptation to qualify your statements with words and phrases like "somewhat" and "sort of." Try to avoid repeating what you have just said unless it is to add new insight. In addition, follow these guidelines:

Use one word instead of several. Instead of "at this point in time" say *then* or *now*. Instead of "due to the fact that" say *because*.

Don't overmodify. Let your nouns and verbs carry the main burden. Be sparing with adjectives and adverbs.

Avoid the passive voice. Use the active voice unless you want to emphasize the receiver of the action. "The fire was finally brought under control" is fine, but "This sentence was written by me" sounds silly.

Clear away clutter. Don't say, "In my opinion, I think Nick Carraway was the real, true protagonist and main character of the book, *The Great Gatsby*." Say, "Nick Carraway is the protagonist of *The Great Gatsby*."

5. Capture Your Reader's Attention

Franz Kafka's "The Metamorphosis" begins with a classic sentence: "As Gregor Samsa awoke one morning from uneasy dreams he found himself transformed in his bed into a gigantic insect." Of course, in your general writing such a bizarre opening would be out of place, but that doesn't mean you have to settle for, "In my paper I am going to write about . . . ." Instead, launch into your subject in a vivid, inviting fashion. If a personal anecdote or something that you have read elsewhere is appropriate, use it.

6. Strive for Freshness

"Avoid clichés like the plague" is a good rule to follow even though it satirically violates itself. Try not to use overworked metaphors and similes. If you've heard a comparison before, it's probably a cliché. Be original but not outlandish. "The road was as slippery as an eel" is tired and probably inappropriate. "The road had a treacherous varnish of bottle-green ice" is better. But "The road was slicker than possum spit on a hickory limb" is going too far.

7. Be Sparing in Emphasis

There are better ways to achieve emphasis than merely to pepper your writing with exclamation points. Consider the following:

Use emphatic words. Choose words and phrases that are precise and powerful in themselves, and you won't need emphatic punctuation. See, for example, how vivid are the verbs in Narayan's story "Such Perfection" (page 868): "Lightning *flashed,* thunder *roared,* and fire *poured* down from the sky. . . . The population of ten villages *crammed* in that village. . . . Women and children *shrieked* and *wailed.* . . . The two lakes, over which the village road ran, *filled, swelled,* and *joined* over the road."

Emphasize through rhythm. Variety in the length and complexity of sentences in a paragraph produces rhythm. A short, compact sentence within a series of longer sentences can grab a reader's attention like a gunshot or a trout leaping in a still pond.

Emphasize through position. Remember that the beginning and the end of a sentence are the places of highest interest. The same goes for paragraphs and entire essays. For this reason, the writing of opening and closing paragraphs in a composition may require more care and attention than the writing of body paragraphs.

Inverting the word order in a sentence (anastrophe) is another way to achieve emphasis. "Sweetbreads I tolerate, but liver I abhor" is more emphatic than "I can tolerate sweetbreads, but I really don't like liver." (Notice, also, the effect of rhythm in the first sentence.)

Emphasize through repetition. Carelessly used, repetition can be boring; skillfully used, repetition can achieve amazing effects. Note the grace—and at the same time, strength—of this passage from the Book of Ruth in the King James Bible:

> "Entreat me not to leave thee or to return from following after thee: for whither thou goest, I will go; and where thou lodgest, I will lodge: thy people shall be my people, and thy God my God: where thou diest, will I die, and there will I be buried . . . ."

For any writer, developing an effective style is a lifelong endeavor requiring discipline and constant effort. You must be willing to practice and experiment, revise and polish. Take care and pride in the craft of composition as you would if you were tuning the engine of a racing car or painting a community mural.

Any one of these techniques, overworked, can become a detriment instead of an asset. As with salt, pepper, and garlic, there can be too much of a good thing. Keep matters of style in mind as you review and evaluate your writing. Refer to the revision checklist on page 980. In addition, ask yourself the following questions:

- Does the opening sentence attract a reader's attention?
- Is the language strong, direct, and concise?
- Is the tone polite—neither flattering, condescending, nor dogmatic?
- Are imagery and figurative language carefully chosen to contribute to the overall effect?
- Are sentence patterns varied?
- Are ideas expressed clearly and forcefully?

You will find this article helpful in completing the assignment on page 62, and most of the other composition assignments in this book.

WRITER'S HANDBOOK

Writing to Persuade an Audience

Good literature presents ideas and issues that are open to various interpretations—many of them defensible. In a sense, all expository writing based on literature is persuasive, for you as a writer attempt to win your reader's confidence in your interpretation, to gain respect for your scholarship and understanding. In addition, writing assignments on literature may offer a statement, judgment, or position with which you are to agree or disagree. Then you must carefully consider various positions, decide which one makes the best sense to you, and persuade your readers that your conclusion is a valid one by providing reasons for your opinion.

PREWRITING

Sample Assignment

In his essay "On Friendship," Cicero states that "friendship can exist only between good men." In a composition of at least three paragraphs, tell whether you think this statement is valid, invalid, or irrelevant to young people in the twentieth century. Defend your position with an argument as measured and reasonable as Cicero's, and support your statements with examples from your own knowledge or experience.

1. Go to the Source

Don't take a stand or make any decisions until you have carefully reviewed the selection to be sure you understand what the statement means. As you read, look for evidence—details, examples, allusions, and so on that will help you support an interpretation. Take notes on these items. Try to be sensitive to where the ideas lead you. You may change your own mind back and forth several times by the end of your research. There is nothing wrong in that; it should, in fact, make your final position the stronger for being more carefully considered.

2. State Your Position

Once you know your material thoroughly, take a stand and stick by it. This may seem obvious, but actually many persuasive papers fail because the writer appears undecided.

Suppose that, after careful consideration, you decide to support Cicero. Your job is now to convince your reader that his statement is valid. First write a position statement, making it perfectly clear to your reader what your stance is.

Cicero's statement that "friendship can exist only between good men" remains valid even today, although his definition of "good men" requires some modification to make the statement relevant to people of our century.

This statement may eventually be refined into your thesis statement, but for now it functions as a focus to help you pick out statements from Cicero that need explaining and examples from your own knowledge and experience that will support your contention.

3. Consider Your Audience

Ask yourself what knowledge and what kinds of opinions your intended readers have. Then ask what kind of approach will best convince them. Avoid an approach that might offend or sound insincere—badgering, excessive flattering, condescending, and so on. Be cautious in appeals to emotion, but on the other hand, don't just disregard your audience's emotions and possible biases. For example, it is unlikely that Cicero meant the term *men* generically—to mean both men and women. How can you convince readers who may be in sympathy with today's feminist movement that his statement nevertheless has validity for all people?

4. Adopt a Tone

Decide on a tone before beginning to write. Don't attempt to bludgeon or attack other positions with sarcasm. An open and direct tone, showing respect for other positions but firmly maintaining your own, is always good.

WRITING

Here are some points to consider as you actually begin writing.

5. Order Your Argument

You should have firmly in mind, or on paper, a list of points you want to emphasize in supporting your view. Remember that the places of emphasis are first and last. If you start off with a solid piece of evidence, be sure you keep something equally persuasive in reserve to close with.

In presenting any logical argument, you have different organizational strategies to choose from. You could begin each paragraph with a general statement and then give evidence to support it (a deductive organization), or you could give your examples first and then draw a conclusion from them (an inductive organization). In this case, you would want to devote at least one paragraph to defining Cicero's statement and putting it in a historical context.

6. Refute Opposing Viewpoints

Properly done, this should *not* leave the impression that you are undecided, unable to choose your position. In fact, by becoming aware of other viewpoints—and what validity they might have—you are better able to defend your own. In your writing, acknowledge those other viewpoints but refute, or disprove, them by showing that yours is more valid. The overall effect will be to strengthen your position by demonstrating that you are fair, open minded, and capable of judging evidence by its merits.

7. Differentiate Between Fact and Opinion

The best evidence comes straight from the text. Ask yourself, "Does the text say this, or do I just think it?" Inferences can be used as evidence—particularly in compositions about literature—but be sure that your inferences are valid. Reject unsupported opinions and sweeping generalizations signaled by words like *never* and *everyone*.

8. Use Evidence Fairly

Do not try to give yourself an advantage by quoting out of context or twisting statements around to mean what you want them to mean, instead of what the author intended.

9. Finish Strong and Fast

After presenting your main points, conclude with some kind of summary, in fresh language, of your position. Do not repeat or weakly echo the first paragraph. Leave your reader with a sense of closure.

Model

Cicero does not anywhere specifically define *virtue,* but he depends instead on his audience's recognition of the goodness of Gaius Fabricius and the other "good men" he mentions. Cicero does, nevertheless, describe these good men: "There are men who behave and live in such a way that they are regarded as models of honor, integrity, justice, and generosity . . . men of unwavering conviction." Further description is phrased negatively: "men who have no vestige of avarice, lustfulness, or insolence."

REVISING

Evaluate your rough draft, using the checklist on page 980. Also consider the following questions:
• Does the paper take a firm and clear stand?
• Are the main points in the argument clearly expressed in topic sentences in each paragraph?
• Do the points seem to flow in a definite direction?
• Is each paragraph adequately developed? Are there unsupported generalizations that need either shoring up or deletion?
• Reread the first and last paragraphs. Are the promises made in the first fulfilled? Does the last draw a conclusion?

You will find this article helpful in completing assignments on pages 551 and 682.

WRITER'S HANDBOOK

Writing Notes and Summaries

Notes and summaries are in a sense part of the preparation for writing about literature. They serve as a kind of shorthand for evaluating and selecting materials, for condensing and storing information and ideas. They are also ways of learning, for with such writing you attempt to get at the essential, to choose the important and give it order for use later, and to dig out ideas and clarify them by paraphrasing—putting them into your own words. While summarizing usually serves as a prewriting skill, an assignment such as a book review may request that you briefly summarize a work before you focus on some specific aspect of it.

PREWRITING

Sample Assignment

Write a summary of the last five paragraphs of Pericles' funeral oration from the *History of the Peloponnesian War*.

1. Read Carefully

Reread the selection quickly to get the overall meaning. Then go back through it, focusing your attention on key words and connectives and checking the meaning of words you don't know. You can't afford to omit anything just because it is difficult or you don't understand it at first.

2. Take Notes

For a plot summary, list the major actions and events in the narrative. Be sure to include causes and effects. For nonfiction selections, list major ideas with subordinating ideas underneath. Notes can take different forms:

List. Jot down words, details, images, and so on that you find significant.

Chart. Classify your notes under headings that are significant to your plan.

Generalization. Jot down your reactions, questions, and comments as they occur to you.

Outline. You can use the same outline form for taking notes that you use for planning a paper. (See the model outline on page 980.) One advantage of an outline is that it lets you show in easily recognizable form how ideas are related—that is, which ideas are parallel and coordinate and which ideas are subordinate. An outline can be as sketchy or as detailed as you need it to be for your purposes.

Direct quotation. Copy the author's exact words in the order in which they appear. Use quotation marks and identify the source. Use elipses (. . .) to show where words have been left out. When you quote poetry, use a slash to indicate the end of a line. For example, compare this quotation from Mistral's poem "Fear" with the original on page 826: ". . . I would like even less/that one day they crown her queen./They would raise her to a throne. . . . I could not rock her to sleep/when nighttime came."

Paraphrase. A paraphrase is a restatement or simplification in your own words, to help your reader (or yourself) understand a passage or selection. A paraphrase runs parallel to the original but simplifies it, making it useful for working with short units, especially those you want to integrate into your literature paper. A paraphrase is not necessarily longer or shorter than the original, in contrast to a summary, which is always much shorter than the original.

Whatever form of notes you take, always record your exact source—page, act, poetic line, and so on. Especially for notes from secondary sources (library research), recording complete information now will save you time later.

A few sheets of paper will provide adequate notes for many assignments. If you plan on taking a lot of notes, however, use notecards. The extra trouble it takes to identify each card will be repaid by the ease with which you can organize them in different ways.

3. Organize Your Notes

Use the requirements of the assignment as a guide to organizing your notes. You might find grouping or clustering sufficient for your purposes. Otherwise, construct an outline with as much detail as you need.

4. Write a Summary

As far as possible, avoid the phrasing of the original, although you will have to use certain key words because they are essential to the meaning. Follow these guidelines:

Be brief. Make every word count. Decide what information is essential to your summary and eliminate all superfluous details. Never include dialogue or quotations, and eliminate most description. If your summary need include only certain aspects of a work—for example, the sample assignment asks for five paragraphs only—choose your material accordingly.

Be complete. An idea summary should include all the major ideas and represent accurately the author's position. A plot summary should include only major actions; you might be surprised, however, to discover how few actions can convey the overall sense of a plot.

Use the present tense. In summarizing literary works, use the present tense throughout to help avoid awkward tense shifts.

WRITING

Here is a response to the sample assignment about Pericles' Funeral Oration. Notice that it is organized in five paragraphs, according to the paragraphs of the original.

Model

By the manner in which these men have gone to their deaths, they have defined the term "manliness." Any faults they may have had are erased by their gallantry in defense of their homeland. They set aside personal concerns to defend their country, and in meeting death as they did they have earned the crown of glory and honor.

You survivors must preserve the patriotic spirit of these dead. The greatness of Athens is a result of its adventurous and courageous citizens who gave their lives in order to repulse foes. Their sepulcher is the entire world, and their memory is inscribed in the hearts and minds of all people. You must emulate their courage, for a life of cowardice is a more painful prospect than death.

I shall not weep with the parents of these fallen heroes; rather I shall comfort them.

Those of child-bearing age should have more children to bring them joy and solace and to serve Athens. Those too old to have children should find comfort in the fame of their dead sons. Honor does not grow old. The respect of one's fellow men is more valuable to the aged than is money.

The sons and brothers of the fallen heroes will have a difficult time living up to the reputation of the dead, who no longer have to struggle and compete for honor.

The widows among you should maintain your glory by remaining inconspicuous. The city will finance the raising of the children of the dead until they come of age. Now mourn for your loved ones and go home.

REVISING

This model could probably be condensed still further; almost anything can be. But be sure you have not left out anything important. Check also to see that you have not changed the author's ideas or colored them with your own interpretation.

In addition to using the checklist on page 980, ask yourself these questions:

- Have you a good reason for including a summary or paraphrase? Have you made that reason clear?
- In nonfiction, are the main ideas and the author's purpose made clear?
- In fiction, are the important elements of setting, character identification and relationships, and the main events of the plot made clear?
- Have you deleted non-essential examples and details?
- Can your summary be made tighter by more economical phrasing?

You will find this article helpful in completing the assignment on page 295.

WRITER'S HANDBOOK

Writing About Plot and Plot Devices

The **plot** of a piece of narrative fiction usually comprises the following elements: *exposition*, the establishment of setting, characters, and any background information necessary to understanding the story; *conflict*, an interior or exterior struggle involving the main character or characters; *rising action*, a series of events leading to the climax; *climax*, the turning point or point of greatest tension; *falling action* and *resolution*, the working out of the conflict. Assignments on writing about plot may ask you to discuss the plot as a whole or to focus on a single element of it. In either case, you will need to understand the whole story, novel, or play and its plot components before responding to the assignment.

PREWRITING

Sample Assignment

Write a three or four paragraph composition describing the exposition in *Oedipus the King*. What information does the audience need to know? How—and at what stages in the play—is it imparted?

1. Examine the Plot Components

First review the elements of plot to be sure you understand them and how they function together. (See PLOT in the Handbook of Literary Terms, page 962.) As you reread the work to discover the plot elements, ask yourself the following questions.

How is exposition presented? What are you told about setting, characters, and what has gone on before? How are you told? (You may learn such information directly, from a narrator, or indirectly, through dialogue or other devices. Or you may be shown directly, through flashbacks.) Answering this question is necessary to fulfilling the sample assignment, but the question is a useful one to ask of any work. You may ask further: Why has the author chosen this particular point and not another to begin the action of the story? This question may or may not be significant to other works, but it is vital to *Oedipus the King*.

What conflict or conflicts arise? What causes the conflict? Is the conflict between characters, between a character and an outside force, or within a character? (Some works may have all three kinds.) In what ways does the conflict create or influence the other events that make up the plot? Often the motivations of several char-

acters will conflict; to the extent that motivation drives the plot, you must consider characterization as well.

What is the climax of the action? At what point do events reach a climax and conflicts begin to be resolved? Is there preparation for the resolution, so that the ending seems fitting? You should be aware that the very concept of plot has undergone changes over the years. The classical dramatists, including Sophocles, and many who followed them adhered rather closely to established models. These included the *classical unities* of time and place—the notion that the action of a play should take place in one location and be confined to a twenty-four-hour period. To facilitate these unities, many classical works begin *in medias res*, in the middle of the action. Later writers do not necessarily follow the same models; the climax of a twentieth-century novel, for example, may come at the very end. In some dramas and short stories there may be little conflict and no climax in the traditional sense at all.

2. Analyze the Plot Structure

How does the story develop? How are the events related? Is there a frame story or flashbacks? Many works are not written in chronological order; if so, how does the author make clear the order of events and the relationships among them? Even when an assignment focuses on certain elements of plot, you need to understand the entire structure. To do this, you might find it helpful to construct a chronology of some sort, listing the events as they happen. The following list shows the major events in *Oedipus the King*. Note where the exposition ends and the sequence of events (the play itself) begins.

Exposition
1. Laius, King of Thebes, learns from an oracle that he and Jocasta will have a son who will kill Laius.
2. Oedipus is born and abandoned on a mountainside to die.
3. A shepherd takes pity on him and delivers him to Polybus, the childless King of Corinth, who raises Oedipus as his son.
4. Oedipus later learns from an oracle that he is fated to slay his father and marry his mother.
5. He tries to avoid the prophecy by leaving Corinth, never to return.
6. Oedipus meets and quarrels with Laius, unknowingly slaying his real father.
7. Oedipus arrives at Thebes, where he solves the riddle of the sphinx, thus delivering the country from the monster.
8. Oedipus marries Jocasta and becomes King of Thebes.
9. Oedipus and Jocasta have children.
10. A plague descends on Thebes.
11. Oedipus sends Creon to consult an oracle.

Sequence of Events
12. Thebans appeal to Oedipus for relief from the plague.
13. Creon returns from the oracle saying that Laius's killer must be found and expelled.
14. Oedipus begins investigations to find Laius's killer.

Climax and Resolution
15. Oedipus's questions reveal that he himself is the slayer of his real father and the son of his present wife.
16. Jocasta hangs herself.
17. Oedipus blinds himself and is exiled.

3. Look for Chains of Cause and Effect

In a well-plotted narrative, events do not simply occur; they are *caused*. An action by one character will cause another character to act; that character's action will cause further actions; and so on throughout the entire plot. In skillful hands, such plotting can seem entirely natural

and inevitable. As you analyze a plot, look for chains of cause and effect. Tracing them may become an important part of your analysis.

4. Consider Possible Subplots

In a long story or novel, there may be more than one plot. If so, how do the main plot and subplot(s) relate? How does the author show connections between them?

WRITING

The following paragraph is part of an essay written to fulfill the sample assignment.

Model

Oedipus the King seems rather like a modern detective story in that almost all the action of the play is given over to discovering the exposition. In fact, finding out just who everyone really is and what has gone on before provides Oedipus's main motivation, since the oracle has stated that Laius's killer must be found and expelled from Thebes before the plague will be lifted. Most of Sophocles' audience already knew the story of *Oedipus the King,* however, and so were not kept in suspense as to exposition. Instead, they could appreciate the great dramatic irony of Oedipus's drive to learn, through his unrelenting questioning of one character after another, the very information that will cause his downfall.

REVISING

In addition to the checklist on page 980, ask yourself these questions:
- Is the connection between events made clear to the reader?
- Have any unusual aspects of plot structure, such as a frame story or flashbacks, been accounted for?
- Are conflicts sufficiently explained?
- Is the climax identified?
- Are sufficient examples from the text given to support any generalizations?

You will find this article helpful in completing the assignment on page 303.

Writing About Characters

Several different procedures may be involved in writing about fictional characters. An assignment may ask you to describe a character as a human being, relating physical characteristics, personality, actions, motivations, reactions to other characters, and so on, or to explain how that character changes during the course of the story. Often, you will be asked to compare and contrast one character with another. Or, you may be asked to analyze the techniques of **characterization** a writer uses to create believable characters in a work.

PREWRITING

Sample Assignment

Analyze the character of Riabovich in Chekhov's "The Kiss." How are direct methods of characterization supported by indirect methods? In what sense are the minor characters, Lobytko and Merzliakov, *foils* to the main character?

1. Think It Through

First review the techniques of characterization available to writers. (See CHARACTERIZATION in the Handbook of Literary Terms, page 944.) As you look back through the story, take notes on what you learn about the different characters and the ways in which you learn these things. Consider these questions.

What methods of characterization are used? Is there physical description? Are you directly told what kind of person you are reading about? Do other characters provide information by what they say or how they act toward the main character? What do you infer about a character from what he or she says and does and the manner in which he or she speaks and acts?

Is the character flat or round? Flat characters may be stereotypes, quickly sketched in because they are easily recognizable embodiments of greed, stupidity, machismo, weakness, and so forth. Round characters, on the other hand, are multi-dimensional and individual, and—like human beings—they cannot be neatly pigeon-holed as mere representatives of a type.

Is the character static or dynamic? Dynamic characters grow and change as a result of what happens in a story. Static characters remain unchanged in nature despite conflicts that develop and are resolved around them.

Is the character believable? Are the character's actions consistent and clearly motivated? Does what the character says and does seem consistent with what you have learned about the character so far?

What function does the character serve? If the character you are analyzing is not a protagonist or antagonist, consider how that character functions in the work as a whole: as a commentator? as a *foil* to the main character, highlighting his or her characteristics through similarity or contrast? as a plot device to help develop the conflict to its climax?

2. Take Notes

To support your conclusions, you need evidence about the character as exhibited in what he or she says and does as well as what the narrator tells about the character directly. Here is a possible scheme of prewriting notes about Riabovich in "The Kiss."

Author's Description

Riabovich the "most awkward of all" at the party.

"Short, round-shouldered, spectacled. . . . whiskered like a lynx."

Appearance and bearing "seemed to explain: 'I am the most timid, modest, undistinguished officer in the whole brigade.' "

Victim of psychical blindness. Stands with wallflowers. Gets in the way in the billiard room.

Mistaken kiss in darkened room transforms his self-image. Constructs composite girl from those at supper. Fantasies sustain him during boring military maneuvers.

Return to the scene of the romantic incident brings only disillusionment.

Character's Statements and Thoughts

Becomes uncharacteristically chatty and affable after the kiss. "What a charming house you have."

Thinking of romantic involvements of other soldiers, he reflects, "I, like the rest, must go through it all sooner or later."

Tries to describe his encounter to Lobytko and Merzliakov. Can't convey the romance. Annoyed at Lobytko's claim of a similar experience.

Comparison/Contrast with Other Characters

Riabovich's social ineptitude is set off by the suavity of the von Rabbeks.

Lobytko, "the setter," is obvious foil. Considers himself a ladies' man.

Merzliakov, bored intellectual, very different from Riabovich.

3. Write a Thesis Statement

After you have organized your notes, draw from them generalizations about your character that you can use in your writing. Then put these generalizations into a thesis statement. The following statement is a response to the sample assignment.

Riabovich, the central character of Chekhov's "The Kiss," is a painfully shy person who compensates for his actual insignificance by living in a world of his imagination.

WRITING

The following paragraphs show how direct methods of characterization are supported by indirect methods and analyze the function of Lobytko and Merzliakov as foils.

Model

Riabovich, of Chekhov's "The Kiss," is a vivid portrait of a timid, insignificant young man. This impression is conveyed directly when the narrator tells us that he is "short, round-shouldered, spectacled. . . . [and] whiskered like a lynx." Everything about his appearance and behavior proclaims, " 'I am the most timid, modest, undistinguished officer in the whole brigade.' "

His actions at the von Rabbek's are consistent with the sort of person the narrator describes. He can't carry on a conversation, he gets in the way in the billiard room, and he is "Amazed at the daring of men who in sight of a crowd could take unknown women by the waist" and dance with them. It is not surprising that such a person constructs—from no more than an accidental encounter in a dark room—a romantic experience, not with a real woman but an imagined composite, and that fantasies of "war and parting . . . then reunion, the first supper together, children . . ." occupy him during subsequent military maneuvers.

Minor characters act as foils to Riabovich. Lobytko is known in the brigade as "the setter," who can sense the presence of women in a neighborhood. "Drop me on the moon," he says, "and in five minutes I'll find both beer and women." Unlike the shy Riabovich, he dances and speaks "unentertaining nonsense" to various women at the von Rabbek's. He responds to the story of Riabovich's adventures with a story of his own, probably a lie, which annoys Riabovich because of its unromantic tawdriness. Another recognizable type, Merzliakov is the bored intellectual with his nose deep in *The Messenger of Europe*. He represents the rational person who can see through the lying boasts of Lobytko but who would never comprehend the intensity and significance of a moment of mistaken identity that has become the climax of Riabovich's emotional life.

REVISING

Evaluate your first draft, either by yourself or with others. In addition to the checklist on page 980, consider these points:
- Does the thesis statement mention the character or characters to be discussed and the points about them to be covered?
- Is the character accurately presented as he or she appears in the story?
- Are examples from the story included to support the character traits discussed?
- Are quotations exact and accurate?

You will find this article helpful in completing assignments on pages 236, 448, and 507.

Writing About Point of View

Point of view refers to the relationship between the narrator of a story and the characters and action. The author's choice of point of view determines what the reader will see through the narrator's eyes. Depending upon the point of view, a narrator may be an active participant in the events that make up the plot, or may be distanced from the action.

Poetry is also said to have a point of view; here, the person narrating the story or presenting his or her thoughts or feelings is called the *speaker*. The speaker may be a character, or *persona*, or may be unidentified.

PREWRITING

Writing assignments about point of view may ask you to analyze what that point of view is, or else to show how the author's choice of point of view affects characterization, plot, theme, or some other element.

Sample Assignment

Write a composition in which you show how the point of view in Walker's "Everyday Use" serves not only to characterize Maggie, Dee, and Hakim-a-barber, but Mama as well.

1. Think It Through

Review what you know about point of view. (See POINT OF VIEW in the Handbook of Literary Terms, page 963.)

The first-person point of view. The person who tells the story also plays a part in it. The narrator will use pronouns such as *I* and *we. Life on the Mississippi* (page 684) is told from the first-person point of view.

The third-person omniscient point of view. The narrator is not a participant in the story, but is able to read the thoughts and feelings of all the characters. "The Artist" (page 766) has an omniscient narrator.

The third-person limited point of view. The narrator is limited to reading the thoughts and feelings of only one character. Also, the action will tend to follow that character; that is, usually only events that happen in the character's presence are described, with other outside events reported through dialogue. "The Kiss" (page 754) is restricted in this way to the perceptions of the main character.

The third-person objective or dramatic point of view. The narrator is like a video camera, see-

ing and hearing all but making no comment or interpretation and unable to read the minds of the characters. The Book of Ruth (page 27) is related in this manner.

2. Analyze the Point of View

Who is the narrator? Is the narrator a major or minor character in the story? If not, into whose thoughts is the reader admitted?

What kind of character is the narrator? If the story is told in the first person, can you trust everything the narrator says, or do the narrator's perceptions slant the information presented about other characters and events, so that you must infer the truth?

Does the point of view affect plot or characterization? Having the rather plodding Dr. Watson narrate the Sherlock Holmes stories, for example, allows A. Conan Doyle to withhold the solutions of the mysteries until the final moment. Also, the bumbling narrator provides an effective foil for the remarkable intellect of Holmes.

Does the point of view affect the theme? A story about the U. S. Civil War narrated by a front-line soldier would probably have a different theme from one narrated by a general safely removed from the action. Authors generally choose narrators to reflect their themes.

Does the point of view change? Sometimes the same incident may be told from the point of view of more than one character. In that case you must infer what information is slanted because of the characters' personal motivations and biases.

3. Imagine an Alternate Point of View

Some assignments require you to do this, but it is a useful approach for any assignment. For example, how would "The Kiss" be changed if Riabovich told his own story, rather than the narrator? How would the story be changed if an omniscient narrator told the thoughts and feelings of all the characters? Why did Chekhov choose the point of view he did?

WRITING

In the model paragraphs that follow, note the discussion of direct and indirect characterization of both the narrator and other characters.

Model

Early in the story Mama Johnson describes herself; her three-room, tin-roofed house; and her family. The reader quickly gets acquainted with the "large, big-boned woman with rough, man-working hands." We recognize her honesty as she shares with us her fantasies about being on a television program "a hundred pounds lighter, my skin like an uncooked barley pancake," but also admits that she is uneasy around white people and that she would never be able to exchange witty remarks with Johnny Carson.

Mama tells us directly about the shy Maggie and about Dee, for whom " 'no' is a word the world never learned to say to her." We first hear Dee's sophisticated voice when Mama remembers Dee's remark that orchids are "tacky" flowers. "Tacky" is a trendy word that would not be in Mama's vocabulary. Mama respects Dee's beauty and educational accomplishments, but she is also aware of how Dee has always patronized her mother and sister and has felt superior to her home environment and early friends. We are prepared to meet Dee in person, and we are not surprised to see what sort of person she has become.

Mama describes Dee's dress, jewelry, and hair style in vivid detail. When we hear the Muslim greetings and the newly adopted names, it becomes clear how far Dee (now calling herself Wangero) has separated herself from her real roots in her attempt to adopt African roots about which she knows nothing. Mama displays her own intelligence and tenacity when she insists on learning how to pronounce the Muslim names, even though her

word choice ("Ream it out again") and syntax ("I wanted to ask him was he a barber") are in amusing contrast to the language of her sophisticated daughter and her male friend.

Maggie, whose scarred, ungainly body and pathetic shyness Mama also describes vividly, is a foil to Dee. When the car bearing her sister arrives, Maggie first tries to flee and then "stops and tries to dig a well in the sand with her toe." There is humor in Mama's description of Maggie avoiding Hakim-a-barber's hug of greeting and the failure to manage what is undoubtedly a modern, elaborate handshake routine. It seems totally in character that Maggie should defer to her sister's request to take possession of the quilts that had been promised to Maggie. But when Dee makes her request (in a voice "sweet as a bird"), Mama hears "something fall in the kitchen, and a minute later the kitchen door slammed." She shrewdly interprets Maggie's feelings. . . .

REVISING

In addition to the checklist on page 980, consider the following questions:

- Is the point of view specifically—and correctly—identified?
- Has the character of the narrator been considered, along with any possible limitations or bias?
- Is the effect of the point of view shown on appropriate aspects of the story?
- Is the term *narrator* or *speaker* (not *author*) used consistently throughout?
- Do quotations or specific references to the story support the general statements?

You will find this article helpful in completing the assignment on page 650.

Writing About Theme

The underlying meaning of a work of literature is its **theme.** Do not confuse theme, which is usually a generalization about life, with the subject or with a plot summary. Seldom is a theme stated explicitly; instead, it may be implied through characterization, the working out of the plot, symbolism, and so on. You can come to grasp the theme of a work by extracting the central idea of that work.

PREWRITING

Writing assignments about theme may ask you to identify the theme of a literary work, or they may state the theme and ask you to explain how the author has reinforced this theme through particular literary devices.

Sample Assignment

The Book of Ruth is generally considered to illustrate two themes—loving devotion to a relative and its rewards, and acceptance of foreigners. Which of these do you consider to be the main theme of the book and why?

1. Think It Through

Be sure you understand how to tell the theme of a work. (See THEME in the Handbook of Literary Terms, page 975.) The clearest examples of theme can be seen in fables and parables, where the theme is often stated at the end in the form of a lesson or moral. For example, one of the "Three Fables" by Marie de France (page 302) ends with the lines "Reaching for goals unwisely cherished,/Many have suffered, many have perished." La Fontaine's fable "The Lion and the Rat" (page 509) ends with the lines "By time and toil we sever/What strength and rage could never." Fables and parables, however, are usually written expressly to convey a theme. In most works of literature there is no such tidy expression of meaning.

The theme of a piece of literature is closely related to the author's purpose in writing. It may be serious or whimsical. In some cases, such as when an author merely wants to create horror, suspense, laughter, or excitement, there may be no theme at all. Theme exists only when an author has set out to record or illustrate a truth about human existence or to present a view of the world and the people in it.

2. Review the Work

Remember that you need to make a generalization about life based on the work. Don't confuse theme with subject matter or plot. For example, Ibsen's play *A Doll House* (page 712) is about a young wife who walks out on her family. That is an accurate, if colorless, statement of what happens at the end of the play. The theme, however, is the insight that a viewer or reader gets from Nora's realization of the petted nonentity she has become—and what she does about it. It is the realization that a woman deserves to be a person and should not have to define herself simply as a wife and mother in a society dominated by males.

As you review the work, ask yourself the following questions.

Is the title a clue? Although themes are seldom stated, the title of a work often provides a strong clue to its theme; for example, Catullus's poem "Lesbia, Let Us Live and Love" (see page 234). The opening and closing paragraphs may also contain clues or outright thematic statements.

Do characterization and plot suggest clues? Ask yourself what the main characters want and whether or not they get it—and how they get it. Often, these elements contribute strongly toward the theme of a work. In Anouilh's play *Antigone* (page 874), for example, the heroine chooses death even after Creon repeatedly offers her a chance to go on living. If she had accepted Creon's offers, if she had been put to death immediately, or if Creon had found other ways to resolve the conflict happily, the theme of the play—that a life of compromise, acceptance, and hypocrisy is not worth living—would have been different.

How do imagery, figurative language, and symbolism contribute? A recurring image or symbol may be a strong clue to theme, especially if it represents something the main character wants or does or something that influences the outcome of the plot.

2. State the Theme

Try to state the theme in one declarative sentence. Do not make it too broad ("Kindness pays off") or too narrow ("If a woman listens to and obeys her mother-in-law, she will eventually be rewarded with a loving husband and child"). Don't resort to clichés such as "love and youth are wasted on the young" or "the sins of the fathers are visited upon the sons." Remember that sometimes the theme is stated by the author; if the work contains such a statement, you need to find and identify it. Don't fall into the trap, however, of accepting any moralizing by a character—or even by a narrator—as the underlying theme of the whole work. For example, in Anouilh's play, Creon says, "Life is nothing more than the happiness that you get out of it," but Antigone counters with, "I want everything of life, I do . . . total, complete: otherwise I reject it!" Both statements are true to their characters, but neither statement sums up the play *as a whole.*

3. Relate Each Part to the Whole

As you analyze the work, recognize how each element relates to the theme. Part of your job is not only to identify the theme but to explain how you have arrived at that theme from synthesizing all the elements of the piece of literature, including characterization, plot, and various literary devices. (Note, in the sample assignment, the all-important *why* at the end.)

WRITING

Use your statement of theme as part of your thesis statement. Note how this is worked in naturally in the paragraph that follows, the opening paragraph of a composition responding to the sample assignment.

Model

In The Book of Ruth considerable stress is given to the fact that Ruth is a Moabitess and thus a foreigner to the people of Bethlehem. Thus the original purpose of the story may have been a plea for the inclusion of foreigners in the assembly of Israel. To modern readers, however, the main theme of the story concerns the trust and affection between Ruth and her mother-in-law, which brings about Naomi's conversion from bitterness to joy and rewards Ruth with a loving husband and a son.

REVISING

Have a classmate evaluate your rough draft in terms of how well you have understood the theme and how clearly and concisely you have stated it. Use the checklist on page 980, and, in addition, ask yourself these questions:

- Is the theme stated? If so, have you correctly identified the statement of theme?
- Is the theme implied? If so, does your paper state it clearly?
- Is the theme distinguished from mere subject or plot summary?
- Is the thesis statement supported by reference to literary techniques and devices such as symbolism, imagery, setting, characterization, and so on?
- Is each part of the work related to the theme of the whole?

You will find this article helpful in completing assignments on pages 63, 219, and 481.

WRITER'S HANDBOOK

Writing to Analyze an Author's Style

Style is the distinct and individual way an author handles language. When you say that you like a particular author, or that you find another author difficult to read, you are probably responding—at least in part—to style. When you are asked to analyze an author's style or to compare it to the style of another author, you will need to consider first all the elements that were discussed in Lesson 2, "Developing Your Style." (See also STYLE in the Handbook of Literary Terms, page 973.) In addition, you will need to consider literary devices such as point of view, theme, tone, mood, and symbolism. Most importantly, note the choice of words, the way they are arranged, and the sounds and images they convey.

PREWRITING
Sample Assignment

Analyze James Joyce's style in the excerpt from *A Portrait of the Artist as a Young Man.* Explain how the style is particularly appropriate to the subject matter—the thoughts and feelings of a young man and budding artist as he becomes conscious of the world and his place in it.

1. Think It Through

In preparing to analyze an author's style, reread the selection and make notes. As you read, ask yourself the following questions.

What diction does the author use? Diction is the choice of words and phrases, usually involving the connotations as well as the denotations of words. Is the level of vocabulary plain, difficult, obscure, formal? Does the author use specific, concrete words, or is the language general and abstract? Is the use of words vivid and fresh or dull, even turgid?

What kinds of syntax are used? Syntax refers to sentence structure. Are sentences long or short, simple or complex? What can you determine about number, kinds, and placement of modifiers? word order for emphasis? use of parallelism to balance thoughts? economy and repetition? Joyce tends to mix short, simple sentences with very long, complex ones and to employ a great deal of repetition. Why? Your job is to figure out how this syntax is appropriate for the subject matter.

What use is there of imagery and figurative language? How do sense impressions contribute to description, mood, and so on? Are some images repeated? to what effect? Is there a pattern of images that can be identified? What types of figurative language do you find? What is its effect?

Is there any symbolism? Do some images or figures take on significance as symbols? If so, are these obvious or subtle? Do they occur singly or repeatedly? to what effect?

How does tone affect the style? Is the voice serious, satiric, objective, didactic, reportorial, bitter, happy, sad? Joyce's tone here seems almost indistinguishable from the mood; that is, the narrator seems as emotionally involved as his subject, Stephen Dedalus.

How much dialogue is there and how often? Long passages of narration create a style very different from one in which there is much interchange of dialogue. Ask yourself whether the dialogue seems natural or artificial, and what makes it seem so. Does it further the plot and reflect the characters as individuals? Note how, in this excerpt, there is not only very little dialogue, but the speakers are not identified. The effect created is rather as if a babble of unimportant words is intruding upon Stephen's thoughts.

What is the effect of sound and rhythm? Read a passage or two aloud. Identify features of sound—alliteration, assonance, onomatopoeia, and so on—and words that describe sounds. Determine the pace and fluency of prose, the rhyme or meter of poetry.

2. Put the Style in Context

No one writes in a vacuum. Although an author's style may be distinctive and individual, it nevertheless has a cultural context. An author may adopt the diction and literary conventions of his or her period in history or may choose to rebel against them—or again may choose to adopt a deliberately archaic style. An author's specific audience and purpose also influence style. You may or may not like certain types of literary styles, but it is not fair to judge a selection ineffective because of a style that is unfamiliar to you.

The same things may be said about translators. For example, the translation of the *Odyssey* by Robert Fitzgerald (see page 126) is very much a product of the twentieth century. This work has been translated innumerable times over the centuries, however, and each translation has employed a somewhat different style. A translation by Alexander Pope in the eighteenth century, for example, was written in then-popular heroic couplets. (See also the Reader's Note "Translating Homer" on page 154.)

3. Develop Your Thesis Statement

By now you have some terms you can use to describe different aspects of style. Now describe the overall effect. Is it plain or flowery, spare or poetic, lean or fat? Use your chosen descriptive terms in a thesis statement that also incorporates the aspects of the work that you will analyze to demonstrate your description.

WRITING

The following paragraphs illustrate how quotations can be used to prove a point.

Model

One excess of style is a tendency toward repetition, as if the narrator, in sympathy with Stephen's subconscious, has struck a word-chord that seems perfectly to embody his idea or mood, and he wants to hear it again and again.

He drew forth a phrase from his treasure and spoke it softly to himself: —A day of dappled seaborne clouds.

The opening sentence, "He could wait no longer," establishes a mood of youthful impulsiveness, and it is repeated at the end of the paragraph. Such repetitions form a recurrent pattern. For example,

He heard a confused music within him as of memories and names which he was almost conscious of but could not capture even for an instant; then the music seemed to recede, to recede, to recede: and from each receding trail of nebulous music there fell always one long-drawn calling note, piercing like a star the dusk of silence. Again! Again! Again! A voice from beyond the world was calling.

Sometimes the narrator's sentences break in the middle and repeat themselves in reverse order, as though the youthful artist-in-words Stephen had exhausted his palette.

Her bosom was as a bird's soft and light, slight and soft as the breast of some dark plumaged dove. But her long fair hair was girlish: and girlish, and touched with the wonder of mortal beauty, her face.

The narrative style that Joyce adopts thus reflects the incipient genius—as well as the youthful excesses—of the protagonist Stephen Dedalus.

REVISING

In addition to the checklist on page 980, ask yourself the following questions:

- Is the style concisely described in a word or phrase?
- If such things as commentary on plot or characterization appear, are they employed for a purpose?
- Are the points in the thesis statement adequately illustrated with quotes or specific references to the text?
- Is any analysis of style given some historical context?
- Does the title reflect the content?

You will find this article helpful in completing assignments on pages 852 and 864.

WRITER'S HANDBOOK

Writing About Poetry and Poetic Devices

Assignments on writing about poetry may ask you to analyze an entire poem and explain what makes it work, or they may focus on one or more specific elements in a poem. A full analysis of all the elements of a literary work and how they function together is called an *explication*. To explicate a poem, you must—in effect—pull it completely apart to examine each line and each device and then put it back together again to show the overall effect that is created by all these elements working together.

PREWRITING

Sample Assignment

Many poets before and after Milton have used blank verse, but Milton put his own individual stamp upon the verse that he used in *Paradise Lost*. Analyze the use and effect of Milton's blank verse, considering as well what you believe to be the two most important literary devices that make his poem distinctly "Miltonic."

1. Think It Through

Poetry has been called the language of compression. Writing assignments about poetry usually require closer scrutiny of individual words and phrases than do assignments about prose. Most assignments will not require a full explication, but the approach outlined here is also useful for focusing on specific elements.

Understand the terms. In the Handbook and Glossary of Literary Terms there are more than two dozen terms that could be called poetic devices. Not all of them will apply to a given poem, but you need to familiarize yourself with the terms and their meanings in order to know which of them operate in the poem you are writing about. (See especially BLANK VERSE and FIGURATIVE LANGUAGE in the Handbook of Literary Terms, pages 943 and 947.) Your task in this sample assignment is to decide what poetic devices Milton uses in his blank verse.

2. Read the Work Closely

Begin, as with any paper about literature, with a close reading. With poems—especially those that seem difficult at first—this means reading slowly and thoughtfully more than once. Read-ing aloud will help you hear the rhythm and sound devices, such as alliteration and consonance. Ask yourself these questions.

What is the poem about? Determine the subject and what is being said about the subject?

Who is the speaker? How do you know? Remember that the speaker is not the same as the poet, although it can be hard to distinguish between them, for many poems are quite autobiographical. Sometimes the poet creates a *persona*, a character who can be identified. To be on the safe side, use the term *speaker* unless you are discussing the poet's writing techniques.

What is the dramatic situation, controlling image, or overall mood? Milton's poem is a narrative—it has characters and a plot, which not all poems have. It is furthermore an epic, and so contains specific elements that contribute to its epic nature.

For lyric poetry, you will need instead to look for imagery and the way that one or more images contribute to the mood or to the ideas being expressed.

What is the poetic form? The blank verse that Milton uses throughout helps him to achieve certain things, but it puts certain limits on him as well. Consider *why* the poet chose this specific poetic form.

What instances are there of figurative language, allusion, and other literary devices? Carefully note each literary technique you find. Its presence is deliberate; your job is to figure out why the poet included it and what it contributes to the effect of the entire poem. Finally, you will need to choose the two literary devices that are most important to *Paradise Lost*.

What do diction and sentence structure tell you?

Note the presence in *Paradise Lost* of lofty, eloquent diction and of long, syntactically complex sentences. Both of them are appropriate for the elevated subject matter.

3. Organize Your Thoughts

You may decide that simile and anastrophe are the two poetic devices that you want to focus on in this poem. If you haven't already done so, you need now to go back through the poem to find the best examples of each of these to cite in your writing.

WRITING

The following paragraphs analyze Milton's blank verse and his use of simile.

Model

Although most popular poetry of his time was written in heroic couplets, a closed form that lent itself to succinct, epigrammatic statements, Milton felt that the best medium for English heroic verse was unrhymed iambic pentameter. He strove to imitate Homer and Virgil in avoiding the constraints and the jingling sounds of end rhymes. A narrative of such length also called for the absence of stanza breaks. The iamb is the most natural foot pattern in English, just as pentameter is the most natural line length. What elevates blank verse above conversational language is the regularizing foot and line length, combined with the freedom to use run-on or enjambement lines which allow thought to move freely from verse to verse. The selection from the Invocation provides a good example of the suitability of blank verse for Milton's purpose. The twenty-six lines of elevated diction comprise only two sentences.

Paradise Lost also abounds in similes, many of them extended through a dozen or more lines. One effect of these elaborate comparisons is to add richness and complexity to the thought as it is reflected by imagery. Another effect is to suspend the sense and slow down the movement of the verse, giving it a majestic, measured quality. For example, the extended simile beginning at line 634 describes the hope and joy of the serpent as he leads Eve to the forbidden tree:

> . . . as when a wandering fire . . .
> Which oft, they say, some evil spirit
>   attends . . .
> Misleads the amazed night-wanderer
>   from his way. . . .
> So glistered the dire snake, and into fraud
>   Led Eve. . . .

More than just vivid description, the simile adds an extra dimension to the characterization of Satan. The mention of fire recalls the "fiery gulf" that is his domain. But this is not just fire but *ignis fatuus,* the false fire seen at night in swampy areas and believed to be caused by vapors from rotting organic matter. Legend has associated the phenomenon with evil spirits who lure night-wanderers to death by drowning in ponds or pools. The long, rhythmic simile rolls along like the serpent it describes, reinforcing both the glistering beauty and the "dire" and "delusive" quality shared by both elements of the comparison.

REVISING

The most important thing to look for as you reread your paper is whether you have addressed the assignment exactly. If the assignment asks you to focus your discussion on a single element, determining how that element functions within the structure of the poem, don't try to do more. If, however, the assignment asks for a full analysis, be sure you have at least considered all the poetic devices that appear in the particular work you are analyzing. In addition to the checklist on page 980, here are some other points to look for:

- Does the thesis statement mention or at least summarize all the elements that will be considered in the paper?
- Are your statements adequately supported by carefully chosen quotations?
- Are quotations exactly worded and signaled by quotation marks or indentation?
- Have you stayed within reasonable limits in your interpretation of the poem's meaning and of the connotative force of the words?
- Does the conclusion put back together the elements that have been taken apart for analysis?

You will find this article helpful in completing assignments on pages 63, 331, and 386.

WRITER'S HANDBOOK

Writing About Drama

Writing about drama shares many characteristics with writing about other narrative fiction. A play, however, presents its own challenges: usually the story is told entirely through dialogue and action, and there is no narrator to provide exposition, description, conflict, characterization, and so on. Writing assignments may ask you to concentrate on any of these elements of narrative fiction, or they may ask you to consider the dramatic conventions of a particular play.

WRITER'S HANDBOOK

PREWRITING
Sample Assignment

Write a composition to show how the set, props, and lighting, as described by Ibsen in his stage directions, all contribute to the theme of *A Doll House*.

1. Think It Through

Many of the elements a dramatist uses in writing a play are the same as those used by, for example, a short-story writer. Yet to a reader the differences between a short story and a play may seem more striking than the similarities. A play is, after all, almost always written for some sort of presentation by actors. When you watch a play, you are confronted with the physical setting of the stage and with the actors, whose voices and gestures tell the story. When you read a play, you must supply many of these things from your imagination. To do this, you must know what to look for in the author's descriptions of set, lighting, placement of actors, and so on, and also how the playwright goes about developing and presenting the characters. As you reread the play, keep these questions in mind.

Who are the major characters? In writing about classical and Shakespearean drama especially, you may refer to the main character as the protagonist and to the opposing character as the antagonist. In modern drama, main characters may not have a protagonist/antagonist relationship, but may rather serve as foils—opposites that emphasize each other's traits by contrast.

Who are the minor characters? What function do they serve? In Shakespeare you will find many characters that do not speak. Usually they fill crowd scenes or serve as attendants. Modern drama usually contains fewer minor characters, and those that remain are more likely to serve

important dramatic functions, as do Mrs. Linde and Dr. Rank in *A Doll House*.

What is the setting? Classical and Shakespearean drama was played on a comparatively bare stage, with very little in the way of props. The viewer had to imagine setting from the action and dialogue. Modern drama, on the other hand, tends more toward realism—and so you are more likely to find detailed descriptions of setting, costumes, properties, and so on. In Ibsen, for example, the carefully described setting contributes largely to the audience's understanding of the social context of the characters.

Does the plot development fit traditional patterns? Shakespearean drama adheres rather closely to a traditional pattern of exposition, conflict, rising action, climax, falling action, and resolution. Modern drama may or may not fit this pattern. For example, the conflict may begin before the opening of the play, and exposition may be presented throughout. Ibsen was one of the first dramatists to present exposition in a natural, seemingly casual manner, and in *A Doll House* the climax comes almost at the very end.

What dramatic conventions are employed? Classical and Shakespearean drama used many dramatic conventions, such as the chorus in Sophocles and the use of soliloquy and asides in Shakespeare. Dramatic conventions may be harder to spot in modern, realistic drama because we are more familiar with them. Yet the realistic box set with its open "fourth wall" and the use of act breaks to signal the passage of time are also dramatic conventions.

What is the theme? Is the dramatist's purpose to reflect or comment on society and its values? Do any characters or events carry symbolic meaning?

2. Organize Your Thoughts

Reread the assignment to be sure of what you are supposed to do. Then plan how you will present your material. For the sample assignment, you would probably want to devote at least one paragraph each to set, props, and lighting.

WRITING

The paragraphs that follow are a partial response to the sample assignment.

Model

The title of Ibsen's play tells us that the Helmer household is going to be the subject of the drama. It is not surprising then that the set, properties, and lighting should play significant roles in conveying the playwright's ideas and the theme of the play.

The description that begins Act One depicts a comfortable middle-class dwelling. The room contains four doors, two of which figure significantly in the play. The door leading to Torvald's study allows Torvald to separate himself from the world of the children and his child-wife. The door to the entryway becomes a focus of interest when Krogstad's letter and Dr. Rank's announcement of his imminent death lie side by side in the letter-box. The final and climactic statement of the play is the slamming of that door.

At the beginning a cheerful mood is established by the entrance of a Christmas tree and gift packages. Nora's listening at the door to Torvald's study while she eats forbidden macaroons are parts of the stage picture that convey to us the nature of the household before any words are exchanged between husband and wife. The warm setting is chilled by the successive entrances of the dispirited Mrs. Linde and the ominous Krogstad, as we understand when Nora stirs the fire in the stove. Later, when Krogstad threatens the stability of the household, Nora tries to disregard the threat by having the Christmas tree moved to the center of the room.

As the curtain goes up on Act Two, we see that the Christmas tree "now stands stripped of ornament, burned-down candle stubs on its ragged branches." The set thus conveys the gradual destruction of family happiness and unity.

Lighting serves an important function in Act Two. During the conversation between Nora and Dr. Rank, the stage directions tell us that "during what follows it begins to grow dark." Nora is powerless to stave off the onset of gloom and the fact of physical and moral corruption represented by Rank and herself. The teasing with the stockings shows Nora momentarily resorting to the sexual manipulations that have been her only means of getting her way in her previous life. When she realizes the true nature of Rank's feelings for her, Nora abandons her scheme of utilizing the doctor's friendship and good will. She asks Helene to bring in a lamp, the light of which dispels the romantic quality of the scene. Nora exhibits heroic strength of character in deciding against using her feminine wiles to take advantage of Rank and solve her problem. "Aren't you a little bit ashamed, now that the lamp is here?" she asks, in a question that might as well have been addressed to herself. . . .

REVISING

Use the checklist on page 980 and the following questions to evaluate your first draft:
• Are all the elements of narrative fiction taken into account?
• Are the specific elements of drama dealt with that are called for in the assignment?
• Are interpretations supported with persuasive evidence from the text?
• Are quotations exact, word-for-word?
• Are quotations or paraphrases introduced in such a way that the reader understands their relevance?

You will find this article helpful in completing assignments on pages 197 and 448.

WRITER'S HANDBOOK

Writing About Mood or Tone

Mood and tone are related, but the two are different. **Tone** is the author's attitude as it is reflected in the work; you sense it in the writing "voice." **Mood** is the overall atmosphere of a literary work; it is the effect the work has on a reader, rather as a piece of music may put you in a happy mood or make you feel sad. This doesn't just happen; an author may use many literary devices to elicit a certain response from a reader. When you write about mood in literature, it is your job not only to identify the mood, but also to analyze how it is created.

PREWRITING

Sample Assignments

The mood of Anna Akhmatova's poem "Requiem" is summed up in the title. In a brief composition, discuss the images and the choice of language that contribute to the mood of the poem.

In the selection from *The Pillow Book*, Sei Shōnagon employs many different tones, from nostalgic to ironical. (She even describes herself as *flippant* at one point.) What tone seems to predominate? Describe it, and cite examples to support its predominance.

1. Think It Through

Be sure you understand the terms. (See MOOD, page 958, or TONE, page 976 in the Handbook of Literary Terms.) Mood can be described by any number of words from *light* and *playful* to *somber* or *tragic*. Tone can generally be described by those same words, but also by words like *objective* or *emotional*, *optimistic* or *pessimistic*, *formal* or *informal*, *ironical* or *cynical*. Reread the work holistically—to get a feeling for the whole—before attempting any close analysis. Does any of the above descriptive words come to mind? If so, it is a good candidate for the descriptive word you want. Trust your instincts. Just as you can usually tell when someone in conversation is being sarcastic, dryly humorous, and so on, you can often sense the same thing in writing. In addition, ask yourself the following questions.

What is the original language? Mood and tone are dependent upon word choice and phrasing, and so writing about them can be further complicated when the work in question has been translated from another language. Unless you have two or more translations of the same work to compare, however, you are justified in assuming that the translator has faithfully captured the mood and tone of the original.

Does the work maintain the same mood or tone throughout? If not, try to define the shifting moods or tones, as for the sample assignment on *The Pillow Book*. See if you can spot where these shifts occur. This will help you figure out the reasons for them.

Is there any external evidence to suggest that a particular work is satirical? Consider the author, title, and reading context. Once you know that Jonathan Swift, for example, is renowned as a satirist, you will be ready *not* to accept everything he says at face value. Satire has been popular at different periods in history; many of the writings of twentieth-century authors contain elements of satire.

Is there any internal evidence to suggest satire? Recognizing that a work has satirical elements such as irony, hyperbole, understatement, and so on, may help you understand passages that may otherwise seem puzzling or even outrageous. Such elements are not always easy to spot, but they are vital to your understanding of a work.

What does the tone or mood add to your understanding of the work? Depending upon the type of writing, either tone or mood can be vital to comprehension, or either can be so far in the background as to be practically unnoticeable.

2. Gather Your Evidence

Because both mood and tone are qualities that you sense in reading, pinpointing their causes may be particularly challenging. While all the elements in a work may help produce a certain effect, pay attention to the author's (or translator's) diction—particularly to the use of connotative language or "loaded" words. Vivid imagery and figurative language contribute greatly as well.

A good prewriting strategy for the sample assignment on "Requiem" would be to categorize images and connotative language that help to generate mood. Here is a listing from the first two sections of "Requiem."

Visual Images	*Positive Connotation*
prison queues	shelter of other
lips blue with cold	wings
smile . . . face	fresh wind blows
moon's circle	the sunset basks
	hope still sings

Sound Images	*Negative Connotation*
whispered in my ear	prison queues
we all spoke in whispers	convicts' holes
clank of keys	deathly sadness
	repellent clank
Images of Touch or Feeling	savage capital
lips blue with cold	more lifeless than
numbness	the dead
fresh wind blows	life . . . wrenched
	from her heart
	smashed flat on her
	back
	hellish years
	Siberian blizzard

WRITING

Even though mood and tone are general qualities that may permeate a work, there is no need for you to be vague in writing about them. When you have done your best job of describing them and of pinpointing the words, phrases, images, figures of speech—even sentence structure—that contribute to them, take a stand. State your opinion firmly and support it. Use direct quotations, pointing out the qualities they possess or the effects they create.

The following paragraph is a partial response to the sample assignment on "Requiem."

Model

The second section is entitled "Dedication," but it is also a "farewell greeting" to the "chance friends/of my two hellish years" whom the speaker has left behind. The mood is one of almost unbearable sadness and oppression; it is so strong that even "The mountains bend before this grief." The mood in this section is not subtle. Almost every line contains images or language connoting this sadness and oppression: "deathly sadness" . . . "repellent clank of keys" . . . "heavy steps of the soldiers" . . . "savage capital." The image of the isolated woman staggering on alone, "as though her life had been wrenched from her heart," summarizes the lives of all the prisoners. Yet, curiously, "in the distance hope still sings," although there is nothing yet to suggest the nature or the source of this hope. . . .

REVISING

As you evaluate your first draft, consider whether or not you have managed to be specific about a topic that may in itself be vague. In addition to the checklist on page 980, ask yourself these questions:

- Is the mood or tone described by a carefully chosen word or phrase?
- Are ideas supported with evidence (including quotations) from the work?
- Are quotations exact?
- Are quotations explained in terms of significance or application to the thesis?
- Do any sections tend to ramble or to repeat the same thing in different words?
- Would the author of the work agree with your analysis?

You will find this article helpful in completing the assignment on page 591.

Writing About Irony and Satire

Irony is not what it appears to be; what is presented literally is not what is meant. It is this contrast that makes irony a useful device for satire. For **satire,** instead of criticizing its subject directly, does so indirectly, through ridicule. Because of this two-sided nature of irony and satire, there are always at least two things to consider in writing about them: the literal meaning and the satirical subtext, or *real* meaning. Satire makes use of more than just irony: hyperbole, understatement, and other literary devices may also serve a satirical function.

PREWRITING

Writing assignments dealing with irony may ask you to identify and explain an ironical statement or situation or to point out how irony contributes to the overall meaning or theme. Assignments dealing with satire may ask you to point out satirical elements in a work, to explain the purpose of the satire, or to analyze the satire by examining the author's technique and use of various literary devices. (See IRONY, page 955, and SATIRE, page 968, in the Handbook of Literary Terms.)

Sample Assignment

Analyze Swift's "A Modest Proposal" to show how irony is put to the service of satire. What kinds of irony are present? What is the purpose and nature of the satire?

1. Think It Through

Read the work closely. Be aware and wary. As you read, ask yourself the following questions.

What external evidence is there of irony or satire? Consider the title, author, and the general reading context. A majority of the writers from the Neoclassical period made some use of satire, and a large number of twentieth-century writers make use of irony and satire as well. Once you know that Swift was one of the foremost satirists of his age, you will be inclined *not* to take what he says at face value.

What internal evidence is there? Look especially for statements that don't seem to mean what they say or that suggest a reversal or twist of other statements in the work. Hyperbole, understatement, and paradox are clues, as are seemingly outrageous statements made with a straight face. Humor often (but not always) suggests the presence of irony or satire. Generally speaking, when the overall effect of a work is different from what might be suggested by a plot summary, suspect a satirical approach by the author.

Is the satire obvious or subtle? Readers have been known to miss the fact that a work is satirical, thereby misunderstanding that work completely. Swift's "A Modest Proposal" has caused much outrage among readers for just that reason. You may not be able to pinpoint just where an author is being satirical, or just what devices that author uses. Your feeling about the overall effect of a work may be all you have to go on.

What is the tone of the work? Satire can range from harsh and biting to light and amusing. Not all satire is amusing, and not all humor is satirical. Try to determine what the tone contributes to the work. For example, the tone of "A Modest Proposal" is grim and bitter, made doubly so by the earnest, genial voice of the persona, a social "projector." In contrast, the irony in Mark Twain's descriptions in *Life on the Mississippi* convey gentle—even affectionate—mockery of himself and his associates.

What is the purpose of the satire? Much satire throughout history has been written to correct personal or social evils, but satire may also poke gentle fun at individuals or institutions, with little purpose beyond entertaining.

2. Organize Your Thoughts

Refer to the original assignment, to be sure you are covering all the elements of the work that you are supposed to cover. If the assignment asks for an analysis, be sure to consider the subject of the satire (including, if appropriate, the historical context), the purpose of the satire, and the various literary techniques used by the author. Note especially words, sentences, and paragraphs where you can pinpoint the use of a certain literary device, such as hyperbole.

3. Test Your Thesis

You can use an evaluation by a peer or classmate at any point in the writing process and with any assignment, but such an evaluation might be particularly useful here. Ask your reader—who should be familiar with the selection—how well you have understood the selection and whether you have missed any important points you should include.

WRITING

Notice how the irony and satire are shown to be interrelated in these paragraphs, based on the sample assignment.

Model

"A Modest Proposal" is ostensibly written by a social "projector," or analyst. The ironical fact that this persona seems blithely unaware of the horror of the suggestions he is making results in our feeling as much disgust for this character—or for the attitudes he personifies—as for the proposal itself.

We respond sympathetically to the reasoned and benevolent tone of the first three paragraphs of the essay. Thereafter we begin to understand that what the projector considers "a melancholy object" is not the suffering poor but the waste and inconvenience that they cause. He projects a humanitarian image with phrases like "helpless infants" and his desire to make them "sound, useful members of the commonwealth," but retrospection shows the ambiguity of his words.

At paragraph four we begin to perceive the satirical mask differentiating the projector from Swift. Our disaffection for the projector and his proposal begins when he makes reference to "a child just dropped from its dam" and builds quickly as he mentions the "lawful occupation of begging." We feel the irony in

paragraph five when he decries abortions and the murder of illegitimate children and speaks of the shame " which would move tears and pity in the most savage and inhuman breast," although we are not prepared for the absolute horror of what he is about to propose.

Once his suggestion of cannibalism is presented, we are outraged by the offhand, business-like tone he maintains as he cites statistics and puts forth a number of "advantages" to his proposal. The ironical contradiction lies in the fact that the projector is unconscious of the hideousness of what he suggests and considers himself humane and philanthropic. His ingrained inhumanity extends beyond meat-producing children to the aged and infirm, about whom "it is very well known, that they are dying every day and rotting, by cold, and famine, and filth, and vermin, as fast as can be reasonably expected." The final stroke in the projector's self-delusion comes when he reassures us of his financial disinterestedness in the project, since "I have no children by which I can propose to get a single penny; the youngest being nine years old and my wife past child bearing."

REVISING

In addition to the checklist on page 980, ask yourself these questions:
- Have you identified the author's purpose?
- Have you kept any plot summary to the essentials and explained its significance?
- Have you given a context for each quotation and explained its meaning?
- Have you identified literary devices—hyperbole, paradox, and so on—wherever possible?
- Have you discussed the overall effect of the irony or satire?

You will find this article helpful in completing assignments on pages 197 and 693.

Writing About Symbolism

Interpreting symbolism requires you to look for more than appears on the surface of a work. **Symbolism** begins with a relatively concrete object, action, character, scene, and so on—which then takes on another dimension of meaning. This meaning will be relatively abstract, a concept or idea that goes beyond the literal meaning on the page. Arriving at that symbolic meaning depends on your sensitivity as a reader and on your ability to follow the writer's intent.

PREWRITING

Some writing assignments on symbolism may tell you what symbol to look for and ask you to interpret it. Other assignments may ask you to find the symbol. Still other assignments may simply ask you to interpret a work; then it is up to you to spot whether there is a symbol, as well as what it means. (See SYMBOL in the Handbook of Literary Terms, page 974.)

Sample Assignment

Analyze the symbolism in Cavafy's poem "Ithaka." What does Ithaka stand for—and why, in the last line of the poem, does the speaker mention plural "Ithakas"? Why might he advise, ". . . don't hurry the journey at all./Better if it lasts for years"?

1. Read the Work Closely

What elements invite a symbolic interpretation? Are certain images or word combinations stressed or repeated, or do they otherwise stand out? Does any character in the work (or the speaker in a poem) seem to feel particular significance in an object, action, and so on? As you carefully examine "Ithaka," you should note that several elements seem to function as symbols: the road/journey, Phoenician trading stations, Egyptian cities, fine things ("mother of pearl . . . perfumes"), and so on.

Is it a symbol, or merely an example? As with similes and metaphors, the actuality of a symbol must be different from what it symbolizes. Nora Helmer of *A Doll House* is an example of an overly petted and protected woman, but she is not a symbol.

What does the symbol stand for? A symbol is economical, for a few words can carry a wealth

of meaning. If a character seems to place particular significance in an object, that significance may be the symbolic meaning of the object. Consider then *why* the object might be symbolic to the character. But a symbol can also be ambiguous, meaning different things to different people. Part of the challenge in writing about symbols is to come up with a sound interpretation and then to support it with evidence from the work. In some cases you may want to offer more than one interpretation, showing the strengths and weaknesses of each.

Is the symbol repeated? Often you will find a symbol recurring, gaining new dimensions with each appearance. In some works, a symbol might in the end take on a completely different significance from what it had in the beginning. Be sure you note each recurrence throughout.

How does the symbolic meaning extend through the rest of the work? A symbol and its meaning may apply to only a small section of a work, or it may have application to a part of the work far removed. If that is the case, an author will usually—but not always—repeat the symbol in some form or other.

Is a symbolic interpretation justified? Not every work carries symbolic meanings. Many authors prefer plain, straightforward writing. Don't try to assign meaning to a work by hunting for symbols where they are not intended.

Also, don't confuse symbolism with metaphor. A writer uses metaphor to imply a comparison, to equate two things, both of which are usually concrete. In using a symbol, the writer lets an object stand for an abstraction.

Is the symbolic meaning traditional or original? Some literary symbols are traditional; for example, a road is often used to mean "life" and a ring—which has no beginning and no end—to mean "eternity." Ask yourself if a symbolic meaning seems clear because others have used it, because the meaning is part of a cultural context. (By the same token, the meaning of a symbol may be unclear if it is part of a cultural context that you don't share; for example, the peach trees in "The Peach-Blossom Fountain.") Keep in mind also that an author may use a traditional symbol, but give it a new twist, one that you should take into account.

2. Organize Your Thoughts

Any or all of the above questions may apply to the work you are analyzing. The most important thing about symbols is the way in which their meanings add depth and complexity to a work. If you can show that this is true, perhaps you need not concern yourself with *why* an author chose to use symbolism.

WRITING

In your introduction, establish immediately the identity of the symbol or symbols you will discuss. Then begin your analysis by showing how and in what context each symbol is introduced. The rest of your paper will be devoted to what the symbol means in detail, how that meaning is reflected throughout the work, and possibly to how you arrived at that meaning.

In the model that follows, note how many possible symbolic interpretations are discussed and rejected before one is chosen.

Model

But if the road symbolizes one's life—a fairly straightforward and traditional symbol —what, then, does Ithaka symbolize? There are many possible interpretations to this rather ambiguous symbol. "Death" can be rejected at once; even though the speaker tells us to hope that the "road [one's life] is a long one," the speaker clearly implies that life continues after the attainment of Ithaka. Besides, living one's life with "Ithaka [if death] always in your mind" seems to negate the kind of full, pleasurable life the speaker talks of so enthusiastically.

Further, "Arriving [at Ithaka] is what you're destined for," but "Destiny" seems too vague an interpretation. Likewise, "Old Age," "Success," and "Wisdom" can all be rejected as interpretations. In the lines, "Better if it lasts for years,/so you're old by the time you reach the island,/wealthy with all you've gained on the way" the word *if* implies that one might reach the island without being either old or wealthy. In the same sense, one *might not* automatically become wise, unless the journey has lasted for years—therefore, the speaker says, ". . . don't hurry the journey at all." If success and/or wisdom could be attained by reaching Ithaka, shouldn't one *want* to get there as quickly as possible?

Rather, Ithaka seems to symbolize a goal— something to strive for but not necessarily to attain, because it is in the striving itself that significance (with its attendant "wealth" and "wisdom") lies. Furthermore, Ithaka is an *individual* goal; everyone has his or her own, and an individual may have several Ithakas during a lifetime. That would explain the plural in the final line, ". . . you'll have understood by then what these Ithakas mean."

REVISING

Symbolic meanings can be complex, but that doesn't mean that your analysis should be so complex that it is difficult for a reader to follow. Have a classmate evaluate your first draft for clarity; then go over it yourself, using the checklist on page 980. Also consider these questions:
• Is the focus on symbolism and not on plot?
• Is the initial appearance of the symbol described? Is each recurrence discussed?
• Is there justification for a symbolic interpretation instead of a literal one?
• Is there consideration of what significance the symbol has to the character(s), and perhaps why?
• Is there a demonstration of how the symbolic meaning reflects on the meaning of the work as a whole?

You will find this article helpful in completing the assignment on page 338.

WRITER'S HANDBOOK

Writing About a Period or Trend

History, as it is lived, does not divide itself neatly into periods; yet, with the advantage of retrospect, we often can classify people, events, and works of art according to certain shared characteristics. The units in this book represent such classification. Assignments on writing about a literary period may ask you to describe a literary trend (fashion; style; vogue) and choose writings to exemplify it. Or, you may be asked to trace the evolution of a trend, showing what caused it and how it progressed to a final stage or culmination. At other times, you may be given several authors or works and asked to observe a trend—to find and define features common to the works and to give a name to their commonality.

PREWRITING

Sample Assignment

Write a composition in which you define the term Naturalism and show how naturalistic tendencies are exhibited in various works of literature that you have read.

1. Think It Through

A historical period may be easy enough to define; it is usually set off by specific beginning and end dates. A literary trend, on the other hand, is a generalization arrived at by examining the shared characteristics of a number of works. A trend may have no clear beginning and end and may exist during the same period as other trends; for example, the kind of gothic romanticism that reached a peak of popularity in the late eighteenth and early nineteenth centuries is still very much in evidence in the novels and movies of today.

The sample assignment implies, first of all, that you understand the term *Naturalism*. You will find the term defined in the Glossary of Literary Terms and in the Background article for Unit 7. Then, because literary works are the product of the time in which their authors lived, review the rest of the Background article and the time line. Just as the relics of ancient cultures and civilizations inform archaeologists about the day-to-day life of the people, so do works of literature reflect the social, political, moral, and philosophical realities of a particular time and place. The more you understand about the historical period in which Naturalism flourished,

the better you will be able to understand the causes, development, and characteristics of this literary trend. As you review these materials, ask yourself the following questions.

What are the important characteristics of the trend? List these characteristics as you find them. Be sure to distinguish Naturalism from the other literary trends dealt with in the same unit. What sets Naturalism apart?

What causes and effects can you find? Any information you can glean about what prompted an author to write about a certain subject or why that author wrote in a certain form or style might be useful. You may or may not be able to use the information in your paper, but at the least it will contribute to your own general understanding of the period or trend.

What do author biographies reveal? The biographical sketches that precede the selections will inform you of pertinent facts about the lives and experiences of the authors that you are considering. Remember also that the year of publication is given at the end of each selection; a given author's creative period will sometimes span more than one literary period.

2. Gather Your Evidence

The sample assignment asks that you cite works of literature. Stop now to consider which works that you have read fit the definition of Naturalism. Review them and take notes on their special characteristics. Once you have identified an author whose works fit the definition, you may want to read other works by that author. If you are examining the important writing of a particular period, you may want to learn something about authors not represented in this text. Secondary sources, such as encyclopedias and works of literary criticism, may provide extra, useful information about time periods and trends.

Keep in mind that literary trends and periods blend into one another and that there are always countercurrents working. During the heyday of Naturalism, for instance, there were also authors writing in an optimistic Romantic vein.

3. Organize Your Thoughts

Because you are dealing with a generalization (the period or trend) and perhaps with many specific examples that support that generalization, it will pay you to plan your paper carefully. The assignment itself may suggest an organizational pattern—here, you may decide to devote one paragraph to a definition and separate paragraphs to works or groups of works that fit the definition. Be sure that your final paragraph comes to some conclusion and does not just summarize what you have written earlier.

WRITING

In the following paragraphs, written to respond to the sample assignment, note how the term is defined and how different works are cited.

Model

Naturalism describes an artistic movement that grew out of nineteenth-century Realism. The Realists had expressed faith in science and liberalism in place of the imagination and religion. Realistic literature tended to focus on the middle and lower classes. Gustave Flaubert's *Madame Bovary* and *A Simple Heart* are often referred to as masterworks of European Realism.

In the last two decades of the nineteenth century, spurred by the theoretical writings of Hippolyte Taine and the fiction of Emile Zola, the emerging Naturalists emphasized a more militantly scientific approach to human behavior. This scientific approach was expressed through examination of causes and effects (although the fact that accidents occur in nature was not overlooked) and in careful reporting of realistic details. As part of this approach, heredity and environment were seen as the dominating forces controlling human destiny. In practice, the subject matter of the Naturalists tended toward the sordid. Instead of being guided by a benignant deity or even being the master of one's own fate, humankind seemed to the Naturalists to be caught in the maddening whirl of a universe that was at best uncaring but more often malign.

The Norwegian dramatist Henrik Ibsen might be considered a bridge figure between Realism and Naturalism. A central theme of *A Doll House* is the influence that parents can have on their children. Dr. Rank is dying because of a disease contracted by his father. Torvald discourses on parental influences and uses Nora's father as a negative example. Nora herself comes to believe that her children will be better off if she removes herself from the premises.

In France, Guy de Maupassant displayed the Naturalists' jaundiced view of human nature. His pessimism is exhibited in his most famous story, "The Necklace," and in "The False Gems," both ironic commentaries on social appearances and snobbery. . . .

REVISING

Evaluate your first draft, using the checklist on page 980. Also consider the following questions:
• Is the purpose clearly introduced in the opening paragraph?
• Are there any vague statements that can be made more specific?
• Are there graceful transitions between the paragraphs?
• Are the literary works related to actual historical events where appropriate?
• Are titles and authors' names spelled correctly? Are titles indicated by underlining (for complete works) or quotation marks (for individual poems and shorter works)?

You will find this article helpful in completing assignments on pages 392, 513, and 752.

WRITER'S HANDBOOK

Writing About Nonfiction

Basically, fiction deals with imaginary people and happenings; nonfiction deals with real people and happenings. **Nonfiction** is a very broad term, however, encompassing biography and autobiography; essays; journals, diaries, and letters; and various kinds of explanatory texts. Assignments on writing about nonfiction may direct you to any of these genres and ask you to consider content and ideas, form and structure, or style and literary devices. Or, you may be asked to respond to the ideas in a piece of writing with ideas of your own.

PREWRITING

Sample Assignment

Choose one section from Machiavelli's *The Prince* for close analysis. Summarize briefly the ideas expressed in that section. Then analyze how Machiavelli has expressed them; his reasons for including them; his arguments supporting them; his use of cause-effect, analogy, historical and mythical allusion; and his conclusions.

1. Think It Through

Your preparation should always begin with a close reading of the work. As you read, ask yourself the following questions.

What is the author's purpose? Much fiction is written primarily to entertain, but nonfiction may have a variety of purposes, including information, persuasion, or preservation of thoughts and experience. To identify an author's purpose, it may help to consider the audience he or she was writing for.

From Machiavelli's biography (page 393) you will learn that he began *The Prince* while in exile and—in hopes of a political position—dedicated it to the very man who had caused his downfall. Using his own experience as well as his extensive knowledge of history, he wrote to show aspiring princes how to achieve and retain autocratic power.

How is the purpose reflected in the structure and development of the work? Purpose can shape both choice of subject and method of organization. Examples of different methods of organization include the following: (1) deductive—a statement or explanation, followed by supporting details or examples; (2) inductive—a number of examples or anecdotes, from which a conclusion is drawn; (3) an analysis of causes and effects, including a discussion of why other causes and effects are not applicable; (4) an account of events in chronological order; (5) a comparison or contrast—as of two books in a review or two types of government in an essay.

Has the author adopted a persona? Why? More often than in other types of writing, the voice in nonfiction may be the author's own. There are exceptions, as with Swift's persona of a social planner in "A Modest Proposal." Even though the nonfiction writer usually speaks as and for himself or herself, be aware that the writer *always* selects, choosing what to put in and what to leave out to give the impression desired. In biography and autobiography, for example, you need to ask if the writer is honest, fully or partially revealing, selective for a purpose, or even biased.

What elements of style are most apparent? Generally, nonfiction style will be straightforward, but great differences are still possible. Consider, for example, the differences between Tacitus (see page 257), who reports his history as a simple narrative, and Thucydides (see page 213), who dramatizes his history, even inventing speeches for his characters. Here, the styles are influenced by the subjects and the historical periods as well as by the authors' personalities.

Style may be a special problem in literature in translation. Generally, you are safe in assuming that a translator has made an effort to transmit the effect of an author's style as well as the thought content.

What ideas are put forth? An assignment may ask you to analyze ideas and the arguments used to support them, as in the sample assignment, or may ask you to respond to the ideas with your own ideas. In either case, be sure you understand the ideas expressed. The technique of paraphrase may be especially helpful here. (See "Writing Notes and Summaries" on page 986 in the Writer's Handbook.)

2. Form Your Thesis

Review the assignment to make sure you understand exactly what aspect of the literature you are supposed to consider. Now may be a good time to form a thesis statement. You can change it later if you want to, but it will help give direction to your next steps.

3. Gather Your Evidence

The type of evidence you need depends to a large extent on your thesis statement. If you are discussing an author's ideas, for example, you will need illustrations of those ideas. Go back through the selection, taking careful notes. Since the assignment asks for a summary of Machiavelli's thought, as well as an analysis of his supporting material, you would probably find it helpful to outline the essay.

In your research, you may occasionally find that you are having trouble finding evidence to support your thesis statement as it stands; if so, consider changing your thesis to fit the evidence on hand.

4. Organize Your Thoughts

The outline form of organization is particularly useful for this type of writing. Your outline should reflect the major divisions in your thesis statement.

WRITING

The following paragraphs respond to the sample assignment. Note the analysis of how Machiavelli has supported his conclusions.

Model

While Machiavelli acknowledges that it is "praiseworthy" for one to keep his word, "to live with integrity and not by guile," he nevertheless urges that a "prudent prince" neither can nor should do so. If all men were good, he argues, "this precept would not be valid; but

since they are sorry creatures and would not keep faith with you, no obligation binds you to observe it toward them." In other words, do unto others *before* they do unto you. Such an attitude may offend our twentieth-century sensibilities, but it seems to have been a coldly realistic response to the belligerently competitive people of the Italian Renaissance who were attempting to forge new social and political structures out of the disintegration of medieval feudalism.

Having established—at least for his own purposes—that a prince must "of necessity" maintain this attitude, Machiavelli proceeds to instruct the reader in how to fight. One way, "by the laws," is proper to men, but Machiavelli has already dismissed this. The other way is as a beast, and here he alludes to Achilles' being taught by the centaur Chiron to prove this "truth." There are, then, two models of "bestial nature" that a prince should follow: the fox, who uses stealth, and the lion, who uses force. Both models are set forth as appropriate in different situations, but Machiavelli clearly prefers the former. For, he says, in the "innumerable examples" of the clash between good faith and infidelity, "the one who has known how to act the fox has always come off the better."

REVISING

In addition to the checklist on page 980, consider these questions:

- Are the author's ideas presented accurately and fairly and not taken out of context?
- If you have included a summary, does it contain unneeded description or elaboration that could be eliminated?
- If you have included a paraphrase, does it accurately reflect the meaning of the original passage?
- If you have included your personal opinion, have you given reasons for it?
- Have you introduced quotations by giving their context or explaining their significance?

You will find this article helpful in completing the assignment on page 818.

GLOSSARY OF LITERARY TERMS

Words within entries in SMALL CAPITAL LETTERS refer to other entries in the Glossary of Literary Terms. Some entries are followed by a cross-reference to the Handbook of Literary Terms, where a more detailed explanation may be found.

For pronunciation symbols, see the pronunciation key on page 1023.

GLOSSARY OF LITERARY TERMS

alexandrine (al′ig zan′drən), a line of IAMBIC HEXAMETER. (The first FOOT below is a TROCHEE.)

"Bárons, / my lords," / begán / the em- / peror / Carlon . . .

Song of Roland, page 284

allegory (al′ə gôr′ē), a NARRATIVE in either VERSE or prose, in which characters, action, and sometimes SETTING represent abstract concepts apart from the literal sense of the story. This underlying meaning may have moral, social, religious, or political significance, and the characters are often PERSONIFICATIONS of abstract ideas such as charity, hope, greed, or envy. Dante's *Inferno* (page 316) is an example from the Middle Ages.

alliteration (ə lit′ə rā′shən), the repetition of consonant sounds at the beginnings of words or within words, particularly in accented syllables. It can be used to reinforce meaning, to unify thought, or simply to produce a musical effect. These lines from *The Lay of Thrym* (page 305) alliterate two different sounds:

Henceforth no god shall get it back
Till you fetch me Freya for my future bride.

See also the Handbook of Literary Terms.

allusion (ə lü′zhən), a reference to a person, event, place, work of art, etc., such as the references to historical events in Akhmatova's *Requiem 1935–1940* (page 820). See also the Handbook of Literary Terms.

analogy (ə nal′ə jē), a comparison made between two objects, situations, or ideas that are somewhat alike but unlike in most respects. Frequently an unfamiliar or complex object or idea will be explained through comparison to a familiar or simpler one. Thus Swift compares the feuding factions in Ireland to groups of fanatics in Jerusalem (page 557). See also the Handbook of Literary Terms.

anapest (an′ə pest), a three-syllable metrical FOOT consisting of two unstressed syllables followed by a stressed syllable, as in the word "interfere." The following line, except for the first foot, is in anapestic TETRAMETER:

The mas- / ter, the swab- / er, the boat- / swain and I . . .

The Tempest, page 443

anastrophe (See INVERSION.)

antagonist (an tag′ə nist), a character in a story or play who opposes the chief character, or PROTAGONIST. In Milton's *Paradise Lost* (page 500), Satan is the antagonist. See also Protagonist in the Handbook of Literary Terms.

aphorism (af′ə riz′əm), a brief saying embodying a moral, such as Pope's "Know then thyself, presume not God to scan; / The proper study of mankind is man," from *An Essay on Man* (page 571).

apostrophe (ə pos′trə fē), a figure of speech in which an absent person, an abstract concept, or an inanimate object is directly addressed. Marlowe's Faustus addresses inanimate objects when he pleads, "Stand still, you ever-moving spheres of heaven, / That time may cease and midnight never come" (page 487). See also the Handbook of Literary Terms.

archetype (är′kə tīp), a symbol, story pattern, or character type that recurs frequently in literature and evokes strong, often unconscious, associations in the reader. For example, the wicked witch and the enchanted prince are character types widely dispersed throughout folk tales and literature. The story of a hero who undertakes a dangerous quest, as in *Sir Gawain and the Green Knight* (page 340), is a recurrent story pattern. See also the Handbook of Literary Terms.

argument, literally a "making clear." A summary or synopsis, usually in prose, of what is in a story or play, with regard both to PLOT and to meaning. There is an argument at the beginning of each book of *Paradise Lost* (page 500).

assonance (as′n əns), the repetition of similar vowel sounds followed by different consonant sounds in stressed syllables or words. It is often used instead of RHYME. "Hate" and "great" are examples of rhyme; "hate" and "grade" are examples of assonance. In Pope's *An Essay on Man* (page 570), these two lines have four assonant sounds: "Cease then, nor order imperfection name: / Our proper bliss depends on what we blame." See also the Handbook of Literary Terms.

autobiography (See BIOGRAPHY.)

ballad, a NARRATIVE passed on, or composed, in the oral tradition. It often makes use of REPETITION and DIALOGUE. If the author of a ballad in unknown, it is called a *folk ballad;* if the author is known, it is called a *literary ballad.* Heine's "The Loreley" (page 619) is a literary ballad.

ballad stanza, a STANZA usually consisting of four alternating lines of IAMBIC TETRAMETER and TRIMETER and rhyming the second and fourth lines:

I cannot explain the sadness
That's fallen on my breast.
An old, old fable haunts me,
And will not let me rest.

> "The Loreley," page 619

biography, an account of a person's life. An example is Plato's account of the life of Socrates in the *Apology* (page 221). Autobiography is the story of all or part of a person's life written by the person who lived it. Dinesen's *Out of Africa* (page 814) is an autobiography.

blank verse, unrhymed IAMBIC PENTAMETER:

Ĭ máy / ăssért / Ētĕr- / năl Prŏv- / ĭdénce,
Ănd jús- / tĭfý / thĕ wáys / ŏf Gód / tŏ mén.

> Milton, *Paradise Lost,* page 501

The Tempest (page 415) is written in blank verse. See also the Handbook of Literary Terms.

cacophony (kə kof′ə nē), a succession of harsh, discordant sounds in either poetry or prose, used to achieve a specific effect. Note the harshness of sound and rhythm in these lines:

No more dams I'll make for fish,
  Nor fetch in firing
  At requiring,
Nor scrape trenchering, nor wash dish.
  'Ban, 'Ban, Ca–Caliban
Has a new master, get a new man.

> Shakespeare, *The Tempest,* page 445

caesura (si zhŭr′ə, si zyŭr′ə), a pause in a line of VERSE, usually near the middle. It most often reflects the sense of the line and is greater than a normal pause between words. It is used to add variety to regular METER and therefore to add emphasis to certain words. A caesura can be indicated by punctuation, by the grammatical construction of a sentence, or by the placement of lines on the page. For purposes of study, the mark indicating a caesura is two short, vertical lines.

Born but to die, ‖ and reas'ning but to err;
Alike in ignorance, ‖ his reason such,
Whether he thinks too little, ‖ or too much. . . .

> Pope, *An Essay on Man,* page 571

The caesura was a particularly important device in Anglo-Saxon poetry, where it coexisted with ALLITERATION. However, it is a technique used in many forms of poetry, such as the SONNET, the HEROIC COUPLET, and BLANK VERSE.

canto, one of the main divisions of a long poem. Dante's *Inferno* (page 316) is divided into cantos.

caricature (kar′ə kə chŭr), exaggeration of prominent features of appearance or personality. When we first see him in *Sir Gawain and the Green Knight,* the Green Knight is a caricature of appearance (page 340).

carpe diem (kär′pe dē′əm), Latin for "seize (enjoy) the day," the name applied to a MOTIF frequently found in LYRIC poetry: take life's pleasures now, while you are able. An example is Catullus's "Lesbia, Let Us Live and Love" (page 234).

chanson de geste (shäN sôN′ də zhest), literally, a song of deeds. An epic-like poem of heroic endeavors set in the era of Charlemagne. The oldest and best known of the *chansons de geste* is the *Song of Roland* (page 284).

characterization, the methods an author uses to develop the personality of a character in a literary work. These methods include a character's actions, such as those of Prospero (page 415); the dialogue between characters, such as that between Oedipus and Tiresias (page 174); and the speech of a chorus or character commenting on the characters, as in Anouilh's *Antigone* (page 874). Any or all of these methods may be used in the same work. See also the Handbook of Literary Terms.

chorus, in Greek tragedy, a group of actors who sing and dance their commentary on the dialogue taking place in the drama (as in *Oedipus the King,* page 165). Later drama has abandoned the chorus as a group of dancing singers, but has not entirely abandoned the convention of a chorus as a commentator on the play, though that commentator is likely to be one speaker only, as in Anouilh's *Antigone* (page 874).

Classicism, the style of literature created by the ancient Greeks and Romans, characterized by attention to form; by order, restraint, and balance in the treatment of content (in Greek tragedy, for instance, no actions take place on the stage); and by an absence of the values associated with Romanticism. *Oedipus the King* (page 165) is a distinguished example, and so is Catullus's poem to his brother (page 235). Many modern authors have been influenced by Classicism, and it flourished especially during the Neoclassical period (see Unit 5). Pope's *Essay on Man* (page 570) is an example of Neoclassicism.

climax, the decisive point in a story or play, after which the action changes course and begins to resolve itself. In *Paradise Lost* (page 500), the climax occurs when Eve eats the forbidden fruit. But not every story or play has this kind of dramatic climax. Sometimes a character may simply resolve a problem in his or her mind, and at some point that is not entirely clear to us. If *The Tempest* (page 415) concerns Prospero's self-reformation, it is difficult to say exactly when that change occurs. At times there is no resolution of the PLOT; the climax then comes when a character realizes that a resolution is impossible. "Climax" is also used to mean the point of greatest interest in a work, where the reader or audience has the most intense emotional response. See also Plot in the Handbook of Literary Terms.

comedy, a play or other work written primarily to amuse the reader or audience. In addition to arousing laughter, comic writing often appeals to the intellect. Thus the comic mode has often been used to "instruct" the audience about the follies of certain social conventions and human foibles. Molière does this in *Tartuffe* (page 516). When used in this way, the comedy tends toward SATIRE.

comic relief, an amusing episode in a serious or tragic literary work, especially a drama, that is introduced to relieve tension.

conflict, the struggle between two opposing forces. The five basic kinds of conflict are: a person against another person, or ANTAGONIST, as in the *Song of Roland* (page 284); a person against nature, as in *The Epic of Gilgamesh* (page 9); a person against society, as in Molière's *Tartuffe* (page 516); a person against fate, as in *Oedipus the King* (page 165); and two elements within a person struggling for mastery, as in Joyce's *A Portrait of the Artist as a Young Man* (page 778). See also Plot in the Handbook of Literary Terms.

connotation (kon′ə tā′shən), the emotional associations surrounding a word, as opposed to the word's literal meaning, or DENOTATION. If a word has connotations, they are usually either negative or positive. Thus "horse" is a neutral, denotative word, "nag" has negative connotations, and "steed" has positive connotations (though the denotations of all three words are the same). See also the Handbook of Literary Terms.

consonance (kon′sə nəns), the repetition of consonant sounds that are preceded by different vowel sounds.

"Hope" is the thing with feathers—
That perches in the soul—
And sings the tune without the words—
And never stops—at all—. . .
    "Hope is the Thing with Feathers," page 680

Consonance is an effective device for linking sound, MOOD, and meaning. In the lines above, the *l* sounds in the words "soul" and "all" provide an example of consonance. See also the Handbook of Literary Terms.

couplet, a pair of rhyming lines with identical METER:

Know then thyself, presume not God to scan;
The proper study of mankind is man.
    Pope, *An Essay on Man*, page 571

(See also HEROIC COUPLET.)

dactyl (dak′tl), a three-syllable metrical FOOT consisting of a stressed syllable followed by two unstressed syllables, as in the word "odyssey." In the following lines the first two feet are dactyls:

Merrily, / merrily / shall I / live now
Under the / blossom that / hangs on / the bough.
    The Tempest, page 473

denotation (dē′nō tā′shən), the strict, literal (dictionary) meaning of a word. See also CONNOTATION.

dénouement (dā′nü mäN′), the resolution of the PLOT. The word is derived from a French word meaning "to untie." See also Plot in the Handbook of Literary Terms.

dialect, a form of speech characteristic of a particular region or class, differing from the standard language in pronunciation, vocabulary, and grammatical form. In Walker's "Everyday Use" (page 922) one can distinguish the dialect of Southern blacks.

dialogue, conversation between two or more people in a literary work. Dialogue can serve many purposes: CHARACTERIZATION of those speaking and those spoken about, as in the "Prologue in Heaven" in Goethe's *Faust* (page 609); the creation of MOOD or atmosphere, as in *The Damask Drum* (page 98); the advancement of the PLOT, as in *Oedipus the King* (page 165); and the development of a THEME, as in Prospero's talks with Ariel in *The Tempest* (page 415).

diary (See JOURNAL.)

diction, the author's choice of words and phrases in a literary work. This choice involves both the CONNOTATION and DENOTATION of a word as well as levels of usage. In *The Tempest* (page 415), Shakespeare makes use of a wide variety of dictions when he has each character speak in a way that is appropriate to his or her education and background.

drama, a literary work in verse or prose, usually written to be acted, that tells a story through the speeches and actions of the characters, rather than through a narrator. A drama may be a TRAGEDY, such as *Oedipus the King* (page 165), or a COMEDY, such as *Tartuffe* (page 516). There are also tragicomedies, histories, and other kinds of dramas.

dramatic convention, any of several devices that the audience accepts as reality in a dramatic work. For instance, the audience accepts that an interval between acts may represent hours, days, weeks, months, or years; that a bare stage may represent a meadow or an inner room; that the three walls of a stage can represent a four-walled room; that audible dialogue is supposed to represent whispered conversation; or that a blackout signals the end of a scene, just as a falling curtain does.

dramatic monologue (mon′l ôg), a LYRIC poem in which the speaker addresses someone whose replies are not recorded. Sometimes the one addressed seems to be present, sometimes not. An example is "The River-Merchant's Wife: A Letter" (page 84), as is Mistral's "To My Husband" (page 829).

elegy, a solemn, reflective poem, usually about death, written in a formal style. An example is Catullus's "At His Brother's Grave" (page 235). Gilgamesh's lament for Enkidu (page 10) has some of the qualities of an elegy.

end rhyme, the rhyming of words at the ends of lines of poetry. (See RHYME.) See also Rhyme in the Handbook of Literary Terms.

end-stopped line, a line of poetry that contains a complete thought, thus necessitating the use of a semicolon, colon, period, or exclamation mark at the end:

Great Lord of all things, yet a Prey to all;
Sole Judge of Truth, in endless Error hurl'd:
The Glory, Jest, and Riddle, of the World!

> Pope, *An Essay on Man,* page 571

(Compare RUN-ON LINE.)

epic, a long NARRATIVE poem (originally handed down in oral tradition—later a literary form) dealing with great heroes and adventures; having a national, world-wide, or cosmic setting; involving supernatural forces; and written in a deliberately ceremonial STYLE. Examples are the *Odyssey* (page 126), the *Aeneid* (page 242), and *Paradise Lost* (page 500).

epigram, any short, witty VERSE or saying, often ending with a wry twist.

The hungry judges soon the sentence sign,
And wretches hang that jurymen may dine . . .

> *The Rape of the Lock,* page 563

See also the Handbook of Literary Terms.

epigraph, a motto or quotation at the beginning of a story, book, poem, or chapter, often suggesting the THEME. "The Circular Ruins" (page 847) has an appropriate epigraph from *Through the Looking Glass.*

epilogue, a concluding section added to a work in order to round it out or to comment on it. Akhmatova's *Requiem 1935–1940* (page 820) concludes with an "Epilogue" as a memorial to the poet's fellow-sufferers.

epiphany (i pif′ə nē), literally "a showing forth," and a holy day in the Christian calendar; as a literary term coined by James Joyce, it is a moment of enlightenment in which the underlying truth, essential nature, or real meaning of something is suddenly made clear to character and/or reader. Many episodes in Joyce build up to an epiphany. Thus in *A Portrait of the Artist as a Young Man* (page 778), the girl in the water reveals Stephen's vocation to himself in an epiphany.

epistle, in general, any letter; specifically, a long, formal, and instructional composition in prose or VERSE. Pope's *Essay on Man* (page 570) consists of four verse epistles.

epitaph, a brief statement commemorating a dead person, often inscribed on a tombstone. Sappho's "Someone, I Tell You" (page 160) is, in part, an epitaph, as is Catullus's poem to his brother (page 235).

epithet, a descriptive expression, sometimes repeated, usually mentioning a quality or attribute of the person or thing being described. Homer (page 126) uses the "wine-dark sea," "grey-eyed Athena," "rosy-fingered dawn," and "Odysseus the great tactician" as epithets. Neoclassical poets tried to be more elaborate. Thus Pope uses "glittering forfex" as an epithet for scissors in *The Rape of the Lock* (page 563).

essay, a brief composition that presents a personal viewpoint. An essay may present a viewpoint through formal analysis and argument, as in Cicero's "On Friendship" (page 230), or it may be more informal in style, as in Camus's "Between Yes and No" (page 932).

exposition, background information about the SETTING, characters, and other elements of a story or play. Often this information about the past is brought out in the dialogue. See also Plot in the Handbook of Literary Terms.

extended metaphor, a METAPHOR that is developed at great length, often through a whole work or a great part of it. It is common in poetry but is used in prose as well. The images of sight and blindness are an extended metaphor in *Oedipus the King* (page 165). See also Figurative Language in the Handbook of Literary Terms.

fable, a brief TALE in which the characters' actions point out a moral truth, as in Tolstoy's "How Much Land Does a Man Need?" (page 669). Often the characters are animals, as in the fables of La Fontaine (page 509).

GLOSSARY OF LITERARY TERMS

falling action, the resolution of a dramatic PLOT, which takes place after the CLIMAX. See also Plot in the Handbook of Literary Terms.

fantasy, a work that takes place in an unreal world, concerns incredible characters, or employs FICTIONAL scientific principles. "The Circular Ruins" (page 847) is an example.

fiction, a type of literature drawn from the imagination of the author that tells about imaginary people and happenings. NOVELS and SHORT STORIES are fiction. Examples are *Don Quixote* (page 406) and "The Metamorphosis" (page 785).

figurative language, language used in a nonliteral way for the purpose of emphasis, clarification, or a special effect. The more common examples of figurative language (figures of speech) are SIMILE, METAPHOR, PERSONIFICATION, HYPERBOLE, and SYNECDOCHE. See also the Handbook of Literary Terms.

foil, a character whose traits are different from those of a comparable character, and who thus points up the strengths or weaknesses of the other character. Antigone and Ismene are foils to each other in Anouilh's *Antigone* (page 874).

folk literature, a type of early literature passed orally from generation to generation, and written down later. The authorship of folk literature is unknown. Folk literature includes MYTHS, FABLES, fairy tales, EPICS, and LEGENDS. Examples are the *Odyssey* (page 126) and *Thorstein the Staff-Struck* (page 308).

foot, a group of syllables in VERSE, usually consisting of one stressed syllable and one or more unstressed syllables. A foot may occasionally, for variety, have two stressed syllables (a SPONDEE) or two unstressed syllables. In the following lines the feet are divided by slashes:

Stand still, / you ev- / er mov- / ing spheres /

of heaven,

That time / may cease / and mid- / night

nev- / er come. . . .

Marlowe, *Doctor Faustus*, page 487

The most common line lengths are five feet (PENTAMETER), four feet (TETRAMETER), and three feet (TRIMETER). The lines quoted above are IAMBIC pentameter. (See also RHYTHM.) See also Rhythm in the Handbook of Literary Terms.

foreshadowing, a clue given to the reader or audience of what is to come. In *Madame Bovary* (page 661), Emma Bovary's behavior after her return from the ball is a foreshadowing of her forthcoming rebellion. See also the Handbook of Literary Terms.

frame, a NARRATIVE device presenting a story or group of stories within the frame of a larger narrative. In *The Decameron* (page 388), Boccaccio creates a frame by having fugitives from the plague gather and tell the stories.

free verse, a type of poetry that differs from conventional VERSE forms in being "free" from a fixed pattern of METER and RHYME, but using RHYTHM and other poetic devices. An example is Whitman in "Song of Myself" (page 652). See also the Handbook of Literary Terms.

ghazal (gaz′əl), a type of lyric popular in eastern literature, especially Arabic and Persian, but occasionally imitated in the West. It has a minimum of five couplets, rhymed *aa, ba, ca, da,* etc. Usually the topic is wine and women. In the last couplet, the poet mentions his own name. "The Crier," by Hafiz (page 54), is an example.

haiku (hī′kü), a three-line poem in Japanese, usually describing some aspect of nature, and having a prescribed number of syllables in each line: five in the first line, seven in the second, and five in the third. The *haiku* by Bashō (page 102) are examples.

hero, the central character in a NOVEL, SHORT STORY, DRAMA, or other work of literature. When the central character is a woman, she is usually called the *heroine.* Faust is the hero of Goethe's *Faust* (page 609). See also Protagonist in the Handbook of Literary Terms.

heroic couplet, a pair of rhymed VERSE lines in IAMBIC PENTAMETER:

For wit's false mirror held up nature's light;
Shew'd erring pride *Whatever is,* is *right.* . . .
                    Pope, *An Essay on Man,* page 571

See also Couplet in the Handbook of Literary Terms.

hexameter, a metrical line of six FEET, like this line from the *Song of Roland,* page 284:

"Barons, / my lords," / began / the em- /

peror / Carlon . . .

See also Rhythm in the Handbook of Literary Terms.

humor, in literature, writing whose purpose is to amuse, to evoke laughter, or to manipulate the attitudes of the audience or reader. Humorous writing can be sympathetic to human nature or can be satirical. Some forms of humor are IRONY, SATIRE, PARODY, and CARICATURE.

hyperbole (hī pėr′bə lē) a figure of speech involving great exaggeration. The effect may be serious or comic. The excerpt from Mark Twain's *Life on the Mississippi* (page 684) makes use of hyperbole for comic effect. See also the Handbook of Literary Terms.

iamb (ī′am), a two-syllable metrical FOOT consisting of

an unstressed syllable followed by a stressed syllable, as in the word "until." The following line is in iambic PENTAMETER:

How man- / y good- / ly crea- / tures are
there here!

Shakespeare, The Tempest, page 415

See also Rhythm in the Handbook of Literary Terms.

imagery, the sensory details that provide vividness in a literary work and tend to arouse emotions in a reader that abstract language would not. Prospero's speech in *The Tempest* beginning "Ye elves of hills, brooks, standing lakes, and groves" (page 472) is rich in specific, concrete details that appeal to the senses. See also the Handbook of Literary Terms.

inference, a reasonable conclusion about the behavior of a character or the meaning of an event, drawn from the limited information presented by the author. Dramas in particular require you to use your powers of inference. In reading *The Tempest* (page 415), you may want to make inferences about whether Prospero is trying to reform himself; he himself makes no such statements. See also the Handbook of Literary Terms.

in medias res (in mä′dē äs räs′), Latin for "into the middle of things." In a traditional EPIC the opening scene often begins in the middle of the action. In the ARGUMENT of Book I of *Paradise Lost* (page 500), Milton says that "the Poem hastes into the midst of things," opening with Satan and his angels already defeated and in Hell. Later in the poem, Milton tells the story of the battle between Satan and the forces of Heaven, which led to this defeat. This device may be used in any NARRATIVE form.

internal rhyme, the rhyming of words or stressed syllables within a line that may or may not have a RHYME at the end as well, as in this line from *The Tempest*, page 445: " 'Ban, 'Ban, Ca–Caliban . . ." See also Rhyme in the Handbook of Literary Terms.

inversion (also called *anastrophe*), an inverting of the usual order of the words or parts of a sentence, primarily for emphasis or to achieve a certain rhythm or rhyme. In this example, both lines contain inversion:

A heavenly image in the glass appears,
To that she bends, to that her eye she rears . . .

Pope, The Rape of the Lock, page 561

invocation (in′və kā′shən), the summoning of a deity or muse (the classical goddess who inspired a poet) for help and inspiration. It is found at the beginning of traditional EPIC poems. In *Paradise Lost* (page 500) Milton invokes the "heavenly muse" instead of one of the classical muses of poetry.

irony, the term used to describe a contrast between what

is claimed to be and what really is. In *verbal irony*, the intended meaning of a statement is different from (often the opposite of) what the statement literally says. An example is Orgon's statement to Cléante in *Tartuffe*, page 522: "You harbor all the insight of the age./You are our one clear mind, our only sage." *Dramatic irony* refers to a situation in which events or facts not known to a character on stage or in a fictional work are known to the audience or reader. *Oedipus the King* (page 165) is one of the most famous examples. In *structural irony*, the irony is sustained over the whole work. In this type of irony there is sometimes a naive spokesman, who is not aware of the discrepancy between what he says and what the author intends. Swift's *A Modest Proposal* (page 553) is a celebrated example. See also the Handbook of Literary Terms.

journal, a formal record of a person's daily experiences. It is less intimate or personal than a diary and more chronological than an AUTOBIOGRAPHY.

lay or *lai*, a short NARRATIVE poem, especially one written in French during the Middle Ages and based on LEGEND. Marie de France's "The Lay of the Werewolf" (page 297) is an example.

legend, a story handed down from the past, often associated with some period in the history of a people. A legend differs from a MYTH in having some historical truth and often less of the supernatural. *Thorstein the Staff-Struck* (page 308), for example, is based on Icelandic history.

literary ballad (See BALLAD.)

lyric, a poem, usually short, that expresses the emotion or state of mind of only one speaker. It usually creates a single impression. It may be RHYMED or unrhymed. A SONNET is a lyric poem. Other examples of lyrics are Ariel's songs in *The Tempest* (page 415) and Mistral's "To My Husband" (page 829). See also the Handbook of Literary Terms.

masque, a short amateur dramatic court entertainment with more emphasis on music, costumes, and scenery than on poetry, frequently given in England in the 1500s and 1600s. The term is also used for a PLAY written for such an entertainment. *The Tempest* (page 415) contains a masque.

maxim (See APHORISM.)

memoir (mem′wär, mem′wôr), a form of AUTO-BIOGRAPHY that is more concerned with personalities, events, and actions of public importance than with the private life of the writer. The *Babur-nama* (page 64) is an example of a memoir.

metaphor, a figure of speech that establishes an identity between two basically unlike things. This identity may be stated (She was a stone) or implied (Her stony silence filled the room). In Mistral's "To My Husband" (page 829), the speaker declares her whole body to be "nothing but a veil." (See also SIMILE and FIGURATIVE LANGUAGE.) See also the Handbook of Literary Terms.

meter, the pattern of stressed and unstressed syllables in POETRY. (See RHYTHM.) See also Rhythm in the Handbook of Literary Terms.

metonymy (mə ton′ə mē), a figure of speech in which a term closely associated with a person or thing is made to stand for it. An example is in Genesis (page 25): "In the sweat of thy face shalt thou eat bread." Here, "sweat" is used to represent hard physical labor.

miracle play, a type of PLAY produced during the late medieval and early Renaissance periods, based on the life of Jesus, on stories from the Bible, or especially on legends of the saints. *Mystery plays* are more often based on Scripture.

mock epic, a poem using the form and style—and especially the conventions—of an EPIC poem to treat a trivial incident. Pope's *The Rape of the Lock* (page 560) is a mock epic.

monologue (See SOLILOQUY and DRAMATIC MONOLOGUE.)

mood, the overall atmosphere or prevailing emotional aura of a work, sometimes established at the beginning. See the words above the gate to Hell in Canto III of Dante's *Inferno* (page 318). Mood is important in arousing a reader's expectations about what is to come. (See TONE for a comparison.) See also the Handbook of Literary Terms.

moral, the lesson or inner meaning to be learned from a FABLE, TALE, or other story. The moral of Tolstoy's "How Much Land Does a Man Need?" (page 669) is stated in the last two paragraphs, and is almost explicit. The moral of La Fontaine's "The Acorn and the Pumpkin" (page 509) is explicit, and is stated at both beginning and end.

morality play, a type of PLAY popular in the 1400s and 1500s in which the characters are PERSONIFICATIONS of abstract qualities such as vice, virtue, mercy, shame, wealth, knowledge, ignorance, poverty, and perseverance.

motif (mō tēf′), a situation that recurs in various works or in various parts of the same work. In Renaissance poetry, painful love is a common motif. See Petrarch's sonnet "Blest Be the Day" (page 381). See Theme in the Handbook of Literary Terms.

motivation, the process of presenting a convincing cause for the actions of a character in a dramatic or fictional work in order to justify those actions. Motivation usually involves a combination of external events and the character's psychological traits, as in the excerpts from Flaubert (page 661) and Joyce (page 778).

mystery play (See MIRACLE PLAY.)

myth, a traditional story connected with the beliefs of a people, usually attempting to account for something in nature or history. A myth has less historical background than a LEGEND. Milton's *Paradise Lost* (page 500) has mythic elements in its attempts to account for aspects of the cosmos, nature, and human life.

narrative, a story or account of an event or a series of events. It may be told either in POETRY or in prose, and it may be either fictional or true. Tacitus's *Annals* (page 258) and Milton's *Paradise Lost* (page 500) are narratives.

narrative poetry, poetry that tells a story or recounts a series of events. It may be either long or short, but is usually long. EPICS and ROMANCES are types of narrative poetry.

narrator, the teller of a story. The teller may be a character in the story, as in Book Two of the *Aeneid* (page 242); an anonymous voice outside the story, as in *Madame Bovary* (page 661); or the author, as in *Out of Africa* (page 814). A narrator's attitude toward his or her subject is capable of much variation; it can range from one of indifference to one of extreme conviction and feeling. (See also PERSONA and POINT OF VIEW.) See also Point of View in the Handbook of Literary Terms.

Naturalism, writing that depicts events as rigidly determined by the forces of heredity and environment, which are conceived of as being indifferent to human desires. The worlds depicted in such works tend to be bleak. Ibsen's *A Doll House* (page 712) and Maupassant's *The False Gems* (page 689) have elements of naturalism.

Neoclassicism, writing of a later period that shows the influence of the Greek and Roman classics. The term is often applied to literature of the eighteenth century. (See also CLASSICISM and Unit 5.)

No **play,** a traditional form of DRAMA in Japan, deriving from religious rite; it uses symbolic scenery, masked actors, and nonrealistic acting and events. *The Damask Drum* (page 98) is an example.

nonfiction, any writing that is not FICTION; any type of prose that deals with real people and happenings. BIOGRAPHY and history are types of nonfiction, and so is the personal essay, such as the one by Camus (page 932).

novel, a long work of NARRATIVE prose fiction dealing with characters, situations, and SETTINGS that imitate those of real life instead of trying to elevate them to higher levels, as a ROMANCE does. Among the authors in this text who have written novels are Hugo, Gogol, Flaubert, Tolstoy, Twain, and Joyce.

novella (nō vel′ə), a story that is longer than a SHORT STORY, but shorter than a NOVEL. "The Metamorphosis" (page 785) is an example.

ode, a LYRIC poem, formal in style and complex in form, often written in commemoration or celebration of a special quality, object, or occasion. The poems by Horace (page 238) are odes.

onomatopoeia (on′ə mat′ə pē′ə), a word or words used in such a way that the sound imitates the sound of the thing spoken of. Some single words in which sound suggests meaning are "hiss," "smack," "buzz," and "hum." Milton uses words with *s* sounds to represent Satan (the serpent) in *Paradise Lost* (for example, page 503, lines 149–152).

parable, a brief fictional work that concretely illustrates an abstract idea or teaches some lesson or truth. It differs from a FABLE in that its characters are generally people rather than animals, and it differs from an ALLEGORY in that its characters do not necessarily represent abstract qualities. Rumi's "The Man Who Fled from Azrael" (page 48) is a parable also.

paradox, a statement or situation that seems to be self-contradictory but has valid meaning. Thus Petrarch, in the sonnet "Blest Be the Day" (page 381), blesses his own pain because it is the pain of loving Laura. See also the Handbook of Literary Terms.

parallelism, an arrangement of parts of a sentence, paragraph, or other unit of composition in which one element equal in importance to another is similarly developed and phrased. Whitman's "A Noiseless Patient Spider" (page 656) has many examples of parallelism.

parody, a humorous imitation of serious writing. It follows the form of the original, but often changes the sense to ridicule the writer's STYLE. Cervantes's *Don Quixote* (page 406) parodies romances of chivalry; Swift's *A Modest Proposal* (page 553) parodies political and economic pamphlets of Swift's time. (See also SATIRE.)

pastoral, a conventional form of LYRIC poetry presenting an idealized picture of rural life. There are elements of pastoralism in the 23rd Psalm (page 33), *The Tempest* (page 415), and *Paradise Lost* (page 500).

pentameter (pen tam′ə tər), a metrical line of five FEET. Here is a line of IAMBIC pentameter:

Bē nót / dĭstúrbed / wĭth mý / ĭnfír- / mĭtý.

Shakespeare, *The Tempest*, page 467

See also Rhythm in the Handbook of Literary Terms.

persona (pər sō′nə), the mask of the author as expressed by an important character in a particular work. Jonathan Swift is the author of *A Modest Proposal* (page 553), but even though the essay is written in the *first-person* POINT OF VIEW, we are not to assume that Swift is expressing his personal opinions. Rather, he has created a persona in the form of the spokesman. (See also NARRATOR and POINT OF VIEW.)

personification (pər son′ə fə kā′shən), the representation of abstractions, ideas, or inanimate objects as living, or even human, beings, as when a medieval playwright names a character Death or Good Deeds or Confession. Personification is one kind of FIGURATIVE LANGUAGE. See also the Handbook of Literary Terms.

play (See DRAMA.)

plot, in the simplest sense, a series of related happenings in a literary work. The term is also used to refer to the action as it is organized around a CONFLICT and builds through complication to a CLIMAX followed by a DÉNOUEMENT, or resolution. You can see this structure in *Oedipus the King* (page 165). See also the Handbook of Literary Terms.

poetry, a type of literature that creates its emotional response by the imaginative use of words patterned (in lines of a certain length) to produce a desired effect through RHYTHM, sound, and the meanings of the words. Poetry may be RHYMED or unrhymed. Among the many forms of poetry are the EPIC, ODE, LYRIC, SONNET, BALLAD, ELEGY, BLANK VERSE, and FREE VERSE.

point of view, the narrative situation a writer uses to present the actions and characters of a story. The story may be narrated by one of its characters (the *first-person* point of view), as in Colette's "The Little Bouilloux Girl" (page 833), or the story may be told by a NARRATOR who does not participate in the action (the *third-person* point of view). Further, the third-person narrator may be *omniscient* (om-nish′ənt)—able to see into the minds of all the characters, as in *Madame Bovary* (page 661). Or the third-person narrator may be *limited*—confined to a single character's perceptions, as in Chekhov's "The Kiss" (page 754). An author who describes only what can be seen, like a newspaper reporter, is said to use an *objective* point of view. (See also NARRATOR and PERSONA.) See also the Handbook of Literary Terms.

prologue, a section preceding the main body of a work and serving as an introduction to it, sometimes with thematic importance. An example is the "Prologue in Heaven" to Goethe's *Faust* (page 609).

protagonist (prō tag′ə nist), the leading character or HERO (heroine) in a literary work. In *Madame Bovary* (page 661) it is Emma. (See also ANTAGONIST.) See also the Handbook of Literary Terms.

proverb, a short, well-known saying, often handed down from the past, that expresses an obvious truth or familiar observation about life. "Haste makes waste" is an example.

psalm (säm, sälm), a song or poem in praise of God. The term is most often applied to the songs or hymns in the Book of Psalms in the Bible, such as those beginning on page 33.

quatrain (kwot′rān), a verse STANZA of four lines. This stanza may take many forms, according to line lengths and RHYME patterns. Akhmatova's "Lot's Wife" (page 820) is in quatrains.

Rationalism, a philosophy that emphasizes the role of reason rather than of experience or of faith in answering the basic questions of human existence. It was most influential during the Age of Reason (1660–1780) and influenced such writers of that period as Voltaire, Molière, Swift, and Pope, most of whom satirized Rationalism.

Realism, a way of representing life that emphasizes ordinary people in believable experiences. *Madame Bovary* (page 661) is an example of Realism.

refrain, the REPETITION of one or more lines in each STANZA of a poem. Some of the songs in *The Tempest* (page 415) have a refrain, or "burden."

repetition, a poetic device in which a sound, word, or phrase is repeated for style or emphasis. An example is these lines from *Paradise Lost* (page 501): "A mind not to be changed by place or time./The mind is its own place, and in itself/Can make a heaven of Hell, a hell of Heaven."

resolution (See FALLING ACTION.) See also Plot in the Handbook of Literary Terms.

rhyme, the exact repetition of sounds in at least the final accented syllables of two or more words:

Hither the heroes and the nymphs resort,
To taste awhile the pleasures of a court.
Pope, *The Rape of the Lock,* page 562

(See also RHYME SCHEME, INTERNAL RHYME, END RHYME, and SLANT RHYME.) See also the Handbook of Literary Terms.

rhyme royal, a seven-line, iambic pentameter stanza rhyming *ababbcc.* See Wordsworth's "Resolution and Independence," page 697.

rhyme scheme, any pattern of rhyme in a STANZA. For purposes of study, the pattern is labeled as shown below, with the first rhyme word and all the words rhyming with it labeled *a,* the second rhyme word and all the words rhyming with it labeled *b,* and so on.

God's works are good. This truth to prove	a
Around the world I need not move;	a
I do it by the nearest pumpkin.	b
"This fruit so large, on vine so small,"	c
Surveying once, exclaimed a bumpkin—	b
"What could He mean who made us all? . . ."	c

La Fontaine,
"The Acorn and the Pumpkin," page 509

See also Rhyme in the Handbook of Literary Terms.

rhythm, in verse, the arrangement into patterns of stressed and unstressed sounds. Rhythm, or METER, may be regular, or it may vary within a line or work. The four most common meters are IAMBIC (⏑ ′), TROCHAIC (′ ⏑), ANAPESTIC (⏑ ⏑ ′), and DACTYLIC (′ ⏑ ⏑). See also the Handbook of Literary Terms.

rising action, the part of a dramatic PLOT that leads up to the CLIMAX. In the rising action, the complication caused by the CONFLICT of opposing forces is developed. See also Plot in the Handbook of Literary Terms.

romance, a long NARRATIVE in poetry or prose that originated in the medieval period. Its main elements are adventure, love, and magic. *Sir Gawain and the Green Knight* (page 340) is an example.

Romanticism, a type of literature that, unlike REALISM, tends to portray the uncommon. The material selected tends to deal with people in unusual settings having unusual experiences. In Romantic literature there is often a stress on the superiority of the past over the present and of nature over the city. Examples are Goethe's *Faust* (page 609) and Pushkin's *The Bridegroom* (page 624).

rubai (rü′bä ē′), the typical QUATRAIN of the type of Persian poem best known outside of Persia. The usual RHYME SCHEME is *aaba,* but occasionally the poet uses *aaaa.* You can see both schemes in FitzGerald's translation of Omar Khayyám's *Rubáiyát,* page 45. (*Rubáiyát* is the plural of *rubai,* which means "quatrain.")

run-on line, a line in which the thought continues beyond the end of the line of verse:

We are such stuff
As dreams are made on, and our little life
Is rounded with a sleep.
Shakespeare, *The Tempest,* page 467

saga (sä′gə), a medieval Scandinavian prose account of the battles and ways of a legendary Norse family or hero, placing much emphasis on genealogy and featuring violent men and outspoken women. *Thorstein the Staff-Struck* (page 308) is a complete, though short, Icelandic saga.

satire, the literary form that employs wit to ridicule characters in a work who represent some social institution or human foible, with the intention of inspiring self-reform. IRONY and sarcasm are often used in writing satire, and PARODY is a related technique. Swift's *A Modest Proposal* (page 553) and Pope's *The Rape of the Lock* (page 560) both provide examples of satire. See also the Handbook of Literary Terms.

scansion (skanʹshən), the result of *scanning*, or marking off lines of POETRY into FEET and indicating the stressed and unstressed syllables. (See RHYTHM and FOOT.) See also Rhythm in the Handbook of Literary Terms.

setting, the time, place, and social situation in which the action of a work occurs. The setting may be suggested through DIALOGUE and action, or it may be described by the NARRATOR or one of the characters. Setting contributes strongly to the MOOD, atmosphere, and plausibility of a work. The setting is important in "Chu-ch'ēn Village" (page 90) and *A Portrait of the Artist as a Young Man* (page 778). See also the Handbook of Literary Terms.

short story, a short prose NARRATIVE that is carefully crafted and usually tightly constructed. The modern short story form developed in the 1800s. This book includes short stories by Tolstoy, Maupassant, Chekhov, Colette, Singer, Narayan, Walker, and others.

simile (simʹə lē), a figure of speech involving a direct comparison, using "like" or "as," between two basically unlike things that are asserted to have something in common. Rilke's "Sense of Something Coming" (page 776) provides a good example of a simile. (See METAPHOR for comparison.) See also the Handbook of Literary Terms.

slant rhyme, rhyme in which the vowel sounds are not quite identical, as in the second and fourth lines below:

I like to see it lap the miles—
And lick the valleys up—
And stop to feed itself at Tanks—
And then—prodigious step . . .

Dickinson, page 680

(See also CONSONANCE.) See also Rhyme in the Handbook of Literary Terms.

soliloquy (sə lilʹə kwē), a DRAMATIC CONVENTION that allows a character alone on stage to speak his or her thoughts aloud. If someone else is on stage but cannot hear the character's words, the soliloquy becomes an *aside*. *The Tempest* (page 415) has examples of soliloquy. (Compare with DRAMATIC MONOLOGUE.)

sonnet, a LYRIC poem with a traditional form of fourteen IAMBIC PENTAMETER lines. Sonnets fall into two groups, according to their RHYME SCHEMES. The *Italian* or *Petrarchan* sonnet, named after the Italian poet Petrarch (page 380), is usually rhymed *abba abba cde cde* (with variations permitted in the *cde cde* rhyme scheme). It forms basically a two-part poem of eight lines (the *octave*) and six lines (the *sestet*). These two parts are played off against each other in a great variety of ways. The *English* or *Shakespearean* sonnet is usually rhymed *abab cdcd efef gg*, presenting a four-part structure in which an idea or theme is developed in three QUATRAINS and then brought to a conclusion in the COUPLET. Shakespeare's sonnets are examples of this type. See also the Handbook of Literary Terms.

speaker, the person who is speaking in a poem. He or she may be an unidentifiable figure, as in Akhmatova's "Lot's Wife" (page 820), or a central character in the poem, as in "To My Husband," by Mistral (page 829). (See also NARRATOR.)

spondee (sponʹdē), a metrical FOOT of two stressed syllables, as in "Great Scott!" It serves occasionally as a substitute to vary the meter, as in the first foot of this line:

Wounds, charms, / and ar- / dors were /
no soon- / er read . . .

Pope, *The Rape of the Lock*, page 560

See also Rhythm in the Handbook of Literary Terms.

stage directions, directions given by the author of a PLAY to indicate the action, costumes, SETTING, arrangement of the stage, and so on. For examples of stage directions, see *The Tempest* (page 415), where they are printed in italic type.

stanza, a group of lines that are set off to form a division in a poem, sometimes linked with other stanzas by a RHYME SCHEME. In BLANK VERSE poetry, stanzas are rare, because there is no rhyme.

stereotype (sterʹē ə tīpʹ, stirʹē ə tīpʹ), a conventional, over-simplified character, PLOT, or SETTING that possesses little or no individuality but that may be used for a purpose. See also the Handbook of Literary Terms.

stream of consciousness, the recording or re-creation of a character's flow of thought. Raw images, perceptions, and memories come and go in seemingly random fashion, much as they do in people's minds; but in this literary technique, the flow is actually controlled by the author. James Joyce (page 777) often used stream of consciousness in his writings.

style, the distinctive handling of language by an author. It involves the specific choices made with regard to DICTION, syntax, FIGURATIVE LANGUAGE, and so on. For a comparison of two very different styles, see *Doctor Faustus* (page 485) and Pope's *Rape of the Lock* (page 560). See also the Handbook of Literary Terms.

symbol, a concrete image, such as an object, action, character, or scene, that signifies something bigger, such as a concept or idea. Several works in this book use the symbol of dust to represent death, as in Genesis, Chapter 3 (page 25). See also the Handbook of Literary Terms.

synecdoche (si nek′də kē), a figure of speech in which a part stands for the whole, as in "hired hand." "Hand" (the part) stands for the whole (one who does manual labor, who works with the hands). See also Figurative Language in the Handbook of Literary Terms.

tale, a simple prose or verse NARRATIVE, either true or fictional, in which the main interest is in the events themselves, rather than in the structure or the meaning of the events. An example is the Book of Ruth (page 27).

terza rima (ter′tsä rē′mä), a VERSE form with a three-line STANZA rhyming *aba, bcb, cdc,* and so on. Dante's *Inferno* (page 316) is in *terza rima.*

tetrameter (te tram′ə tər), a metrical line of four FEET:

Tell all / the Truth / but tell / it slant. . . .

Dickinson, page 680

See also Rhythm in the Handbook of Literary Terms.

theme, the underlying meaning of a literary work. A theme may be directly stated but more often is implied. In Goethe's *Faust* (page 609) one of the themes (implied) is that a man who promises to keep striving, without enjoying the passing moment, will never experience love. See also the Handbook of Literary Terms.

tone, the author's attitude, either stated or implied, toward his or her subject matter and toward the

audience. In Shakespeare's *The Tempest* (page 415), the tone is sympathetic, ironic, humorous, and compassionate. (See MOOD for a comparison.) See also the Handbook of Literary Terms.

tragedy, dramatic or NARRATIVE writing in which the main character suffers disaster after a serious and significant struggle, but faces his or her downfall in such a way as to attain heroic stature. An example is *Oedipus the King* (page 165).

trimeter (trim′ə tər), a metrical line of three FEET:

The Truth's / superb / surprise . . .

Dickinson, "Tell All the Truth . . . ," page 680

See also Rhythm in the Handbook of Literary Terms.

trochee (trō′kē), a metrical FOOT made up of one stressed syllable followed by an unstressed syllable, as in the word "answer." In the following line the first foot is a trochee:

Slight is / the sub- / ject, but / not so /

the praise . . .

Pope, *The Rape of the Lock,* page 560

See also Rhythm in the Handbook of Literary Terms.

verse, in its most general sense a synonym for POETRY. "Verse" may also be used to refer to poetry carefully composed as to RHYTHM and RHYME SCHEME, but having less literary value, or a less serious THEME, than "poetry." Sometimes the word "verse" is used to mean a line or STANZA of poetry.

verisimilitude (ver′ə sə mil′ə tüd), the appearance of truth or reality in fiction. For example, Virgil achieves verisimilitude in Book Two of the *Aeneid* (page 242) by using searing details so that his fictional account has the authenticity of real horror.

Glossary

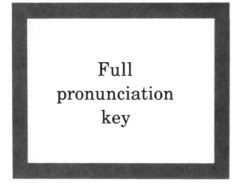

Full
pronunciation
key

The pronunciation of each word is shown just after the word, in this way: **ab bre vi ate** (ə brē′vē āt). The letters and signs used are pronounced as in the words below. The mark ′ is placed after a syllable with primary or heavy accent, as in the example above. The mark ′ after a syllable shows a secondary or lighter accent, as in **ab bre vi a tion** (ə brē′vē ā′shən).

Some words, taken from foreign languages, are spoken with sounds that do not otherwise occur in English. Symbols for these sounds are given in the key as "foreign sounds."

a	hat, cap	j	jam, enjoy	u	cup, butter	**foreign sounds**
ā	age, face	k	kind, seek	ù	full, put	
ä	father, far	l	land, coal	ü	rule, move	Y as in French *du.*
		m	me, am			Pronounce (ē) with the lips
b	bad, rob	n	no, in	v	very, save	rounded as for (ü).
ch	child, much	ng	long, bring	w	will, woman	
d	did, red			y	young, yet	à as in French *ami.*
		o	hot, rock	z	zero, breeze	Pronounce (ä) with the lips
e	let, best	ō	open, go	zh	measure, seizure	spread and held tense.
ē	equal, be	ô	order, all			
ėr	term, learn	oi	oil, voice	ə	represents:	œ as in French *peu.*
		ou	house, out		a in about	Pronounce (ā) with the lips
f	fat, if				e in taken	rounded as for (ō).
g	go, bag	p	paper, cup		i in pencil	
h	he, how	r	run, try		o in lemon	N as in French *bon.*
		s	say, yes		u in circus	The N is not pronounced,
i	it, pin	sh	she, rush			but shows that the vowel
ī	ice, five	t	tell, it			before it is nasal.
		th	thin, both			
		ŦH	then, smooth			H as in German *ach.*
						Pronounce (k) without
						closing the breath passage.

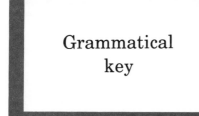

Grammatical
key

adj.	adjective	*prep.*	preposition
adv.	adverb	*pron.*	pronoun
conj.	conjunction	*v.*	verb
interj.	interjection	*v.i.*	intransitive verb
n.	noun	*v.t.*	transitive verb
sing.	singular	*pl.*	plural
pt.	past tense	*pp.*	past participle

a bash (ə bash**'**), *v.t.* embarrass and confuse; make uneasy and somewhat ashamed; disconcert. [< Old French *esbaïss-*, a form of *esbaïr* astonish] —**a bash'ment**, *n.*

ab hor (ab hôr**'**), *v.t.,* **-horred, -hor ring.** regard with horror or disgust; hate completely; detest; loathe. [< Latin *abhorrere* < *ab-* from + *horrere* to shudder, shrink] —**ab hor'rer**, *n.*

ab ject (ab**'**jekt, ab jekt**'**), *adj.* **1** so low or degraded as to be hopeless; wretched; miserable. **2** deserving contempt; despicable. **3** slavish. [< Latin *abjectum* cast down < *ab-* down + *jacere* to throw] —**ab ject'ly**, *adv.* —**ab ject'ness**, *n.*

ab jure (ab jùr**'**), *v.t.,* **-jured, -jur ing. 1** swear to give up; renounce. **2** retract formally or solemnly; repudiate. **3** refrain from; avoid. [< Latin *abjurare* < *ab-* away + *jurare* swear] —**ab'ju ra'tion**, *n.* —**ab jur'er**, *n.*

ab lu tion (ab lü**'**shən), *n.* Often, **ablutions,** *pl.* **1** a washing of one's person. **2** a washing or cleansing as a religious ceremony of purification. [< Latin *ablutionem* < *ab-* away + *lavere* to wash]

a bom i na tion (ə bom**'**ənā**'**shən), *n.* **1** something that arouses strong disgust. **2** a feeling of disgust; loathing.

ab ra ca dab ra (ab**'**rə kə dab**'**rə), *n.* **1** a word supposed to have magical power, used in incantations or as a charm to ward off disease. **2** meaningless talk; gibberish. [< Latin]

ab ste mi ous (ab stē**'**mē əs), *adj.* **1** sparing in eating, drinking, etc.; moderate; temperate. **2** very plain; restricted. [< Latin *abstemius*] —**ab ste'mi ous ly**, *adv.* —**ab ste'mi ous ness**, *n.*

a bysm (ə biz**'**əm), *n.* abyss.

a byss (ə bis**'**), *n.* **1** a bottomless or very great depth; chasm. **2** anything too deep or great to be measured; lowest depth. **3** the chaos before the Creation. [< Late Latin *abyssus* < Greek *abyssos* < *a-* without + *byssos* bottom]

ac cost (ə kôst**'**, ə kost**'**), *v.t.* approach and speak to first; address. [< Middle French *accoster* < Latin *ad-* to + *costa* side, rib]

ac quaint (ə kwānt**'**), *v.t.* **1** make aware; inform. **2 be acquainted with,** have personal knowledge of; know. **3 become acquainted with,** get to know. [< Old French *acointer*, ultimately < Latin *ad-* to + *cognoscere* know]

ac qui esce (ak**'**wē es**'**), *v.i.,* **-esced, -esc ing.** give consent by keeping silent or by not making objections; accept (the conclusions or arrangements of others); accede. [< Latin *acquiescere* < *ad-* to + *quies* rest, quiet]

ac quit tal (ə kwit**'**l), *n.* an acquitting; discharge; release.

a cu men (ə kyü**'**mən), *n.* sharpness and quickness in seeing and understanding; keen insight; discernment. [< Latin < *acuere* sharpen]

ad der (ad**'**ər), *n.* **1** a small, poisonous snake of Europe and the only poisonous snake in England. **2** hognose snake. **3** puff adder. [Old English *nædre*; in Middle English *a nadder* came to be understood and written as *an adder*]

ad dle (ad**'**l), *v.,* **-dled, -dling,** *adj.* —*v.t., v.i.* **1** make or become muddled. **2** make or become rotten. —*adj.* **1** muddled; confused. **2** rotten. [Old English *adela* muck]

ad duce (ə düs**'**, ə dyüs**'**), *v.t.,* **-duced, -duc ing.** offer as a reason in support of an argument; give as proof or evidence for consideration; cite as pertinent or conclusive. [< Latin *adducere* < *ad-* to + *ducere* bring, lead] —**ad duc'er**, *n.*

ad mo ni tion (ad**'**mə nish**'**ən), *n.* act of admonishing; gentle reproof or warning. [< Latin *admonitionem* < *ad-* to + *monere* warn]

a do (ə dü**'**), *n.* **1** noisy activity; bustle. **2** trouble; difficulty. [Middle English *at do* to do]

ad vent (ad**'**vent), *n.* **1** a coming; arrival. **2 Advent, a** the season of devotion including the four Sundays before Christmas. **b** the birth of Christ. [< Latin *adventum* < *ad-* to + *venire* come]

ad vo cate (*v.* ad**'**və kāt; *n.* ad**'**və kit, ad**'**və kāt), *v.,* **-cat ed, -cat ing,** *n.* —*v.t.* speak or write in favor of; recommend publicly (a measure, policy, etc.); support. —*n.* **1** person who defends, maintains, or publicly recommends a proposal, belief, theory, etc.; supporter. **2** lawyer who pleads the cause of anyone in certain courts of law. [< Latin *advocatum* summoned < *ad-* to + *vocare* to call] —**ad'vo ca'tion**, *n.* —**ad'vo ca'tor**, *n.*

adz or **adze** (adz), *n., pl.* **adz es.** a cutting tool for shaping heavy timbers, similar to an ax but with a blade set across the end of the handle and curving inward. [Old English *adesa*]

aer ie or **aer y** (er**'**ē, ar**'**ē, ir**'**ē), *n., pl.* **aer ies. 1** the nest of an eagle, hawk, or other bird of prey, usually built in a lofty place. **2** house, castle, etc., placed high on a rock or mountainside. Also, **eyrie, eyry.** [< Medieval Latin *aeria* < Old French *aire* < Latin *area* area]

af fi da vit (af**'**ə dā**'**vit), *n.* statement written down and sworn to be true, usually before a notary public or other authorized official. [< Medieval Latin, he has stated on oath]

af fin i ty (ə fin**'**ə tē), *n., pl.* **-ties. 1** a natural attraction to a person or liking for a thing. **2** relation; connection. **3** relationship by marriage. **4** resemblance between species, genera, etc., that makes a common ancestry probable. **5** force that attracts certain chemical elements to others and keeps them combined. [< Latin *affinitatem* relation < *affinis* related, bordering on < *ad-* on + *finis* border]

a ghast (ə gast**'**), *adj.* struck with surprise or horror; filled with shocked amazement. [past participle of obsolete *agast* terrify < Old English *on-* on + *gæstan* frighten. Related to GHOST.]

a gue (ā**'**gyü), *n.* **1** a malarial fever with chills and sweating that alternate at regular intervals. **2** any fit of shaking or shivering; chill. [< Middle French *ague* < Latin *(febris) acuta* severe (fever)]

a lar um (ə lar**'**əm, ə lär**'**əm), *n.* ARCHAIC. alarm.

al be it (ôl bē**'**it), *conj.* even though; even if; although. [Middle English *al be it* although it be]

al lay (ə lā**'**), *v.t.,* **-layed, -lay ing. 1** put at rest; quiet. **2** relieve (pain, trouble, thirst, etc.); alleviate. [Old English *ālecgan* < *ā-* away, off + *lecgan* to lay] —**al lay'er**, *n.*

al le lu ia (al**'**ə lü**'**yə), *interj., n.* the Latin and liturgical form of **hallelujah.**

al lo cu tion (al**'**ə kü**'**shən), *n.* a speech; an encouraging or authoritative speech.

al lot (ə lot**'**), *v.t.,* **-lot ted, -lot ting. 1** divide and distribute in parts or shares. **2** give as a share, task, duty, etc.; assign. **3** appropriate (anything) to a special purpose; allocate. [< Middle French *allotir* < *a-* to + *lot* lot] —**al lot'ter**, *n.*

al loy (*n.* al**'**oi, ə loi**'**; *v.* ə loi**'**), *n.* **1** metal made by melting and mixing two or more metals, or a metal and a nonmetal, to secure some desirable quality or qualities, as toughness, resistance to wear, etc. Brass is an alloy of copper and zinc. **2** an inferior metal mixed with a more valuable one. **3** any injurious addition; impurity. —*v.t.* **1** make into an alloy. **2** make less valuable by mixing with a cheaper metal. **3** make worse by mixing with something bad; debase. [< Middle French *aloi* < *alier* unite < Latin *alligare* bind to. Doublet of ALLY.]

al mon er (al**'**mə nər, ä**'**mə nər), *n.* person who distributes alms for a king, a monastery, or a person of rank.

alms (ämz, älmz), *n. sing.* or *pl.* money or gifts given freely to help the poor; charity. [Old English *ælmysse* < Latin *eleemosyna* < Greek *eleēmosynē* pity, alms < *eleos* pity]

al pac a (al pak**'**ə), *n., pl.* **-pac as** or **-pac a. 1** a domesticated mammal of South America with long, soft, silky hair or wool. It is closely related to but somewhat smaller than the llama. **2** its wool. **3** cloth made from this wool. **4** a glossy, wiry cloth made of sheep's wool and cotton, usually black. **5** imitation of this made of rayon or cotton. [< Spanish < Quechua]

a me na ble (ə mē**'**nə bəl, ə men**'**ə bəl), *adj.* **1** open to influence, suggestion, advice, etc.; responsive; submissive. **2** accountable or answerable to some jurisdiction or authority. [< Middle French *amener* lead to < *a-* to + *mener* to lead] —**a me'na ble ness**, *n.* —**a me'na bly**, *adv.*

am e thyst (am**'**ə thist), *n.* **1** a purple or violet variety of quartz, used for jewelry. **2** a violet-colored corundum, used for jewelry. **3** a purple or violet color. —*adj.* purple; violet. [< Greek *amethystos* < *a-* not + *methy* wine; thought to prevent intoxication]

am or ous (am**'**ər əs), *adj.* **1** inclined to love; fond of making love. **2** in love; enamored. **3** showing love; loving. **4** having to do with love or courtship. [< Old French < *amour* love < Latin *amor*] —**am'or ous ly**, *adv.* —**am'or ous ness**, *n.*

am or ti za tion (am**'**ər tə zā**'**shən, ə môr**'**tə zā**'**shən), *n.* **1** an amortizing of a debt. **2** money regularly set aside for this.

a mour (ə mùr′), *n.* a love affair, especially a secret love affair. [< Old French < Latin *amor* love]

a nal o gous (ə nal′ə gəs), *adj.* **1** similar in certain qualities, circumstances, or uses; comparable. **2** (in biology) corresponding in function, but not in structure and origin. [< Greek *analogos* proportionate < *ana logon* according to due ratio] **—a nal′o gous ly,** *adv.* **—a nal′o gous ness.** *n.*

an gle (ang′gəl), *v.,* **-gled, -gling.** to turn, bend, or move at an angle.

an i mos i ty (an′ə mos′ə tē), *n., pl.* **-ties.** keen hostile feelings; active dislike or enmity; ill will.

an ise (an′is), *n.* **1** plant of the same family as the parsley, grown especially for its fragrant seeds. **2** the seed. [ultimately < Greek *anison*]

an ni hi late (ə nī′ə lāt), *v.t.,* **-lat ed, -lat ing.** destroy completely; wipe out of existence. **—v.i.** cease to be; vanish; disappear. [< Late Latin *annihilatum* brought to nothing < Latin *ad-* to + *nihil* nothing] **—an ni′hi la′tive.** *adj.* **—an ni′hi la′tor,** *n.*

a non (ə non′), *adv.* ARCHAIC. **1** in a little while; soon. **2** at another time; again. **3 ever and anon,** now and then. [Old English *on ān* into one]

ape (āp), *n., v.,* **aped, ap ing.** —*v.t.* imitate; mimic. [Old English *apa*] **—ape′like′,** *adj.* **—ap′er,** *n.*

ap pease (ə pēz′), *v.t.,* **-peased, -peas ing. 1** put an end to by satisfying (an appetite or desire). **2** make calm or quiet; pacify. **3** give in to the demands of (especially those of a potential enemy). [< Old French *apaisier* < *a-* to + *pais* peace] **—ap peas′er,** *n.* **—ap peas′ing ly,** *adv.*

ar a ble (ar′ə bəl), *adj.* (of land) suitable for producing crops which require plowing and tillage. [< Latin *arabilis* able to be plowed < *arare* to plow]

ar dor (är′dər), *n.* **1** warmth of emotion; passion. **2** great enthusiasm; eagerness; zeal. [< Latin < *ardere* to burn]

ar du ous (är′jü əs), *adj.* hard to do; requiring much effort; difficult. [< Latin *arduus* steep] **—ar′du ous ly,** *adv.* **—ar′du ous ness,** *n.*

ar mi stice (är′mə stis), *n.* a stop in fighting, by agreement on all sides; temporary peace; truce. [< New Latin *armistitium* < Latin *arma* arms + *sistere* to stand, stand still]

ar raign (ə rān′), *v.t.* **1** bring before a court of law to answer an indictment. **2** call to account; find fault with; accuse. [< Anglo-French *arainer* < Old French *a-* to + *raisnier* speak] **—ar raign′er,** *n.* **—ar raign′ment,** *n.*

ar ras (ar′əs), *n.* **1** a rich tapestry fabric, with figures and scenes in color. **2** curtain, screen, or hangings of tapestry. [< *Arras*, city in northern France]

ar tic u late (*adj.* är tik′yə lit; *v.* är tik′yə lāt), *adj., v.,* **-lat ed, -lat ing.** —*adj.* **1** uttered in distinct syllables of words. **2** able to put one's thoughts into words easily and clearly. **3** consisting of sections united by joints; jointed. —*v.t.* **1** speak distinctly; express in clear sounds and words. **2** unite by joints. —*v.i.* **1** express oneself in words. **2** fit together in a joint. **—ar tic u late-ly** (är tik′yə lit lē), *adv.* **—ar tic u late ness** (är tik′yə lit nis), *n.* **—ar tic′u la′tor,** *n.*

ar ti fice (är′tə fis), *n.* **1** a clever device or trick. **2** trickery; craft. **3** skill or ingenuity. [< Latin *artificium* < *artem* art + *facere* make]

a skance (ə skans′), *adv.* **1** with suspicion or disapproval. **2** to one side; sideways. [origin uncertain]

as perse (ə spėrs′), *v.t.,* **-persed, -pers ing.** spread damaging or false reports about; slander. [< Latin *aspersum* sprinkled on < *ad-* on + *spargere* to sprinkle] **—as pers′er,** *n.*

as sent (ə sent′), *v.i.* express agreement; agree; consent. [< Latin *assentire* < *ad-* along with + *sentire* feel, think] **—as sen′tor, as sent′er,** *n.*

as sig na tion (as′ig nā′shən), *n.* **1** a secret meeting of lovers. **2** the appointment of a time and place for such a meeting. **3** an allotting; apportionment.

as suage (ə swāj′), *v.t.,* **-suaged, -suag ing. 1** make (angry or excited feelings, etc.) less intense; calm or soothe. **2** make (physical or mental pain) easier or milder; relieve or lessen. **3** satisfy or appease (appetites or desires). [< Old French *assuagier*, ultimately < Latin *ad-* + *suavis* sweet] **—as suag′er,** *n.* **—as-**

---

a hat	i it	oi oil	ch child	a in about
ā age	ī ice	ou out	ng long	e in taken
ä far	o hot	u cup	sh she	ə = i in pencil
e let	ō open	ù put	th thin	o in lemon
ē equal	ô order	ü rule	ŦH then	u in circus
ėr term			zh measure	< = derived from

suage′ment, *n.*

a sun der (ə sun′dər), *adv.* in pieces; into separate parts. —*adj.* apart or separate from each other. [Old English *on sundran*]

a thwart (ə thwôrt′), *adv.* across from side to side; crosswise. —*prep.* **1** across. **2** across the line or course of. **3** in opposition to; against.

au da cious (ô dā′shəs), *adj.* **1** having the courage to take risks; recklessly daring; bold. **2** rudely bold; impudent. **—au da′cious ly,** *adv.* **—au da′cious ness,** *n.*

au gur y (ô′gyər ē), *n. pl.* **-gur ies. 1** prediction; sign; omen.

au gust (ô gust′), *adj.* inspiring reverence and admiration; majestic; venerable. [< Latin *augustus* < *augere* to increase] **—au gust′ly,** *adv.* **—au gust′ness,** *n.*

au re o la (ô rē′ə lə), *n.* aureole.

au re ole (ôr′ē ōl), *n.* **1** ring of light surrounding a figure or object, especially in religious paintings. **2** ring of light surrounding the sun. [< Late Latin *aureola* golden < Latin *aurum* gold]

aus pi cious (ô spish′əs), *adj.* **1** with signs of success; favorable. **2** prosperous; fortunate. **—aus pi′cious ly,** *adv.* **—aus pi′cious ness,** *n.*

aus tere (ô stir′), *adj.* **1** stern in manner or appearance; harsh. **2** severe in self-discipline; strict in morals. **3** severely simple. **4** grave; somber; serious. [< Greek *austēros* < *auos* dry] **—aus tere′ly,** *adv.* **—aus tere′ness,** *n.*

av ar ice (av′ər is), *n.* too great a desire for money or property; greed for wealth. [< Old French < Latin *avaritia* < *avarus* greedy]

av id (av′id), *adj.* extremely eager or enthusiastic; greatly desirous. [< Latin *avidus* < *avere* desire eagerly] **—av′id ly,** *adv.* **—av′id ness,** *n.*

awn ing (ô′ning), *n.* piece of canvas, metal, wood, or plastic spread over or before a door, window, porch, deck, or patio for protection from the sun or rain. [origin uncertain]

az ure (azh′ər), *n.* the clear blue color of the unclouded sky; sky blue. —*adj.* sky-blue. [< Old French *l'azur* the azure < Arabic *lāzuward* < Persian *lajward* lapis lazuli]

Ba bel (bā′bəl, bab′əl), *n.* **1 Tower of Babel,** (in the Bible) a high tower whose builders hoped to reach heaven. God punished them by changing their language into several new and different languages so that they could not understand one another and had to leave the tower unfinished. **2 babel, a** noise; confusion. **b** place of noise and confusion.

bait (bāt), *n.* **1** anything, especially food, used to attract fish or other animals so that they may be caught. **2** thing used to tempt or attract; temptation. —*v.t.* **1** put bait on (a hook) or in (a trap). **2** tempt; attract. **3** set dogs to attack. **4** attack; torment. **5** torment or worry by unkind or annoying remarks. **6** ARCHAIC. give food and water to (a horse or other animal), especially on a journey. [< Scandinavian (Old Icelandic) *beita* cause to bite]

bale ful (bāl′fəl), *adj.* **1** full of hurtful or deadly influence; destructive. **2** full of misfortune; disastrous. **—bale′ful ly,** *adv.* **—bale′ful ness,** *n.*

bal last (bal′əst), *n.* **1** something heavy placed in the hold of a ship to steady it. **2** bags of sand or other heavy material carried in a balloon or dirigible to steady it or regulate its ascent. **3** anything which steadies a person or thing. **4** gravel or crushed rock used in making the bed for a road or railroad track. —*v.t.* **1** furnish or steady with ballast. **2** put gravel or crushed rock on. [apparently < Scandinavian (Old Danish) *barlast*]

balm (bäm, bälm), *n.* **1** a fragrant, oily, sticky substance obtained from certain kinds of trees, used to heal or to relieve pain; balsam. **2** an ointment or similar preparation that heals or soothes. **3** a healing or soothing influence. **4** a fragrant ointment or oil used in anointing. **5** sweet odor; fragrance. **6** a fragrant plant of the mint family. [< Old French *basme* < Latin *balsamum* < Greek *balsamon.* Doublet of BALSAM.]

ba nal i ty (bə nal′ə tē), *n., pl.* **-ties. 1** commonplaceness; triteness; triviality. **2** a banal remark, idea, etc.

ban ter (ban′tər), *n.* playful teasing; joking. —*v.t.* tease playfully; make fun of. —*v.i.* talk in a joking way. [origin uncertain] —**ban′ter er,** *n.* —**ban′ter ing ly,** *adv.*

bark (bärk), *n.* **1** a three-masted ship, square-rigged on the first two masts and fore-and-aft-rigged on the other. **2** ARCHAIC. boat; ship. Also, **barque.** [< Middle French *barque* < Italian *barca* < Late Latin]

barque (bärk), *n.* bark.

bat ter y (bat′ər ē), *n., pl.* **-ter ies. 1** set of similar pieces of equipment, such as mounted guns, searchlights, mortars, etc., used as a unit. **2** any set of similar or connected things. **3** a military unit of artillery, usually commanded by a captain. A battery corresponds to a company or troop in other branches of the army.

bay (bā), *adj.* reddish-brown. —*n.* a reddish-brown horse with black mane and tail. [< Old French *bai* < Latin *badius*]

be-, *prefix.* **1** thoroughly; all around: *Bespatter = spatter thoroughly.* **2** make; cause to seem: *Belittle = cause to seem little.* **3** provide with: *Bespangle = provide with spangles.* **4** at; on; to; for; about; against: *Bewail = wail about.* [Old English *be-,* unstressed form of *bī* by]

beam (bēm), *n.* **1** a large, long piece of timber, ready for use in building. **2** a similar piece of metal, stone, reinforced concrete, etc. **3** any of the main horizontal supports of a building or ship. —*v.t.* **1** throw out or radiate (beams or rays of light); emit in rays. **2** direct (a broadcast). —*v.i.* **1** shine radiantly. **2** look or smile brightly. [Old English *bēam* tree, piece of wood, ray of light]

be di zen (bi dī′zn, bi diz′n), *v.t.* dress or ornament with showy finery. [< *be-* + *dizen*] —**be di′zen ment,** *n.*

Be el ze bub (bē el′zə bub), *n.* **1** (in the Bible) the Devil; Satan. **2** a devil.

beeves (bēvz), *n. pl.* of **beef.**

be guile (bi gīl′), *v.t.,* **-guiled, -guil ing.** trick or mislead (a person); deceive; delude. —**be guile′ment,** *n.* —**be guil′er,** *n.*

be hest (bi hest′), *n.* command; order. [Old English *behæs* promise]

be hoove (bi hüv′), *v.,* **-hooved, -hoov ing.** —*v.t.* **1** be necessary for. **2** be proper for. —*v.i.* be proper or due. [Old English *behōfian*]

be hove (bi hōv′), *v.t., v.i.,* **-hoved, -hov ing.** BRITISH. behoove.

be nev o lence (bə nev′ə ləns), *n.* **1** desire to promote the happiness of others; goodwill; kindly feeling. **2** act of kindness; something good that is done; generous gift. **3** (formerly) a forced loan to an English king, now illegal. [< Latin *benevolentia* < *bene* well + *velle* to wish]

be seech (bi sēch′), *v.t.,* **-sought** or **-seeched, -seech ing.** ask earnestly; beg; implore. [Middle English *bisechen* < *be-* thoroughly + *sechen* seek] —**be seech′er,** *n.* —**be seech′ing ly,** *adv.*

bes tial (bes′chəl), *adj.* **1** like a beast; beastly. **2** sensual; obscene. **3** of beasts. [< Latin *bestialis* < *bestia* beast] —**bes′tial ly,** *adv.*

be times (bi tīmz′), *adv.* ARCHAIC. **1** early. **2** before it is too late. **3** in a short time; soon.

be wail (bi wāl′), *v.t.* mourn for; weep for; complain of. —*v.i.* wail; mourn; complain. [*be-* + *wail*]

bier (bir), *n.* a movable stand or framework on which a coffin or dead body is placed before burial. [Old English *bēr.* Related to *beran* bear.]

big ot (big′ət), *n.* person who is bigoted; intolerant person. [< Middle French]

bit (bit), *n.* the part of a bridle that goes in a horse's mouth and to which the reins are attached. [Old English *bite* a bite < *bītan* to bite]

black guard (blag′ärd, blag′ərd), *n.* a low, contemptible person; scoundrel. —*v.t.* abuse with vile language; revile. —*v.i.* behave like a blackguard.

blas pheme (bla sfēm′), *v.t., v.i.,* **-phemed, -phem ing.** speak about (God, sacred things, etc.) with abuse or contempt; utter blasphemy. [< Old French *blasfemer* < Latin *blasphemare.* Doublet of BLAME.] —**blas phem′er,** *n.*

blithe (blīᴛʜ, blīth), *adj.* happy and cheerful; gay; joyous. [Old English *blīthe*] —**blithe′ly,** *adv.* —**blithe′ness,** *n.*

blow (blō), *n., v.,* **blew, blown, blow ing.** —*n.* a state of blossoming; bloom. [Old English *blōwan*]

bo gy (bō′gē, bug′ē), *n., pl.* **-gies. 1** evil spirit; goblin. **2** person or thing, usually imaginary, that is feared without reason; bugbear; bugaboo. Also, **bogey, bogie.** [probably < obsolete *bog* bugbear]

Bo he mi an (bō hē′mē ən, bō hē′myən), *adj.* carefree and unconventional. —*n.* **1** artist, writer, etc., who lives an unconventional, carefree sort of existence. **2** gypsy.

boon[1] (bün), *n.* **1** great benefit; blessing. **2** ARCHAIC. something asked for or granted as a favor. [< Scandinavian (Old Icelandic) *bōn* petition]

boon[2] (bün), *adj.* **1** full of cheer; jolly; merry. **2** kindly; pleasant. [< Old French *bon* good < Latin *bonus*]

boot less (büt′lis), *adj.* of no benefit or profit; useless. [< *boot*] —**boot′less ly,** *adv.* —**boot′less ness,** *n.*

bound er (boun′dər), *n.* INFORMAL. a rude, vulgar person; cad.

bow er (bou′ər), *n.* **1** shelter of leafy branches. **2** summerhouse or arbor. [Old English *būr* dwelling]

bow stave (bō′stāv′), *n. Archery* a trimmed rod of wood to be made into a bow.

brace (brās), *n.* a pair; couple. [< Old French, the two arms < Latin *bracchia,* plural of *bracchium* arm < Greek *brachīōn*]

bray (brā), *v.t.* to pound, beat, rub, or grind small or fine.

bra zen (brā′zn), *adj.* **1** having no shame; shameless; impudent. **2** loud and harsh; brassy. [Old English *bræsen* < *bræs* brass] —**bra′zen ly,** *adv.* —**bra′zen ness,** *n.*

bra zier (brā′zhər), *n.* a large metal pan or tray to hold burning charcoal or coal. Braziers are used in some countries for heating rooms. [< Old French *brasier* < *breze* hot coals]

brev i ty (brev′ə tē), *n., pl.* **-ties. 1** shortness in time. **2** shortness in speech or writing; conciseness. [< Latin *brevitatem* < *brevis* short]

brim stone (brim′stōn′), *n.* sulfur. [Middle English *brinston* < *brinn-* burn + *ston* stone]

broach (brōch), *v.t.* begin conversation or discussion about; introduce. [< Old French *broche* < Latin *broccus* projecting] —**broach′er,** *n.*

bruit (brüt), *n.* ARCHAIC. report; rumor. [< Old French, a roar < *bruire* to roar]

brusque (brusk), *adj.* abrupt in manner or speech; blunt. [< French < Italian *brusco* coarse] —**brusque′ly,** *adv.* —**brusque′ness,** *n.*

buck ler (buk′lər), *n.* a small, round shield used to parry blows or thrusts.

buf fet (buf′it), *n.* **1** a blow of the hand or fist. **2** a knock, stroke, or hurt. [< Old French, diminutive of *buffe* blow] —**buf′fet er,** *n.*

bulk head (bulk′hed′), *n.* one of the upright partitions dividing a ship into compartments.

bur eau crat (byu̇r′ə krat), *n.* **1** official in a bureaucracy. **2** a government official who insists on rigid routine. [< *bureau* + *(auto)crat*]

burg (bėrg), *n.* INFORMAL. town or city. Also, **burgh.** [variant of *borough*]

bur sar (bėr′sər, bėr′sär), *n.* treasurer, especially of a college or university. [< Medieval Latin *bursarius* < *bursa*]

bulkhead (def. 1)
A, dividing;
B, watertight

caf tan (kaf′tən, käf tän′), *n.* **1** a long-sleeved, ankle-length tunic with a girdle, worn under the coat by men in Turkey, Egypt, etc. **2** a similar garment, worn especially by women in Western countries. Also, **kaftan.** [< Turkish *kaftan*]

cai tiff (kā′tif), *n.* ARCHAIC. a mean, cowardly person. [< Old French *caitif*, ultimately < Latin *captivus* captive. Doublet of CAPTIVE.]

cal dron (kôl′drən), *n.* a large kettle or boiler. Also, **cauldron.** [< Old French *caudron* < Late Latin *caldaria* < Latin *calidus* hot]

ca lèche (kä lesh′), *n.* a two-wheeled vehicle with a folding hood or top.

cal i co (kal′ə kō), *n., pl.* **-coes** or **-cos,** *adj.* —*n.* a cotton cloth that usually has colored patterns printed on one side. [< *Calicut*, India]

cal um ny (kal′əm nē), *n., pl.* **-nies.** a false statement made to injure someone's reputation; slander. [< Latin *calumnia*. Doublet of CHALLENGE.]

cam ou flage (kam′ə fläzh), *v.,* **-flaged, -flag ing.** —*v.t.* give a false appearance to in order to conceal; disguise. [< French < *camoufler* to disguise] —**cam′ou flag′er,** *n.*

cam phor (kam′fər), *n.* a white, crystalline substance with a strong odor, usually obtained from the camphor tree and used in medicine and to protect clothes from moths. *Formula:* C₁₀H₁₆O [< Medieval Latin *camphora* < Arabic *kāfūr* < Malay *kāpūr*]

can non (kan′ən), *v.* act of caroming, striking, rebounding, or colliding.

can ton (kan′tən, kan′ton, kan ton′), *n.* a small part or political division of a country. [< French < Italian *cantone* < *canto* corner < Popular Latin *cantus*.]

ca pa cious (kə pā′shəs), *adj.* able to hold much; large and roomy; spacious. —**ca pa′cious ly,** *adv.* —**ca pa′cious ness,** *n.*

ca pri cious (kə prish′əs, kə prē′shəs), *adj.* likely to change suddenly without reason; changeable; fickle. —**ca pri′cious ly,** *adv.* —**ca pri′cious ness,** *n.*

car (kär), *n.* **1** any vehicle that moves on wheels. **2** chariot. [< Old North French *carre* wagon < Medieval Latin *carra* < Latin *carrus*] —**car′less,** *adj.*

card (kärd), *n.* a toothed tool or wire brush, such as that used to separate, clean, and straighten the fibers of wool before spinning or to clean the grooves of a metal file. —*v.t.* clean or comb with such a tool. [< Middle French *carde*, ultimately < Latin *carduus* thistle] —**card′er,** *n.*

car nage (kär′nij), *n.* slaughter of a great number of people.

car nel ian (kär nē′lyən), *n.* a red or reddish-brown stone used in jewelry. It is a kind of quartz. Also, **cornelian.** [< Old French *corneline*]

carp (kärp), *v.t.* find fault; complain. [< Scandinavian (Old Danish) *karpa* to boast] —**carp′er,** *n.*

car riage (kar′ij), *n.* manner of holding the head and body; bearing. [< Old French *cariage* < *carier*.]

cart wright (kärt′rīt), *n.* maker of carts; a cartwright.

cast (kast), *v.,* **cast, cast ing,** *n., adj.* —*v.t.* **1** throw, fling, or hurl. [< Scandinavian (Old Icelandic) *kasta*]

ca tas tro phe (kə tas′trə fē), *n.* a sudden, widespread, or extraordinary disaster; great calamity or misfortune. A big earthquake, flood, or fire is a catastrophe. [< Greek *katastrophē* an overturning < *kata-* down + *strephein* to turn]

caul dron (kôl′drən), *n.* caldron.

cen so ri ous (sen sôr′ē əs, sen sōr′ē əs), *adj.* too ready to find fault; severely critical. —**cen so′ri ous ly,** *adv.* —**cen so′ri ous ness,** *n.*

cen sure (sen′shər), *n., v.,* **-sured, -sur ing.** —*n.* **1** expression of disapproval; unfavorable opinion; criticism. **2** penalty, as a public rebuke or suspension from office. —*v.t.* express disapproval of; find fault with; criticize. [< Latin *censura* < *censere* appraise] —**cen′sur er,** *n.*

cen taur (sen′tôr), *n.* (in Greek myths) a monster that had the head, arms, and chest of a man, and the body and legs of a horse. [< Greek *kentauros*]

cere ment (sir′mənt), *n.* Often, **cerements,** *pl.* cloth or garment in which a dead person is wrapped for burial.

a hat	i it	oi oil	ch child	⎧ a in about
ā age	ī ice	ou out	ng long	⎪ e in taken
ä far	o hot	u cup	sh she	ə = ⎨ i in pencil
e let	ō open	u̇ put	th thin	⎪ o in lemon
ē equal	ô order	ü rule	ᵺ then	⎩ u in circus
ėr term			zh measure	< = derived from

chafe (chāf), *v.,* **chafed, chaf ing,** *n.* —*v.t.* rub so as to wear away, scrape, or make sore. [< Old French *chaufer* to warm < Latin *calefacere* < *calere* be warm + *facere* make]

chaff (chaf), *v.t., v.i.* make fun of in a good-natured way to one's face; banter. —*n.* good-natured joking about a person to his or her face. [origin uncertain]

cha grin (shə grin′), *n.* a feeling of disappointment, failure, or humiliation. [< French, apparently < *chat* cat + *grigner* to purse (the lips)]

chap let (chap′lit), *n.* string of beads. [< Old French *chapelet*, diminutive of *chapel* headdress]

char la tan (shär′lə tən), *n.* person who pretends to have expert knowledge or skill; quack. [< French < Italian *ciarlatano* < *cerretano* person from *Cerreto (di Spoleto)*, town in Italy where street hucksters were common in the Middle Ages]

chat tel (chat′l), *n.* **1** piece of property that is not real estate; any movable possession. Furniture, automobiles, and animals are chattels. **2** slave or bondman. [< Old French *chatel* < Latin *capitale,* neuter of *capitalis.* Doublet of CAPITAL, CATTLE.]

cheek (chēk), *n.* INFORMAL. saucy talk or behavior; impudence. [Old English *cēce*]

chic or y (chik′ər ē), *n., pl.* **-or ies.** **1** any of a genus of plants of the composite family with deep, hard roots and blue, purple, or white flowers, whose leaves are used as salad. **2** plant of this genus with bright-blue flowers; succory. **3** its root, roasted and used as a substitute for coffee or in a mixture with ground coffee. [< Middle French *chicoree* < Latin *cichoreum* < Greek *kichoreion*]

chide (chīd), *v.,* **chid ed, chid, chid ing.** —*v.t.* find fault with; reproach or blame; scold. [Old English *cīdan*] —**chid′er,** *n.* —**chid′ing ly,** *adv.*

chi gnon (shē′nyon; *French* shē nyôn′), *n.* a large knot or roll of hair worn at the back of the head by women. [< French]

chol er (kol′ər), *n.* an irritable disposition; anger. [< Late Latin *cholera* bile < Latin, cholera]

churl (chėrl), *n.* **1** a rude, surly person; boor. **2** person of low birth; peasant. **3** person stingy in money matters; miser. **4** (in Anglo-Saxon and medieval England) a freeman of the lowest rank; ceorl. [Old English *ceorl*]

chute (shüt), *n.* a steep slope or sloping passage. [apparently blend of French *chute* fall (of water) and English *shoot*]

cir cum ci sion (sėr′kəm sizh′ən), *n.* **1** act of circumcising. **2** a Jewish ritual in which a boy is circumcised when he is eight days old as a symbol of the covenant which, according to the Bible, God made with Abraham.

cir cum spec tion (sėr′kəm spek′shən), *n.* caution or prudence; care.

cit a del (sit′ə del, sit′ə dəl), *n.* **1** fortress commanding a city. **2** a strongly fortified place; stronghold. [< Middle French *citadelle* < Italian *cittadella*, diminutive of *città* city < Latin *civitatem*.] —**citadelled,** *adj.*

ci vil i ty (sə vil′ə tē), *n., pl.* **-ties.** **1** polite behavior; courtesy. **2** act or expression of politeness or courtesy.

clair voy ant (kler voi′ənt, klar voi′ənt), —*n.* person who has, or claims to have, the power of seeing or knowing things that are out of sight. [< French < *clair* clear + *voyant,* present participle of *voir* to see] —**clair voy′ant ly,** *adv.*

clam ber (klam′bər), *v.i., v.t.* climb, using both hands and feet; climb awkwardly or with difficulty; scramble. —*n.* an awkward or difficult climb. [Middle English *clambren.* Related to CLIMB.]

clan des tine (klan des′tən), *adj.* arranged or made in a stealthy or underhanded manner; concealed; secret. [< Latin *clandestinus* < *clam* secretly]

clave (klāv), *v.* ARCHAIC. a pt. of **cleave**[2].

cleave[1] (klēv), *v.*, **cleft** or **cleaved** or **clove**, **cleft** or **cleaved** or **clo ven**, **cleav ing.** —*v.t.* **1** cut, divide, or split open. **2** pass through; pierce; penetrate. —*v.i.* **1** split, especially into layers. **2** pass; penetrate. [Old English *clēofan*] —**cleav′a ble,** *adj.*

cleave[2] (klēv), *v.i.*, **cleaved** or (ARCHAIC) **clave, cleav ing.** hold fast; cling; adhere. [Old English *cleofian*]

clout (klout), *v.t.* INFORMAL. hit with the hand; rap; knock; cuff. —*n.* INFORMAL. a hit with the hand; rap; knock; cuff. [Old English *clūt* small piece of cloth or metal]

clove (klōv), *v.* a pt. of **cleave**[1].

cloy (kloi), *v.t., v.i.*, **cloyed.** **1** make or become weary by too much, too sweet, or too rich food. **2** make or become weary by too much of anything pleasant. [Middle English *acloyen, ancloyen* drive a nail into, stop up, fill full < Old French *encloyer* < *en-* in + *clou* nail] —**cloy′ing ly,** *adv.* —**cloy′ing ness,** *n.*

cod dle (kod′l), *v.t.*, **-dled, -dling.** treat tenderly; pamper. [origin uncertain]

col on nade (kol′ə nād′), *n.* series of columns set the same distance apart, usually supporting a roof, ceiling, cornice, etc. [< French < Italian *colonnata* < *colonna* column < Latin *columna*]

come ly (kum′lē), *adj.*, **-li er, -li est.** **1** pleasant to look at; attractive. **2** fitting; suitable; proper. [Old English *cȳmlic*]

com mend (kə mend′), *v.t.* **1** speak well of; praise. **2** recommend. **3** hand over for safekeeping; entrust. [< Latin *commendare* < *com-* + *mandare* commit, command]

com men sur ate (kə men′shər it, kə men′sər it), *adj.* in the proper proportion; proportionate. [< Late Latin *commensuratum* < Latin *com-* together + *mensura* measure]

com mis e rate (kə miz′ə rāt′), *v.t., v.i.*, **-rat ed, -rat ing.** feel or express sorrow for another's suffering or trouble; sympathize with; pity. [< Old French *commiseratum* pited < *com-* + *miser* wretched] —**com mis′e ra′tion,** *n.*

com punc tion (kəm pungk′shən), *n.* uneasiness of the mind because of wrongdoing; pricking of conscience; remorse. [< Late Latin *compunctionem* < Latin *compungere* to prick, sting < *com-* + *pungere* to prick]

com rade (kom′rad), *n.* **1** companion and friend. **2** person who shares in what another is doing; fellow worker; partner. **3** a fellow member of a union, political party, etc. [< Middle French *camarade* < Spanish *camarada* roommate < *cámara* room < Latin *camera*]

con (kon), *v.t.*, **conned, con ning.** **1** learn well enough to remember; study. **2** examine carefully; pore over. [Old English *cunnian* test, examine]

con cen tric (kən sen′trik), *adj.* having the same center. —**con cen′tri cal ly,** *adv.*

con dign (kən dīn′), *adj.* deserved; adequate; fitting. [< Middle French *condigne* < Latin *condignus* very worthy < *com-* + *dignus* worthy] —**con dign′ly,** *adv.*

con gen ial (kən jē′nyəl), *adj.* **1** having similar tastes and interests; getting on well together. **2** agreeable; suitable. [< *con-* + Latin *genialis* < *genius* spirit] —**con gen′ial ly,** *adv.*

con jure (kon′jər, kun′jər *for v.t. 1-3, v.i.*; kən jur′ *for v.t. 4*), *v.*, **-jured, -jur ing.** —*v.t.* **1** compel (a spirit, devil, etc.) to appear or disappear by a set form of words. **2** cause to appear or happen as if by magic. **3** cause to appear in the mind. **4** make a solemn appeal to; request earnestly; entreat. —*v.i.* **1** summon a devil, spirit, etc. **2** practice magic. **3** perform tricks by skill and quickness in moving the hands. [< Old French *conjurer* < Latin *conjurare* make a compact < *com-* together + *jurare* swear]

con sci en tious (kon′shē en′shəs), *adj.* **1** careful to do what one knows is right; controlled by conscience. **2** done with care to make it right; painstaking. —**con′sci en′tious ly,** *adv.* —**con′sci en′tious ness,** *n.*

con so nant (kon′sə nənt) —*adj.* in agreement; in accord; harmonious. [< Latin *consonantem* harmonizing < *com-* together + *sonare* to sound] —**con′so nant ly,** *adv.*

con sum ma tion (kon′sə mā′shən), *n.* completion; fulfillment.

con ten tious (kən ten′shəs), *adj.* **1** fond of arguing; given to disputing; quarrelsome. **2** characterized by contention. —**con ten′tious ly,** *adv.* —**con ten′tious ness,** *n.*

con tra band (kon′trə band), *n.* goods imported or exported contrary to law; smuggled goods. [< Spanish *contrabando* < Italian < *contra-* against + *bando* edict, ban]

con trive (kən trīv′), *v.t.*, **-trived, -triv ing.** **1** plan with cleverness or skill; invent; design. **2** plan; scheme; plot. **3** manage. **4** bring about. [< Old French *controver* < Late Latin *contropare* compare] —**con triv′a ble,** *adj.* —**con triv′er,** *n.*

con verse (kon′vėrs′), *n.* thing that is opposite or contrary. [< Latin *conversum* turned around, converted]

con vo lu tion (kon′və lü′shən), *n.* **1** a coiling, winding, or twisting together. **2** a coil; winding; twist.

co quette (kō ket′), *n.* woman who tries to attract men; flirt. [< French, feminine of *coquet,* diminutive of *coq* cock]

co quet tish (kō ket′ish), *adj.* **1** of a coquette. **2** like a coquette; like a coquette's. —**co quet′tish ly,** *adv.* —**co quet′tish ness,** *n.*

co que try (kō′kə trē, kō ket′rē), *n., pl.* **-tries.** **1** flirting. **2** trifling.

cor nice (kôr′nis), *n.* **1** an ornamental, horizontal molding along the top of a wall, pillar, building, etc. **2** a molding around the walls of a room just below the ceiling or over the top of a window. [< French *corniche* < Italian *cornice*]

cor tege or **cor tège** (kôr tezh′, kôr tāzh′), *n.* procession [< French *cortège* < Italian *corteggio* < *corte* court < Latin *cohortem* crowd, enclosure.]

cos mog o ny (koz mog′ə nē), *n., pl.* **-nies.** **1** origin of universe. **2** theory, system, or account of its origin. [< Greek *kosmogonia* < *kosmos* world + *gonos* birth] —**cos mog′o nist,** *n.*

co til lion (kə til′yən), *n.* **1** a dance with complicated steps and much changing of partners, led by one couple. **2** an early French social dance for couples. **3** any large social dance. [< French *cotillon,* originally, petticoat]

couch (kouch), *v.t.* lower into a level position ready to attack. [< Old French *couche* < *coucher* lay in place < Latin *collocare* < *com-* together + *locus* a place]

coun te nance (koun′tə nəns), *n., v.*, **-nanced, -nanc ing.** —*n.* **1** expression of the face. **2** face; features. **3** approval; encouragement. **4** calmness; composure. **5** keep one's countenance, **a** be calm; not show feeling. **b** keep from smiling or laughing. —*v.t.* approve or encourage; sanction. [< Old French *contenance* < Medieval Latin *continentia* demeanor < Latin, self-control < *continere.*] —**coun′te nanc er,** *n.*

coun ty (koun′tē), *n., pl.* **-ties.** the officials of a country. [< Anglo-French *counté* territory of a count < *counte* count, variant of Old French *conte.*]

cou pé (kü pā′), *n.* a four-wheeled, closed carriage with a seat for two people inside and a seat for the driver outside.

cov ert (*adj.* kō′vərt, kuv′ərt; *n.* kuv′ərt, kō′vərt), *adj.* kept from sight; concealed; secret; hidden. [< Old French, past participle of *covrir.*] —**cov′ert ly,** *adv.* —**cov′ert ness,** *n.*

cov et (kuv′it), *v.t.* desire eagerly (something that belongs to another). [< Old French *coveitier* < Popular Latin *cupiditare* < Latin *cupiditatem.*]

cov et ous (kuv′ə təs), *adj.* desiring things that belong to others. —**cov′et ous ly,** *adv.* —**cov′et ous ness,** *n.*

cow er (kou′ər), *v.i.* **1** crouch in fear or shame. **2** draw back tremblingly from another's threats, blows, etc. [apparently < Scandinavian (Old Icelandic) *kūra* doze, lie quiet]

coz en (kuz′n), *v.t., v.i.* deceive or trick; cheat; beguile. [perhaps < Italian *cozzonare* play the crafty knave] —**coz′en er,** *n.*

crag (krag), *n.* a steep, rugged rock or cliff rising above others. [< Celtic (Gaelic) *creag*] —**crag′like,** *adj.*

crane (krān), *v.*, **craned, cran ing.** —*v.t.* stretch (the neck) as a crane does, in order to see better. [Old English *cran*] —**crane′like,** *adj.*

cra vat (krə vat′), *n.* necktie, especially a wide one. [< French *cravate,* special use of *Cravate* Croat (Croatian mercenaries in France wore these)]

cra ven (krā′vən), *adj.* cowardly. —*n.* coward. [< Old French *cravente* overcome < Popular Latin *crepantare* < Latin *crepare* crush; burst] —**cra′ven ly,** *adv.* —**cra′ven ness,** *n.*

cred u lous (krej′ə ləs), *adj.* too ready to believe; easily deceived. —**cred′u lous ly,** *adv.* —**cred′u lous ness,** *n.*

cro ny (krō′nē), *n., pl.* **-nies.** a very close friend; chum. [earlier *chrony* < Greek *chronios* lasting < *chronos* time]

crouch (krouch), *v.i.* **1** stoop low with bent legs like an animal ready to spring. **2** shrink down in fear. **3** bow down in a timid or slavish manner; cower. —*v.t.* bend low. —*n.* **1** act or state of crouching. **2** a crouching position. [perhaps blend of *couch* and *crook*]

crup per (krup′ər), *n.* strap attached to the back of a harness and passed under a horse's tail to prevent the harness from slipping forward. [< Old French *cropiere* < *crope, croupe* croup]

cu bit (kyu′bit), *n.* an ancient measure of length, about 18 to 22 inches (46 to 56 centimeters). [< Latin *cubitum* elbow, cubit]

cuck old (kuk′əld), *n.* husband of an unfaithful wife. —*v.t.* make a cuckold of. [< Old French *cucuault* < *coucou* cuckoo]

cull (kul), *v.t.* **1** pick out; select. **2** pick over; make selections from. —*n.* something picked out as inferior or worthless. Poor fruit, stale vegetables, and animals not up to standard are called culls. [< Old French *coillir* < Latin *colligere* collect] —**cull′er,** *n.*

cul mi na tion (kul′mə nā′shən), *n.* **1** the highest point; climax. **2** a reaching of the highest point.

cu ne i form (kyü nē′ə fôrm, kyü′nē ə fôrm), *adj.* **1** wedge-shaped. **2** composed of cuneiform characters or inscriptions. — *n.* the wedge-shaped characters used in the writing of ancient Babylonia, Assyria, Persia, etc. [< Latin *cuneus* wedge + English *-form*]

cup (kup), *n., v.,* **cupped, cup ping.** —*n.* **1** as much as a cup holds; cupful. **2** drink or food served in a cup. **3 in one's cups,** drunk. [Old English *cuppe* < Late Latin *cuppa* < Latin *cupa* tub]

cur (ker), *n.* **1** a dog of mixed breed; mongrel. **2** a surly, contemptible person. [< Middle English *curre,* probably < Scandinavian (Old Icelandic) *kurra* snarl]

cur ate (kyūr′it), *n.* clergyman who assists a pastor, rector, or vicar. [< Medieval Latin *curatus* < *cura* cure of souls < Latin *cura* care.]

curb (kerb), *n.* chain or strap fastened to a horse's bit and passed under its lower jaw. When the reins are pulled tight, the curb checks the horse. [< Middle French *courbe* < Latin *curvus* bent, curved]

cur ry (ker′ē), *v.* to cajole, or smooth down, as with flattery.

curt (kert), *adj.* rudely brief; short; abrupt. [< Latin *curtus* cut short] —**curt′ly,** *adv.* —**curt′ness,** *n.*

Cy clops (sī′klops), *n., pl.* **Cy clo pes** (sī klō′pēz). (in Greek legends) one of a race of giants, each having only one eye in the center of the forehead. [< Latin < Greek *Kyklōps* < *kyklos* circle + *ōps* eye]

cy clo ram a (sī′klə ram′ə), *n.* a large picture of a landscape, battle, etc., on the wall of a circular room. [< Greek *kyklos* circle + *horama* spectacle]

da is (dā′is; *British* dās), *n.* a raised platform at one end of a hall or large room for a throne, seats of honor, a lectern, etc. [< Old French *deis* < Latin *discus* quoit, dish < Greek *diskos.* Doublet of DESK, DISCUS, DISH, and DISK.]

dam ask (dam′əsk), *n.* **1** a firm, shiny, reversible linen, silk, or cotton fabric with woven designs, used especially for tablecloths and napkins. **2** a rose color; pink. —*adj.* **1** made of damask. **2** rose-colored; pink. —*v.t.* **1** damascene. **2** weave with the design of damask fabric. [< Greek *Damaskos* Damascus]

dam sel (dam′zəl), *n.* ARCHAIC. a young girl; maiden. [< Old French *dameisele,* ultimately < Latin *domina* lady]

dan dy (dan′dē), *n., pl.* **-dies,** *adj.,* **-di er, -di est.** —*n.* man who is too concerned about his clothing and appearance; fop. [perhaps < *Dandy,* a variant of *Andrew*]

dar kle (där′kəl), *v.* to lurk or loom in the dark; to render obscure; to grow dark.

a hat	i it	oi oil	ch child	(a in about
ā age	ī ice	ou out	ng long	⎧ e in taken
ä far	o hot	u cup	sh she	ə = ⎨ i in pencil
e let	ō open	u̇ put	th thin	⎪ o in lemon
ē equal	ô order	ü rule	ŦH then	⎩ u in circus
ėr term			zh measure	< = derived from

dark ling (därk′ling), *adv.* in the dark. —*adj.* dark; dim; obscure.

daunt less (dônt′lis, dänt′lis), *adj.* not to be frightened or discouraged; brave. —**daunt′less ly,** *adv.*

dearth (dėrth), *n.* **1** too small a supply; great scarcity or lack. **2** scarcity of food; famine. [Middle English *derthe*]

de bauch (di bôch′), *v.t.* lead away from duty, virtue, or morality; corrupt or seduce. —*v.i.* indulge excessively in sensual pleasures, eating, drinking, etc. [< French *débaucher* entice from duty] —**de bauch′er,** *n.*

deb o nair or **deb o naire** (deb′ə ner′, deb′ə när′), *adj.* pleasant, courteous, and cheerful. [< Old French *debonaire* < *de bon aire* of good disposition] —**deb′o nair′ly,** *adv.* —**deb′o nair′ness,** *n.*

de cant er (di kan′tər), *n.* a glass bottle with a stopper, used for serving wine, liquor, or other liquids.

de ci sive (di sī′siv), *adj.* **1** having or giving a clear result; settling something beyond question or doubt. **2** having or showing decision; resolute. —**de ci′sive ly,** *adv.* —**de ci′sive ness,** *n.*

de cree (di krē′), *n., v.,* **-creed, -cree ing.** —*n.* **1** something ordered or settled by authority; official decision. **2** a decision or order of a court or judge. —*v.t.* **1** order or settle by authority. **2** decide; determine. —*v.i.* decide; determine. [< Old French *decre* < Latin *decretum* < *de-* + *cernere* distinguish, separate]

de fame (di fām′), *v.t.,* **-famed, -fam ing.** attack the good name of; harm the reputation of; speak evil of; slander or libel. —**de fam′er,** *n.*

de file (di fīl′), *v.t.,* **-filed, -fil ing. 1** make filthy or dirty; make disgusting in any way. **2** destroy the purity or cleanness of (anything sacred); desecrate. **3** stain; dishonor. **4** ARCHAIC. ravish. [< Old French *defouler* trample down or violate] —**de file′ment,** *n.* —**de fil′er,** *n.*

de lude (di lüd′), *v.t.,* **-lud ed, -lud ing.** mislead the mind or judgment of; trick or deceive. [< Latin *deludere* < *de-* + *ludere* to play] —**de lud′er,** *n.* —**de lud′ing ly,** *adv.*

de mean (di mēn′), *v.t.* lower in dignity or standing; humble; degrade. [< *de-* down + *mean*]

de mure (di myūr′), *adj.,* **-mur er, -mur est. 1** artificially proper; assuming an air of modesty; coy. **2** reserved or composed in demeanor; serious and sober. [< *de-* + Old French *meür* discreet, mature < Latin *maturus*] —**de mure′ly,** *adv.* —**de mure′ness,** *n.*

de praved (di prāvd′), *adj.* morally bad; corrupt; perverted. —**de praved′ly,** *adv.* —**de praved′ness,** *n.*

de ri sion (di rizh′ən), *n.* **1** scornful laughter; ridicule. **2** object of ridicule. [< Latin *derisionem* < *deridere*]

de rog a to ry (di rog′ə tôr′e, di rog′ə tōr′ē), *adj.* having the effect of lowering in honor or estimation; disparaging. —**de rog′a to′ri ly,** *adv.* —**de rog′a to′ri ness,** *n.*

der vish (dėr′vish), *n.* member of a Moslem religious order that practices self-denial and devotion. Some dervishes dance and spin about violently. [< Turkish *derviş* < Persian *darvīsh* poor man] —**der′vish like′,** *adj.*

de scry (di skrī′), *v.t.,* **-scried, -scry ing. 1** catch sight of; be able to see; make out. **2** discover by observation; detect. [< Old French *descrier* proclaim < *des-* dis- + *crier* to cry]

des e crate (des′ə krāt), *v.t.,* **-crat ed, -crat ing.** treat or use without respect; disregard the sacredness of; profane. [< *de-* + *(con)secrate*] —**des′e crat′er, des′e cra′tor,** *n.* —**des′e cra′tion,** *n.*

de sist (di zist′), *v.i.* stop doing something; cease. [< Latin *desistere* < *de-* + *sistere* to stop]

de spite (di spīt′), *prep.* in spite of. —*n.* **1** insult or injury. **2** malice; spite. **3** contempt; scorn. **4 in despite of,** in spite of. [< Old French *despit* < Latin *despectum* spite < *despicere* despise]

de spoil (di spoil′), *v.t.* strip of possessions; rob; plunder. [< Latin *despoliare* < *de-* + *spolium* armor, booty]

de spond (di spond′), *v.i.* lose heart, courage, or hope. —*n.* despondency. [< Latin *despondere* < *de-* + *spondere* to promise]

des pot ic (des pot′ik), *adj.* of a despot; having unlimited power; tyrannical. —**des pot′i cal ly,** *adv.*

des tri er (des′tri ər, des trēr′), *n.* ARCHAIC. a war horse.

des ul to ry (des′əl tôr′ē, des′əl tōr′ē), *adj.* jumping from one thing to another; without aim or method; unconnected. [< Latin *desultorius* of a leaper, ultimately < *de-* down + *salire* to leap] —**des′ul to′ri ly,** *adv.* —**des′ul to′ri ness,** *n.*

de tect (di tekt′), *v.t.* **1** discover (a person) in the performance of some act. **2** discover the presence, existence, or fact of. [< Latin *detectum* uncovered < *de-* + *tegere* to cover]

de tour (dē′tùr, di tùr′), *n.* **1** road that is used when the main or direct road cannot be traveled. **2** a roundabout way or course. —*v.i.* use a detour. —*v.t.* cause to use a detour. [< French *détour* < *détourner* turn aside]

dex ter ous (dek′stər əs), *adj.* **1** skillful in using the hands or body. **2** having or showing skill in using the mind; clever. Also, **dextrous.** —**dex′ter ous ly,** *adv.* —**dex′ter ous ness,** *n.*

di a lec tic (dī′ə lek′tik), *n.* **1** Often, **dialectics,** *pl.* art or practice of logical discussion as a means of examining critically the truth of a theory or opinion. **2** discussion or debate on the basis of logic of the truth of an opinion or theory. —*adj.* **1** having to do with dialectics; dialectical. [< Greek *dialektikē (technē)* dialectic (art) < *dialektos*] —**di′a lec′ti cal ly,** *adv.*

dil i gence (dil′ə jəns), *n.* constant and earnest effort to accomplish what is undertaken; industry.

dim i nu tion (dim′ə nü′shən, dim′ə nyü′shən), *n.* a diminishing; lessening; reduction; decrease.

din (din), *n.* a continuing loud, confused noise. [Old English *dynn*]

dire (dīr), *adj.*, **dir er, dir est.** causing great fear or suffering; dreadful. [< Latin *dirus*] —**dire′ly,** *adv.* —**dire′ness,** *n.*

dirge (dėrj), *n.* a funeral song or tune. [contraction of Latin *dirige* direct! (first word in office for the dead)] —**dirge′like′,** *adj.*

dis cern ment (də zėrn′mənt, də sėrn′mənt), *n.* **1** keenness in seeing and understanding; good judgment; shrewdness. **2** act of discerning.

dis con so late (dis kon′sə lit), *adj.* without hope; forlorn; unhappy. [< Medieval Latin *disconsolatus* < Latin *dis-* + *consolari* to console] —**dis con′so late ly,** *adv.* —**dis con′so late ness,** *n.*

dis course (*n.* dis′kôrs, dis′kōrs; *v.* dis kôrs′, dis kōrs′), *n.*, *v.*, **-coursed, -cours ing.** —*n.* **1** a formal or extensive speech or writing. **2** talk; conversation. —*v.i.* **1** speak or write formally or at length on some subject. **2** talk; converse. [< Latin *discursus* a running about < *dis-* + *cursus* a running]

dis cre tion (dis kresh′ən), *n.* quality of being discreet; great carefulness in speech or action; good judgment; wise caution.

di shev eled or **di shev elled** (də shev′əld), *adj.* not neat; rumpled; mussed; disordered.

dis in gen u ous (dis′in jen′yü əs), *adj.* lacking in frankness; insincere. —**dis′in gen′u ous ly,** *adv.* —**dis′in gen′u ous ness,** *n.*

dis par age (dis par′ij), *v.t.*, **-aged, -ag ing.** **1** speak slightingly of; belittle. **2** lower the reputation of; discredit. [< Old French *desparagier* match unequally < *des-* dis- + *parage* rank, lineage < *par* peer[1]] —**dis par′age ment,** *n.* —**dis par′ag er,** *n.* —**dis par′ag ing ly,** *adv.*

dis qui si tion (dis′kwə zish′ən), *n.* a long or formal speech or writing about a subject; dissertation. [< Latin *disquisitionem* < *disquirere* inquire < *dis-* + *quaerere* seek]

dis ser ta tion (dis′ər tā′shən), *n.* a formal oral or written discussion of a subject, especially the thesis of a candidate for a doctor's degree. [< Latin *dissertationem* < *dissertare* discuss often < *disserere* discuss < *dis-* + *serere* join words]

dis sim u late (di sim′yə lāt), *v.*, **-lat ed, -lat ing.** —*v.t.* disguise or hide under a pretense; dissemble. —*v.i.* hide the truth;

dissemble. —**dis sim′u la′tion,** *n.* —**dis sim′u la′tor,** *n.*

dis so lu tion (dis′ə lü′shən), *n.* **1** a breaking up or ending of an association of any kind. **2** ruin; destruction. **3** death.

dis suade (di swād′), *v.t.*, **-suad ed, -suad ing.** **1** persuade not to do something. **2** advise against. [< Latin *dissuadere* < *dis-* against + *suadere* to urge]

dis taff (dis′taf), *n.* **1** a stick, split at the tip, to hold wool or flax for spinning by hand. **2** staff on a spinning wheel for holding wool or flax. **3** woman's work or affairs. [Old English *distæf* < *dis-* flax + *stæf* staff]

dith er (diⱦ′ər), *n.* a confused, excited condition. —*v.t.* act in a nervous, excited, or indecisive way; waver fearfully. [origin uncertain]

dith y ram bic (diⱦ′ə ram′bik), *adj.* **1** of a dithyramb. **2** wild and vehement.

di van (dī′van, də van′), *n.* a long, low, soft couch or sofa. [< Turkish *divān* < Persian *dēvān*]

di vers (dī′vərz), *adj.* more than one; several different; various. [< Old French < Latin *diversum* turned aside, diverted]

di vine (də vīn′), *v.*, **-vined, -vin ing.** —*v.t.* **1** foresee or foretell by inspiration, by magic, or by signs and omens; predict. **2** guess correctly. [< Old French *divin* < Latin *divinum* < *divus* deity] —**di vin′er,** *n.*

doc ile (dos′əl; *British* dō′sīl, dos′īl), *adj.* easily managed or trained; obedient. [< Middle French < Latin *docilem* < *docere* teach] —**doc′ile ly,** *adv.*

dock et (dok′it), *n.* label or ticket giving the contents of a package, document, etc.

dole ful (dōl′fəl), *adj.* very sad or dreary; mournful; dismal. —**dole′ful ly,** *adv.* —**dole′ful ness,** *n.*

dol or ous (dol′ər əs, dō′lər əs), *adj.* **1** full of or expressing sorrow; mournful. **2** causing or giving rise to sorrow; grievous; painful. —**dol′or ous ly,** *adv.* —**dol′or ous ness,** *n.*

Don Juan (don wän′; don hwän′; don jü′ən), **1** a legendary Spanish nobleman who led an immoral life. **2** man leading an immoral life; libertine. —**Don Juanesque,** *adj.*

dough ty (dou′tē), *adj.*, **-ti er, -ti est.** strong and bold; stout; brave; hearty. [Old English *dohtig* < *dugan* be of use] —**dough′ti ly,** *adv.* —**dough′ti ness,** *n.*

dove cote (duv′kōt′), *n.* a small house or shelter for doves or pigeons.

draught (draft), *n.*, *v.t.*, *adj.* draft. —**draught′er,** *n.*

dray (drā), *n.* a strong cart or wagon for carrying heavy loads. [Old English *dræge* dragnet < *dragan* to draw]

dregs (dregz), *n.pl.* **1** the solid bits of matter that settle to the bottom of a liquid. **2** the least desirable part. [< Scandinavian (Old Icelandic) *dregg,* singular]

driv el (driv′əl), **-eled, -el ing** or **-elled, -el ling,** *n.* silly talk; nonsense. [Old English *dreflian*] —**driv′el er, driv′el ler,** *n.*

drove (drōv), *n.* **1** group of cattle, sheep, hogs, etc., moving or driven along together; flock; herd. [Old English *drāf*]

drowse (drouz), *v.*, **drowsed, drows ing,** *n.* a being half asleep; sleepiness. [Old English *drūsian* to sink]

dudg eon (duj′ən), *n.* **1** a feeling of anger or resentment. **2 in high dudgeon,** very angry; resentful.

dun (dun), *v.*, **dunned, dun ning,** *n.* —*v.t.* **1** demand payment of a debt from (someone) again and again. **2** pester or plague constantly. [< obsolete *dun* make a din < Scandinavian (Old Icelandic) *duna* to thunder]

dupe (düp, dyüp), *n.*, *v.*, **duped, dup ing.** —*n.* **1** person easily deceived or tricked. **2** one who is being deluded or tricked. —*v.t.* deceive or trick. [< French] —**dup′er,** *n.*

ebb (eb), *n.* a growing less or weaker; decline; decay. [Old English *ebba*]

ec stat ic (ek stat′ik), *adj.* **1** full of ecstasy. **2** caused by ecstasy. —**ec stat′i cal ly,** *adv.*

ed dy (ed′ē), *n.*, *pl.* **-dies,** *v.*, **-died, -dy ing.** —*n.* water, air, smoke, etc., moving against the main current, especially when having a whirling motion; small whirlpool or whirlwind. [perhaps < Scandinavian (Old Icelandic) *itha*]

e dict (ē′dikt), *n.* decree or law proclaimed by a king or other ruler on his or her sole authority. [< Latin *edictum* < *edicere* proclaim < *ex-* out + *dicere* say]

ed i fice (ed′ə fis), *n*. a building, especially a large or impressive one, such as a cathedral, palace, or temple. [< Old French < Latin *aedificium* < *aedificare* build < *aedis* a dwelling, temple + *facere* make]

ed i fy (ed′ə fī), *v.t.*, **-fied, -fy ing.** improve morally; benefit spiritually; instruct and uplift. [< Old French *edifier* < Latin *aedificare* build] —**ed′i fi′er,** *n*.

ef fi gy (ef′ə jē), *n., pl.* **-gies.** image or statue, usually of a person. [< Latin *effigies* < *effingere* to fashion < *ex-* out + *fingere* to form]

ef ful gence (i ful′jəns), *n*. a shining forth of light, etc.; great luster or brilliance; splendor.

e lix ir (i lik′sər), *n*. **1** substance supposed to have the power of changing lead, iron, etc., into gold or of lengthening life indefinitely. **2** cure-all. **3** medicine made of drugs or herbs mixed with alcohol and syrup. [< Medieval Latin < Arabic *al-iksīr*]

el o quence (el′ə kwəns), *n*. **1** flow of speech that has grace and force. **2** power to win by speaking; the art of using language so as to stir the feelings.

el o quent (el′ə kwənt), *adj*. **1** having eloquence. **2** very expressive. [< Latin *eloquentem* speaking out < *ex-* out + *loqui* speak] —**el′o quent ly,** *adv*.

e ma ci ate (i mā′shē āt), *v.t.*, **-at ed, -at ing.** make unnaturally thin; cause to lose flesh or waste away. [< Latin *emaciatum* made lean < *ex-* + *macies* leanness] —**e ma′ci a′tion,** *n*.

e man ci pate (i man′sə pāt), *v.t.*, **-pat ed, -pat ing.** release from slavery or restraint; set free. [< Latin *emancipatum* set free < *ex-* away + *manus* hand + *capere* to take] —**e man′ci pa′tor,** *n*.

em bay (em bā′), *v.t.* **1** to shut in, or shelter, as in a bay; to encircle, surround. **2** to form into a bay.

em bel lish (em bel′ish), *v.t.* **1** add beauty to; decorate; adorn; ornament. **2** make more interesting by adding real or imaginary details; elaborate. [< Old French *embelliss-*, a form of *embellir* embellish < *en-* in + *bel* handsome] —**em bel′lish ment,** *n*.

em brace (em brās′), *v.*, **-braced, -brac ing.** —*v.t.* **1** clasp or hold in the arms to show love or friendship; hug. **2** take up; take for oneself; accept. **3** take in; include; contain. **4** surround; enclose. —*v.i.* hug one another. —*n*. a clasping in the arms; hug. [< Old French *embracer*, ultimately < Latin *in-* in + *brachium* arm] —**em brace′a ble,** *adj.* —**em brace′ment,** *n*. —**em brac′er,** *n*.

em i nent (em′ə nənt), *adj*. above all or most others; outstanding; distinguished. [< Latin *eminentem* standing out, prominent < *ex-* out + *minere* jut] —**em′i nent ly,** *adv*.

em u late (em′yə lāt), *v.t.*, **-lat ed, -lat ing.** **1** copy or imitate in order to equal or excel the achievements or qualities of an admired person. **2** vie with; rival. [< Latin *aemulatum* rivaled < *aemulus* striving to equal] —**em′u la′tion,** *n*. —**em′u la′tor,** *n*.

en cum brance (en kum′brəns), *n*. **1** something useless or in the way; hindrance; burden. **2** claim, mortgage, etc., on property. Also, **incumbrance.**

en due (en dü′, en dyü′), *v.t.*, **-dued, -du ing.** **1** provide with a quality or power; furnish; supply. **2** clothe. Also, **indue.** [< Old French *enduire* < Latin *inducere* lead into, induce]

en gen der (en jen′dər), *v.t.* **1** bring into existence; produce; cause. **2** beget. [< Old French *engendrer* < Latin *ingenerare* < *in-* in + *generare* create]

e nig ma (i nig′mə), *n*. **1** a baffling or puzzling problem, situation, person, etc. **2** a puzzling statement; riddle. [< Latin *aenigma* < Greek *ainigma* < *ainissesthai* speak in riddles < *ainos* riddle, fable]

en mi ty (en′mə tē), *n., pl.* **-ties.** the feeling that enemies have for each other; hostility or hatred. [< Old French *enemistie* < Popular Latin *inimicitatem* < Latin *inimicus*]

en no ble (en nō′bəl), *v.t.*, **-bled, -bling.** **1** raise in the respect of others; make noble; dignify; exalt. **2** raise to a noble rank; give a title of nobility to. **3** make finer or more noble in nature; elevate. —**en no′ble ment,** *n*. —**en no′bling ly,** *adv*.

en tail (en tāl′), *v.t.* impose or require. [< *en-* + Old French

a hat	i it	oi oil	ch child		a in about
ā age	ī ice	ou out	ng long		e in taken
ä far	o hot	u cup	sh she	ə =	i in pencil
e let	ō open	u̇ put	th thin		o in lemon
ē equal	ô order	ü rule	ᴛʜ then		u in circus
ėr term			zh measure		< = derived from

taille cutting, tax < *taillier* to cut] —**en tail′ment,** *n*.

en trails (en′trālz, en′trəlz), *n.pl.* **1** the inner parts of the body of a human being or animal. **2** the intestines; bowels. [< Old French *entrailles* < Medieval Latin *intralia*, alteration of Latin *interanea* things inside < *inter* within]

en treat y (en trē′tē), *n., pl.* **-treat ies.** an earnest request; prayer or appeal.

é pée or **e pee** (ā pā′, e pā′), *n*. sword used in fencing and dueling, especially one with a sharp point and no cutting edge. [< French *épée*]

eq uer ry (ek′wər ē), *n., pl.* **-ries.** **1** officer of a royal or noble household who has charge of the horses. **2** attendant upon a member of the British royal household. [< Old French *escuerie* stable]

eq ui ty (ek′wə tē), *n*. a being equal or fair; fairness; justice.

es chew (es chü′), *v.t.* keep away from; avoid; shun. [< Old French *eschiver*] —**es chew′er,** *n*.

es cu lent (es′kyə lənt), *adj*. suitable for food; edible. —*n*. anything that is fit for food, especially vegetables. [< Latin *esculentus* < *esca* food]

es py (e spī′), *v.*, **-pied, -py ing.** see at a distance; catch sight of; spy. [< Old French *espier*]

es teem (e stēm′), *v.t.* **1** have a very favorable opinion of; think highly of. **2** think; consider. —*n*. a very favorable opinion; high regard. [< Old French *estimer* < Latin *aestimare* to value]

e ta gère (ā tä zher′), *n*. an open-shelved cabinet.

e ven (ē′vən), *n*. ARCHAIC. evening. [Old English *ǣfen*]

e ven song (ē′vən sông′, ē′vən song′), *n*. vespers. [Old English *ǣfensang*]

ex e crate (ek′sə krāt), *v.*, **-crat ed, -crat ing.** —*v.t.* **1** feel intense loathing for; abhor; detest. **2** pronounce a curse upon. —*v.i.* curse. [< Latin *exsecratum* declared accursed < *ex-* out + *sacer* sacred] —**ex′e cra′tor,** *n*.

ex hor ta tion (eg′zôr tā′shən, ek′sôr tā′shən), *n*. strong urging; earnest advice or warning.

ex or bi tant (eg zôr′bə tənt), *adj*. exceeding what is customary, proper, or reasonable; unreasonably excessive. [< Latin *exorbitantem* going out of the track < *ex-* out of + *orbita* track] —**ex or′bi tant ly,** *adv*.

ex pe di ent (ek spe′dē ənt), *n*. means of bringing about a desired result.

ex pi a tion (ek′spē ā′shən), *n*. **1** a making amends for a wrong, sin, etc.; atonement. **2** means of atonement; amends.

ex tir pate (ek′stər pāt, ek stėr′pāt), *v.t.*, **-pat ed, -pat ing.** **1** remove completely; destroy totally. **2** tear up by the roots. [< Latin *exstirpatum* uprooted < *ex-* out + *stirps* root] —**ex′tir pa′tion,** *n*. —**ex′tir pa′tor,** *n*.

ex tol or **ex toll** (ek stōl′, ek stol′), *v.t.*, **-tolled, -tol ling.** praise highly; commend. [< Latin *extollere* < *ex-* up + *tollere* to raise] —**ex tol′ler,** *n*. —**ex tol′ment,** *n*.

ex tort (ek stôrt′), *v.t.* obtain (money, a promise, etc.) by threats, force, fraud, or illegal use of authority. [< Latin *extortum* twisted out < *ex-* + *torquere* twist] —**ex tort′er,** *n*.

ex tor tion (ek stôr′shən), *n*. **1** an extorting.

ex trav a gant (ek strav′ə gənt), *adj*. beyond the bounds of reason; excessive. [< Medieval Latin *extravagantem* < Latin *extra-* outside + *vagari* to wander] —**ex trav′a gant ly,** *adv*.

eyr ie or **eyr y** (er′ē, ar′ē, *or* ir′ē), *n., pl.* **eyr ies.** aerie.

fa cade or **fa çade** (fə säd′), *n*. **1** the front part of a building. **2** any side of a building that faces a street or an open space. **3** outward appearance. [< French *façade*, ultimately < Latin *facies* a form, face]

1031

fa cil i tate (fə sil′ə tāt), *v.t.*, **-tat ed, -tat ing.** make easy; lessen the labor of; help bring about; assist; expedite. **—fa cil′i ta′tion,** *n.* **—fa cil′i ta′tor,** *n.*

fain (fān), *adj.* ARCHAIC. eager. [Old English *fægen*]

fa kir (fə kir′, fā′kər), *n.* **1** a Moslem holy man who lives by begging. **2** dervish. **3** a Hindu ascetic. Fakirs sometimes do extraordinary things, such as lying upon sharp knives. [< Arabic *faqīr* poor (man)]

fane (fān), *n.* ARCHAIC. temple; church. [< Latin *fanum* temple]

far thing (fär′ᴛʜing), *n.* a former British coin equal to a fourth of a British penny. [Old English *fēorthung* < *fēortha* fourth]

fast (fast), *adj.* ARCHAIC. close; near.

fas tid i ous (fa stid′ē əs), *adj.* hard to please; dainty in taste; easily disgusted. [< Latin *fastidiosus* < *fastidium* loathing] **—fas tid′i ous ly,** *adv.* **—fas tid′i ous ness,** *n.*

fath om (faᴛʜ′əm), *n., pl.* **fath oms** or **fath om,** *v.* **—n.** unit of measure equal to 6 feet, used mostly in measuring the depth of water and the length of ships' ropes, cables, etc. **—v.t.** **1** measure the depth of (water); sound. **2** get to the bottom of; understand fully. [Old English *fæthm* width of the outstretched arms] **—fath′om a ble,** *adj.*

fat u ous (fach′ü əs), *adj.* stupid but self-satisfied; foolish; silly. [< Latin *fatuus*] **—fat′u ous ly,** *adv.* **—fat′u ous ness,** *n.*

fawn (fôn), *v.i.* **1** try to get favor or notice by slavish acts. **2** (of dogs, etc.) show fondness by crouching, wagging the tail, licking the hand, etc. [Old English *fagnian* < *fægen* fain] **—fawn′ing ly,** *adv.*

fe al ty (fē′əl tē), *n., pl.* **-ties. 1** loyalty and duty owed by a vassal to his feudal lord. **2** loyalty; faithfulness; allegiance. [< Old French *feauté* < Latin *fidelitatem.* Doublet of fidelity.]

fear some (fir′səm), *adj.* **1** causing fear; frightful. **2** afraid; timid. **—fear′some ly,** *adv.* **—fear′some ness,** *n.*

feign (fān), *v.t.* **1** put on a false appearance of; make believe; pretend. **2** make up to deceive; invent falsely. **—v.i.** make oneself appear; pretend (to be). [< Old French *feign-*, a form of *feindre* feign < Latin *fingere* to form] **—feign′er.** *n.*

feint (fānt), *n.* movement intended to deceive; sham attack; pretended blow. [< French *feinte* < *feindre* feign]

fe lic i ty (fə lis′ə tē), *n., pl.* **-ties.** great happiness; bliss. [< Latin *felicitatem* < *felicem* happy]

fell¹ (fel), *n.* **1** a mountain. **2** an elevated wild field; moor; down.

fell² (fel), *adj.* **1** fierce; savage; ruthless. **2** deadly; destructive. [< Old French *fel* < *felon* felon]

fen (fen), *n.* low, marshy land covered wholly or partially with shallow, often stagnant water. [Old English *fenn*]

fen nel (fen′l), *n.* **1** a tall, perennial European plant with yellow flowers, of the same family as the parsley. **2** its fragrant seeds, used in medicine and cooking. [Old English *fenol,* ultimately < Latin *fenum* hay]

fe ro cious (fə rō′shəs), *adj.* **1** savagely cruel or destructive; fierce. **2** INFORMAL. extremely intense. [< Latin *ferocem* fierce] **—fe ro′cious ly,** *adv.* **—fe ro′cious ness,** *n.*

fete or **fête** (fāt; *French* fet), *n., v.,* **fet ed, fet ing** or **fêt ed, fêt ing. —n.** festival or party, especially an elaborate one and often one held outdoors. [< French *fête* feast, ultimately < Latin *festus* festal, joyous]

fet ish (fet′ish, fē′tish), *n.* **1** any material object worshiped by primitive people for its supposed magic powers. **2** anything regarded with unreasoning reverence or blind devotion. [< French *fétiche* < Portuguese *feitiço* charm, originally adjective, artificial < Latin *factitius*]

fet ter (fet′ər), *n.* chain or shackle for the feet to prevent escape. [Old English *feter.* Related to foot]

fick le (fik′əl), *adj.* **1** likely to change or give up a loyalty, attachments, etc., without reason; inconstant [Old English *ficol* deceitful] **—fick′le ness,** *n.*

fief (fēf), *n.* piece of land held on condition of giving military and other services to the feudal lord owning it, in return for his protection and the use of the land; feudal estate; feud; fee. Also, **feoff.** [< Old French; of Germanic origin]

fil let (fil′it), *n.* a narrow band, ribbon, etc., worn around the head to hold the hair in place or as an ornament. [< Old French *filet,* diminutive of *fil* thread < Latin *filum*]

fir ma ment (fėr′mə mənt), *n.* arch of the heavens; sky. [< Latin *firmamentum,* ultimately < *firmus* firm]

flank (flangk), *n.* **1** the fleshy or muscular part of the side of an animal or person between the ribs and the hip. **2** the far right or the far left side of an army, fleet, or fort. [< Old French *flanc* < Germanic]

flay (flā), *v.t.* **1** strip off the skin or outer covering of; skin. **2** scold severely; criticize without pity or mercy. [Old English *flēan*]

fleer (flir), *v.i., v.t., n.* jeer. [Middle English *fleryen, fliren*]

flib ber ti gib bet (flib′ər tē jib′it), *n.* a frivolous, flighty person. [probably imitative]

flin ders (flin′dərz), *n.pl.* small pieces; fragments; splinters. [perhaps < Scandinavian (Norwegian) *flindra*]

flip pant (flip′ənt), *adj.* smart or pert in speech or manner; not respectful; impertinent; saucy. **—flip′pant ly,** *adv.*

flout (flout), *v.t.* treat with contempt or scorn; scoff at; mock. [variant of *flute,* verb] **—flout′er,** *n.* **—flout′ing ly,** *adv.*

flum mer y (flum′ər ē), *n., pl.* **-mer ies.** an empty compliment; nonsense. [< Welsh *llymru*]

fore done (fôr dun′), *adj.* done, or made, previously.

for ti tude (fôr′tə tüd, fôr′tə tyüd), *n.* courage in facing pain, danger, or trouble; firmness of spirit. [< Latin *fortitudo* strength < *fortis* strong]

fort night (fôrt′nīt, fôrt′nit), *n.* two weeks. [Middle English *fourtenight* fourteen nights]

fosse (fôs, fos), *n.* ditch, trench, or moat. [< Old French < Latin *fossa* ditch]

frank in cense (frang′kən sens), *n.* a fragrant gum resin from certain Asian or African trees of the same family as myrrh. It gives off a sweet, spicy odor when burned. [< Old French *franc encens* pure incense]

fret (fret), *n., v.,* **fret ted, fret ting. —n.** an ornamental pattern made of straight lines bent or combined at angles. **—v.t.** decorate with fretwork. [< Old French *frete*]

fret work (fret′wėrk′), *n.* ornamental openwork or carving.

frip per y (frip′ər ē), *n., pl.* **-per ies. 1** cheap, showy clothes; gaudy ornaments. **2** a showing off; foolish display; pretended refinement. [< Middle French *friperie,* ultimately < Old French *frepe* rag]

frowst (froust), *n.* stale, stuffy atmosphere; offensive or musty odor.

fru gal (frü′gəl), *adj.* avoiding waste; tending to avoid unnecessary spending; saving; thrifty. [< Latin *frugalis* < *frugi* temperate, useful, ultimately < *fructus* fruit, produce.]

fur or (fyur′ôr), *n.* **1** wild enthusiasm or excitement. **2** craze; mania. **3** a rage; fury. [< Latin *fuere* to rage]

fur tive (fėr′tiv), *adj.* **1** done quickly and with stealth to avoid being noticed; secret. **2** sly; stealthy. [< Latin *furtivus* < *furtum* theft < *fur* thief] **—fur′tive ly,** *adv.* **fur′tive ness,** *n.*

fu tile (fyü tl, fyü tīl), *adj.* **1** not successful; useless; ineffectual. **2** not important; trifling. [< Latin *futilis* pouring easily, worthless < *fundere* pour] **—fu′tile ly,** *adv.*

gad fly (gad′flī′), *n., pl.* **-flies. 1** fly that bites cattle, horses, and other animals. The horsefly and botfly are two kinds. **2** person who goads others to action by irritating or annoying remarks.

gall¹ (gôl), *n.* INFORMAL. too great boldness; impudence. [Old English *gealla*]

gall² (gôl), *v.t.* make sore by rubbing. [< Latin *galla* gall] **—galled,** *v.*

ga lore (gə lôr′, gə lōr′), *adv.* in abundance. [< Irish *go leór* to sufficiency]

gar net (gär′nit), *n.* a deep red. **—adj.** deep-red. [Middle English *gernet* < Old French *grenat* of pomegranate color < (*pomme*) *grenate* pomegranate] **—gar′net like′,** *adj.*

gar rote (gə rot′, gə rōt′), *n., v.,* **-rot ed, -rot ing. —n.** a method of execution in which a person is strangled with an iron collar. The collar is fastened to a post and tightened by a screw.

—*v.t.* execute by garroting. Also, **garotte**. [< Spanish] **garrot′er**, *n.*

gauge (gāj), *v.,* **gauged, gaug ing.** —*v.t.* **1** measure accurately; find out the exact measurement of with a gauge. **2** determine the capacity or content of (a cask, etc.). **3** estimate; judge. Also, **gage.** [< Old North French *gauger*] —**gauge′a ble,** *adj.*

ge ne a log i cal (jē′nē ə log′ə kəl, jen′ē ə loj′ə kəl), *adj.* having to do with genealogy. A genealogical table or chart is called a family tree. —**ge′ne a log′i cal ly,** *adv.*

gen u flect (jen′yə flekt), *v.i.* bend the knee as an act of reverence or worship. [< Medieval Latin *genuflectere* < Latin *genu* knee + *flectere* bend] —**gen′u flec′tion,** *n.*

gib bet (jib′it), *n.* **1** an upright post with a projecting arm at the top, from which the bodies of criminals were hung after execution. **2** gallows. [< Old French *gibet,* diminutive of *gibe* club]

gir dle (gėr′dl), *n., v.,* **-dled, -dling.** —*n.* belt, sash, cord, etc., worn around the waist. [Old English *gyrdel* < *gyrdan* gird] —**gir′dler,** *n.*

glean (glēn), *v.t.* **1** gather (grain) left on a field by reapers. **2** gather little by little. —*v.i.* gather grain left on a field by reapers. [< Old French *glener* < Late Latin *glennare*] —**glean′er,** *n.*

glean ing (glē′ning), *n.* Usually, **gleanings,** *pl.* anything that is gleaned.

gloam ing (glō′ming), *n.* evening twilight; dusk. [Old English *glōmung* < *glōm* twilight]

glow er (glou′ər), *v.i.* stare angrily; scowl fiercely. —*n.* an angry stare; fierce scowl. [Middle English *gloren*] —**glow′er ing ly,** *adv.*

Gnos tic (nos′tik), *adj.* of or having to do with Gnosticism or the Gnostics. [< Greek *gnōstikos* of knowledge < *gignōskein* know]

Gnos ti cism (nos′tə siz′əm), *n.* a mystical religious and philosophical doctrine of early Christian times, according to which spiritual knowledge, rather than faith, was essential to salvation.

goad (gōd), *n.* **1** a sharp-pointed stick for driving cattle; gad. **2** anything which drives or urges one on. —*v.t.* drive or urge on; act as a goad to. [Old English *gād*] —**goad′like′,** *adj.*

gos sa mer (gos′ə mər), *n.* **1** film or thread of cobweb spun by small spiders, which is seen floating in the air in calm weather. **2** a very thin, light cloth or coat. **3** anything very light and thin. —*adj.* like gossamer; very light and thin; filmy. [Middle English *gossomer* goose summer, name for "Indian summer," as the season for goose and cobwebs]

gra da tion (grā dā′shən), *n.* **1** a change by steps or stages; gradual change. **2** step, stage, or degree in a series. **3** act or process of grading.

graft (graft), *n.* **1** dishonest gains or unlawful profits made by a person in and through an official position, especially in connection with politics or government business. **2** money dishonestly and improperly taken. —*v.i.* make money by dishonest or unlawful means. [origin uncertain] —**graft′er,** *n.*

gran dee (gran dē′), *n.* **1** a Spanish or Portuguese nobleman of the highest rank. **2** person of high rank or great importance. [< Spanish and Portuguese *grande*]

gran di ose (gran′dē ōs), *adj.* **1** grand in an imposing or impressive way; magnificent. **2** grand in a showy or pompous way; not really magnificent, but trying to seem so. [< French < Italian *grandioso*] —**gran′di ose ly,** *adv.*

grape shot (grāp′shot′), *n.* cluster of small iron balls formerly used as a projectile for cannon.

grat is (grat′is, grā′tis), *adv., adj.* for nothing; free of charge. [< Latin, ablative plural of *gratia* favor]

gra tu i tous (grə tü′ə təs, grə tyü′ə təs), *adj.* without reason or cause; unnecessary; uncalled for. —**gra tu′i tous ly,** *adv.* —**gra tu′i tous ness,** *n.*

griev ous (grē′vəs), *adj.* **1** hard to bear; causing great pain or suffering; severe. **2** very evil or offensive; outrageous. —**griev′ous ly,** *adv.* —**griev′ous ness,** *n.*

groat (grōt), *n.* **1** an old English silver coin worth fourpence. **2** a very small sum. [< Middle Dutch *groot,* literally thick (coin)]

grudge (gruj), *n., v.,* **grudged, grudg ing.** give or let have unwillingly. [< Old French *groucher* to murmur, grumble. Doublet of GROUCH.] —**grudge′less,** *adj.* —**grudg′er,** *n.*

—**grudg′ing ly,** *adv.*

guer don (gėrd′n), *n., v.t.* reward. [< Old French *guerdoner* to reward < *guerdon* a reward < Old High German *widarlōn* repayment]

guile (gīl), *n.* crafty deceit; sly tricks; cunning. [< Old French; of Germanic origin. Related to WILE.]

guile ful (gīl′fəl), *adj.* crafty and deceitful; sly and tricky. —**guile′ful ly,** *adv.* —**guile′ful ness,** *n.*

guise (gīz), *n.* style of dress; garb. [< Old French; of Germanic origin. Related to WISE.]

gul let (gul′it), *n.* **1** esophagus. **2** throat. [< Old French *goulet,* ultimately < Latin *gula* throat]

gul li ble (gul′ə bəl), *adj.* easily deceived or cheated. [< *gull*] —**gul′li bly,** *adv.*

gut (gut), *n.* catgut. [Old English *guttas,* plural.]

guz zle (guz′əl), *v.,* **-zled, -zling.** —*v.t.* **1** drink or eat greedily; drink or eat too much. **2** use, especially in excessive amounts. —*v.i.* drink greedily; drink too much. [probably < Old French *gosiller* to vomit] —**guz′zler,** *n.*

haft (haft), *n.* handle, especially that of a knife, sword, dagger, etc. —*v.t.* furnish with a handle or hilt; set in a haft. [Old English *hæft*]

hal berd (hal′bərd), *n.* weapon of the 1400s and 1500s used both as a spear and as a battle-ax. [< Middle French *hallebarde* < Italian *alabarada*]

hal le lu jah or **hal le lu iah** (hal′ə lü′yə), *interj.* praise ye the Lord! —*n.* song of praise. Also, **alleluia.** [< Hebrew *halēlūyāh* praise ye Jehovah]

ham string (ham′string′), *n., v.,* **-strung** or **-stringed, -string ing.** —*n.* **1** either of two tendons at the back of the knee in human beings. **2** the great tendon at the back of the hock in a four-footed animal. —*v.t.* **1** cripple by cutting the hamstring. **2** destroy the activity, efficiency, etc., of; cripple; disable.

hap (hap), *n., v.,* **happed, hap ping.** ARCHAIC. —*n.* chance; luck. —*v.i.* happen. [< Scandinavian (Old Icelandic) *happ*]

ha rangue (hə rang′), *n., v.,* **-rangued, -rangu ing.** —*n.* **1** a noisy, vehement speech. **2** a long, pompous, formal speech. [< Middle French] —**ha rangu′er,** *n.*

har lot (här′lət), *n.* prostitute. [< Old French, vagabond]

har o (har′ō; ha rō′), *interj.* ARCHAIC. exclamation of alarm or distress.

har row (har′ō), *v.t.* **1** hurt; wound. **2** cause pain or torment to; distress. [Middle English *harwe*]

har row ing (har′ō ing), *adj.* that harrows; very painful or distressing.

hart (härt), *n., pl.* **harts** or **hart.** a male deer, especially the male European red deer after its fifth year; stag. [Old English *heorot*]

Ha sid ic (hə sid′ik), *adj.* of or having to do with the Hasidim or with Hasidism.

Has i dim (has′i dim; *Hebrew* Hä sē′dim), *n.pl.* of **Has id** (has′id; *Hebrew* Hä sēd′). members of a Jewish sect founded in the 1700s in Poland. Hasidim believe in mysticism and emphasize religious piety and devotion over formal learning. [< Hebrew *hasidhim* pious ones]

hau berk (hô′bėrk), *n.* a long coat of mail worn in the 1100s and 1200s; habergeon. [< Old French *hauberc* < Germanic]

haugh ty (hô′tē), *adj.,* **-ti er, -ti est.** too proud and scornful of others. [Middle English *haute* < Middle French *haut* < Latin *altus* high] —**haugh′ti ly,** *adv.* —**haugh′ti ness,** *n.*

ha ven (hā′vən), *n.* place of shelter and safety. [Old English *hæfen*]

a hat	i it	oi oil	ch child	a in about
ā age	ī ice	ou out	ng long	e in taken
ä far	o hot	u cup	sh she	ə = i in pencil
e let	ō open	ů put	th thin	o in lemon
ē equal	ô order	ü rule	ŦH then	u in circus
ėr term			zh measure	< = derived from

haw ser (hô′zər, hô′sər), *n.* a large, stout rope or thin steel cable, used for mooring or towing ships. [< Old French *haucier* to hoist < Popular Latin *altiare* < Latin *altus* high]

head y (hed′ē), *adj.,* **head i er, head i est. 1** hasty; rash; headlong. **2** apt to affect the head and make one dizzy; intoxicating. **—head′i ly,** *adv.* **—head′i ness,** *n.*

hedge hog (hej′hog′, hej′hôg′), *n.* **1** any of a genus of small nocturnal, insectivorous mammals of Europe, Asia, and Africa, that have spines on their backs. **2** any of several similar animals, such as the porcupine.

heed (hēd), *v.t.* give careful attention to; take notice of; mind. [Old English *hēdan*] **—heed′er,** *n.*

helm (helm), *n.* ARCHAIC. helmet. [Old English]

helve (helv), *n.* handle of a tool or weapon, such as an ax or hammer. [Old English *hielfe*]

hemp (hemp), *n.* **1** a tall annual plant of the same family as the mulberry, native to Asia and extensively cultivated elsewhere for its tough fibers, which are made into heavy string, rope, coarse cloth, etc.; cannabis. **2** the tough fibers obtained from the bark of this plant. **3** hashish or some other narcotic drug obtained from this plant. [Old English *henep*] **—hemp′like′,** *adj.*

hie (hī), *v.,* **hied, hie ing** or **hy ing. —***v.i.* go quickly; hasten; hurry. **—***v.t.* cause to hasten. [Old English *hīgian*]

hi er o glyph ic (hī′ər ə-glif′ik), *n.* **1** picture, character, or symbol standing for a word, idea, or sound; hieroglyph. The ancient Egyptians used hieroglyphics instead of an alphabet like ours. **2** letter or word that is hard to read. **3 hieroglyphics,** *pl.* **a** system of writing that uses hieroglyphics. **b** writing that is hard to read. **4** a secret symbol. **—***adj.* **1** of or written in hieroglyphics. **2** hard to read. [< Late Latin *hieroglyphicus* < Greek *hieroglyphikos* < *hieros* sacred + *glyphē* a carving] **—hi′er o glyph′i cal ly,** *adv.*

A KINGLY	
GIFT OF AN	
OFFERING TABLE	
TO	
RA-HORUS	
THE GREAT	
GOD	
LORD OF	
HEAVEN	

hieroglyphic (def. 1) Egyptian hieroglyphics

hind (hīnd), *n., pl.* **hinds** or **hind.** a female deer, especially a female red deer in and after its third year. [Old English]

hin ny (hin′ē), *n., pl.* **-nies.** a hybrid animal resembling a mule that is the offspring of a male horse and a female ass. [< Latin *hinnus*]

hin ter land (hin′tər land′), *n.* **1** land or district behind a coast. **2** region far from towns and cities; thinly settled country.

his tri o (his′trē ō), *n.* an actor.

hith er to (hĭтн′ər tü′), *adv.* until now.

hoar (hôr, hōr), *adj.* hoary. **—***n.* hoarfrost. [Old English *hār*]

hoar frost (hôr′frôst′, hôr′frost′; hōr′frôst′, hōr′frost′), *n.* the white, feathery crystals of ice formed when dew freezes; rime.

hol o caust (hol′ə kôst), *n.* **1** complete destruction by fire, especially of animals or human beings. **2** great or wholesale destruction. [< Greek *holokaustos* < *holos* whole + *kaustos* burned]

hol o graph (hol′ə graf), *n.* wholly written in the handwriting of the person in whose name it appears. **—***n.* a holograph manuscript, letter, document, etc. [< Greek *holographos* < *holos* whole + *graphē* a writing]

hood wink (hud′wingk), *v.t.* mislead by a trick; deceive. **—hood′wink er,** *n.*

hor ren dous (hô ren′dəs, ho ren′dəs), *adj.* causing horror; horrible. **—hor ren′dous ly,** *adv.*

ho san na (hō zan′ə), *interj., n.* **1** a shout of praise to God. **2** any shout of praise or approval. [< Greek *hōsanna* < Hebrew *hōshī′āhnnā* save, we pray]

how be it (hou bē′it), *adv.* ARCHAIC. nevertheless. **—***conj.* though.

hum bug (hum′bug′), *n., v.,* **-bugged, -bug ging,** **—***n.* **1** person who tries to deceive or cheat; fraud; impostor. **2** cheat; sham. **3** deception or pretense. **—***v.t.* deceive with a sham; cheat. [origin unknown]

hur i (hur′ē, hoŏ′rē), *n.* one of the young, eternally beautiful women of the Moslem paradise. [< Persian *ḥūrī* < Arabic *ḥūr* black-eyed]

hus band (huz′bənd), **—***v.t.* manage carefully; be saving of. [Old English *hūsbŏnda* < Scandinavian (Old Icelandic) *hūsbōndi* < *hūs* house + *bōndi* freeholder]

hy giene (hī′jēn), *n.* science that deals with the maintenance of health; system of principles or rules for preserving or promoting health. [< French *hygiène,* ultimately < Greek *hygiēs* healthy]

hyp o crite (hip′ə krit), *n.* **1** person who pretends to be very good or religious. **2** person who is not sincere; pretender. [< Greek *hypokritēs* actor < *hypo-* under + *kritēs* a judge]

hyp o crit i cal (hip′ə krit′ə kəl), *adj.* of or like a hypocrite; insincere. **—hyp′o crit′i cal ly,** *adv.*

hys ter i a (hi stir′ē ə, hi ster′ē ə), *n.* unrestrained excitement or emotion. [< New Latin < Greek *hystera* uterus; because originally only women were thought to be affected]

i bex (ī′beks), *n.* any of a genus of wild goats of mountainous regions of Europe, Asia, and Africa. The male has very large horns which curve backward. [< Latin]

ig no min y (ig′nə min′ē), *n., pl.* **-min ies. 1** public shame and disgrace; dishonor. **2** shameful action or conduct. [< Latin *ignominia* < *in-* not + *nominis* name]

il lic it (i lis′it), *adj.* not permitted by law; forbidden. **—il lic′it ly,** *adv.* **—il lic′it ness,** *n.*

il lu mine (i lü′mən), *v.t.,* **-mined, -min ing.** make bright; illuminate.

im mu ni ty (i myü′nə tē), *n., pl.* **-ties.** freedom; exemption.

im mure (i myür′), *v.t.,* **-mured, -mur ing. 1** shut up within walls; put into prison; confine. [< Medieval Latin *immurare* < Latin *in-* in + *murus* wall] **—im mure′ment,** *n.*

im pal pa ble (im pal′pə bəl), *adj.* **1** that cannot be felt by touching; intangible. **2** very hard to understand; that cannot be grasped by the mind. **—im pal′pa bly,** *adv.*

im per ish a ble (im per′i shə bəl), *adj.* not perishable; unable to be destroyed; lasting forever; enduring. **—im per′ish a ble ness,** *n.* **—im per′ish a bly,** *adv.*

im per ti nent (im pèrt′n ənt), *adj.* not pertinent; not to the point; out of place. **—im per′ti nent ly,** *adv.* **—im per′ti nent ness,** *n.*

im pet u ous (im pech′ü əs), *adj.* acting or done with sudden or rash energy; hasty. **—im pet′u ous ly,** *adv.* **—im pet′u ous ness,** *n.*

im pi ous (im′pē əs, im pī′əs), *adj.* not pious; not having or not showing reverence for God; wicked; profane. **—im′pi ous ly,** *adv.* **—im′pi ous ness,** *n.*

im pla ca ble (im plā′kə bəl, im plak′ə bəl), *adj.* unable to be appeased; refusing to be reconciled; unyielding. **—im pla′ca ble ness,** *n.* **—im pla′ca bly,** *adv.*

im por tune (im′pôr tün′, im′pôr tyün′, im pôr′chən), *v.,* **-tuned, -tun ing,** *adj.* **—***v.t.* ask urgently or repeatedly; annoy with pressing demands. **—***adj.* importunate. [< Latin *importunus* inconvenient] **—im′por tune′ly,** *adv.* **—im′por tun′er,** *n.*

im po tence (im′pə təns), *n.* condition or quality of being impotent.

im po tent (im′pə tənt), *adj.* **1** not having power; helpless. **2** (of males) incapable of having sexual intercourse. **—im′po tent ly,** *adv.*

im preg nate (im preg′nāt), *v.t.,* **-nat ed, -nat ing. 1** spread through the whole of; fill; saturate. **2** fill the mind of; inspire. [< Late Latin *impraegnatum* made pregnant < Latin *in-* + *praegnas* pregnant] **—im′preg na′tion,** *n.* **—im preg′na tor,** *n.*

im pu dence (im′pyə dəns), *n.* **1** a being impudent; shameless boldness; great rudeness; insolence. **2** impudent conduct or language.

im pu dent (im′pyə dənt), *adj.* shamelessly bold; very rude and

insolent. [< Latin *impudentem* < *in-* not + *pudere* be modest]
—**im′pu dent ly,** *adv.*

in-, *prefix.* in; within; into; toward: *Indoors = within doors. Inland = toward land.* [Old English]

in can ta tion (in′kan tā′shən), *n.* **1** set of words spoken as a magic charm or to cast a magic spell. **2** the use of such words. [< Latin *incantationem* < *incantare* enchant < *in-* against + *cantare* to chant]

in cen di a rism (in sen′dē ə riz′əm), *n.* **1** crime of setting property on fire intentionally. **2** the deliberate stirring up of strife, violence, or rebellion.

in cense (in sens′), *v.t.,* **-censed, -cens ing.** make very angry; fill with rage. [< Latin *incensum* inflamed, enraged, set on fire < *in-* (intensive) + *candere* glow white] —**in cense′ment,** *n.*

in cer ti tude (in sėr′tə tüd, in sėr′tə tyüd), *n.* uncertainty; doubt.

in ces sant (in ses′nt), *adj.* never stopping; continued or repeated without interruption; continual. [< Late Latin *incessantem* < Latin *in-* not + *cessare* cease] —**in ces′sant ly,** *adv.* —**in ces′sant ness,** *n.*

in cred u lous (in krej′ə ləs), *adj.* not ready to believe; doubting; skeptical. —**in cred′u lous ly,** *adv.*

in di gence (in′də jəns), *n.* extreme need; poverty.

in dis cre tion (in′dis kresh′ən), *n.* **1** a being indiscreet; lack of good judgment; unwiseness; imprudence. **2** an indiscreet act or remark.

in ex tri ca ble (in ek′strə kə bəl), *adj.* **1** that one cannot get out of. **2** that cannot be disentangled or solved. —**in ex′tri ca bil′i ty,** *n.* —**in ex′tri ca bly,** *adv.*

in fa my (in′fə mē), *n., pl.* **-mies.** **1** a very bad reputation; public disgrace. **2** shameful badness; extreme wickedness. **3** an infamous or disgraceful act. [< Latin *infamia* < *infamis* of ill fame < *in-* without + *fama* fame, reputation]

in fat u ate (in fach′ü āt), *v.t.,* **-at ed, -at ing.** **1** inspire with a foolish or extreme passion. **2** make foolish. [< Latin *infatuatum* made foolish < *in-* + *fatuus* foolish]

in fer nal (in fėr′nl), *adj.* **1** of or having to do with hell. **2** of the lower world which the ancient Greeks and Romans thought of as the abode of the dead. **3** fit to have come from hell; hellish; diabolical. **4** INFORMAL. hateful; shocking; abominable; outrageous. [< Late Latin *infernalis* < *infernus* hell < Latin, lower < *inferus* situated below] —**in fer′nal ly,** *adv.*

in fi del (in′fə dəl), *n.* **1** person who does not believe in religion. **2** person who does not accept a particular faith. During the Crusades, Moslems called Christians infidels. **3** person who does not accept Christianity. —*adj.* not believing in religion. [< Latin *infidelis* unfaithful < *in-* not < *fides* faith]

in fra hu man (in fra hyü′mən), *adj.* (of animals) beneath human beings in evolutionary development.

in gen u ous (in jen′yü əs), *adj.* **1** free from restraint or reserve; frank and open; sincere. **2** simple and natural; innocent; naïve. [< Latin *ingenuus*, originally, native < *in-* in + *gignere* beget] —**in gen′u ous ly,** *adv.* —**in gen′u ous ness,** *n.*

in grate (in′grāt), *n.* an ungrateful person. [< Latin *ingratus* ungrateful < *in-* not + *gratus* grateful]

in iq ui ty (in ik′wə tē), *n., pl.* **-ties.** **1** gross injustice or unrighteousness; wickedness; sin. **2** a wicked or unjust act. [< Latin *iniquitatem* < *iniquus* unjust < *in-* not + *aequus* just]

in qui si tion (in′kwə zish′ən), *n.* **1** a thorough investigation; searching inquiry. **2** an official investigation; judicial inquiry. **3 the Inquisition,** court appointed by the Roman Catholic Church in the 1200s to discover and suppress heresy. It was abolished in the 1800s. [< Latin *inquisitionem* < *inquirere*]

in quis i tor (in kwiz′ə tər), *n.* **1** person who makes an inquisition; official investigator; judicial inquirer. **2 Inquisitor,** member of the Inquisition.

in sa ti ate (in sā′shē it), *adj.* never satisfied. —**in sa′ti ate ly,** *adv.* —**in sa′ti ate ness,** *n.*

in so lence (in′sə ləns), *n.* bold rudeness; insulting behavior or speech.

in so lent (in′sə lənt), *adj.* boldly rude; intentionally disregarding the feelings of others; insulting. [< Latin *insolentem* arrogant, contrary to custom < *in-* not + *solere* be accustomed] —**in′so lent ly,** *adv.*

a hat	i it	oi oil	ch child	(a in about
ā age	ī ice	ou out	ng long	e in taken
ä far	o hot	u cup	sh she	ə = { i in pencil
e let	ō open	ù put	th thin	o in lemon
ē equal	ô order	ü rule	ŦH then	u in circus
ėr term			zh measure	< = derived from

in som ni a (in som′nē ə), *n.* inability to sleep, especially when chronic; sleeplessness. [< Latin < *in-* not + *somnus* sleep]

in ter po late (in tėr′pə lāt), *v.,* **-lat ed, -lat ing.** —*v.t.* insert or introduce (something additional or different) between other things or in a series. —*v.i.* make insertions or interpolations. [< Latin *interpolatum* freshened up < *inter-* between + *polire* make smooth] —**in ter′po lat′er, in ter′po la′tor,** *n.* —**in ter′po la′tion,** *n.*

in ter ro gate (in ter′ə gāt), *v.,* **-gat ed, -gat ing.** —*v.t.* ask questions of; examine or get information from by asking questions; question thoroughly or in a formal manner. —*v.i.* ask a series of questions. [< Latin *interrogatum* interrogated < *inter-* between + *rogare* ask] —**in ter′ro ga′tor,** *n.*

in trac ta ble (in trak′tə bəl), *adj.* **1** hard to manage; stubborn. **2** not easily treated. —**in trac′ta ble ness,** *n.* —**in trac′ta bly,** *adv.*

in tro spec tion (in′trə spek′shən), *n.* examination of one's own thoughts and feelings.

in vei gle (in vē′gəl, in vā′gəl), *v.t.,* **-gled, -gling.** mislead by trickery; entice; lure. [apparently alteration of Old French *aveugler* make blind < *aveugle* blind < Popular Latin *aboculus* < Latin *ab-* without + *oculus* eye] —**in vei′gle ment,** *n.* —**in vei′gler,** *n.*

in vet er ate (in vet′ər it), *adj.* long and firmly established; deeply rooted. [< Latin *inveteratum* grown old, long established < *in-* in + *vetus, veteris* old] —**in vet′er ate ly,** *adv.*

in vin ci ble (in vin′sə bəl), *adj.* unable to be conquered; impossible to overcome; unconquerable. [< Latin *invincibilis* < *in-* not + *vincere* conquer] —**in vin′ci ble ness,** *n.* —**in vin′ci bly,** *adv.*

in vi o la ble (in vī′ə lə bəl), *adj.* **1** that must not be violated or injured; sacred. **2** that cannot be violated or injured. —**in vi′o la bly,** *adv.*

in vi o late (in vī′ə lit, in vī′ə lāt), *adj.* not violated; uninjured; unbroken. —**in vi′o late ly,** *adv.* —**in vi′o late ness,** *n.*

in vul ner a ble (in vul′nər ə bəl), *adj.* that cannot be wounded or hurt; safe from attack. —**in vul′ner a ble ness,** *n.* —**in vul′ner a bly,** *adv.*

ire (īr), *n.* anger; wrath. [< Old French < Latin *ira*]

ire ful (īr′fəl), *adj.* angry; wrathful. —**ire′ful ly,** *adv.*

ir ref u ta ble (i ref′yə tə bəl, ir′i fyü′tə bəl), *adj.* that cannot be refuted or disproved; undeniable; unanswerable. —**ir ref′u ta bly,** *adv.*

jade (jād), *n.,* an inferior or worn-out horse.

jeer (jir), *v.i.* make fun rudely or unkindly; mock; scoff. —*v.t.* speak to or treat with scornful derision. —**jeer′er,** *n.* —**jeer′ing ly,** *adv.*

jet sam (jet′səm), *n.* goods which are thrown overboard to lighten a ship in distress and often afterwards washed ashore. [variant of *jettison*]

joc und (jok′ənd, jō′kənd), *adj.* feeling, expressing, or communicating mirth or cheer; cheerful; merry; gay. [< Latin *jocundus, jucundus* pleasant < *juvare* please] —**joc′und ly,** *adv.*

joust (joust, just, jüst), *n.* combat between two knights on horseback, armed with lances, especially as part of a tournament. [< Old French *jouste* < *jouster* to joust < Popular Latin *juxtare* be next to < Latin *juxta* beside]

jug gler y (jug′lər ē), *n., pl.* **-gler ies.** **1** skill or tricks of a juggler; sleight of hand. **2** trickery; deception; fraud.

ka pok (kā′pok), *n.* the silky fibers around the seeds of a tropical silk-cotton tree, used for stuffing pillows, mattresses, and life preservers, for insulation, etc.; silk cotton. [< Malay]

kine (kīn), *n.pl.* ARCHAIC OR DIALECT. cows or cattle. [earlier *kyen* (formed after pattern of *oxen*) < Old English *cȳ*, plural of *cū* cow]

knave (nāv), *n.* **1** a tricky, dishonest man; rogue; rascal. **2** jack (def. 2). **3** ARCHAIC. a male servant or any man of humble birth or position. [Old English *cnafa* boy]

knav er y (nā′vər ē), *n., pl.* **-er ies. 1** behavior of a knave or rascal; trickery; dishonesty. **2** a tricky, dishonest act.

knish (knish), *n.* pastry made of dough, wrapped around a stuffing of potato, cheese, etc. [< Yiddish]

knoll (nōl), *n.* a small, rounded hill; mound. [Old English *cnoll*]

ko peck or **ko pek** (kō′pek), *n.* unit of money in the Soviet Union, a coin worth ¹⁄₁₀₀ of a ruble. Also, **copeck.** [< Russian *kopeika*]

lack ey (lak′ē), *n., pl.* **-eys,** *v.* —*n.* **1** a male servant; footman. **2** a slavish follower; toady. —*v.t.* **1** wait on. **2** be slavish to. [< Middle French *laquais* < Spanish *lacayo* foot soldier]

la ment (lə ment′), *v.t.* **1** express grief for; mourn for. **2** regret. —*v.i.* express grief; mourn; weep. —*n.* **1** expression of grief or sorrow; wail. **2** poem, song, or tune that expresses grief. [< Latin *lamentari* < *lamentum* a wailing] —**la ment′er,** *n.* —**la ment′ing ly,** *adv.*

lam en ta tion (lam′ən tā′shən), *n.* **1** loud grief; cries of sorrow; mourning; wailing. **2 Lamentations,** book of the Old Testament. According to tradition it was written by Jeremiah.

lan guor (lang′gər), *n.* **1** lack of energy; weakness; weariness. **2** lack of interest or enthusiasm; indifference. **3** softness or tenderness of mood. **4** quietness; stillness. **5** lack of activity; sluggishness. [< Latin < *languere* be faint]

lan yard (lan′yərd), *n.* a short cord with a small hook used in firing certain kinds of cannon. Also, **laniard.** [< Middle French *laniere* thong]

lap is laz u li (lap′is laz′yə lī; lap′is laz′yə lē), **1** a deep blue, opaque semiprecious stone used for an ornament. **2** deep blue. [< Medieval Latin < Latin *lapis* stone + Medieval Latin *lazulum* lapis lazuli < Arabic *lāzuward.*]

lar der (lär′dər), *n.* **1** place where meat and other foods are kept; pantry. **2** stock of food.

lar gess or **lar gesse** (lär′jis), *n.* **1** a generous giving. **2** a generous gift or gifts. [< Old French *largesse* < *large* generous]

las civ i ous (lə siv′ē əs), *adj.* **1** feeling lust. **2** showing lust. **3** causing lust. [< Late Latin *lasciviosus* < Latin *lascivia* playfulness < *lascivus* playful] —**las civ′i ous ly,** *adv.* —**las civ′i ous ness,** *n.*

laud a ble (lô′də bəl), *adj.* worthy of praise; commendable. —**laud′a ble ness,** *n.* —**laud′a bly,** *adv.*

lav ish (lav′ish), *adj.* very free or too free in giving or spending; extravagant; prodigal. [< Old French *lavasse* flood < *laver* to wash < Latin *lavare*] —**lav′ish er,** *n.* —**lav′ish ly,** *adv.* —**lav′ish ment,** *n.* —**lav′ish ness,** *n.*

league (lēg), *n.* measure of distance, varying at different periods and in different countries, usually about 3 miles (5 kilometers). [< Late Latin *leuga;* of Celtic origin]

leath er y (leŦH′ər ē), *adj.* resembling leather in appearance or texture; tough. —**leath′er i ness,** *n.*

lech er y (lech′ər ē), *n.* gross indulgence of lust; lewdness.

lee (lē), *n.* **1** shelter; protection. **2** side or part sheltered or away from the wind. [Old English *hlēo*]

len ien cy (lē′nyən sē, lē′nē ən sē), *n.* lenient quality; mildness; gentleness; mercy.

lev i ty (lev′ə tē), *n., pl.* **-ties.** lightness of mind, character, or behavior; lack of proper seriousness or earnestness; flippancy; frivolity. [< Latin *levitatem* < *levis* light]

li ba tion (lī bā′shən), *n.* **1** a pouring out of wine, water, etc., as an offering to a god. **2** the wine, water, etc., offered in this way. [< Latin *libationem* < *libare* pour out]

li bel (lī′bəl), *n., v.,* **-beled, -bel ing** or **-belled, -bel ling.** —*n.* **1** a written or published statement, picture, etc., tending to damage a person's reputation or subject someone to public ridicule and disgrace. **2** any false or damaging statement about a person. [< Old French, a formal written statement < Latin *libellus,* diminutive of *liber* book] —**li′bel er, li′bel ler,** *n.*

lib e ral i ty (lib′ə ral′ə tē), *n., pl.* **-ties.** tolerant and progressive nature; broad-mindedness.

liege (lēj), *n.* in the Middle Ages: lord having a right to the homage and loyal service of his vassals. [< Old French, ultimately of Germanic origin]

lim ber (lim′bər), *n.* the detachable front part of the carriage of a field gun. [Middle English *lymor*]

lim pid (lim′pid), *adj.* **1** clear or transparent. **2** free from obscurity; lucid. [< Latin *limpidus,* related to *lympha* clear water] —**lim′pid ly,** *adv.* —**lim′pid ness,** *n.*

lin e age (lin′ē ij), *n.* **1** descent in a direct line from a common ancestor. **2** the descendants of a common ancestor. **3** family or origin. [Middle English *linage* < Old French]

list less (list′lis), *adj.* seeming too tired to care about anything; not interested in things; not caring to be active; languid. —**list′less ly,** *adv.* —**list′less ness,** *n.*

lit ter (lit′ər), *n.* **1** stretcher for carrying a sick, injured, or wounded person. **2** framework supported on long poles and carried on men's shoulders or by beasts of burden, with a couch usually enclosed by curtains. [< Anglo-French *litere* < Medieval Latin *lectaria* < Latin *lectus* bed]

litter (def. 2)

liv id (liv′id), *adj.* **1** having a dull-bluish or grayish color, as from a bruise. **2** very pale. **3** flushed; reddish. **4** very angry. [< Latin *lividus* < *livere* be bluish] —**liv′id ly,** *adv.* —**liv′id ness,** *n.*

loam (lōm), *n.* rich, fertile earth in which much humus is mixed with clay and sand. [Old English *lām*]

loath some (lōŦH′səm, lōth′səm), *adj.* making one feel sick; disgusting. —**loath′some ly,** *adv.* —**loath′some ness,** *n.*

lu cid (lü′sid), *adj.* **1** marked by clearness of reasoning, expression, or arrangement; easy to follow or understand. **2** shining; bright; luminous. [< Latin *lucidus* < *lucere* to shine] —**lu′cid ly,** *adv.* —**lu′cid ness,** *n.*

lu cid i ty (lü sid′ə tē), *n.* lucid quality or condition.

lu di crous (lü′də krəs), *adj.* causing derisive laughter; amusingly absurd; ridiculous. [< Latin *ludicrus* < *ludus* sport] —**lu′di crous ly,** *adv.* —**lu′di crous ness,** *n.*

lu mi nar y (lü′mə ner′ē), *n., pl.* **-nar ies,** *adj.* —*n.* **1** a heavenly body that gives or reflects light. **2** anything that gives light. [< Late Latin *luminarium* < Latin *lumen* light]

lynx (lingks), *n., pl.* **lynxes** or **lynx.** any of a genus of wildcats with short tails, rather long legs, and tufts of hair at the end of their ears, especially a large, shaggy species of Canada and the northern United States. [< Latin < Greek] —**lynx′like′,** *adj.*

lyre (līr), *n.* an ancient stringed musical instrument somewhat like a small harp. [< Latin *lyra* < Greek]

mach i na tion (mak′ə nā′shən, mash′ə nā′shən), *n.* **1** evil or artful plotting; scheming against authority. **2** Usually, **machinations,** *pl.* an evil plot; secret or cunning scheme.

mag is trate (maj′ə strāt, maj′ə strit), *n.* a government official who has power to apply the law and put it in force. [< Latin *mag-*

istratus, ultimately < *magister* master < *magnus* great]

mal ice (mal′is), *n.* **1** active ill will; wish to hurt or make suffer; rancor. **2** (in law) intent to commit an act which will result in harm to another person without justification. [< Old French < Latin *malitia* < *malus* bad, evil]

ma lign (mə līn′), *v.t.* speak evil of; slander. [< Late Latin *malignare* < Latin *malignus* disposed to evil < *malus* evil + *-gnus* born] —**ma lign′er,** *n.* —**ma lign′ly,** *adv.*

ma lin ger (mə ling′gər), *v.i.* pretend to be sick, injured, etc., in order to escape work or duty; shirk. [< French *malingre* sickly] —**ma lin′ger er,** *n.*

mal o dor ous (mal ō′dər əs), *adj.* smelling bad; unsavory; fetid. —**mal o′dor ous ly,** *adv.* —**mal o′dor ous ness,** *n.*

man i fest (man′ə fest), *adj.* apparent to the eye or to the mind; plain; clear. —*v.t.* **1** show plainly; reveal; display. **2** put beyond doubt; prove. —*n.* list of cargo of a ship or aircraft. [< Latin *manifestus* palpable < *manus* hand + *-festus* (able to be) seized] —**man′i fest′er,** *n.* —**man′i fest′ly,** *adv.*

man i fold (man′ə fōld), *adj.* **1** of many kinds; many and various. **2** having many parts or forms. **3** doing many things at the same time. [Old English *manigfeald*] —**man′i fold′ly,** *adv.* —**man′i fold′ness,** *n.*

man na (man′ə), *n.* **1** (in the Bible) the food miraculously supplied to the Israelites in the wilderness. **2** food for the soul or mind. **3** any necessity unexpectedly supplied. [Old English < Late Latin < Greek < Hebrew *mān*]

ma raud (mə rôd′), *v.i.* go about in search of plunder. —*v.t.* plunder. [< French *marauder*] —**ma raud′er,** *n.*

mar shal (mär′shəl), *v.,* **-shaled, -shal ing** or **-shalled, -shal ling.** —*v.t.* **1** arrange in proper order. **2** conduct with ceremony. [< Old French *mareschal;* of Germanic origin]

mar ten (märt′n), *n., pl.* **-tens** or **-ten.** **1** any of various slender carnivorous mammals of the same family as and resembling the weasel, but larger. Several species are valued for their brown fur. **2** their fur. [< Old French *martrine;* ultimately, of Germanic origin]

mas ti cate (mas′tə kāt), *v.t., v.i.,* **-cat ed, -cat ing.** grind (food) to a pulp with the teeth; chew. [< Late Latin *masticatum* chewed < Greek *mastichan* gnash the teeth] —**mas′ti ca′tion,** *n.* —**mas′ti ca′tor,** *n.*

mas tiff (mas′tif), *n.* any of a breed of large, powerful dogs having a short, thick coat, drooping ears, and hanging lips. [< Old French *mastin;* influenced by Old French *mestif* mongrel]

ma tins (mat′nz), *n.pl.* **1** first of the seven canonical hours in the breviary of the Roman Catholic Church. **2** service for this hour, often joined to lauds. **3** morning prayer in the Church of England and other churches of the Anglican communion. Also, **mattins** for 2. [< Old French *matines* < Latin *matutinus* of or in the morning]

maud lin (môd′lən), *adj.* **1** sentimental in a weak, silly way. **2** tearfully silly because of drunkenness or excitement. [alteration of Mary *Magdalene,* often painted as weeping]

maul (môl), *n.* a very heavy hammer or mallet for driving stakes, piles, or wedges. —*v.t.* beat and pull about; handle roughly. [< Old French *mail* < Latin *malleus*] —**maul′er,** *n.*

ma zur ka or **ma zour ka** (mə zėr′kə, mə zur′kə), *n.* **1** a lively Polish folk dance in moderately quick triple rhythm. **2** music for it. [< Polish *mazurka,* originally, woman of *Mazovia* in Poland]

mel an chol y (mel′ən kol′ē), *n., pl.* **-chol ies,** *adj.* —*n.* **1** condition of sadness and low spirits; gloominess; dejection. **2** sober thoughtfulness; pensiveness. —*adj.* **1** depressed in spirits; sad; gloomy. **2** causing sadness; depressing. **3** lamentable; deplorable. **4** soberly thoughtful; pensive. [< Greek *melancholia* < *melanos* black + *cholē* bile]

mel o dra ma (mel′ə drä′mə, mel′ə dram′ə), *n.* a sensational drama with exaggerated appeal to the emotions and, usually, a happy ending. [< French *mélodrame* < Greek *melos* music + *drama* drama]

men di cant (men′də kənt), *adj.* begging. Mendicant friars ask alms for charity. —*n.* **1** beggar. **2** member of a mendicant religious order. [< Latin *mendicantem* < *mendicus* beggar]

met a mor pho sis (met′ə môr′fə sis), *n., pl.* **-ses** (-sēz′). **1** a marked change in the form, and usually the habits, of an animal

a hat	**i** it	**oi** oil	**ch** child		a in about
ā age	**ī** ice	**ou** out	**ng** long		e in taken
ä far	**o** hot	**u** cup	**sh** she	**ə** =	i in pencil
e let	**ō** open	**ù** put	**th** thin		o in lemon
ē equal	**ô** order	**ü** rule	**ŦH** then		u in circus
ėr term			**zh** measure		**<** = derived from

in its development after the embryonic stage. Tadpoles become frogs by metamorphosis; they lose their tails and grow legs. **2** change of form, structure, or substance by or as if by witchcraft; transformation. **3** form, shape, substance, etc., resulting from any such change. **4** a noticeable or complete

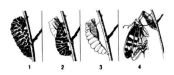

metamorphosis (def. 1) of a butterfly
1 Caterpillar prepares to change form.
2 It sheds skin, exposing chrysalis.
3 Chrysalis is entirely exposed.
4 Adult emerges from the chrysalis.

change of character, appearance, circumstances, etc. [< Greek *metamorphōsis,* ultimately < *meta-* after + *morphē* form]

me tic u lous (mə tik′yə ləs), *adj.* extremely or excessively careful about details. [< Latin *meticulosus* fearful, timid < *metus* fear] —**me tic′u lous ly,** *adv.* —**me tic′u lous ness,** *n.*

mi as ma (mī az′mə, mē az′mə), *n., pl.* **-mas, -ma ta** (-mə tə). **1** a bad-smelling vapor rising from decaying organic matter in swamps. It was formerly thought to cause disease. **2** anything considered to resemble this in its ability to spread and poison. [< Greek, pollution < *miainein* pollute] —**mi as′mal,** *adj.* —**mi as′mic,** *adj.*

milk sop (milk′sop′), *n.* person who lacks courage; coward.

mi na (mī′nə), *n., pl.* **mi nae** (mī′nē), **mi nas.** unit of weight and value used by the ancient Greeks, Egyptians, and others, equal to ⅟₆₀ of a talent. [< Latin < Greek *mna,* of Semitic origin]

min is tra tion (min′ə strā′shən), *n.* **1** service as a minister of a church. **2** help; aid.

mire (mīr), *n., v.,* **mired, mir ing.** —*n.* **1** soft, deep mud; slush. **2** wet, swampy ground; bog. [< Scandinavian (Old Icelandic) *myrr*]

mite (mīt), *n.* anything very small; little bit. [< Middle Dutch]

mi ter (mī′tər), *n.* a tall, pointed, folded cap worn as the official headdress of bishops, abbots, and other ecclesiastics. Also, **mitre.** [< Greek *mitra* headband]

mock (mok), *v.t.* laugh at scornfully; make fun of; ridicule. [< Middle French *mocquer*] —**mock′er,** *n.* —**mock′ing ly,** *adv.*

mold (mōld), *n.* loose, broken, or crumbly earth, especially fine, soft soil rich in decayed leaves, manure, or other organic matter, suitable for the cultivation of plants. Also, **mould.** [Old English *molde*]

mon ey chang er (mun′ē chān′jər), *n.* person whose business is to exchange money, usually that of one country for that of another.

mo rass (mə ras′), *n.* **1** piece of low, soft, wet ground; swamp; marsh. **2** a difficult situation; puzzling mess. [< Dutch *moeras*]

mo ri on (môr′ē on, mōr′ē on), *n.* helmet without a visor, shaped like a hat, with a comb-shaped crest and an upturned rim forming a peak in front. [< French]

mo rose (mə rōs′), *adj.* gloomy; sullen; ill-humored. [< Latin *morosus,* originally, set in one's ways < *morem* custom, habit] —**mo rose′ly,** *adv.* —**mo rose′ness,** *n.*

mor tal (môr′tl), *adj.* to the death; implacable; relentless. [< Latin *mortalis* < *mortem* death]

mor ti fy (môr′tə fī), *v.,* **-fied, -fy ing.** —*v.t.* wound the feelings of; make feel humbled and ashamed; humiliate. [< Old French *mortifier* < Latin *mortificare* to kill < *mortem* death + *facere* to make] —**mor′ti fi′er,** *n.*

moun te bank (moun′tə bangk), *n.* **1** person who sells quack medicines in public, appealing to the audience by tricks, stories, etc. **2** anybody who tries to deceive people by tricks, stories, etc.; charlatan. [< Italian *montambanco* < *montare in banco* mount on a bench]

mum mer y (mum′ər ē), *n.*, *pl.* **-mer ies. 1** performance of mummers. **2** any useless or silly show or ceremony.

Muse (myüz), *n.* **1** (in Greek myths) one of the nine goddesses of the fine arts and sciences. **2** Sometimes, **muse**. spirit that inspires a poet, composer, writer, etc.; source of inspiration.

myrrh (mėr), *n.* a fragrant gum resin with a bitter taste, used in medicine as an astringent tonic, in perfumes, and in incense. It is obtained from certain small trees, of the same family as frankincense, that grow in southern Arabia and eastern Africa [Old English *myrre* < Latin *myrrha* < Greek; of Semitic origin]

myr tle (mėr′tl), *n.* **1** any of a genus of shrubs of the myrtle family, especially an evergreen shrub of southern Europe with shiny leaves, fragrant white flowers, and black berries. **2** periwinkle. [< Old French *mirtile* < Latin *myrtus* < Greek *myrtos*]

na dir (nā′dər, nā′dir), *n.* **1** the point in the celestial sphere directly beneath the observer or a given place; the point opposite the zenith. **2** the lowest point. [< Old French < Arabic *nazīr* opposite (that is, to the zenith)]

na tal (nā′tl), *adj.* **1** of or having to do with one's birth. **2** native. [< Latin *natalis*, ultimately < *nasci* be born. Doublet of NOEL.]

na tiv i ty (nə tiv′ə tē, nā tiv′ə tē), *n.*, *pl.* **-ties.** a being born; birth.

nau se ate (nô′zē āt, nô′shē āt, nô′zhē āt), *v.*, **-at ed, -at ing.** —*v.t.* **1** cause nausea in; make sick. **2** cause to feel loathing. —*v.i.* feel nausea; become sick. —**nau′se at′ing ly,** *adv.*

neb u lous (neb′yə ləs), *adj.* hazy; vague; confused. —**neb′u lous ly,** *adv.* —**neb′u lous ness,** *n.*

nec tar (nek′tər), *n.* (in Greek and Roman myths) the drink of the gods. [< Latin < Greek *nektar*] —**nec′tar like′,** *adj.*

net tle (net′l), *v.*, **-tled, -tling.** —*v.t.* sting the mind of; irritate; provoke; vex. [Old English *netele*] —**net′tle like′,** *adj.* —**net′tler,** *n.*

nig gard (nig′ərd), *n.* a stingy person; miser. —*adj.* stingy. [< Scandinavian (Old Icelandic) *hnöggr* stingy]

nock (nok), *v.t.* fit (an arrow) to the bowstring ready for shooting. [Middle English *nocke*]

non de script (non′də skript), *adj.* not easily classified; not of any one particular kind. —*n.* a nondescript person or thing. [<*non-* + Latin *descriptum* (to be) described]

non pa reil (non′pə rel′), *adj.* having no equal. —*n.* **1** person or thing having no equal. **2** painted bunting. **3** a small chocolate drop covered with tiny white pellets of sugar. [< Middle French < *non-* not + *pareil* equal]

nose gay (nōz′gā′), *n.* bunch of flowers; bouquet. [< *nose* + obsolete *gay* something gay or pretty]

nul li fy (nul′ə fī), *v.t.*, **-fied, -fy ing. 1** make not binding; render void. **2** make of no effect; make unimportant, useless, or meaningless; destroy; cancel; wipe out.

nymph (nimf), *n.* **1** (in Greek and Roman myths) one of the lesser goddesses of nature, who lived in seas, rivers, fountains, springs, hills, woods, or trees. **2** a beautiful or graceful young woman. [< Greek *nymphē*] —**nym′phal,** *adj.* —**nymph′like′,** *adj.*

o bei sance (ō bā′sns, ō bē′sns), *n.* **1** movement of the body expressing deep respect or reverence; deep bow or curtsy. **2** deference; homage. [< Old French *obeissance* obedience < *obeir* obey]

ob scene (əb sēn′), *adj.* offending modesty or decency; impure; filthy; vile. [< Latin *obscenus*] —**ob scene′ly,** *adv.* —**obscene′ness,** *n.*

ob sti nate (ob′stə nit), *adj.* not giving in; stubborn. [< Latin *obstinatum* determined < *ob-* by + *stare* to stand] —**ob′sti nate ly,** *adv.* —**ob′sti nate ness,** *n.*

o di ous (ō′dē əs), *adj.* very displeasing; hateful; offensive. [< Latin *odiosus* < *odium* odium] **o′di ous ly,** *adv.* **o′di ous ness,** *n.*

o gle (ō′gəl), *v.*, **o gled, o gling.** —*v.t.*, *v.i.* look at with desire; make eyes at. [probably < Low German *oeglen* < *oegen* look at < *oog* eye] —**o′gler,** *n.*

o gre (ō′gər), *n.* **1** (in folklore and fairy tales) giant or monster that supposedly eats people. **2** person like such a monster in appearance or character. [< French]

om nip o tent (om nip′ə tənt), *adj.* **1** having all power; almighty. **2** having very great power or influence. —*n.* **the Omnipotent,** God. —**om nip′o tent ly,** *adv.*

om nis cient (om nish′ənt), *adj.* knowing everything; having complete or infinite knowledge. —**om nis′cient ly,** *adv.*

o ra cle (ôr′ə kəl), *n.* **1** (in ancient Greece and Rome) an answer believed to be given by a god through a priest or priestess to some question. It often had a hidden meaning that was ambiguous or hard to understand. **2** place where the god was believed to give such answers. A famous oracle was at Delphi. **3** the priest, priestess, or other means by which the god's answer was believed to be given. **4** a very wise person. [< Latin *oraculum* < *orare* speak formally]

o ra tion (ô rā′shən, ō rā′shən), *n.* a formal public speech, especially one delivered on a special occasion. [< Latin *orationem* < *orare* speak formally, pray. Doublet of ORISON.]

o ra tor (ôr′ə tər, or′ə tər), *n.* **1** person who makes an oration. **2** person who can speak very well in public and often with great eloquence.

or gan dy or **or gan die** (ôr′gən dē′), *n.*, *pl.* **-dies.** a fine, thin, stiff, transparent muslin, used for dresses, curtains, etc. [< French *organdi*]

os ten ta tion (os′ten tā′shən), *n.* a showing off; display intended to impress others. [< Latin *ostentationem*, ultimately < *ob-* toward + *tendere* to stretch]

os ten ta tious (os′ten tā′shəs), *adj.* **1** done for display; intended to attract notice. **2** showing off; liking to attract notice. —**os′ten ta′tious ly,** *adv.* —**os′ten ta′tious ness,** *n.*

-ous, *suffix forming adjectives from nouns.* **1** full of; having much; having. **2** characterized by. **3** having the nature of. **4** of or having to do with. **5** like. **6** committing or practicing. **7** inclined to. **8** (in chemistry) indicating the presence in a compound of the designated element in a lower valence than indicated by the suffix *-ic*, as in *stannous, ferrous, sulfurous.* [< Old French *-os, -us* < Latin *-osum*]

o ver ween ing (ō′vər wē′ning), *adj.* thinking too much of oneself; conceited; self-confident; presumptuous. —**o′ver ween′ing ly,** *adv.* —**o′ver ween′ing ness,** *n.*

pa lav er (pə lav′ər), *n.* **1** parley or conference, especially between Europeans and peoples of other cultures, whose customs required the formal exchange of compliments, gifts, etc., before the bringing up of any matter of business. **2** unnecessary or idle words; mere talk. [< Portuguese *palavra* < Late Latin *parabola* speech. Doublet of parable, PARABOLA, PARLEY, parole.] —**pa lav′er er,** *n.*

pal frey (pôl′frē), *n.*, *pl.* **-freys.** ARCHAIC. a gentle riding horse, especially one used by women. [< Old French *palefrey* < Late Latin *paraveredus* horse for outlying districts]

pal i sade (pal′ə sād′), *n.*, *v.*, **-sad ed, -sad ing.** —*n.* **1** a long, strong wooden stake pointed at the top end. **2** a strong fence of such stakes set firmly and closely together in the ground to enclose or defend. [< Middle French *palissade* < Provençal *palissada* < Latin *palus* stake]

pal let (pal′it), *n.* bed of straw; small or poor bed. [< Old French *paillet* < *paille* straw < Latin *palea*]

pal lid (pal′id), *adj.* lacking normal color; wan; pale. [< Latin *pallidum*]

pang (pang), *n.* **1** a sudden, short, sharp pain.

pa pist (pā′pist), *n.*, *adj.* (often considered offensive) Roman Catholic. [< Late Latin *papa* pope]

pa py rus (pə pī′rəs), *n., pl.* **-ri** (-rī). **1** a tall aquatic sedge, from which the ancient Egyptians, Greeks, and Romans made a kind of paper to write on. **2** a writing material made from the pith of the papyrus plant by laying thin strips of it side by side, the whole being then soaked, pressed, and dried. **3** an ancient record written on papyrus. [< Latin < Greek *papyros*. Doublet of PAPER.]

pa rab o la (pə rab′ə lə), *n.* a plane curve formed by all the points equally distant from a fixed line and from a fixed point not on that line. A parabola is also produced by the intersection of a right circular cone with a plane parallel to a side of the cone. The trajectory of a missile is a parabola. [< Greek *parabolē* comparison, juxtaposition. Doublet of PALAVER, PARABLE, PARLEY, PAROLE.]

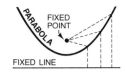

par a mount (par′ə mount), *adj.* chief in importance; above others; supreme. [< Anglo-French *paramount* above < Old French *par* by + *amont* up]

par bleu (pär blœ′), *interj.* a corruption of *par Dieu* (by God), a French oath.

pare (per, par), *v.t.*, **pared, par ing. 1** cut, trim, or shave off the outer part of; peel. **2** cut away (an outer layer, part, etc.). **3** cut away little by little. [< Old French *parer* arrange, dispose < Latin *parare* make ready. Doublet of PARRY.] —**pare′a ble,** *adj.*

par ley (pär′lē), *n., pl.* **-leys. 1** conference or informal talk. **2** an informal discussion with an enemy during a truce about terms of surrender, exchange of prisoners, etc. [< Old French *parlee*, past participle of *parler* speak < Late Latin *parabolare* < *parabola* speech, story. Doublet of PALAVER, PARABLE, PARABOLA, PAROLE.] —**par′ley er,** *n.*

par ry (par′ē), *v.,* **-ried, -ry ing,** *n., pl.* **-ries.** —*v.t.* meet and turn aside (an awkward question, a threat, etc.); avoid; evade. —*n.* act of parrying, avoiding. [< French *parez,* imperative of *parer* ward off < Italian *parare* < Latin, prepare. Doublet of PARE.] —**par′ri a ble,** *adj.* —**par′ri er,** *n.*

par si mo ny (pär′sə mō′nē), *n.* extreme economy; stinginess. [< Latin *parsimonia* < *parcere* to spare]

pate (pāt) *n.* top of head; head, [Middle English]

pâ té de foie gras (pä tā′ də fwä grä′), FRENCH. patty or paste made with livers of specially fattened geese and usually finely chopped truffles.

pa thos (pā′thos), *n.* **1** quality in speech, writing, music, events, or a scene that arouses a feeling of pity or sadness; power of evoking tender or melancholy emotion. **2** a pathetic expression or utterance. [< Greek, suffering, feeling < *path-,* stem of *paschein* suffer]

pa tri arch (pā′trē ärk), *n.* a highly respected elderly man, especially the elder of a village, community, etc. [< Latin *patriarcha* < Greek *patriarchēs* < *patria* family, clan + *archos* leader]

pat ri mo ny (pat′rə mō′nē), *n., pl.* **-nies. 1** property inherited from one's father or ancestors. **2** any heritage. [< Latin *patrimonium* < *pater* father]

peck (pek), *n.* unit of dry measure, 8 quarts or ¼ of a bushel. [Middle English *pek*]

ped a gog ic (ped′ə goj′ik, ped′ə gō′jik), *adj.* of teachers or teaching; of pedagogy. —**ped′a gog′i cal ly,** *adv.*

ped a gog i cal (ped′ə goj′ə kəl, ped′ə gō′jə kəl), *adj.* pedagogic.

ped a go gy (ped′ə gō′jē, ped′ə goj′ē), *n.* **1** teaching. **2** science or art of teaching.

ped ant (ped′nt), *n.* **1** person who makes an unnecessary or tiresome display of knowledge or who puts great stress on minor points of learning. **2** a dull, narrow-minded teacher or scholar. [< Italian *pedante*]

pelf (pelf), *n.* money or riches, thought of as bad or degrading. [< Old French *pelfre* spoils]

pell-mell or **pell mell** (pel′mel′), *adv.* **1** in a rushing, tumbling mass or crowd. **2** in headlong haste. [< French *pêle-mêle*]

pen e tra tion (pen′ə trā′shən), *n.* sharpness of intellect; insight.

a hat	i it	oi oil	ch child		a in about
ā age	ī ice	ou out	ng long		e in taken
ä far	o hot	u cup	sh she	ə =	i in pencil
e let	ō open	ù put	th thin		o in lemon
ē equal	ô order	ü rule	ŦH then		u in circus
ėr term			zh measure		< = derived from

pen sive (pen′siv), *adj.* **1** thoughtful in a serious or sad way. **2** melancholy. [< Old French *pensif* < *penser* think < Latin *pensare* ponder < *pendere* weigh] —**pen′sive ly,** *adv.* —**pen′sive ness,** *n.*

pe num bra (pi num′brə), *n., pl.* **brae** (-brē) **-bras.** the partial shadow outside of the complete shadow formed by the sun, moon, etc., during an eclipse. [< Latin *paene* almost + *umbra* shadow] —**pe num′bral,** *adj.*

per di tion (pər dish′ən), *n.* **1** loss of one's soul and the joys of heaven; damnation. **2** hell. **3** utter loss or destruction; complete ruin. [< Latin *perditionem* < *perdere* destroy < *per-* to destruction + *dare* to give]

pe remp tor y (pə remp′tər ē, per′əmp tôr′ē, per′əmp tōr′ē), *adj.* **1** leaving no choice; decisive; final; absolute. **2** allowing no denial or refusal. **3** imperious; dictatorial. [< Latin *peremptorius* that puts an end to, ultimately < *per-* to the end + *emere* to take] **pe remp′tor i ly,** *adv.* —**pe remp′tor i ness,** *n.*

per fid i ous (pər fid′ē əs), *adj.* deliberately faithless; treacherous. —**per fid′i ous ly,** *adv.* —**per fid′i ous ness,** *n.*

per force (pər fôrs′, pər fōrs′), *adv.* by necessity; necessarily. [< Old French *par force* by force]

per jur y (pėr′jər ē), *n., pl.* **-jur ies.** act or crime of willfully giving false testimony or withholding evidence while under oath; a swearing falsely.

per pen dic u lar (pėr′pən dik′yə lər), *adj.* **1** standing straight up; vertical; upright. **2** very steep; precipitous. **3** at right angles to a given line, plane, or surface. [< Latin *perpendicularis* < *perpendiculum* plumb line < *per-* thoroughly + *pendere* hang] —**per′pen dic′u lar ly,** *adv.*

pet u lance (pech′ə ləns), *n.* a being petulant; peevishness.

pew (pyü), *n.* bench in a church for people to sit on, fastened to the floor and provided with a back. [< Old French *puie* < Latin *podia,* plural of *podium* balcony]

phan tas ma go ri a (fan taz′mə gôr′ē ə, fan taz′mə gōr′ē ə), *n.* a shifting scene of real things, illusions, imaginary fancies, deceptions, and the like. [< Greek *phantasma* image, ultimately < *phainein* to show]

phy lac ter y (fə lak′tər ē), *n., pl.* **-ter ies.** either of two small leather cases containing texts from the Jewish law, worn by Orthodox Jewish males during weekday morning prayers, to remind them to keep the law. One is strapped to the forehead, the other to the left arm. [< Greek *phylaktērion* safeguard, ultimately < *phylax* watchman]

pick et (pik′it), *n.* a small body of troops, or a single soldier, posted at some place to watch for the enemy and guard against surprise attacks. [< French *piquet,* diminutive of *pic* a pick] —**pick′et er,** *n.*

pi e ty (pī′ə tē), *n., pl.* **-ties.** a being pious; reverence for God; devotion to religion; godliness; devoutness. [< Old French *piete* < Latin *pietatem* < *pius* pious. Doublet of PITY.]

pin a fore (pin′ə fôr′, pin′ə fōr′), *n.* **1** a child's apron that covers most of the clothes. **2** a light dress without sleeves. [< *pin,* verb + *afore*]

pin na cle (pin′ə kəl), *n.* **1** a high peak or point of rock, ice, etc. **2** the highest point. **3** a slender turret or spire. [< Old French *pinacle* < Latin *pinnaculum,* diminutive of *pinna* wing, point]

pi ous (pī′əs), *adj.* **1** having or showing reverence for God; righteous. **2** done under pretense of religion or of serving a good cause. **3** sacred rather than secular. [< Latin *pius*] —**pi′ous ly,** *adv.* —**pi′ous ness,** *n.*

pique (pēk), *n., v.,* **piqued, pi quing.** —*n.* a feeling of anger at being slighted; wounded pride. —*v.t.* **1** cause a feeling of anger in; wound the pride of. **2** arouse; stir up [< French < *piquer* to prick, sting]

plac er (plas′ər), *n.* deposit of sand, gravel, or earth in the bed of a stream, containing particles of gold or other valuable minerals. [< Spanish]

plait (plāt, plat *for 1;* plāt, plēt *for 2*), *n., v.t.* **1** braid. **2** pleat. [< Old French *pleit,* ultimately < Latin *plicare* to fold]

plash (plash), *v.t., v.i., n.* splash.

plum met (plum′it), *n.* plumb. —*v.i.* plunge; drop. [< Old French *plommet* < *plomb* lead < Latin *plumbum*]

poign ant (poi′nyənt), *adj.* very painful; piercing. [< Old French, present participle of *poindre* to prick < Latin *pungere*] —**poign′ant ly,** *adv.*

po made (pə mād′), *n., v.,* **-mad ed, -mad ing.** —*n.* a perfumed ointment for the scalp and hair. [< Middle French *pommade,* ultimately < Latin *pomum* fruit]

pomp (pomp), *n.* **1** a stately display; splendor; magnificence. **2** a showy display; boastful show. [< Greek *pompē* parade]

pop ish (pō′pish), *adj.* (often considered offensive) having to do with the Roman Catholic Church. —**pop′ish ly,** *adv.*

pop py cock (pop′ē kok′), *n., interj.* INFORMAL. nonsense; bosh.

por tent (pôr′tent, pōr′tent), *n.* **1** a warning of coming evil; sign; omen. **2** ominous significance. [< Latin *portentum* indicated beforehand]

por ter (pôr′tər, pōr′tər), *n.* a heavy, dark-brown beer. [short for *porter's ale,* apparently < *porter* (who perhaps originally drank it)]

por ti co (pôr′tə kō, pōr′tə kō), *n., pl.* **-coes** or **-cos.** roof supported by columns, forming a porch or a covered walk. [< Italian < Latin *porticus.* Doublet of PORCH.]

Po sei don (pə sīd′n), *n.* (in Greek myths) the god of the sea, identified with the Roman god Neptune.

poul tice (pōl′tis), *n., v.,* **-ticed, -tic ing.** —*n.* a soft, moist mass of mustard, herbs, etc., applied to the body as a medicine. —*v.t.* put a poultice on. [< Latin *pultes,* plural of *puls* mush]

prac ti ca ble (prak′tə kə bəl), *adj.* that can be done; capable of being put into practice; feasible. —**prac′ti ca ble ness,** *n.* —**prac′ti ca bly,** *adv.*

pre cept (prē′sept), *n.* rule of action or behavior; guiding principle. [< Latin *praeceptum* < *praecipere* instruct, anticipate < *prae-* pre- + *capere* to take]

pre cep tor (pri sep′tər, prē′sep tər), *n.* instructor; teacher; tutor.

pre cur sor (pri kėr′sər, prē′kər sər), *n.* forerunner. [< Latin *praecursor* < *praecurrere* run before < *prae-* pre- + *currere* run]

pre mo ni tion (prē′mə nish′ən, prem′ə nish′ən), *n.* notification or warning of what is to come; forewarning. [< Latin *praemonitionem* < *praemonere* warn beforehand < *prae-* pre- + *monere* warn]

pre pos ter ous (pri pos′tər əs), *adj.* contrary to nature, reason, or common sense; absurd; senseless. [< Latin *praeposterus* with the posterior in front < *prae-* pre- + *posterus* coming after, behind] —**pre pos′ter ous ly,** *adv.* —**pre pos′ter ous ness,** *n.*

pre rog a tive (pri rog′ə tiv), *n.* special superiority of right or privilege, such as may derive from an official position, office, etc. [< Latin *praerogativa* allotted to vote first < *praerogare* ask for a vote first < *prae-* pre- + *rogare* ask]

pres age (pres′ij; *also* pri sāj′ *for v.*), *n., v.,* **pre saged, pre sag ing.** —*n.* **1** sign felt as a warning; omen. **2** a feeling that something is about to happen; presentiment; foreboding. —*v.t.* **1** give warning of; predict. **2** have or give a presentiment or prophetic impression of. [< Latin *praesagium* < *prae-* pre- + *sagus* prophetic] —**pre sag′er,** *n.*

pre sci ence (prē′shē əns, presh′ē əns; prē′shəns, presh′əns), *n.* knowledge of things before they exist or happen; foreknowledge; foresight. [< Late Latin *praescientia* < Latin *praescientem* foreknowing < *prae-* pre- + *scire* know]

pre sen ti ment (pri zen′tə mənt), *n.* a feeling or impression that something, especially something evil, is about to happen; vague sense of approaching misfortune; foreboding.

pre tense (prē′tens, pri tens′), *n.* **1** make-believe; pretending. **2** a false appearance. **3** a false claim. **4** claim. **5** a showing off; display; ostentation. **6** anything done to show off. Also, **pretence.**

pre ten sion (pri ten′shən), *n.* **1** claim. **2** a putting forward of a claim; laying claim to. **3** a doing things for show or to make a fine appearance; showy display.

pre text (prē′tekst), *n.* a false reason concealing the real reason; misleading excuse; pretense. [< Latin *praetextum,* literally, woven in front, alleged as an excuse < *prae-* pre- + *texere* to weave]

pre var i cate (pri var′ə kāt), *v.i.,* **-cat ed, -cat ing.** turn aside from the truth in speech or action; lie. [< Latin *praevaricatum* deviated < *prae-* pre- + *varicus* straddling < *varus* crooked] —**pre var′i ca′tor,** *n.*

prime (prīm), *v.t.,* **primed, prim ing.** equip (a person) with information, words, etc.

prod (prod), *v.,* **prod ded, prod ding,** *n.* a sharp-pointed stick; goad. —**prod′der,** *n.*

prod i gal (prod′ə gəl), *n.* person who is wasteful or extravagant; spendthrift. [< Latin *prodigus* wasteful < *prodigere* drive forth, squander < *prod-, pro-* forth + *agere* to drive] —**prod′i gal ly,** *adv.*

pro di gious (prə dij′əs), *adj.* wonderful; marvelous. [< Latin *prodigiosus* < *prodigium* prodigy, omen] —**pro di′gious ly,** *adv.* —**pro di′gious ness,** *n.*

prog e ny (proj′ə nē), *n., pl.* **-nies.** children or offspring; descendants. [< Latin *progenies,* ultimately < *pro-* forth + *gignere* beget]

pro lif ic (prə lif′ik), *adj.* **1** producing offspring or fruit abundantly. **2** highly productive; fertile. **3** conducive to growth, fruitfulness, etc. [< Medieval Latin *prolificus* < Latin *proles* offspring + *facere* to make] —**pro lif′i cal ly,** *adv.* —**pro lif′ic ness,** *n.*

prop a ga tion (prop′ə gā′shən), *n.* the breeding of plants or animals.

pro pi ti ate (prə pish′ē āt), *v.t.,* **-at ed, -at ing.** prevent or reduce the anger of; win the favor of; appease or conciliate (one offended or likely to be). [< Latin *propitius*] —**pro pi′ti a′tor,** *n.*

pro pi tious (prə pish′əs), *adj.* **1** holding well; favorable. **2** favorably inclined; gracious. [< Latin *propitius,* originally, falling forward < *pro-* forward + *petere* go toward] —**pro pi′tious ly,** *adv.* —**pro pi′tious ness,** *n.*

pro sa ic (prō zā′ik), *adj.* like prose; matter-of-fact; ordinary; not exciting. —**pro sa′i cal ly,** *adv.* —**pro sa′ic ness,** *n.*

pros e lyt ize (pros′ə lə′tīz, pros′ə lī tīz), *v.,* **-ized, -iz ing.** —*v.i.* make converts. —*v.t.* make a proselyte of; convert. —**pros′e lyt iz′er,** *n.*

pros trate (pros′trāt), *v.,* **-trat ed, -trat ing,** *adj.* lying flat with face downward. [< Latin *prostratum* thrown down flat < *pro-* forth + *sternere* spread out]

pro tract (prō trakt′), *v.t.* **1** draw out; lengthen in time; prolong. **2** slide out; thrust out; extend. **3** draw by means of a scale and protractor. [< Latin *protractum* drawn out < *pro-* forward + *trahere* to draw] —**pro tract′i ble,** *adj.*

prow ess (prou′is), *n.* **1** bravery; daring. **2** brave or daring acts. **3** unusual skill or ability. [< Old French *proece* < *prod* valiant]

puce (pyüs), *n.* a purplish brown. *adj.* purplish-brown. [< French]

pul chri tude (pul′krə tüd, pul′krə tyüd), *n.* physical beauty. [< Latin *pulchritudo* < *pulcher* beautiful]

punt (punt), *n.* a shallow, flat-bottomed boat with square ends, usually moved by pushing with a pole against the bottom of a river, etc. [< Latin *ponto* pontoon] —**punt′er,** *n.*

quack (kwak), *n.* **1** a dishonest person who pretends to be a doctor. **2** an ignorant pretender to knowledge or skill of any sort; charlatan. —*adj.* **1** used by quacks. **2** not genuine. [short for *quacksalver*]

qua dran gu lar (kwo drang′gyə lər), *adj.* like a quadrangle; having four corners or angles.

qua drille (kwə dril′), *n.* **1** a square dance for four couples that usually has five parts. **2** music for such a dance. [< French < Spanish *cuadrilla* troop < *cuadro* battle square < Latin *quadrus* square]

qualm (kwäm, kwälm), *n.* a sudden disturbing feeling in the mind; uneasiness; misgiving; doubt. [origin unknown]

quar rel (kwôr′əl, kwor′əl), *n.* bolt or arrow used with a crossbow. [< Old French < Medieval Latin *quadrellus,* ultimately < Latin *quadrum* a square]

quar ry[1] (kwôr′ē, kwor′ē), *n., pl.* **-ries,** *v.* **-ried, -ry ing.**
—*n.* place where stone, slate, etc., is dug, cut, or blasted out for use in building. [< Medieval Latin *quareia, quadraria* < Latin *quadrum* a square] **—quar′ri er,** *n.*

quar ry[2] (kwôr′ē, kwor′ē), *n., pl.* **-ries.** **1** animal chased in a hunt; game; prey. **2** anything hunted or eagerly pursued. [< Middle French *cuiree* < *cuir* skin, hide < Latin *corium*]

qua ver (kwā′vər), *v.i.* shake tremulously; tremble. [frequentative form of earlier *quave* to shake] **—qua′ver er,** *n.* **—qua′ver ing ly,** *adv.*

queen (kwēn), *v.i.* act like a queen. [Old English *cwēn*] **—queen′like′,** *adj.*

queue (kyü), *n., v.,* **queued, queu ing** or **queue ing.** —*n.* a line of people, automobiles, etc. [< French < Latin *coda, cauda* tail] **—queu′er,** *n.*

quire (kwīr), *n.* 24 or 25 sheets of paper of the same size and quality. [< Old French *quaier,* ultimately < Latin *quaterni* four each]

quit tance (kwit′ns), *n.* **1** a release from debt or obligation. **2** the paper certifying this; receipt. **3** repayment or retaliation.

quiv er (kwiv′ər), *v.i.* shake with a slight but rapid motion; shiver; tremble. —*n.* act of quivering; tremble. [Old English *cwifer* nimble] **—quiv′er er,** *n.* **—quiv′er ing ly,** *adv.*

rab bi (rab′ī), *n.* an ordained preacher and teacher of the Jewish law and religion, usually serving as the spiritual leader of a Jewish congregation; Jewish clergyman. [< Hebrew *rabbī* my master]

ra gout (ra gü′), *n.* a highly seasoned stew of meat and vegetables. [< French *ragoût* < *ragoûter* restore the appetite, ultimately < Latin *re-* back + *ad-* to + *gustus* taste]

rail (rāl), *v.i.* complain bitterly; use violent and reproachful language. [< Middle French *railler* to mock, ridicule, ultimately < Late Latin *ragere* to bray, brawl] **—rail′er,** *n.*

rai ment (rā′mənt), *n.* ARCHAIC. clothing; garments. [short for *arraiment* < *array*]

rake (rāk), *v.,* **raked, rak ing.** —*v.t., v.i.* slant or cause to slant.

ram part (ram′pärt), *n.* **1** a wide bank of earth, often with a wall on top as a fortification, built around a fort to help defend it. **2** anything that defends; defense; protection. [< Middle French *rempart* < *remparer* fortify]

ran cor (rang′kər), *n.* bitter resentment or ill will; extreme hatred or spite. [< Late Latin, rankness < Latin *rancere* be rank]

ran cor ous (rang′kər əs), *adj.* bitterly malicious; spiteful. **—ran′cor ous ly,** *adv.* **—ran′cor ous ness,** *n.*

rank (rangk), *n.* **1** row or line, especially of soldiers, placed side by side. **2 ranks,** *pl.* **a** army; soldiers. **b** rank and file. [< Old French *rang;* of Germanic origin] **—rank′er,** *n.*

ra pa cious (rə pā′shəs), *adj.* **1** seizing by force; plundering. **2** grasping; greedy. [< Latin *rapacem* grasping < *rapere* seize] **—ra pa′cious ly,** *adv.* **—ra pa′cious ness,** *n.*

rap ine (rap′ən), *n.* a robbing by force and carrying off; plundering. [< Latin *rapina* < *rapere* seize]

rau cous (rô′kəs), *adj.* hoarse; harsh-sounding. [< Latin *raucus*] **—rau′cous ly,** *adv.* **—rau′cous ness,** *n.*

rav en ing (rav′ə ning), *adj.* greedy and hungry.

rav ish (rav′ish), *v.t.* **1** fill with delight. **2** carry off by force. **3** rape. [< Old French *raviss-,* a form of *ravir* ravish < Latin *rapere* seize] **—rav′ish er,** *n.* **—rav′ish ment,** *n.*

raze (rāz), *v.t.,* **razed, raz ing.** tear down; destroy completely; demolish. [< Middle French *raser* to scrape, ultimately < Latin *radere*]

re al (rē′əl; Spanish rä äl′), *n., pl.* **re als, re a les** (rä ä′lās). a former small silver coin of Spain and Spanish America. [< Spanish *real (de plata)* royal (coin of silver) < Latin *regalis* regal. Doublet

a hat	i it	oi oil	ch child	(a in about
ā age	ī ice	ou out	ng long	e in taken
ä far	o hot	u cup	sh she	ə = { i in pencil
e let	ō open	u̇ put	th thin	o in lemon
ē equal	ô order	ü rule	ŦH then	u in circus
ėr term			zh measure	< = derived from

of REGAL, ROYAL, RIAL.]

re buke (ri byük′), *v.,* **-buked, -buk ing,** *n.* —*v.t.* express disapproval of; reprove. [< Anglo-French *rebuker* < Old French *rebuchier* < *re-* back + *buchier* to strike] **—re buk′er,** *n.* **—re buk′ing ly,** *adv.*

re cal ci trance (ri kal′sə trəns), *n.* refusal to submit, conform, or comply.

rec og nize (rek′əg nīz), *v.t.,* **-ized, -niz ing.** **1** be aware of (someone or something) as already known; know again. **2** identify. **3** acknowledge acquaintance with; greet. **4** acknowledge; accept; admit. **5** take notice of. **6** show appreciation of. **7** acknowledge and agree to deal with. [< Old French *reconoistre* < Latin *recognoscere* < *re-* again + *com-* (intensive) + *(g)noscere* learn, come to know. Doublet of RECONNOITER.]

re com pose (rē kəm pōz′), *v.t.* to compose again; to form anew.

rec re ant (rek′rē ənt), *adj.* **1** lacking courage; cowardly. **2** unfaithful to duty, etc.; disloyal; traitorous. [< Old French, confessing oneself beaten, ultimately < Latin *re-* back + *credere* believe]

rec ti tude (rek′tə tüd, rek′tə tyüd), *n.* **1** upright conduct or character; honesty; righteousness. **2** direction in a straight line; straightness. [< Late Latin *rectitudo* < Latin *rectus* straight]

re fur bish (rē fėr′bish), *v.t.* polish up again; do up anew; brighten; renovate. **—re fur′bish ment,** *n.*

ref u ta tion (ref′yə tā′shən), *n.* disproof of a claim, opinion, or argument.

reive (rēv), *v.* to seize, plunder, steal.

re lin quish (ri ling′kwish), *v.t.* give up; let go; release. [< Old French *relinquiss-,* a form of *relinquir* leave behind < Latin *relinquere* < *re-* + *linquere* to leave] **—re lin′quish er,** *n.* **—re lin′quish ment,** *n.*

re mon strate (ri mon′strāt), *v.i.,* **-strat ed, -strat ing.** speak, reason, or plead in complaint or protest. [< Medieval Latin *remonstratum* pointed out, ultimately < Latin *re-* back + *monstrum* sign] **—re mon stra tion** (rē′mən strā′shən), *n.* **—re mon′stra′tor,** *n.*

re nowned (ri nound′), *adj.* having fame; famed.

re pine (ri pīn′), *v.i.,* **-pined, -pin ing.** be discontented; fret; complain. **—re pin′er,** *n.*

rep re hend (rep′ri hend′), *v.t.* reprove, rebuke, or blame. [< Latin *reprehendere,* originally, pull back < *re-* back + *prehendere* to grasp]

rep re hen si ble (rep′ri hen′sə bəl), *adj.* deserving reproof, rebuke, or blame. **—rep′re hen′si bil′i ty,** *n.* **—rep′re hen′si ble ness,** *n.* **—rep′re hen′si bly,** *adv.*

re pu di ate (ri pyü′dē āt), *v.t.,* **-at ed, -at ing.** **1** refuse to accept; reject. **2** refuse to acknowledge or pay. **3** cast off; disown. [< Latin *repudiatum* divorced < *repudium* divorce] **—re pu′di a′tion,** *n.* **—re pu′di a′tor,** *n.*

re pug nant (ri pug′nənt), *adj.* **1** disagreeable or offensive; distasteful; objectionable. **2** contrary; averse; opposed. [< Latin *repugnantem* resisting, opposing < *re-* back + *pugnare* to fight] **—re pug′nant ly,** *adv.*

re pute (ri pyüt′), *n., v.,* **-put ed, -put ing.** —*n.* **1** reputation. **2** good reputation. [< Latin *reputare* consider < *re-* over + *putare* think]

req ui si tion (rek′wə zish′ən), *n.* act of requiring. —*v.t.* demand or take by authority.

re quite (ri kwīt′), *v.t.,* **-quit ed, -quit ing.** **1** pay back; make return for. **2** make return to; reward. **3** make retaliation for; avenge. [< *re-* + *quite,* variant of *quit*] **—re quit′er,** *n.*

res in ous (rez′n əs), *adj.* containing resin; full of resin.

re splend ent (ri splen′dənt), *adj.* very bright; shining; splendid.

GLOSSARY

[< Latin *resplendentem* < *re-* back + *splendere* to shine] **—resplend′ent ly,** *adv.*

res ti tu tion (res′tə tü′shən, res′tə tyü′shən), *n.* **1** the giving back of what has been lost or taken away; return. **2** act of making good any loss, damage, or injury; reparation; amends. [< Latin *restitutionem,* ultimately < *re-* again + *statuere* set up]

ret i cence (ret′ə səns), *n.* tendency to be silent or say little; reserve in speech.

ret ri bu tion (ret′rə byü′shən), *n.* a deserved punishment; return for wrongdoing. [< Latin *retributionem,* ultimately < *re-* back + *tribuere* assign]

ret ro grade (ret′rə grād), *adj., v.,* **-grad ed, -grad ing.** —*adj.* **1** moving backward; retreating. **2** becoming worse; declining; deteriorating. [< Latin *retrogradus* < *retro-* back + *gradi* go] **—ret′ro gra da′tion,** *n.*

re vere (ri vir′), *v.t.,* **-vered, -ver ing.** love and respect deeply; honor greatly; show reverence for. [< Latin *revereri* < *re-* back + *vereri* stand in awe of, fear]

re vile (ri vīl′), *v.,* **-viled, -vil ing.** —*v.t.* call bad names; abuse with words. —*v.i.* speak abusively. [< Old French *reviler* despise < *re-* again + *vil* vile] **—re vile′ment,** *n.* **—re vil′er,** *n.*

re vul sion (ri vul′shən), *n.* **1** a sudden, violent change or reaction, especially of disgust. **2** a drawing or a being drawn back or away, especially suddenly or violently. [< Latin *revulsionem* < *re-* back + *vellere* tear away]

road stead (rōd′sted), *n.* place near the shore where ships may anchor; road.

rogue (rōg), *n.* **1** a dishonest or unprincipled person; scoundrel; rascal. **2** a mischievous person; scamp.

rook (rúk), *n.* a common European bird, of the same genus as and closely resembling the crow; that often nests in large flocks in trees near buildings. [Old English *hrōc*]

Rosh Ha sha nah (rosh′ hə shä′nə), the Jewish New Year, usually occurring in September. [< Hebrew *rōsh hashshānāh,* literally, head of the year]

rout (rout), *v.t.* put to flight in disorder. [< Middle French, detachment < Popular Latin *rupta* dispersed soldiers, ultimately < Latin *rumpere* to break]

row (rou), *n.* a noisy quarrel or disturbance; squabble. —*v.i.* quarrel noisily; squabble.

ruck (ruk), *v.t.* to rake into a heap.

ru di men tar y (rü′də men′tər ē), *adj.* **1** to be learned or studied first; elementary. **2** in an early stage of development; undeveloped. **—ru′di men′tar i ly,** *adv.* **—ru′di men′tar i ness,** *n.*

ru mi nate (rü′mə nāt), *v.,* **-nat ed, -nat ing.** —*v.i.* **1** chew the cud. **2** think or ponder; meditate; reflect. —*v.t.* **1** chew again (food which has been previously chewed and swallowed). **2** turn over in the mind; meditate on. **—ru′mi na′tor,** *n.*

run nel (run′əl), *n.* a small stream or brook; rivulet; runlet. [Old English *rynel* < *rinnan* to run]

rut (rut), *n.* **1** sexual excitement of male deer, goats, sheep, etc.; occurring at regular intervals, usually annually. **2** period during which it lasts. [< Old French *ruit* < Latin *rugitus* a bellowing < *rugire* bellow]

Sab bath (sab′əth), *n.* **1** day of the week used for rest and worship. Sunday is the Sabbath for most Christians; Saturday is the Jewish Sabbath. **2 sabbath,** period of rest, quiet, etc. —*adj.* of or belonging to the Sabbath. [< Latin *sabbatum* < Greek *sabbaton* < Hebrew *shabbāth* < *shābath* to rest]

sa ber (sā′bər), *n.* a heavy, curved sword with a sharp edge, used especially by cavalry. —*v.t.* strike, wound, or kill with a saber. Also, **sabre.** [< French *sabre,* alteration of *sable* < earlier German *Sabel,* ultimately < Hungarian *szabni* to cut]

sack (sak), *v.t.* plunder (a captured city); loot and despoil; pillage. —*n.* a plundering of a captured city. [< Middle French *(mettre à) sac* (put to the) sack < Italian *sacco* sack < Latin *saccus*] **—sack′er,** *n.*

sac ri lege (sak′rə lij), *n.* an intentional injury to anything sacred; disrespectful treatment of anyone or anything sacred. [< Latin *sacrilegium* temple robbery < *sacrum* sacred object + *legere* pick up, gather]

saf fron (saf′rən), *n.* **1** an autumn crocus with purple flowers having orange-yellow stigmas. **2** an orange-yellow coloring matter obtained from the dried stigmas of this crocus. Saffron is used to color and flavor candy, drinks, etc. **3** an orange yellow. —*adj.* orange-yellow. [< Old French *safran,* ultimately < Arabic *za′farān*]

sage (sāj), *adj.,* **sag er, sag est.** —*adj.* **1** showing wisdom or good judgment. **2** wise. [< Old French, ultimately < Latin *sapere* be wise] **—sage′ly,** *adv.* **—sage′ness,** *n.*

sal a ble (sā′lə bəl), *adj.* that can be sold; fit to be sold, easily sold. Also, **saleable.**

sal low (sal′ō), *adj.* having a sickly, yellowish or brownish-yellow color. [Old English *salo*] **—sal′low ness,** *n.*

sal ly (sal′ē), *v.,* **-lied, -ly ing.** —*v.i.* **1** go suddenly from a defensive position to attack an enemy. **2** rush forth suddenly; go out. **3** set out briskly or boldly. [< Old French *saillie* a rushing forth < *saillir* to leap < Latin *salire*] **—sal′li er,** *n.*

sal va tion (sal vā′shən), *n.* **1** a saving. **2** a being saved. **3** person or thing that saves. **4** a saving of the soul; deliverance from sin and from punishment for sin. [< Late Latin *salvationem,* ultimately < Latin *salvus* safe] **—sal va′tion al,** *adj.*

sal vo (sal′vō), *n., pl.* **-vos** or **-voes.** **1** the discharge of several guns at the same time as a broadside or as a salute. **2** the release at the same time of several bombs, rockets, etc. **3** round of cheers or applause. **4** barrage. [< Italian *salva* salute, volley < Latin *salve* hail!, be in good health!]

sam o var (sam′ə vär, sam′ə vär′), *n.* a metal urn used for heating water for tea. [< Russian, literally, self-boiler]

sanc ti mo ni ous (sangk′tə mō′nē əs), *adj.* making a show of holiness; putting on airs of sanctity. **—sanc′ti mo′ni ous ly,** *adv.* **—sanc′ti mo′ni ous ness,** *n.*

san guine (sang′gwən), *adj.* **1** naturally cheerful and hopeful. **2** (in old physiology) having an active circulation, a ruddy color, and a cheerful and ardent disposition. [< Latin *sanguineus* < *sanguinem* blood] **—san′guine ly,** *adv.*

sate (sāt), *v.t.,* **sat ed, sat ing.** **1** satisfy fully (any appetite or desire). **2** supply with more than enough, so as to disgust or weary. [alteration of *sade* (Old English *sadian* to glut) under influence of Latin *satiare* satiate]

sa teen (sa tēn′), *n.* a cotton cloth made to imitate satin, often used for lining sleeves. [variant of *satin*]

sa ti e ty (sə tī′ə tē), *n.* the feeling of having had too much; disgust or weariness caused by excess; satiated condition.

sau cy (sô′sē), *adj.,* **-ci er, -ci est.** **1** showing lack of respect; impudent; rude. **2** pert; smart. [< *sauce*] **—sau′ci ly,** *adv.* **—sau′ci ness,** *n.*

scathe (skāᴛʜ), *v.,* **scathed, scath ing,** *n.* —*v.t.* ARCHAIC. injure; damage. —*n.* ARCHAIC. a hurt; harm. [< Scandinavian (Old Icelandic) *skathi* injury]

scourge (skėrj), *n.* some thing or person that causes great trouble or misfortune. [< Old French *escorge,* ultimately < Latin *ex-* out + *corium* a hide] **—scourg′er,** *n.*

scru ple (skrü′pəl), *n.* a feeling of uneasiness that keeps a person from doing something. [< Latin *scrupulus* a feeling of uneasiness, originally diminutive of *scrupus* sharp stone, figuratively, uneasiness, anxiety]

scru pu lous (skrü′pyə ləs), *adj.* **1** very careful to do what is right; conscientious. **2** attending thoroughly to details; very careful. **—scru′pu lous ly,** *adv.* **—scru′pu lous ness,** *n.*

scul ler y (skul′ər ē), *n., pl.* **-ler ies.** a small room where the dirty, rough work of a kitchen is done. [< Old French *escuelerie,* ultimately < Latin *scutella,* diminutive of *scutra* platter]

scythe (sīᴛʜ), *n., v.,* **scythed, scyth ing.** —*n.* a long, thin, slightly curved blade on a long handle, for cutting grass, etc. —*v.t.* cut or mow with a scythe. [Old English *sithe;* spelling influenced by Latin *scindere* to cut]

sear (sir), *v.t.* **1** burn or char the surface of. **2** make hard or unfeeling. **3** dry up; wither. —*v.i.* become dry, burned, or hard. —*n.* mark made by searing. —*adj.* sere. [Old English *sēarian*

< *sēar,* adjective]

sea wrack (sē rak), *n.* seaweed.

sec u lar (sek′yə lər), *adj.* **1** not religious or sacred; worldly. **2** living in the world; not belonging to a religious order. **3** occurring once in an age or century. **4** lasting through long ages; going on from age to age. [< Latin *saecularis* < *saeculum* age, world] —**sec′u lar ly,** *adv.*

sedge (sej), *n.* any of a large family of monocotyledonous herbs growing chiefly in wet places, resembling grasses but having solid, three-sided stems and small, inconspicuous flowers usually in spikes or heads. [Old English *secg*]

seethe (sēŦH), *v.,* **seethed, seeth ing.** —*v.i.* **1** be excited; be disturbed. **2** bubble and foam. **3** ARCHAIC. boil. —*v.t.* **1** soak; steep. **2** boil. [Old English *sēothan*] —**seeth′ing ly,** *adv.*

sem blance (sem′blans), *n.* **1** outward appearance. **2** likeness. [< Old French < *sembler* seem < Latin *similare* make similar < *similis* similar]

sep ul cher (sep′əl kər), *n.* place of burial; tomb; grave. Also, **sepulchre.** [< Old French < Latin *sepulcrum* < *sepelire* bury]

se pul chral (sə pul′krəl), *adj.* deep and gloomy; dismal; suggesting a tomb. —**se pul′chral ly,** *adv.*

ser aph (ser′əf), *n., pl.* **-aphs** or **-a phim.** one of the highest order of angels. [< *seraphim,* plural, < Late Latin < Hebrew *sĕrāphīm*]

sere (sir), *adj.* ARCHAIC. dried; withered. Also, **sear.** [Old English *sēar*]

serf (sèrf), *n.* **1** (in the feudal system) a slave who could not be sold off the land, but passed from one owner to another with the land. **2** person treated almost like a slave; person who is mistreated, underpaid, etc. [< French < Latin *servus* slave] —**serf′like′,** *adj.*

ser rate (ser′āt, ser′it), *adj.* notched like the edge of a saw; toothed. [< Latin *serratus* < *serra* a saw]

ses terce (ses′tèrs′), *n.* an ancient Roman coin of small value. [< Latin *sestertius,* originally, two and a half < *semis* half + *tertius* third]

shade (shād), *n.* ghost; spirit. [Old English *sceadu*]

Shah or **shah** (shä), *n.* title of the former rulers of Iran. [< Persian *shāh*]

sheaf (shēf), *n., pl.* **sheaves.** —*n.* **1** one of the bundles in which grain is bound after reaping. **2** bundle of things of the same sort bound together or so arranged that they can be bound together. [Old English *scēaf*] —**sheaf′like′,** *adj.*

shend (shend), *v.* to be injured or ruined. [Anglo-Saxon *sceand, sceond* disgrace, shame]

shoal (shōl), *n.* **1** place in a sea, lake, or stream where the water is shallow. **2** sandbank or sandbar that makes the water shallow, especially one which can be seen at low tide. —*adj.* shallow. —*v.i.* become shallow. [Old English *sceald* shallow, adjective]

shoe (shü), **shoon,** *v.,* **shod, shoe ing. 1** put shoes on; furnish with a shoe or shoes. **2** protect or arm at the point; edge or face with metal. [Old English *scōh*] —**shoe′less,** *adj.*

shrew (shrü), *n.* a bad-tempered, quarrelsome woman. [Old English *scrēawa*] —**shrew′like′,** *adj.*

shroud (shroud), *n.* **1** cloth or garment in which a dead person is wrapped or dressed for burial. **2** something that covers, conceals, or veils. —*v.t.* **1** wrap or dress for burial. **2** cover; conceal; veil. [Old English *scrūd*] —**shroud′like′,** *adj.*

shut tle (shut′l), *n., v.,* **-tled, -tling.** —*n.* device that carries the thread from one side of the web to the other in weaving. [Old English *scytel* a dart < *scēotan* to shoot]

shy (shī), *v.,* **shied, shy ing,** *n., pl.* **shies.** —*v.t., v.i.* throw; fling. —*n.* a throw; fling. [origin uncertain]

si dle (sī′dl), *v.,* **-dled, -dling,** *n.* —*v.i.* **1** move sideways. **2** move sideways slowly so as not to attract attention. —*n.* movement sideways. [< *sideling,* variant of *sidelong*] —**si′dling ly,** *adv.*

sim u la crum (sim′yə lā′krəm), *n., pl.* **-cra** (-krə), **-crums. 1** a faint, shadowy, or unreal likeness; mere semblance. **2** image. [< Latin < *simulare* simulate < *similis* like]

skein (skān), *n.* **1** a small, coiled bundle of yarn or thread. There are 120 yards in a skein of cotton yarn. **2** a confused tangle.

a hat	i it	oi oil	ch child	(a in about
ā age	ī ice	ou out	ng long	e in taken
ä far	o hot	u cup	sh she	ə = { i in pencil
e let	ō open	ů put	th thin	o in lemon
ē equal	ô order	ü rule	ŦH then	(u in circus
ėr term			zh measure	< = derived from

[< Old French *escaigne*]

skit tles (skit′lz), *n.* game in which the players try to knock down nine wooden pins by rolling or throwing wooden disks or balls at them. [< Scandinavian (Danish) *skyttel* shuttle]

slake (slāk), *v.,* **slaked, slak ing.** —*v.t.* cause to be less active, vigorous, intense, etc. —*v.i.* become less active, vigorous, intense, etc. [Old English *slacian* slacken < *slæc* slack]

slan der (slan′dər), *n.* **1** a false statement spoken with intent to harm the reputation of another. **2** the spreading of false reports. —*v.t.* talk falsely about. —*v.i.* speak or spread slander. [< Old French *esclandre* scandal < Latin *scandalum.* Doublet of SCANDAL.] —**slan′der er,** *n.*

sledge (slej), *n., v.,* **sledged, sledg ing.** —*n.* a heavy sled or sleigh, usually pulled by horses. —*v.i.* ride in a sledge. —*v.t.* carry on a sledge. [< Dutch *sleedse*]

slop (slop), *n.* Often, **slops,** *pl.* dirty water; liquid garbage. [Middle English *sloppe*]

sloth ful (slôth′fəl, slōth′fəl), *adj.* unwilling to work or exert oneself; lazy; idle. —**sloth′ful ly,** *adv.* —**sloth′ful ness,** *n.*

slough (sluf), *v.* drop off; throw off; shed. [Middle English *slouh*]

sluice (slüs), *n., v.,* **sluiced, sluic ing.** —*n.* **1** structure with a gate or gates for holding back or controlling the water of a canal, river, or lake. **2** gate that holds back or controls the flow of water. When the water behind a dam gets too high, the sluices are opened. [< Old French *escluse* < Late Latin *exclusa* barrier to shut out water < Latin *excludere* shut out]

slur (slėr), *n.* blot or stain (upon reputation); insulting or slighting remark.

smite (smīt), *v.,* **smote, smit ten** or **smote, smit ing.** —*v.t.* **1** give a hard blow to (a person, etc.) with the hand, a stick, or the like; strike. **2** give or strike (a blow, stroke, etc.). **3** strike with a weapon, etc., so as to cause serious injury or death. **4** attack with a sudden pain, disease, etc. **5** impress suddenly with a strong feeling, sentiment, etc. **6** punish severely; chasten. —*v.i.* **1** deliver a blow or blows, a stroke, etc., with or as with a stick, weapon, etc.; strike. **2** come with force *(upon).* [Old English *smītan*] —**smit′er,** *n.*

smit ten (smit′n), *adj.* hard hit; struck. —*v.* a pp. of **smite.**

smote (smōt), *v.* pt. and a pp. of **smite.**

smut ty (smut′ē), *adj.,* **-ti er, -ti est.** indecent; nasty; obscene. —**smut′ti ly,** *adv.* —**smut′ti ness,** *n.*

snipe (snīp), *n., pl.* **snipes** or **snipe.** *n.* any of various marsh birds with long bills, of the same family as the sandpipers, frequently hunted as game. [< Scandinavian (Old Icelandic) *snīpa*]

sniv el (sniv′əl), *v.,* **-eled, -el ing** or **-elled, -el ling,** *n.* —*v.i.* **1** cry with sniffling; whimper. **2** put on a show of grief; whine. [Middle English *snivelen,* related to Old English *snofl* mucus] —**sniv′el er, sniv′el ler,** *n.*

soi ree or **soi rée** (swä rā′), *n.* an evening party or social gathering. [< French *soirée* < *soir* evening]

so journ (*v.* sō′jèrn′, sō jėrn′; *n.* sō′jèrn′), *v.i.* stay for a time. —*n.* a brief stay. [< Old French *sojorner,* ultimately < Latin *sub* under + *diurnus* of the day] —**so′journ′er,** *n.*

sol ace (sol′is), *n.* **1** comfort or relief. **2** that which gives comfort or consolation. [< Latin *solacium* < *solari* to console]

-some, *suffix forming adjectives.* **1** tending to _____: *Meddlesome = tending to meddle.* **2** causing _____: *Troublesome = causing trouble.* **3** _____to a considerable degree: *Lonesome = lone to a considerable degree.* [Middle English < Old English *-sum*]

so no rous (sə nôr′əs, sə nōr′əs), *adj.* **1** giving out or having a deep, loud sound. **2** full and rich in sound. **3** having an impres-

sordid

sive sound; high-sounding. [< Latin *sonorus* < *sonare* to sound < *sonus* sound] —**so no′rous ly,** *adv.* —**so no′rous ness,** *n.*

sor did (sôr′did), *adj.* dirty; filthy. [< Latin *sordidus* dirty < *sordere* be dirty < *sordes* dirt] —**sor′did ly,** *adv.* —**sor′did-ness,** *n.*

spake (spāk), *v.* ARCHAIC. a pt. of **speak.**

spawn (spôn), *n.* **1** the eggs of fish, frogs, shellfish, etc. **2** the young newly hatched from such eggs. **3** offspring, especially a large number of offspring. **4** product or result. [< Old French *espandre* spread out < Latin *expandere.* Doublet of EXPAND.] —**spawn′er,** *n.*

spe cious (spē′shəs), *adj.* **1** seeming desirable, reasonable, or probable, but not really so; apparently good, but without real merit. **2** making a good outward appearance in order to deceive. [< Latin *speciosus* < *species* appearance, sort] —**spe′cious ly,** *adv.* —**spe′cious ness,** *n.*

sphinx (sfingks), *n.* (in Greek myths) a monster with the head of a woman, the body of a lion, and wings. The Sphinx proposed a riddle to every passer-by and killed those unable to answer it. [< Greek]

spite (spīt), *v.,* **spit ed, spit ing.** —*v.t.* show ill will toward; annoy; irritate. [Middle English, short for *despite*] —**spite′less,** *adj.*

spleen (splēn), *n.* **1** a ductless, glandlike organ at the left of the stomach in human beings, and near the stomach or intestine in other vertebrates, that stores blood, disintegrates old red blood cells, and helps filter foreign substances from the blood. **2** bad temper; spite; anger. **3** low spirits. [< Greek *splēn*]

springe (sprinj), *n.* snare for catching small game. [apparently < Old English *sprengan* cause to spring]

sprite (sprīt), *n.* fairy. [< Old French *esprit* spirit < Latin *spiritus.*]

spurn (spėrn), *v.t.* refuse with scorn; scorn. [Old English *spurnan*] —**spurn′er,** *n.*

squall (skwôl), *n.* a sudden, violent gust of wind, often with rain, snow, or sleet. [apparently related to Swedish *skval* sudden rush of water]

squire (skwīr), *n.* **1** a young man of noble family who attended a knight till he himself was made a knight. **2** a male personal attendant, especially of a sovereign or noble personage. [< Old French *esquier* < Latin *scutarius* shield-bearer < *scutum* shield] —**squire′like′,** *adj.*

stal wart (stôl′wərt), *adj.* **1** strongly built; sturdy; robust. **2** strong and brave; valiant. **3** firm; steadfast. —*n.* **1** a stalwart person. **2** a loyal supporter of a political party. [Old English *stælwierthe* serviceable < *stathol* position + *wierthe* worthy] —**stal′wart ly,** *adv.* —**stal′wart ness,** *n.*

stead ing (sted′ing), *n.* a homestead, esp. a humble one, as of a herdsman or small farmer.

steep (stēp), *n.* a steep slope. [Old English *stēap*] —**steep′ly,** *adv.* —**steep′ness,** *n.*

stir rup (stėr′əp, stir′əp), *n.* loop or ring of metal or wood that hangs from a saddle to support a rider's foot. [Old English *stigrāp* < *stige* climbing + *rāp* rope]

strand (strand), *n.* shore; land bordering a sea, lake, or river. [Old English]

strat a gem (strat′ə jəm), *n.* scheme or trick for deceiving an enemy; trickery. [< Greek *stratēgēma* < *stratēgein* be a general < *stratēgos* general.

strew (strü), *v.t.,* **strewed, strewed** or **strewn, strew ing.** **1** scatter or spinkle. **2** cover with something scattered or sprinkled. **3** be scattered or sprinkled over. [Old English *strēowian*]

strow (strō), *v.t.* ARCHAIC. pt. and pp. of **strew.**

strum pet (strum′pit), *n.* prostitute. [Middle English]

stu pe fy (stü′pə fī, styü′pə fī), *v.t.,* **-fied, -fy ing. 1** make stupid, dull, or senseless. **2** overwhelm with shock or amazement; astound. [< Latin *stupefacere* < *stupere* be amazed + *facere* to make] —**stu′pe fi′er,** *n.* —**stu′pe fy′ing ly,** *adv.*

sub ter fuge (sub′tər fyüj), *n.* trick, excuse, or expedient used to

escape something unpleasant. [< Late Latin *subterfugium,* ultimately < Latin *subter-* from under + *fugere* flee]

sub tile (sut′l, sub′təl), *adj.* subtle. —**sub′tile ly,** *adv.*

sub tle (sut′l), *adj.,* **-tler, -tlest. 1** delicate; thin; fine. **2** so fine or delicate as to elude observation or analysis. **3** faint; mysterious. **4** discerning; acute. **5** sly; crafty; tricky. **6** skillful; clever; expert. **7** working unnoticeably or secretly; insidious. Also, **subtile, subtil.** [< Old French *soutil* < Latin *subtilis,* originally, woven underneath] —**sub′tle ness,** *n.* —**sub tly** (sut′lē, sut′l ē), *adv.*

suc cor (suk′ər), *n.* person or thing that helps or assists; help; aid. —*v.t.* help, assist, or aid (a person, etc.). [< Old French *sucurs,* ultimately < Latin *succurrere* run to help < *sub-* up to + *currere* to run] —**suc′cor er,** *n.*

suf fer ance (suf′ər əns), *n.* **1** permission or consent given only by a failure to object or prevent. **2** power to bear or endure; patient endurance.

Su fi (sü′fē), *n.* **1** member of an ascetic Moslem sect practicing a form of mysticism that began in Persia. **2** the sect itself. [< Arabic *sūfī,* literally, (man) of wool < *sūf* wool]

suit (süt), *n.* request; asking; wooing. [< Anglo-French *suite* a following < Popular Latin *sequita* < Latin *sequi* follow. Doublet of SUITE.]

Suk koth or **Suk kot** (sūk′əs, sūk′ōt, sūk′ōs), *n.* a Jewish festival of either eight or nine days celebrated in September or October by building temporary booths in remembrance of those the Israelites used during their wanderings in the desert. Also, **Succoth.** [< Hebrew *sukkōth* tabernacles]

sul tan (sult′n), *n.* ruler of a Moslem country. Turkey was ruled by a sultan until 1922. [< Arabic *sulṭān* ruler]

sump ter (sump′tər), *n.* ARCHAIC. horse or mule for carrying baggage. [< Old French *sommetier,* ultimately < Latin *sagma* pack-saddle]

sun der (sun′dər), *v.t., v.i.* put asunder; separate; sever; split. —*n.* **in sunder,** apart. [Old English *sundrian* < *sundor* apart]

sun dry (sun′drē), *adj.* several; various. [Old English *syndrig* separate < *sundor* apart]

su per cil i ous (sü′pər sil′ē əs), *adj.* haughty, proud, and contemptuous; disdainful; showing scorn or indifference because of a feeling of superiority. [< Latin *superciliosus* < *supercilium* eyebrow, pride < *super-* above + *-cilium* (< *celare* to cover, conceal)] —**su′per cil′i ous ly,** *adv.* —**su′per cil′i ous ness,** *n.*

su per flu i ty (sü′pər flü′ə tē), *n., pl.* **-ties. 1** a greater amount than is needed; excess. **2** something not needed.

su per flu ous (sù pèr′flü əs), *adj.* needless; unnecessary. [< Latin *superfluus,* ultimately < *super-* over + *fluere* to flow] —**su per′flu ous ly,** *adv.* —**su per′flu ous ness,** *n.*

sup pli ant (sup′lē ənt), *n.* person who asks humbly and earnestly. [< Middle French, present participle of *supplier* supplicate]

sup pli ca tion (sup′lə kā′shən), *n.* **1** a supplicating. **2** Usually, **supplications,** *pl.* a humble prayer addressed to God or a deity.

sur e ty (shûr′ə tē), *n., pl.* **-ties.** person who agrees to be legally responsible for the debt, default, etc., of another.

sur feit (sėr′fit), *n.* disgust or nausea caused by too much of anything. [< Old French *surfait,* originally, overdone < *sur-* over + *faire* to do]

sur mise (sər mīz′, sėrmīz), *n.* formation of an idea with little or no evidence; a guessing. [< Old French, accusation, ultimately < *sur-* upon + *mettre* to put]

sus cep ti ble (sə sep′tə bəl), *adj.* **1** easily influenced by feelings or emotions; very sensitive. **2 susceptible of,** capable of receiving, undergoing, or being affected by. [< Late Latin *susceptibilis,* ultimately < Latin *sub-* up + *capere* to take] —**sus cep′ti ble ness,** *n.* —**sus cep′ti bly,** *adv.*

sward (swôrd), *n.* a grassy surface; turf. [Old English *sweard* skin]

swarth y (swôr′ᴛʜē, swôr′thē), *adj.,* **swarth i er, swarth i-est.** having a dark skin. —**swarth′i ly,** *adv.* —**swarth′i-ness,** *n.*

swell (swel), *v.,* **swelled, swelled** or **swol len, swell ing,** *n.,* *adj.* —*v.i., v.t.* become or make proud or conceited. [Old English *swellan*]

sylph (silf), *n.* **1** a slender, graceful girl or woman. **2** a spirit of

the air. [< New Latin *sylphes,* plural; a coinage of Paracelsus]
—**sylph′like′** *adj.*
syn a gogue or **syn a gog** (sin′ə gôg, sin′ə gog), *n.* **1** building used by Jews for reglious worship and instruction. **2** a Jewish congregation. [< Greek *synagōgē* assembly, ultimately < *syn-* together + *agein* bring]

a hat	i it	oi oil	ch child	⎧a in about
ā age	ī ice	ou out	ng long	e in taken
ä far	o hot	u cup	sh she	ə = ⎨ i in pencil
e let	ō open	ù put	th thin	o in lemon
ē equal	ô order	ü rule	ŦH then	⎩u in circus
ėr term			zh measure	< = derived from

tab er nac le (tab′ər nak′əl), *n.* **1** a temporary dwelling; tent. **2** recess covered with a canopy and used as a shrine. **3** container for something holy or precious. [< Latin *tabernaculum* tent < *taberna* cabin]
tac i turn (tas′ə tèrn′), *adj.* speaking very little; not fond of talking. [< Latin *taciturnus* < *tacitum* unspoken, tacit] —**tac′i-turn′ly,** *adv.*
tac ti cian (tak tish′ən), *n.* an expert in tactics.
ta'en (tān), *v.* ARCHAIC. taken.
tan gi ble (tan′jə bəl), *adj.* **1** that can be touched or felt by touch. **2** real; actual; definite. **3** whose value can be accurately appraised. [< Late Latin *tangibilis* < *tangere* to touch] —**tan′gi-bil′i ty,** *n.* —**tan′gi ble ness,** *n.* —**tan′gi bly,** *adv.*
tar an tel la (tar′ən tel′ə), *n.* **1** a rapid, whirling southern Italian dance in very quick rhythm, usually performed by a single couple. **2** music for this dance. [< Italian < *Taranto,* the seaport]
tar nish (tär′nish), *v.t.* **1** dull the luster or brightness of. **2** bring disgrace upon (a reputation, one's honor, etc.); sully; taint. —*v.i.* lose luster or brightness. —*n.* **1** loss of luster or brightness. **2** a discolored coating, especially on silver. [< Middle French *terniss-,* a form of *ternir* to dull] —**tar′nish a ble,** *adj.*
tar ry (tar′ē), *v.,* **-ried, -ry ing.** —*v.i.* delay leaving; remain; stay. —*v.t.* ARCHAIC. wait for. [Middle English *tarien*] —**tar′ri er,** *n.*
taw dry (tô′drē), *adj.,* **-dri er, -dri est.** showy and cheap; gaudy; garish. [short for *(Sain)t Audrey('s lace),* sold at the fair of Saint Audrey in Ely, England] —**taw′dri ly,** *adv.* —**taw′dri-ness,** *n.*
taw ny (tô′nē), *adj.,* **-ni er, -ni est,** *n., pl.* **-nies.** —*adj.* brownish-yellow. —*n.* a brownish yellow. [< Old French *tane,* past participle of *taner* to tan] —**taw′ni ly,** *adv.* —**taw′ni ness,** *n.*
te mer i ty (tə mer′ə tē), *n.* reckless boldness; rashness; foolhardiness. [< Latin *temeritatem* < *temere* heedlessly]
tem per ance (tem′pər əns), *n.* **1** a being moderate in action, speech, habits, etc.; self-control. **2** a being moderate in the use of alcoholic drinks. **3** the principle and practice of not using alcoholic drinks at all.
tem por al (tem′pər əl), *adj.* **1** of time. **2** lasting for a time only; temporary. **3** of this life only; earthly. **4** not religious or sacred; worldly; secular. [< Latin *temporalis* < *tempus* time] —**tem′por al ly,** *adv.* —**tem′por al ness,** *n.*
te nac i ty (ti nas′ə tē), *n.* **1** firmness in holding fast. **2** stubbornness; persistence.
ten ure (ten′yər), *n.* **1** a holding or possessing. **2** length of time of holding or possessing. **3** manner of holding land, buildings, etc., from a feudal lord or superior. **4** conditions, terms, etc., on which anything is held or occupied. **5** permanent status, granted after a period of trial, especially to a member of a faculty. [< Old French, ultimately < Latin *tenere* to hold]
ter res tri al (tə res′trē əl), *adj.* of the earth; not of the heavens. [< Latin *terrestris* < *terra* earth] —**ter res′tri al ly,** *adv.*
ter tian (tèr′shən), *n.* fever, such as malaria, which recurs every other day. [< Latin *tertiana (febris)* third (fever)]
tête-à-tête (tāt′ə tāt′), *n.* a private conversation between two people. [< French, head to head]
thwart (thwôrt), *v.t.* prevent from doing something, particularly by blocking the way; oppose and defeat. —*n.* **1** seat across a boat, on which a rower sits. **2** brace between the gunwales of a canoe. —*adj.* lying or passing across. —*adv.* across; crosswise; athwart. [< Scandinavian (Old Icelandic) *thvert* across] —**thwart′er,** *n.*
tim or ous (tim′ər əs), *adj.* **1** easily frightened; timid. **2** characterized by or indicating fear. [< Latin *timor* fear < *timere* to fear] —**tim′or ous ly,** *adv.* —**tim′or ous ness,** *n.*
-tion, *suffix added to verbs to form nouns.* **1** act or process of

_____ing: *Addition* = *act or process of adding.* **2** condition of being _____ed: *Exhaustion* = *condition of being exhausted.* **3** result of _____ing: *Reflection* = *result of reflecting.* [< Latin *-tionem*]
tip pet (tip′it), *n.* **1** scarf for the neck and shoulders with ends hanging down in front. **2** a long, narrow, hanging part of a hood, sleeve, or scarf. **3** band of silk or other material worn around the neck by certain clergymen. [probably < *tip*]
tithe (tīŦH), *n., v.,* **tithed, tith ing.** —*n.* **1** one tenth. **2** one tenth of one's yearly income paid as a donation or tax for the support of the church. **3** a very small part. **4** any small tax, levy, etc. —*v.t.* **1** put a tax or a levy of a tenth on. **2** pay or pledge a tithe on. —*v.i.* give or pledge one tenth of one's income to the church or to charity. [Old English *tēotha* tenth < *tēn* ten] —**tith′er,** *n.*
toi let (toi′lit), *n.* **1** process of dressing. Bathing, combing the hair, and putting on one's clothes are all part of one's toilet. **2** a person's dress; costume. [< Middle French *toilette* a cover for the clothes < *toile* cloth < Latin *tela* web]
To rah or **to rah** (tôr′ə, tōr′ə), *n.* **1** the entire body of Jewish law and tradition. **2** the first five books of the Old Testament; the Pentateuch. **3** scroll on which the Pentateuch is written. [< Hebrew *tōrāh* teaching]
tor sion (tôr′shən), *n.* **1** act or process of twisting. **2** state of being twisted. **3** the twisting or turning of a body by two equal and opposite forces. [< Late Latin *torsionem* < Latin *torquere* to twist]
trac ta ble (trak′tə bəl), *adj.* **1** easily managed or controlled; easy to deal with; docile. **2** easily handled or worked; malleable. [< Latin *tractabilis* < *tractare* to handle] —**trac′ta bil′i ty,** *n.* —**trac′ta ble ness,** *n.* —**trac′ta bly,** *adv.*
tra jec tor y (trə jek′tər ē), *n., pl.* **-tor ies.** the curved path of a projectile, comet, planet, etc. [< Medieval Latin *trajectorius* throwing across, ultimately < Latin *trans-* across + *jacere* to throw]
tram (tram), *n.* **1** BRITISH. streetcar. **2** an overhead or suspended carrier traveling on a cable. [< Middle Dutch *trame* beam] —**tram′less,** *adj.*
tram mel (tram′əl), *v.,* **-meled, -mel ing** or **-melled, -mel -ling.** —*v.t.* **1** hinder; restrain. **2** catch in or as if in a trammel; entangle. [< Old French *tramail* < Late Latin *trimaculum* < Latin *tri-* three + *macula* mesh]
trans-, *prefix.* **1** across; over; through, as in *transcontinental, transmit.* **2** on the other side of; beyond, as in *transatlantic.* **3** in or to a different place, condition, etc., as in *transmigration, transform.* **4** (in chemistry) having certain atoms on the opposite side of a plane: *a trans-isomeric compound.* [< Latin < *trans* across]
trans fix (tran sfiks′), *v.t.* make motionless or helpless (with amazement, terror, grief, etc.). —**trans fix′ion,** *n.*
trans gres sion (trans gresh′ən, tranz gresh′ən), *n.* a transgressing or being transgressed; breaking a law, command, etc.; sin.
tran sient (tran′shənt), *adj.* **1** passing soon; fleeting; not lasting. **2** passing through and not staying long. [< Latin *transientem* going through < *trans-* + *ire* go] —**tran′sient ly,** *adv.*
tra vail (trə vāl′, trav′āl), *n.* **1** toil; labor. **2** trouble, hardship, or suffering. **3** severe pain; agony; torture. **4** the labor and pain of childbirth. —*v.i.* **1** toil; labor. **2** suffer the pains of childbirth; be in labor. [< Old French < Late Latin *trepalium* torture device, ultimately < Latin *tri-* three + *palus* stake]
treach er y (trech′ər ē), *n., pl.* **-er ies.** **1** a breaking of faith; treacherous behavior; deceit. **2** treason. [< Old French *trecherie* < *trechier* to cheat]

tremulous

GLOSSARY

trem u lous (trem′yə ləs), *adj.* **1** trembling; quivering. **2** timid; fearful. **3** that wavers; shaky. [< Latin *tremulus* < *tremere* to tremble] —**trem′u lous ly,** *adv.* —**trem′u lous ness,** *n.*
tri dent (trīd′nt), *n.* a three-pronged spear. —*adj.* three-pronged. [< Latin *tridentem* < *tri-* three + *dentem* tooth]
tripe (trīp), *n.* the walls of the first and second stomachs of an ox, steer, or cow, used as food. [< Old French, entrails]
troth (trôth, trōth), *n.* ARCHAIC. **1** faithfulness or fidelity; loyalty. **2** promise. [Old English *trēowth* < *trēow* faith]
trou ba dour (trü′bə dôr, trü′bə dōr, trü′bə dùr), *n.* one of a class of knightly lyric poets and composers of southern France, eastern Spain, and northern Italy from the 1000s to the 1200s, who wrote mainly about love and chivalry. [< French < Provençal *trobador* < *trobar* compose]
truf fle (truf′əl, trü′fəl), *n.* an edible fungus with a black, warty exterior, that grows underground and varies in size between that of a walnut and that of a potato. It is a native of central and southern Europe. [< Old French *truffe,* ultimately alteration of Latin *tuber* tuber]
trull (trul), *n.* a trollop; strumpet.
tryst (trist), *n.* **1** appointment to meet at a certain time and place, especially one made by lovers. **2** an appointed meeting. [< Old French *triste*]
tulle (tül), *n.* a thin, fine net, usually of silk, used for veils, etc. [< *Tulle,* town in France, where it was first made]
tum brel or **tum bril** (tum′brəl), *n.* cart that carried prisoners to be executed during the French Revolution. [< Old French *tomberel* cart < *tomber* to fall; of Germanic origin]
tu mult (tü′mult, tyü′mult), *n.* **1** noise or uproar; commotion. **2** a violent disturbance or disorder. **3** a violent disturbance of mind or feeling; confusion or excitement. [< Latin *tumultus*]
Tus can (tus′kən), *adj.* of or having to do with Tuscany, its people, or their language. —*n.* **1** native or inhabitant of Tuscany. **2** dialect of Tuscany, regarded as the standard form of Italian.
tus sore (tus′ôr), *n.* seashell pink color.
tu te lage (tü′tl ij, tyü′tl ij), *n.* **1** office or function of a guardian; guardianship; protection. **2** instruction. **3** a being in the charge of a guardian or tutor. [< Latin *tutela* protection]
twain (twān), *n., adj.* ARCHAIC. two. [Old English *twēgen*]

un bow el (un bou′əl), *v.t.* open up; disclose; display.
un couth (un küth′), *adj.* **1** not refined; awkward; clumsy; crude. **2** unusual and unpleasant; strange. [Old English *uncūth* < *un-* + *cūth* known] —**un couth′ly,** *adv.* —**un couth′ness,** *n.*
un mit i ga ble (un mit′i gə bəl), *adj.* not able to be lessened in force or intensity; not able to be appeased.
un ut ter a ble (un ut′ər ə bəl), *adj.* **1** that cannot be expressed in words; unspeakable. **2** that cannot be pronounced. —**un ut′ter a bly,** *adv.*
up braid (up brād′), *v.t.* find fault with; blame; reprove. [Old English *upbregdan* < *up* up + *bregdan* to weave, braid] —**up braid′er,** *n.*
ur chin (ėr′chən), *n.* **1** a small child. **2** a mischievous child. **3** a poor, ragged child. [< Old French *irechon* < Latin *ericius* hedgehog < *er* hedgehog]
urn (ėrn), *n.* **1** vase with a foot or pedestal. Urns were used in ancient Greece and Rome to hold the ashes of the dead. **2** coffeepot or teapot with a faucet, used for making or serving coffee or tea at the table. [< Latin *urna*]
u surp (yü zėrp′, yü sėrp′), *v.t.* seize and hold (power, position, authority, etc.) by force or without right. —*v.i.* commit usurpation. [< Latin *usurpare* < *usu* through use + *rapere* seize] —**u surp′er,** *n.*

vac il late (vas′ə lāt), *v.i.,* **-lat ed, -lat ing. 1** waver in mind or opinion. **2** move first one way and then another; waver. [< Latin *vacillatum* wavered] —**vac′il lat′ing ly,** *adv.* —**vac′il la′tion,** *n.*

vale (vāl), *n.* valley. [< Old French *val* < Latin *vallis*]
van (van), *n.* the front part of an army, fleet, or other advancing group. [short for *vanguard*]
van guard (van′gärd′), *n.* **1** the front part of an army; soldiers marching ahead of the main part of an army to clear the way and guard against surprise. **2** the foremost or leading position. **3** leaders of a movement. [< Old French *avangarde* < *avant* before + *garde* guard]
van quish (vang′kwish, van′kwish), *v.t.* **1** conquer, defeat, or overcome in battle or conflict. **2** overcome or subdue by other than physical means. [< Old French *vainquiss-,* a form of *vainquir* vanquish < Latin *vincere*] —**van′quish a ble,** *adj.* —**van′quish er,** *n.*
var let (vär′lit), *n.* a low, mean fellow; rascal. [< Old French *varlet, vaslet* page, squire < *vassal.* See VASSAL.]
vas sal (vas′əl), *n.* **1** (in the feudal system) a person who held land from a lord or superior, to whom in return he gave homage and allegiance, usually in the form of military service. **2** person in the service of another; servant. [< Old French < Medieval Latin *vassallus* < *vassus* servant; of Celtic origin]
ve he ment (vē′ə mənt), *adj.* **1** having or showing strong feeling; caused by strong feeling; eager; passionate. **2** forceful; violent. [< Latin *vehementem* being carried away < *vehere* carry] —**ve′he ment ly,** *adv.*
ven e ra tion (ven′ə rā′shən), *n.* a feeling of deep respect; reverence.
ver dure (vėr′jər), *n.* **1** fresh greenness. **2** a fresh growth of green grass, plants, or leaves. [< Old French < *verd* green < Latin *viridis* < *virere* be green]
verst (vėrst), *n.* a Russian measure of distance equal to about 3500 feet (1067 meters). [< Russian *versta*]
ver tig i nous (vər tij′ə nəs), *adj.* **1** whirling; rotary; revolving. **2** fickle; unstable. —**ver tig′i nous ly,** *adv.*
ves per (ves′pər), *n.* **1** evening. **2** an evening prayer, hymn, or service. **3** an evening bell. [< Latin]
ves tige (ves′tij), *n.* a slight remnant; trace; mark. [< French < Latin *vestigium* footprint]
vest ment (vest′mənt), *n.* something that covers as a garment; covering. [< Latin *vestis* garment]
ves ture (ves′chər), *n.* covering.
vex (veks), *v.t.* **1** anger by trifles; annoy; provoke. **2** worry; trouble; harass. [< Latin *vexare*] —**vex′ing ly,** *adv.*
vi al (vī′əl), *n.* a small glass or plastic bottle for holding medicines or the like; phial. [variant of *phial*]
vi and (vī′ənd), *n.* **1** article of food. **2 viands,** *pl.* articles of choice food. [< Old French *viande* < Late Latin *vivenda* things for living < Latin, to be lived < *vivere* to live]
vice roy (vīs′roi), *n.* **1** person ruling a country or province as the deputy of the sovereign. **2** an American butterfly whose coloration and markings closely resemble those of the monarch butterfly. [< French *vice-roi* < *vice* vice + *roi* king]
vi cis si tude (və sis′ə tüd, və sis′ə tyüd), *n.* **1** change in circumstances, fortune, etc. **2** change; variation. **3** regular change. [< Latin *vicissitudo* < *vicis* turn, change]
vie (vī), *v.i.,* **vied, vy ing.** strive for superiority; contend in rivalry; compete. [short for Middle French *envier* to wager, challenge < Latin *invitare* invite] —**vi′er,** *n.*
vig il (vij′əl), *n.* a staying awake for some purpose; a watching; watch. [< Latin *vigilia* < *vigil* watchful]
vile (vīl), *adj.,* **vil er, vil est. 1** very bad. **2** foul; disgusting; obnoxious. **3** evil; low; immoral. [< Latin *vilis* cheap] —**vile′ly,** *adv.* —**vile′ness,** *n.*
vin di ca tion (vin′də kā′shən), *n.* a vindicating or a being vindicated; defense; justification.
vint ner (vint′nər), *n.* dealer in wine; wine merchant.
vir tu os i ty (vėr′chü os′ə tē), *n., pl.* **-ties.** character or skill of a virtuoso.
vir tu o so (vėr′chü ō′sō), *n., pl.* **-sos, -si** (-sē), *adj.* —*n.* person skilled in the techniques of an art, especially in playing a musical instrument. —*adj.* showing the artistic qualities and skills of a virtuoso. [< Italian, learned, virtuous]
vis age (viz′ij), *n.* **1** face. **2** appearance or aspect. [< Old French < *vis* face < Latin *visus* sight < *videre* to see]

1046

vis cid (vis′id), *adj.* thick like heavy syrup or glue; sticky; viscous. [< Late Latin *viscidus* < Latin *viscum* birdlime] —**vis′cid ly,** *adv.* —**vis′cid ness,** *n.*

vis cous (vis′kəs), *adj.* **1** thick like heavy syrup or glue; sticky. **2** having the property of viscosity. [< Latin *viscosus* < *viscum* birdlime] —**vis′cous ly,** *adv.* —**vis′cous ness,** *n.*

vo lup tu ar y (və lup′chü er′ē), *n., pl.* **-ar ies,** *adj.* —*n.* person who cares much for luxurious or sensual pleasures.

vo lup tu ous (və lup′chü əs), *adj.* caring much for the pleasures of the senses. [< Latin *voluptuosus* < *voluptas* pleasure] —**vo lup′tu ous ly,** *adv.* —**vo lup′tu ous ness,** *n.*

vo tar y (vō′tər ē), *n., pl.* **-tar ies.** **1** person bound by vows to a religious life; monk or nun. **2** person devoted to something; devotee. [< Latin *votum* vow]

vouch safe (vouch sāf′), *v.t.,* **-safed, -saf ing.** be willing to grant or give; deign (to do or give).

vul pine (vul′pīn, vul′pən), *adj.* of or like a fox; cunning; sly. [< Latin *vulpinus* < *vulpes* fox]

wail (wāl), *v.i.* lament; mourn. —*v.t.* **1** grieve for or because of; bewail. **2** utter (a wailing cry, bad news, etc.). [< Scandinavian (Old Icelandic) *væla*] —**wail′er,** *n.*

wane (wān), *v.,* **waned, wan ing,** *n.* —*v.i.* **1** lose size; become smaller gradually. **2** decline in strength or intensity. **3** draw to a close. —*n.* act or process of waning. [Old English *wanian*]

wan gle (wang′gəl), *v.,* **-gled, -gling.** INFORMAL. —*v.t.* manage to get by schemes, tricks, persuasion, etc. [origin uncertain] —**wan′gler,** *n.*

wan ton (won′tən), *adj.* **1** reckless, heartless, or malicious. **2** without reason or excuse. **3** not moral; not chaste. **4** frolicsome; playful. **5** not restrained. —*n.* a wanton person. —*v.i.* act in a wanton manner. —*v.t.* waste foolishly; squander. [Middle English *wantowen* < Old English *wan-* not, lacking + *togen* brought up] —**wan′ton ly,** *adv.* —**wan′ton ness,** *n.*

wast rel (wā′strəl), *n.* **1** spendthrift. **2** an idle, disreputable person; good-for-nothing.

wa ver (wā′vər), *v.i.* **1** move to and fro; flutter. **2** vary in intensity; flicker. **3** be undecided; hesitate. **4** become unsteady; begin to give way. —*n.* act of wavering. [ultimately < *wave*] —**wa′ver er,** *n.* —**wa′ver ing ly,** *adv.*

weal (wēl), *n.* well-being; prosperity. [Old English *wela* wealth, welfare]

wean (wēn), *v.t.* accustom (a person) to do without something; cause to turn away. [Old English *wenian*]

weed (wēd), *n.* **1 weeds,** *pl.* mourning garments. **2** ARCHAIC. garment. [Old English *wǣd*]

ween (wēn), *v.t., v.i.* ARCHAIC. think; suppose; believe; expect. [Old English *wēnan*]

wel kin (wel′kən), *n.* ARCHAIC. the sky; the vault of heaven. [Old English *wolcen* cloud]

well a day (wel′ə dā′), *interj.* ARCHAIC. alas!

wel ter (wel′tər), *v.i.* (of waves, the water, or sea) surge. —*n.* **1** a rolling or tumbling about. **2** a surging or confused mass. [< Middle Dutch and Middle Low German *welteren*]

wend (wend), *v.,* **wend ed** or **went, wend ing.** —*v.t.* direct (one's way). —*v.i.* go. [Old English *wendan*]

weth er (weŦH′ər), *n.* a castrated ram. [Old English]

whelp (hwelp), *n.* **1** puppy or cub; young dog, wolf, bear, lion, tiger, etc. **2** an impudent young person. —*v.i., v.t.* give birth to (whelps). [Old English *hwelp*]

wher ry (hwer′ē), *n., pl.* **-ries.** **1** a light, shallow rowboat for carrying passengers and goods on rivers, used especially in England. **2** a light rowboat for one person, used for racing. **3** any of several types of boats used locally in England, such as a barge, fishing vessel, sailboat, etc. [origin unknown]

whet (hwet), *v.,* **whet ted, whet ting,** *n.* —*v.t.* sharpen by rubbing. [Old English *hwettan*] —**whet′ter,** *n.*

a hat	**i** it	**oi** oil	**ch** child		a in about
ā age	**ī** ice	**ou** out	**ng** long		e in taken
ä far	**o** hot	**u** cup	**sh** she	ə =	i in pencil
e let	**ō** open	**ů** put	**th** thin		o in lemon
ē equal	**ô** order	**ü** rule	**ŦH** then		u in circus
ėr term			**zh** measure	**<** = derived from

whorl (hwėrl, hwôrl), *n.* anything that circles or turns on or around something else. People can be identified by the whorls of their fingerprints. [Middle English *whorle,* apparently variant of *whirl*]

wight (wīt), *n.* ARCHAIC. a human being; person. [Old English *wiht*]

will ful (wil′fəl), *adj.* **1** wanting or taking one's own way; stubborn. **2** done on purpose; intended. —**will′ful ly,** *adv.* —**will′ful ness,** *n.*

win now (win′ō), *v.t.* **1** blow off the chaff from (grain); drive or blow away (chaff). **2** sort out; separate; sift. **3** fan (with wings); flap (wings). —*v.i.* blow chaff from grain. [Old English *windwian* < *wind* wind]

with ers (wiŦH′ərz), *n.pl.* the highest part of a horse's or other animal's back, between the shoulder blades.

wiz ened (wiz′nd, wē′znd), *adj.* dried up; withered; shriveled. [Old English *wisnian* dry up, shrivel]

wraith (rāth), *n.* **1** ghost of a person seen before or soon after the person's death. **2** specter; ghost. [origin uncertain] —**wraith′like′,** *adj.*

wretch (rech), *n.* **1** a very unfortunate or unhappy person. **2** a very bad person. [Old English *wrecca* exile]

wroth (rôth, roth), *adj.* angry. [Old English *wrāth*]

wrought (rôt), *v.* ARCHAIC. a pt. and a pp. of **work.** —*adj.* **1** made. **2** formed with care; not rough or crude. **3** manufactured or treated; not in a raw state. **4** (of metals or metalwork) formed by hammering.

wry (rī), *adj.,* **wri er, wri est.** **1** turned to one side; twisted. **2** ironic. [ultimately < Old English *wrīgian* to turn] —**wry′ly,** *adv.* —**wry′ness,** *n.*

ye shi va (yə shē′və), *n., pl.* **ye shi vas, ye shi voth** (yə shē′vōt′). **1** a Jewish school for higher studies, often a rabbinical seminary. **2** a Jewish elementary school or high school in which both religious and secular subjects are taught. [< Hebrew *yĕshībā,* literally, a sitting]

yew (yü), *n.* **1** any of a genus of evergreen coniferous trees, especially a common species of Europe and Asia having heavy, elastic wood. **2** the wood of this tree, especially as the material of bows. **3** an archer's bow made of this. [Old English *īw*]

yoke (yōk), *n., v.,* **yoked, yok ing.** —*n.* **1** a wooden frame to fasten two work animals together. **2** something that holds people in slavery or submission. **3** rule; dominion. [Old English *geoc*] —**yoke′less,** *adj.*

Yom Kip pur (yom kip′ər, yom ki pùr′), a Jewish fast day of atonement for sins; Day of Atonement. It occurs ten days after Rosh Hashanah, the Jewish New Year. [< Hebrew *yōm kippūr* day of atonement]

zeal (zēl), *n.* eager desire or effort; earnest enthusiasm; fervor. [< Latin *zelus* < Greek *zēlos*]

zeal ous (zel′əs), *adj.* full of zeal; eager; earnest; enthusiastic. [< Medieval Latin *zelosus* < Latin *zelus* zeal < Greek *zēlos*] —**zeal′ous ly,** *adv.* —**zeal′ous ness,** *n.*

ze nith (zē′nith), *n.* **1** the point in the heavens directly overhead; point opposite the nadir. **2** the highest point; apex. [< Old French or Medieval Latin *cenith* < Arabic *samt (ar-rās)* the way (over the head)]

GLOSSARY

INDEX OF AUTHORS, TRANSLATORS, AND TITLES

INDEX OF FEATURES

INDEX OF LITERATURE SKILLS

INDEX OF THINKING SKILLS

INDEX OF VOCABULARY EXERCISES

INDEX OF COMPOSITION ASSIGNMENTS

INDEX OF ENRICHMENT ACTIVITIES

INDEX OF GENRES

INDEX OF THEMES

This index is partly based on the "Themes in World Literature" articles appearing on pages 104–105, 263–264, 363–364, 483–484, 593–594, 695–696, 831–832, and 930–931. Selections are shown in the order in which they appear in the text. Many selections are shown under more than one theme. A few works are omitted. The date in parentheses following most works is either the date of composition (indicated by an asterisk), the date of publication, or, in the case of plays, the date of the first performance.

INDEX OF GRAPHIC AIDS

INDEX OF ARTISTS

TEXT ACKNOWLEDGMENTS

UNIT 1

9 Excerpts from *The Epic of Gilgamesh*, translated with an introduction by N. K. Sandars (Penguin Classics, 1960, 1964), pp. 61, 94–96, 108–113, 114 and 116–117. Copyright © 1960, 1964 by N. K. Sandars. Reprinted by permission of Penguin Books Ltd. **17–18** from "A Dialogue of a Man with His Soul" and "Akhenaton's Hymn to the Sun" from *Most Ancient Verse* selected and translated by Thorkild Jacobsen and John A. Wilson, with an introduction by David Grene, The Oriental Institute of The University of Chicago, The University of Chicago Press, Chicago, Illinois. Copyright © 1963 The University of Chicago (Oriental Institute), pp. 35, 37, 45, 47. Reprinted by permission. **20** "I Was Simply Off to See Nefrus My Friend" and "I Think I'll Go Home and Lie Very Still" by John L. Foster from *Love Songs of the New Kingdom*. Copyright © 1974 John L. Foster. Reprinted with the permission of Charles Scribner's Sons, a div. of Macmillan, Inc. **44** "Lament for His Son" from *The Epic of the Kings* trans. by Reuben Levy. Reprinted by permission of Ehsan Yarshater, Columbia University. **47** From *The Rubaiyat of Omar Khayyam* trans. by Edward FitzGerald and E. H. Whinfield, prose version by Justin Huntly McCarthy. Copyright 1932 by Walter J. Black, Inc. Reprinted by permission. Excerpts from *The Rubaiyyat of Omar Khayaam* translated by Robert Graves and Omar Ali-Shah. Copyright © 1967 by Robert Graves and Omar Ali-Shah. Reprinted by permission of A. P. Watt, Ltd. From *The Ruba'iyat of Omar Khayyam* translated by Peter Avery and John Heath-Stubbs (Penguin Classics, 1979). Copyright © 1979 by Peter Avery and John Heath-Stubbs. Reprinted by permission of Penguin Books Ltd. **48–49** "The Man Who Fled from Azrael," "The Elephant in the Dark House," and "The Soul of Goodness in Things Evil" from *Rumi Poet and Mystic* by Rumi, translated by Reynold A. Nicholson. Reprinted by permission of George Allen & Unwin Ltd. **49** Excerpt by Peter Avery from the introduction to *The Ruba'iyat of Omar Khayyam* translated by Peter Avery and John Heath-Stubbs. Penguin Books, 1981. **50** "The Greek and the Chinese Artists, on the Difference Between Theologians and Mystics" from *Tales from the Masnavi* translated by A. J. Arberry. Copyright © 1961 by George Allen & Unwin, Ltd. Reprinted by permission. **52** Excerpts from *The Gulistan or Rose Garden of Sadi* translated by Edward Rehatsek, edited by W. G. Archer. Copyright © 1964 by George Allen & Unwin Ltd. Reprinted by permission of G. P. Putnam's Sons and Unwin & Hyman Ltd. **54** "If That Shirazi Turk . . . ," translated by R. H. Rehder cited in *Anthology of Islamic Literature* by James Kritzeck, New American Library, 1964. "The Crier" from *Fifty Poems of Hafiz* ed. by A. J. Arberry. Reprinted by permission of Cambridge University Press. **58** "Hymn of the Thoughts of Men" from *Hymns from the Rig-Veda*, translated and introduced by Jean Le Mee. Text copyright © 1975 by Jean Le Mee. Reprinted by permission of Alfred A. Knopf, Inc. and Jonathan Cape Ltd. **58–59** "Night" and "Prayer in Sickness" from *Ancient Poetry from China, Japan & India* rendered into English verse by Henry W. Wells. Copyright © 1968 by the University of South

Carolina Press. Reprinted by permission. **60** From the *Bhagavad Gita* translated by Juan Mascaró (Penguin Classics, 1962). Copyright © 1962 by Juan Mascaró. Reprinted by permission. **62** Excerpts from *Shakuntala* translated by A. W. Ryder (Everyman's Library). Reprinted by permission of J. M. Dent & Sons Ltd., Publishers. **64** F. G. Talbot, *Memoirs of Babur Emperor of India: First of the Great Moghuls*. London: Arthur L. Humphrey's, 1909. **75** Excerpts from *The Analects of Confucius* translated by Arthur Waley. Copyright 1938 by George Allen & Unwin Ltd. Reprinted by permission of Macmillan Publishing Company and George Allen & Unwin Ltd. **76** Excerpts from *Chuang Tzu* translated by Burton Watson. Copyright © 1964 Columbia University Press. Reprinted by permission. **79** "I Built My Cottage Among the Habitations of Men" from An *Introduction to Chinese Literature* by Liu Wu-chi, pg. 64. Copyright © 1966 by Liu Wu-chi. Reprinted by permission of Indiana University Press. "Two Poems on Returning to Dwell in the Country" translated by William Acker from *T'ao the Hermit: Sixty Poems by T'ao Ch'ien*. Reprinted by permission of the publisher, The Vanguard Press, Inc. and Thames and Hudson Ltd. **83** Excerpts from "Lu Chi: Wen Fu (The Art of Writing)" translated and with an introduction by Sam Hamill from Breitenbush. Copyright © 1987 by Sam Hamill. Reprinted by permission. **84** "The River-Merchant's Wife: A Letter" by Ezra Pound, *Personae*. Copyright 1926 by Ezra Pound. Reprinted by permission of New Directions Publishing Corporation and Faber and Faber Limited. "Addressed Humorously to Tu Fu" from *The Works of Li Po* by Li Po, translated by Shigeyoshi Obata. Copyright 1922 by E. P. Dutton, renewed 1950 by E. P. Dutton. Reprinted by permission of the publisher, E. P. Dutton, a division of NAL Penguin Inc. **85** "Fighting South of the Ramparts" from *The Poetry and Career of Li Po* by Arthur Waley. Copyright 1956 by Allen & Unwin Ltd. Reprinted by permission. **86** "Parting at a Wine-Shop in Nan-king" from *The Jade Mountain: A Chinese Anthology*, translated by Witter Bynner from the texts of Kiang Kang-Hu. Copyright 1929 and renewed 1957 by Alfred A. Knopf, Inc. Reprinted by permission of Alfred A. Knopf, Inc. **87** "Sent to Li Po as a Gift" from *Fir Flower Tablets* edited by Amy Lowell and translated by Florence Ayscough. Copyright 1921 by Florence Ayscough and Amy Lowell. Copyright renewed 1949. Reprinted by permission of Houghton Mifflin Company. "A Night Abroad" from *The Jade Mountain: A Chinese Anthology*, translated by Witter Bynner from the texts of Kiang Kang-Hu. Copyright 1929 and renewed 1957 by Alfred A. Knopf, Inc. Reprinted by permission of Alfred A. Knopf, Inc. **88** From *Translations from the Chinese*, translation with preface by Arthur Waley. Copyright 1919 and renewed 1947 by Arthur Waley. Reprinted by permission of Alfred A. Knopf, Inc. and Unwin Hyman Ltd. **94** Excerpts from *The Pillow Book of Sei Shonagon* translated and edited by Ivan Morris. Copyright © 1967 by Ivan Morris. Reprinted by permission of Oxford University Press. **95** Excerpt from "The Diary of Murasaki Shikibu" pp. 134–135 from *Diaries of Court*

Ladies of Old Japan, edited and translated by Annie Shepley Omori and Kocki Doi, published by Kenkyusha Ltd., Tokyo, 1935. Reprinted by permission. **98** "The Damask Drum" attributed to Seami, translated by Arthur Waley. Copyright © 1957 by Arthur Waley. Reprinted by permission of Grove Press, Inc. and Unwin Hyman Ltd. **101** From *Anthology of Japanese Literature*, edited by Donald Keene, pp. 258–259. Copyright © 1955 by Grove Press. Reprinted by permission of Georges Borchardt, Inc. for the Estate of Ivan Morris. **102** Nine Haiku Poems by Basho from *An Introduction to Haiku* edited by Harold G. Henderson. Copyright © 1958 by Harold G. Henderson. Reprinted by permission of Doubleday & Company, Inc.

UNIT 2

126 Excerpts from Homer's *The Odyssey* translated by Robert Fitzgerald. Copyright © 1961 by Robert Fitzgerald. Reprinted by permission of Doubleday & Company, Inc. and William Heinemann Ltd. **155** Excerpt from *The Odyssey of Homer* translated by Richmond Lattimore. Copyright © 1965, 1967 by Richmond Lattimore. Reprinted by permission of Harper & Row, Publishers, Inc. **156** "Loss of Shield" by Archilochus, translated by Richmond Lattimore from *Greek Lyrics*, 1960, p. 75. Copyright © 1960 by The University of Chicago. Reprinted by permission. **156–158** Excerpts from *Archilochus, Sappho, Alkman: Three Lyric Poets of the Late Greek Bronze Age* translated by Guy Davenport. Copyright © 1980 by The Regents of the University of California. Reprinted by permission. **158** "The Doublecross" translated by Willis Barnstone from *Greek Lyric Poetry*. Copyright © 1962, 1967 by Willis Barnstone. Reprinted by permission of Schocken Books, Inc. **159** From *Greek Lyric Poetry* translated by Willis Barnstone. Copyright © 1962, 1967 by Willis Barnstone. Reprinted by permission of Schocken Books Inc. **165** "Oedipus the King," from *The Three Theban Plays* by Sophocles, translated by Robert Fagles. Copyright © 1977, 1979, 1982 by Robert Fagles. All rights reserved. Reprinted by permission of Viking Penguin, Inc. **214** "Pericles' Funeral Oration" from *The History of the Peloponnesian War* by Thucydides, translated by Rex Warner (Penguin Classics, 1954, 1972), pp. 143–151. Copyright 1954, 1972 by Rex Warner. Reprinted by permission of Penguin Books Ltd. **221** "Apology" reprinted from *The Dialogues of Plato* translated by Benjamin Jowett (4th ed. 1953) by permission of Oxford University Press. **230** Excerpt from *Cicero: On Old Age and On Friendship* translated by Frank O. Copley. Copyright © 1967 by The University of Michigan. Reprinted by permission. **234** From *Catullus: The Complete Poems for American Readers* translated by Reney Myers and Robert J. Ormsby. Copyright © 1970 by Reney Myers and Robert J. Ormsby. Reprinted by permission of the publisher, E. P. Dutton, a division of NAL Penguin Inc. **235** From *Catullus* translated by G. P. Goold. Copyright © 1983 by G. P. Goold. Reprinted by permission of Gerald Duckworth & Company Ltd. **238** Excerpts from *The Odes and Ephodes of Horace* translation by Joseph P. Clancy, pp. 35, 37, 54, 76, 106. Copyright © 1960 by The University of Chicago Press. Reprinted by permission. **242** Rolfe Humphries, trans., *The Aeneid of Virgil*. New York: Charles Scribner's Sons. **254** Excerpts from *Metamorphoses* by Ovid, pp. 61–64 and 84–86 translated by Rolfe Humphries. Copyright © 1955 by Indiana University Press. Reprinted by permission. **258** Excerpt from *The Annals of Tacitus—An English Translation* by George Gilbert Ramsay. Reprinted by permission of John Murray, Ltd. **265** Excerpts from Homer's *The Odyssey* translated by Robert Fitzgerald. Copyright © 1961 by Robert Fitzgerald. Reprinted by permission of Doubleday & Company, Inc. and William Heinemann Ltd.

UNIT 3

284 Excerpts from *The Song of Roland* translated by Dorothy L. Sayers. Copyright © 1957 by Executors of Dorothy L. Sayers. Reprinted by permission of David Higham Associates Limited. **297** "The Lay of the Werewolf" from *Lays of Marie de France and Other French Legends* translated by Eugene Mason (Everyman's Library). Reprinted by permission of J. M. Dent & Sons Ltd., Publishers. **301** From *Fables From Old French: Aesop's Beasts and Bumpkins* translated by Norman R. Shapiro. Copyright © 1982 by Norman R. Shapiro. Reprinted by permission of Wesleyan University Press. **305** "The Lay of Thrym" from *The Elder Edda* translated by W. H. Auden and Paul B. Taylor. Copyright © 1969 by W. H. Auden and Paul B. Taylor. Reprinted by permission of Curtis Brown Ltd. **308** "Thorstein the Staff-Struck" from *Hrafnkel's Saga and Other Icelandic Stories*, translated with an introduction by Hermann Palsson (Penguin Classics, 1971), pp. 72–81. Copyright © 1970 by Hermann Palsson. Reprinted by permission of Penguin Books Ltd. **316** From the *Inferno* by Dante Alighieri, translated by John Ciardi. Copyright 1954, 1982 by John Ciardi. Reprinted by arrangement with NAL Penguin Inc., New York, NY and by permission of the Estate of John Ciardi. **325** From Dante's *Inferno* translated by Dorothy L. Sayers. Copyright 1949 by the Estate of Dorothy L. Sayers. Reprinted by permission of David Higham Associates Limited. From *The Divine Comedy of Dante Alighieri: Inferno*, translated by Allen Mandelbaum. English translation copyright © 1980 by Allen Mandelbaum. Reprinted by permission of Bantam Books. All rights reserved. **340** Excerpts from *The Story of Sir Gawain and the Green Knight* translated by M. R. Ridley. Reprinted by permission of William Heinemann Ltd. **359** John Gardner, *The Complete Works of the Gawain-Poet*. Chicago: The University of Chicago Press, 1965. Brian Stone, "The Common Enemy of Man" from *Sir Gawain and the Green Knight*. London: Penguin Books, Ltd., 1959. **360** Heinrich Zimmer, *The King & the Corpse: Tales of the Soul's Conquest of Evil*. Princeton, New Jersey: Princeton University Press, 1957. **365** From the *Inferno* by Dante Alighieri, translated by John Ciardi. Copyright 1954, 1982 by John Ciardi. Reprinted by arrangement with NAL Penguin Inc., New York, NY and by permission of the Estate of John Ciardi.

UNIT 4

381 "It Was the Morning" and "Blest Be the Day" by Francis Petrarch, translated by Joseph Auslander from *The Continental Edition of World Masterpieces*, vol. 1, Maynard Mack, ed. New York: W. W. Norton & Company, Inc., 1956. **382–383** "Alas, That Gentle Look," "Life Hurries On," and "Go, Grieving Rimes of Mine" from *Petrarch and His World*, translations and text by Morris Bishop. Copyright © 1963 by Indiana University Press. Reprinted by permission of Indiana University Press. "The Eyes I Spoke of Once" and

"I Keep Lamenting Over Days Gone By" used by permission from *Petrarch: Selected Poems*, English translation by Anthony Mortimer. Copyright © 1977 by The University of Alabama Press. **385** "Love who within my thought does live and reign" from *Petrarch: Sonnets & Songs* translated by Anna Maria Armi. New York: AMS Press, Inc. "Love, who reigns in my thought and keeps his principal" from *Petrarch's Lyric Poems* translated by Robert M. Durling. Copyright © 1976 by Robert M. Durling. Reprinted by permission of Harvard University Press. "Love, who within my thoughts still lives and reigns" used by permission from *Petrarch: Selected Poems*, English translation by Anthony Mortimer. Copyright © 1977 by The University of Alabama Press. **388** Excerpt reprinted from *The Decameron* by Giovanni Boccaccio. A Norton Critical Edition, selected, translated, and edited by Mark Musa and Peter E. Bondanella. Copyright © 1977 by W. W. Norton & Company, Inc. Reprinted by permission of W. W. Norton & Company, Inc. **394** From *The Prince* by Machiavelli translated by A. Robert Caponigri. Copyright © 1963 Henry Regnery Company. Reprinted by permission. **403** Andrew Lang, trans., "Of His Lady's Old Age" from *The Poetical Works of Andrew Lang*. London: Longman Group Ltd. "When You Are Old" from *Collected Poems* by William Butler Yeats. Reprinted by permission of A. P. Watt Ltd. on behalf of Michael B. Yeats and Macmillan London Ltd. **406** Excerpts from *Don Quixote* translated by Walter Starkie. Copyright © 1957 by Macmillan & Co., Ltd., London. Reprinted by permission of Macmillan London & Basingstoke. **446** From "Of Cannibals" from *Michel de Montaigne: Selected Essays* trans. by Donald M. Frame. Copyright 1943 by Walter J. Black, Inc. Reprinted by permission.

UNIT 5

509 *The Fables* of Jean de La Fontaine translated by Elizur Wright. **511** "The Camel and the Flotsam" from *The Fables of La Fontaine* translated by Marianne Moore. Copyright 1954 by Marianne Moore, renewed © 1982 by Lawrence E. Brinn and Louise Crane, Executors of the Estate of Marianne Moore. Reprinted by permission of Viking Penguin Inc. "The Camel and the Driftwood" from *Selected Fables and Tales of La Fontaine* translated by Marie Ponsot. Copyright © 1966 by Marie Ponsot. Reprinted by arrangement with NAL Penguin Inc., New York, New York. "The Camel and the Driftwood" by Jean de La Fontaine from *Selected Fables*, translated by Eunice Clark. Reprinted by permission of George Braziller, Inc. **512** *The Fables* of Jean de La Fontaine translated by Elizur Wright. **516** Molière's *Tartuffe*, translated by Richard Wilbur. Copyright © 1961, 1962, 1963 by Richard Wilbur. Reprinted by permission of Harcourt Brace Jovanovich, Inc. Caution: Professionals and amateurs are hereby warned that this translation, being fully protected under the copyright laws of the United States of America, the British Empire, including the Dominion of Canada, and all other countries which are signatories to the Universal Copyright Convention and the International Copyright Union, is subject to royalty. All rights, including professional, amateur, motion picture, recitation, lecturing, public reading, radio broadcasting, and television, are strictly reserved. Inquiries on professional rights should be addressed to Mr. Gilbert Parker, Curtis Brown Ltd, 10 Astor Place, New York NY 10003. Inquiries on translation rights should be addressed to Harcourt Brace Jovanovich, Inc., Copyrights and Permissions Department, Orlando, FL 32887. **572** Excerpt from *The Flamingo's Smile: Reflections in Natural History* by Stephen Jay Gould. Copyright © 1985 by Stephen Jay Gould. Reprinted by permission of W. W. Norton & Company, Inc. **575** From *Candide* by Voltaire, translated by Tobias Smollett, rev. by James Thornton, published by E. P. Dutton & Co., Inc., New York and J. M. Dent and Sons, Ltd., London. **595** From *Montesquieu: The Persian Letters*, edited and translated by J. Robert Loy (Columbus, Ohio: World Publishing Company, 1961). Reprinted by permission of Anna Gerbeth for the estate of J. Robert Loy.

UNIT 6

609 Excerpts from *Goethe's Faust*, parts I and II translated by F. Louis MacNeice. Copyright 1951 by Louis MacNeice; copyright renewed 1979 by Hedli MacNeice. Reprinted by permission of Oxford University Press, Inc. and Faber and Faber Ltd. **619** "My Songs, You Say" from *Heinrich Heine: Paradox and Poet, The Poems* by Louis Untermeyer. Copyright 1937 by Harcourt Brace Jovanovich, Inc.; renewed 1965 by Louis Untermeyer. Reprinted by permission of the publisher. "The Loreley" and "The Silesian Weavers" by Heinrich Heine, translated by Aaron Kramer from *The Poetry and Prose of Heinrich Heine*, selected and edited with an introduction by Frederic Ewen. Copyright 1948 by The Citadel Press. Reprinted by permission of The Citadel Press, Inc. **621** "Ich weiss nicht, was soll es bedeuten" from *Poems of Heinrich Heine* by Louis Untermeyer. Copyright 1923, 1952 by Louis Untermeyer. Reprinted by permission of Harcourt Brace Jovanovich, Inc. Excerpt from "The Homecoming 1823–1824" from The Complete Poems of Heinrich Heine translated by Hal Draper. Copyright © 1982 by Hal Draper. Reprinted by permission of Suhrkamp Publishers. Heinrich Heine, "Ich weiss nicht was soll es bedeuten" translated by Alexander Macmillan. **624** "The Bridegroom" from *The Bronze Horseman and Other Poems* by Alexander Pushkin, translated with an introduction by D. M. Thomas (Penguin Books, 1982), copyright © D. M. Thomas, 1982, pp. 129–135. Reprinted by permission of Penguin Books Ltd. and John Johnson Ltd. **627** "The Prophet" translated by Babette Deutsch from *Two Centuries of Russian Verse* ed. by Avrahm Yarmolinsky. Copyright 1949, © 1965, 1966 by Avrahm Yarmolinsky. Reprinted by permission of Adam Yarmolinsky. **629** "Russia 1812" by Victor Hugo from *Imitations* by Robert Lowell. Copyright © 1958, 1959, 1960, 1961 by Robert Lowell. Reprinted by permission of Farrar, Straus and Giroux, Inc. and Faber and Faber Limited. **632** From *The Diary of a Madman and Other Stories* by Nikolai Gogol, translated by Andrew R. MacAndrew. Copyright © 1960 by Andrew R. MacAndrew. Reprinted by arrangement with NAL Penguin Inc, New York, NY. **661** From *Madame Bovary* by Gustave Flaubert, translated by Mildred Marmur. Copyright © 1964 by Mildred Marmur. Reprinted by arrangement with NAL Penguin Inc., New York, NY. **669** "How Much Land Does a Man Need?" reprinted from *Twenty-Three Tales* by Leo Tolstoy, translated by Louise and Aylmer Maude (1906) by permission of Oxford University Press.

680 Reprinted by permission of the publishers and the Trustees of Amherst College from *The Poems of Emily Dickinson*, edited by Thomas H. Johnson, Cambridge, Mass.: The Belknap Press of Harvard University Press, Copyright 1951, © 1955, 1979, 1983 by The President and Fellows of Harvard College.

UNIT 7
712 "A Doll House" from *The Complete Major Prose Plays* by Henrik Ibsen, translated by Rolf Fjelde. Copyright © 1965, 1970, 1975, by Rolf Fjelde. Reprinted by arrangement with NAL Penguin Inc., New York, NY. **754** "The Kiss" by Anton Chekhov from *The Kiss and Other Stories* translated by R. E. C. Long. **766** "The Artist" by Rabindranath Tagore. Reprinted by Visva-Bharati, Publishing Department, Calcutta. **770** From *C. P. Cavafy: Selected Poems* translated by Edmund Keeley and Philip Sherrard, edited by George Savidis. Copyright © 1972 by Edmund Keeley and Philip Sherrard. Reprinted by permission of Princeton University Press and Chatto & Windus. **775** "The Cadet Picture of My Father" from *Imitations* by Robert Lowell. Copyright © 1958, 1959, 1960, 1961 by Robert Lowell. Reprinted by permission of Farrar, Straus and Giroux, Inc. and Faber and Faber Limited. **776** Excerpt from *Selected Poems of Rainer Maria Rilke* translated from the German by Robert Bly. Copyright © 1981 by Robert Bly. Reprinted by permission of Harper & Row, Publishers, Inc. **778** From *A Portrait of the Artist as a Young Man* by James Joyce. Copyright 1916 by B. W. Huebsch. Copyright 1944 by Nora Joyce. Copyright © 1964 by the Estate of James Joyce. Reprinted by permission of Viking Penguin Inc., Jonathan Cape Ltd. and the Executors of the James Joyce Estate. **785** "The Metamorphosis" translated by Willa and Edwin Muir. Copyright 1948 and renewed 1976 by Schocken Books, Inc. Reprinted from *Franz Kafka: The Complete Stories* by Franz Kafka, edited by Nahum N. Glatzer, by permission of Schocken Books, published by Pantheon Books, a Division of Random House, Inc. and Martin Secker & Warburg Limited. **814** From *Out of Africa* by Isak Dinesen. Copyright 1937 by Random House, Inc. and renewed © 1965 by Rungstedlundfonden. Reprinted by permission of Random House, Inc. and The Rungstedlund Foundation. **820** "Hands Clenched Under My Shawl" by Anna Akhmatova translated by Robert Tracy. Reprinted by permission of Robert Tracy. "Lot's Wife" by Anna Akhmatova from *Walking to Sleep* by Richard Wilbur. Copyright © 1961 by Richard Wilbur. Reprinted by permission of Harcourt Brace Jovanovich, Inc. and Faber and Faber Limited. "Requiem" from *Selected Poems* by Anna Akhmatova, translated by Richard McKane (Penguin Classics, 1969). Copyright © 1969 by Richard McKane. Reprinted by permission of Penguin Books Ltd. **826** "Rocking" from *Selected Poems of Gabriela Mistral* translated by Doris Dana. Copyright © 1961, 1964, 1970, 1971 by Doris Dana. Reprinted by permission of Joan Daves. **827** "Rocking" by Gabriela Mistral translated by Muriel Kittel from *An Anthology of Spanish Poetry from Garcilaso to Garcia Lorca in English Translation with Spanish Originals* edited by Angel Flores, Doubleday & Company, Inc., 1961. Reprinted by permission of Angel Flores. "Rocking" by Gabriela Mistral translated by Seymour Resnick. Reprinted by permission of Seymour Resnick. **827–829** From *Selected Poems of*

Gabriela Mistral translated by Langston Hughes. Copyright © 1957 by Indiana University Press. Reprinted by permission of Joan Daves. **833** "The Little Bouilloux Girl" from *My Mother's House and Sido* by Colette, translated by Una Vicenzo Troubredge and Enid McLeod. Copyright 1953, renewed copyright © 1981 by Farrar, Straus and Giroux, Inc. Reprinted by permission of Farrar, Straus and Giroux, Inc. and Martin Secker & Warburg Limited.

UNIT 8
847 "The Circular Ruins" by Jorge Luis Borges, *Labyrinths*. Copyright © 1962, 1964 by New Directions Publishing Corporation. Reprinted by permission of New Directions and Laurence Pollinger Limited. **855** "And Suddenly It's Evening" by Salvatore Quasimodo translated by A. Michael de Luca from *Selections from Italian Poetry* by A. Michael de Luca and William Guiliano. Copyright © 1966 by Harvey House, Inc. Reprinted by permission of Evelyn Singer Agency. **855** From *The Selected Writings of Salvatore Quasimodo* edited and translated from the Italian by Allen Mandelbaum (Arnold Mondadori Editore). Reprinted by permission of Anvil Press Poetry Ltd., London. **858** "The Old Man" from *Gimpel the Fool* by Isaac Bashevis Singer. Copyright © 1957 by Isaac Bashevis Singer. Reprinted by permission of Farrar, Straus and Giroux, Inc. and Jonathan Cape Ltd. **866** "Cable Ship" by Harry Martinson translated by Richard Vowles from *20th Century Scandinavian Poetry*. Reprinted by permission of Albert Bonniers Förlag. "March Evening" by Harry Martinson translated by Robert Bly from *Friends, You Drank Some Darkness: Three Swedish Poets, Harry Martinson, Gunnar Ekelöf and Tomas Tranströmer* chosen and translated by Robert Bly. Copyright © 1975 by Robert Bly. Copyright © 1970 by the Seventies Press. Swedish text copyright © 1974 by Harry Martinson. Reprinted by permission of Robert Bly. **868** "Such Perfection" from *Malgudi Days* by R. K. Narayan. Copyright © 1982 by R. K. Narayan. Reprinted by permission of Viking Penguin Inc. and William Heinemann Ltd. **874** *Antigone* by Jean Anouilh, adapted and translated by Lewis Galantière. Copyright 1946 by Random House, Inc. and renewed 1974 by Lewis Galantière. Reprinted by permission of Random House, Inc. and Methuen and Company Ltd. **905** Selections from *The Dark Child* by Camara Laye. Copyright 1954, copyright renewed © 1982 by Camara Laye. Reprinted by permission of Farrar, Straus and Giroux, Inc. and Collins Publishers, London. **916** "Parabolic Ballad," from *Antiworlds and the Fifth Ace*, poetry by Andrei Voznesensky. Edited by Patricia Blake and Max Hayward. Copyright © 1963 by Encounter Ltd. Copyright © 1966, 1967 by Basic Books, Inc. Reprinted by permission of the publisher. **920** "I'm Goya" by Andrei Voznesensky translated by Babette Deutsch from *Two Centuries Of Russian Verse* ed. by Avrahm Yarmolinsky. Copyright 1949, © 1965, 1966 by Avrahm Yarmolinsky. Reprinted by permission. "Goya" by Andrei Voznesensky translated by Anselm Hollo from *Red Cats*. Copyright © 1962 by Anselm Hollo. Reprinted by permission of City Lights Books. "I Am Goya," from *Antiworlds and the Fifth Ace*, poetry by Andrei Voznesensky. Edited by Patricia Blake and Max Hayward. Copyright © 1963 by Encounter Ltd. Copyright © 1966, 1967 by Basic Books, Inc. Reprinted by permission of the publisher. "I—Am Goya" from *Voznesensky: Selected Poems* translated by Herbert

HANDBOOK OF LITERARY TERMS

ILLUSTRATION ACKNOWLEDGMENTS

All photographs not credited are the property of Scott, Foresman.

Cover: Bridgeman Art Library/Art Resource, NY.

UNIT 1

1 Alex Greely/Alpha/FPG. **2** (all) Hirmer Fotoarchiv, Munich. **3** (l) Courtesy of the Trustees of the British Museum; (c) Courtesy of The Oriental Institute of The University of Chicago; (r) The Hebrew University, Jerusalem. Photo by Helene Bieberkraut. **7** Erich Lessing/Magnum. **8** Giraudon/Art Resource, NY. **17** Courtesy of the Trustees of the British Museum. **18** Hirmer Fotoarchiv, Munich. **19** Courtesy of the Trustees of the British Museum. **20** Robert Frerck/Odyssey Productions, Chicago. **25** Erich Lessing/Magnum. **29** M.638 f.18 The Pierpont Morgan Library, New York. **33** Courtesy of The Oriental Institute of The University of Chicago. **36** (l) Jehangir Gazdar/Woodfin Camp & Assoc.; (c) Robert Frerck/Odyssey Productions, Chicago; (r) The Seattle Art Museum, Eugene Fuller Memorial Collection, Inll.29. **37** (l) The Metropolitan Museum of Art, Fletcher Fund, 1934; (c) Courtesy of the Freer Gallery of Art, Smithsonian Institution, Washington, D.C. 30.60; (r) Bibliothèque Nationale, Paris. **42** The British Library. **43** (t) The British Library, Royal Asiatic Society loan 5; (c) The British Library; (b) The Metropolitan Museum of Art, Gift of Alexander Smith Cochran, 1913. **47** Courtesy of The Harvard University Art Museums, Arthur M. Sackler Museum, Private Collection. **48** M.500 f. 13 The Pierpoint Morgan Library, New York. **50** The Metropolitan Museum of Art, Rogers Fund, 1918. **56** Jehangir Gazdar/ Woodfin Camp & Assoc. **57** (t) V. Punjabi/Shostal Associates; (b) Roland Michaud/Woodfin Camp & Assoc. **61** Used by permission of the publisher Harry N. Abrams, Inc., NY, from the book *Treasures of the Library of Congress* by Charles A. Goodrum. © 1980 Harry N. Abrams, Inc. All rights reserved. **65** By Courtesy of the Trustees of the Victoria and Albert Museum. **68** (l) Courtesy of the Freer Gallery of Art, Smithsonian Institution, Washington, D.C. 61.22; (c) Andy Bernhaut/FPG; (r) Courtesy of the Trustees of the British Museum. **69** (l) International Society for Educational Information, Inc., Tokyo; (c) National Palace Museum, Taipei, Taiwan, Republic of China; (r) Lee Boltin. **72** The Seattle Art Museum, Eugene Fuller Memorial Collection, 50.120. **74** Courtesy, Field Museum of Natural History, Chicago. **78** Tokyo National Museum. **79** National Palace Museum, Taipei, Taiwan, Republic of China. **81** The Metropolitan Museum of Art, The Sackler Fund, 1969. **83** Honolulu Academy of Arts. **85** Courtesy of the Cultural Relics Bureau, Beijing and The Metropolitan Museum of Art, New York. **89** Courtesy, Museum of Fine Arts, Boston. **93** (t) Collection Kimiko and John Powers. Photo: Fogg Art Museum, Harvard University; (b) The Mary and Jackson Burke Collection. Photo: Otto E. Nelson. **96** The Mary and Jackson Burke Collection, Photo: Otto E. Nelson. **100** Tokyo National Museum. **103** Cliché des Musées Nationaux, Paris. **105** Honolulu Academy of Arts. **107** Courtesy, Museum of Fine Arts, Boston.

UNIT 2

110 (l) Hirmer Fotoarchiv, Munich; (c) Lee Boltin; (r) Scala/Art Resource, NY. **111** (l) Museo Nazionale di Villa Giulia, Rome; (c) Scala/Art Resource, NY.; (r) Roman Baths Museum, Bath, England. Photo by Stephen Bird. **117** Robert Frerck/Odyssey Productions, Chicago. **119** Alinari/Art Resource, NY. **122** Ronald Sheridan/Ancient Art & Architecture Collection. **124, 127, 139, 148** Erich Lessing/ Magnum. **155** Alinari/Art Resource, NY. **157** Courtesy of the Trustees of the British Museum. **159** (t) Ronald Sheridan/Ancient Art & Architecture Collection; (b) The Metropolitan Museum of Art, Fletcher Fund, 1936. **162** Ronald Sheridan/Ancient Art & Architecture Collection. **163** Scala/Art Resource, NY. **167, 170** Courtesy of the Trustees of the British Museum. **173** Staatliche Museen Preussischer Kulturbesitz, Antikenmuseum, Berlin. **174** Courtesy of the Trustees of the British Museum. **177** Alinari/Art Resource, NY. **179** Courtesy of the Trustees of the British Museum. **181** Staatliche Museen Preussischer Kulturbesitz, Antikenmuseum, Berlin. **183** Martin-von-Wagner Museum, University of Würzburg. Photo: K. Oehrlein. **185, 189** Courtesy of the Trustees of the British Museum. **191, 193** Alinari/Art Resource, NY. **203** Museo Archeologico Nazionale, Naples. **207** Bulloz. **211** Staatliche Museen Preussischer Kulturbesitz, Antikenmuseum, Berlin. **213, 215** Scala/Art Resource, NY. **220** Ronald Sheridan/Ancient Art & Architecture Collection. **229, 234, 238** Scala/Art Resource, NY. **241** Musée du Bardo, Tunis. **245** Bibliothèque Nationale, Paris. **250** The Metropolitan Museum of Art, Fletcher Fund, 1956. **255** Städelsches Kunstinstitut, Frankfurt-am-Main. Photo: Ursula Edelmann. **262** Museo della Civiltà Romana. **264** Ronald Sheridan/Ancient Art & Architecture Collection.

UNIT 3

272 (l) Cathedral Treasury, Aachen. Photo by Ann Münchow; (c) The British Library; (r) Werner Forman Archive, London. **273** (l) Bibliothèque Municipale, Boulogne/Weidenfeld & Nicolson Archives; (c) The British Library; (r) The Bodleian Library, Oxford. MS. Bodley 264, folio 218r Marco Polo. **279** Helga Schmidt-Glassner. **280** Scala/Art Resource, NY. **282, 285** Giraudon/Art Resource, NY. **291** Musée Condé, Chantilly. **293** Cathedral Treasury, Aachen. Photo by Ann Münchow. **300** The British Library. **301** M.820 f. 12 The Pierpont Morgan Library, New York. **306** Werner Forman Archive, London. **313** Scala/Art Resource, NY. **314** Biblioteca Apostolica Vaticana, Rome. **319** William Blake 1757–1827, British. Illustration to Dante's *Divine Comedy* 1824–27. *Inferno*, Canto III. *The Vestibule of Hell and the Souls Mustering to Cross the Acheron.* Watercolor. 37.3 × 52.8 cm. National Gallery of Victoria, Felton Bequest, 1920. **322** The Tate Gallery, London. **335** Courtesy of the Trustees of the British Museum. **343** The British Library. **346** M.805 f. 48 The Pierpont Morgan Library, New York. **351** The British Library. **364** The Bodleian Library, Oxford. MS. Douce 215, folio 14r.

UNIT 4

370 (l) Alinari/Art Resource, NY; (c) Library of Congress; (r) National Gallery of Art, Washington, Samuel

H. Kress Collection; **371** (1) Bibliothèque de l'Institut de France, Paris; (c) Rare Books Division, The New York Public Library, Astor, Lenox and Tilden Foundations; (r) Courtesy A. H. Robins Company. **375, 378** Scala/Art Resource, NY. **380** Biblioteca Nazionale Marciana, Venice. Photo by Foto Toso. **383** Giraudon/Art Resource, NY. **387** Scala/Art Resource, NY. **391** Spencer Collection, The New York Public Library, Astor, Lenox and Tilden Foundations. **393, 395, 397, 399** Scala/Art Resource, NY. **402** Lauros-Giraudon/Art Resource, NY. **403** Bibliothèque Nationale, Paris. **405** ARXIU MAS. **409** Berg Collection, The New York Public Library, Astor, Lenox and Tilden Foundations. **413** National Portrait Gallery, London. **415** Devonshire Collection, Chatsworth, Reproduced by permission of the Chatsworth Settlement Trustees. **417** By permission of the Folger Shakespeare Library. **429, 442** Bridgeman Art Library/Art Resource, NY. **446** Giraudon/Art Resource, NY. **447** (both), **460** (1) Courtesy of the Trustees of the British Museum. **461** Scale drawing by Irwin Smith from *Shakespeare's Globe Playhouse: A Modern Reconstruction in Text and Scale Drawings* by Irwin Smith. Charles Scribner's Sons, New York, 1956. Hand colored by Cheryl Kucharzak. **482, 484** Scala/Art Resource, NY.

UNIT 5

490 (1) Cliché des Musées Nationaux, Paris; (c) Pepys Library, by permission of the Master and Fellows, Magdalene College, Cambridge. **491** (1) The Bettmann Archive; (c) The Trustees of Sir John Soane's Museum; (r) National Geographic Society Photographer George F. Mobley. Courtesy U.S. Capitol Historical Society. **495** The Metropolitan Museum of Art, The Jules Bache Collection, 1949. **497** Yale Center for British Art, Paul Mellon Collection. **499** National Portrait Gallery, London. **503** Courtesy, Museum of Fine Arts, Boston. **508** Bulloz. **512** Jean-Loup Charmet. **514, 516** Bulloz. **519, 529, 534, 540, 547** Dawn Murray. **552** National Portrait Gallery, London. **559** The Bodleian Library, Oxford. Poole portrait of Alexander Pope. **561, 563, 565, 569** (both) The British Library. **572** By permission of the Houghton Library, Harvard University. **574** Bulloz. **584, 587** Jean-Loup Charmet. **592** Bibliothèque Nationale, Paris. **594** Galerie St. Etienne, New York.

UNIT 6

598(1) Scala/Art Resource, NY; (c) The Bettmann Archive; (r) The Royal College of Surgeons of England, Darwin Museum, Down House, Kent. **599** (1) The Granger Collection, New York; (r) Gettysburg National Military Park. **603** Bulloz. **605** Staatliche Museen Preussischer Kulturbesitz, Nationalgalerie, Berlin. **606** Courtauld Institute Galleries/Bridgeman Art Library/Art Resource, NY. **608** Detail, *Goethe in the Campagna* by Johann Tischbein, 1787. Städelsches Kunstinstitut, Frankfurt-am-Main. Photo: Blauel/Gnamm/Artothek. **613** Reproduced by permission of the Trustees of the Wallace Collection. **618** The Granger Collection, New York. **619** Staatliche Museen Preussischer Kulturbesitz, Kupferstichkabinett, Berlin. **623** The Bettman Archive. **625** State Russian Museum, Leningrad. **628** Bulloz. **629** Musée des Beaux-Arts, Rouen. **631** The Granger Collection, New York. **636, 643** State

Russian Museum, Leningrad. **651** Rare Books Division, The New York Public Library, Astor, Lenox and Tilden Foundations. **653** The National Gallery of Art, Washington, Gift of Mrs. Huttleston Rogers. **660** Giraudon/Art Resource, NY. **663** Harlingue-Viollet. **665** Cliché des Musées Nationaux, Paris. © ARS NY/SPADEM, 1988. **668** The Granger Collection, New York. **671** State Russian Museum, Leningrad. **675** Elsie Timbey Collection, Society for Cultural Relations with the USSR. **679** Trustees of Amherst College. **681** Museum of Fine Arts, Springfield, Massachusetts, The Horace P. Wright Collection. **683** Mark Twain Home Board. **685** The Harry T. Peters Collection, Museum of the City of New York. **688** The Granger Collection, New York. **690** Potter Palmer Collection (Bequest of Berthe Honoré Palmer), 1922.410. © 1988 The Art Institute of Chicago. All Rights Reserved. **694** Brown Brothers. **696** Bulloz.

UNIT 7

702 (1) Library of Congress; (c) The Bettmann Archive; (r) Hedrich-Blessing. **703** (1) Trustees of the Imperial War Museum, London; (c) Sovfoto; (r) The Museum of Modern Art/Film Stills Archive. **706** Bridgeman Art Library/Art Resource, NY. **709** Josef S. Martin/Artothek. **710** The Granger Collection, New York. **713, 719, 726, 729, 739** Kobal/SuperStock. **753** The Bettmann Archive. **762** Novosti Press Agency. **765** Mansell Collection. **767** Collection of Betty LaDuke, Ashland, Oregon. **770, 775** The Granger Collection, New York. **777** National Portrait Gallery, London. **784** The Bettmann Archive. **813, 815, 819, 825** The Granger Collection, New York. **829** The Saint Louis Art Museum. **830** From *Caught in the Web of Words* by K. M. Elisabeth Murray, Yale University Press. **832** Bridgeman Art Library/Art Resource, NY.

UNIT 8

838 (1) The Museum of Modern Art/Film Stills Archive; (r) The Granger Collection, New York. **839** (1) Bob Adelman; (c) NASA; (r) Bill Fitz-Patrick/The White House. **843** *Broadway Boogie Woogie* by Piet Mondrian, 1942–43. Oil on canvas, 50 × 50″. Collection, The Museum of Modern Art, New York. Given Anonymously. **844** Edgar Kaufmann Restricted Fund, 1970.1100. © 1988 The Art Institute of Chicago. All Rights Reserved. **846** Organization of American States. **849** Kunsthaus Zürich. © ARS NY/SPADEM, 1988. **853, 857** The Granger Collection, New York. **860** From *Polish Jews: A Pictorial Record* by Roman Vishniac. Copyright © 1947 and renewed 1975 by Schocken Books Inc. Reprinted by permission of Shocken Books, published by Pantheon Books, a division of Random House, Inc. **865** The Granger Collection, New York. **867** © Joyce Ravid. **869** The Nelson-Atkins Museum of Art, Kansas City, Missouri (Nelson Fund). **872** The Granger Collection, New York. **874** Agence de Presse Bernand. **877, 880, 883, 887, 897** © Gerry Goodstein. **904** Librairie Plon, Paris. **913** Lee Boltin. **915** Tass/Sovfoto. **919** The Metropolitan Museum of Art, Bequest of Michael Dreicer, 1921. **921** L. A. Hyder. **926** Lee Boltin. **929** Milt & Joan Mann/Cameramann International, Ltd. **931** Agence de Presse Bernand.

HANDBOOK OF LITERARY TERMS
937 Bridgeman Art Library/Art Resource, NY. **939** Cartoon by Anthony Gilbert from *The English Comic Album*, edited by Leonard Russell and Nicolas Bentley. Michael Joseph Ltd., London, 1948. **950** Harley Schwadron. **952** Courtesy of the Trustees of the British Museum.

WRITER'S HANDBOOK
977 From *Haiku Painting* by Leon M. Zolbrod. Copyright © 1982 by Kodansha International Ltd. All rights reserved.

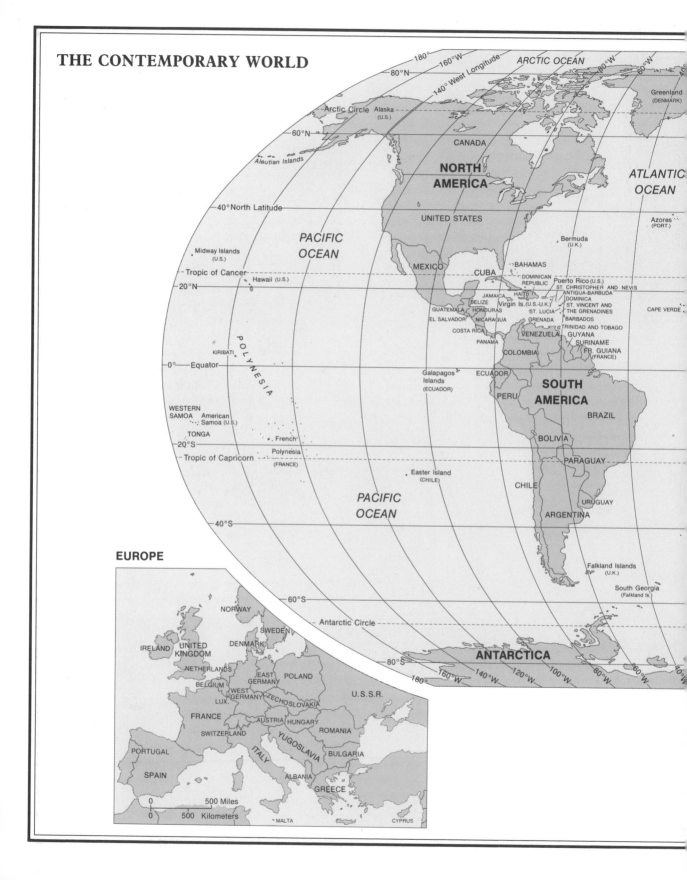

THE CONTEMPORARY WORLD

ARCTIC OCEAN

180°
160°W
140° West Longitude
80°N
80°W
60°W
40°

Greenland
(DENMARK)

Arctic Circle   Alaska
(U.S.)

60°N

Aleutian Islands

CANADA

NORTH
AMERICA

ATLANTIC
OCEAN

40° North Latitude

UNITED STATES

Azores
(PORT.)

PACIFIC
OCEAN

Midway Islands
(U.S.)

Bermuda
(U.K.)

Tropic of Cancer
20°N
Hawaii (U.S.)

MEXICO
CUBA
BAHAMAS
DOMINICAN
REPUBLIC
Puerto Rico (U.S.)
ST. CHRISTOPHER AND NEVIS
ANTIGUA-BARBUDA
DOMINICA
ST. VINCENT AND
THE GRENADINES
BARBADOS
TRINIDAD AND TOBAGO
JAMAICA
HAITI
Virgin Is. (U.S.-U.K.)
GUATEMALA
BELIZE
HONDURAS
EL SALVADOR
NICARAGUA
ST. LUCIA
GRENADA
COSTA RICA
PANAMA

CAPE VERDE

KIRIBATI

VENEZUELA
COLOMBIA
GUYANA
SURINAME
FR. GUIANA
(FRANCE)

POLYNESIA

0°   Equator

Galapagos
Islands
(ECUADOR)
ECUADOR

PERU

SOUTH
AMERICA

BRAZIL

WESTERN
SAMOA   American
Samoa (U.S.)
TONGA
French
20°S
Polynesia
(FRANCE)

BOLIVIA

Tropic of Capricorn

PARAGUAY

Easter Island
(CHILE)

CHILE

URUGUAY

PACIFIC
OCEAN

ARGENTINA

40°S

EUROPE

Falkland Islands
(U.K.)

South Georgia
(Falkland Is.)

60°S

Antarctic Circle

NORWAY

SWEDEN

ANTARCTICA

80°S
160°W
140°W
120°W
100°W
80°W
60°W
40°W
180°

IRELAND   UNITED
KINGDOM
DENMARK

NETHERLANDS
BELGIUM
LUX.
WEST
GERMANY
EAST
GERMANY
POLAND
CZECHOSLOVAKIA

U.S.S.R.

FRANCE
AUSTRIA
SWITZERLAND
HUNGARY
ROMANIA

PORTUGAL
ITALY
YUGOSLAVIA
BULGARIA

SPAIN
ALBANIA

GREECE

0   500 Miles

0   500 Kilometers

MALTA
CYPRUS